Excel 2013

the missing manual®

The book that should have been in the box®

Matthew MacDonald

O'REILLY®

Beijing | Cambridge | Farnham | Köln | Sebastopol | Tokyo

Excel 2013: The Missing Manual

by Matthew MacDonald

Published by O'Reilly Media, Inc.,
1005 Gravenstein Highway North, Sebastopol, CA 95472.

O'Reilly books may be purchased for educational, business, or sales promotional use. Online editions are also available for most titles (*http://my.safaribooksonline.com*). For more information, contact our corporate/institutional sales department: (800) 998-9938 or *corporate@oreilly.com*.

April 2013: First Edition.

Revision History for the Nth Edition:

2013-04-10 First release

See *http://oreilly.com/catalog/errata.csp?isbn=9781449357276* for release details.

ISBN-13: 978-1-449-35727-6

[LSI]

Contents

The Missing Credits

ABOUT THE AUTHOR

Matthew MacDonald (author) is a four-time Microsoft MVP and a technology writer with well over a dozen books to his name. Office geeks can follow him into the world of databases with *Access 2013: The Missing Manual*. Web fans can build an online home with him in *Creating a Website: The Missing Manual*. And human beings of all description can discover just how strange they really are in the quirky handbooks *Your Brain: The Missing Manual* and *Your Body: The Missing Manual*.

ABOUT THE CREATIVE TEAM

Peter McKie (editor) graduated from Boston University's School of Journalism and lives in New York City. In his spare time, he manages the Facebook page and website that chronicle the history of his summer community. Email: *pmckie@oreilly.com*.

Melanie Yarbrough (production editor) lives and works in Cambridge, MA. When not ushering books through production, she's sewing, writing, and baking whatever she can think up. Email: *myarbrough@oreilly.com*.

Julie Hawks (indexer) is an indexer for the Missing Manual series. She is currently pursuing a master's degree in Religious Studies while discovering the joys of warm winters in the Carolinas. Email: *juliehawks@gmail.com*.

Carla Spoon (proofreader) is a freelance writer and copy editor. An avid runner, she works and feeds her tech gadget addiction from her home office in the shadow of Mount Rainier. Email: *carla_spoon@comcast.net*.

Zack Barresse (technical reviewer) is a Microsoft Excel MVP and has held that title for seven consecutive years. He works as a full-time firefighter in his hometown of Boardman, Oregon, where he resides with his wife and four children.

Stephanie Dukes (technical reviewer) lives in San Francisco, and works for a software company that supports the global finance industry. When she isn't crunching numbers and reverse-engineering SQL databases, she spends her time in the El Dorado National Forest skiing, hiking, and kayaking with her partner and dog, or volunteering with her favorite dog rescue, Muttville Senior Dog Rescue (*www.Muttville.org*) in San Francisco.

ACKNOWLEDGMENTS

Writing a book about a program as sprawling and complex as Excel is a labor of love (love of pain, that is). I'm deeply indebted to a whole host of people who helped out with this edition and the three previous ones. They include Peter McKie, Nellie McKesson, Brian Sawyer, Peter Meyers, Sarah Milstein, and technical reviewers Zack Barresse, and Stephanie Dukes. I also owe thanks to many people who worked to get this book formatted, indexed, and printed—you can meet many of them in the section "About the Creative Team," above.

Completing this book required a few sleepless nights (and many sleep-deprived days). I extend my love and thanks to my daughters Maya and Brenna, who put up with it without crying most of the time, my dear wife Faria, who mostly did the same, and our moms and dads (Nora, Razia, Paul, and Hamid), who contributed hours of babysitting, tasty meals, and general help around the house that kept this book on track. So thanks everyone—without you half of the book would still be trapped inside my brain!

— Matthew MacDonald

THE MISSING MANUAL SERIES

Missing Manuals are witty, superbly written guides to computer products that don't come with printed manuals (which is just about all of them). Each book features a handcrafted index and cross-references to specific pages (not just chapters). Recent and upcoming titles include:

- *Access 2010: The Missing Manual* by Matthew MacDonald
- *Access 2013: The Missing Manual* by Matthew MacDonald
- *Adobe Edge Animate: The Missing Manual* by Chris Grover
- *Buying a Home: The Missing Manual* by Nancy Conner
- *Creating a Website: The Missing Manual, Third Edition* by Matthew MacDonald
- *CSS3: The Missing Manual* by David Sawyer McFarland
- *David Pogue's Digital Photography: The Missing Manual* by David Pogue
- *Dreamweaver CS6: The Missing Manual* by David Sawyer McFarland
- *Droid 2: The Missing Manual* by Preston Gralla
- *Droid X2: The Missing Manual* by Preston Gralla
- *Excel 2010: The Missing Manual* by Matthew MacDonald
- *Excel 2013: The Missing Manual* by Matthew MacDonald
- *FileMaker Pro 12: The Missing Manual* by Susan Prosser and Stuart Gripman
- *Flash CS6: The Missing Manual* by Chris Grover
- *Galaxy S II: The Missing Manual* by Preston Gralla

- *Galaxy Tab: The Missing Manual* by Preston Gralla
- *Google+: The Missing Manual* by Kevin Purdy
- *HTML5: The Missing Manual* by Matthew MacDonald
- *iMovie '11 & iDVD: The Missing Manual* by David Pogue and Aaron Miller
- *iPad: The Missing Manual, Fifth Edition* by J.D. Biersdorfer
- *iPhone: The Missing Manual, Fifth Edition* by David Pogue
- *iPhone App Development: The Missing Manual* by Craig Hockenberry
- *iPhoto '11: The Missing Manual* by David Pogue and Lesa Snider
- *iPod: The Missing Manual, Tenth Edition* by J.D. Biersdorfer and David Pogue
- *JavaScript & jQuery: The Missing Manual, Second Edition* by David Sawyer McFarland
- *Kindle Fire HD: The Missing Manual* by Peter Meyers
- *Living Green: The Missing Manual* by Nancy Conner
- *Mac OS X Lion: The Missing Manual* by David Pogue
- *Microsoft Project 2010: The Missing Manual* by Bonnie Biafore
- *Microsoft Project 2013: The Missing Manual* by Bonnie Biafore
- *Motorola Xoom: The Missing Manual* by Preston Gralla
- *Netbooks: The Missing Manual* by J.D. Biersdorfer
- *NOOK HD: The Missing Manual* by Preston Gralla
- *Office 2010: The Missing Manual* by Nancy Conner and Matthew MacDonald
- *Office 2011 for Macintosh: The Missing Manual* by Chris Grover
- *Office 2013: The Missing Manual* by Nancy Conner and Matthew MacDonald
- *OS X Mountain Lion: The Missing Manual* by David Pogue
- *Personal Investing: The Missing Manual* by Bonnie Biafore
- *Photoshop CS6: The Missing Manual* by Lesa Snider
- *Photoshop Elements 11: The Missing Manual* by Barbara Brundage
- *PHP & MySQL: The Missing Manual, Second Edition* by Brett McLaughlin
- *QuickBooks 2012: The Missing Manual* by Bonnie Biafore
- *QuickBooks 2013: The Missing Manual* by Bonnie Biafore
- *Switching to the Mac: The Missing Manual, Lion Edition* by David Pogue
- *Switching to the Mac: The Missing Manual, Mountain Lion Edition* by David Pogue

- *Windows 7: The Missing Manual* by David Pogue
- *Windows 8: The Missing Manual* by David Pogue
- *WordPress: The Missing Manual* by Matthew MacDonald
- *Your Body: The Missing Manual* by Matthew MacDonald
- *Your Brain: The Missing Manual* by Matthew MacDonald
- *Your Money: The Missing Manual* by J.D. Roth

For a full list of all Missing Manuals in print, go to *www.missingmanuals.com/library.html.*

Introduction

Most people don't need much convincing to use Excel, perhaps the world's premier spreadsheet software. Its overwhelming popularity, especially in the business world, makes it the obvious choice for millions of number crunchers. But despite its wide use, few people know where to find Excel's most impressive features or why they'd want to use them in the first place. *Excel 2013: The Missing Manual* fills that void, explaining everything from basic Excel concepts to the fancy tricks of the trade.

This book teaches you how Excel works, and shows you how to use Excel's tools to answer real-world questions like "How many workdays are there between today and my vacation?", "How much money do I need in the bank right now to retire a millionaire?", and "Statistically speaking, who's smarter—Democrats or Republicans?" Best of all, you'll steer clear of obscure options that aren't worth the trouble to learn, while homing in on the hidden gems that will win you the undying adoration of your coworkers, your family, and your friends—or at least your accountant.

What You Can Do with Excel

Excel and Word are the two powerhouses of the Microsoft Office family. While Word lets you create and edit documents, Excel specializes in letting you create, edit, and analyze *data* that's organized into lists or tables. This grid-like arrangement of information is called a *spreadsheet*. Figure I-1 shows an example.

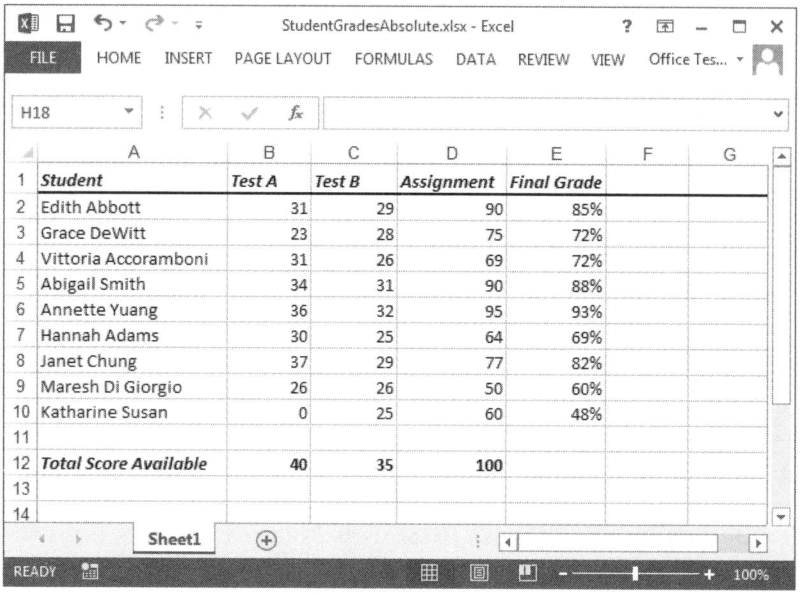

FIGURE I-1

This spreadsheet lists nine students, each of whom has two test scores and an assignment grade. Using Excel formulas, it's easy to calculate the final grade for each student. And with a little more effort, you can calculate averages and medians, and determine each student's rank in the class. Chapter 8 looks at how to perform these calculations.

NOTE Excel shines when it comes to *numerical* data, but the program doesn't limit you to calculations. While it has the computing muscle to analyze stacks of numbers, it's equally useful for keeping track of the Blu-rays in your personal movie collection.

Some common types of spreadsheet include:

- **Business documents** like financial statements, invoices, expense reports, and earnings statements.
- **Personal documents** like weekly budgets, catalogs of your *Star Wars* action figures, exercise logs, and shopping lists.
- **Scientific data** like experimental observations, models, and medical charts.

These examples just scratch the surface. Resourceful spreadsheet gurus use Excel to build everything from cross-country trip itineraries to logs of every Ben Stiller movie they've ever seen.

Of course, Excel really shines in its ability to help you *analyze* a spreadsheet's data. For example, once you enter a list of household expenses, you can start crunching numbers with Excel's slick formula tools. Before long you'll have totals, subtotals, monthly averages, a complete breakdown of cost by category, and maybe even some predictions for the future. Excel can help track your investments and tell you how long until you'll have saved enough to buy that weekend house in Vegas.

The bottom line is that once you enter raw information, Excel's built-in smarts can help compute all kinds of useful figures. Figure I-2 shows a sophisticated spreadsheet that's designed to help identify hot-selling product categories.

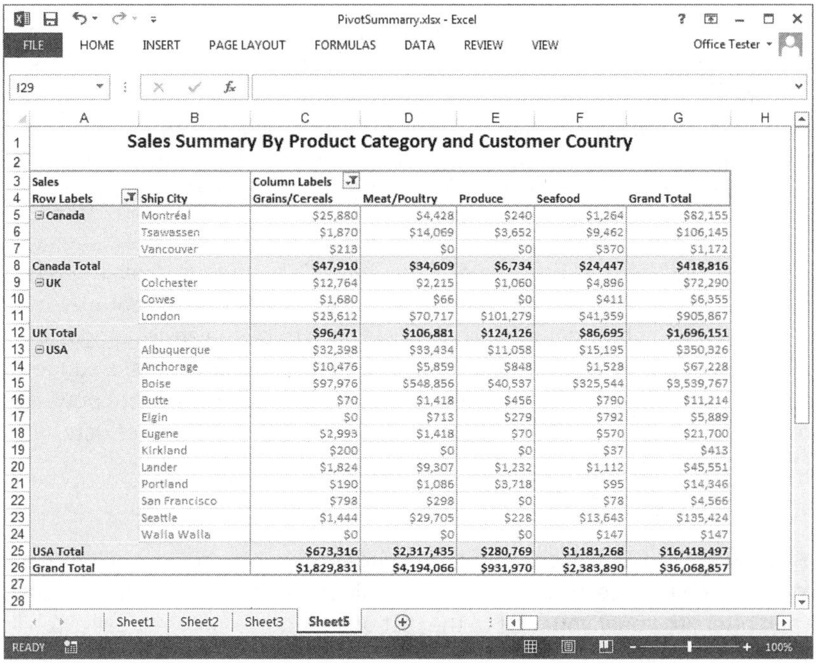

Sales Summary By Product Category and Customer Country

Sales		Column Labels				
Row Labels	Ship City	Grains/Cereals	Meat/Poultry	Produce	Seafood	Grand Total
Canada	Montréal	$25,880	$4,428	$240	$1,264	$82,155
	Tsawassen	$1,870	$14,069	$3,652	$9,462	$106,145
	Vancouver	$213	$0	$0	$370	$1,172
Canada Total		**$47,910**	**$34,609**	**$6,734**	**$24,447**	**$418,816**
UK	Colchester	$12,764	$2,215	$1,060	$4,896	$72,290
	Cowes	$1,680	$66	$0	$411	$6,355
	London	$23,612	$70,717	$101,279	$41,359	$905,867
UK Total		**$96,471**	**$106,881**	**$124,126**	**$86,695**	**$1,696,151**
USA	Albuquerque	$32,398	$33,434	$11,058	$15,195	$350,326
	Anchorage	$10,476	$5,859	$848	$1,528	$67,228
	Boise	$97,976	$548,856	$40,537	$325,544	$3,539,767
	Butte	$70	$1,418	$456	$790	$11,214
	Elgin	$0	$713	$279	$792	$5,889
	Eugene	$2,993	$1,418	$70	$570	$21,700
	Kirkland	$200	$0	$0	$37	$413
	Lander	$1,824	$9,307	$1,232	$1,112	$45,551
	Portland	$190	$1,086	$3,718	$95	$14,346
	San Francisco	$798	$298	$0	$78	$4,566
	Seattle	$1,444	$29,705	$228	$13,643	$135,424
	Walla Walla	$0	$0	$0	$147	$147
USA Total		**$673,316**	**$2,317,435**	**$280,769**	**$1,181,268**	**$16,418,497**
Grand Total		**$1,829,831**	**$4,194,066**	**$931,970**	**$2,383,890**	**$36,068,857**

FIGURE I-2

This spreadsheet summarizes a company's total sales. It groups the information based on where the company's customers live, and it further divides items according to product category. Summaries like these can help you spot profitable product categories and identify items popular in specific cities. This advanced example uses pivot tables, which are described in Chapter 22.

NOTE Keen eyes will notice that neither Figure I-1 nor Figure I-2 include the omnipresent Excel ribbon, which usually sits atop the window, stacked with buttons. That's because it's been collapsed neatly out of the way to let you focus on the spreadsheet. You'll learn how to use this trick yourself on page 15.

Excel is not just a math wizard. If you want to add a little life to your data, you can inject color, apply exotic fonts, and even create *macros* (automated sequences of steps) to help speed up repetitive formatting or editing chores. And if you're bleary-eyed from staring at rows and rows of spreadsheet numbers, you can use Excel's many chart-making tools to build everything from 3-D pie charts to more exotic scatter graphs. (See Chapter 17 to learn about all of Excel's chart types.) Excel can be as simple or as sophisticated as you want it to be.

Finally, it's important to understand that you can use Excel to analyze other people's data—for example, the sales records in a massive company database. That's because Excel has built-in *data connection* features that can pull information out of different sources, from a data feed on a website to a database server in a big company. Once you bring that information into Excel, you can examine it with formulas and charts, just as you would analyze the information in an ordinary workbook. You'll see this side of Excel in Chapters 27 and 28.

The New Features in Excel 2013

For Excel 2007 and Excel 2010, Microsoft spent most of its time rebuilding the spreadsheet program's user interface, replacing the clutter of old-fashioned toolbars with a unified ribbon, and creating a new backstage view where you can open, save, and print files. The visual changes in Excel 2013 are much less dramatic. Excel 2013 tweaks the program's looks, but just a little, changing the capitalizing of toolbar tabs and toning down the color scheme. But the modern Excel window (which you'll tour in Chapter 1) stays essentially the same.

That's not to say that the creators of Excel haven't been busy over the past few years. In fact, they've introduced a range of refinements and new features, most of which fall into two categories. First, Excel 2013 aims to be the easiest, most intuitive version of Excel yet, with several new features that offer help or make suggestions as you work with batches of data. Second, Excel 2013 has grown more powerful, so it can act as a data analysis tool for big businesses with boatloads of data.

You'll learn about all of Excel's changes in this book. Here's a preview of the most significant new features:

- **Flash Fill.** Tired of making repetitive changes to a whole column of information? With Flash Fill, Excel watches you make minor changes, learns the pattern, and then offers to apply your edit to the rest of your data—automatically. You'll put it to work on page 66.
- **Quick Analysis.** Excel always had plenty of great features, but you need to click your way through layers of buttons and menus to find them. But Excel's new Quick Analysis feature gives you easy access to the most useful charting, summarizing, and data visualization options. Just select your data, click a simple smart tag, and pick one of the convenient choices Excel offers. Quick Analysis is particularly handy for basic charts (page 489), but you'll see it crop up throughout this book.
- **Slicers and timelines.** Excel pros know all about Excel's list and pivot table features, which let you filter masses of data to find the information you need. Now Excel sweetens the pie with *slicers*, which let you switch filtering options on or off with the click of a fancy floating button; and *timelines*, which let you select a range of dates in a handy slider widget. By using both tools, you can turn an ordinary Excel worksheet into a slick data dashboard (page 815).

- **The new data model.** Excel has always been a brilliant tool for pulling in data from a database and crunching the numbers. Now, Excel integrates the Power-Pivot add-in, giving it the ability to handle millions of rows of data. You'll learn more in Chapter 27.
- **Worksheet reporting.** The Inquire add-in is a bonus that ships with the Office Professional Plus version of Excel. It lets you compare different versions of the same workbook, and discover how the formulas in sheets and workbook files link together, among other tricks. You'll try it out on page 696.

Of course, this list is by no means complete. Excel 2013 is chock-full of refinements, tweaks, and tune-ups that make it easier to use than any previous version. You'll learn all the best tricks throughout this book.

The Office 365 Subscription Service

Along with the changes covered above, Microsoft has been busy tweaking the way it *sells* Office. Excel 2013 is available in the usual array of desktop packages, as well as through a subscription service called Office 365, which is aimed at businesses, educational institutions, and government workers. When a company signs up, they give each of their employees a separate Office 365 account that they can use to run Office (either online or on the desktop, if the subscription plan includes desktop use). Depending on the plan, the Office 365 subscription may also include other online services, such as email, messaging, document sharing, project tracking, and more.

The drawback to Office 365 is that each person who uses it needs a separate subscription plan, and each subscription plan entails a monthly payment to Microsoft (ranging from $4 to over $20 per month). For big businesses, the cost of giving their employees Office 365 subscriptions is often less than buying multiple copies of the shrink-wrapped Office software, and it saves them many administrative tasks, because Microsoft manages most of the administration, from spam filtering to setting up SharePoint. However, Office 365 probably won't interest families, hobbyists, or self-employed people.

To learn more about Office 365 and compare the different subscription plans, visit *http://office.microsoft.com.*

Office RT: Office for Tablets

Excel doesn't just live on ordinary Windows PCs. Now, Microsoft gives Excel lovers a way to run their favorite program on a Windows 8 tablet (see below), or in a web browser (see the next section).

To run Office applications on a Windows 8 tablet, you use a slightly different version of the productivity suite called Office 2013 RT. (Oddly enough, no one knows exactly what the "RT" stands for. The name appears to be inspired by WinRT, the new runtime in Windows 8 that powers tile-based apps. However, Office RT doesn't use WinRT, so go figure.)

Office RT looks almost identical to the desktop version of Office, but it has a number of changes under the hood. For example, it's optimized to conserve battery life and save disk space. It also turns on *touch mode*, which makes it easier to scroll around and use the ribbon with your fingers instead of the traditional mouse pointer.

Although this book is written with the full desktop version of Excel in mind, you can also use it to feel your way around the Office RT version of Excel. However, you'll find that the instructions in this book are unashamedly mouse-centric (we talk about "right-clicking" but not "double-tapping," for example). You should also know that there are a small set of significant Excel features that aren't available in Office RT. These include macros, Visual Basic programming, plug-ins, and the new data model that lets you work with related tables and huge amounts of data.

NOTE Most Excel pros will continue to use desktop versions of Excel for hardcore spreadsheet work. They may switch to Office RT when they need to collect data on the go, or carry their latest analysis into a company meeting.

The Office Web Apps

The Office Web Apps are an interesting new direction in the Office world. They provide a way to run sophisticated Office applications, like Excel, in an ordinary browser and on virtually any computer. However, the Office Web Apps have only a sliver of the features of their desktop cousins, and you can't use them at all unless you have a SharePoint server or you're willing to upload your documents to SkyDrive (Microsoft's free document-hosting service). The online version of Excel is called the Excel Web App.

NOTE Overall, the Excel Web App is designed for collecting data and viewing Excel spreadsheets, not creating them. For example, you can view workbooks that use common Excel ingredients like sparklines and pivot tables, but you can't add them yourself.

Microsoft introduced the Excel Web App at the same time as Excel 2010. When the company released Excel 2013, they also updated the Excel Web App, giving it the new Excel 2013 color scheme and tweaking its chart drawing to be just a bit crisper. However, the only completely new feature you'll find in the Excel 2013 Web App is the ability to create surveys (page 733).

Interestingly, the desktop version of Excel 2013 now has slightly better integration with the Excel Web App. It's easier than ever to upload your work to SharePoint or SkyDrive, and you can even send out a link to your work through social media sites like Facebook, Twitter, and LinkedIn, all without leaving the Excel window. You'll consider these minor frills, and the Excel Web App, in Chapter 23.

About This Book

Despite the many improvements in software over the years, one feature hasn't improved a bit: Microsoft's documentation. In fact, with Office 2013, you get no printed user guide at all. To learn about the thousands of features included in this software collection, Microsoft expects you to read its online help.

Occasionally, the online help is actually helpful, like when you're looking for a quick description explaining a mysterious new function. On the other hand, if you're trying to learn how to, say, create an attractive chart, you're stuck with terse and occasionally cryptic instructions.

The purpose of this book, then, is to serve as the manual that should have accompanied Excel 2013. In these pages, you'll find step-by-step instructions and tips for using almost every Excel feature, including those you may not even know exist.

About the Outline

This book is divided into eight parts, each containing several chapters.

- **Part One: Worksheet Basics.** In this part, you'll get acquainted with Excel's interface and learn the basic techniques for creating spreadsheets and entering and organizing data. You'll also learn how to format your work to make it more presentable, and how to create sharp printouts.
- **Part Two: Formulas and Functions.** This part introduces you to Excel's most important feature—formulas. You'll learn how to perform calculations ranging from the simple to the complex, and you'll tackle specialized functions for dealing with all kinds of information, including scientific, statistical, business, and financial data.
- **Part Three: Organizing Your Information.** The third part covers how to organize and find what's in your spreadsheet. First, you'll learn to search, sort, and filter large amounts of information by using tables. Next, you'll see how to boil down complex tables using grouping and outlining. Finally, you'll turn your perfected spreadsheets into reusable templates.
- **Part Four: Charts and Graphics.** The fourth part introduces you to charting and graphics, two of Excel's most popular features. You'll learn about the wide range of different chart types available and when it makes sense to use each one. You'll also find out how you can use pictures to add a little pizazz to your spreadsheets.
- **Part Five: Sharing Data with the Rest of the World.** The sixth part explores ways you can share your spreadsheets with other people. You'll learn how to collaborate with colleagues to revise a spreadsheet, without letting mistakes creep in or losing track of who did what. You'll also learn how to copy Excel tables and charts into other programs (like Word) and how to use the Excel Web App to share and edit spreadsheets on the Web.

- **Part Six: Advanced Data Analysis.** In this brief part, you'll tackle some of Excel's most advanced features. You'll see how to study different possibilities with scenarios, use goal-seeking and the Solver add-in to calculate "backward" and fill in missing numbers, and create multi-layered summary reports with pivot tables. You'll also learn how to use Excel's data connection features to pull information out of databases, websites, and XML files.
- **Part Seven: Programming Excel.** This part presents a gentle introduction to the world of Excel programming, first by recording macros and then by using the full-featured VBA (Visual Basic for Applications) language, which lets you automate complex tasks.
- **Part Eight: Appendix.** The end of this book wraps up with an appendix that shows you how to customize the ribbon to get easy access to your favorite commands.

About→These→Arrows

Throughout this book, you'll find sentences like this one: "Choose Insert→Illustrations→Picture." This is a shorthand way of telling you how to find a feature in the Excel ribbon. It translates to the following instructions: "Click the Insert tab of the toolbar. On that tab, look for the Illustrations section. In the Illustrations box, click the Picture button." Figure I-3 shows the button you want.

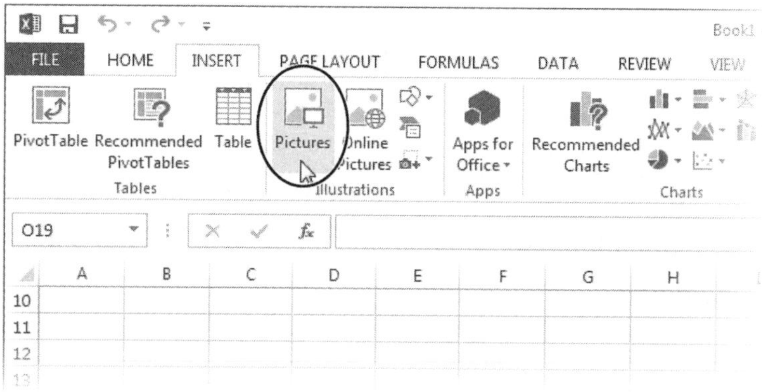

FIGURE I-3

In this book, arrow notations help simplify ribbon commands. For example, "Choose Insert→Illustrations→Picture" leads to the highlighted button shown here.

NOTE The ribbon adapts itself to different screen sizes. Depending on the size of your Excel window, it's possible that the button you need to click will include a tiny picture but no text. In this situation, you can hover over the mystery button to see its name before deciding whether to click it.

CONTEXTUAL TABS

There are some tabs that appear in the ribbon only when you work on specific tasks. For example, when you create a chart, a Chart Tools section appears with two new tabs (see Figure I-4).

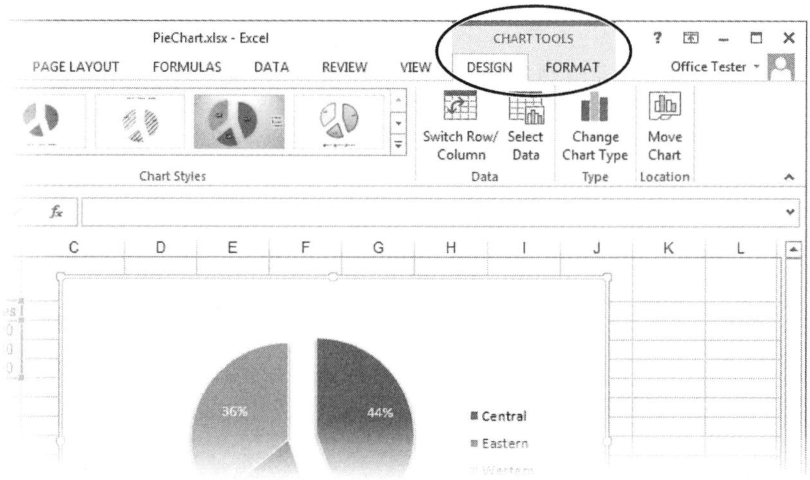

FIGURE I-4

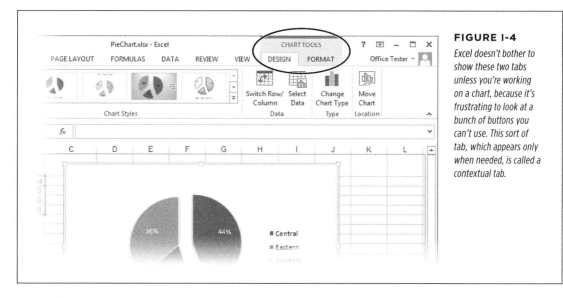

Excel doesn't bother to show these two tabs unless you're working on a chart, because it's frustrating to look at a bunch of buttons you can't use. This sort of tab, which appears only when needed, is called a contextual tab.

When dealing with contextual tabs, the instructions in this book always include the title of the tab section (it's Chart Tools in Figure I-4, for example). Here's an example: "Choose Chart Tools | Design→Type→Change Chart Type." Notice that the first part of this instruction includes the tab section title (Chart Tools) and the tab name (Design), separated by the | character. That way, you can't mistake the Chart Tools | Design tab for a Design tab in some other group of contextual tabs.

NOTE Excel adds contextual tabs after the standard tabs, so you'll always see them on the right side of the Excel window.

BUTTONS WITH MENUS

From time to time, you'll encounter buttons in the ribbon that have short menus attached to them. Depending on the button, this menu might appear as soon as you click the button, or it might appear only if you click the button's drop-down arrow, as shown in Figure I-5.

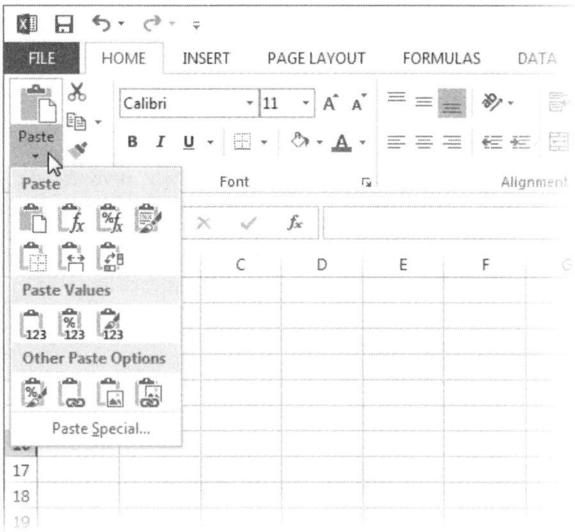

FIGURE I-5

There are several options for pasting text from the Clipboard. Click the top part of the Paste button to perform a plain-vanilla paste (with all the standard settings), or click the bottom part to see the menu of choices shown here.

When dealing with this sort of button, the last step of the instructions in this book tells you what to choose from the drop-down menu. For example, say you're directed to "Home→Clipboard→Paste→Paste Special." That tells you to select the Home tab, look for the Clipboard section, click the drop-down part of the Paste button (to reveal the menu with extra options), and then choose Paste Special from the menu.

TIP Be on the lookout for drop-down arrows in the ribbon—they're tricky at first. You need to click the *arrow* part of the button to see the full list of options. When you click any other part of the button, you don't see the list. Instead, Excel fires off the standard command (the one Excel thinks is the most common choice) or the command you used most recently.

DIALOG BOX LAUNCHERS

As powerful as the ribbon is, you can't do everything using the buttons it provides. Sometimes you need to use a good ol'-fashioned dialog box. (A *dialog box* is a term used in the Windows world to describe a small window with a limited number of options. Usually, dialog boxes are designed for one task and aren't resizable, although software companies like Microsoft break these rules all the time.)

There are two ways to get to a dialog box in Excel. First, some ribbon buttons take you there straightaway. For example, if you choose Home→Clipboard→Paste→Paste Special, you always get a dialog box. There's no way around it.

The second way to get to a dialog box is through something called a *dialog box launcher*, which is just a nerdified name for the tiny square-with-arrow icon that sometimes appears in the bottom-right corner of a section of the ribbon. The easiest way to learn how to spot a dialog box launcher is to look at Figure I-6.

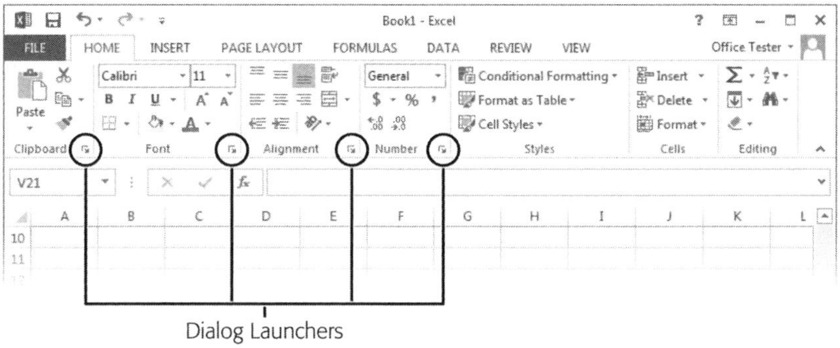

FIGURE I-6

As you can see here, the Clipboard, Font, Alignment, and Number sections all have dialog box launchers. The Styles, Cells, and Editing sections don't.

When you click a dialog box launcher, the related dialog box appears. For example, click the dialog box launcher for the Font section and you get a full Font dialog box that lets you scroll through all the typefaces on your computer, choose a size and color, and so on.

In this book, there's no special code word that tells you to use a dialog box launcher. Instead, you'll see an instruction like this: "To see more font options, look at the Home→Font section and click the dialog box launcher (the small icon in the bottom-right corner)." Now that you know what a dialog box launcher is, that makes perfect sense.

BACKSTAGE VIEW

If you see an instruction that includes arrows but starts with the word File, it's telling you to go to Excel's backstage view. For example, the sentence "Choose File→New" means click the File button (which appears just to the left of ribbon's Home tab) to switch to backstage view, then click the New command (which appears in the narrow list on the left side of the window). You'll take your first look around backstage view on page 23.

ORDINARY MENUS

There are a couple of other cases where you'll use the familiar Windows menu. One is when you use the Visual Basic editor (in Chapter 29). In this case, the arrows refer to menu levels. For example, the instruction "Choose File→Save" means "Click the File menu heading. Then, on the File menu, click the Save command."

About Shortcut Keys

Every time you take your hand off the keyboard to move the mouse, you lose a few microseconds. That's why many experienced computer fans use keystroke combinations instead of toolbars and menus wherever possible. Ctrl+S, for example, is a keyboard shortcut that saves your current work in Excel (and most other programs).

When you see a shortcut like Ctrl+S in this book, it's telling you to hold down the Ctrl key and, while it's down, press the letter S, and then release both keys. Similarly, the finger-tangling shortcut Ctrl+Alt+S means hold down Ctrl, and then press and hold Alt, and then press S (so that all three keys are held down at once).

Online Resources

As the owner of a Missing Manual, you've got more than just a book to read. As you read this book, you'll see a number of examples that demonstrate Excel features and techniques for building good spreadsheets. Most of these examples are available as downloadable Excel workbook files. Just surf to *http://missingmanuals.com/cds/excel2013mm/* to visit a page where you can download a ZIP file that includes the examples, organized by chapter.

Registration

If you register this book at *www.oreilly.com*, you'll be eligible for special offers—like discounts on future editions of this book. If you buy the ebook from oreilly.com and register your purchase, you get free lifetime updates for this edition of the ebook; we'll notify you by email when updates become available. Registering takes only a few clicks. Type *www.oreilly.com/register* into your browser to hop directly to the Registration page.

Feedback

Got questions? Need more information? Fancy yourself a book reviewer? On our Feedback page, you can get expert answers to questions that come to you while reading, share your thoughts on this Missing Manual, and find groups for folks who share your interest in Dreamweaver. To have your say, go to *www.missingmanuals.com/feedback*.

Errata

To keep this book as up to date and accurate as possible, each time we print more copies, we'll make any confirmed corrections you suggest. We also note such changes on the book's website, so you can mark important corrections into your own copy of the book, if you like. And if you bought the ebook from us and registered your purchase, you'll get an email notifying you when you can download a free updated version of this edition of the ebook. Go to *http://tinyurl.com/excel2013errata* to report an error and view existing corrections.

Examples

As you read this book, you'll see a number of examples that demonstrate Excel features and techniques for building good spreadsheets. Most of these examples are available as Excel workbook files in a separate download. Just surf to *www.missingmanuals.com/cds* and click the link for this book to visit a page where you can download a ZIP file that includes the examples, organized by chapter.

Safari© Books Online

Safari© Books Online is an on-demand digital library that lets you easily search over 7,500 technology and creative reference books and videos to find the answers you need quickly.

With a subscription, you can read any page and watch any video from our library online. Read books on your cellphone and mobile devices. Access new titles before they're available for print, and get exclusive access to manuscripts in development and post feedback for the authors. Copy and paste code samples, organize your favorites, download chapters, bookmark key sections, create notes, print out pages, and benefit from tons of other time-saving features.

O'Reilly Media has uploaded this book to the Safari Books Online service. To have full digital access to this book and others on similar topics from O'Reilly and other publishers, sign up for free at *http://my.safaribooksonline.com*.

PART 1

Worksheet Basics

CHAPTER

1

Creating Your First Spreadsheet

Every Excel grandmaster needs to start somewhere. In this chapter, you'll learn how to create a basic spreadsheet. First, you'll find out how to move around Excel's grid of cells, typing in numbers and text as you go. Next, you'll take a quick tour of the Excel ribbon, the tabbed toolbar of commands that sits above your spreadsheet. You'll learn how to trigger the ribbon with a keyboard shortcut, and collapse it out of the way when you don't need it. Finally, you'll go to Excel's *backstage view*, the file-management hub where you can save your work for posterity, open recent files, and tweak Excel options.

Starting a Workbook

When you first fire up Excel, you'll see a welcome page where you can choose to open an existing Excel spreadsheet or create a new one (Figure 1-1).

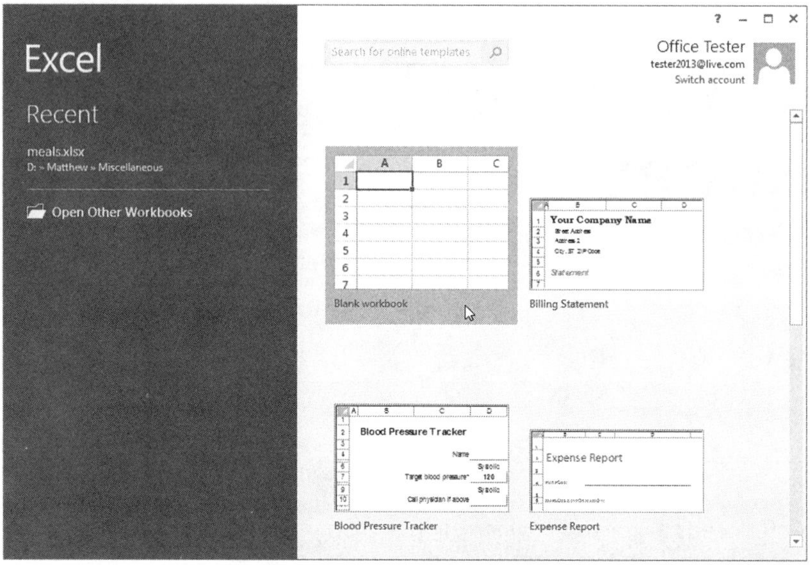

FIGURE 1-1

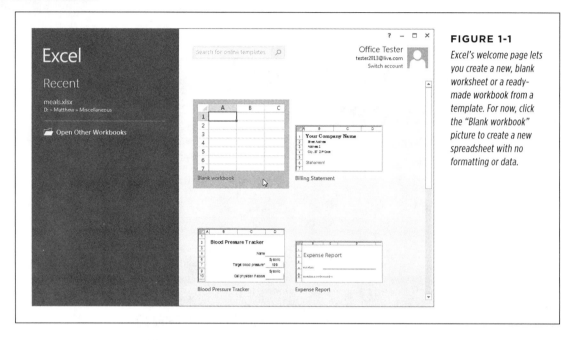

Excel's welcome page lets you create a new, blank worksheet or a ready-made workbook from a template. For now, click the "Blank workbook" picture to create a new spreadsheet with no formatting or data.

Excel fills most of the welcome page with templates, spreadsheet files preconfigured for a specific type of data. For example, if you want to create an expense report, you might choose Excel's "Travel expense report" template as a starting point. You'll learn lots more about templates in Chapter 16, but for now, just click "Blank workbook" to start with a brand-spanking-new spreadsheet with no information in it.

NOTE *Workbook* is Excel lingo for "spreadsheet." Excel uses this term to emphasize the fact that a single work*book* can contain multiple work*sheets*, each with its own grid of data. You'll learn about this feature in Chapter 4, but for now, each workbook you create will have just a single worksheet of information.

You don't get to name your workbook when you first create it. That happens later, when you *save* your workbook (page 26). For now, you start with a blank canvas that's ready to receive your numerical insights.

Adding Information to a Worksheet

When you click "Blank workbook," Excel closes the welcome page and opens a new, blank *worksheet*, as shown in Figure 1-2. A worksheet is a grid of cells where you type in information and formulas. This grid takes up most of the Excel window. It's where you'll perform all your work, such as entering data, writing formulas, and reviewing the results.

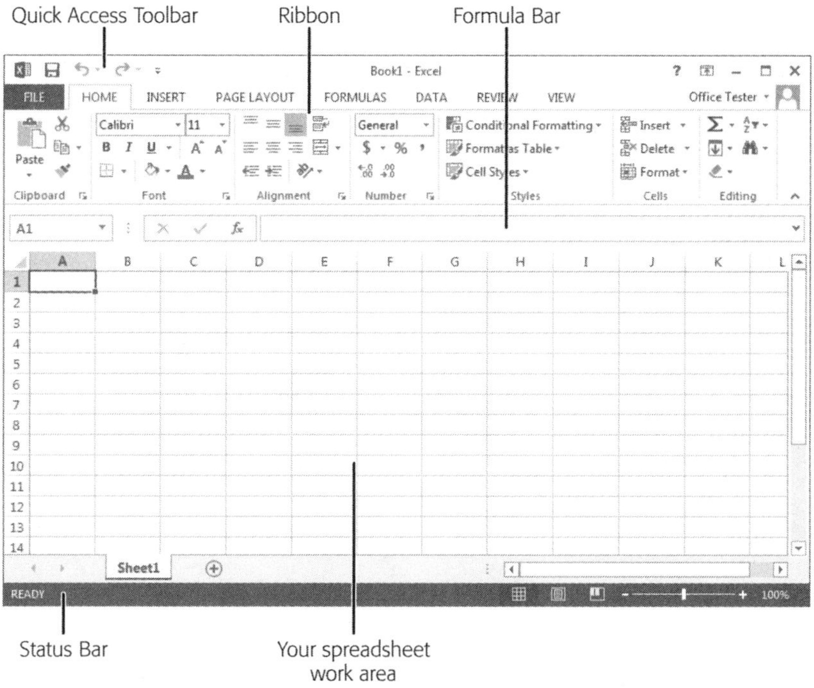

FIGURE 1-2

The largest part of the Excel window is the worksheet grid, where you type in your information.

Here are a few basics about Excel's grid:

- **The grid divides your worksheet into rows and columns.** Excel names columns using letters (A, B, C...), and labels rows using numbers (1, 2, 3...).
- **The smallest unit in your worksheet is the cell.** Excel uniquely identifies each cell by column letter and row number. For example, C6 is the address of a cell in column C (the third column) and row 6 (the sixth row). Figure 1-3 shows this cell, which looks like a rectangular box. Incidentally, an Excel cell can hold approximately 32,000 characters.
- **A worksheet can span an eye-popping 16,000 columns and 1 million rows.** In the unlikely case that you want to go beyond those limits—say, if you're tracking blades of grass on the White House lawn—you'll need to create a new worksheet. Every spreadsheet file can hold a virtually unlimited number of worksheets, as you'll learn in Chapter 4.
- **When you enter information, enter it one cell at a time.** However, you don't have to follow any set order. For example, you can start by typing information into cell A40 without worrying about filling any data in the cells that appear in the earlier rows.

NOTE Obviously, once you go beyond 26 columns, you run out of letters. Excel handles this by doubling up (and then tripling up) letters. For example, after column Z is column AA, then AB, then AC, all the way to AZ and then BA, BB, BC—you get the picture. And if you create a ridiculously large worksheet, you'll find that column ZZ is followed by AAA, AAB, AAC, and so on.

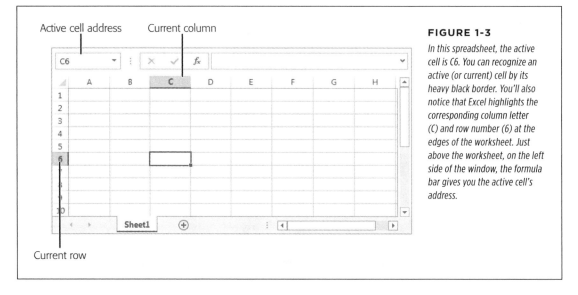

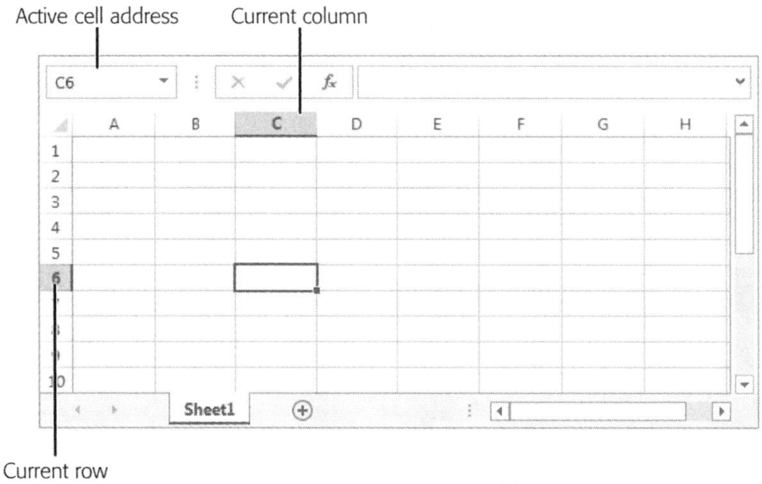

FIGURE 1-3

In this spreadsheet, the active cell is C6. You can recognize an active (or current) cell by its heavy black border. You'll also notice that Excel highlights the corresponding column letter (C) and row number (6) at the edges of the worksheet. Just above the worksheet, on the left side of the window, the formula bar gives you the active cell's address.

The best way to get a feel for Excel is to dive right in and start putting together a worksheet. The following sections cover each step that goes into assembling a simple worksheet. This one tracks household expenses, but you can use the same approach with any basic worksheet.

Adding Column Titles

Excel lets you arrange information in whatever way you like. There's nothing to stop you from scattering numbers left and right, across as many cells as you want. However, one of the most common (and most useful) ways to arrange information is in a table, with headings for each column.

It's important to remember that with even the simplest worksheet, the decisions you make about what's going to go in each column can have a big effect on how easy it is to manipulate your information. For example, in a worksheet that stores a mailing list, you *could* have two columns: one for names and another for addresses. But if you create more than two columns, your life will probably be easier because you can separate first names from street addresses from ZIP codes, and so on. Figure 1-4 shows the difference.

	A	B	C	D	E
1	**Name**	**Address**			
2	Michel DeFrance	3 Balding Pl., Gary, IN, 46403			
3	Johnson Whit	10932 Bigge Rd., Menlo Park, CA, 94025			
4	Marjorie Green	309 63rd St. #411, Oakland, CA, 94618			
5	Cheryl Carson	589 Darwin , Berkeley, CA, 94705			
6	Michael O'Leary	22 Cleveland Av. #14, San Jose, CA, 95128			
7	Dean Straight	5420 College Av., Oakland, CA, 94609			
8	Meander Smith	10 Mississippi Dr., Lawrence, KS, 66044			
9	Abraham Bennet	6223 Bateman St., Berkeley, CA, 94705			
10	Ann Dull	3410 Blonde St., Palo Alto, CA, 94301			

Sheet1

	A	B	C	D	E	F	G
1	**First Name**	**Last Name**	**Address**	**City**	**State**	**Zip**	
2	Michel	DeFrance	3 Balding Pl.	Gary	IN	46403	
3	Johnson	Whit	10932 Bigge Rd.	Menlo Park	CA	94025	
4	Marjorie	Green	309 63rd St. #411	Oakland	CA	94618	
5	Cheryl	Carson	589 Darwin	Berkeley	CA	94705	
6	Michael	O'Leary	22 Cleveland Av. #14	San Jose	CA	95128	
7	Dean	Straight	5420 College Av.	Oakland	CA	94609	
8	Meander	Smith	10 Mississippi Dr.	Lawrence	KS	66044	
9	Abraham	Bennet	6223 Bateman St.	Berkeley	CA	94705	
10	Ann	Dull	3410 Blonde St.	Palo Alto	CA	94301	

Sheet1

FIGURE 1-4

Top: If you enter both first and last names in a single column, you can sort the column only by first name. And if you clump the addresses and ZIP codes together, you have no way to count the number of people in a certain town or neighborhood.

Bottom: The benefit of a six-column table is significant: It lets you break down (and therefore analyze) information granularly, For example, you can sort your list according to people's last names or where they live. This arrangement also lets you filter out individual bits of information when you start using functions later in this book.

You can, of course, always add or remove columns. But you can avoid getting gray hairs by starting a worksheet with all the columns you think you'll need.

The first step in creating a worksheet is to add your headings in the row of cells at the top of the sheet (row 1). Technically, you don't need to start right in the first row, but unless you want to add more information before your table—like a title for the chart or today's date—there's no point in wasting space. Adding information is easy—just click the cell you want and start typing. When you finish, hit Tab to complete your entry and move to the cell to the right, or click Enter to head to the cell just underneath.

NOTE The information you put in an Excel worksheet doesn't need to be in neat, ordered columns. Nothing stops you from scattering numbers and text in random cells. However, most Excel worksheets resemble some sort of table, because that's the easiest and most effective way to manage large amounts of structured information.

For a simple expense worksheet designed to keep a record of your most prudent and extravagant purchases, try the following three headings:

- **Date Purchased.** Stores the date when you spent the money.
- **Item.** Stores the name of the product that you bought.
- **Price.** Records how much it cost.

Right away, you face your first glitch: awkwardly crowded text. Figure 1-5 shows how to adjust the column width for proper breathing room.

FIGURE 1-5

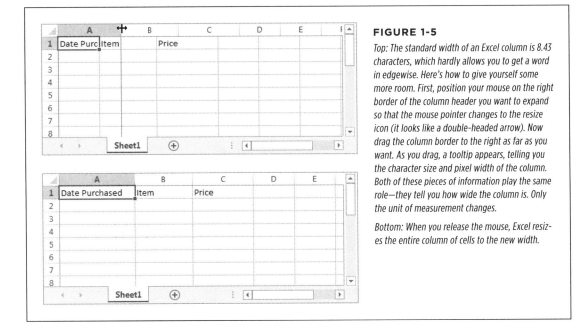

Top: The standard width of an Excel column is 8.43 characters, which hardly allows you to get a word in edgewise. Here's how to give yourself some more room. First, position your mouse on the right border of the column header you want to expand so that the mouse pointer changes to the resize icon (it looks like a double-headed arrow). Now drag the column border to the right as far as you want. As you drag, a tooltip appears, telling you the character size and pixel width of the column. Both of these pieces of information play the same role—they tell you how wide the column is. Only the unit of measurement changes.

Bottom: When you release the mouse, Excel resizes the entire column of cells to the new width.

NOTE A column's character width doesn't really reflect how many characters (or letters) fit in a cell. Excel uses *proportional* fonts, in which different letters take up different amounts of room. For example, the letter W is typically much wider than the letter I. All this means is that the character width Excel shows you isn't a real indication of how many letters can fit in the column, but it's a useful way to compare column widths.

Adding Data

You can now begin adding your data: Simply fill in the rows under the column titles. Each row in the expense worksheet represents a separate purchase. (If you're familiar with databases, you can think of each row as a separate *record*.)

As Figure 1-6 shows, the first column is for dates, the second stores text, and the third holds numbers. Keep in mind that Excel doesn't impose any rules on what you type, so you're free to put text in the Price column. But if you don't keep a consistent kind of data in each column, you won't be able to easily analyze (or understand) your information later.

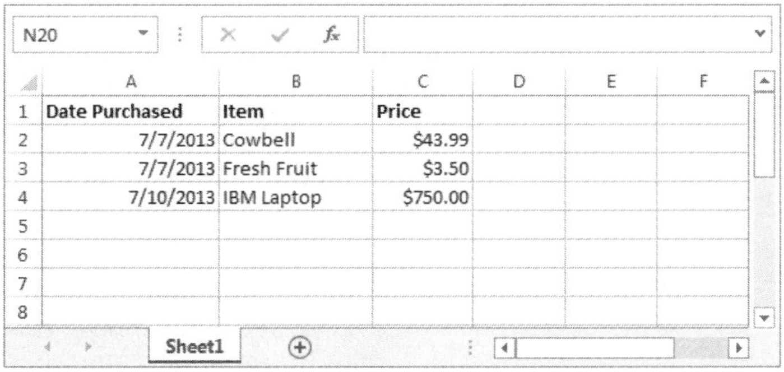

FIGURE 1-6

This rudimentary expense list has three items in it (in rows 2, 3, and 4). By default, Excel aligns the items in a column according to their data type. It aligns numbers and dates on the right, and text on the left.

That's it. You've now created a living, breathing worksheet. The next section explains how you can edit the data you just entered.

Editing Data

Every time you start typing in a cell, Excel erases any existing content in that cell. (You can also quickly remove the contents of a cell by moving to the cell and pressing Delete, which clears its contents.)

If you want to *edit* cell data instead of replacing it, you need to put the cell in *edit mode*, like this:

1. **Move to the cell you want to edit.**

   Use the mouse or the arrow keys to get to the correct cell.

2. **Put the cell in edit mode by pressing F2 or by double-clicking inside it.**

   Edit mode looks like ordinary text-entry mode, but you can use the arrow keys to position your cursor in the text you're editing. (When you aren't in edit mode, pressing these keys just moves you to another cell.)

3. **Complete your edit.**

   Once you modify the cell content, press Enter to confirm your changes or Esc to cancel your edit and leave the old value in the cell. Alternatively, you can click on another cell to accept the current value and go somewhere else. But while you're in edit mode, you can't use the arrow keys to move out of the cell.

TIP If you start typing new information into a cell and you decide you want to move to an earlier position in your entry (to make an alteration, for instance), just press F2. The cell box still looks the same, but now you're in edit mode, which means that you can use the arrow keys to move within the cell (instead of going from cell to cell). Press F2 again to return to data entry mode, where you can use the arrow keys to move to other cells.

As you enter data, you may discover the Bigtime Excel Display Problem (known to aficionados as BEDP): Cells in adjacent columns can overlap one another. Figure 1-7 illustrates the problem. One way to fix BEDP is to manually resize the column, as shown in Figure 1-5. Another option is to turn on text wrapping so you can fit multiple lines of text in a single cell, as described on page 151.

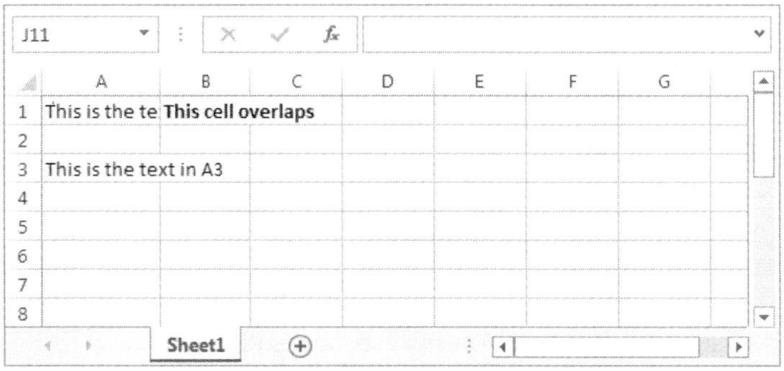

FIGURE 1-7

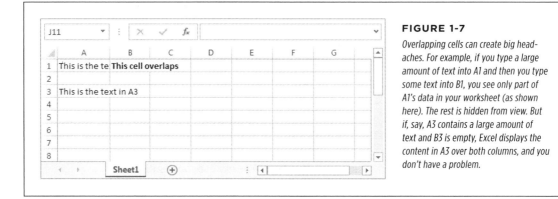

Overlapping cells can create big headaches. For example, if you type a large amount of text into A1 and then you type some text into B1, you see only part of A1's data in your worksheet (as shown here). The rest is hidden from view. But if, say, A3 contains a large amount of text and B3 is empty, Excel displays the content in A3 over both columns, and you don't have a problem.

Editing Cells with the Formula Bar

Just above the worksheet grid but under the ribbon is an indispensable editing tool called the *formula bar* (Figure 1-8). It displays the address of the active cell (like A1) on the left edge, and it shows you the current cell's contents.

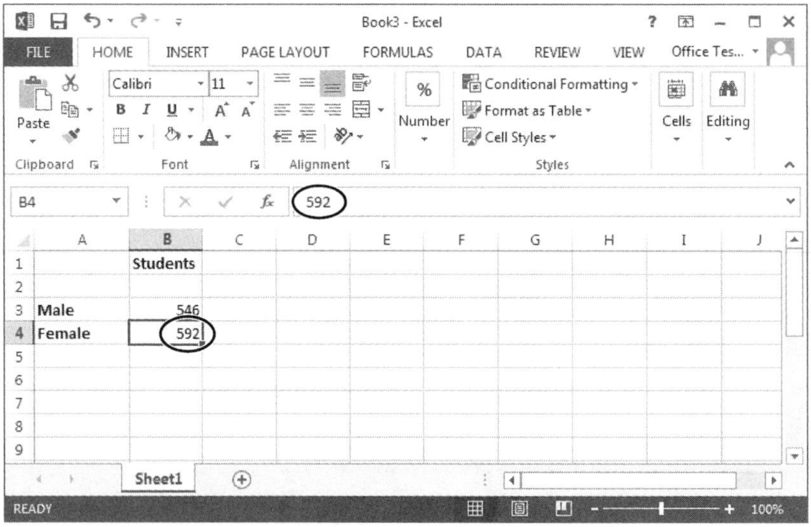

FIGURE 1-8

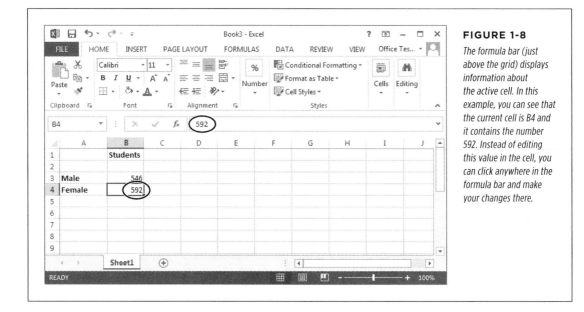

The formula bar (just above the grid) displays information about the active cell. In this example, you can see that the current cell is B4 and it contains the number 592. Instead of editing this value in the cell, you can click anywhere in the formula bar and make your changes there.

You can use the formula bar to enter and edit data instead of editing directly in your worksheet. This is particularly useful when a cell contains a formula or a large amount of information. That's because the formula bar gives you more work room than a typical cell. Just as with in-cell edits, you press Enter to confirm formula bar edits or Esc to cancel them. Or you can use the mouse: When you start typing in the formula bar, a checkmark and an "X" icon appear just to the left of the box where you're typing. Click the checkmark to confirm your entry or "X" to roll it back.

Ordinarily, the formula bar is a single line. If you have a *really* long entry in a cell (like a paragraph's worth of text), you need to scroll from one side to the other. However, there's another option—you can resize the formula bar so that it fits more information, as shown in Figure 1-9.

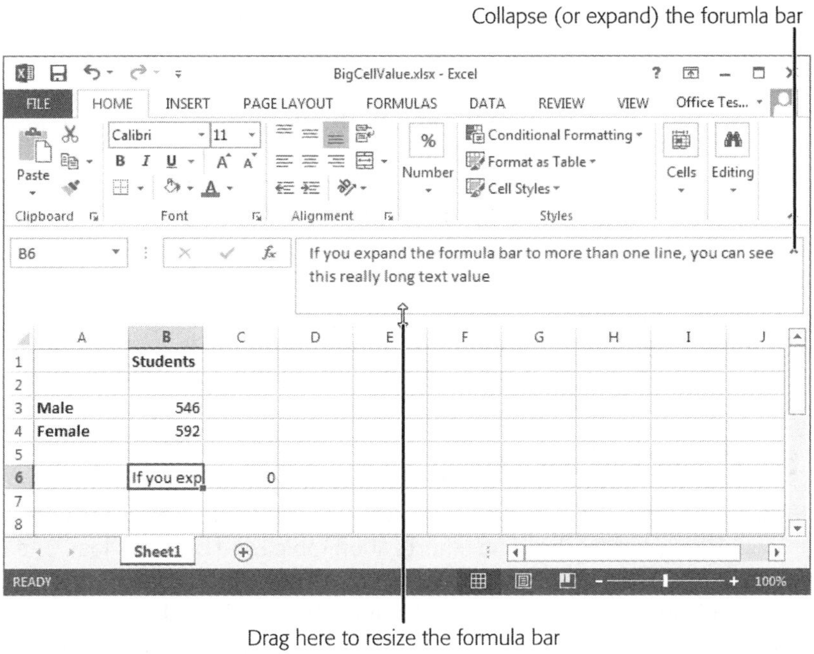

FIGURE 1-9

To enlarge the formula bar, click the bottom edge and pull down. You can make it two, three, four, or many more lines large. Best of all, once you get the size you want, you can use the expand/collapse button to the right of the formula bar to quickly expand it to your preferred size and collapse it back to the single-line view.

POWER USERS' CLINIC

Using R1C1 Reference Style

Most people like to identify columns with letters and rows with numbers. This system makes it easy to tell the difference between the two, and it lets you use short cell addresses like A10, B4, and H99. When you first install Excel, it uses this style of cell addressing.

However, Excel lets you use another cell addressing system called *R1C1*. In R1C1 style, Excel identifies both rows and columns with numbers. That means the cell address A10 becomes R10C1 (read this as Row 10, Column 1). The letters R and C tell you which part of the address represents the row number and which part is the column number. The R1C1 format reverses the order of conventional cell addressing.

R1C1 addressing isn't all that common, but it can be useful if you need to deal with worksheets that have more than 26 columns. With normal cell addressing, Excel runs out of letters after column 26, and it starts using two-letter column names (as in AA, AB, and so on). But this approach can get awkward. For example, if you want to find cell AX1, it isn't immediately obvious that cell AX1 is in column 50. On the other hand, the R1C1 address for the same cell—R1C50—gives you a clearer idea of where to find the cell.

To use R1C1 for a spreadsheet, select File→Options. This shows the Excel Options window, where you can change a wide array of settings. In the list on the left, choose Formulas to hone in on the section you need. Then, look under the "Working with formulas" heading, and turn on the "R1C1 reference style" checkbox.

R1C1 is a file-specific setting, which means that if someone sends you a spreadsheet saved using R1C1, you'll see the R1C1 cell addresses when you open the file, regardless of what type of cell addressing you use in your own spreadsheets. Fortunately, you can change cell addressing at any time using the Excel Options window.

Using the Ribbon

The focal point of the Excel window is the worksheet grid. It's where you enter and edit information, whether that's an amortization table for a business loan or a catalog of your rare Spider-Man comics. However, it won't be long before you need to direct your attention upwards, to the super-toolbar that sits at the top of the Excel window. This is the *ribbon*, and it ensures that even the geekiest Excel features are only a click or two away.

The Tabs of the Ribbon

Everything you'll ever want to do in Excel—from picking a fancy background color to pulling information out of a database—is packed into the ribbon. To accommodate all these buttons without becoming an over-stuffed turkey, the ribbon uses *tabs*. You start out with seven tabs. When you click one, you see a whole new collection of buttons (Figure 1-10).

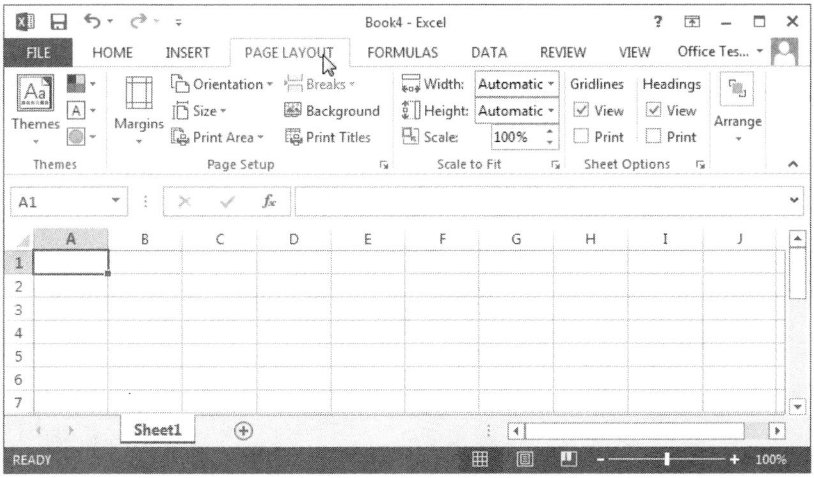

FIGURE 1-10

When you launch Excel, you start at the Home tab. But here's what happens when you click the Page Layout tab. Now, you have a slew of options for tasks like adjusting paper size and making a decent printout. Excel groups the buttons within a tab into smaller sections for clearer organization.

The ribbon makes it easy to find features because Excel groups related features under the same tab. Even better, once you find the button you need, you can often find other, associated commands by looking at the other buttons in the tab. In other words, the ribbon isn't just a convenient tool, it's also a great way to explore Excel.

The ribbon is full of craftsman-like detail. For example, when you hover over a button, you don't see a paltry two- or three-word description in a yellow rectangle. Instead, you see a friendly pop-up box with a mini-description of the feature and (often) a shortcut that lets you trigger the command from the keyboard. Another nice detail is the way you can jump from one tab to another at high velocity by positioning your mouse pointer over the ribbon and rolling the scroll wheel (if your mouse has a scroll wheel). And you're sure to notice the way the ribbon rearranges its buttons when you change the size of the Excel window (see Figure 1-11).

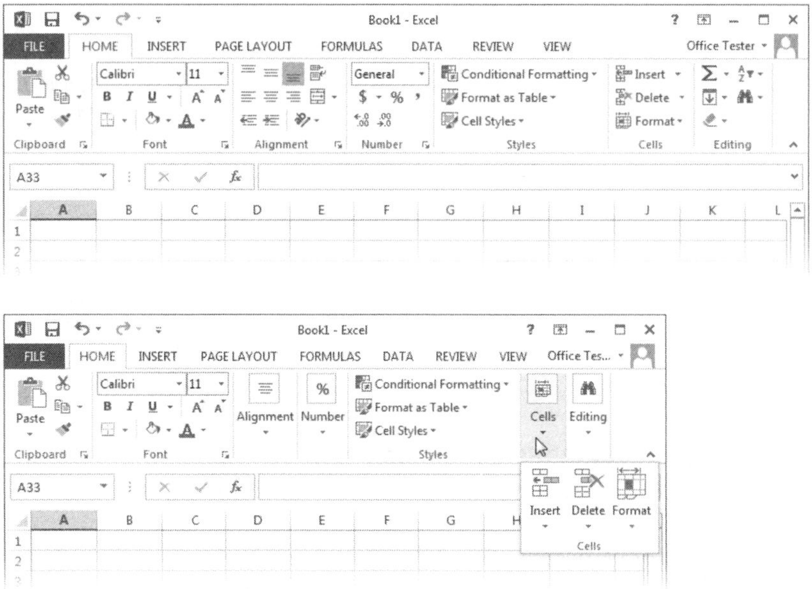

FIGURE 1-11

Top: A large Excel window gives you plenty of room to play. The ribbon uses the space effectively, making the most important buttons bigger.

Bottom: When you shrink the Excel window, the ribbon shrinks some buttons or hides their text to make room. Shrink small enough, and Excel starts to replace cramped sections with a single button, like the Alignment, Cells, and Editing sections shown here. Click the button and the missing commands appear in a drop-down panel.

Throughout this book, you'll dig through the ribbon's tabs to find important features. But before you start your journey, here's a quick overview of what each tab provides.

- **File** isn't really a toolbar tab, even though it appears first in the list. Instead, it's your gateway to Excel's backstage view, as described on page 23.
- **Home** includes some of the most commonly used buttons, like those for cutting and pasting text, formatting data, and hunting down important information with search tools.
- **Insert** lets you add special ingredients to your spreadsheets, like tables, graphics, charts, and hyperlinks.
- **Page Layout** is all about getting your worksheet ready for printing. You can tweak margins, paper orientation, and other page settings.
- **Formulas** are mathematical instructions that perform calculations. This tab helps you build super-smart formulas and resolve mind-bending errors.
- **Data** lets you get information from an outside data source (like a heavy-duty database) so you can analyze it in Excel. It also includes tools for dealing with large amounts of information, like sorting, filtering, and subgrouping data.

- **Review** includes the familiar Office proofing tools (like the spell-checker). It also has buttons that let you add comments to a worksheet and manage revisions.
- **View** lets you switch on and off a variety of viewing options. It also lets you pull off a few fancy tricks if you want to view several separate Excel spreadsheet files at the same time; see page 200.

NOTE In some circumstances, you may see tabs that aren't in this list. Macro programmers and other highly technical types use the Developer tab. (You'll learn how to reveal this tab on page 916.) The Add-Ins tab appears when you open workbooks created in previous versions of Excel that use custom toolbars. And finally, you can create a tab of your own if you're ambitious enough to customize the ribbon, as explained in the Appendix.

Collapsing the Ribbon

Most people are happy to have the ribbon sit at the top of the Excel window, with all its buttons on hand. But serious number-crunchers demand maximum space for their data—they'd rather look at another row of numbers than a pumped-up toolbar. If this describes you, then you'll be happy to find out that you can *collapse* the ribbon, which shrinks it down to a single row of tab titles, as shown in Figure 1-12. To collapse it, just double-click the current tab title. (Or click the tiny up-pointing icon in the top-right corner of the ribbon, right next to the help icon.)

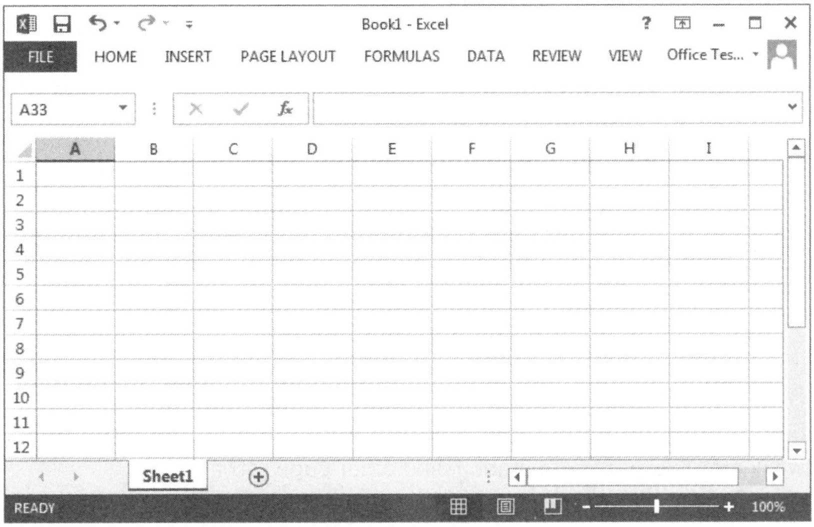

FIGURE 1-12

Do you want to use every square inch of screen space for your cells? You can collapse the ribbon (as shown here) by double-clicking any tab. Click a tab to pop it open temporarily, or double-click a tab to bring the ribbon back for good. And if you want to perform the same trick without lifting your fingers from the keyboard, use the shortcut Ctrl+F1.

Even if you collapse the ribbon, you can still use all its features. All you need to do is click a tab. For example, if you click Home, the Home tab pops open over your worksheet. As soon as you click the button you want in the Home tab (or click a cell in your worksheet), the ribbon collapses again. The same trick works if you trigger a command in the ribbon using the keyboard, as described in the next section.

If you use the ribbon only occasionally, or if you prefer to use keyboard shortcuts, it makes sense to collapse the ribbon. Even then, you can still use the ribbon commands—it just takes an extra click to open the tab. On the other hand, if you make frequent trips to the ribbon or you're learning about Excel and like to browse the ribbon to see what features are available, don't bother collapsing it. The two or three spreadsheet rows you'll lose are well worth it.

Using the Ribbon with the Keyboard

If you're an unredeemed keyboard lover, you'll be happy to hear that you can trigger ribbon commands with the keyboard. The trick is using *keyboard accelerators*, a series of keystrokes that starts with the Alt key (the same key you used to use to get to a menu). When you use a keyboard accelerator, you *don't* hold down all the keys at the same time. (As you'll soon see, some of these keystrokes contain so many letters that you'd be playing Finger Twister if you tried.) Instead, you hit the keys one after the other.

The trick to keyboard accelerators is understanding that once you hit the Alt key, there are two things you do, in this order:

1. **Pick the ribbon tab you want.**
2. **Choose a command in that tab.**

Before you can trigger a specific command, you *must* select the correct tab (even if it's already selected). Every accelerator requires at least two key presses after you hit the Alt key. You need to press even more keys to dig through submenus.

By now, this whole process probably seems hopelessly impractical. Are you really expected to memorize dozens of accelerator key combinations?

Fortunately, Excel is ready to help you out with a feature called KeyTips. Here's how it works: When you press Alt, letters magically appear over every tab in the ribbon. Once you hit the corresponding key to pick a tab, letters appear over every button in that tab (Figure 1-13). Once again, you press the corresponding key to trigger the command (Figure 1-14).

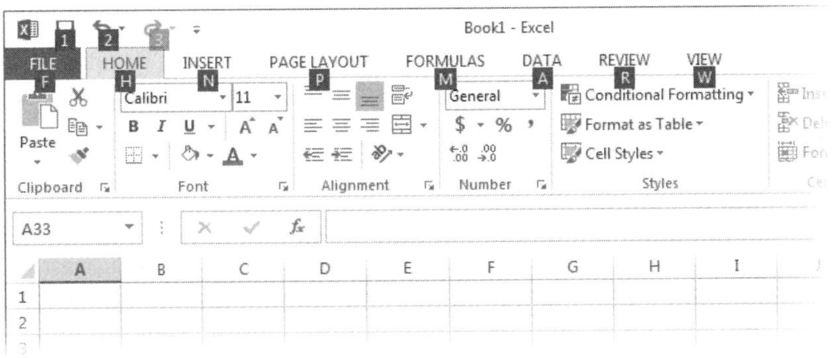

FIGURE 1-13

When you press Alt, Excel displays KeyTips next to every tab, over the File menu, and over the buttons in the Quick Access toolbar. If you follow up with M (for the Formulas tab), you'll see letters next to every command in that tab, as shown in Figure 1-11.

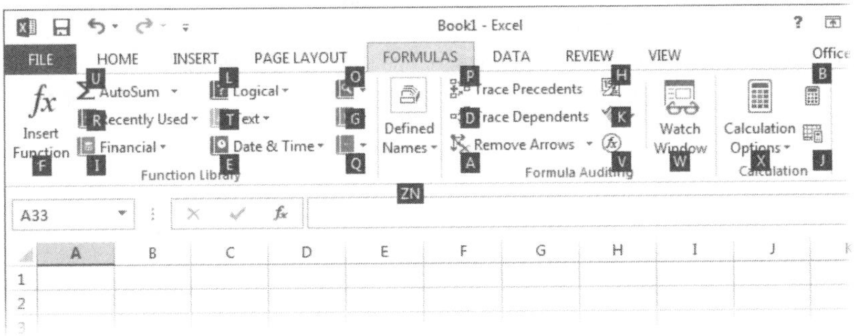

FIGURE 1-14

You can now follow up with F to trigger the Insert Function button, U to get to the AutoSum feature, and so on. Don't bother trying to match letters with tab or button names—there are so many features packed into the ribbon that in many cases the letters don't mean anything at all.

Sometimes, a command might have two letters, in which case you need to press both keys, one after the other. (For example, the Find & Select button on the Home tab has the letters FD. To trigger it, press Alt, then H, then F, and then D.)

TIP You can go back one step in KeyTips mode by pressing Esc. Or, you can stop cold without triggering a command by pressing Alt again.

Excel gives you other shortcut keys that don't use the ribbon. These are key combinations that start with the Ctrl key. For example, Ctrl+C copies highlighted text, and Ctrl+S saves your work. Usually, you find out about a shortcut key by hovering over a command with your mouse. For example, hover over the Paste button in the ribbon's Home tab, and you see a tooltip that tells you its timesaving shortcut key, Ctrl+V. And if you worked with a previous version of Excel, you'll find that Excel 2013 uses almost all the same shortcut keys.

NOSTALGIA CORNER

Excel 2003 Menu Shortcuts

If you've worked with an old version of Excel, you might have trained yourself to use menu shortcuts—key combinations that open a menu and pick out the command you want. For example, if you press Alt+E in Excel 2003, the Edit menu pops open. You can then press the S key to choose the Paste Special command.

At first glance, it doesn't look like these keyboard shortcuts will amount to much in Excel 2013. After all, Excel 2013 doesn't even have a corresponding series of menus! Fortunately, Microsoft went to a little extra trouble to make life easier for longtime Excel aficionados. The result is that you can still use your menu shortcuts, but they work in a slightly different way.

When you hit Alt+E in Excel 2013, you see a tooltip appear over the top of the ribbon (Figure 1-15) that lets you know you've started to enter an Excel 2003 menu shortcut. If you go on to press S, you wind up at the familiar Paste Special window, because Excel knows what you're trying to do. It's almost as though Excel has an invisible menu at work behind the scenes.

Of course, this feature can't help you out all the time. It doesn't work if you try to use one of the few commands that don't exist any longer. And if you need to see the menu to remember what key to press next, you're out of luck. All Excel gives you is the tooltip.

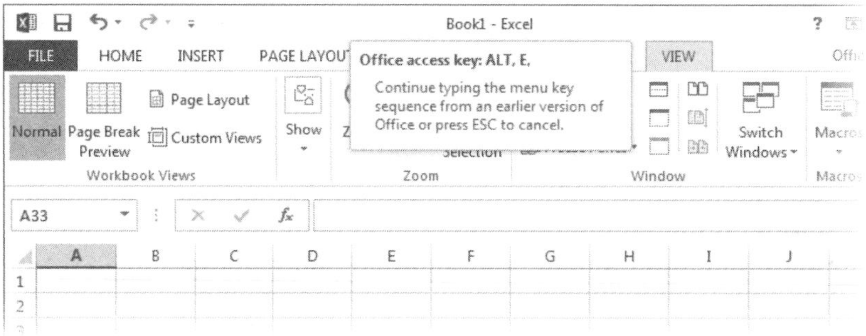

FIGURE 1-15

When you press Alt+E in Excel 2013, you trigger the "imaginary" Edit menu originally in Excel 2003 and earlier. You can't actually see the menu, because it doesn't exist in Excel 2013, but the tooltip lets you know that Excel is paying attention. You can now complete your action by pressing the next key for the menu command you're nostalgic for.

The Quick Access Toolbar

Keen eyes will have noticed the tiny bit of screen real estate just above the ribbon. It holds a series of tiny icons, like the toolbars in older versions of Excel (Figure 1-16). This is the Quick Access toolbar (or QAT, to Excel nerds).

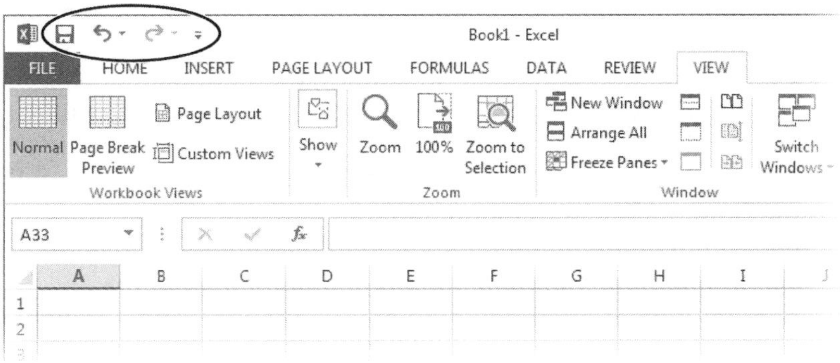

FIGURE 1-16

The Quick Access toolbar puts the Save, Undo, and Redo commands right at your fingertips. Excel provides easy access to these commands because most people use them more frequently than any others. But as you'll learn in the Appendix, you can add any commands you want here.

If the Quick Access toolbar were nothing but a specialized shortcut for three commands, it wouldn't be worth the bother. But it has one other notable attribute: You can customize it. In other words, you can remove commands you don't use and add your own favorites. The Appendix of this book (page 945) shows you how.

Microsoft has deliberately kept the Quick Access toolbar very small. It's designed to provide a carefully controlled outlet for those customization urges. Even if you go wild stocking the Quick Access toolbar with your own commands, the rest of the ribbon remains unchanged. (And that means a co-worker or spouse can still use Excel, no matter how dramatically you change the QAT.)

Using the Status Bar

Though people often overlook it, Excel's status bar (Figure 1-17) is a good way to monitor the program's current state. For example, if you save or print a document, the status bar shows the progress of the save operation or print job. If your task is simple, the progress indicator may disappear before you even have a chance to notice it. But if you're performing a time-consuming operation—say, printing an 87-page table of the hotel silverware you happen to own—you can look to the status bar to see how things are coming along.

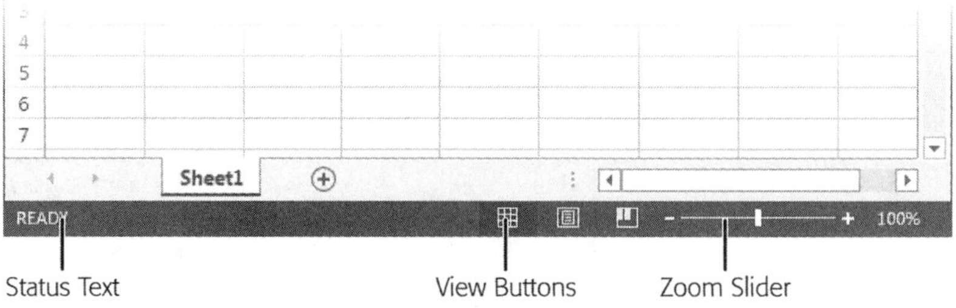

FIGURE 1-17

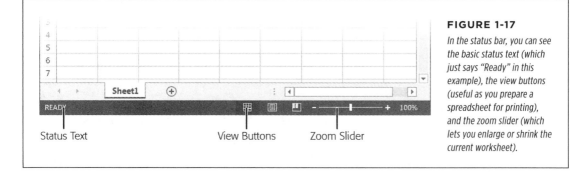

In the status bar, you can see the basic status text (which just says "Ready" in this example), the view buttons (useful as you prepare a spreadsheet for printing), and the zoom slider (which lets you enlarge or shrink the current worksheet).

The status bar combines several types of information. The leftmost area shows Cell Mode, which displays one of three indicators:

- **Ready** means that Excel isn't doing anything much at the moment, other than waiting to execute a command.
- **Enter** appears when you start typing a new value into a cell.
- **Edit** means you currently have the cell in edit mode, and pressing the left and right arrow keys moves through the data within a cell, instead of moving from cell to cell. You can place a cell in edit mode or take it out of edit mode by pressing F2.

Farther to the right of the status bar are the view buttons, which let you switch to Page Layout view or Page Break Preview. These help you see what your worksheet will look like when you print it. They're covered in Chapter 7.

The zoom slider is next to the view buttons, at the far right edge of the status bar. You can slide it to the left to zoom out (which fits more information into your Excel window) or slide it to the right to zoom in (and take a closer look at fewer cells). You can learn more about zooming on page 190.

In addition, the status bar displays other miscellaneous indicators. If you press the Scroll Lock key, for example, a Scroll Lock indicator appears in the status bar (next to the "Ready" text). This indicator tells you that you're in *scroll mode*, where the arrow keys don't move you from one cell to another, but scroll the entire worksheet up, down, or to the side. Scroll mode is a great way to check out another part of your spreadsheet without leaving your current position.

You can control what indicators appear in the status bar by configuring it. To see the list of possibilities, right-click the status bar (Figure 1-8). Table 1-2 describes the options.

TABLE 1-1 *Status bar indicators*

INDICATOR	MEANING
Cell Mode	Shows Ready, Edit, or Enter depending on the state of the current cell.
Flash Fill Blank Cells and Flash Fill Changed Cells	Shows the number of cells that were skipped (left blank) and the number of cells that were filled after a Flash Fill operation (page 65).
Signatures, Information Management Policy, and Permissions	Displays information about the rights and restrictions of the current spreadsheet. These features come into play only if you use a SharePoint server to share spreadsheets among groups of people (usually in a corporate environment).
Caps Lock	Indicates whether you have Caps Lock mode on. When it is, Excel automatically capitalizes every letter you type. To turn Caps Lock on or off, hit the Caps Lock key.
Num Lock	Indicates whether Num Lock mode is on. When it is, you can use the numeric keypad (typically on the right side of your keyboard) to type in numbers more quickly. When this sign's off, the numeric keypad controls cell navigation instead. To turn Num Lock on or off, press Num Lock.
Scroll Lock	Indicates whether Scroll Lock mode is on. When it's on, you can use the arrow keys to scroll through a worksheet without changing the active cell. (In other words, you can control your scrollbars by just using your keyboard.) This feature lets you look at all the information in your worksheet without losing track of the cell you're currently in. You can turn Scroll Lock mode on or off by pressing Scroll Lock.
Fixed Decimal	Indicates when Fixed Decimal mode is on. When it is, Excel automatically adds a set number of decimal places to the values you enter in any cell. For example, if you tell Excel to use two fixed decimal places and you type the number 5 into a cell, Excel actually enters 0.05. This seldom-used featured is handy for speed typists who need to enter reams of data in a fixed format. You can turn this feature on or off by selecting File→Options, choosing the Advanced section, and then looking under "Editing options" to find the "Automatically insert a decimal point" setting. Once you turn this checkbox on, you can choose the number of decimal places displayed (the standard option is 2).
Overtype Mode	Indicates when you have Overwrite mode turned on. Overwrite mode changes how cell edits work. When you edit a cell with Overwrite mode on, the new characters that you type overwrite existing characters (rather than displacing them). You can turn Overwrite mode on or off by pressing Insert.

INDICATOR	MEANING
End Mode	Indicates that you've pressed End, which is the first key in many two-key combinations; the next key determines what happens. For example, hit End and then Home to move to the bottom-right cell in your worksheet.
Macro Recording	Macros are automated routines that perform some task in an Excel spreadsheet. The Macro Recording indicator shows a record button (which looks like a red circle superimposed on a worksheet) that lets you start recording a new macro. You'll learn more about macros in Chapter 29.
Selection Mode	Indicates the current Selection mode. You have two options: normal mode and extended selection. When you press the arrows keys with Extended selection on, Excel automatically selects all the rows and columns you cross as you move around the spreadsheet. Extended selection is a useful keyboard alternative to dragging your mouse to select swaths of the grid. To turn Extended selection on or off, press F8. You'll learn more about selecting cells and moving them around in Chapter 3.
Page Number	Shows the current page and the total number of pages (as in "page 2 of 4"). This indicator appears only in Page Layout view (as described on page 209).
Average, Count, Numerical Count, Minimum, Maximum, Sum	Show the result of a calculation on selected cells. For example, the Sum indicator totals the value of all the numeric cells selected. You'll take a closer look at this handy trick on page 88.
Upload Status	Does nothing (that we know of). Excel does show a handy indicator in the status bar when you're uploading files to the Web, as you'll learn in Chapter 26. However, Excel always displays the upload status when needed, and this setting doesn't seem to have any effect.
View Shortcuts	Shows the three view buttons that let you switch between Normal view, Page Layout view, and Page Break Preview.
Zoom	Shows the current zoom percentage (like 100 percent for a normal-sized spreadsheet, and 200 percent for a spreadsheet that's blown up to twice the magnification).
Zoom Slider	Lets you zoom in (by moving the slider to the right) or out (by moving it to the left) to see more information at once.

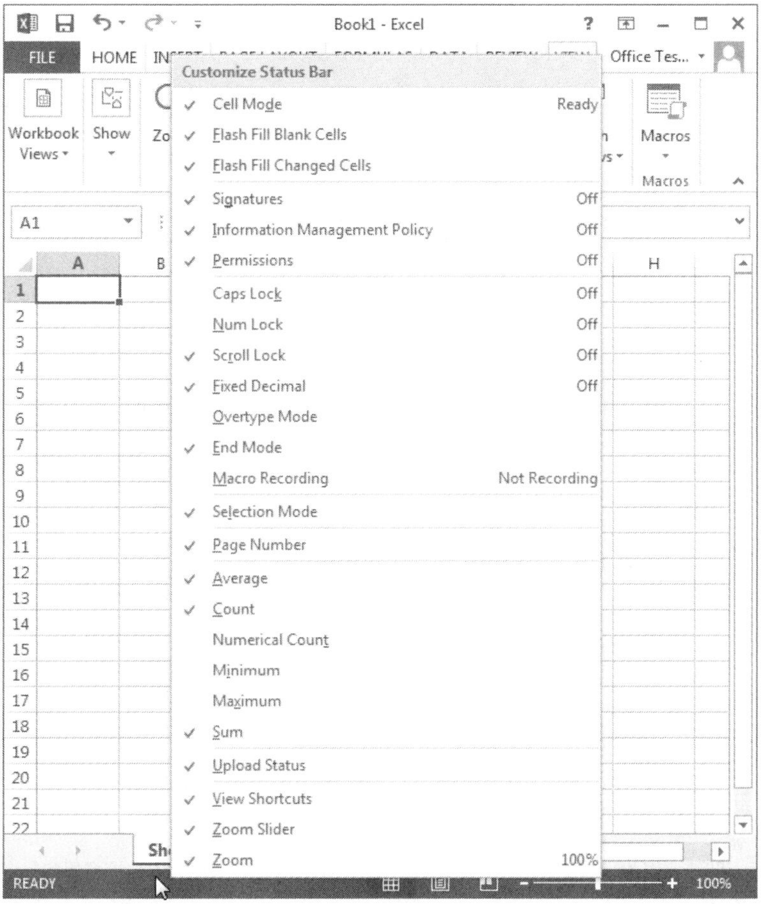

FIGURE 1-18

Every item that has a checkmark appears in the status bar when you need it. For example, if you choose Caps Lock, the text "Caps Lock" appears in the status bar whenever you hit the Caps Lock key. The text that appears on the right side of the list tells you the current value of the indicator. In this example, Caps Lock mode is currently off and the Cell Mode text says "Ready."

Going Backstage

Your data is the star of the show. That's why the creators of Excel refer to your worksheet as being "on stage." The auditorium is the Excel main window, which—as you've just seen—includes the handy ribbon, formula bar, and status bar. Sure, it's a strange metaphor. But once you understand it, you'll realize the rationale for Excel's *backstage view*, which temporarily takes you away from your worksheet and lets you concentrate on other tasks that don't involve entering or editing data. These tasks include saving your spreadsheet, opening more spreadsheets, printing your work, and changing Excel's settings.

To switch to backstage view, click the File button to the left of the Home ribbon tab. Excel temporarily tucks your worksheet out of sight (although it's still open and waiting for you). This gives Excel the space it needs to display information related to the task at hand, as shown in Figure 1-19. For example, if you plan to print your spreadsheet, Excel's backstage view previews the printout. Or if you want to open an existing spreadsheet, Excel can display a detailed list of files you recently worked on.

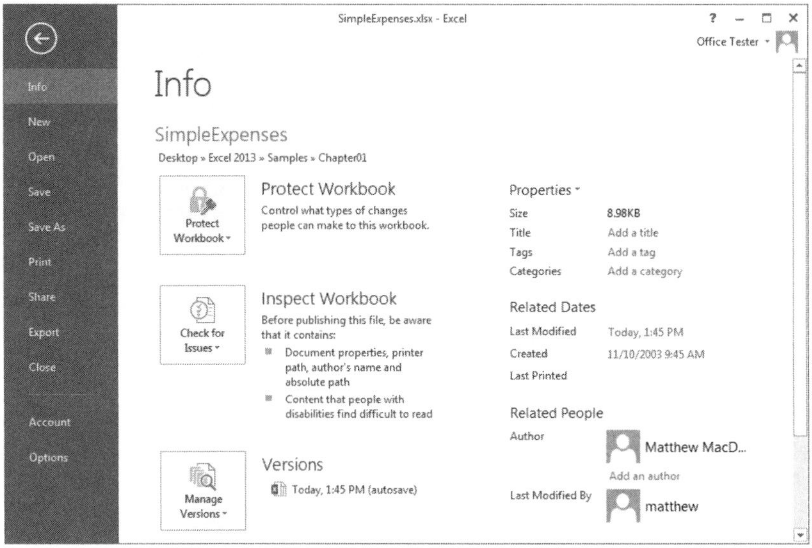

FIGURE 1-19

When you first switch to backstage view, Excel shows the Info page, which provides basic information about your workbook file, its size, when it was last edited, who edited it, and so on (see the column on the far right). The Info page also provides the gateway to three important features: document protection (Chapter 21), compatibility checking (page 31), and AutoRecover backups (page 38). To go to another section, click a different command in the column on the far left.

To get out of backstage view and return to your worksheet, press Esc or click the arrow-in-a-circle icon in the top-right corner of backstage view.

The key to using backstage view is the menu of commands that runs in a strip along the left side of the window. You click a command to get to the page for the task you want to perform. For example, to create a new spreadsheet (in addition to the one you're currently working on), you begin by clicking the New command, as shown in Figure 1-20.

TIP You don't need to go to backstage view to create a new, blank spreadsheet. Instead, hit the shortcut key Ctrl+N while you're in the worksheet grid. Excel will launch a new window, with a new, blank worksheet at the ready.

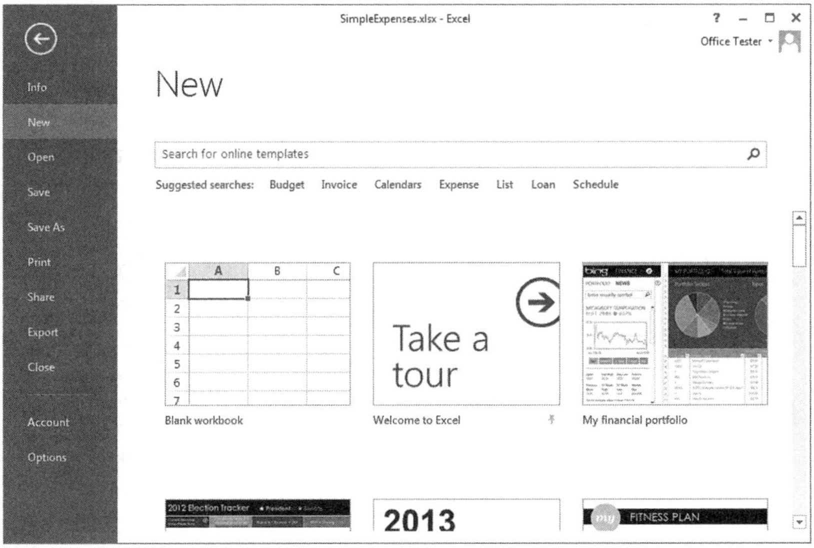

FIGURE 1-20

When you click New, you see a page resembling the welcome page that greets you when you start Excel. To create a new, empty workbook, click "Blank workbook." Excel opens the workbook in a new window, so that it's separate from your current workbook, which Excel leaves untouched.

Here are some of the things you'll do in Excel's backstage view:

- **Work with files** (create, open, close, and save them) with the help of the New, Open, Save, and Save As commands. You'll spend the rest of this chapter learning the fastest and most effective ways to save and open Excel files.
- **Print your work** (Chapter 7) and **email** it to other people (Chapter 25) using the Print and Share commands.
- **Prepare a workbook** you want to share with others. For example, you can check its compatibility with older versions of Excel (Chapter 1) and lock your document to prevent other people from changing numbers (Chapter 24). You find these options under the Info command.
- **Configure your Office account**—that's the email address and password you use to access Microsoft's SkyDrive service for storing spreadsheets online (page 706) or for your Office 365 account (if you're a subscriber; see page xvii). To do this, click the Account command.
- **Configure how Excel behaves.** Once you're in backstage view, click Options to launch the Excel Options window, an all-in-one place for configuring Excel.

Saving Files

As everyone who's been alive for at least three days knows, you should save your work early and often. Excel is no exception. To save a file for the first time, choose File→Save or File→Save As. Either way, you end up at the Save As page in backstage view (Figure 1-21).

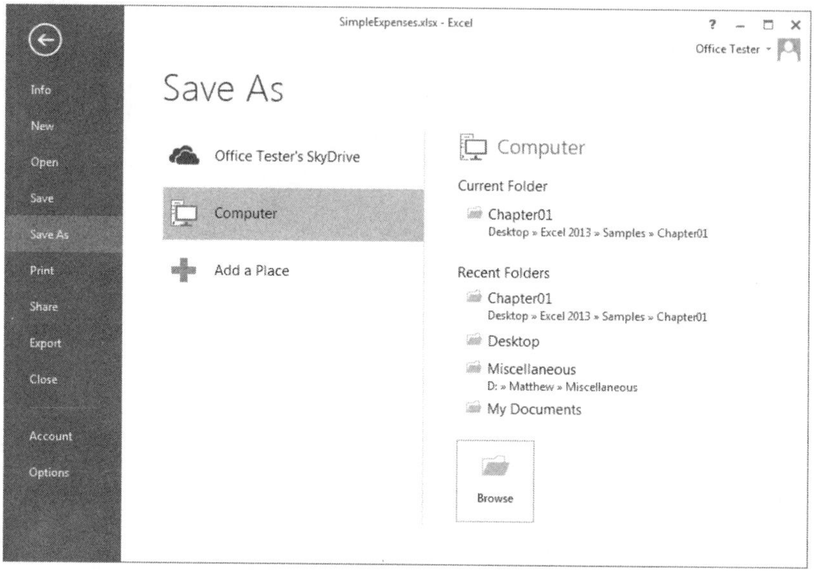

FIGURE 1-21

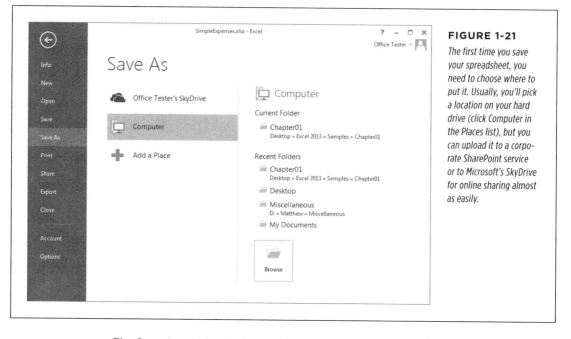

The first time you save your spreadsheet, you need to choose where to put it. Usually, you'll pick a location on your hard drive (click Computer in the Places list), but you can upload it to a corporate SharePoint service or to Microsoft's SkyDrive for online sharing almost as easily.

The Save As window includes a list of *places*—locations where you can store your work. The exact list depends on how you configured Excel, but here are some of the options you're likely to see:

- **Computer.** Choose this to store your spreadsheet somewhere on your computer's hard drive. This is the most common option. When you click Computer, Excel lists the folders where you recently saved or opened files (see Figure 1-21, on the right). To save a file to one of these locations, select the folder. Or, click the big Browse button at the bottom to find a new location. Either way, Excel opens the familiar Save As window, where you type in a name for your file (Figure 1-22).

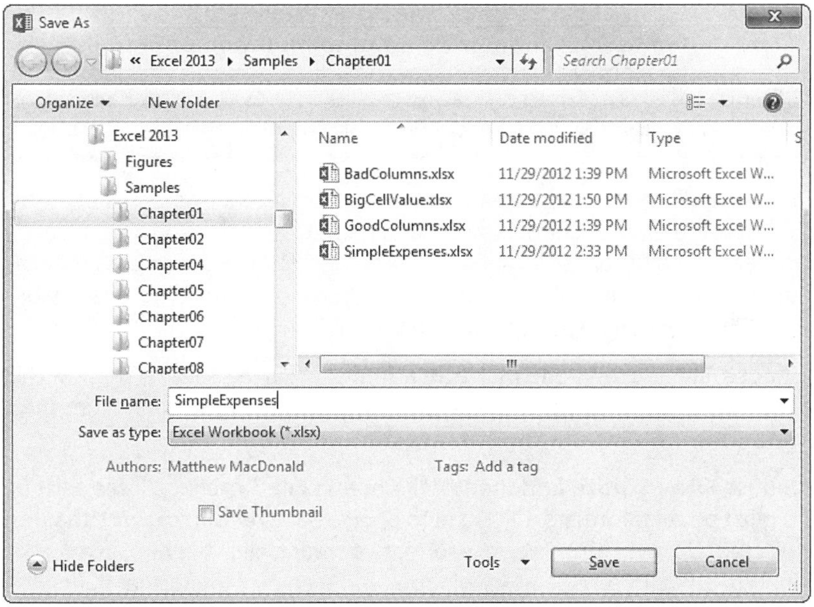

FIGURE 1-22

Once you pick a location for your file, you need to give it a name. This window won't surprise you, because it's the same Save As window that puts in an appearance in almost every document-based Windows application.

- **SkyDrive.** When you set up Excel, you can supply the email address and password you use for Microsoft services like Hotmail, Messenger, and SkyDrive, Microsoft's online file-storage system. Excel features some nifty SkyDrive integration features. For example, you can upload a spreadsheet straight to the Web by clicking your personalized SkyDrive item in the Places list, and then choosing one of your SkyDrive folders.

NOTE The advantage of putting a file on SkyDrive is that you can open and edit it from another Excel-equipped computer, without needing to worry about copying or emailing the file. The other advantage is that other people can edit your file with the Excel Web App. You'll learn more about SkyDrive and the Excel Web App in Chapter 23.

- **SharePoint.** If you're running a computer on a company network, you may be able to store your work on a SharePoint server. Doing so not only lets you share your work with everyone else on your team, it lets you tap into SharePoint's excellent workflow features. (For example, your organization could have a process set up where you save expense reports to a SharePoint server, and they're automatically passed on to your boss for approval and then accounting for payment.) A SharePoint server won't necessarily have the word "SharePoint" in its place name, but it will have the globe-and-server icon to let you know it's a web location.

After you save a spreadsheet once, you can quickly save it again by choosing File→Save, or by pressing Ctrl+S. Or look up at the top of the Excel window in the Quick Access toolbar for the tiny Save button, which looks like an old-style diskette. To save your spreadsheet with a new name or in a new place, select File→Save As, or press F12.

TIP Saving a spreadsheet is an almost instantaneous operation, and you should get used to doing it regularly. After you make any significant change to a sheet, hit Ctrl+S to store the latest version of your data.

Ordinarily, you'll save your spreadsheets in the modern .xlsx format, which is described in the next section. However, sometimes you'll need to convert your spreadsheet to a different type of file—for example, if you want to pass them along to someone using a very old version of Excel, or a different type of spreadsheet program. There are two ways you can do this:

- **Choose File→Save As and pick a location.** Then, in the Save As window (Figure 1-22), click "Save as type" and then pick the format you want from the long drop-down list.
- **Choose File→Export, and then click Change File Type.** You'll see a list of the 10 most popular formats. Click one to open a Save As window with that format selected. Or, if you don't see the format you want, click the big Save As button underneath to open a Save As window, and then pick the format yourself from the "Save as type" drop-down list.

Excel lets you save your spreadsheet in a variety of formats, including the classic Excel 95 format from more than a decade ago. If you want to look at your spreadsheet using a mystery program, use the CSV file type, which produces a comma-delimited text file that almost all spreadsheet programs can read (comma-delimited means that commas separate the information in each cell). And in the following sections, you'll learn more about sharing your work with old versions of Excel (page 31) or putting it in PDF form so anyone can view and print it (page 34). But first, you need to take a closer look at Excel's standard file format.

The Excel File Format

Modern versions of Excel, including Excel 2013, use the *.xlsx* file format (which means your saved spreadsheet will have a name like *HotelSilverware.xlsx*). Microsoft introduced this format in Excel 2007, and it comes with significant advantages:

- **It's compact.** The .xlsx format uses ZIP file compression, so spreadsheet files are smaller—as much as 75 percent smaller than Excel 2003 files. And even though the average hard drive is already large enough to swallow millions of old-fashioned Excel files, a more compact format is easier to share online and via email.

- **It's less error-prone.** The .xlsx format carefully separates ordinary content, pictures, and macro code into separate sections. That means that if a part of your Excel file is damaged (due to a faulty hard drive, for example), there's a good chance that you can still retrieve the rest of the information. (You'll learn about Excel disaster recovery on page 38.)
- **It's extensible.** The .xlsx format uses XML (the eXtensible Markup Language), which is a standardized way to store information. (You'll learn more about XML in Chapter 28.) XML storage doesn't benefit the average person, but it's sure to earn a lot of love from companies that use custom software in addition to Excel. As long as you store the Excel documents in XML format, these companies can create automated programs that pull the information they need straight out of the spreadsheet, without going through Excel itself. These programs can also generate made-to-measure Excel documents on their own.

For all these reasons, .xlsx is the format of choice for Excel 2013. However, Microsoft prefers to give people all the choices they could ever need (rather than make life really simple), and Excel file formats are no exception. In fact, the .xlsx file format actually comes in *two* additional flavors.

First, there's the closely related .xls*m*, which lets you store macro code with your spreadsheet data. If you add macros to a spreadsheet, Excel prompts you to use this file type when you save your work. (You'll learn about macros in Chapter 29.)

Second, there's the optimized .xls*b* format, which is a specialized option that might be a bit faster when opening and saving gargantuan spreadsheets. The .xlsb format has the same automatic compression and error-resistance as .xlsx, but it doesn't use XML. Instead, it stores information in raw *binary* form (good ol' ones and zeros), which is speedier in some situations. To use the .xlsb format, choose File→Export, click Change File Type, and then choose "Binary Workbook (.xlsb)" from the drop-down list.

Most of the time, you don't need to think about Excel's file format. You can just create your spreadsheets, save them, and let Excel take care of the rest. The only time you need to stop and think twice is when you share your work with other, less fortunate people who have older versions of Excel, such as Excel 2003. You'll learn how to deal with this challenge in the following sections.

TIP Don't use the .xlsb format unless you try it out and find that it really does give you better performance. Usually, .xlsx and .xlsb are just as fast. And remember, the only time you'll see any improvement is when you load or save a file. Once you open your spreadsheet in Excel, everything else (like scrolling around and performing calculations) happens at the same speed.

POWER USERS' CLINIC

Under the Hood with .xlsx Files

Here's a shocking secret: The .xlsx file format is actually a ZIP file in disguise. It's composed of several files that are compressed and then packaged together as a single unit. With a little know-how, you can take a look at these hidden files-within-a-file, which makes for a great Excel party trick. Here's how:

1. Save your Excel spreadsheet in .xlsx format.
2. Browse to the file (using Windows Explorer or your favorite file-management tool). If you're lazy, you can save the file to your desktop so you can manipulate it right there.
3. Right-click the file, and then choose Rename.
4. Change the file extension to .zip. So if you start with *BlackMarketDinnerware.xlsx*, change it to *BlackMarketDinnerware.zip*.
5. Open the ZIP file by double-clicking the file name.
6. Now you can see the files hidden inside your Excel file. Excel organizes them into several folders (Figure 1-23). To find the actual content from your spreadsheet, head to xl→worksheets→sheet1.xml. Double-click the file name to open it and take a look at what's inside.
7. When you finish, rename the file using the .xlsx extension so you can open it in Excel.

To learn way more about the technical details of XML file storage, read the Microsoft white paper at *http://tinyurl.com/xmlfileformats*.

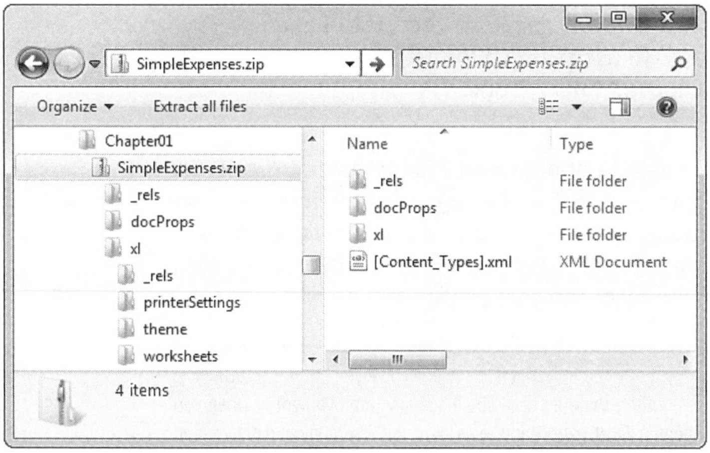

FIGURE 1-23

Inside every .xlsx file lurks a number of compressed files, each with different information. For example, separate files store printer settings, text styles, the name of the person who created the document, the composition of your workbook, and the individual worksheets themselves.

Sharing Your Spreadsheet with Older Versions of Excel

As you just learned, Excel 2013 uses the same .xlsx file format as Excel 2010 and Excel 2007. That means that an Excel 2013 fan can exchange files with an Excel 2010 devotee, and there won't be any technical problems.

However, a few issues can still trip you up when you share spreadsheets between different versions of Excel. For example, Excel 2013 introduces a few new formula functions, such as BASE (page 286). If you write a calculation in Excel 2013 that uses BASE(), the calculation won't work in Excel 2010. Instead of seeing the numeric result you want, your recipient will see an error code mixed in with the rest of the spreadsheet data.

To avoid this sort of problem, you need the help of an Excel tool called the Compatibility Checker. It scans your spreadsheet for features and formulas that will cause problems in Excel 2010 or Excel 2007.

To use the Compatibility Checker, follow these steps:

1. **Choose File→Info.**

   Excel switches into backstage view.

2. **Click the Check for Issues button, and choose Check Compatibility.**

   The Compatibility Checker scans your spreadsheet, looking for signs of trouble. It reports problems to you (Figure 1-24).

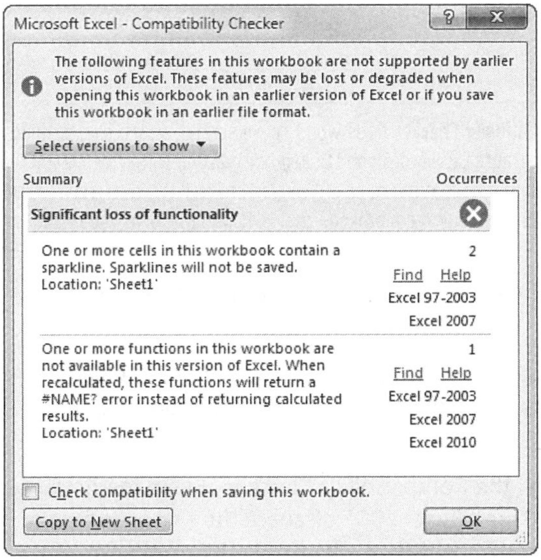

FIGURE 1-24

In this example, the Compatibility Checker found two potential problems. The first affects people using Excel 2007 or older, while the other affects people using Excel 2010 or older.

3. **Optionally, you can choose to hide compatibility problems that don't affect you.**

   The Compatibility Checker reports on three types of problems:

   - Problems that affect old—really old—versions of Excel (Excel 97 to Excel 2003).
   - Problems that affect Excel 2007 or earlier.
   - Problems that affect Excel 2010 or earlier.

   You don't necessarily need to worry about all these versions of Excel. For example, if you plan to share your files with Excel 2010 users but not with people using Excel 2007 or older, you don't need to pay attention to the first two categories, because they don't affect your peeps.

   To choose what errors the Compatibility Checker reports on, click the "Select versions to show" button and turn off the checkboxes next to the versions of Excel you don't want to consider. For example, you can turn off "Excel 97-2003" if you don't want to catch problems that affect only these versions of Excel.

4. **Review the problems.**

   You can ignore the Compatibility Checker issues, click Find to hunt each one down, or click Help to figure out the exact problem. You can also click "Copy to New Sheet" to insert a full compatibility report into your spreadsheet as a separate worksheet. This way, you can print it up and review it in the comfort of your cubicle. (To get back to the worksheet with your data, click the Sheet1 tab at the bottom of the window. Chapter 4 has more about how to use and manage multiple worksheets.)

NOTE The problems that the Compatibility Checker finds won't cause serious errors, like crashing your computer or corrupting your data. That's because Excel is designed to *degrade gracefully*. That means you can still open a spreadsheet that uses newer, unsupported features in an old version of Excel. However, you may receive a warning message and part of the spreadsheet may seem broken—that is, it won't work as you intended.

5. **Optionally, you can set the Compatibility Checker to run automatically for this workbook.**

   Turn on the "Check compatibility when saving this workbook" checkbox. Now, the Compatibility Checker runs each time you save your spreadsheet, just before Excel updates the file.

Once your work passes through the Compatibility Checker, you're ready to save it. Because Excel 2013, Excel 2010, and Excel 2007 all share the same file format, you don't need to perform any sort of conversion—just save your file normally. But if you want to share your spreadsheet with Excel 2003, follow the instructions in the next section.

Saving Your Spreadsheet for Excel 2003

Sharing your workbook with someone using Excel 2003 presents an additional consideration: Excel 2003 uses the older .xls format instead of the current-day .xlsx format.

There are two ways to resolve this problem:

- **Save your spreadsheet in the old format**. You can save a copy of your spreadsheet in the traditional .xls standard Microsoft has supported since Excel 97. To do so, choose File→Export, click Change File Type, and choose "Excel 97-2003 Workbook (*.xls)" from the list of file types.

NOTE If you keep your spreadsheet in Excel 2013 and share it with an Excel 2003 user, the sheet might look a little different when your recipient opens it. That's because, if Excel 2003 finds features it doesn't support, it simply ignores them.

- **Use a free add-in for older versions of Excel**. People stuck with Excel 2000, Excel 2002, or Excel 2003 *can* read your Excel 2013 files—they just need a free add-in from Microsoft. This is a good solution because it doesn't require you to do extra work, like saving both a current and a backward-compatible version of the spreadsheet. People with past-its-prime versions of Excel can find the add-in by surfing to *www.microsoft.com/downloads* and searching for "compatibility pack file formats" (or use the secret shortcut URL *http://tinyurl.com/y5w78r*). However, you should still run the Compatibility Checker to find out if your spreadsheet uses features that Excel 2003 doesn't support.

TIP If you save your Excel spreadsheet in the Excel 2003 format, make sure to keep a copy in the standard .xlsx format. Why? Because the old format isn't guaranteed to retain all your information, particularly if you use newer chart features or data visualization.

As you already know, each version of Excel introduces a small set of new features. Older versions don't support these features. The differences between Excel 2010 and Excel 2013 are small, but the differences between Excel 2003 and Excel 2013 are more significant.

Excel tries to help you out in two ways. First, whenever you save a file in .xls format, Excel automatically runs the Compatibility Checker to check for problems. Second, whenever you open a spreadsheet in the old .xls file format, Excel switches into *compatibility mode*. While the Compatibility Checker points out potential problems after the fact, compatibility mode is designed to prevent you from using unsupported features in the first place. For example, in compatibility mode you'll face these restrictions:

- Excel limits you to a smaller grid of cells (65,536 rows instead of 1,048,576).
- Excel prevents you from using really long or deeply nested formulas.
- Excel doesn't let you use some pivot table features.

In compatibility mode, these missing features aren't anywhere to be found. In fact, compatibility mode is so seamless that you might not even notice its limitations. The only clear indication that you're in Compatibility Mode appears at the title bar at the top of the Excel window. Instead of seeing something like CateringList.xlsx, you'll see "CateringList.xls [Compatibility Mode]."

NOTE When you save an Excel workbook in .xls format, Excel won't switch into compatibility mode right away. Instead, you need to close the workbook and reopen it.

If you decide at some point that you're ready to move into the modern world and convert your file to the .xlsx format favored by Excel 2013, you can use the trusty File→Save As command. However, there's an even quicker shortcut. Just choose File→Info and click the Convert button. This saves an Excel 2013 version of your file with the same name but with the extension .xlsx, and reloads the file so you get out of compatibility mode. It's up to you to delete your old .xls original if you don't need it anymore.

Saving Your Spreadsheet As a PDF

Sometimes you want to save a copy of your spreadsheet so that people can read it even if they don't have Excel (and even if they're running a different operating system, like Linux or Apple's OS X). One way to solve this problem is to save your spreadsheet as a PDF file. This gives you the best of both worlds—you keep all the rich formatting (for when you print your workbook), and you let people who don't have Excel (and possibly don't even have Windows) see your work. The disadvantage is that PDFs are for viewing only—there's no way for you to open a PDF in Excel and start editing it.

UP TO SPEED

Learning to Love PDFs

You've probably heard about PDFs, files saved in Adobe's popular format for sharing formatted, print-ready documents. People use PDFs to pass around product manuals, brochures, and all sorts of electronic documents. Unlike a document format like .xlsx, PDF files are designed to be viewed and printed, but not edited.

The best part about PDFs is that you can view them on just about any computer using the free Adobe Reader. You can download Adobe Reader at *http://get.adobe.com/reader*, but you probably don't need to. Most computers come with it installed because so many of today's programs use it (usually so you can view their electronic documentation). It's also widespread on the Web.

Incidentally, PDF isn't the only kid on the block. The Windows operating systems includes another electronic paper format called XPS, which works just as well as PDF for creating print-ready files. However, PDF is dramatically more popular and widespread, so it's the one to stick with for now. (If you're interested in saving an Excel document as an XPS file, you can do that, too—just choose XPS from the "Save as type" list.)

To save your spreadsheet as a PDF, select File→Export, click Create PDF/XPS Document (in the "File Types" section), and then click the Create PDF/XPS button. Excel opens a modified version of the Save As window that has a few additional options (Figure 1-25).

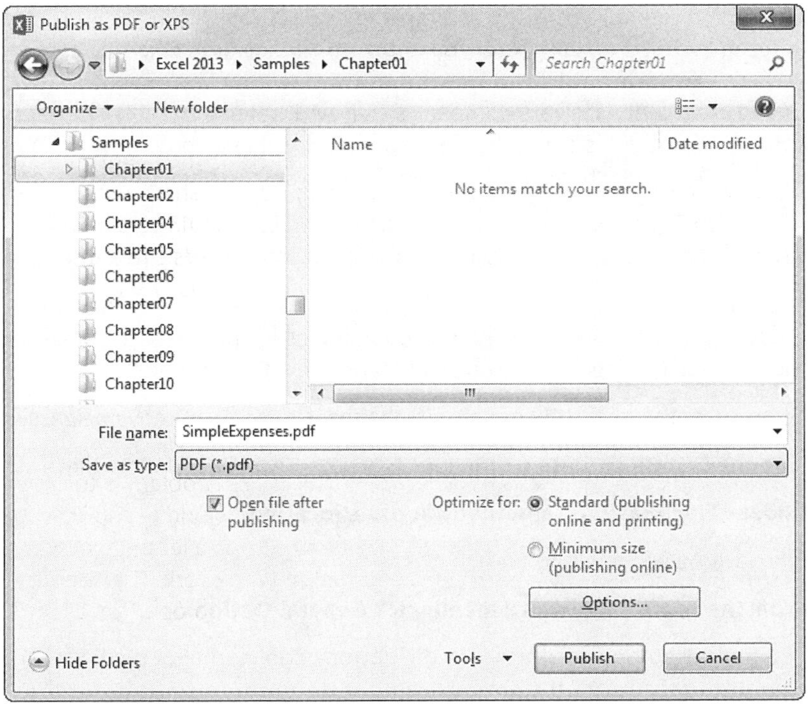

FIGURE 1-25

You can save PDF files at different resolutions and quality settings (which mostly affect graphics in your workbook, like pictures and charts). Normally, you use higher-quality settings if you want to print your PDF file, because printers use higher resolutions than computers.

The "Publish as PDF" window gives you some control over the quality of your printout using the "Optimize for" options. If you're just saving a PDF copy so other people can *view* your workbook, choose "Minimum size (publishing online)" to cut down on the storage space required. On the other hand, if people reading your PDF might want to print it out, choose "Standard (publishing online and printing)" to save a slightly larger PDF that makes for a better printout.

You can switch on the "Open file after publishing" setting to tell Excel to open the PDF file in Adobe Reader (assuming you have it installed) after it saves the file. That way, you can check the result.

Finally, if you want to publish only a portion of your spreadsheet as a PDF file, click the Options button to open a window with even more settings. You can publish just a fixed number of pages, just selected cells, and so on. These options mirror the choices you see when you print a spreadsheet (page 202). You also see a few more cryptic options, most of which you can safely ignore (they're intended for PDF nerds). One exception is the "Document properties" option—turn this off if you don't want the

PDF to keep track of certain information that identifies you, like your name. (Excel document properties are discussed in more detail on page 668.)

Password-Protecting Your Spreadsheet

Occasionally, you might want to add confidential information to a spreadsheet—a list of the hotels from which you've stolen spoons, for example. If your computer is on a network, the solution may be as simple as storing your file in the correct, protected location. But if you're afraid you might email the spreadsheet to the wrong people (say, executives at Four Seasons), or if you're about to expose systematic accounting irregularities in your company's year-end statements, you'll be happy to know that Excel provides a tighter degree of security. It lets you *password-protect* your spreadsheets, which means that anyone who wants to open them has to know the password you set.

Excel actually has two layers of password protection you can apply to a spreadsheet:

- You can prevent others from *opening* your spreadsheet unless they know the password. This level of security, which scrambles your data for anyone without the password (a process known as *encryption*), is the strongest.
- You can let others *read* but not *modify* the sheet unless they know the password.

To apply one or both of these restrictions to your spreadsheet, follow these steps:

1. **Choose File→Save As, and then choose a location.**

   The Save As window opens.

2. **From the Tools drop-down menu, pick General Options.**

   The Tools drop-down menu sits in the bottom-right corner of the Save As window, just to the left of the Save button.

   The General Options window appears.

3. **Type a password next to the security level you want to turn on (as shown in Figure 1-26), and then click OK.**

   The General Options window also gives you a couple of other unrelated options:

   - Turn on the "Always create backup" checkbox if you want a copy of your file in case something goes wrong with the first one (think of it as insurance). Excel creates a backup with the file extension *.xlk*. For example, if you save a workbook named *SimpleExpenses.xlsx* with the "Always create backup" option on, Excel creates a file named "Backup of *SimpleExpenses.xlk*" every time you save your spreadsheet. You can open the .xlk file in Excel just as you would an ordinary Excel file. When you do, you see that it is an exact copy of your work.

- Turn on the "Read-only recommended" checkbox to prevent other people from accidentally making changes to your spreadsheet. With this option, Excel displays a message every time you (or anyone else) opens the file. It politely suggests that you open the spreadsheet in *read-only mode*, which means that Excel won't let you make any changes to the file. Of course, it's entirely up to the person opening the file whether to accept this recommendation.

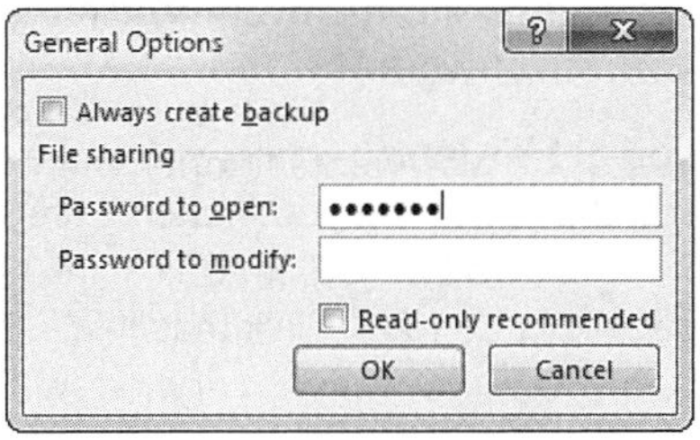

FIGURE 1-26

You can use any sequence of letters and numbers as a password. Passwords are case-sensitive (which means that PanAm is different from panam), and masked (which means that, when you type in the password, Excel displays just a series of asterisks).

4. **Click Save to store the file.**

   If you use a password to restrict people from opening the spreadsheet, Excel prompts you to supply the "password to open" the next time you open the file (Figure 1-27, top).

If you use a password to restrict people from modifying the spreadsheet, the next time you open this file, Excel gives you the choice, shown in Figure 1-27 bottom, to open it in *read-only mode* (which requires no password) or to open it in full edit mode (in which case you'll need to supply the "password to modify").

FIGURE 1-27

Top: You can give a spreadsheet two layers of protection. Assign a "password to open," and you'll see this window when you open the file.

Bottom: If you assign a "password to modify," you'll see the choices in this window. If you use both passwords, you'll see both windows, one after the other.

Disaster Recovery

The corollary to the edict "Save your data early and often" is the truism "Sometimes things fall apart quickly...before you even had a chance to back up." Fortunately, Excel includes an invaluable safety net called AutoRecover.

AutoRecover periodically saves backup copies of your spreadsheet while you work. If you suffer a system crash, you can retrieve the last backup even if you never managed to save the file yourself. Of course, even the AutoRecover backup won't necessarily have *all* the information you entered in your spreadsheet before the problem occurred. But if AutoRecover saves a backup every 10 minutes (the standard), at most you'll lose 10 minutes' worth of work.

If your computer does crash, when you get it running again, you can easily retrieve your last AutoRecover backup. In fact, the next time you launch Excel, it automatically checks the backup folder and, if it finds a backup, it adds a link named Show Recovered Files to Excel's welcome page (Figure 1-28). Click that link, and Excel adds a panel named Document Recovery to the left side of the Excel window (Figure 1-29).

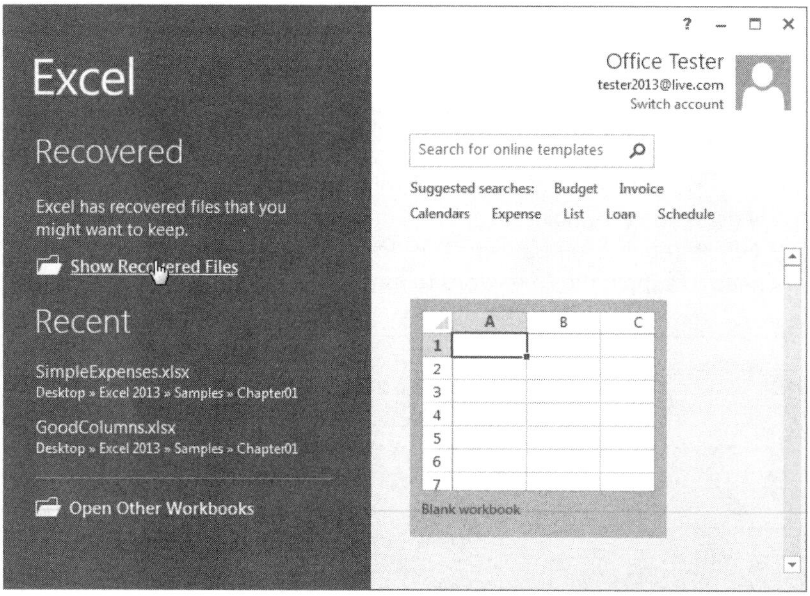

FIGURE 1-28

Excel's got your back—click Show Recovered Files to see what files it's rescued.

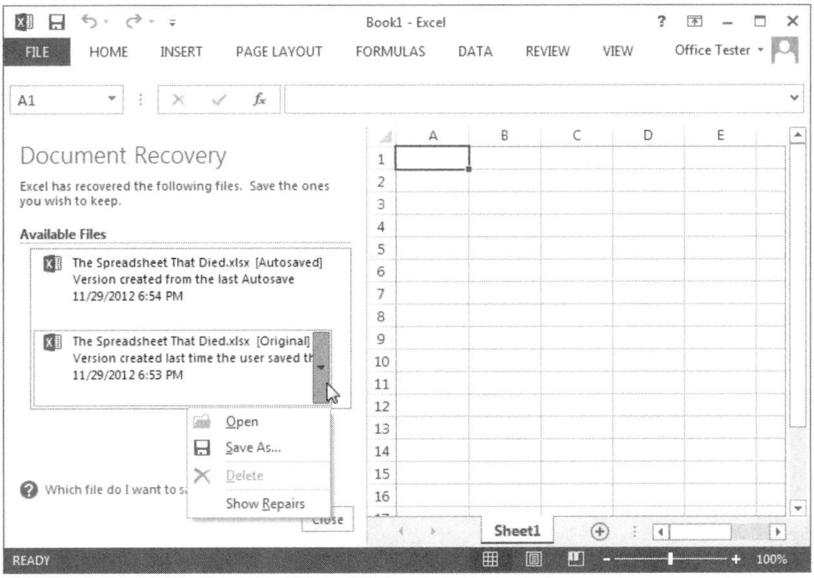

FIGURE 1-29

You can save or open an AutoRecover backup just as you would an ordinary Excel file; simply click the item in the list. Once you deal with all the backup files, close the Document Recovery window by clicking the Close button. If you haven't saved the backup, Excel asks you whether you want to save it permanently or delete it.

If your computer crashes mid-edit, the next time you open Excel you may see the same file listed twice in the Document Recovery window, as shown in Figure 1-29. The difference is in the status: "[Autosaved]" indicates the most recent backup Excel created, while "[Original]" means the last version of the file *you* saved (which is safely stored on your hard drive, right where you expect it).

To open a file in the Document Recovery window, just click it. You can also use a drop-down menu with additional options (Figure 1-29). If you find a file you want to keep permanently, make sure to save it. If you don't, the next time you close Excel it asks if it should throw the backups away.

If you attempt to open a backup file that's somehow been scrambled (technically known as *corrupted*), Excel attempts to repair it. You can choose Show Repairs to display a list of any changes Excel made to recover the file.

AUTORECOVER SETTINGS

AutoRecover comes switched on when you install Excel, but you can tweak its settings. Choose File→Options, and then choose the Save section. Under the "Save workbooks" section, make sure you have "Save AutoRecover information" turned on.

You can make a few other changes to AutoRecover:

- You can adjust the backup frequency in minutes. (See Figure 1-30 for tips on timing.)

- You can control whether Excel keeps a backup if you create a new spreadsheet, work on it for at least 10 minutes, and then close it without saving your work. This sort of AutoRecover backup is called a *draft*, and it's discussed in more detail on page 73. Ordinarily, the setting "Keep the last Auto Recovered file if I exit without saving" is switched on, and Excel keeps drafts. (To find all the drafts that Excel has saved for you, choose File→Open, and scroll to the end of the list of recently opened workbooks, until you see the Recover Unsaved Workbooks button. Click it.)

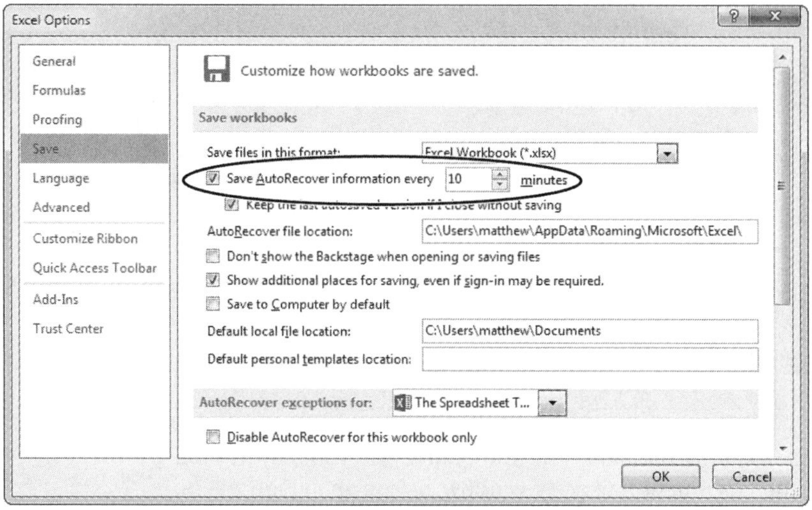

FIGURE 1-30

You can configure how often AutoRecover backs up your files. There's really no danger in being too frequent. Unless you work with extremely complex or large spreadsheets—which might suck up a lot of computing power and take a long time to save—you can set Excel to save a document every 5 minutes with no appreciable slowdown in performance.

- You can choose where you want Excel to save backup files. The standard folder works fine for most people, but feel free to pick some other place. Unfortunately, there's no handy Browse button to help you locate the folder, so you need to find the folder in advance (using a tool like Windows Explorer), write it down somewhere, and then copy the full folder path into this window.

- Under the "AutoRecover exceptions" heading, you can tell Excel not to bother saving a backup of a specific spreadsheet. Pick the spreadsheet name from the list (which shows all the currently open spreadsheet files), and then turn on the "Disable AutoRecover for this workbook only" setting. This setting is exceedingly uncommon, but you might use it if you have a gargantuan spreadsheet full of data that doesn't need to be backed up. For example, this spreadsheet might hold records you pulled out of a central database so you can take a closer look. In such a case, you don't need to create a backup because your spreadsheet is just a copy of the data in the database. (If you're interested in learning more about this scenario, check out Chapter 27.)

Opening Files

To open files in Excel, you begin by choosing File→Open (or using the keyboard shortcut Ctrl+O). This takes you to the Open page in Excel's backstage view. The left side of the page includes the Places list, which matches the list in the Save As page with one addition: Recent Workbooks. Click this, and you'll see up to 25 of the most recent spreadsheet files you worked on. If you find the file you want, click it to open it.

NOTE When you open a file, Excel loads it into a new window. If you already have a workbook on the go, that workbook remains open in a separate Excel window.

The best part about the Recent Documents list is the way you can *pin* a document so it stays there forever, as shown in Figure 1-31.

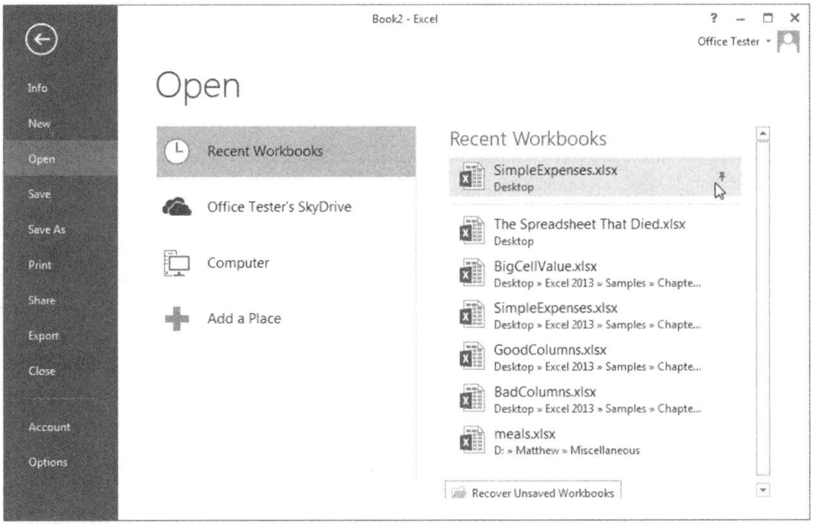

FIGURE 1-31

To keep a spreadsheet on the Recent Documents list, click the thumbtack on the right. Excel moves your workbook to the top of the list and pins it in place. That means it won't ever leave the list, no matter how many documents you open. If you decide to stop working with the file later on, just click the thumbtack again to release it. Pinning is a great way to keep your most important files at your fingertips.

TIP Do you want to hide your recent editing work? You can remove any file from the recent document list by right-clicking it and choosing "Remove from list." And if the clutter is keeping you from finding the workbooks you want, pin the important files, then right-click any file and choose "Clear unpinned workbooks." This action removes every file that isn't pinned down.

If you don't see the file you want in the list of recent workbooks, you can choose one of the other locations in the Places list. Choose Computer to see a list of locations on your hard drive.

As with recently opened workbooks, you can pin your favorite locations so they remain on this list permanently. To open a file in one of these locations, click the folder (or click the Browse button underneath to look somewhere else). Either way, Excel opens the familiar Open window, where you can pick the file you want.

TIP The Open window also lets you open several spreadsheets in one step, as long as they're all in the same folder. To use this trick, hold down the Ctrl key and click to select each file. When you click Open, Excel puts each one in a separate window, just as if you'd opened them one after the other.

Opening Files in Other Formats

Excel can open many file types other than its native .xlsx format. To open files in another format, begin by choosing File→Open, and then pick a location. When the Open window appears, pick the type of format you want from the "Files of type" list at the bottom.

If you want to open a file but don't know what format it's in, try using the first option in the list, "All Files." Once you choose a file, Excel scans the beginning of the file and informs you about the type of conversion it will attempt (based on the type of file Excel thinks it is).

NOTE Depending on your computer settings, Windows might hide file extensions. That means that instead of seeing the Excel spreadsheet file *MyCoalMiningFortune.xlsx*, you'll just see the name *MyCoalMiningFortune* (without the .xlsx part on the end). In this case, you can still tell what type of file it is by looking at the icon. If you see a small Excel icon next to the file name, that means Windows recognizes the file as an Excel spreadsheet. If you see something else (like a tiny paint palette, for example), you need to make a logical guess as to what type of file it is.

Protected View

Even something that seems as innocent as an Excel file can't always be trusted. Protected view is an Excel security feature that aims to keep you safe. It opens potentially risky Excel files in a specially limited Excel window. You'll know you're in protected view because Excel doesn't let you edit any of the data in the workbook, and it displays a message bar at the top of the window (Figure 1-32).

Excel automatically uses protected view when you download a spreadsheet from the Web or open it from your email inbox. This is actually a huge convenience, because Excel doesn't need to hassle you with questions when you try to view the file (such as "Are you sure you want to open this file?"). Because Excel's protected view has bullet-proof security, it's a safe way to view even the most suspicious spreadsheet.

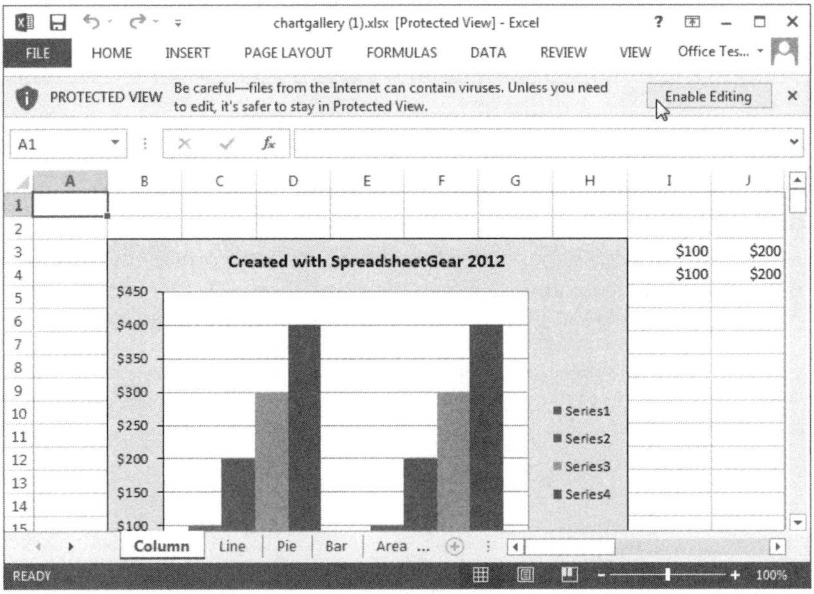

FIGURE 1-32

Currently, this file is in protected view. If you decide that it's safe and you need to edit its content, click the Enable Editing button to open the file in the normal Excel window with no security safeguards.

At this point, you're probably wondering about the risks of rogue spreadsheets. Truthfully, they're quite small. The most obvious danger is *macro code*: miniature programs stored in a spreadsheet file that perform Excel tasks. Poorly written or malicious macro code can tamper with your Excel settings, lock up the program, and even scramble your data. But before you panic, consider this: Excel macro viruses are very rare, and the .xlsx file format doesn't even allow macro code. Instead, macro-containing files must be saved as .xlsm or .xlsb files.

The more subtle danger here is that crafty hackers could create corrupted Excel files that might exploit tiny security holes in the program. One of these files could scramble Excel's brains in a dangerous way, possibly causing it to execute a scrap of malicious computer code that could do almost anything. Once again, this sort of attack is extremely rare. It might not even be possible with the up-to-date .xlsx file format. But protected view completely removes any chance of an attack, which helps corporate bigwigs sleep at night.

Opening Files—With a Twist

The Open window harbors a few tricks. To see these hidden secrets, first select the file you want to use (by clicking it once, not twice), and then click the drop-down arrow on the right-side of the Open button. A menu with several options appears, as shown in Figure 1-33.

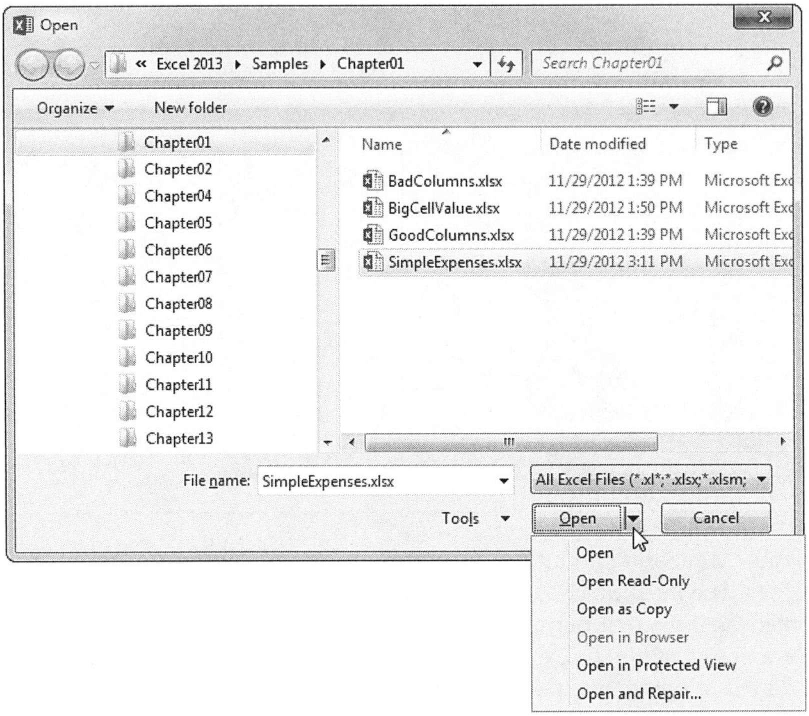

FIGURE 1-33

Why settle for the plain-vanilla Open command when you have all these choices?

Here's what these different choices do:

- **Open** opens the file in the normal way.
- **Open Read-Only** opens the file, but won't let you *save* changes. This option is great if you want to make sure you don't accidentally overwrite an existing file. (For example, if you're using last month's sales invoice as a starting point for this month's invoice, you might use Open Read-Only to make sure you can't accidentally wipe out the existing file.) If you open a document in read-only mode, you can still make changes—you just have to save the file with a new file name (choose File→Save As).
- **Open as Copy** creates a copy of the spreadsheet in the same folder. If you named your file *Book1.xlsx*, the copy will be named *Copy of Book1.xlsx*. This feature comes in handy if you're about to start editing a spreadsheet and want to be able to look at the last version you saved. Excel won't let you open the

same file twice, but you can load the previous version by selecting the same file and using "Open as Copy." (Of course, this technique works only when you have changes you haven't saved yet. Once you save the current version of a file, Excel overwrites the older version and it's lost forever.)

- **Open in Browser** is only available when you select an HTML file. This option lets you open the HTML file in your computer's web browser. It's part of an old Excel feature that allows you to save spreadsheets as web pages, which has now been replaced by Excel's Web App (page 705).
- **Open in Protected View** prevents a potentially dangerous file from running any code. However, you'll also be restrained from editing the file, as explained on page 42.
- **Open and Repair** is useful if you need to open a file that's corrupted. If you try to open a corrupted file by just clicking Open, Excel warns you that the file has problems and refuses to open it. To get around this, you can open the file using the "Open and Repair" option, which prompts Excel to make the necessary corrections, display them for you in a list, and then open the document. Depending on the type of problem, you might not lose any information at all.

Working with Multiple Open Spreadsheets

As you open multiple spreadsheets, Excel creates a new window for each one. Although this helps keep your work separated, it can cause a bit of clutter and make it harder to track down the window you really want. Fortunately, Excel provides a few shortcuts that are indispensable when dealing with several spreadsheets at a time:

- To jump from one spreadsheet to another, find the window in the View→Window→Switch Windows list, which includes the file name of all the currently open spreadsheets (Figure 1-34).

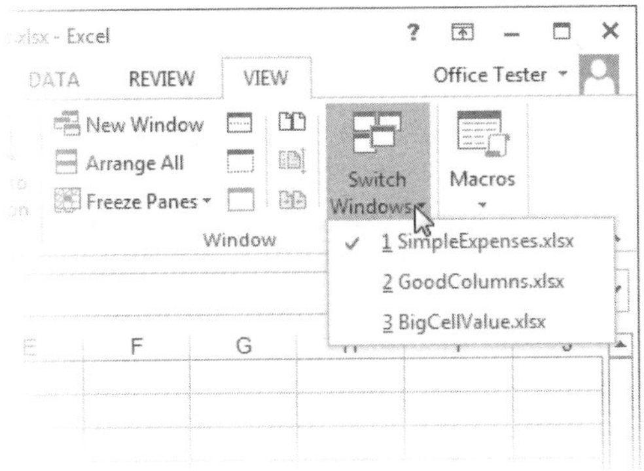

FIGURE 1-34

When you have multiple spreadsheets open at the same time, you can easily move from one to the other using the Switch Windows list.

- To move to the next spreadsheet, use the keyboard shortcut Ctrl+Tab or Ctrl+F6.
- To move to the previous spreadsheet, use the shortcut key Ctrl+Shift+Tab or Ctrl+Shift+F6.

NOTE One of the weirdest limitations in Excel occurs if you try to open more than one file with the same name. No matter what steps you take, you can't coax Excel to open both of them at once. It doesn't matter if the files have different content or if they're in different folders or even on different drives. When you try to open a file that has the same name as a file that's already open, Excel displays an error message and refuses to go any further. Sadly, the only solution is to open the files one at a time, or rename one of them.

POWER USERS' CLINIC

Handy Options for Opening and Saving Files

If you're in the habit of configuring your programs to get the most out of them, you'll be happy to hear that Excel has several useful details to tweak. To see them, choose File→Options.

Here are the most useful things you can do:

- **Adjust your starting point.** When you open a file or save it for the first time, Excel starts you off in your personal documents folder. This is a Windows-specific folder that many programs assume you use for all your files. If you don't use this folder, you can tell Excel to look elsewhere when it saves and opens files. Choose the Save section, and then look under the "Save workbooks" heading for the "Default file location" text box. You can modify it so that it points to the folder where you usually store your files (as in *C:\John Smith\MyExcel Files*). Sadly, you can't browse and pick the path from a window—instead, you need to type it in by hand.
- **Keep track of more recent documents.** Why stick with 25 recent documents when you can show scores? If you want to keep track of more recent work and aren't deterred by a long Recent Documents list, choose the Advanced section, scroll down to the Display group of settings, and then change the "Show this number of Recent Workbooks." You can pick any number from 0 to 50.
- **Change the standard file type.** Most Excel fans prefer the new .xlsx file format, which Excel uses every time you save a new file (unless you explicitly choose another option in the "Save as type" list). But if you decide that something else suits you better, like the binary .xlsb format (page 29) or the legacy .xls format, you can tell Excel to save files using that format. Choose the Save section, look under the "Save workbooks" heading, and then change the "Save files in this format" setting by choosing another file type from the list.
- **Get started with a bang.** You can tell Excel to automatically open a whole group of spreadsheet files every time it starts up. To find this setting, choose the Advanced section, and then scroll to the General group of settings. You can use the "At startup, open all files in" text box to specify a folder where you put all the Excel files on which you're currently working. Then, the next time you start Excel, it automatically opens (in separate windows) every Excel file it finds. Of course, if you decide to use this option, make sure you don't clutter your in-progress folder with too many files, or Excel will open a dizzying number of windows when it launches.

CHAPTER

2

Adding Information to Worksheets

Now that you've created a basic worksheet, and you've become familiar with Excel's spiffy interface, it's time to get down and dirty by adding data to your spreadsheet. Whether you want to plan your household budget, build a sales invoice, or graph your soaring (or plunging) net worth, you first need to understand how Excel interprets the information you give it.

Depending on what kind of data you type into a cell, Excel classifies it as a number, a date, or a piece of text. In this chapter, you'll learn how Excel makes up its mind and how you can make sure it decides correctly.

After that, you'll learn how to use some of Excel's best data-entry timesavers. You'll zip around your worksheet with shortcut keys and the Go To feature, save time with AutoComplete and AutoCorrect, and use Excel's new Flash Fill feature to automate tedious editing jobs. You'll also master the indispensable Undo feature and Excel's handy spell-checker. Finally, you'll consider a completely different editing task: adding a web-style hyperlink to your worksheet.

Adding Different Types of Data

One of Excel's most important features is its ability to distinguish between different types of information. A typical worksheet contains both text and numbers. There isn't a lot you can do in Excel with ordinary text (other than alphabetize a list, perform a simple spell-check, and apply some basic formatting). On the other hand, Excel gives you a wide range of options when it comes to numeric data. You can, for example, string numbers together to create complex calculations and formulas, or you can graph spreadsheet data on a chart. Programs that don't distinguish between text and numbers—like Microsoft Word, for example—can't provide these features.

Most of the time, when you enter information in Excel, you don't explicitly indicate the type of data it is. Instead, Excel examines the information you type in and, based on your formatting and other clues, Excel classifies it automatically. Excel distinguishes between four core data types:

- **Ordinary text.** This data type includes column headings, descriptions, and any other content that Excel can't identify as one of the other data types.
- **Numbers.** This data type includes currency, integers, fractions, percentages, and every other type of numeric data. Numbers are the basic ingredient of most Excel worksheets.
- **Dates and times.** This data type includes dates (like Oct 3, 2013), times (like 4:30 p.m.), and combined date and time information (like Oct 3, 2013, 4:30 p.m.). You can enter date and time values in a variety of formats.
- **True or false values.** This data type (known in geekdom as a *Boolean* value) contains one of two values: TRUE or FALSE (displayed in uppercase letters). You don't need Boolean data types in most worksheets, but they're useful in worksheets that include Visual Basic macro code (see Chapter 30) or complex formulas that evaluate conditions (see Chapter 13).

One useful way to tell how Excel interprets your data is to look at how it aligns it in a cell, as explained in Figure 2-1.

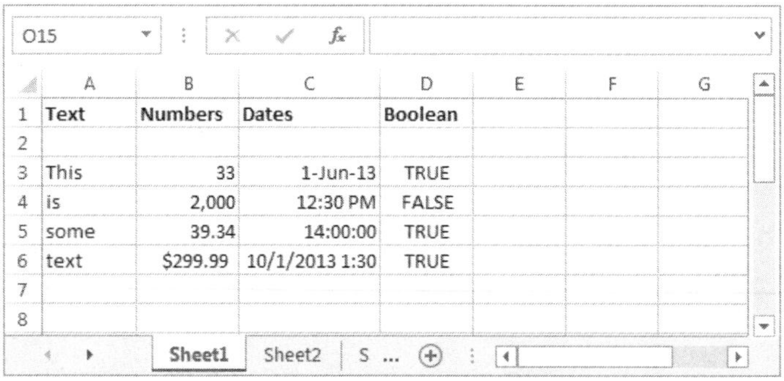

FIGURE 2-1

Unless you explicitly change the alignment, Excel always left-aligns text (that is, it lines it up against the left edge of a cell), as in column A. On the other hand, it always right-aligns numbers and dates, as in columns B and C. And it centers Boolean values, as in column D.

NOTE The standard alignment of text and numbers doesn't just represent the whims of Excel—it also matches the behavior you want most of the time. For example, when you type in text, you usually want to start at the left edge so that subsequent entries in a column line up. But when entering numbers, you usually want their *decimal points* aligned so it's easier to scan a list of numbers and quickly spot small and large values. Of course, if you don't like Excel's standard formatting, you're free to change it, as you'll see in Chapter 5.

As Figure 2-1 shows, Excel can display numbers and dates several ways. Some of the numbers in Figure 2-1, for example, include decimal places, one uses a comma, and one has a currency symbol. Similarly, one of the time values uses a 12-hour clock, while another uses a 24-hour clock. Some entries include dates only, while others contain both date and time information.

When you type a number into a cell, you assume it'll appear exactly as you typed it. For example, when you type 3-comma-0-0-0 you expect to see 3,000. But the number you type isn't necessarily what Excel displays. To see why, try this test. First, type *3,000* into a cell. It shows up exactly the way you entered it. Then, type over that value with *2000*, omitting the comma as you do. The new number appears as "2,000". In this example, Excel remembered your first entry in this cell and assumed you wanted to use "thousand separators" for this cell, *all the time*.

These quirks may make formatting a workbook seem like a spreadsheet free-for-all, but don't despair—you can easily tell Excel how to format your numbers and dates. (In fact, that's the subject of Chapter 5.) At this point, though, all you need to know is that the values Excel *stores* in each cell don't necessarily reflect how it *displays* those values. For example, Excel could format the number 4300 as plain old 4300 or as the dollar amount $4,300. But at its core, Excel treats all raw numbers the same way, no matter how it formats them for display. That works to your benefit because you can combine them in calculations.

Figure 2-2 shows you how to find the underlying stored value of a cell.

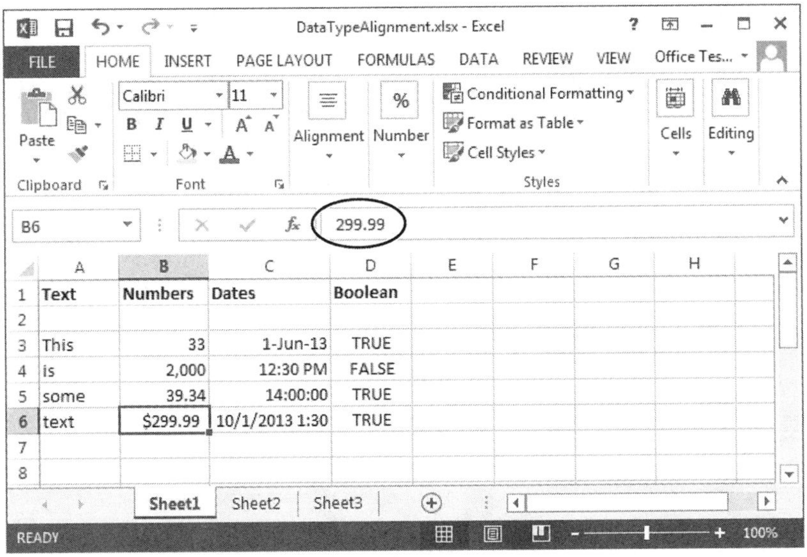

FIGURE 2-2

You can see the underlying value that Excel stores for a cell by selecting the cell and glancing at the formula bar. In this sheet, you can see that Excel stores the value $299.99 without the currency symbol, which Excel adds only when it displays the number in a spreadsheet. Similarly, Excel stores the number 2,000 without the comma, the date 1-Jun-13 as 6/1/2013, the time 12:30 p.m. as 12:30:00 PM, and the time 14:00:00 as 2:00:00 PM.

NOTE Excel assigns data types to each cell in your worksheet, and you can't mix more than one data type in the same cell. For example, when you type in *44 fat cats*, Excel interprets the whole thing as text because it includes letters. If you want to treat 44 as a number (so that you can perform calculations with it, say), you need to split this content into two cells—one that contains the number 44 and one that contains the text.

By looking at cell alignment, you can easily tell how Excel interprets your data. But what happens when Excel's interpretation is at odds with your wishes? For example, what if you type in something you consider a *number* but Excel freakishly treats it as *text*, or vice versa? The first step to solving this problem is grasping the logic behind Excel's decision-making process.

How Excel Identifies Text

If the content of a cell meets any of the following criteria, Excel treats it as ordinary text:

- **It contains any letters.** Thus, C123 is text, not a number.
- **It contains any punctuation that Excel can't interpret numerically.** Punctuation allowed in numbers and dates includes the comma (,), the decimal point (.), and the forward slash (/) or dash (-) for dates. When you type in any other punctuation, Excel treats the contents of the cell as text. Thus, 14! is text, not a number.

Occasionally, Excel reads your data the wrong way. For example, you may have a value—like a Social Security number or a credit card number—made up entirely of numeric characters, but you want Excel to treat it like text because you don't ever want to perform calculations with it. In this case, Excel doesn't know what you're up to, so it automatically treats the value as a number. You can also run into problems when you precede text with the equal sign (which tells Excel that you started writing a formula), or when you use a series of numbers and dashes that you don't intend to be part of a date (for example, you want to enter 1-2-3 but you don't want Excel to read it as January 2, 2003—which is what it wants to do).

In cases like these, the solution's simple. Before you type in the cell value, start by typing in an apostrophe ('). That tells Excel to treat the cell's content as text. Figure 2-3 shows you how this works.

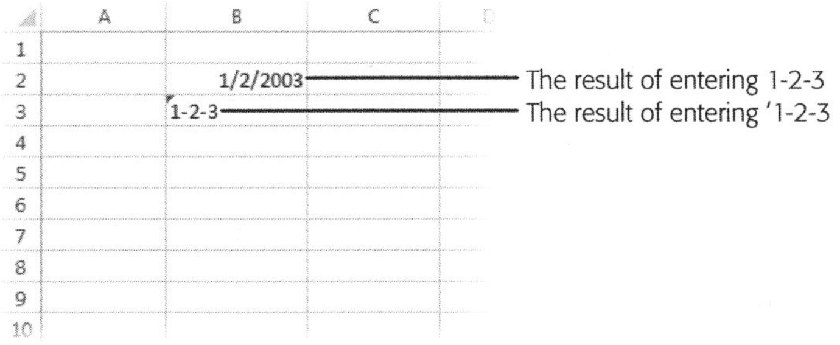

FIGURE 2-3

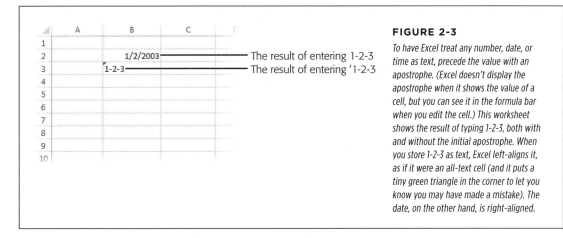

To have Excel treat any number, date, or time as text, precede the value with an apostrophe. (Excel doesn't display the apostrophe when it shows the value of a cell, but you can see it in the formula bar when you edit the cell.) This worksheet shows the result of typing 1-2-3, both with and without the initial apostrophe. When you store 1-2-3 as text, Excel left-aligns it, as if it were an all-text cell (and it puts a tiny green triangle in the corner to let you know you may have made a mistake). The date, on the other hand, is right-aligned.

When you precede a numeric value with an apostrophe, Excel checks out the cell to see what's going on. When it determines that it can represent the content as a number, it places a green triangle in the top-left corner of the cell and gives you a few options for dealing with it, as shown in Figure 2-4.

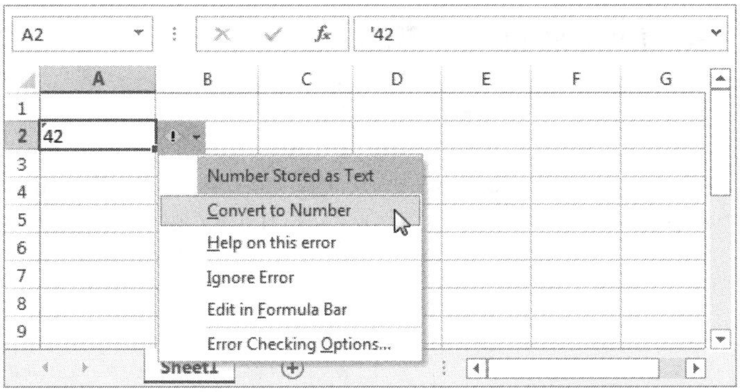

FIGURE 2-4

In this worksheet, Excel stores the number 42 as text, thanks to the apostrophe preceding it. Excel notices the apostrophe, wonders if it's an unintentional error, and flags the cell by putting a tiny green triangle in the top-left corner. If you move to the cell, an exclamation mark appears and, if you click it, a menu appears, letting you either convert the number or ignore the issue for this cell. Excel provides a similar menu if you enter a text date that has a two-digit year, as in '1-1-13. In this case, the menu lets you convert the two-digit date to a four-digit date that has a year starting with 19 or 20.

TIP When you type in either *false* or *true* (using any capitalization you like), Excel automatically recognizes the data type as a Boolean value instead of text, converts it to the uppercase word FALSE or TRUE, and centers it in the cell. If you want to make Excel treat a cell that contains *false* or *true* as text and *not* as Boolean data, start by typing an apostrophe (') at the beginning of the cell.

How Excel Identifies Numbers

Excel automatically interprets any cell that contains only numeric characters as a number. In addition, you can add the following nonnumeric characters to a number without causing problems:

- One decimal point (but not two). For example, 42.1 is a number, but 42.1.1 is text.
- One or more commas, provided you use them to separate groups of three numbers (like thousands, millions, and so on). Thus 1,200,200 is a valid number, but 1,200,20 is text.
- A currency sign ($ for U.S. dollars), provided it's at the beginning of the number.
- A percent symbol at the beginning or end of the number (but not both).
- A plus (+) or minus (-) sign before the number. You can also create a negative number by putting it in parentheses. In other words, entering (33) is the same as entering -33.
- An equal sign at the start of the cell. This tells Excel that you're starting a formula (page 221).

The most important thing to understand about entering numbers is that when you choose to add other details, like commas or dollar signs, you're actually doing two things at once: entering a value for the cell *and* setting the format for the cell, which affects how Excel displays the value. Chapter 5 has more on number styles, and shows you how you can completely control cell formatting.

How Excel Identifies Dates and Times

When you type in a date, you have a choice of formats. You can type in the full date (like *July 4, 2013*) or an abbreviated date, using dashes or slashes (like *7-4-2013* or *7/4/2013*), which is generally easier. If you enter numbers formatted as a date but the date you entered doesn't exist (like the 30th day in February or the 13th month), Excel interprets the entry as text. Figure 2-5 shows you the options.

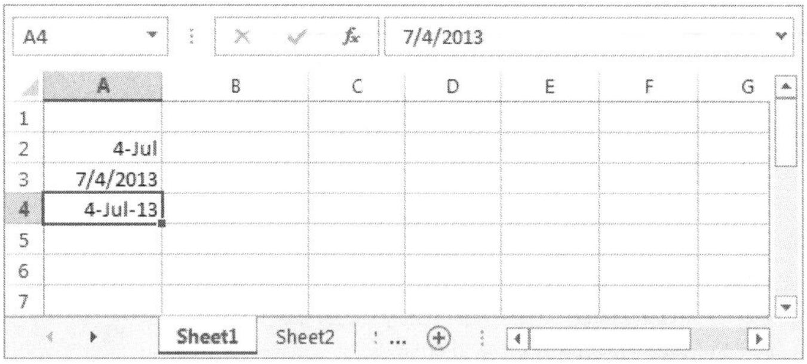

FIGURE 2-5

Whichever way you type the date in a cell, it always appears the same way in the formula bar (the specific way Excel displays dates in the formula bar depends on your computer's regional settings, as explained next). To fine-tune how the date appears in a worksheet, use the formatting features discussed on page 137.

Because you can represent dates a few ways, working with them can be tricky, and you're likely to encounter some unexpected behavior from Excel. Here are some tips for using dates, trouble-free:

- **Instead of using a number for the month, you can use a three-letter month abbreviation, but you must put the month in the middle.** In other words, you can use *7/4/2013* and *4/Jul/2013* interchangeably.
- **When you use a two-digit year as part of a date, Excel tries to guess whether the first two digits should be 20 or 19.** When you type in a two-digit year of from 00 to 29, Excel assumes it belongs to the 21st century. If the year is from 30 to 99, Excel plants it in the 1900s. In other words, Excel translates 7/4/29 into 7/4/2029, while 7/4/30 becomes 7/4/1930.

TIP If you're a mere mortal and forget where the cutoff point is, enter the year as a four-digit number, which prevents any confusion.

- **If you don't type in any year at all, Excel automatically assumes you mean the current year.** For example, when you enter 7/4, Excel inserts the date 7/4/2013 (assuming it's currently 2013 on your computer's internal clock). When you enter a date this way, the year doesn't show up in the cell, but Excel still stores it in the worksheet (and it's visible in the formula bar).
- **Excel understands and displays dates differently depending on the regional settings on your computer.** Windows has a setting that determines how your computer interprets dates (see the next section, "Regional Dating"). On a computer configured with U.S. settings, Month-Day-Year is the standard date format. But on a UK-configured computer, Day-Month-Year is the deal. For example, in the U.S., either 11-7-13 or 11/7/13 is shorthand for November 7, 2013. In the UK or Canada, the same notations refer to July 11, 2013.

  Thus, if your computer has U.S. regional settings turned on and you type in *11/7/13*, Excel understands it as November 7, 2013, and the formula bar displays 11/7/2013.

NOTE The way Excel recognizes and displays dates varies according to the regional settings on your computer, but the way Excel *stores* dates does not. This feature comes in handy when you save a worksheet on one computer and then open it on a computer with different regional settings. Because Excel stores every date the same way, the date information remains accurate on the new computer, and Excel displays it according to the current regional settings.

Typing in times is more straightforward than typing in dates. You simply use numbers, separated by a colon (:). You need to include an hour and minute component at minimum (as in 7:30), but you can also add seconds (as in 7:30:10). You can use values from 1 to 24 for the hour part, though if your system's set to use a 12-hour clock, Excel converts the time accordingly (in other words, 19:30 becomes 7:30 PM).

If you want to use the 12-hour clock when you type in a time, follow your time with a space and the letters P or PM (or A or AM).

Finally, you can create cells that have both date and time information. To do so, just type the date portion first, followed by a space, and then the time portion. For example, Excel happily accepts this combo: 7/4/2013 1:30 PM.

Behind the scenes, Excel stores dates as *serial numbers*. It considers the date January 1, 1900 to be day 1. January 2, 1900 is day 2, and so on, up through the year 9999. This system is quite nifty, because if you use Excel to subtract one date from another, you actually end up calculating the difference in days, which is exactly what you want. On the other hand, it means you can't enter a date in Excel that's earlier than January 1, 1900 (if you do, Excel treats your date as text).

Similarly, Excel stores times as fractional numbers from 0 to 1. The number 0 represents 12:00 a.m. (the start of the day) and 0.99999 represents 11:59:59 p.m. (the end of the day). As with dates, this system lets you subtract one time value from another. (See Chapter 11 for more on performing calculations that use dates and times.)

Regional Dating

Windows has regional settings for your computer, which affect the way Microsoft programs understand things like dates and currency. You can change the settings, and they don't have to correspond to where you live—you can set them to your company headquarters' time zone on another continent, for instance. But keep in mind that regional settings affect *all* the programs on your computer, not just Office.

Every version of Windows uses the same system for regional settings. However, every version also puts them in a slightly different place. Here's the easiest way to find them:

- **If you use Windows 7:** Click the Start button and then, in the search box at the bottom of the Start menu, type *region*. When "Region and Language" appears in the list of matches, click it.
- **If you use Windows 8:** In desktop view, move your mouse to the bottom-left corner of the screen. Right-click the Start tile and choose Control Panel. When the Control Panel window appears, click Language. Then, click the link on the left that says "Change date, time, or number formats."

Either way, the Region and Language window appears (see Figure 2-6). The most important setting is in the first box, which has a drop-down list where you can pick the region you want, like English (United States) or Swedish (Finland).

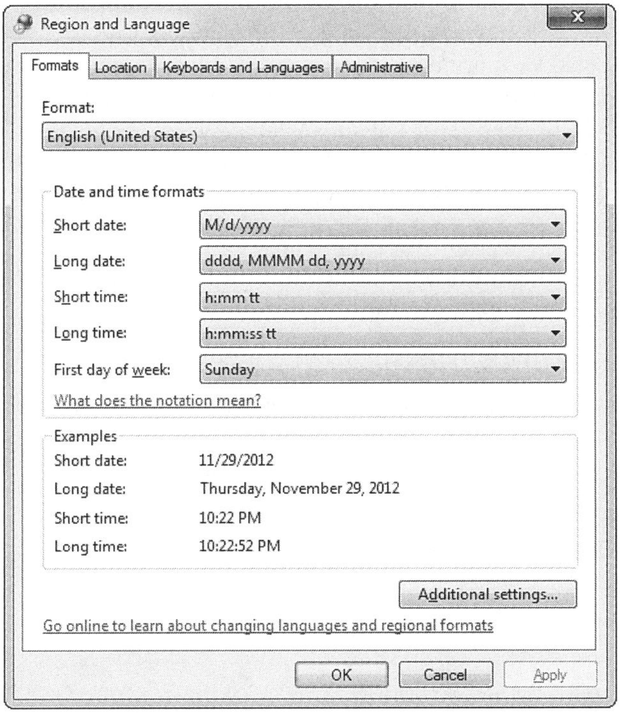

FIGURE 2-6

In the Region and Language window, you choose a geographical region and your computer stores a set of preferences about number and date display. Excel heeds these settings.

Underneath the Format box, you can fine-tune the settings for your region, such as how dates are written. You might decide to customize your settings if you have a particular preference that doesn't match the standard options. For example, you might decide that you want U.K.-formatted dates on a computer set to use U.S. regional settings for everything else.

TIP No matter what your regional settings, you can always use the international date standard when you type dates into Excel. That standard is Year/Month/Day, though you must supply a four-digit year (as in 2013/7/4). If you use a two-digit year, Excel assumes you're trying to use the Month-Day-Year or the Day-Month-Year pattern.

Handy Timesavers

Some of Excel's frills can make life easier when you enter data in a worksheet. In the following sections, you'll explore several timesaving features.

First, you'll learn to hustle around the worksheet grid with shortcut keys and the Go To feature. Next, you'll consider AutoComplete and AutoCorrect, two features that do things to your spreadsheets *automatically.* Sometimes that's cool and convenient, other times it can send you running for the old manual typewriter. Fortunately, you can turn off both. You'll also learn about AutoFit and AutoFill, two "auto" features that really aren't that automatic. They never run on their own—instead, you call them into action when you need to resize a column or flesh out a list.

Finally, you'll learn to use Excel's new Flash Fill feature, which recognizes patterns in your data and finishes simple editing tasks.

Moving Around the Grid with Shortcut Keys

Learning how to move around the Excel grid quickly and confidently is an indispensable skill. You already know how to get around by using the keyboard or clicking the mouse. But sometimes you want to cover ground a little quicker.

Excel provides a number of handy key combinations that transport you across your worksheet in leaps and bounds (see Table 2-1). The most useful include the Home key combinations, which bring you back to the beginning of a row or the top of your worksheet.

NOTE Shortcut key combinations that use the + sign must be entered together. For example, "Ctrl+Home" means you hold down Ctrl and press Home at the same time. Key combinations with a comma work in sequence. For example, the key combination "End, Home" means press End first, release it, and then press Home.

TABLE 2-1 *Shortcut keys for moving around a worksheet*

KEY COMBINATION	RESULT
→ (or Tab)	Moves one cell to the right.
← (or Shift+Tab)	Moves one cell to the left.
↑	Moves one cell up.
↓ (or Enter)	Moves one cell down.
Page Up	Moves up one screen. Thus, if the grid shows 10 cells at a time, this key moves to a cell in the same column, 10 rows up (unless you're already at the top of the worksheet).

KEY COMBINATION	RESULT
Page Down	Moves down one screen. Thus, if the grid shows 10 cells at a time, this key moves to a cell in the same column, 10 rows down.
Home	Moves to the first cell (column A) of the current row.
Ctrl+Home	Moves to the first cell in the top row, which is A1.
Ctrl+End (or End, Home)	Moves to the last column of the last occupied row. This cell is at the bottom-right edge of your data.

Excel also lets you cross great distances in a single bound using *Ctrl+arrow key* combinations. These combinations jump to the *edges* of your data. For example, if you press Ctrl+→ while you're inside a group of cells with information in them, you skip to the right, over all the filled cells, and stop just before the next blank cell. If you press Ctrl+→ again, you'll skip over all the nearby blank cells and land in the next cell to the right that has information in it. If there aren't any more cells on the right that have data, you wind up on the very edge of your worksheet.

The *Ctrl+arrow key* combinations are useful if you have more than one table of data in the same worksheet. For example, imagine you have two tables of data, one at the top of a worksheet and one at the bottom. If you're at the top of the first table, you can use Ctrl+↓ to jump to the bottom of the first table, skipping all the rows in between. Press Ctrl+↓ again, and you leap over all the blank rows, winding up at the beginning of the second table.

The Go To Feature

If you're fortunate enough to know exactly where in a spreadsheet you need to go, you can use the Go To feature to make the jump. Go To moves you to the cell address you specify. It comes in useful for extremely large spreadsheets, where just scrolling through the worksheet takes half a day.

To bring up the Go To window (shown in Figure 2-7), choose Home→Editing→Find & Select→Go To. Or do yourself a favor and just press Ctrl+G. Enter the cell address (such as C32), and then click OK.

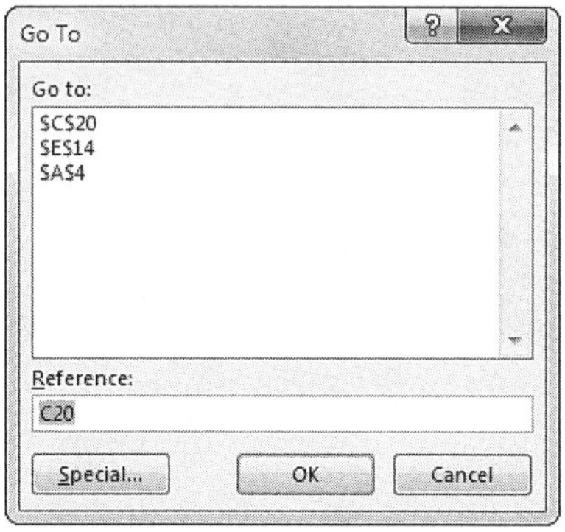

FIGURE 2-7

You'll notice that, in the Go To list, cell addresses include dollar signs before the row number and column letter. Thus, C20 becomes $C$20, which is simply the convention Excel uses for fixed cell references. (You'll learn much more about the different types of cell references in Chapter 8.)

The Go To feature becomes more useful the more you use it. That's because the Go To window maintains a list of the most recent cell addresses you entered. In addition, every time you open the Go To window, Excel automatically adds the current cell to the list. This feature makes it easy to jump to a far-off cell and quickly return to your starting location.

The Go To window isn't your only option for leaping through a worksheet in a single bound. If you look at the Home→Editing→Find & Select menu, you'll find more specialized commands that let you jump straight to cells that contain formulas, comments, conditional formatting, and other advanced Excel ingredients you haven't learned about yet. And if you want to hunt down cells that have specific text, you need the popular Find command (Home→Editing→Find & Select→Find), which is covered on page 118.

AutoComplete

Some worksheets require that you type in the same information row after row. For example, if you're creating a table to track the value of all your Sesame Street collectibles, you can type in *Kermit* only so many times before you start turning green. Excel tries to help you out with its AutoComplete feature, which examines what you type, compares it against previous entries in the same column, and, if it recognizes the beginning of an existing word, fills in the rest.

For instance, in your Sesame Street worksheet, if you already have Kermit in the Characters column, when you start typing a new entry in that column beginning with the letter K, Excel automatically fills in the whole word Kermit. Excel then highlights the letters it added (in this case, *ermit*). You now have two options:

- **If you want to accept the AutoComplete text, move to another cell.** For example, when you hit the right arrow key or press Enter to move down, Excel leaves the word Kermit behind.

- **If you want to blow off Excel's suggestion, just keep typing.** Because Excel automatically selects the AutoComplete portion of the word (*ermit*), your next keystrokes type over that text. Or, if you find the AutoComplete text distracting, press Delete to remove it right away.

TIP When you want to change the AutoComplete text slightly, press F2. That drops you into edit mode, so you can use the arrow keys to move through the cell and make modifications.

AutoComplete has a few limitations. It works only with text entries, ignoring numbers and dates. It doesn't pay any attention to the entries in other columns. And if there's a blank row between the cell you're working on and the values above it, Excel ignores the values, assuming they're part of a different list that just happens to use the same column.

Finally, Excel won't give you a suggestion unless the text you typed matches the value in another cell *unambiguously*. That means that when your column contains two words that start with K, like Kermit and kerplop, Excel doesn't make any suggestion when you type K into a new cell, because it can't tell which of those two words is the one you might want. But once you type *Kerm*, Excel realizes that kerplop isn't a candidate, and it supplies the AutoComplete suggestion Kermit.

If you find AutoComplete annoying, you can get it out of your face with a mere click of the mouse. Choose File→Options, select the Advanced section, and look under the "Editing options" heading for the setting "Enable Auto-Complete for cell values." Turn this setting off to banish AutoComplete from your life.

AutoCorrect

As you type text in a cell, AutoCorrect cleans up behind you—fixing things like incorrectly capitalized letters and common misspellings. AutoCorrect is subtle enough that you may not even realize it's monitoring your every move. To get a taste of its magic, look for behaviors like these:

- If you type *HEllo*, AutoCorrect changes it to *Hello*.
- If you type *friday*, AutoCorrect changes it to *Friday*.
- If you scramble the letters of a common word (for example, typing *thsi* instead of *this*, or *teh* instead of *the*), AutoCorrect replaces the word with the proper spelling.
- If you accidentally hit the Caps Lock key and then type *jOHN sMITH* when you really wanted to type *John Smith*, Excel not only fixes the mistake, it switches off Caps Lock, too.

NOTE AutoCorrect doesn't correct most misspelled words, just common typos. To correct other mistakes, use the spell-checker described on page 75.

For the most part, AutoCorrect is harmless and even occasionally useful, as it can spare you from delivering minor typos in a major report. But if you need to type irregularly capitalized words, or if you have a garden-variety desire to rebel against standard English, you can turn off some or all of AutoCorrect's actions.

To reach the AutoCorrect settings, click File→Options. Choose the Proofing section, and then click the AutoCorrect Options button. (All AutoCorrect options are language-specific, and the title of the window that opens indicates the language you're currently using.) Most of the actions are self-explanatory, and you can turn them off by turning off their checkboxes. Figure 2-8 explains the "Replace text as you type" option, which isn't just for errors.

FIGURE 2-8

Under "Replace text as you type" is a long list of symbols and commonly misspelled words (the column on the left) that Excel automatically replaces with something else (the column on the right). But what if you want the copyright symbol to appear as a C in parentheses? You can remove individual corrections (select one, and then click Delete), or you can change the replacement text. And you can add your own rules. For example, you might want to be able to type PESDS and have Excel insert Patented Electronic Seltzer Delivery System. Simply type in the "Replace" and "With" text, as shown here, and then click OK.

TIP For really advanced AutoCorrect settings, use the Exceptions button to define cases where Excel *won't* use AutoCorrect. When you click this button, the AutoCorrect Exceptions window appears with a list of exceptions. For example, the list contains abbreviations that include a period but shouldn't be capitalized (like pp.) and words where mixed capitalization is allowed (like WordPerfect).

AutoFit

Page 8 explains how you can drag the edge of a column to resize it. For greater convenience, Excel also provides an AutoFit feature that automatically enlarges or shrinks a column to fit its content.

AutoFit springs into action in three situations:

- When you type a number or date that's too wide to fit into a cell, Excel automatically widens the column to accommodate the new content. (Excel doesn't automatically expand columns when you type in text, however.)
- If you double-click the right edge of a column header, Excel automatically sizes the column to fit the widest entry it contains. This trick works for all types of data, including dates, numbers, and text.
- If you choose Home→Cells→Format→AutoFit Column Width, Excel automatically sizes the column to fit the content in the current cell. Or you can select a group of cells (see page 85) and use this command to size the column to fit the widest value in the group.

Although AutoFit automatically widens columns when you type a number or date into a cell, you can still *shrink* a column after you enter your information. You can even make a column too small to fit its contents. Excel deals with this situation differently, depending on the type of information in your cells. If your cells contain *text*, it's entirely possible for one cell to overlap (and thereby obscure) another, a problem first described in Chapter 1. But Excel never truncates a number or date. Instead, if you shrink a cell so that its number can't fit, Excel fills the cell with a series of number signs (like #####). This is Excel's way of telling you that you're out of space, and it avoids potential confusion. (If Excel truncated *numbers* like it truncates text, the result could be seriously deceiving. For example, you might squash a cell with the price of espresso makers so that they appear to cost $2 instead of $200.)

Once you enlarge the column by hand (or by using AutoFit), the original number reappears. (Until then, you can see the number by looking in the formula bar.)

GEM IN THE ROUGH

A Few More Ways to Adjust Column Width

Excel lets you control column widths precisely. To change the width of a column, right-click the header and then choose Column Width. Excel's standard unadjusted column size is a compact 8.43 characters, but you can change that to any number. (Remember that, because different fonts use different size letters, the number of characters you specify here probably won't correspond exactly to the number of characters you see in your column.)

You can also adjust multiple column widths simultaneously. Just select the columns (click the first column header, and then drag to the left or to the right to select more columns). Now, when you apply a new width, Excel applies it to all the selected columns.

Finally, you can customize the standard width for columns, which is the width that Excel assigns columns for every new worksheet you create. To set the standard width, choose Home→Cells→Format→Default Width and then change the number.

AutoFill

AutoFill is a quirky yet useful feature that lets you create a whole column or row of values based on the value in just a few cells—Excel extrapolates those values into a series. Put another way, AutoFill looks at the cells you've filled in in a column or row, and makes a reasonable guess about the cells you want to add. People commonly use AutoFill for sequential numbers, months, or days.

Here are a few examples of lists that AutoFill can and can't work with:

- The series 1, 2, 3, 4 is easy for Excel to interpret—it's a list of steadily increasing numbers. The series 5, 10, 15 (numbers increasing by 5) is just as easy. Both of these are great AutoFill candidates.
- The series of part numbers CMP-40-0001, CMP-40-0002, CMP-40-0003 may seem more complicated because it mingles text and numbers. But clever Excel can spot the pattern, as long as the numbers are at the end of the value (so CMP-40-A won't work).
- Excel readily recognizes series of months (*January, February, March*) and days (*Sun, Mon, Tue*), either written longhand or as three-letter abbreviations.
- A list of numbers like 47, 345, 6 doesn't seem to follow a regular pattern. But by doing some analysis, Excel can guess at a relationship and generate more numbers that fit the pattern. There's a good chance, however, that these won't be the numbers you want, so take a close look at whatever Excel comes up with in cases like these.

Bottom line: AutoFill is a great tool for generating simple lists. When you work with a complex sequence of values, it's no help—unless you're willing to create a custom list (page 63) that spells it out for Excel.

TIP AutoFill doubles as a quick way to copy a cell value multiple times. For example, if you select a cell in which you typed *Cookie Monster*, you can use AutoFill to fill every cell in that row or column with the same text.

To use AutoFill, follow these steps:

1. **Fill in a couple of cells in a row or column to start off the series.**

   You can opt to fill in only one cell, but Excel is more reliable when it has a little more data to work with.

2. **Select the cells you entered, and then click and hold the small black square at the bottom-right corner of the selected box.**

   You can tell that your mouse is in the correct place when the pointer changes to a plus symbol (+).

3. **Drag the mouse down (if you're filling a column of items) or to the right (if you're filling a row of items).**

   As you drag, a tooltip appears, showing the text that Excel is generating for each cell.

   While you're dragging, you can hold down Ctrl to affect the way that Excel fills a list. When you've filled in at least *two* cells, Ctrl tells Excel to just copy the list multiple times, rather than look for a pattern. When you want to expand a range based on just *one* cell, Ctrl does the opposite: It tells Excel to try to predict a pattern, rather than just copy it.

   When you release the mouse, Excel automatically fills in the additional cells, and a special AutoFill icon appears next to the last cell in the series, as shown in Figure 2-9.

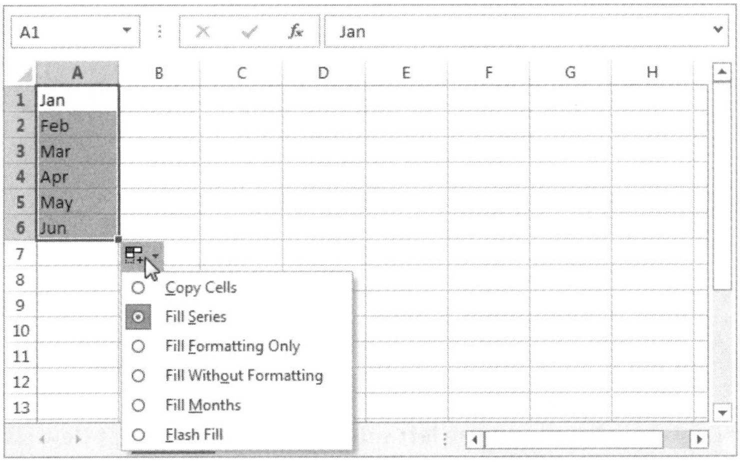

FIGURE 2-9

After AutoFill does its magic, Excel displays a menu that lets you fill the series without copying the formatting, or copy the formatting without filling the series. You can also choose to copy values instead of generating a list. For example, if you choose to copy values—or Copy Cells, as Excel calls it—then, in the two-item series Jan, Feb, you end up with Jan, Feb, Jan, Feb, rather than Jan, Feb, Mar, Apr.

CUSTOM AUTOFILL LISTS

Excel stores a collection of AutoFill lists that it refers to every time you use the feature. You can add your own lists to the collection, which extends the series Auto-Fill recognizes. For example, Excel doesn't come set to understand Kermit, Cookie Monster, and Snuffleupagus as a series, but you can add it to the mix.

Why bother to add custom lists to Excel's collection? After all, if you need to type in the whole list before you use it, is AutoFill really saving you any work? The benefit occurs when you need to create the same list in *multiple* worksheets, in which case you type it in just once and then use AutoFill to recreate it as often as you like. You can also use custom lists to tell Excel how to sort data, as you'll learn on page 428.

To create a custom list:

1. **Choose File→Options.**

   The familiar Excel Options window appears.

2. **Choose the Advanced section, scroll down to the General heading and then, at the bottom of that section, click Edit Custom Lists.**

   Here, you can take a gander at Excel's predefined lists and add your own (Figure 2-10).

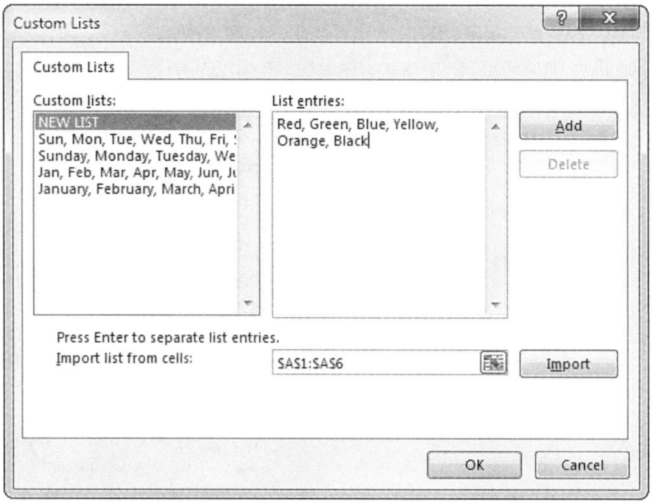

FIGURE 2-10

Here, you're adding a custom list of colors.

3. **In the "Custom lists" box on the left side of the window, select New List.**

   This tells Excel that you're ready to create a new list.

4. **In the "List entries" box on the right side of the window, type in your list.**

   Separate each item with a comma or by pressing Enter. The list in Figure 2-10 shows a series of color names separated by commas.

   If you already typed your list into your worksheet, you can save some work. Instead of retyping the list, click inside the text box labeled "Import list from cells." Then click the worksheet and select the cells that contain the list. (Each item in the list must be in a separate cell, and the whole list should be in a series of adjacent cells in a single column or single row.) When you finish, click Import, and Excel copies the cell entries into the list you're creating.

5. **Click Add to store your list.**

   You can return to this window any time, select the saved list, and modify it in the window on the right. Just click Add to commit your changes after making a change, or Delete to remove the list entirely.

6. **Click OK to close the Custom Lists window and OK again to close the Excel Options window.**

   You can now start using the list with the current worksheet or in a new worksheet. Just type the first item in your list and then follow the AutoFill steps outlined in the previous section.

Flash Fill

Excel's Flash Fill feature is similar to AutoFill in that it attempts to determine a pattern so it can fill in new cells based on data you already entered. The difference is that Flash Fill doesn't limit itself to a single column or row of values. Instead, it looks at all the surrounding cells and attempts to recognize more complex patterns.

Flash Fill is ideal for common data-entry tasks. It shines when you need to clean up long lists of information—for example, splitting the text in one column into multiple columns, or combining text from multiple columns into a single column. To understand how Flash Fill works, it helps to consider a basic example, like the worksheet of names shown in Figure 2-11.

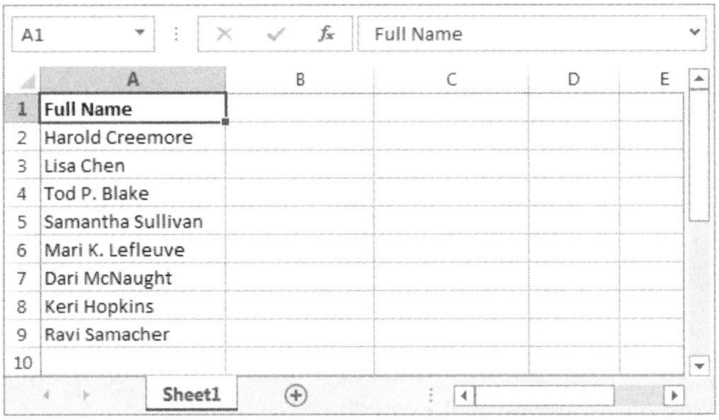

FIGURE 2-11

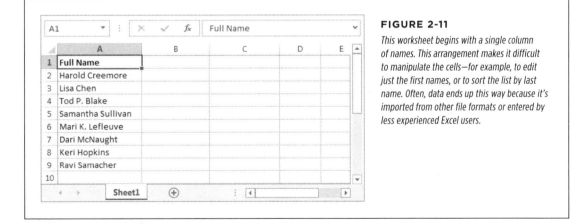

This worksheet begins with a single column of names. This arrangement makes it difficult to manipulate the cells—for example, to edit just the first names, or to sort the list by last name. Often, data ends up this way because it's imported from other file formats or entered by less experienced Excel users.

To clean up this worksheet, you might decide to split the name information into three columns: one for the first name, one for the middle initial, and one for the last name. Doing this manually can be quite a chore, especially if your list stretches to hundreds of names.

This is where Flash Fill becomes truly useful. With it, you make the first change, and then ask Excel to finish the job. Here's how:

1. **Start a new column. At the top of the column, add the heading.**

   FlashFill likes consistency. If you have a heading on the left column (like "Full Name", in cell A1), then you should have a heading on the right one (like "Last Name", in cell B1).

2. **Enter the edited value for the first item in your new column.**

   In the example in Figure 2-11, you need to create a new column of last names. Copy the first full name from A2 to B2, and then edit the copy so that just the last name remains (Figure 2-12).

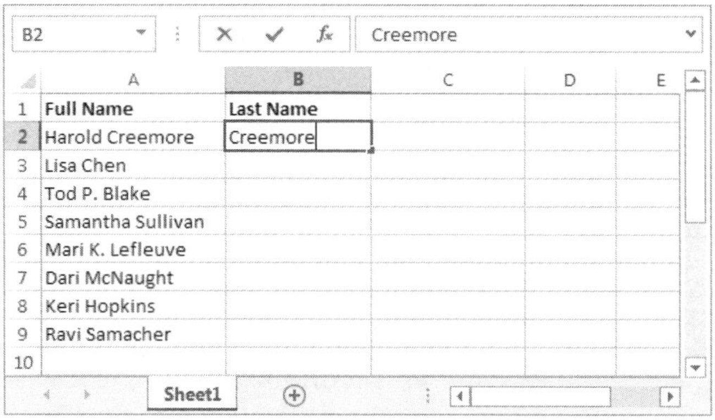

FIGURE 2-12

The job has only just begun. So far, you've extracted just one last name from just one cell.

NOTE Flash Fill works when you add new cells that use other cells in some way (for example, the new cell might combine content from other cells, or extract just part of the content in other cells). Flash Fill doesn't work if you're *editing* the original data. For example, it won't help if you're changing the original names in column A in Figure 2-12.

3. **Move to the next item, but don't add any more data yet.**

   In the current example, that means moving down to cell B3.

4. **Now it's time to put Flash Fill to work. Press Ctrl+E (or choose Home→Editing→Fill→Flash Fill, if you prefer mouse clicks to keyboard shortcuts).**

   Excel looks at the surrounding data and takes its best guess about what belongs in the empty cell. But it doesn't stop there—instead, it attempts to fill the whole column to match (Figure 2-13).

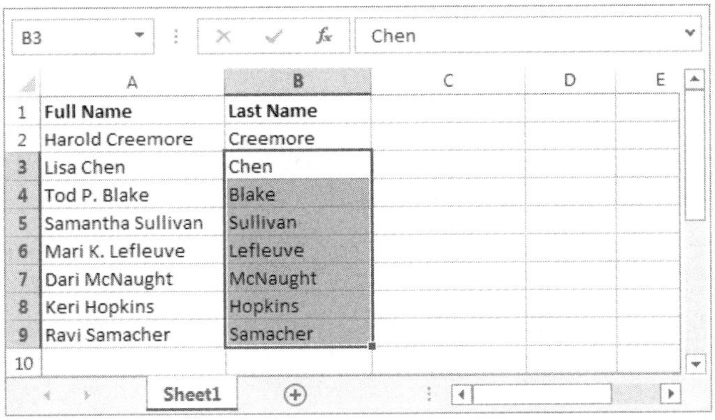

FIGURE 2-13

Press Ctrl+E once and Excel extracts the last name from every other cell in column A, and copies it into the blank cells in column B.

5. **Repeat the process to add all the columns you need.**

   So far, you've extracted just the last names. Now, move to column C to extract the first names. As before, you simply need to enter the first name for the first row, jump down to the cell below, and hit Ctrl+E.

   The next logical step is to move to column D and work on middle initials. Here, you'll run into a problem. Because not all the names have a middle initial, FlashFill's pattern matching system is confused. In cases like these, FlashFill may make mistakes (for example, extracting a different letter for names that don't include a middle initial) or it may refuse to work at all (in which case Excel gives you the message "We looked at all the data next to your selection and didn't see a pattern" when you press Ctrl+E). Quirks like these are unavoidable because FlashFill, smart as it is, can't deal with any inconsistencies in your data.

6. **If you don't need the original data anymore, you can delete it now.**

   Once you extract the first names and last names, you may not want column A, which combines them. To remove it, click the column header (the letter A at the top of the column) and choose Home→Cells→Delete→Delete Sheet Rows.

When Flash Fill works, it seems almost miraculous. Here are some examples of the editing patterns it understands:

- **Extracting part of a cell.** You saw how Flash Fill can grab first names and last names. This works because it pays attentions to spaces and uses them to separate a text value into distinct words. Flash Fill identifies words separated by periods or commas equally well. It can also grab a certain number of characters by position (for example, the first 12 characters in every cell).

- **Changing case.** For example, you can take a name in all-caps (JOE BLOW) and change it to initial-caps (Joe Blow). Or, you can turn an all-caps sentence ("OPEN THE DOOR!") into proper sentence case ("Open the door!").
- **Combining cells.** Instead of splitting cells, you can combine them. For example, if you have first and last names in separate columns, you can create a third column that puts the two together (in any order), and Flash Fill will finish the job.
- **Adding text to cells.** Maybe you want to take an existing value and add some text around it. For example, you can take a cell that contains the number 43.75 and use it to create another column with the text "Current Price: $43.75."
- **Extracting part of a date or number.** For example, you can get the decimal portion from a number (like 13 from 172.13) or part of a date (like 23 from January 23, 2013). However, remember that Flash Fill is a one-time operation. If you use it to get part of a number or date and you later change the original number or date, your Flash-Fill copy won't change.

NOTE Flash Fill is ideal when you want to take some data, create a cleaned-up copy, and then delete your original data. Flash Fill isn't a good choice if you want to keep your original data around, because there's no way to make sure the Flash-Filled copy stays in sync with the original data. (If that's what you want to do, you're better off writing formulas that can grab and manipulate the content in other cells *dynamically*. You'll learn how to do that in Part Two of this book.)

- **A combination of the above.** You can perform more than one of these changes at once, and Flash Fill can usually keep up. For example, you can extract the last name from a full name and change its capitalization, all in one step.

Figure 2-14 shows several more examples of Flash Fill at work.

	A	B	C	D	E	F	G	H	I
1	Full Date	Month		Price	Tag Text		First Initial	Last Name	Combined
2	1-Sep-13	SEP		$43.99	The full price is $43.99		H	Creemore	H. Creemore
3	16-May-88			$159.75			L	Chen	
4	12-Dec-14			$23.00			T	Blake	
5	29-Jun-06			$69.99			S	Sullivan	
6	1-Jan-14			$12.50			M	Lefleuve	
7	12-Jan-14			$23.44			D	McNaught	
8	30-Jan-14			$299.75			K	Hopkins	
9	9-Apr-13			$101.00			R	Samacher	
10									

Sheet1

	A	B	C	D	E	F	G	H	I
1	Full Date	Month		Price	Tag Text		First Initial	Last Name	Combined
2	1-Sep-13	SEP		$43.99	The full price is $43.99		H	Creemore	H. Creemore
3	16-May-88	MAY		$159.75	The full price is $159.75		L	Chen	L. Chen
4	12-Dec-14	DEC		$23.00	The full price is $23.00		T	Blake	T. Blake
5	29-Jun-06	JUN		$69.99	The full price is $69.99		S	Sullivan	S. Sullivan
6	1-Jan-14	JAN		$12.50	The full price is $12.50		M	Lefleuve	M. Lefleuve
7	12-Jan-14	JAN		$23.44	The full price is $23.44		D	McNaught	D. McNaught
8	30-Jan-14	JAN		$299.75	The full price is $299.75		K	Hopkins	K. Hopkins
9	9-Apr-13	APR		$101.00	The full price is $101.00		R	Samacher	R. Samacher
10									

Sheet1

FIGURE 2-14

Top: Here are three in-progress editing tasks that share one thing in common—Flash Fill can automate them all.

Below: Here's the same worksheet after Flash Fill completes each of the three tables.

Dealing with Change: Undo, Redo, and AutoRecover

While editing a worksheet, an Excel guru can make as many (or more) mistakes as a novice. These mistakes include copying cells to the wrong place, deleting something important, or just making a mess of the cell formatting. Excel masters can recover much more quickly, however, because they rely on Excel's Undo and Redo commands. Get in the habit of calling on these features, and you'll be well on your way to Excel gurudom.

Undo and Redo

As you create your worksheet, Excel records every change you make. Because today's computer has vast resources of memory and computing power (that is, when it's not running the latest three-dimensional real-time action game), Excel can keep this log without slowing your computer down one bit.

If you make a change to your worksheet that you don't like (say you inadvertently delete your company's payroll plan), you can use Excel's Undo command to reverse the change. In the Quick Access toolbar, simply click the Undo button (Figure 2-15) or press the super-useful keyboard shortcut Ctrl+Z. Excel immediately restores your worksheet to its state just before the last change. If you change your mind again, you can revert to the changed state (known to experts as "undoing your undo") by choosing Edit→Redo, or pressing Ctrl+Y.

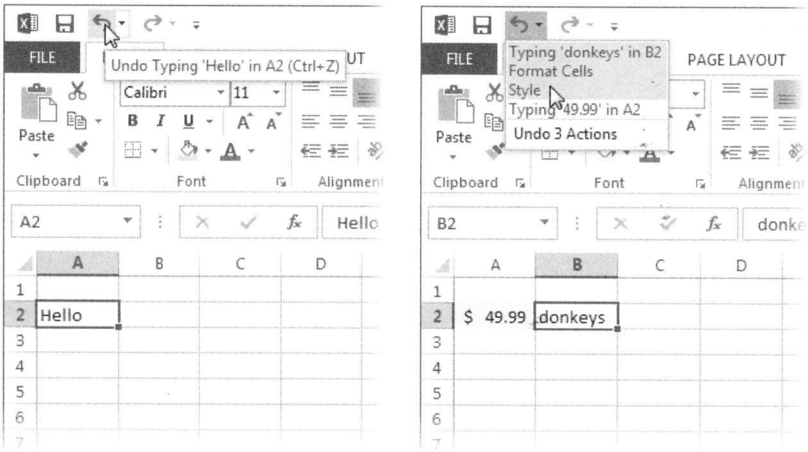

FIGURE 2-15

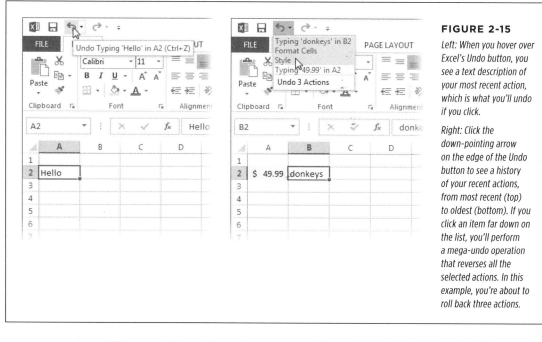

Left: When you hover over Excel's Undo button, you see a text description of your most recent action, which is what you'll undo if you click.

Right: Click the down-pointing arrow on the edge of the Undo button to see a history of your recent actions, from most recent (top) to oldest (bottom). If you click an item far down on the list, you'll perform a mega-undo operation that reverses all the selected actions. In this example, you're about to roll back three actions.

Things get interesting when you want to go farther back than just the previous change, because Excel doesn't just store one change in memory—it tracks your last *100* actions. And it tracks just about anything you do to a worksheet, including cell edits, cell formatting, cut and paste operations, and much more. As a result, if you make a series of changes you don't like, or if you discover a mistake a little later down the road, you can step back through the entire series of changes, one at a time. Every time you press Ctrl+Z, you go back one change in the history. This makes Undo one of the most valuable features ever added to a software package.

NOTE The Undo feature means you don't need to be afraid to make a change that may not come out as you want. Excel experts often try out new actions, and then simply reverse them if the actions don't have the desired effect.

The Undo feature raises an interesting dilemma: When you can go back 100 edits, how do you know exactly what changes you're reversing? Most people don't remember the previous 100 changes they made to a worksheet, which makes it all too easy to reverse a change you really *want*. Excel provides the solution by not only keeping track of old worksheet versions, but also by keeping a simple description of each change. You don't see this description if you use the Ctrl+Z and Ctrl+Y shortcuts.

But you do see it when you hover over the Undo and Redo buttons in the Quick Access toolbar.

For example, consider what happens if you type *Hello* into cell A2 and then clear the cell by pressing the Delete key. Now, when you hover over the Undo button in the Quick Access toolbar, it says "Undo Clear (Ctrl+Z)". If you click Undo, the word *Hello* returns. And if you hover over the Undo button again, it now says, "Undo Typing 'Hello' in A2 (Ctrl+Z)", as shown in Figure 2-15, left.

Incidentally, Excel doesn't clear the Undo history when you save your spreadsheet. Instead, the Undo history remains until you close your workbook file.

NOTE If you're editing an extremely complex worksheet, Excel may not be able to keep an old version of your worksheet in memory. This situation is extremely rare, but if Excel hits this point, it warns you and gives you the chance to either cancel your edit or continue without the possibility of undoing the change. In this rare situation, you may want to cancel the change, save your worksheet as a backup copy, and then continue.

GEM IN THE ROUGH

Using "Repeat" to Automate Tasks

Redo is commonly used to reverse an Undo. In other words, if you cancel an action and then change your mind, you can use Redo to quickly reapply the change. But Redo has a much more interesting relative called Repeat, which lets you repeat any action multiple times. The neat thing is that you can repeat this action *on other cells*.

For example, imagine you hit Ctrl+B to change a cell's formatting to bold. If you move to another cell and hit Ctrl+Y, Excel *repeats* your operation and applies bold formatting to the new cell.

In this case, you're not saving much effort, because it's just as easy to use Ctrl+B to set bolding. But imagine you finish an operation that applies a set of sophisticated formatting changes to a cell. For example, say you go to the Home→Font section of the ribbon, click the dialog launcher to get to the Format Cells window, and then increase the font size, boldface the text, and apply a border around the cell (Chapter 5 tells you how to do all these things). Now, when you move to another cell and press Ctrl+Y, Excel applies all these formatting changes at once—which is much easier than calling up the Format Cells window again and selecting the same options.

The trick to using Repeat is making sure you don't perform another action until you finish repeating your changes. For example, if you make some formatting changes and then stop to delete an incorrect cell value, you can no longer use Repeat to apply formatting because Excel applies the last change you made—in this case, clearing the cell. (Of course, when you mistakenly apply Repeat, you can always call on Undo to get out of the mess.)

If you're ever in doubt about what will happen when you use Repeat, just hover over the Undo button in the Quick Access toolbar. You'll see a text description, like Undo Font or Undo Format Cells, which describes your last action.

AutoRecover

Undo and Redo are undeniably useful, but there's another data-saving trick that just might save your sanity (and your job) if you need it in a pinch: AutoRecover.

In Chapter 1, you learned how AutoRecover can help you out in the event of catastrophe—for example, if Excel crashes or your computer loses power. If that happens, Excel opens your automatically backed-up workbook the next time you start the program. However, you can also use AutoRecover when the problem is your fault—for example, if you just realized you wiped out a critical column of numbers 20 minutes ago.

The solution? Open one of the automatically saved versions of your spreadsheet in a separate Excel window, find the missing or modified data, and then copy it back to the current version of your spreadsheet. Or, if you really made a mess of things, you can revert to the older version.

TIP AutoRecover is perfect in situations where Undo isn't enough—for example, if you made the change long ago and it isn't in the Undo history anymore, or if you don't want to reverse every change you made after your mistake in order to fix the problem.

To see the AutoRecover files for your current workbook, choose File→Info. Excel switches into backstage view and shows the info page. At the bottom, next to the Manage Versions button, is a list with all the automatically saved copies of your work (Figure 2-16).

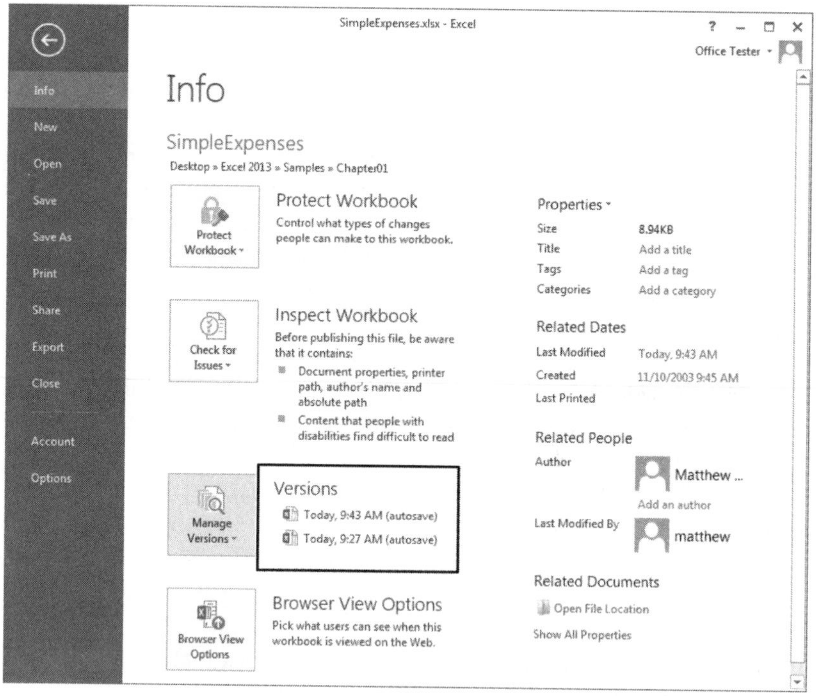

FIGURE 2-16

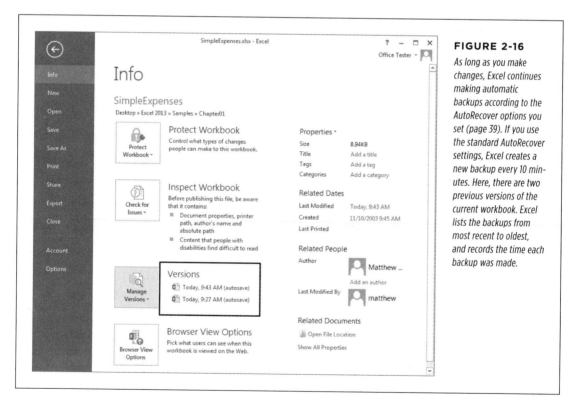

As long as you make changes, Excel continues making automatic backups according to the AutoRecover options you set (page 39). If you use the standard AutoRecover settings, Excel creates a new backup every 10 minutes. Here, there are two previous versions of the current workbook. Excel lists the backups from most recent to oldest, and records the time each backup was made.

To take a look at an AutoRecover backup, just click the file you want in the Versions list. Excel opens the backup in a new window, but adds a helpful warning to make sure you don't confuse it with the current version (Figure 2-17).

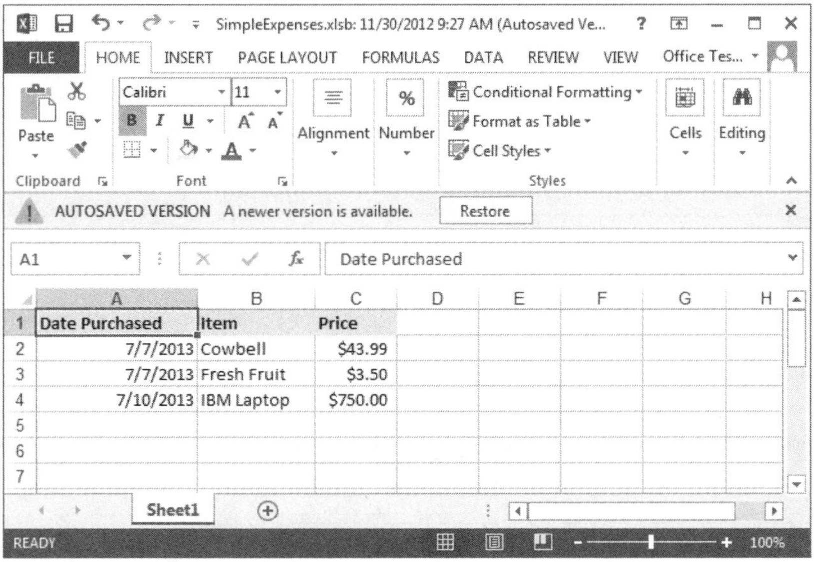

FIGURE 2-17

The yellow bar at the top of the worksheet indicates that this is an autosaved version of the workbook. You can copy data from this window to the window that has your current version, or you can click Restore to abandon your current version and use this in its place.

NOTE Ordinarily, Excel deletes AutoRecover files when you close a workbook, but there's one significant exception. If you close a workbook without saving it, the last AutoRecover version remains on your computer. To get it back, open the file again and look at the list of old versions (choose File→Info, as shown in Figure 2-16). You'll see just one backed-up copy, with the note "(when I closed without saving)" next to its name. This is the version of your spreadsheet that you didn't save.

Interestingly, if you start a new workbook, work on it long enough for Excel to create an AutoRecover backup, and then exit without saving it, the AutoRecover file will *still* remain, even though you haven't saved your work even once. A similar thing happens if you open a file, edit it for a while, and close it without saving your changes. Excel calls this sort of file a *draft*, and you can usually find it in the recent files list (choose File→Open). Or, to dig it up later, choose File→Info, click the Manage Versions button, and choose Recover Unsaved Workbooks. An Open window appears with a list of drafts (Figure 2-18).

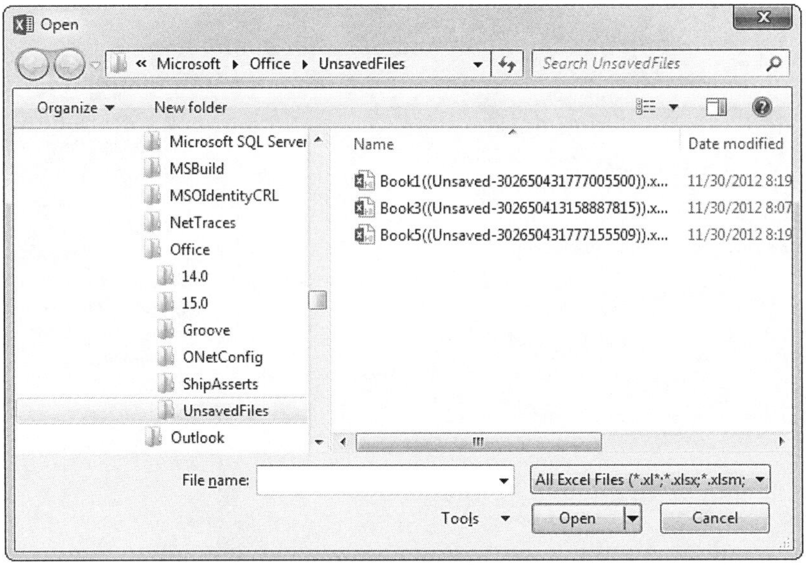

FIGURE 2-18

Here, Excel is storing three unsaved workbooks. The file name is the name Excel originally gave the new document (like Book1), followed by a unique string of numbers. To open a workbook, select it and then click Open, or double-click the file name.

You shouldn't depend on Excel to keep copies of unsaved work. After all, the AutoRecover file is a temporary backup, and Excel can delete it any time. Instead, think of AutoRecover as an emergency measure, there to bail you out if you make a serious blunder. For example, almost every Excel guru has a horror story that runs like this: "It was 3:00 a.m. and I had just finished a long bout of number-crunching, with eight Excel windows open. Relieved that my job was done, I saved my file, closed the program, and hit Don't Save a few times to get rid of my temporary work—only to realize I had another spreadsheet open with all the company financials in it, and I'd just banished it into oblivion." Fortunately, you won't face this nightmare. If you act fast, you'll find that your abandoned file is still available in the recent files list.

NOTE Excel files usually aren't that big, so you don't need to worry about drafts cluttering up your computer's hard drive. If you want to clear them out anyway, choose File→Info, click Manage Versions, and choose Delete All Unsaved Workbooks.

Incidentally, Excel stores its AutoRecover backups in a specific location, based on the person currently logged on to the computer. For example, if you're logged in as cindy_k, your AutoRecover backups are stored in a hidden folder like this: *C:\Users\cindy_k\AppData\Roaming\Microsoft\Excel.* (Excel creates a separate folder there for each workbook, so each workbook can keep its own carefully separated set of backups.) Excel stores drafts—the AutoRecover files for workbooks you've never saved—in a folder like *C:\Users\cindy_k\AppData\Roaming\Microsoft\DraftFiles*. You can change this location and other AutoRecover settings by clicking File→Options, and then choosing the Save category. Page 39 has a detailed description of AutoRecover settings.

Spell-Check

A spell-checker in Excel? Is that supposed to be for people who can't spell 138 correctly? The fact is that more and more people cram text—column headers, boxes of commentary, lists of favorite cereal combinations—into their spreadsheets. And Excel's designers have graciously responded by providing the very same spell-checker you've probably used with Microsoft Word. As you might expect, Excel's spell-checker only examines text as it sniffs its way through a spreadsheet.

To start the spell-checker, follow these steps:

1. **Move to where you want to start checking your spelling.**

   If you want to check the entire worksheet from start to finish, move to the first cell. Otherwise, move to the location where you want to start spell-checking. Or, if you want to check only a portion of a worksheet, select the cells you want to check.

   Excel's spell-checker checks only one worksheet at a time.

2. **Choose Review→Proofing→Spelling, or press F7.**

   The Excel spell-checker gets to work immediately, starting with the current cell and moving to the right, going from column to column. After it finishes the last column of the current row, it continues with the first column of the next row.

   If you don't start at the first cell (A1) in your worksheet, when Excel reaches the end of the worksheet, it asks if it should continue checking from the beginning of the sheet. If you say yes, it checks the remaining cells and stops when it reaches your starting point (having made a complete pass through all your cells).

When the spell-check finishes, a window informs you that Excel has checked all the cells. If your data passes the spell-check, this window is the only confirmation you'll see. On the other hand, if Excel discovers potential spelling errors, it displays a Spelling window with the offending word and a list of suggestions (as shown in Figure 2-19).

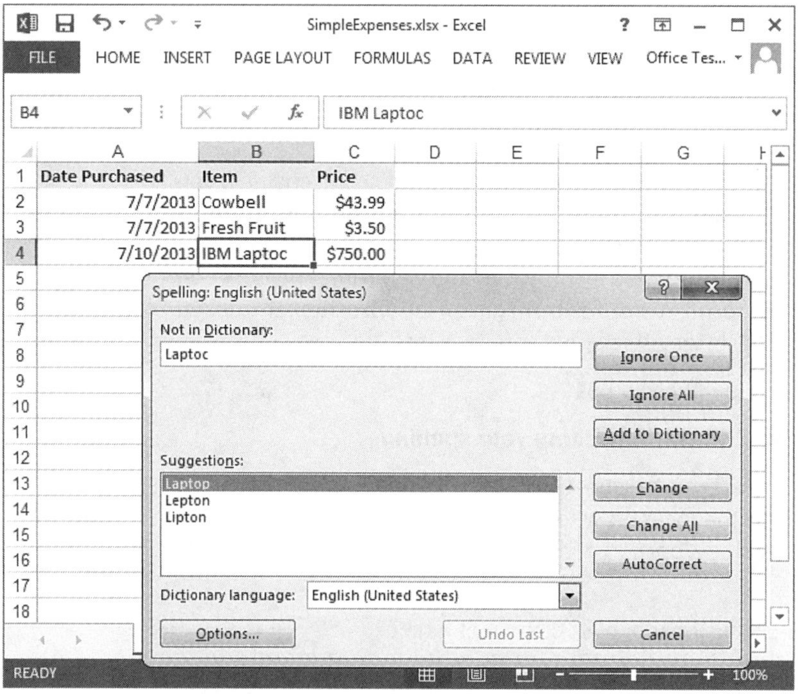

FIGURE 2-19

When Excel encounters a word it thinks you misspelled, it displays the Spelling window. The cell containing the word—but not the actual word itself—gets highlighted with a black border. Excel doesn't let you edit your spreadsheet with the Spelling window active, but if you don't see the word you want in the list of suggestions, you can type a replacement in the "Not in Dictionary" box and click Change.

The Spelling window offers a range of choices. If you want to correct an error, you have four options:

- Click one of the words in the list of suggestions, and then click Change to replace your text with the proper spelling. Double-clicking the correct word has the same effect.
- Click one of the words in the list of suggestions, and then click Change All to replace your text with the proper spelling. If Excel finds the same mistake elsewhere in your worksheet, it repeats the change automatically.

- Click one of the words in the list of suggestions, and then click AutoCorrect. Excel makes the change for this cell and for any other similarly misspelled words. In addition, Excel adds the correction to its AutoCorrect list (described on page 60). That means that if you type the same unrecognized word into another cell (or even another workbook), Excel automatically corrects your entry. This option is useful if you frequently make the same mistake.
- Type your own correction into the "Not in Dictionary" box and hit Enter. This is the approach to use if Excel spots an error but doesn't give you the correct spelling in its list of suggestions.

On the other hand, if Excel warns you about a word that doesn't contain a mistake (like your company name or some specialized term), you can click one of the following buttons:

- **Ignore Once** skips the word and continues the spell-check. If the same word appears elsewhere in your spreadsheet, Excel again prompts you for a correction.
- **Ignore All** skips the current word and all other instances of it in your spreadsheet. You might use Ignore All to force Excel to disregard something you don't want to correct, like a person's name. The nice thing about Ignore All is that Excel doesn't prompt you again if it finds the same name, but it does prompt you if it finds a different spelling (for example, if you spelled the name as "MacDonald" the first time, but as "McDonald" the second time).
- **Add to Dictionary** adds the word to Excel's custom dictionary. Adding a word is great if you plan to keep using it. For example, a company name makes a good addition to the custom dictionary. Not only does Excel ignore any occurrences of this word, but if it finds a similar but slightly different variation, it provides the custom word in its list of suggestions. Even better, Excel uses the custom dictionary on every workbook you spell-check.
- **Cancel** stops the spell-checking operation altogether. You can then correct the cell manually (or do nothing) and resume the spell-check later.

Spell-Checking Options

Excel lets you tweak a few basic spell-checker options, like the language the dictionary uses and which, if any, custom dictionaries Excel examines. To set these options (or to just take a look at them), choose File→Options and then select the Proofing section (Figure 2-20). Or click the Spelling window's Options button when a spell-check is underway.

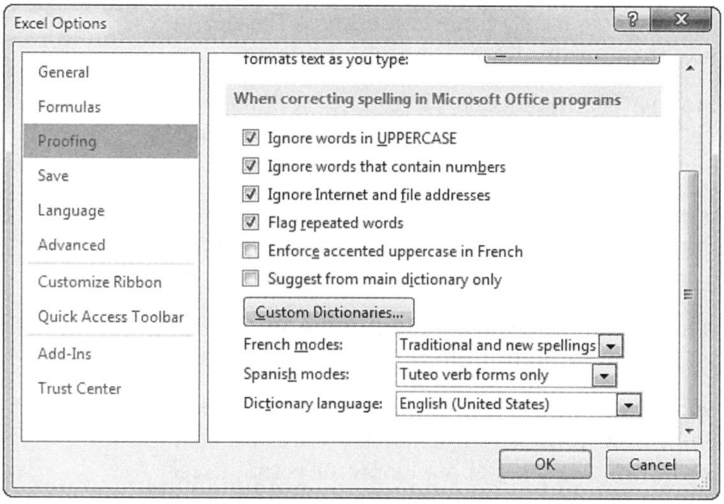

FIGURE 2-20

The spell-checker options lets you specify the dictionary's language and a few other settings. This figure shows Excel's standard settings.

The most important spell-check setting is the language (at the bottom of the window), which determines what dictionary Excel uses. Depending on your version of Excel and the choices you made while installing it, you might be using one or more languages during a spell-check.

Some other spelling options you can set include:

- **Ignore words in UPPERCASE.** Excel won't bother checking any word written in all capital letters (which is helpful when your text contains lots of acronyms).
- **Ignore words that contain numbers.** Excel won't check words that contain numeric characters, like *Sales43* or *H3ll0*. If you don't choose this option, Excel flags these entries as errors unless you added them to the custom dictionary.
- **Ignore Internet and file addresses.** Excel ignores words that appear to be file paths (like *C:\Documents and Settings*) or website addresses (like *http://FreeSweatSocks.com*).
- **Flag repeated words.** Excel treats the same words appearing consecutively ("the the") as an error.
- **Suggest from main dictionary only.** The spell checker won't suggest words from the custom dictionary. However, it still *accepts* a word that matches one of the custom dictionary entries.

You can also choose the file Excel uses to store custom words—the unrecognized words that you add to the dictionary with a spell-check underway. Excel automatically creates a custom dictionary for you, but you might want to use another file if you're sharing someone else's custom dictionary. (You can use more than one custom dictionary at a time. If you do, Excel combines them to get a single list of custom words.) Or, you might want to edit the list of words if you mistakenly added something that shouldn't be there.

To perform any of these tasks, click the Custom Dictionaries button, which opens the Custom Dictionaries window (Figure 2-21). From there, you can remove your custom dictionary, edit it, or add a new one.

FIGURE 2-21

Excel starts you off with two custom dictionary files: RoamingCustom.dic (the default) and custom.dic (for backward compatibility with old versions of Excel). To add a custom dictionary that already exists, click Add and browse to the file. Or click New to create a new, blank custom dictionary. You can also edit the list of words a dictionary contains (select it and click Edit Word List). Figure 2-22 shows an example of editing the default dictionary.

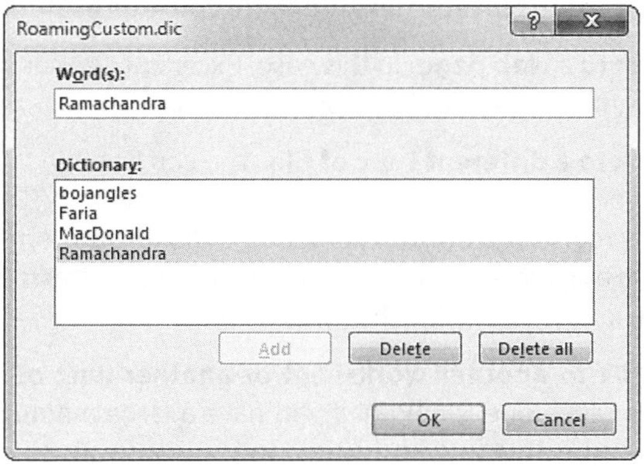

FIGURE 2-22

This custom dictionary is fairly modest. It contains three names and an unusual word. Excel lists the words in alphabetical order. You can add a new word directly from this window (type in the text and click Add), remove one (select it and click Delete), or go nuclear and remove them all (click Delete All).

NOTE All custom dictionaries are ordinary text files with the extension *.dic*. Unless you tell it otherwise, Excel assumes that custom dictionaries are located in a folder named *AppData\Roaming\UProof* inside the folder Windows uses for user-specific settings. For example, if you're logged in under the user account Brad_Pitt, you'd find the custom dictionary at *C:\Users\Brad_Pitt\AppData\Roaming\UProof*.

GEM IN THE ROUGH

Other Proofing Tools

Spreadsheet spell-checking is a useful proofing tool, but Excel doesn't stop there. It piles on a few questionable extras to help you enhance your workbooks. Along with the spell-checker, Excel offers the following goodies. All of them require an Internet connection.

- **Research.** Click Review→Proofing→Research to open a Research window, which appears on the right side of the Excel window and lets you retrieve all kinds of information from the Web. The Research window provides a small set of Internet-driven services, including the ability to search a dictionary for a detailed definition, look in the Encarta encyclopedia, or get a delayed stock market quote from MSN Money.
- **Thesaurus.** Itching to promulgate your prodigious prolixity? (Translation: Wanna use big words?) The thesaurus can help you take ordinary language and transform it into clear-as-mud jargon. Or, it can help you track down a synonym that's on the edge of your tongue. Either way, use this tool with care. To get started, click Review→Proofing→Thesaurus.
- **Translate.** Click this button to translate words or short phrases from one language into another. Behind the scenes, a free web service (like *www.worldlingo.com*) does the actual translation. To try it out, click Review→Language→Translate.

Adding Hyperlinks

Web browsers aren't the only programs that use *hyperlinks*, those underlined pieces of text that let you easily travel around the Web. You may be surprised to find out that hyperlinks are quite useful in Excel, letting you link together different types of content and even navigate large spreadsheets. Here are three common examples:

- **You can create a hyperlink to a web page.** In this case, Excel opens your web browser in a new window and points it to the appropriate page.
- **You can create a hyperlink to a different type of file.** You can link to a Word document or a PowerPoint presentation, among other things. In this case, Excel opens whatever program is registered on your computer to handle this type of file. For example, if you have a link to a .doc or .docx file and have Word installed, Excel opens a new Word window to display the document.
- **You can create a hyperlink to another worksheet or another part of the current spreadsheet.** This technique is helpful if you have a large amount of data and you want people to be able to quickly jump to the important places.

In Excel, you can place a maximum of one hyperlink in each cell.

TIP Excel can create web page hyperlinks automatically. If you type some text that clearly corresponds to a web address (like text that starts with "http://" or "www."), Excel converts it to a hyperlink. When you're done typing, a smart tag appears, which you can click to undo this automatic adjustment, converting the cell back to ordinary text.

Creating a Link to a Web Page or Document

To insert a hyperlink into a cell, follow these steps:

1. **Move to the cell where you want to place the hyperlink.**

2. **Choose Insert→Links→Hyperlink (or press the shortcut key Ctrl+K).**

   The Insert Hyperlink window appears, as shown in Figure 2-23.

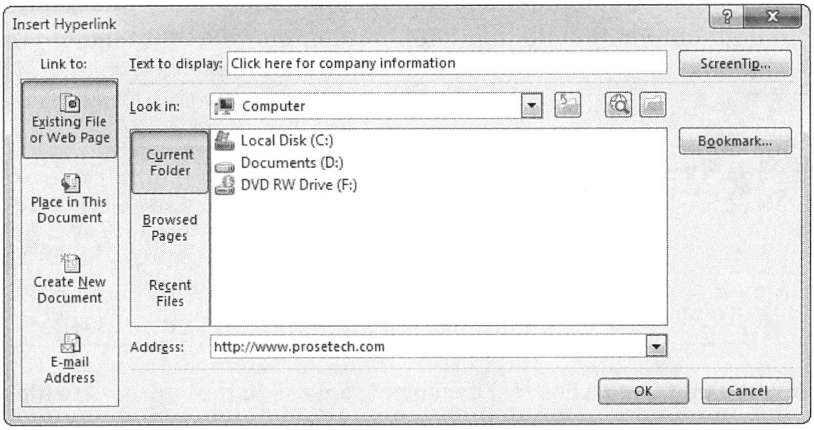

FIGURE 2-23

In this example, you're about to create a new hyperlink. It'll appear in the worksheet with the text "Click here for company information" (which, of course, you can edit to say anything you want) and will take the clicker to the website www.prosetech.com.

TIP You can also create a hyperlink on a picture object, so that the web page opens when you click the image. To do so, right-click the picture box, choose Hyperlink, and then continue with step 3. (For help inserting the picture in the first place, see Chapter 19.)

3. **Click Existing File or Web Page on the left side of the window.**

   You can also select Create New Document to create a new file and a link to it in one step. The trick is remembering to add the correct file extension so that Windows knows what program to open so you can view and edit the file. If you want to create a new Word document, you need to add .docx to the end of the file name. If you use this feature, you can also select "Edit this document now" to immediately open the file in the appropriate program, once Excel creates it.

4. **At the top of the window, in the "Text to display" box, type in whatever you want the link to say.**

   Common choices include the actual web address (like *www.mycompany.com*) or a descriptive message (like "Click here to go to my company's website"). If the current cell already contains text, that text appears in the "Text to display" text box. If you change it, the new text replaces the cell's current content.

5. **To set a custom tooltip for this hyperlink, click the ScreenTip button. Type in your message and click OK (see Figure 2-24).**

   A custom tooltip is a little message-bearing window that appears above a hyperlink when you hover over a link. If you don't specify a custom tooltip, Excel displays the link's full path or URL.

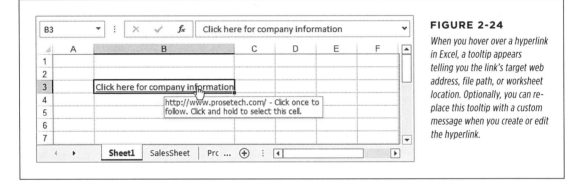

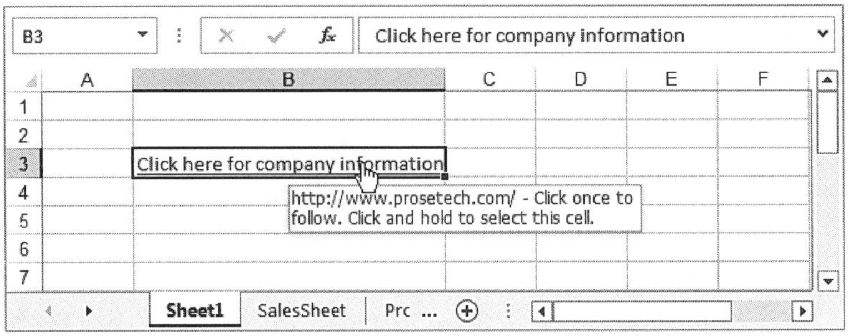

FIGURE 2-24

When you hover over a hyperlink in Excel, a tooltip appears telling you the link's target web address, file path, or worksheet location. Optionally, you can replace this tooltip with a custom message when you create or edit the hyperlink.

6. **If you want to add a link to a document, browse to the appropriate file and select it. If you want to add a link to a web page, type the URL address into the Address text box.**

   If you're adding a link to a document, Excel sets the address to the full file path, as in *C:\MyDocuments\Resume.doc*. You can type this path in manually, and if you're on a network, you can use a UNC (Universal Naming Convention) path to point to a file on another computer, as in *\\SalesComputer\Documents\CompanyPolicy.doc*.

NOTE When you add a hyperlink to a spreadsheet, you're free to point to a file on your computer or on a network drive. Just remember that when you click the link, Excel looks in the exact location you specify. That means that if you move the target file to a new location, Excel won't be able to follow the link.

7. **Click OK to insert the hyperlink.**

   When you insert a hyperlink, Excel formats the cell with blue lettering and adds an underline, so it looks like a web browser hyperlink. If you like, you can reformat the cell using the Home→Font section of the ribbon.

To use a hyperlink, just click it. You'll notice that the mouse pointer changes to a pointing hand as soon as you hover over the link. To move to a cell that contains a hyperlink without activating it, use the arrow keys or click *and hold* the cell for about 1 second.

Creating a Link to a Worksheet Location

Hyperlinks also make for helpful navigational aids. If you have a worksheet with multiple tables of data, you can use a hyperlink to jump to a specific cell. If you create a spreadsheet that splits its data over multiple worksheets (a trick you'll pick up in Chapter 4), you can use a hyperlink to jump from worksheet to worksheet.

To create a hyperlink that uses a worksheet location as its target, follow these steps:

1. **Make note of the target location.**

   A worksheet hyperlink points to a specific cell.

   If you're a bit more advanced, you can create a link that moves to a new worksheet. For example, the reference Sheet2!A1 moves to cell A1 in Sheet2. (To learn more about worksheets and how to create them, see Chapter 4.)

   If you're feeling really slick, you can create a link that points to a *named cell reference*—a descriptive cell shortcut that you create and name. (To learn how to create a named cell reference, see page 384.)

2. **Move to the cell where you want to place the hyperlink.**

3. **Choose Insert→Links→Hyperlink (or press the shortcut key Ctrl+K).**

   The Insert Hyperlink window appears.

4. **Click the "Place in This Document" option on the left side of the window.**

   Excel displays a tree that represents the layout of your current workbook. When you link to another location in the workbook, you need to supply a cell reference (see Figure 2-25).

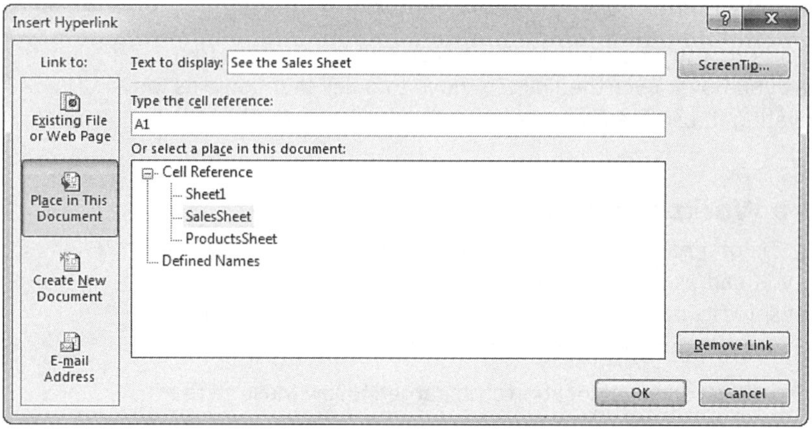

FIGURE 2-25

Excel gives you a convenient tree that represents your workbook. You can choose any of the worksheets in your workbook, or you can choose a predefined named range (page 384).

5. **If you want to jump to another worksheet, select the worksheet from the list.**

   All the worksheet names in your workbook appear under the Cell Reference heading.

6. **Type the cell reference in the "Type the cell reference" text box.**

   Excel jumps to this location when somebody clicks the link.

7. **At the top of the window, in the "Text to display" box, enter whatever you want the link to say.**

   Dealer's choice here.

8. **If you want to set a custom tooltip for this hyperlink, click the ScreenTip button. Type in your message and then click OK.**

9. **Click OK to insert the hyperlink.**

   Admire your handiwork.

TIP To edit a hyperlink, move to the relevant cell and choose Insert→Links→Hyperlink again (or press Ctrl+K). The same window appears, although now it has the title Edit Hyperlink.

CHAPTER

3

Moving Data

Simple spreadsheets are a good way to get a handle on Excel. But in the real world, you often need a spreadsheet that's more sophisticated—one that can grow and change as you track more information. For example, on the expenses worksheet you created in Chapter 1, you might want to add the name of the stores you shopped in. Or you may want to swap the order of your columns. To make changes like these, you need to add a few more skills to your Excel repertoire.

This chapter covers the basics of spreadsheet modification, including how to select cells, how to move data from one place to another, and how to change the structure of your worksheet. What you learn here will make you a master of spreadsheet manipulation.

Selecting Cells

First things first: Before you can make changes to an existing worksheet, you need to select the cells you want to modify. Happily, selecting cells in Excel—try saying that five times fast—is easy. You can do so many ways, and it's worth learning them all. Different selection techniques come in handy in different situations, and if you master all of them in conjunction with the formatting features you'll learn in Chapter 5, you'll be able to transform the look of any worksheet in seconds.

Making Continuous Range Selections

The simplest type of selection you can make is a continuous range selection. A *continuous range* is a block of cells that has the shape of a rectangle (high-school math reminder: a square is a kind of rectangle), as shown in Figure 3-1. The easiest way to select a continuous range is to click the top-left cell you want, and then drag to the right (to select more columns) or down (to select more rows). As you go, Excel highlights the selected cells. Once you highlight all the cells you want, release the mouse button. Now you can perform an action, like copying the selected cells' contents, formatting the cells, or pasting new values into the cells.

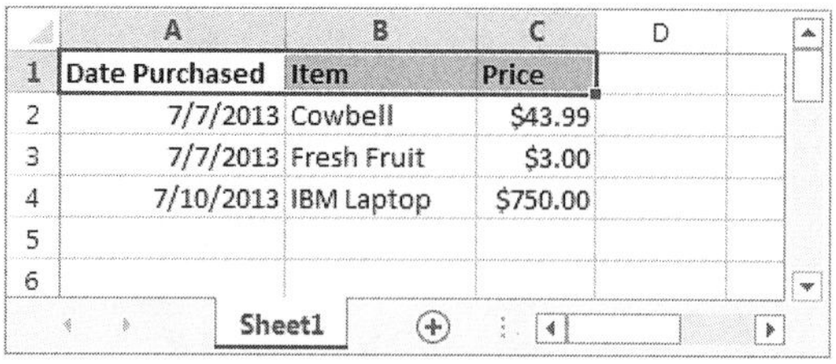

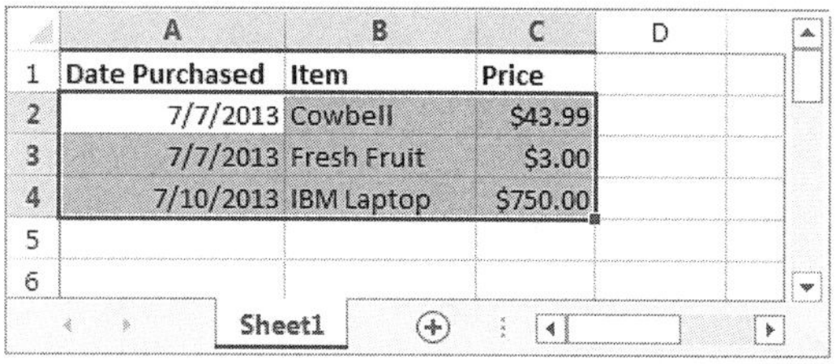

FIGURE 3-1

Top: The three selected cells (A1, B1, and C1) cover the column titles.

Bottom: This selection covers the nine cells that make up the rest of the worksheet. Notice that Excel doesn't highlight the first cell you select. In fact, Excel knows you selected it (as you can see by the thick black border that surrounds it), but gives it a white background to indicate that it's the active cell. When you start typing, Excel inserts your text into this cell.

In the simple expense worksheet from Chapter 1, for example, you could select the cells in the top row and then apply bold formatting to make the column titles stand out. (Select the top three cells and then press Ctrl+B, or chose Home→Font→Bold.)

Excel offers a few useful shortcuts for making continuous range selections (some illustrated in Figure 3-2):

- Instead of clicking and dragging to select a range, you can use a two-step technique: First, click the top-left cell. Then hold down the Shift key and click the cell in the bottom-right corner of the area you want to select. Excel highlights all the cells in between. This technique works even if both cells aren't visible at the same time; just scroll to the second cell using the scroll bars, and make sure you don't click any other cell on your way there.

- To select an entire column, click the header at the top of the column (as shown in Figure 3-2). For example, to select the second column, click the gray "B" box above the column. Excel selects all the cells in this column, right down to row 1,048,576.

- To select an entire row, click the numbered header on the left edge of the row. For example, you select the second row by clicking the gray "2" box to the left of the row. Excel highlights all the columns in row 2.

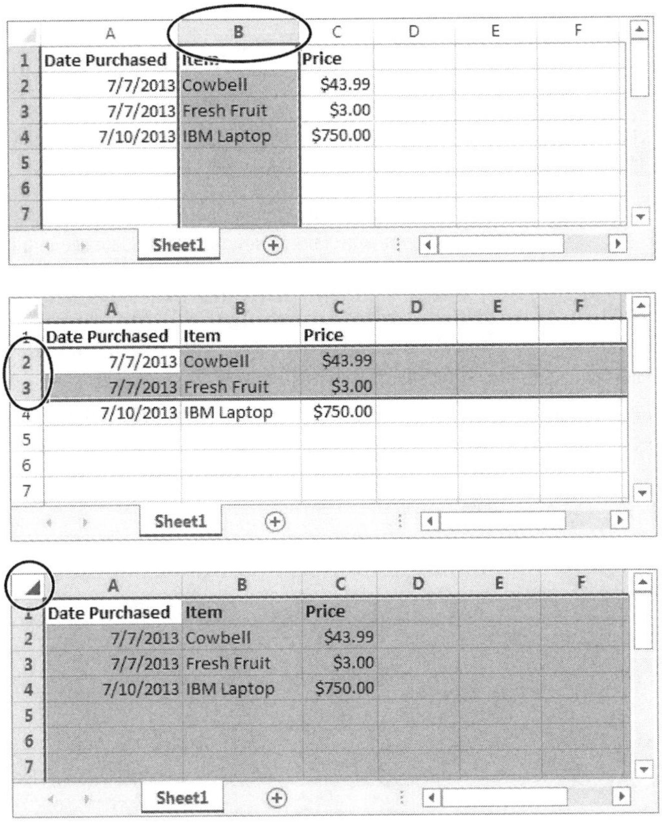

FIGURE 3-2

Top: Click a column header to select the entire column.

Middle: Click a row number to select an entire row.

Bottom: To select every cell in a worksheet, click the triangle in the top-left corner.

- To select multiple adjacent columns, click the leftmost column header and then drag to the right until you select all the columns you want. As you drag, a tooltip appears indicating how many columns you've selected. For example, if you select three columns, the tooltip displays the text "3C" (C stands for "column").
- To select multiple adjacent rows, click the topmost row header and then drag down until you select all the rows you want . As you drag, a tooltip tells you how many rows you've selected. For example, if you select two rows, the tooltip says "2R" (R stands for "row").
- To select all the cells in a worksheet, click the blank gray box just outside the top-left corner, immediately to the left of the column headers and just above the row headers.

TIP When you select multiple rows or columns of a spreadsheet, make sure you click *between* the column header's left and right edges, not *on* either edge. When you click the right edge of a column header, you end up resizing the column instead of making a selection.

GEM IN THE ROUGH

A Truly Great Calculation Trick

Excel provides a seriously nifty calculation tool in the status bar. Just select two or more cells and look down at the status bar; you'll see the number of cells you selected (the *count*) along with their sum and average (shown in Figure 3-3).

To choose what calculations appear in the status bar, right-click anywhere in the status bar and then, in the menu that appears, choose one of the following options:

- **Average.** The average of the selected numbers or dates.
- **Count.** The number of selected cells that contain some type of content (in other words, cells that aren't blank).
- **Numerical Count.** The number of selected cells that contain numbers or dates.
- **Minimum.** The selected number or date with the smallest value (for dates, this means the earliest date).
- **Maximum.** The selected number or date with the largest value (for dates, this means the latest date).
- **Sum.** The sum of all selected numbers. Although you can use Sum with date values, adding up dates generates meaningless results.

If you select cells that have both date and numeric information, most of the status bar calculations won't work properly. Why? Excel gets tripped up when you ask it to do a calculation based on both real numbers and dates. That's because it internally stores date values as numbers (page 54), and a combination of date numbers and real numbers gives you a result that, alas, doesn't really mean anything.

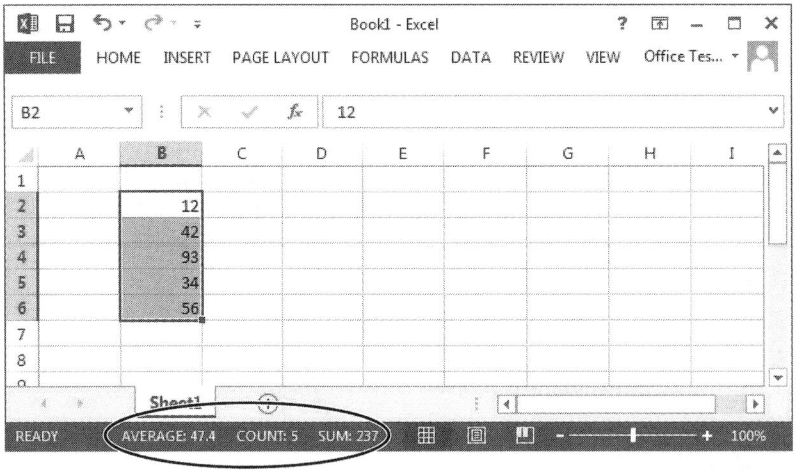

FIGURE 3-3

The status bar displays the results of several classic math operations. Here, you see the count, average, and sum of the selected cells.

If you select a group of cells that isn't completely blank (it has to have at least two values), a small icon appears next to the bottom right-corner of your selection. This icon is the Quick Analysis smart tag. Click it, and a small window pops open with shortcuts for some of Excel's most popular features, like sums, conditional formatting, and charts. You'll use the Quick Analysis icon throughout this book—for example, page 489 puts it to work with charts.

Making Noncontiguous Selections

In some cases, you may want to select *noncontiguous* cells (also known as nonadjacent cells), which means they don't form a neat rectangle. For example, you might want to select columns A and C, but not column B. Or you might want to select a handful of cells scattered throughout your worksheet.

The trick to noncontiguous cell selection is the Ctrl key. All you need to do is select the cells you want while holding down Ctrl. You can select individual cells by Ctrl-clicking them, and you can select multiple blocks of cells in different parts of a sheet by clicking and dragging while holding down Ctrl. You can also combine the Ctrl key with any of the shortcuts discussed earlier to select entire columns or rows. Excel highlights the cells you select (except for the last cell, which, as shown in Figure 3-4, it doesn't highlight because it becomes the active cell).

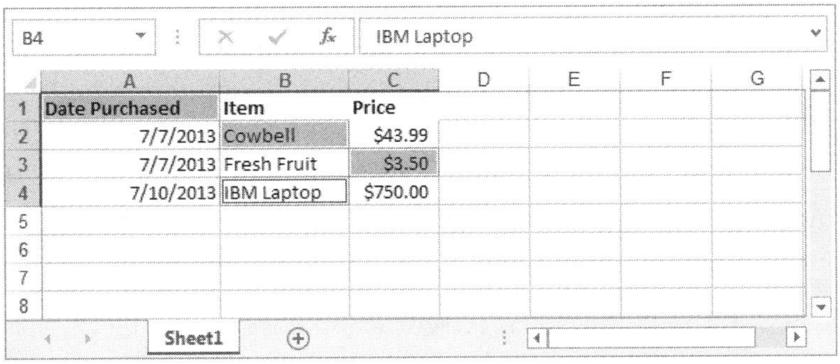

FIGURE 3-4

This figure shows a noncontiguous selection that includes four cells (A1, B2, C3, and B4). Excel doesn't highlight the last cell you select (B4) because it's the active cell. This behavior is a little different from a continuous selection, in which the first cell you select is always the active cell. With a noncontiguous selection, the last cell you select becomes the active cell. Either way, the active cell is still a part of the selection.

Automatically Selecting Your Data

Excel provides a nifty shortcut that can help you select a series of cells without dragging or Shift-clicking anything. It's called AutoSelect, and its special power is to select all the cell values in a given row or column until it encounters an empty cell.

To use AutoSelect, follow these steps:

1. **Move to the first cell you want to select.**

   Before continuing, decide which direction you want to extend the selection.

2. **Hold down the Shift key. Double-click whichever edge of the active cell corresponds to the direction you want to AutoSelect.**

   For example, to select the cells below the active cell, double-click its bottom edge. (You'll know you're in the right place when the mouse pointer changes to a four-way arrow.)

3. **Excel completes your selection automatically.**

   AutoSelect selects every cell in the direction you choose until it reaches the first blank cell. It doesn't select the blank cell (or any cells beyond it).

Making Selections with the Keyboard

The mouse can be an intuitive way to navigate a worksheet and select cells. It can also be a tremendous time-suck, especially for nimble-fingered typists who've grown fond of the keyboard shortcuts that let them speed through actions in other programs.

Fortunately, you can use keyboard shortcuts with Excel, too. One lets you select cells in a worksheet. Just follow these steps:

1. **Move your cursor to the first cell you want to select.**

   Whichever cell you begin on becomes the anchor point from which your selection grows. Think of this cell as the corner of a rectangle you're about to draw.

2. **Hold down the Shift key and, using the arrow keys, move to the right or left (to select more columns) or down or up (to select more rows).**

   Instead of holding down the Shift key, you can press F8 once, which turns on extend mode and displays the text "Extend Selection" in the status bar. As you move, Excel selects cells just as though you were holding down the Shift key. Once you finish marking your range, turn off extend mode by pressing F8 again.

TIP If you really want to perform some selection magic, you can throw in one of Excel's powerful keyboard shortcuts. Use Ctrl+Space to select an entire column, or Shift+Space to select an entire row. Or use the remarkable Ctrl+Shift+Space, which selects a block that includes the current cell and all the nearby contiguous cells (stopping only at the edges where it finds a blank cell). Finally, you can hit Ctrl+Shift+Space twice in a row to select the entire worksheet.

Making a noncontiguous selection is almost as easy. The trick is switching between extend mode and another mode called add mode. Just follow these steps:

1. **Move to the first cell you want to select.**

   You can add cells to a noncontiguous range one at a time or add multiple continuous ranges. Either way, you start with the first cell you want to select.

2. **Press F8.**

   This key turns on extend mode and displays "Extend Selection" in the Status bar.

3. **To select more than one cell, use the arrow keys to extend your selection.**

   If you just want to select the currently active cell, do nothing; you're ready to go on to the next step. When you want to add a whole block of cells, you can mark out your selection now. Remember, at this point you're still selecting a continuous range. In the steps that follow, you can add several distinct continuous ranges to make a noncontiguous selection.

4. **Press Shift+F8 to add the highlighted cells to your noncontiguous range.**

   When you hit Shift+F8, you switch to add mode, and you see the text "Add to Selection" in the status bar.

5. **You now have two choices: You can repeat steps 1 to 4 to add more cells to your selection, or you can perform an action on the current selection, like applying new formatting.**

   You can repeat steps 1 to 4 as many times as necessary to add to your noncontiguous range. These new cells (either individual cells or groups of cells) don't need to be near each other or in any way connected to the other cells you select. If you decide you don't want to do anything with your selection after all, press F8 twice—once to move back into extend mode and again to return to normal mode. Now, the next time you press an arrow key, Excel releases the current selection.

POWER USERS' CLINIC

Selecting Cells with the Go To Feature

In Chapter 1 (on page 57), you learned how to use the Go To feature to jump from one position in a cell to another. A little-known Excel secret lets you use the Go To feature to select a *range* of cells, too.

It works like this: Start off in the top-left cell of the range you want to select. Open the Go To window by selecting Home→Editing→Find & Select→Go To or by pressing Ctrl+G. Type in the address of the bottom-right cell in the selection you want to highlight. Now, here's the secret: Hold down Shift when you click the OK button. This action tells Excel to select the range of cells as it moves to the new cell.

For example, if you start in cell A1 and use the Go To window to jump to B3, you'll select a block of six cells: A1, A2, A3, B1, B2, and B3.

TIP You can also use the keyboard to activate AutoSelect. Just hold down the Shift key and use one of the shortcut key combinations that automatically jumps over a range of cells. For example, when you hold down Shift and then press Ctrl+↓, you'll automatically jump to the last occupied cell in the current row with all the cells in between selected. For more information about shortcut keys, refer to Table 2-1 on page 57.

Moving Cells Around

One of the most common reasons to select groups of cells in a worksheet is to copy or move them from one place to another. Excel is a champion of the basic cut-and-paste operation, and it gives you enhancements that let you do things like drag and drop blocks of cells and copy multiple selections to the Clipboard.

Before you start shuffling data from one place to another, here are a few points to keep in mind:

- Excel lets you cut or copy a single cell or a continuous range of cells. Ordinarily, when you cut or copy a cell, *everything* goes with it, including the data and formatting. But Excel also lets you copy data without formatting (or even *just* the formatting). You'll learn about those options on page 96.
- When you paste cells into your worksheet, you have two basic choices: To paste the cells into a new, blank area of the worksheet, or to paste them in a place that already contains data. In the second case, Excel overwrites the existing cells with the newly pasted data.
- Cutting and copying cells works almost exactly the same way. The only difference is that when you *cut* and paste information (as opposed to *copying* and pasting it), Excel erases the source data. However, it doesn't remove the source cells from the worksheet, it just leaves them empty. (Page 103 shows you what to do if you do want to remove or insert cells, not just the data they contain.)

A Simple Cut-and-Paste or Copy-and-Paste

Here's the \basic procedure for any cut-and-paste or copy-and-paste operation:

1. **Select the cells you want to cut or copy.**

   You can use any of the tricks you learned in the previous section to highlight a continuous range of cells. (You can't cut and paste noncontiguous selections.)

   When you want to cut or copy only a single cell, just move to the cell—you don't actually need to select it.

2. **If you want to cut your selection, choose Home→Clipboard→Cut (or Ctrl+X). To copy your selection, choose Home→Clipboard→Copy (or Ctrl+C).**

   Excel highlights your selection with a *marquee border* (Figure 3-5), so-called because it blinks like the twinkling lights of an old-style movie marquee. At the same time, the text "Select destination and press ENTER or choose Paste" appears in the status bar (if it fits).

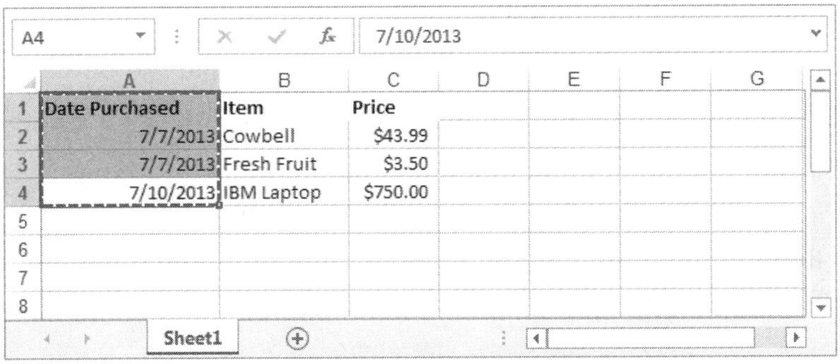

FIGURE 3-5

In this example, you copied cells A1 to A4. The next step is to position your cursor where you want to paste the cells and then press Enter to complete the operation. Excel treats cut and copy operations the same way. In both cases, the selection remains on the spreadsheet, surrounded by the marquee border. When you cut cells, Excel doesn't empty the original ones until you paste the cut cells somewhere else.

3. **Move to the location where you want to paste the cells.**

   If you selected just one cell, move to the cell where you want to place the data. If you selected multiple cells, move to the top-left corner of the area where you want to paste your selection. If you have data below or to the right of that cell, Excel overwrites it with the content you paste.

   It's perfectly acceptable to paste over the data you're copying. For example, you could make a selection that consists of columns A, B, and C and paste that selection starting at column B. In this case, the pasted data appears in columns B, C, and D, and Excel overwrites the original content in these columns (although the original content remains in column A).

TIP In some cases, you want to paste without overwriting part of your worksheet. For example, you might want to paste a column in a new position and shift everything else out of the way. To pull this trick off, you need the Insert Copied Cells command, which is described on page 104.

4. **Paste the data by selecting Home→Clipboard→Paste (or press Ctrl+V or Enter on the keyboard).**

   If you're cutting and pasting data, Excel removes the original data from the spreadsheet just before pasting it in the new location.

   If you're copying and pasting info, Excel displays a tiny Clipboard icon in the bottom-right corner of the pasted cells, with the text "(Ctrl)" next to it. Click this icon to get a menu of specialized paste options (described on page 97).

A Quicker Cut-and-Paste or Copy-and-Paste

If you want a really quick way to cut and paste data, use Excel's drag-and-drop feature. It works like this:

1. **Select the cells you want to move.**

   Drag your pointer over the block of cells you want to select.

2. **Click the border of the selection box and don't release the mouse button.**

   You'll know you're in the right place when the mouse pointer changes to a four-way arrow. You can click any edge, but *don't* click in the corner.

3. **Drag the selection box to its new location.** If you want to copy (not move) the text, hold down the Ctrl key while you drag.

   As you drag, a light-gray box shows you where Excel will paste the cells.

4. **Release the mouse button to move the cells.**

   If you drop the cells into a region that overlaps with other data, Excel prompts you to make sure that you want to overwrite the existing cells. You don't get this convenience with ordinary cut-and-paste operations. (Excel uses it for drag-and-drop operations because it's all too easy to inadvertently drop your cells in the wrong place, especially while you're still getting used to this feature.)

TIP Excel has a hidden dragging trick that impresses even the most seasoned users. To use it, follow the steps listed above, but click on the border of the selection box with the *right* mouse button instead of the left. When you release the mouse button to finish the operation, a pop-up menu appears with a slew of options. Using this menu, you can perform a copy instead of a move, shift the existing cells out of the way, or use a special pasting option to copy values, formats, or links (page 97).

FREQUENTLY ASKED QUESTION

The Mysterious Number Signs

What does it mean when I see ####### in a cell?

A series of number signs is Excel's way of telling you that a column isn't wide enough to display the number or date that it contains (see Figure 3-6). Sometimes these signs appear when you copy a big number into a narrow cell.

The problem here is that Excel needs a certain amount of space to display your number. It's not acceptable to show just the first two digits of the number 412, for example, because that will look like the completely different number 41. However, Excel will trim off decimal places, if it can, which means that it will show 412.22344364 as 412.223 in a narrow column, while storing the full value behind the scenes. But when a column is too narrow to fit a whole number, or if you set a required number of decimal places for a cell (page 131) and the column's too narrow to accommodate them, Excel displays the number signs to flag the problem.

Fortunately, the issue's easy to resolve—just position the mouse pointer at the right edge of the cell header and drag it to the right to enlarge the column. Provided you've made the column large enough, the missing number reappears. For a quicker solution, double-click the right edge of the column to automatically make it large enough.

You don't usually see this error the first time you enter information because Excel automatically resizes columns to accommodate any numbers you type in. The problem is more likely to crop up if you shrink a column afterward, or if you cut some numeric cells from a wide column and paste them into a much narrower one. To verify the source of your problem, move to the offending cell and then check the formula bar to see your complete number or date. Excel doesn't use the number signs with text cells—if those cells aren't large enough to hold their data, the words simply spill over to the adjacent cell (if it's blank) or become truncated (if the adjacent cell has content in it).

There's one other situation that can cause a cell to display #######. If you create a formula that subtracts one time from another (as described in Chapter 11), and the result is a *negative* time value, you see the same series of number signs. But in this case, column resizing doesn't help.

FIGURE 3-6

Cell C4 holds a wide number in an overly narrow column. You can see the mystery number if you move to the cell and check out the formula bar (it's 10,042.01), or you can expand the column to a more reasonable width.

Fancy Pasting Tricks

When you copy cells, *everything* comes along for the ride, including text, numbers, and formatting. For example, if you copy a column that has one cell filled with bold text and several other cells filled with dollar amounts (including the dollar sign), when you paste this column into its new location, the numbers will still have the dollar sign and the text will still have bold formatting. If you want to change this behavior, you can use one of Excel's fancy paste options.

On their own, these options can seem intimidatingly complex. But Excel helps out with a *paste preview* feature so you see what your cells will look when you actually paste them into your worksheet.

Here's how to try it out. First, copy your cells in the normal way. (Don't cut them, or the Paste Special feature won't work.) Then, move to where you want to paste the information, go to the Home→Clipboard section of the ribbon, and click the drop-down arrow at the bottom of the Paste button. You'll see a menu full of tiny pictures, each of which represents a different type of paste (see Figure 3-7).

Here's where things get interesting. When you hover over one of these pictures (but don't click it), the name of the paste option pops up, and Excel shows you a preview of what the pasted data will look in your worksheet. If you're happy with the result, click the picture to finish the paste. Otherwise, move your mouse over a different option to preview *its* results. And if you get cold feet, you can call the whole thing off by clicking any cell in the worksheet, in which case the preview disappears and the worksheet returns to its previous state.

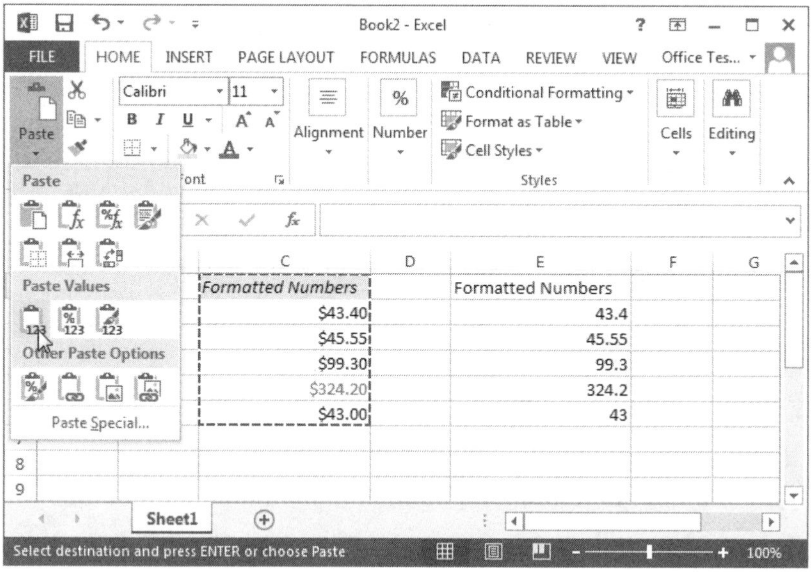

FIGURE 3-7

In this example, the original data is in cells C1 to C6. The paste preview is shown in cells E1 to E6. Here, Excel previews the Values paste option, which copies all the numbers in a selection, but none of the formatting. You can move to a different paste option and get a different preview or click a cell in the worksheet to banish the preview and cancel the paste operation.

When you copy Excel cells (as opposed to data from another program), the list of paste options includes 14 choices arranged in three groups. The first group, named Paste, includes these choices:

- **Paste.** This option is the same as a normal paste operation, and it pastes both formatting and numbers.
- **Formulas.** This option pastes only cell content—numbers, dates, and text—without any formatting. If your source range includes any formulas, Excel also copies the formulas.
- **Formulas and Number Formatting.** This option is the same as Formulas, except that it retains the formatting for any numbers you copy. So Excel will retain currency signs, percentage signs, and thousands separators in numbers, but it drops the formatting for fancy fonts, colors, and borders.
- **Keep Source Formatting.** This option copies all of a cell's data and formatting. In fact, it's the same as the ordinary Paste option, making it a minor Excel quirk.
- **No Borders.** This option copies all the data and formatting (just like an ordinary Paste), except that it ignores any borders you drew around the cells. (Page 158 describes adding borders to cells.)
- **Keep Source Column Widths.** This option copies all the data and formatting (just like an ordinary Paste command), but it also adjusts the columns in the pasted region so that they match the widths of the source columns.
- **Transpose.** This option inverts your information before it pastes it, so that all the columns become rows and the rows become columns. Figure 3-8 shows an example.

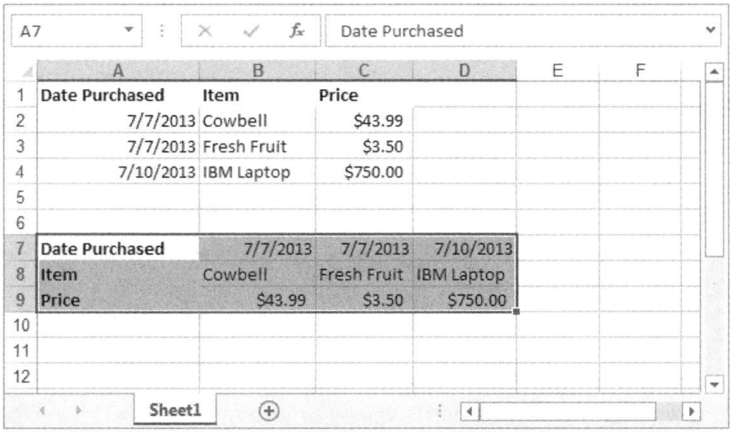

FIGURE 3-8

With the Transpose option (from the Paste Special window), Excel pastes the table at the top and transposes it on the bottom.

The second group of paste options, called Paste Values, includes three choices:

- **Values.** This option pastes only cell content—numbers, dates, and text—without any formatting. If your source range includes any formulas, Excel pastes the *result* of those formulas (the calculated number) but not the actual formulas. (You'll learn everything you need to know about formulas in Chapter 8.)
- **Values and Number Formatting.** This option pastes the cell content and the formatting settings that control how numbers appear. If your source range includes any formulas, Excel pastes the calculated result of those formulas but not the actual formulas.
- **Values and Source Formatting.** This option is the same as a normal paste operation, except that it doesn't copy formulas. Instead, it pastes the calculated result of any formula.

The third group of paste options, called Other Paste Options, includes four choices that are a little more specialized and a little less common:

- **Formatting.** This option applies the formatting from the source selection, but it doesn't actually copy any data.
- **Paste Link.** This option pastes a *link* in each cell that points to the original data. (By comparison, an ordinary paste creates a duplicate *copy* of the source content.) If you use this option and then modify a value in one of the source cells, Excel automatically modifies the copy, too. (In fact, if you take a closer look at the copied cells in the formula bar, you'll find that they don't contain the actual data. Instead, they contain a formula that points to the source cell. For example, if you paste cell A2 as a link into cell B4, then cell B4 contains the reference =A2. You'll learn more about cell references and get to the bottom of this strange behavior in Chapter 8.)
- **Picture.** This option pastes a *picture* of your cell, which is more than a little odd. Excel puts the picture right in the worksheet, with the formatting and borders you'd expect. In fact, if you don't look closely, this picture looks almost exactly like ordinary Excel data. The only way you'll know that it isn't is to click it. Unlike ordinary Excel data, you can't edit the data in a picture; instead, you're limited to resizing it, dragging it around your worksheet, and changing its borders. (You'll pick up these picture-manipulation skills in Chapter 19.)

NOTE Although it might make sense to copy a picture of your worksheet into other programs (a feat you'll master in Chapter 24), there's little reason to use the picture-pasting feature inside an Excel spreadsheet.

- **Linked Picture.** This option is the same as Picture, except that Excel regenerates the picture whenever you modify the values or formatting of the source cells. This way, the picture always matches the source cells. Excel experts sometimes use this feature to create a summary that shows the important parts of a massive spreadsheet in one place. But in the wrong hands, this feature is a head-scratching trick that confuses everyone.

At the very bottom of the paste options is a command named Paste Special. This brings up another window, with more esoteric pasting options. You'll take a peek at those in the next section.

Once you become familiar with the different paste options, you don't need to rely on the ribbon to use them. Instead, you can use them after a normal copy-and-paste. After you insert your data (by pressing Enter or using the Ctrl+V shortcut), look for the small paste icon that appears near the bottom-right corner of the pasted region. (Excel geeks know this icon as a *smart tag*.) If you click the icon (or press the Ctrl key), Excel pops open a menu (Figure 3-9) with the same set of paste options you saw earlier.

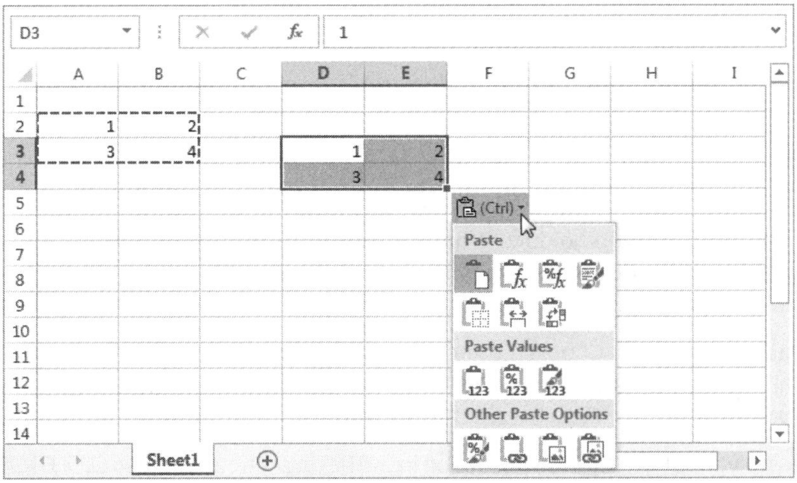

FIGURE 3-9

The paste icon appears after every paste operation, letting you control a number of options, including whether the cell's format matches the source or destination cells. You can change the type of paste you use until you get exactly the result you want. The only disadvantage is that this menu doesn't have the same preview feature that the ribbon offers.

NOTE The paste icon appears only after a copy-and-paste operation, not a cut-and-paste operation.

Paste Special

The paste options in the ribbon are practical and powerful. But Excel has even more paste options for those who have the need. To see them all, choose Home→Clipboard→Paste→Paste Special to pop open a window with a slew of options (Figure 3-10).

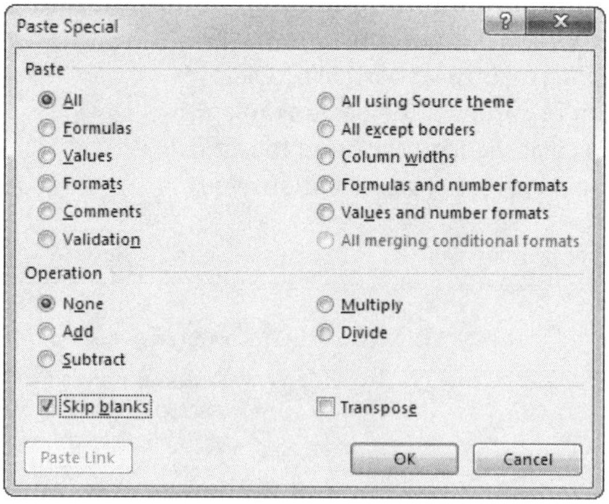

FIGURE 3-10

The Paste Special window lets you choose exactly what Excel pastes, and apply a few other settings. The big drawback is that you don't get a preview, and some of the options are less than clear. In this example, Excel will perform an ordinary paste with a twist—it won't bother to copy any blank cells.

Paste Special is a bit of a holdover from the past. Many of its options are duplicated in the ribbon's drop-down Paste menu. However, the Paste Special window lets you do a few things the ribbon won't, including:

- **Paste comments.** Choose Comments in the Paste section, and then click OK. This leaves all the text and formatting behind but copies any comments you added to the cells. (You'll learn about comments on page 674.)
- **Paste validation.** Choose Validation in the Paste section, and then click OK. This leaves all the text and formatting behind but copies any validation settings you applied to the cells. (You'll learn about validation on page 640.)
- **Combine source and destination cells.** Choose All in the Paste section, choose Add, Subtract, Multiply, or Divide from the Operation section, and then click OK. For example, if you choose Subtract and paste the number 4 into a cell that currently has the number 6, Excel changes the cell to 2 (because *6–2=4*). It's an intriguing idea, but few people use the Operation settings, because they're not intuitive (the settings, not the people).
- **Refrain from copying blank cells.** Choose All in the Paste section, turn on the "Skip blanks" checkbox at the bottom of the window, and then click OK. Now, if any of the cells you're copying are blank, Excel ignores them and leaves the contents of the destination cell intact. (With an ordinary paste, Excel would overwrite the existing value, leaving a blank cell.)

Copying Multiple Items with the Clipboard

In Windows' early days, you could copy only a single piece of information at a time. If you copied two pieces of data, only the most recent item you copied would remain in the Clipboard, a necessary way of life in the memory-starved computing days of yore. But nowadays, Excel boasts the ability to hold 24 separate cell selections in the Office Clipboard. This information remains available as long as you have at least one Office application open.

NOTE Even though the Office Clipboard holds 24 pieces of information, you won't be able to access all of them in Windows applications that aren't part of the Office suite. If you want to paste Excel data into a non-Office application, you'll have access only to the data you added to the Clipboard most recently.

When you use the Home→Clipboard→Paste command (or Ctrl+V), you're using the ordinary Windows clipboard. That means you always paste the item most recently added to the Clipboard. But if you fire up the Office Clipboard, you can choose from many more paste possibilities. Go to the Home→Clipboard section of the ribbon and then click the window launcher (the small arrow-in-a-square icon in the bottom-right corner) to open the Clipboard panel. Now Excel adds all the information you copy to *both* the Windows Clipboard and the more capacious Office Clipboard. Each item you copy appears in the Clipboard panel (Figure 3-11).

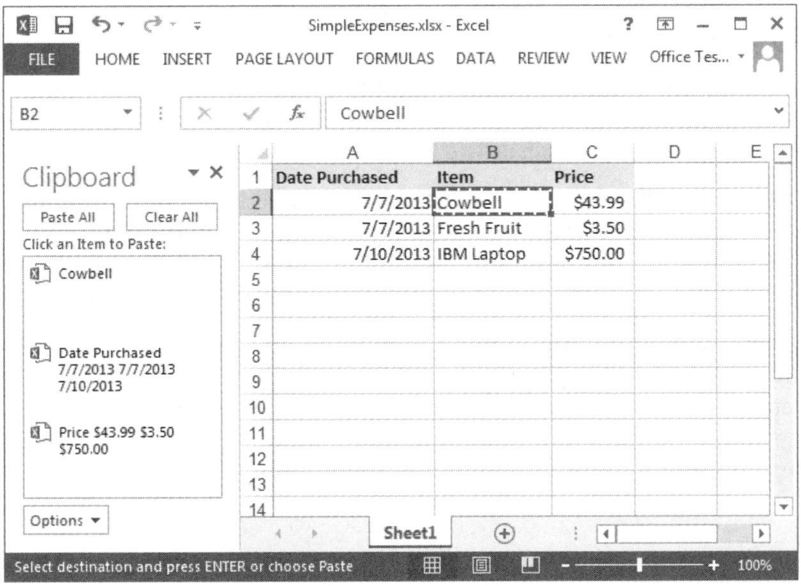

FIGURE 3-11

The Clipboard panel lists all the items you copied to the Office Clipboard since you opened it (up to a limit of 24 items). Each item shows the combined content for all the cells in the selection. For example, the first item in this list includes four cells: the Price column title followed by the three prices. If you're using multiple Office applications at the same time, you may see scraps of Word documents, PowerPoint presentations, or pictures in the Clipboard along with your Excel data. The icon next to the item always tells you which program the information came from.

Using the Clipboard panel, you can do the following:

- **Click Paste All to paste all the selections into your worksheet.** Excel pastes the first selection into the current cell and pastes the next selection starting in the first row underneath that, and so on. As with all paste operations, the pasted cells overwrite any existing content in the cells.
- **Click Clear All to remove all the selections from the Clipboard.** This is a useful approach if you want to add more data to the Clipboard but don't want to confuse this information with what was there before.
- **Click a selection in the list to paste it into the current location in the worksheet.**
- **Click the drop-down arrow to the right of a selected item to see a menu letting you paste the item or remove it from the Clipboard.**

Depending on your settings, the Clipboard panel may automatically spring into action. To configure this behavior, click the Options button at the bottom of the panel to display a menu of settings. They include:

- **Show Office Clipboard Automatically.** If you turn on this option, the Clipboard panel automatically appears if you copy more than one piece of information to the Clipboard. (Remember, without the Clipboard panel, you can access only the last piece of information you copied.)
- **Show Office Clipboard When Ctrl+C Pressed Twice.** If you turn on this option, the Clipboard panel appears when you press Ctrl+C twice in a row.
- **Collect Without Showing Office Clipboard.** If you turn on this option, it overrides the previous two settings, ensuring that the Clipboard panel never appears automatically. You can still call up the panel manually, of course.
- **Show Office Clipboard Icon on Taskbar.** If you turn on this option, a Clipboard icon appears in the system tray to the right of the taskbar. Double-click it to display the Clipboard panel from any Office application. Right-click the icon to change Clipboard settings or to tell the Office Clipboard to stop collecting data.
- **Show Status Near Taskbar When Copying.** If you turn on this option, you'll see a tooltip in the bottom-right corner of your screen whenever you copy data in Excel. The icon for the Office Clipboard is a Clipboard, and it displays a message like "4 of 24 -Item Collected" (which indicates you just copied a fourth item to the Clipboard).

UP TO SPEED

Cutting or Copying Part of a Cell

Excel's cut-and-paste and copy-and-paste features let you move data in one or more cells. But what if you simply want to take a snippet of text from a cell and transfer it to another cell or even another application? It's possible, but you need to work a little differently.

First, move to the cell that contains the content you want to cut or copy. Place the cell in edit mode by double-clicking it with the mouse, clicking in the formula bar, or pressing F2. You can now scroll through the cell's content using the arrow keys. Move to the position where you want to start chopping or copying, hold down the Shift key, and then arrow over to the right. Keep moving until you select all the text you want to cut or copy. Then hit Ctrl+C to copy the text, or Ctrl+X to cut it. (When you cut text, it disappears immediately, just as it does in any other Windows application.) Hit Enter to exit edit mode when you finish.

The final step is to paste your text. You can move to another cell that has data in it already, press F2 to enter edit mode again, move to the correct position in that cell, and then press Ctrl+V. However, you can also paste the text directly into a cell by moving to the cell and pressing Ctrl+V without placing it in edit mode. In this case, the data you paste overwrites the content currently in the cell.

Adding and Moving Columns or Rows

The cut-and-paste and copy-and-paste operations let you move data from one cell (or group of cells) to another. But what if you want to make some *major* changes to your worksheet? For example, imagine you have a spreadsheet with 10 filled columns (A to J) and you decide you want to add a new column between columns C and D. You could cut all the columns from D to J and then paste them starting at E. That would solve the problem and leave column C free for your new data. But the actual task of selecting these columns can be a little awkward, and it only becomes more difficult as your spreadsheet grows in size.

A much easier option is to use two dedicated Excel commands designed for inserting columns and rows into an existing spreadsheet. If you use these features, you won't need to disturb your existing cells at all.

Inserting Columns

To insert a new column, follow these steps:

1. **Find the column immediately to the *right* of where you want to place the new column.**

   That means that if you want to insert a new, blank column between columns A and B, start with the existing column B.

2. **Right-click the column header (the gray box with the column letter in it), and then choose Insert.**

   Excel inserts a new column and automatically moves all the other columns to the right. So if you add a column after column A, the old column B becomes column C, the old column C becomes column D, and so on.

Inserting Rows

Inserting rows is just as easy as inserting columns:

1. **Find the row immediately *below* where you want to place the new row.**

   That means that if you want to insert a new, blank row between rows 6 and 7, start at row 7.

2. **Right-click on the row header (the numbered box at the far left of the row), and then choose Insert.**

   Excel inserts a new row, and all the rows beneath it automatically move down one row.

NOTE In the unlikely event that you have data at the extreme right edge of a spreadsheet, in column XFD, Excel doesn't let you insert a new column *anywhere* in the sheet because the data would be pushed off into the region beyond the spreadsheet's edges. Similarly, if you have data in the very last row (row 1,048,576), Excel doesn't let you insert more rows.

Inserting Copied or Cut Cells

Usually, inserting entirely new rows and columns is the most straightforward way to change the structure of your spreadsheet. You can then cut and paste new information into the blank rows or columns. In some cases, however, you may simply want to insert cells into an *existing* row or column.

To do so, begin by copying or cutting a cell or group of cells and then select the spot you want to paste into. Next, choose Home→Cells→Insert→Insert Copied Cells (or Home→Cells→Insert→Insert Cut Cells if you're cutting instead of copying). Unlike the cut-and-paste feature, when you insert cells, you won't overwrite the existing data. Instead, Excel asks you whether you want the existing cells shifted down or to the right to make way for the new cells (as shown in Figure 3-12).

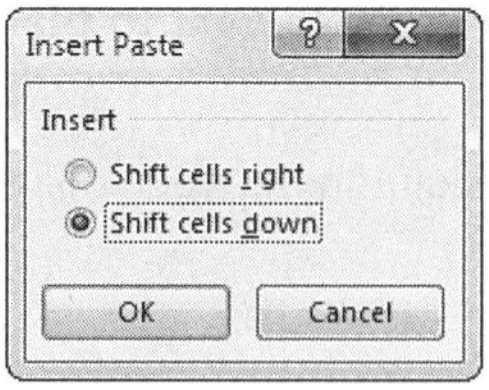

FIGURE 3-12

When you insert copied cells, Excel asks whether it should move the existing cells down or to the right.

You need to be careful when you use the Insert Copied Cells feature. Because you're shifting only certain *parts* of your worksheet, it's possible to mangle your data, splitting the information that should be in one row or one column into multiple rows or columns (see Figure 3-13)! Fortunately, you can always back out of a tight spot with the Undo command (page 69).

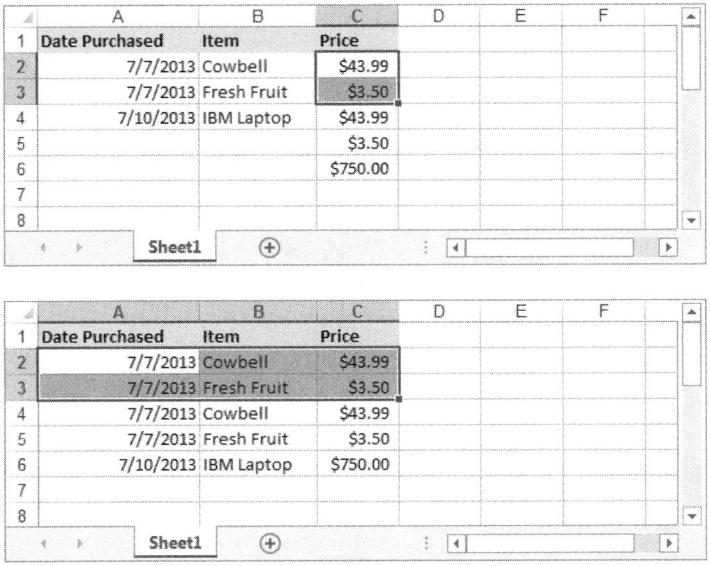

FIGURE 3-13

Top: Here, two price cells ($43.99 and $3.50) were copied and pasted before this picture was taken, and the existing price cells were shifted down to accommodate the new entries. But the prices now no longer line up with the appropriate item names, which is probably not what you want.

Bottom: It makes much more sense to use the Insert Copied Cells command when you copy a row's worth of data. Here's a worksheet where you pasted two new rows while Excel politely moved the original set of items out of the way.

Deleting Columns and Rows

In Chapter 1, you learned that you can quickly remove cell values by moving to the cell and hitting the Delete key. You can also delete an entire range of values by selecting multiple cells and hitting Delete. Using this technique, you can quickly wipe out an entire row or column.

However, Delete simply clears the cell content; it doesn't remove the cells themselves or change the structure of your worksheet. If you want to simultaneously clear cell values *and* adjust the rest of your spreadsheet to fill in the gap, you need to use the Home→Cell→Delete command.

For example, if you select a column by clicking the column header, you can either clear all the cells (by pressing Delete) or remove the column (by choosing Home→Cells→Delete). Deleting a column like this is the reverse of inserting one. Excel moves all the columns to the right of the removed column one column to the left to fill in the gap left by the column you removed. Thus, if you delete column B, column C becomes the new column B, column D becomes column C, and so on. If you take out row 3, row 4 moves up to fill the void, row 5 becomes row 4, and so on.

Usually, you use Home→Cells→Delete to remove entire rows or columns. But you can also use it to remove just some cells in a column or row. In such a case, Excel asks if you want to fill in the gap by moving cells in the current column up or by moving cells in the current row to the left. This feature is the reverse of the Insert Copied Cells feature, and you need to take special care to make sure you don't scramble the structure of your spreadsheet when you use this approach.

CHAPTER

4

Managing Worksheets

So far, you've learned how to create a basic worksheet with a table of data in it. That's great for getting started, but as power users, professional accountants, and other Excel jockeys quickly learn, some of the most compelling reasons to use Excel involve *multiple* tables that share information and interact with each other.

For example, say you want to track the performance of your company. You create one table summarizing your firm's yearly sales, another listing expenses, and a third analyzing profitability and making predictions for the coming year. If you create these tables in different spreadsheets, you must copy the information you want the sheets to share from one location to another, all without misplacing a number or making a mistake. What's worse is that, with your data scattered in multiple places, you're missing the chance to use some of Excel's niftiest charting and analytical tools. But cramming a bunch of tables onto the same worksheet page isn't the solution. Not only are you likely to lose your spot in the avalanche of data, you'll face a host of formatting and cell-management problems.

Fortunately, a better solution exists. Excel lets you create spreadsheets with multiple pages of data, each of which can conveniently exchange information with other pages. Each page is called a worksheet, and a collection of one or more worksheets is called a *workbook* (which is also sometimes called a *spreadsheet file*).

In this chapter, you'll learn how to manage the worksheets in a workbook. You'll also take a look at Find and Replace, an Excel tool for digging through worksheets in search of specific data.

Worksheets and Workbooks

Many workbooks contain more than one table of information. For example, you might have a list of your bank account balances and a list of items repossessed from your home in the same financial planning spreadsheet. You might find it a bit challenging to arrange these tables. You could stack them (Figure 4-1) or place them side by side (Figure 4-2), but neither solution is perfect.

	A	B	C	D	E
1	2013 Purchases				
2	Date Purchased	Item	Price		
3	7/7/2013	Cowbell	$43.99		
4	7/7/2013	Fresh Fruit	$3.00		
5	7/10/2013	IBM Laptop	$750.00		
6					
7	2012 Purchases				
8	Date Purchased	Item	Price		
9	1/8/2012	Gorilla Suit	$140.25		
10	5/30/2012	Crayons	$2.99		
11	8/30/2012	Sofa	$599.00		
12					

FIGURE 4-1

Stacking tables on top of each other is usually a bad idea. If you add a new column of data to the top table, you'll mess up the bottom table. You'll also have trouble properly resizing or formatting columns because each one contains data from two different tables.

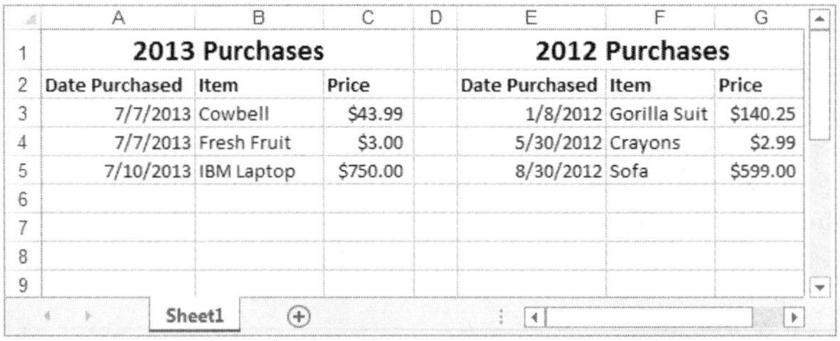

	A	B	C	D	E	F	G
1	2013 Purchases				2012 Purchases		
2	Date Purchased	Item	Price		Date Purchased	Item	Price
3	7/7/2013	Cowbell	$43.99		1/8/2012	Gorilla Suit	$140.25
4	7/7/2013	Fresh Fruit	$3.00		5/30/2012	Crayons	$2.99
5	7/10/2013	IBM Laptop	$750.00		8/30/2012	Sofa	$599.00
6							
7							
8							
9							

FIGURE 4-2

You're somewhat better off putting tables side by side, separated by a blank column, than you are stacking them, but side-by-side columns present their own limitations if you need to add more columns to the first table. It also makes for a lot of side-to-side scrolling.

Most Excel masters agree that the best way to arrange different tables of information is to use separate worksheets for each table. When you create a new workbook, you start with a single worksheet, named Sheet1. However, Excel gives you the ability to add plenty more.

NOTE In old versions of Excel, every workbook began with three blank worksheets. Excel 2013 abandons this practice, but you'll still find the extra worksheets in older spreadsheet files. Often, these worksheets will be left blank—in fact, the person who created the spreadsheet might not even know they're there.

Adding and Removing Worksheets

When you start a fresh workbook in Excel, you get a single blank worksheet. To add more sheets, you need to click the "New sheet" button, which is a small plus-in-a-circle icon that appears immediately to the right of your last worksheet tab (Figure 4-3). You can also use the Home→Cells→Insert→Insert Sheet command, which works the same way but inserts a new worksheet immediately to the *left* of the current worksheet. (Don't panic: page 113 shows how you can rearrange worksheets after the fact.) Each worksheet contains a fresh grid of cells—from A1 all the way to XFD1048576.

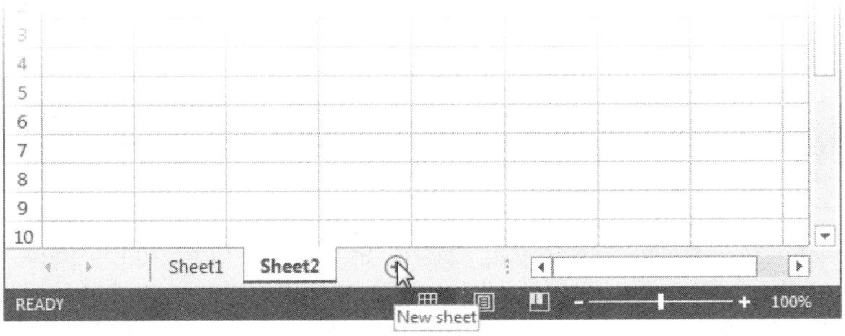

FIGURE 4-3

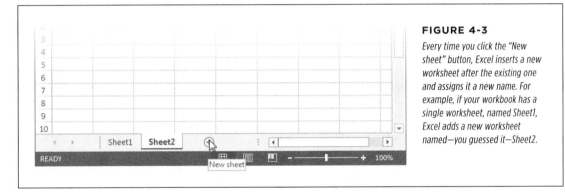

Every time you click the "New sheet" button, Excel inserts a new worksheet after the existing one and assigns it a new name. For example, if your workbook has a single worksheet, named Sheet1, Excel adds a new worksheet named—you guessed it—Sheet2.

If you continue adding worksheets, you'll eventually find that all the worksheet tabs won't fit at the bottom of your workbook window. Excel uses an ellipsis (...) to indicate the next tab that doesn't fit. For example, if you workbook has worksheets named Sheet1, Sheet2, and Sheet3, and the tab for Sheet3 doesn't quite fit into view at the end of the list, you'll see the ellipsis instead. (You can click it to select Sheet3.)

If you have way more worksheets than fit into the tab list, you'll need to use the scroll buttons, which are immediately to the left of the worksheet tabs) to review the list of worksheets. Figure 4-4 shows the scroll buttons and the ellipsis.

FIGURE 4-4

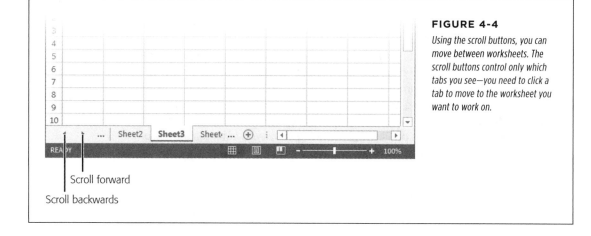

Using the scroll buttons, you can move between worksheets. The scroll buttons control only which tabs you see—you need to click a tab to move to the worksheet you want to work on.

TIP If you have a huge number of worksheets and they don't all fit in the strip of worksheet tabs, there's an easy way to jump around. Right-click the scroll buttons to pop up a list of all your worksheets, then move to the worksheet you want by clicking its name.

Removing a worksheet is just as easy as adding one. Simply move to the sheet you want to get rid of, and then choose Home→Cells→Delete→Delete Sheet (you can also right-click a tab, and then choose Delete). Excel won't complain if you ask it to remove a blank worksheet, but if you try to remove a sheet that contains data, Excel displays a warning message asking for your confirmation. Also, if you're down to one last worksheet, Excel won't let you remove it. Doing so would create a tough existential dilemma for Excel—a workbook that holds no worksheets—so the program prevents you from taking this step.

WARNING Be careful when you delete a worksheet, because you can't use Undo (Ctrl+Z) to reverse this change!

Excel starts you off with one worksheet for each workbook, but changing this setting is easy. You can configure Excel to start with up to 255 worksheets. Select File→Options, and then choose the General section. Under the heading "When creating new workbooks," change the number in the "Include this many sheets" box, and then click OK. This setting takes effect the next time you create a new workbook.

NOTE Although Excel limits you to 255 sheets in a new workbook, it doesn't limit the number of worksheets you can add *after* you create a workbook. Ultimately, the only factor that limits the number of worksheets your workbook can hold is your computer's memory. But today's computers can easily handle even the most ridiculously large, worksheet-stuffed workbook.

Moving Between Worksheets

To move from one worksheet to another, you have a few choices:

- Click the worksheet tabs at the bottom of Excel's grid window (just above the status bar).
- Press Ctrl+Page Down to move to the next worksheet. For example, if you're currently in Sheet1, this key sequence jumps you to Sheet2 (assuming your sheets are in order).
- Press Ctrl+Page Up to move to the previous worksheet. For example, if you're currently in Sheet2, this key sequence takes you to Sheet1.

Excel keeps track of the active cell in each worksheet. That means that if you're in cell B9 in Sheet1, and then move to Sheet2, when you jump back to Sheet1, you'll automatically return to cell B9.

TIP Excel includes some interesting viewing features that let you look at two different worksheets at the same time, even if these worksheets are in the same workbook. You'll learn more about custom views in Chapter 7.

Hiding Worksheets

Deleting worksheets isn't the only way to tidy up a workbook or get rid of information you don't want. You can also *hide* a worksheet temporarily.

When you hide a worksheet, its tab disappears, but the worksheet itself remains part of your workbook file, available whenever you choose to unhide it. You can't print a hidden worksheet, either.

To hide a worksheet, right-click the worksheet tab, and then choose Hide. (Or, for a more long-winded approach, choose Home→Cells→Format→Hide & Unhide→Hide Sheet.)

To redisplay a hidden worksheet, right-click any worksheet tab, and then choose Unhide. The Unhide window appears along with a list of all hidden sheets, as shown in Figure 4-5. Select a sheet from the list, and then click OK to unhide it. (Once again, the ribbon can get you to the same window—point yourself to Home→Cells→Format→Hide & Unhide→Unhide Sheet.)

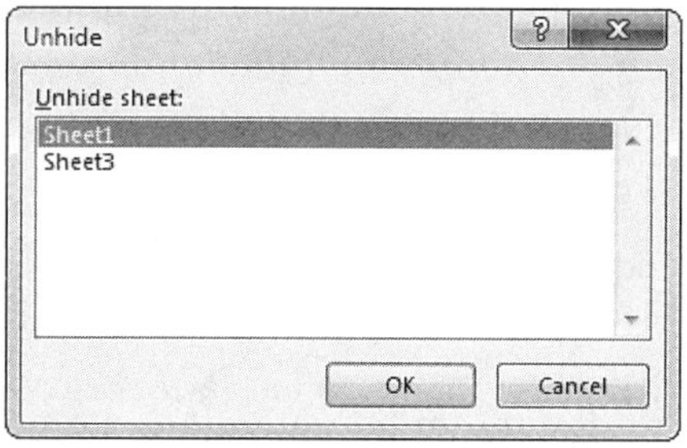

FIGURE 4-5

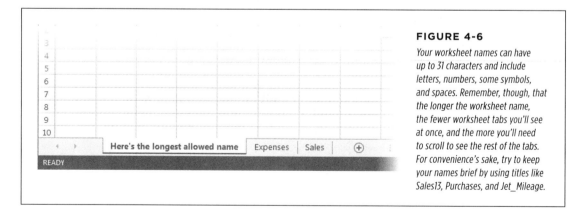

This workbook contains two hidden worksheets. To restore one, select it from the list, and then click OK. Unfortunately, if you want to show multiple hidden sheets, you must tap the Unhide Sheet command multiple times—Excel has no shortcut for unhiding multiple sheets at once.

Naming and Rearranging Worksheets

The standard names Excel assigns new worksheets—Sheet1, Sheet2, Sheet3, and so on—aren't very helpful for identifying what they contain. They become even less helpful if you start adding new worksheets, since the new sheet numbers (Sheet2, and so on) don't necessarily indicate the position of the sheets, just the order in which you created them.

For example, if you're on Sheet 3 and you add a new worksheet (by choosing Home→Cells→Insert→Insert Sheet), then the worksheet tabs read: Sheet1, Sheet2, Sheet4, Sheet3. (That's because the Insert Sheet command inserts the new sheet just before your current sheet.) Excel doesn't expect you to stick with these auto-generated names. You can rename them by right-clicking the worksheet tab and selecting Rename, or by just double-clicking the sheet name. Either way, Excel highlights the worksheet tab, and you can type a new name directly in the tab. Figure 4-6 shows worksheet tabs with better names.

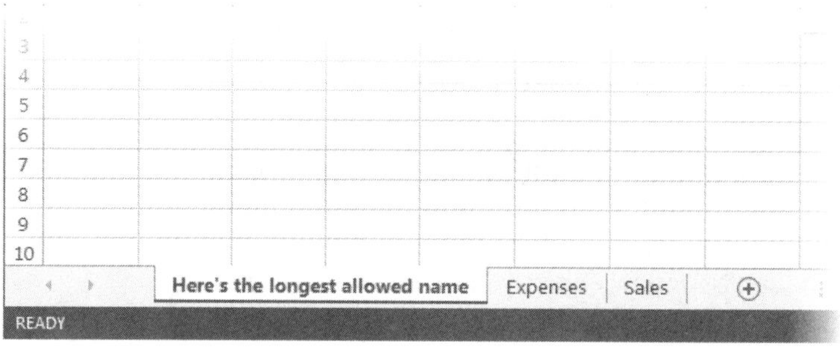

FIGURE 4-6

Your worksheet names can have up to 31 characters and include letters, numbers, some symbols, and spaces. Remember, though, that the longer the worksheet name, the fewer worksheet tabs you'll see at once, and the more you'll need to scroll to see the rest of the tabs. For convenience's sake, try to keep your names brief by using titles like Sales13, Purchases, and Jet_Mileage.

NOTE Excel reserves a small set of worksheet names that you can never use. To witness this problem, try to create a worksheet named History. Excel doesn't let you, because it uses the History worksheet as part of its change-tracking feature (page 685). Use this Excel oddity to impress your friends.

Sometimes Excel refuses to insert new worksheets exactly where you'd like them. Fortunately, you can easily rearrange any of your sheets just by dragging their tabs from one place to another, as shown in Figure 4-7.

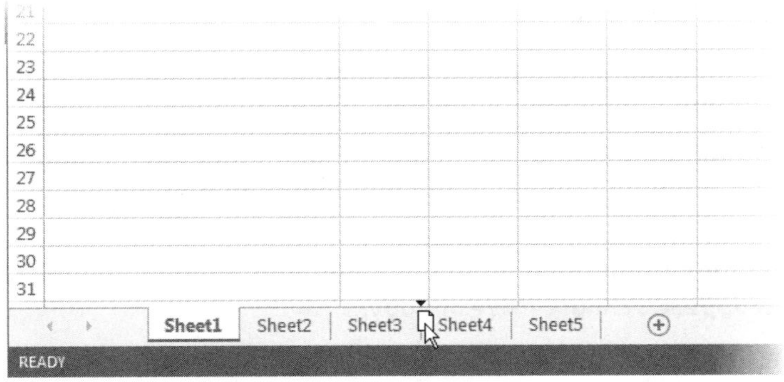

FIGURE 4-7

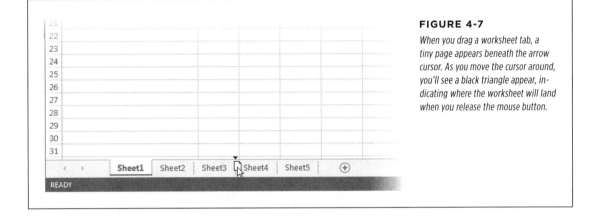

When you drag a worksheet tab, a tiny page appears beneath the arrow cursor. As you move the cursor around, you'll see a black triangle appear, indicating where the worksheet will land when you release the mouse button.

TIP You can use a similar technique to create *copies* of a worksheet. Click the worksheet tab and begin dragging, just as you would to move the worksheet. Before you release the mouse button, press the Ctrl key (you'll see a plus sign [+] appear). Keep holding the Ctrl key until you release the mouse button, at which point Excel creates a copy of the worksheet in the new location. The original worksheet remains in its original location. Excel gives the new worksheet a name with a number in parentheses. For example, a copy of Sheet1 is named Sheet1 (2). As with any other worksheet tab, you can change this name.

GEM IN THE ROUGH

Colorful Worksheet Tabs

Names aren't the only thing you can change when it comes to newly added worksheets. Excel lets you modify a worksheet tab's background color, too. This minor convenience has no effect on your data or printout, but it can help you quickly find an important worksheet if it has lots of neighbors.

To change the background color of a worksheet tab, right-click the tab, and then select Tab Color (or move to the appropriate worksheet and select Home→Cells→Format→Tab Color). A list of color choices appears; click the color you want.

Moving Worksheets from One Workbook to Another

Once you get the hang of creating worksheets for different types of information, your Excel files can quickly fill up with more sheets than the bedding department at Macy's. What happens when you want to shift some of these worksheets around? For instance, you may want to move (or copy) a worksheet from one Excel file to another. Here's how:

1. **Open both spreadsheet files.**

   The file that contains the worksheet you want to move or copy is called the *source* file; the other file (the one where you want to place the worksheet copy) is the *destination* file.

2. **Go to the source workbook.**

   Remember, you can move from one window to another using the Windows task bar, or by choosing the file's name from the ribbon's View→Windows→Switch Windows list.

3. **Right-click the worksheet you want to transfer, and then, from the shortcut menu that appears, choose Move or Copy.**

   To transfer multiple worksheets at once, hold down the Ctrl key, and then select all the worksheets you want to move or copy. Excel highlights all the worksheets you select (and groups them together). Right-click the selection, and then choose Move or Copy.

   When you move or copy a worksheet, Excel launches the Move or Copy window (shown in Figure 4-8).

4. **Choose the destination file from the "To book" drop-down list.**

   The "To book" menu shows all the currently open workbooks (including the source workbook).

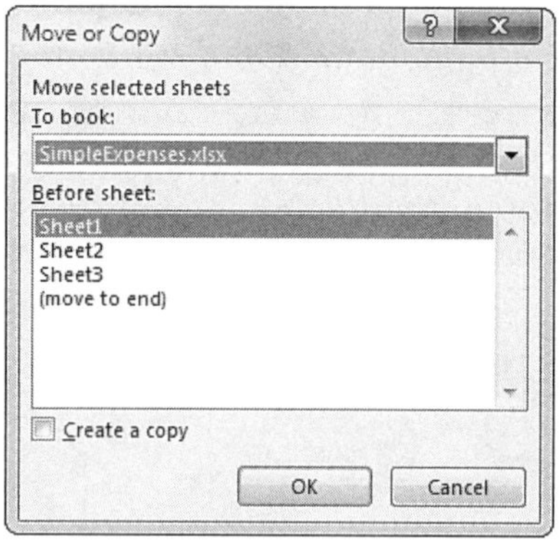

FIGURE 4-8

Here, you're about to move the selected worksheet into the SimpleExpenses.xlsx workbook. (The source workbook isn't shown.) The SimpleExpenses workbook already contains three worksheets (named Sheet1, Sheet2, and Sheet3). Excel inserts the new worksheet just before the first sheet. Because you didn't turn on the "Create a copy" checkbox, Excel removes the worksheet from the source workbook when it completes the transfer.

TIP Excel also lets you move worksheets to a new workbook, which it automatically creates for you. To do so, choose "(new book)" in the "To book" list. The resulting workbook has only the worksheets you transferred to it.

5. **Specify where you want to insert the worksheet.**

   Choose a destination worksheet from the "Before sheet" list. Excel places the copied worksheets just *before* the worksheet you select. If you want to place the worksheets at the end of the destination workbook, select "(move to end)." Of course, you can always rearrange the worksheets after you transfer them, so you don't need to worry too much about getting the perfect placement.

6. **If you want to copy the worksheet, turn on the "Create a copy" checkbox at the bottom of the window.**

   With this option turned off, Excel copies a worksheet to the destination workbook and removes the original from the source workbook. If you *do* turn this option on, you'll end up with a copy of the worksheet in both workbooks.

7. **Click OK.**

   This final step closes the Move or Copy window and transfers the worksheet(s).

NOTE If Excel encounters a worksheet name conflict, it adds a number in parentheses after the moved sheet's name. For example, if you try to copy a worksheet named Sheet1 to a workbook that already has a Sheet1, Excel names the copied worksheet Sheet1 (2).

Grouping Worksheets

As you saw in previous chapters, Excel lets you work with more than one column, row, or cell at a time. The same holds true for worksheets. You can select multiple worksheets and perform an operation on all of them at once. The process of selecting multiple sheets is called *grouping*, and it's helpful if you need to hide or format several worksheets (for example, to make sure all your worksheets start with a bright yellow first row), and you don't want the hassle of selecting them one at a time. Grouping sheets doesn't let you do anything you couldn't do ordinarily—it's just a nifty timesaver.

Here are some operations—all of which are explained in detail below—that you can simultaneously perform on worksheets grouped together:

- Move, copy, delete, or hide the worksheets.
- Apply formatting to individual cells, columns, rows, or even entire worksheets.
- Enter new text, change text, or clear cells.
- Cut, copy, and paste cells.
- Adjust some page layout options, like paper orientation (on the Page Layout tab).
- Adjust some view options, like gridlines and the zoom level (on the View tab).

To group worksheets, hold down Ctrl while clicking multiple worksheet tabs. When you finish, release the Ctrl key. Figure 4-9 shows an example.

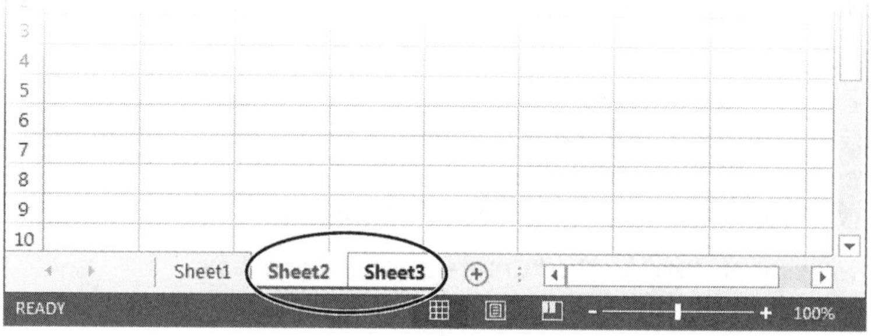

FIGURE 4-9

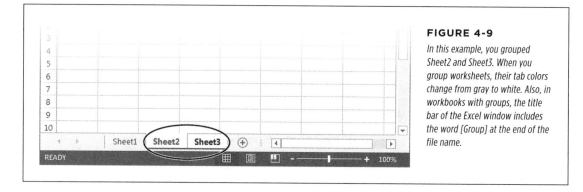

In this example, you grouped Sheet2 and Sheet3. When you group worksheets, their tab colors change from gray to white. Also, in workbooks with groups, the title bar of the Excel window includes the word [Group] at the end of the file name.

TIP As a shortcut, you can select all the worksheets in a workbook by right-clicking any tab, and then choosing Select All Sheets.

To ungroup worksheets, right-click one of the tabs and then select Ungroup Sheets, or just click one of the worksheet tabs that isn't in your group. You can also remove a single worksheet from a group by clicking it while holding down Ctrl. However, this technique works only if the worksheet you want to remove from the group is *not* the currently active worksheet.

MANAGING GROUPED SHEETS

As your workbook grows, you'll often need better ways to manage the collection of worksheets you've accumulated. For example, you might want to temporarily hide a number of worksheets, or move a less important batch of them from the front (that is, the left side) of the worksheet tab holder to the end (the right side). And if a workbook's got way too many worksheets, you might even want to relocate several of them to a brand-new workbook.

You can easily perform an action on a group of worksheets. For example, you can drag a group of selected worksheets from one location to another using the worksheet tab holder. To delete or hide a group of sheets, just right-click one of the worksheet tabs in your group, and then choose Delete or Hide. Excel then deletes or hides *all* the selected worksheets (provided that action leaves at least one visible worksheet in your workbook).

NOTE Excel keeps track of print and display settings on a per-worksheet basis. In other words, when you set the zoom to 50 percent in one worksheet, it doesn't affect the zoom in another worksheet. However, when you make the change for a *group* of worksheets, that change affects all the sheets in the same way.

FORMATTING GROUPED SHEETS

When you format cells inside *one* grouped worksheet, it triggers the same changes in the cells in the *other* grouped worksheets. So you have another tool you can use to apply consistent formatting over a batch of worksheets. It's mainly useful when you structure all your worksheets the same way.

For example, imagine you create a workbook with 10 worksheets, each representing a different customer order. If you group all 10 worksheets together and then format just the first one, Excel formats all the worksheets in exactly the same way. Or say you group Sheet1 and Sheet2, and then change the font of column B in Sheet2—Excel automatically changes the font in column B in Sheet1, too. The same is true if you change the formatting of individual cells or the entire worksheet—Excel replicates these changes across the group. (To change the font, select your cells and pick what you want from the Home→Font section of the ribbon. You'll learn much more about the different types of formatting in Chapter 5.)

NOTE It doesn't matter which worksheet you modify in a group. For example, if Sheet1 and Sheet2 are grouped, you can modify the formatting of both in either worksheet. Excel automatically applies the changes to the other sheet.

ENTERING DATA IN GROUPED SHEETS

With grouped worksheets, you can also modify the contents of individual cells, including entering or changing text and clearing cell contents. For example, if you enter a new value in cell B4 of Sheet2, Excel enters the same value in cell B4 of the grouped Sheet1. Even more interesting, if you modify a value in a cell in Sheet2, the same value appears in the same cell in Sheet1, even if Sheet1 didn't previously have a value in that cell. Similar behavior happens when you delete cells.

Editing a group of worksheets at once isn't as useful as moving and formatting them, but it does have its moments. Once again, it makes most sense when all the worksheets have the same structure. For example, you could use this technique to put the same copyright message in cell A1 on every worksheet, or to add the same column titles to multiple tables (assuming you arranged them in *exactly* the same way). One example where grouped sheets make sense is if you have a different worksheet for every month of a year, but each one has the same overall structure.

WARNING Be careful to remember the magnified power your keystrokes possess when you work on grouped sheets. For example, imagine you're in cell A3 of Sheet1, which happens to be empty. If you click Delete, you see no change. However, if any of the other worksheets have data in cell A3 , that data in now gone. Groupers beware.

Cut and paste operations work the same way as entering or modifying grouped cells. When you take an action on one grouped sheet, Excel performs the same action on the other grouped sheets. For example, consider what happens if you group Sheet1 and Sheet2, and you copy cells A1 to A2 in Sheet1. The same action takes place in

Sheet2—in other words, Excel copies the contents of cell A1 in Sheet2 to cell A2 in Sheet2. Obviously, the contents of cells A1 and A2 in Sheet1 may differ from the contents of cell A1 and A2 in Sheet2—the grouping simply means that whatever was in cell A1 will now also be in cell A2.

Find and Replace

When you deal with great mounds of information, you may have a tough time ferreting out the nuggets of data you need. Fortunately, Excel's Find feature is great for locating numbers or text, even when it's buried within massive workbooks holding dozens of worksheets. And if you need to make changes to a bunch of identical items, the find-and-replace option can be a real timesaver.

The Find and Replace feature includes both simple and advanced options. In its basic version, you're only a quick keystroke combo away from a word or number you *know* lurks somewhere in your data pile. With the advanced options turned on, you can do things like search for cells that have certain formatting characteristics and apply changes automatically. The next few sections dissect these features.

The Basic Find

Excel's Find feature is a little like the Go To tool (page 57), which lets you move across a large expanse of cells in a single bound. The difference is that Go To moves to a *known* location, using the cell address you specify. The Find feature, on the other hand, searches every cell until it finds the content you asked Excel to look for. Excel's search works similarly to the search feature in Microsoft Word, but it's worth keeping in mind a few additional details:

- When Excel searches, it compares the content you enter with the content in each cell. If you search for the word *Date*, for example, Excel identifies as a match the cell containing the phrase *Date Purchased*.
- When you search for cells with numeric or date information, Excel always searches the cell *content*, not the display text. (For more information on the difference between the way Excel displays a numeric value and the underlying value Excel actually stores, see page 52.)
- Say a cell displays dates using the day-month-year format, like *2-Dec-13*. Internally, Excel stores that date as *12/2/2013*, which you'll see if you move to the cell and look up in the formula bar. Thus, if you search for *2013* or *12/2* you'll find the cell, because your search text matches part of the stored content. But if you search for *Dec* or *2-Dec-13*, you won't find a match. You see similar behavior with numbers. For example, the search string *$3* won't match the currency value *$3.00*, because the dollar sign isn't part of the stored cell value—it's just a formatting detail. You can change this behavior and search for what the cell actually displays using the "Look in" setting described on page 122.
- Excel searches one cell at a time, from left to right. When it reaches the end of a row, it moves to the first column of the next row.

To use the Find feature, follow these steps:

1. **Move to the cell where you want to begin the search.**

   If you start halfway down the worksheet, for example, the search covers the cells from there to the end of the worksheet, and then "loops over" and starts at cell A1. If you select a group of cells, Excel restricts the search to just those cells. You can search across a set of columns, rows, or even a noncontiguous group of cells.

2. **Choose Home→Editing→Find & Select→Find, or press Ctrl+F.**

   The Find and Replace window appears, with the Find tab selected.

NOTE To assist frequent searches, Excel lets you keep the Find and Replace window hanging around (rather than forcing you to use it or close it, as is the case with many other windows).

3. **In the "Find what" combo box, enter the word, phrase, or number you're looking for.**

   If you recently searched for a term, Excel makes it easy to search for the same term again later—it keeps a temporary record of your search terms in the "Find what" list. Choose the search term you want from the drop-down menu.

4. **Click Find Next.**

   Excel jumps to the next matching cell, which becomes the active cell. However, Excel doesn't highlight the matched text or in any way indicate *why* it decided the cell was a match. (That's a bummer if you've got, say, 200 words crammed into a cell.) If it doesn't find a matching cell, Excel displays a message telling you it couldn't find the requested content.

   If the first match isn't what you're looking for, keep looking by clicking Find Next again to move to the next match. Keep clicking Find Next to move through the worksheet. When you reach the end, Excel resumes the search at the beginning, potentially bringing you back to a match you've already seen. When you finish searching, click Close to get rid of the Find and Replace window.

Find All

One of the problems with searching in Excel is that you're never quite sure how many matches there are in a worksheet. Sure, clicking Find Next gets you from one cell to the next, but wouldn't it be easier for Excel to let you know right away how many matches it found?

Enter the Find All feature. With Find All, Excel searches the entire worksheet in one go, and compiles a list of matches, as shown in Figure 4-10.

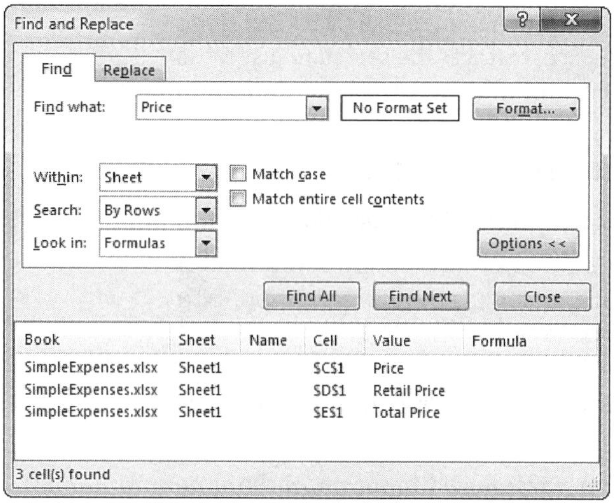

FIGURE 4-10

In the example shown here, the search for "Price" matched three cells in the worksheet. The list shows you the matching cell's complete text and cell reference number (for example, $C$1 is a reference to cell C1).

The Find All button doesn't lead you through the worksheet like the Find feature does. It's up to you to select one of the results in the list, at which point Excel automatically moves you to the matching cell.

Excel keeps the text and numbers in your Find All list synchronized with any changes you make in the worksheet. For example, if you change cell D5 to Total Price, the change appears in the Value column in the found-items list *automatically*. This tool is great for editing a worksheet because you can keep track of multiple changes at a single glance. However, Excel won't pick up on new matches if you add data to your worksheet—for that, you need to run a new search.

Finally, the Find All feature is the heart of another great Excel trick: It gives you another way to change multiple cells at once. After you finish the Find All search, select all the entries you want to change from the list by clicking them while holding down Ctrl (so you can select several at once). Click the formula bar, and then start typing in the new value. When you finish, hit Ctrl+Enter to apply your changes to every selected cell. Voilà—it's like Find and Replace, but you're in control!

More Advanced Searches

Basic searches are fine if all you need to find is a glaringly unique phrase or number (*Pet Snail Names* or *10,987,654,321*). But Excel's advanced search feature gives you lots of ways to fine-tune your searches or even search more than one worksheet. To conduct an advanced search, begin by clicking the Options button in the Find and Replace window, as shown in Figure 4-11.

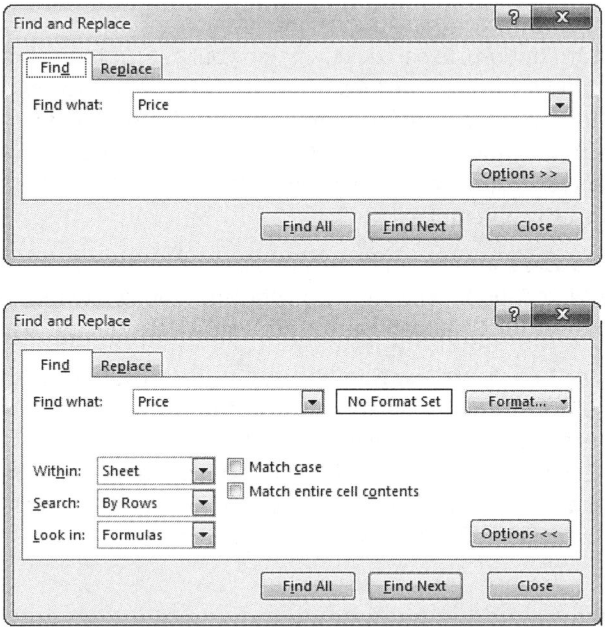

FIGURE 4-11

In the standard Find and Replace window (top), when you click Options, Excel gives you a slew of additional settings (bottom) so you can configure things like search direction, case sensitivity, and format-matching.

You can set any or all of the following options:

- **The Within box** controls the span of your search. The standard option, Sheet, searches all the cells in the currently active worksheet. If you want to continue the search on the other worksheets in your workbook, choose Workbook. When Excel searches a workbook, it examines your worksheets from left to right, starting with the current one. When it finishes searching the last worksheet in your workbook, it loops back and starts again at the first worksheet.

- **The Search box** chooses the direction of the search. The standard option, By Rows, searches each row from top to bottom before moving on to the next one. That means that if you start in cell B2, Excel first searches C2, D2, E2, and so on. Once it moves through every column in the second row, it moves on to the third row and searches from left to right.

  On the other hand, if you choose By Columns, Excel searches all the rows in the current column before moving to the next column. That means that if you start in cell B2, Excel searches B3, B4, and so on, until it reaches the bottom of the column, and then starts at the top of the next column (column C).

NOTE The search direction tells Excel where to start out, but ultimately it traverses every cell in your worksheet. (Or, if you've selected a group of cells, the search continues until it's checked out every cell in that selection.)

- **The "Look in" box** tells Excel what to examine in each cell. If you choose Formulas (the standard option), Excel tries to match your search term and the cell's *content* (for example, the number 3.5 or the date 12/2/2013). If you choose Values, Excel tries to match your search term and the cell's *display text* (for example, the formatted number $3.50 or the formatted date 2-Dec-10). And if you choose Comments, Excel searches any comments attached to a cell (page 674), but ignores the cell content itself.
- **The "Match case" option** specifies whether capitalization is important. If you select "Match case," Excel finds only words or phrases whose capitalization matches. Thus, searching for *Date* matches the cell value *Date*, but not *date*.
- **The "Match entire cell contents" option** lets you restrict your searches to the entire contents of a cell. Excel ordinarily looks to see if your search term is contained anywhere inside a cell. So, if you specify the word *Price*, Excel finds cells containing text like *Current Price* and even *Repriced Items*. Similarly, a number like 32 will match cell values like 3253, 10032, and 1.321. Turning on the "Match entire cell contents" option forces Excel to be precise.

POWER USERS' CLINIC

Using Wildcards

Sometimes you sorta, kinda know what you're looking for—for example, a cell with some version of the word "date" in it (as in "date" or "dated" or "dating"). What you really need is a search tool that's flexible enough to keep its eyes open for results that are *similar* but not exactly alike. Power searchers will be happy to know that Excel lets you use *wildcards* in your searches. Wildcards are symbols that stand in for any character or characters in a search term.

The asterisk wildcard (*) represents a group of one or more characters. A search for s*nd finds any word that begins with the letter s and ends with the letters nd; it would find words like sand, sound, send, or even the bizarre series of characters *sgrthdnd*. The question mark (?) wildcard represents any *single* character. For example, a search for *f?nd* turns up *find* or *fund*, but not *friend*.

Wildcards are particularly useful when you use the "Match entire cell contents" option. For example, if you turn it on and enter the search term *date** you'll find any cell that starts with the word *date*. In contrast, if you execute the same search without turning on the "Match entire cell contents" option, you'd find any cell *containing* the word *date*.

If you want to search for special characters, like the asterisk or the question mark, you need to use a tilde (~) before the wildcard. For example, the search string ~* searches for cells that contain the asterisk symbol.

Finding Formatted Cells

Excel's Find and Replace feature is an equal opportunity search tool: It doesn't care what the contents of a cell look like. But what if you know, for example, that the data you're looking for is formatted in bold, or that it's a number that uses the Currency format? You can use these formatting details to help Excel find the cells you want and ignore irrelevant ones.

To use formatting details as part of your search criteria, follow these steps:

1. **Launch the Find tool.**

   Choose Home→Editing→Find & Select→Find, or press Ctrl+F. Click the Options button to make sure the Find and Replace window displays the advanced settings.

2. **Decide how you want to specify the formatting.**

   You have two options, and they both involve the Format button next to the "Find what" search box.

   The quickest way to target a cell's format is to copy the format information from another cell. To do that, click the arrow to the right of the Format button to pop open a menu with additional options, and then click Choose Format From Cell. The mouse pointer changes to a plus symbol with an eyedropper next to it. Next, click any cell that has the formatting you want to match. Keep in mind that when you use this approach, you copy *all* the format settings.

   A more controlled approach is to specify the exact formatting settings you want to hunt down. To do this, click the Format button. The Find Format window appears (Figure 4-12). Using the Find Format box, you can specify any combination of settings for number format, alignment, font, fill pattern, and borders. (Chapter 5 explains these settings in detail.) You can also search for protected and locked cells, which are described in Chapter 21. When you finish, click OK to return to the Find and Replace window.

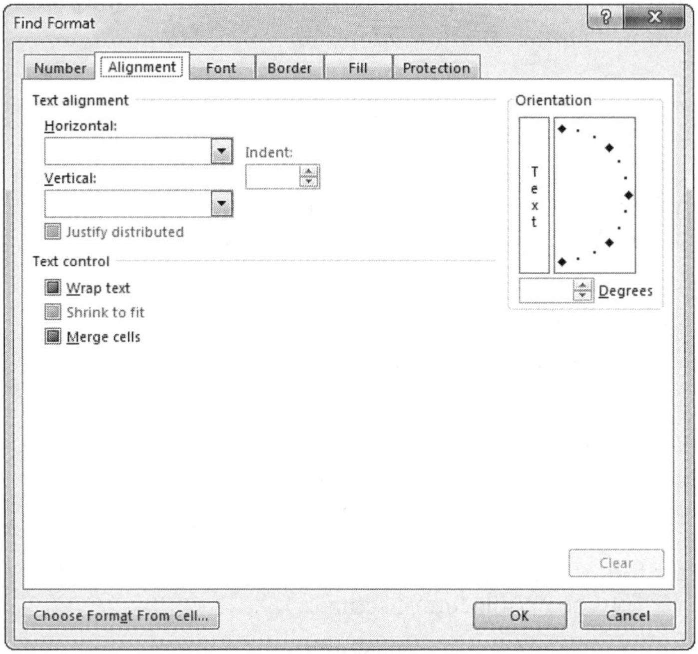

FIGURE 4-12

In the Find Format window, Excel won't use the formatting option as part of its search criteria if it's blank or grayed out. For example, here, Excel won't search based on alignment because it's blank. Checkboxes are a little different—if they look like they're filled with a solid square (as with the "Wrap text" setting in this example), Excel won't use them as part of its search.

3. **Review your formatting and start your search.**

   Next to the "Find what" search box, a preview appears indicating the format of the cells you want to find, as shown in Figure 4-13. If everything checks out, click Find All or Find Next to get started.

   To remove these formatting restrictions in subsequent searches, click the arrow on the right of the Format button, and then choose Clear Find Format.

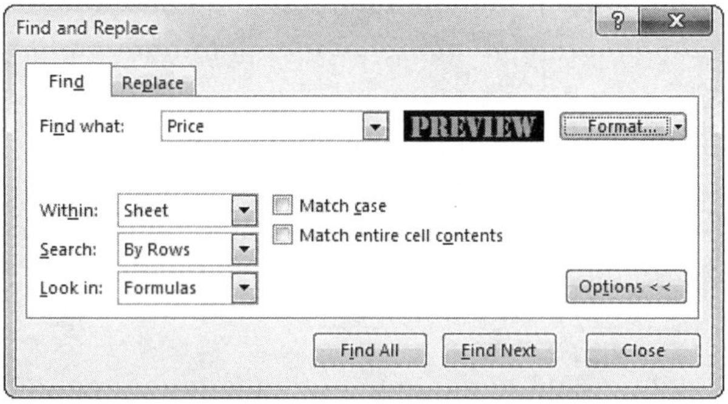

FIGURE 4-13

The Find Format window previews your formatting choices. In this example, the search will find cells that contain the word "price" and that also use orange lettering, a black background, and the Stencil font.

Finding and Replacing Values

You can use Excel's search muscles to find not only the information you're interested in, but to modify cells quickly and easily, too. You can make two types of changes using Excel's *Replace* tool:

- **Automatically change cell content.** For example, you can replace the word *Colour* with *Color* or the number *$400* with *$40*.
- **Automatically change cell formatting.** For example, you can search for every cell that contains the word *Price* or the number *$400* and change the fill color. Or, you can search for every cell that uses a specific font, and then change that font.

Here's how to replace characters in a cell. Once you mastered this technique, check out the box on page 126, which describes some super-handy tricks this process lets you do.

1. **Move to the cell where you want to start the search.**

   Remember, if you don't want to search the entire spreadsheet, select a range of cells (page 85).

2. **Choose Home→Editing→Find & Select→Replace, or press Ctrl+H.**

   The Find and Replace window appears, with the Replace tab selected, as shown in Figure 4-14.

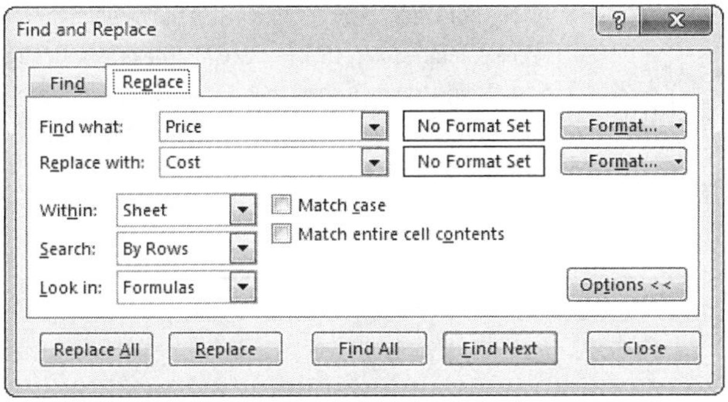

FIGURE 4-14

The Replace tab looks like the Find tab—even the advanced options are the same. The only difference is that with Replace, you need to specify the substitute text for your search term.

3. **In the "Find what" box, enter your search term. In the "Replace with" box, enter the replacement text.**

   Type the replacement text exactly as you want it to appear. If you want to set any advanced options, click Options (see the earlier sections page 121 for more on your choices).

4. **Execute the search.**

   You've got three options here. *Replace All* changes all the matches your search identifies. *Find All* works just like the Find All feature described earlier (page 119)—it searches the entire worksheet in one go, and compiles a list of matches. *Find Next* moves to the next match, where you can click Replace to drop in your new characters and keep going, or Find Next to skip to the next match without making any changes. The replace options are good if you're confident you want to make a change; the find options work well if you first want to see what changes you're about to make (although you can reverse either option using Ctrl+Z to fire the Undo command).

NOTE It's possible for a single cell to contain more than one match. In such a case, clicking Replace replaces every occurrence of the matched text in the entire cell.

POWER USERS' CLINIC

Mastering the Art of Replacement

You can use the Find and Replace feature in many imaginative ways. Here are just a few:

- **You can automatically delete a specific piece of text**. Just enter the appropriate "Find what" text, and leave the "Replace with" box blank.
- **You can change the formatting in specific cells**. Just type the same text in both the "Find what" and "Replace with" text, and then click the Format button next to the "Replace with" combo box to set some formatting attributes. (You don't need to specify any formatting settings for your "Find what" search criteria.)
- **You can change the formatting in a series of cells**. Imagine you have a worksheet in which you have several cells bolded. Say you want to change the font in those cells. First, leave both the "Find what" and "Replace with" boxes blank. Then set the format search criteria to look for the bold font attribute, and select the new font as the replacement format. Click Replace All. The cells with bold formatting acquire the new font. You might find mastering this technique tricky, but it's one of the most powerful formatting tricks around.

CHAPTER

5

Formatting Cells

When you create a basic workbook, you've taken only the first step toward mastering Excel. If you plan to print your data, email it to colleagues, or show it off to friends, you need to think about whether you formatted your worksheets in a viewer-friendly way. The careful use of color, shading, borders, and fonts can make the difference between a messy glob of data and a worksheet that's easy to work with and understand.

But formatting isn't just about deciding, say, where and how to make text bold. It's about formatting numerical values, too. In fact, two aspects of formatting are fundamental in any worksheet:

- **Appearance formatting.** Cell appearance formatting is all about cosmetic details like color, typeface, alignment, and borders. When most people think of formatting, they think of the cell's appearance first.
- **Value formatting.** Cell value formatting controls the way Excel displays numbers, dates, and times. For numbers, it includes details like whether to use scientific notation, the number of decimal places displayed, and the use of currency symbols, percent signs, and commas. With dates, cell value formatting determines what parts of the date the cell displays, and in what order.

In many ways, cell value formatting is more significant than cell appearance formatting, because it can change the meaning of your data. For example, even though 45%, $0.45, and 0.450 are all the same number (just formatted differently), your spreadsheet readers will see a failing test score, a cheap price for chewing gum, and a world-class batting average.

NOTE Keep in mind that regardless of how you *format* your cell values, Excel maintains an unalterable *value* for every number entered. For more on how Excel internally stores numbers, see the box on page 52.

In this chapter, you'll learn about cell value formatting, and then unleash your inner artist with cell appearance formatting.

Formatting Cell Values

The basic principle behind cell value formatting is this: The cell value that Excel *stores* doesn't necessarily match the cell value it *displays*. This gives you the best of both worlds: Your cells can store super-accurate values, but you don't need to clutter your worksheet with numbers that have 13 decimal places.

To make your worksheet as clear and readable as possible, you need to make sure that it displays values in a form that makes sense for your spreadsheet. Figure 5-1 shows how Excel can show the same number in a variety of ways.

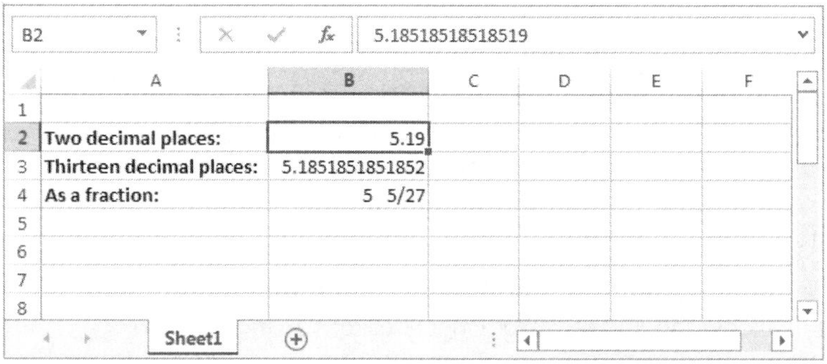

FIGURE 5-1

This worksheet shows how formatting affects the appearance of your data. Here, cells B2, B3, and B4 contain the same number: 5.18518518518519. (You can see this number in the formula bar, where Excel always displays a cell's actual content.) But look at how dramatically different that number appears in the worksheet, where each of the three cells use different formatting.

The first time you type a number or date into a blank cell, Excel makes an educated guess about what format you want. For example, if you type in a currency value like $34.99, Excel assumes you want a number format that uses the dollar sign. If you then type a new number in the same cell without a dollar sign (say, 18.75), Excel adds the dollar sign automatically (making it $18.75).

Changing the Cell Value Format

Before long, you'll need to change a cell value format, or you'll want to fine-tune it. The basic process unfolds like this:

1. **Select the cells you want to format.**

   You can apply formatting to individual cells or a collection of cells. Usually, you'll want to format an entire column at once because all the values in a column typically contain the same type of data. Remember, to select a column, you simply click the column header (the gray box at the top with the column letter in it) or press Ctrl+Space.

NOTE Usually, a column contains *two* types of data: the values you store in the cells and the column header in the topmost cell (where the text is). However, you don't need to worry about unintentionally formatting the column title because Excel applies number formats only to numeric cells (cells that contain dates, times, or numbers). It doesn't format the column header cell as a number because it contains text.

2. **Select Home→Cells→Format→Format Cells, or just right-click the selection, and then choose Format Cells.**

   In either case, the Format Cells window appears, as shown in Figure 5-2.

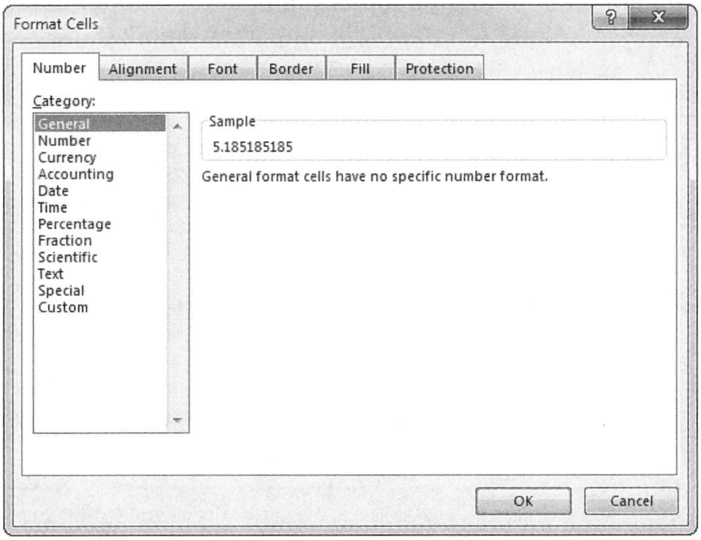

FIGURE 5-2

The Format Cells window provides one-stop shopping for cell value and cell appearance formatting. The first tab, Number, lets you specify the format for numeric values. You can use the Alignment, Font, Border, and Fill tabs to control the cell's appearance. Finally, the Protection tab lets you prevent changes to the worksheet and hide formulas. (You'll learn about worksheet protection in Chapter 21.)

3. **Set the format options.**

   The Number tab's options let you choose how Excel translates the cell value into a display value. For example, you can change the number of decimal places Excel uses when it displays the number. (The next section covers number formatting choices in much more detail.)

   Most of the other tabs in the Format Cells window are for cell appearance formatting, which is covered later in this chapter.

NOTE Once you apply formatting to a cell, it retains that formatting even if you clear the cell's contents (by selecting it, and then pressing Delete). In addition, formatting comes along for the ride if you copy a cell, so if you copy the content from cell A1 to cell A2, the formatting comes with it. Formatting includes both cell value formatting *and* cell appearance.

The only way to remove formatting is to highlight the cell and select Home→Editing→Clear→Clear Formats. This command removes the formatting, restoring the cell to its original, General number format (which you'll learn more about next), but it doesn't remove any of the cell's content.

4. **Click OK.**

   Excel applies your formatting changes to the selected cells.

You'll spend a lot of time in this chapter in the Format Cells window. As you saw earlier, the most obvious way to get there is to choose Home→Format→Cells→Format Cells. However, your mouse finger's sure to tire out with that method. Fortunately, there's a quicker route—you can use one of three *window launchers*. Figure 5-3 shows the way.

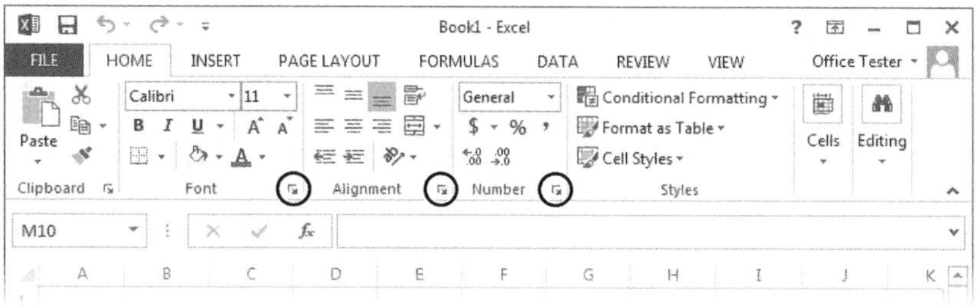

FIGURE 5-3

The ribbon's Home tab lets you open the Format Cells window from three spots: the Font tab, the Alignment tab, and the Number tab.

TIP If you don't want to take your fingers off the keyboard, you can use the shortcut Ctrl+1 to launch the Format Cells window at any time.

Formatting Numbers

In the Format Cells window, the Number tab lets you control how Excel displays numeric data in a cell. Excel gives you a lengthy list of predefined formats (as shown in Figure 5-4), and also lets you design your own formats. Remember, Excel uses number formats when the cell contains only numeric information. Otherwise, Excel simply ignores the number format. For example, if you enter *Half past* 12 in a column full of times, Excel considers it plain ol' text—although, under the hood, the cell's numerical formatting stays put, and Excel uses it if you change the cell content to a time.

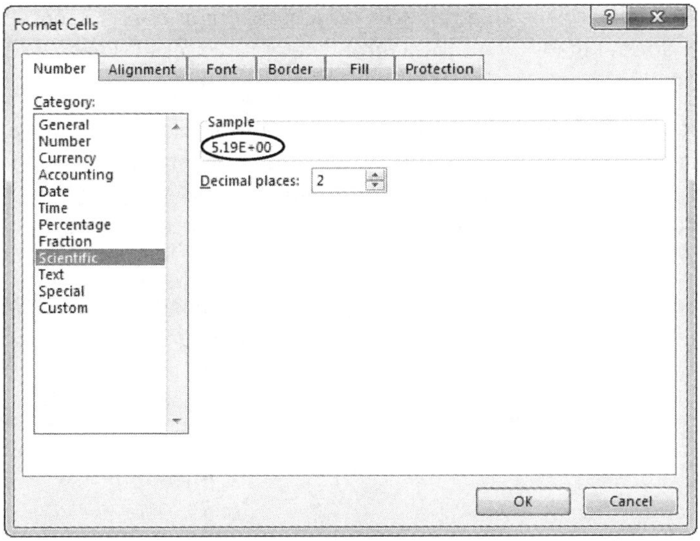

FIGURE 5-4

You can learn about the different number formats by selecting a cell that already has a number in it, and then choosing a new format from the Category list (Home→Cells→Format→Format Cells). When you do, Excel uses the Format Cells window to preview the number in that format. In this example, the cell value 5.18518518518519 will appear as 5.19E+00, which is scientific notation with two decimal places.

When you create a new spreadsheet, every cell starts out with the same number format: General. This format comes with a couple of basic rules:

- If a number has any decimal places in it, Excel displays them, providing they fit in the column. If the number has more decimal places than Excel can display, it leaves out the numbers that don't fit. (It rounds up the last displayed digit, when appropriate.) If you change a column width, Excel automatically adjusts the amount of digits it displays.
- Excel removes leading and trailing zeros. Thus, 004.00 becomes 4. The only exception is for numbers between –1 and 1, which retain the 0 before the decimal point. For example, Excel displays the number .42 as 0.42.

As you saw in Chapter 2, the way you type in a number can change a cell's formatting. For example, if you enter a number with a currency symbol, the number format of the cell changes automatically to Currency. Similarly, if you enter three numbers separated by dashes (-) or forward slashes (/), Excel assumes you're entering a date, and adjusts the number format to Date.

However, rather than rely on this automatic process, it's far better to enter ordinary numbers and then set the formatting for the whole column—that prevents you from having different formats in different cells (which can confuse even the sharpest spreadsheet reader), and it makes sure you get exactly the formatting and precision you want. You can apply formatting to a column before or after you enter the numbers. And it doesn't matter if a cell is currently empty; Excel still keeps track of the number format you apply.

Different number formats provide different options. For example, if you choose the Currency format, you can choose from dozens of currency symbols. When you use the Number format, you can choose to add commas (to separate groups of three digits) or parentheses (to indicate negative numbers). And most number formats let you set the number of decimal places.

The following sections give you a quick tour of the predefined number formats available in the Number tab of the Format Cells window. Figure 5-5 gives you an overview of how different number formats affect similar numbers.

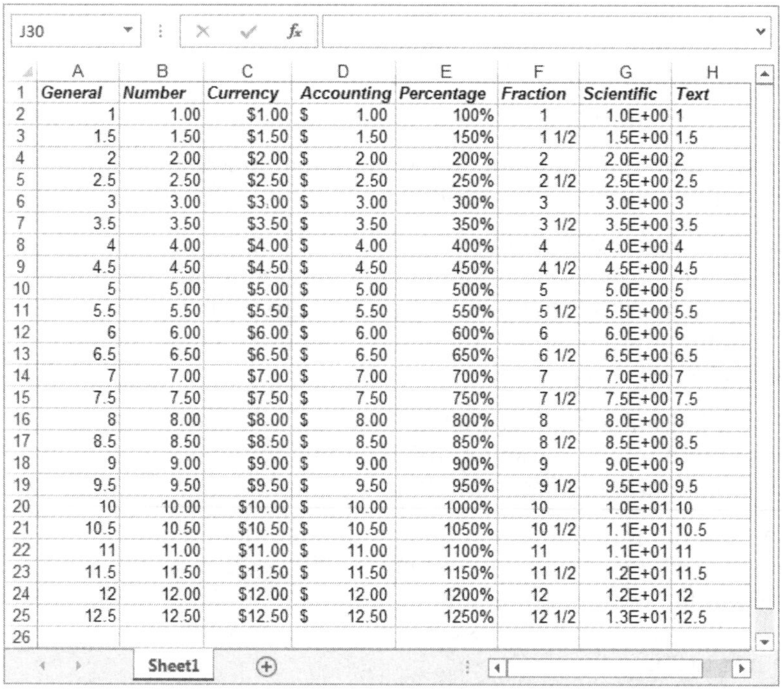

	A	B	C	D	E	F	G	H
1	General	Number	Currency	Accounting	Percentage	Fraction	Scientific	Text
2	1	1.00	$1.00	$ 1.00	100%	1	1.0E+00	1
3	1.5	1.50	$1.50	$ 1.50	150%	1 1/2	1.5E+00	1.5
4	2	2.00	$2.00	$ 2.00	200%	2	2.0E+00	2
5	2.5	2.50	$2.50	$ 2.50	250%	2 1/2	2.5E+00	2.5
6	3	3.00	$3.00	$ 3.00	300%	3	3.0E+00	3
7	3.5	3.50	$3.50	$ 3.50	350%	3 1/2	3.5E+00	3.5
8	4	4.00	$4.00	$ 4.00	400%	4	4.0E+00	4
9	4.5	4.50	$4.50	$ 4.50	450%	4 1/2	4.5E+00	4.5
10	5	5.00	$5.00	$ 5.00	500%	5	5.0E+00	5
11	5.5	5.50	$5.50	$ 5.50	550%	5 1/2	5.5E+00	5.5
12	6	6.00	$6.00	$ 6.00	600%	6	6.0E+00	6
13	6.5	6.50	$6.50	$ 6.50	650%	6 1/2	6.5E+00	6.5
14	7	7.00	$7.00	$ 7.00	700%	7	7.0E+00	7
15	7.5	7.50	$7.50	$ 7.50	750%	7 1/2	7.5E+00	7.5
16	8	8.00	$8.00	$ 8.00	800%	8	8.0E+00	8
17	8.5	8.50	$8.50	$ 8.50	850%	8 1/2	8.5E+00	8.5
18	9	9.00	$9.00	$ 9.00	900%	9	9.0E+00	9
19	9.5	9.50	$9.50	$ 9.50	950%	9 1/2	9.5E+00	9.5
20	10	10.00	$10.00	$ 10.00	1000%	10	1.0E+01	10
21	10.5	10.50	$10.50	$ 10.50	1050%	10 1/2	1.1E+01	10.5
22	11	11.00	$11.00	$ 11.00	1100%	11	1.1E+01	11
23	11.5	11.50	$11.50	$ 11.50	1150%	11 1/2	1.2E+01	11.5
24	12	12.00	$12.00	$ 12.00	1200%	12	1.2E+01	12
25	12.5	12.50	$12.50	$ 12.50	1250%	12 1/2	1.3E+01	12.5
26								

FIGURE 5-5

Each column contains the same list of numbers. Although this worksheet shows you an example for each number format (except dates and times), it doesn't show all your options. That's because each number format has its own set of options, like the number of decimal places it displays.

UP TO SPEED

The Relationship Between Formatting and Values

The format that you choose for a number doesn't affect Excel's internal storage of that number. For example, if a cell contains the fraction 1/3, then Excel stores this value as 0.333333333333333. (The exact number of decimal places varies, depending on the number you entered, due to the slight approximations computers need to make when converting fractional numbers into 0s and 1s.) When deciding how to format a cell, you may choose to show only two decimal places, in which case the number appears in your worksheet as 0.33. Or maybe you choose just one decimal place, in which case the number is simply 0.3. In both cases, Excel still keeps the full 15 or so decimal places on hand. To tell the difference between the displayed number and the real number—the one Excel stores behind the scenes—just move to the cell and then look at the formula bar, which always displays the real deal.

Because of the difference between the stored value and the displayed number, there may be times when you think Excel's making a mistake. For example, imagine you have three cells, and each stores 0.333333333333333 but displays only 0.3. When you add these three cell values together, you won't end up with 0.3 + 0.3 + 0.3 = 0.9. Instead, Excel adds the more precise stored values and you end up with a number that's infinitesimally close to, but not quite, 1. Excel rounds this number up to 1.

This is almost always the way you want Excel to work, because you know full well that if you add up 1/3 three times you end up with 1. But, if you need to, you can change this behavior.

To do so, select File→Options, choose the Advanced section, and then scroll down to the "When calculating this workbook" group of settings. A "Set precision as displayed" checkbox appears. When you turn on this checkbox, Excel adjusts all the values in your current spreadsheet so that the stored value matches the displayed value. Unfortunately, with this choice, you get less precise data. For example, if you use this option with the 1/3 example, Excel stores the display value 0.3 instead of 0.333333333333333. Because you can't reverse this change, Excel warns you and asks for a final confirmation when you try to apply the "Precision as displayed" setting.

GENERAL

The General format is Excel's standard number format; it applies no special formatting. General is the only number format (other than Text) that doesn't limit your data to a fixed number of decimal places. That means that if you want to display numbers that differ wildly in precision (like 0.5, 12.334, and 0.120986398), it makes sense to use the General format. On the other hand, if your numbers have a similar degree of precision (for example, if you log the number of miles you run each day), the Number format makes more sense.

NUMBER

The Number format is like the General format, but with three refinements. First, it uses a fixed number of decimal places (which you set). That means that the decimal points always line up, assuming you format the entire column. The Number format also lets you use commas as separators between groups of three digits, which is handy if you work with really long numbers. Finally, you can choose to have negative numbers displayed with the negative sign, in parentheses, or in red lettering.

CURRENCY

The Currency format closely matches the Number format, with two differences. First, you can choose a currency symbol (like the dollar sign, pound symbol, or euro symbol) from an extensive list; Excel displays the currency symbol before the number. Second, the Currency format always includes commas. It also supports a fixed number of decimal places (chosen by you), and lets you customize how Excel displays negative numbers.

ACCOUNTING

The Accounting format is based on the Currency format. Like the Currency format, the Accounting format lets you choose a currency symbol, use commas, and display a fixed number of decimal places. However, the Accounting format aligns numbers slightly differently. The currency symbol is always at the far left of the cell (away from the number), and there's always an extra space that pads the right side of the cell. Also, the Accounting format always shows negative numbers in parentheses, which is an accounting standard. Finally, the Accounting format never displays the number 0. Instead, it uses a dash (-) in its place. There's really no reason to prefer the Currency or the Accounting format. Think of it as a personal decision, and choose whichever looks nicest on your worksheet. The only exception is if you happen to *be* an accountant, in which case you really have no choice in the matter—stick with your namesake.

PERCENTAGE

The Percentage format displays fractional numbers as percentages. For example, if you enter 0.5, that translates to 50 percent. You can choose the number of decimal places to display.

There's one trick to watch out for with the Percentage format. If you forget to start your number with a decimal point, Excel quietly "corrects" your numbers. For example, if you type 4 into a cell that uses the Percentage format, Excel interprets this as 4 percent. As a result, it stores the value 0.04. A side-effect of this quirkiness is that if you want to enter percentages larger than 100 percent, you can't enter them as decimals. For example, to enter 200 percent, you need to type in 200 (not 2.00).

FRACTION

The Fraction format displays your number as a fraction instead of a number with decimal places. That doesn't mean you must enter the number as a fraction (although you can if you want, by using the forward slash, like 3/4). Instead, it means that Excel converts any number you enter and displays it as a fraction. Thus, to have 1/4 appear, you can either enter .25 or 1/4.

NOTE If you try to enter 1/4 and you *haven't* formatted the cell to use the Fraction format, you won't get the result you want. Excel assumes you're trying to enter a date (in this case, January 4 of the current year). To avoid this misunderstanding, change the number format *before* you type in your fraction. Or, enter it as *0 1/4* (zero and one quarter).

People often use the Fraction format for stock market quotes, but it's also handy for certain types of measurements (like weights and temperatures). When you use the Fraction format and type in a number, Excel does its best to calculate the closest fraction. That depends on a few factors, including whether an exact match exists for the number (entering .5 always gets you 1/2, for example) and what level of precision you specified for the formatting.

You can choose to have fractions with three digits (for example, 100/200), two digits (10/20), or just one digit (1/2) using the top three choices in the Type list. For example, if you enter the number 0.51, Excel displays it as 1/2 in one-digit mode, and the more precise 51/100 in three-digit mode. In some cases, you may want all your numbers to use the same denominator (the bottom number in a fraction) so you can easily compare numbers. (Don't you wish Excel had been around when you were in grammar school?) In this case, you can display fractions as halves (with a denominator of 2), quarters (a denominator of 4), eighths (8), sixteenths (16), tenths (10), and hundredths (100). For example, the number 0.51 displays as 2/4 if you choose quarters.

TIP Entering a fraction in Excel can be awkward, because Excel may attempt to convert it to a date. To prevent this from happening, always start by entering 0, and then a space. For example, instead of typing 2/3, enter 0 2/3 (which means zero and two-thirds). If you type in a whole number and a fraction, like 1 2/3, you also duck the date confusion.

FREQUENTLY ASKED QUESTION

Just How Precise Are Excel's Numbers, Anyway?

Can I enter a number with 10 decimal places? How about 20?

Here's a handy way to find out: Type the fraction *2/3* into a cell, and then check the formula bar, which shows you the number Excel has stored. Turns out Excel thinks of 2/3 as 0.666666666666667.

This test shows that Excel is limited to 15 significant digits, and it rounds the last digit. You may be slightly unnerved by the word "about," but in the binary world of computers, fractional numbers don't have a fixed number of digits and may just be approximations with very slight rounding errors. You can find a good (but technical) explanation of this phenomenon in the online encyclopedia Wikipedia at *http://en.wikipedia.org/wiki/Floating_point*.

Because Excel doesn't store fractions as precisely as they exist in the world of real math, you may occasionally experience minor rounding errors in calculations with more than 14 significant digits. (Recall from high-school math that the number of significant digits is the number of digits starting with the first nonzero digit and ending with the last nonzero digit. Essentially, the significant digits hold all the information in your number.) This behavior shouldn't cause you to panic—it's a limitation of nearly all computers, based on the way they manipulate numbers.

SCIENTIFIC

The Scientific format displays numbers using scientific notation, which is ideal when you need to handle numbers that range widely in size (like 0.0003 and 300) *in the same column*. Scientific notation displays the first nonzero digit of a number, followed by a fixed number of digits, and then indicates what power of 10 that number needs to be multiplied by to generate the original number. For example, 0.0003 becomes 3.00×10^{-4} (displayed in Excel as 3.00E-04, with the E standing for "exponent"). The number 300, on the other hand, becomes 3.00×10^{2} (displayed in Excel as 3.00E02). Scientists—surprise, surprise—like the Scientific format for recording things like experimental data or creating mathematical models to predict when an incoming meteor will strike the Earth.

TEXT

Few people use the Text format for numbers, but it's certainly possible to do so. The Text format simply displays a number as though it were text, although you can still perform calculations with it. Excel shows the number exactly as it stores it internally, positioning it against the left edge of the column. You can get the same effect by placing an apostrophe before the number (although this approach won't let you use the number in calculations).

TIMESAVING TIP

Shortcuts in the Ribbon

You don't need to waste hours jumping between your worksheet and the Format Cells window. The ribbon gets you to some of the most commonly used number formats in the Home→Number section.

The Home→Number section's most prominent part is the drop-down list of number formats (Figure 5-6). Just underneath are buttons that let you quickly apply common number formats, like Accounting and Percent. Just to the right are two buttons that let you increase or decrease the number of decimal places that Excel displays.

One of the neatest features is the list of currency options for the Accounting format. If you click the drop-down arrow on the Accounting button (which looks like a dollar sign), you see a list of currency symbols from which you can choose (like pounds, euros, Chinese yuan, and so on). But if you click the *other* portion of the Accounting button (not the arrow), you get the currency symbol that matches the regional settings for your computer.

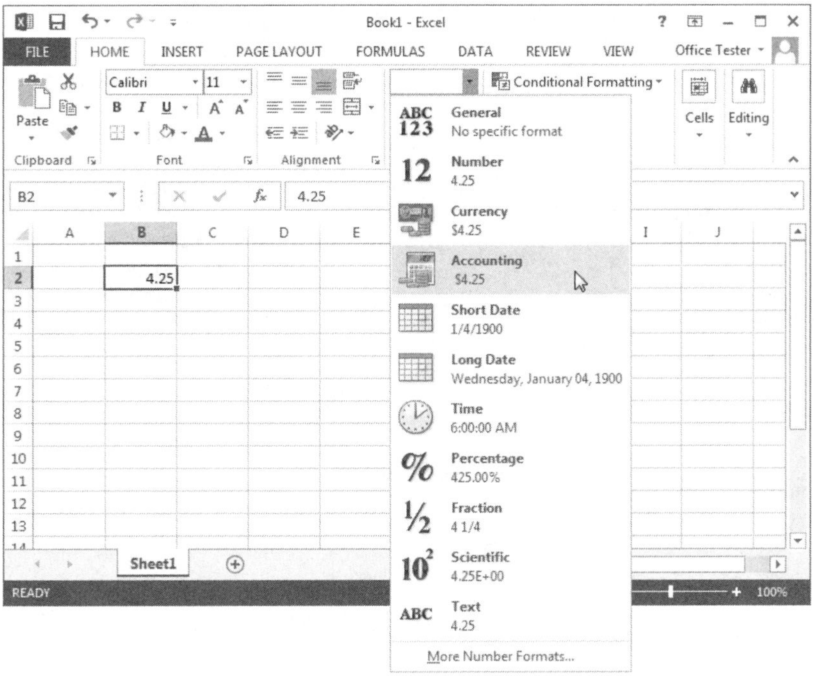

FIGURE 5-6

The all-around quickest way to apply a number format is to select some cells, and then, from the number format list, choose an option. Best of all, you see a small preview of what the value in the first selected cell will look like should you apply the format.

Formatting Dates and Times

Excel gives you lots of options here. You can use everything from compact styles like 3/23/13 to longer formats that include the day of the week, like Saturday, March 23, 2013. Time formats give you a similar range of options, including the ability to use a 12-hour or 24-hour clock, show seconds, show fractional seconds, and include the date information.

To format dates and times, first open the Format Cells window, shown in Figure 5-7 (Home→Cells→Format→Format Cells). Choose Date or Time from the column on the left, and then choose the format from the list on the right. Date and Time both provide a slew of options.

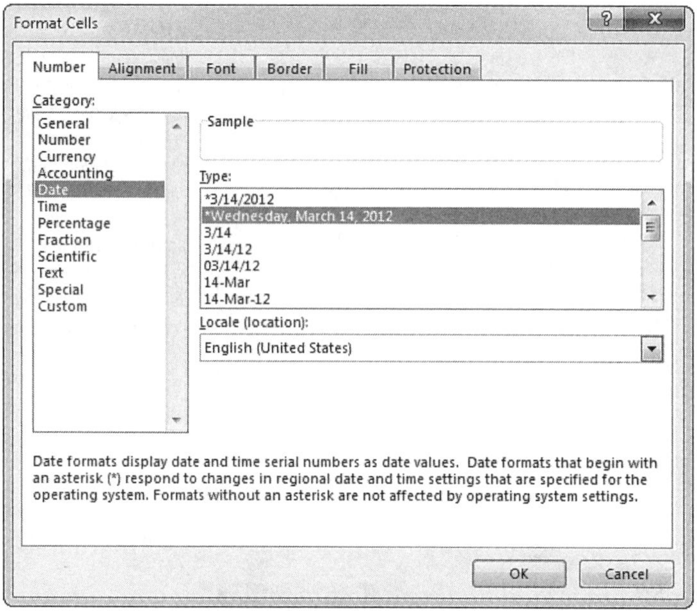

FIGURE 5-7

Excel gives you dozens of ways to format dates and times. You can choose a format that modifies the date's appearance depending on the regional settings of the computer viewing the Excel file, or you can choose a fixed date format. When using a fixed date format, you don't need to stick to the U.S. standard. Instead, choose the appropriate region from the Locale list box. Each locale provides its own set of customized date formats.

Excel has essentially two types of date and time formats:

- **Formats that take the regional settings of the spreadsheet viewer's computer into account**. With these formats, dates display differently depending on the computer that's running Excel. This choice is a good one, because it lets everyone see dates in just the way they want to, which means no time-consuming arguments about month-day-year or day-month-year ordering.
- **Formats that ignore the regional settings of individual computers**. These formats define a fixed pattern for month, day, year, and time components, and display date-related information in exactly the same way on all computers. If you need to absolutely make sure a date is in a certain format, use one of these formats.

The first group (the formats that rely on a computer's regional settings) offers the fewest number of formats. It includes two date formats (a compact, number-only format, and a long, more descriptive format) and one time format. Excel puts these numbers at the top of the Type list, preceded by an asterisk (see Figure 5-7).

The second group (the formats that are independent of a computer's regional settings) offers many more options. To choose one, first select a region from the Locale list, and then select the appropriate date or time format (that isn't preceded by an asterisk). Some examples of locales include "English (U.S.)" and "English (U.K.)."

If you enter a date without specifying a format for the cell, Excel usually uses the short region-specific date format. That means that the order of the month and year vary depending on the regional settings of the current computer. If you incorporate the month name (for example, January 1, 2013), instead of the month number (for example, 1/1/2013), Excel uses a medium date format that includes a month abbreviation, like 1-Jan-2013.

NOTE You may remember from Chapter 2 that Excel internally stores a date as the cumulative number of days that have elapsed since a certain long-ago date. You can take a peek at this internal number using the Format Cells window. First, enter your date. Then, format the cell using one of the number formats (like General or Number). The underlying date number appears in the cell where the date used to be.

Special Formats for Special Numbers

You wouldn't ever want to perform mathematical operations with some types of numeric information. For example, it's hard to imagine a situation where you'd want to add or multiply phone numbers or Social Security numbers.

When you enter these types of numbers, therefore, you may choose to format them as plain old text. For example, you could enter the text (555) 123-4567 to represent a phone number. Because of the parentheses and the dash (–), Excel won't interpret this information as a number. Alternatively, you could just precede your value with an apostrophe (') to explicitly tell Excel that it should treat the number as text (you might do this if you don't use parentheses or dashes in a phone number).

But whichever solution you choose, you're potentially creating more work for yourself, because you must enter the parentheses and dash for each phone number (or precede the number with an apostrophe). You also increase the likelihood of creating inconsistently formatted numbers, especially if you're entering a long list of them. For example, you may find some phone numbers entered in similar but slightly different formats, like 555-123-4567 and (555)1234567.

To avoid these problems, apply Excel's Special number format (shown in Figure 5-8), which converts numbers into common patterns. And lucky you: In the Special number format, one of the Type options is Phone Number (other formats handle Zip codes and Social Security numbers).

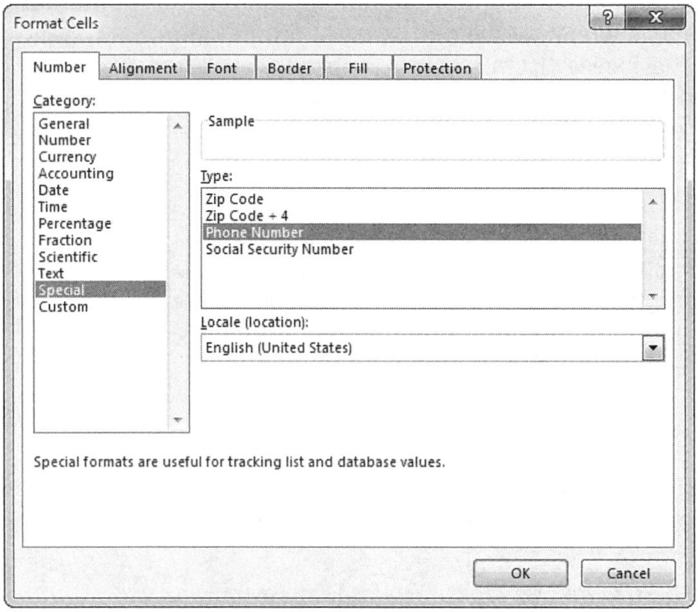

FIGURE 5-8

Special number formats are ideal for formatting sequences of digits into a common pattern. For example, in the Type list, if you choose Phone Number, Excel converts the sequence of digits 5551234567 into proper phone number style—(555) 123-4567—with no extra work on your part.

The Special format is a good idea, but it's limited. Out of the box, Excel provides only a small set of special types you can use. However, there's no reason you can't handle similar problems by creating a custom format, as you'll do in the next section.

Custom Formats

As versatile as Excel is, it can't read your mind. You'll find some situations where you want to format numbers in a special way that Excel just doesn't expect. For example, you may want to use the ISO (International Organization for Standardization) format for dates, which a wide range of scientific and engineering documents use. This format is year-month-day (as in 2013-12-25). Although it's fairly straightforward, Excel doesn't provide this format as a standard option.

Or maybe you want to type in short versions of longer numbers. For example, say your company, International Pet Adventures, uses an employee number to identify each worker, in the format 0521-1033. It may be that 0521- is the company's code for the Travel department. To save effort, you want to be able to enter 1033 and have Excel automatically insert the leading 0521-.

The solution lies in creating a *custom format*. Custom formats are a powerful tool for taking control of how Excel formats your numbers. Unfortunately, they aren't exactly easy to master.

The basic concept behind custom formats is that you define the format using a string of special characters and placeholders. This *format string* tells Excel how to format a number or date, including details like how many decimal places it should include, and how it should treat negative numbers. You can also add fixed characters that never change, like the departmental code just described.

CREATING A CUSTOM FORMAT

Here's the easiest way to apply a custom format:

1. **Select the cells you want to format.**

   You can include any combination of cells, columns, rows, and so on. To make life easier, make sure the first cell you select contains a value you want to format. That way, you'll be able to use the Format Cells window to preview your custom format.

NOTE Excel saves any custom format strings you create as part of your workbook file. Once you perfect a format string, you can apply it to as many cells as you want.

2. **Select Home→Cells→Format→Format Cells, or just right-click the selection, and then choose Format Cells.**

   The Format Cells window appears, as shown in Figure 5-2.

3. **Choose a format that's similar to the format you want.**

   For example, if you want to apply a custom date format, begin by selecting the Date number format, and then choosing the appropriate style. To apply a custom currency format, begin by selecting the Currency number format, and then specifying the appropriate options (like the number of decimal places).

   To create the International Pet Adventures employee code, it makes sense to first select the Number format, and then choose 0 decimal places (because the number format you're looking to model—0521-1033—doesn't use any decimal places).

4. **At the bottom of the Category list, click Custom.**

   Now you see a list of custom number strings. A highlighted format string, based on the format you chose in step 3, tops the list. You just need to edit the string to create a custom format. (Make sure you don't accidentally select another format before you click Custom, or you won't end up with the right format string.)

   If you're creating the International Pet Adventures employee code, you'll see a 0. That means you can use any number without a decimal place. However, what you really want is an employee number that always starts with 0521- followed by four more digits. You'll specify your new format in the next step.

5. **Enter your custom string.**

   Type your custom string into the box below the Type label, as shown in Figure 5-9. The correct format string for the International Pet Adventures example is as follows:

   ```
   "0521-"0000
   ```

   This string tells Excel to begin all cells that use the Custom format with the digits 0521-, and then follow them with whatever four numbers you enter into the cell (if you don't enter any numbers, Excel adds four zeros after the 0521-). The following sections explain all the ingredients you can use in your custom format.

TIP Remember, you can preview your custom format in the Sample section of the Format Cells window. As you adjust the format string, the Sample box shows you what the current cell would look like if you applied the custom format to it.

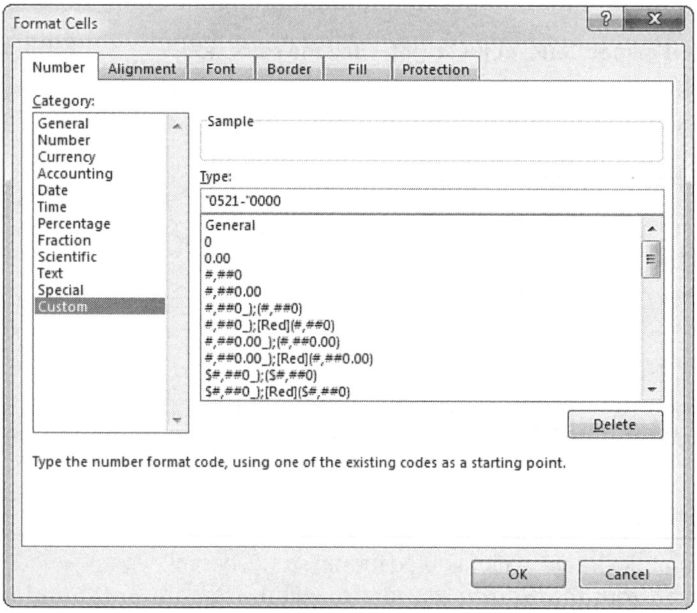

FIGURE 5-9

Custom number strings let you format a number in almost any way, but you need to explicitly spell out your intentions using Excel's cryptic codes. In the example shown here, the custom format string is "0521-"0000. The "0521-" is a fixed string of characters that Excel adds to the beginning of every number. The four zeros indicate that the cell's expecting four digits. If you provide a one-, two-, or three-digit number, Excel adds the zeros needed to create a four-digit number. For example, Excel automatically displays the number 4 as the employee code 0521-0004.

6. **Click OK to commit your changes.**

   If the results aren't quite what you want, you can start over. But this time, skip step 3 because you want to change the *current* format string rather than replace it with a new format string.

7. **To use the Custom format you created, select one or more cells, launch the Format Cells window (by right-clicking the cells, and then choosing Format Cells), and then select your new Custom format.**

   Excel lists newly created Custom formats in the Custom category, at the bottom of the Type list. To use the new International Pet Adventures employee code, click OK after you select your new format, and then begin entering the four digits specific to each employee. For example, if you format a cell with the new Custom format, and then type 6754 into the cell, you'll see *0521-6754*. Remember, despite your crafty formatting, the actual number is still 6754, which is important to know if you use the number in a calculation.

CUSTOM FORMAT STRING CODES

The tricky part about Custom formats is creating the right format string. To the untrained eye, the format string looks like a cryptic jumble of symbols—which it is. But these symbols, or *formatting codes* in Excel lingo, actually have very specific and clear meanings.

For example, the format string $#,##0.00 translates into the following series of instructions:

$ tells Excel to add a currency symbol before the number.

#,## tells Excel to use commas to separate thousands.

0.00 tells Excel to always include a single digit and two decimal places, no matter what the number is.

In fact, $#,##0.00 is the format string for the basic Currency format. Once you understand what the codes stand for and how they work together, you can create some really useful Custom format strings.

You have three types of codes at your disposal for creating format strings: those used to format dates and times; those used to format numbers; and those used to format ordinary text. The following three sections tackle each type of code.

DATE AND TIME FORMAT STRINGS

Date and time format strings are built out of pieces. Each piece represents a single part of the date, like the day, month, year, minute, hour, and so on. You can combine these pieces in whatever order you want, and you can insert your own custom text along with these values.

NOTE Keep in mind that none of these formatting codes actually generate or insert the date in your worksheet for you. That is, simply formatting an empty cell with one of these custom strings isn't going to cause the date to appear. Instead, these format strings take the dates *you* enter and make sure they all appear in a uniform style.

Table 5-1 shows the basic ingredients for a date or time format string. These strings are placeholders that represent the different parts of the date. If you want to include fixed text along with the date, put it in quotation marks.

TABLE 5-1 *Date and time formatting codes*

CODE	DESCRIPTION	EXAMPLE VALUE DISPLAYED ON WORKSHEET
D	The day of the month, from 1 to 31, with the numbers between 1 and 9 appearing without a leading 0.	7
dd	The day of the month, from 01 to 31, with a leading 0 added to numbers from 1 to 9.	07
ddd	A three-letter abbreviation for the day of the week.	Thu
dddd	The full name of the day of the week.	Thursday
m	The number value, from 1 to 12, of the month (no leading 0 used).	1
mm	The number value, from 01 to 12, of the month, with a leading 0 used for the values 01 to 09.	01
mmm	A three-letter abbreviation for the month.	Jan
mmmm	The full name of the month.	January
yy	A two-digit abbreviation for the year.	13
yyyy	The year with all four digits.	2013
h	The hour, from 0 to 23 (no leading 0 used).	15
hh	The hour, from 00 to 23, with a leading 0 used for numbers from 00 to 09.	15
:m	The minute, from 0 to 59.	5
:mm	The minute, from 0 to 59 (leading 0 used for the values 00 to 09).	05
:s	The second, from 0 to 59 (no leading 0 used). If you want to add tenths, hundredths, or thousandths of a second, follow this with .0 or .00 or .000, respectively. For example, :s.0	5
:ss	The second, from 0 to 59 (leading 0 used for numbers from 00 to 09). If you want to add tenths or hundredths of a second, follow this with .0 or .00, respectively.	05

CODE	DESCRIPTION	EXAMPLE VALUE DISPLAYED ON WORKSHEET
AM/PM	Tells Excel to use a 12-hour clock, including the AM or PM tag.	PM
A/P	Tells Excel to use a 12-hour clock, with just an A or P tag.	P
[ ]	Tells Excel that a given time component (hour, minute, or second) shouldn't "roll over." For example, Excel's standard approach is to have seconds become minutes once they hit the 60 mark, and minutes become hours at the 60 mark. Similarly, hours roll over into a new day when they hit 24. But if you don't want this to happen—for example, if you're tracking the total time on a music playlist—you could use a format string like [mm]:ss or [h]:mm:ss. The first format string shows the total time in minutes and seconds (without rolling over to hours), while the second shows the total time in hours, minutes, and seconds (without rolling over to days).	133:12 (for the format string [mm]:ss and a value of just over two hours)

For example, consider the following format string:

```
yyyy-mm-dd
```

If you apply this string to a cell that contains a date, you end up with the following in your worksheet (assuming you entered the date January 15, 2013): *2013-01-15*.

Regardless of how you type in a date, once you format a cell using a Custom format string, Excel always overrides the format you use when you type in the date. In other words, it doesn't matter whether you type *1/15/13* or *January 15, 2013* in the cell—Excel displays it as 2013-01-15 if that's what your custom format dictates.

NOTE Date and time formatting strings are case sensitive. That means if you make the mistake of typing in YYYY-MM-DD instead of yyyy-mm-dd, your format won't work.

Now if you format the same value with this format string:

```
"Day "yyyy-mm-dd
```

You'll see this in your worksheet:

```
Day 2013-01-15
```

And remember, whatever information you choose to display or hide, Excel always *internally* stores the date the same way.

NOTE You'll learn much more about date and time calculations in Chapter 11.

NUMBER FORMAT STRINGS

Custom number formats are more challenging than Custom date formats, because Excel gives you lots of flexibility when it comes to customizing number formats. Table 5-2 shows the different codes you can use. The most important ones are the digit placeholders 0, ?, and #. You use these to tell Excel where it should slot in the various digits of the number currently in the cell (or that you're typing in). For example, a format string that looks like this:

```
#,###.00
```

displays the numbers 45 and 4,500 like this:

```
   45.00
4,500.00
```

In this format string, the # character is a placeholder that lets you put the comma wherever you want it. The 0 character is a placeholder that makes sure trailing zeros appear, even if you display a whole number. Table 5-2 reveals many more tricks of the trade.

TABLE 5-2 *Number formatting codes*

CODE	DESCRIPTION	EXAMPLE
0	This digit placeholder forces a zero to appear whenever a number isn't provided.	0.000 displays .3 as 0.300.
?	This digit placeholder forces a space to appear whenever a number isn't provided.	?.??? displays .3 as " .3 " (quotations used to indicate spacing).
#	This digit placeholder indicates where you can place a number, but doesn't automatically insert a 0 or space if there isn't a number in this position. You can use this symbol to set the precision of decimal values or to indicate where commas should go.	###.# displays .3 as .3 and #,### displays 9999 as 9,999.
.	The period, or decimal point, determines where the decimal place will go. You use it in conjunction with the digit placeholders 0, ?, and #.	#.## truncates 1.23456 to 1.23.

CODE	DESCRIPTION	EXAMPLE
,	The comma causes the thousands separator to appear. Here again, you use it with the digit placeholders 0, ?, and #. You can also use it to scale a number. For example, if you place one comma at the end of a format string, Excel displays the number rounded to thousands. Add two commas to the end, and Excel displays the number only in millions (and so on).	#,### displays 3000 as 3,000. #,###,###, displays 123456789 as 123,457 (rounded to thousands).
/	The forward slash formats a number as a fraction. You use this symbol in conjunction with the digit placeholders ? and # to indicate the number of digits you want in your fraction.	?/? displays 1.75 as 7/4, while # ?/? formats the same number as 1 3/4.
E+	This code formats numbers using scientific notation. You use this symbol in conjunction with the digit placeholders 0, ?, and #.	#.## E+## means Excel displays 12345 as 1.23 E+4.
[color]	Applies a specified color to the text that follows the closing bracket. The color name goes inside the square brackets. Excel supports eight colors: [black], [blue], [cyan], [green], [magenta], [red], [white], and [yellow].	[red]#,### displays the number that follows the brackets in red lettering.
_	The underscore character, when followed by any other character, inserts a space equal to the width of that other character. This code is occasionally used when aligning complex formatting codes.	_W inserts a space as wide as the capital letter W.
*	The asterisk, when followed by any other character, inserts that other character in a cell until the cell is filled.	#,###*- displays 9999 as 9,999------ (with the dashes appearing until the cell is filled).

NOTE Excel uses custom number formats to decide how to round off displayed numbers, and how to format them (by adding commas, currency symbols, and so on). But no matter what format string you use, you can't coax Excel into shaving off digits that appear to the *left* of the decimal place—and for good reason: doing so would mangle your numbers beyond recognition.

It helps to keep a few pointers in mind when you use the number formatting codes listed in Table 5-2:

- **Use 0** to tell Excel that there *must* be a number in that spot—if a number doesn't naturally occur there, Excel automatically inserts a 0. For example, the format string 0.00 would display the number .3 as 0.30. And the format string 00.00 would format the same value as 00.30.
- **The question mark (?)** works similarly, but if there's no number in the spot, it turns into a space instead of a zero. Although spaces might seem somewhat useless (because you can't see them), they can help you align the digits in a column. For example, ??.?? displays the number 3 as " 3." (without the quotation marks).
- **The # symbol** lets you indicate where a number *can* exist but doesn't *have to* exist. For example, the format string 0.0# indicates that the first digit before the decimal place and the first digit after the decimal place must be present (that's what the zeros tell Excel), but the second number after the decimal place is optional. With this format string, Excel rounds additional digits, starting with the third decimal place. Thus, the format string 0.0# displays the value .3 as 0.3, .34 as 0.34, and .356 as 0.36. You can also use the # symbol to indicate where commas should go, as in the format string #,###.00. This string displays the value 3639 as 3,639.00.

NOTE Remember, custom format strings control how Excel displays values. They aren't meant to control what values someone can enter in a cell. To set rules for allowed data, you need a different Excel feature—data validation, described on page 640.

Excel also lets you use codes that apply currency symbols, percent symbols, and colors. As with date values, you can insert fixed text—also known as *literals*—into a number-formatting string using quotation marks. For example, you could add "USD" at the end of the format string to indicate that the number represents a denomination in U.S. dollars. Excel automatically recognizes some characters as literals, including currency symbols, parentheses, plus (+) and minus (–) symbols, backward slashes (\), and spaces, which means you don't need to use quotation marks to have those characters appear.

Finally, if you want your worksheet to display different types of values (like negative numbers versus positive numbers) differently, you can create a collection of four custom format strings to style the four types of data you can enter into a cell. Collectively, these four format strings tell Excel how to deal with positive values, negatives values, zeros, and text values. You have to write the format strings in this order and separate each with a semicolon. Here's an example:

```
#,###; [red]#,###; "---"; @
```

Excel uses the first format string (#,###) if the cell contains a positive number. It uses the second format string ([red]#,###) to display negative numbers—in this example, it's the same format as the one for positive numbers, except that it displays the text in red. The third format string ("---") applies to zero values. It inserts three dashes into a cell when the cell contains the number 0. (If the cell is empty, Excel doesn't apply a format string, and the cell remains blank.) Finally, Excel uses the last format (@) if you enter text into a cell. The @ symbol tells Excel to simply display whatever text the cell contains.

TIP For a real trick, use the empty format string ;;; to puzzle friends and coworkers. This string specifies that no matter what the content in the cell (positive number, negative number, zero, or text), Excel shouldn't display it. You can add information to the cell (and see it in the formula bar), but it doesn't appear in your worksheet or in printouts.

TEXT FORMAT STRINGS

Good news: Text format strings are extremely simple. Usually, you use a text format string to repeatedly insert the same text in a large number of cells. For example, you may want to add the word note before a collection of entries. To do this, your format string needs to define the literal text you want to use—in this case, the word "NOTE"—and place the text within quotation marks (including any spaces you wish to appear). Use the @ symbol to indicate which side of the string the cell contents should go. For example, if you set the format string:

```
"NOTE: "@
```

And then you type *Transfer payment* into the cell, Excel displays it as note *Transfer payment*. If the cell is empty, however, it stays blank, and Excel doesn't add the note text.

Formatting Cell Appearance

Formatting cell values is important, because it helps maintain consistency among your numbers. But to really make your spreadsheet readable (and even beautiful), you need to enlist some of Excel's tools for controlling things like alignment, color, borders, and shading.

You can format a cell's appearance two ways. You can find the button you need on the Home tab of the ribbon, or you can go back to the more comprehensive Format Cells window. Just select the cell or group of cells you want to work with, and then choose Home→Cells→Format→Format Cells. Or, right-click the selection, and then choose Format Cells. The following sections walk you through the options in the Format Cells window.

TIP Even a small amount of formatting can make a worksheet easier to interpret by drawing the viewer's eye to important information. Of course, as with formatting a Word document or designing a web page, a little goes a long way. Don't feel the need to bury your worksheet in exotic colors and styles just because you can.

Alignment and Orientation

As you learned in the previous chapter, Excel automatically aligns cells according to the type of information you enter. But what if *you* want to control the alignment? Fortunately, the Alignment tab has you covered.

Excel lets you control the position of content between a cell's left and right borders, known as the *horizontal alignment*. It offers the following choices for horizontal alignment, some of which are shown in Figure 5-10:

- **General** is the standard type of alignment; it aligns cells to the right if they hold numbers or dates, and to the left if they hold text. You learned about this type of alignment in Chapter 2.
- **Left (Indent)** tells Excel to always line up content with the left edge of the cell. You can also choose an indent value to add some extra space between the content and the left border.
- **Center** tells Excel to always center content between the left and right edges of the cell.
- **Right (Indent)** tells Excel to always line up content with the right edge of the cell. You can set an indent value here, too, to add some extra space between the content and the right border.
- **Fill** copies content multiple times across the width of the cell, which is almost never what you want.
- **Justify** is the same as Left if the cell content fits on a single line. When you insert text that spans more than one line, Excel justifies every line except the last one, which means that Excel adjusts the space between the words in each line of text to try and ensure that both the right and left edges of the text block line up.
- **Center Across Selection** is a bit of an oddity. When you apply this option to a single cell, it has the same effect as Center. If you select more than one adjacent cell in a row (for example, cells A1, A2, and A3), this option centers the value in the first cell so that it appears to be centered over the full width of all the cells. However, this happens only as long as the other cells are blank. This setting may confuse you a bit at first, because Excel can end up displaying one cell's value across empty adjacent cells. Another approach to centering long titles and headings is to merge the content-bearing cell with its adjacent cells (as described in the box on page 153), but Excel purists prefer Center Across Selection, because it doesn't muck with the worksheet's structure.
- **Distributed (Indent)** is the same as Center—if the cell contains a numeric value or a single word. If you add more than one word, Excel increases the space between words so that the text precisely fills the cell (from left edge to right edge).

Vertical alignment controls the position of content between the top and bottom border of a cell. Vertical alignment becomes important only if you enlarge a row's height so that it becomes taller than the content it contains. To change the height of a row, click the bottom edge of the row header (the numbered cell on the left side of the worksheet), and drag it up or down. As you resize the row, the content stays fixed at the bottom, which is Excel's default for vertical alignment. You can change that using the vertical alignment setting.

Excel gives you the following vertical alignment choices, some of which are shown in Figure 5-10:

- **Top** tells Excel that it should display the first line of text at the top of the cell.
- **Center** tells Excel to center the block of text between the top and bottom border of the cell.
- **Bottom** tells Excel that the last line of text should end at the bottom of the cell. If the text doesn't fill the cell exactly, then Excel adds some padding to the top.
- **Justify** is the same as Top for a single line of text. When you have more than one line of text, Excel increases the space between each line so that the text fills the cell completely, from the top edge to the bottom edge.
- **Distributed** is the same as Justify for multiple lines of text. If you have a single line of text, this is the same as Center.

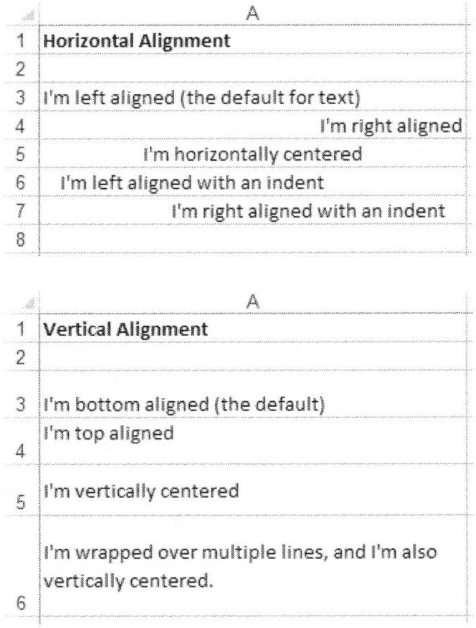

FIGURE 5-10

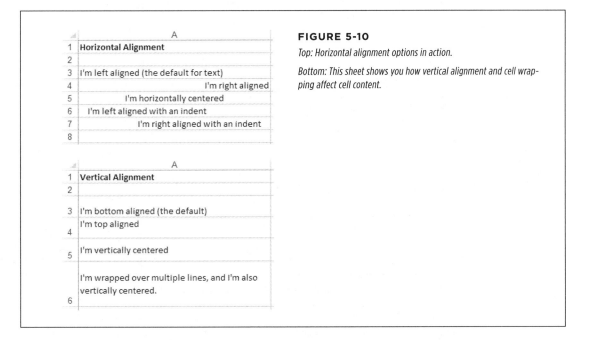

Top: Horizontal alignment options in action.

Bottom: This sheet shows you how vertical alignment and cell wrapping affect cell content.

If you have a cell containing a lot of text, you may want to increase the row's height so you can display multiple lines of text. Unfortunately, enlarging a cell doesn't automatically make the text flow from one line to another and fill the newly available space. But there's a simple solution: Turn on the "Wrap text" checkbox (on the Alignment tab of the Format Cells window). Now, long passages of text flow across multiple lines. You can use this option in conjunction with the vertical alignment setting to control whether Excel centers a block of text, or lines it up at the bottom or top of the cell. Another option is to explicitly split your text into lines. Whenever you want to insert a line break, just press Alt+Enter, and then start typing the new line.

TIP After you expand a row, you can shrink it back by double-clicking the bottom edge of the row header. Assuming you haven't turned on text wrapping, this action shrinks the row back to its standard single-line height.

Finally, the Alignment tab lets you rotate content in a cell up to 180 degrees, as shown in Figure 5-11. You can set the number of degrees in the Orientation box on the right of the Alignment tab. Rotating cell content automatically changes the size of the cell. Usually, you'll see it become narrower and taller to accommodate the rotated content.

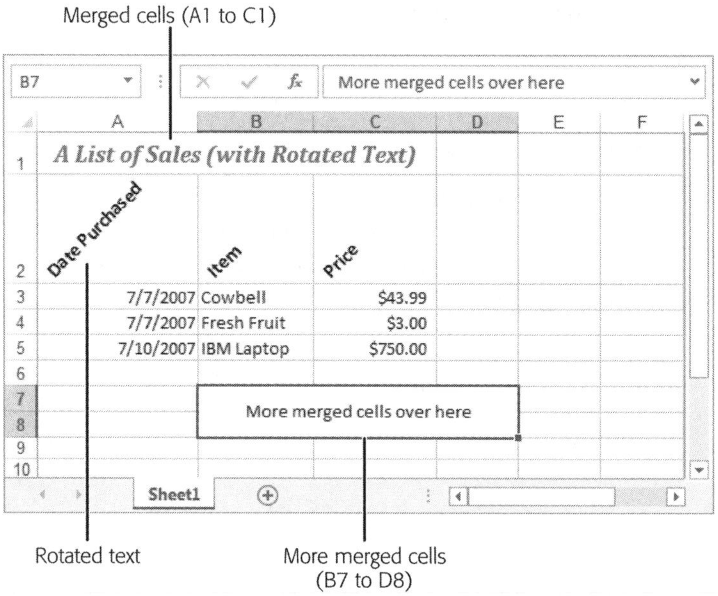

FIGURE 5-11

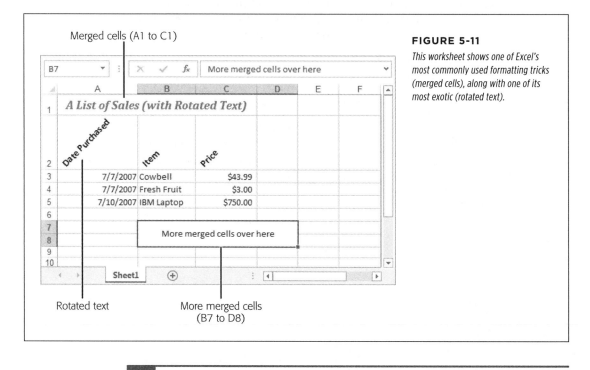

This worksheet shows one of Excel's most commonly used formatting tricks (merged cells), along with one of its most exotic (rotated text).

TIP You can use the Home→Alignment section of the ribbon to quickly change alignment, indenting, rotation, and wrapping, without opening the Format Cells window.

FREQUENTLY ASKED QUESTION

Shrinking Text and Merging Cells So You Can Fit More Text into a Cell

I'm frequently writing out big chunks of text that I'd love to scrunch into a single cell. Do I have any options other than text wrapping?

You betcha. When you need to store a large amount of text in one cell, text wrapping is a good choice, but it's not your only option. You can also shrink the size of the text or merge multiple cells, both from the Alignment tab in the Format Cells window.

To shrink a cell's content, select the "Shrink to fit" checkbox. Be warned, however, that if you have a small column that doesn't use wrapping, this option can quickly reduce your text to vanishingly small proportions.

Joining multiple cells together removes the cells' shared borders and creates one mega-sized cell. Usually, you merge cells to accommodate a large amount of content that can't fit in a single cell (like a long title that you want to display over several columns). For example, if you merge cells A1, B1, and C1, you end up with a single cell named A1 that stretches over the full width of the A, B, and C columns, as shown in Figure 5-11.

To merge cells, select the cells you want to join, choose Home→Cells→Format→Format Cells, and then, on the Alignment tab, turn on the "Merge cells" checkbox. There's no limit to how many cells you can merge. (In fact, you can actually convert your entire worksheet into a single cell if you want to go crazy.) And if you change your mind, don't worry—you simply need to select the single merged cell, choose Home→Cells→Format→Format Cells again, and then turn off the "Merge cells" checkbox to redraw the original cells.

Fonts and Color

As in almost any Windows program, you can customize the text in Excel, applying a dazzling assortment of colors and fancy typefaces. You can do everything from enlarging headings to colorizing big numbers. Here are the individual font details you can change:

- **The font style.** For example, Arial, Times New Roman, or something a little more shocking, like Futura Extra Bold. Calibri is the standard font for new worksheets. If you have an old-school workbook created by Excel 2003, you'll notice that it uses 10-point Arial instead.
- **The font size, in points.** The standard point size is 11, but you can choose anything from a minuscule 1-point to a monstrous 409 points. Excel automatically enlarges the row height to accommodate the font.
- **Various font attributes, like italics, underlining, and bold.** Some fonts have complementary italic and bold typefaces, while others don't (in which case Windows uses its own algorithm to make the font bold or italic).
- **The font color.** This option controls the color of the text. (Page 158 covers how to change the background color of a cell.)

To change font settings, first highlight the cells you want to format, choose Home→Cells→Format→Format Cells, and then click the Font tab (Figure 5-12).

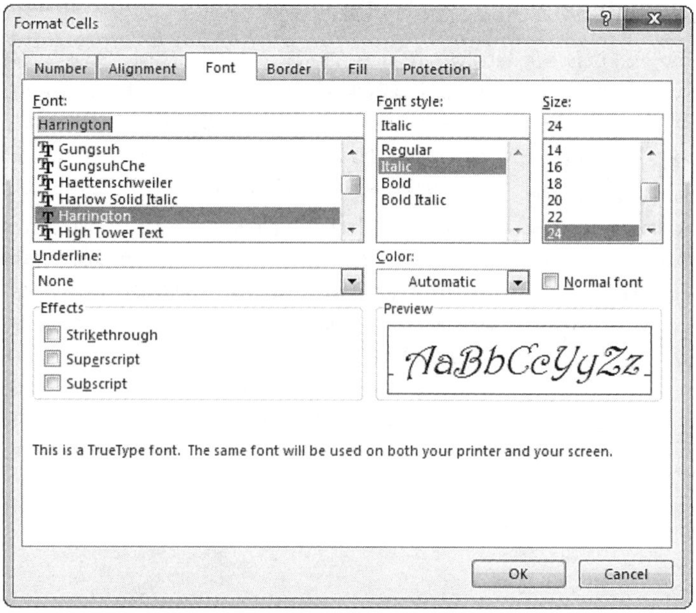

FIGURE 5-12

Here's an example of applying an exotic font using the Format Cells window. Keep in mind that when you display data, and especially numbers, sans-serif fonts usually look clearer and more professional than serif fonts. (Serif fonts have little embellishments, like tiny curls, on the ends of the letters; sans-serif fonts don't.) Calibri, Excel's default font, is sans-serif.

TIP Thanks to Excel's handy Redo feature, you can repeatedly apply a series of formatting changes to different cells. After you make your changes in the Format Cells window, simply select the new cell you want to format in the same way, and then hit Ctrl+Y to repeat the last action.

Rather than heading to the Format Cells window every time you want to tweak a font, you can use the ribbon's handy shortcuts. The Home→Font section displays buttons for changing the font and font size. You also get a load of tiny buttons that let you apply font basics like bold, italic, and underlined text; style cell borders; and change a cell's text and background colors. (Truth be told, you'll probably find the formatting toolbar way more convenient for setting fonts than the Format Cells window. That's because the toolbar's drop-down menu shows a long list of fonts at once, whereas the Format Cells window displays an impossibly restrictive six fonts at a time. Scrolling through that cramped space is like reading the phone book on index cards.)

Without a doubt, the ribbon's most useful formatting feature is *live preview*, a frill that shows you the result of a change *before* you apply it. Figure 5-13 shows live preview in action.

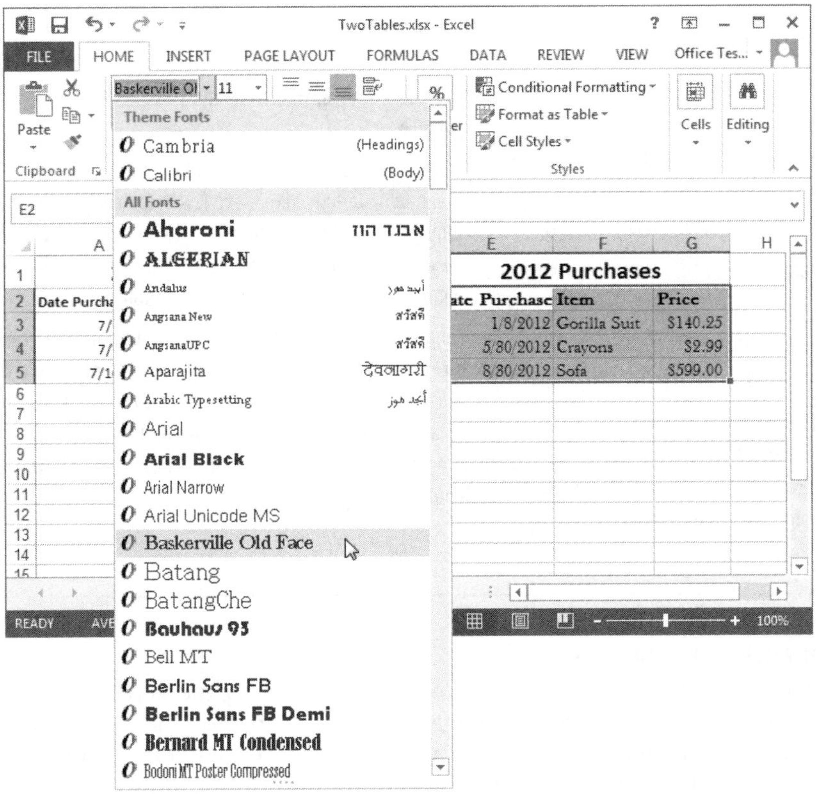

FIGURE 5-13

Right now, this spreadsheet's creator is just thinking about using the stylish Baskerville font for the highlighted table. However, the moment she hovers over Algerian (higher up in the font list), Excel switches the font in the selected cells, giving her a preview of the change. The best part: When she moves the mouse pointer away from a font name, the formatting disappears instantaneously. To make the changes stick, all she needs to do is click the font. This live preview feature works with font names, font sizes, and colors.

NOTE No matter what font you apply, Excel, thankfully, always displays the cell contents in the formula bar in easy-to-read Calibri font. That makes things easier if you're working with cells you formatted with difficult-to-decipher script fonts, or really large or small text sizes.

POWER USERS' CLINIC

Formatting Individual Characters

The ribbon lets you perform one task that you can't with the Format Cells window: apply formatting to just *part* of a cell. For example, if a cell contains the text "New low price", you could apply a new color or bold format to the word "low."

To apply formatting to a portion of a cell, follow these steps:

1. **Move to the appropriate cell, and then put it into edit mode by pressing F2.**

   You can also put a cell into edit mode by double-clicking it, or by moving to it, and then clicking the text inside the formula bar.

2. **Select the text you want to format.**

   You can select the text by highlighting it with the mouse, or by holding down Shift while using the arrow keys to mark your selection.

3. **Choose a font option from the ribbon's Home→Font section**

   You can also change the size, color, or attributes (bold, italic, or underline) of the text. If you don't want to waste time choosing the Home tab if you're currently somewhere else in the ribbon, simply right-click the selected text to launch a pop-up toolbar with font options.

Applying multiple types of formatting to the same cell can get tricky. The formula bar doesn't show what fonts your cell is using, and, when you edit the cell, you may end up entering text in a font you don't want. Also, be careful that you don't apply new font formatting to the cell later; if you do, you'll wipe out all the earlier styling.

SPECIAL CHARACTERS

Most fonts contain not only digits and the common letters of the alphabet, but some special symbols you can type in directly from your keyboard. One is the copyright symbol ©, which you can insert by entering the text *(C)* and letting AutoCorrect do its work. Other symbols, however, aren't as readily available. One is the special arrow character, →. To enter it, you need to tap Excel's library of symbols. Simply follow these steps:

1. **Choose Insert→Symbols→Symbol.**

   The Symbol window opens, as shown in Figure 5-14. Now it's time to hunt for the symbol you need.

2. **Choose the font and subset (the group of symbols you want to explore).**

   If you're looking for a fairly common symbol (like a mathematical sign, an arrow, an accented letter, or a fraction), you probably don't need to change your current font. In the Font box, keep the automatic selection of "(normal text)", and then, from the Subset box at the right, choose the type of symbol you want. For example, choose the Arrows subset to see arrow symbols that point in different directions.

   If you want funkier alternatives, choose a fancy font from the Font box on the left. You should be able to find at least one version of the Wingdings font in the list. Wingdings has the most interesting symbols to use. It's also the most likely to be on other people's computers, which makes a difference if you plan to email your worksheet to other people. If you get your symbols from a really bizarre font that other people don't have, they won't be able to see your symbols.

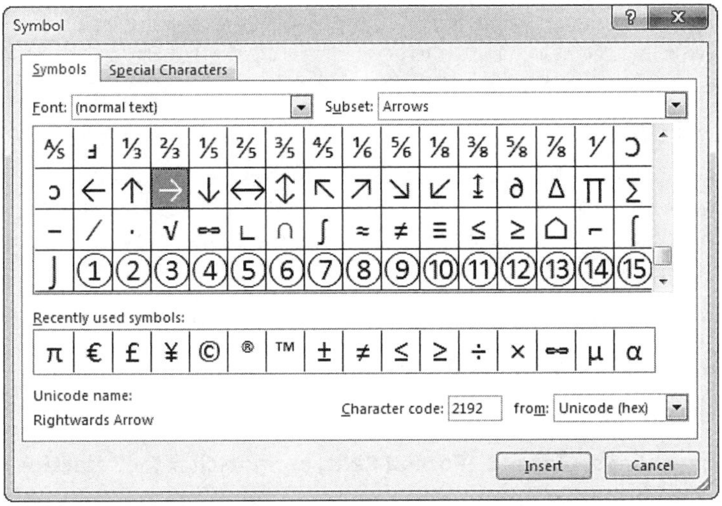

FIGURE 5-14

The Symbol window lets you insert one or more special characters. You can choose extended characters that most fonts support (like currency symbols, non-English letters, arrows, and so on). Or you can use a font that's all about fancy characters, like the Wingdings font, which is chock-full of tiny graphical icons.

3. **Select the character you want, and then click Insert.**

   Alternatively, if you need to insert multiple special characters, double-click each one; doing so inserts the symbol right next to the previous one in the same cell without you having to close the window.

TIP If you're looking for an extremely common special character (like the copyright symbol), you can shorten this whole process. Instead of using the Symbols tab, click over to the Special Characters tab in the Symbol window. Then, look through the small list of commonly used symbols. If you find what you want, select it, and then click Insert.

There's one idiosyncrasy you should be aware of if you insert a symbol from another font. For example, if you insert a symbol from the Wingdings font into a cell that already has text in it, you actually end up with a cell that has two fonts—one for the symbol character and one for the rest of your text. This system works perfectly well, but it can cause some confusion. For example, if you apply a new font to the cell after you insert a special character, Excel adjusts the entire contents of the cell to use the new font, and your symbol changes into the corresponding character in the new font (which usually isn't what you want). These problems can crop up any time you deal with a cell that uses more than one font.

On the other hand, if you kept the font selection on "(normal text)" when you picked your symbol, you won't see this behavior. That's because you picked a more commonplace symbol that's included in the font you're already using. In this case, Excel doesn't need to use two fonts at once.

NOTE When you look at the cell contents in the formula bar, you always see the cell data in the standard Calibri font. This consistency means, for example, that a Wingdings symbol doesn't appear as the icon that shows up in your worksheet. Instead, you see an ordinary letter or some type of extended non-English character, like æ.

Borders and Fills

The best way to call attention to important information isn't to change fonts or alignment, however. It's to place borders around key cells or groups of cells and then use shading to highlight the important columns and rows. Excel provides dozens of ways to outline and highlight any selection of cells.

Once again, the trusty Format Cells window is your control center. Follow these steps:

1. **Choose the cells you want to fill or outline.**

   Excel highlights the selected cells.

2. **Select Home→Cells→Format→Format Cells, or right-click the selection and then choose Format Cells.**

   The Format Cells window appears.

3. **Head directly to the Border tab. (If you don't want to apply any borders, skip to step 4.)**

   Applying a border is a multistep process (see Figure 5-15). Begin by choosing the line style you want (dotted, dashed, thick, double, and so on), followed by the color. ("Automatic" picks black.) You find both options on the left side of the Border window. Next, choose where you want the border lines to appear. The Border box (the square that contains the word "Text") functions as a nifty interactive test canvas that previews your choices. Make your selection either by clicking one of the eight Border buttons (which contain a single bold horizontal, vertical, or diagonal line), or click directly inside the Border box. If you change your mind, click a border line to make it disappear.

   For example, if you want to apply a border to the top of your selection, click the top of the Border box. To apply a line between columns inside the selection, click between the cell columns in the Border box. The line that appears reflects the border style you chose earlier.

TIP The Border tab also provides two shortcuts in the tab's Presets section. To apply a border style around all the cells you selected, choose Outline after you've chosen a border style and color. Choose Inside to apply the border between the rows and columns of the selected cells. Choose None to remove all border lines.

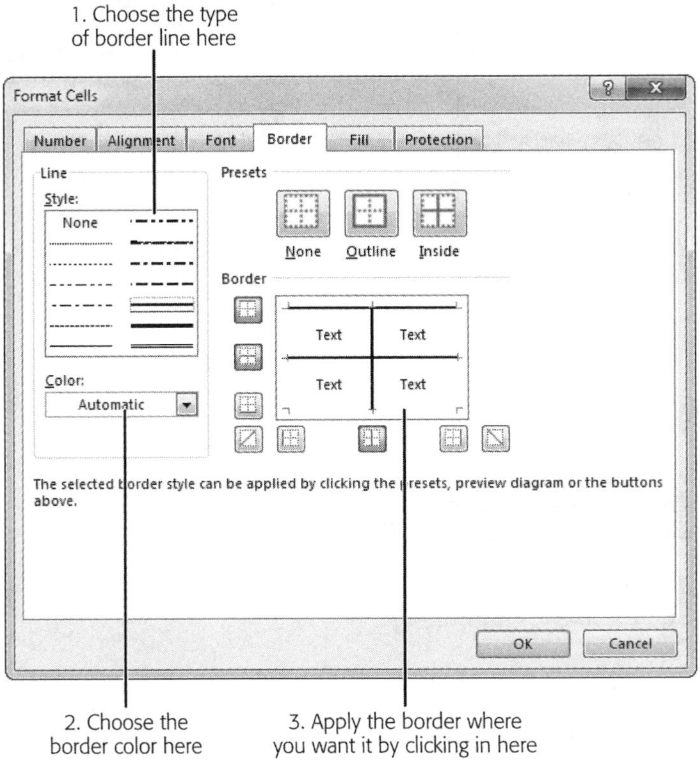

FIGURE 5-15

Follow the numbered steps in this figure to choose a border style and color, and then click within the Border box to specify which borders you want styled. Here, Excel will apply a solid border between the columns and at the top edge of the selected cells.

4. **Click the Fill tab.**

   Here, you can select the background color, pattern color, and pattern style to apply to the selected cells (see Figure 5-16). Click the No Color box to clear any current color or pattern in the selected cells. When you pick a pattern color, you may notice certain colors described as *theme colors*. Theme colors are sets of coordinated hues that change whenever you pick a new theme for your workbook, as described in on page 172.

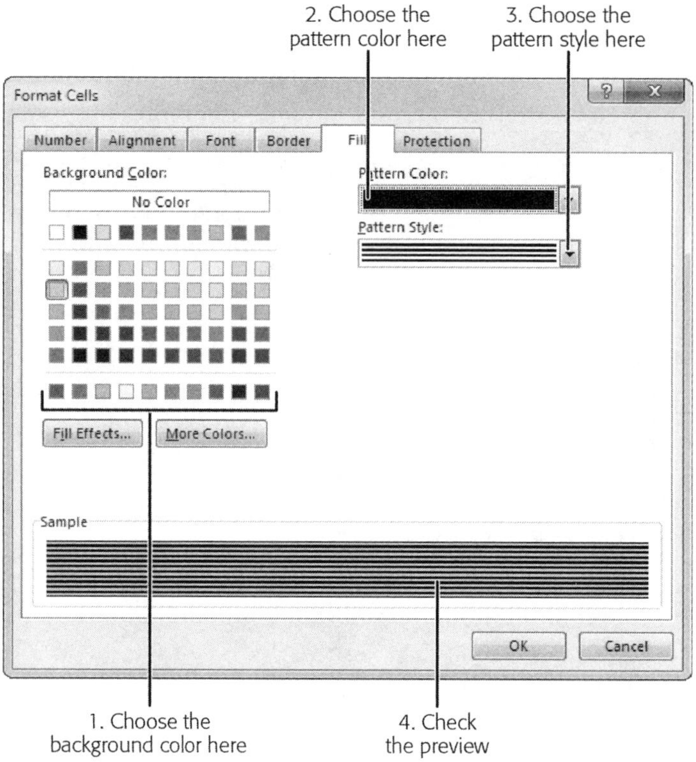

FIGURE 5-16

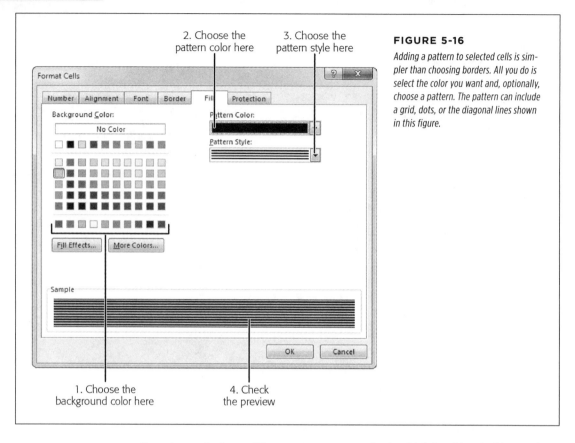

Adding a pattern to selected cells is simpler than choosing borders. All you do is select the color you want and, optionally, choose a pattern. The pattern can include a grid, dots, or the diagonal lines shown in this figure.

To get a really fancy fill, you can use a *gradient*, which is a blend of two colors. For example, with gradients you can create a fill that starts out white on one side of a cell and gradually darkens to blue on the other. To use a gradient fill, click the Fill Effects button, and then follow the instructions in Figure 5-17.

5. **Click OK to apply your changes.**

If you don't like the modifications you just made, roll back time by pressing Ctrl+Z, which triggers the indispensable Undo command.

TIP You can remove a worksheet's gridlines, which is handy when you want to more easily see any custom borders you added. To do so, select View→Show→Gridlines. (This action affects only the current worksheet in the current workbook file.)

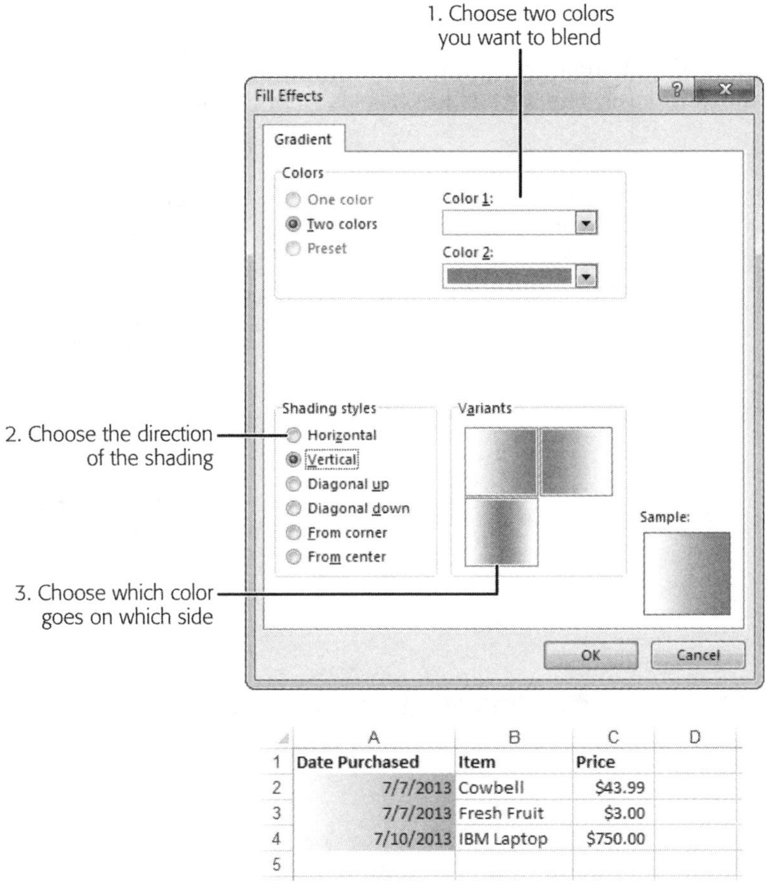

FIGURE 5-17

Top: To create a gradient, you need to pick the starting and ending colors that create the gradient, and you need to choose the way Excel does the blending (from one side to another, from top to bottom, and so on). When you apply a gradient fill to a stack of cells, a vertical fill makes the most sense, because that way the gradients in each cell line up and look like one seamless shaded region. When you apply a gradient fill to a row of cells, a horizontal fill looks better, for the same reason.

Bottom: A gradient fill on cells A2 to A5.

Drawing Borders by Hand

If you need to add a border around a cell or group of cells, the Border tab in the Format Cells window does the trick (see Figure 5-15). However, you could have a hard time getting the result you want, particularly if you want to add a combination of different borders around different cells. In this situation, you have a major project on your hands that requires several trips back to the Format Cells window.

Fortunately, there's a little-known secret that lets you avoid the hassle: Excel's Draw Border feature. It lets you draw border lines directly in your worksheet. The process is a little like working with a painting program; you pick the border style, color, and thickness, and then you drag to draw the line between the appropriate cells. When you draw, Excel applies the formatting settings to each affected cell, just as if you'd used the Borders tab.

Here's how it works:

1. **Look in the ribbon's Home→Font section for the "border" button.**

   The name of the border button changes to reflect whatever you used it for last. You can most easily find it by its position, as shown in Figure 5-18.

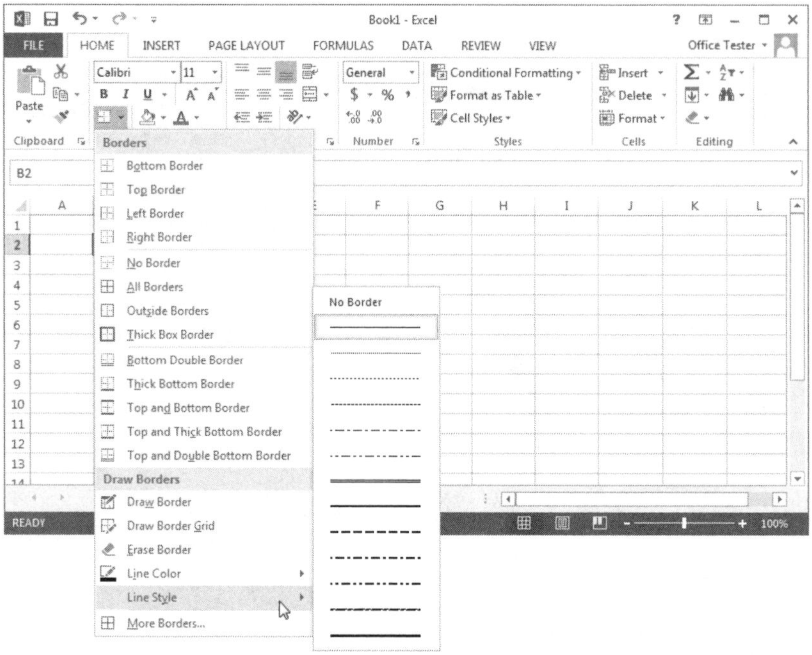

FIGURE 5-18

The border button is at the bottom-left of the Home→Font section. When you click it, you see a list of commands. Before you draw any borders, it makes sense to customize the border style. For example, choose Line Style to dictate the border's look, as shown here, and choose Line Color to set its hue.

2. **Click the border button, choose Line Style, and then pick the type of line you want.**

   You can use dashed and solid lines of different thicknesses, just as you can in the Borders tab of the Format Cells window.

3. **Click the border button, choose Line Color, and then pick the color you want.**

   Now you're ready to start drawing.

4. **Click the border button, and then choose Draw Border.**

   When you do, your mouse pointer changes into a pencil icon.

5. **Using the border pencil, click the grid line where you want to place your border (Figure 5-19).**

   You can also drag side to side or up and down to draw a longer horizontal or vertical line. And if you drag your pointer down *and* to the side, you create an outside border around a whole block of cells.

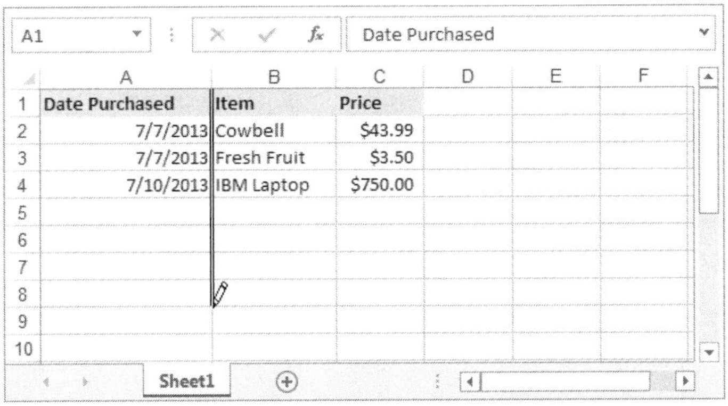

FIGURE 5-19

Here, you're drawing a double-line border between columns A and B.

6. **To stop drawing, head back to the border menu, and then choose Draw Border again.**

   If you make a mistake, you can use an "eraser" to tidy it all up. Just click the border button, and then choose Erase Border. The mouse pointer changes to an eraser. Now click the border you want to remove.

TIP If you don't want to use the Draw Border feature, you can still make good use of the border button. First pick a line style and line color, select some cells, and then choose an option from the border menu. For example, if you pick Bottom Border, Excel applies a border with the color and style you chose to the bottom of the current cell selection.

DESIGN TIME

A Designer Worksheet

Cells aren't the only part of a worksheet you can tweak. A little-known feature in Excel lets you change the appearance of the entire worksheet by applying a custom *picture* as a background. Just select Page Layout→Page Setup→Background, and then choose a picture file. (Excels supports just about any image format.) Excel takes your image and spreads it like tiles across your worksheet surface to fill the whole working area.

The picture background feature is really just for fun, and the image doesn't show up if you print out your worksheet. To remove a background, choose Page Layout→Page Setup→Delete Background.

CHAPTER

6

Smart Formatting Tricks

In the previous chapter, you took a comprehensive tour of Excel's formatting fundamentals. But of course, just because those features exist doesn't mean they're easy to use. Digging through your options and applying a range of formatting settings can be a tedious task. Fortunately, Excel includes a few timesavers that speed up many formatting jobs.

In this chapter, you'll try out the essential formatting techniques that every Excel guru loves. They include:

- **The Format Painter**, which provides a quick-and-dirty way to transfer formatting from one cell to another.
- **Styles**, which let you standardize your favorite formatting choices so you can use them again and again.
- **Themes**, which give you a toolkit with a collection of ready-to-use styles that can jazz up the dullest worksheet.
- **Conditional formatting**, which gets Excel to do the hard work of finding values you're interested in and then highlighting them with custom formatting.

Once you master these four timesavers, you'll have the secret to making great-looking worksheets.

The Format Painter

The Format Painter is a simple yet elegant tool that lets you copy all of a cell's format settings—including fonts, colors, background fill, borders, and even the number format—from one cell to another. (Apparently, the Excel team decided that the more accurate label "Format Copier" wasn't nearly as exciting as the name Format Painter.)

To use the Format Painter, follow these steps:

1. **Move to a cell that has the formatting you want to copy.**

   You can use the Format Painter to copy formatting from either one cell or a whole group of cells. For example, you could copy the format from two cells that use different fill colors, and paste that format to a whole range of new cells. The new cells will alternate between the two fill colors. Although this is a powerful trick, in most cases, it's easiest to copy the format from a single cell.

2. **Choose Home→Clipboard→Format Painter to switch into "format painting" mode.**

   The pointer changes so that it now includes a paintbrush icon, indicating that Excel is ready to copy the format.

3. **Click the cell where you want to apply the format.**

   The moment you release your mouse button, Excel applies the formatting, and your pointer changes back to its normal appearance. If you want to copy the selected format to several cells at once, just drag to select a group of cells, rows, or columns, instead of clicking a single cell.

Excel doesn't let you get too carried away with format painting—as soon as you copy the format to a new cell or selection, you exit format painting mode. If you want to copy the desired format to another cell, you must backtrack to the cell that has your format, and start over again. However, there's a neat trick you can use if you want to repeatedly apply the same format to a bunch of cells. Instead of single-clicking the Format Painter button, double-click it. You'll remain in format painting mode until you single-click the Format Painter button again (or press Esc) to switch it off.

NOTE The Format Painter is a good tool for quickly copying formatting, but it's no match for another Excel feature called *styles*. With styles, you define a group of formatting settings, and then apply them wherever you want. Best of all, if you change the style after you create it, Excel automatically updates all the cells you formatted using that style. The next section describes styles in more detail.

Styles and Themes

Styles let you create a customized collection of format settings, give that collection a name, and save it, ready for use, as part of your spreadsheet file. You can then apply these settings anywhere you need them in your workbook. For example, you could create a style called Great Big Header that uses the Cambria font, pumps up the font size to 46 points, and colors the text bright red.

Every Excel spreadsheet starts off with a collection of prebuilt styles. Microsoft designed them with two goals in mind: to give you quick access to the most common and practical formatting choices, and to make great-looking documents. To take a look at the styles waiting for you, choose Home→Styles→Cell Styles. Figure 6-1 shows the gallery of options you'll see.

NOTE If your Excel window is very wide, the Home→Styles→Cell Styles button disappears, and you'll see a scrollable gallery of styles in the Home→Styles section instead. This change saves you a click, but doesn't alter the way styles work.

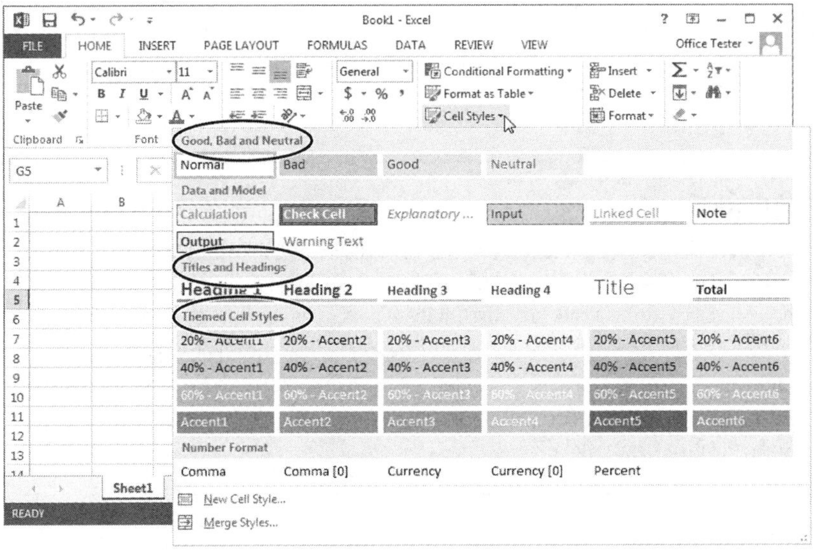

FIGURE 6-1

Excel divides its built-in styles into categories, according to how you might use them. For example, the "Good, Bad and Neutral" category lets you separate good news (a net profit!) from bad (an $11 million tax penalty!) using carefully shaded versions of the universal colors red, yellow, and green. The Titles and Headings category adds border formatting (page 158) to make great titles. And the Themed Cell Styles category gives you a range of differently colored, differently shaded cells that blend harmoniously with one another.

You can apply more than one style to the same cell to get just the right combination of formatting options. For example, you could use the Currency style to get the right number format, and then pick the Bad style to flag a huge debt with a light red background fill. (Bad is simply the name of a prebuilt style that applies a light red background fill and a dark red font.) If you apply more than one style and they conflict (for example, both styles use a different background color), the style you applied last takes over.

Styles use Excel's live preview feature, which gives you try-before-you-buy formatting. When you select a group of cells and then hover over one of the styles in the ribbon, your selected cells change instantaneously to reflect that style. Run your mouse over the different style options, and you see a quickly changing series of formatting choices. To actually apply a style, click it.

If this was all that styles offered—a handy way to reuse good-looking formatting presets—they'd be quite useful. But wait, there's more: Excel styles come with two more invaluable features. First, you can create your own styles and reuse them time and again. Second, you can use *themes* to swap one set of styles for another. You'll learn both these techniques in the following sections.

NOTE At the bottom of the style list (Figure 6-1) is the Number Format group of styles. These styles simply apply a different number format (page 128) to a cell, like Currency, Percentage, and so on. They don't do any other formatting. However, they're still useful. For example, you could use Currency style for all the dollar figures in your worksheet and then, at some later point, modify that style to use a different currency symbol, set a different alignment, or change the number of decimal places. This one change updates every cell that uses the Currency style—in this case, all the prices across your entire worksheet.

TIMESAVING TIP

A Quicker Way to Apply Styles

The ribbon makes it fairly easy to work with styles. However, sometimes you may be in the middle of working with another ribbon tab and find it's just too inconvenient to jump back to the Home tab.

If you're in this situation, you can make your life more pleasant by adding the style gallery to the Quick Access toolbar. To do so, choose Home→Styles→Cell Styles, right-click any style, and then choose Add Gallery to Quick Access Toolbar. This adds a Cell Styles button to the toolbar, so it's always available to you. Click the Cell Styles button and you'll see the familiar style gallery.

If you get tired of the Cell Styles button on the Quick Access toolbar, right-click it, and then choose Remove from Quick Access Toolbar.

Custom Styles

Styles really shine in complex worksheets where you need to apply different formatting to different groups of cells. For example, say you've got a worksheet that tracks your company's fiscal performance. You're confident that most of the data is reliable, but know that a few rows come from your notoriously hopeful sales department. To highlight these sales projections, you decide to use a combination of a bold font with a hot pink fill. And since these figures are estimated and aren't highly precise, you decide to use a number format without decimal places and precede the number with a tilde (~), the universal symbol for "approximately right."

You *could* implement all these changes manually, but that'll take fourscore and seven years. Better to set up a style that includes all these settings, and then apply it with a flick of your wrist whenever you need it. Styles are efficiency monsters in a few ways:

- They let you reuse your formatting easily, with just a mouse click.
- They free you from worry about being inconsistent, because the style includes all the formatting you want.

- Excel automatically saves styles with your spreadsheet file, and you can transfer styles from one workbook to another.
- If you decide to change a style, you can do so with just a few mouse clicks. Then Excel automatically adjusts every cell that uses the style.

Here's how you create a new style:

1. **Begin by moving to a cell in your worksheet that has the formatting you want for your style.**

   The quickest way to create a new style is to start with an existing one. However, you can also create a new style from scratch. To do that, move to a blank, unformatted cell in your worksheet.

2. **Select Home→Styles→Cell Styles→New Cell Style.**

   The Style window appears, which lets you design your own styles.

3. **In the "Style name" box, type a name for your new style.**

   For example, if you want to create a new style for column titles, enter the style name ColumnTitle. Each style in your workbook has to have a unique name.

4. **Choose the style options you want.**

   Styles don't need to format every aspect of a cell. For example, you might want to create a style that applies new font and fill settings, but keeps the current Number format (page 128), alignment, and border details. When you create this style, you'd clear the Number, Alignment, and Border checkboxes, so these details aren't included in your new style. Figure 6-2 shows an example.

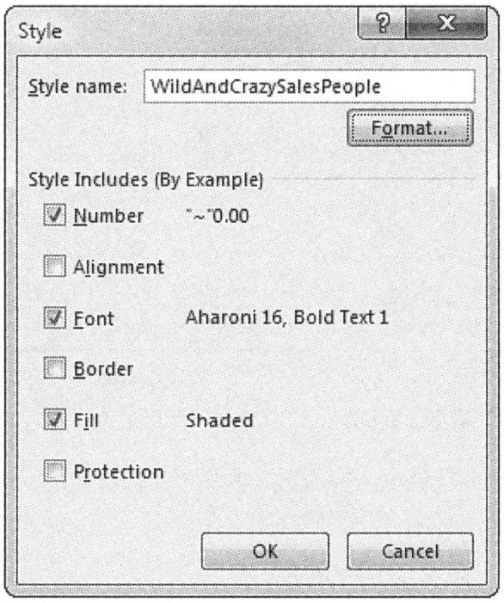

FIGURE 6-2

Here, you're about to create a new style, named WildAndCrazySales-People. This style defines a Number format as well as font and fill settings. If you don't want your style to include some of these settings, turn off the appropriate checkboxes. For example, if you want to create a style that applies a new font, fill, and border, but you want to keep the existing alignment and number format, turn off the Number and Alignment checkboxes. As a general rule, if you don't need to explicitly set a specific style characteristic, turn off the corresponding checkbox.

NOTE When you select many style checkboxes, you create a pumped-up style that does a lot at once. When you select only one or two style checkboxes, you create a less powerful style, but one that's more flexible. You can use it in a variety of cells that already have customized formatting, without changing the formatting characteristics you want to keep.

5. **Click Format to specify the formatting options for the style.**

   When you click Format, the familiar Format Cells window appears. Use this window to change the formatting just as if you were formatting an individual cell. Click OK to close the Format Cells window when you finish.

6. **Click OK to close the Style window.**

   Once you've created a style, applying it is just a matter of a few mouse clicks. Select the cell or cells you want to modify, choose Home→Styles→Cell Styles, and then choose your style from the list (Figure 6-3).

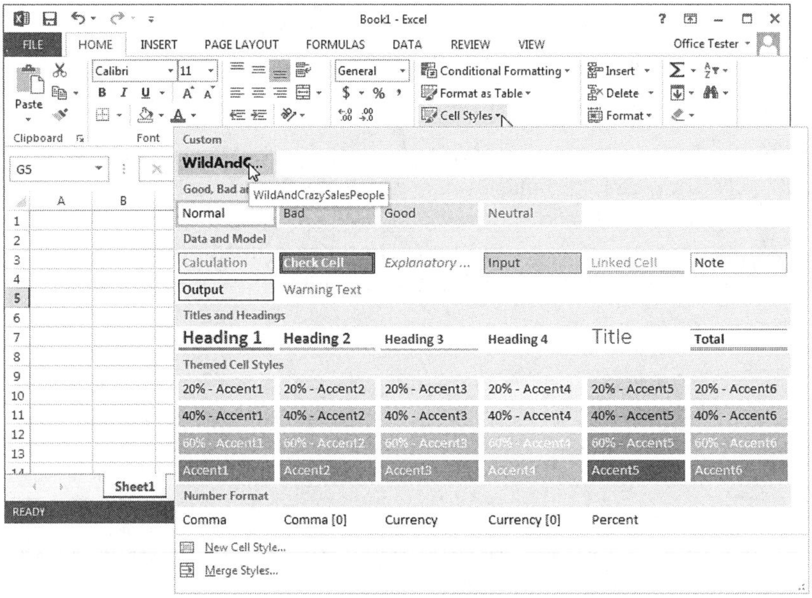

FIGURE 6-3

The styles you create appear in a Custom group at the top of the list of styles. (If you haven't created any styles, you won't see the Custom group at all.)

TIMESAVING TIP

Turning Off Live Preview

Most of the time, live preview is a great way for wishy-washy spreadsheet writers to see formatting possibilities without committing. However, if you have a heavily formatted workbook, you might find the live preview feature slows you down as you're scrolling through a lot of options. In this case, it might make sense to turn off live preview.

To do so, choose File→Options, and then pick the General section. Under the "User Interface options," turn off the Enable Live Preview setting, and then click OK. Now you can zip around the ribbon, but you need to actually *apply* a formatting change (by clicking the appropriate button in the ribbon) before you see what it looks like.

Modifying Styles

Keep in mind that you can modify a cell's formatting even after you apply a style. But if you find yourself overriding a style fairly frequently, and always in the same way, that probably means your style isn't quite right. Either create more than one version of the same style, each with the appropriate settings, or clear some of the style checkboxes so that your style doesn't apply formatting settings that you commonly change:

- **To modify a style**, choose Home→Styles→Cell Styles, find the style you want in the gallery, right-click it, and then choose Modify. You wind up back at the familiar Style window (Figure 6-2), where you can tweak the style to your heart's content. You can use this approach to revise your own custom styles, or to change the built-in styles that Excel adds to every workbook.
- **To duplicate a style**, choose Home→Styles→Cell Styles, find the style you want in the gallery, right-click it, and then choose Duplicate. The Styles window appears with the style you chose. Change the formatting as desired, choose a better name, and then click OK to add this style to the Custom category.
- **To delete a style** you don't want anymore, choose Home→Styles→Cell Styles, find the style, right-click it, and then choose Delete. Excel removes the formatting from all the cells that used that style.

Transferring Styles Between Workbooks

Once you create a few useful styles, you'll probably want to reuse them in a variety of spreadsheet files. To do that, you need to copy the style information from one workbook to another. Excel makes this fairly straightforward:

1. **Open both files in Excel.**

   You need both the source workbook (the one that has the styles you want to copy) and the destination workbook (the one where you want to copy the styles).

2. **Go to the destination workbook.**

3. **Choose Home→Styles→Cell Styles→Merge Styles.**

   The Merge Styles window appears with a list of all the files you currently have open in Excel.

4. **Select the file that has the styles you want to copy into your active workbook, and then click OK.**

   If two or more styles have the same name, Excel displays a warning message, informing you that it will overwrite the current styles with the styles you're importing. Click OK to continue.

   You can now use the styles you imported. They're independent copies of the styles in the source workbook. If you change the styles in one workbook, you won't affect the styles in the other, unless you merge the changed styles back into it.

TIP To automatically include custom styles in new workbooks, consider creating a template that includes those styles. Chapter 16 has the full story.

Themes: A Package of Styles

As nice as Excel's prebuilt styles are, they don't suit everyone. For example, the standard style colors favor subdued shades of blue, orange, and gray, which make sense for the company accountant but aren't the most exciting choice for an urban hipster. To jazz things up, you can choose a different *theme* that features livelier colors. When you do, your entire worksheet gets an immediate facelift—you don't need to track down each individual cell and reformat it.

Technically, a theme is a combination of three ingredients:

- **Fonts.** Every theme has one font that's used for headings and another one that's used for everything else. These two fonts might be different sizes of the same typeface, or two complementary typefaces.
- **Colors.** Every theme has a palette of 12 complementary colors. The cell styles that appear under the Themed Cell Styles heading (see Figure 6-1) draw upon these colors for text and background fills. Best of all, these colors don't reflect the preferences of Cheeto-munching programmers. Instead, bona-fide artsy types chose them—in this case, professional designers on the Microsoft payroll.
- **Effects.** Effects are fine alterations that pretty up shapes and other hand-drawn graphics you can create with Excel's drawing tools (Chapter 19). If you don't have any shapes on your worksheet, the effect settings don't do anything.

To choose a theme, choose Page Layout→Themes→Themes to see a gallery of choices (Figure 6-4).

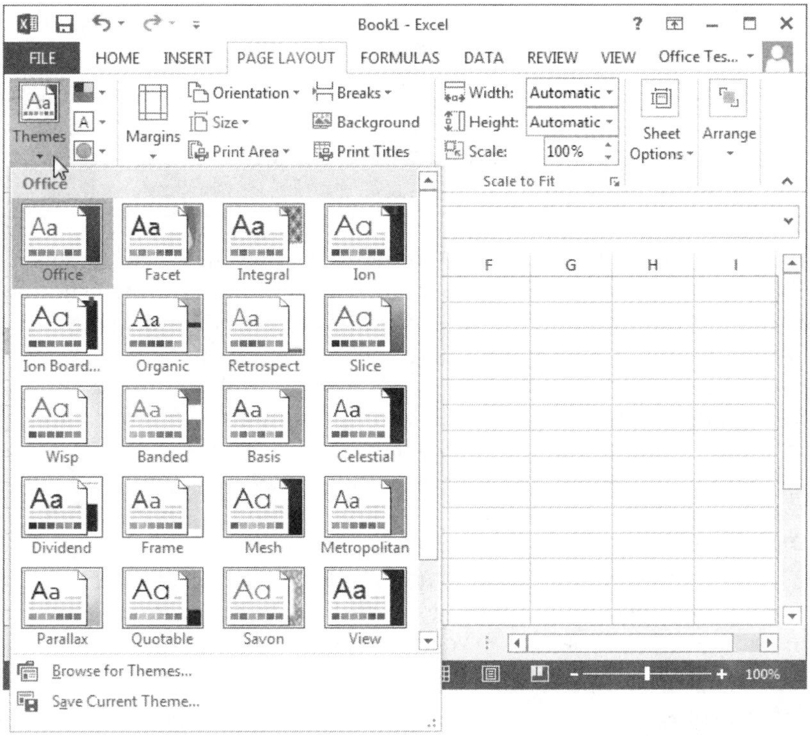

FIGURE 6-4

Every workbook begins using the crowd-pleasing Office theme, but you have a long list of other options. As you hover over a new theme, your workbook adjusts itself automatically, thanks to the magic of Excel's live preview feature.

The secret to understanding themes is realizing how changing a theme affects your worksheet. In other words, how does Excel apply a theme's fonts, colors, and effects to your worksheet? The following sections break it down.

FONTS

Every workbook has a standard *body font* that it uses in every cell, which comes from the Normal style. Excel uses this standard font unless you explicitly choose a different one using the ribbon's Home→Font section or the Format Cells window.

In a brand-new Excel spreadsheet, everything you type starts out in easy-on-the-eyes 11-point Calibri font. If you apply a new theme, you get a new Normal style and a new standard font. For example, switch to the traditionally styled Organic theme, and you'll get the elegant Garamond font instead.

NOTE All the fonts used in Excel themes are installed as part of Microsoft Office.

The same sort of magic works with the *heading font*, but it's more limited—in fact, the only style that uses the heading font is Title. If you use the Title cell style and switch from one theme to another, Excel updates your cell to use the heading font from that style. In Excel's prebuilt themes, the heading font is the same as the standard body font. However, this isn't necessarily the case if you pick a different set of fonts or create a custom theme (page 177).

NOTE You might assume that the heading styles (Heading 1, Heading 2, Heading 3, and so on) use the heading font. Oddly enough, that's not how it works. All the heading styles use the theme's body font. Title is the only style that uses the heading font.

If you're feeling a bit reckless, you can override the font that Excel automatically uses for all new workbooks. To do so, select File→Options, and then choose the General section. Under the "When creating new workbooks" heading is a "Use this font" and a "Font size" setting where you can set the standard font and font size. Ordinarily, the automatic font isn't set to a specific font at all—instead, it's set to the special value Body Font. This tells Excel to apply the standard font from the current theme. Usually, this is the choice you want, because it lets you quickly adapt your entire spreadsheet to a theme of your choosing.

COLORS

Every theme relies on 12 key colors. When you move from one theme to another, Excel swaps in the new set of colors. However, Excel doesn't alter any *other*, non-theme colors you may have used in your worksheet.

NOTE Although each theme has only 12 base colors, Excel varies the saturation of the color to make it bolder or lighter, based on the style you use. For example, the Office theme includes a steel blue color that you can use at full strength (with the style named Accent 1) or lighten to a faint gray-blue mist (with the style named *20% - Accent1*).

To make this system a bit clearer, imagine that a designer runs amok, formatting cells with different background fills. He fills some of the cells with theme colors, and others with custom colors. (Figure 6-5 shows the difference.) When you switch themes, Excel changes the cells that use theme colors, and leaves all the other cells unchanged.

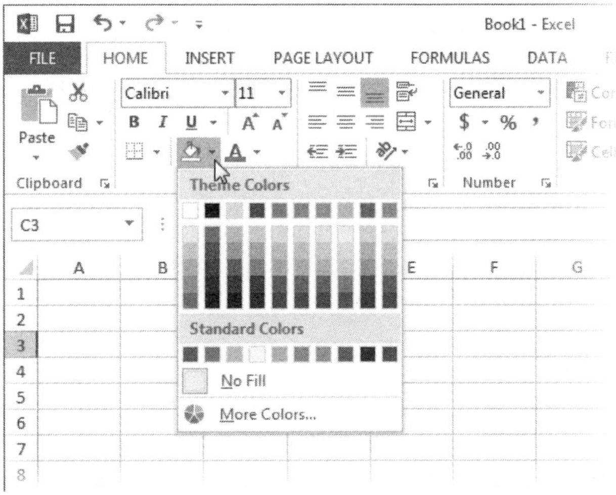

FIGURE 6-5

When you set the background fill in a cell, you can pick one of the theme colors (at different saturations), use a standard color (which gives you the standard red-green-blue lineup), or click More Colors to pick a custom color. You have the same choices when picking the foreground color for your text.

TIP You're always better off using theme colors rather than picking a custom color. That way, you can give your workbook a facelift simply by switching from one theme to another, and the colors will still match. Also, if you choose custom colors that look nice with a specific theme, they're likely to clash horribly if you change themes.

Experienced Excel workers rarely waste time picking background and foreground colors out of the ribbon. Instead, they use styles. Any time you use one of the styles from the Themed Cell Styles category (Home→Styles→Cell Styles; see Figure 6-1), you're applying a theme-specific color. As a result, if you pick another theme, all the themed cell styles change to the new color.

The theme system works well because each color in a theme plays a specific role. In other words, some colors are intended for text, while others are designed to play the role of a complementary background; a few more add eye-catching accents. To see the intended purpose of each color, hover over it in the ribbon (Figure 6-6).

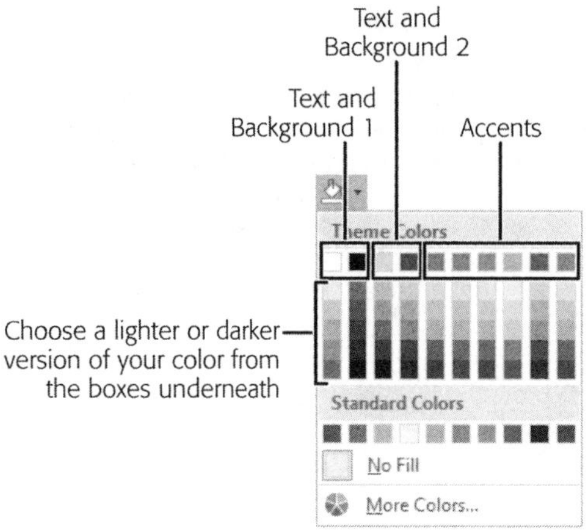

FIGURE 6-6

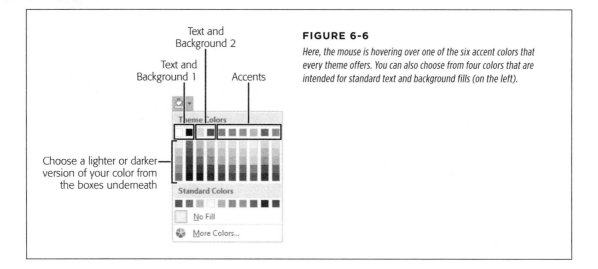

Here, the mouse is hovering over one of the six accent colors that every theme offers. You can also choose from four colors that are intended for standard text and background fills (on the left).

■ EFFECTS

Effects are the simplest part of any theme, because Excel applies them with no work on your part (all you need to do is switch themes, and then the effects kick in). Excel automatically applies effects to any graphics you create. You'll learn more about creating shapes and other illustrations in Chapter 19.

Modifying Themes

Excel lets you use just part of a theme. For example, you might want the modern fonts from the Savon theme paired with the rich orangey reds of the Wood Type theme. The Excel designers might cringe at your combination, but there's no reason for you to hesitate—from the Page Layout→Themes→Themes gallery, choose the Savon theme, and then, from the Page Layout→Themes→Colors list, pick the Orange Red colors (Figure 6-7).

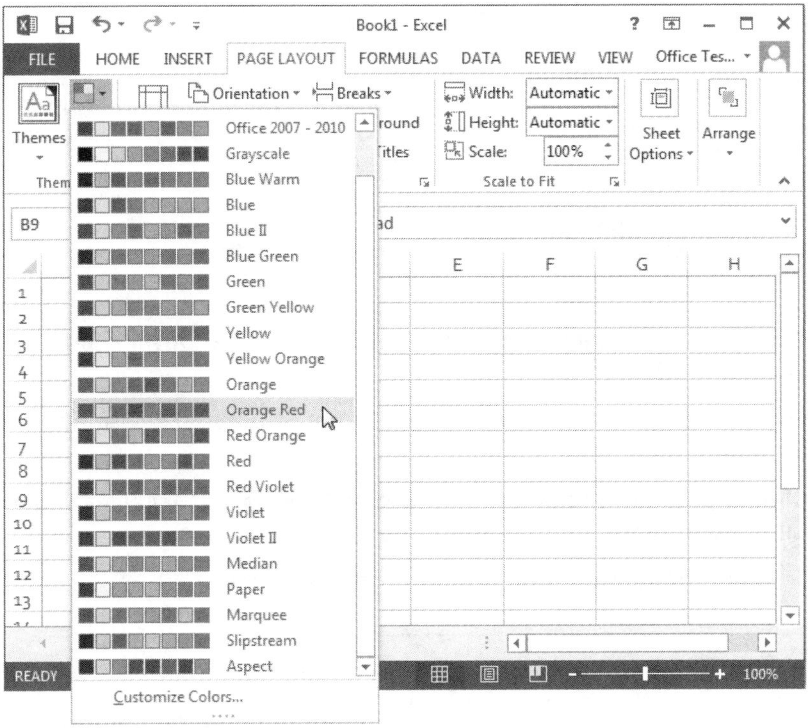

FIGURE 6-7

Using the ribbon, you can apply just the colors (as shown here), just the fonts, or just the effects from a theme of your choosing. This technique lets you mix and match different theme parts (which is a bit of a no-no for the artistically minded).

A more interesting possibility is the way Excel lets you create a brand-new, custom theme with your own personalized combination of colors and fonts. Here's how:

1. **From the Page Layout→Themes→Themes gallery, choose the theme you want to use as a starting point.**
2. **Choose your favorite body and heading font by going to Page Layout→Themes→Fonts→Customize Fonts.**

   The Create New Theme Fonts window appears (Figure 6-8).

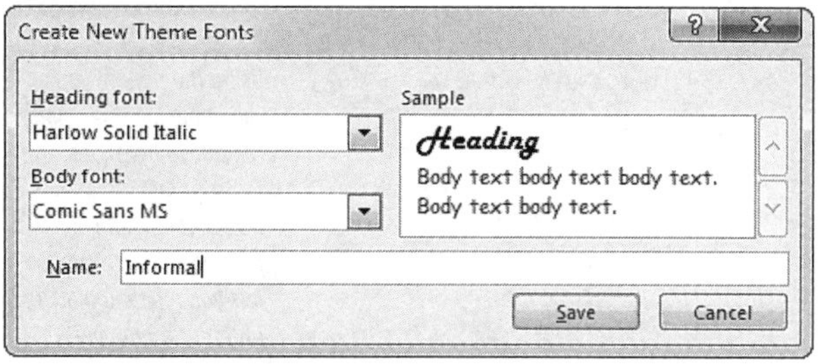

FIGURE 6-8

The Create New Theme Fonts window doesn't let you choose font sizes, but you can pick two complementary typefaces: one for body text and one for headings. Before you click Save, enter a descriptive new name for your font combo.

3. **Choose your fonts, enter a name for your font combination (like "Informal"), and then click Save.**

   Your font selection appears in the Page Layout→Themes→Font list, so you can use it with any theme.

4. **Choose your favorite colors by going to Page Layout→Themes→Colors→Customize Colors.**

   The Create New Theme Colors window appears (Figure 6-9).

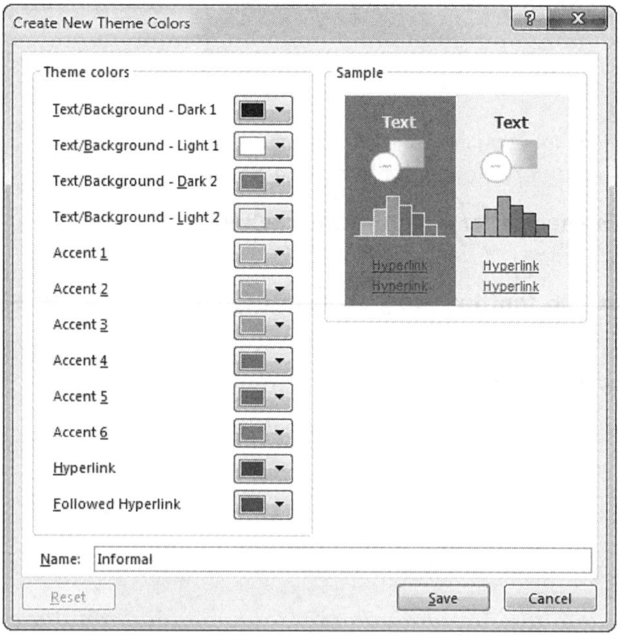

FIGURE 6-9

The Create New Theme Colors window shows all 12 theme colors, and lets you adjust each. Microsoft designed the first two colors as complementary foreground and background colors. The second two colors offer an alternate foreground and background pair. The next six are accent colors for cell backgrounds (so you can highlight important values), and the final two colors are for web-style links (page 80). As you adjust colors, Excel updates the tiny preview pictures.

5. **Choose your colors, enter a name for your color combination (like "Wacky Office Temp"), and then click Save.**

   Your new color palette appears in the Page Layout→Themes→Colors list, so you can use it with any theme.

6. **Optionally, save your work to a *.thmx* file by choosing Page Layout→Themes→Themes→Save Current Theme.**

   If you want to reuse your theme in other workbooks (or share it with friends), you can save your fonts and colors as a .thmx theme file. To apply your custom theme later on, just choose Page Layout→Themes→Themes→Browse for Themes, browse to your .thmx file, and then choose it.

POWER USERS' CLINIC

Different Office Programs, Same Good Style

Excel shares its theming system with Microsoft Word and PowerPoint. That means you can create a .thmx theme file in Excel, and then use it to set document colors in Microsoft Word, or vice versa. That way, you can create memos in Word, presentations in PowerPoint, and reports in Excel that share the same hot colors.

In fact, you don't even need to create a .thmx file to use this feature (although it's always a good idea). Your theme settings are stored directly in your document file, whether it's an Excel spreadsheet (.xlsx), a Word document (.docx), or a PowerPoint slide deck (.pptx). To pull theme settings directly out of one of these files and place them in your current Excel spreadsheet, choose Page Layout→Themes→Themes→Browse for Themes, and then select the file whose theme you want to use.

Conditional Formatting

A good worksheet highlights the most important information, thereby making it easy to spot. For example, if you look at a worksheet that shows the last year of a company's sales, you want to be able to find underperforming products without having to hunt through hundreds of cells. And even if you're not using Excel in the business world, you need to be able to home in on key details in a spreadsheet—whether that's a budget-busting dinner in your monthly expense worksheet or a skipped week at the gym in your exercise log. All too often, these essential details are buried in an avalanche of data.

As you learned in Chapter 5, you can use formatting tricks to make important data stand out from the crowd. The problem with that is that it's up to *you* to track down the cells you want formatted. Not only is this a time-devouring task, you also run into trouble when you start using formulas (as discussed on page 221). Formulas let you set up elaborate calculations that link cells together, which means that a change to a single cell can cascade through your worksheet, altering data everywhere else. If you're highlighting important information by hand, you just might need to repeat the whole formatting process each time a value changes.

Fortunately, Excel has a feature that's designed to spare you the drudgery. It's called *conditional formatting*, and it lets Excel automatically find and highlight important information. In this section, you'll learn to master conditional formatting to make important bits of data stick out for all to see.

NOTE In this chapter, you'll learn how to use basic conditional formatting, which applies the formatting settings you learned about in Chapter 5 to make important cells stand out. In Chapter 20, you'll learn about three more advanced types of conditional formatting that build on this system: data bars, color scales, and icon sets. They let you use other formatting tricks, like shaded bars and tiny pictures, to create a *graphical representation* of different values.

The Basics of Conditional Formatting

In Chapter 5, you learned to create custom format strings. As you saw, Excel lets you supply up to three different format strings for the numbers in a single cell (page 141). For example, you can define a format string for positive numbers, a format string for negative numbers, and another format string for zero values. Using this technique, you could create a worksheet that automatically uses red text for negative numbers, while leaving nonnegative numbers in black.

This ability to treat negative numbers differently from positive numbers is quite handy, but it's obviously limited. For example, what if you want to flag extravagant expenses that top $100, or you want to flag a monthly sales total if it exceeds the previous month's sales by 50 percent? Custom format strings can't help you there, but conditional formatting fills the gap.

With conditional formatting, you set a condition that, if true, prompts Excel to apply additional formatting to a cell. This new formatting can change the text color, or use some of the other formatting tricks you saw in Chapter 5, including modifying fill colors and fonts. You can also use other graphical tricks, like data bars (shaded bars that grow or shrink based on the number in a cell) and icons.

Highlighting Specific Values

To see how conditional formatting can highlight important values, consider the daily calorie intake log shown in Figure 6-10.

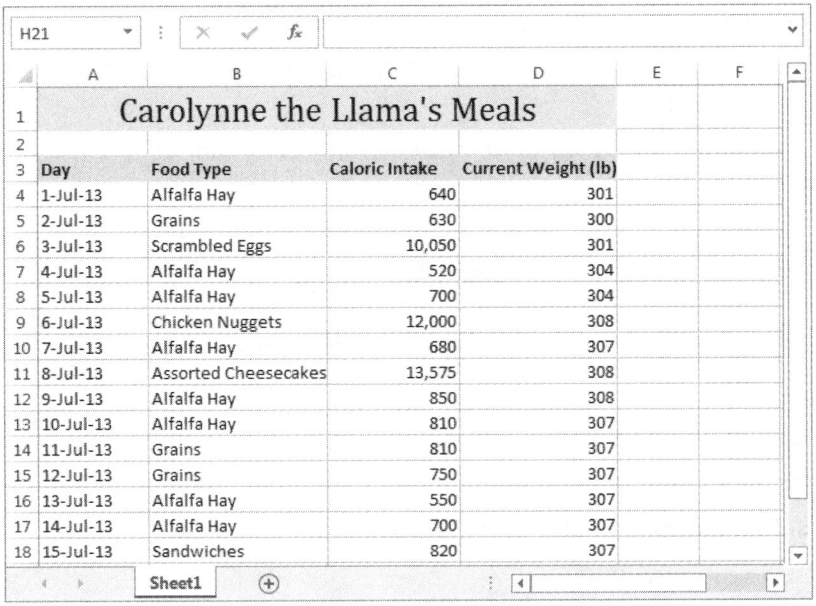

	A	B	C	D
1	Carolynne the Llama's Meals			
2				
3	Day	Food Type	Caloric Intake	Current Weight (lb)
4	1-Jul-13	Alfalfa Hay	640	301
5	2-Jul-13	Grains	630	300
6	3-Jul-13	Scrambled Eggs	10,050	301
7	4-Jul-13	Alfalfa Hay	520	304
8	5-Jul-13	Alfalfa Hay	700	304
9	6-Jul-13	Chicken Nuggets	12,000	308
10	7-Jul-13	Alfalfa Hay	680	307
11	8-Jul-13	Assorted Cheesecakes	13,575	308
12	9-Jul-13	Alfalfa Hay	850	308
13	10-Jul-13	Alfalfa Hay	810	307
14	11-Jul-13	Grains	810	307
15	12-Jul-13	Grains	750	307
16	13-Jul-13	Alfalfa Hay	550	307
17	14-Jul-13	Alfalfa Hay	700	307
18	15-Jul-13	Sandwiches	820	307

FIGURE 6-10

This worksheet tracks the caloric intake of Carolynne, the pet llama, over several weeks. Carolynne's owners have noticed a dramatic weight gain over the same period, but they're at a loss as to when the over-eating actually took place. Fortunately, conditional formatting can highlight the problem areas.

To apply conditional formatting, select the cells you want to examine and format. Next, pick the right conditional formatting rule. A *rule* is an instruction that tells Excel when to apply conditional formatting to a cell and when to ignore it. For example, a typical rule might state, "If the cell value is greater than 10,000, apply bold formatting."

Excel has a wide range of conditional formatting rules, and they fall into two categories (each of which has a separate menu):

- **Highlight specific values.** If your cell contains numbers or dates, you can set a minimum, a maximum, or a range of values that you want Excel to highlight. In the case of text, you can highlight cells that contain specific text, start with specific text, and so on. In the case of dates, you can pick values that fall within certain ranges (last week, last month, next week, and so on). To see all your choices, choose Home→Styles→Conditional Formatting→Highlight Cells Rules.
- **Highlight values based on where they fall in a series.** These options get Excel to highlight the top values, bottom values, or values that fall above or below average. To see your choices, choose Home→Styles→Conditional Formatting→Top/Bottom Rules.

For example, here's how you quickly identify the days when Carolynne indulged her appetite (Figure 6-10):

1. **Select all the cells in the Caloric Intake column.**

   Click the C column's header to choose the whole column.

2. **Go to Home→Styles→Conditional Formatting→Highlight Cells Rules→Greater Than.**

   A window appears where you can set the cutoff number and formatting (Figure 6-11).

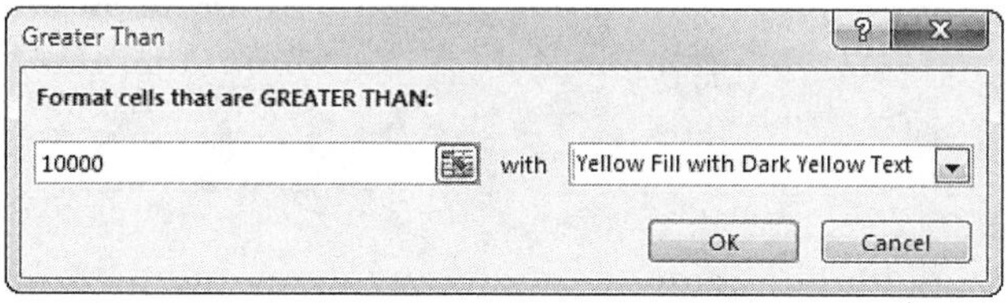

FIGURE 6-11

Each time Carolynne consumes more than 10,000 calories, Excel highlights the cell with a yellow shaded background.

3. **Set your minimum value in the text box on the left.**

   In this case, use 10000.

NOTE Usually, conditional formatting compares a cell value to a fixed number. However, you can also create conditions that compare the cell value to *other* cells in your worksheet. To take this step, click inside the text box that usually holds the comparison number, and then click the cell in the worksheet that you want to use for comparison. Excel automatically inserts a cell reference (like $D$2 for cell D2) into the text box.

4. **Choose the type of formatting from the list box on the right.**

   You can choose from several presets (like Red Text, Red Border, Red Fill with Dark Red Text, and so on), or you can define your own formatting.

   To define your own format settings, choose Custom Format. An abbreviated version of the Format Cells window appears. Excel has turned a few settings off, because you can't apply them conditionally. For example, you can't conditionally change the font or font size, but you can conditionally set other font characteristics, like the use of bold, italic, and underlining. Aside from these limitations, the tabs are exactly the same as the ones you're familiar with from the full-blown Format Cells window (page 149). Click OK when you finish choosing your format options.

NOTE Imaginative Excel fans can do a lot with the Format Cells window and conditional formatting. For example, you can highlight specific values by drawing a border around them, adding a different color fill, or changing the number format to add more decimal places.

5. **Click OK.**

   As soon as you click OK, Excel evaluates the conditions and adjusts the formatting as needed. Every time you open your spreadsheet, or change the value in one of the conditional cells, Excel evaluates the condition and adds or removes the formatting as required.

   Figure 6-12 shows the result.

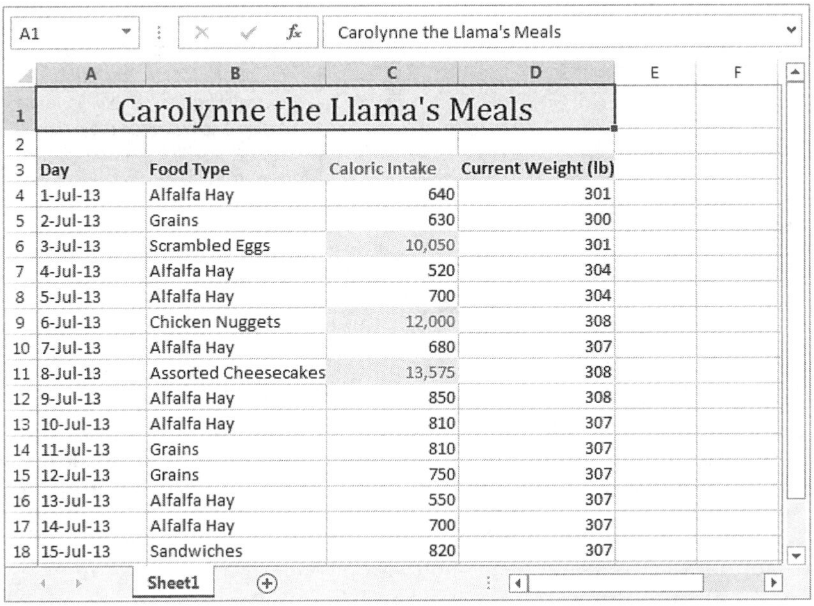

	A	B	C	D
1	Carolynne the Llama's Meals			
2				
3	Day	Food Type	Caloric Intake	Current Weight (lb)
4	1-Jul-13	Alfalfa Hay	640	301
5	2-Jul-13	Grains	630	300
6	3-Jul-13	Scrambled Eggs	10,050	301
7	4-Jul-13	Alfalfa Hay	520	304
8	5-Jul-13	Alfalfa Hay	700	304
9	6-Jul-13	Chicken Nuggets	12,000	308
10	7-Jul-13	Alfalfa Hay	680	307
11	8-Jul-13	Assorted Cheesecakes	13,575	308
12	9-Jul-13	Alfalfa Hay	850	308
13	10-Jul-13	Alfalfa Hay	810	307
14	11-Jul-13	Grains	810	307
15	12-Jul-13	Grains	750	307
16	13-Jul-13	Alfalfa Hay	550	307
17	14-Jul-13	Alfalfa Hay	700	307
18	15-Jul-13	Sandwiches	820	307

FIGURE 6-12

Now Carolynne's days of indulgence stand out. The highlights you see here are the result of the settings you applied on page 182.

TIP To remove any type of conditional formatting, select your cells, and then choose Home→Styles→Conditional Formatting→Clear Rules→Clear Rules from Selected Cells. To wipe all the conditional formatting from your entire worksheet, use Home→Styles→Conditional Formatting→Clear Rules→Clear Rules from Entire Sheet. (Or, to be more selective about the rules you remove, you can investigate them with the Conditional Formatting Rules Manager, which you'll meet on page 186.)

The ribbon is packed with useful conditional formatting choices. However, a few possibilities don't appear in the Highlight Cells Rules and Top/Bottom Rules lists. To see every choice, you must create your conditional formatting rule by hand. Just choose Home→Styles→Conditional Formatting→New Rule. You see the New Formatting Rule window (Figure 6-13).

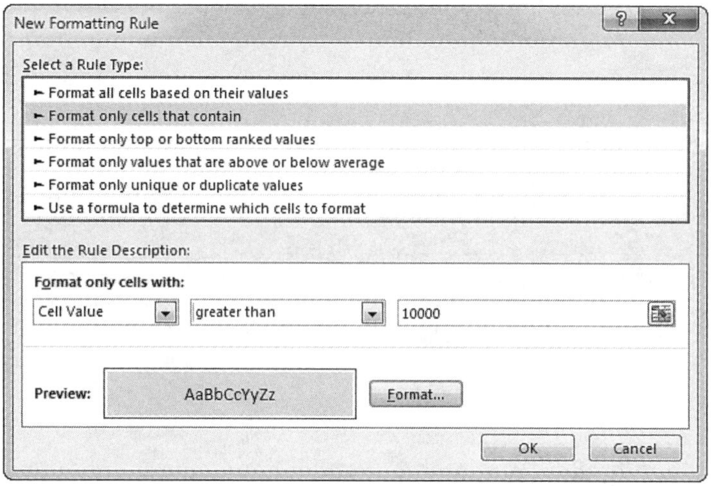

FIGURE 6-13

The New Formatting Rule window has two sections. The top section lets you choose the type of rule. (Ignore the first one, "Format all cells based on their values," because that applies to data bars, color scales, and icon sets—three features you'll consider a little later in this chapter.) The bottom section lets you define all the rule settings. In this example, you're creating a rule that formats any cell with a value greater than 10,000.

The New Formatting Rule window is surprisingly intuitive (translation: It's not just for tech jockeys). The "Format only cells that contain" rule is by far the most versatile. It lets you pick out specific numbers, dates, blank cells, cells with errors, and so on. Most people find that this rule satisfies most of their conditional formatting needs.

Two rules work well with values that change frequently; these are "Format only top or bottom ranked values" and "Format only values that are above or below average." Both of these rules highlight values that stand out in relationship to other cell values. For example, if you didn't know that 10,000 calories is the threshold for llama overeating, you might use one of these rules to find Carolynne's largest meals, as shown in Figure 6-14.

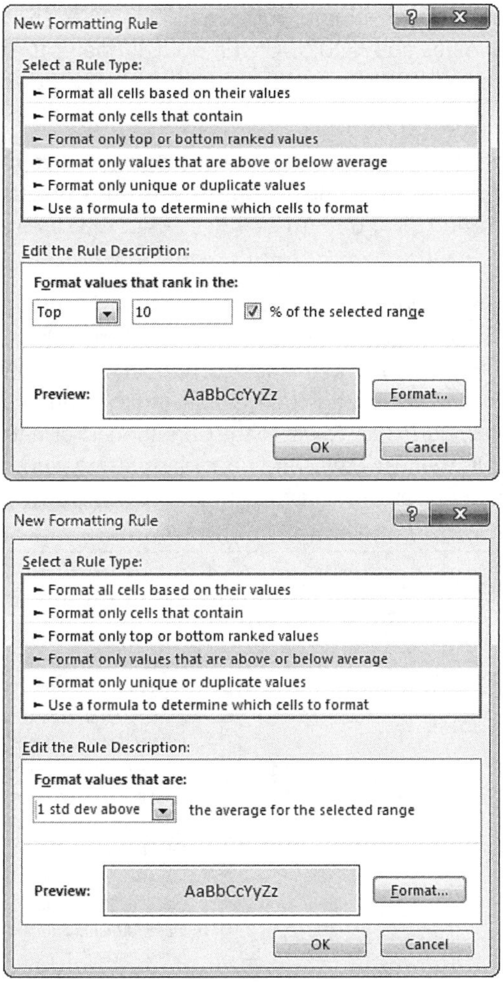

FIGURE 6-14

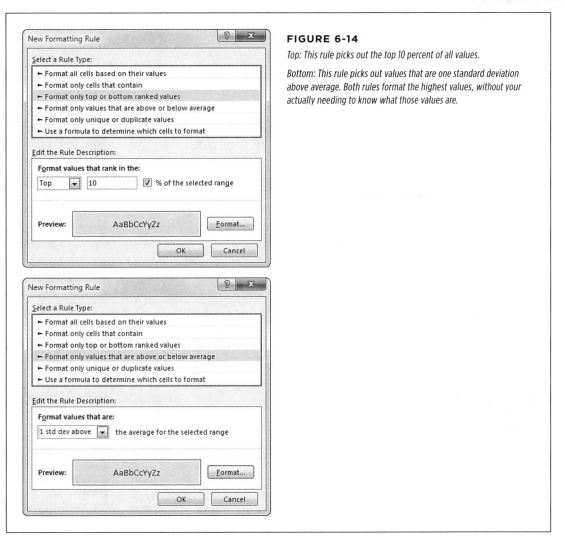

Top: This rule picks out the top 10 percent of all values.

Bottom: This rule picks out values that are one standard deviation above average. Both rules format the highest values, without your actually needing to know what those values are.

These rules are the foundation of conditional formatting. In the following sections, you'll learn about three more specialized conditional formatting features that use unique formatting to distinguish between values.

Using Multiple Rules

So far, you've seen examples that use only one conditional formatting rule. However, there's no limit to the number of rules you can apply simultaneously.

Excel gives you two basic ways to use multiple rules:

- You can create rules that format different subsections of data. This lets you apply several layers of conditional formatting to highlight different values.
- You can create rules that overlap. For example, you can highlight the top five values with red lettering and values above 10,000 with bold. If one of the top five values has a value above 10,000, it gets the combined formatting, and Excel displays it in bold red.

If you use conditional rules that overlap, there's always the possibility of a conflict. For example, one conditional formatting rule might apply a red background fill while another sets a yellow background fill. If both these rules affect the same cell, only one can win.

Which one? That all depends on the *order* in which Excel applies the conditional formatting rules. If there's a conflict, rules that Excel applied later override the rules it applied earlier. Ordinarily, Excel applies rules in the same order that you created them, but if this isn't what you want, you can change things up using the Conditional Formatting Rules Manager, shown in Figure 6-15. To get to the Conditional Formatting Rules Manager, select one of the cells that uses the conditional formatting, and then choose Home→Styles→Conditional Formatting→Manage Rules.

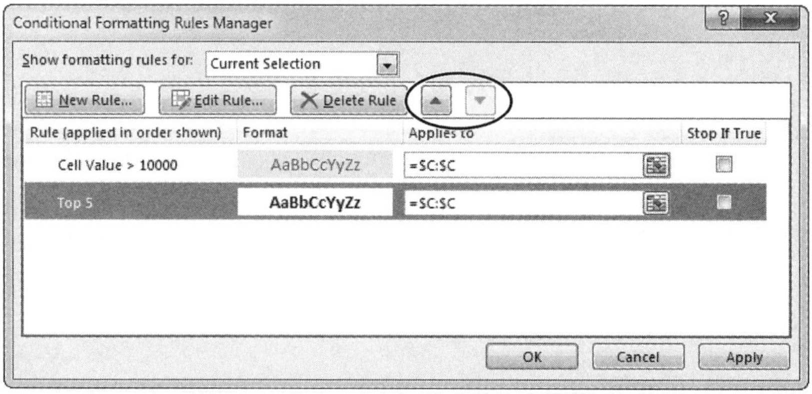

FIGURE 6-15

To reorder a rule, select it, and then click the up or down arrow button (circled). Excel applies the rules at the top of the list first. In this example, Excel applies the Cell Value > 10000 rule before the Top 5 rule. As a result, the Top 5 rule formatting will override the Cell Value > 10000 formatting if the two rules conflict.

NOTE Ordinarily, the Conditional Formatting Rules Manager shows only the conditional formatting rules for the currently selected cell or cells. But you can see the formatting rules for an entire *worksheet* by choosing the worksheet from the "Show formatting rules for" list. That's a nice way to review all the rules you created, but it can be a little confusing, too. That's because you need to remember that the order of rules you see isn't important if the rules apply to different sets of cells.

The Conditional Formatting Rules Manager isn't just for reordering your rules. It also lets you:

- Create rules (click New Rule)
- Modify rules (select a rule in the list, and then click Edit Rule)
- Delete rules (select a rule, and then click Delete Rule)

Finally, there's one easily overlooked gem: the Stop If True column. You use this setting to tell Excel to stop evaluating the conditional formatting rules on a cell. For example, imagine you create two rules: a Top 5 rule that gives cells a black background and white bold text, and a Cell Value > 10000 rule that gives cells red text. If you put the Top 5 rule first and switch on Stop If True setting, you ensure that the rules will never overlap. If a cell value is both in the Top 5 *and* greater than 10000, it will get only the Top 5 formatting—which is good, because red text is difficult to read on a black background.

CHAPTER

7

Viewing and Printing Worksheets

The previous chapters have given you all the tools you need to create nicely formatted worksheets. That's all well and good, but as you use those features to build intricate worksheets, you may quickly find yourself buried in an avalanche of data. If you want to see more than one part of your workbook at once, or if you want an overview of the entire worksheet, you must seize control of Excel's viewing features.

These features include zooming, which lets you fit more information into your Excel window; panes, which let you see more than one part of a worksheet at once; and freezing, which lets you keep certain cells visible at all times (like column titles). This chapter teaches you how to use these tools, store a custom view, and even save a *workspace* (a configuration that lets you edit multiple files in one window).

No matter what your worksheets look like on a screen, sometimes the best way to review them is in print. The second half of this chapter tackles printing your worksheets. You'll learn Excel's basic printing options and a few tricks that can help you preview page breaks and make sure large amounts of data get divided the way you want.

Controlling Your View

So far, most of the worksheets in this book have included only a small amount of data. But as you cram your worksheets with dozens of columns, and hundreds or even thousands of rows, editing becomes much trickier. The most challenging problems are keeping track of where you are in an ocean of information and making sure the data you want stays visible. Double that if you have multiple large worksheets in a single workbook.

The following sections introduce the basic tools you can use to view your data, along with a few tips for managing large worksheets.

Zooming

Excel's zoom feature lets you control how much data you see in your worksheet. When you *reduce* the zoom percentage—say, from 100 percent to 10 percent—Excel shrinks your worksheet, letting you see more cells at once, which also makes it harder to read the data. Very small zoom percentages are ideal for looking at the overall layout of a worksheet. When you *increase* the zoom percentage—say, from 100 percent to 200 percent—Excel magnifies your worksheet, letting you see more detail but fewer cells. Larger zoom percentages are good for editing.

NOTE Excel lets you zoom in to 400 percent and out all the way to 10 percent.

You can most easily adjust the zoom percent using the zoom slider in the bottom-right part of the Status bar. The slider also displays the current zoom percentage. But if you want to specify the exact zoom level by hand (say, 142 percent), you can choose View→Zoom→Zoom (or click the zoom percentage next to the zoom slider). A Zoom window appears (shown in Figure 7-1).

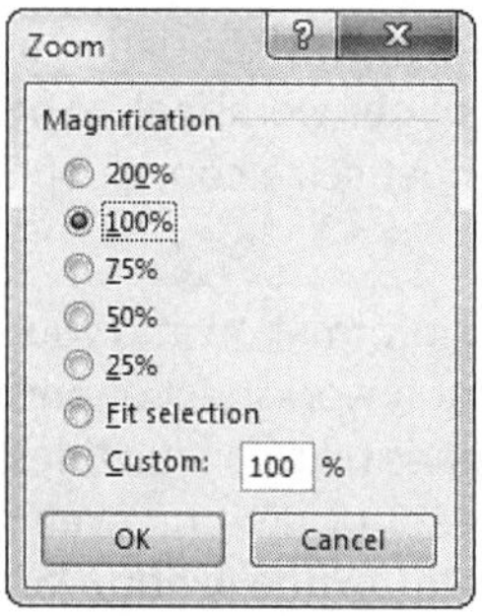

FIGURE 7-1

Using the Zoom window, you can select a preset magnification or, in the Custom box, type in your own percentage. However, using the Zoom slider (on the right side of the status bar) is almost always faster than making frequent trips to the Zoom window.

The standard zoom setting is 100 percent, although other factors, like the size of the font you're using and the size and resolution of your computer screen, help determine how many cells fit into Excel's window. As a rule of thumb, every time you double the zoom, Excel cuts in half the number of rows you can see. Thus, if you can see 20 rows at 100 percent, you'll see roughly 10 rows at 200 percent.

NOTE Changing the zoom affects how your data appears in the Excel window, but it doesn't have any effect on how your data is printed or calculated.

You can also zoom in on a specific range of cells. This is a handy trick if you've zoomed out to get a bird's-eye view of all your data and you want to swoop in on just a particular section, To try it out, first select some cells (Figure 7-2), and then choose View→Zoom→Zoom to Selection (Figure 7-3). (You can perform this same trick by highlighting some cells, opening the Zoom window, and then choosing "Fit selection.") Make sure you select a large section of the worksheet—if you select a small group, you'll end up with a truly jumbo-sized zoom.

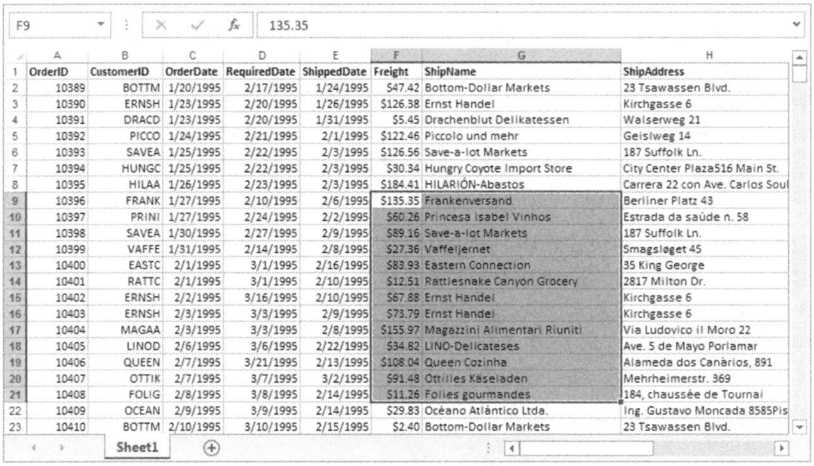

FIGURE 7-2

To magnify just a range of cells, select them as shown here, and then choose View→Zoom→Zoom to Selection to have Excel expand the range to fill the entire window, as shown in Figure 7-3.

FIGURE 7-3

Here, Excel increased the selected cells' zoom to 97 percent (from 57 percent in Figure 7-2).

TIP If your mouse has a scroll wheel, you can zoom in and out using the wheel. Place your mouse pointer over the worksheet (anywhere will do), hold down the Ctrl key, and then roll the scroll wheel up (to zoom in) or down (to zoom out).

Viewing Distant Parts of a Spreadsheet at Once

Zooming is an excellent way to survey a large expanse of data or focus on just the important cells, but it won't help if you want to simultaneously view cells that aren't near each other. For example, if you want to focus on both row 1 and row 138 at the same time, zooming won't help. Instead, try splitting your Excel window into multiple *panes*—separate frames that each provide a different view of the same worksheet. You can split a worksheet into two or four panes, depending on how many different parts you want to see. When you split a worksheet, each pane contains an identical replica of the entire worksheet. When you make a change to the worksheet in one pane, Excel automatically applies the same change in the other panes. The beauty of panes is that you can look at different parts of the same worksheet simultaneously.

You can split a window horizontally or vertically (or both). To compare different *rows* in the same worksheet, use a horizontal split. To compare different *columns* in the same worksheet, use a vertical split. And if you want to be completely crazy and see four different parts of your worksheet at once, you can use a horizontal *and* a vertical split—but that's usually too confusing to be much help.

Here's how to split the Excel window:

1. **Choose where you want to create the split by selecting a row or column.**

   To split the window into an upper and lower portion, select a row in the middle of the worksheet (by clicking a row button in the left margin), as shown in Figure 7-4.

   To split the window into a left and right portion, select a column in the middle of the worksheet (by clicking a column header above the worksheet).

   Don't worry about picking exactly the right row or column, because you'll resize your split after you create it.

NOTE If for any reason you *do* want to split the window into four panes, don't select anything. Just move to a cell that's roughly in the middle of the worksheet grid.

	A	B	C	D	E	F	G
1	OrderID	CustomerID	OrderDate	RequiredDate	ShippedDate	Freight	ShipName
2	10389	BOTTM	1/20/1995	2/17/1995	1/24/1995	$47.42	Bottom-Dollar Marke
3	10390	ERNSH	1/23/1995	2/20/1995	1/26/1995	$126.38	Ernst Handel
4	10391	DRACD	1/23/1995	2/20/1995	1/31/1995	$5.45	Drachenblut Delikate
5	10392	PICCO	1/24/1995	2/21/1995	2/1/1995	$122.46	Piccolo und mehr
6	10393	SAVEA	1/25/1995	2/22/1995	2/3/1995	$126.56	Save-a-lot Markets
7	10394	HUNGC	1/25/1995	2/22/1995	2/3/1995	$30.34	Hungry Coyote Impo
8	10395	HILAA	1/26/1995	2/23/1995	2/3/1995	$184.41	HILARIÓN-Abastos
9	10396	FRANK	1/27/1995	2/10/1995	2/6/1995	$135.35	Frankenversand
10	10397	PRINI	1/27/1995	2/24/1995	2/2/1995	$60.26	Princesa Isabel Vinh
11	10398	SAVEA	1/30/1995	2/27/1995	2/9/1995	$89.16	Save-a-lot Markets
12	10399	VAFFE	1/31/1995	2/14/1995	2/8/1995	$27.36	Vaffeljernet
13	10400	EASTC	2/1/1995	3/1/1995	2/16/1995	$83.93	Eastern Connection

FIGURE 7-4

Here, you selected row number 7. Excel will create the split just above this row.

2. **Choose View→Window→Split.**

   Excel splits the window into two separately scrollable regions (or four, if you didn't select anything in step 1).

3. **If you want to resize the panes, drag the splitter bar to a new location.**

   In the case of a horizontal split, click the splitter bar and drag it up or down. For a vertical split, drag it to the left or right.

4. **Within each pane, scroll to the cells you want to see.**

   For example, if you have a 100-row table that you split horizontally in order to compare the top five rows and the bottom five rows, scroll to the top of the upper pane, and then scroll to the bottom of the lower pane. (Again, the two panes are replicas of each other; Excel is just showing you different parts of the same worksheet.)

NOTE To remove a split, choose View→Window→Split again.

Using the scroll bars in panes can take some getting used to. When you split a worksheet, Excel changes the way you can scroll within it. For example, if you split a window into top and bottom halves, Excel gives you just one *horizontal* scroll bar (at the bottom of the screen), which controls both panes (Figure 7-5). Thus, when you scroll to the left or right, Excel moves both panes horizontally. On the other hand, Excel gives you separate *vertical* scroll bars for each pane, letting you independently move up and down within each pane.

FIGURE 7-5

Here, you can see the data in rows 1 through 6 and rows 709 through 715 at the same time. As you move from column to column, both panes move in sync, letting you see, for instance, the phone number information in both panes at once. (You can scroll up or down separately in each pane.)

TIP If you want the data in one pane—for example, column titles—to remain in place, you can freeze that pane. The next section tells you how.

The reverse is true with a vertical split; in this case, you get one vertical scroll bar and two horizontal bars, and Excel synchronizes both panes when you move up or down. With four panes, life gets a little more complicated. In this case, when you scroll left or right, the frame that's just above or just below the current frame moves, too. When you scroll up or down, the frame that's to the left or right moves with you. Try it out.

NOTE If you use Excel's worksheet navigation tools—like the Go To and Find commands—*all* your panes move to the newly found spot. For example, if you use the Find command in one pane to move to a new cell, the other panes display the same cell.

Freezing Columns or Rows

Excel has another neat trick up its sleeve to help you manage large worksheets: *freezing*. Freezing is a simpler way to make sure a specific set of rows or columns remains visible at all times. When you freeze data, it remains fixed in place in the Excel window, even as you move to another location in the worksheet in a different pane. For example, say you want to keep visible the first row in a worksheet because it contains your column titles. When you freeze that row, you can always tell what's in each column beneath—even when you scroll down several screens' worth of cells. Similarly, if your first column holds identifying labels, you may want to freeze it so that, when you scroll off to the right, you don't lose track of what you're looking at.

TIP Excel lets you print out worksheets with a particular row or column fixed in place. Page 209 tells you how.

You can freeze rows at the top of your worksheet, or columns at the left of your worksheet, but Excel does limit your freezing options in a few ways:

- You can freeze rows or columns only in groups. That means you can't freeze columns A and C without freezing column B. (You can, of course, freeze just one row or column.)
- If a row or column isn't visible and you freeze it, you can't see it until you unfreeze it. For example, if you scroll down so that row 100 appears at the top of the worksheet grid, and then freeze the top 100 rows, you can't see rows 1 to 99 anymore. This may be the effect you want, or it may be a major annoyance.

To freeze a row or set of rows at the top of your worksheet, just follow these steps:

1. **Make sure the row or rows you want to freeze are visible and at the top of your worksheet.**

   For example, if you want to freeze rows 2 and 3 in place, make sure they're visible at the top of your worksheet. Remember, Excel freezes rows starting at row 1. That means that if you scroll down so that row 1 isn't visible, and you freeze row 2 and row 3 at the top of your worksheet, then Excel also freezes row 1—and keeps it hidden so you can't scroll up to see it.

2. **Move to the first row you want *unfrozen*, and then move left to column A.**

   At this point, you're getting into position so that Excel knows where to create the freeze.

3. **Select the seemingly redundant View→Window→Freeze Panes→Freeze Panes.**

   Excel splits the worksheet, but instead of displaying a gray bar (as it does when you create panes), it uses a solid black line to divide the frozen rows from the rest of the worksheet. As you scroll down the worksheet, the frozen rows remain in place.

   To unfreeze the rows, select View→Freeze Panes→Unfreeze Panes.

Freezing columns works the same way:

1. **Make sure the column or columns you want to freeze are visible and at the left of your worksheet.**

   For example, if you want to freeze columns B and C in place, make sure they're visible at the edge of your worksheet. Remember, columns are frozen starting at column A. That means that if you scroll over so that column A isn't visible, and you freeze columns B and C on the left side of your worksheet, Excel also freezes column A—and keeps it hidden so you can't scroll over to see it.

2. **Move to the first column you want *unfrozen*, and then move up to row 1.**

   At this point, you're getting into position so that Excel knows where to create the freeze.

3. **Select View→Window→Freeze Panes→Freeze Panes.**

   Excel splits the worksheet, but instead of displaying a gray bar (as it does when you create panes), it uses a solid black line to divide the frozen columns from the rest of the worksheet. As you scroll across the worksheet, the frozen columns remain in place.

   To unfreeze the columns, select View→Window→Freeze Panes→Unfreeze Panes.

TIP If you want to freeze just the first row or the leftmost column, there's no need to go through this whole process. Instead, use the handy View→Window→Freeze Panes→Freeze Top Row or View→Window→Freeze Panes→Freeze First Column.

You can also freeze columns and rows *at the same time*, which is useful when you have identifying information you need to keep visible both on the left and at the top of your worksheet. Figure 7-6 shows an example.

	A	E	F	G	H
1	OrderID	ShippedDate	Freight	ShipName	ShipAddress
149	10367	1/2/1995	$13.55	Vaffeljernet	Smagsløget 45
150	10368	1/2/1995	$101.95	Ernst Handel	Kirchgasse 6
151	10369	1/9/1995	$195.68	Split Rail Beer & Ale	P.O. Box 555
152	10370	1/27/1995	$1.17	Chop-suey Chinese	Hauptstr. 31
153	10371	1/24/1995	$0.45	La maison d'Asie	1 rue Alsace-Lorraine
154	10372	1/9/1995	$890.78	Queen Cozinha	Alameda dos Canàrios,
155	10373	1/11/1995	$124.12	Hungry Owl All-Night Grocers	8 Johnstown Road
156	10374	1/9/1995	$3.94	Wolski Zajazd	ul. Filtrowa 68
157	10375	1/9/1995	$20.12	Hungry Coyote Import Store	City Center Plaza516 Ma
158	10376	1/13/1995	$20.39	Mère Paillarde	43 rue St. Laurent
159	10377	1/13/1995	$22.21	Seven Seas Imports	90 Wadhurst Rd.
160	10378	1/19/1995	$5.44	Folk och fä HB	Åkergatan 24

FIGURE 7-6

Here, both column A and row 1 are frozen, and thus always remain visible. The easiest way to create these frozen regions is to scroll to the top of the worksheet, make cell B2 the active cell by selecting it, and then choose View→Window→Freeze Panes→Freeze Panes. Excel then automatically freezes the rows above and the columns to the left in separate panes.

Hiding Data

In some cases, your problem isn't that you need to keep data visible, but that you need to *hide* it. For example, say you have a column of numbers that you need only for a calculation but don't want to see when you edit or print the sheet. Excel provides the perfect solution: *hiding* rows and columns. Hiding doesn't delete information; it just temporarily tucks it out of view. You can restore hidden information any time you need it.

Technically, hiding a row or column is just a special type of resizing. When you instruct Excel to hide a column, it simply shrinks the column down to a width of 0. Similarly, when you hide a row, Excel compresses the row height.

NOTE You can also hide an entire worksheet of data. See Chapter 4 for details.

You can hide data in a few ways:

- **To hide a column**, right-click the column header (the letter button on the top of the column), and then choose Hide. Or, put your cursor in any row in that column, and then select Home→Cells→Format→Hide & Unhide→Hide Columns.
- **To hide a row**, right-click the row header (the number button at the left of the row), and then choose Hide. Or, put your cursor in any column in that row, and then select Home→Cells→Format→Hide & Unhide→Hide Rows.
- **To hide multiple rows or columns**, select the ones you want to disappear before choosing Hide.

To unhide a column or row, select the *range* that includes the hidden cells. For example, if you hid column B, select columns A and C by dragging over the numeric row headers. Then right-click the selection and choose Unhide. Excel makes the missing columns or rows visible, and then highlights them so you can see which information you restored.

TIP To unhide all columns (or rows) in a worksheet, select the entire worksheet (by clicking the square in the top-left corner of the grid), and then select Home→Cells→Format→Hide & Unhide→Unhide Columns (or Unhide Rows).

Forgetting that you've hidden data is as easy as forgetting where you put your keys. While Excel doesn't include a hand-clapper to help you locate your cells, it does offer a clue that some of your row numbers or column letters are missing, as shown in Figure 7-7.

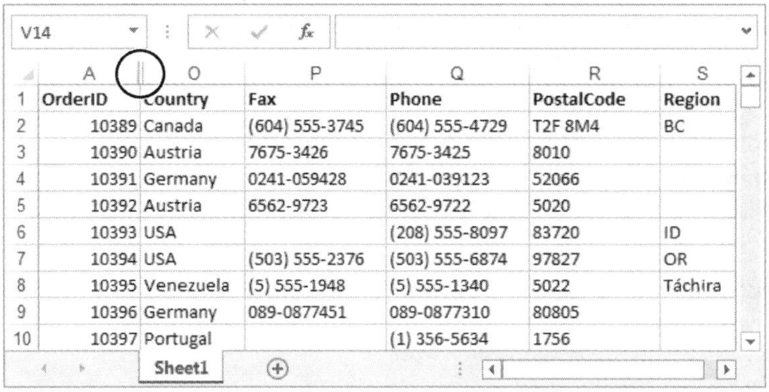

FIGURE 7-7

This worksheet jumps directly from column A to column O, which tells you that columns B through N are hidden.

TIP Excel doesn't let you hide individual cells. However, Excel gurus use workarounds. The first one is to format the cell so that the text's white (because white lettering on a white background is invisible). Another solution is to format the cell with the custom number format ;;; (which doesn't show anything for positive, negative, or text values; see page 146 for more on custom formatting). When you use either of these tricks, you can still see the cell content by moving to the cell and looking in the formula bar.

Saving View Settings

If you regularly tweak things in Excel like changing the zoom level, hiding or showing columns, and creating panes, you can easily spend more time adjusting your worksheet than editing it. Fortunately, Excel lets you save your view settings with *custom views*. Custom views let you save a combination of view settings in a workbook. You can store as many views as you want. When you want to use a particular view, simply select it from a list and Excel applies your settings.

Custom views are particularly useful when you frequently switch views for different tasks, like editing and printing. For example, if you like to *edit* with several panes open and all your data visible, but you like to *print* your data in one pane with some columns hidden, custom views let you quickly switch between the two layouts.

NOTE You can't save a custom view for one worksheet, and then apply it to another.

Custom views can save the following settings:

- The location of the active cell. (In other words, your position in the worksheet. For example, if you scroll to the bottom of a 65,000-row spreadsheet and save a custom view, Excel will take you back to that cell when you open the view.)
- The currently selected cell (or cells).

- Column widths and row heights, including hidden columns and rows.
- Split panes (page 200).
- View settings, like the zoom percentage, which you set using the ribbon's View tab.
- Print settings (page 203), like page margins.
- Filter settings, which affect what information Excel shows in a data list (see Chapter 14).

WARNING Excel does have one restriction on custom views. You can't use views with Excel's very useful table feature, which is described in Chapter 14. In fact, once you add a table to your worksheet, Excel turns the Custom Views button off.

To create a custom view, follow these steps:

1. **Adjust an open worksheet for your viewing pleasure.**

   Set the zoom, hide or freeze columns and rows, and move to the place in the worksheet where you want to edit.

2. **Choose View→Workbook Views→Custom View.**

   The Custom Views window appears, showing you a list of all the views defined for this workbook. If you haven't created any yet, this list is empty.

3. **Click the Add button.**

   The Add View window appears.

4. **Type in a name for your custom view.**

   You can use any name, but consider something that'll remind you of your view settings (like "50 Percent Zoom"), or the task that this view is designed for (like "All Data at a Glance"). A poor choice is one that won't mean anything to you later ("View One" or "Zoom with a View") or something obscure like '"57 Chevy."

   The Add View window also gives you the chance to specify print settings or hidden rows and columns that Excel *shouldn't* save as part of the view. Turn off the appropriate checkboxes if you don't want to retain this information. Say you hide column A, but you clear the "Hidden rows, columns, and filter settings" checkbox because you don't want to save this as part of the view. The next time you restore the view, Excel won't make any changes to the visibility of column A. If it's hidden, it stays hidden; if it's visible, it stays visible. On the other hand, if you want column A to always be hidden when you apply your new custom view, then keep the "Hidden rows, columns, and filter settings" checkbox turned on when you save it.

   After you name your view and dealt with the inclusion settings, click OK to create the view. Excel adds it to the views list.

5. **Click Close.**

   You're now ready to use your shiny new view or add another (readjust your settings and follow this procedure again).

Applying views is a snap. Simply select View→Workbook Views→Custom Views to return to the Custom Views window (Figure 7-8), select your view from the list, and then click Show. Because Excel stores views with the workbook, they'll always be available when you open the file, even if you take that file to another computer.

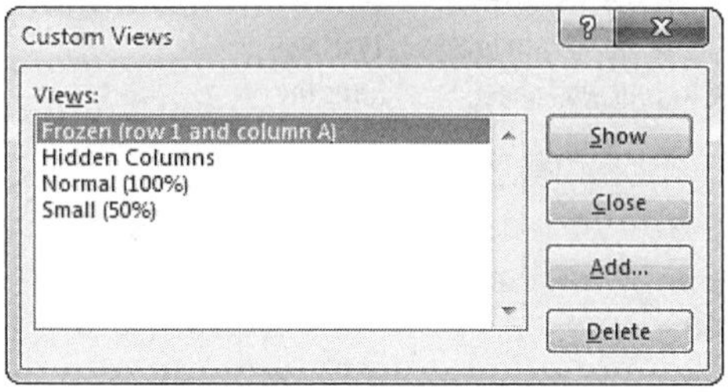

FIGURE 7-8

You can use the Custom Views window to show or delete existing views or to create new ones (click Add, and then follow the preceding procedure from step 4).

TIP Visit this book's Missing CD page at *www.missingmanuals.com/cds/excel2013mm* for some examples of custom views in action, and download CustomViews.xls, a sample spreadsheet with an array of custom views already set up.

Viewing Multiple Workbooks at Once

Every time you open a new spreadsheet, Excel uses a separate window. If you want to compare two or more workbooks, you need to switch between these windows, or arrange them next to each other. Positioning them in the right spot, so they don't overlap one another, can be a bit finicky.

But Excel has a shortcut to help you out. It automatically positions all your open Excel windows in a neat side-by-side, top-to-bottom, or tiled arrangement. That way, you can see all your data at once. (The disadvantage is that the more windows you have open, the smaller each window is.) Figure 7-9 shows an arrangement of three spreadsheets.

TIP If you're arranging Excel windows next to each other, you'll probably want to collapse the ribbon in each one (to do that, double-click any one of the tabs). Otherwise, you'll use up a lot of screen real estate that could be better used to show data. In the past, Excel had a feature that let you tile multiple documents in a single, larger Excel window with a single toolbar, but Microsoft removed that feature in Excel 2013.

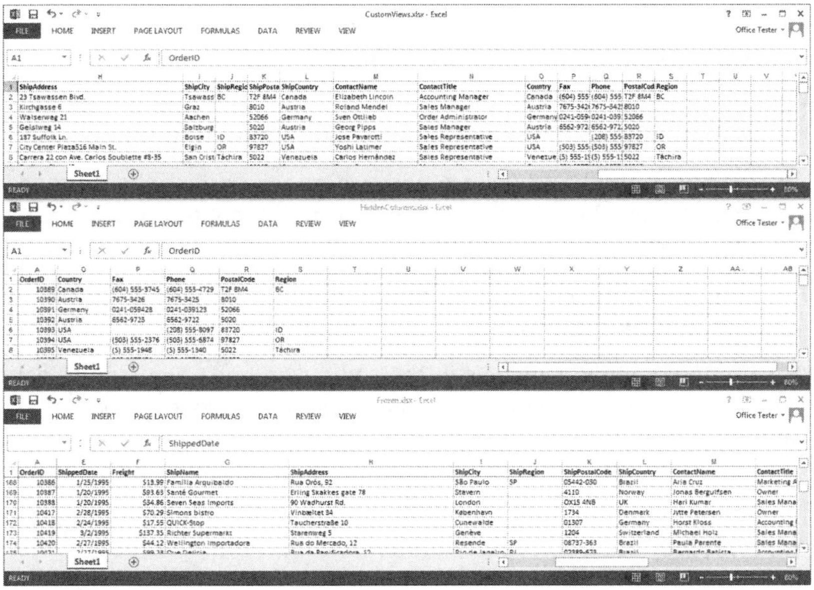

FIGURE 7-9

These three spreadsheets have been arranged horizontally, in separate Excel windows. In each window, the ribbon is collapsed, maximizing the space for displaying data.

Here's how to get Excel to arrange its windows:

1. **Open all the spreadsheet files you want to make part of your workspace. Close all other Excel files.**

   Should you want different worksheets from the *same* workbook to be part of your workspace, you must open duplicate versions of the workbook. To do this, go to the workbook and select View→Window→New Window. Excel opens a second (or third, or fourth...) window with the same workbook in it. Don't worry though—any change you make in one window automatically appears in the others, because there's still just one open workbook. You can tell that you have more than one window open for the same workbook by looking at the title bar of the window, which adds a colon and a number. For example, when you open a second view of MyBeanieBabies.xlsx, the title bar will say MyBeanieBabies.xlsx:2.

   If you lose track of your windows (or you want to quickly jump from one to another), you can use the View→Window→Switch Windows list, which shows all the currently open windows.

2. **Choose View→Window→Arrange All.**

   The Arrange Windows window appears.

3. **Choose an Arrange option, and then click OK.**

   Excel gives you four choices for window-arranging:

   - **Horizontal**, as shown in Figure 7-9, stacks the windows from top to bottom. Excel arranges the windows one above the other, each occupying the full width of the Excel window (similar to when you split a worksheet with the horizontal splitter bar).
   - **Vertical** instructs Excel to tile the windows from left to right.
   - **Tiled** arranges the windows in a grid whose composition changes depending on the number of files you're arranging. This option is great if you have a huge monitor.
   - **Cascade** layers the windows on top of each other with just a smidge of each window showing.

   If you open multiple windows in the same workbook, you can select the "Windows of active workbook" option to tell Excel to ignore any other open workbooks.

Printing

Printing in Excel is pretty straightforward—as long as your spreadsheet fits on a normal 8.5 x 11-inch piece of paper. If you're one of the millions of spreadsheet owners who don't belong to that club, welcome to the world of Multiple Page Disorder: the phenomenon in which pages and pages of apparently unrelated and noncontiguous columns start spewing from your printer. Fortunately, Excel comes with a slew of print-tweaking tools designed to help you control what you print. First off, though, it helps to understand the standard settings Excel uses.

NOTE You can change most of the settings listed; this is just a list of what happens if you *don't* adjust any settings before printing a spreadsheet.

- When printing a worksheet, Excel retains any formatting characteristics you applied to your cells, including fonts, fills, and borders. However, Excel's gridlines, row headers, and column headers *don't* appear in the printout.
- If you have too many rows or columns to fit on one page, Excel prints the worksheet on multiple pages. If your data is both too long *and* too wide, Excel prints in the following order: all the rows for the first set of columns that fit on a printed page, then all the rows for the next set of columns that fit, and so on (this is known as "down, then over"). When printing on multiple pages, Excel never prints part of an individual column or row.
- Excel prints your file in color if you use colors and you have a color printer.

- Excel sets margins to 0.75 inches at the top and bottom of the page, and 0.7 inches on the left and right. Ordinarily, Excel doesn't include headers and footers (so you don't see any page numbers).
- Excel doesn't include hidden rows or columns in the printout.

How to Print an Excel File

Excel uses its backstage view to make printing a whole lot less confusing. Its key feature is a built-in preview that shows you what your printout will look like before you actually click Print.

If you're in a tremendous hurry to get your printout and you're not interested in playing with print settings, just choose File→Print, and then click the big Print button shown in Figure 7-10.

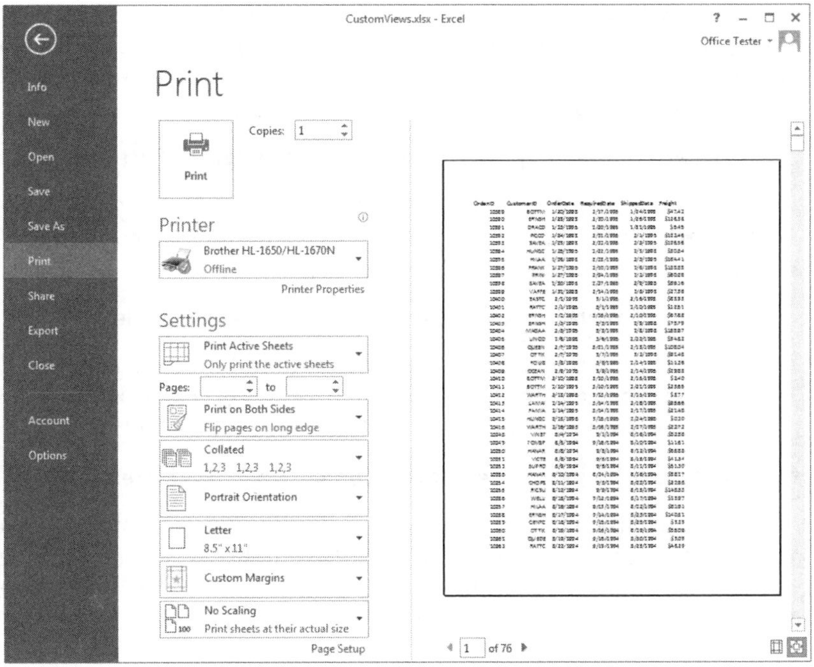

FIGURE 7-10

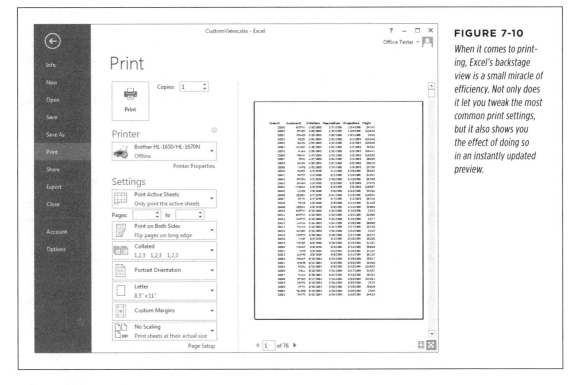

When it comes to printing, Excel's backstage view is a small miracle of efficiency. Not only does it let you tweak the most common print settings, but it also shows you the effect of doing so in an instantly updated preview.

If this no-fuss printing approach doesn't give you the results you want, you need to take a closer look at the print settings you can tweak. Here's a walkthrough of your options:

1. **Choose File→Print (or press Ctrl+P).**

   Excel switches to backstage view, where you see printing options on the left and a print preview on the right (Figure 7-10).

2. **To print multiple copies of your data, use the Copies box.**

   Excel normally prints just a single copy of your work; to change that, change the number in the Copies box.

   If you're printing more than one copy and your worksheet has multiple pages, you should also review the collating setting, which appears farther down. This setting determines whether Excel duplicates each page separately. For example, if you print 10 pages and your printout is set to Uncollated, Excel prints 10 copies of page 1, 10 copies of page 2, and so on. If your printout is set to Collated, Excel prints the entire 10-page document, then prints out another copy, and so on; you still end up with 10 copies of each page, but they'll be grouped together for added convenience.

3. **Select a printer from the drop-down list under the Printer heading.**

   Excel automatically selects your regular printer. If you want to use a different one, you need to select it yourself. You can also adjust the printer settings by clicking the Printer Properties link. Every printer has its own set of options, but common Properties settings include print quality and paper handling (like double-sided printing for those with a printer that supports it).

4. **Choose what you want to print from the first list under the Settings heading.**

   - **Print Active Sheets** prints the current worksheet. If you grouped two or more worksheets together using the techniques described on page 115, Excel prints all the selected sheets, one after the other.
   - **Print Entire Workbook** prints all the worksheets in your file.
   - **Print Selection** prints out just a portion of a worksheet. To make this feature work, you need to start by selecting a range of cells, columns, or rows before you start your print out, and *then* choose File→Print.

5. **If you want to print just some pages, use the two Pages boxes.**

   By default, Excel uses as many pages as it needs to to print your data. Alternately, you can choose a range of pages using the Pages option. For example, you can choose to print only the first three pages by typing 1 into the first box and 3 in the second. You can also print just the fourth page by printing from 4 to 4.

NOTE To use the "Print range" box effectively, you need to know how many pages your worksheet requires and what data will appear on each page. You can step through all the pages using the handy print preview shown in Figure 7-10.

6. **Set the orientation and paper size.**

   Orientation is one of the all-time most useful print settings. It lets you control whether you print on pages that are upright (choose Portrait Orientation) or turned horizontally on their sides (choose Landscape Orientation). If Excel splits your rows across multiple pages when you print your worksheet, it makes good sense to switch to landscape orientation. That way, Excel prints your columns across a page's long edge, which accommodates more columns (but fewer rows per page).

If you're fed up with trying to fit all your data on an ordinary sheet no matter which way you turn it, you may be tempted to try using a longer sheet of paper, like legal size paper. You can then tell Excel what paper you've decided to use by choosing it from the list just under the orientation setting. (Of course, the paper needs to fit into your printer.) Letter is the standard 8.5 x 11-inch sheet size, while Legal is another common choice—it's just as wide but comes in a bit longer at 8.5 x 14 inches.

7. **Adjust your margins.**

   Beneath the options for page orientation and paper size is the margin setting, which determines the amount of space between your worksheet content and the edges of the page.

   You can set the margins two ways. The easiest is to pick one of the presets (Normal, Wide, or Narrow), as shown in Figure 7-11.

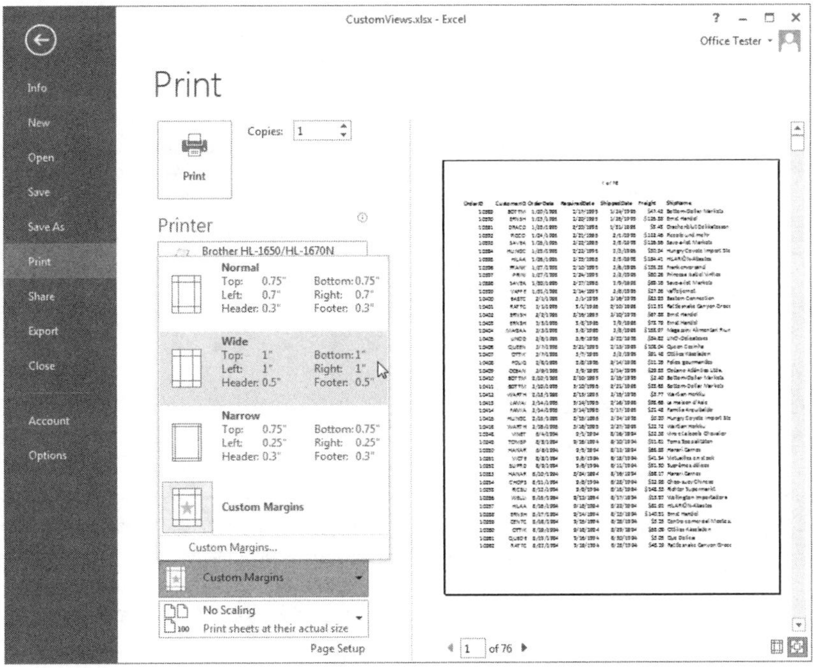

FIGURE 7-11

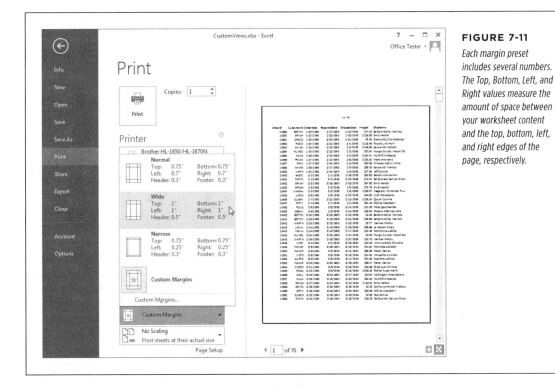

Each margin preset includes several numbers. The Top, Bottom, Left, and Right values measure the amount of space between your worksheet content and the top, bottom, left, and right edges of the page, respectively.

For more control, you can choose Custom Margins and fill in your own values (Figure 7-12). Logically enough, when you reduce the size of your margins, you can accommodate more information. However, you can't *completely* eliminate your margins. Most printers require at least a little space (usually no less than 0.25 inches) to grip onto the page, and you won't be able to print on this part (the very edge of the page). If you try to make the margins too small, Excel won't inform you of the problem; instead, it sticks with the smallest margin your printer allows.

If you have only a few rows or columns of information, you may want to use one of the "Center on page" options. Select Horizontally to center your columns between the left and right margins. Select Vertically to center your data between the top and bottom of the page.

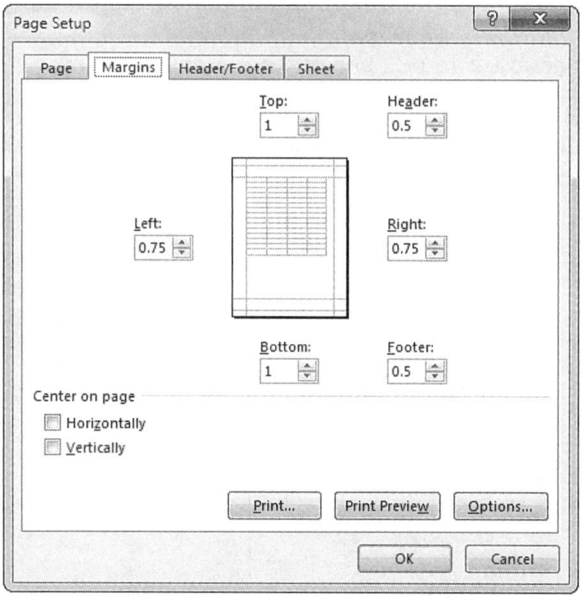

FIGURE 7-12

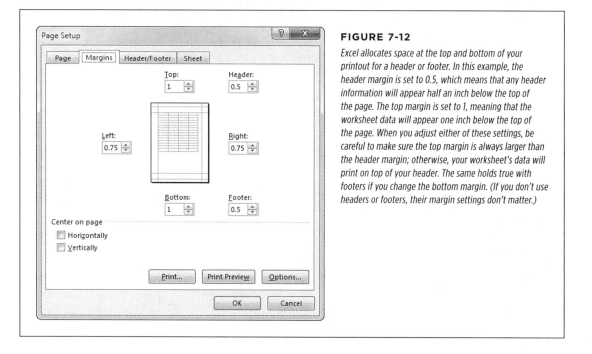

Excel allocates space at the top and bottom of your printout for a header or footer. In this example, the header margin is set to 0.5, which means that any header information will appear half an inch below the top of the page. The top margin is set to 1, meaning that the worksheet data will appear one inch below the top of the page. When you adjust either of these settings, be careful to make sure the top margin is always larger than the header margin; otherwise, your worksheet's data will print on top of your header. The same holds true with footers if you change the bottom margin. (If you don't use headers or footers, their margin settings don't matter.)

TIP A good rule of thumb is to adjust your margins symmetrically (printouts tend to look nicest that way). Thus, if you shrink the left margin to 0.5, make the same change to the right margin. Generally, if you want to fit in more data and you don't need any header or footer space, you can safely reduce all your margins to 0.5. If you really want to cram in the maximum amount of data you can try 0.25, but that's the minimum margin that most printers allow.

8. **If you need to shrink your printout and cram more information into each page, pick a scaling option.**

   No matter how drastically you reduce your margins, you'll only be able to fit a few extra rows and columns on a page. A more powerful approach for fitting mass amounts of data into a smaller number of pages is to use *scaling*. Page 215 gives you more detail, but for now, try one of these handy scaling presets:

- **Fit All Columns on One Page** squashes your page width-wise, making it narrower. This way, the columns won't leak off the edge and onto a separate page.
- **Fit All Rows on One Page** squashes your page height-wise, making it shorter. This way, all your rows will appear on the same page.
- **Fit Sheet on One Page** squashes your page both ways, making sure all your data fits on a single sheet.

NOTE Excel performs scaling by reducing the font size in the printout. If you try to cram too much data into too small a space, your text might shrink into near-oblivion. It can be hard to judge just how small your text is from the print preview, so you might need to print a test page to see how much scaling is too much.

9. **If you want still more printout options, click the Page Setup link.**

   That launches the Page Setup window (Figure 7-13), which holds a few of Excel's more specialized print settings. The Page Setup window is organized into several tabs. The Page and Margins tabs duplicate the settings you find in backstage view. The Header/Footer tab isn't the most convenient way to add a header or footer (instead, see page 212). However, the Sheet tab has a number of options you won't find anywhere else:

   - **Print area** lets you specify the range of cells you want to print. While this tool definitely gets the job done, it's easier to use the Print Area tool (described in the box on page 209). And some people find that the Print window's Selection setting (step 4) offers an easier way for you to print small groups of cells.
   - **Print titles** lets you print specific rows at the top of every page, or specific columns on the left side of every page. For example, you could use this setting to print column titles at the top of every page.

NOTE Due to a strange Excel quirk, you can't modify the "Print area" or "Print titles" settings while Excel previews your printout. Instead, you need to close backstage view (press Esc), head to the Page Layout→Sheet Options section of the ribbon, and click the window launcher. This gives you the same Page Setup window, but with all its options enabled.

   - **Gridlines** prints the grid of lines that separate columns and rows in your on-screen worksheet.
   - **Row and column headings** prints the column headers (which contain the column letters) at the top of each page and the row headers (with the row numbers) on the left side of each page.
   - **Black and white** tells Excel to render all colors as a shade of gray, regardless of your printer settings.

- **Draft quality** tells Excel to use lower-quality printer settings to save ink or toner and speed up printing—assuming your printer has these features, of course.
- **Comments** lets you print the comments you added to a worksheet. Excel can either append them to the cells in the printout or add them at the end of the printout, depending on the option you select. For the lowdown on comments, see page 674.
- **Cell errors** lets you configure how Excel prints a cell if it contains a formula with an error in it. You can choose to print the error that's shown (the standard option), or replace the error with a blank value, two dashes (--), or the error code #N/A (meaning "not available"). You'll learn much more about formulas in Chapter 8.
- **Page order** sets the way Excel handles a worksheet that's too wide and too long for the printed page's boundaries. When you choose "Down, then over" (the standard option), Excel starts by printing all the rows in the first batch of columns. Once it finishes that batch, it moves on to the next set of columns, and prints those columns for all the rows in your worksheet, and so on. When you choose "Over, then down," Excel moves across your worksheet first. That means it prints all the columns in the first set of rows, and then moves to the next set of rows, and so on.

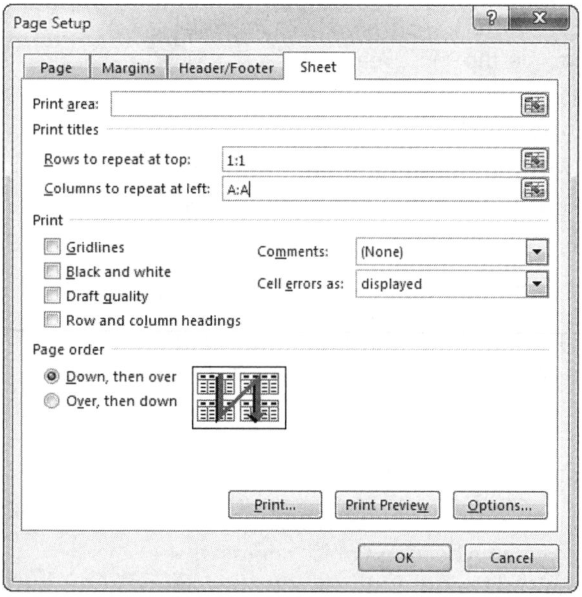

FIGURE 7-13

In this example, you're using the "Print titles" options to print the first row and the first column of the spreadsheet on every page.

10. **Now that you finished setting print options, click the Print button to send the spreadsheet to the printer.**

    Excel prints your document using your settings.

    If you're printing a very large worksheet, Excel shows a Printing window for a few seconds as it sends the pages to the printer. If you decide to cancel the printing process—and you're quick enough—you can click the Cancel button to stop the operation. If you lack the cat-like reflexes for this, you can open your printer queue to cancel the print job. Look for your printer icon in the notification area at the bottom-right of your screen, and double-click that icon to open a print window. Select the offending print job in the list, and then press Delete (or choose Document→Cancel from the print window's menu). Some printers offer a cancel button on the printer itself, which lets you stop a print job even after it leaves your computer.

GEM IN THE ROUGH

Printing Parts of a Spreadsheet

When you work with large worksheets, you'll often want to print only a small portion of your data. Excel gives you several ways to limit your printout. You can hide the rows or columns you aren't interested in, or you can select the cells you want to print, and, in the Print window's "Print what" box, choose Selection. But if you frequently need to print the same area, you're better off defining and using a *print area*.

A print area designates a portion of your worksheet as the only region that Excel will print. (The one exception is if you choose Selection from the "Print what" box, in which case Excel prints the selected cells, not the print area.) Once you define a print area, Excel retains it until you change or remove it. That means you can edit, save, close, and open your spreadsheet, and the print area remains the same.

To set a print area, select the rows, columns, or group of cells you want, and then choose Page Layout→Page Setup→Print Area→Set Print Area. The portion of the worksheet you highlighted now has a thin dashed outline, indicating that this is the only region Excel will print. You can only have one print area per worksheet, and setting a new one always clears the previous one. To remove your print area so that you can print the entire worksheet, choose Page Layout→Page Setup→Print Area→Clear Print Area.

Page Layout View: A Better Print Preview

When you're preparing to print that 142-page company budget monstrosity, there's no reason to go in blind. Instead, prudent Excel fans use Page Layout view to preview their printouts.

Page Layout view is a bit like the print preview that you saw backstage (Figure 7-11), but it's more powerful. First, Page Layout view is bigger and easier to navigate than backstage view. More importantly, it lets you do a few things backstage view doesn't, like setting headers and footers, editing cell values, and tweaking other page layout settings from the ribbon.

To see Page Layout view for a worksheet, choose View→Workbook Views→Page Layout View. For a quicker alternative, use the tiny Page Layout View button in the Status bar, which appears immediately to the left of the zoom slider. Either way, you see a nicely formatted preview (Figure 7-14).

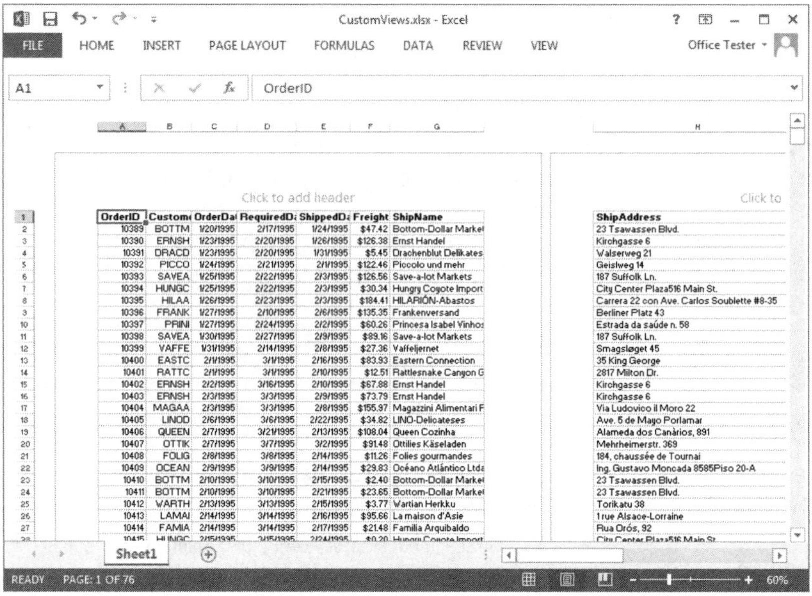

FIGURE 7-14

Page Layout view previews how the first (and part of the second) page of this worksheet's 76 pages will look in print. This worksheet has 19 columns, but since they're wider than the width of a single printed page, the first page includes only the leftmost seven columns, as shown here. You can scroll to the right to see the additional columns that'll turn up on other pages, or scroll down to see more rows.

How does Page Layout view differ from Excel's normal worksheet grid? For starters, Page Layout view:

- **Paginates your data.** You see exactly what fits on each page, and how many pages your printout requires.
- **Reveals any headers and footers you've added.** These details don't appear in the Normal worksheet view.
- **Shows the margins that Excel will use for your pages.**
- **Doesn't show anything that Excel won't print (like the letters at the top of each column).** The only exception is the cell gridlines, which are shown to help you move around your worksheet.
- **Includes a bit of text in the Status bar that tells you where you are, page-wise, in a large spreadsheet.** For example, you might see the text "Page: 5 of 26."

NOTE Don't confuse Page Layout view with an ordinary print preview (like the one you see when you choose File→Print). A print preview provides a fixed "snapshot" of your printout. You can look, but you can't touch. Page Layout view is vastly better because it shows what your printout will look like *and* it lets you edit data, change margins, set headers and footers, create charts, draw pictures, and so on. In fact, you can do everything you do in Normal view in Page Layout view. The only difference is you can't squeeze quite as much data into the view at once.

If you aren't particularly concerned with your margin settings, you can hide your margins in Page Layout view so you can fit more information into the Excel window. Figure 7-15 shows you how.

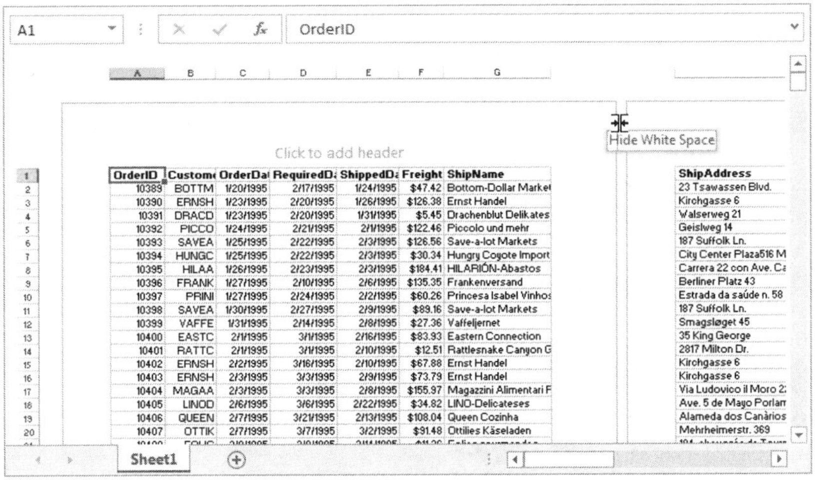

FIGURE 7-15

Move your mouse between the "pages," and your pointer changes to this strange two-arrow beast. You can then click to hide the margins in between pages (as shown here), and click again to show them (as shown in Figure 7-14). Either way, you see an exact replica of your printout. The only difference is whether you see the empty margin space.

Here are some of the things you can do in Page Layout view:

- **Tweak print settings and see the effect.** Choose the Page Layout tab in the ribbon. The most important print-related sections are Page Setup (which lets you change orientation and margin settings), Scale to Fit (which lets you cram more information into your printed pages), and Sheet Options (which lets you control whether gridlines and column headers appear on your printout).
- **Move from page to page.** You can use the scroll bar at the side of the window, or use keyboard keys (like Page Up, Page Down, and the arrow keys). When you reach the edge of your data, you see shaded pages with the text "Click to add data" superimposed. If you want to add information further down the worksheet, just click one of these pages, and then start typing.
- **Adjust the page margins.** First make sure you can see Excel's reference ruler by turning on the View→Show→Ruler checkbox. Then, drag one of the margin lines on the ruler, as shown in Figure 7-16. If you want to set page margins by typing in the exact margin width, use the Page Layout tab of the ribbon instead.

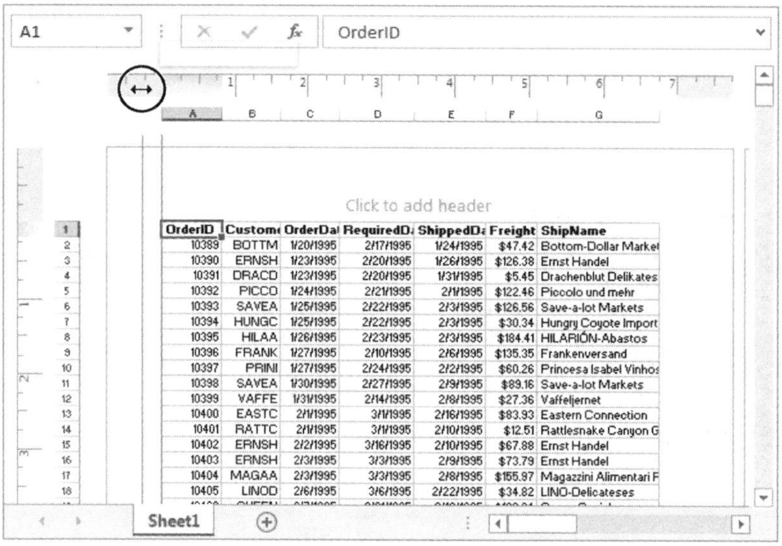

FIGURE 7-16

The Page Layout view lets you set margins by dragging the margin edge with your mouse. Here, you're about to narrow the left margin (circled) down to 0.58 inches. If you're also using a header or footer (see the section below), make sure you don't drag the page margin above the header or below the footer. If you do, your header or footer will overlap your worksheet's data.

When you're ready to return to the Normal worksheet view, choose View→Workbook Views→Normal (or just click the Status bar's tiny Normal View button).

Creating Headers and Footers

A *header* is a bit of text at the top of every page in your printout. A *footer* is a bit of text printed at the bottom of every page. You can use one, both, or neither in a printout.

Ordinarily, every new workbook starts out without a header or footer. However, Page Layout view gives you an easy way to add either or both. Scroll to the top of any page to create a header (or to the bottom to create a footer), and then look for the box with the text "Click to add header" or "Click to add footer." Click inside this box, and then type the header or footer you want.

NOTE You won't see the header or footer boxes if you drastically compress your margins, because they won't fit. To get them back, make your margins larger. When you're finished adding the header or footer you want, you can try adjusting the margins again to see just how small you can get them.

Of course, a good header or footer isn't just an ordinary piece of text. Instead, it can contain dynamically changing information, like the worksheet's file name, current page, or the date you printed it. You can get these pieces of information using specialized header and footer *codes*, which are distinguished by their use of square brackets. For example, if you type the code *&[Page]* into a footer, Excel replaces it with the current page number. If you use the code *&[Date]*, Excel substitutes the current date (when you fire off your printout). Of course, no one wants to memorize a long list of cryptic header and footer codes. To help you get the details right, Excel adds a new tab to the ribbon named Header & Footer Tools | Design (Figure 7-17) when you edit a header or footer.

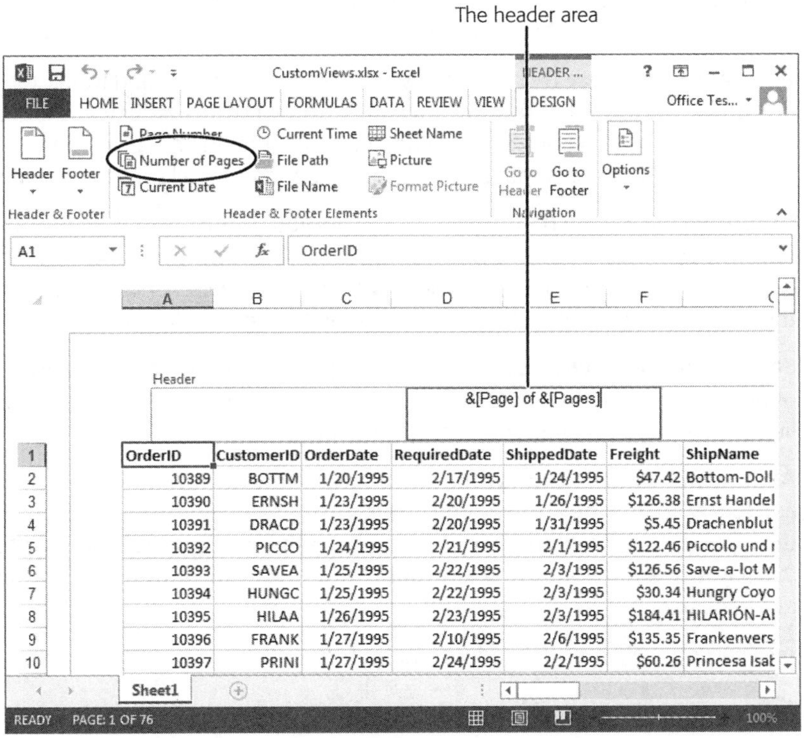

FIGURE 7-17

The Header & Footer Tools | Design tab is chock-full of useful ingredients you can add to a header or footer. Click a button in the Header & Footer Elements section to insert a special Excel code that represents a dynamic value, like the current and total number of pages in your printout (circled).

The quickest way to get a header or footer is to go to the Header & Footer Tools | Design→Header & Footer section (shown in Figure 7-17), and then choose one of the Header or Footer list's ready-made options. Those options include:

- Page numbering (for example, Page 1 or Page 1 of 10).
- Worksheet name (for example, Sheet 1).
- File name (for example, *myfile.xlsx* or *C:\MyDocuments\myfile.xlsx*).
- The person who created the document, and the date it was created.
- A combination of this information.

Oddly enough, the options for the header and footer are the same. It's up to you to decide whether you want a title at the top and the page numbering at the bottom, or vice versa.

If none of the standard options match what you need, you can edit the automatic header or footer, or you can create your own from scratch. Start typing in the header or footer box, and use the buttons in the Header & Footer Elements section to paste in the code you need for a dynamic value. Then, if you want to get creative, switch to the Home tab of the ribbon, and use the formatting buttons to change the font, size, alignment, and color of your header or footer.

Finally, Excel gives you a few high-powered options in the Header & Footer Tools | Design→Options section. These include:

- **Different First Page.** This option lets you create one header and footer for the first page, and use a different pair for all subsequent pages. After you check this option, fill in the first page's header and footer on the first page, and then head to the second page to create a new header and footer for all subsequent pages.
- **Different Odd & Even pages.** This option lets you create two different headers (and footers)—one for all even-numbered pages and one for all odd-numbered pages. Use the first page to fill in the odd-numbered header and footer, and use the second page to fill in the even-numbered header and footer.
- **Scale with Document.** If you select this option, then, when you change the print scale to fit in more or less information on your printout (page 215), Excel adjusts the headers and footers proportionately.
- **Align with Page Margins.** With this option selected, Excel moves the header and footer so that they're centered in relation to the margins. If you don't select this option, Excel centers them in relation to the whole page. The only time you'll notice a difference is when your left and right margins are significantly different sizes.

All these settings affect both headers and footers.

Controlling Pagination

Sooner or later it will happen—you'll face an intimidatingly large worksheet that, when printed, is hacked into dozens of apparently unconnected pages. You could spend a lot of time assembling this jigsaw printout (using a bulletin board and lots of tape), or you could take control of the printing process and tell Excel exactly where to split your data into pages. In the following sections, you'll learn several techniques to do just that.

Page Breaks

One of Excel's often overlooked but surprisingly handy features is *manual page breaks.* The idea is that you tell Excel explicitly where to start a new page. For example, you can tell Excel to start a new page between tables in a worksheet (rather than print a page that has the end of one table and the beginning of the next one).

To insert a page break, move to the leftmost column (column A), and then scroll down to the first cell that you want to appear on the new page. Then, choose Page Layout→Page Setup→Breaks→Insert Page Break. Excel inserts a solid line where it will break the page (Figure 7-18).

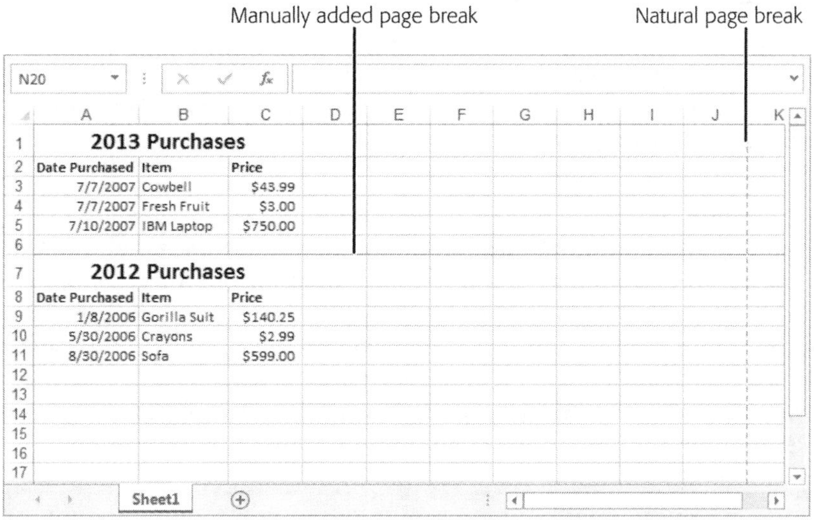

FIGURE 7-18

Using a page break, you can make sure the second table (2012 Purchases) always begins on a new page. Excel denotes page breaks you add with a solid line, and shows naturally falling breaks (based on your settings for margins, page orientation, and paper size) with a dotted line.

NOTE There's no limit to how many page breaks you can add to a worksheet—if you have a dozen tables that appear one after the other, you can place a page break after each one to make sure they all start on a new page.

You can also insert page breaks to split your worksheet vertically into pages. This is useful if your worksheet is too wide to fit on a single page, and you want to control exactly where the page break will fall. To do so, move to the first row, scroll to the column where the new page should begin, and then choose Page Layout→Page Setup→Breaks→Insert Page Break.

You can remove page breaks one at a time by moving to an adjacent cell and choosing Page Layout→Page Setup→Breaks→Remove Page Break. Or you can clear them all using Page Layout→Page Setup→Breaks→Reset All Page Breaks.

Scaling

Page breaks are a nifty feature for making sure you paginate your printouts just the way you want them. However, they can't help you fit more information on a page. They simply let you place page breaks earlier than they would ordinarily appear, so they fall in a more appropriate place.

If you want to fit more info on a page, you need to shrink your information down to a smaller size. Excel includes a scaling feature that lets you do that easily, without having to reformat your worksheet.

Scaling lets you fit more rows and columns on a page, by shrinking everything proportionally. For example, if you reduce scaling to 50 percent, you fit twice as many columns and rows on a page. Conversely, you can use scaling to enlarge your data.

To change the scaling percentage, type a new percentage into the Page Layout→Scale to Fit→Scale box. The data appears normally in your worksheet on screen, but Excel shrinks or expands it in the printout. To gauge the effect, use the Page Layout view (page 209) to preview your printout.

Rather than fiddling with the scaling percentage (and then seeing what its effect is on your worksheet by trial and error), you may want to force your data to fit into a fixed number of pages. To do this, you set the values in the Page Layout→Scale to Fit→Width box and the Page Layout→Scale to Fit→Height box. Excel performs a few behind-the-scenes calculations and adjusts the scaling percentage accordingly. For example, if you choose "1 page(s) tall" and "1 page(s) wide," Excel shrinks your entire worksheet so that everything fits into one page. It's tricky to get the scaling right (and can lead to hopelessly small text), so make sure you review your worksheet in the Page Layout view before you print it.

TIP Page Break Preview mode, described next, gives you yet another way to squeeze more data onto a single page.

Page Break Preview: A Bird's-Eye View of Your Worksheet

You don't need to be a tree-hugging environmentalist to want to minimize the number of pages you print. Enter the Page Break Preview, which gives you a bird's-eye view of how an entire worksheet's going to print. Page Break Preview is particularly useful if your worksheet has lots of columns. That's because Page Break Preview zooms out so you can see a large amount of data at once, and it uses thick blue dashed lines to show you where page breaks will occur, as shown in Figure 7-19. In addition, the Page Break Preview numbers every page, placing the label "Page X" (where "X" is the page number) in large gray lettering in the middle of each page.

To preview the page breaks in your worksheet, select View→Workbook Views→Page Break Preview, or use the tiny Page Break Preview button in the Status bar. A window appears, informing you that you can use Page Break Preview mode to move page breaks. You can choose whether you want to see this message each time you use this feature; if not, turn on the "Do not show this dialog again" checkbox before clicking OK.

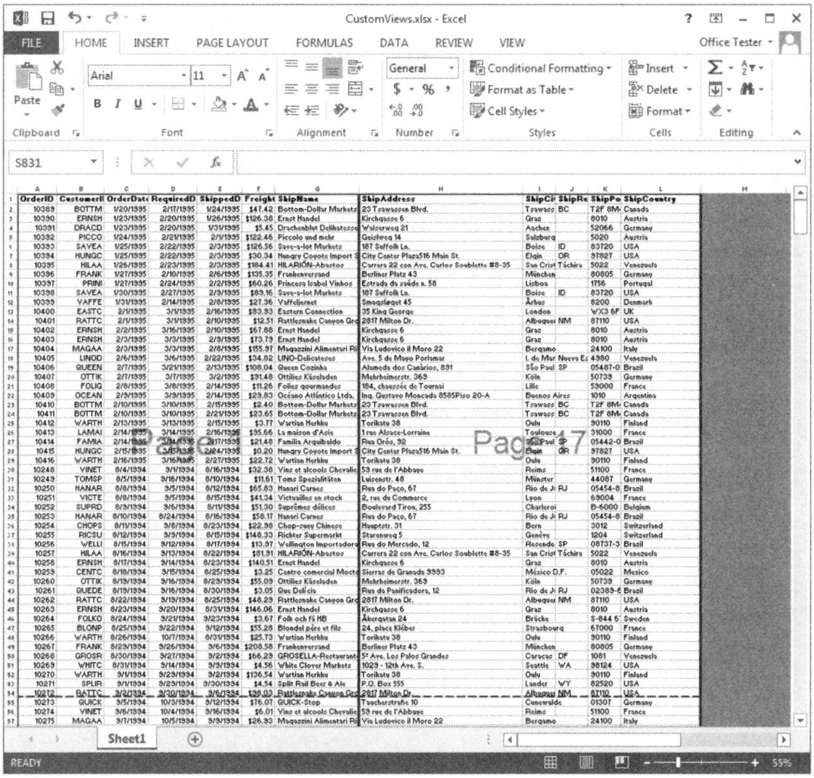

FIGURE 7-19

This example shows a large worksheet in Page Break Preview mode. The worksheet is too wide to fit on one page (at least in portrait orientation), and the thick dotted line clearly indicates that the page will break after column G and after row 54. (Excel never breaks a printout in the middle of a column or row.)

Once you're in Page Break Preview mode, you can do all the things you can do in Normal view mode, including editing data, formatting cells, and changing the zoom percentage to reveal more or fewer pages. You can also click the blue dashed lines that represent page breaks, and drag them to include more or fewer rows and columns in your page.

Excel lets you make two types of changes using page breaks:

- **You can make less data fit onto a page.** To do so, drag the bottom page break up or the right-side page break to the left. Usually, you'll take one of these steps if you notice that a page break is in an awkward place, like just before a row with some kind of summary or subtotal.
- **You can make more data fit onto a page.** To do so, drag the bottom page break down or the right-side page break to the right.

Of course, everyone wants to fit more information in their printouts, but there's only so much space on a page. So what does Excel do when you expand a page by dragging the page break? It simply adjusts the scaling setting you learned about earlier (page 215). The larger you make the page, the smaller the Scaling percentage setting becomes. That means your printed text may end up too tiny for you to read. (The text on your computer's display doesn't change, so you don't have any indication of just how small your text is until you print out your data, or take a look at it in Page Layout view.)

NOTE Scaling affects all the pages in your printout. That means that when you drag one page break to expand the size of a page, you actually end up compressing the data on *all* the pages in your workbook.

PART

2

Formulas and Functions

CHAPTER

8

Building Basic Formulas

Most Excel fans don't turn to the world's leading spreadsheet software just to create nicely formatted tables. Instead, they rely on Excel's industrial-strength computing muscle, which lets you reduce reams of numbers to neat subtotals and averages. Performing these calculations is the first step in extracting meaningful information from raw data.

Excel provides a number of ways to build formulas, letting you craft them by hand or by pointing-and-clicking them into existence. In this chapter, you'll learn all of Excel's formula-building techniques. You'll start by examining the basic ingredients that make up any formula, and then take a close look at the rules Excel uses when evaluating a formula.

Creating a Basic Formula

First things first: What exactly do formulas do in Excel? A *formula* is a series of instructions that you place in a cell in order to perform some kind of calculation. These instructions may be as simple as telling Excel to sum up a column of numbers, or they may incorporate advanced statistical functions to spot trends and make predictions. But no matter your end goal, all formulas share the same basic characteristics:

- You enter each formula into a single cell.
- Excel calculates the result of a formula every time you open a spreadsheet or change the data a formula uses.
- Most formula results are numbers, but you can create formulas that have text or Boolean (true or false) results, too.

- To view any formula (for example, to gain some insight into how Excel produced a displayed result), you must move to the cell containing the formula, and then look in the *formula bar* (see Figure 8-1). The formula bar also doubles as a handy tool for editing your formulas.
- You can build formulas with ordinary numbers (that you type in) or, more powerfully, by using the contents in other cells.

One of the simplest formulas you can create is this one:

```
=1+1
```

The equal sign is how you tell Excel that you're entering a formula (as opposed to a string of text or numbers). The formula that follows is what you want Excel to calculate. Note that the formula doesn't include the *result*. When creating a formula in Excel, you write the question, and Excel coughs up the answer, as shown in Figure 8-1.

FIGURE 8-1

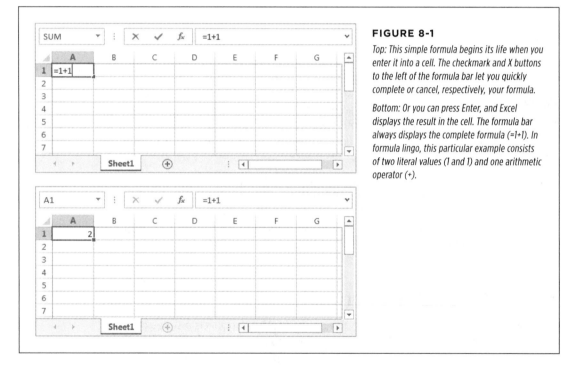

Top: This simple formula begins its life when you enter it into a cell. The checkmark and X buttons to the left of the formula bar let you quickly complete or cancel, respectively, your formula.

Bottom: Or you can press Enter, and Excel displays the result in the cell. The formula bar always displays the complete formula (=1+1). In formula lingo, this particular example consists of two literal values (1 and 1) and one arithmetic operator (+).

All formulas use some combination of the following ingredients:

- **The equal sign (=).** Every formula must begin with the equal sign. It signals to Excel that the cell contains a formula, not just ordinary text.
- **The simple operators.** These ingredients include everything you fondly remember from high-school math class, including addition (+), subtraction (–), multiplication (*), division (/), exponentiation (^), and percent (%). Table 8-1 lists these ingredients, also known as *arithmetic operators*.

- **Numbers.** These ingredients are known as constants or *literal values*, because they never change (unless you edit the formula).
- **Cell references.** These references point to another cell, or a range of cells, that you need data from in order to perform a calculation. For example, say you have a list of 10 numbers. To calculate the average of those numbers, you tell Excel to get the value from each cell, add them up, and then divide by 10.
- **Functions.** Functions are specialized formulas built into Excel that let you perform a wide range of calculations. For example, Excel provides dedicated functions that calculate sums and averages, standard deviations, yields, cosines and tangents, and much more. The next four chapters describe these functions, which span every field from financial accounting to trigonometry.
- **Spaces.** Excel ignores these. However, you can use them to make formulas easier to read. For example, you can write the formula *=3*5+6*2* as *=3*5 + 6*2*. (The only exception to this rule applies to cell ranges, where spaces have a special meaning. You'll see this described on page 231.)

TABLE 8-1 *Excel's arithmetic operators*

OPERATOR	NAME	EXAMPLE	RESULT
+	Addition	=1+1	2
-	Subtraction	=1-1	0
*	Multiplication	=2*2	4
/	Division	=4/2	2
^	Exponentiation	=2^3	8
%	Percent	=20%	0.20

NOTE The percentage (%) operator divides a number by 100.

Excel's Order of Operations

For computer programs and human beings alike, one of the basic challenges when it comes to reading and calculating formulas is figuring out the *order of operations*—mathematician-speak for deciding which calculations to perform first when there's more than one calculation in a formula. For example, given the formula:

```
=10 - 8 * 7
```

the result, depending on your order of operations, is either 14 or –46. Fortunately, Excel abides by the standard rules for the order of operations, meaning it doesn't necessarily process your formulas from left to right. Instead, it evaluates complex formulas piece-by-piece, in this order:

1. Parentheses (Excel always performs any calculations in parentheses first)
2. Percent
3. Exponents
4. Division and Multiplication
5. Addition and Subtraction

NOTE When Excel encounters formulas that contain operators of equal *precedence* (that is, the same order-of-operation priority level), it evaluates these operators from left to right. However, in basic mathematical formulas, this has no effect on the result.

For example, consider the following formula:

```
=5 + 2 * 2 ^ 3 - 1
```

To arrive at the answer of 20, Excel first performs the exponentiation (2 to the power of 3):

```
=5 + 2 * 8 - 1
```

And then the multiplication:

```
=5 + 16 - 1
```

And then the addition and subtraction:

```
=20
```

To control this order, you can add parentheses. For example, notice how adding parentheses affects the result in the following formulas:

```
5 + 2 * 2 ^ (3 - 1) = 13

(5 + 2) * 2 ^ 3 - 1 = 55

(5 + 2) * 2 ^ (3 - 1) = 28

5 + (2 * (2 ^ 3)) - 1 = 20
```

You must always use parentheses in pairs (one open parenthesis for every closing parenthesis). If you don't, Excel gets confused and lets you know you need to fix things, as shown in Figure 8-2.

TIP Remember, when you're working with a lengthy formula, you can expand the formula bar to see several lines of the formula at once. To do so, click the down arrow at the far right of the formula bar (to make it three lines tall), or drag the bottom edge of the formula bar to make it as many lines long as you like. Page 11 shows an example.

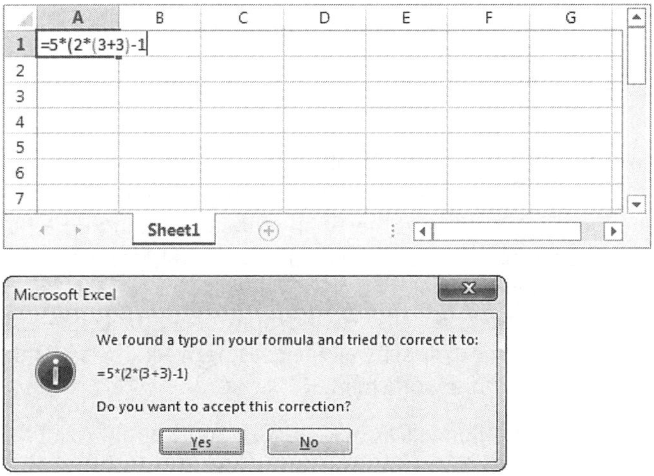

FIGURE 8-2

Top: If you create a formula with a mismatched number of opening and closing parentheses (like this one), Excel won't accept it.

Bottom: Excel offers to correct the formula by adding the missing parenthesis at the end. You may not want this addition, though. If not, cancel the suggestion, and then edit your formula by hand. Excel helps a bit by highlighting matched sets of parentheses. For example, as you move to the opening parenthesis, Excel automatically bolds both the opening and closing parentheses in the formula bar.

GEM IN THE ROUGH

Excel As a Pocket Calculator

Sometimes you need to calculate a value before you enter it into your worksheet. Before you reach for your pocket calculator, you may like to know that Excel lets you enter a formula in a cell, and then use the result in that same cell. This way, the formula disappears and you're left with the result of the calculated value.

Start by typing your formula into the cell (for example *=65*88*). Next, press F9 to perform the calculation. Finally, just hit Enter to insert this value into the cell.

Remember, when you use this technique, you replace your formula with the calculated value. If your calculation is based on the values of other cells, then Excel won't update the result if you change those other cells' values. That's the difference between a cell that has a value, and a cell that has a formula.

Excel has a similar trick that's helpful if you want to take a whole batch of formulas (in different cells), and replace them all with values. It's the Paste Values command. To try it out, select the cells that have the formulas you want to change, copy them (Home→Clipboard→Copy), and then paste them somewhere in your worksheet using the Home→Clipboard→Paste→Paste Values command. The pasted cells display the formulas' calculated values, not the formulas themselves.

Cell References

Excel's formulas are handy when you want to perform a quick calculation. But if you want to take full advantage of Excel's power, you're going to want to perform calculations on the information that's already in your worksheet. To do that, you need to write formulas that use *cell references*—Excel's way of pointing to one or more cells in a worksheet.

For example, say you want to calculate the cost of your Amazonian adventure holiday, based on information like the number of days your trip will last, the price of food and lodging, and the cost of vaccination shots at a travel clinic. If you use cell references, you can enter all this information into different cells, and then write a formula that calculates a grand total. This approach buys you unlimited flexibility because you can change the cell data whenever you want (for example, turning your three-day getaway into a month-long odyssey), and Excel automatically refreshes the formula results.

Cell references are a great way to save a *ton* of time. They come in handy when you want to create a formula that involves a bunch of widely scattered cells whose values frequently change. For example, rather than manually adding up a bunch of subtotals to create a grand total, you can create a grand total formula that uses cell references to point to a handful of subtotal cells. They also let you refer to large groups of cells by specifying a *range* of cells. For example, using the cell reference lingo you'll learn on page 231, you can specify all the cells between the second and 100th rows in the first column of your worksheet.

Every cell reference points to another cell. For example, if you want to point to cell A1 (the cell in column A, row 1), you'd use this cell reference:

```
=A1
```

In Excel-speak, this translates to "get the value from cell A1, and insert it into the current cell." So if you put this formula in cell B1, it displays whatever value's currently in cell A1. In other words, these two cells are now linked.

You can use cell references in formulas the same way you'd use regular numbers. For example, the following formula calculates the sum of two cells, A1 and A2:

```
=A1+A2
```

NOTE In Excel lingo, A1 and A2 are *precedents*, which means they contain information that another cell needs to perform a calculation. Cell B1, which contains the formula, is called the *dependent*, because it depends on the values in cells A1 and A2 to do its work. These terms become important when you need to hunt for errors in a complex calculation using Excel's error-checking tools (page 407).

Provided both cells contain numbers, you'll see the total appear in the cell that contains the formula. If one of the cells contains text, you'll see an error code that starts with a # symbol instead. Errors are described in more detail on page 234.

NOTE This chapter focuses on performing calculations using cells that contain ordinary numbers. Excel also lets you manipulate other types of content in a formula, like text and dates. You'll learn more about these topics in Chapter 11.

How Excel Formats Cells That Contain Cell References

As you learned in Chapter 5, the way you format a cell affects how Excel displays the cell's value. When you create a formula that references other cells, Excel attempts to simplify your life by applying automatic formatting. It reads the number format that the *source cells* (that is, the cells being referred *to*) use, and applies that format to the cell that contains the formula. So if you add two numbers and you formatted both source cells with the Currency number format, your result will have the Currency format, too. Of course, you're always free to change the formatting of the cell after you enter the formula.

Usually, Excel's automatic formatting is quite handy. Like all automatic features, however, it's a little annoying if you don't understand how it works when it springs into action. Here are a few points to consider:

- Excel copies only the number format to the formula cell. It ignores other details, like fonts, fill colors, alignment, and so on. (Of course, you can manually copy formats using the Format Painter, as discussed on page 165.)
- If your formula uses more than one cell reference, and the different cells use different number formats, Excel uses its own rules of precedence to decide which number format to use. For example, if you add a cell that uses the Currency number format with one that uses the Scientific number format, the destination cell has the Scientific number format. Sadly, these rules aren't spelled out anywhere, so if you don't see the result you want, it's best to just set your own formatting.
- If you change the formatting of the source cells *after* you enter the formula, it won't have any effect on the formula cell.
- Excel copies source cell formatting only if the cell that contains the formula uses the General number format (the format that all cells begin with). If you apply another number format to the cell *before* you enter the formula, Excel doesn't copy any formatting from the source cells. Similarly, if you change a formula to refer to new source cells, Excel doesn't copy the format information from the new source cells.

Functions

A good deal of Excel's popularity is due to the collection of *functions* it provides. Functions are built-in, specialized algorithms that you can incorporate into your own formulas to perform powerful calculations. Functions work like miniature computer programs—you supply the data, and the function performs a calculation and gives you the result.

In some cases, functions just simplify calculations that you could probably perform on your own. For example, most people know how to calculate the average of several values, but when you're feeling a bit lazy, Excel's built-in AVERAGE() function automatically gives you the average of any cell range. Even more usefully,

Excel functions perform feats that you probably wouldn't have a hope of coding on your own, including complex mathematical and statistical calculations that predict *trends*—hidden relationships in your data that you can use to make educated guesses or predict the future.

TIP You can create your own Excel functions by writing a series of instructions using VBA (Visual Basic for Applications) code. Chapter 30 shows you how.

Every function provides a slightly different service. For example, one of Excel's statistical functions is named COMBIN(). It's a specialized tool used by probability mathematicians to calculate the number of ways a set of items can be combined. Although this sounds technical, even ordinary folks can use COMBIN() to get some interesting information. For example, you can use the COMBIN() function to count the number of possible outcomes in certain games of chance.

The following formula uses COMBIN() to calculate how many different five-card combinations there are in a standard deck of 52 playing cards:

```
=COMBIN(52,5)
```

Functions are always written in all capitals. (More in a moment on what those numbers inside the parentheses are doing.) However, you don't need to worry about the capitalization of function names, because Excel automatically capitalizes them after you type them in and hit Enter.

UP TO SPEED

Learning New Functions

This book will introduce you to dozens of Excel functions. Sometimes you'll start off by looking at a sample formula that uses the function, but for more complex functions, start by considering the *function description*. You can find function descriptions in Excel; page 247 tells you where to look.

The function description assigns a name to each argument. You can learn about the type of data the function requires before you start wading into an example with real numbers. For example, here's the function description for the COMBIN() function:

```
COMBIN(number_in_set, number_chosen)
```

You can tell the difference between a sample formula and a function description because the function description doesn't include the initial equal sign (=) that you need in all formulas.

Sometimes a function takes an *optional argument*. The argument isn't required, but it may be important depending on the behavior you want. Optional arguments are always shown in square brackets. (Excel uses the same convention in its help and formula tooltips.)

You'll see plenty of function descriptions in this book.

Using a Function in a Formula

Functions alone don't actually *do* anything in Excel. To produce a result, they need to be part of a formula. For example, COMBIN() is a function name. But it only *does* something—that is, give you a result—when you insert it into a formula, like so: *=COMBIN(52,5)*.

Whether you use the simplest or the most complicated function, the function's *syntax*—the rules for including the function in a formula—is always similar. To use a function, you start by typing in the function's name. Excel then helps you out by displaying a pop-up list of matching names as you type, as shown in Figure 8-3. This handy feature is called Formula AutoComplete.

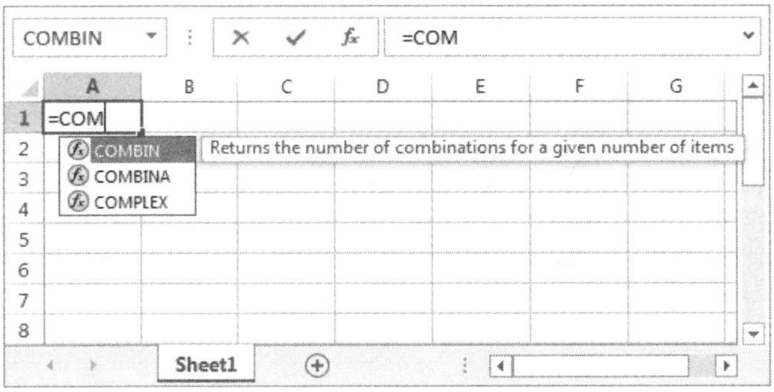

FIGURE 8-3

After you type =COM, Excel helpfully points out that it knows only three functions that start that way: COMBIN(), COMBINA(), and COMPLEX(). If your fingers are getting tired, use the arrow keys to pick the right one out of the list, and then click Tab to pop it into your formula. (Or just double-click the function name.)

After you type the function name, add a pair of parentheses. Then, inside the parentheses, put all the information the function needs to perform its calculations.

In the case of COMBIN(), Excel needs two pieces of information, or *arguments*. The first is the number of items in the set (the 52-card deck), and the second's the number of items you're randomly selecting (in this case, 5). Most functions, like COMBIN(), require two or three arguments. However, some can accept many more, while a few don't need any arguments at all. Once again, Formula AutoComplete guides you by telling you what arguments you need, as shown in Figure 8-4.

Once you type this formula into a cell, the result (2598960) appears in your worksheet. In other words, there are 2,598,960 different possible five-card combinations in any deck of cards. Rather than having to calculate this fact using probability theory—or, heaven forbid, trying to count out the possibilities manually—the COMBIN() function handled it for you.

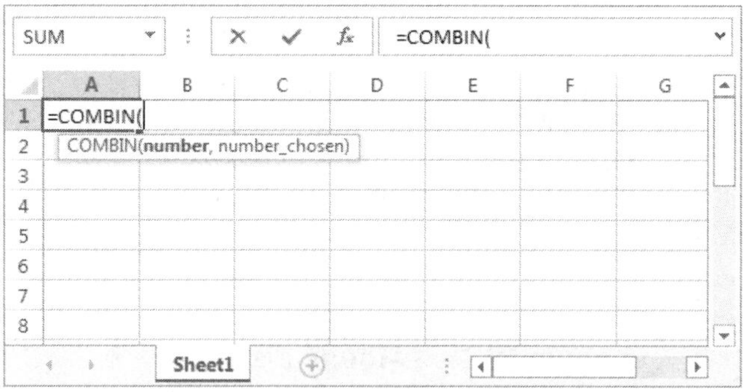

FIGURE 8-4

When you type the opening parenthesis after a function name, Excel displays a tooltip showing you the arguments the function requires. As you type, Excel boldfaces the argument you need to enter next. The argument names aren't crystal clear, but if you already know how the function works, they're usually descriptive enough to jog your memory.

NOTE Even if a function doesn't take any arguments, you still need to supply an empty set of parentheses after the function name. One example is the RAND() function, which generates a random fractional number. The formula =RAND() works fine, but if you forget the parentheses and merely enter *=RAND*, Excel displays an error message (*#NAME?*) that's Excelian for: "Hey! You got the function's name wrong." See Table 8-2 for more on Excel's error messages.

UP TO SPEED

Understanding Functions

Even though it's relatively easy to understand the basics behind how functions work and how to combine them in a formula, that doesn't mean you'll understand what all of Excel's functions do and *why* you should use a particular one. If you don't already know a little probability theory, for instance, then the COMBIN() function may not be very useful. Excel's packed full of advanced functions like COMBIN() that are tailored for statisticians, accountants, and mathematicians. You'll probably never need to use most of them.

But for functions you *are* most likely to use, this book explains them completely. For example, you may not know the financial term *net present value*, but you'll probably still be interested in using Excel's NPV() function to calculate the value of your investments. On the other hand, if you don't know the meaning of a *complex conjugate*—an abstract concept used in some engineering calculations—you won't be interested in the IMCONJUGATE() function.

This book won't explain the math behind these more specialized functions. (In fact, properly explaining some of these concepts would require a book of its own.) Instead, you'll see these arcane functions briefly described in a note or table in the relevant chapter. That way, you can easily find these functions if they're relevant to your work and you already know the underlying math or statistical concepts that power them.

Using Cell References with a Function

One of the particularly powerful things about functions is that they don't necessarily need to use literal values in their arguments. They can also use cell references. For example, you could rewrite the five-card combination formula mentioned earlier so that it specifies the number of cards that'll be drawn from the deck based on a number that you typed in somewhere else in the spreadsheet. Assuming this information is in cell B2, for example, the five-card formula would be:

```
=COMBIN(52, B2)
```

Building on this formula, you can calculate the probability (albeit astronomically low) of getting the exact hand you want in one draw:

```
=1/COMBIN(52,B2)
```

You could even multiply this number by 100 or use the Percent number style to see your percentage chance of getting the cards you want.

TIP Excel offers a detailed guide to its functions, although it doesn't make for light reading (for the most part, it's in IRS-speak). You'll learn more about this reference on page 247.

Using Cell Ranges with a Function

In many cases, you don't want to refer to just a single cell, but rather to a *range* of cells. A range is simply a grouping of multiple cells. They may be next to each other (say, a range that includes all the cells in a single column), or they could be scattered across your worksheet. Ranges are useful for computing averages, totals, and many other calculations.

To group together a series of cells, use one of these three reference operators:

- **The comma (,) separates more than one cell.** For example, the series *A1, B7, H9* is a cell range that contains three cells. The comma's known as the *union operator.* You can add spaces before or after a comma, but Excel just ignores or removes them (depending on its mood).
- **The colon (:) separates the top-left and bottom-right corners of a block of cells.** You're telling Excel: "Hey, use **this** block of cells in my formula." For example, *A1:A5* is a range that includes cells A1, A2, A3, A4, and A5. The range *A2:B3* is a grid that contains cells A2, A3, B2, and B3. The colon is the *range operator*—by far the most powerful way to select multiple cells.
- **The space can find cells that are common to two or more cell ranges.** For example, the expression *A1:A3 A1:B10* is a range that consists of only three cells: A1, A2, and A3 (because those three cells are the only ones found in both ranges). The space is technically the *intersection operator,* and it's not used terribly often.

TIP As you might expect, Excel lets you specify ranges by selecting cells with your mouse, instead of typing in the range manually. You'll see this trick later in this chapter, on page 241.

You can't enter ranges directly into formulas that just use the simple operators. For example, the formula *=A1:B1+5* doesn't work, because Excel doesn't know what to do with the range A1:B1. (Should it sum up the range? Average it? Excel has no way of knowing.) Instead, you need to use ranges with functions that know how to use them. For instance, one of Excel's most basic functions is *SUM()*; it calculates the total for a group of cells. To use the SUM() function, you enter its name, an open parenthesis, the cell range you want to add up, and then a closing parenthesis.

Here's how you can use the SUM() function to add the cells A1, A2, and A3:

```
=SUM(A1,A2,A3)
```

And here's a more compact syntax that performs the same calculation using the range operator:

```
=SUM(A1:A3)
```

A similar SUM() calculation's shown in Figure 8-5. Clearly, if you want to total a column with hundreds of values, it's far easier to specify the first and last cell using the range operator than it is to include each cell reference in your formula!

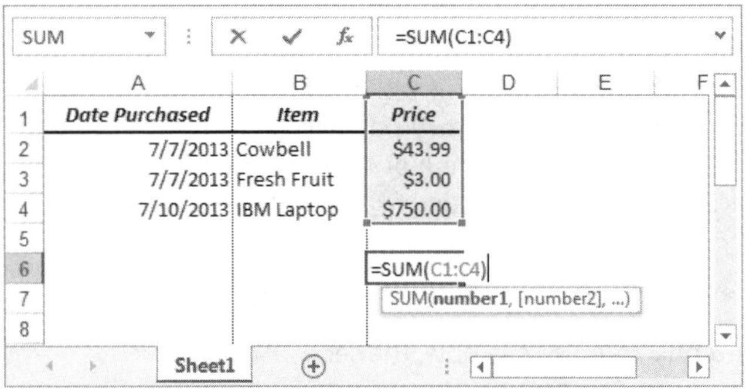

FIGURE 8-5

Using a cell range as the argument in the SUM() function is a quick way to add up a series of numbers in a column. Note that when you enter or edit a formula, Excel highlights all the cells the formula uses with a colored border. In this example, you see the range of cells C2, C3, and C4 in a blue box.

Sometimes your worksheet may have a list with unlimited growth potential, like a list of expenses or a catalog of products. In this case, you can code your formulas to include an *entire* column by leaving out the row number. For example, the range A:A includes all the cells in column A (and, similarly, the range 2:2 includes all the cells in row 2).

The range A:A also includes any heading cells, which isn't a problem for the SUM() function (because it ignores text cells), but could cause problems for other functions. If you don't want to include the top cell, you need to think carefully about how you write the reference. You could create a normal range that stretches from the second cell to the last cell using the mind-blowingly big range A2:A1048576. However, this could cause a problem with older versions of Excel, which don't support as many rows. You're better off creating a table (described in Chapter 14). Tables expand automatically, updating any linked formulas.

Excel Compatibility Functions

Some of Excel's functions use extraordinarily complex logic behind the scenes. Over the years, Excel experts have found minor flaws and quirks in some functions, like cases where the functions deviate from mathematical standards.

Correcting these problems is a bit messy. If different versions of Excel use subtly different calculation logic, you could find that your numbers change unpredictably—for example, when you upgrade your software or when you pass your spreadsheet to a colleague who has a different version of Excel. In such cases, consistency is more important than absolute, theoretical accuracy.

To avoid this sort of situation, Excel's designers rarely change an existing function. Instead, they add a new, similarly named function that replaces the old one. You can recognize a new function by the fact that it has a similar name but incorporates a period. For example, the RANK.AVG() and RANK.EQ() functions replace the old-school RANK() function. Although RANK() still works, Microsoft recommends you use one of its replacements in new worksheets. (If you're curious, the replacements change how Excel ranks tied values, as you'll learn on page 272.) Because RANK() is kicking around only to ensure that old worksheets keep working, it's called a *compatibility function.*

So how do you recognize compatibility functions, to make sure you don't accidentally use one when you actually want the modern replacement? The trick is to read the function tooltip, which clearly identifies compatibility functions, as shown in Figure 8-6.

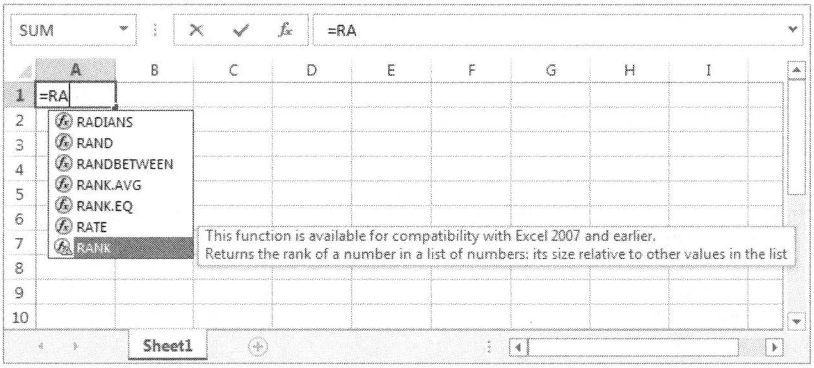

FIGURE 8-6

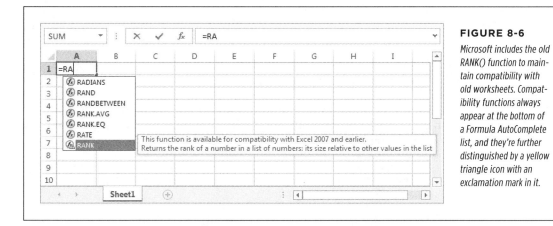

Microsoft includes the old RANK() function to maintain compatibility with old worksheets. Compatibility functions always appear at the bottom of a Formula AutoComplete list, and they're further distinguished by a yellow triangle icon with an exclamation mark in it.

Unfortunately, the case for ditching compatibility functions isn't as clear-cut as it seems. The problem is that the new functions won't work in older versions of Excel. For example, imagine you use a function like RANK.EQ() and send your spreadsheet to a colleague who's using Excel 2007. Because Excel 2007 doesn't know anything about this function, it can't evaluate the formula. Instead, it shows the infamous #NAME? error (page 236) in the cell.

So what do you do? If you plan to keep your work to yourself, or share it with other Excel 2013 fans (but not people using older versions of Excel), you should avoid the compatibility functions in favor of their replacements. But if you need to share work with older versions of Excel, the compatibility functions are the safest choice.

NOTE Almost all the functions you'll learn about in the following chapters are traditional functions that have been with Excel for generations. You'll get a clear warning when we discuss new functions introduced in Excel 2010 or Excel 2013, so you don't use them unknowingly. And if you're still paranoid, you can use the Compatibility Checker (page 31) to scan your worksheet for potential issues, including new functions that won't work in old versions of Excel.

FREQUENTLY ASKED QUESTION

Making Sure Your Formulas Work with Excel 2010

My spreadsheets need to work with Excel 2010, but not necessarily Excel 2007. Should I use the compatibility functions?

Microsoft has introduced new replacement functions in Excel twice—first in Excel 2010, and again in Excel 2013. You can recognize these new functions by the period in their names. However, you can't tell the difference between the replacement functions added in Excel 2013 and those added in Excel 2010.

This is a problem if you plan to share your work with Excel 2010 users. Limiting yourself to using only compatibility functions is unnecessarily restrictive, because there are a number of replacement functions that *do* work in Excel 2010. The only way to find out if Excel 2010 supports the function you want to use is to add the function to a formula and then run the Compatibility Checker (page 31). When the Compatibility Checker spots a new, potentially unsupported function, it tells you which versions of Excel it works with: either Excel 2007 *and* Excel 2010 (which means the function is off-limits), or just Excel 2007 (in which case you can still use the function without causing problems for Excel 2010 users).

Formula Errors

If you make a syntax mistake when entering a formula (like leaving out a function argument or including a mismatched number of parentheses), Excel lets you know right away. Moreover, like a stubborn schoolteacher, it won't accept the formula until you correct it.

It's also possible, though, to write a perfectly legitimate formula that doesn't return a valid answer. Here's an example:

```
=A1/A2
```

If both A1 and A2 have numbers, this formula works without a hitch. However, if you leave cell A2 blank, or if you enter text instead of numbers, Excel can't evaluate the formula, and it reminds you with an error message.

Excel's error messages use an *error code* that begins with the number sign (#) and ends with an exclamation point (!), as shown in Figure 8-7. To continue working, you need to track down the problem and resolve it, which may mean correcting the formula or changing the cells it references.

In addition to the error code, Excel sticks a tiny green triangle in the problematic cell's upper-left corner. When you move to the cell to see what's up, Excel displays a yellow Yield-sign icon with an exclamation point in it. Click the exclamation mark, and you see a menu of choices (as shown in Figure 8-7):

- **Help On This Error** pops open Excel's online help, with a (sometimes cryptic) description of the problem and what could have caused it.
- **Show Calculation Steps** pops open the Evaluate Formula window, where you can work your way through a complex formula one step at a time. Page 401 describes how this advanced feature works.
- **Ignore Error** tells Excel to stop bothering you about this problem, in any worksheet you create. You won't see the green triangle for this error again (although you'll still see the error code in the cell).
- **Edit in Formula Bar** brings you to the formula bar, where you can change the formula to fix a mistake.

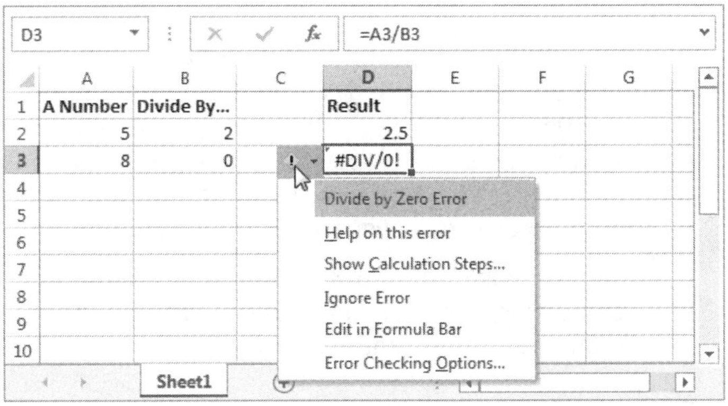

FIGURE 8-7

When Excel spots an error, it inserts a tiny green triangle into the cell's top-left corner. When you move to the offending cell, Excel displays an exclamation mark icon next to it (a smart tag). Hover over the exclamation mark to view a description of the error (which appears in a tooltip), or click the exclamation icon to see a list of menu options.

- **Error Checking Options** opens the Excel Options window, and brings you to the section where you can configure Excel's error-checking and notification settings. You can turn off *background error checking*, for example, or change the color of the tiny error triangles using the settings under the Error Checking heading. (Background error-checking is the feature that plants the tiny green triangle in problematic cells.) You can also tell Excel to start paying attention to errors you previously told it to ignore by clicking the Reset Ignored Errors button. Underneath that button is a section named "Error checking rules" that lets you set options for specific types of errors. For example, you can have Excel ignore numbers stored as text, formulas that ignore part of a range, and other situations that technically aren't errors, but usually indicate that you've done something you didn't mean to. Excel *always* reports genuine errors, like #VALUE! and #NAME?, regardless of the choices you make in this window.

NOTE Sometimes a problem isn't an error, but simply the result of data that hasn't yet been entered. In this case, you can solve the problem by using a conditional *error-trapping formula*. This conditional formula checks to see whether the data's present, and performs the calculation only if it is. The next section shows you one way to use an error-trapping formula.

Table 8-2 lists Excel's error codes.

TABLE 8-2 *Excel's error codes*

ERROR CODE	DESCRIPTION
#VALUE!	You used the wrong type of data. Maybe your function expects a single value and you submitted a whole range. Or, more commonly, you used a function or created a simple arithmetic formula with a cell that contains text instead of numbers.
#NAME?	Excel can't find the name of the function you used. This error code usually means you misspelled a function's name, although it can indicate you used text without quotation marks or left out the empty parentheses after the function name. (Chapter 11 shows you how to use text in a formula.) This error will also occur if you try to use a new function in older versions of Excel (page 31).
#NUM!	There's a problem with one of the numbers you're using. For example, this error code appears when a calculation produces a number that's too large or too small for Excel to deal with.
#DIV/0	You tried to divide by zero. This error code also appears if you try to divide by a cell that's blank, because Excel treats a blank cell as though it contains the number 0 for the purpose of simple calculations with the arithmetic operators. (Some functions, like AVERAGE(), are a little more intelligent and ignore blank cells.)

ERROR CODE	DESCRIPTION
#REF!	Your cell reference is invalid. This error can crop up when you delete or paste over cells you were using in a formula, or when you copy a formula from one worksheet to another. (For information about creating formulas that span worksheets and workbooks, refer to Chapter 13.)
#N/A	The value isn't available. You'll see this error if you try to perform certain types of lookup or statistical functions that work with cell ranges. For example, if you use a function to search a range and it can't find what you need, you may get this result. (You'll learn about lookup functions in Chapter 12.) Sometimes people enter a #N/A value manually in order to tell Excel to ignore a particular cell when creating charts and graphs. However, the easiest way to do this is to use the NA() function (rather than entering the text #N/A, which isn't the same thing at all).
#NULL!	You used the intersection operator (page 231) incorrectly. Remember, the intersection operator finds cells that two ranges have in common. This error results if there are no cells in common. Oftentimes, people use the intersection operator by accident, as the operator's just a single-space character.
########	This code isn't actually an error condition—in all likelihood, Excel has successfully calculated your formula. However, it can't display the result because the number's too wide to fit in the cell using the cell's current number format. To solve this problem, you can widen the column, or change the number format (page 128) if you require a certain number of fixed decimal places.

TIP Chapter 13 describes a collection of Excel tools designed to help you track down the source of an error in a complex formula—especially one where the problem isn't immediately obvious.

TROUBLESHOOTING MOMENT

Circular References

One of the more aggravating errors you might see is the infamous *circular reference*. A circular reference occurs when you create a formula that depends, indirectly or directly, on its own value. For example, consider what happens if you enter the following formula in cell B1.

```
=B1+10
```

For this formula to work, Excel needs to take the current value of B1 and add 10. However, this operation *changes* the value of B1, which means Excel needs to calculate the formula all over again. If unchecked, this process would continue in an endless loop without ever producing a result.

You may encounter more subtle forms of circular references, too. For example, you can create a formula in one cell that refers to a cell in another cell that refers back to the original cell. This is what's known as an *indirect circular reference*, but the problem is the same.

Ordinarily, Excel doesn't allow circular references. When you enter a formula that contains a circular reference, Excel displays an error message and forces you to edit the formula until you remove the reference. However, you can configure Excel to allow circular references by modifying the calculation settings in the Formulas section of the Excel Options window. In this case, Excel repeats the loop a fixed number of times, or until the value seems to settle down and stop changing. You might find this technique useful for calculating certain types of approximations in advanced formulas. But in most cases, this approach is rather dangerous, because it means you don't catch accidental circular references, which can lead to invalid data. A better approach is to use the Solver add-in (page 776), or write a custom function that performs a calculation in a loop using Visual Basic, as described in Chapter 30.

Logical Operators

So far, you've seen the basic arithmetic operators (which are used for addition, subtraction, division, and so on) and the cell reference operators (used to specify one or more cells). There's one final category of operators you'll find useful when creating formulas: *logical operators.*

Logical operators let you build conditions into your formulas so the formulas produce different values depending on the value of the data they encounter. You can use a condition with cell references or literal values.

For example, the condition A2=A4 is true if cell A2 contains the same value as cell A4. On the other hand, if these cells contain different values (say 2 and 3), the formula generates a false value. Using conditions is a stepping-stone to using conditional logic. Conditional logic lets you perform different calculations based on different scenarios.

For example, you can use conditional logic to see how large an order is, and provide a discount if the total order cost's over $5,000. Excel *evaluates* the condition, meaning it determines if the condition is true or false. You can then tell Excel what to do, based on that that evaluation.

Table 8-3 lists all the logical operators you can use to build formulas.

TABLE 8-3 *Logical operators*

OPERATOR	NAME	EXAMPLE	RESULT
=	Equal to	1=2	FALSE
>	Greater than	1>2	FALSE
<	Less than	1<2	TRUE
>=	Greater than or equal to	1>=1	TRUE
<=	Less than or equal to	1<=1	TRUE
<>	Not equal to	1<>1	FALSE

You can use logical operators to build standalone formulas, but that's not particularly useful. For example, here's a formula that tests whether cell A2 contains the number 3:

```
=(A2=3)
```

The parentheses aren't actually required, but they make the formula a little bit clearer, emphasizing the fact that Excel evaluates the condition first, and then displays the result in the cell. If you type this formula into a cell, Excel displays, in uppercase, either the word TRUE or FALSE, depending on the content in cell A2.

On their own, logical operators don't accomplish much. But they really shine when you start combining them with other functions to build conditional logic. For example, you can use the SUMIF() function, which totals the value of certain rows, depending on whether the row matches a set condition. Or you can use the IF() function to determine what calculation you should perform.

The IF() function has the following function description:

```
IF(condition, [value_if_true], [value_if_false])
```

In English, this line of code translates to: If the condition is true, display the second argument in the cell; if the condition is false, display the third argument.

Consider this formula:

```
=IF(A1=B2, "These numbers are equal", "These numbers are not equal")
```

This formula tests to see whether the value in cell A1 equals the value in cell B2. If it does, Excel displays the message "These numbers are equal" in the cell. Otherwise, you'll see "These numbers are not equal."

NOTE If you see a quotation mark in a formula, it's because that formula uses text. You must surround all literal text values with quotation marks. (Numbers are different: You can enter them directly into a formula.)

People often use the IF() function to prevent Excel from performing a calculation if some of the data is missing. Consider the following formula:

```
=A1/A2
```

This formula causes a divide-by-zero error if A2 is empty or contains a 0 value. Excel then displays an error code in the cell. To prevent this from happening, you can replace this formula with the conditional formula shown here:

```
=IF(A2=0, 0, A1/A2)
```

This formula checks to see if cell A2 is empty or contains a 0. If so, the condition's true, and the formula simply gives you a 0. If it isn't, the condition's false, and Excel performs the calculation A1/A2.

Practical examples of conditional logic abound in Chapters 12 and 13.

FREQUENTLY ASKED QUESTION

Showing and Printing Formulas

How in the world do I print out formulas that appear in my cells?

When you print a worksheet, Excel prints the calculated value in each cell rather than any formula that happens to be inside the cell. Usually, that's what you want to happen. But in some cases, you want to see or print the calculations that generated the results.

Excel lets you do that by choosing Formulas→Formula Auditing→Show Formulas. Now, Excel displays the cells' formulas instead of the results—but on the current worksheet only. (Excel simultaneously widens the columns to show more information, since formulas tend to be longer than their results.) Choose Formulas→Formula Auditing→Show Formulas again to return to normal life.

Formula Shortcuts

So far, you've learned how to build a formula by entering it manually. That's a good way to start out because it forces you to understand the basics of formula-writing. But writing formulas by hand is a drag; plus, it's easy to type in the wrong cell address. For example, if you type A2 instead of A3, you can end up with incorrect data, and you won't necessarily notice your mistake.

As you become more comfortable with formulas, you'll find that Excel gives you a few tools—like point-and-click formula creation and the Insert Function button—to speed up your formula writing and reduce your mistakes. You'll learn about these features in the following sections.

Point-and-Click Formula Creation

Instead of entering a formula by typing it out letter-by-letter, Excel lets you create formulas by clicking the cells you want to use. For example, consider this simple formula that totals the numbers in two cells:

```
=A1+A2
```

To build this formula by clicking, just follow these steps:

1. **Move to the cell where you want to enter the formula.**

   This cell's where the result of your formula's calculation will appear. While you can pick any cell on the worksheet, A3 works nicely because it's directly below the two cells you're adding.

2. **Press the equal sign (=) key.**

   The equal sign tells Excel you're entering a formula.

3. **Move to the first cell you want to use in your formula (in this case, A1).**

   You can move to this first cell by pressing the up arrow key twice, or by clicking the cell with the mouse. You'll notice that moving to another cell doesn't cancel your edit, as it would normally, because Excel recognizes that you're building a formula. When you move to the new cell, the cell reference appears automatically in the formula (which Excel displays in cell A3, as well as in the formula bar just above your worksheet). If you move to another cell, Excel changes the cell reference accordingly.

4. **Press the + key.**

   Excel brings you back to the cell with the formula (A3) and adds the + sign. Now the formula reads *=A1+*.

5. **Finish the formula by moving to cell A2, and then pressing Enter.**

   Again, you can move to A2 either by pressing the up arrow key or by clicking the cell directly. Remember, you can't just finish the formula by moving somewhere else; you need to press Enter to tell Excel you're finished writing the formula. Another way to complete your edit is to click the checkmark that appears on the formula bar, to the left of the current formula. Even experienced Excel fans get frustrated with this step. If you click another cell before you press Enter, you won't move to the cell—instead, Excel inserts the cell into your formula.

TIP You can use this technique with any formula. Just type in the operators, function names, and so on, and use the mouse to select the cell references. If you need to select a range of cells, then just drag your mouse to highlight the whole group of cells. You can practice this technique with the SUM() function. Start by typing *=SUM(* into the cell, and then selecting the range of cells you want to add. Finish by adding a final closing parenthesis, and then press Enter.

Point-and-Click Formula Editing

You can use a similar approach to edit formulas, although it's slightly trickier.

1. **Move to the cell that contains the formula you want to edit, and then put it in edit mode by double-clicking it or pressing F2.**

   Excel highlights the borders of any cell used in this formula with a colored outline. Excel's even clever enough to use a helpful color-coding system: It displays each of the cell references using the same color it used to outline the cell itself. This helps you quickly identify the original cell.

2. **Click the outline of the cell you want to change. (Your pointer changes from a fat plus sign to a four-headed arrow when you're over the outline.) With the mouse button still held down, drag this outline over to the new cell (or cells) you want to use.**

   Excel updates the formula automatically. You can also expand and shrink cell range references. To do so, put the formula-holding cell into edit mode, and then click any corner of the border that surrounds the range you want to change. Next, drag the border to change the size of the range. If you want to move the range, click any part of the range border, and then drag the outline in the same way as you would with a cell reference.

3. **Press Enter or click the formula bar checkmark to accept your changes.**

   That's it.

The Formulas Tab

Excel's ribbon offers a few buttons that make formula-writing easier. To take a look, click the Formulas tab.

The most important commands under the Formulas tab reside in the Function Library section at the left. It includes the indispensable Insert Function button, which you'll take for a spin in the next section. It also includes many more buttons that set out Excel's vast catalog of functions in related categories for easier access. Figure 8-8 shows how it works.

The Formulas→Function Library section of the ribbon lets you pick a function from one of the following categories:

- **AutoSum** has a few shortcuts that let you quickly add, average, or otherwise deal with a list of numbers. You'll see how they work on page 268.
- **Recently Used** has exactly what you'd expect—functions you recently used in a formula. If you're just starting out with functions, you'll see that Excel fills the Recently Used list with a small set of commonly used functions, like SUM().
- **Financial** functions let you track your car loan payments and calculate how many more years until you can retire rich. You'll tackle them in Chapter 10.

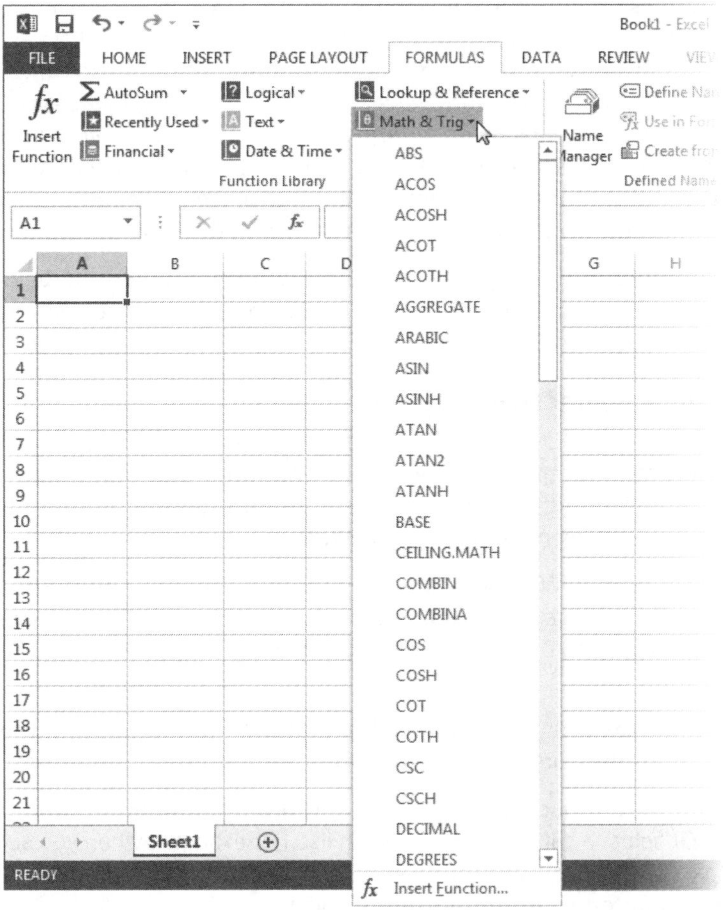

FIGURE 8-8

Each button in the Function Library (other than Insert Function) pops up a mini menu of Excel functions. Choose one, and Excel inserts that function into the current formula. You can use this technique to find functions you've used recently, or to browse the main function categories. This example shows some of the functions in the Math & Trig section, which you'll explore in the next chapter.

- **Logical** functions let you add conditional logic to formulas. You already had a quick introduction to conditional logic earlier in this chapter, but you'll get more details in Chapter 13.
- **Text** functions manipulate words, sentences, and other non-numeric information. Chapter 11 has the scoop.
- **Date & Time** functions perform calendar math, and can help you sort out ages, due dates, and more. You'll try them out in Chapter 11.
- **Lookup & Reference** functions perform the slightly mind-bending feat of searching for information in other cells. You'll see why they're so useful in Chapter 12.

- **Math & Trig** functions are the mathematic basics, including sums, rounding, and all the other high-school trigonometry you're trying to forget. Chapter 9 explores this section.
- **More Functions** groups together some heavy-duty Excel functions intended for specialized purposes. This category includes high-powered statistical and engineering functions. It also includes *cube* functions, which are designed for working in highly technical OLAP (*online analytical processing*) databases, and information functions, which get "information" about the other cells in your worksheet. You won't see all these functions used in this book, because some are reserved for true specialists, but you'll dip your toe into a few statistical functions in Chapter 9, and you'll explore information functions in Chapter 12.

The Function Library isn't the only part of the Formulas tab you'll use. To the right of the Function section are buttons for using named cells, tracking down errors, and changing calculation settings (three techniques you'll pick up in Chapter 13).

Using the Insert Function Button

Excel provides more than 300 built-in functions. But to use a function, you need to type its name *exactly*. That means that every time you want to employ a function, you need to refer to this book, call on your own incredible powers of recollection, or click over to the convenient Insert Function button.

To use the Insert Function feature, choose Formulas→Function Library→Insert Function. However, formula pros skip straight to the action by clicking the *fx* button that appears just to the left of the formula bar. (Or they press the Shift+F3 shortcut key.)

No matter which approach you use, Excel displays the Insert Function window (shown in Figure 8-9), which offers three ways to search for and insert any of Excel's functions.

- If you're looking for a function, the easiest way to find one is to choose a category from the "Or select a category" drop-down list. For example, when you select the Math & Trig category, you see a list of functions with names like SIN() and COS(), which perform basic trigonometric calculations.
- If you choose the Most Recently Used category, you'll see a list of functions you recently picked from the ribbon or the Insert Function window.
- If you're really ambitious, you can type a couple of keywords into the "Search for a function" box and then click Go to execute the search. Excel gives you a list of functions that match your keywords.

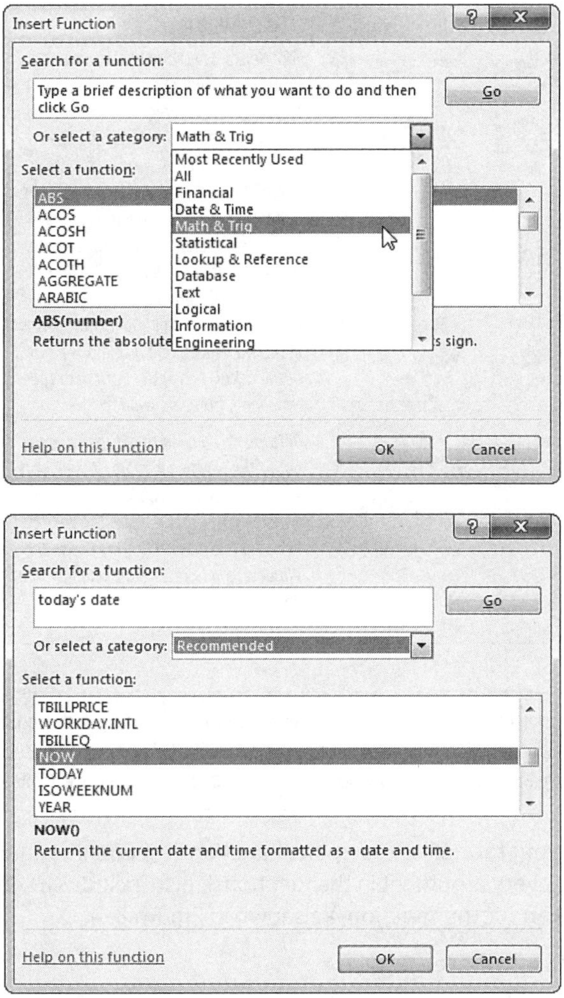

FIGURE 8-9

Top: The Insert Function window lets you quickly find the function you need. You can choose a category that seems likely to have the functions you're interested in.

Bottom: You can also try to search by entering keywords in the "Search for a function" box. Either way, when you click one of the functions in the list, Excel presents you with a description of the function at the bottom of the window.

When you spot a function that looks promising, click it once to highlight its name. Excel displays a brief description of the function at the bottom of the window. For more information, you can click the "Help on this function" link in the bottom-left corner of the window. To build a formula using this function, click OK.

Excel then inserts the function into the currently active cell, followed by a set of parentheses. Next, it closes the Insert Function window, and then opens the Function Arguments window (Figure 8-10).

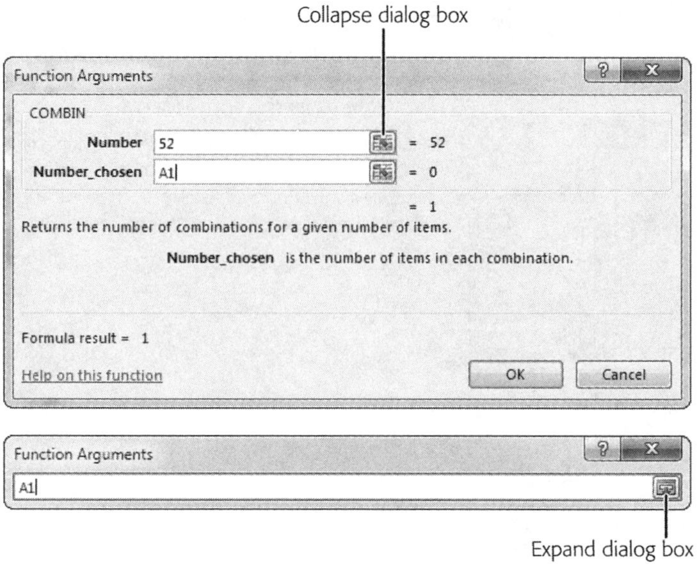

FIGURE 8-10

Top: Here's what happens when you insert the COMBIN() function. Because the COMBIN() function requires two arguments (Number and Number_chosen), the Function Arguments window shows two text boxes. The first argument uses a literal value (52), while the second uses a cell reference (A1). (You can use literal values or a cell reference for either argument—it's up to you.) As you enter the arguments, Excel updates the formula in the worksheet, and displays the result of the calculation at the bottom of the Function Arguments window.

Bottom: If you need to get the window out of the way to see more of your worksheet and select cells, click the Collapse Window icon—that reduces the window to a single text box. Click the Expand Window icon to restore the window to its normal size.

NOTE Depending on the function you use, Excel may make a (somewhat wild) guess about which arguments you want to supply. For example, if you use the Insert Function window to add a SUM() function, you'll see that Excel picks a nearby range of cells. If that isn't what you want, just replace the range with the correct values.

Now you can finish creating your formula by using the Function Arguments window, which includes a text box for every argument in the function. It also includes a "help" link for detailed information about the function, as shown in Figure 8-11.

To complete your formula, follow these steps:

1. **Click the text box for the first argument.**

   A brief sentence describing the argument appears in the Function Arguments window.

   Some functions don't require any arguments. In such a case, you won't see any text boxes, although you still see some basic information about the function. Skip directly to step 4.

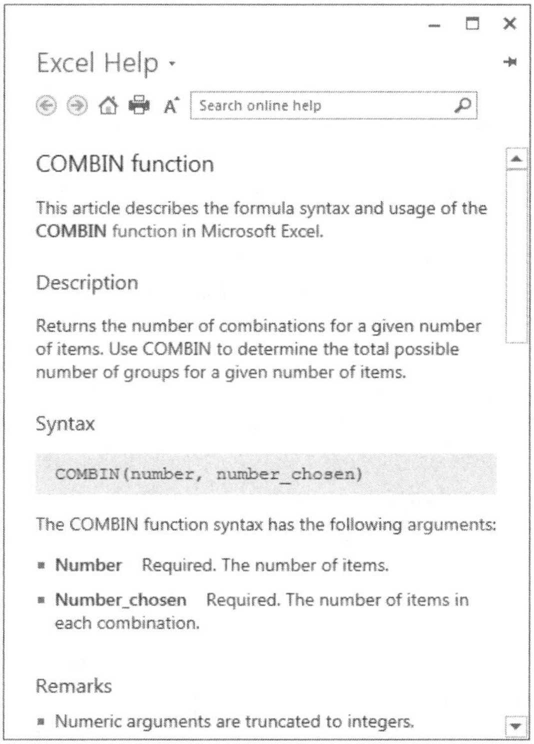

FIGURE 8-11

Both the Insert Function and Function Arguments windows make it easy to get detailed information on any function by clicking the "Help on this function" link at the bottom left of the window, seen in Figure 8-10. The help page includes a brief description, important notes, and a couple of sample formulas that use the function, complete with results.

2. **Enter a value for the argument.**

   If you want to enter a literal value (like the number 52), type it in now. To enter a cell reference, you can type it in manually, or click the appropriate cell in the worksheet. To enter a range of cells, drag your cursor to select a group of cells.

   You may need to move the Function Arguments window to the side to expose the part of the worksheet you want to click. The Collapse Window icon (located to the immediate right of each text box) is helpful since clicking it shrinks the window's size. This way, you'll have an easier time selecting cells from your worksheet. To return the window to normal, click the same button, which has changed to an Expand Window icon.

3. **Repeat step 2 for each argument in the function.**

   As you enter the arguments, Excel updates the formula automatically.

4. **Once you specify a value for every required argument, click OK.**

   Excel closes the window and returns you to your worksheet.

POWER USERS' CLINIC

Functions That Return Arrays

A few exotic functions actually give you *multiple* results, so rather than simply generating a single value, as a function like SUM() would, these functions generate more than one value. To use these functions properly, you need to create a special type of formula called an *array formula*. (In Excel geek-speak, an array is a group of numbers, and an array formula is a formula whose result is an array .)

To create an array formula, you begin by selecting all the cells that Excel should use to display the results. (The exact number of cells you need depends on the function you're using and the calculation you're performing.) Then, with all these cells selected, you type in the formula you want and press Ctrl+Shift+Enter. It's this final keystroke that actually creates the array formula and links the selected cells together. Usually, you'll see a different result appear in each cell.

You can recognize an array formula by inspecting any of the linked cells it in the formula bar. Unlike normal formulas, array formulas are wrapped in curly braces { }. If you try to edit one of these cells, Excel warns you that you can't change just part of an array. Instead, you need to select all the cells in the array, edit the formula, and then press Ctrl+Shift+Enter to recreate it.

To get a better feel for array formulas, try one out for yourself. Some functions that require array formulas include FREQUENCY (page 276), TREND (page 294), and TRANSPOSE (page 363) .

Copying Formulas

Sometimes you need to perform similar calculations in different cells throughout a worksheet. For example, say you want to calculate sales tax on each item in a product catalog, the monthly sales in each store of a company, or the final grade for each student in a class. In this section, you'll learn how Excel makes it easy with *relative cell references*. Relative cell references are those that Excel updates automatically when you copy them from one cell into another. They're the standard kind of references that Excel uses (as opposed to absolute cell references, which are covered in the next section). In fact, all the references you've used so far have been relative references, but you haven't yet seen how they work with copy-and-paste operations.

Consider the worksheet in Figure 8-12, which represents a teacher's grade book. In this example, each student has three grades: two tests and one assignment. A student's final grade is based on the following percentages: 25 percent for each of the two tests, and 50 percent for the assignment.

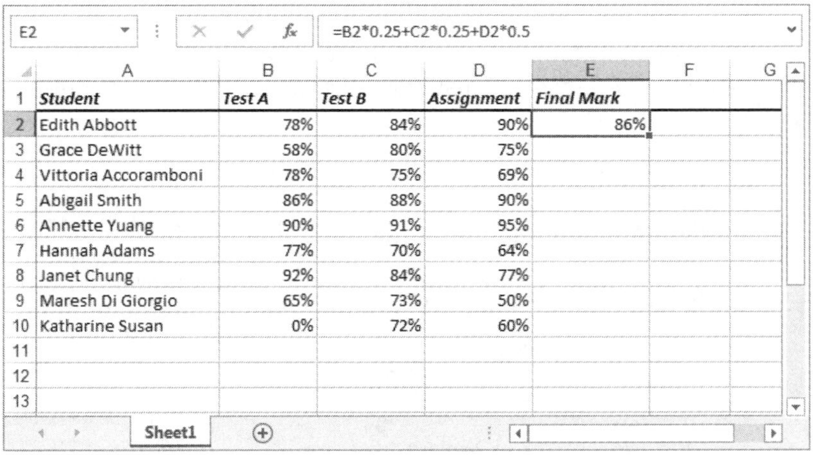

E2 =B2*0.25+C2*0.25+D2*0.5

	A	B	C	D	E	F	G
1	*Student*	*Test A*	*Test B*	*Assignment*	*Final Mark*		
2	Edith Abbott	78%	84%	90%	86%		
3	Grace DeWitt	58%	80%	75%			
4	Vittoria Accoramboni	78%	75%	69%			
5	Abigail Smith	86%	88%	90%			
6	Annette Yuang	90%	91%	95%			
7	Hannah Adams	77%	70%	64%			
8	Janet Chung	92%	84%	77%			
9	Maresh Di Giorgio	65%	73%	50%			
10	Katharine Susan	0%	72%	60%			
11							
12							
13							

FIGURE 8-12

This worksheet shows a list of students in a class, and calculates the final grade for each student using two test scores and an assignment score. So far, the only formula that's been added is for the first student (in cell E2).

The following formula calculates the final grade for the first student (Edith Abbott):

```
=B2*25% + C2*25% + D2*50%
```

The formula that calculates the final mark for the second student (Grace DeWitt) is almost identical. The only change is that all the cell references are offset by one row, so that B2 becomes B3, C2 becomes C3, and D2 becomes D3:

```
=B3*25% + C3*25% + D3*50%
```

You may get fed-up entering all these formulas by hand. A far easier approach is to copy the formula from one cell to another. Here's how:

1. **Move to the cell containing the formula you want to copy.**

   In this example, you'd move to cell E2.

2. **Copy the formula to the Clipboard by pressing Ctrl+C.**

   You can also copy the formula by choosing Home→Clipboard→Copy.

3. **Select the range of cells you want to copy the formula into.**

   Select cells E3 to E10.

4. **Paste in the new formulas by pressing Ctrl+V.**

   You can also paste the formula by choosing Home→Clipboard→Paste.

   When you paste a formula, Excel magically copies an appropriate version of the formula into each of the cells from E3 to E10. Excel makes these automatic adjustments for any formula, whether the formula uses functions or just simple operators. Excel then automatically calculates and displays the results, as shown in Figure 8-13.

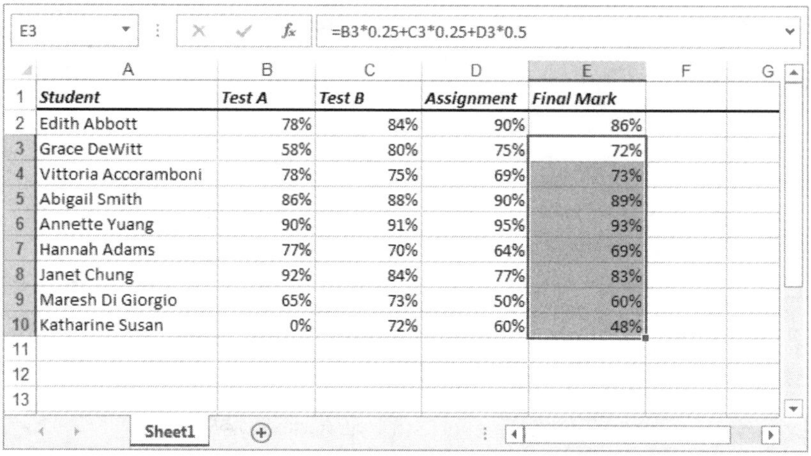

E3
=B3*0.25+C3*0.25+D3*0.5
Student
Test A
Test B
Assignment
Final Mark
Edith Abbott 78% 84% 90% 86%
Grace DeWitt 58% 80% 75% 72%
Vittoria Accoramboni 78% 75% 69% 73%
Abigail Smith 86% 88% 90% 89%
Annette Yuang 90% 91% 95% 93%
Hannah Adams 77% 70% 64% 69%
Janet Chung 92% 84% 77% 83%
Maresh Di Giorgio 65% 73% 50% 60%
Katharine Susan 0% 72% 60% 48%
Sheet1

FIGURE 8-13

When you paste the formula into one or more new cells, each Final Grade formula operates on the data in its own row. This means that you don't need to tweak the formula for each student. Here, the formula bar shows the formula in cell E3.

TIP There's an even quicker way to copy a formula to multiple cells—the AutoFill feature introduced in Chapter 2 (page 62). In the student grade example, you start by moving to cell E2, which contains the original formula. Click and hold the small square at the bottom-right corner of the cell outline, and then drag the outline down until it includes all the destination cells, from E3 to E10. When you release the mouse button, Excel inserts copies of the formula in the AutoFill region.

POWER USERS' CLINIC

Cell Formulas "Under the Hood"

To understand how Excel adjusts copied formulas, you need to know a little more about how Excel stores formulas. Internally, Excel formulas are actually stored using a system called R1C1 reference (page 12). With R1C1 referencing, when you create a formula, it doesn't contain cell references; instead, it contains cell *offsets*. Offsets tell Excel how to find a cell based on its position relative to the current cell, as you'll see below.

For example, in the student grade calculation shown in Figure 8-11, the formula:

```
=B2*25% + C2*25% + D2*50%
```

looks like this in R1C1 representation:

```
=RC[-3]*25% + RC[-2]*25% + RC[-1]*50%
```

Notice that Excel has translated the cell reference B2 into the notation RC[-3], which means "get the number in the same row, but three columns to the left." If the formula were using a number from the row above, you'd see an R1C1 reference like R[-1]C[-3], which would tell Excel to go one row up and three columns to the left. Negative numbers in relative cell referencing indicate movement to the left (for columns) or up (for rows); positive numbers indicate movement to the right (columns) or down (rows).

When you copy a formula from one cell to another, Excel actually copies the R1C1 formula, rather than the formula you entered (unless you instructed Excel to use absolute cell references, as explained in the section below this box). To view your formulas in R1C1 style, you can temporarily change the type of cell addressing your spreadsheet uses. (See page 12 for instructions.) You'll probably want to turn this mode off when you're about to create a formula, as it's almost always easier to write formulas using Excel's standard cell addressing.

Absolute Cell References

Relative references are a true convenience since they let you create formula copies that don't need the slightest bit of editing. But you've probably already realized that relative references don't always work. For example, what if you have a value in a specific cell that you want to use in multiple calculations? You may have a currency conversion ratio that you want to use in a list of expenses. Each item in the list needs to use the same cell to perform the conversion correctly. But if you make copies of the formula using relative cell references, Excel adjusts this reference automatically and the formula ends up referring to the wrong cell (and therefore the wrong conversion value).

Figure 8-14 shows the problem with the worksheet of student grades. In this example, the test and assignment scores aren't all graded out of 100 possible points; each test and assignment has a different total score (listed in row 12). To calculate the percentage score a student earned on a test, you need to divide the test score by the total score available. This formula, for example, calculates the percentage for Edith Abbott's performance on Test B:

```
=B2/B12*100%
```

To calculate Edith's final grade for the class, you use the following formula:

```
=B2/B12*25% + C2/C12*25% + D2/D12*50%
```

Like many formulas, this one contains a mix of cells that should be relative (the individual scores in cells B2, C2, and D2) and those that should be absolute (the possible totals in cell B12, C12, and D12). As you copy this formula to subsequent rows, Excel incorrectly changes all the cell references, causing a calculation error.

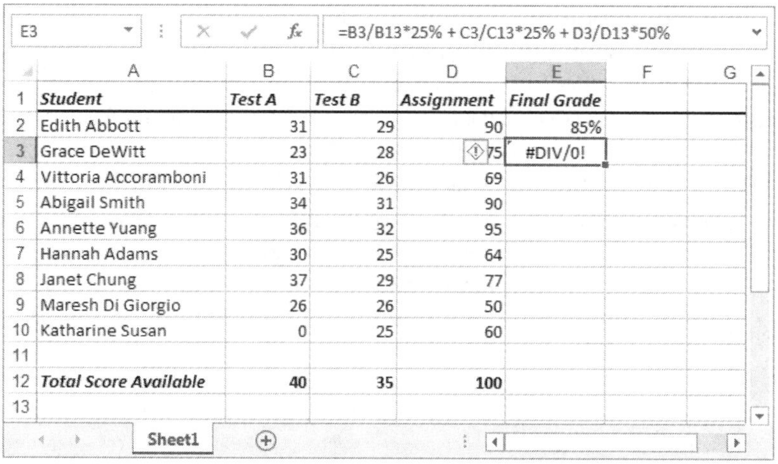

	A	B	C	D	E
1	*Student*	*Test A*	*Test B*	*Assignment*	*Final Grade*
2	Edith Abbott	31	29	90	85%
3	Grace DeWitt	23	28	75	#DIV/0!
4	Vittoria Accoramboni	31	26	69	
5	Abigail Smith	34	31	90	
6	Annette Yuang	36	32	95	
7	Hannah Adams	30	25	64	
8	Janet Chung	37	29	77	
9	Maresh Di Giorgio	26	26	50	
10	Katharine Susan	0	25	60	
11					
12	***Total Score Available***	**40**	**35**	**100**	
13					

FIGURE 8-14

In this version of the student gradebook, both the tests and the assignment are graded on different scales (as listed in row 12). Thus, the formula for calculating the final class grade uses the values in cells B12, C12, and D12. When you copy the Final Grade formula from the first row (cell E2) to the rows below it, Excel offsets the formula to use B13, C13, and D13—none of which exist. Thus, you run into a problem—shown here as a divide-by-zero error. To fix this, you need to use absolute cell references.

Fortunately, Excel provides a perfect solution. It lets you use *absolute cell references*—cell references that always refer to the same cell. When you create a copy of a formula that contains an absolute cell reference, Excel doesn't change the reference (as it does when you use *relative* cell references; see the previous section). To indicate that a cell reference is absolute, you use the dollar sign ($) character in the reference. For example, to change B12 into an absolute reference, you add the $ character twice, once in front of the column and once in front of the row, which changes it to $B$12.

Here's the corrected class grade formula for Edith, using absolute cell references:

```
=B2/$B$12*25% + C2/$C$12*25% + D2/$D$12*50%
```

This formula still produces the same result for the first student. However, you can now copy it correctly for use with the other students. To copy this formula into all the cells in column E, use the same procedure described in the previous section on relative cell references.

Partially Fixed References

You might wonder why you need to use the $ character twice in an absolute reference (before the column letter *and* the row number). The reason is that Excel lets you create *partially* fixed references. To understand partially fixed references, it helps to remember that every cell reference consists of a column letter and a row number.

With a partial fixed reference, Excel updates one component (say, the column part) but not the other (the row) when you copy the formula. If this sounds complex (or a little bizarre), consider a few examples:

- You have a loan rate in cell A1, and you want all loans on an entire worksheet to use that rate in calculations. If you refer to the cell as $A$1, its column and row always stay the same when you copy the formula to another cell.
- You have several rows of loan information. The first column of a row always contains the loan rate for the loans on that row. In your formula cell, if you refer to cell $A1, then, when you copy the formula across columns and rows, the row changes (to 2, 3, 4, and so on) but the column doesn't (so your formula will reference cells A2, A3, A4, and so on).
- You have a table of loan rates organized by the length of the loan (10-year, 15-year, 20-year, and so on) along the top of a worksheet. Excel calculates the loans in each column using the rate specified at the top of that column. If you refer to the rate cell as A$1 in your first column's formula, the row stays constant (1), but the column changes (B1, C1, D1, and so on) as you copy the formula across columns and down rows.

TIP You can quickly change formula references into absolute or partially fixed references. First, put the cell into edit mode by double-clicking it or pressing F2. Then move through the formula and highlight the appropriate cell reference. Now, press F4 to change the cell reference. Each time you press F4, the reference changes. If the reference is A1, for instance, it becomes $A$1, then A$1, then $A1, and then A1 again.

UP TO SPEED

Creating an Exact Formula Copy

There's another way to copy a formula that prevents Excel from automatically changing the formula's cell references. The trick is to copy the formula itself rather than copy the whole cell (which is what you do when you use a basic copy-and-paste operation on a formula).

The process takes a few more steps, and it lets you paste only one copy at a time, but it can still come in handy if you don't want Excel to use relative references. Here's how it works:

1. First, move to the cell that contains the formula you want to copy.
2. In the formula bar, select all the text in the cell. You can use the mouse, or you can use the arrow keys (just hold down Shift as you scroll from the beginning to the end of the cell).
3. Once you select the complete formula, press Ctrl+C to copy it.
4. Press Esc to leave edit mode.
5. Move to the new cell, and then press Ctrl+V to paste the formula.

Keep in mind that when you use this approach, you create an exact copy of the formula. That means that this technique doesn't help in situations where some cell references need to be absolute, and others need to be relative.

Referring to Other Worksheets

To reference a cell in another worksheet, you simply need to preface the cell with the worksheet name, followed by an exclamation mark. For example, say you created a formula to double the value of the number in cell A1 in a worksheet named Sheet1. You'd use this formula:

```
=A1*2
```

If you want to use the same formula in another worksheet (in the same workbook), you'd insert this formula in the new worksheet:

```
=Sheet1!A1*2
```

NOTE If you use the point-and-click method to build formulas, you'll find that you don't need to worry about the syntax for referring to cells on other worksheets. If you switch to another worksheet, and then click a cell in it as you build a formula, Excel automatically inserts the correct reference, complete with the worksheet name.

Referring to Other Workbooks

It's fairly common for one worksheet to reference another within the same workbook file. (For a refresher on the difference between worksheets and workbooks, see page 108.) On page 369, you'll see an example where one worksheet includes a product catalog, and a second one builds an invoice. In that example, the second worksheet uses formulas that refer to data in the first sheet.

It's less common for a worksheet to refer to data in another *file*. The potential problem with this type of link is that there's no way to guarantee that referenced files will always be available—if you rename the referenced file or move it to a different folder, the link breaks. Fortunately, Excel doesn't leave you completely stranded in this situation—instead, it continues with the most recent version of the data it was able to retrieve. You can also tweak the link to point to the new location of the file.

To create a link to a cell in another workbook, you need to put the file name at the beginning of the reference, and then enclose it in square brackets. You follow the file name with the sheet name, an exclamation mark, and then the cell address. Here's an example:

```
=[SimpleExpenses.xlsx]Sheet1!B3
```

If the file name or the sheet name contains any spaces, you need to enclose the whole initial portion inside apostrophes, like so:

```
='[Simple Expenses.xlsx]Sheet1'!B3
```

When you enter this formula, Excel checks to see if this file is already open in another Excel window. If not, Excel attempts to find the file in the current folder (that is, the folder that holds the workbook you're editing). If it can't find the file, it shows a standard Open window. You can use this window to browse to the file you want to use. Once you select the file, Excel updates the formula accordingly.

NOTE Once again, if you use point-and-click formula creation (for example, start entering a formula in one workbook, and then click a cell in another workbook), Excel will add the right cell reference, complete with the appropriate file name.

Excel performs a little sleight of hand with formulas that reference other files. If the referenced workbook's currently open, the formula displays only the file name. However, once you close the referenced file, the formula changes so that it includes the full folder path. Excel makes this change automatically, whether you type a file name in by hand or build the formula by pointing and clicking cells in another open workbook.

Here's an example of what the full formula looks like when you close the file that contains the Sheet1 worksheet:

```
='[C:\Users\Matthew\Documents\Simple Expenses.xlsx]Sheet1'!B3
```

UPDATING LINKS

As you know, the point of a reference is to get the latest information out of a cell. But when you create a formula that references a cell in another workbook, life gets a bit more complicated.

As long as your linked workbook is currently open, Excel spots any changes right away. For example, imagine you have a workbook named Summary.xlsx that refers to cell B3 in a workbook named SimpleExpenses.xlsx (as shown in the previous example). When you modify the number in B3 in SimpleExpenses.xlsx, Excel recalculates the linked formula in Summary.xlsx immediately.

It's a different story if you work with both files *separately*. For example, imagine you close Summary.xlsx, change the total in SimpleExpenses.xlsx, and then close SimpleExpenses.xlsx. The next time you open Summary.xlsx, Excel is in a difficult position. It needs to get the updated information in SimpleExpenses.xlsx, but it doesn't want to open the file to do so (at least not without your OK). So instead, the Summary.xlsx file uses the most recent information—the value it pulled out of cell B3 the last time SimpleExpenses.xlsx was open.

The first time you open a workbook with linked formulas, Excel shows a message bar just above the grid of cells, warning you that it hasn't retrieved the latest information from the referenced workbook (Figure 8-15).

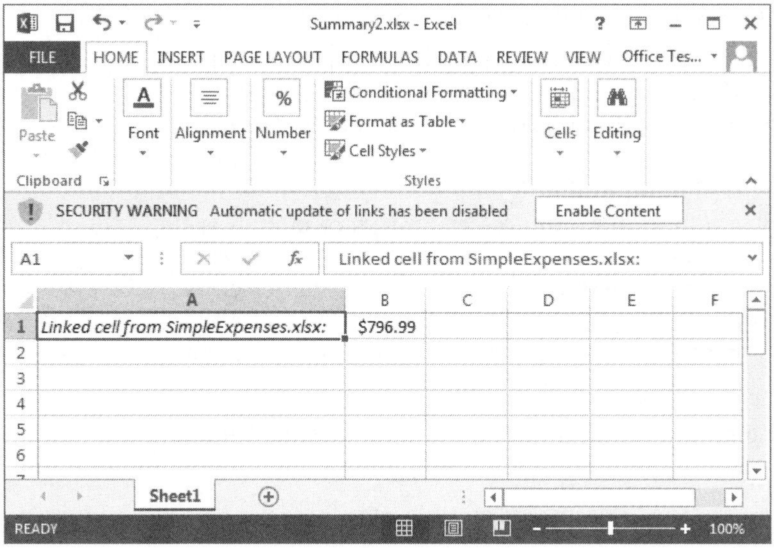

FIGURE 8-15

This security warning tells you that the workbook you just opened has linked cells, but Excel hasn't tried to update them. That's because updating them involves opening another file, which ultra-paranoid Excel isn't ready to do.

Before you can do anything about this problem, you need to tell Excel to trust your workbook. To do that, click the Enable Content button in the message bar. Excel opens the linked workbook (in this case, SimpleExpenses.xlsx) behind the scenes, and then uses the latest information to recalculate your formula.

Now, here's the tricky bit. Once you click Enable Content, your workbook is trusted, and you won't see the warning message again. (To learn more about Excel's trusted document system, see page 904.) However, even though Excel trusts your workbook, it won't automatically update your linked formulas the *next* time you open your workbook. Instead, Excel asks for your guidance (Figure 8-16).

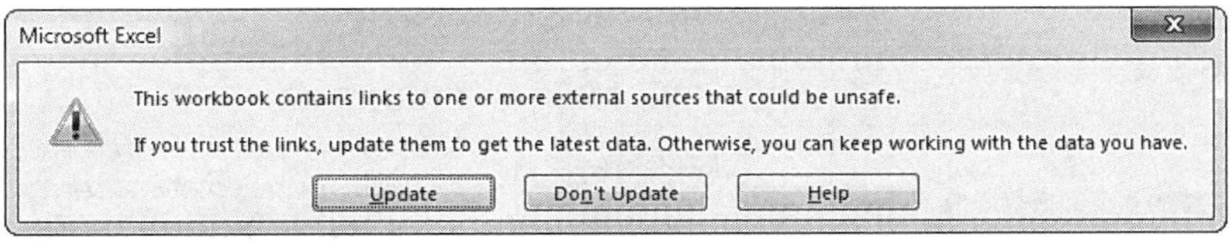

FIGURE 8-16

Every time you open a trusted workbook that links to another file, Excel shows this window. If you click Update, Excel silently opens the linked workbook and updates your links. If you click Don't Update, Excel keeps the old data, but lets you update the links later.

If you don't want to update links right away (and you click Don't Update), you can still update your links later, using one of two approaches. The first approach is to open the workbook you're linking *to*, while you have the original workbook open. In this case, Excel updates the links automatically. The second approach is to use the Edit Links window, described in the next section.

NOTE Confused? Here's the executive summary. The first time you open a workbook with linked formulas, you see the security message (Figure 8-16) and you must click Enable Content to update the links. Any time you open the workbook afterwards, you see the link message (Figure 8-17) and you must click Update to update the links. Keep reading to learn how you can tweak this behavior.

TROUBLESHOOTING LINKS

Sometimes, despite the best of intentions, your formula points to a workbook that Excel can't find. You'll run into this problem if, for example, you rename SimpleExpenses.xlsx or move it to another folder. In this situation, Excel gives you an error message when you attempt to update your links (Figure 8-17).

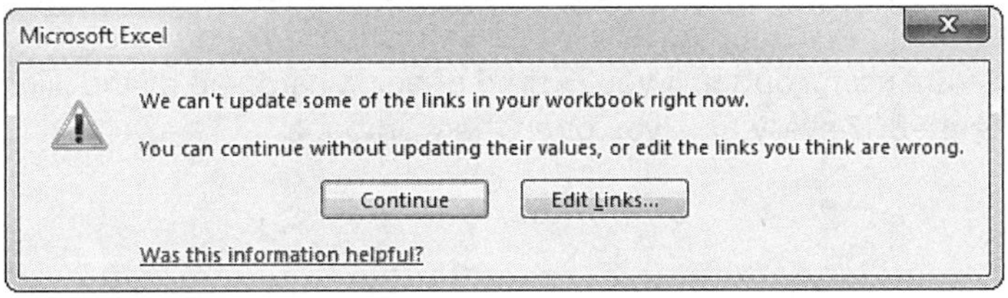

FIGURE 8-17

If Excel can't find the workbook you reference, it displays an error message giving you the choice to continue working with what you have (click Continue), or relinking the workbook to the correct file (click Edit Links and see Figure 8-18).

If you know that a link's gone bad, you've got a problem—depending on how many linked formulas your workbook has, you could be stuck updating dozens of cells.

Fortunately, the Edit Links window (shown in Figure 8-18) gives you an easier alternative. Rather than changing each formula by hand, you can relink everything by pointing Excel to the right file.

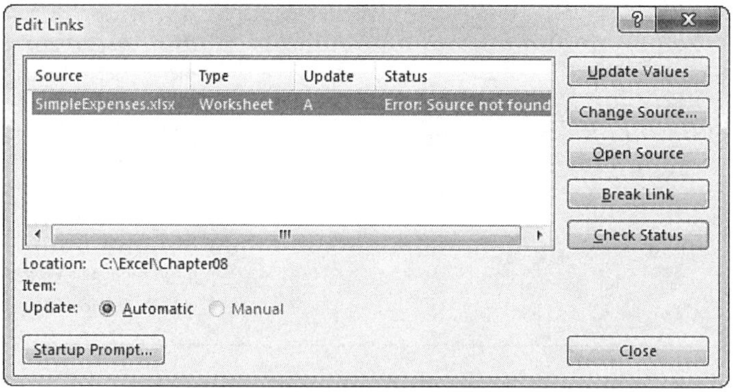

FIGURE 8-18

In this example, Excel can't find the linked file SimpleExpenses.xlsx. You can select the link, and then click Change Source to browse for the linked workbook (click OK when you find it), or you can click Break Link to make your workbook independent, and just use whatever data Excel extracted the last time it updated the links.

THE EDIT LINKS WINDOW

The Edit Links window is invaluable for fixing broken links, but it lets you work with linked files in other ways, too, including:

- **Update Values** refreshes the formulas that use linked cells. This is useful if you chose not to update your links when you first opened the workbook.
- **Open Source** opens the linked workbook in another Excel window, so you can really see what's going on. This also has the side effect of updating all the linked formulas in your current workbook.
- **Break Link** severs your ties with the linked workbook. Excel replaces any linked formulas with the most recent data.
- **Check Status** rechecks the linked workbook, and updates the Status column to let you know whether it exists, whether it's currently open, and so on.
- **Startup Prompt** opens a Startup Prompt window where you can choose the behavior Excel uses when it opens the current workbook. You have three choices: refresh the linked cells automatically, never refresh, or ask you (the standard setting). This is a useful option if you're tired of being harassed by the window shown in Figure 8-17 every time you open the workbook.

FREQUENTLY ASKED QUESTION

How Changing the Location of Cells Affects Formulas

OK, I know how Excel adjusts a formula when I copy it to another location. But what happens if I move cells around after I create a formula?

No worries. It turns out that Excel is surprisingly intelligent. Consider the following simple formula:

```
=B1+A2
```

If you cut and paste the contents of A2 to A3, Excel automatically updates your formula to point to the new cell, without complaining once. It performs the same automatic cleanup if you drag the contents of a cell to another location (although if you simply make a duplicate copy of the cell, Excel won't change your formula). Excel is also on the ball when you insert and delete rows and columns.

If at any time Excel can't find your cells, the formula changes to show the error code #REF!. You can then take a closer look at the formula to find out what really went wrong. For example, if you delete column B from your spreadsheet (by selecting the column and using the Home→Cells→Delete command), the formula changes to this:

```
=#REF!+A2
```

Even though there's still a B1 cell in your worksheet (it's the cell that was formerly named C1), Excel modifies the formula to make it clear that the formula has lost track of your original data.

CHAPTER

9

Math and Statistical Functions

Excel is packed with dozens of mathematical functions. Some of these functions are for specialist audiences, like engineers or statisticians, while others are so useful they can turn up in almost any civilian's spreadsheet.

In this chapter, you'll take a tour of two of the largest categories in Excel's function library, namely the Math & Trig and Statistical functions. Rather than slog through each function one by one, this chapter covers the most useful functions in each category. It starts by looking at a bunch of functions that help round, add, and count numbers. Then it explains how to find averages, medians, and percentiles, which are helpful when you want to compare groups of data. Toward the end of the chapter, you'll see some of the more specialized functions that showcase Excel's skill with trigonometry and advanced statistics—great for math lovers, accounting jockeys, or political-polling wonks interested in double-checking statistical significance claims.

Rounding Numbers

Most people don't devote enough thought to *rounding*, the process by which you adjust fractional numbers so they're less precise but more manageable. For example, rounding can transform the unwieldy number 1.984323125 to 2. Excel lets you round numbers two ways:

- **Modify the number format of the cell.** With this method, Excel rounds the displayed value, but doesn't change the underlying value. The advantage to this approach is that you can use the value in other calculations without losing any precision. When Excel rounds your numbers using this method, it simply rounds to the last displayed digit (rounding up if the next digit is 5 or greater).

For example, if you tell Excel to show the number 3.145 using two decimal places, Excel displays the rounded value of 3.15. (Cell value formatting is described in Chapter 5.)

- **Use a rounding function.** This approach gives you more control. For example, you can round a number *before* you use it in another calculation, and you can round numbers to a multiple you choose, like 500 or 1,000. The drawback is that when you use a rounding function, you may lose precision. This doesn't happen when you change the number format, which simply tweaks the way Excel displays the number.

With classic overkill, Microsoft includes no fewer than 10 functions designed for rounding numbers, from the basic ROUND() function, to the more flexible MROUND(), and then to the quirky EVEN() and ODD().

ROUND(), ROUNDDOWN(), ROUNDUP(): Rounding Numbers

The most basic (and most commonly used) of Excel's rounding functions is ROUND(), which rounds a numeric value to whatever level of precision you choose. The ROUND() function needs two arguments: the actual number you want to round, and the number of digits you want to keep to the right of the decimal point. Here's what it looks like:

```
ROUND(number_to_round, number_of_digits)
```

For example, the following formula rounds the number 3.987 to two decimal places. The result is 3.99.

```
=ROUND(3.987, 2)
```

If you specify 0 for the number of digits, Excel rounds to the nearest whole number. Interestingly, you can also round to the nearest 10, 100, 1000, and so on by using negative numbers for the second argument. For example, if you use –2 for the number of digits, Excel rounds two digits to the *left* of the decimal place, which means your number gets rounded to the nearest 100.

Here's an example:

```
=ROUND(34655.7, -2)
```

This formula produces a result of 34,700.

NOTE The ROUND() function always rounds the positive values 1 through 4 *down* and 5 through 9 *up*. If you round 1.5 to the nearest whole number, for instance, the result is 2. When dealing with negative numbers, Excel rounds the digits 5 through 9 down (toward the larger negative value). Similarly, –1 through –4 get rounded up. For example, –1.5 gets rounded to –2, while –1.4 gets rounded up to –1.

The ROUNDDOWN() and ROUNDUP() functions work similarly to ROUND(). Like ROUND(), they take two arguments: the number you want to round, and the number of decimal places you want the final, rounded number to use. The difference is that ROUNDDOWN() always rounds numbers down, while ROUNDUP() always rounds them up.

For example, the result of ROUNDUP(1.1, 0) is 2, even though 1.1 is only slightly above 1. Similarly, the result of ROUNDDOWN(1.9, 0) is 1, even though 1.9 is almost 2. The only time that ROUNDUP() and ROUNDDOWN() don't change a number is if it's already rounded to the appropriate precision. For example, the result of ROUNDUP(2, 0) and ROUNDDOWN(2, 0) is the same: 2.

When most people learn about ROUNDUP() and ROUNDDOWN(), they wonder why anyone would want to use a rounding function that's *less* precise than ol' reliable ROUND(). The answer, not surprisingly, must do with making more money. If you're selling discounted Beanie Babies, say, then you might set the price at 60 percent of the original list price. However, this formula produces prices like $8.43423411 that you need to round to the nearest penny. Rather than rounding down (and giving up your fractional cents), you can use ROUNDUP() to make sure the price is always rounded up, ensuring that you keep every last penny and even collect a few extra. Never say Microsoft didn't try to help you make a buck.

MROUND(), CEILING(), and FLOOR(): More Rounding Functions

While you may not necessarily think of the ROUND() function as letting you round a number to any multiple of a *power of 10* you'd like, that's actually what's going on under the hood. But in some cases, you might want to round your numbers to something that *isn't* a power of 10. For example, you might want to round a number to the nearest multiple of 5 or 50 or 100.

In these cases, you need to use Excel's MROUND() function. MROUND() takes two arguments: the number you want to round, and the multiple you want to use:

```
MROUND(number_to_round, multiple)
```

Here it is in action, as the following formula rounds the number 653 to the nearest multiple of 5. The result is 655.

```
=MROUND(653, 5)
```

CEILING() and FLOOR() work like MROUND(), except that they let you control whether the rounding goes up (in which case you'd use CEILING) or down (FLOOR). In other words, the CEILING() function is really a combination of MROUND() and ROUNDUP(). The FLOOR() function, meanwhile, is a combination of MROUND() and ROUNDDOWN().

Consider the following formula. It rounds the number 653 to the nearest multiple of 5, but, because it uses the FLOOR() function, it rounds *downward*. The result is 650:

```
=FLOOR(653, 5)
```

Compare that with the following formula, which produces a result of 700. This formula uses the CEILING() function, which means it always rounds up, unless the number is already rounded to the appropriate multiple, of course.

```
=CEILING(653, 50)
```

The CEILING() function is handy if you need to calculate an item's price in more than one currency. Consider a U.S.-based company that's trying to figure out how to price its products in Canada (Figure 9-1). The company would probably start by setting the price in U.S. dollars, and then use a currency conversion ratio to produce a set of Canadian prices. However, this approach produces prices that, in effect, leave a little money on the table. (Most people willing to pay $153.16 for a product are probably also willing to pay $153.99—whether it's Canadian or American dollars.) Using a function like MROUND(), the company could make sure that prices are always rounded to the nearest 25- or 50-cent multiple. That's fine, but there's a possibility that margins might be shaved too thin if you round prices down—so the CEILING() function is a better choice. And if you want to get particularly fancy, why not use CEILING() to round up to the nearest dollar and then subtract a single cent, giving attention-grabbing prices that always end with .99?

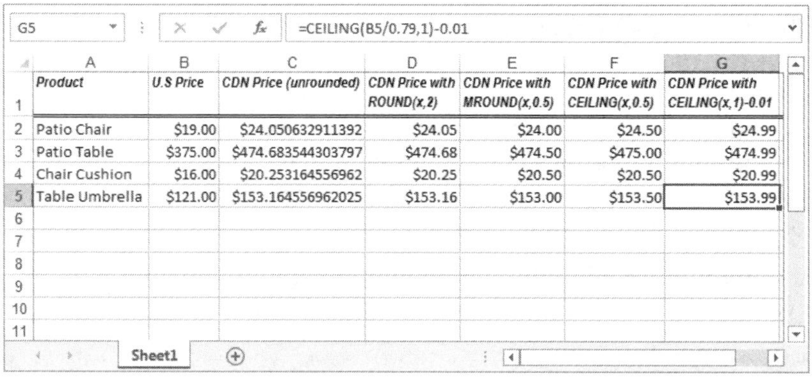

G5 =CEILING(B5/0.79,1)-0.01

	A	B	C	D	E	F	G
1	Product	U.S Price	CDN Price (unrounded)	CDN Price with ROUND(x,2)	CDN Price with MROUND(x,0.5)	CDN Price with CEILING(x,0.5)	CDN Price with CEILING(x,1)-0.01
2	Patio Chair	$19.00	$24.050632911392	$24.05	$24.00	$24.50	$24.99
3	Patio Table	$375.00	$474.683544303797	$474.68	$474.50	$475.00	$474.99
4	Chair Cushion	$16.00	$20.253164556962	$20.25	$20.50	$20.50	$20.99
5	Table Umbrella	$121.00	$153.164556962025	$153.16	$153.00	$153.50	$153.99

Sheet1

FIGURE 9-1

The CEILING() function in action. Notice how different approaches to rounding net different prices.

POWER USERS' CLINIC

Rounding Negative Numbers

The rounding functions don't necessarily treat negative numbers the way you'd expect. ROUNDUP() and ROUNDDOWN() ignore the minus sign entirely. If you use ROUNDUP() to round to 0 decimal places and the number is –4.5, you end up with –5; if you use ROUNDDOWN(), you get –4. On the other hand, FLOOR() rounds negative numbers away from 0 (so –4.5 becomes –5) and CEILING() rounds toward 0 (so –4.5 becomes –4), which is probably what you expect.

Interestingly, Excel 2013 introduces two new functions that are intended to eventually replace FLOOR() and CEILING(), called FLOOR.MATH() and CEILING.MATH(). The only difference is that they accept an optional *mode* argument, which controls how Excel rounds negative numbers. Supply a value of –1, and the rounding direction of negative numbers is reversed. For example, this formula rounds –4.5 to –4:

```
=FLOOR.MATH(-4.5, 1, -1)
```

Whereas these two formulas are equivalent, and round to –5:

```
=FLOOR(-4.5, 1)
=FLOOR.MATH(-4.5, 1)
```

INT() and TRUNC(): Chopping Off Non-Whole Numbers

INT() and TRUNC() are two functions that simply shorten your numbers, removing extra digits without performing any rounding. INT() is the simpler of the two, as it always rounds to whole numbers (a.k.a. integers). You need only specify the number you want rounded. The formula here, for example, works out to 2:

```
=INT(2.5)
```

You'd get the same answer for INT(2), INT(2.9), INT(2.7509630), and so on. In each case, Excel discards the decimal portion.

TRUNC() is similar to INT(), except that it uses a second argument specifying the number of decimal places you want to *preserve*. This argument is optional, and if you leave it out, TRUNC() and INT() behave the same way with positive numbers.

```
TRUNC(number_to_round, [number_of_digits])
```

In real life, you'll find reasons to round numbers far more often than you have reasons to truncate them.

One of the few instances in which you'd truncate a number is when you want to *ignore* the digits of a number that you don't want, rather than *change* them. For example, imagine you want to start memorizing the digits of the mathematical constant pi (3.14159265...). Using the following formula, you can truncate pi to the first three decimal places so you can get started:

```
=TRUNC(PI(), 3)
```

This formula gives you the number 3.141 (note that Excel lets you use the PI() function to insert the constant pi). If you used the ROUND() function, you'd end up with 3.142, because Excel would round the last digit.

You might also use TRUNC() to give you just the whole number portion of a value. This approach is reasonable when the decimal portion doesn't have any real meaning. For example, you might calculate that your furniture factory produces 5.6 chairs per day when you average the monthly production. Unfortunately, this still means you can rely on having only five chairs to sell at the end of the day. You can make a similar case for using the ROUNDUP() function. For example, maybe you know your friends tend to eat 1.3 pumpkin pies each time they come for dinner, so you'd do best to round up and make sure you slide two pies into the oven.

EVEN() and ODD(): Rounding Up to Even or Odd Values

EVEN() and ODD() are the last of Excel's rounding functions. They accept a single number and round it up to the nearest even or odd number. As simple as this sounds, these functions can cause a bit of confusion because many people assume that the functions will return the *closest* odd or even number. But they don't. Since the functions round *up*, the closest correct number may be, numerically speaking, a confusingly long ways away.

To understand these quirky functions a little better, consider the following formula:

```
=ODD(2.6)
```

This formula produces the expected result: It rounds 2.6 up to the closest odd number, 3. Now consider:

```
=ODD(3.6)
```

This formula also rounds up to the nearest odd number, which in this case is 5.

In fact, ODD() always rounds up, unless you begin with a whole odd number. That means that the result of the following formula is also 5, even though 3.1 is clearly much closer to 3 than 5:

```
=ODD(3.1)
```

The EVEN() function behaves similarly. Thus, the result of the following formula is 4:

```
=EVEN(2.1)
```

The EVEN() and ODD() functions aren't useful too often. For most people, they simply represent an interesting footnote in Excel functions.

POWER USERS' CLINIC

Excel's Rounding May Not Be Good Enough

Even though Excel provides 10 rounding functions, they all work in exactly the same way. They use a technique called *arithmetic rounding*, which always rounds the number 5 up. Although this may seem like the only option, accountants and statisticians are well aware that there are a variety of approaches to rounding numbers, and that they all have their own particular problems.

The key difficulty is deciding how to round the number 5. For example, consider 1.5, which lies exactly halfway between the numbers 1 and 2. In arithmetic rounding, 1.5 is always rounded up to 2. This convention can bias your results if you're rounding a large group of numbers and then adding them together (since the five digits 5, 6, 7, 8, and 9 always get rounded up, versus the four digits 1, 2, 3, and 4, which always get rounded down).

The best way to understand the problem is to think of the sales tax you pay on a typical restaurant bill. Sales tax is supposed to be calculated as a percentage of the total, and then rounded arithmetically. However, imagine what would happen if the sales tax were calculated separately on each item you ordered, *rounded up* separately, and then added. You'd pay more than if the tax were calculated from the total.

So how can you avoid rounding biases? The best option is to calculate first, and round later. Never add numbers that you've already rounded. Or, you could use a different type of rounding. One example is *banker's rounding*, which rounds 5 up sometimes and down other times, depending on whether it's paired with an even or odd number. For example, 1.5 is rounded up to 2, but 2.5 is rounded down to 2, 3.5 is rounded up to 4, and so on. This eliminates rounding bias, allowing you to sum up a long column of rounded numbers without skewing the result.

You can use banker's rounding in Excel, but Microsoft makes it available only to the VBA (Visual Basic for Applications) programming language. Translation: You need to write a custom macro or function to access it. You'll learn about how you can use banker's rounding with VBA on page 942. In the meantime, you can learn more about the various aspects of rounding, and see what types of rounding Microsoft uses in different products in the technical support note at *http://tinyurl.com/d6taz*.

Groups of Numbers

You can use spreadsheets to distill a few important pieces of information out of several pages of data. For example, say you want to hunt through a column looking for minimums and maximums, in order to find the lowest-priced product or best sales quarter. Or maybe you want to calculate averages, means, and percentile rankings to help grade a class of students. In either case, Excel provides a number of useful functions. Most are part of the Statistical group, although the SUM() function is actually part of the Math & Trig group.

SUM(): Summing Up Numbers

Almost every Excel program in existence has been called on at least once to do the same thing: Add a group of numbers. This task falls to the wildly popular SUM() function, which simply adds everything in it. The SUM() function takes over 200 arguments, each of which can be a single cell reference or a range of cells.

Here's a SUM() formula that adds two cells:

```
=SUM(A1,A2)
```

And here's a SUM() formula that adds the range of 11 cells from A2 to A12:

```
=SUM(A2:A12)
```

And here's a SUM() formula that adds a range of cells along with a separately referenced cell, and two literal values:

```
=SUM(A2:A12,B5,429.1,35000)
```

NOTE The SUM() function automatically ignores blank cells and any cells in its range that have text in them. However, SUM() doesn't ignore dates (which are actually specially formatted numbers, as you saw on page 54). Therefore, make sure you don't sum a range of cells that includes a date.

POWER USERS' CLINIC

Creating Formulas Quickly with AutoSum

People so often sum a row or column of values that Excel has a button dedicated to just that purpose: the AutoSum button. To find it, choose Formulas→Function Library→AutoSum. The button has a picture of the Greek letter Σ (capital sigma), which means sum to mathematicians.

When you click the AutoSum button, Excel makes an educated guess about what cells you want to total (as shown in Figure 9-2). For example, if you're at the end of a row, Excel assumes you want to add all the numeric values in all the columns on the left. If you're at the bottom of a column of numbers, Excel assumes you want to add the values above.

The AutoSum feature isn't just for summing. You can also use it to calculate averages, counts, maximums, and minimums. To do so, don't click the top part of the AutoSum button. Instead, click the drop-down arrow at the bottom of the AutoSum button to get a list of calculation options, including summing, averaging, counting, and finding the maximum or minimum. When you pick an option from the AutoSum menu, Excel inserts the appropriate function into your cell and uses the auto-guess strategy described above to pick out the nearby cells for the calculation.

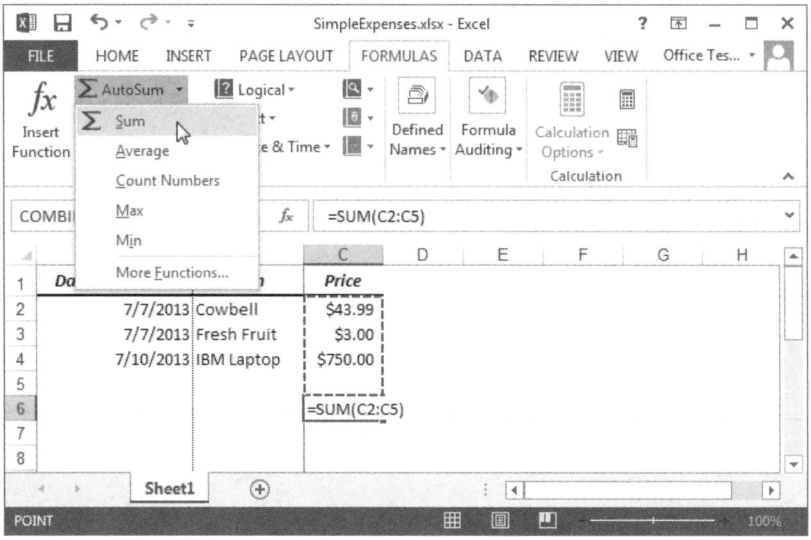

FIGURE 9-2

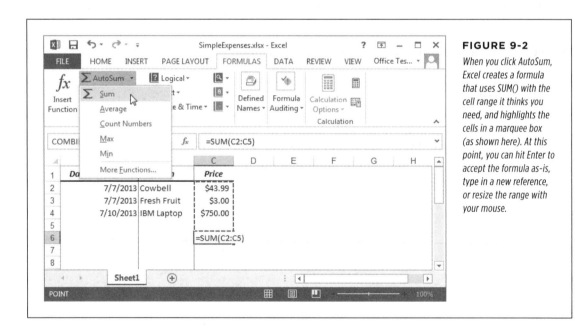

When you click AutoSum, Excel creates a formula that uses SUM() with the cell range it thinks you need, and highlights the cells in a marquee box (as shown here). At this point, you can hit Enter to accept the formula as-is, type in a new reference, or resize the range with your mouse.

COUNT(), COUNTA(), and COUNTBLANK(): Counting Items in a List

Sometimes you don't need to add the values in a series of cells, but instead want to know how many values there are. That's the purpose of Excel's straightforward counting functions: COUNT(), COUNTA(), and COUNTBLANK(). COUNT() and COUNTA() operate similarly to the SUM() function in that they accept over 200 arguments, each of which can be a cell reference or range of cells.

The COUNT() function counts the number of cells that have numeric input (including dates). The COUNTA() function counts cells with any kind of content. And finally, the COUNTBLANK() function takes a single argument—a range of cells—and gives you the number of empty cells in that range (see Figure 9-3).

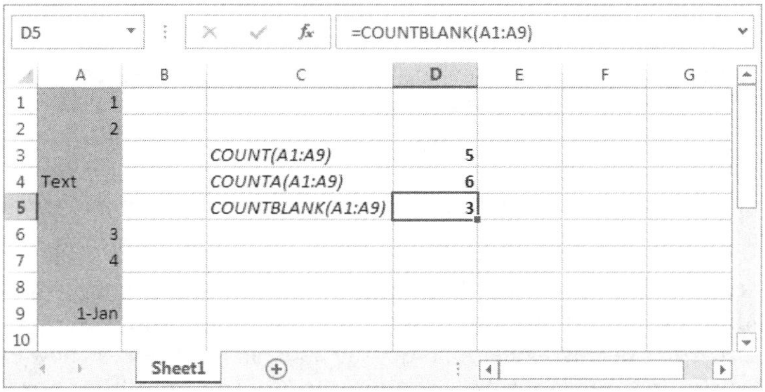

FIGURE 9-3

This worksheet shows Excel's counting functions in action on a range of cells, from A1 to A9. The function names are in column C; the formulas containing the functions are in column D. The COUNT() function includes the date cell A9, while the COUNTA() function includes all cells that have any kind of information in them.

Here's how you could use the COUNT() function with a range of cells:

```
=COUNT(A2:A12)
```

For an example of when COUNT() comes in handy, consider the following formula, which determines the average of a group of cells, without requiring that you manually input the total number of values:

```
=SUM(A2:A12)/COUNT(A2:A12)
```

This formula finds the average of the cells in the range A2:12 that have values. Because it uses COUNT(), the average remains correct even if the range includes empty cells (which Excel simply ignores). Of course, Excel's AVERAGE() function does the same task, but you still might find COUNT() useful in long lists of data that may contain missing information. For example, imagine you create a worksheet with a list of customer charges. One of the columns in your list is Discount Amount. Using the COUNT() function on the discount column, you can find out how many customers got a discount. When you want to get a little fancier, use COUNT() on the Customer Name column to find out how many customers you actually have. Then you can divide the number of discount sales by the number of total customers to find out the percentage of sales that result from selling something at a reduced price.

You can also combine counting functions to calculate additional pieces of potentially useful information. If you subtract COUNT() from COUNTA(), for example (that is, if your formula reads something like *=COUNTA(A1:A10)–COUNT(A1:A10)*), you end up with the number of text cells in the range.

TIP You can also use SUMIF() and COUNTIF() functions to sum or count cells that meet specific criteria. For more information on using conditional logic, as well as the SUMIF() and COUNTIF() functions, see page 375.

MAX() and MIN(): Finding Maximum and Minimum Values

The MAX() and MIN() functions pick the largest or smallest value out of a series of cells. This tool's great for picking important values (best-selling products, failing students, or historically high temperatures) out of a long list of information. As with COUNT() and SUM(), the MAX() and MIN() functions accept over 200 cell references or ranges.

For example, the following formula examines four cells (A2, A3, B2, and B3) and tells you the largest value in that grid:

```
=MAX(A2:B3)
```

The MAX() and MIN() functions ignore any nonnumeric content, which includes text, empty cells, and Boolean (true or false) values.

Excel includes dates in MAX() and MIN() calculations because it stores them internally as the number of days that have passed since a particular date. (For Windows versions of Excel, this date is January 1, 1900; see page 54 for details on how Excel handles dates.) For this reason, it makes little sense to use MAX() or MIN() on a range that includes both dates and ordinary numeric data. On the other hand, you may want to use MAX() to find the latest (that is, the largest) date or MIN() to find the oldest (or smallest) date. Just make sure you format the cell containing the formula using the Date number format, so that Excel displays the result as a date as well.

Excel also provides MAXA() and MINA() functions, which work just like MAX() and MIN(), except for the way in which they handle text and Booleans. MAXA() and MINA() always assume TRUE values equal 1 and FALSE values equal 0. Excel treats all text values as 0. For example, if you have a list of top professionals with a Salary column, and some cells say "Undisclosed," it makes sense to use MAX() and MIN() to ignore these cells altogether. On the other hand, if you have a list of items you've tried to auction off on eBay with a Sold For column, and some cells say "No Bids," you may use MINA() and MAXA() to treat this text as a 0 value.

LARGE(), SMALL(), and RANK(): Ranking Numbers

MAX() and MIN() let you grab the largest and smallest numbers, but what if you want to grab something in between? For example, you might want to create a top10 list of best-selling products, instead of picking out just the single best. In these cases, consider the LARGE() and SMALL() functions, which identify values that aren't *quite* the highest or lowest. In fact, these functions even let you specify how *far* from the top and bottom you want to look. Here's how they work.

Both the LARGE() and SMALL() functions require two arguments: the range you want to search, and the item's position in the list. The list position is where the item would fall if the list were ordered from largest to smallest (for LARGE()), or from smallest to largest (for SMALL()). Here's what LARGE() looks like:

```
LARGE(range, position)
```

For example, if you specify a position of 1 with the LARGE() function, you get the largest item on the list, which is the same result as using MAX(). If you specify a position of 2, as in the following formula, you get the second-largest value:

```
=LARGE(A2:A12, 2)
```

Here's an example formula that adds the three largest entries in a range:

```
=LARGE(A2:A12,1) + LARGE(A2:A12,2) + LARGE(A2:A12,3)
```

Assuming the range A2:A12 contains a list of monthly expenses, this formula gives you the total of your three most extravagant splurges.

SMALL() performs the opposite task by identifying the number that's the smallest, second-smallest, and so on. For example, the following formula gives you the second-smallest number:

```
=SMALL(A2:A12, 2)
```

And finally, Excel lets you approach this problem in reverse. Using the RANK() function, you can find where a specific value falls in the list. The RANK() function requires two parts: the number you're looking for and the range you're searching. In addition, you can supply a third parameter that specifies how Excel should order the values before searching. (Excel automatically searches values from highest to lowest.) Here's what the RANK() formula looks like:

```
RANK(number, range, [order_type])
```

For example, imagine you have a range of cells from A2 to A12 that represent scores on a test. Somewhere in this range is a score of 77. You want to know how this compares to the other marks, so you create the following formula using the RANK() function:

```
=RANK(77, A2:A12)
```

If this formula works out to 5, you know that 77 is the fifth-highest score in the range you indicated. But what if more than one student scored 77? Excel handles duplicates in much the same way as it deals with tied times in races. If three students score 77, for example, then they all tie for fifth place. But the next lowest grade (say, 75) gets a rank of eight—three positions down the list.

If you want to rank values in the reverse order, you need to include a third argument of 0. This orders them from highest to lowest (so that the lowest grade gets a rank of 1):

```
=RANK(77, A2:A12, 0)
```

NOTE If you use RANK() to rank a number that doesn't exist in the data series, Excel gives you the #N/A error code in the cell, telling you it can't rank the number because the number isn't there.

You can do a neat trick and rank all your numbers in a list. For example, assume you have a list of grades in cells A2 to A12. You want to show the rank of each grade in the corresponding cells B2 to B12. Calculate the rank for A2 like so:

```
=RANK(A2, $A$2:$A$12)
```

This formula uses absolute references for the list. That means you can copy this formula to cells B3 through B12 to calculate the rank for the remaining grades, and Excel automatically adjusts the formula to what you need.

POWER USERS' CLINIC

RANK.EQ() and RANK.AVG()

Microsoft has recast the original RANK() as a compatibility function (page 233). RANK() still works in all versions of Excel, but Excel is replacing it with two new versions of the function, RANK.EQ() and RANK.AVG(), which differ in how they handle tied values.

RANK.EQ() works the same way as RANK(): It assigns the next available rank to all the tied values. So if two students tie for second place, they both get a rank of 2 and the next student is ranked 4. No one gets the third-place ranking.

RANK.AVG() calculates an *average* rank for tied values. So if two students tie for second place, they both get a rank of 2.5 (because that's the average of rank 2 and the skipped rank 3). If three students tied for second place, the average rank is 3, because that's the result of the average rank calculation *(2+3+4)/3*.

The average ranking system has the advantage of keeping tied values from rating quite as highly as standalone performers. This lets you avoid the illusion that a large number of people are better than average because they've all tied for a high rank.

Just remember, the RANK.EQ() and RANK.AVG() functions require Excel 2010 or Excel 2013. They won't work if you open your spreadsheet in Excel 2007.

AVERAGE() and MEDIAN(): Finding Average or Median Values

Excel makes it easy for you to find the average value for a set of numbers. The AVERAGE() function doesn't accomplish anything you couldn't do on your own using COUNT() and SUM() together, but, well, you could also bake your own bread. Bottom line: AVERAGE()is a real timesaver.

The AVERAGE() function uses just one argument—the cell range you want to average:

```
=AVERAGE(A2:A12)
```

It ignores empty cells or those with text values. For example, if the preceding formula had only three numbers in the range A2:A12, then Excel would add these values and divide them by 3. If this isn't the behavior you want, you can use the AVERAGE() function, which counts all text cells as though they contain the number 0 (but still ignores blank cells). (To see when you should and shouldn't treat text as a 0 value, see the discussion about the MAXA() and MINA() functions on page 270.)

TIP In some cases, you may want to perform an average that *ignores* certain values. For example, when determining the average score of all students on a test, you may want to disregard students who scored 0 because they may have been absent. In this case, you can use AVERAGEIF() function, as described on page 381.

Excel can also help you identify the *median* value for a set of numbers. If you were to order your range of numbers from lowest to highest, the median is the number that falls in the middle position. (If you have an even number of numbers, Excel averages the two middle numbers to generate the median.)

You calculate the median (see Figure 9-4) the same way you calculate an average:

```
=MEDIAN(B2:B10)
```

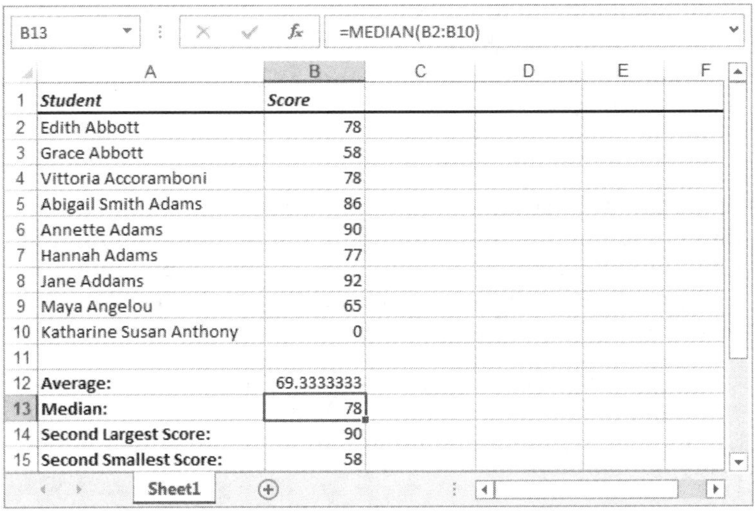

B13 =MEDIAN(B2:B10)

	A	B	C	D	E	F
1	*Student*	*Score*				
2	Edith Abbott	78				
3	Grace Abbott	58				
4	Vittoria Accoramboni	78				
5	Abigail Smith Adams	86				
6	Annette Adams	90				
7	Hannah Adams	77				
8	Jane Addams	92				
9	Maya Angelou	65				
10	Katharine Susan Anthony	0				
11						
12	**Average:**	69.3333333				
13	**Median:**	78				
14	**Second Largest Score:**	90				
15	**Second Smallest Score:**	58				

Sheet1

FIGURE 9-4

When comparing test scores and class grades, people often use medians instead of averages. The reason? Averages can be unnaturally skewed if one or more values are extremely high or low. For example, if one student turns in a blank test and receives a 0, the average may be unnaturally low, and not truly representative of a class's performance. You get unnaturally low averages, for instance, when averaging a small set of numbers. Usually, however, the median's quite close to the average.

TIP Remember, Excel has a quick shortcut for five of its most popular functions—SUM(), AVERAGE(), COUNT(), MAX(), and MIN(). Just choose Formulas→Function Library→AutoSum to quickly sum any group of selected cells. When you click the drop-down arrow on this button, you see a list of functions that let you quickly unleash any of the other four functions.

PERCENTILE() and PERCENTRANK(): Advanced Ranking Functions

If you really want to dissect the test scores from the worksheet in Figure 9-4, you don't need to stop with simple averages, medians, and rankings. You can take a closer look at the overall grade distribution by using the PERCENTILE() and PERCENTRANK() functions.

People often use percentiles to split groups of students into categories. (Technically, a percentile is a value on a scale of 1 to 100, indicating the percentage of scorers in any given ranking who are equal to, or below, the scorer in question.) For example, you might decide that the top 10 percent of all the students in your class will gain admission to an advanced class the following semester. In other words, a student's final grade must be better than 90 percent of his or her classmates' final grade. Students at this prestigious level occupy the 90th percentile.

That's where the PERCENTILE() function comes in handy. You supply the cell range, the percentile (as a fraction from 0 to 1), and the function reveals the numeric grade the student needs to have to match that percentile. For example, here's how you calculate the minimum grade needed to enter the 90th percentile (assuming the grades are in cells B2 to B10):

```
=PERCENTILE(B2:B10, 0.9)
```

Percentiles make the most sense when you have a large number of values because the larger the number of values, the more regular the distribution of those values. In other words, a wider range of test scores gives you values that are well spread out, with no "clumping" that may skew your results. Percentiles don't work as well with small amounts of data.

PERCENTRANK() performs the inverse task. It takes a range of data and a number from 1 to 100, and gives you the fraction indicating the number's percentile. The following formula, for instance, returns the percentile of the grade 81 (as it compares to a list of other grades):

```
=PERCENTRANK(B2:B13, 81)
```

Using the data shown in Figure 9-5, this formula gives you the fraction 0.727 (or 72.7%, if you've applied the Percent number style). This indicates that a grade of 81 falls into the 72nd percentile (and almost hits the 73rd percentile). That means it's a better score than 72 percent of all the other students, and a lower score than the other 28 percent. In this case, you can also apply the rounding functions explained earlier in this chapter because percentiles are (by convention) whole numbers. You can use ROUND() to round the result of the formula to the closest percentile (73rd), or use TRUNC() to return the highest percentile that the student actually reached (72nd), which is the conventional approach.

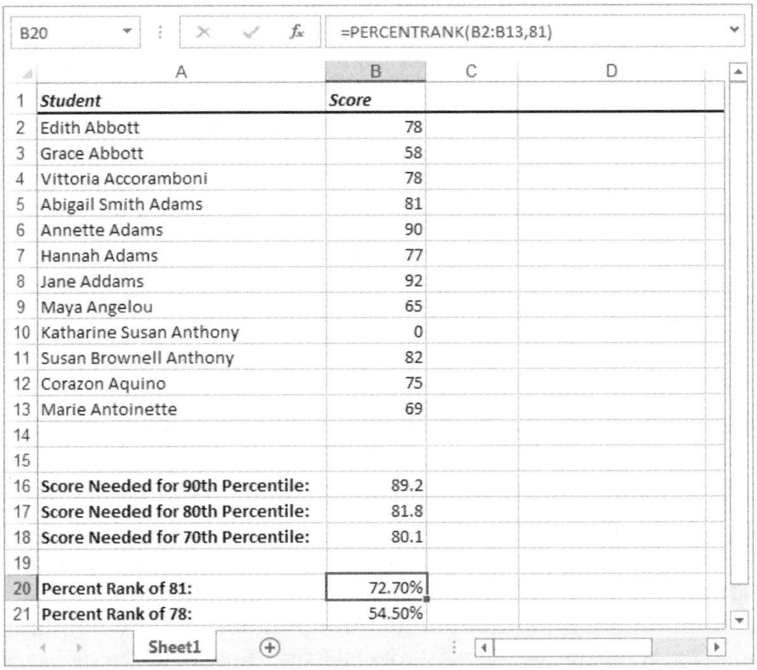

B20 =PERCENTRANK(B2:B13,81)

	A	B	C	D
1	***Student***	***Score***		
2	Edith Abbott	78		
3	Grace Abbott	58		
4	Vittoria Accoramboni	78		
5	Abigail Smith Adams	81		
6	Annette Adams	90		
7	Hannah Adams	77		
8	Jane Addams	92		
9	Maya Angelou	65		
10	Katharine Susan Anthony	0		
11	Susan Brownell Anthony	82		
12	Corazon Aquino	75		
13	Marie Antoinette	69		
14				
15				
16	**Score Needed for 90th Percentile:**	89.2		
17	**Score Needed for 80th Percentile:**	81.8		
18	**Score Needed for 70th Percentile:**	80.1		
19				
20	**Percent Rank of 81:**	72.70%		
21	**Percent Rank of 78:**	54.50%		

Sheet1

FIGURE 9-5

Percentiles make a lot of sense when you want to see where one value fits into a large range. For example, using these student scores, you can tell that students need an 89.2 to enter the 90th percentile. Ideally, you'd use a much larger series of data to calculate percentiles, as a small sample like this generates widely varying percentiles each time you enter a new score. Keep in mind that percentiles also work wonders for figuring wages, survey data, and even physical characteristics like heights and weights.

POWER USERS' CLINIC

A Different Way to Calculate Percentiles

It's a shady secret in statistics that there's no universally accepted definition for percentiles. Excel's approach is to designate the smallest number in your sample as the 0th percentile and the highest number as the 100th percentile. In the student grading spreadsheet shown in Figure 9-5, that means the 0th percentile is represented by a test score of 0 and the 100th percentile is represented by a test score of 92.

Excel's approach makes sense for the student score example, because you have all the values. But it doesn't work as well for, say, a researcher gathering data in the field. In this situation, the data in the worksheet is a small sample of the total population, and the range of your sample probably isn't as great as the range of the full population.

For example, imagine you're studying the average length of a certain type of lake trout. In all likelihood, the biggest fish you capture won't be the biggest fish in the lake. Similarly, the smallest fish you capture won't be the smallest fish in the lake.

To deal with this situation, statistical pros make an estimate of what the 100th and 0th percentile should be, based on the data they have. The 100th percentile value will be slightly higher than the largest value in the sample, and the 0th percentile value will be slightly smaller than the smallest sample value.

Excel includes two newer functions that let you apply this correction to percentile calculations: PERCENTILE.EXC() and PERCENTRANK.EXC(). The *EXC* stands for excluded, because the 0th and 100th percentile values are *excluded* (they're not part of the sample data you use for your calculation). Excel also includes the PERCENTILE.INC() and PERCENTRANK.INC() functions, where the *INC* stands for *included*. They use the same logic as the traditional PERCENTILE() and PERCENTRANK() functions, which are now designated as compatibility functions (page 233). The only caveat is that all the new functions require Excel 2010 or Excel 2013—they won't work if the spreadsheet is opened in Excel 2007.

FREQUENCY(): Putting Numbers into Grouped Ranges

The FREQUENCY() function is the last statistical function you'll learn about in this section. Like the functions you've seen so far, FREQUENCY() helps you analyze numbers based on the way they're distributed within a group of other numbers. For example, PERCENTILE() and PERCENTRANK() let you examine how a single test score ranks in comparison to other students' scores. Functions like AVERAGE(), RANK(), and MEDIAN() give you other tools to compare how different values stack up against one another.

FREQUENCY() is different from these functions in one key way: It doesn't compare values against each other. Instead, it lets you define multiple ranges, and then, after chewing through a list of numbers, tells you how many values on the list fall into each range. For example, you could use FREQUENCY() to examine a list of incomes in order to see how many belong in a collection of income ranges that you identify.

FREQUENCY() is a little more complicated than the other functions you've seen in this chapter because it gives you what's known as an *array* (a list of separate values). When a function gives you an array, it returns multiple results that Excel must display in different cells.

To use the FREQUENCY() function properly, you first need to create an *array formula*, which displays its results in a group of cells. (Put another way: A plain-vanilla formula occupies *one* cell; an array formula spans *multiple* cells.)

A worksheet filled with student test scores, like the one shown in Figure 9-6, provides an ideal place to learn how the FREQUENCY() function works, showing you how many students aced a test and how many botched it. Here's how to use the FREQUENCY() function to generate the results shown in cells F6 through F10:

1. **Figure out which cells have the numbers you want to analyze.**

   If you were creating the worksheet in Figure 9-6, you'd fill in the first two columns with student names and scores, and then enter the words *Grade, Maximum*, and *Frequency* in columns D, E, and F. You'd also enter the relevant grade ranges in cells D6 to D10—not because the FREQUENCY() function uses them, but to help you remember what each grade range includes. The important part is the maximum scores you enter in cells E6 to E10. The FREQUENCY() function uses these maximums to create each grade range. For the first grade range, it starts at 0 and includes grades up to the maximum value in cell E6 (that's 59). For the second grade range, the FREQUENCY() function starts just after the previous maximum (at 60), and continues to the maximum in cell E7 (69). This process continues until the FREQUENCY() function has processed all the cells and created all the grade ranges. (The ranges and scores in Figure 9-6 represent traditional values, but, of course, you can enter any range you want.)

TIP If you want to calculate the values that fall in a range with no upper maximum (one that simply captures all values from the previous maximum up), leave the cell that defines the maximum value blank. This category must be the last one you define. For instance, in the student grade example, you could leave cell E10 blank, although there's no reason to take this step, because you know a student can't score higher than 100.

   The FREQUENCY() function also needs a set of numbers to *analyze*. These are the student scores you entered in cells B2 through B12. The FREQUENCY() formula itself goes into cells F6 to F10, as explained in the next step.

2. **Select the cells where you want to enter the formula (which is also where the results will appear).**

   One result appears in each cell. In this example, you'd select cells F6 to F10.

3. **Type in the formula.**

   The FREQUENCY() function requires two arguments: the cells you want to analyze (B2:B13) and the cells that set the upper limit of each range (E6:E10). You can manually type in the function arguments, or enter them by clicking in the worksheet itself.

   Here's the actual formula used in this example:

   ```
   =FREQUENCY(B2:B13,E6:E10)
   ```

4. **When you finish entering the formula, press Ctrl+Shift+Enter.**

   You can't simply press Enter, because that just enters the formula into the first selected cell. Instead, you need to press Ctrl+Shift+Enter to copy the formula into *all* the result cells. When you do, you'll see the results shown in Figure 9-6.

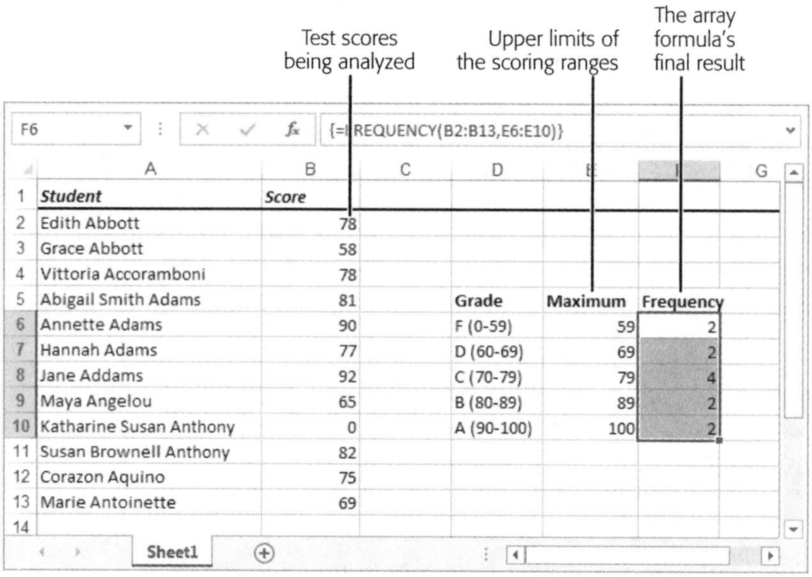

FIGURE 9-6

This worksheet shows the results of the FREQUENCY() function's analysis of student grades. It indicates that four students received a C, while only two received an A. As with any other formula, if you modify the scores or the category maximums, you see the results change automatically. If you want to change your FREQUENCY() formula, make sure you select all the cells in the array, so that you update all of the cells.

MODE(): Finding Numbers That Frequently Occur in a List

MODE() is an interesting function that gives you the most frequently occurring value in a series of values. For example, if you use MODE() with the worksheet shown in Figure 9-6 like this: *=MODE(B2:B10)*, you get the number 78. That's because the score 78 occurs twice, unlike all the other scores, which appear just once.

MODE() does have a few limitations, though. It ignores text values and empty cells, so you can't use it to get the most common text entry. It also returns the error code #N/A if no value appears at least twice. And if more than one value repeats the same number of times, MODE() shows just one of them—the one that has its items occur first in the list.

This last limitation led the creators of Excel to turn MODE() into a compatibility function and introduce two new variants, which work in Excel 2010 and Excel 2013. MODE.SNGL() works the same way as the existing MODE(), which means that it always gives you just a single result. MODE.MULT() is craftier: It returns multiple results, if you have multiple values that tie for first place. For example, if you have a list with three occurrences of 64 and three occurrences of 78, you can capture both values with MODE.MULT(). The trick is that you need to enter MODE.MULT() as an array function. Here's how:

1. **First, decide how many results you want. Select that many cells, either in a continuous row or column.**

   For example, if you select three cells, you'll get up to three results, but not more. You may get fewer, because the exact number of results depends on how many values tie for first place.

2. **With the cells selected, begin typing the formula that uses the MODE.MULT() function.**

   For example, *=MODE.MULT(B2:B10)* searches for repeated values in the column of cells from B2 to B10.

3. **Press Ctrl+Shift+Enter to insert an array formula in all the selected cells.**

   The list of most frequently repeated values will appear. If you have more result cells than results, the extra cells will show the error code #N/A. For example, if your list has two numbers that tie for status as most-frequently-repeated-number, and you use MODE.MULT() in *three* cells, you'll see those two numbers and one #N/A.

General Math Functions

Excel's Math & Trig category contains functions that go a step beyond the basic mathematical operators (like +,-, /, *, and ^) to help you figure out things like absolute values and greatest (and least) common denominators.

TIP Poker fan alert: The COMBIN() and PERMUT() functions may help you keep your game sharp even when you're away from the table.

This section covers 14 of the most commonly used functions in this category.

PRODUCT(), FACT(), POWER(), and SQRT(): Products, Factorials, Powers, and Square Roots

These four functions actually offer the same services many of the simple operators covered in the last chapter provide, but, in some cases, they come with a few twists that may save you time.

The PRODUCT() function takes a list of numbers, multiplies them together, and gives you the result. For example, the following formula multiplies 2*3*3, and arrives at 18:

```
=PRODUCT(2,3,3)
```

One interesting characteristic of the PRODUCT() function is that in addition to accepting *individual* cell references, it also supports cell *ranges*. You can use PRODUCT() to multiply all the numbers in a range the same way you use SUM() to add numbers. Here's an example:

```
=PRODUCT(A2:A12)
```

You can use the FACT() function to calculate a *factorial*, which is a sequence of numbers (starting at 1), each of which is multiplied together to arrive at the result. For example, 5! (pronounced "five factorial") translates to 5*4*3*2*1, which works out to 120. Rather than typing in all these numbers and their accompanying multiplication symbols, you can use the following convenient formula:

```
=FACT(5)
```

People use factorials in many areas of math, including probability theory and calculus. On the other hand, you aren't likely to find factorials cropping up in financial statements or expense reports.

POWER() is a straightforward function used for working with exponents. For example, if you want to calculate 4^3, you can use one of two approaches. You can use the exponentiation operator:

```
=4^3
```

Or you can opt for the POWER() function:

```
=POWER(4,3)
```

The POWER() function is useful if you frequently use cube roots—or any other exponential expressions whose exponent is a fraction—because it lets you write clearer formulas. For example, imagine you want to find the cube root of 4, which, on paper, would be written as $4^{1/3}$. Here's the operator-based expression for that:

```
=4^(1/3)
```

If you perform the same calculation with the POWER() function, you don't need to use parentheses around the exponent (and, more important, you have no chance of getting the wrong answer because you forgot to use them):

```
=POWER(4,1/3)
```

If you simply want to calculate the square root of a number, you can use the POWER() function, or you can summon the SQRT() function, which requires only a single argument. Here's a sample formula that gives you 3:

```
=SQRT(9)
```

QUOTIENT() and MOD(): Higher Division

QUOTIENT() and MOD() are handy for fancy division problems (see Figure 9-7).

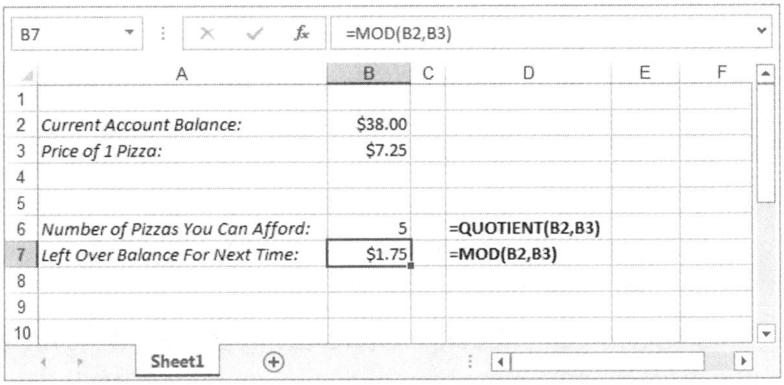

FIGURE 9-7

The QUOTIENT() and MOD() functions let you break a number down into two pieces. In this case, the worksheet uses QUOTIENT() to find out how many pizzas you can afford with a set amount of money, and MOD() to find out how much money you'll have left over.

QUOTIENT() performs *integer* division, which means it ignores any remainder, and gives you just the whole-number result. For example, consider the following formula:

```
=QUOTIENT(7,2)
```

This formula performs the calculation 7/2, and gives you a result of 3. Excel discards the remainder of 1. If you performed this division using the division operator, you'd end up with the fractional value 3.5. Sure, you could truncate the remainder portion using a function like TRUNC(), but the QUOTIENT() function saves you the trouble.

The MOD() function gives you the remainder (also known as the *modulus*) that's left over when you divide a number. For instance, the following formula gives you 1, which is what remains after dividing 7 by 2 using integer division:

```
=MOD(7,2)
```

ABS() and SIGN(): Absolute Value and Determining a Number's Sign

ABS() is a straightforward function that gives you the *absolute value* of a number. The absolute value is the number stripped of any negative sign. Thus, the absolute value of -3 is 3. Here's how that function would look:

```
=ABS(-3)
```

The ABS() function doesn't change a positive number. For example, the absolute value of 8 is just 8. Absolute value calculations work equally well with whole numbers or fractional values. Often, people use ABS() to make sure that a number isn't negative. For example, Excel's financial functions (see Chapter 10) sometimes use negative numbers when you don't expect it—like when you calculate the monthly payment on a loan—to represent the fact that money's leaving your hands. However, to avoid confusing the person reading the spreadsheet, you can use ABS() to make sure that all the information you display is positive, which tends to be what most people understand best.

SIGN() is a related, but less useful, function that lets you quickly determine whether a number is positive or negative. SIGN() gives you a 1 if the number's positive, a 0 if the number's 0 (or the cell's blank), and a –1 if the number's negative (as in the following case):

```
=SIGN(-3)
```

People don't use SIGN() too often, because it's usually just as easy to use a condition like A1<0 to check whether a number's negative.

RAND() and RANDBETWEEN(): Generating Random Numbers

The RAND() function gives you a random fractional number that's less than 1, but greater than or equal to 0 (like 0.778526443457398).

```
=RAND()
```

You can use this function to calculate values in any range. For example, if you want a random value between 0 and 50, multiply the RAND() result by 50, as in this formula:

```
=RAND()*50
```

NOTE Technically, random numbers from a computer aren't really random. Instead, they're either generated from an algorithm or drawn from a list of pseudo random numbers that the computer has stored in its hardware. When generating a random number, most programs look at the current millisecond value of your computer's clock to decide where to start in this list. Despite these limitations, however, Excel's random numbers still suffice for most spreadsheets—just don't count on using them for advanced statistical models or secret-sauce encryption tools.

Converting a RAND()-generated number into an integer is pretty easy: You just use it in conjunction with the INT() function. For example, here's how to get a random whole number from 1 to 6:

```
=INT(RAND()*6)+1
```

For added efficiency, you can save a step with the RANDBETWEEN() function. This function takes two arguments, indicating the minimum and maximum between which you want your randomly selected value to fall. For example, consider the following:

```
=RANDBETWEEN(1,6)
```

This formula generates a random number from 1 to 6, just like the previous formula.

The RAND() and RANDBETWEEN() functions are *volatile functions*, meaning that their results change every time Excel recalculates one of the formulas in the worksheet. This behavior can be quite distracting, as actions like inputting new data, editing a cell, or even undoing an action can trigger recalculation—at which point any random values in your worksheet change. If you want to use the RAND() or RANDBETWEEN() function to generate a set of random numbers and then keep these numbers fixed, you need to do a little more work. Here's the deal:

1. **Create one or more random numbers using the RAND() or RANDBETWEEN() function.**

   For example, you might want to fill a column using RANDBETWEEN(1,6) to simulate the outcome of rolling a die multiple times.

2. **Select the cells with the random values, and copy them by selecting Home→Clipboard→Copy (Ctrl+C).**

   The next step pastes the cell content back into the same location—but with a twist.

3. **Choose Home→Clipboard→Paste→Paste Values.**

   This step overwrites the formulas and permanently inserts the calculated random numbers—permanent, that is, until you decide to change them.

One neat trick involves using the RAND() function to perform a random sort, which is helpful if, say, you need help deciding which of your 12 sisters to call. To do this, you begin by adding a new column next to the column listing their names. Then, put a random number into each cell, as shown in Figure 9-8.

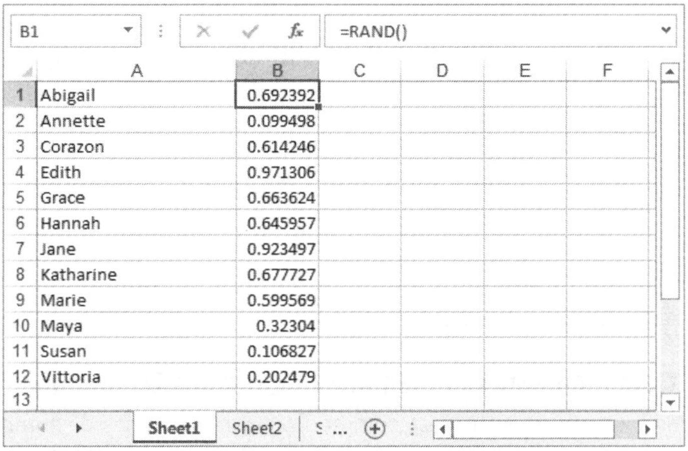
B1 =RAND()

	A	B	C	D	E	F
1	Abigail	0.692392				
2	Annette	0.099498				
3	Corazon	0.614246				
4	Edith	0.971306				
5	Grace	0.663624				
6	Hannah	0.645957				
7	Jane	0.923497				
8	Katharine	0.677727				
9	Marie	0.599569				
10	Maya	0.32304				
11	Susan	0.106827				
12	Vittoria	0.202479				
13						

Sheet1 Sheet2

FIGURE 9-8

Insert a random value next to each item you want to sort randomly. To speed this process up, you can use the AutoFill feature (page 62) to copy your formula.

Next, select all the cells you want to sort and the accompanying random values. (In this example, that's cells A1 through B12.) Choose Data→Sort & Filter→Sort, and then create a sort order that uses the random values; Figure 9-9 explains how to do so.

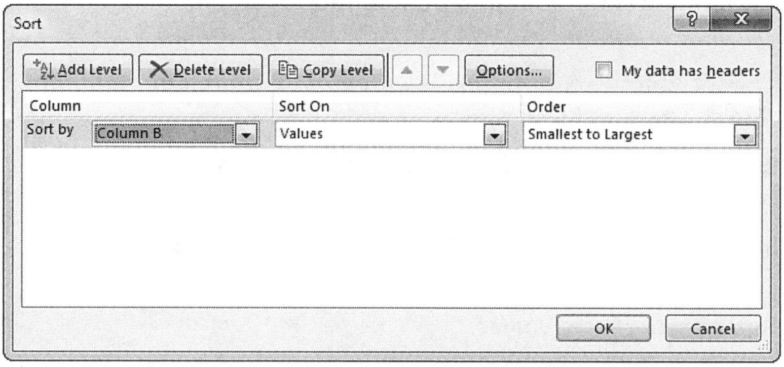

FIGURE 9-9

In the "Sort by" box, choose the column that has the random values (in this case, Column B). Leave the rest of the settings untouched, and then click OK. (You can check out page 424 for more detail on Excel's sort feature.) The final result is shown in Figure 9-10.

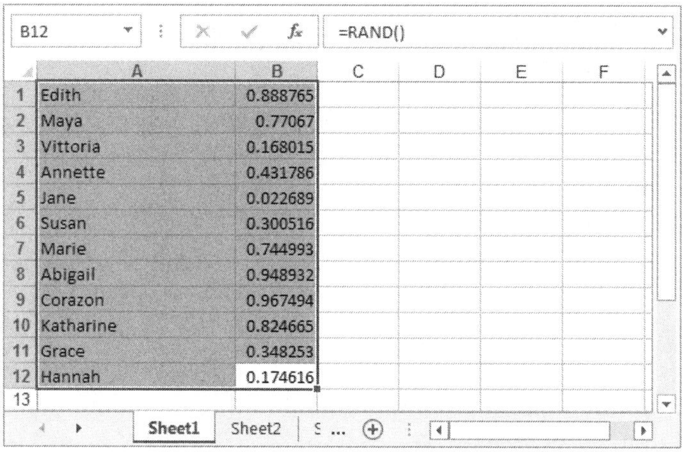

FIGURE 9-10

The final result is a randomly ordered list of names and, oddly enough, a new set of random numbers, because Excel recalculates your random numbers at the end of every sort operation. If you want a different random sort, you can simply re-sort the list (choose Data→Sort & Filter→Sort again).

GCD() and LCM(): Greatest and Least Common Denominator

The GCD() function returns the greatest common divisor in a series of numbers you specify. For example, consider the numbers 12 and 8. Both numbers share the divisor 4 (12/4 = 3 and 8/4 = 2). Therefore 4 is the greatest common divisor of 12 and 8. You can also divide the number 12 by 6, but it isn't possible to divide 8 by 6 without generating a fraction.

Here's how you find the greatest common divisor of 12 and 8 using the GCD() function:

```
=GCD(12,8)
```

Consider a few points about GCD(). If you use fractional values, GCD() simply ignores the fractional part of the number. That means that it calculates GCD(12.5,8.1) the same way that it calculates GCD(12,8). Also, Excel always finds a common divisor, as all whole numbers are divisible by 1, even if they don't have any other divisors.

The LCM(), or least common multiple function, works slightly differently. It considers the multiples of every number you supply, and looks for the smallest multiple that they all have in common. For example, consider 12 and 8 again. The multiples of 12 are 12, 24, 36, and so on. The multiples of 8 are 8, 16, 24, 34, and so on. The smallest multiple that 12 and 8 have in common is 24, which is exactly what LCM() calculates in this formula:

```
=LCM(12,8)
```

No matter what numbers you use, they always have a common multiple that LCM() can find. (If nothing else, you can always multiply your numbers together to create a common multiple. For example, 12*8 produces a number that's guaranteed to be a multiple of both 12 and 8, although, in this case, it's not the *lowest* multiple.)

COMBIN() and PERMUT(): Figuring Combinations and Permutations

People use the COMBIN() and PERMUT() functions in probability theory, to count the number of possible outcomes when randomly choosing items from a set. COMBIN() and PERMUT() are short for *combinations* and *permutations*, which are mathematical terms for the number of distinct combinations you can make from a set of items. The main difference lies in the way they consider the order of items in a set (more on that in a moment).

One reason you might use COMBIN() and PERMUT() is to assess the odds in a game of chance. You could use COMBIN() to help you figure out, say, the odds of being dealt an ace of spades from a deck of cards. And people often use both these functions to calculate the occurrence of other random events, like winning the lottery or being hit by a falling anvil.

Both COMBIN() and PERMUT() take two arguments. The first is the number of items in your set. The second argument is the number of items you want to randomly "draw" from the set. For example:

```
COMBIN(number_in_set, number_chosen)
```

The key difference between COMBIN() and PERMUT() is that PERMUT() assumes order is important, while COMBIN() assumes it isn't. For example, say you want to count how many possible ways you can *draw* five cards from a 52-card deck.

You'd use the PERMUT() function as shown here:

```
=PERMUT(52,5)
```

PERMUT() generates a whopping result of *311,875,200*, because it counts every group of five cards as unique, even if the difference is only a matter of card order. Thus, PERMUT() considers the set 1, 2, 3, 4, 5 different from the set 5, 4, 3, 2, 1. By contrast, when COMBIN() evaluates those same parameters, it returns a value of *2,598,960*.

As you can see, permutations are far more plentiful than combinations. In fact, you can convert the number of combinations into the number of permutations by multiplying it by 5! (5*4*3*2*1), which is a measure of how many different ways you can arrange the order of five items.

To go much further with PERMUT() and COMBIN(), you'll need a refresher course in probability theory. However, you may be interested to know that you can find the *probability* of an event by dividing the number of satisfactory outcomes (the number of outcomes that meet your criteria) into the number of total outcomes (the total number of possibilities). For example, the chance of your getting a specific hand of cards is expressed like so:

```
=1/COMBIN(52,5)
```

Here, you're only interested in a single outcome (a hand that has every card you want). Thus, there's one satisfactory outcome. You can use the COMBIN() function to find the total number of possibilities by counting the different possible draws. To see your percentage chance of getting the cards you want, you can multiply the result by 100 or use the Percentage number style.

If you aren't completely cross-eyed over probability yet, you'll be interested to learn that Excel 2013 adds two new functions to the mix: PERMUTATIONA() and COMBINA(), for solving slightly different problems. Both functions allow duplicate picks. For example, say you write this formula:

```
=PERMUTATIONA(52,5)
```

Now Excel calculates how many different possibilities there are if you pick one card at random, then put it back in the pile, and then pick again, repeating the process five times. There are now more possibilities because the cards you pick aren't excluded—they're returned to the pile and can be picked again. The result of this formula reflects this difference, indicating *380,204,032* possible permutations rather than *311,875,200*, which is the total if you keep your hand of five cards separate.

NOTE As always, be cautious when using new functions, because PERMUTATIONA() and COMBINA() won't work on older versions of Excel.

BASE() and DECIMAL(): Converting Numbers to Different Bases

As all mathematicians and computer geeks know, humans count using a base-10 numbering system. That means there are exactly 10 different digits (that's 0, 1, 2, 3, 4, 5, 6, 7, 8, and 9). Once you use them all—say, by counting from 0 to 9—you need to add another digit and start counting all over again (as in 10, 11, 12, 13, and so on).

Having 10 fingers, most of us are quite comfortable with this counting system. However, it's easy to cook up a number system that uses a different base. Sometimes, different bases are used to solve certain types of problems more easily. In the computer world, they're used to match the physical characteristics of the underlying hardware. For example, you've probably heard of binary counting, which uses a base-2 number system that includes just two digits: 0 and 1. Counting to 10 in binary goes like this: 1, 10, 11, 100, 101, and so on, eventually arriving at 1010.

You can also use numbering systems that have more than 10 digits, provided you swap in some other symbol or letter. For example, the hexadecimal system used to store data in computer memory is base-16, which means it allows digits from 1 to 10 and then A to F. The number 124 in the decimal system becomes 7C in hexadecimal notation.

Excel has two functions that can make these sort of conversions for you automatically. The first is BASE(), which converts a normal decimal number into a different base. It has this syntax:

```
BASE(number, base)
```

So here's how you convert 482 to binary (base-2):

```
=BASE(482, 2)
```

And here's how you convert it to hexadecimal (base-16):

```
=BASE(482, 16)
```

The DECIMAL() function does the reverse, converting a number from the base you indicate into a plain-Jane decimal number. Here's how to decode a binary number:

```
=DECIMAL("111100010", 2)
```

You need to put the number you want to convert in quotation marks. Otherwise, Excel attempts to treat it as an ordinary base-10 number, which will cause an error if your binary string is very long or your number includes non-numeric characters (like letters in a hexadecimal number).

Here's an example formula that converts a hexadecimal number into decimal representation:

```
=DECIMAL("1E2",16)
```

In both the examples above, the answer is the same: 482.

NOTE BASE() and DECIMAL() are new functions, introduced in Excel 2013. They won't work if you open your spreadsheet in an older version of Excel. However, Excel includes a number of better-supported functions for conversions to and from binary, octal, and hexadecimal number systems, with names like DEC2HEX() and BIN2DEC(). You can find them in the ribbon by choosing Formulas→Function Library→More Functions→Engineering.

ROMAN() and ARABIC(): Using Roman Numerals

Excel provides two bizarre functions that work with an even more exotic number system: Roman numerals. You use ROMAN() to convert an ordinary number (from 1 to 3999) into Roman numerals.

```
ROMAN(number, [form])
```

For example, ROMAN(4) returns the text *IV*. You may find large Roman numerals very confusing, so use the optional form argument to tell Excel to simplify the Roman numeral by applying a kind of rounding off effect. Form can range from 0 (which generates the unrounded Roman numeral) to 4 (which generates a much shorter but slightly less precise version). Search Excel's Help for *ROMAN* for a complete explanation.

The ARABIC() function is the counterpart to ROMAN(). It converts a Roman numeral stored as text (like *IV*) into the corresponding Arabic number (4). Unlike ROMAN(), ARABIC() is supported only in Excel 2013.

Trigonometry and Advanced Math

People sometimes describe trigonometry as the science of circles and angles. It's trigonometry that helps you calculate the hypotenuse of a triangle or the diameter of a circle. However, when you use trigonometry in Excel, you probably won't be worrying about shapes; instead, you'll be using some type of formula from a scientific field that requires common trigonometric calculations, like the cosine or tangent.

Students of the sciences know that trigonometry turns up anywhere you need to think about space, including geography, astronomy, kinematics, and optics. Less direct applications turn up in just about every other scientific field—from chemistry to social science.

Excel's trigonometry functions work just as any other Excel functions do. Knowing *when* to use these functions is another issue, and it may require a refresher course in mathematics. Table 9-1 lists the functions you can use. Figure 9-11 shows how you can use trigonometry to solve a common high-school math problem: You have the distance to a tree (which you can easily measure), and the angle between your current position and the top of the tree (which you can estimate). The problem is, you have no way to judge the height of the tree.

TABLE 9-1 *Trigonometry functions*

FUNCTION	SYNTAX	DESCRIPTION
ACOS()	ACOS(number)	Calculates the inverse cosine (also known as the arccosine) of a number.
ACOSH()	ACOSH(number)	Calculates the inverse hyperbolic cosine of a number.
ASIN()	ASIN(number)	Calculates the inverse sine (also known as the arcsine) of a number.
ATAN()	ATAN(number)	Calculates the inverse tangent (also known as the arctangent) of a number.
ATANH()	ATANH(number)	Calculates the inverse hyperbolic tangent of a number.
COS()	COS(angle)	Calculates the cosine of an angle.
COSH()	COSH(angle)	Calculates the hyperbolic cosine of an angle.
DEGREES()	DEGREES(angle)	Converts an angle in radians into degrees. 360 degrees equals 2ϖ radians.
EXP()	EXP(power)	Calculates e (the natural logarithm constant), raised to the power you specify.
LN()	LN(number)	Calculates the natural logarithm of a number (which is the logarithm with the base of e).
LOG()	LOG(number, base)	Calculates the logarithm of a number with the base you specify.
LOG10()	LOG10(number)	Calculates the base 10 logarithm of a number.
PI()	PI()	Returns the mathematical constant pi (ϖ), which is approximately 3.14.
RADIANS()	RADIANS(degrees)	Converts an angle in degrees into an angle in radians. 360 degrees equals 2ϖ radians.
SIN()	SIN(angle)	Calculates the sine of an angle.
SINH()	SINH(angle)	Calculates the hyperbolic sine of an angle.
TAN()	TAN(angle)	Calculates the tangent of an angle.
TANH()	TANH(angle)	Calculates the hyperbolic tangent of an angle.

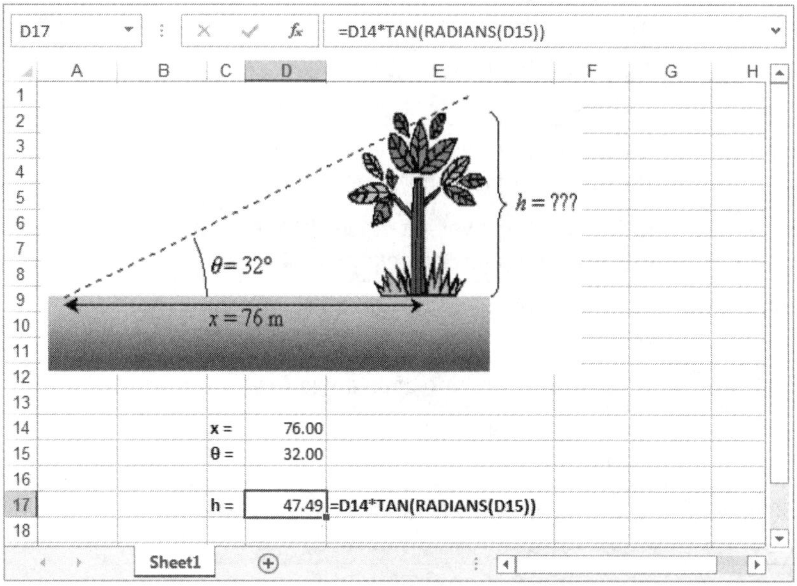

FIGURE 9-11

*You can solve this problem by using the trigonometric identity tan = h/x. You can rearrange this formula to find h (the height of the tree) so that h = x*tan. Be aware that Excel calculates the tangent using radians, which are a measure of an angle, like degrees. Fortunately, Excel provides a RADIANS() function, making it easy to convert degrees to radians. (You can do the reverse—convert radians to degrees—using Excel's DEGREES() function.) In this example, you use the RADIANS() function to convert degrees into radians, and then use the result of that calculation as the argument in the TAN() function.*

In addition to its trigonometric functions, Excel includes a number of specialized mathematical functions, like those used with matrices. Table 9-2 summarizes them.

TABLE 9-2 *Miscellaneous math functions*

FUNCTION	SYNTAX	DESCRIPTION
FACTDOUBLE()	FACTDOUBLE(number)	Calculates the double factorial of a number. The double factorial's like a factorial, but it skips every second number. Thus, 5!! is 5*3*1 (whereas 5! is 5*4*3*2*1).
MDETERM()	MDETERM(range)	Calculates the determinant of a matrix.
MINVERSE()	MINVERSE(range)	Returns the inverse of a matrix. This is an array function that returns multiple results.
MMULT()	MMULT(range1, range2)	Returns the result of multiplying two matrixes. This function's an array function that returns multiple results.
MULTINOMIAL()	MULTINOMIAL(range)	Returns the multinomial of a set of numbers. The multinomial's the ratio of the factorial of a sum of values to the product of factorials.
SERIESSUM()	SERIESSUM(x, n, m, coefficients)	Calculates the sum of a power series, where x is the base of the power series, n is the initial power to raise x to, m is the increment to the power for each term in the series, and co are the coefficients by which each successive power of x is multiplied. For more gory mathematical details, check out a detailed example of the series formula in Excel's function reference (choose Formulas→Function Library→Insert Function, find the function, and then click the "Help on this function" link).
SQRTPI()	SQRTPI(number)	Multiplies a number by pi (ϖ), and then calculates the square root of the result.

POWER USERS' CLINIC

An Advanced Engineering Toolkit

Excel includes an Engineering category of functions with some very specialized mathematical functions. To take a look, select Formulas→Function Library→More Functions→Engineering.

These functions tackle several specialized mathematical problems, including those using imaginary numbers (numbers that incorporate *i*, the square root of –1), Bessel functions, bit-shifting operations, error functions, and number conversions between binary, decimal, and octal representations. These functions come in handy for advanced mathematical spreadsheets, but if you don't know the difference between a complex conjugate and a vector, they probably aren't very useful.

Excel hasn't cornered the market on advanced math features. You can get many more specialized functions if you install add-ins from other vendors. (Google "Excel add-ins" to start searching.) And in Chapter 30, you'll learn how to write the custom logic for your own functions using Visual Basic for Applications (VBA).

Advanced Statistics

Excel offers a smorgasbord of number-crunching tools; in fact, it has more than 50 advanced statistical functions that this chapter hasn't even mentioned. Many of these will appeal only to those who already understand concepts like standard deviation, theoretical distributions, and dimensionless Pearson product moment correlation coefficients (a subject of keen interest to all six people in the world who currently use such numbers).

But even if you don't understand *any* of these concepts (and if you're still wondering whether your inner mathematician may yet emerge), Excel has two advanced statistical functions—FORECAST() and TREND()—that give you a taste of all that awaits the advanced statistician. While both FORECAST() and TREND() rely on some complex, behind-the-scenes computations, you can use them quite easily, even if you're not a specialist.

The FORECAST() and TREND() functions predict missing values based on existing data. These "missing" values may represent experimental data you didn't collect, or future sales numbers for dates that haven't yet occurred. Excel examines the data you have so far (the more the better), and uses a mathematical technique known as the *method of least squares* to generate a trend line. Excel then uses this trend line to generate the other values you requested.

Both FORECAST() and TREND() work similarly and produce the same answers. However, FORECAST() calculates just a single value; TREND(), on the other hand, is an array function that gives you multiple values. It works a little like the FREQUENCY() function described on page 276.

The FORECAST() and TREND() analyses work by spotting relationships between two sets of numbers, designated as the X-axis and Y-axis. To predict a new value using the FORECAST() function, for instance, you supply the function with a new X value. It then uses the known relationship between the X and Y values to guess the corresponding new Y value. The syntax is as follows:

```
FORECAST(x, known_y_values, known_x_values)
```

For example, imagine you're trying to study the relationship between the number of product inquiries received during one month and the actual sales recorded in the next month. You have plenty of historical data, and you'd like to use that to predict how many sales you should expect next month (based on the number of inquiries you've received during the current month). The existing inquiry numbers are the first set of known values, so they make up the X-axis values (the cells A2:A9, as shown in Figure 9-12). The second set of known values is the actual recorded sales in the following month (the Y-axis values, shown in cells B2:B9). You want to predict a new Y-axis value for expected sales based on the current inquiries (cell A12). Here's the final formula:

```
=FORECAST(A12,B2:B9,A2:A9)
```

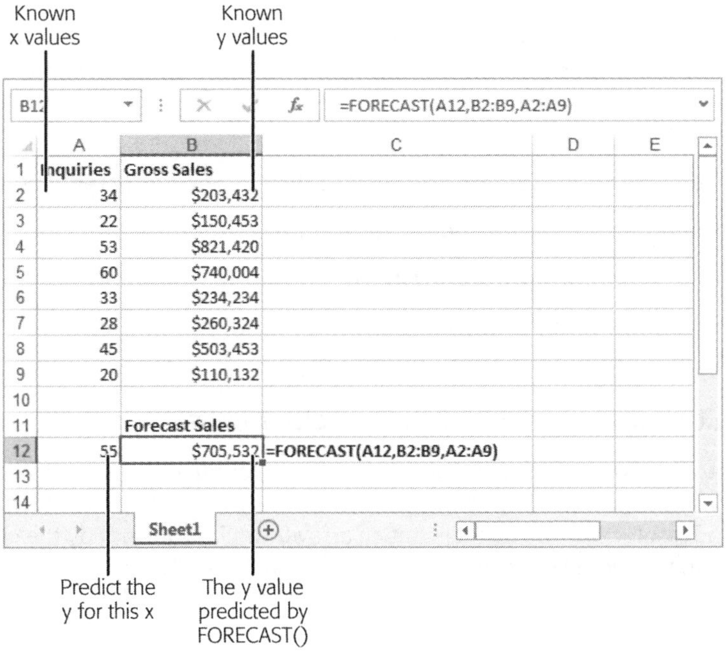

FIGURE 9-12

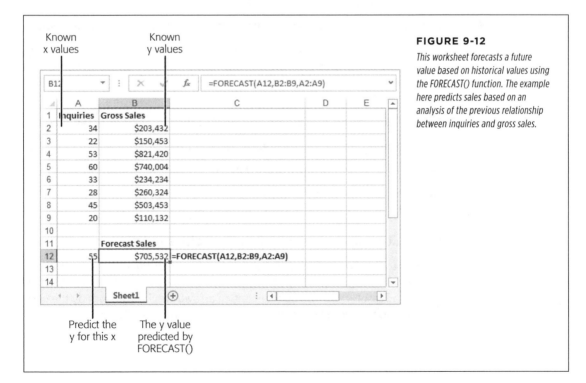

This worksheet forecasts a future value based on historical values using the FORECAST() function. The example here predicts sales based on an analysis of the previous relationship between inquiries and gross sales.

NOTE The FORECAST() and TREND() functions can always find some sort of relationship using your data. However, if your data doesn't have a real correlation, then the values they predict will be meaningless. For example, the number of product inquiries may not be an effective predictor of future sales, especially when you consider other factors. Determining where correlations exist and what relationships are statistically significant is a much more subtle and complex issue than just using the FORECAST() and TREND() functions. An understanding of basic statistics will set you down the right path.

You can also use the TREND() function to generate expected sales based on multiple inquiry numbers (as opposed to the single sales value that FORECAST() generates). Using the previous example, you could theoretically use TREND() to predict sales for the next six months. In truth, that approach doesn't really make sense because, while you have previous sales data to draw from, you don't know how many inquiries you'll receive in future months.

You're better off using TREND() to project future sales based on a slightly different set of data. You still use previous sales, but rather than using *inquiries* as your second known factor, you use the *progression of time*. In effect, you're asking TREND() if your sales over periods 1, 2, and 3 were 100, 150, and 200, what would sales look like over periods 4, 5, and 6? Without further ado, here's what you need to generate new, predicted sales figures using the TREND() function:

1. **Make sure your worksheet has all the data your TREND() formula needs.**

   As shown in Figure 9-13, you need three groups of numbers: known y-values (historical sales figures), known x-values (previous time periods), and the new x-values (known, new time periods). You want the formula to figure out the new y-values (that is, the sales figures).

2. **Select the range of cells where you want to display the predicted values.**

   In this example, four new sales figures appear in cells C11:C14.

3. **Enter the array formula using the TREND() function.**

   Here's the formula used in this example:

   ```
   =TREND(C2:C9, A2:A9, A11:A14)
   ```

4. **When you finish typing in the formula, hit Ctrl+Shift+Enter.**

   You can't simply press Enter, as that enters only the formula into the first selected cell. Instead, you need to press Ctrl+Shift+Enter to copy the array formula into all the result cells. You can tell that an array formula is at work by the curly braces {} in the formula bar, which Excel adds automatically.

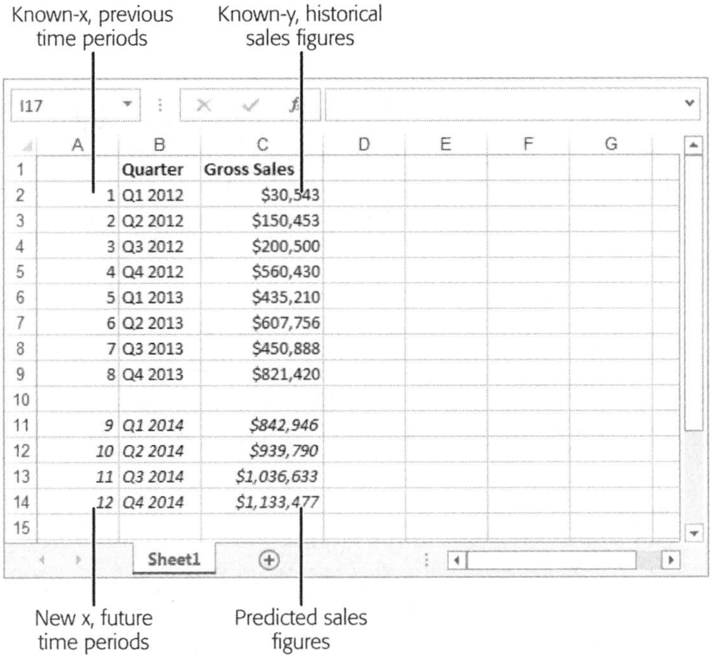

FIGURE 9-13

All signs point to a strong year. Based on the previous growth in sales, Excel cheerily predicts four more quarters of escalating growth. (Excel has predicted the italicized cells.) Keep in mind, of course, that Excel generated these numbers using the pattern of the last two years. Various other factors could make the predicted trend irrelevant.

Excel provides many more advanced statistical functions. For the full list, refer to the Formulas→Formula Library→More Functions→Statistical group. Table 9-3 outlines some of the more commonly used functions in this group.

TABLE 9-3 *Advanced statistical functions*

FUNCTION	SYNTAX	DESCRIPTION
AVEDEV()	AVEDEV(range)	Calculates the average deviation, which is the average of how much a series of data points deviate from the mean.
CORREL()	CORREL(range1, range2)	Calculates the correlation coefficient between two sets of data, which is a measure of how the sets are related. The correlation coefficient's always between –1 and 1 (the closer to 1, the stronger the correlation, while 0 means no correlation at all).

FUNCTION	SYNTAX	DESCRIPTION
COVAR()	COVAR(range1, range2)	Calculates the covariance, which is the average of the products of deviation for each data point pair. Covariance determines whether a relationship exists between data sets.
LINEST()	LINEST(known_y_values, known_x_values)	Calculates the best-fit line using the least squares method. This array function returns both the slope and the y-intercept.
NORMDIST()	NORMDIST(x, mean, standard_dev)	Calculates the normal cumulative distribution for a specified mean and standard deviation.
NORMINV()	NORMINV(probability, mean, standard_deviation)	Calculates the inverse of the normal cumulative distribution for a specified mean and standard deviation.
SLOPE()	SLOPE(known_y, known_x)	Calculates a regression line through the supplied data points, and returns its slope.
STDEV()	STDEV(range)	Calculates the standard deviation of a data set. Excel ignores blank cells and cells that have text in them.
STDEVA()	STDEVA(range)	Calculates the standard deviation of a data set. Excel assigns text cells a value of 0, but ignores blank cells.
VAR()	VAR(range)	Estimates the variance of a sample population. Excel ignores blank cells and cells that have text in them.
VARA()	VARA(range)	Estimates the variance of a sample population. Excel assigns text cells a value of 0, but ignores blank cells.

CHAPTER

10

Financial Functions

Calculating cosines and analyzing statistical trends may seem like a great way to tap Excel's brainpower, but what if you want help tracking the movement of small pieces of green paper from one bank account to another? Fortunately, Excel's no slouch when it comes to dealing with money. In fact, it comes with a slew of financial functions that can help you figure out the bottom line like a pro.

Most of Excel's financial functions help you determine how numbers change over time. With them, you can track soaring assets or mounting debts. In this chapter, you'll start by learning basic financial concepts, like *present value* and *payment period*, which Excel bases all of its financial functions on. Afterward, you'll take a close look at some of the most useful financial functions, complete with examples that answer common questions about mortgages, loans, and investments.

The World of Finance

Before you start using Excel's financial functions, it helps to understand the financial concepts that lie at the heart of many of these operations. Here are some terms that those wacky accountants love to use:

- **Present Value (PV).** The value of an investment or loan at the very beginning of its life. (Hopefully, after this point, the investment will rise or you'll begin to pay off the loan.) This number's also called the *principal*.
- **Future Value (FV).** The value of an investment or loan at some point in the future.

- **Rate.** The rate at which an investment or loan will increase or decrease. A typical investment could have an annual interest rate of 5 percent, which means that after one year, the future value will be 5 percent larger than the present value.
- **Payment (PMT).** An amount of money you contribute to an investment or loan. It's a regular contribution, usually made at the same time as the interest on the investment or loan is calculated.
- **Number of Payment Periods (NPER).** The total number of payment periods between the present value and the future value of an investment or loan. If you've got a three-year car loan (with payments due monthly), the NPER equals 36—in other words, there are 12 payment periods each year, for 3 years.

Usually, you'll use one of Excel's financial formulas when you have *some* of the information from the list above, but not all of it. Maybe you want to discover how much an investment will increase in value over a set amount of time. Or perhaps you want to determine what rate of savings you need to maintain in order to collect a certain amount of money for retirement.

UP TO SPEED

Knowing When to Use Positive and Negative Numbers

Since Excel lets you use the same functions whether you're calculating investments or loans, the big thing to remember—and one of the hardest—is whether to use positive or negative numbers in your formulas. The rules of thumb are as follows:

- If it's money that's leaving your hands, whether it's a deposit *to* an account or a payment *for* a loan, then the number should be negative.
- If it's money that's coming *to* you, whether you're receiving a loan or an investment that's matured, the number should be positive.

Be on the lookout for numbers bearing an incorrect sign. If the results of your formula indicate an unusually large monthly payment, a shrinking investment, or a growing loan balance, numbers with incorrect signs may be at fault. The easiest way to see is to slightly modify your formula, and watch how it changes. If you *decrease* the amount of money you want to borrow and the monthly payment *increases*, one of your numbers probably has the wrong sign.

Financial Functions

Excel includes several dozen financial formulas, but non-accountants use only a handful of these regularly. These all-purpose functions, described in the following sections, are remarkably flexible. You can use them to make projections about how investments or loans will change over time, or to answer hypothetical questions about investments or loans. Perhaps you want to determine the interest rate or length of time you need to reach an investment goal or pay off a loan.

FV(): Future Value

The FV() function lets you calculate the future value of an investment, assuming a fixed interest rate. Perhaps the FV() function's most convenient feature is that it lets you factor in regular payments, which makes it perfect for calculating how money's accumulating in a retirement or savings account.

To understand how FV() works, it helps to start out by considering what life would be like without FV(). Imagine you invested $10,000 that's earning a fixed interest rate of 5 percent over one year. You want to know how much your investment's going to be worth at the end of the year. You can tackle this problem quite easily with the following formula:

```
=10000*105%
```

This calculation provides you with the future value—that is, the initial 100 percent of the principal you invested plus an additional 5 percent in interest income.

It's just as easy to determine what happens if you keep your money invested for two years, reinvesting the 5 percent interest payment for an additional year. Here's the formula for that:

```
=10000*105%*105%
```

In the end, you wind up with a tidy $11,025.

Clearly, for these simple calculations, you don't need any help from Excel's financial functions. However, real accounts aren't always this simple. Here are two common problems that can make the aforementioned calculation a lot more difficult to solve using a do-it-yourself formula:

- You invest your money in a savings account that pays interest monthly. Even though the annual rate of interest's the same as in the earlier examples, your money accumulates faster, thanks to *compound interest* (that is, interest earned on the interest you previously earned).
- You make regular deposits to the investment account. You can't calculate this extra amount of money separately because it also accumulates interest, starting from the date on which you deposit it.

All of a sudden, this calculation isn't so easy. Of course, you could solve it on your own, but the formula you'd need to write is startlingly complex. At this point, the FV() function becomes a lot more attractive. Here's how the function breaks down (remember, brackets indicate optional arguments):

```
FV(rate, nper, payment, [pv], [type])
```

- The *rate* is the interest rate your investment's earning.
- The *nper* is the number of interest payments. If your investment distributes interest once a year and you invest your money over a two-year period, the nper is 2. If you make regular contributions, this value also specifies the number of contributions you make. FV() assumes that you make every contribution on

the same day the interest is paid, which is an unfortunate limitation. (You can get around this limitation by using FV() several times to calculate the value of individual contributions, and then adding those contributions together.)

- The *payment* is the amount of the contribution you want to make regularly. Set this to 0 if you don't want to add anything.
- The *pv* is the present value, or the initial balance, in your account. If you omit this value, Excel assumes you start with nothing. As a result, you need to include a value other than 0 for the payment argument. (There's no sense tracking a nonexistent investment.)
- The *type* indicates the timing of the payment. If you specify 0 (or omit this value), Excel assumes you'll make the payment at the end of the period. If you specify 1, Excel assumes you'll make the payment at the beginning of the period, giving your interest just a little bit more time to compound.

The only trick—some would say Bizarro World element—with FV() is that you need to make sure both the payment and the initial balance (*pv*) are *negative* numbers (or zero values). Huh? Isn't this money that's *accumulating* for you? Here's what's going on: In Excel's thinking, the initial balance and the regular contributions represent money you're *handing over*, so these numbers need to be negative. The final value is positive because that's the total you get back.

Continuing with the earlier example, here's how you'd rewrite the formula that calculates the return on a $10,000 investment after one year of earning five percent annual interest:

```
=FV(5%, 1, 0, -10000)
```

NOTE The formula knows that this is a one-year investment because the 5% is an *annual* interest rate, and you've indicated (through the second argument) that there's only one interest payment being made.

This calculation returns the expected value of $10,500. But what happens if you switch to an account that pays *monthly* interest? You now have 12 interest payment periods per year, and each one pays 1/12th of the total 5 percent interest (see Figure 10-1). Here's the revised formula:

```
=FV(5%/12, 12, 0, -10000)
```

Note that two numbers are different from the original formula: the interest (divided by 12 because it's calculated per payment period) and the number of payment periods. The new total earned is a slightly improved $10,511.62.

NOTE The interest rate and the number of payment periods always must use the same time scale. If payments are monthly, then you must use a monthly interest rate. (Remember, to calculate the monthly interest rate, just take the yearly interest rate and divide by 12.)

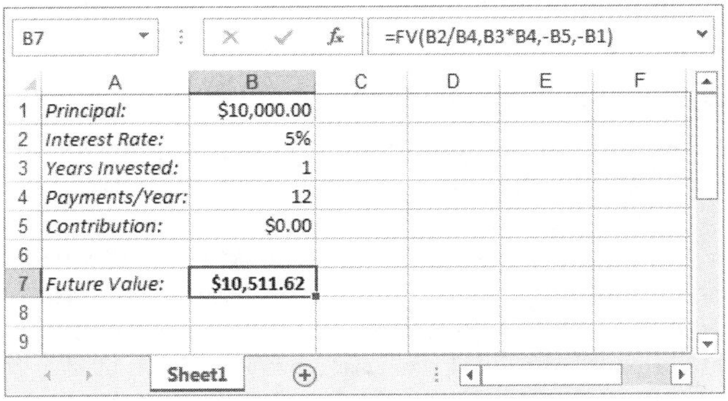

FIGURE 10-1

This worksheet depicts a future value calculation using the FV() function and the information in cells B1 to B5. In this example, the initial balance is $10,000, the interest is 5 percent (paid monthly), and you don't make any additional contributions. Note that, in the formula bar, Excel calculates the nper (number of interest payments) by multiplying Years Invested by Payments/Year.

Finally, here's the calculation over two years. The only number that changes is the number of payment periods.

```
=FV(5%/12, 24, 0, -10000)
```

And while you're at it, why not check to see what happens if you make a monthly contribution of $100 to top up the fund? In this case, you'll make payments at the beginning of the month. The formula for this scenario is:

```
=FV(5%/12, 24, -100, -10000, 1)
```

Now, the total tops $13,000 ($13,578.50 to be precise). Not bad for a little number-crunching!

Incidentally, FV() works just as well on loan payments. Say you take out a $10,000 loan and decide to repay $200 monthly. Interest is set at 7 percent and calculated monthly. The formula that tells you your *outstanding* balance after three years—that is, the amount you still owe—is as follows:

```
=FV(7%/12, 3*12, -200, 10000)
```

Note that the balance begins positive, because it's money you *received*, while the payment is negative, because it's money you pay out. After three years, you'll probably be disappointed to learn that the loan hasn't been paid off. The FV() function returns –4,343.24, which is the balance you owe.

NOTE The FV() function simply can't solve some of the more complex financial problems. It can't take into account, for example, payments that change, interest rates that change, or payments that aren't made on the same date as the interest date. You can sometimes deal with an interest rate that varies from one year to another by using the FV() function more than once, to calculate the years separately. Excel includes some advanced functions to help you here—if you have an advanced accounting degree. If not, you may be interested in checking out a heavyweight reference book like *Financial Analysis with Microsoft Excel* (South-Western College Pub, 2011).

FREQUENTLY ASKED QUESTION

Monthly Versus Annual Interest Rates

How do I compare monthly and annual interest rates?

A dollar may always be a dollar, but a five percent interest rate may not always pay what you expect. The important factor is how often your interest's *compounded*, which all depends on how often the interest payments are paid to your account (or calculated against your loan). As you've seen with the FV() function examples, if 5 percent interest is compounded monthly, you have a chance to make a little extra cash. That's because your interest payments make it into your account before the year's over, giving you the chance to earn some additional interest on the amount of interest you've received so far.

When comparing different types of investments, it's often important to get a feeling for how much difference compound interest makes. Say you need to know which investment option is better—one that pays 5 percent after one year, or a savings account that pays a monthly interest of 4.75 percent. To answer this question, you can run the numbers with FV(), or you can use a shortcut, available courtesy of the EFFECT() function. This financial function calculates the effective annual interest for an interest rate that's compounded multiple times. All you need to do is specify two arguments: the rate and the number of times it'll be compounded. In the case of a 4.75 percent rate compounded 12 times over the course of the year, here's your formula:

```
=EFFECT(4.75%, 12)
```

This formula returns a result of 0.485, or 4.85 percent. In other words, 4.75 percent compounded monthly is equivalent to 4.85 percent compounded annually, provided you don't make any more payments during the lifetime of the investment. Assuming you don't need early access to your money, the 5 percent fixed investment's still the better deal. How much better? Well, once again, you could use FV() to calculate the future value. But seeing as you've used EFFECT() so far, why not just try the following shortcut?

```
=(5%-EFFECT(4.75%,12)) * 10000
```

Keeping in mind Excel's precedence rules (page 224), which specify that expressions inside parentheses get evaluated first, here's what's happening: first, the EFFECT() function repeats the calculation just performed, returning a value of 0.0485. Excel then subtracts this value from 5 percent (0.05), leaving you with the difference between the two rates: about 0.15 percent. Once you multiply that by the total amount of money you invested ($10,000), you get the extra bit of money you make.

In this example, the difference between the fixed investment and the savings account is a modest $14.52, which may be a price worth paying for flexibility.

PV(): Present Value

The PV() function calculates the initial value of an investment or loan (which is also called the present value). The PV() function takes almost the same arguments as the FV() function, except that Excel replaces the optional *pv* argument with an optional *fv* (or future value) argument:

```
PV(rate, nper, payment, [fv], [type])
```

At first glance, the PV() function may not seem as useful as FV(). Using future information to calculate a value from the past somehow seems counterintuitive. Can't people just dig up the principal value from their own records?

Yes, but the real purpose of PV() is to answer hypothetical questions. If you know what interest rate you can get for your money, how long you'll be invested, and what future value you hope to attain, you can pose the following question: What initial amount of money do I need to come up with? The PV() function can provide the answer.

Consider this formula:

```
=PV(10%/12, 25*12, 0, 1000000)
```

The question Excel answers here is: In order to end up with $1,000,000, how much money do I need to invest initially, assuming a 10 percent annual interest rate (compounded monthly) and a maturation period of 25 years? The PV() function returns a modest result of $82,939.75. (Technically, the result is negative, which indicates that you need shell out this money at the beginning.)

NOTE If you don't have that much cash on hand, you can supplement your principal with a regular investment. The following formula assumes a monthly payment of $200, paid at the beginning of each month. Note that you should type in a negative number for the monthly payment, because it's money you're giving up:

```
=PV(10%/12, 25*12, -200, 1000000)
```

This change decreases the principal you need to a cool $60,930.30.

See Figure 10-2 for a much larger collection of PV formulas designed to answer the popular question: Who wants to be a millionaire? These formulas assume no monthly payment, and display the initial investment you need to make to reach a cool million. Sharp eyes will notice that the formula uses partially fixed references (like $A9 instead of A9). That means you can copy the formula from one cell to another without mangling the cell reference. $A9 tells Excel that it can change the row but not the column. As a result, no matter where you paste it, this formula always retrieves a number from column A of the current row, which is the interest rate.

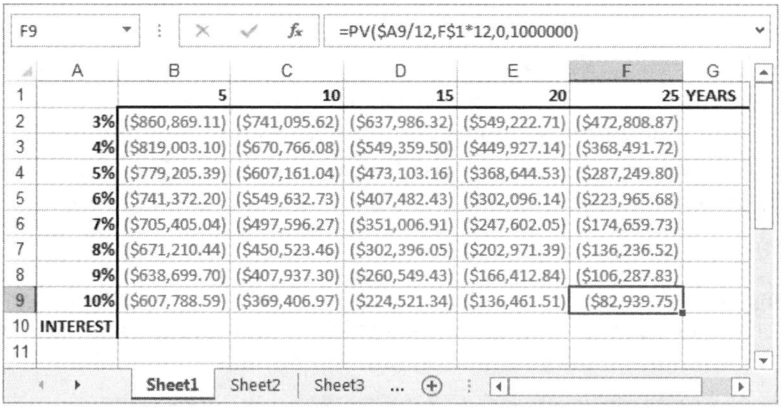
F9 =PV($A9/12,F$1*12,0,1000000)

	A	B	C	D	E	F	G
1		5	10	15	20	25	YEARS
2	3%	($860,869.11)	($741,095.62)	($637,986.32)	($549,222.71)	($472,808.87)	
3	4%	($819,003.10)	($670,766.08)	($549,359.50)	($449,927.14)	($368,491.72)	
4	5%	($779,205.39)	($607,161.04)	($473,103.16)	($368,644.53)	($287,249.80)	
5	6%	($741,372.20)	($549,632.73)	($407,482.43)	($302,096.14)	($223,965.68)	
6	7%	($705,405.04)	($497,596.27)	($351,006.91)	($247,602.05)	($174,659.73)	
7	8%	($671,210.44)	($450,523.46)	($302,396.05)	($202,971.39)	($136,236.52)	
8	9%	($638,699.70)	($407,937.30)	($260,549.43)	($166,412.84)	($106,287.83)	
9	10%	($607,788.59)	($369,406.97)	($224,521.34)	($136,461.51)	($82,939.75)	
10	INTEREST						
11							

FIGURE 10-2

With the right amount of money and a sufficient amount of time, anyone can become a millionaire. This table shows the effect that different interest rates and investment periods have on your goal of reaching $1,000,000. The selected cell shows that if you invest for 25 years and realize 10 percent interest per year, you need to start out with $82,939.75 to hit the millionaire mark.

If you don't have the patience to wait for accruing money, you may be more interested in using PV() to determine how much money you can afford to borrow *now*. Assuming you can pay $250 a month for a three-year loan at a 7 percent annual interest rate, here's how you calculate the size of the loan:

```
=PV(7%/12, 3*12, -250, 0)
```

The answer? $8,096.62. In this example, the future value *(fv)* is 0, because you want to pay the loan off completely.

PMT(), PPMT(), and IPMT(): Calculating the Number of Payments You Need to Make

The PMT() function calculates the dollar amount of regular payments you need to make, either to pay off a loan or to achieve a desired investment target. Its list of arguments closely resembles the FV() and PV() functions you just learned about. You specify the present value and future value of the loan or investment and the rate of interest over its lifetime, and the function returns the payment you need to make in each time period. Here's how the function breaks down:

```
PMT(rate, nper, pv, [fv], [type])
```

If you don't specify a future value, Excel assumes it's 0 (which is correct if you want to see how long it'll take to pay off a loan). Once again, the *type* argument indicates whether you make payments at the beginning of the payment period (1) or at the end (0).

To consider a few sample uses of the PMT() function, you simply need to rearrange the formulas you used in the FV() and PV() sections. If you have a 7 percent interest rate (compounded monthly) and a starting balance of $10,000, how much do you need to pay monthly to top it up to $1,000,000 in 30 years? The PMT() function provides your answer:

```
=PMT(7%/12, 12*30, -10000, 1000000)
```

The result—$753.16—is a negative number, because this is money you're *giving up* each month.

A loan calculation is just as easy, although in this case, the present value becomes positive, since it represents money you receive when you take out the loan. To determine the payments you need to make to pay back a $10,000 loan (that comes with a 10 percent annual interest rate) over five years, you need this formula:

```
=PMT(10%/12, 12*5, 10000, 0)
```

Assuming you make payments at the end of each month, the monthly payment is $212.47. If you decide to pay at the beginning of the month, add a *type* argument of 1 to the formula above, and your monthly payments decrease to $210.71.

The PPMT() and IPMT() functions let you take a closer look at how you repay your loan, as they both analyze a single loan payment. PPMT() calculates the amount of a payment that goes toward paying down the loan's principal, while IPMT() calculates the amount of a payment that pays back accrued interest. You'll find both functions extremely useful if you need to figure, for tax purposes, what portion of your monthly loan payment is paying interest, versus what portion is paying off a loan's principal (see Figure 10-3).

	A	B	C	D	E
1	***A Mortgage***				
2					
3	*Principal:*	$300,000			
4	*Interest:*	6%			
5	*Term (years):*	25			
6	*Payments:*	300			
7					
8	***Payment***	*Total (PMT)*	*Interest (IPMT)*	*Principal (PPMT)*	
9	1	($1,932.90)	($1,500.00)	($432.90)	
10	2	($1,932.90)	($1,497.84)	($435.07)	
11	3	($1,932.90)	($1,495.66)	($437.24)	
12	4	($1,932.90)	($1,493.47)	($439.43)	
13	5	($1,932.90)	($1,491.28)	($441.63)	
302	294	($1,932.90)	($66.32)	($1,866.59)	
303	295	($1,932.90)	($56.99)	($1,875.92)	
304	296	($1,932.90)	($47.61)	($1,885.30)	
305	297	($1,932.90)	($38.18)	($1,894.72)	
306	298	($1,932.90)	($28.71)	($1,904.20)	
307	299	($1,932.90)	($19.19)	($1,913.72)	
308	300	($1,932.90)	($9.62)	($1,923.29)	
309					
310	**Total:**	($579,871.26)	($279,871.26)	($300,000.00)	
311					

FIGURE 10-3

Top: A home mortgage is an ideal reason to use the PMT(), PPMT(), and IPMT() functions. This worksheet depicts each of the 300 mortgage payments you'd make over the course of a 25-year $300,000 mortgage at 6 percent interest. The first payment contributes a measly $432.90 to paying off the principal.

Bottom: This table shows that the total of all the payments you make will come to $579,871.26—that's what you'll actually spend to repay your $300,000 loan. This type of table is known as an amortization table.

NOTE Over the course of a loan, the amount you pay toward your principal will gradually increase, and the amount going to pay interest will decrease (see Figure 10-3). But for each payment, it's always true that *PMT = PPMT + IPMT*. In other words, your total monthly payment remains the same until you pay off the loan.

The PPMT() and IPMT() functions take the same arguments as the PMT() function with one difference: you need to specify the period, or *per*, of the loan or investment. This argument tells Excel which payment you want to analyze. For example, a *per* of 1 examines the first payment. A *per* of 6, meanwhile, analyzes the sixth payment, which, assuming you pay back the loan on a monthly basis, occurs halfway through your first year of repayment. Here are both functions:

```
PPMT(rate, per, nper, pv, [fv], [type])
```

```
IPMT(rate, per, nper, pv, [fv], [type])
```

As a quick example, consider the first payment of the $10,000 loan analyzed earlier using the PMT() function. You already know that each payment is $212.47. But what portion of this goes toward paying down your principal? For the first payment, you can calculate the answer as follows:

```
=PPMT(10%/12, 1, 12*5, 10000, 0, 0)
```

The answer's a relatively minute $129.14—about 60 percent of your $212.47 payment. For your last payment, however, the situation improves:

```
=PPMT(10%/12, 12*5, 12*5, 10000, 0, 0)
```

Now a full $210.71 goes toward paying off the last of your balance.

NOTE Clearly, the PPMT() and IPMT() functions don't work if you specify an argument of *per* that's greater than *nper*. In other words, you can't analyze a payment you don't make! Should you ever make this mistake, the function returns a #NUM! error value.

POWER USERS' CLINIC

Cumulative Interest and Principal Payments

The PPMT() and IPMT() functions let you analyze how much of a single payment pays a loan's principal, as well as the amount that pays its interest. But what if you want to calculate the principal or interest payments over a *range* of payments? You can build an amortization table, like the one in Figure 10-3, or you can opt for a simpler choice: the *CUMIPMT()* and *CUMPRINC()* functions (which stand for cumulative interest payments and cumulative principal, respectively).

The CUMIPMT() function calculates the amount of money paid toward interest over a range of payments. Just specify the first and last payment you want to consider:

```
CUMPIPMT(rate, nper, pv, first_per,last_
per, type)
```

The following formula calculates the amount of interest you'll pay over the first year (payments 1 through 12) of a $300,000 mortgage with a 25-year term and 6 percent interest.

```
=CUMIPMT(6%/12, 25*12, 300000, 1, 12, 0)
```

The CUMPRINC() function performs a similar, but complementary task. It uses the same syntax, but calculates the amount of money paid toward the *principal* over a range of payments.

NPER(): Figuring Out How Much Time You Need to Pay Off a Loan or Meet an Investment Target

The NPER() function calculates the amount of time it will take you to pay off a loan or meet an investment target, provided you already know the initial balance, the interest rate, and the amount you're prepared to contribute to each payment. Here's what the function looks like:

```
NPER(rate, pmt, pv, [fv], [type])
```

If you're ready to contribute $150 a month to a savings account that pays 3.5 percent interest, you can use the following formula to determine how long it'll take you to afford a new $4,500 high-definition television, assuming you start off with an initial balance of $500:

```
=NPER(3.5%/12, -150, -500, 4500)
```

So you'll have to make 25.48 payments before you can buy your new TV. Remember, a payment period in this example is one month, so you'll need to save for more than two years.

If you just want to wait for interest to do its magic, with no additional payments, leave the payment amount blank:

```
=NPER(3.5%/12, , -500, 4500)
```

Now it takes a far longer 754.43 payments—roughly 63 years—for your $500 to grow to your target of $4,500. In the meantime, you missed all 5,983 episodes of "Downton Abbey."

A similar calculation can tell you how long it'll take to pay off a line of credit. Assuming the line of credit's $10,000 at 6 percent, and you pay $500 monthly, here's the formula you'd use:

```
=NPER(6%/12, -500, 10000, 0)
```

In this case, the news isn't so good: It'll take just over 21 months before you're debt-free.

RATE(): Calculating the Interest Rate You Need to Achieve a Target

The RATE() function determines the interest rate you need to achieve a certain future value, given an initial balance, and a set value for regular contributions. The function looks like this:

```
RATE(nper, pmt, pv, [fv], [type], [guess])
```

The math underlying the RATE() function is trickier than the calculations used in the financial functions mentioned above. In fact, there's no direct way to determine the desired interest rate if you want to make more than one payment. Instead, Excel uses an *iterative approach* (otherwise known as *trial and error*). In most cases, Excel can quickly spot the answer, but if it comes up empty after 20 iterations, the formula fails and returns the dreaded #NUM! error code.

You can always supply an optional *guess* argument, which tells Excel what interest rate to try first. If you don't specify a rate, Excel assumes 10 percent, and works from there. The guess must use the appropriate time scale, so if you make monthly payments, remember to divide the yearly interest rate by 12. The number returned by the RATE() function uses the same time scale.

TIP It's all too easy to unintentionally ask an impossible question using the RATE() function. So make sure you use realistic numbers with this function. Say you want to find the interest rate you need to find to pay off a $10,000 loan in two years by making monthly payments of $225. If you attempt this calculation, you'll get a negative value, indicating that there's no way to meet your goal unless the loan pays *you* interest.

You could have avoided this mix up if you calculated the total amount of your monthly contributions ($225*24), which add up to only $5,625.00. Clearly, this amount of money isn't enough to even pay off the $10,000 principal, let alone the interest!

Imagine you have a starting balance of $10,000. You make regular payments of $150, and you're hoping to double your money to $20,000 in three years. To determine the interest rate you need to make this a reality, use the following formula:

```
=RATE(3*12, -150, -10000, 20000)
```

This calculation returns a monthly interest rate of 0.88 percent. You can generate the *annual* rate from this number by multiplying it by 12 (which gives you 10.5 percent, compounded monthly).

RATE() lends itself similarly well to loan calculations. Say you want to pay off a $5,000 loan in two years by making $225 payments each month. Here's the formula that determines the maximum annual rate you can afford.

```
=RATE(2*12, -225, 5000, 0)*12
```

In this case, you need to find a loan that charges less than 7.5 percent annual interest.

RRI(): Calculating the Interest Rate Your Investments Achieve

The RRI() function is a straightforward bit of math. It takes an initial value and a future value, and tells you the rate of return over some period of time. For example, if you started with $5,000 three years ago, and you have $7,433 now, the RRI function can tell you the interest you earned annually.

The RRI() function has this syntax:

```
RRI(nper, pv, fv)
```

And here's an example that puts it to work:

```
=RRI(3, 5000, 7433)
```

This returns 0.14, suggesting an impressive 14% rate of return.

The RRI() function isn't meant to calculate the interest rate of a standard bank account deposit (after all, you already know that). Instead, it's meant to help examine one of your investments and evaluate how well it's done (or how well it's projected to do), by comparing it to a fixed-rate deposit.

NOTE Only Excel 2013 supports RRI(). Don't use the function if you share your spreadsheet with people using older versions of Excel.

The RRI() function handles simple scenarios, where you know the value of an investment at the outset and at the end of the investment period. In more sophisticated scenarios, the calculations are a bit foggier, because you need to deal with expenses or earnings during the course of your investment. For example, if you buy a property to rent, you have to think about both the appreciating value of that property and the rent you're collecting. To handle these scenarios, you need the more complex NPV() and IRR() functions, described in the next section.

NPV() and IRR(): Net Present Value and Internal Rate of Return

NPV() is a more specialized function that can help you decide whether to make an investment or embark on a business venture by calculating *net present value*. To understand net present value, you first need to understand the concept of *present value*, which is the value that a projected investment has *today*. If you have an investment that earns 5 percent monthly interest and is worth $200 at maturity (after one month), its present value is $190.48.

You tackled present values with the PV() function described earlier in this chapter. Net present value is the same concept, except that it applies to a series of *cash flows* (the profit, or loss, generated by an investment), rather than an investment with a fixed interest rate (like a bond or Certificate of Deposit).

Practically speaking, people almost always use the NPV() function to compare the present value of an investment or business (sometimes called the *venture investment*) to an investment with a fixed rate of return. The basic idea is simple: To be worthwhile, the venture investment must exceed a specific rate of return. If you know that you can get a 5 percent fixed rate of return from your bank, you won't consider using the money to open a coffee shop that's projected to make only 3 percent annually. (As always, Excel's financial functions take only cold, hard money into account—if opening a coffee shop is a lifelong dream, you may think differently.)

The NPV() function works by examining cash flow over a series of years. You specify how much the venture investment cost you, or how much you received during each period, and NPV() calculates how that compares with a fixed-rate investment. To make this comparison, you must choose an interest rate for the venture investment. (Accountants call that interest rate the *discount rate*.) If the final NPV() value is negative, you'd have been better off with the fixed investment. If the NPV() value is positive, your venture will exceed the payback of a fixed-rate investment.

Imagine you want to open a new coffee shop. You're prepared to invest $25,000 at the start, and you expect to realize profits of $2,000 in the first year. In the following three years, you project a profit of $6,500, $10,000, and $12,500. Simple addition tells you that this business will earn $31,000 over four years (and a net profit of $6,000). However, you also need to account for the interest you could realize by investing your profits at 5 percent as soon as they become available. Based on this scenario, how would your business (the venture investment) compare to a fixed security that earns 5 percent each year? You can answer that question using NPV().

The NPV() function (see Figure 10-4) requires the discount rate, and then a series of payments (or a cell range that contains a series of payments). Here's how to calculate the net present value of the four-year investment:

```
=NPV(5%, 2000, 6500, 10000, 12500)
```

Excel counts each cash flow as one period. Thus, this formula covers four periods. Because the calculation uses an *annual* interest rate (5%), each period represents a full year. The formula returns a result of $26,722.61. In other words, to generate the same amount of money as your business will, you'd need to invest $26,722.61 initially at an annual interest rate of 5 percent. This amount's more than the outlay required by our hypothetical business (which needs only $25,000 to get off the ground), so the business is a better place to put your money.

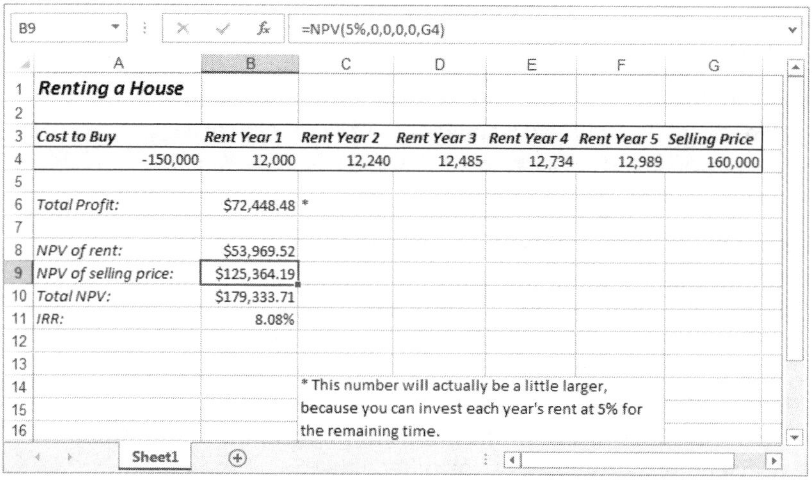
B9 =NPV(5%,0,0,0,0,G4)

	A	B	C	D	E	F	G
1	**Renting a House**						
2							
3	Cost to Buy	Rent Year 1	Rent Year 2	Rent Year 3	Rent Year 4	Rent Year 5	Selling Price
4	-150,000	12,000	12,240	12,485	12,734	12,989	160,000
5							
6	Total Profit:	$72,448.48	*				
7							
8	NPV of rent:	$53,969.52					
9	NPV of selling price:	$125,364.19					
10	Total NPV:	$179,333.71					
11	IRR:	8.08%					
12							
13							
14			* This number will actually be a little larger,				
15			because you can invest each year's rent at 5% for				
16			the remaining time.				

Sheet1

FIGURE 10-4

This worksheet helps you figure out whether it makes more sense to invest $150,000 at a fixed rate, or to use that money to buy and rent out a property.

Put another way, the value of the business *today* (in other words, its present value) is $26,722.61, even though you haven't ordered a sign or chosen a name. Because it costs only $25,000 to build the business, you'll be ahead of the game as soon as you set up shop (assuming, of course, you meet your profit projections).

Another way to look at net present value is to calculate the total amount of money you'd realize if you subtracted the cost of your initial investment, as shown here:

```
=NPV(5%, 2000, 6500, 10000, 12500) - 25000
```

In this case, as long as the result is greater than $0, the investment is a go. In this example, the difference is $1,722.61. The business is worth this much today, over and above what you spent to get it started.

NOTE In this example, the business made money each and every year. But even if you're projecting a negative cash flow for some of the years, you can still use NPV() to determine the current value of your business.

TROUBLESHOOTING MOMENT

Subtle Problems with NPV()

No one ever said that financial accounting is easy. In fact, the NPV() function is a good example of accounting's limitations, as it's littered with caveats that can easily trip you up.

For instance, you'll see that, in order to calculate the real net present value, you need to subtract the initial investment after you use the function. You might wonder why you can't include the cost of $25,000 as one of the cash flows for NPV(), like this:

```
=NPV(5%, -25000, 2000, 6500, 10000, 12500)
```

This formula assumes that you incur the $25,000 cost *during* the first period, which is incorrect. Also, the NPV() function now assumes that five years have elapsed, instead of four, further skewing the answer. These problems happen because NPV() is sensitive to the *time value* of money. Time value is an expression economists use to emphasize the fact that $95 dollars today isn't worth the same as $95 next year—because the earlier you get the money, the more time you have to earn interest. Adding arguments or changing their order can cause a different result.

Another problem with NPV() is that it assumes you're able to reinvest your business's earnings at a rate comparable to the set interest rate you're using to calculate NPV (in this case, 5 percent). However, if you're unable to invest the profit at 5 percent (perhaps because you need a shorter-term investment, which will earn less), you're not generating as much profit as the NPV() calculation indicates.

The NPV() function is particularly useful for evaluating prospective real estate investments. Consider what happens if you buy a condominium, rent it out for several years, and then sell it for the original price. If you take the rent money you earn (or predict you're going to earn), NPV()can tell you whether you'd be better off investing your money at a fixed interest rate.

Figure 10-4 shows an example. In it, NPV() suggests that the rent you collect (a total of $62,448.48, calculated by summing the rent collected in each year) is worth about $53,970 today. But you need to factor in the value of the property, which may increase or decrease. In this case, the property's estimated selling price ($160,000, which represents a measly gain of $10,000) makes it equivalent to having $125,364.19 to invest today at 5 percent interest. Thus, you're losing money on the value of the property (versus the rate of return you could get in the bank), but you more than make up for it in the rent you collect. By adding these two factors (property value and rent) together, you get a total net present value of $179,333.71. And because you purchased the property for only $150,000, this is very good news. If you still have doubts, look at the internal rate of return in cell B11. It shows that you earned the equivalent of 8.08 percent—significantly more than 5 percent—from your real estate dealings.

The IRR() function is closely related to NPV(). The main difference is that while NPV() calculates the value of a business or investment today, IRR() calculates how fast the business or rate *appreciates* in value (its rate of return). Technically, IRR() calculates the *internal rate of return,* which is the effective return rate based on your cash flows. To perform this calculation, you need to include your initial investment and the business's cash flow. In fact, you need to supply all the values as a range, like so:

```
=IRR(A4:G4)
```

This calculation returns 7.35 percent for the coffee shop business introduced on page 309, and 8.08 percent for the rental property scenario shown in Figure 10-4.

WARNING The IRR() function is dangerous! While the NPV() function assumes you can reinvest your money at a rate you specify (in the first argument), the IRR() function assumes that you can reinvest your money in the business and achieve the same rate of return, which often isn't possible. Both NPV() and IRR() calculations are just estimates, and you need to carefully evaluate them.

POWER USERS' CLINIC

A Better NPV()

Excel provides versions of NPV() and IRR() that don't assume that you make payments (or realize profits) on fixed dates, once per period. These functions are XIRR() and XNPV(). Using them is a little bit more complicated because you need to supply not only the cash flows, but the dates when each transaction took place. You do this by submitting two cell ranges: the first includes the cash flows, and the second specifies the dates.

```
XNPV(rate, cashflow_range, date_range)
XIRR(cashflow_range, date_range)
```

The two ranges must be exactly the same size (that is, they must include the same number of cells), and must line up logically. In other words, Excel assumes that the first cash flow in the cash flow range is deposited on the first date in the date range.

Depreciation

Another common calculation in the world of finance is *depreciation*. Simply stated, depreciation is how much the value of an asset decreases over time. All assets that depreciate begin with a certain value (which you determine) and then depreciate over the course of a lifetime (which you specify). At the end of an asset's life, from an accounting perspective, the asset is deemed to be useless and without value.

Excel gives you four basic depreciation functions (explained below), which can help you determine how much value your asset has lost at any given point in time. You use these values if you want to sell the asset, or if you want to calculate the current net worth of a business. Depreciation can also figure into tax calculations and business losses; a company could write off a loss based on the value an asset has lost.

NOTE The depreciation of an asset isn't as straightforward as interest calculations. You use a certain amount of guesswork when you decide what an asset is worth and how rapidly its value declines. An asset can include almost anything, from a piece of equipment or property to a patented technology. It may depreciate due to wear and tear, obsolescence, or market conditions (like decreased demand and increased supply).

To assign a value to a depreciated asset, Excel makes a logical guess about the way in which the asset depreciates. You can use any of a number of accepted ways to make this guess (or estimate, as financial types prefer to call it). The easiest way to depreciate an asset is the *straight-line depreciation* method, where the value of the asset decreases regularly from its starting value to its final value. However, this approach isn't necessarily realistic for all assets.

Each of Excel's four basic depreciation functions figures depreciation in a slightly different way:

- **SLN()** uses simple *straight-line depreciation*, where you take the cost of the asset minus its *scrap value* (the value of the asset if sold purely as raw material) and divide that number by the life span of the asset. In other words, if your asset's life span is 10 years, the book value of the asset is depreciated by 10 percent of its original value each year. SLN() is the only form of depreciation that proceeds regularly. All other types of depreciation are *accelerated depreciation* functions, because they assume that the asset's greatest loss in value happens early on, rather than evenly over several years. As a result, these accelerated depreciation functions are often more realistic.
- **SYD()** uses the *sum-of-years-digits* depreciation method. It depreciates the value of your asset more quickly than SLN() at the beginning of the asset's lifetime, and gradually reduces the rate of depreciation as the asset becomes less valuable. SYD() is a good all-around choice for most depreciation calculations.
- **DDB()** uses the *double declining balance* depreciation method, which is like straight-line depreciation on steroids. It reduces an asset's value by doubling the depreciation that the SLN() method uses, which makes for a fast reduction in value (and a hefty tax write-off). In other words, if the life span is 10 years, the book value of the asset depreciates by 20 percent of the original value each year.

NOTE The DDB() approach has one flaw, however: Eventually the asset will dip below its final value (and even become a negative number). Accountants handle this problem by imposing an additional rule: As soon as the DDB() depreciation in any given year falls *below* what the straight-line depreciation would be, you must abandon the DDB() method and start calculating depreciation with SLN(). And it's up to you to be aware of this rule and check for the condition. If that sounds messy—well, it is.

- **DB()** uses the *declining balance* method, where an asset declines in value by a fixed percentage of its book value every year. Like the SYD() and the DDB() approaches, this method is an accelerated depreciation function. However, it has a different limitation: You can't specify the final value the asset (its salvage value) at the end of its lifetime.

These functions work with more of less the same arguments as the other depreciation methods, but they produce different results. Here's a look at the syntax of all four functions:

```
SLN(cost, salvage, life)

SYD(cost, salvage, life, period)

DB(cost, salvage, life, period, [month])

DDB(cost, salvage, life, period, [factor])
```

- The *cost* is the initial value of the asset.
- The *salvage* argument is the value of the asset at the end of its depreciation. If it's lost all value, this number is 0.
- The *life* is the number of periods over which the asset depreciates. It's also known as the *useful life* of the asset.
- The *period* is a number that indicates the period in which you want to calculate depreciation; it must use the same unit of measure as the life. If you're depreciating an asset over three years, a period of 3 will get you the amount of money that the asset depreciated in the third year. The SLN() function doesn't require a period argument because depreciation is the same in every period.
- The *month* is an optional argument in the DB() function. It specifies the number of months that the asset's in use for the first year. If you leave this out, Excel assumes 12 months of service.
- The *factor* is an optional argument in the DDB() function. You multiply the factor by the expected straight-line depreciation to get the actual depreciation. If you omit this argument, Excel assumes a value of 2 (which is why it's known as *double* declining depreciation).

As an example, imagine a company purchases a top-of-the-line computer for $10,000. The computer has a salvage value of $200 after its useful life of five years. To compute its second-year depreciation using the popular SYD() method, you'd use the following calculation:

```
=SYD(10000, 200, 5, 2)
```

This calculation indicates that the computer loses $2,613.33 of its value in the second year. However, to calculate the total depreciation so far, you need to add the depreciation for both the first and second year, and subtract that from the initial value, as shown here:

```
=10000-SYD(10000, 200, 5, 1)-SYD(10000, 200, 5, 2)
```

This formula takes the $10,000 total and subtracts the first- and second-year depreciation ($3,266.67 and $2,613.33, respectively), which gives you a current value of $4,120. You'll notice that with the SYD() function, most of the depreciation takes place in the first year; for each year after that, the asset loses a smaller amount of its value.

The easiest way to see depreciation at work is to build a worksheet that compares the results of these four functions. Figure 10-5 shows an example.

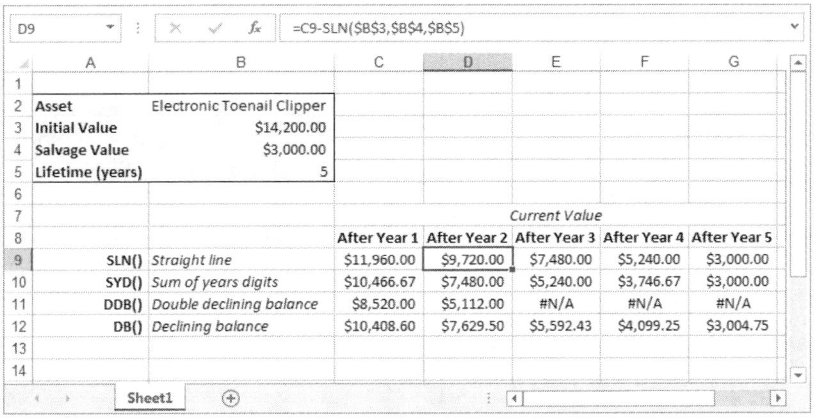

D9 =C9-SLN($B$3,$B$4,$B$5)

	A	B	C	D	E	F	G
1							
2	Asset	Electronic Toenail Clipper					
3	Initial Value	$14,200.00					
4	Salvage Value	$3,000.00					
5	Lifetime (years)	5					
6							
7					Current Value		
8			After Year 1	After Year 2	After Year 3	After Year 4	After Year 5
9	SLN()	Straight line	$11,960.00	$9,720.00	$7,480.00	$5,240.00	$3,000.00
10	SYD()	Sum of years digits	$10,466.67	$7,480.00	$5,240.00	$3,746.67	$3,000.00
11	DDB()	Double declining balance	$8,520.00	$5,112.00	#N/A	#N/A	#N/A
12	DB()	Declining balance	$10,408.60	$7,629.50	$5,592.43	$4,099.25	$3,004.75
13							
14							

Sheet1

FIGURE 10-5

This worksheet shows you how the value of an investment depreciates over time. Once you set the investment's initial value, lifetime value, and salvage value, you can calculate its depreciation. As you can see, some methods produce faster depreciation than others.

In Figure 10-5, the straight-line depreciation is the slowest of all, which makes it less realistic for dealing with the plummeting values of aging high-tech parts. The sum-of-years-digits depreciation provides faster depreciation, yet still ends up with the desired salvage value of $3,000. The last two methods are a little trickier. You can use the double-declining balance approach for only the first two years. In the third year, the investment's value ($2,044.8) is less than its sum-of-years depreciation value ($2,240), so it's time to switch methods. To underscore that fact, the following cells display the #N/A code. The declining-balance approach works well initially, but then tops out in the last year. In this case, you'll probably want to ignore the last calculated value and just use the salvage value of $3,000.

NOTE When you use the double-declining balance depreciation, it's your responsibility to spot when the method no longer applies. Excel doesn't tell you; instead, it cheerily continues calculating depreciation values, even if the depreciation exceeds the total value of the asset. In Figure 10-5, the #N/A values were typed in by hand.

Other Financial Functions

Excel includes dozens more financial functions. People like stockbrokers, bond traders, and chief financial officers, who regularly depend on the functions' abilities to deal with complex financial transaction procedures, use most of these functions. Table 10-1 provides an overview.

TIP For more info on non-Excel-specific investing, depreciation, and financial concepts, check out *http://beginnersinvest.about.com/od/investinglessons*.

TABLE 10-1 *Specialized financial functions*

FUNCTION	DESCRIPTION
ACCRINT()	Returns the accrued interest for a security that pays periodic interest.
ACCRINTM()	Returns the accrued interest for a security that pays interest at maturity.
AMORDEGRC()	Returns the depreciation for each accounting period.
COUPDAYBS()	Returns the number of days from the beginning of the coupon period to the settlement date.
COUPDAYS()	Returns the number of days in the coupon period that contains the settlement date.
COUPDAYSNC()	Returns the number of days from the settlement date to the next coupon date.
COUPNCD()	Returns the next coupon date after the settlement date.
COUPNUM()	Returns the number of coupons payable between the settlement date and maturity date.
COUPPCD()	Returns the previous coupon date before the settlement date.
DISC()	Returns the discount rate for a security.
DURATION()	Returns the annual duration of a security with periodic interest payments.
FVSCHEDULE()	Returns the future value of an initial principal after applying a series of compound interest rates.
INTRATE()	Returns the interest rate for a fully invested security.
MDURATION()	Returns the Macaulay modified duration for a security with an assumed par value of $100.
MIRR()	Returns the internal rate of return where positive and negative cash flows are financed at different rates.
NOMINAL()	Returns the annual nominal interest rate.
ODDFPRICE()	Returns the price per $100 face value of a security with an odd first period.
ODDFYIELD()	Returns the yield of a security with an odd first period.
ODDLPRICE()	Returns the price per $100 face value of a security with an odd last period.
ODDLYIELD()	Returns the yield of a security with an odd last period.

FUNCTION	DESCRIPTION
PDURATION()	Returns the number of periods needed to meet an investment goal or pay off a loan when there are no additional regular payments. Although this function works perfectly well, only Excel 2013 supports it, and you can get the same information by using NPER() and setting the *pmt* argument to 0 (page 306).
PRICE()	Returns the price per $100 face value of a security that pays periodic interest.
PRICEDISC()	Returns the price per $100 face value of a discounted security.
PRICEMAT()	Returns the price per $100 face value of a security that pays interest at maturity.
RECEIVED()	Returns the amount received at maturity for a fully invested security.
TBILLEQ()	Returns the bond-equivalent yield for a Treasury bill.
TBILLPRICE()	Returns the price per $100 face value for a Treasury bill.
TBILLYIELD()	Returns the yield for a Treasury bill.
VDB()	Returns the depreciation of an asset for a specified or partial period using a declining balance method.
YIELD()	Returns the yield on a security that pays periodic interest.
YIELDDISC()	Returns the annual yield for a discounted security, like a Treasury bill.
YIELDMAT()	Returns the annual yield of a security that pays interest at maturity.

CHAPTER

11

Manipulating Dates, Times, and Text

Most of the functions you've learned so far focus on crunching raw numbers. But Excel also provides functions that work with *other* types of data, including dates, times, and ordinary text. For text, for example, you may want Excel to pull first and last names from two different columns and join them in a single column. Or you may want to find and remove a word that appears in a bunch of column titles. Similarly, you may want to replace a character in a word, capitalize a name, or count the number of letters in a cell. Excel provides specialized text functions for all these tasks, and you'll learn about them in this chapter.

Excel also gives you specialized functions for dates and times. These functions perform some indispensable tasks, like retrieving the current time and determining what day of the week a given date falls on. In addition, Excel lets you perform calculations with dates and times just as you would with ordinary numbers. This chapter introduces these techniques, too, and explains how Excel stores dates and times behind the scenes.

Manipulating Text

You can't use arithmetic operators like + and – with text. If you try to, Excel displays a *#VALUE* error message. However, there's one operator you *can* use: the *concatenation* operator (&), which joins together text. For example, imagine you have an individual's first name in cell A1, and the last name in cell B1. You could join the values from these two cells to create a full name with this formula:

```
=A1 & B1
```

This approach has one drawback: In all likelihood, the first- and last-name cells don't include any leading or trailing spaces. That means that when you join the two names, Excel will fuse them into a single word, like JohnSmith. One solution is to explicitly add a space (between quotation marks) into your formula, like so:

```
=A1 & " " & B1
```

The important concept in this example is that you can enter *string literals*—fixed pieces of text (including spaces)—as easily as you can enter literal numbers. The only difference between entering literal text and literal numbers is that you have to place text between quotation marks. You can stitch together as many pieces of text as you want; there's no limit. The next group of functions showcases the many ways that Excel lets you manipulate text.

Concatenation also works with cells that contain numbers. In these cases, the "text" is simply the cell content formatted with the General number format, no matter what number format the cell uses. For example, if you format the number 43.2 so it appears as the currency value $43.20 in a cell, that number automatically reverts to the ordinary 43.2 when you join it to a piece of text using concatenation. This is often a different result from the one you want, particularly if the cell contains date information, which Excel displays as a serial number in the General number format. (For more on how number formats affect the appearance of dates, see page 137.) To avoid these problems, use the TEXT() function described on page 325.

CONCATENATE(): Joining Strings of Text Together

The CONCATENATE() function lets you join text in exactly the same way as the concatenation operator (&) does. CONCATENATE() joins all the parameters you supply into one long piece of text, in the order you specify them.

Here's how you rewrite the name-joining formula shown earlier using CONCATENATE() with two pieces of text:

```
=CONCATENATE(A1, " ", B1)
```

LEFT(), MID(), and RIGHT(): Copying Portions of a Text String

Just as you can join pieces of text, so you can split up a string of text. The LEFT(), MID(), and RIGHT() functions let you extract a portion of text from a larger text string. For example, the LEFT() function takes two arguments: the text you want to examine, and the number of characters that Excel should extract, starting from the string's left side:

```
LEFT(text, num_characters)
```

To take the first four letters from the text in cell A1, you'd use the formula:

```
=LEFT(A1, 4)
```

Assuming the cell contains the text *tofurkey*, this formula would give you *tofu*.

The RIGHT() function performs the same operation, but extracts letters starting from the right side of the string. For example, consider the following formula:

```
=RIGHT(A1, 5)
```

If you use this function with the same text string, you end up with the text *urkey*.

The MID() function is more powerful than the LEFT() and RIGHT() functions, as it has the ability to extract a consecutive series of characters from anywhere inside a string. When using the MID() function, you need to supply *three* arguments: the text you're evaluating, the starting position of the extraction, and the number of characters you want to retrieve. Excel numbers each letter and space in a string, starting with 1 for the first character, 2 for the second character, and so on. That means that if you specify a starting position of 3 and a length of 2, Excel extracts the third and fourth characters from a string. The basic formula looks like this:

```
MID(text, start_position, number_of_characters)
```

Here's an example that copies characters from the middle of a string. If the cell A1 contains the text *Swanky Franks*, the following formula returns the value *Frank*.

```
=MID(A1, 8, 5)
```

NOTE LEFT(), MID(), and RIGHT() all pluck out the string you specify, but leave the cell's original content unchanged.

LEN(), FIND(), and SEARCH(): Counting Characters in a String

The LEFT(), RIGHT(), and MID() functions let you copy specified segments of a string. But what happens if you don't know the exact length of the string you're searching? For example, if you're interested in retrieving last names from a column that contains full names, none of these functions help you since last names vary in length.

Fortunately, Excel provides some other tools that can help you out. Three of these, LEN(), FIND(), and SEARCH(), give you numeric information about text. This section explains how to use each of these functions, and then shows how to combine them with the LEFT(), RIGHT(), and MID() functions to perform some really powerful operations.

To begin with, LEN()—short for LENgth—counts the number of characters in a string of text. For example, the result of the following formula is 5:

```
=LEN("Hello")
```

The FIND() function is more sophisticated. It gives you a number representing the position of a given character or series of characters. For example, it can tell you where a space is located in a phrase. If there's more than one match, the FIND() function returns the position of only the first match. The FIND() function can take an optional third parameter that tells the function where to begin the search—if you leave it out, Excel starts searching at the beginning of the text. Here's what the basic formula looks like:

```
FIND(find_text, within_text, [start_position])
```

Now consider the following example. It gives you a result of 5, indicating that the first space in the phrase "Mind the Gap" is in position 5.

```
=FIND(" ", "Mind the Gap")
```

SEARCH() works in almost exactly the same way, and it takes the same two or three arguments. The only difference is that FIND() performs a *case-sensitive* search, which means that it looks for upper- and lowercase letters that match those in your search term, whereas SEARCH() doesn't care about matching cases.

The LEN(), FIND(), and SEARCH() functions all become even more useful when you combine them with the LEFT(), RIGHT(), and MID() functions. For example, say you have a column of full names, as shown in Figure 11-1, and you want to copy the first and last names into their own new columns.

The first step is to use the FIND() function to find the space that separates the first name from the last name. You can then take that number and subtract 1 from it to get the length of the first name. Finally, you can use the newly calculated length with the LEFT() function to snip out the first name. Here's the formula that puts all these steps together:

```
=LEFT(A2,FIND(" ", A2)-1)
```

You can see the result in cell B2 of Figure 11-1.

You use a similar trick to get the last name, but with the RIGHT() function:

```
=RIGHT(A2,LEN(A2)-FIND(" ", A2))
```

Figure 11-1 uses this formula in cell C2. At first glance, the formula might look a bit overwhelming, so it helps to remember the two arguments that the RIGHT() function uses. The first argument is the cell to evaluate (A2). The second argument is the number of characters that RIGHT() should take from the right side of the text, using the calculation LEN(A2)–FIND(" ", A2). Here's how the second argument breaks down: First, the FIND() function locates the space between the first and last names. Next, the LEN() function determines how many characters (including spaces) make up the full name. Finally, Excel subtracts the FIND() result from the LEN() result to determine the length of the last name, which is what the RIGHT() function needs to do its job.

TIP The previous example uses a custom formula to split text, but Excel has a feature designed for just this purpose, called the Text to Columns feature. Simply select the cells you want to change, and then choose DataData ToolsText to Columns. Excel launches the Convert Text to Columns Wizard, which lets you choose how to carve up text into separate columns (either by fixed position, or by using a recognized delimiter character, like a space or a comma). The Convert Text to Columns Wizard is based on the Text Import Wizard, which you'll explore in detail on page 754.

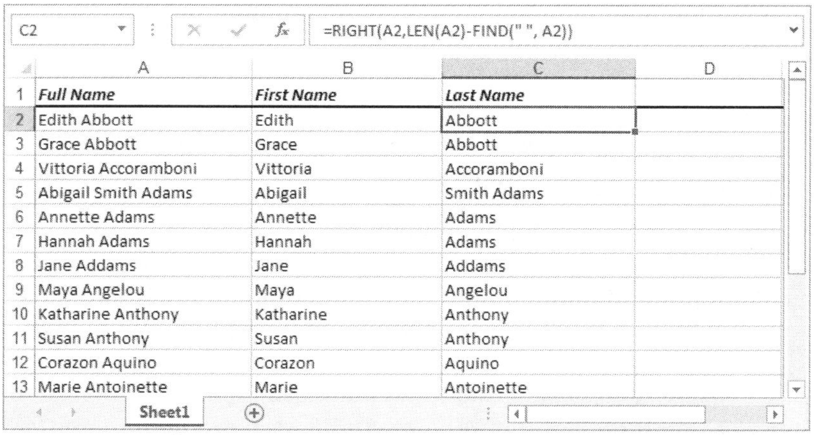

C2 =RIGHT(A2,LEN(A2)-FIND(" ", A2))

	A	B	C	D
1	*Full Name*	*First Name*	*Last Name*	
2	Edith Abbott	Edith	Abbott	
3	Grace Abbott	Grace	Abbott	
4	Vittoria Accoramboni	Vittoria	Accoramboni	
5	Abigail Smith Adams	Abigail	Smith Adams	
6	Annette Adams	Annette	Adams	
7	Hannah Adams	Hannah	Adams	
8	Jane Addams	Jane	Addams	
9	Maya Angelou	Maya	Angelou	
10	Katharine Anthony	Katharine	Anthony	
11	Susan Anthony	Susan	Anthony	
12	Corazon Aquino	Corazon	Aquino	
13	Marie Antoinette	Marie	Antoinette	

Sheet1

FIGURE 11-1

This worksheet shows the LEFT(), RIGHT(), FIND(), and LEN() functions at work. Excel uses these functions to extract the first and last names from the full names in column A.

UPPER(), LOWER(), and PROPER(): Changing Capitalization

Another way to manipulate text is by changing its case. Excel provides three functions for this purpose (see Figure 11-2):

- **UPPER()** converts text to all capitals.
- **LOWER()** converts text to all lowercase.
- **PROPER()** converts text to initial-case. That means every letter is lowercase, except for the first letter in each word. (Excel identifies words by looking for the spaces between them.)

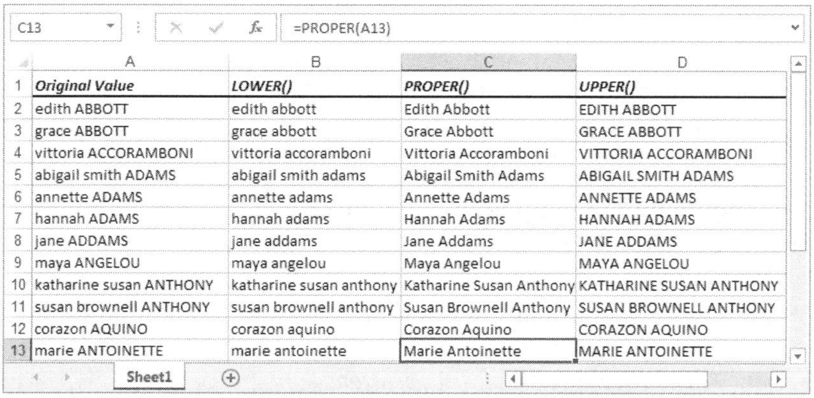

C13 =PROPER(A13)

	A	B	C	D
1	*Original Value*	*LOWER()*	*PROPER()*	*UPPER()*
2	edith ABBOTT	edith abbott	Edith Abbott	EDITH ABBOTT
3	grace ABBOTT	grace abbott	Grace Abbott	GRACE ABBOTT
4	vittoria ACCORAMBONI	vittoria accoramboni	Vittoria Accoramboni	VITTORIA ACCORAMBONI
5	abigail smith ADAMS	abigail smith adams	Abigail Smith Adams	ABIGAIL SMITH ADAMS
6	annette ADAMS	annette adams	Annette Adams	ANNETTE ADAMS
7	hannah ADAMS	hannah adams	Hannah Adams	HANNAH ADAMS
8	jane ADDAMS	jane addams	Jane Addams	JANE ADDAMS
9	maya ANGELOU	maya angelou	Maya Angelou	MAYA ANGELOU
10	katharine susan ANTHONY	katharine susan anthony	Katharine Susan Anthony	KATHARINE SUSAN ANTHONY
11	susan brownell ANTHONY	susan brownell anthony	Susan Brownell Anthony	SUSAN BROWNELL ANTHONY
12	corazon AQUINO	corazon aquino	Corazon Aquino	CORAZON AQUINO
13	marie ANTOINETTE	marie antoinette	Marie Antoinette	MARIE ANTOINETTE

Sheet1

FIGURE 11-2

This worksheet shows how the UPPER(), LOWER(), and PROPER() functions change the capitalization of the names in column A.

All three of these functions need just one argument, which is a string of text (a short bit of text, anywhere from a few letters to a lengthy phrase). For the argument, you can reference a cell that contains text, or type in a piece of literal text—as long as you remember the quotation marks. For example, the following formula displays the text contained in cell A1, but changes all the characters to lowercase:

```
=LOWER(A1)
```

GEM IN THE ROUGH

Using Text Functions to Clean Up Your Data

Usually, functions like UPPER(), LOWER(), and PROPER() transform the appearance of text that's already in your spreadsheet. But you could have a tricky time figuring out exactly how to do this transformation.

Say you've got a list of first and last names in column A (beginning in cell A1) whose letters are all uppercase. You want to change these names so that only the first letter of each name is capitalized. Here's what to do: First, insert a new column B. Next, enter the formula *=PROPER(A1)* in cell B1, and then copy this formula to the rest of the cells in column B. Because this formula uses a *relative* cell reference (as explained on page 251), Excel automatically adjusts the formula for each cell that you paste it into.

Once you take this step, Excel displays the properly capitalized names in column B. But you can't just copy and paste these reformatted names into column A because the formulas in column B reference the cells in column A. Instead, you need to select the corrected names from column B, copy them (Home→Clipboard→Copy), move to cell A1, and then choose Home→Clipboard→Paste→Values (not the plain-vanilla Home→Clipboard→Paste command).

This technique provides a quick way to clean up a number of problems. For example, you can use this approach with many other text functions, like TRIM(), CLEAN(), SUBSTITUTE(), TEXT(), FIXED(), DOLLAR(), all of which are explained in this chapter.

TRIM() and CLEAN(): Removing Unwanted Spaces and Non-Printing Characters

The TRIM() and CLEAN() clean up any strings of text you run through them. TRIM() removes any leading and trailing spaces; it also changes any series of more than one space to a single space. Thus, if you use TRIM() on the text string " Hello There " the altered text becomes "Hello There." TRIM() can be quite handy for fixing erratic spacing.

CLEAN() simply removes non-printable characters from a text string. Non-printable characters, which usually appear as empty-box icons in your text, tend to appear only if you import text that uses a format that Excel has difficulty understanding.

SUBSTITUTE(): Replacing One Sequence of Characters with Another

The SUBSTITUTE() function replaces a sequence of characters in a string with another set of characters. The function has three parts: the text you want to modify, the characters you're looking to replace, and the replacement text you want to insert. In addition, you can supply an optional *occurrence number* parameter, which Excel uses if it finds more than one match. For example, if Excel matches your search text three times and you supply 2 for the occurrence number, Excel changes only the second occurrence of the matched text. If you don't supply the occurrence number, Excel changes all occurrences. Here's what the function looks like:

```
SUBSTITUTE(text, old_text, new_text, [occurrence_number])
```

Consider the case where cell A1 contains the text *It was the best of times; it was the worst of times.* You could use the following formula to change the word "times":

```
=SUBSTITUTE(A1, "times", "nanoseconds")
```

The result is the string *It was the best of nanoseconds; it was the worst of nanoseconds.*

On the other hand, the following formula explicitly replaces just the second occurrence of "times." The resulting string is *It was the best of times; it was the worst of crimes.*

```
=SUBSTITUTE(A1, "times", "crimes", 2)
```

NOTE The SUBSTITUTE() function always performs a case-sensitive search. That means that if you try using SUBSTITUTE() to replace the word *it*, in the previous example, Excel won't match *It*.

TEXT(), VALUE(), FIXED(), and DOLLAR(): Converting Text to Numbers and Vice Versa

Sometimes, you may need to convert text into a number, or vice versa. For example, imagine you have a cell that contains the sentence "A good sandwich costs $5.95." Using the MID() function, you could copy just the part of this text that has the price—"5.95." However, even though this text contains numeric information, to Excel it's still a piece of text, so you can't perform mathematical operations with it (like adding tax). On the other hand, you may have the reverse problem: You might want to show a string of text that includes a number from another cell. In these cases, the data conversion functions TEXT() and VALUE() are useful.

TEXT() converts an ordinary number into formatted text using the format you specify. It always requires two arguments:

```
TEXT(number, format)
```

The first argument is the number you're converting; the second is the format you want to use. You can use any of the date, time, or numeric formatting codes described in Chapter 5 (in particular, Table 5-2 on page 146). For example, the following formula converts the number 434.2 to the formatted text $434.20.

```
=TEXT(434.2,"$#,##0.00")
```

On its own, this method may not seem very practical. After all, you already learned how to control cell formatting using the Format Cells window. What's the point of doing the same job with a formula? The answer is that you may find it handy when you want to perform some fancy text processing with your number.

For example, imagine you have the price of a product in cell A1 (which happens to be 300). You could use the following formula to change the number to formatted text, and then put it into a complete sentence, like *$300.00 is way too expensive.*

```
=TEXT(A1,"$#,##0.00") & " is way too expensive"
```

Now compare what happens if you try to do the same thing without using the TEXT() function:

```
=A1 & " is way too expensive."
```

You end up with an unformatted result (*300 is way too expensive*), regardless of what formatting you used in cell A1.

In other words, you can use text-based functions with numbers, but unless you explicitly perform the conversion using the TEXT() function, Excel always uses General formatting—which may not be what you want.

TIP You can also use the FIXED() or DOLLAR() functions (explained below) to convert content to specific formats without needing to find the right format string.

The VALUE() function does the reverse—it converts a piece of text into a number you can manipulate in a formula. Here's an example:

```
=VALUE(A1)
```

This trick becomes useful if you need to extract a price from a string of text, and then perform a calculation with it. Here's an example that gets the number 300 out of a sentence using the MID() function, and then converts it to a number using the VALUE() function:

```
=VALUE(MID("I suggest a price of $300.00 for the chair.",23,6))
```

NOTE In many cases, you can get by without the VALUE() function, because you can coax Excel into converting text into numbers. However, with some formulas, you need it—and it never hurts to make your formulas clearer by using it.

The VALUE() function is fairly simple to use, but it isn't terribly bright. If you use it with content that contains both numeric characters and letters, like the string of text *42 bananas*, it fails. You'll see the error message #VALUE! instead of the desired content.

The FIXED() and DOLLAR() functions also convert numbers to text. The difference is that they use a set format (described shortly), so you don't need to specify a format for the result, as you would with the TEXT() function.

The FIXED() function actually performs several steps. First, it rounds a number to a specified number of decimal places. Next, it formats the number with a decimal point and, optionally, with commas to separate the thousands. Finally, it converts the number to text. Here's what the function looks like:

```
FIXED(number, [number_of_decimals], [no_commas])
```

You need only the first argument. If you don't specify the other arguments, the FIXED() function automatically uses two decimal places and includes commas if your number's large enough to warrant them.

For example, the following formula gives you the text *5,450.59*:

```
=FIXED(5450.586, 2)
```

If you don't want commas, set the third argument to TRUE.

The DOLLAR() function automatically applies the currency format before it converts a value, so your text appears with a currency symbol before it. If you want, you can specify a number of decimal places, or just accept the default of two decimal places:

```
DOLLAR(number, [number_decimals])
```

NOTE Because the FIXED() and DOLLAR() functions give you text, not numbers, you'll notice that cells bearing these functions are left-aligned (Excel's default alignment for all text). If this bothers you, you can explicitly change the alignment. You'll also notice that if you change the number format for any of these cells, it won't have any effect. That's because the cell contains text, not a number.

Other Text Functions

So far you've toured Excel's most useful text-manipulation functions. The program provides a few lesser-used functions, too, which are outlined in Table 11-1.

TABLE 11-1 *Miscellaneous text functions*

FUNCTION	SYNTAX	DESCRIPTION
CHAR()	CHAR(number)	Returns the character for a specific character code. For example, CHAR(100) corresponds to the lowercase letter d.
CODE()	CODE(text)	Returns the numeric code for the first character in a text string. For example, CODE("d") returns 100.
EXACT()	EXACT(text1, text2)	Compares two pieces of text, and returns TRUE if they match, and FALSE if they don't. Usually, it's just easier to use the IF() function with the equal sign for comparison, as described on page 239.
REPT()	REPT(text, number_of_times)	Creates a text string by repeating the text you specify the number of times you specify. This function's a quick way to repeat one or more characters in a cell.

FUNCTION	SYNTAX	DESCRIPTION
T()	T(value)	Ensures that certain content is in text form. If you use T() with a piece of text, it returns that piece of text. If you use T() with a number, it returns an empty string. Thus, =T("Hello") returns the text *Hello*, while =T(56) returns just a blank value.
N()	N(value)	Ensures that certain content is a number. If you use N() with a numeric value, it returns that number. If you use N() with a text string, it returns 0, even if the text could be converted to a number. Thus, =N(2) returns the number 2, while =N("2") returns 0.
UNICHAR()*	UNICHAR(character_code)	Inserts a symbol, provided you know the *number code* for that number, according to the Unicode standard. For example, the Greek letter and mathematical symbol pi (π) has the number code 960, which means you can display it using the formula =UNICHAR(960). Most of the time, Excel's InsertSymbolsSymbol command is more convenient.
UNICODE()*	UNICODE(character)	For example, if you actually have the symbol for pi (π) in cell A3, the formula =UNICODE(A3) returns the number 960. If you supply a longer bit of text, UNICODE() only examines the first character.

** These functions are new to Excel 2013. Don't use them if you want to share your spreadsheet with people using older versions of Excel.*

Manipulating Dates and Times

To understand how you can use Excel's functions to manipulate dates and times, you need to understand a little more about how Excel stores these values. The reality is that even though many dates look, at least partly, like text entries (for instance, *Mar. 5, 2013*), Excel actually stores them as *serial numbers*. Under this system, Excel designates the date January 1, 1900 as day 1; January 2, 1900 is day 2; and so on.

Thus, if you use Excel to subtract one date from another, you actually end up calculating the difference in days, which, it turns out, is exactly what you want. But this system of date storage leads to some interesting side effects. For example, you can't enter a date in Excel that's earlier than January 1, 1900. Try it—if you do, Excel treats your date like text.

Excel also supports an alternate date system where it designates January 1, 1904 as day 1. Microsoft included this format to ensure compatibility with the Macintosh version of Excel, which uses that date as its baseline. To change your Windows worksheet to use dates that start at 1904, select FileOptions, and then choose the Advanced section. Scroll down the page of settings until you see the heading "When calculating this workbook." Underneath that, turn on the checkbox next to "Use 1904 date system." Dates don't look any different on your worksheet, but their internal representations have changed, and you can't enter a date earlier than January 1, 1904, without Excel converting it to plain text.

TIP The fact that the PC version of Excel uses a different date format than the Mac version won't cause a problem when you transfer files from one system to another, because Excel's smart enough to adjust to the difference between the two formats. However, in a few rare cases, it could be trouble. First, if you cut-and-paste between Excel files that use different date systems, you could get some glitches. And if you use General format on your dates and then transfer files, you could wind up with errors. These cases aren't common—but if they affect you, be on the lookout.

Ordinarily, you won't see these underlying serial values, because Excel always displays dates using the Date number format. However, you can take a look at the underlying number by changing the format of any cell that contains a date. For example, type *1/1/2010* into a worksheet, right-click the cell, and then choose Format Cells. In the Category list, choose General instead of Date. Now you'll see the number 40179 instead of the text date. (Incidentally, you can do the reverse to display a normal number as a date, although doing so doesn't usually make much sense.) For more information about formatting date values, see Chapter 5.

Excel also stores times of day as numbers behind the scenes. In fact, Excel internally stores every time value as a fractional number from 0 to 1. The number 0 represents 12:00 AM (the start of the day) and 0.99999 represents 11:59:59 PM (the end of the day). Because Excel stores times as a single number, it's easy to subtract one time value from another. However, time values can have varying degrees of precision. If your time's accurate down to the millisecond, it includes more decimal places (up to eight). For example, Excel stores 10:30 AM as 0.4375, whereas it stores 10:30:32.34 as 0.437874306.

So now that you know dates are really whole numbers and times of day are fractions, what happens if you enter a number like *40179.50,* and then apply the Date number format? In this case, Excel uses the whole number part (40179) for the date, and the fractional part (0.50) for the time. Excel therefore interprets 40179.50 to mean 40,179 days from January 1, 1900. Thus, the resulting value is the combined date and time of 1/1/2010 12:00:00 PM (see Table 11-2). If you change the number to *40179.40*, you end up with 1/1/2010 9:36:00 AM. At this point, you're probably realizing that there's really no difference between dates and times—they're just different components of a single number.

TABLE 11-2 *The internal representation of dates and times*

WHAT YOU SEE	WHAT EXCEL SEES
January 1, 2010	40179
12:05 PM	0.503472
January 1, 2010 12:05 PM	40179.503472

Math with Dates and Times

On Planet Excel, since dates and times are really just special types of numbers, you can use them in calculations like addition, subtraction, and so on. In the case of dates, the most common operation is to subtract one date from another to calculate the number of days in between. For example, consider this formula:

```
=A2-A1
```

If A2 contains the value 10/30/2013, and A1 contains the value 3/20/2013, the result is 224, which is the number of days between these two dates.

If the dates include time information (for example, if one of them is 10/30/2013 4:25 PM rather than just 10/30/2013), the result of your calculation will be a fractional number (like 224.684 days). This counts the number of full days (224) and the left-over minutes (in other words, 0.684 of a day).

This result makes perfect sense. However, it may not be the result you want. For example, if you're counting the number of days until an important event, you probably want to follow the calendar and ignore the time information. There are two ways to accomplish this. Your first option is to use the DAYS() function, which performs a date subtraction without considering the time information. To use it, you simply supply the end date, followed by the start date, like so:

```
=DAYS(A2, A1)
```

Assuming these two dates are 224 days apart, the DAYS() function always returns the number 224, no matter what time information the dates include.

The DAYS() function has a downside, too: Only Excel 2013 supports it. Fortunately, you can easily duplicate its work with a little Excel know-how. If you have dates that include time information, use the INT() function to strip out the fractional time portion and then perform your calculation:

```
=INT(A2)-INT(A1)
```

With a bit more mathematical gymnastics, you can craft formulas that extract other bits of date or time information. For example, you could take a number that represents a combined date and time value, extract just the fractional time portion, and then round that number to a number of whole hours using the following formula:

```
=ROUND((B10-INT(B10))*24, 0)
```

This formula works on the date in cell B10 of Figure 11-3. Here's how it breaks down: The formula begins by calculating *INT(B10)*. This function truncates the date number, removing the fractional time portion. Then the formula evaluates *B10-INT(B10)*. Now you've got just the fractional time portion of the date. Next, the formula multiplies this fractional part by 24 (the number of hours in a day), and then rounds it to a whole number. You end up extracting just the number of hours from the combined date/time value. Figure 11-3 shows the result of this date calculation (in cell B11), along with several similar date calculations.

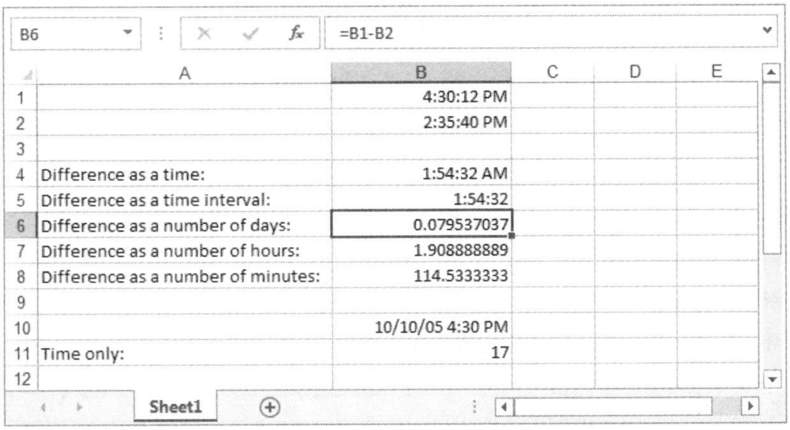

FIGURE 11-3

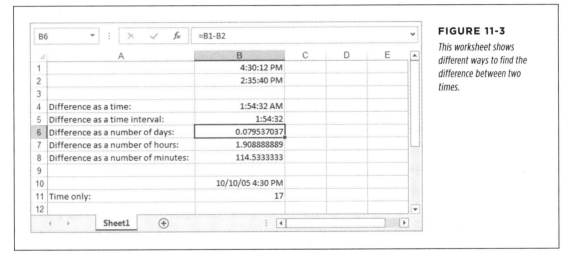

This worksheet shows different ways to find the difference between two times.

In Figure 11-3, the calculation shown in cell B4 (*=B1–B2*) uses the default format, which incorrectly interprets the time difference as a chronological time value. The second calculation (cell B5) uses the same formula, but an interval time format. As a result, Excel displays the result as an interval of time. The next example (cell B6) uses the General format to display the result in terms of the number of fractional days. Finally, the last two examples take the additional step of multiplying the number of fractional days by 24 (to calculate fractional hours) and by 60 (to calculate fractional minutes).

As you'll see in the rest of this chapter, Excel has plenty more specialized date functions that often make calculations easier than this.

NOTE Remember, if you change the number format, you may end up hiding part of the date's information. For example, if you choose to display a combined date and time value using a time-only format, you won't see the date information. However, Excel still uses this date information in any calculations you perform, which could lead to unexpected results. For best results, perform your date manipulation using the date functions described in the next section, rather than writing your own formulas from scratch.

TODAY() and NOW(): Inserting the Current Date and Time

The TODAY() function automatically retrieves the current date. It doesn't require any arguments because it simply examines your computer's internal clock. TODAY() is extremely useful for creating spreadsheets that continuously update themselves (sometimes called *dynamic spreadsheets*). For example, you could create a formula that determines the number of days that a payment is overdue. Here's an example:

```
=TODAY()-A1
```

This formula assumes that cell A1 contains the date a payment was due. As a result, it calculates the number of days between the two dates, which shows up as an ordinary number (like 14 for a payment that's two weeks late). Remember, you need to format the result as an ordinary number (representing the number of days), not as a date.

The NOW() function is similar to TODAY(), except that it retrieves the current date along with the current time. If you use NOW() to display a value in a cell that doesn't have any special formatting applied, Excel uses a custom format that shows the date and time (listed in the 24-hour format; for example, 10/5/2013 19:06).

You can use other formats to hide some of this information. For example, if Excel formats a cell using the custom number format [h]:mm:ss, you'll see only the time portion 19:06, not the date information. (For more on custom number formats, see page 143.) The following formula shows one handy way to calculate the current time by completely removing the date:

```
=NOW()-TODAY()
```

Remember to format the displayed result as a time value.

NOTE Excel recalculates both TODAY() and NOW() when you reopen a spreadsheet or when you explicitly refresh the worksheet by pressing F9. But sometimes, you may want to insert the current date and make sure Excel never updates it again. In these cases, you can use the TODAY() or NOW() functions, but you need to convert the result into a static date. Hit F2 to activate edit mode for the cell, and then press F9 to replace the cell with the calculated result. At this point, you'll see the serial number appear in the cell. Finally, press Enter to commit this value.

DATE() and TIME(): Dates and Times in Calculations

As you've learned over the last few chapters, formulas can include cell references and *literals*, or fixed values. So far, you've seen examples of literal numbers (like 1+1) and literal text. Unfortunately, it's not as easy to insert literal date values into a formula. Although Excel makes it easy to type a single date into a cell (just use a format like 1/7/2013), you can't use the same syntax *inside* a formula.

NOTE If you simply want to calculate the difference between two dates stored in different cells, you can use an ordinary formula, like =A2-A1 (assuming the dates are in cells A1 and A2).

For example, if you enter the formula *=2/9/2013–1/14/2013*, Excel won't recognize this as an attempt to calculate the number of days between January 14, 2013 and February 9, 2013. Instead, it sees the whole chain of numbers and backward slashes, as well as the minus sign, as one long arithmetic operation involving division. And while you *can* enter a literal date value by typing in the corresponding serial number (as explained on page 54), this technique is confusing and error-prone—unless you're keeping track of the number of days that have elapsed since January 1, 1900.

An easier way to enter literal date values is to use the DATE() function. It's a quick and easy way to insert a date into a formula. DATE() accepts three numbers, each of which represent a different component of the date. The function gives you the date's serial number. Here's what it looks like:

```
DATE(year, month, day)
```

In other words, if you enter this formula into a cell:

```
=DATE(2013, 1, 1)
```

Excel displays the date *1/1/2013*. However, you need to watch the formatting you use for the cell. If you use the DATE() function in a cell that uses the General number format, Excel automatically adjusts the cell to use the Date number format. However, if you already applied a specific non-General number format to the cell (like Currency), the DATE() function won't change the format. That means you'll see the familiar date serial number (in this example, *41275*), which isn't what you want.

Similarly, you can use the DATE() function to create a formula that combines date literals and cell references. Here's a formula that determines the number of days between 12/30/2014 and another date (the one contained in cell A1):

```
=A1-DATE(2014, 12, 30)
```

NOTE You can use the DATE() function to take a year number, month number, and day number from three different cells and calculate the resulting date. However, it's unlikely that you'll find a worksheet that splits date information into more than one cell.

The TIME() function performs similar magic with time values. It requires three components: an hour number, a minute number, and a seconds number. If you want, you can use fractional seconds to indicate milliseconds. With this function, you have to enter hours using a 24-hour clock. Here's what the function looks like:

```
TIME(hour, minute, second)
```

For example, the following function calculates how much time exists between now and a deadline at 9:00 p.m. (21:00 in a 24-hour clock):

```
=TIME(21,0,0)-(NOW()-TODAY())
```

As you'll see soon, constructing this formula requires several steps. (For a refresher on the precedence rules Excel uses when determining order of operations, see page 224.)

- First, the formula creates the time literal for 9:00 p.m. using the TIME() function.
- Next, the formula determines the current time using the calculation NOW()–TODAY(). This calculation works because it takes the current date and time (the result of the NOW() function), and removes the current date portion (the result of the TODAY() function).
- Finally, it calculates the difference between 9:00 p.m. and the current time. Excel expresses the result as it does all time values, as a fractional number of days. You could multiply this number by 24 to get the final result as a number of hours, but a better choice is to simply apply a Time number format to the cell.

DAY(), MONTH(), and YEAR(): More Date Calculations

The DAY(), MONTH(), and YEAR() functions are great when you want to calculate dates that fall before or after a certain date you already know. All three functions take a date argument and give you a number representing the day (1 to 31), the month (1 to 12), or the year (1900 to 9999), respectively. For example, if you place the date 1/1/2013 in cell A1, the following formula displays a result of 2013:

```
=YEAR(A1)
```

If you want to use the DAY(), MONTH(), and YEAR() functions with date literals, you need to use these functions in conjunction with the DATE() function. For example, the following formula displays the number 5:

```
=MONTH(DATE(2013,05,20))
```

NOTE The DAY(), MONTH(), and YEAR() functions all require that you put their arguments in the form of a date's underlying serial value, so a formula like *=YEAR(1/1/2010)* won't give you the value you're presumably looking for (that is, 2010). Instead, Excel calculates the result of the division 1/1/2010 (which is 0.000498), and then passes that to the YEAR() function, the result of which has no real meaning. To correct this problem, use the DATE() function to create the serial number for the date you need.

The DAY(), MONTH(), and YEAR() functions really shine when you need to take an existing date and move it forward or backward a set number of days, months, or years. For example, say that, given any date, you want to know what the date will be in two weeks. You could use the DAY(), MONTH(), and YEAR() functions in conjunction with the DATE() function to find out. Here's the formula you'd use (assuming your base date was in cell A1):

```
=DATE(YEAR(A1), MONTH(A1), DAY(A1)+14)
```

Here's how this formula breaks down, assuming that cell A1 contains the date 5/14/2013. The YEAR() and MONTH() functions both generate pretty straightforward results for the DATE() function's first two arguments: 2013 and 5, respectively. The DAY() function gives you a value of 14, which, when added to 14, results in 28, which serves as the third argument in the DATE() function. The final result of the formula, therefore, is 5/28/2013.

Impressively, Excel handles these calculations correctly even if the DAY argument's *greater* than the number of days in the month. For example, if you pass 33 as the third argument to the DATE() function, and the current month has only 31 days, Excel simply rolls over to the next month. (Excel knows how many days are in every month.) The DATE() function performs a similar trick to increment the year if the second argument you use is greater than 12.

NOTE As you may expect, the TIME() function, which uses three arguments (hour, minute, second), works similarly. Namely, if you try to pass the function an hour value that's 24 or greater, or a number value that's 60 or greater, TIME() automatically rolls these values over. Thus, *=TIME(25, 10, 00)* results in 1:10 a.m..

These DAY(), MONTH(), and YEAR() functions are also useful for building conditions. For example, you can use MONTH() to see if a given date falls on a specific month or day, regardless of the year. The following formula displays the heading "First of the month" when the day component of the current date is 1. In all other cases, Excel leaves the cell blank.

```
=IF(DAY(TODAY())=1, "First of the month", "")
```

For much more on using conditional logic, see Chapter 13.

HOUR(), MINUTE(), SECOND(): More Time Calculations

The HOUR(), MINUTE(), and SECOND() functions work the same way as the DAY(), MONTH(), and YEAR() functions, except they each generates a number representing the number of hours, minutes, or seconds in a given timeframe. The hour component always uses a 24-hour clock. For example, if you type 9:30 PM into cell A1 (which Excel stores as the serial number 0.89583), the following formula displays the number 21:

```
=HOUR(A1)
```

And this function shows the minute component, which is the number 30:

```
=MINUTE(A1)
```

UP TO SPEED

Excel's Intentional Date Bug

Most software programmers spend their waking hours struggling to eradicate bugs from their software. So it may come as a bit of a surprise that Microsoft programmers deliberately *inserted* at least one bug into all versions of Excel.

People know this bug affectionately as the *date leap year bug*. As leap year aficionados know, the year 1900 is *not* a leap year. According to Excel, however, the year 1900 *is* a leap year. So if you enter the following formula, Excel won't complain, even though February 29, 1900 isn't an actual date:

```
=DATE(1900,2,29)
```

The reason for this error is compatibility. When Microsoft released Excel, Lotus 1-2-3 was by far the most popular spreadsheet program. Lotus 1-2-3 contained this bug, and by emulating it, Excel could use the same date numbering system, enhancing its compatibility.

This bug also means that the days of the week prior to March 1, 1900, are incorrect, and that date calculations that stretch over this date will also be off by one day.

It's unlikely that Microsoft will ever fix this problem. Most conceivable fixes would change the internal numbering for every date after February 28, 1900, potentially causing problems with every existing spreadsheet that uses dates. Fortunately, this problem's also fairly benign, because few spreadsheets use dates before February 29, 1900.

WEEKDAY(): Determining the Day of the Week

The WEEKDAY() function takes a date and returns a number that represents which day of the week that date falls on. For example, if the date falls on Sunday, the number's 1, on Monday it's 2, right up through Saturday, which is 7. If you need this sort of information, the WEEKDAY() function is indispensable.

Here's what the function looks like:

```
WEEKDAY(date, [return-type])
```

The first argument in WEEKDAY() is the date serial number. The WEEKDAY() function also accepts an optional second parameter, which you can use to change the numbering system. The second parameter can take one of three preset values: 1, 2, or 3. If you specify the number 1, Excel uses the default numbering system described earlier. The number 2 instructs Excel to start counting at 1 for Monday and end at 7 for Sunday. If you specify the number 3, Excel starts counting at 0 for Monday and ends at 6 for Sunday.

Here's a sample formula that returns 2, indicating that January 6, 2014 falls on a Monday:

```
=WEEKDAY(DATE(2014,1,6))
```

It's quite easy to change things if you prefer to show the day's name rather than its number. You simply need a little help from the TEXT() function (page 325), which can convert a number to any number format. In this case, you want to use a custom date format that shows the name of the day. Here's how:

```
=TEXT(WEEKDAY(DATE(2014,1,6)), "dddd")
```

Here, Excel shows the full day name (*Monday*). You can also tweak the format string to show the day's three-letter abbreviation (like *Mon*).

```
=TEXT(WEEKDAY(DATE(2014,1,6)), "ddd")
```

DATEDIF(): Calculating the Difference Between Dates

You've already learned how to use the DATE() function (page 332) to subtract one date from another and display the results in terms of days. But what if you want to calculate the difference in years or months? You could try and break the date up into components using the DAY(), MONTH(), and YEAR() functions, but these types of calculations can get surprisingly complicated. You're better off using Excel's little-known DATEDIF() function. Despite this being a useful gem for many date calculations, Excel's own Help tool neglects to cover this function.

FREQUENTLY ASKED QUESTION

Solving the DATEDIF() Mystery

Why isn't DATEDIF() mentioned in Excel's Help?

DATEDIF() is an Excel oddity. Excel gurus use it, but it's unknown by just about everyone else. But DATEDIF() isn't anything new—in fact, it was introduced in Excel 5.0. Microsoft even documented the DATEDIF() function in Excel 2000, but it removed the documentation from later versions of the program.

The DATEDIF() function has its origins in Lotus 1-2-3. Apparently, Microsoft included it in Excel for compatibility purposes. However, DATEDIF() is useful even in modern spreadsheets, because it fills a gap that other date functions don't address.

If you're still curious, you can read some unofficial DATEDIF() documentation at *www.cpearson.com/excel/datedif.htm.*

DATEDIF() accepts three arguments. The first two are the dates that you want to find the difference between. The smaller (older) date goes first, and the other date comes second. The third argument is a string that indicates the way you want to measure the time interval, such as in days, months, years, and so on. Table 11-3 explains your options. Remember, as with all string arguments, you need to put quotation marks around whatever value you choose. The formula looks like this:

```
DATEDIF(start_date, end_date, interval_type)
```

NOTE Remember, you can't use literal dates in any formula (ever). Instead, use tools like the DATE() function to first transform your date into the type of number you can use inside a formula.

TABLE 11-3 *Interval Strings for DATEDIF()*

CODE	MEANING	DESCRIPTION
"m"	Months	The number of complete months between the two dates.
"d"	Days	The number of days between the two dates.
"y"	Years	The number of complete years between the two dates.
"ym"	Months Excluding Years	The number of months between the two dates, as if they were in the same year.
"yd"	Days Excluding Years	The number of days between the two dates, as if they were in the same year.
"md"	Days Excluding Months and Years	The number of days between the two dates, as if they were in the same month and the same year.

For example, here's how to calculate the number of months that separate a date in the future (stored in cell A1) from the current date:

```
=DATEDIF(TODAY(), A1, "m")
```

Remember that, when using the DATEDIF() function with the "m" argument, you're counting *complete* months. That means that Excel counts the interval from, say, January 6, 2013 to February 6, 2013, as one month, but the interval from January 6, 2013 to February 5, 2013, is still a day shy, and Excel therefore counts it as zero months. Usually, this is the behavior you want. However, you do have another, somewhat more complicated, option, if you want intervals like January 6–February 5 to register as one month: Use the YEAR() and MONTH() functions.

For example, here's the DATEDIF() approach (which has a result of 0):

```
=DATEDIF(DATE(2013,1,6), DATE(2013,2,5), "m")
```

And here's the YEAR() and MONTH() approach, which returns a result of 1 (it works by subtracting the one month number from the other):

```
=MONTH(DATE(2013,2,5))-MONTH(DATE(2013,1,6))
```

And here's a revised approach that works with dates that aren't in the same year:

```
=(YEAR(DATE(2014,2,5))-YEAR(DATE(2013,1,6)))*12 +
MONTH(DATE(2014,2,5))-MONTH(DATE(2013,1,6))
```

Although this formula looks more complicated at first glance, it's really not that difficult. It's long because Excel calculates the year and month components separately. Once you find the difference in year numbers, Excel multiplies that number by 12, and then adds it to the month component. You end up with the total number of months between January 6, 2013 and February 5, 2014 (there are 13 of them).

Unfortunately, this formula assumes that every year is 365 days long, which neglects leap years. This formula is probably right most of the time, but it's likely to fail when you attempt to calculate someone's age in the days just before or after their birthday. (To solve the problem, see the box below.)

POWER USERS' CLINIC

Getting a Birthday Right

Now that you've learned about a wide variety of Excel date functions, it probably seems like it wouldn't be very difficult to calculate a person's age based on the current date and his or her birth date. But, in fact, it can be surprisingly tricky.

One approach is to use Excel's support for date subtraction. The following formula is a good first try (assuming the birthday is stored in cell A1):

```
=INT((NOW()-A1)/365)
```

Unfortunately, this formula assumes that every year has 365 days, which neglects leap years. The formula is probably right most of the time, but it fails in the days just before or after a person's birthday.

The YEAR(), MONTH(), and DAY() functions don't provide a solution—they all suffer from the same problem—none of them take leap years into account. The only real solution is to use DATEDIF(), which does take leap years into account. Here's the DATEDIF() formula you'd need:

```
=DATEDIF(A1,NOW(),"y")
```

You can even get a little fancier with the following formula, which uses some of the text manipulation techniques you saw earlier in this chapter. It displays a person's age in years, months, and days:

```
=DATEDIF(A1,NOW(),"y") & " years, " &
DATEDIF(A1,NOW(),"ym") & " months, " &
DATEDIF(A1,NOW(),"md") & " days"
```

DATEVALUE() and TIMEVALUE(): Converting Dates and Times into Serial Numbers

DATEVALUE() and TIMEVALUE() convert dates and times that Excel has stored as text into serial date numbers. Of course, for this conversion to work, Excel has to be able to interpret the text as a date or time. So if you type *1-1-2010* or *January 1, 2010* into a cell, these functions would be able to convert these values, but if you enter something like *1st January, 2010* or *1,1,2010*, you'd get an error message.

NOTE Keep in mind that the DATEVALUE() and TIMEVALUE() functions don't change the formatting of a cell. Therefore, if you want to see something other than the date serial number, you need to apply a Date number format to the cell.

The rules Excel uses to convert a piece of text into a date with DATEVALUE() are the same ones it uses for recognizing dates and time values when you enter them into a cell. To refresh your memory, see page 52. The only difference is that DATEVALUE() and TIMEVALUE() ignore the initial apostrophe in a text value.

For example, you can type the following text in cell A1. Remember that the apostrophe tells Excel to treat this entry as text even though it's clearly recognizable as a date:

```
'1/1/2010
```

Now another cell can perform a date calculation by first converting this text to a real date:

```
=NOW()-DATEVALUE(A1)
```

This formula calculates the number of days elapsed since January 1, 2010. Because the result is a number of days, you'll want to use the General number format, not a Date number format.

DATEVALUE() and TIMEVALUE() also work with literal text strings. That means that you can use these functions as an alternative to DATE() and TIME() to create a date or time literal. The difference? Whereas DATE() and TIME() create dates and times based on several numeric components you supply, DATEVALUE() and TIMEVALUE() create dates and times from string literals. Here's an example of TIMEVALUE() in action:

```
=TIMEVALUE("19:30:00")
```

This formula converts a static piece of text into the time value 19:30:00 (which Excel represents internally as the fractional number 0.8125). The only drawback to using DATEVALUE() and TIMEVALUE() is that you'll run into trouble if Excel can't interpret the text you supply. For example, the text string *January 1,2010* isn't formatted properly, because there's no space between the comma and the number 2010. This minor glitch is enough to completely stymie the DATEVALUE() function. It's much less likely that you'll make an error if you rely on the DATE() function instead.

DAYS360(): Finding Out the Number of Days Between Two Dates

DAYS360() gives you the number of days between two dates. Unlike simple date subtraction, however, DAYS360() assumes that every month has 30 days (giving the year a total of 360 days). So is this the kind of function you're supposed to use when following some radically alternative calendar system? Sort of. The only reason you'd use DAYS360() is if you were using an accounting system that performs its calculations based on 360-day years, which is common in some payroll systems. (Also, some systems calculate investments by assuming 12 months with 30 days each, for a total of 360 days.) Read on if you're still interested.

Here's what the function looks like:

```
=DAYS360(start_date, end_date, [European_method])
```

The smaller (older) date goes first (unless you want a negative number). The second argument is the date following the first date.

The third argument in DAYS360() is an optional value that you can set to TRUE to use the European version of the DAYS360() calculation. The only difference is how the calculation deals with start or end dates that happen on the 31st day of the month:

- In the default U.S. NASD (National Association of Securities Dealers) method, a starting day of 31 changes to 30. An ending day of 31 is handled differently depending on the start day. If the start day's 30 or 31, then the end date changes to day 30 in the same month. If the start day's earlier than 30, then the end date changes from 31 to the first day of the next month.
- In the European method, both a starting and ending day of 31 change to 30.

EDATE(): Calculating Future Dates

The EDATE() function (short for Elapsed Date) calculates a future date by adding a certain number of months to a date you supply. You specify two parameters: the starting date, and the number of months you want to move forward (use a negative number to move one or more months backward).

Here's an example that calculates a date one month from today:

```
=EDATE(NOW(),1)
```

The EDATE() function would be more useful if it provided a similar ability to advance a date by a set number of days or years. If you need to do that, then you need to resort to using the DAY(), MONTH(), and YEAR() functions, in conjunction with the DATE() function, as described earlier.

YEARFRAC(): Calculating the Percentage of a Year Between Two Dates

The YEARFRAC() function (short for Year Fraction) lets you take a range of days between two dates in the same year and determine what percentage this represents out of the whole year. For example, if you pay for a monthly fitness club membership and cancel it after a few weeks, this function may help you determine what portion of your money the club should refund (provided they'll spare you from the usual Draconian contract clauses).

The YEARFRAC() function requires two parameters: the start date and the end date (which can come from similar or different years). In addition, you can specify a third parameter to indicate how Excel should calculate the fraction. Here's what the function looks like:

```
YEARFRAC(start_date, end_date, [basis])
```

The basis has to be a number from 0 to 4. The meaning of the numbers are as follows:

- **0.** Excel performs the calculation in the same way as the DAYS360() function. The calculation assumes that every month has 30 days, and every year has 360 days. This system is primarily useful for accounting systems that use 360-day years in their calculations.
- **1.** The calculation gives you the fractional amount of a year that exists between two days. This basis counts the actual number of days in the range, and then divides this figure by the number of days in the year. It correctly takes leap years into account.

- **2.** The calculation counts the number of days between your two dates, but divides this total by 360 instead of the actual number of days in the appropriate year.
- **3.** The calculation counts the number of days between your two dates, but divides this total by 365 instead of the actual number of days in the appropriate year. This calculation provides the same answer as basis 1, assuming the year isn't a leap year.
- **4.** The calculation uses the European version of the DAYS360() function.

If you don't specify a basis number, Excel uses a basis of 0.

The following formula calculates the fraction of the year represented by the date range from January 1, 2010 to February 14, 2010:

```
=YEARFRAC(DATE(2010,1,1),DATE(2010,2,14),1)
```

This formula gives you approximately 0.12, or 12 percent, of the year.

EOMONTH(): Finding the Last Day of Any Month

The EOMONTH() function (short for End of Month) calculates the last day of any month in any year. However, it doesn't work quite the way you'd expect. EOMONTH() is designed so that you can look into the future and answer questions like "Two months from now, what's the last day of the month?" This quirk seems confusing at first, but business people like it because it helps them set payment periods and due dates for invoices.

When using EOMONTH(), you need to supply two parameters: the starting date and the number of months you want to look into the future. If you want to look into the past, use a negative value for the number of months (like -2 to go back in time two months). Here's what the basic EOMONTH() function looks like:

```
EOMONTH(start_date, number_of_months)
```

The following formula takes the date 1/1/2013, moves it to the next month (February), and then provides the last day of that month (February 28, 2013):

```
=EOMONTH(DATE(2013,1,1), 1)
```

To find the last day in the current month, you specify 0 for the second parameter. Here's a formula that does just that:

```
=EOMONTH(TODAY(), 0)
```

Like all of Excel's date functions, the EOMONTH() function is intelligent enough to handle leap years correctly.

NETWORKDAYS(): Counting the Number of Business Days

The NETWORKDAYS() function counts the number of business days in a given range. It requires two parameters: a start date and an end date. In addition, you can supply a third parameter to specifies holidays that Excel shouldn't count.

The basic function looks like this:

```
=NETWORKDAYS(start_date, end_date, [holidays])
```

The following formula gives you the number 23, which is the number of working days in January 2013:

```
=NETWORKDAYS(DATE(2013,1,1), DATE(2013,1,31))
```

You can specify holidays several ways. To exclude just a single holiday from your calculation, you can set it as a date literal. Here's how you'd rewrite the earlier example so that January 15, 2013 is designated as a holiday and, therefore, not included in the calculation:

```
=NETWORKDAYS(DATE(2013,1,1), DATE(2013,1,31), DATE(2013,1,15))
```

To specify more than one date, you have to use a messier syntax, which writes each date as a text string in the month/day/year format. Here's an example that excludes January 2, 2013, and January 5, 2013. Note that you need to surround the holidays with curly braces:

```
=NETWORKDAYS(DATE(2013,1,1), DATE(2013,1,31), {"1/2/2013","1/5/2013"})
```

Your final option is to specify holidays as a range of cells in your worksheet. For example, if you enter a holiday schedule in the cells C1:C11, you can use that range in the NETWORKDAYS() function, as shown here:

```
=NETWORKDAYS(DATE(2013,1,1), DATE(2013,1,31), C1:C11)
```

WORKDAY(): Figuring Out When Days Will Fall in the Future

The WORKDAY() function lets you perform date calculations that take workdays, weekends, and holidays into account. Essentially, the WORKDAY() function takes a date you specify, and moves it into the future by a certain number of business days (while automatically skipping over weekends). One of the most common reasons to use WORKDAY() is to estimate a due date by taking the current date and adding the number of business days it should take to complete a given task. The WORKDAY() function accepts three parameters: the start date, the number of days you want to move into the future, and any days that Excel should ignore because they represent holidays. The function looks like this:

```
WORKDAY(start_date, days, [holidays])
```

You can use the optional holiday parameter to specify days that Excel would ordinarily treat as workdays, but which you want it to exclude. You can also supply a reference to a range of cells that contain all the holiday dates.

For example, imagine you want to find out when you'll complete a project if you start working on it today, and it requires 30 days of work. You can use the following formula to estimate the completion date, assuming you don't work on weekends:

```
=WORKDAY(TODAY(), 30)
```

As with many of the date functions, you need to format the cell so that the value Excel generates (the date serial number) appears as a date.

WEEKNUM(): Figuring Out in Which Week a Date Falls

The WEEKNUM() function accepts a date and gives you a number from 1 to 52 to indicate where the date falls in the year. For example, if the cell that WEEKNUM() refers to contains the date 1/1/2014, then the function gives you the value of 1 (indicating the first week in the year). If WEEKNUM() gives you 52, the date falls on the last week of the year.

Ordinarily, WEEKNUM() assumes that every week starts on Sunday. However, the WEEKNUM() function also takes an optional second parameter, called *return_type*, which lets you designate a different day. This strange-sounding feature is used in some accounting scenarios—for example, it's useful if a company needs to create weekly invoices that are always issued on Fridays. To pick a different starting day for your weeks, use a return_type value of 11 for Monday, 12 for Tuesday, 13 for Wednesday, and so on. Here's an example that gets the week number for the date in cell A2, and assumes that Wednesday is the first day of the week:

```
=WEEKNUM(A2, 13)
```

CHAPTER

12

Lookup, Reference, and Information Functions

Excel's lookup, reference, and information functions are quite different from the mathematical functions discussed in the last few chapters. Most math functions take your data as a starting point and use it to calculate some new result. Lookup, reference, and information functions, on the other hand, don't generate any *new* data. Instead, they let you search for and extract important bits of content from your worksheet and then reuse it in ways guaranteed to delight spreadsheet lovers worldwide.

All three types of functions play different but complementary roles. A *lookup function* finds and then copies data from a particular cell in a worksheet. A *reference function* retrieves more general information about groups of cells (like how many columns' worth of data is in your table). It's common to use lookup and reference functions together. You can use a reference function to find out which cell has the data you want to use, and a lookup function to actually retrieve the cell's contents.

Finally, *information functions* let you determine what *kind* of content resides in an individual cell (for instance, a number or text). Knowing that can help you construct extremely powerful *conditional formulas*, which behave differently depending on the type of data they encounter.

All these functions may not immediately seem useful, but they become indispensable in a variety of situations. Consider a few common examples:

- You want to let spreadsheet viewers look up items, and then see these items used in a series of calculations. Say you have a worksheet with a long list of customer records (each of which includes info like their mailing address and how much money they owe your company). You not only want to make the spreadsheet searchable, you also want to present your searchers with a series of calculations about the items they've found, like how much money they owe your company after 30 days plus interest, 60 days plus interest and penalty, and so on. Lookup and reference functions let you turn your spreadsheets into extremely useful, interactive databases. It's kind of like having an accountant-in-waiting for anyone who wants to ask questions about the information in your spreadsheet.

- You want to extract some data from a table and use it in another worksheet. Maybe you have a list of mailing addresses, and you need to extract a specific address and place it at the top of a form letter. Lookup functions are perfect for that.
- Your worksheet has more than one table, and they're all designed to work together. Say you want to pluck out a product's name and price from a massive table of product information, and then use it to create an invoice. This example represents one of the most powerful ways you can use lookup functions.

TIP Excel user groups and online forums are full of problems that you can solve only with lookup functions. Try, for instance, the Excel forum on Microsoft's Community site *http://tinyurl.com/ms-excel-forum*, or third-party discussion groups like *www.msofficeforums.com/excel*.

In this chapter, you'll learn how to use the lookup and information functions, as well as how to overcome some of their limitations. Finally, you'll consider the oddest lookup and reference function of them all: the HYPERLINK() function, which lets you create Web-style hyperlinks in a worksheet cell.

The Basic Lookup

VLOOKUP() and HLOOKUP() are the two most popular lookup functions. They perform the same task—finding and copying data—but they look in different directions:

- **VLOOKUP() is the vertical lookup function.** You use it to find a specific row in a large table of data. VLOOKUP() works by scanning the values in a single column from top to bottom. Once the function finds the entry you're looking for, it can retrieve other information from the same row. VLOOKUP(), examined in closer detail in the next section, is the more commonly used of the two lookup functions.
- **HLOOKUP() is the horizontal lookup function.** You use it to find a specific column in a large table of data. HLOOKUP() works by scanning the values in a single row from left to right. Once the function finds the entry you're looking for, it can retrieve other information from the same column.

Both VLOOKUP() and HLOOKUP() require three parameters, and both have one optional parameter:

```
VLOOKUP(search_for, table_range, column_number, [range_lookup])

HLOOKUP(search_for, table_range, row_number, [range_lookup])
```

The first parameter, *search_for*, is the cell content you're trying to find. The second parameter, *table_range*, is the rectangular grid of cells that contains all the data you're searching through. The *column_number* and *row_number* parameters are known as *offsets*. Once VLOOKUP() or HLOOKUP() finds the data you requested, the offset tells Excel how many cells to move over or down to find the related data you want.

Imagine a spreadsheet filled with customer records, each listed in its own row. You may initially use VLOOKUP() to find a customer's last name, but what you're really interested in is how much money she owes you. To find that crucial info, you'd use the offset argument to retrieve the value from a cell that's a few columns away from the last name column.

Finally, the *range_lookup* parameter is a Boolean (true or false) value. If you specify TRUE, or leave out this parameter, Excel finds approximate matches. If you specify FALSE, Excel gives you either an exact match or, if it finds no match, the error value #N/A. (You can also substitute 1 for TRUE or 0 for FALSE, if you find that's easier.)

VLOOKUP(): Vertical Lookups

The simplest way to understand how lookup functions work is to study one of these functions in action. Looking at VLOOKUP() is a good place to start. Figure 12-1 shows a worksheet that uses VLOOKUP() to let spreadsheet viewers learn more about the products contained in a long list of exotic grocery store items. The idea here is to offer a kind of interactive information dashboard on top of the spreadsheet so that anyone can enter a product's ID number, and then view specific information about the product (like the value of the inventory in stock).

True, you could simply construct your worksheet so that this information appears alongside the product data that's already listed, but when you have multiple scenarios that you want to let people play around with, your spreadsheet can get more crowded than a cross-town bus at 5:30 p.m. The functions in this chapter offer a better way to get customizable views for large amounts of information.

Here's a blow-by-blow breakdown of what's happening in Figure 12-1. The key cells are B2 and cells C4 through C11. B2 is where whoever's reading the spreadsheet types in the product ID. C4 through C8 all contain different versions of the lookup function, which retrieve the product name, unit price, the number of units in stock, the number of units on order, and the reorder level, respectively. The actual calculations, which are pretty straightforward, take place in cells C9, C10, and C11.

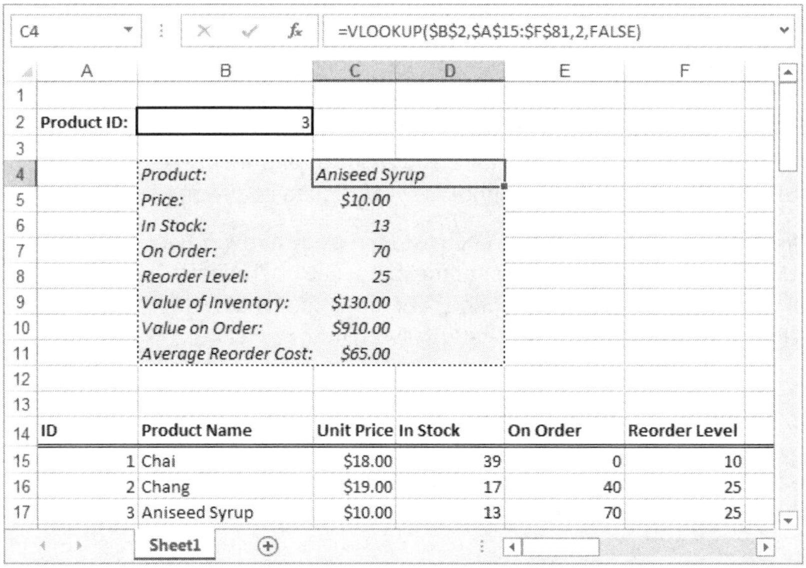

FIGURE 12-1

VLOOKUP() in action: The person using this spreadsheet simply types the appropriate product number in cell B2. Then the lookup formulas in cells C4 through C8 automatically retrieve different kinds of price and inventory data (which starts in row 15). The cells C9 through C11 don't need any lookup functions—they simply use the values from the lookup cells to perform additional calculations.

Consider how Excel retrieves the product name, shown in cell C4. The formula is:

```
=VLOOKUP(B2, A15:F81, 2, FALSE)
```

Here's what you're looking at:

- The first parameter, B2, is the product ID (which the person reading the spreadsheet types in). This is the value VLOOKUP() tries to match.
- The second parameter is the most important: It tells Excel what range of cells to search. This example has 66 product rows (from row 15 to 81) and six columns of data (from column A to column F). The first column in this range must be the column that contains the data you're trying to locate (in this case, the product ID). The other columns contain the remaining information Excel is going to retrieve once it finds a match.
- The third parameter, 2, indicates the position of the data you want to retrieve. Excel numbers each column in the range that you supply from left to right, starting at 1. Thus, 2 represents the Product Name column.
- Finally, FALSE indicates that you're insisting on an exact match to ensure you have the correct product.

Now, if someone typed the product ID *21* into cell B2, for instance, each of the VLOOKUP() functions in cells C4 through C8 finds the requested row, and then gives you the data they're designed to retrieve (product, price, the number of units in stock, and the number of units on order, respectively).

TIP If you supply a range lookup value of TRUE, or if you omit this parameter altogether, Excel accepts a partial match when it performs the search. That is, it attempts to find an ID value that matches exactly, but if it can't, it uses the closest ID that's *less* than the lookup value in B2. As a result, it's always a good idea to explicitly turn off range matching if you're looking for specific items.

Once you retrieve the information you need, it's fairly easy to use it in other ordinary calculations. For example, the formula in cell C9 (Figure 12-1) calculates the total value of all the products on order by multiplying the retrieved unit price by the retrieved number of units on order:

```
=C5*C6
```

NOTE Perhaps the most convenient feature of a worksheet that uses lookup functions is that the worksheet has to store only one copy of the data. So, in the previous example, if you modify the product list, the information you get from any linked lookup formulas updates automatically.

POWER USERS' CLINIC

Advanced Text Lookup

The product lookup example shown in Figure 12-1 searches by product ID, which is a numeric value. You can also use lookup formulas to search *text*. You could modify the product lookup example to conduct searches using a product's name. The price lookup formula would then look like this:

```
=VLOOKUP(B2, B15:F81, 2, FALSE)
```

This version of the price lookup formula has two changes (compared to the one on page 348). First, the range of searched data starts at B15 instead of A15. That's because the column that Excel searches must always be the leftmost column. The second change is the offset. Because the first column is B, the VLOOKUP() function numbers that column as 1, and the adjacent Price column as 2 (instead of 3). Consequently, you need to modify your offset accordingly.

Text lookups are useful, but you may find them a bit cumbersome. As a rule of thumb, when you perform a text search, you should always specify FALSE for the range lookup parameter. Otherwise, the VLOOKUP() function will work erratically on unsorted lists, and it may fail to find the right match.

If you truly *do* need to perform partial text searches, you can use the asterisk (*) wildcard as a workaround. When you add an asterisk to the end of the search value, the VLOOKUP() function finds any cell that starts with this text. For example, if you type in *Queso**, the VLOOKUP() function matches the Queso Cabrales product. You can even go one step further, and change your lookup formulas so they always accept partial matches. The trick is to add the asterisk onto the end of the cell value in your formula, as shown here:

```
=VLOOKUP(B2&"*", B15:F81, 2, FALSE)
```

This formula uses the ampersand (&)—a special operator for joining text. For more information about manipulating text, see Chapter 11.

HLOOKUP(): Horizontal Lookups

Now that you've mastered vertical lookups, horizontal lookups will be a snap. The key distinction is that HLOOKUP() searches *across* the first row in the cell range you supply. You use the offset to retrieve data from other rows in the matching column.

Figure 12-2 shows an example of HLOOKUP() used with a grid of product information:

```
=HLOOKUP(C11,A1:E8,2)*C12
```

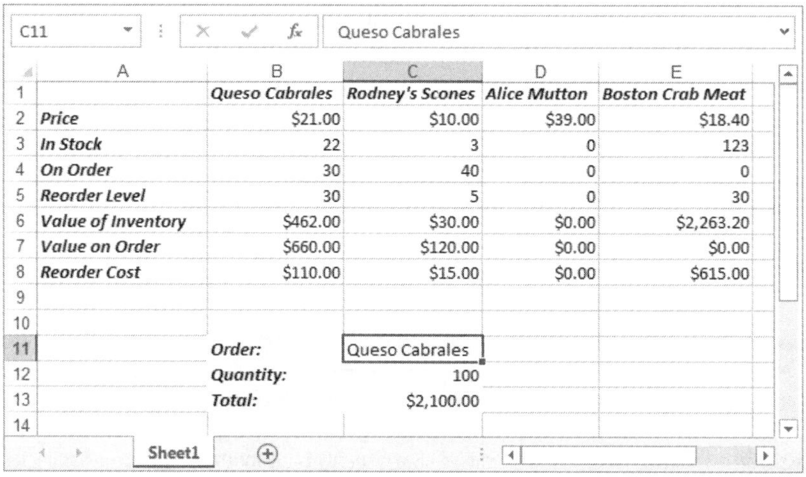

	A	B	C	D	E
1		Queso Cabrales	Rodney's Scones	Alice Mutton	Boston Crab Meat
2	Price	$21.00	$10.00	$39.00	$18.40
3	In Stock	22	3	0	123
4	On Order	30	40	0	0
5	Reorder Level	30	5	0	30
6	Value of Inventory	$462.00	$30.00	$0.00	$2,263.20
7	Value on Order	$660.00	$120.00	$0.00	$0.00
8	Reorder Cost	$110.00	$15.00	$0.00	$615.00
9					
10					
11		Order:	Queso Cabrales		
12		Quantity:	100		
13		Total:	$2,100.00		
14					

FIGURE 12-2

Horizontal lookups are just as straightforward as vertical lookups; the direction is the only thing that changes. Here, Excel uses the function HLOOKUP() to scan the top row of product names.

This formula tells Excel to search the range of cells from A1:E8. Because this is a horizontal lookup, Excel starts out by inspecting the first row (cells A1 to E1), where it attempts to find a cell that matches the content in C11 (*Queso Cabrales*). When Excel finds a match, it uses the offset of 2 to step down to the second row and retrieve the cell value with the product price (*21*). Finally, the formula multiplies the retrieved price by the number of units (*100*), which are listed in cell C12.

IFNA(): Dealing with Failed Lookups

As you already learned, if you use a lookup function to search for something that doesn't exist, the result is the #N/A error code, which means "not available." For example, Figure 12-3 shows what happens if you enter the wrong product ID in the vertical lookup example you considered earlier.

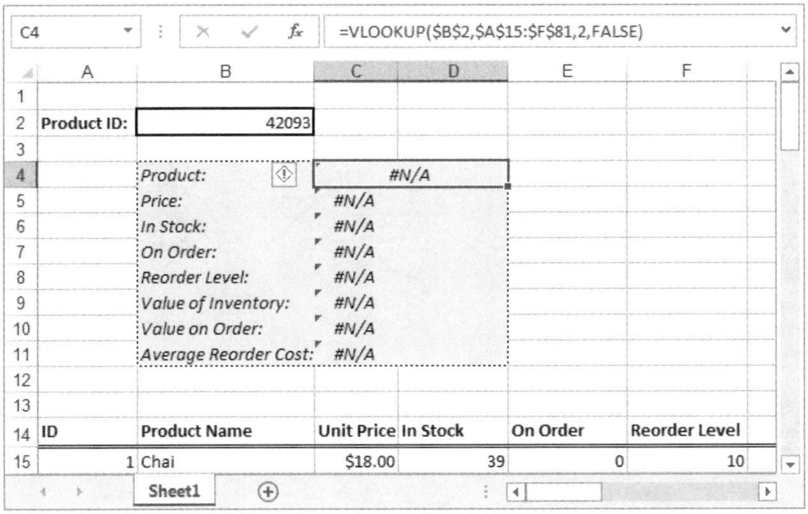

FIGURE 12-3

Excel can't find a product with the ID 42093, so it shows the #N/A error code instead.

This is Excel's standard behavior, and there's nothing wrong with it. After all, the #N/A error code points out that there's a problem with your data. However, it might confuse less experienced Excel users. If you're developing a workbook that other people will use, it's worth taking some extra time to replace the #N/A code with a more meaningful message.

The easiest way to do that is to use Excel's IFNA() function. It checks an expression to see if it causes a #N/A error code. If your lookup succeeds, the IFNA() function simply shows the lookup result. But if the lookup fails and returns the #N/A code, IFNA() swaps in the alternate value you specify.

For example, in Figure 12-3 this function performs the product name lookup:

```
=VLOOKUP(B2, A15:F81, 2, FALSE)
```

To replace the #N/A value with your own message, you wrap the VLOOKUP() function in an IFNA() function, like so:

```
=IFNA(VLOOKUP(B2, A15:F81, 2, FALSE), "[ PRODUCT NOT FOUND ]")
```

Now, when the lookup function can't find the text you want, *[PRODUCT NOT FOUND]* appears in the cell, as shown in Figure 12-4.

NOTE IFNA() is new to Excel 2013. If you need backward compatibility with older versions of Excel, and you want to use the trick described here, you'll need to rely on a more verbose and awkward solution: combining the IF() function (described on page 239) with the ISNA() function. Essentially, you use ISNA() to test for an #N/A value (it returns TRUE or FALSE), and then you use the IF() function to swap in the right value, depending on the result.

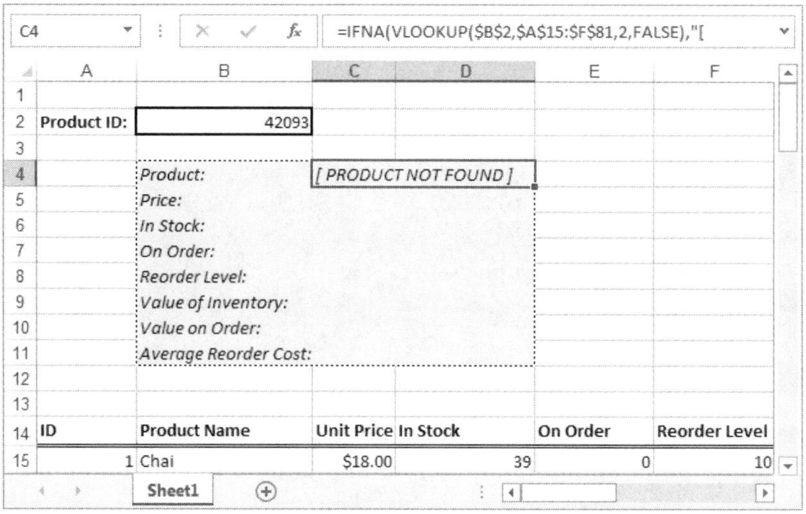

FIGURE 12-4

This lookup function failed to find matching text, but now the worksheet explains what happened in cell C4. It also hides the #N/A error messages that would ordinarily appear in the cells underneath.

You can work similar magic with the lookups for the other product information, including the price and stock numbers. Here, the IFNA() function simply substitutes a blank value (really an empty text string; see the formula below) if the price lookup fails:

```
=IFNA(VLOOKUP(B2, A15:F81, 3, FALSE), "")
```

There's still one minor niggle in this example. When the lookup fails, any other functions that use the lookup data will fail, too, and report an #N/A error. For example, consider the reorder calculation in cell C8, which uses this formula:

```
=C5*C6
```

If the lookup fails, the IFNA() functions in cells C5 and C6 replace the lookups with empty text strings. This causes the reorder calculation to fail, because there's no way to multiply two pieces of text together. So the result of the formula is the #VALUE! error code.

NOTE If you create a formula that uses a true blank cell—one that has never been touched—Excel treats that cell as though it contains the number 0. But once you put something in a cell, there's no way to return it to this blank, virgin state. The best you can do is to put in an empty string, and that will break any formulas that attempt to use the cell in a calculation.

There are two solutions. One is change the IFNA() functions that get the price and stock information. Instead of replacing #N/A values with empty text strings, they should swap in the number 0. That way, the equation won't fail, because *=0*0* is a perfectly reasonable calculation. The only problem is that all these zeros will be visible in your worksheet. To hide them, you can style the cells with the Accounting number format (page 134) or a custom number format that tells it not to show zero values (page 143).

The other option is to use the IFERROR() function to tell Excel to show a blank string (nothing) if the formula fails:

```
=IFERROR(C5*C6, "")
```

The IFERROR() function works the same as the IFNA() function, except it checks the expression for any type of error, not just #N/A values.

Advanced Lookups

VLOOKUP() and HLOOKUP() work well for finding related information in different tables. They also impose a few restrictions, however, including:

- The lookup column has to be the first column or row in the range. That means you can't use VLOOKUP() to retrieve columns to the left of the lookup column, and you can't use HLOOKUP() to retrieve rows above the lookup row.
- You must choose between horizontal and vertical lookups. You can't perform a lookup that finds cells based on a lookup column and a lookup row.

In this section, you'll learn how to skirt these restrictions with the help of other functions.

TIP You simply can't get around certain lookup rules. The lookup functions aren't much use if you have potentially multiple matches. That means you can't use a lookup function to retrieve your top-10 selling products, for example. If you want to use this sort of logic, then you should probably opt for Excel's list feature (Chapter 14), which provides filtering capabilities.

MATCH(): Finding the Position of Items in a Range

The MATCH() function lets you find the position of an item in a range. On its own, MATCH() doesn't accomplish a whole lot, but used in conjunction with some of the functions described later in this section, you'll find it really handy. Here are some MATCH() fundamentals.

To use MATCH(), you simply specify the search value (either a number or text) and the range you want to search:

```
MATCH(search_for, range, [match_type])
```

The range you use must be one-dimensional. That means you can search through the column of cells A1:A10 or the row of cells A1:E1, but you can't search the *grid* of cells A1:E10.

The *match_type* argument is optional, but highly recommended. It can take one of three values:

- **0** gives you the position of the first item that matches exactly.
- **1** gives you the position of the largest value that's equal to or less than the search argument. For this argument to work correctly, you must perform a lookup on a range of numbers or text values arranged in ascending order. If you use the formula *=MATCH(100, {12,23,48,101,321}, 1)*, the result is 3 because the third value in the range (*48*) is the largest number less than 100.
- **–1** gives you the position of the smallest value that's equal to or greater than the search argument. For this argument to work correctly, you must execute a lookup on a range of numbers or text values arranged in descending order. If you use the formula *=MATCH("b", {"doughnut","cracker","banana","apple"},-1)*, the result is 3 because the third value in the range (*banana*) is the smallest text value that falls after b in dictionary order.

NOTE You almost always want to use a match_type of 0. However, the MATCH() function automatically uses a match_type of 1 if you omit the match_type parameter. Consider yourself warned.

If MATCH() finds the value you're searching for, it gives you a number indicating its position. If you're searching the range of cells A1:A10, and the search item's in cell A3, then the MATCH() function returns 3 (because it's the third cell in this range). If it finds no match, MATCH() returns #N/A.

INDEX(): Retrieving the Value from a Cell

You may have already noticed that the MATCH() function really does half the work of the VLOOKUP() and HLOOKUP() functions. It can find the position of the search term, but it gives you the position as an *index number*, instead of returning the actual contents of the cell. (Index 1 is the first item in a range, 2 is the second, and so on.) The MATCH() function becomes useful only when you combine it with another function, like INDEX().

INDEX() is powerful not only because it can retrieve the cell content, but also because it lets you move to any row or column. The next section shows you how useful this feature is. But first, here's a quick look at how INDEX() works.

INDEX() gives you a value from a range of cells, using the index number you specify:

```
INDEX(range, row_number, [column_number]
```

Consider the following formula:

```
=INDEX(A2:A10, 3)
```

It returns the content of the third cell in the range, A4. If you supply a two-dimensional range, you need to give a row and column index. Here's an example:

```
=INDEX(A2:B10, 3, 2)
```

This formula gives you the contents of the cell in the third row of the second column, which is cell B4.

NOTE Remember that the index numbers that MATCH() and INDEX() use are offsets, not actual cell references. In other words, if you specify a range that starts with cell E10, Excel designates E10 as index number 1, E11 as index number 2, and so on. The actual row number in the worksheet doesn't matter.

Performing a "Left Lookup"

On their own, MATCH() and INDEX() are just curiosities. But when you combine them, you have the ability to overcome many of the limitations inherent in VLOOKUP() and HLOOKUP().

Consider the worksheet in Figure 12-5. Here, Excel performs the lookup using column B (the product name), and the formula retrieves information from column A (the product ID). This is an example of a *left lookup*, something the VLOOKUP() function can't handle.

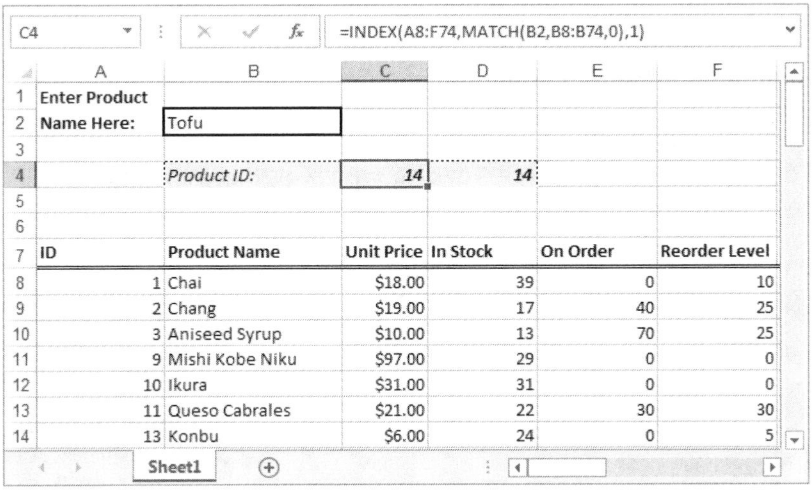

FIGURE 12-5

This worksheet lets you search for a product by name, and then retrieve its corresponding ID. Because the ID info is to the left of the lookup column, VLOOKUP() can't help you. The solution is to combine MATCH() and INDEX(), so that MATCH() gives you the offset row number from the Product Name column. INDEX() then uses that value in the ID column, and Excel displays the final result—the product ID—in cell C4, which contains the formula that's doing all the work. In essence, this formula breaks the problem down into two questions: "How far down is this product name?" and "What product ID is just as far down?" MATCH() answers the first question, while INDEX() answers the second.

To solve this problem, you first use MATCH() to find the position of the product name you're looking for:

```
=MATCH(B2, B8:B74, 0)
```

This formula gives you a value of 8 because the searched-for value (*Tofu*) is located in the eighth row of the cell range you're searching. Next, you can use the value the MATCH() function returned to retrieve the cell content by employing the INDEX() function. The trick is that the INDEX() function uses a *range* that covers all the rows and columns in the table of data:

```
=INDEX(A8:F74, match_result, 1)
```

Here's how you'd combine these functions into a single formula:

```
=INDEX(A8:F74, MATCH(B2,B8:B74,0), 1)
```

TIP Remember, the INDEX() function lets you perform a lookup in a column or a row.

Performing a Double Lookup

Another shortcoming of the VLOOKUP() and HLOOKUP() functions is that you can't use them simultaneously, so they don't help if you want to write a formula that finds a cell at the intersection of a specific column and row heading. Imagine you want to write a formula to find the number of sales recorded in January 2013 at the London location, using the spreadsheet in Figure 12-6. You solve this problem with the INDEX() function, which is much more flexible than either the VLOOKUP() or the HLOOKUP() function.

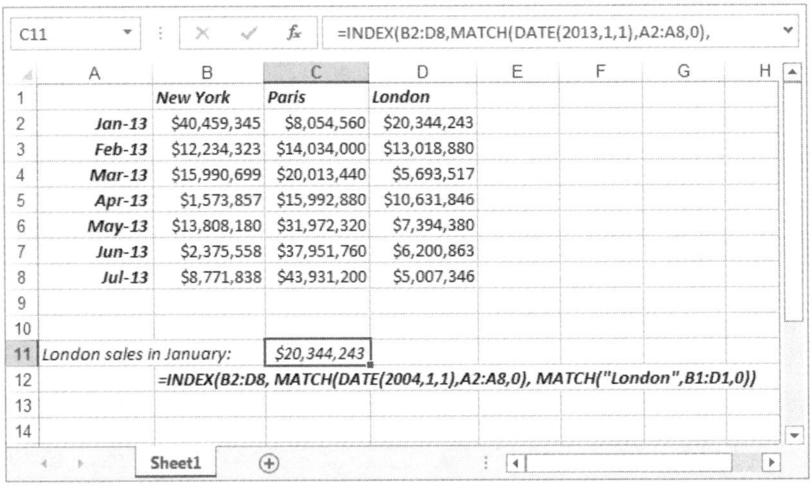

C11
=INDEX(B2:D8,MATCH(DATE(2013,1,1),A2:A8,0),
New York
Paris
London
Jan-13 $40,459,345 $8,054,560 $20,344,243
Feb-13 $12,234,323 $14,034,000 $13,018,880
Mar-13 $15,990,699 $20,013,440 $5,693,517
Apr-13 $1,573,857 $15,992,880 $10,631,846
May-13 $13,808,180 $31,972,320 $7,394,380
Jun-13 $2,375,558 $37,951,760 $6,200,863
Jul-13 $8,771,838 $43,931,200 $5,007,346
London sales in January:
$20,344,243
=INDEX(B2:D8, MATCH(DATE(2004,1,1),A2:A8,0), MATCH("London",B1:D1,0))
Sheet1

FIGURE 12-6

The formula in cell C11 performs a double lookup by using MATCH() twice to get the offsets, and INDEX() once to retrieve the value from the cell. This formula works because the INDEX() function accepts both a row and a column offset.

NOTE With just a tad more work, you can write a formula that lets your spreadsheet readers specify the month and city whose sales figures they want to see. The next section covers these steps.

Because you need to look up the rows *and* columns, you need to use the MATCH() function twice.

First, you use MATCH() to find the row that has the January sales figures:

```
=MATCH(DATE(2013,1,1), A2:A8, 0)
```

NOTE Remember that the DATE() function, as explained on page 332, creates a date without your needing to know its underlying serial number.

Next, you use MATCH() once more to find the column that has the sales figures for the London office:

```
=MATCH("London", B1:D1, 0)
```

With these two pieces of information, you can build an INDEX() function that searches the whole range of cells for the appropriate sales figure:

```
=INDEX(B2:D8, MATCH(DATE(2013,1,1),A2:A8,0), MATCH("London",B1:D1,0))
```

In this example, the search values (the date and store location) are hard-coded in the formula, but you can just as easily retrieve this information from other cells in your worksheet. This allows someone using your spreadsheet to plug in the date and location they want.

OFFSET(): Shifting Cell References

Not surprisingly, Excel gives you another way to solve lookup problems. The OFFSET() function lets you take a cell reference and redirect it to a new location. For example, if you take the cell reference A1, and use OFFSET() to move down two rows, your formula would refer to cell A3.

For the most part, everything you can accomplish with the OFFSET() function you can achieve by combining INDEX() and MATCH(). It's really a matter of preference. Some Excel gurus prefer to use INDEX() and MATCH(), while others find that OFFSET() makes for clearer formulas. Once you finished this section, you'll be able to make your own choice.

The OFFSET() function requires three arguments: the cell reference you want to change, and the number of rows and columns you want to shift that reference by:

```
OFFSET(reference, rows_to_offset, cols_to_offset, [height], [width])
```

The following formula shifts the cell reference from A1 to A3, and then returns whatever content is in cell A3:

```
=OFFSET(A1, 2, 0)
```

To change a cell reference to a row above the original reference or to a column to the left of it, specify a negative number for the *rows_to_offset* or *cols_to_offset* parameter, respectively. You can also use the height and width parameters to change a reference to a *single* cell to a reference to a *range* of cells. Here's one example:

```
=SUM(OFFSET(D2, 0, 0, 7, 1))
```

This formula uses OFFSET() to change the reference from cell D2 to the range of seven cells in D2:D8. The original cell becomes the "anchor point" for a corner of the range. Excel then passes that range to the SUM() function. The end result is equivalent to this formula:

```
=SUM(D2:D8)
```

Now that you understand OFFSET(), you can use it in place of the INDEX() function in most situations. You just need to start at the top-left corner of your table, and use the OFFSET() function to get to the cell you want.

Consider this formula from Figure 12-5, which performs a left lookup on the list of products there:

```
=INDEX(A8:F74, MATCH(B2,B8:B74,0), 1)
```

You can easily rewrite this calculation using the OFFSET() function, as shown here. Cell A8, at the top-left corner of the table, is the starting point:

```
=OFFSET(A8, MATCH(B2,B8:B74,0)-1, 0)
```

Like the formulas you saw in the INDEX() section (page 354), this formula still lets you search through the entire table of data to find the Product Name (using the Product ID value you typed in). In fact, there's really no meaningful difference between the two functions. In most cases, you can use OFFSET() and INDEX() interchangeably. One exception is converting a single-cell reference to a cell range reference; only the OFFSET() function can help you there.

FORMULATEXT(): Getting the Text of a Formula

By now you're well acquainted with how formulas work. You type them into a cell, and the cell shows the formula's *result*. But what if you want to display the actual formula in your worksheet—say, to show the person who's reading your spreadsheet how you got to that result? You could copy the formula and paste it as a bit of text in another cell, so long as you put an apostrophe (') in front of it, which tells Excel to treat the copied formula as plain ol' text. But this approach is a bit clumsy, because it's all too easy for someone to edit the original formula but forget to update the text in the copied formula.

For a situation like that, Excel offers the FORMULATEXT() function. It grabs a formula in any cell and displays it as ordinary text, in your worksheet. For example, imagine cell B12 contains this formula:

```
=1+6
```

Now, add this formula to cell A1:

```
=FORMULATEXT(B12)
```

In cell A1, you'll see the text *=1+6* rather than the result of the formula, 7 (which appears in cell B12).

The FORMULATEXT() function provides a handy way to show the content of a specific formula in your worksheet, but remember that Excel has its own tools for displaying and printing formulas (page 240). These tools make more sense if you want to reveal *all* the calculations in your worksheet.

Finally, before you use FORMULATEXT(), make sure you don't need to support older versions of Excel, because FORMULATEXT() is a new addition to Excel 2013.

Other Reference and Lookup Functions

MATCH(), INDEX(), and OFFSET() are definitely Excel's three most useful reference and lookup functions. But the program provides several similar functions that occasionally come in handy. Table 12-1 gives you a quick tour. Warning: Some of these are very specialized, and a few of them are downright strange.

TABLE 12-1 *Miscellaneous reference and lookup functions*

FUNCTION	SYNTAX	DESCRIPTION
AREAS()	AREAS(reference)	Returns the number of areas in a reference. An area is a single cell or a range of contiguous cells. If you have more than one area, you have to wrap all the areas with double parentheses. For example, *=AREAS(A1)* returns a value of 1; *=AREAS((A1, B3:D5, E8))* returns a value of 3.
COLUMN()	COLUMN(reference)	Returns the column number for a reference. *=COLUMN(B3)* returns the number 2, which represents column B. If you leave out the reference, you get the column number of the current cell (the cell that holds your formula).
COLUMNS()	COLUMNS(range)	Counts the number of columns in a range.
ROW()	ROW(reference)	Returns the row number for a reference. *=ROW(B3)* returns the number 3. If you leave out the reference, you get the row number of the current cell (the cell that holds your formula).

FUNCTION	SYNTAX	DESCRIPTION
ROWS()	ROWS(range)	Counts the number of rows in a range.
CHOOSE()	CHOOSE (index_num, value1, value2,...)	Returns a value from a list depending on the index number. For example, *=CHOOSE(1, A1, A2, B1)* returns the content in cell A1 because that's the first position in the list of values that follows.
LOOKUP()	LOOKUP(search_for, lookup_range, result_range)	LOOKUP() is a slimmed-down version of HLOOKUP() and VLOOKUP(). It searches for a value in one range, and returns the value in the same index position in the second range. Unfortunately, you have no way to enforce strict matching, which reduces the usefulness of this function.
SHEET()*	SHEET(sheet_name)	Looks for the worksheet with the name you specify, and returns its sheet number (1 for the first worksheet, 2 for the second, and so on). For example, using *=SHEET("Sheet1")* in a new workbook returns 1, because the first worksheet is named Sheet1.
SHEETS()*	SHEETS(reference)	Use it with no argument to find the total number of worksheets in the current workbook. Or use it with a range, and the function tells you the number of worksheets in that range (usually, that's 1).

** This function is new to Excel 2013. Don't use it if you want to share your spreadsheet with people using older versions of the program.*

INDIRECT() and ADDRESS(): Working with Cell References Stored As Text

INDIRECT() and ADDRESS() are two of Excel's strangest reference functions. They let you work with cell references stored as text.

The INDIRECT() function retrieves the content from any cell you specify. The twist is that you specify the cell using literal text (a string) to describe the location of the cell. So, where normally you'd add two cells this way:

```
=A1+A2
```

If you were to use INDIRECT() to refer to cell A1, you'd write the formula this way:

```
=INDIRECT("A1")+A2
```

Note the quotation marks around the cell name; they indicate that A1 is just a piece of text, not a cell reference. The INDIRECT() function examines this text and gives you the corresponding cell reference.

The obvious question is why would anyone bother to specify cell references as ordinary text? The most common reason is that you want to create an extremely flexible formula. So, for example, instead of hard coding your cell references (as in *=A1+A2*), you may want your formula to read *another* cell to find out which cell reference it should use. The end result is that the person reading the spreadsheet can change a cell reference used in a calculation, without needing to edit a complex formula. For example, the spreadsheet in Figure 12-7 lets the spreadsheet reader choose which numbers to add, without forcing him to write a SUM() function by hand.

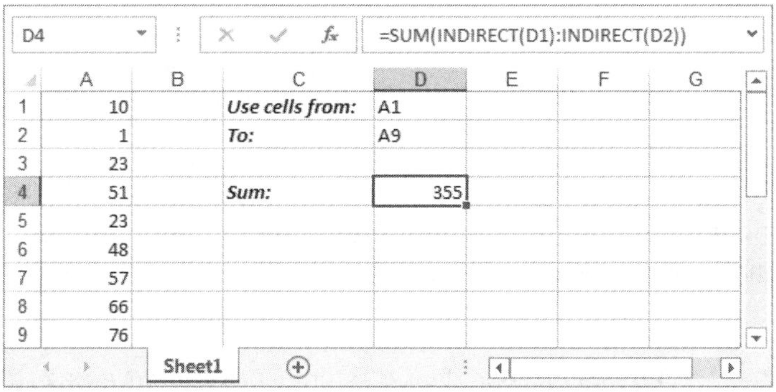

FIGURE 12-7

This worksheet shows the quirky INDIRECT() function at work. Here, a dynamic SUM() formula (in cell D4) adds a range of cells. It uses the INDIRECT() function to read the cell references stored in D1 and D2. It then uses these references to create the range of cells that the formula adds together.

Here's an example of this technique:

```
=INDIRECT(A1)+INDIRECT(A2)
```

This formula does *not* add the content of cells A1 and A2. Instead, it looks in cells A1 and A2 to determine which two cells it *should* add together. If A1 contains the text "B2" and A2 contains the text "D8," the formula becomes:

```
=INDIRECT("B2")+INDIRECT("D8")
```

which is the same as:

```
=B2+D8
```

This formula assumes that there are two cell references, entered as text, in cells A1 and A2. If the cells contain something else, the INDIRECT() function doesn't work. If cell A1 contains a number, for instance, the formula INDIRECT(A1) returns the error code #REF! (which is Excel shorthand for, "I expected a cell reference, but all you gave me was a lousy number"). Figure 12-8 shows what you can—and can't—do with the INDIRECT() function.

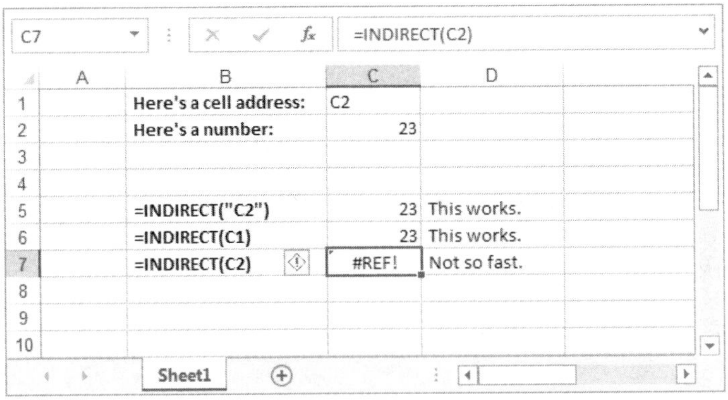

FIGURE 12-8

Cells C5, C6, and C7 show three attempts at using INDIRECT(). The corresponding formulas are shown in cells B5, B6, and B7, for reference.

The formula in C5 uses INDIRECT() with a piece of text ("C2"). The INDIRECT() function understands this, and shows the content from cell C2. The formula in cell C6 use an extra layer of indirection. It grabs the content in C1, which is the piece of text "C2", and then supplies that to the INDIRECT() function. The INDIRECT() function then displays the content from cell C2, as in the previous example. The formula in C7 grabs the content from C2, which isn't a cell reference (it's the number 23). As a result, the INDIRECT() function fails.

The ADDRESS() function performs a similarly strange operation, but in reverse. You supply ADDRESS() with row and column index numbers, and Excel gives you a piece of text that contains the cell reference. The following formula returns $B$1:

```
=ADDRESS(1, 2)
```

Remember, all the ADDRESS() function does is return a cell reference as a string. This piece of text isn't too useful; all you can really do with it is display it in a cell—or, if you're really warped, pass it to the INDIRECT() function to convert it back to a real cell reference.

Consider the example shown in Figure 12-6, which uses a lookup function to find the sales in a particular city on a particular month. The formula looked like this:

```
=INDEX(B2:D8, MATCH(DATE(2013,1,1),A2:A8,0), MATCH("London",B1:D1,0))
```

Instead of displaying the actual sales figures, you could use the ADDRESS() function to display the cell reference for the spreadsheet reader to see, like so:

```
=ADDRESS(MATCH(DATE(2013,1,1),A2:A8,0), MATCH("London",B1:D1,0))
```

This formula displays the text $C$4. If you want to get craftier, you could add some additional text by modifying the formula like this:

```
="The number you are looking for is in cell " &

ADDRESS(MATCH(DATE(2013,1,1),A2:A8,0), MATCH("London",B1:D1,0))
```

This formula displays the text *The number you are looking for is in cell $C$4.* Clearly, you won't use a formula like this often, but it does raise some interesting possibilities.

If you don't want the ADDRESS() function to return a string with an absolute reference (page 251),you can supply a third parameter, called *abs_number*. It takes one of the following values:

- **1** returns an absolute address, as in $B$1
- **2** fixes the row number, as in B$1
- **3** fixes the column, as in $B1
- **4** returns a relative reference, as in B1

TRANSPOSE(): Changing Rows to Columns and Vice Versa

TRANSPOSE() is an interesting function. It lets you change the structure of a table, inverting the data so that all the rows become columns, and all the columns become rows (Figure 12-9). In that respect, it works the same as the Transpose pasting option you can use with Paste Special (page 97). The pasting approach, however, creates a distinct *copy* of the data. The TRANSPOSE() function, on the other hand, creates a linked table that's bound to the original data, which means that if you change the original table, the transposed table also changes. The TRANSPOSE() function is, therefore, ideal for showing more than one representation of the same data.

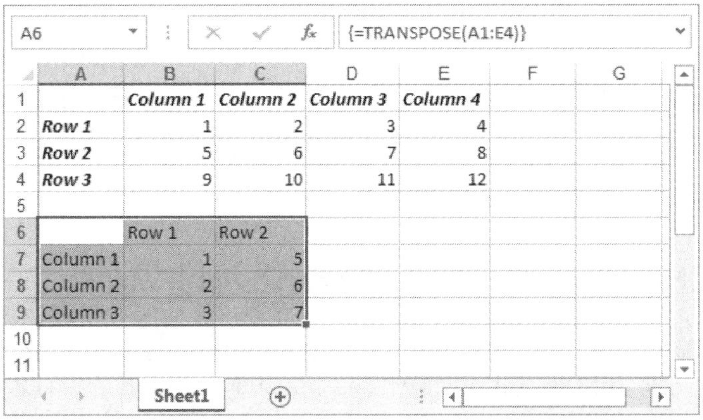

FIGURE 12-9

In this worksheet, the TRANSPOSE() function has inverted most of the data in a table, turning columns into rows and rows into columns.

The best way to get started with TRANSPOSE() is to try a simple example. Follow these steps:

1. **Find a table of cells you want to transpose. Make a note of its size in rows and columns.**

   To determine the size of the transposed table, simply switch the number of rows and columns. That means a table made up of three rows and four columns becomes a table made up of four rows and three columns.

2. **Move to the area where you want to insert the transposed cells, and select the appropriately sized area.**

   To transpose a table with three rows and two columns, you need to select a grid of cells that's two rows high and three columns wide. You need to select all the cells before you begin because you'll be creating an array formula (page 248). (You need an array formula because the TRANSPOSE() function returns a whole table's worth of results.)

3. **Press the equal sign (=) and begin typing the TRANSPOSE() formula.**

   The formula requires one argument, which is the range of cells you want to transpose. Here's an example: *=TRANSPOSE(A1:E4)*. Don't press Enter yet.

4. **Commit the function by pressing Ctrl+Shift+Enter.**

   This step inserts the formula into all the selected cells as an array formula.

TIP Editing array formulas can be a challenge. To remove or replace an array formula, you need to first select *all* the cells that use it. If you have a large array, this can be awkward. One handy-dandy shortcut is to use the Go To command to select the array formula cells. First, move to one of the cells that has the array formula. (You'll know you're in the right place when you see the curly brackets around the formula in the formula bar.) Press Ctrl+G to show the Go To window. Next, click the Special button, choose "Current array," and then click OK. Presto: Excel selects the entire group of cells that uses this array formula.

The HYPERLINK() Function: Creating a Dynamic Link

The lookup and reference category holds an odd collection of functions. In theory, all the functions are unified by a common theme: They extract values or information from another cell. But every once in a while, a function turns up in the lookup and reference category because it isn't accepted anywhere else. The HYPERLINK() function is one such example.

HYPERLINK() has no real similarity to the other information and reference functions. It has a single purpose in life: to create an underlined hyperlink that someone can click. When clicked, this link can open another workbook, jump to somewhere else in the current workbook, or open a website URL in a browser window.

To use the HYPERLINK() function, you supply two arguments: the target (like a web page, the path to a file, or a cell reference) and the text you want to appear in the cell. Here's what the function looks like:

```
HYPERLINK(link_location, [cell_text])
```

Both the link_location and the cell_text arguments are text-based, so you need to use double quotes. Here's a formula that creates a hyperlink to a web page:

```
=HYPERLINK("http://www.prosetech.com", "Click to see company site")
```

The links that the HYPERLINK() function creates behave the same way as the links you can create with Excel's Insert→Hyperlink command (page 80). This fact raises a reasonable question—why would you use a function to accomplish what you can polish off just as easily using Excel's ribbon? In most cases, HYPERLINK() doesn't add any benefit. However, it *does* make sense when you need to create *dynamic* links whose contents vary depending on what's in other cells.

Consider this formula:

```
=HYPERLINK(A20, "Click to see company site")
```

When you click this cell, the hyperlink sends you to whatever web address you entered in cell A20. Imagine you repeat this formula in several places. All you need to do is change one cell—A20—to update all the links.

The HYPERLINK() function also gives you the chance to create some more complex conditional formulas (for more on conditional formulas, see page 376). You may want to send the clicker to a different place depending on the content in other cells. Here's an example:

```
=IF(B2="Acme Company", HYPERLINK("http://www.acme.com", "Click to
see company site"), "")
```

This formula actually generates a quirky—but potentially useful—disappearing link. If cell B2 contains the text "Acme Company", the IF() function calls the HYPERLINK() function and inserts a new link to the company website. But if B2 contains something else, a blank value appears instead of the link. It's not too often that you'll want to combine hyperlinks with these types of special effects, but when you do, the HYPERLINK() function is ready and waiting.

Information Functions

Excel features yet another group of functions closely related to the lookup and reference functions. Called *information functions*, they let you retrieve information about the type of content found in any particular cell you want to examine. You can find the full list of information functions in the Information group (choose Formulas→Function Library→More Functions→Information).

The "IS" Functions: Checking the Value Inside a Cell

The most important information functions are those that start with the word IS. They let you test whether a cell is blank, has numeric content, and so on.

The IS functions are Boolean functions, which means they give you a result of either TRUE or FALSE. On their own, the IS functions aren't too impressive. However, you can combine them with other conditional functions to make simple decisions. (The IF() function tests a condition, and inserts one of two values based on whether the condition's true or false. For a refresher on IF(), see page 239.)

You could use the IF() function in combination with the ISNUMBER() function to avoid performing a calculation if a cell doesn't contain numeric content. Here's the formula you'd use:

```
=IF(ISNUMBER(A1), 10/A1, NA())
```

In this example, if the ISNUMBER() test returns TRUE (that is, if A1 contains a number), Excel uses the first argument. That means the program performs the calculation *10/A1*, and displays the result in the cell. If cell A1 doesn't contain numeric content, the ISNUMBER() function returns FALSE, and Excel uses the second argument. In that case, Excel executes the NA() function, which displays the error code #N/A. Figure 12-10 shows several IS functions at work.

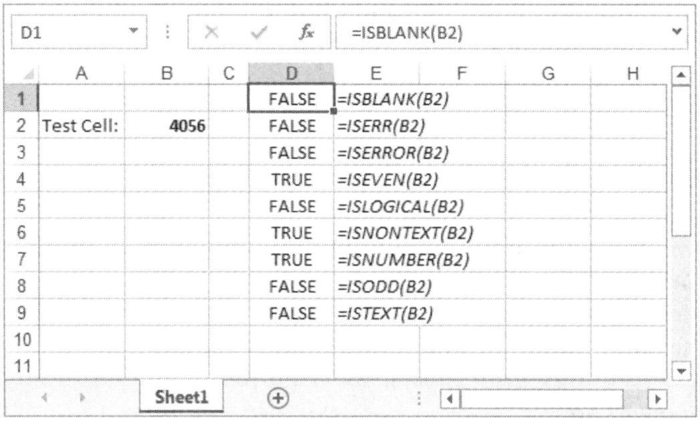

FIGURE 12-10

This worksheet shows the result of a series of tests on a single cell, B2. On their own, these TRUE and FALSE results may not impress you, but they represent building blocks you can use to create powerful conditional formulas.

Here's another example that displays an error message when an error exists in a cell:

```
=IF(ISERROR(D10), "The calculation could not be completed due to an error.",
"")
```

You could insert this formula in cell E10, so it appears right next to the cell that may or may not have an error (cell D10). If there is no error, E10 stays blank. If there is an error, E10 offers a little bit of extra information.

Excel includes a handy shortcut for error-checking: the IFERROR() function. IFERROR() checks the indicated cell for an error. If there's no error, IFERROR() displays the value from that cell. But if the cell contains an error, IFERRROR() displays the alternate value that you supply as an argument. Here's an example that tests cell D10:

```
=IFERROR(D10, "The calculation could not be completed due to an error.")
```

IFERROR() may not save much typing, but it does make for more readable formulas.

Table 12-2 lists the IS functions. Usually, you use the IS functions with a literal value or a cell reference, although you can also use it with a cell range. When you use a range, the value is true only if the condition is satisfied in *all* the cells in the range. That means that *=ISBLANK(A1:A10)* returns TRUE only if all 10 cells in the range are empty.

TABLE 12-2 *The IS functions*

FUNCTION	RETURNS TRUE IF...
ISBLANK()	The cell is empty, meaning it doesn't contain text, numbers, or any other content.
ISERR()	The cell contains an error other than #N/A.
ISERROR()	The cell contains any error, including #N/A.
ISEVEN()	The value is an even number.
ISLOGICAL()	The value is a Boolean (TRUE or FALSE) value.
ISNA()	The cell contains the #N/A error.
ISNONTEXT()	The value isn't text; it could be blank, a number, or a Boolean value.
ISNUMBER()	The value is a number, and not blank.
ISODD()	The value is an odd number.
ISREF()	The value is a cell reference. Thus, ISREF(A1) is true, but ISREF("A1") is not.
ISTEXT()	The value is text, and not blank.
ISFORMULA()	The cell contains a formula (an expression that starts with the equal sign). This function is new to Excel 2013.

TYPE() and ERROR.TYPE(): Finding a Value's Data Type or Error Type

Both the TYPE() and ERROR.TYPE() functions examine a cell and return a number that describes its content. You can use these functions to build conditional formulas (page 239).

The TYPE() function returns a number that represents the type of data in a cell. Possible numbers include:

```
1 (Number)
2 (Text)
4 (Logical Value)
16 (Error)
64 (Range)
```

The ERROR.TYPE() returns a number that represents the type of error in a cell. If the cell doesn't contain an error, the ERROR.TYPE() function returns #N/A. Possible numbers include:

1 (#NULL!)

2 (#DIV/0!)

3 (#VALUE!)

4 (#REF!)

5 (#NAME?)

6 (#NUM!)

7 (#N/A)

To learn how to use these kinds of functions to build conditional logic, see Chapter 13.

INFO() and CELL(): Gathering Info About Your Computer and Your Worksheet's Cells

INFO() and CELL() are two of the strangest information functions out there. While they're useful for stumping coworkers with Excel trivia, they don't solve many practical problems.

The INFO() function provides information related to the computer and operating system that's running Excel. To kick it into gear, you specify a single text argument, which tells Excel what information to retrieve. If you specify "numfile", Excel returns the number of all the worksheets in all the workbook files that are currently open:

```
=INFO("numfile")
```

NOTE *As you can see here, you need to enclose the argument value in quotation marks.*

Table 12-3 lists all the possible arguments you can use with the INFO() function. Possible, of course, doesn't mean any of these make it into heavy rotation.

TABLE 12-3 *Argument values for the INFO() function*

TEXT	GIVES YOU
Directory	The current directory path. This path is usually the last directory you browsed to in the Open or Save windows, which means that it's not necessarily the path where Excel stores the current spreadsheet.
Numfile	The number of all the worksheets in all the workbook files currently open.
Origin	The reference, as text, of the cell in the top-left corner of the currently visible area. The cell reference is prepended with the fixed text $A. This trick is useful for backward compatibility with ancient versions of the Lotus 1-2-3 spreadsheet program.

TEXT	GIVES YOU
Osversion	The version of your computer's operating system.
Recalc	The current recalculation mode, which determines when Excel refreshes formula results. Chapter 13 (page 400) describes the different recalculation modes and how to set them.
Release	The version of Excel you're using.
System	The type of operating system—"pcdos" for a PC, "mac" for a Macintosh.

The CELL() function performs a similar trick, except that it returns information about a cell. It requires two arguments: a string indicating the type of information you want, and a reference pointing to the cell you want to examine. Here's an example that retrieves the number format of the cell A2:

```
=CELL("format", A2)
```

If you omit the cell reference, the CELL() function operates on the cell where the formula exists. The CELL() function is useful primarily for maintaining compatibility with other software. People occasionally use it in add-ins or macros that automate tasks in a worksheet, although most of its features are duplicated by other, more straightforward information and reference functions like ROW(), COLUMN(), INDIRECT(), and ADDRESS(). One interesting piece of information that you can retrieve from CELL(), but not from these other functions, is the file name (including the full file path) of the current spreadsheet:

```
=CELL("filename")
```

For a full list of values you can use with CELL(), refer to the Excel help reference—or just start typing. As soon as you add the CELL() function to a formula and type the opening parenthesis, Excel pops up a list of values you can choose from.

TIP The CELL() and INFO() functions don't refresh automatically. If you need to recalculate these formulas, press F9 to update your worksheet.

Tutorial: Generating Invoices from a Product Catalog

The reference, lookup, and information functions really shine when you want to build worksheets that automatically carry out a series of boredom-inducing tasks. And they let you tie your information together in interesting ways. Maybe you want to determine monthly wages based on billing rates, build a parts list for an order, or create an invoice based on items you ordered from a product catalog. This last task, which is shown in the next example, is sometimes called a *dynamic invoicer.*

It lets sales representatives quickly create an invoice by choosing from a catalog of company products.

The dynamic invoicer employs the following techniques:

- Looking up information from a table using VLOOKUP().
- Referencing data from another worksheet.
- Using absolute references to make it easier to copy formulas.
- Avoiding calculations when data isn't present using IF() and ISBLANK().
- Checking for missing values with IFNA().

First, you build the table filled with your company's products. Figure 12-11 shows you the list for this example.

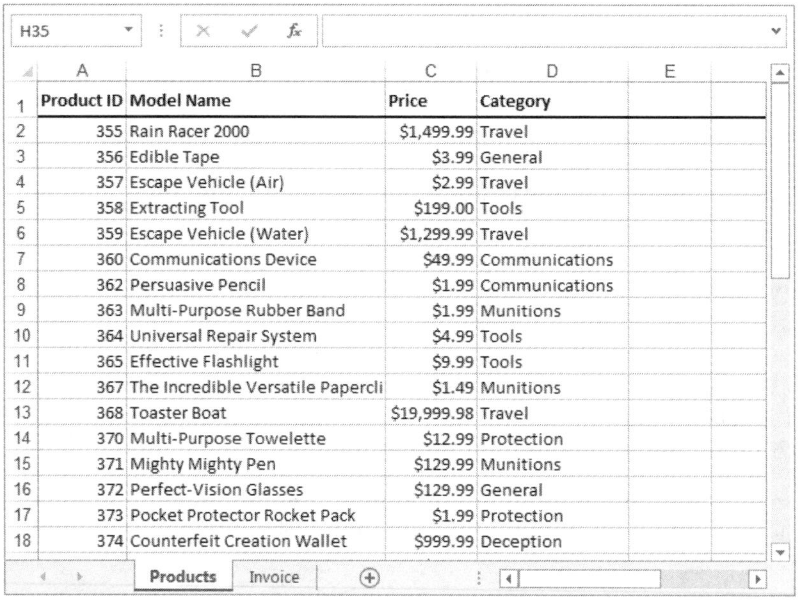

Product ID	Model Name	Price	Category
355	Rain Racer 2000	$1,499.99	Travel
356	Edible Tape	$3.99	General
357	Escape Vehicle (Air)	$2.99	Travel
358	Extracting Tool	$199.00	Tools
359	Escape Vehicle (Water)	$1,299.99	Travel
360	Communications Device	$49.99	Communications
362	Persuasive Pencil	$1.99	Communications
363	Multi-Purpose Rubber Band	$1.99	Munitions
364	Universal Repair System	$4.99	Tools
365	Effective Flashlight	$9.99	Tools
367	The Incredible Versatile Papercli	$1.49	Munitions
368	Toaster Boat	$19,999.98	Travel
370	Multi-Purpose Towelette	$12.99	Protection
371	Mighty Mighty Pen	$129.99	Munitions
372	Perfect-Vision Glasses	$129.99	General
373	Pocket Protector Rocket Pack	$1.99	Protection
374	Counterfeit Creation Wallet	$999.99	Deception

FIGURE 12-11

Here's a product catalog that a sales rep might use to build an invoice. It includes the Product ID (used for the lookup), the Model Name (used to identify the selected products), and the Price (used to calculate the total cost of an order).

Next, you build a worksheet that actually *creates* the invoices. You should probably include space for entering customer information, followed by a large area for the list of items ordered, as shown in Figure 12-12.

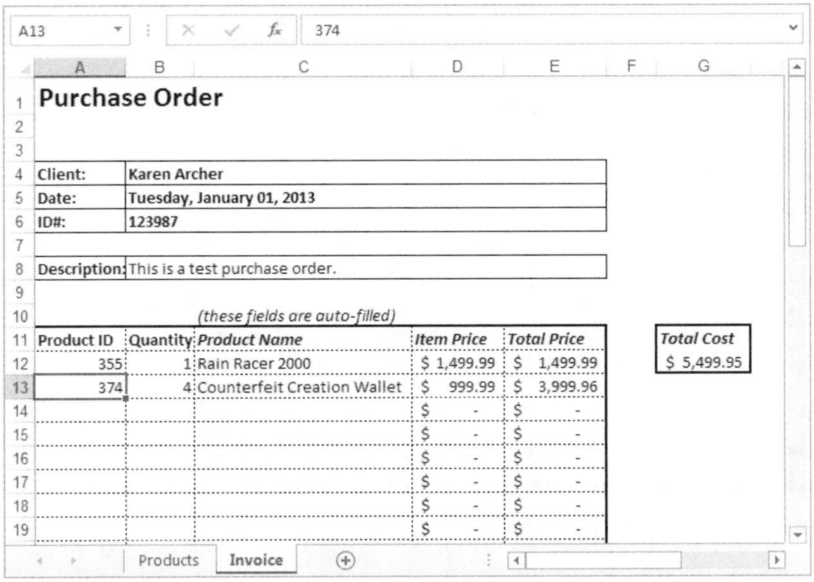

FIGURE 12-12

To add items to this invoice, the sales rep simply types in the product ID and quantity. The lookup functions retrieve the model name and unit price, and then determine the total price.

Here, your best approach is to retrieve an item from the product catalog based on the product ID; this prevents people using the spreadsheet from having to type out full product names. Therefore, you need to write a lookup function to scan the product table for a matching ID. And since the invoice needs to record the product name and its price, you need two lookup functions. Here's the lookup that retrieves the price for the first item in the invoice:

```
=VLOOKUP(A12, Products!$A$2:$D$42, 3, FALSE)
```

The lookup for the model name is the same, but the column offset is 2 instead of 3:

```
=VLOOKUP(A12, Products!$A$2:$D$42, 2, FALSE)
```

The reference to the table of products is preceded by the word *Products* and an exclamation mark. That's because the products table isn't on the invoice worksheet. Instead, it's in a worksheet named Products in the same workbook. (Remember, to perform a calculation with data from another worksheet, you need to preface your cell reference with the name of the worksheet, followed by the exclamation mark. For a refresher on how formulas work across worksheets and workbooks, see page 254.)

You'll also notice that this function uses a mix of absolute and relative references. The reference for the product ID is relative (A12) because each line item in the invoice has its own product ID, which is what the sales rep enters to start filling in the purchase order. The product table is a range made up of two absolute references *($A$2:$D$42)*. This range ensures that, as you copy the formula to subsequent rows on the invoice table, each copy refers to the same product catalog.

Dealing with Blank Values

As written, the VLOOKUP() function still suffers from a problem. If you copy the formula to all the available rows in the invoice, you'll notice that the value #N/A appears in each row where you haven't entered a product ID. This error message appears because VLOOKUP() attempts to look up a product with a product ID of 0, which doesn't exist. The #N/A error message is a significant concern because it prevents you from calculating the total cost of the order with the SUM() function. If the SUM() function attempts to add together a range of cells that includes an #N/A value, it returns the #N/A error code.

To solve this problem, you must use conditional logic to see whether a product ID has been entered. If it hasn't, you can put a blank value in the product name column. If it has, you can use the original VLOOKUP() function to get the product name.

Here's the corrected formula:

```
=IF(ISBLANK(A12), "", VLOOKUP(A12, Products!$A$2:$D$42, 2, FALSE))
```

Similarly, you can use IF() and ISBLANK() to put a 0 in the item price column when there's no product ID:

```
=IF(ISBLANK(A12), 0, VLOOKUP(A12, Products!$A$2:$D$42, 3, FALSE))
```

Excel displays this 0 value as an empty cell with a dash in it, thanks to the Accounting number format.

You can now build an invoice in seconds, just by typing in a few product ID numbers in the leftmost column. The product names appear automatically, and you can calculate the overall total with a simple SUM() function formula:

```
=SUM(E12:E100)
```

Dealing with Incorrect Values

The ISBLANK() function makes sure that empty rows show the right information. But what if the person using the invoice types in a product ID that doesn't correspond to a real product?

Right now the result is the familiar #N/A error, which appears in the Product Name and Item Price columns, indicating two failed lookups. However, Excel errors have a habit of spreading to the formulas that use them. An #N/A in the price column causes the line total for that item to be #N/A, and the SUM() function to fail and also show #N/A.

Of course, this problem disappears the moment the spreadsheet user fixes the problem by typing in a legitimate product ID. However, you can tweak your formulas to make lookup errors cleaner and easier to understand. One good solution is to use the IFNA() function you first met on page 350.

Here's how you use IFNA() in the item price column to tell Excel to substitute a value of 0 if the lookup fails for any reason:

```
=IFNA(VLOOKUP(A12, Products!$A$2:$D$42, 3, FALSE), 0)
```

The product name formula is a bit more complex. Ideally, you should distinguish between bank values (in which case the product name should remain blank) and incorrect product IDs (in which case an error message should appear). To make this happen, you need to stack your conditions, as described on page 377.

The first condition is the check for a blank value. Here's the portion of the formula that does that:

```
...   IF(ISBLANK(A12), "", VLOOKUP(A12, Products!$A$2:$D$42, 2, FALSE)) ...
```

If the cell isn't blank, the second condition checks for an #N/A value. Because it occurs *after* the check for blank values, you need to wrap it around the first function. Here's the complete formula:

```
=IFNA(IF(ISBLANK(A12), "", VLOOKUP(A12, Products!$A$2:$D$42, 2, FALSE)), "[ NO
PRODUCT FOUND ]")
```

To follow this formula through, start with the cell reference (A12). The formula begins by testing to see if it's blank (in which case it shows a blank text string). If it isn't, Excel runs the lookup. The IFNA() function then checks the result of the VLOOKUP() function, and swaps in the text [NO PRODUCT FOUND] if an #N/A error occurs. The result is a formula that neatly handles two possible problems.

NOTE No matter how you write your formulas, the sales rep still needs to know which product ID codes to use when filling out the form (or must look them up on the other worksheet). An even more impressive workbook could automate this process by providing a drop-down list of possible products for the sales rep to pick from. You'll see how to take this step on page 650.

CHAPTER

13

Advanced Formula Writing and Troubleshooting

Over the last five chapters, you've learned how to use Excel's impressive function library to calculate everything from statistical trend lines to payment schedules for home mortgages. Now that you've had a close look at these functions, it's time to consider a few techniques to help you get the most from your formulas.

In this chapter, you'll tackle four new topics that'll make you a formula master:

- How to use conditional logic with functions like SUMIF() and COUNTIF().
- How to make formulas more readable by using named ranges.
- How to control when Excel recalculates your worksheets.
- How to solve mysterious errors by using Excel's formula auditing tools.

Conditions in Formulas

Chapter 8 gave you a first look at using conditional logic in Excel formulas. The basic principles are easy: You construct a condition using the logical operators <, >, =, and <>, and then use that condition with a *conditional function*. So far, you've focused on one conditional function—IF()—which performs different actions depending on the result of a calculation.

Here's an example that uses the IF() function. The following formula carries out the operation in either the second or third argument, depending on the value of cell A20:

```
=IF(A20>10000, A20*5%, A20*3%)
```

Translation: For values greater than 10,000, Excel executes the formula *A20*5%*; otherwise, it carries out the second formula. If A20 contains the dollar amount of a sales invoice, you can use this formula to determine the commission for a sales person. If the sale exceeds the magic $10,000 amount, a larger 5-percent commission kicks in.

Incidentally, the following formula is equivalent, but it shows how you can embed IF() inside a formula, alongside other operations:

```
=A20*IF(A20>10000, 5%, 3%)
```

It's up to you to pick the approach that seems clearest.

IF(): Building Conditional Formulas

IF() is one of the most useful conditional functions, but it's not the only one. In fact, you'll find several more logical functions in the Formulas→Function Library→Logical category. They include the IFERROR() function you tackled on page 366, and the following:

- **TRUE() and FALSE().** These functions don't take any arguments. The TRUE() function simply returns the logical value *true*, and the FALSE() function returns *false*. You can use these functions to enter logical values directly into a cell or formula, but you won't need them often.
- **AND().** This function accepts two (or more) conditions, and then returns *true* if all of them are true. If any condition's false, the AND() function returns *false*.
- **OR().** This function accepts two (or more) conditions, and then returns *true* if any one of them is true. The OR() function returns *false* only if all conditions are false.
- **NOT().** This function accepts a condition and reverses it. Consider the formula *=NOT(ISBLANK(A10))*. Assuming A10 is empty, the ISBLANK() function used by itself returns *true*; by contrast, adding in the NOT() formula returns the reverse—*false*. You rarely need the NOT() function, but sometimes it helps make your logic a little clearer.
- **XOR().** If you use this function with two conditions, it returns *true* if one of them is true, but *false* if both of them are true or both of them are false. If you use this function with more conditions, it acts a bit more strangely, returning *true* if you supply an odd number of true conditions, or *false* if there's an even number of true conditions. A word of caution: XOR() was introduced in Excel 2013, so don't use it if you need to use your spreadsheet on older versions of Excel.

On their own, these logical functions don't do much. But you can combine them in some interesting ways with the IF() function. Imagine you want to make sure that the 5-percent rate (from the sales commission example) kicks in only if the sale exceeds $10,000 *and* the sale takes place after the year 2012, when the new commission rules came into effect. You can rewrite the earlier formula to take this into account using the AND() function. If the invoice date's in cell B4, here's what the formula would look like:

```
=IF(AND(A20>10000,YEAR(B4)>2012), A20*5%, A20*3%)
```

Similarly, you may encounter a situation where you want to alter your logic so that the higher commission kicks in if at least one of two criteria is met. In this case, you'd use the OR() function.

TIP The information functions described in Chapter 12 are also quite useful in conditional statements. The "IS" functions, like ISERROR() and ISBLANK(), especially lend themselves to these statements.

You can also choose between more than two options by *nesting* multiple IF() statements in a single formula. (Nesting is a technique that lets you put one function inside another.) The following formula uses a commission of 2 percent if the sale is under $500, a commission of 5 percent if the total is above $10,000, and a 3 percent commission for all other cases.

```
=IF(A20<500, A20*2%, IF(A20>10000, A20*5%, A20*3%))
```

The formula begins by checking the first condition (whether A20 is less than $500). If the condition is met, Excel carries out the first expression, *A20*2%*. If A20 is *not* less than $500, Excel moves on to the second expression, which is actually another IF() function. It then checks the second condition and chooses between the two remaining commission levels.

Excel allows up to a staggering 64 nested IF() statements in one formula. (This limitation actually applies to all Excel functions. You can't nest functions more than 64 levels deep.) However, it's unlikely that anyone could actually understand a formula with 64 IF() statements. Nesting IF() statements may get the job done, but it can lead to some extremely complicated formulas, so tread carefully.

NOTE In some situations, nesting multiple IF() statements may cause the formula to become too complex and error-prone. In such cases, you may want to consider simplifying your logic by breaking the formula into several linked formulas, or building a custom function using full-fledged VBA (Visual Basic for Applications) code. You'll see an example of that in Chapter 30.

Along with the functions in the Logical category, Excel includes a few more functions that use conditions. They include the COUNTIF() and SUMIF() functions, as described in the next two sections.

COUNTIF(): Counting Only the Cells You Specify

To understand the purpose of COUNTIF() and SUMIF(), you need to remember that the COUNT() and SUM() functions devour everything in their path. But what if you want to pick out *specific* cells in a range and count or sum only those cells? You might try to use COUNT() or SUM() in conjunction with an IF() statement, but that doesn't solve the problem. Consider the following formula:

```
=IF(ISBLANK(A1), 0, COUNT(A1:A10))
```

This formula checks to see if cell A1 is blank. If it is, the formula returns 0. If it isn't, the formula returns the count of all the numeric values from A1 to A10. As you can see, the actual counting operation is an all-or-nothing affair. Excel either counts all the cells or ignores them all. There's no way to count just some of the cells (or, similarly, add just some of the cells). The COUNTIF() and SUMIF() functions address this issue by letting you specify a condition for *each cell*.

The COUNTIF() function is the more straightforward of the two. It takes two parameters: the range of cells you want to count, and the criteria that a cell needs to satisfy in order to be counted:

```
COUNTIF(range, criteria)
```

The criteria argument is the key to unlocking the real power of COUNTIF(). The formula tests every cell in your range to see if it meets your criteria, and counts it *only* if it does. With the criteria, you can:

- Test if a cell matches a specific value.
- Test if a cell is greater or less than a specific number.
- Test if a cell matches, or is greater or less than, a number in another cell.
- Test if a cell contains text that matches a simple pattern.

Consider the list of products in Figure 13-1, which stretches from rows 2 to 42. Counting the number of products is easy—you just use the plain-vanilla count function:

```
=COUNT(A2:A42)
```

This formula returns *41*, which is the total number of nonblank cells in the range. Now, what if you want to count the number of products with a price over $500? This challenge calls for the COUNTIF() function. Here's the formula:

```
=COUNTIF(C2:C42, ">500")
```

Note that, in this case, the formula counts the cells in column C. That's because column C contains the price information for each product, which you need in order to evaluate the condition. (When using the COUNTIF() function, the condition in the second argument's always a string, which means you need to make sure to place it inside quotation marks.)

FIGURE 13-1

This worksheet shows a list of products. The COUNT() function makes it easy to count the products, but COUNTIF() gives you the ability to count only those products that reach a set price threshold or appear in a certain category.

To understand how the criteria argument works, you need to realize that it's *not* a logical condition like the ones used with the IF() statement. Instead, it's a snippet of text that contains *part* of a condition. When COUNTIF() springs into action, it creates a full condition for each cell in its assigned range. In the formula shown earlier, the criteria is *>500*. Each time the COUNTIF() function tests a cell, it uses this criteria to generate a full-fledged condition on the fly. The first cell in the range is C2, so the condition becomes *C2>500*. If the condition is true (and for C2 in Figure 13-1, it is), COUNTIF() counts the cell.

Using this logic, you can easily construct other conditional counting formulas. Here's how you'd count all the products in the Travel category (column D) by examining the cells in the Category column:

```
=COUNTIF(D2:D42, "=Travel")
```

TIP If your condition uses the equal sign, you can omit it. For example, COUNTIF() assumes that the condition *"Travel"* is equivalent to *"=Travel"*.

You can even draw the information you want to use in your condition from another cell. In this case, you simply need to use the text concatenation operator (&) to join the cell value with the conditional operator you want to use. (See page 319 for an explanation of how concatenation works.) If the reader of your spreadsheet enters the category name in cell G1, you could count matching products using the following formula:

```
=COUNTIF(D2:D42, "=" & G1)
```

This formula joins the equal sign to whatever text is in cell G1. Thus, if G1 has the text Tools, the criteria becomes *"=Tools"*.

You can use a similar technique to include a function in the criteria argument. Here's a formula that counts the number of products that are above the average price:

```
=COUNTIF(C2:C42, ">" & AVERAGE(C2:C42))
```

UP TO SPEED

How Excel Compares Different Types of Data

The type of data in a cell—ordinary numbers, text, or dates—influences how Excel compares it in a condition. If you use the greater than (>) and less than (<) symbols with numbers, Excel performs the expected numeric comparison. However, if you use these symbols with text, Excel performs a letter-by-letter alphabetic comparison, which means Excel considers the word *apple* less than *banana* because the first letter, a, comes before b in the alphabet. Comparisons are always case-insensitive, so *tRaVeL* matches *Travel*.

Date and time comparisons work the same as numeric comparisons, although it helps to remember that Excel stores dates as a number of days (see page 54 for an explanation) and times as a fractional number between 0 and 1. In other words, Excel deems that dates or times in the past are smaller than more recent dates in a comparison.

Finally, Excel lets you use the asterisk (*) wildcard when you make text comparisons. The asterisk stands for any sequence of characters. Thus, the criteria *"=T*"* matches any cell that contains text that starts with the letter T. Here's how you'd use it with the COUNTIF() function:

```
=COUNTIF(D2:D42,"=T*")
```

This formula matches any category that starts with the letter T, which includes Travel and Tools.

SUMIF(): Adding Only the Cells You Specify

The SUMIF() function follows the same principle as COUNTIF(). The only difference is that it accepts an optional third argument:

```
SUMIF(test_range, criteria, [sum_range])
```

The first argument is the range of cells you want the criteria to test, the second is the criteria itself, and the third is the range of cells you want to sum. So if the first cell in the *test_range* passes the test (that is, causes the criteria to evaluate as *true*), the function adds whatever the first cell is in the *sum_range* to the total sum. Both the *test_ range* and *sum_range* must have the same number of cells—usually they'll be different columns in the same table.

Imagine you want to calculate the sum of all the products in the Travel category, as shown in Figure 13-1. In this case, you'd want to *test* the cells from the Category column (D2:D42) to see whether they contain the word Travel; these cells constitute your test range. But then you'd want to *add* the cells from the Price column (C2:C42), and those cells would be your sum range. Here's the formula:

```
=SUMIF(D2:D42, "=Travel", C2:C42)
```

The two ranges (D2:D42 and C2:C42 in this example) need to have the same number of cells. For each cell Excel tests in D2:D42, there's a corresponding cell Excel may or may not add from C2:C42. For example, if cell D2 meets the condition, Excel adds cell C2 to the running total. If cell D3 meets the condition, Excel adds C3 to the total, and so on.

If you omit the *sum_range* argument, the SUMIF() function tests *and* sums the range in the *test_ range argument.* You could use this approach to calculate the total value of all products with a price above $500:

```
=SUMIF(C2:C42, ">500")
```

Along with COUNTIF() and SUMIF(), Excel has one more "IF" formula: AVERAGEIF(), which calculates the average of cells that fit the set criteria. Figure 13-2 shows an example.

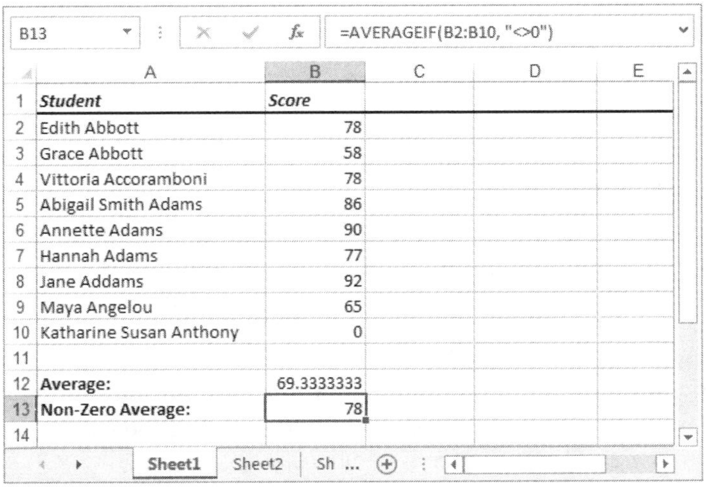

FIGURE 13-2

Here are two approaches to calculating an average. The formula in B13 ignores all scores of 0, which represent students who didn't take the test. The result of 78 percent (returned by the AVERAGEIF() function) is clearly quite a bit higher than the value of 69 percent and change (returned by the AVERAGE() function), but it's a more realistic representation of student performance.

COUNTIFS() and SUMIFS(): Counting and Summing Using Multiple Criteria

The COUNTIF(), SUMIF(), and AVERAGEIF() functions all suffer from one limitation: They can evaluate cells using only one criterion. Fortunately, Excel has a set of matching functions that don't have this restriction. They have the same names as the functions you already learned about, with an *S* added at the end:

- **SUMIFS()** is the same as SUMIF(), except that it accepts multiple conditions.
- **COUNTIFS()** is the same as COUNTIF(), except that it accepts multiple conditions.
- **AVERAGEIFS()** is the same as AVERAGEIF(), except that it accepts multiple conditions.

If you're truly demanding, you'll be happy to know that all three functions accept more than 100 separate conditions.

Earlier in this chapter, you saw how you could use COUNTIF() to either count the number of products over $500 or to count the number of travel products in the list. But what if you want to use *both* conditions at once—in other words, you want to zero in on just those travel products that pass the $500 threshold? In this situation, you need COUNTIFS() to evaluate your two conditions. The following explanation builds the formula you need one piece at a time. (See Figure 13-1 if you need help visualizing the spreadsheet this formula uses.)

The first argument for COUNTIFS() identifies the range you want to use to evaluate your first condition. In this example, this first condition tests whether a product is in the Travel category. To test this condition, you need to grab the entire Category column, like so:

```
=COUNTIFS(D2:D42, ...)
```

Now, you need to fill in the condition against which Excel tests each value. In this case, you need a condition that determines whether the value matches the text "Travel":

```
=COUNTIFS(D2:D42, "=Travel", ...)
```

The fun doesn't stop there. You can use the same technique to fill in the second condition, which looks for prices that exceed $500. Once again, you fill in the range you want to use (this time it's the Price column) and the condition:

```
=COUNTIFS(D2:D42, "=Travel", C2:C42, ">500")
```

This COUNTIFS() function counts only products that meet both conditions. However, you can continue this process by tacking on more and more range and condition arguments to make ridiculously stringent conditions.

NOTE When you use the COUNTIFS() function, all your ranges need to have the same number of cells. If you break this rule, Excel becomes terribly confused and shows you the *#VALUE!* error. After all, the idea is that you're looking at different parts of the same list, and it wouldn't make sense for one column to be longer than another one in the same table.

The SUMIFS() function works similarly, but differs in that the range you want to sum may not match the ranges you want to use to evaluate your conditions. To clear up any confusion, you add an extra argument right at the beginning of the formula, which identifies the cells you want to add up.

The following formula calculates the total of all products between $500 and $1,000—a feat that's impossible with SUMIF().

```
=SUMIFS(C2:C42, C2:C42, ">500", C2:C42, "<1000")
```

Here's how it breaks down. The first range (C2:C42) identifies the cells you want to sum up. The next two arguments check a condition (which cells in C2:C42 are above 500?). And the last two arguments check a *second* condition (which cells in C2:C42 are below 1000?). Only if both conditions are met is the corresponding value added to the sum.

Notice that, in this example, the ranges you use to sum and test the two conditions are the same.

The COUNTIFS() and SUMIFS() functions offer a nifty way to create reports. See the two tables in Figure 13-3 for an example. The first table (rows 1 through 8) has the source data, which is a list of dates that various contractors worked, and the total number of hours they logged. The second table (rows 12 through 14) uses the SUMIFS() function to figure out how many hours each programmer spent either programming or testing.

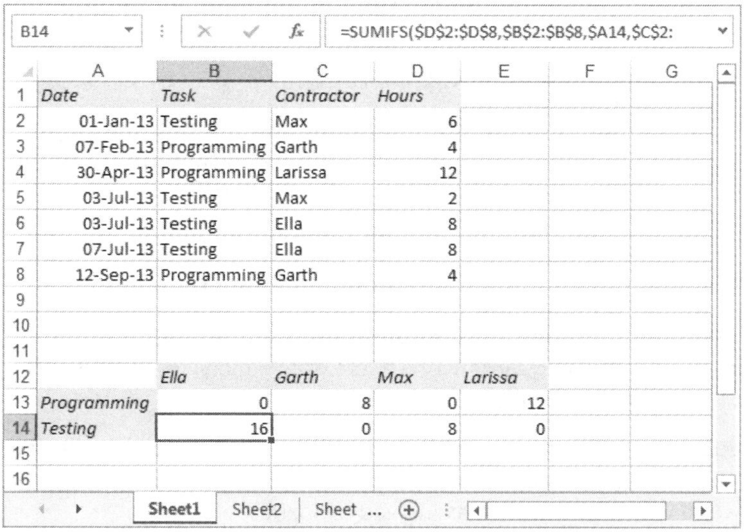
B14 =SUMIFS($D$2:$D$8,$B$2:$B$8,$A14,$C$2:

	A	B	C	D	E	F	G
1	Date	Task	Contractor	Hours			
2	01-Jan-13	Testing	Max	6			
3	07-Feb-13	Programming	Garth	4			
4	30-Apr-13	Programming	Larissa	12			
5	03-Jul-13	Testing	Max	2			
6	03-Jul-13	Testing	Ella	8			
7	07-Jul-13	Testing	Ella	8			
8	12-Sep-13	Programming	Garth	4			
9							
10							
11							
12		Ella	Garth	Max	Larissa		
13	Programming	0	8	0	12		
14	Testing	16	0	8	0		
15							
16							

Sheet1 Sheet2 Sheet ...

FIGURE 13-3

SUMIFS() can be a godsend when boiling down large amounts of information. In the highlighted cell shown here, the formula returns the total number of hours Ella spent testing (16) based on rows that matched two conditions.

Cell B14 answers the question: How many hours did Ella spend testing? The following SUMIFS() formula solves this question using two conditions. First, it scans column C to identify all the rows that have Ella's name in them. Then it scans column B to determine what type of work Ella did. Here's the final formula:

```
=SUMIFS(D2:D8, B2:B8, A14, C2:C8, B12)
```

Note that there are two conditions at work on two different ranges. The first condition determines if the values in cells B2:B8 match the value in cell A14, which identifies the task type (in this case, "Testing"). The second condition checks cells C2:C8 to see if any of them match the value in B12, which has Ella's name.

Descriptive Names for Cell References

One of the obvious problems with Excel formulas is that they don't make for the easiest reading in the world. Consider this formula:

```
=(A1+A2)*B1
```

It's immediately obvious that this formula adds two numbers (those in cells A1 and A2), and then multiplies the result by a third number (in cell B1). However, the formula doesn't tell you anything about the *purpose* of the calculation. There's no way to know whether it's converting currencies, calculating a discount, or measuring the square footage of your llama day-care center. To answer these questions, you need to look at the worksheet and track down the cells this formula references.

On the other hand, consider the next formula, which uses descriptive names in place of cryptic cell references. Although it performs the same calculation, it gives you much more information about what it's trying to do—calculate the retail price of a product:

```
=(ProductCost + ShippingCost) * MarkupPercentage
```

Excel lets you build formulas using such descriptive names, or *named ranges*. All you have to do is define the ranges as you create your worksheet; then you can use those names instead of cell references.

Named ranges provide other benefits besides conveying the meaning of a formula:

- They make complex, nested formulas more understandable.
- They make it easy to quickly find a cell or select a group of cells. That makes them ideal for navigating large worksheets or for applying formatting to cell ranges that frequently change.
- They reduce the likelihood of some types of errors. For example, you're unlikely to notice whether you used A42 instead of A41, but you can spot the wrong name when you use TotalWithTax instead of TaxRate.
- They use absolute references. That way, you don't need to worry about having a formula change when you copy a formula from one cell to another. (Although 99.9 percent of all Excel fans use absolute references for named ranges, this Excel rule is one you can break for some unusual tricks. To learn about them, check out *Excel Hacks* by David and Raina Hawley.)
- They add an extra layer between your formulas and your worksheet. If you change the structure of your worksheet, you don't need to modify your formulas. Instead, you simply edit the named ranges so they point to the new cell locations.

This is particularly useful when you write macros (Chapter 30), because it lets you avoid writing direct cell references in your code.

In the next few sections, you'll learn how to create named ranges. You'll also pick up a few tricks for defining and applying names automatically.

Creating and Using a Named Range

Creating a named range is easy. Just follow these steps:

1. **Select the cells you want to name.**

   You can name a single cell or an entire range of cells.

2. **Look for the box at the left end of the formula bar, which indicates the address of the current cell (for example, C5).** This part of the formula bar is called the *name box*. Click the name box once.

   The text inside (the cell address) is now selected.

3. **Start typing the name you want to use.**

   What you type replaces the cell address (see Figure 13-4).

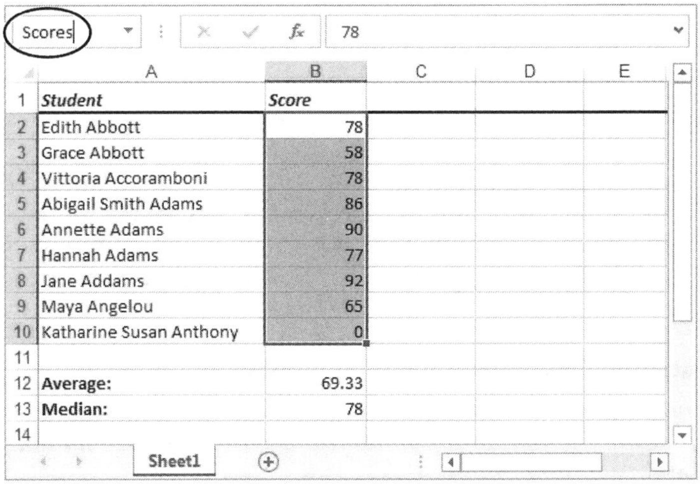

FIGURE 13-4

This worksheet has a named range, Scores, so you can easily use the student grades in your formulas without having to remember the cell range. (It also lets you change the range and update all your formulas in one step, if the worksheet changes.) To define the range for student scores, select the cells with the numeric scores (B2 to B10), and then enter the new name using the name box in the formula bar (circled).

4. **Press Enter to confirm the new name.**

   You can now select the name at any time (see Figure 13-5). To use a name, click the drop-down arrow to the right side of the name box to see the list of names defined in the workbook. When you click a name, Excel jumps to the appropriate position and selects the corresponding cell or range of cells.

NOTE When you name a range, you have to follow certain rules. All names have to start with a letter, and they can't contain spaces or special characters—except the underscore character (_). Also, all names have to be unique. Finally, you can't create a range name that matches a valid cell address. For example, BB10 isn't a valid range name, because every worksheet has a cell with the address BB10.

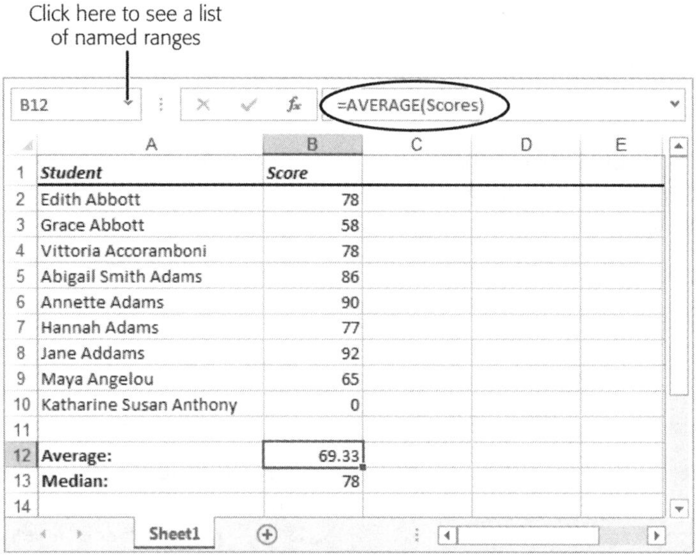

FIGURE 13-5

Once you define and name a cell range, you can use it in formulas (as shown with the AVERAGE() function here). To see a list of all the named ranges in your worksheet, click the drop-down arrow in the box on the left side of the formula bar. (If you pick a name from this list, Excel selects the corresponding cells.)

Once you create a name, you can use it in any formula, just as you would any other cell reference or cell range. As a shortcut, you can pick the name from a handy list. To do so, start entering your formula, and then select Formulas→Defined Names→Use in Formula. You'll see a menu with all the names you defined in your workbook. Select the one you want to use, and Excel inserts it into the formula.

Creating Slightly Smarter Named Ranges

The name box gives you a quick way to give a cell range a name, but you can add additional information, too, like a description. To create a name with this optional information:

1. **Select the cells you want to name.**

2. **Choose Formulas→Defined Names→Define Name.**

   Or, to bypass the ribbon, right-click the selected cells, and then choose Name a Range. Either way, the New Name window appears (Figure 13-6).

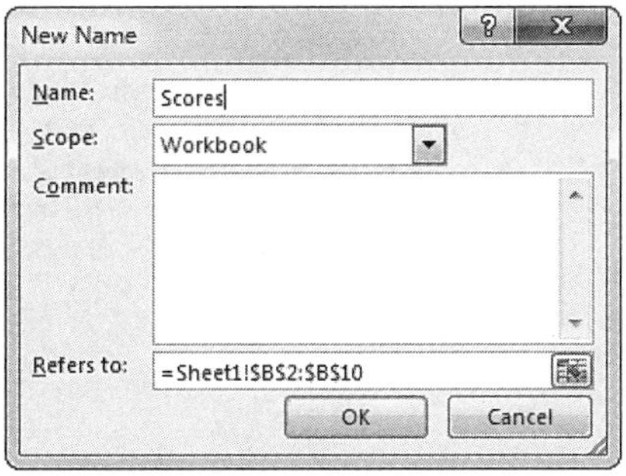

FIGURE 13-6

In the New Name window, you fill in the standard name and cell reference information, along with two extra details: the ever-important Scope setting (which lets you organize names in workbooks with multiple worksheets) and a Comment section (which lets you add descriptive text for the range).

3. **Fill in the information for your named range.**

   The only information you need to add is the name, but you can tweak several settings:

   - **Name** is the name you give the range (like TaxRate).
   - **Scope** lets you control where you can use the name. Ordinarily, names have Workbook scope, which means you can use them on any worksheet in your workbook. However, you may choose to limit the scope to a single, specific worksheet instead. That way, your name lists aren't as cluttered, because you see only the names for the current worksheet. Also, you don't need to worry about using the same name in different worksheets.
   - **Comment** is a description for your named range. This description appears in a tooltip when you enter the name into a formula. You can use any text you want for the comment, but Excel experts use it to describe the type of information in the cells, when the data was last updated, and whether the range depends on information in other workbooks.
   - **Refers to** is a cell reference that indicates the cells you selected in step 1. If you didn't get it quite right, you can modify the range now.

4. **Click OK to create the name.**

   You can now use your name in formulas anywhere. In fact, Excel even helps you out with its Formula AutoComplete feature, as shown in Figure 13-7.

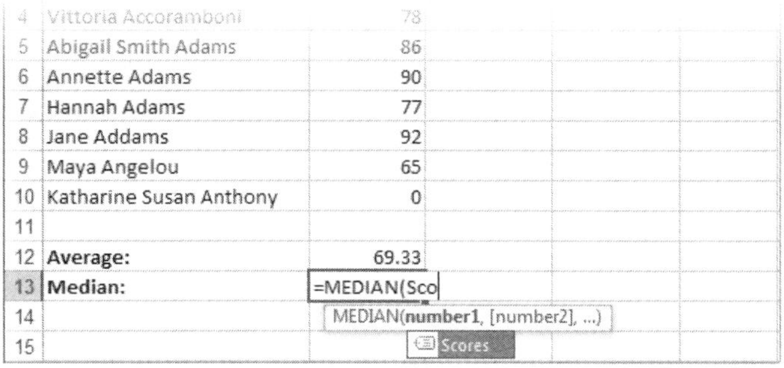

4 Vittoria Accoramboni 78
5 Abigail Smith Adams 86
6 Annette Adams 90
7 Hannah Adams 77
8 Jane Addams 92
9 Maya Angelou 65
10 Katharine Susan Anthony 0
12 Average: 69.33
13 Median: =MEDIAN(Sco
MEDIAN(number1, [number2], ...)
Scores

FIGURE 13-7

Excel's AutoComplete feature doesn't just suggest possible function names—it also shows you the named ranges that match the text you've typed so far. And if your name has a comment, you see that text appear in a tooltip to help you out.

Naming Formulas and Constants

The New Name window also provides the key to unlock additional naming features. Using it, you can create nicknames for frequently used formulas (like "My_Net_Worth"). This section describes how.

Internally, Excel treats all names as formulas. That is, when you create a named range, Excel simply generates a formula that points to that range, like *=$A$1: $A$10*. To check this out, select a few cells, and then choose Formulas→Defined Names→Define Name. In the "Refers to" text box at the bottom of the window, you see a formula with the corresponding cell reference.

Although most names refer to cell ranges, there's no reason why you can't create names with different formulas. You can use this approach to define a fixed constant value that you want to use in several formulas, for example. Here's how:

```
=4.35%
```

To create this constant, first name it in the text box at the top of the New Name window (for example, "SalesCommission"), enter the formula in the "Refers to" text box, click Add, and then click OK. You can now use this name in place of the constant in your worksheet calculations:

```
=A10*SalesComission
```

People often use named constants to make it easier to insert frequently used text. You may want to declare a company name a constant:

```
="Acme Enterprises, Incorporated."
```

You can then use that text in a number of cells. And best of all, if the company name changes, you simply need to update the named formula, no matter how many times it's used in the worksheet!

Similarly, you can create names that reference more complex formulas. These formulas can even use a combination of functions. Here's an example that automatically displays the name of the current day:

```
=TEXT(TODAY(), "dddd")
```

TIP Overall, you'll probably find that the most useful type of name is one that refers to a range of cells. However, don't hesitate to use named constants and named formulas, which are particularly useful if you have static text or numbers that you need to use in multiple places.

Managing Named Ranges

It's all well and good to create named ranges, but sooner or later you'll need to tweak your handiwork by doing things like deleting names you don't need anymore, or editing the ones you regularly use (so that they designate a different range, for example). For these tasks, you need to choose Formulas→Defined Names→Name Manager to show the Name Manager (Figure 13-8) or press Ctrl+F3.

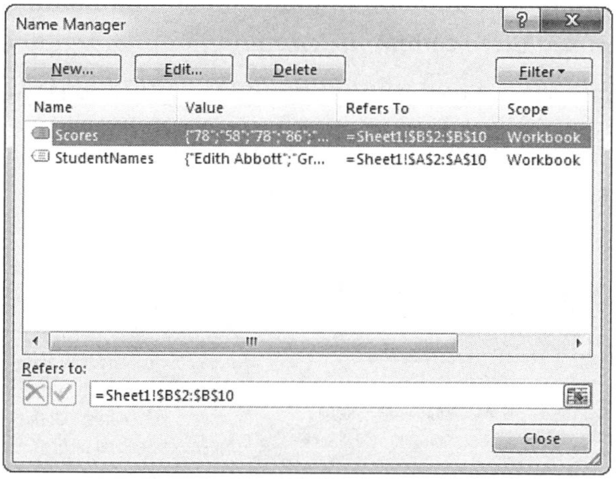

FIGURE 13-8

The Name Manager lists all the named constants in your workbook. For better organization, you can click a column to re-sort the list. You can also resize the window to see more names at once.

The Name Manager is the starting point when you need to add, delete, or edit existing named ranges. Here's what you can do:

- **To add a name**, click New. You get to the familiar New Name window.
- **To remove a name**, select it in the list, and then click Delete. Any formulas using that name display the error code *#NAME?* or *#REF!*, indicating that Excel can't find the named range.

- **To edit a name**, select it in the list, and then click Edit. You see an Edit Name window, which looks exactly the same as the New Name window. Excel's nice enough to keep track of names. If you rename TaxRate to TaxPercentage, Excel adjusts every formula that used TaxRate to now use TaxPercentage, thereby avoiding an error.

TIP If you need to change the cell reference for an existing name but you don't need to change anything else (like its name or comment), Excel's got a quicker solution. Select the name in the list, and then modify the cell reference in the "Refers to" box at the bottom of the window. (Click-lovers can change the cell reference using the mouse. Just click inside the "Refers to" box to highlight the cell reference on the worksheet. Then, drag on the worksheet to draw the new cell reference.)

The Name Manager is a great place to review all the names you're using, check for errors, and make adjustments. Many Excel experts create workbooks with hundreds of names. If you do, too, you may have a hard time finding the names you want. Fortunately, the Name Manager includes a filtering feature that can help.

Filtering cuts down the names list so that it displays only the names you're interested in. The Name Manager lets you use several types of filters:

- You can find names limited to the current worksheet.
- You can find names that point to cells with errors (and those that don't).
- You can find ordinary names, or names used in tables (Chapter 14).

Figure 13-9 shows the filter settings you can choose from.

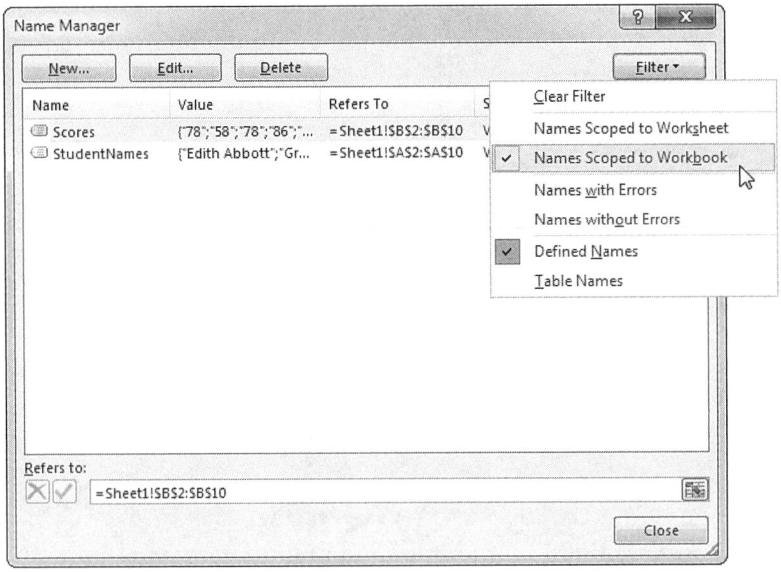

FIGURE 13-9

To apply a filter, click the filter button, and then make a choice from the drop-down menu. You'll notice that this menu has several sections, separated by horizontal lines. Each section represents a separate type of filter, and you can apply more than one filter at once. This example applies two types of filter, resulting in a list of defined names that have workbook scope. In other words, it ignores names generated as part of a table and names tied to a specific worksheet. To get back to normal and show all names, choose Clear Filter.

GEM IN THE ROUGH

Getting a List of Names

After defining dozens of names in a worksheet, you may appreciate an easy way to review them. The Name Manager works well from within Excel, but there's another choice that lets you look over your names from the comfort of your armchair. You paste the list of names into a worksheet, complete with their cell references, print it out, and then remove it from your worksheet.

To generate the list of names, click the cell where you want to start the list. Remember, you need two free columns—one for the range names and one for the range addresses—and you don't want to overwrite any existing data. Once you're at the right place, select Formulas→Defined Names→Use in Formula→Paste Names. When the Paste Name window appears, click the Paste List button.

This name list is static, which means Excel doesn't update it if you add more names to your worksheet. Instead, you need to generate the list again.

Automatically Creating Named Ranges

Excel also has the built-in smarts to automatically generate names for cell ranges. To perform this trick, Excel searches a group of cells you select and, with a little help from you, identifies which cell or cells would offer appropriate names. If you have a column title in cell A1, for example, Excel can use the text in that cell to label the range of cells underneath it.

To use automatic naming, follow these steps:

1. **Select the cells for which you want Excel to create one or more named ranges.**

   Your selection must include the cells that you want to be part of the named range, plus the cell or cells that contain the descriptive text. Figure 13-10 and Figure 13-11 show examples.

2. **Choose Formulas→Defined Names→Create from Selection.**

   The Create Names from Selection window appears.

3. **Specify which part of your selection has the text label (or labels) you want to use by turning on the appropriate checkbox.**

   In order to create a name, Excel has to find some text to use as a label. You use the Create Names from Selection window to tell Excel where that text is. If the text is contained in column headings, then select "Top row." If there are row and column headings, then select "Top row" and "Left column." Excel selects the options that it thinks make sense based on your selection.

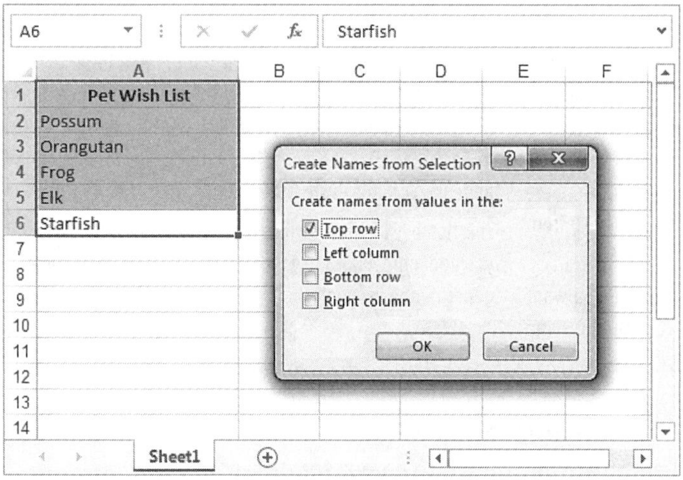

FIGURE 13-10

If you just want to create a single named range (from a vertical list, for example), then you'd pick "Top row" in the Create Names from Selection window. Here, the named range is Pet_Wish_List (Excel automatically inserts underscores in place of spaces), and the included cells in this range are A2 to A6.

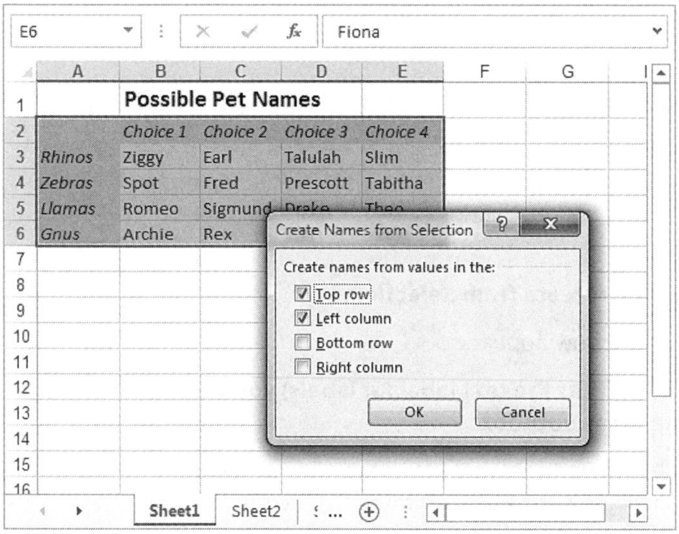

FIGURE 13-11

You can also use Create Names from Selection with a table of data. In this case, by turning on Top Row and Left Column, Excel uses each of the animals in column A as the title for a different named range. The Rhinos range, for example, contains cells B3 to E3. If you turn on the "Top row" checkbox, then Excel also creates named ranges for each column, like Choice_1 (cells B3:B6), Choice_2 (cells C3:C6), and so on.

NOTE It's up to you whether you want to create ranges for row headings, column headings, or both.

4. **Click OK to generate the names.**

   Excel's automatic naming ability seems like a real timesaver, but it can introduce as many problems as it solves. Here are some of the quirks and annoyances to watch out for:

   - The named ranges may not be the ones you want, especially if you use long, descriptive column titles. The name *Length* is more manageable than the name *Length_in_Feet*—which is what Excel sticks you with if your name-containing cell happens to contain the text *Length in Feet*. You could rename your named range after the fact (page 390), but it's extra work.
   - If you frequently use the Create Names from Selection tool, you may suddenly find yourself with dozens of names, depending on your worksheet's complexity. Since you haven't created these names yourself, you won't necessarily know what each one references. One way to figure it out is to use the technique described in the box on page 391.
   - Excel doesn't generate names if your column or row labels contain only numbers. If you have a table with a list of part numbers or customer IDs, then Excel assumes the numbers are a part of the data, and not labels it can use for naming. And if your column or row names are text values that start with a number (like "401K"), Excel adds an underscore at the beginning to make a valid name ("_401K").
   - If you don't have *any* row or column labels, Excel can't generate any names.

Applying Names to Existing Formulas

Named ranges are extremely helpful, but unless you plan out your spreadsheet writing in a careful, orderly manner, you may find that you spend more time managing these names than actually using them. Suppose you write a bunch of formulas that work their magic on a table of data that doesn't use any named ranges. Then, *after* you've written the formulas, you catch the named range bug and apply names to, say, all the columns in your table. Your formulas still work, but they don't use the names you just created.

NOTE There's one thing to remember before you get started with the Apply Names feature. Excel can use named ranges only if you've defined them. If your worksheet doesn't include any named ranges, or if they don't match the ranges used in your formulas, this feature doesn't do anything.

So you either have to go through and manually revise each formula—so that, for example, *=SUM(A2:A85)* becomes *=SUM(My_Stocks)*—or, if you're not a fan of carpal tunnel syndrome, you can use one of Excel's most valuable shortcuts: the ability to automatically replace old-school alphanumeric cell references with reader-friendly named range labels. To use this timesaving technique, follow these steps:

1. **Select the cells that contain the formulas you want to change.**

   Of course, you can only use this shortcut if you've got a bunch of formulas that don't yet use one or more existing named ranges. Select the cells that contain the formulas you want to change. This shortcut can work on more than one formula at a time (even if each formula references a different named range), so it's OK to select a group of formulas.

2. **Select Formulas→Defined Names→Define Name→Apply Names.**

   The Apply Names window appears (Figure 13-12), with a list of all the names in your workbook.

3. **Choose the names you want to use in your formulas.**

   These are the names that Excel will attempt to insert in your formulas, in place of the cell references.

   To select a name, click it once. (Or, if it's already selected, you can click that name to unselect it.) You can select as many names as you want, but you have to pick them one at a time.

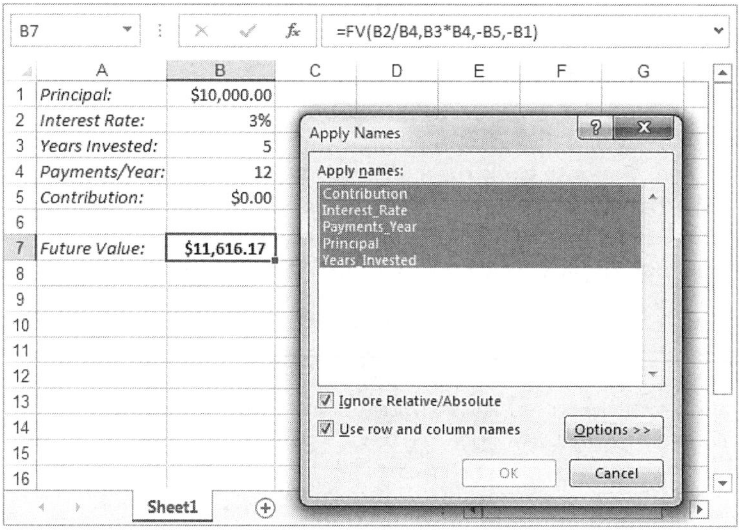

FIGURE 13-12

*When you use the Formulas→Defined Names→Define Name→Apply Names command, the formula in B7 will change from =FV(B2/B4,B3*B4,-B5,-B1) to the more understandable (but longer) formula =FV(Rate/Payments, Years*Payments, -Contribution, -Principal).*

If the Ignore Relative/Absolute checkbox is turned on, Excel changes any matching reference, whether it's absolute or relative. This behavior is usually what you want, because most people writing formulas use relative references (like A2 instead of $A$2)—unless they explicitly need absolute references to make copying and pasting easier. If you don't turn this option on, Excel replaces only absolute references.

You'll also notice the "Use row and column names" checkbox. This setting applies only if you generated names using the Formulas→Named Cells→Create from Selection technique described in the previous section. If you used this technique to create row and column names, you can turn off the "Use row and column names" checkbox to prevent Excel from using these names in your formulas. This is often a good idea, because it prevents Excel from creating horribly complex formulas with the row and column names. (The problem is that, in this situation, Excel uses *range intersection* to identify each cell. For example, consider the grid of pet names in Figure 13-11. If you apply names with the "Use row and column names" checkbox turned on, Excel converts a simple formula like *=B3* into *=RHINOS Choice_1*. In other words, Excel notices that the intersection of the RHINOS range (B3:E3) and the Choice_1 range (B3:B6) is the single cell B3. You may consider this either an elegant adjustment or, more likely, an unnecessary way to complicate your life.)

4. **Click OK to apply the names.**

   Every time Excel finds a range that matches one of the highlighted range names, it replaces the alphanumeric cell reference with the range name.

Variable Data Tables

When you create a formula, you generate a single result based on the operators, functions, and data you use. This makes sense when you're nailing down last year's profit-loss report, but it's not always as handy when you're making projections for the *future*. In these cases, it's often helpful to compare several possibilities. One tool you can use is a *variable data table*.

A variable data table is simply a table that shows multiple results, based on different source data. You could use a variable data table to see how the return of an investment varies based on different interest rates, for example. Because Excel shows you all the results side by side, you can quickly compare them.

You could create your own comparison table without too much trouble. In fact, using the power of relative references, you could create one formula and copy it into several cells to quickly create a table without any formula-tweaking. Some Excel fans prefer this approach. However, when you use variable data tables you save more than a few keystrokes.

NOTE Variable data tables have nothing in common with the similarly named *table feature*, which you'll learn about in Chapter 14.

Creating a One-Variable Data Table

A *one-variable* data table provides a single column of results. It's called one-variable because there's only one input value that changes. For example, if you want to compare how an investment payoff changes based on interest rates, you can create a one-variable data table that uses the interest rate as the changing variable.

Here's how you create a one-variable data table:

1. **Create a sample formula using the calculation you plan to use.**

   When you create this formula, make sure that you use a cell reference for the value you want to change, not a literal value. Otherwise, Excel can't *change* the value to calculate the different possibilities.

   In the example in Figure 13-13, the formula uses the FV() financial function (page 299) to calculate the future value of an investment. The variable is the rate argument, which is stored in cell B3.

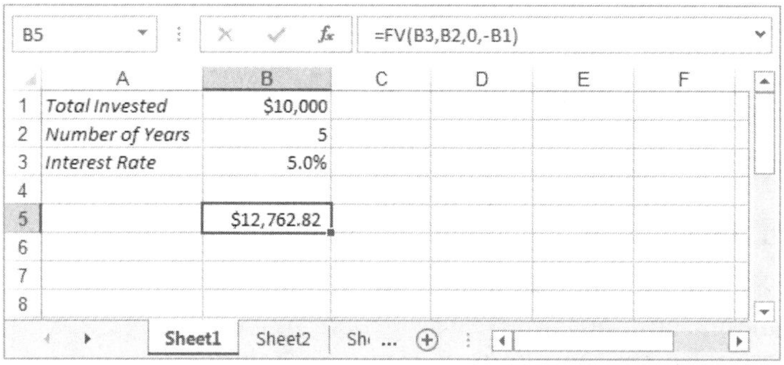

FIGURE 13-13

Before you can create a one-variable data table, you need to start with a formula that calculates the result, using cell references. In this example, the formula is in cell B5, and it calculates the value of a $10,000 investment after five years at 5 percent interest.

2. **Set up the table.** To do so, create a column that has each value you want to test.

   In this example, you need to create a column with different interest rates. The calculated results appear in the column on the right. You may find getting the correct arrangement a little tricky. You need to make sure the formula you want to modify is just above the column where the results will appear, as shown in Figure 13-14.

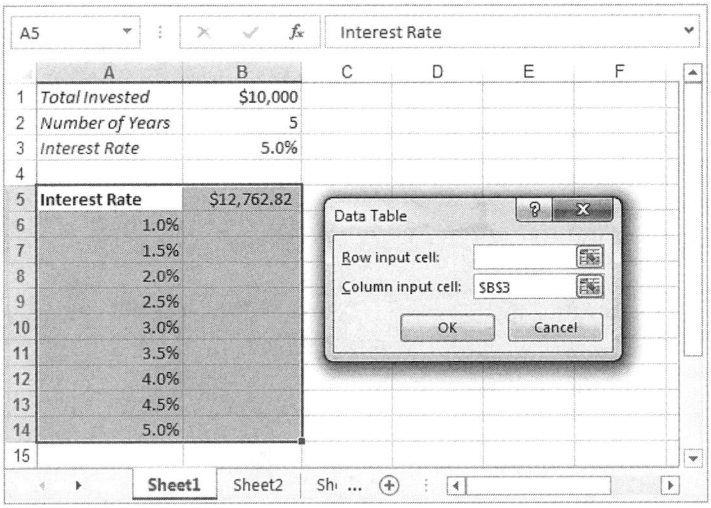

FIGURE 13-14

In the Data Table window, specify the cell that has the changing value, and then click OK.

3. **Generate the table by selecting the whole table, and then choosing Data→Data Tools→What-If Analysis→Data Table.**

   The Data Table window appears (Figure 13-14).

4. **In the "Column input cell" box, type the address of the cell that has the value you want to change.**

   This part is tricky. Excel needs to figure out which part of the formula it's supposed to modify to generate the results that'll appear in the table. In this example, the formula's *=FV(B3,B2,0,–B1)*. The cell B3 supplies the rate (currently 5 percent). This is the piece of information you want to change, so enter B3 in the "Column input cell" text box. (When Excel generates the data table, it looks at the first column, gets the new rate value, and substitutes this value for the value referenced in B3.)

5. **Click OK to create the table.**

   Excel displays all the results—in this example, the value of the investment based on different interest rates (Figure 13-15). If you actually look at the content of each cell, you'll find that it uses an array formula with the TABLE() function to work its magic.

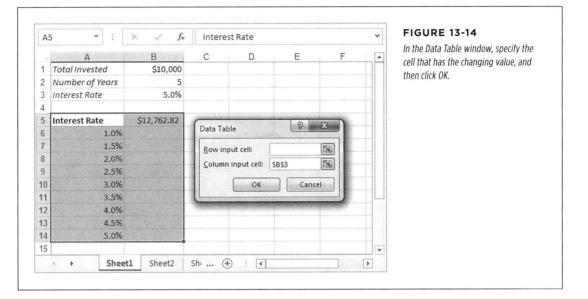

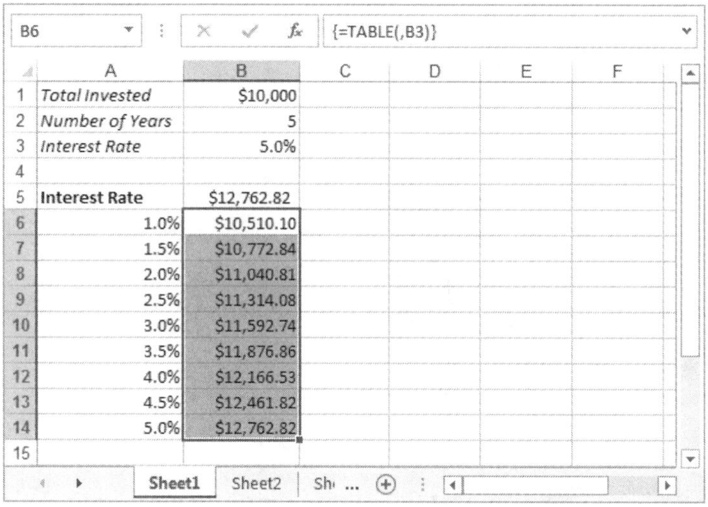

FIGURE 13-15

The end result of a one-variable data table: a table of investment profits based on different interest rates.

Creating a Two-Variable Data Table

It's almost as easy to create a *two-variable* data table, where two different values change. In this case, you place one set of changing values in the column on the left, and the other set of changing values in the row on the top. Figure 13-16 shows an example.

Next, select the whole table and choose Data→Data Tools→What-If Analysis→Data Table. This time, fill out both text boxes (the top row provides an investment period value in place of cell B2, and the leftmost cell provides the interest rate in place of cell B3). When you click OK, Excel generates the complete table (Figure 13-17).

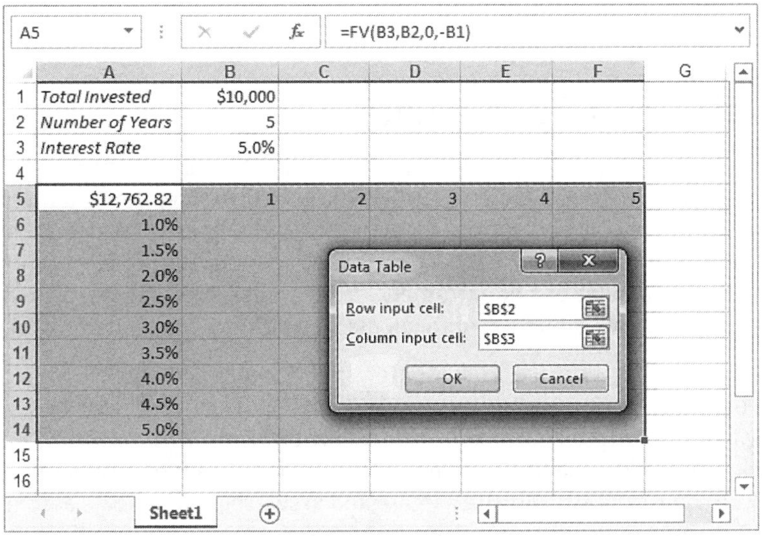

FIGURE 13-16

This two-variable data table studies how an investment performs for different interest rates and different investment periods (in years). The row of values in cells B5 to F5 represent the number of years, while the column of values in cells A6 to A14 represent the interest rate. You need to enter the formula in the top-left corner of the table.

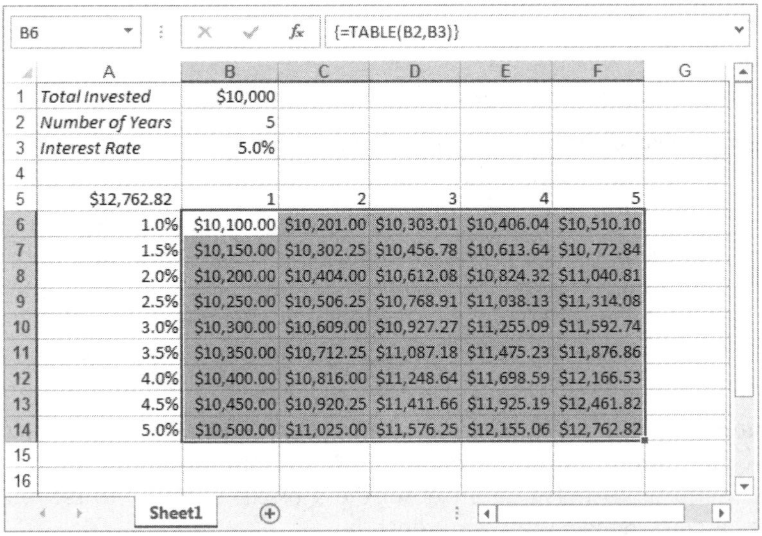

FIGURE 13-17

The final table shows how the money you make changes based on the time you wait and the interest rate.

TIP What-if analysis is the art of exploring possibilities with your numbers. The goals of what-if analysis are many—you might want to discover hidden relationships, set new targets, or prepare for future outcomes. For some more sophisticated ways to perform what-if analyses, you can read about scenarios and goal-seeking in Chapter 25.

Controlling Recalculation

Ordinarily, Excel recalculates a formula whenever you change any of the cells the formula uses, and whenever you open the workbook containing the formula. This behavior is extremely convenient because it ensures that your information never gets out of date. However, it can cause trouble if your worksheet contains time-consuming calculations or extremely large tables of data. In this situation, life can slow to a crawl while Excel recalculates and updates all its formulas.

With the exponential increase in computer speed (and Microsoft's continuous tweaking of Excel's performance), large worksheets aren't the problem they used to be. However, some Excel aficionados still report problems when crunching data that's thick with formulas. If you're using Excel to plot the path of orbital satellites or to analyze census data, you may be interested in switching off Excel's automatic calculation to make your worksheet more responsive.

To select the calculation mode, choose Formulas→Calculation→Calculation Options, and then pick an option from the menu.

- **Manual** turns off all automatic calculation.
- **Automatic** is the standard way of life for Excel spreadsheets. Excel recalculates formulas whenever cell changes affect them.
- **Automatic Except Data Tables** uses automatic recalculation for all formulas except those in data tables (Chapter 14).

In manual recalculation mode, Excel calculates most simple formulas when you enter them. However, if you modify cells that the formula uses, the program doesn't recalculate the formula—instead, it keeps displaying the old result. When you see the word *Calculate* in the Status bar, that's your clue that Excel would have ordinarily performed a recalculation, but didn't because of your settings. It means that some data's changed, and a recalculation's a good idea to refresh your formula results.

When you decide you do want to recalculate your workbook, you can choose Formulas→Calculation→Calculate Now (or hit F9). Alternatively, you can choose Formulas→Calculation→Calculate Sheet (or the shortcut Shift+F9) to recalculate just those formulas in the current worksheet.

NOTE Unfortunately, the recalculation settings are program-wide. When you switch off automatic calculation for one worksheet, it affects any other worksheets you're using. If you don't remember that you switched off automatic recalculation, you may end up using and printing stale data.

Solving Formula Errors

Errors ... they happen in the most unexpected places, transforming rows of calculations into unhelpful error codes like *#NAME?*, *#VALUE!*, and *#MORON!* (OK, that last one doesn't actually appear in Excel, but it might as well, given the sense of defeat and frustration these error codes can give you.) In some cases, you can see how to fix an error just by looking at the formula. However, sometimes the problem isn't so easy to solve, especially if your formulas perform calculations using the results of *other* formulas. In such cases, you can have a tough time tracking down the original error.

Excel provides some interesting *formula auditing tools*—a handful of features that you can use to inspect broken formulas or figure out what's going on in really complex ones. These tools make it much easier to fix errors.

With any error, your first step is to identify the error code by using the information listed in Table 8-2 on page 236. If the problem isn't immediately obvious, you can use the Formula Auditing tools to do the following:

- Evaluate an expression step-by-step, until you hit the error. That way, you know exactly what part of the formula's causing the error.
- Trace the *precedents* of a formula that gives you an error. Precedents are the cells that a particular formula references. In the formula *=A1+B1*, both A1 and B1 are precedents. If either of these cells contains an error, the error gets fed into—and trips up—the formula.
- Trace the *dependents* of a cell. Dependents are other cells that use the current cell. If one cell has the formula *=A1+B1*, and another cell contains *=A1*10*, both these cells are dependents of cell A1. If A1 has an error, it infects both formulas.
- Perform an error check on the entire worksheet. Excel's error checker is like a spell checker. One by one, it takes you to each cell that has an unresolved problem.

To perform any of these tasks, seek out the Formulas tab's Formula Auditing section. The following sections explain how you use it to find errors, evaluate formulas piece-by-piece, and trace relationships.

Step-by-Step Evaluation

Complex formulas usually include multiple *sub-expressions*. Each sub-expression is a piece of any formula that Excel evaluates separately. It may be an arithmetic operation in parentheses, a nested function, or even just a cell reference. To understand why your formula's generating an error, you need to know which sub-expression caused the problem.

Excel's solution is to provide a feature—called the Evaluate Formula tool—that evaluates your formula one sub-expression at a time. Using this tool, you can watch as Excel computes your formula, up until the point where the error occurs.

To watch the step-by-step execution of a formula that contains an error, follow these steps:

1. **Move to the cell that contains the formula that's producing the error.**

   You don't need to highlight the formula, you just need to be in the offending cell.

2. **Choose Formulas→Formula Auditing→Evaluate Formula.**

   The Evaluate Formula window appears (Figure 13-18), with the formula in a large, multiline textbox.

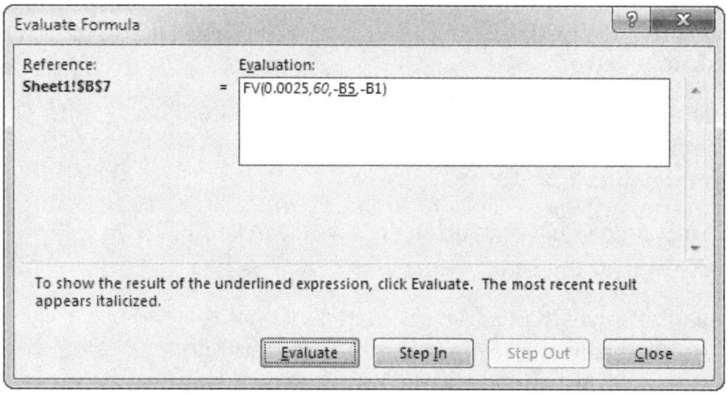

FIGURE 13-18

Excel has evaluated the first two arguments in this formula. (The second argument [60] is italicized, indicating that Excel calculated it in the last step.) The next time you click Evaluate, Excel evaluates the third argument, which is underlined. If you want to show the contents of this cell before evaluating it, you can click Step In.

3. **Excel underlines the part of the formula that it's about to evaluate. Click the Evaluate button.**

   Excel evaluates the sub-expression and replaces it with the calculated value. It might replace a cell reference with the cell's actual value, evaluate an arithmetic operator, or execute a function. The value appears in italic, indicating that it's the most recent value that Excel calculated.

4. **Repeat step 3 until the sub-expression that generates the error occurs.**

   When the error occurs, you'll see the error code appear in your formula. When you click Evaluate again, the error code spreads, encompassing the whole expression or the function that uses it. Consider the ill-fated formula *=1+5/0*. The first step (the division) creates a divide-by-zero error, and the formula appears as *=1+#DIV/0!*. But you can't add 1 to an error, so, in the next step, the error spreads to the whole formula, which becomes *=#DIV/0!* in the end.

5. **When the calculation process ends, you can click Restart to repeat the calculation from the beginning.**

   You can also click Close to stop evaluating the formula and return to your worksheet at any time.

TIP Step-by-step evaluation isn't just for solving errors. It can also help you understand *why* a formula doesn't produce the result you expect. You can use the Evaluate Formula window with a formula that doesn't cause an error in exactly the same way as one that does. By watching the calculation proceed step-by-step, you may realize that the order of operations Excel follows is subtly different from the order you expected. You can then edit the formula accordingly.

GEM IN THE ROUGH

Digging Deeper into Linked Formulas

In problematic formulas, even if you discover the sub-expression that's causing the trouble, you still may not have found the root of the problem. If the sub-expression that's causing the error is a reference, it may point to another cell that contains another formula. If it does, you need to evaluate *that* formula step-by-step to find the real mistake.

To evaluate the second formula, you can move to the appropriate cell and start the step-by-step evaluation process by clicking the Evaluate Formula button. However, Excel provides a useful shortcut that lets you jump from one formula into another. The secret is the Step In and Step Out buttons in the Evaluate Formula window (Figure 13-19).

When you use the Evaluate Formula window, the Step In button becomes available just before you evaluate a sub-expression containing a cell reference. If you click the Step In button at this point, Excel adds a new text box to the window underneath the first one. This new text box shows the contents of the referenced cell. Excel also informs you if the cell contains a formula or a constant (just read the label at the bottom of the Evaluate Formula window). If the cell contains a constant or there's no calculation left to perform, you need to click Step Out to return to the original formula. If the cell does contain a formula, you can click the Evaluate button to start evaluating *it*—one sub-expression at a time—and then click Step Out once you finish.

In fact, Excel lets you dig even deeper into chains of linked formulas. Every time you find a cell reference that points to another formula-holding cell, you can click Step In to show the formula in a new text box. You can continue this process with no practical limit. If you exceed the space available in the Evaluate Formula window, Excel just adds a scroll bar to help you out.

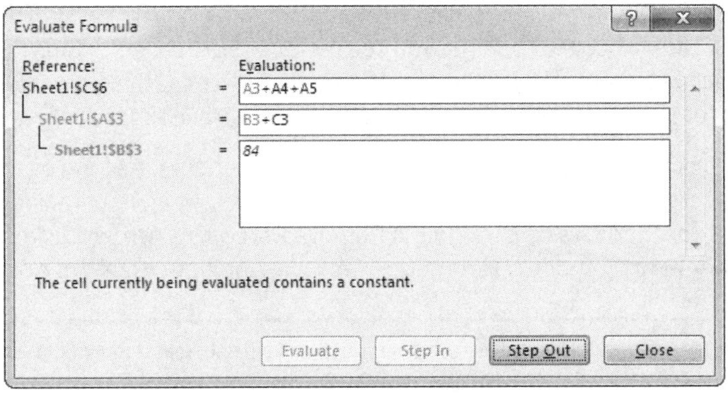

FIGURE 13-19

In this example, the Step In button has taken you three levels deep into a formula. The formula it's evaluating is in the first box; it's A3+A4+A5. However, clicking Step In adds a second box, which reveals that cell A3 itself contains a formula (B3+C3). Finally, another click of Step In shows a third box, which zooms in on the first part of the second formula (B3), and shows that the cell it points to holds the number 84.

Tracing Precedents and Dependents

The Evaluate Formula window is one way to examine complex formulas' anatomy. However, depending on the complexity of your formulas, you can end up having to move through a long series of steps before you find the problem. In this case, you may be interested in using a different approach, one that uses Excel's ability to graphically trace linked cells. This feature isn't any better or worse than the Evaluate Formula window—it's just another tool you can use to resolve problems, depending on the situation and your own preference.

First, here's a quick review of how Excel thinks about precedents and dependents. Consider the following formula:

```
=A1+B1
```

If this formula is in cell C1, that makes A1 and B1 *precedents* of C1. In other words, C1 relies on the values in A1 and B1 in order to do its work. If either of these cells contains an error, the problem spreads to C1. You can say that C1 is the *dependent* of both A1 and B1.

Excel's tracing features graphically represent these relationships—in the form of blue arrows—right on your worksheet without relying on another window or window.

To see tracing in action, move to a cell that contains one or more cell references, and then choose Formulas→Formula Auditing→Trace Precedents. Excel displays solid blue arrows that link the cells together. If you click Trace Precedents in the cell C1 that contains that formula *=A1+B1*, you see two arrows. One points from A1 to C1, and the other points from B1 to C1. Figure 13-20 and Figure 13-21 show examples.

NOTE If a formula references a cell in another worksheet or workbook, Excel draws a dotted line linking your cell to a small grid icon. This icon represents the other worksheet or workbook and can't see the actual cell that the formula links to.

The first time you click Trace Precedents, you see the *direct precedents*. These cells are the ones directly referenced by the current formula. However, these precedents may themselves refer to other cells. To see *these* cells, click Trace Precedents again.

There's no limit to how many times you can click Trace Precedents. As long as there are more indirect precedents, Excel continues adding arrows. At any point, you can remove a single level of arrows by clicking the Remove Precedent Arrows button, or you can clear everything by choosing Formulas→Formula Auditing→Remove Arrows.

TIP Nothing prevents you from tracing the precedents for a bunch of different cells: Just move to another cell and repeat the process for each cell you want to trace, one after the other. You can see all the arrows at once, which can make for a tangled worksheet. When you click Remove Arrows, Excel removes all the precedent arrows and any dependent arrows for every cell you've traced. You can remove the arrows for just one cell by moving to it, and then choosing Formulas→Formula Auditing→Remove Precedent Arrows.

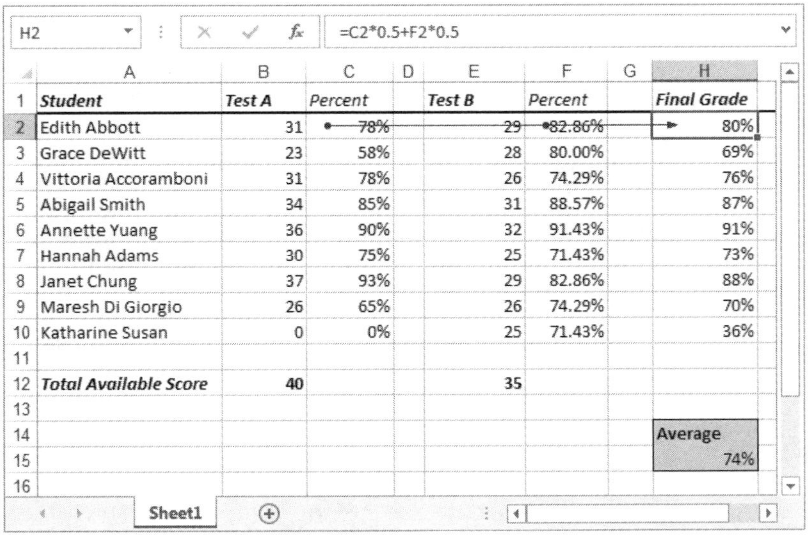

H2 =C2*0.5+F2*0.5

	A	B	C	D	E	F	G	H
1	*Student*	*Test A*	*Percent*		*Test B*	*Percent*		*Final Grade*
2	Edith Abbott	31	78%		29	82.86%		80%
3	Grace DeWitt	23	58%		28	80.00%		69%
4	Vittoria Accoramboni	31	78%		26	74.29%		76%
5	Abigail Smith	34	85%		31	88.57%		87%
6	Annette Yuang	36	90%		32	91.43%		91%
7	Hannah Adams	30	75%		25	71.43%		73%
8	Janet Chung	37	93%		29	82.86%		88%
9	Maresh Di Giorgio	26	65%		26	74.29%		70%
10	Katharine Susan	0	0%		25	71.43%		36%
11								
12	*Total Available Score*	40			35			
13								
14								Average
15								74%
16								

Sheet1

FIGURE 13-20

This example shows the direct precedents of cell H2. As you can see, H2 calculates the student's final grade based on the test results stored in cells C2 and F2. Because these two arrows overlap, they appear as one, but you can clearly see two circles, each of which represents the starting point of an arrow (one each on cells C2 and F2).

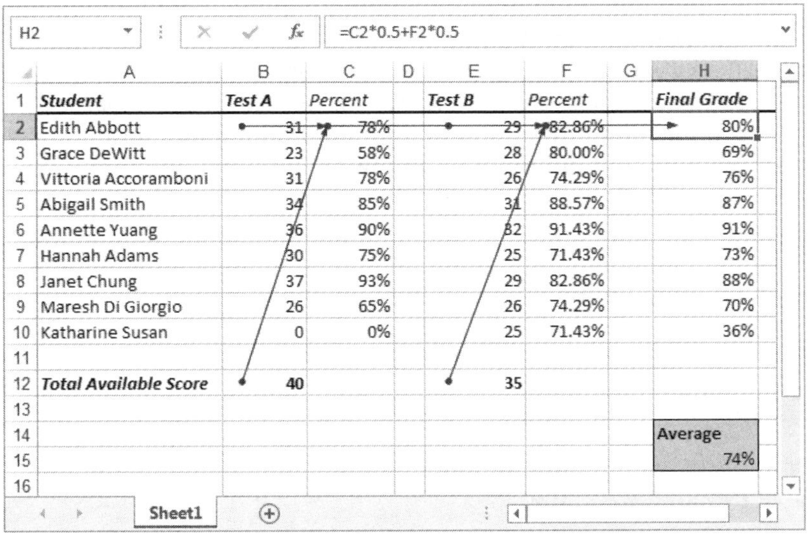

H2 =C2*0.5+F2*0.5

	A	B	C	D	E	F	G	H
1	*Student*	*Test A*	*Percent*		*Test B*	*Percent*		*Final Grade*
2	Edith Abbott	31	78%		29	82.86%		80%
3	Grace DeWitt	23	58%		28	80.00%		69%
4	Vittoria Accoramboni	31	78%		26	74.29%		76%
5	Abigail Smith	34	85%		31	88.57%		87%
6	Annette Yuang	36	90%		32	91.43%		91%
7	Hannah Adams	30	75%		25	71.43%		73%
8	Janet Chung	37	93%		29	82.86%		88%
9	Maresh Di Giorgio	26	65%		26	74.29%		70%
10	Katharine Susan	0	0%		25	71.43%		36%
11								
12	*Total Available Score*	40			35			
13								
14								Average
15								74%
16								

Sheet1

FIGURE 13-21

Excel also lets you trace multiple levels of relationships. Just click the Trace Precedents button again to see whether the precedent cells have other precedents. Here you can see that the test result cells are themselves calculations that rely on other cells. C2 makes its calculations using cells B2 and B12.

You can trace dependents in the same way that you trace precedents—just choose Formulas→Formula Auditing→Trace Dependents (see Figure 13-22). If you click Trace Dependents and cell A1 is selected, Excel adds an arrow connecting A1 to any other cells that *refer* to A1.

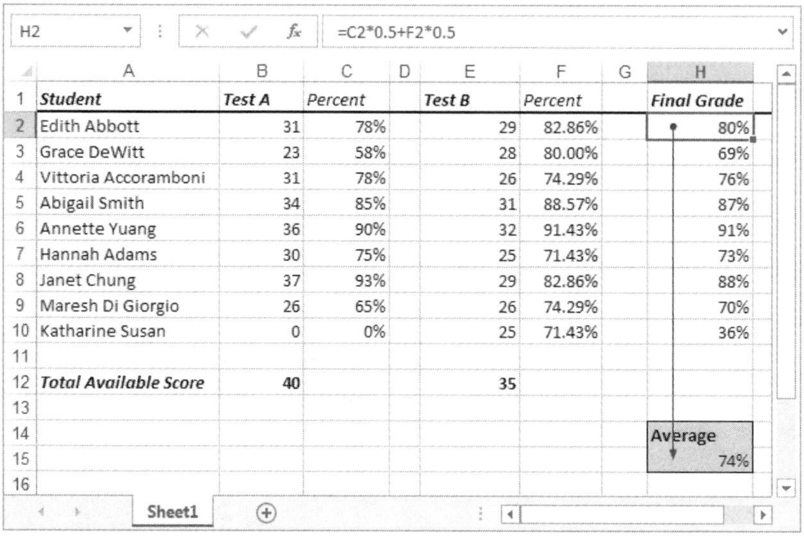

FIGURE 13-22

If you click Trace Dependents in cell H2, you can see that Excel uses this cell in the average calculation in cell H15. However, H2 isn't the only value cell H15 uses. To see all its precedents, you need to move to H15, and then click Trace Precedents.

There really isn't a difference between precedent and dependent arrows—they're just two different ways of looking at the same idea. In fact, every arrow Excel draws connects one precedent to one dependent. Finally, Excel's tracing tools also work with formulas that *aren't* working (which is important, after all, when it comes to troubleshooting). Figure 13-23 shows you how the tool works when your formulas generate error codes.

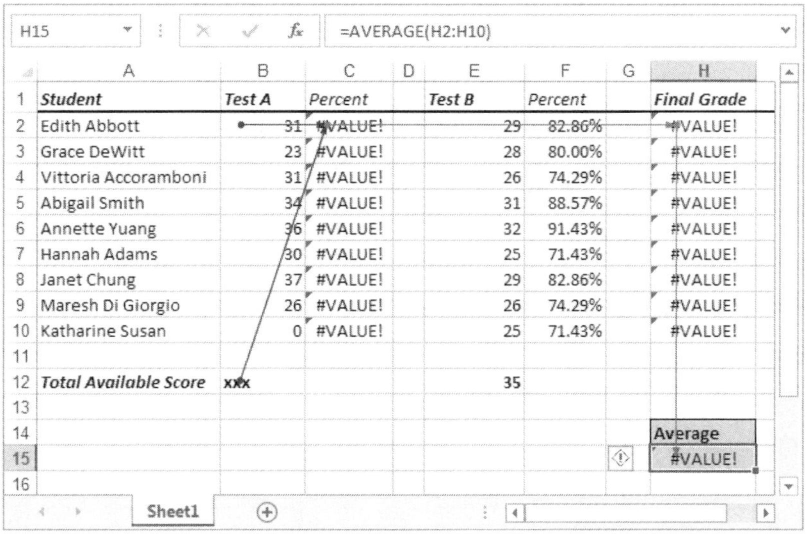

FIGURE 13-23

Excel's tracing features work with any formulas—whether or not they contain an error. But Excel also includes a related feature, Trace Error, which works only with formulas that result in error values. When you select a cell with an error code and then choose Trace Error, Excel traces all the precedents that lead back to the error using blue arrows. Then, Excel uses red arrows to indicate how the error spread. In this example, two blue arrows show the precedents of cell C2, where the error occurred. The error then spread to cell H2 and, finally, to the current cell, H15.

TIP If you have the Office Professional Plus edition of Excel, you have access to another tracing tool: the Inquire add-in. Inquire can create detailed diagrams that make it easier to navigate a dense thicket of formulas in a large, complex worksheet. Page 702 shows you how to use Inquire's diagramming feature.

Error-Checking

Sometimes, you may have a large worksheet containing a number of errors that are widely distributed. Rather than hunt for these errors by scrolling endlessly, you can jump straight to the offending cells using Excel's error-checking feature.

To perform an error check, follow these steps:

1. **Move to the position where you want to start the error check.**

   If you want to check the worksheet from start to finish, click the first cell. Otherwise, go to the location where you want to start checking. As with a spell check, Excel moves from column to column first, and then from row to row. However, the error checker automatically loops back to the beginning of your worksheet, making sure to check every cell before it stops.

2. **Choose Formulas→Formula Auditing→Error Checking.**

   If Excel doesn't find any errors in your worksheet, it displays a message indicating that its work is complete. Otherwise, you see the Error Checking window, as shown in Figure 13-24, which indicates the offending cell and formula. This box also provides a number of options.

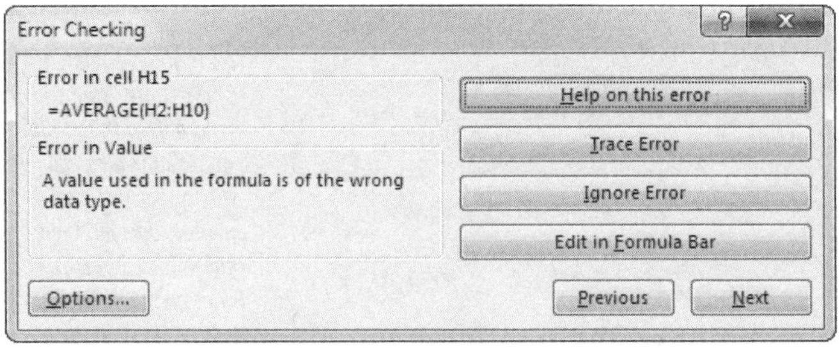

FIGURE 13-24

Excel's error checker helps you scan through a worksheet and quickly jump to the cells that contain errors. You can click the Trace Error button to quickly jump to the Evaluate Formula window and start analyzing the problem.

The Error Checking window contains the following options:

- **Next or Previous.** Use these buttons to move from one error to the next.
- **Help on this Error.** Click this button to jump to Excel's online help, which lists common causes of specific errors. It may give you some insight into your own troubles.
- **Trace Error.** Use this button to open the Evaluate Formula window, where you can move one step at a time through the evaluation of the formula.
- **Ignore Error.** Click this button to skip the error, and ignore the cell from this point onward. If you want the error checker to pay attention to a cell you previously decided to ignore, click the Options button, and then click Reset Ignored Errors.
- **Edit in Formula Bar.** Use this button to start editing the formula. This choice doesn't close the error checker—you can click Resume to get back to checking other errors once you make your change.
- **Options.** Click this button to open the Excel Options window, with the Formulas section selected. The Formulas section includes a small set of error-checking options under the headings "Error checking" and "Error checking rules" (page 235). Ordinarily, you don't need to change any of these options, as the factory settings are stringent enough to ensure that Excel catches all problems.

GEM IN THE ROUGH

Follow the Arrow

If you have a complex number-laden spreadsheet with formulas that pull values from all over the place, you may need to scroll around to find the precedents or dependents that interest you. Excel has a trick to help you out—just double-click the appropriate arrow to follow it back to its source cell, no matter where it lies.

If you've got a particularly tricky worksheet, it may contain formulas that draw upon values in other worksheets or workbooks. If you double-click the arrow in this situation, Excel pops up the Go To window (page 57), with the information about the source cell already filled in at the top of the list. To follow the arrow to the new worksheet or file, just select the reference (something like, *[SuperSecretValues.xlsx]Sheet1!$A$3*), and then click OK.

PART

3

Organizing Your Information

CHAPTER

14

Tables: List Management Made Easy

Excel's grid-like main window gives you lots of freedom to organize your information. As you've seen in the chapters so far, tables of data can assume a variety of shapes and sizes—from complex worksheets that track expenses, to a simple list of dishes your guests are bringing to a potluck dinner.

Some tables are sophisticated, with multiple levels, subtotals, and summary information. (You'll learn how to manage these multi-tiered creations in the next chapter.) But in many cases, your table consists of nothing more than a long list of data, with a single row at the top that provides descriptive column headings. These types of tables are so common that Excel provides a set of features designed exclusively for managing them. These tools let you control your tables in style—sorting, searching, and filtering your information with just a couple of mouse clicks. Excel even includes a group of functions expressly designed to analyze the information in tables. But before you can use any of these tools, you have to convert your garden-variety table into a *structured table*.

In this chapter, you'll learn more about what, exactly, a structured table is, how to create one, and how to make use of all its features and frills.

NOTE Don't confuse structured tables with the variable data tables you used for what-if analysis. These tables have a similar moniker but nothing else in common.

The Basics of Tables

An Excel table is really nothing more than a way to store a bunch of information about a group of items. Each item occupies a separate row, and different kinds of information about the item reside side by side in adjacent columns. In database terminology, the rows are *records*, and the columns of information are *fields*. For example, the records could represent customers, and the fields could contain things like name, address, purchase history, and so on.

Excel tables have a number of advantages over ordinary worksheet data:

- **They grow and shrink dynamically.** As you add data to adjacent rows and columns, the table grows to include the new cells. And as a table changes size, any formulas that use the table adjust themselves accordingly. In other words, if you have a formula that calculates the sum of a column in a table, the range that the SUM() function uses expands when you add a new record to the table.
- **They have built-in smarts.** You can quickly select rows and columns, apply a custom sort order, and search for important records. And if you add a formula for one row, Excel fills it in for all the rest, including any new rows that you add afterwards.
- **They excel (ahem) at dealing with large amounts of information.** If you need to manage vast amounts of information, you may find ordinary worksheet data a little cumbersome. If you put the same information in a table, you can apply *custom filtering*, which means you see only the records that interest you.
- **They look sharp.** Thanks to table styles, you can quickly format tables with a wide variety of colors, add gridlines, and use banding (shading that appears in alternate rows).
- **They can link to databases.** Tables are perfectly useful in standalone worksheets, but they can also double as indispensable tools for navigating information in a database. In Chapter 27, you'll learn how to get information *out of* a database and *into* an Excel table.

Creating a Table

Creating a table is easy. Here's how:

1. **Choose the row where you want your table to start.**

   If you're creating a new table, the worksheet's first row is a good place to begin. (You can always shift the table down later by putting your cursor in the top row, and then choosing Home→Cells→Insert→Insert Sheet Rows.) This first row of the table is where you enter any column titles you want to use, as explained in the next step.

NOTE Be careful when placing content in the cells directly *beneath* your table. If your table expands too far down, you'll run up against these filled-up cells. Although you can use commands like Home→Cells→Insert→Insert Sheet Rows to add some extra space when things get crowded, it's always better to start off with plenty of breathing room.

2. **Enter the column titles for your table, one column title for each category you want to create.**

   If you want, you can start to add entries underneath the column headings now (in the row directly below the column titles). Or just jump straight to the next step to create the table.

TIP To create the perfect table, you need to divide your data into categories. For example, if you're building a table of names and addresses, you probably want your columns to hold the standard info you see on every form ever created: First Name, Last Name, Street, City, and so on. The columns you create are the basis for all the searching, sorting, and filtering you'll do later. For instance, if you have First Name and City columns, you can sort your contacts by first name or by city.

3. **Make sure your cursor is currently positioned somewhere inside the table (anywhere in the column title row works well), and then choose Insert→Tables→Table.**

   Excel scans the nearby cells, and then selects all the cells that it thinks are part of your table. Once Excel determines the bounds of your table, the Create Table window appears, as shown in Figure 14-1.

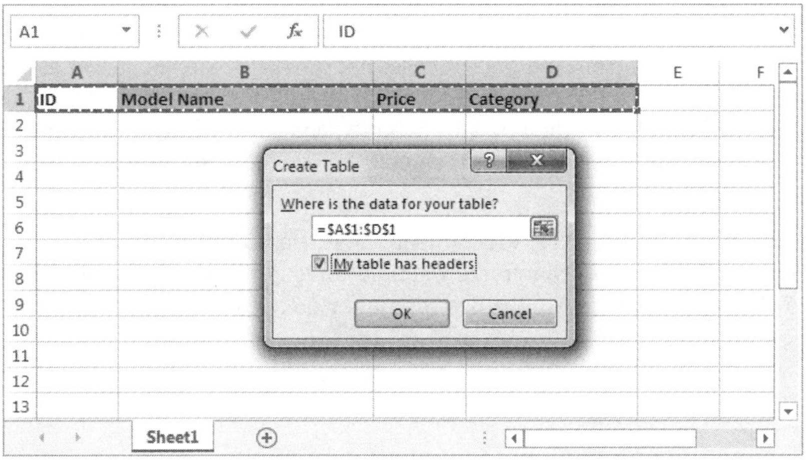

FIGURE 14-1

The Create Table window displays the cell references for the currently selected range. In this example, the selection includes only the headings (there's no data yet). You can type in a new range. Or, click the worksheet icon at the right end of the cell range box and then select the cells you want on the worksheet.

4. **Make sure the "My table has headers" checkbox is turned on. This option tells Excel you're using the first row just for column headers. Then click OK.**

   Excel transforms your cells into a table, like the one shown in Figure 14-2. You can tell that your ordinary range of cells has become a genuine table by a few telltale signs. First, tables start out with automatic formatting that gives each row a shaded background (alternating between blue and white). Second, the column headings appear in white letters on a blue background, and each one includes a drop-down arrow that you can use for quick filtering (a feature you'll explore on page 430).

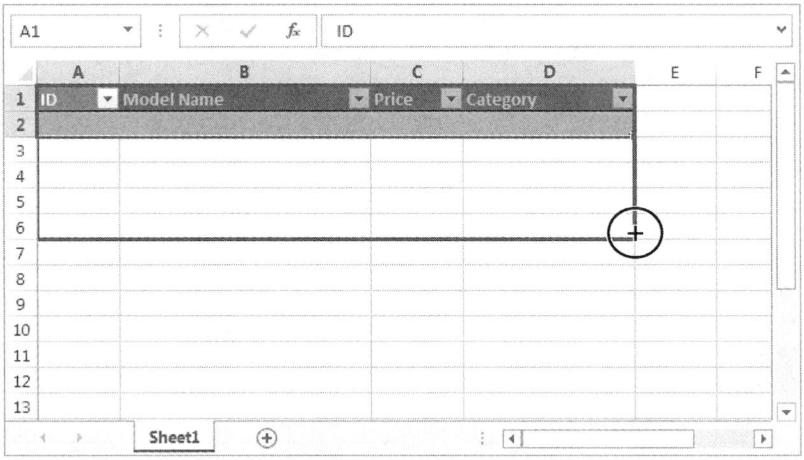

FIGURE 14-2

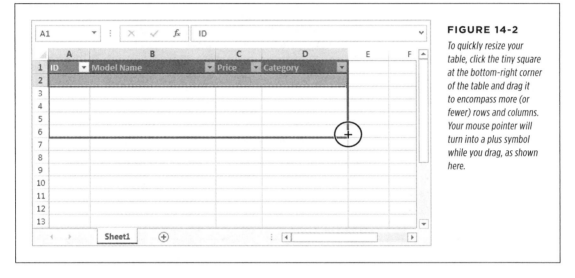

To quickly resize your table, click the tiny square at the bottom-right corner of the table and drag it to encompass more (or fewer) rows and columns. Your mouse pointer will turn into a plus symbol while you drag, as shown here.

If you create a table from a group of cells that don't include column titles, don't turn on the "My table has headers" checkbox. When you create the table, Excel adds a row of columns at the top with generic names like Column1, Column2, and so on. You can click these cells, and then edit the column titles, to something more descriptive (Figure 14-3).

Tables have a fixed structure, which means that every row has exactly the same number of columns. You can create multiple tables in the same worksheet, but you're often better off placing them in separate worksheets so you can more easily manage them.

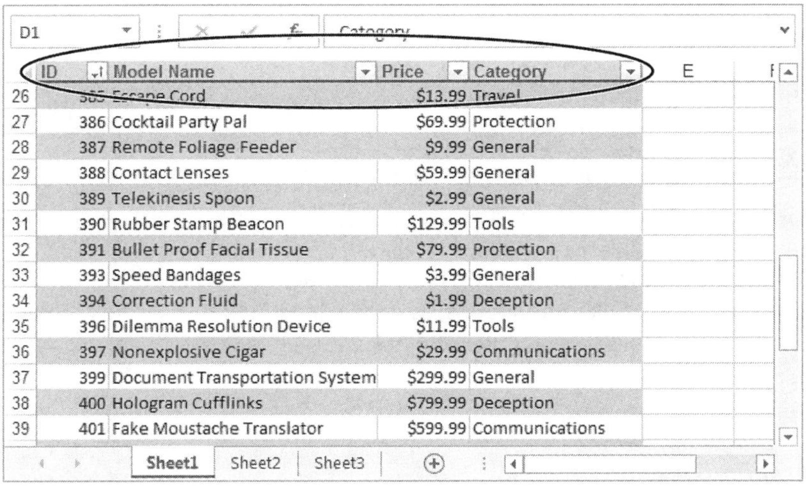

FIGURE 14-3

Here's one unsung frill in every table. When you can't see the column headers any longer (because you scrolled down the page), the column buttons atop the worksheet grid change from letters (like A, B, C) to your custom headers (like Product ID, Model Name, and Price). This way, you never forget what column you're in, and, because the drop-down column menus come along for the ride, you don't need to scroll up to use the columns' sorting and filtering features.

Formatting a Table

When you move to a cell in a table, Excel adds a new tab to the ribbon—the Table Tools | Design tab. This tab has five sections:

- **Properties**, which lets you rename and resize your table. (The table name is important only if you choose to use it in a formula, as described on page 442.)
- **Tools**, which lets you use pivot tables (described in Chapter 26), find duplicate rows (page 436), and convert your table back to ordinary cells.
- **External Table Data**, which lets you work with external data (like records drawn from a database) using an Excel table. (You'll learn more about this in Chapter 27.)
- **Table Style Options** and **Table Styles**, which help you make your table look pretty.

Every table starts out with some basic formatting, and you can use the ribbon and the Format Cells window (as discussed in Chapter 5) to further change its appearance. However, Excel gives you an even better option—you can use *table styles.*

A table style is a collection of formatting settings that apply to an entire table. The nice part about table styles is that Excel remembers your style settings. If you add new rows to a table, Excel automatically adds the right cell formatting. Or, if you delete a row, Excel adjusts the formatting of all the cells underneath to make sure the *banding* (the alternating pattern of cell shading that makes each row easier to read) stays consistent.

When you first create a table, you start out with a fairly ordinary set of colors: a gray-blue combination that makes your table stand out from the rest of the worksheet. By choosing another table style, you can apply a different set of colors and borders to your table.

NOTE Excel's standard table styles don't change the fonts in a table. To change fonts, you can change the theme (page 172), or select some cells, and then, from the ribbon's Home→Font section, pick the font you want.

To choose a new table style, head to the ribbon's Table Tools | Design→Table Styles section. You'll see a gallery of options, as shown in Figure 14-4. As you move over a table style, Excel uses its live preview feature to change the table, giving you a sneak peak at how your table would look with that style.

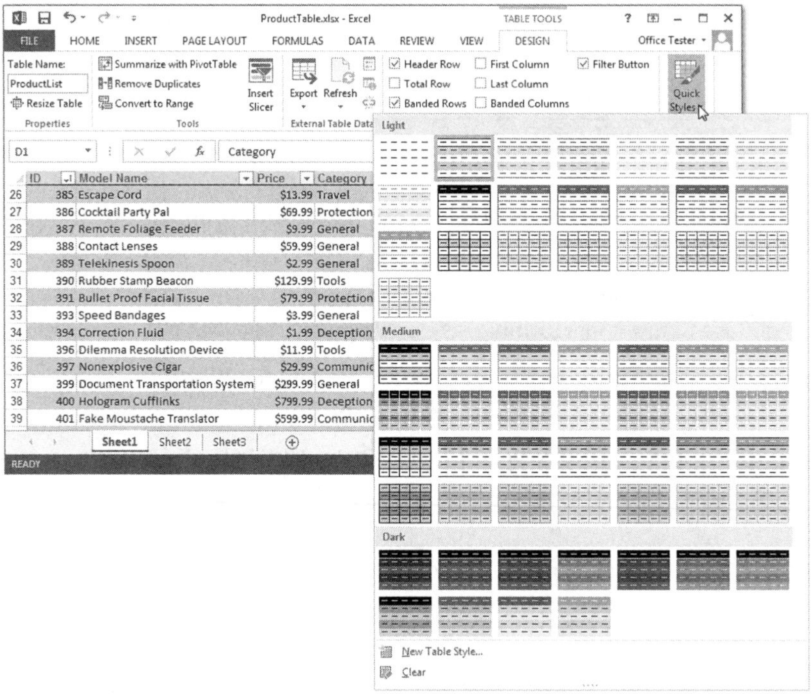

FIGURE 14-4

Depending on your Excel window's width, you may see the table style gallery in the ribbon. If there's not enough room, you see a Quick Styles button that you need to click to display a drop-down style gallery (as shown here).

NOTE Notice that some table styles use banding, while others don't.

Table styles work like cell styles, which you learned about on page 166. Like cell styles, they let you standardize and reuse formatting. Table styles, however, include a whole package of settings that tell Excel how to format different portions of the table, including the headers, first and last columns, the summary row (page 444), and so on. To get a better feel for the variety of options in a table style, you can create your own by clicking the drop-down arrow in the Table Tools | Design→Table Styles section, and then choosing New Table Style. You'll see a New Table Quick Style window that lets you go through the somewhat painstaking process of tweaking the formatting for each part of a table (Figure 14-5).

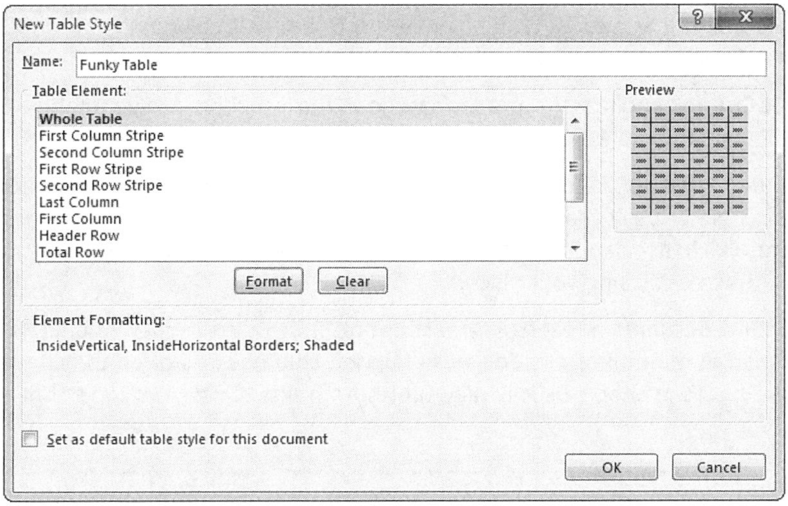

FIGURE 14-5

To set the formatting for part of a table, select the part in the Table Element list, and then click Format. Excel opens a slimmed-down Format Cells window that includes only the Font, Border, and Fill tabs. For example, to change the font for a whole table, select Whole Table, click Format, and then make your changes. If you think you've created the perfect table style, you can turn on the "Set as default table quick style" checkbox so Excel uses it whenever you create a new table in this workbook.

The new styles you create appear in the table style gallery, under the heading "Custom." To modify one of your custom styles, right-click it and choose Modify.

NOTE You can't edit the built-in table styles. However, you can create a duplicate copy of a built-in style, and then change that. To do so, right-click a built-in style in the gallery, and choose Duplicate.

Most of the time, it's not worth creating your own table styles because it's simply too much work (and the prebuilt table styles give you a good selection of formatting choices). However, you'll notice that the built-in table styles have a limited set of colors. Excel limits them because table styles use colors from the current theme, which ensures that your table meshes well with the rest of your worksheet (assuming you've been sticking to theme colors elsewhere). To get different colors for your tables, you can choose a new theme by selecting Page Layout→Themes→Themes gallery. Page 172 has more about themes.

Along with the table style and theme settings, you have a few more options to fine-tune your table's appearance. Head over to the ribbon's Table Tools | Design→Table Style Options section, where you see a group of checkboxes, each of which lets you toggle on or off different table elements:

- **Header Row** lets you show or hide the row with column titles at the top of the table. You'll rarely want to remove this option. Not only are the column headers informative, they include the drop-down lists for sorting and filtering your table, as you'll explore in this later.
- **Total Row** lets you show or hide the row that displays summary calculations at the bottom of your table. You'll learn how to configure this row on page 444.
- **First Column** applies different formatting to the first column in your table, if it's defined in the table style.
- **Last Column** applies different formatting to the last column in your table, if it's defined in the table style.
- **Banded Rows** applies different formatting to every other row, if it's defined in the table style. Usually, the banded row appears with a background fill. Large-table lovers like to use banding because it makes it easier to scan a full row from right to left without losing your place.
- **Banded Columns** applies different formatting to every other column, if it's defined in the table style. Folks use banded columns less often than banded rows, because people usually read tables from side to side, not top to bottom.

UP TO SPEED

The Difference Between Excel Worksheets and Databases

An Excel table uses some of the same concepts as a database—namely, the idea of records and fields. However, databases and Excel worksheets are two very different entities.

For starters, databases—which programs like Microsoft Access and SQL Server let you create—have much stricter rules than Excel worksheets. Before you can add any data to a table in a database, you must carefully define the table. You need to specify not only the name of each field, but also the type of information the field can contain. Although Excel provides some of these so-called data validation features (which you'll explore in Chapter 21), the program isn't nearly as strict about it—validation is completely optional. Also, unlike Excel, most modern databases are *relational*, which means they contain multiple tables that have specific links to one another. For example, a relational database might tie together customers in one table and their order history in another. In Excel, a worksheet can hold multiple tables of data, but it's up to you to try to combine their data.

Most importantly, databases play a dramatically different role in the world of business. Typically, Excel is an *end user* program, which means ordinary mortals who generally know how to create an Excel file, design what it's going to look like, and then fill it up with data can use it. Ex-math majors, on the other hand, usually create databases, and they store information, behind the scenes, that non-programmer types end up using. For example, every time you use Google or search on Amazon for something to buy, you're actually seeing answers that have been stored in, and generated by, massive and powerful databases. In Chapter 27, you'll see how you can use Excel to retrieve information from a database, and then analyze it in a worksheet.

Editing a Table

Once you create a table, you can perform three basic editing tasks:

- **Edit a record.** This part's easy. Just modify cell values as you would in any ordinary worksheet.
- **Delete a record.** First, go to the row you want to delete (you can be in any column), and then choose Home→Cells→Delete→Delete Table Rows. Excel removes the row and shrinks the table automatically. For faster access that bypasses the ribbon altogether, just right-click a cell in the appropriate row, and then choose Delete→Table Rows.
- **Add a new record.** To add a record, head to the bottom of the table, and then type a new set of values just underneath the last row in the table. Once you finish typing the first value, Excel expands the table automatically, as shown in Figure 14-6.

If you want to insert a row but don't want it to be at the bottom of the table, you can head to your chosen spot, and then choose Home→Cells→Insert→Insert Table Rows Above (or right-click, and then choose Insert→Table Rows Above). Excel inserts a new blank row immediately *above* the current row.

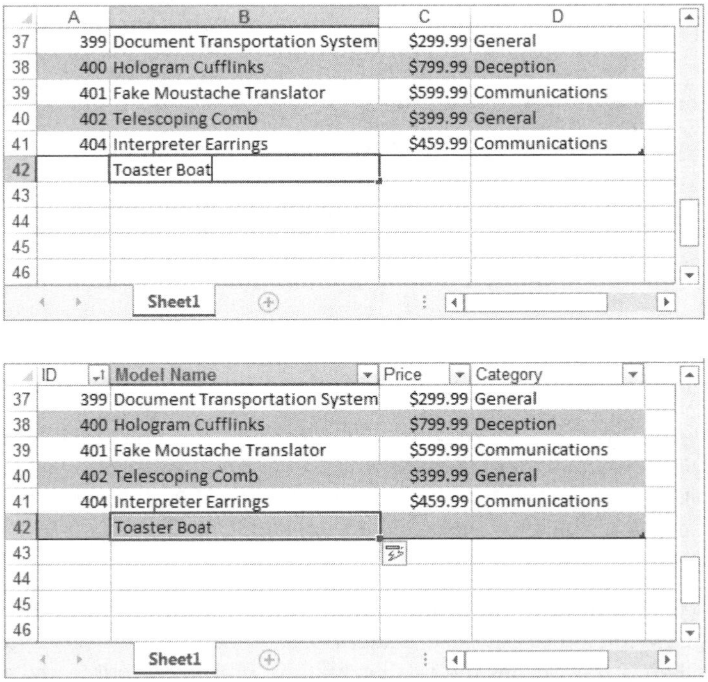

FIGURE 14-6

Top: Here, you're adding a new record just under the current table.

Bottom: Once you enter at least one column of information and move to another cell, Excel adds the new row to the table and formats it. Don't worry—if Excel expands a table against your wishes, you aren't completely powerless. To correct Excel's mistake, click the smart tag icon that appears immediately next to the newly added column (it looks like a lightning bolt) and choose Undo Table AutoExpansion (to return your table to its previous size) or Stop Automatically Expanding Tables (to turn off this behavior altogether).

NOTE Notice that when you insert or remove rows, you're inserting or removing *table* rows, not *worksheet* rows. For example, if you have a table with three columns and you delete a row, Excel removes three cells, and then shifts up any table row underneath. But any information in the same row that exists *outside* the table (say, in the columns to the right of it) is unaffected.

You may also decide to change the structure of your table by adding or removing columns. Once again, you'll find this task is like inserting or removing columns in an ordinary worksheet. (The big difference, as shown in Figure 14-7, is that any rows or columns *outside* your table remain unaffected when you add new rows or columns.)

FIGURE 14-7

Excel makes an effort to leave the rest of your worksheet alone when you change your table's structure. For example, when you expand a table vertically or horizontally, Excel moves cells out of the way only when it absolutely needs more space. The example here is a case in point. Compare the before (top) and after (bottom) pictures: Even though the table in the bottom figure has a new column, it hasn't affected the data underneath the table, which still occupies the same column. The same holds true when you delete columns.

If you want to add a column to the right side of the table, just start typing in the blank column immediately to the right of the table. When you finish, Excel automatically merges that column into the table, in the same way that it expands to include new rows. Excel automatically gives the new column a generic title, like Column1, which you can then edit.

To add a new column somewhere inside your table, move to the column where you want your new column to go. Then, select Home→Cells→Insert→Insert Table Columns to the Left. Excel pushes the existing column over to the right—and also bumps any other columns that are to the right of that column further over—to make room for your new column.

To delete a column, move to one of its cells, and then choose Home→Cells→ Delete→Delete Table Column.

Finally, you can always convert your snazzy table back to an ordinary collection of cells. Just click anywhere in the table, and then choose Table Tools | Design→Tools→ Convert to Range. But then, of course, you don't get to play with your table toys anymore.

Selecting Parts of a Table

Once you create a table, Excel provides you with some nice time-saving tools. For example, Excel makes it easy to select a portion of a table, like an individual row or column. Here's how it works:

- **To select a column**, position your mouse cursor over the column header. When it changes to a down-pointing arrow, click once to select all the values in the column. Click a second time to select all the values plus the column header.
- **To select a row**, position your mouse cursor over the left edge of the row until it turns to a right-pointing arrow, and then click once.
- **To select the entire table**, position your mouse at the top-left corner until it turns into an arrow that points down and to the right. Click once to select all the values in the table, and click twice to select all the values plus the column headers.

Figure 14-8 shows an example.

	ID	Model Name	Price	Category
2	355	Rain Racer 2000	$1,499.99	Travel
3	356	Edible Tape	$3.99	General
4	357	Escape Vehicle (Air)	$2.99	Travel
5	358	Extracting Tool	$199.00	Tools
6	359	Escape Vehicle (Water)	$1,299.99	Travel
7	360	Communications Device	$49.99	Communications
8	362	Persuasive Pencil	$1.99	Communications
9	363	Multi-Purpose Rubber Band	$1.99	Munitions
10	364	Universal Repair System	$4.99	Tools
11	365	Effective Flashlight	$9.99	Tools
12	367	The Incredible Versatile Paperclip	$1.49	Munitions

FIGURE 14-8

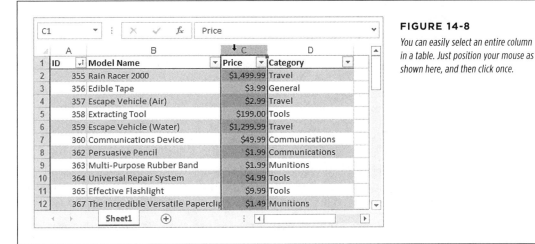

You can easily select an entire column in a table. Just position your mouse as shown here, and then click once.

Once you select a row, column, or the entire table, you can apply extra formatting, or use another Excel feature like validation (page 640) or charting (Chapter 17). However, changing a part of a table isn't exactly like changing a bunch of cells. For example, if you give 10 cells a hot pink background fill, that's all you get—10 hot pink cells. But if you give a column a hot pink background fill, your formatting change may initially affect 10 cells, but every time you add a new value in that column, it also gets the hot pink background. This behavior—where Excel recognizes that you changed parts of a table and goes on to apply those same changes to any new rows and columns—is called *stickiness*.

Sorting a Table

Sorting lets you order the items in your table alphabetically or numerically according to the information in a column. By using the correct criteria, you can make sure the information you're interested in appears at the top of the column, making it easier to find items in your table.

Before you can sort your data, you need to choose a *sorting key*—the piece of information that Excel uses to order your records. For example, to sort a table of products so the cheapest (or most expensive) products appear at the top of the table, you'd use the Price column as the sorting key.

In addition to choosing a sorting key, you also need to decide whether you want to use ascending or descending order. Ascending order, which is most common, organizes numbers from smallest to largest, dates from oldest to most recent, and text in alphabetical order. (If you have more than one type of data in the same column—which is rarely a good idea—text appears first, followed by numbers and dates, then true or false values, and finally error values.) In descending order, the order is reversed.

NOTE Remember, it's technically possible to have numbers in Excel that are stored as text, as described in Chapter 2; simply prefix these values with an apostrophe ('). For example, you might store a number as text if you're entering numeric content that doesn't convey a numeric value, like a Social Security number. Excel sorts these values alphabetically, which means that it looks at the text string one character at a time until it finds a difference. Thus, even though 42 is less than 102 in a numeric sort, the text *42* is greater than *102* in an alphabetic sort, because the first character *4* comes after *1*.

Applying a Simple Sort Order

To apply a new sort order, choose the column you want to use as your sort key. Click the drop-down box at the right side of the column header, and then choose one of the menu commands that starts with the word "Sort." The exact wording depends on the type of data in the column, as follows:

- **If your column contains numbers**, you see "Sort Smallest to Largest" and "Sort Largest to Smallest."
- **If your column contains text**, you see "Sort A to Z" and "Sort Z to A" (see Figure 14-9).
- **If your column contains dates**, you see "Sort Oldest to Newest" and "Sort Newest to Oldest."

When you choose an option, Excel immediately reorders the records, and then places a tiny arrow in the column header to indicate that you used this column for your sort. However, Excel doesn't keep re-sorting your data when you make changes or add new records (after all, it would be pretty distracting to have your records jump around unexpectedly). If you make changes and want to reapply the sort, go to the column header menu and choose the same sort option again.

If you click a second column, and then choose Sort Ascending or Sort Descending, the new sort order replaces your previous sort order. In other words, the column headers let you sort your records quickly, but you can't sort by more than one column at a time.

Sorting with Multiple Criteria

Simple table sorting runs into trouble when you have duplicate values. Take the product table sorted by category in Figure 14-9, for example. All the products in the Communications category appear first, followed by products in the Deception category, and so on. However, Excel doesn't make any effort to sort products that are in the *same* category. For example, if you have a bunch of products in the Communications category, they appear in whatever order they were in in your worksheet, which may not be what you want. In this case, you're better off using *multiple sort criteria.*

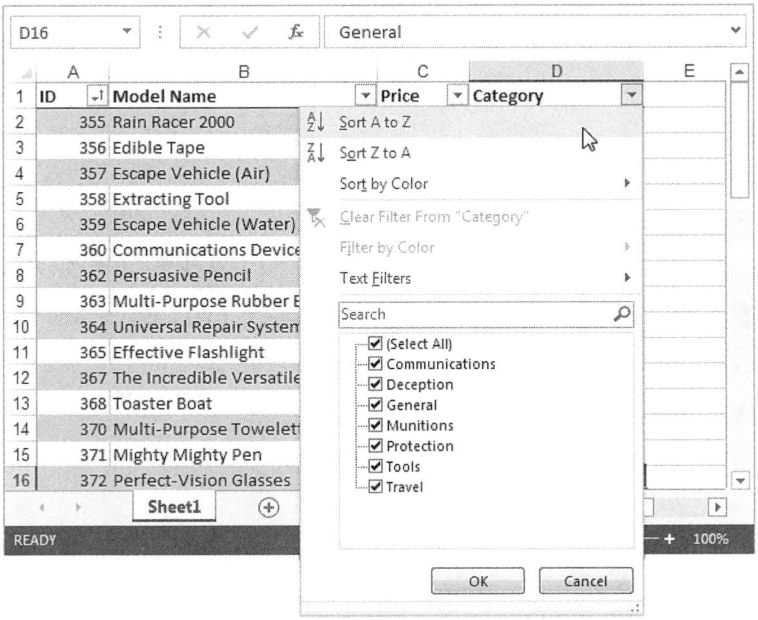

FIGURE 14-9

A quick click is all it takes to order records in ascending order by their category names. You don't need to take any action to create these handy drop-down lists—Excel automatically provides them for every table.

With multiple sort criteria, Excel orders a table using more than one sorting key. The second sorting key springs into action only if there are duplicate values in the first sorting key. For example, if you sort by Category and Model Name, Excel first separates the records into alphabetically ordered category groups. It then sorts the products in each category in order of their model name.

To use multiple sort criteria, follow these steps.

1. **Move to any one of the cells in your table, and then choose Home→Editing→Sort & Filter→Custom Sort.**

   Excel selects all the data in your table, and then displays the Sort window (see Figure 14-10) where you can specify the sorting keys you want to use.

TIP You can use the Home→Editing→Sort & Filter→Custom Sort command with any row-based data, including information that's not in a table. When you use it with non-table data, Excel automatically selects the range of cells it believes constitutes your table.

2. **Fill in the information for the first sort key in the Column, Sort On, and Order columns.**

   Figure 14-10 shows how it works.

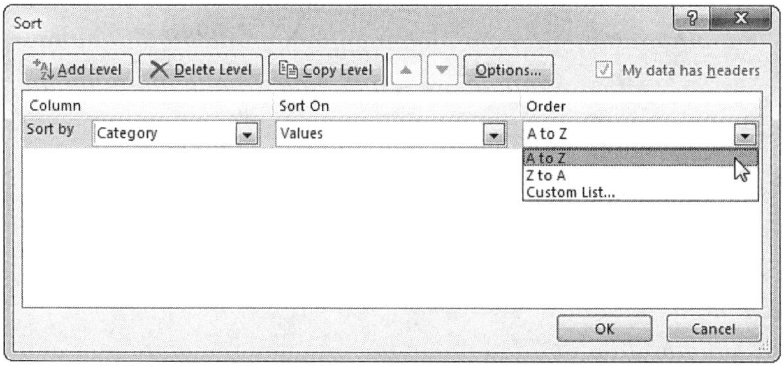

FIGURE 14-10

To define a sorting key, you need to identify the column you want Excel to use (in this example, Category). Next, pick the information you want to sort from that column, which is almost always the actual cell values (Values). Finally, you need to choose the order for arranging values, which depends on the type of data. For text values, as in this example, you can pick A to Z, Z to A, or Custom List (page 63).

3. **To add another level of sorting, click Add Level, and then follow the instructions in step 2 to configure it.**

   You can repeat this step to add as many sorting levels as you want (Figure 14-11). Remember, it makes sense to add more levels of sorting only if there's a possibility of duplicate value in the levels you've added so far. For example, if you've sorted a bunch of names by last name, you want to sort by first name, because some people may share the same last name. However, it's probably not worth it to add a third sort on the middle initial, because very few people share the same first and last name.

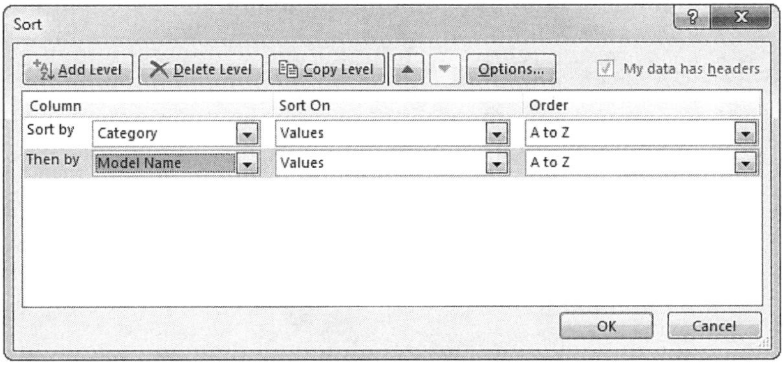

FIGURE 14-11

This example shows two sorting keys: the Category column and the Model Name column. The Category column may contain duplicate entries, which Excel sorts in turn according to the text in the Model Name column. When you use multiple sort keys, make sure they're in the right order. If you need to rearrange your sorting, select a sort key, and then click the arrow buttons to move it up the list (so it's applied first) or down the list (so it's applied later).

4. **Optionally, click the Options button to configure a few finer points about how Excel sorts your data.**

   For example, you can turn on case-sensitive sorting, which is ordinarily switched off. If you switch it on, *travel* appears before *Travel*.

5. **Click OK.**

   Excel sorts your entire table based on the criteria you so carefully specified (Figure 14-12).

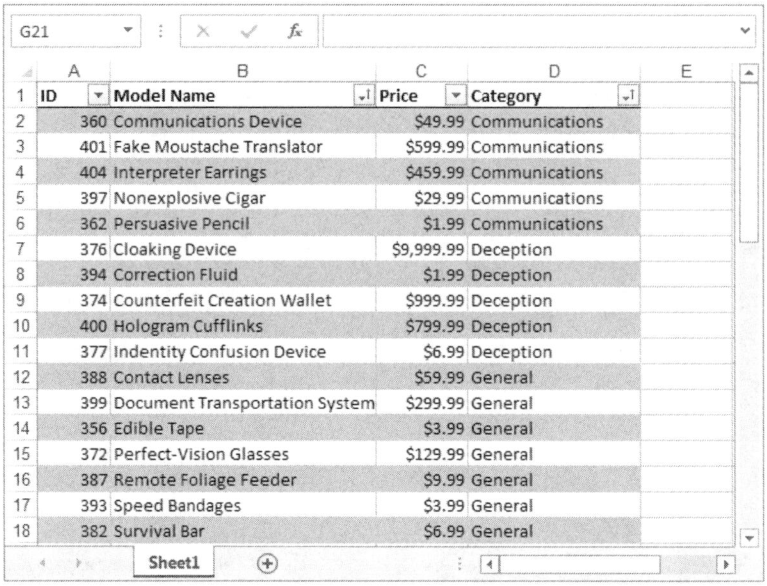

	ID	Model Name	Price	Category
2	360	Communications Device	$49.99	Communications
3	401	Fake Moustache Translator	$599.99	Communications
4	404	Interpreter Earrings	$459.99	Communications
5	397	Nonexplosive Cigar	$29.99	Communications
6	362	Persuasive Pencil	$1.99	Communications
7	376	Cloaking Device	$9,999.99	Deception
8	394	Correction Fluid	$1.99	Deception
9	374	Counterfeit Creation Wallet	$999.99	Deception
10	400	Hologram Cufflinks	$799.99	Deception
11	377	Indentity Confusion Device	$6.99	Deception
12	388	Contact Lenses	$59.99	General
13	399	Document Transportation System	$299.99	General
14	356	Edible Tape	$3.99	General
15	372	Perfect-Vision Glasses	$129.99	General
16	387	Remote Foliage Feeder	$9.99	General
17	393	Speed Bandages	$3.99	General
18	382	Survival Bar	$6.99	General

FIGURE 14-12

This worksheet is the result of the following sort settings: alphabetically ordered categories, each of which contains a subgroup of products that are themselves in alphabetical order.

POWER USERS' CLINIC

Sorting with a Custom List

Most of the time, you'll want to stick with the standard sorting orders. For example, you'll put numbers in numeric order, dates in chronological order, and text in alphabetical order. But not always. You might, for instance, have good reason to arrange the categories in Figure 14-12 in a different order that puts more important categories at the top of the table. Or you may have text values that have special meaning and are almost always used in a specific non-alphabetical order, like the days of the week (Sunday, Monday, Tuesday, and so on) or calendar months (January, February, March, April, and so on).

You can deal with these scenarios with a custom list that specifies your sort order. In the Order column, choose Custom List. This opens the Custom List window, where you can choose an existing list or create a new one by selecting NEW LIST, and then typing in your values. (Page 63 has more on creating specialized lists.) Figure 14-13 shows an example.

Custom list sorting works best when you have a relatively small number of values that never change. If you have dozens of different values, it's probably too tedious to type them all into a custom list.

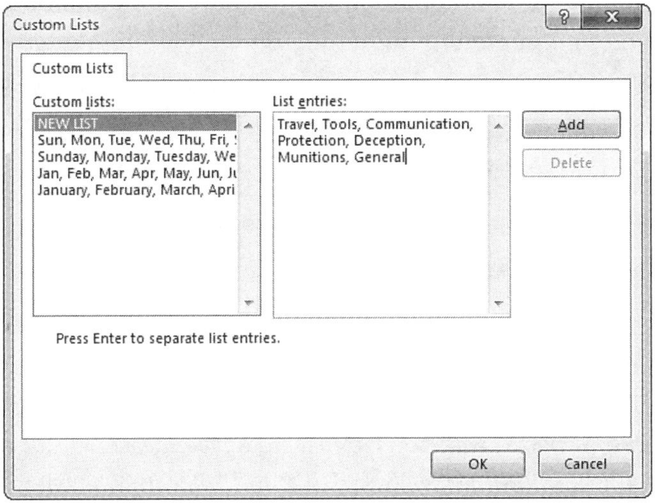

FIGURE 14-13

Using a custom list for your sort order, you can arrange your categories so that Travel always appears at the top, as shown here. Once you finish creating a custom list, click Add to store the list for future use.

Sorting by Color

One of Excel's weirdest sorting options is Sort By Color, which lets you arrange records based on the *color* of each cell. For example, with color sorting you can make cells with a hot pink background stick to the top of your table.

You can color-sort by background color or by font color. Either way, the first step is to make sure that some of your cells have a different color from the rest. You can change the color of a cell by hand—just select it and use the Home→Font→Fill Color command (for the background) or the Home→Font→Font Color command (for the font). But color sorting is really designed to work in conjunction with conditional formatting (page 179). Typically, you'll create a conditional format that changes the foreground or background color of the cells you're interested in, and you'll then use color sorting to make sure those cells appear first in your table.

The quickest way to color-sort is to pick just one background color or font color. The cells with that color are then sent to the top of your table. To sort this way, open the drop-down column list, choose Sort By Color, and then choose your color. Excel helps out by letting you pick from a list of all the background colors that are currently applied to cells in that column. (This list doesn't include the background color that's applied from the table style.)

If you want to get a bit more sophisticated, you can sort with *multiple* colors. To do this, you need to create a custom sort and add a separate sort key for each color. So if you want to sort cells in the order red, green, yellow, and then no color, you need to add three sorting keys. Choose Data→Sort & Filter→Sort, and then add three rules, as shown in Figure 14-14. Using the Sort On column, you can choose to sort using the background color (choose Cell Color) or the font color (Font Color).

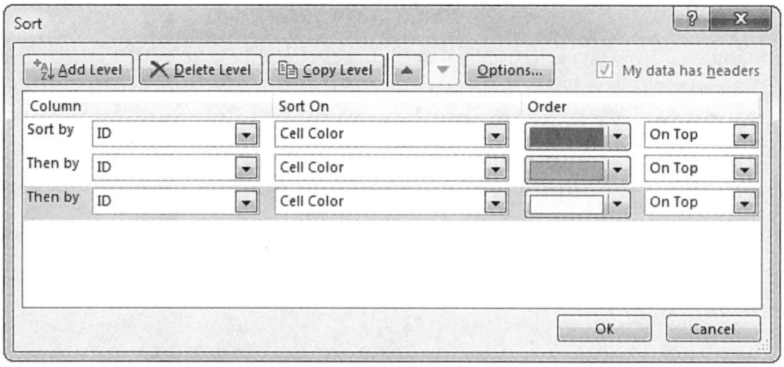

FIGURE 14-14

In this table, rows with a red background appear at the top of the sorted column, followed by green and then yellow rows (followed by any rows without a background color). To send a color to the bottom of a table instead of the top, change On Top to On Bottom.

The custom sort feature also works with icon sets, a feature that's described on page 623. In this case, you must choose Cell Icon from the Sort On column. Same idea, but instead of picking a color that should rise to the top of the list, you pick one of the icons from your icon set.

Filtering a Table

Sorting is great for ordering your data, but it may not be enough to tame large piles of info. You can try another useful technique, *filtering*, which lets you limit the data a table displays so you see only the info you want. Filtering may seem like a small convenience, but if your table contains hundreds or thousands of rows, filtering is vital for your day-to-day worksheet sanity.

Here are some situations where filtering is especially useful:

- To pluck out important information, like the number of accounts that currently have a balance due. Filtering lets you see just the information you need, saving you hours of headaches.
- To print a report that shows only the customers who live in a specific city.
- To calculate information, like sums and averages, for products in a specific group. You can use a function like the totals row (page 444) or the SUBTOTAL() function (page 445), to perform calculations using only cells that are currently visible.

There are several ways to filter a table, and the following sections explain them all.

Hiding Specific Values

Simple filtering, like sorting, uses the drop-down column headings at the top of your table. When you click the drop-down arrow, Excel shows a list of all the distinct values in that column. Figure 14-15 and Figure 14-16 show how filtering works on the Category column.

To remove a filter, open the drop-down column menu, and then choose Clear Filter.

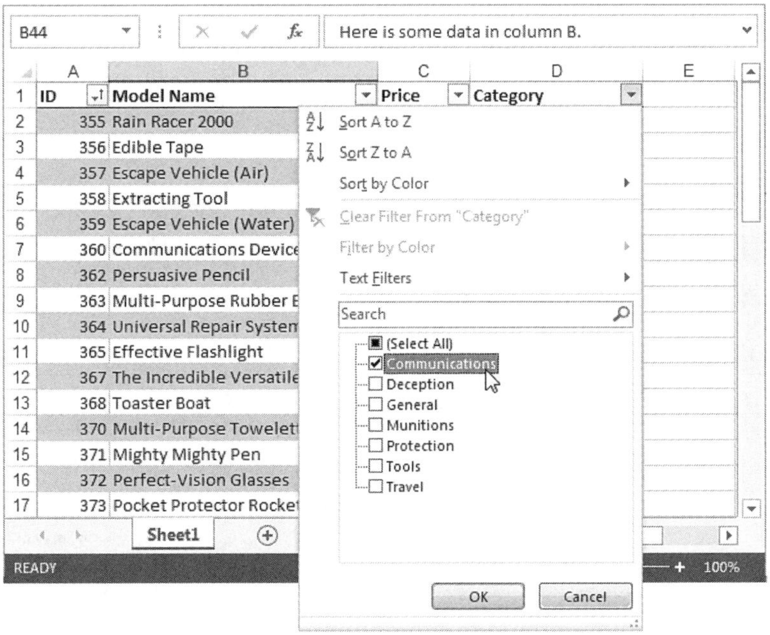

FIGURE 14-15

Initially, each value has a checkmark next to it. Clear the checkmark to hide rows with that value. To home in on just a few items, clear the Select All checkmark to remove all the checkmarks, and then choose just the rows you want to see in your table. Either way, remember to click OK to make your choices take effect.

FIGURE 14-16

If you select Communications and nothing else from the Category list in the product table example, the table displays only the five products in the Communications category. Excel takes several steps to make the situation more apparent. First, it adds a strange funnel icon to the Category header. Second, it switches the color of the row numbers next to your table from black to blue. Third, Excel adds a status bar message that indicates the number of filtered matches and the total number of records in the list.

The drop-down column lists give you an easy way to filter out specific rows. However, in many situations you'll want a little more intelligence in your filtering. For example, imagine you filter a list of products to focus on those that top $100. You could scroll through the list of values, and remove the checkmark next to every price that's lower than $100. What a pain in the neck that would be.

Thankfully, Excel has more filtering features that can really help you out here. Based on the type of data in your column (text, a number, or date values), Excel adds a range of useful filter options to the drop-down column lists. You'll see how this all works in the following sections.

Filtering Dates

You can filter dates that fall before or after another date, or you can use preset periods like last week, last month, next month, year-to-date, and so on.

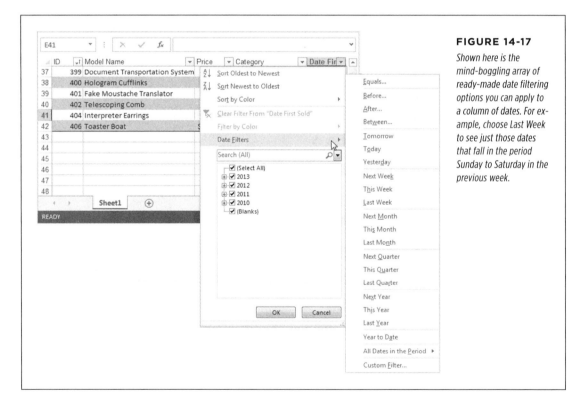

To filter by date, open the drop-down column list, and then choose Date Filters. Figure 14-17 shows what you see.

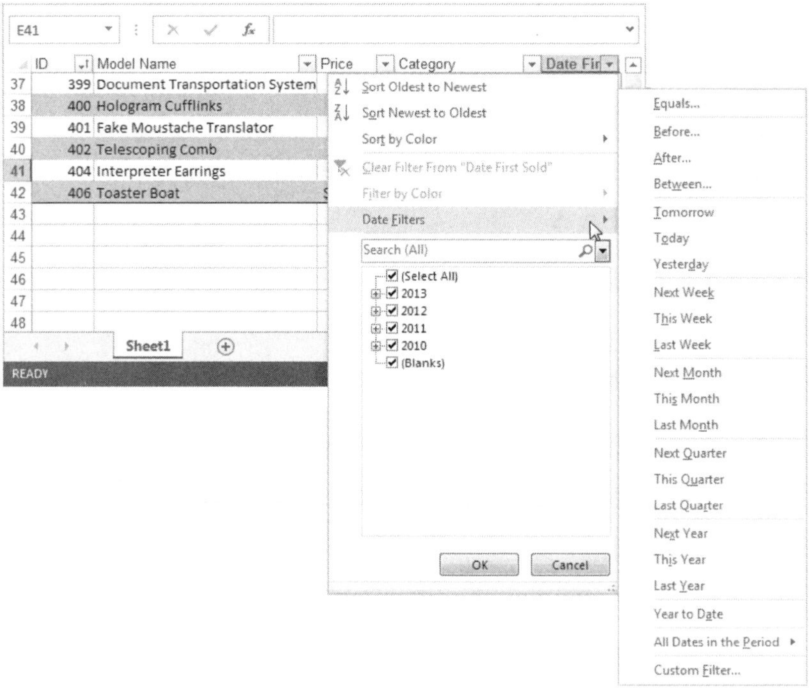

FIGURE 14-17

Shown here is the mind-boggling array of ready-made date filtering options you can apply to a column of dates. For example, choose Last Week to see just those dates that fall in the period Sunday to Saturday in the previous week.

WORKAROUND WORKSHOP

The Disappearing Cells

Table filtering has one quirk. When you filter a table, Excel hides the rows that contain the filtered records. For example, in Figure 14-16 notice that the row numbers jump straight from 8 to 36, indicating that all the rows in between are hidden. In fact, all Excel really does is shrink each of these rows to have a height of 0 so they're neatly out of sight. The problem? When Excel hides a row, it hides all the data in that row, *even if the data isn't a part of the table.*

That means that if you place a formula in one of the cells to the right of the table, this formula may disappear from your worksheet temporarily when you filter the table! This behavior is quite a bit different from what happens if you delete a row, in which case cells outside the table aren't affected.

If you frequently use filtering, you may want to circumvent this problem by putting your formulas underneath or above the table. Generally, putting the formulas above the table is the most convenient choice, because the cells don't move as the table expands or contracts.

Filtering Numbers

For numbers, you can filter values that match exactly, numbers that are smaller or larger than a specified number, or numbers that are above or below average.

To use number filtering, open the drop-down column list, choose Number Filters, and then pick one of the filter options. For example, imagine you're trying to show just the most expensive products in the product list. You can accomplish this quite quickly with a number filter. Open the drop-down column list for the Price column, and then choose Number Filters→Greater Than Or Equal To. A window appears where you can apply the $100 minimum (Figure 14-18).

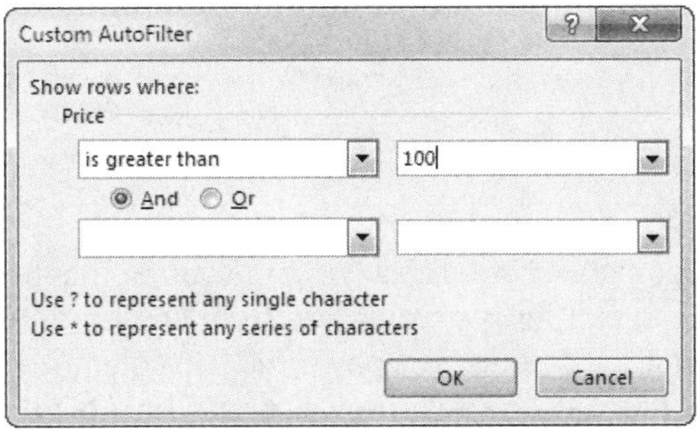

FIGURE 14-18

This window lets you complete the Greater Than Or Equal To filter. It matches all products that are $100 or more. You can use the bottom portion of the window (left blank in this example) to supply a second filter condition that either further restricts (choose And) or supplements (choose Or) your matches.

Filtering Text

For text, you can filter values that match exactly, or values that contain a piece of text. To apply text filtering, open the drop-down column list, and then choose Text Filters.

When you filter text, you can get even more versatile results using wildcards. The asterisk (*) matches any series of characters, while the question mark (?) matches a single character. So the filter expression *Category equals T** matches any category that starts with the letter T. The filter expression *Category equals T????* matches any five-letter category that starts with T.

Applying Filters with Slicers

You just learned the traditional way to filter a table—pick a column, click its drop-down arrow, and adjust the filtering options. Most of the time, this is the way Excel pros operate.

However, Excel also has a specialized tool, called *slicers*, that gives you another way to apply filtering: using a floating panel that you position anywhere you want on your worksheet (Figure 14-19).

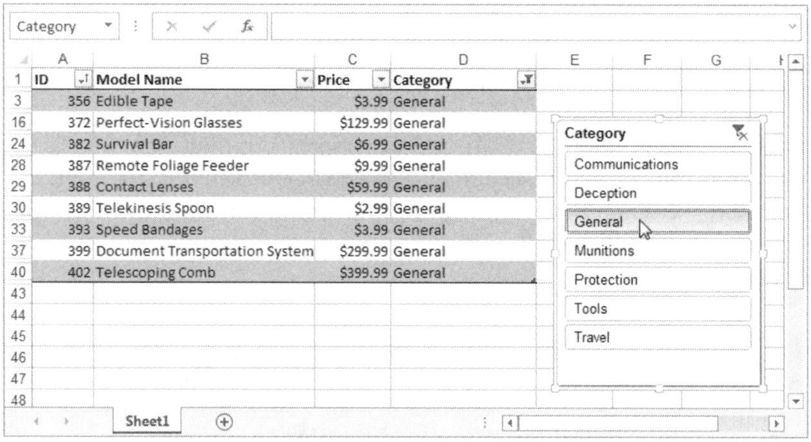

FIGURE 14-19

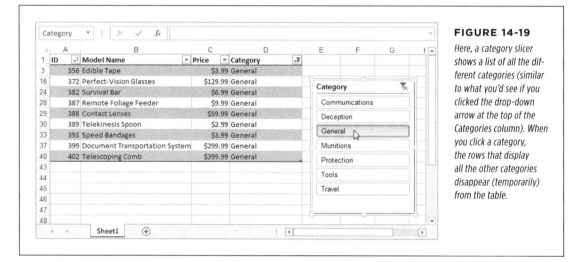

Here, a category slicer shows a list of all the different categories (similar to what you'd see if you clicked the drop-down arrow at the top of the Categories column). When you click a category, the rows that display all the other categories disappear (temporarily) from the table.

Slicers look attractive enough on your worksheet, but why would you bother using them? After all, clicking categories in a slicer is no different from choosing them from the list in a column header. In fact, slicers are *less* powerful than column filters because they don't let you exclude ranges of values. They also take up a fair bit of space on your worksheet.

The real role of slicers is to let you create a sort of personalized filter "control panel." For example, imagine you're preparing a spreadsheet for your boss, who wants to review the sales of different stores. Rather than force her to click column headers and learn the finer points of tables, you can slap a tailor-made slicer for the Stores column right next to the table. Then, your boss can investigate the data for different stores with just a few quick and convenient clicks on the slicer, no Excel expertise required.

NOTE Slicers make the most sense when you have huge amounts of information—for example, thousands of records that you extract from a database (as described in Chapter 27).

Here's how to create a slicer:

1. **Click somewhere inside your table.**

2. **Choose Table Tools | Design→Tools→Insert Slicer.**

   The Insert Slicers window appears. It lists all the fields in your table, with a checkbox next to each one.

3. **Add a checkmark next to the field you want to use for filtering.**

   For example, to create the category slicer in Figure 14-19, you would add a checkmark next to the Category column. To add several slicers at once, just add a checkmark next to several fields.

4. **Click OK.**

   Excel adds a separate floating window for each slicer.

5. **Position your slicer.**

   To move a slicer, move your mouse pointer over the border, so it turns into a four-way arrow. Then, drag the slicer to the position where you want it. If possible, put the slider in a place where it won't obscure your worksheet data.

   To resize a slicer, move the mouse pointer to a corner or the middle of an edge so it turns into a two-way resize arrow. Then, drag the slicer's border to resize it.

   To remove a slicer, select it and press Delete.

6. **Apply your filter.**

   You can now use your slicer to filter the table:

   - To filter the table to a single value, click the corresponding button in the slicer. For example, if you click Beverages, Excel shows only the rows with that category. (When you click a value, Excel changes its shading in the slicer so you can tell which value you picked.)
   - To filter the table to show multiple values, hold down the Ctrl key while you click each value you want to show.
   - To clear the filter (and show everything), click the tiny funnel-with-an-X icon in the top-right corner of the slicer window.

   You can also change the filter settings in the column headers. The column header checkboxes and the slicers always stay in perfect sync.

NOTE Microsoft initially introduced slicers for pivot tables, an advanced data analysis tool you'll consider in Chapter 26. To learn about more options for formatting your slicers (so they look extra snazzy), jump to page 820.

Dealing with Duplicate Rows

Hard-core table types know that every once in a while, despite the utmost caution, a duplicate value slips into a table. Fortunately, Excel has tools that let you find duplicates, wherever they're hiding, and remove them.

Highlighting Duplicates

It's not too hard to fish out these duplicates—one option is to use sorting (described earlier) on the column where you suspect a duplicate exists. Then, if you spot two identical values, you can delete one of the table rows (page 421). Of course, for this technique to work, you have to be ready to scroll through all the records and check each one. In a supremely long list, that could take some time.

Fortunately, Excel has another solution—conditional formatting. You already used conditional formatting to highlight important data (in Chapter 6), but you can also use it to make repeating values stand out like sore thumbs. Here's how:

1. **Select the table column you want to check for duplicate values.**

   For example, you could select the Product ID column to look for products that have the same ID value.

NOTE You can highlight more than one column, but if you do, Excel highlights identical values that appear in more than one column. For example, if the same number appears in the Product ID column and in the Price column, Excel highlights it even though it isn't really a duplicate.

2. **Choose Home→Styles→Conditional Formatting→Highlight Cells Rules→ Duplicate Values.**

   When the Duplicate Values window appears, choose the type of formatting you'd like to use to highlight repeated values. People often choose to change the background color.

3. **Click OK.**

   Excel changes the background color of all values that appear more than once in the selected column (or columns), as shown in Figure 14-20. Conditional formatting keeps working even *after* you apply it. So, if you add a new record that duplicates the value of an existing record in the column you're checking, Excel immediately highlights it. It's like having a duplicate value cop around at all times.

TIP If you have an extremely large table, you may like to use color-based sorting (page 429) to bring the duplicate records to the top of the table. For example, if you highlighted duplicate Product ID values with a light red background fill, you click the Product ID column's drop-down arrow, choose Sort By Color, and then pick the same color (which automatically appears in the menu).

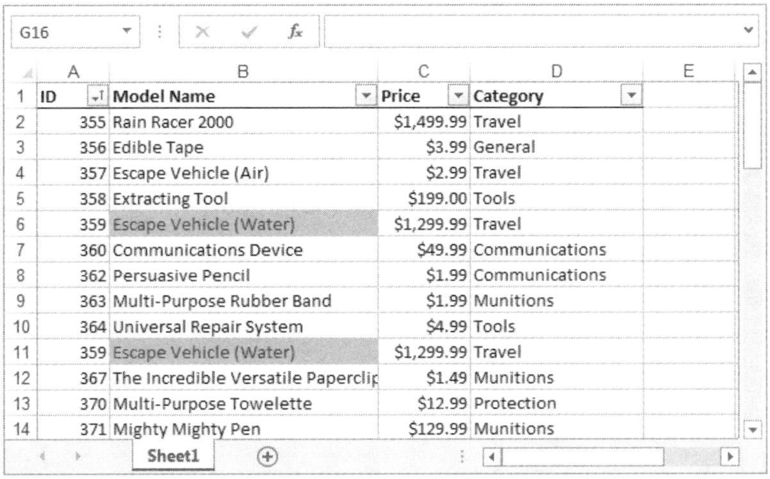

FIGURE 14-20

Conditional formatting helps smoke out a product with the same name—"Escape Vehicle (Water)"—that happens to be in two different places in the table.

Removing Duplicates Automatically

Once you find duplicate records, it's up to you to decide what you want to do with them. You can leave them in your table or delete them by hand. If you do want to remove them, Excel has a quick solution, thanks to a built-in feature that hunts for duplicates and automatically removes the offending rows. Here's how to use it:

1. **Move to any one of the table cells.**

   Although you can technically use the duplicate removal feature with any range of cells, it works best with tables because you don't need to select the full range of data yourself.

2. **Choose Data→Data Tools→Remove Duplicates.**

   Excel launches the Remove Duplicates window, where you can choose which columns to search for duplicates.

3. **Decide how many columns need to match in order for Excel to consider the record a duplicate. Add a checkmark next to each column you want to inspect.**

   For example, you may decide that any record with the same Product ID is a duplicate. When Excel scans the table, it removes any subsequent record that has the same Product ID as an earlier record, even if the rest of the data is different.

   On the other hand, you may decide that you want to match several columns to prevent the possibility of error. For example, two different products may share the same Product ID due to a minor typo. To avoid this possibility, you can select several columns (as shown in Figure 14-21), so that Excel removes only records that have matches in multiple columns. (You can't do this with conditional formatting and the Highlight Duplicates rule. When you use conditional formatting, you're limited to finding duplicates in *one* column—if you include more than one column, Excel treats them as one big batch of cells.)

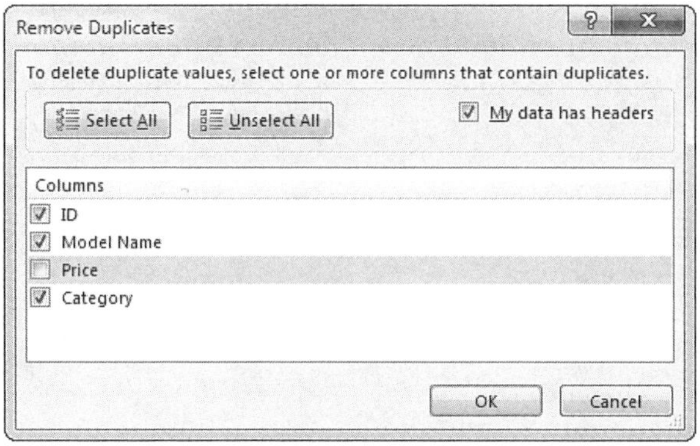

FIGURE 14-21

For data in this table to be considered a duplicate, the record has to have the same Product ID, Model Name, and Category (the Price can vary). If you need to select all the columns in a hurry, use the Select All button.

4. **Click OK to remove the duplicates.**

   Excel scans your table looking for duplicates. If it finds any, it keeps the first copy and deletes those that appear later. When Excel is finished, it pops up a message box telling you how many rows it removed and how many remain.

   You don't get a chance to confirm the deletion process, but you can reverse it by using the Undo feature (hit Ctrl+Z) immediately after Excel finishes.

Remember, when using the Remove Duplicates feature, you have no way of knowing what records Excel has deleted. For this reason, people often use the Highlight Duplicates rule first to check out the duplicates and make sure they don't belong.

NOTE The Remove Duplicates feature and the Highlight Duplicates rule don't work in exactly the same way. For instance, Remove Duplicates treats repeated empty cells (blank values) as duplicates, and removes them. The Highlight Duplicates feature ignores empty cells and doesn't highlight them.

Performing Table Calculations

Excel tables have several nifty features that help you perform calculations on the data inside a table.

One example is the way automatic expansion works when you add new columns that contain calculations. For example, say you've got a table with three columns: Product ID, Model Name, and Price. If you want to add a new column that tracks the discounted price of each product (say, 90 percent of the regular price), then a table's a great timesaver. Once you create the new discount price column for one row (see Figure 14-22), Excel adds the same calculation to every other row (Figure 14-23). You wind up with a table that shows the discounted price of every product, no copying and pasting required.

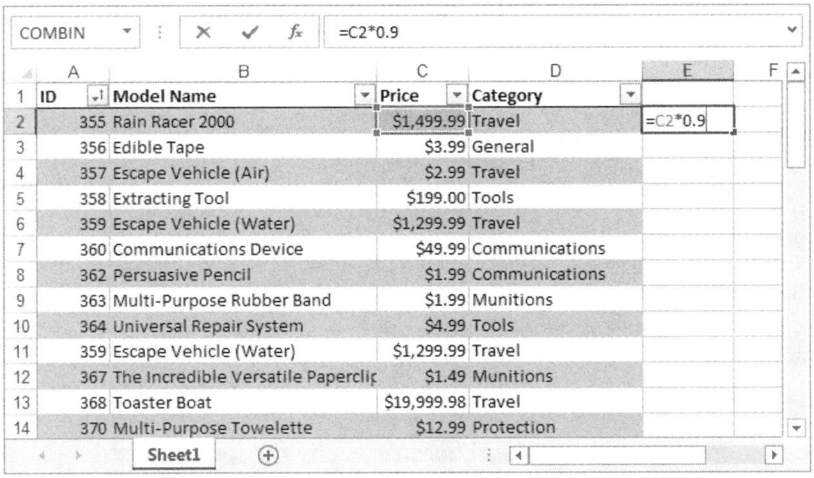

COMBIN | =C2*0.9

	A	B	C	D	E	F
1	ID	Model Name	Price	Category		
2	355	Rain Racer 2000	$1,499.99	Travel	=C2*0.9	
3	356	Edible Tape	$3.99	General		
4	357	Escape Vehicle (Air)	$2.99	Travel		
5	358	Extracting Tool	$199.00	Tools		
6	359	Escape Vehicle (Water)	$1,299.99	Travel		
7	360	Communications Device	$49.99	Communications		
8	362	Persuasive Pencil	$1.99	Communications		
9	363	Multi-Purpose Rubber Band	$1.99	Munitions		
10	364	Universal Repair System	$4.99	Tools		
11	359	Escape Vehicle (Water)	$1,299.99	Travel		
12	367	The Incredible Versatile Paperclip	$1.49	Munitions		
13	368	Toaster Boat	$19,999.98	Travel		
14	370	Multi-Purpose Towelette	$12.99	Protection		

Sheet1

FIGURE 14-22

This worksheet shows a new column with a formula that's in the process of being entered. See Figure 14-23 for what happens next.

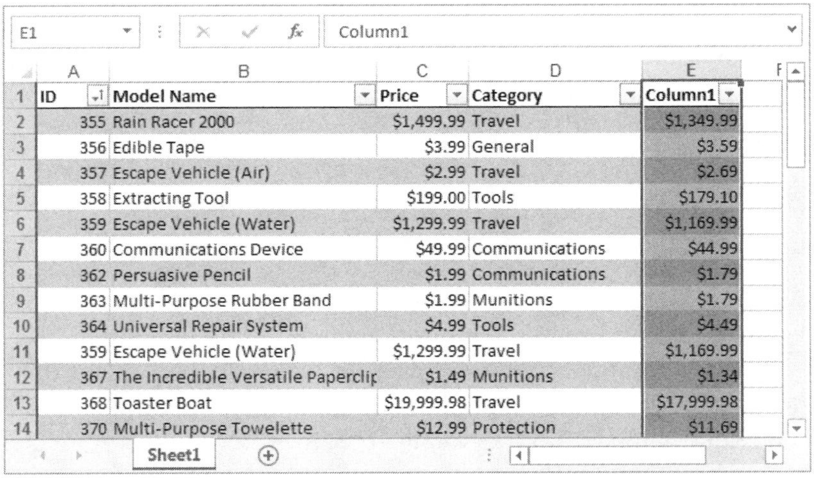

E1 | Column1

	A	B	C	D	E	F
1	ID	Model Name	Price	Category	Column1	
2	355	Rain Racer 2000	$1,499.99	Travel	$1,349.99	
3	356	Edible Tape	$3.99	General	$3.59	
4	357	Escape Vehicle (Air)	$2.99	Travel	$2.69	
5	358	Extracting Tool	$199.00	Tools	$179.10	
6	359	Escape Vehicle (Water)	$1,299.99	Travel	$1,169.99	
7	360	Communications Device	$49.99	Communications	$44.99	
8	362	Persuasive Pencil	$1.99	Communications	$1.79	
9	363	Multi-Purpose Rubber Band	$1.99	Munitions	$1.79	
10	364	Universal Repair System	$4.99	Tools	$4.49	
11	359	Escape Vehicle (Water)	$1,299.99	Travel	$1,169.99	
12	367	The Incredible Versatile Paperclip	$1.49	Munitions	$1.34	
13	368	Toaster Boat	$19,999.98	Travel	$17,999.98	
14	370	Multi-Purpose Towelette	$12.99	Protection	$11.69	

Sheet1

FIGURE 14-23

Once you finish the formula shown in Figure 14-22 and then hit Enter, Excel expands the table to include the new column, and then adds the formula to every other row. And if you scroll to the bottom of the table and start adding a new row, Excel is intelligent enough to automatically copy this new formula into the new row. In other words, once you add a formula to a column, that formula is sticky.

Once you added a new column that has a formula, the only thing left to do is to give the column a good name. Click the column header cell (which will say something like Column1), and then type in something more relevant (like Discount Price).

Dynamic Calculations

One of Excel tables' nicest features is the way they handle calculations. You can build formulas that use the data in a table, and Excel adjusts them automatically as the table grows or shrinks.

For example, imagine creating a table that stretches from row 1 to row 5. The first row contains the column headers, followed by four product rows. You create the following formula to add the total price of all the items:

```
=SUM(C2:C5)
```

If you now add a new item (that is, a new row) to the table, Excel automatically updates your formula so it includes this new item:

```
=SUM(C2:C6)
```

The same magic happens if your table shrinks because you've deleted an item. You just need to make sure that your range includes the whole column when you first create the formula. For example, consider the following formula, which omits the first item in the table:

```
=SUM(C3:C5)
```

If you expand the table now, Excel doesn't modify the formula. Fortunately, the program's got your back: It'll remind you if you create a formula that includes only a portion of your table by showing a green triangle in the corner of the missing cell(s), which is Excel code for "Is this really what you want to do?" When you move to the cell, an exclamation mark icon appears. Click it, and you get a short explanation and a menu of error-fixing options, as shown in Figure 14-24. Rather than worry about this sort of issue, it's always better to use table and column names to build your formulas, as described on page 441.

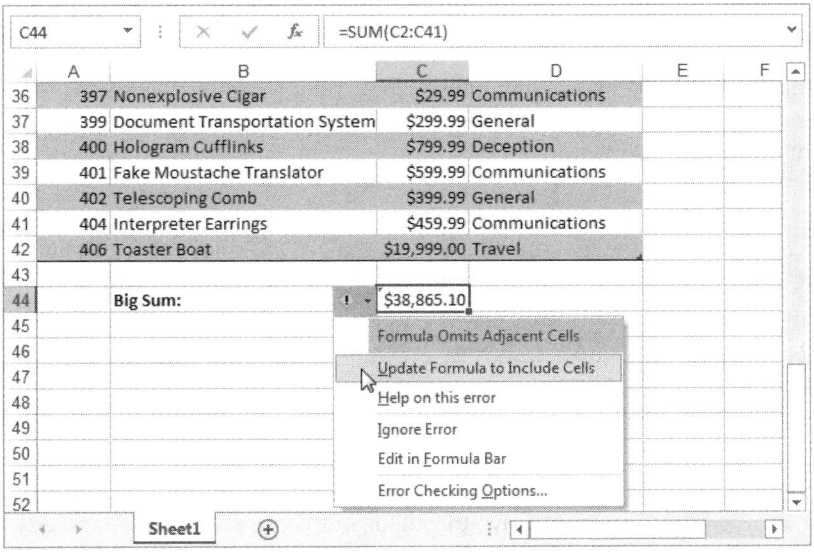

FIGURE 14-24

Excel warns you if you create a function that leaves out part of the information in a table. For example, the formula in C44 mistakenly left out cell C42. Excel offers to remedy the problem—just choose Update Formula to Include Cells.

Filtering settings don't affect your formulas. If you filter a table so that only some products are visible, the SUM() function still produces the same result, which is the total price of all products. If you don't want this behavior, you can use the *total row* (page 444) or Excel's SUBTOTAL() function (page 445).

Column Names

So far, the table calculation examples you've seen have ignored a super-convenient feature called *column names*. You already learned how Excel lets you create your own named ranges to refer to frequently used parts of your worksheet. (Page 384 has the full story.) But even if you don't create any named ranges of your own, you'll find that Excel equips every table with some built-in names.

First of all, Excel creates column names that you can use when you write formulas inside your table. For example, look back at Figure 14-22, which uses this formula to discount the current price:

```
=C2*0.9
```

When Excel copies this formula down the table, it adjusts the formula automatically using the familiar magic of relative references (page 284), so that each discounted price refers to the product price in the same row. For example, in row 10 (technically, the ninth row of data), the formula becomes:

```
=C10*0.9
```

But there's a shortcut. Instead of referring to the specific cell, you can use the name of the column preceded by an *at sign* (@) and inside square brackets. That shortcut means you can write the formula like this:

```
=[@Price]*0.9
```

To Excel, the @ symbol means "the current row", so [@Price] automatically refers to the value of the Price column in the current row, no matter where in the table you stick it.

NOTE The column name is based on whatever text you place in the column header. If the column header has the text "Price", then the column name in a formula is [@Price].

It's considered good practice to always use the @ sign before a column name. However, Excel allows you to leave this detail out if you're lazy, which means you can also write table formulas that look like this:

```
=[Price]*0.9
```

If a column name has a space in it, Excel adds a second set of square brackets around the name. So to refer to the Tax Rate column in the current row, you'd write this:

```
[@[Tax Rate]]
```

Column names aren't only major timesavers, they also make your worksheets much easier to understand and they reduce the likelihood of errors. After all, who could mistake the purpose of the following formula?

```
=[@Price] * [@[Tax Rate]] + [@[Shipping Charge]]
```

NOTE If you use Excel's point-and-click formula creation, Excel uses the column names rather than the cell reference.

Table Names

You've just seen how you can write formulas inside a table using column names. Excel also lets you use this technique in the cells *outside* your table. However, you need to first identify the table you want to use by its *table name*.

The table name is a reference that points to your entire table, and you can use it anywhere on your worksheet. This raises one excellent question—namely, how does Excel decide what name your table should have? When you first create a table, Excel picks a rather unexciting name, like Table1, Table2, and so on. To change this, click anywhere inside your table, and then edit the text in the Table Tools | Design→Properties→Table Name box. For example, ProductList makes a good name.

On its own, your table name refers to the entire range of cells that contains the data for your table. That means it includes the entire table, minus the column headers and total row. You may want to use these cells with a lookup function like VLOOKUP(), as described on page 347. For example, if you want to get the price (from the third column) of the product named Persuasive Pencil, you can use this easy-to-read formula:

```
=VLOOKUP("Persuasive Pencil", ProductList, 3, FALSE)
```

Excel includes another treat that lets you dig deeper into your table. You can use the table name in conjunction with a column name to get the range of cells that holds the data for just one column. Here's an example:

```
=SUM(ProductList[Price])
```

This gets the ProductList table, pulls out the cells in the Price column, and then passes them to the familiar SUM() function, which generates a total. Notice that you don't add the @ symbol character before the Price reference, because this formula is referring to the *entire* column, not the current row. Figure 14-25 shows you how Excel helps you create formulas like these with its Formula AutoComplete feature.

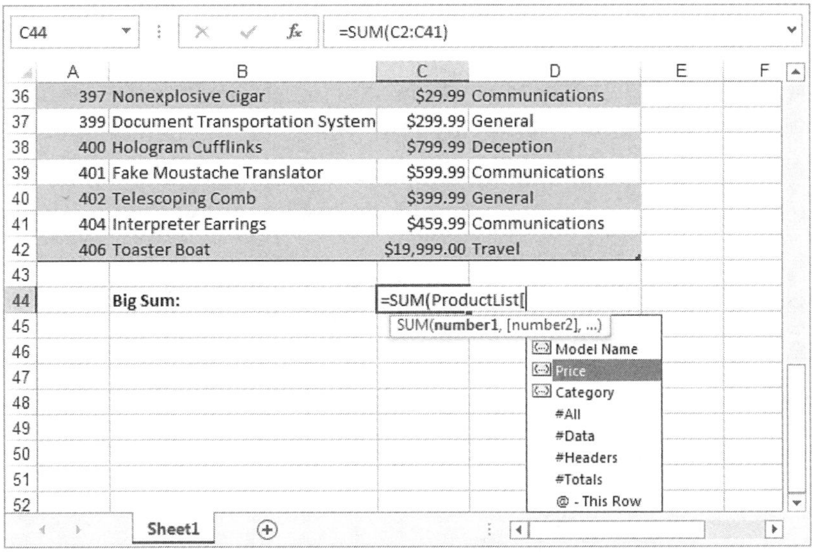

FIGURE 14-25

Once you type a table name followed by an open bracket, Excel displays a list of columns in that table. You can select one using the up and down arrow keys, and then insert it into your formula by pressing Tab.

Table names and column names are called *structured table references*, and Excel has a few more specialized ones that you'll recognize because they incorporate a number sign (#). Here's how to get a range with all the header cells in a table:

```
ProductList[#Headers]
```

Or the total row (if it's visible):

```
ProductList[#Totals]
```

Or everything else (the table data):

```
ProductList[#Data]
```

Or the whole shebang, headers, data, total row, and all:

```
ProductList[#All]
```

TIP Table and column names let you get hold of the parts of your table quickly and efficiently. Best of all, these references are rock-solid reliable, and they continue to work flawlessly when you add new rows to the table or rearrange columns. For these reasons, you should always use table and column names instead of cell references when creating formulas that use table data.

The Total Row

Excel tables make it easy to calculate totals, averages, standard deviations, and other common formulas by using a dedicated summary row. To show this row, select Table Tools | Design→Table Style Options→Total Row. Excel adds an extra row at the bottom of the table.

When the total row first appears, it includes only one piece of information: the number of records currently displayed. If you want to show some other type of information, choose a column, and then click the total row cell at the bottom of that column. A drop-down list appears with preset options. Choose one, and the total row displays the calculation in that cell, as shown in Figure 14-26.

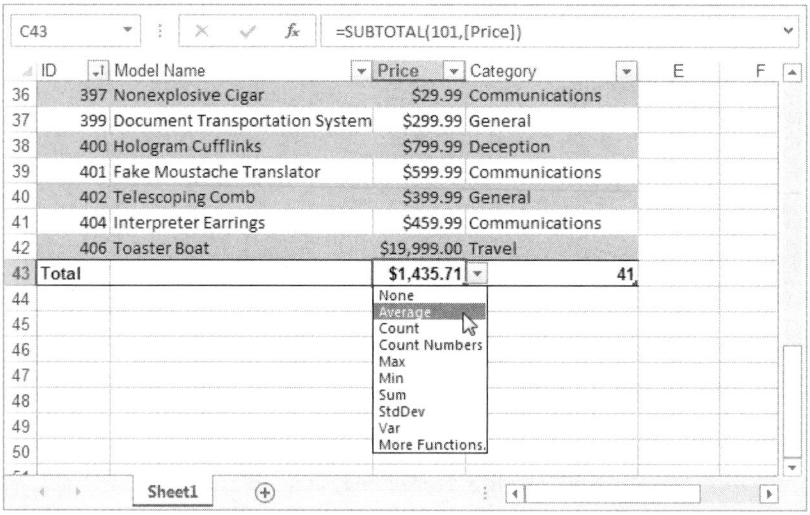

FIGURE 14-26

The Total row lets you perform common calculations with a single mouse click. In this example, the total row displays the average price of the records that match the filter condition.

NOTE When the total row is showing, you can't add a new row to the table by typing underneath it. Fortunately, there are two good workarounds. First, you can add a new row by right-clicking the last table row and choosing Insert→Table Row Below. Or, if your table doesn't have any filtering applied, you can add a row by moving to the cell in the bottom-right corner of your table and pressing the Tab key.

Of course, you can create your own formulas to display the same information as the total rows do. However, the total row requires no work. It also uses only the rows that are currently visible, ignoring all filtered rows. You may or may not want this behavior. (It's great if you want to calculate totals for a small subset of filtered data, but it's not so good if you want to create grand totals that include everything.) If you want a different behavior, you can write your own summary formula using functions like SUM(), COUNT(), and AVERAGE().

The SUBTOTAL() Function

The total row conveniently works only with the currently visible rows in a table. To see this phenomenon in action, simply click one of the cells in the total row. If you look in the formula bar, you see that these cells use the SUBTOTAL() function to perform their calculations. That's because the SUBTOTAL() function is the only Excel function that takes table filtering into account.

The SUBTOTAL() function is the perfect solution for all the calculations in the total row, including sums, averages, counts, and more. The trick is that the first argument of the SUBTOTAL() function is a numeric code that tells Excel what type of calculation it should perform, while the second argument is the range of cells for the entire table column, from the first row to the last.

```
SUBTOTAL(function_code, column_range)
```

Table 14-1 lists all the function codes you can use with SUBTOTAL(). Note that each calculation type actually has two function codes associated with it. Function codes *above* 100 ignore hidden rows (rows that you hid using the Home→Cells→Format→Hide & Unhide→Hide Rows command). These function codes are the ones the total row uses. Function codes *under* 100 don't ignore hidden rows, but they still ignore rows you filtered out. Figure 14-27 shows the SUBTOTAL() function in action.

TABLE 14-1 *Function codes for SUBTOTAL()*

FUNCTION USED FOR CALCULATION	CODE THAT IGNORES HIDDEN ROWS	CODE THAT INCLUDES HIDDEN ROWS
AVERAGE()	101	1
COUNT()	102	2
COUNTA()	103	3
MAX()	104	4
MIN()	105	5
PRODUCT()	106	6

FUNCTION USED FOR CALCULATION	CODE THAT IGNORES HIDDEN ROWS	CODE THAT INCLUDES HIDDEN ROWS
STDEV()	107	7
STDEVP()	108	8
SUM()	109	9
VAR()	110	10
VARP()	111	11

In Figure 14-27, compare the results of the SUBTOTAL() functions in cells C2 to C6 to the formulas in cells D2 to D6, which just use the regular functions, like AVERAGE(), SUM(), MAX(), MIN(), and so on. In this figure, the formulas show the totals after filtering limits the table to items in the Communications category.

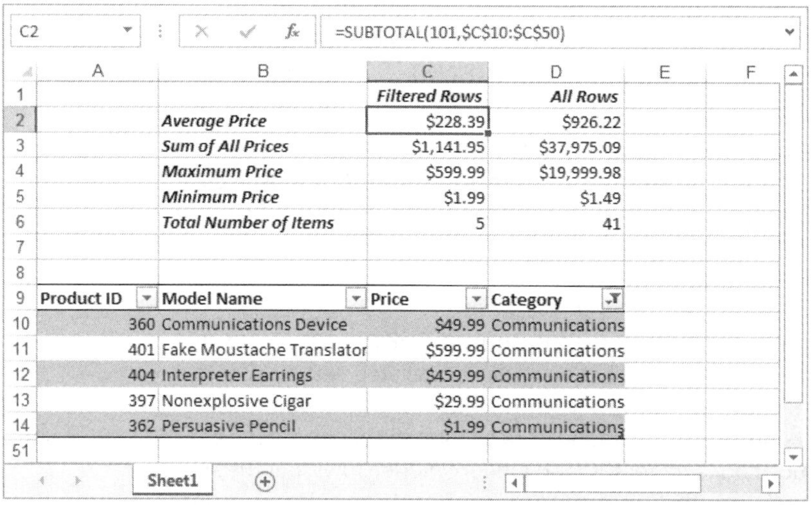

FIGURE 14-27

This worksheet puts the SUBTOTAL() function to work calculating averages, sums, and more. The formulas that use the SUBTOTAL() function are in cells C2 to C6, while the formulas that use the closest ordinary Excel function (and don't take filtering into account) are in cells D2 to D6.

The Database Functions

Excel also includes functions exclusively for use with long tables. These are the *database functions*, a set of 11 functions that let you analyze groups of data.

The database functions are similar to basic statistical functions like SUM(), AVERAGE(), and COUNT(). In fact, the database functions have the exact same names, but with an initial letter D—so you find a DSUM(), DAVERAGE(), DCOUNT(), and so on. The database functions differ from their non-database counterparts in that they can selectively filter out rows. In other words, when you use DSUM(), you can specify a set of criteria that a record must match in order to be included in the sum. (The filtering that you apply with the AutoFilter feature makes no difference to the database functions. They don't ignore hidden rows.)

Table 14-2 lists the database functions, along with their comparable statistical functions.

TABLE 14-2 *Database functions*

FUNCTION	SIMILAR TO	DESCRIPTION
DAVERAGE()	AVERAGE()	Calculates the average in rows that meet the specified criteria.
DCOUNT()	COUNT()	Counts the number of rows that meet the specified criteria.
DCOUNTA()	COUNTA()	Calculates the number of non-blank values in rows that meet the specified criteria.
DGET()	No equivalent	Returns the value that meets the specified criteria. If more than one value matches, DGET() returns the *#NUM!* error. If no records match, it returns the *#VALUE!* error.
DMAX()	MAX()	Returns the maximum value in rows that meet the specified criteria.
DMIN()	MIN()	Returns the minimum value in rows that meet the specified criteria.
DPRODUCT()	PRODUCT()	Calculates the product produced by multiplying all values in rows that meet the specified criteria.
DSTDEV()	STDEV()	Calculates the standard deviation in rows that meet the specified criteria.
DSUM()	SUM()	Calculates the sum of values in rows that meet the specified criteria.
DVAR()	VAR()	Estimates the variance of a sample population in the rows that meet the specified criteria.
DVARP()	VARP()	Estimates the variance of an entire population in the rows that meet the specified criteria.

DGET() is the only function without a statistical counterpart. It works a little like the VLOOKUP() and HLOOKUP() functions (page 346), and it returns a single value in a row that meets the specified criteria.

Each database function uses the same three parameters:

```
DFUNCTION(table_range, field, criteria)
```

- The *table_range* is the range the function uses. The table range should include the entire table, including the column you want to use for your calculation and the columns for your criteria. The table range has to include the column headers, because that's how the database functions identify each column and match it up with the criteria. That means you can't use the automatically generated table names you learned about earlier (page 442).
- The *field* is the name of the column you want to use for the calculation. For example, if you're using DSUM(), the field is the column you want to total. Excel scans the column headers until it finds the column that has the same name. (Instead of using column names, you can use column *numbers*, but this is approach a lot riskier, because it means that your formulas will break if you decide to rearrange the table.)
- The *criteria* is a range of cells that specifies all the conditions that rows must meet to be included in the calculation. This range can be as large as you want, and you're free to define conditions for multiple columns, or multiple conditions that apply to the same column. If the range contains only empty cells, the database function operates on all the items in the table.

To use a database function successfully, you need to create a suitable range of cells that you can use for criteria. Excel expects this range of cells to be in a strict arrangement. Here are some rules you need to follow:

- Each condition requires two cells. One cell specifies the name of the field, and the other specifies the filter condition. For example, you can enter "Category" for the field name and "Tools" for the filter condition.
- The cell with the filter condition must be directly under the cell with the field name. If you put them side by side, the database function gives you an error.
- You can apply more than one filter condition to the same field. Just place all the conditions in a neat stack under the cell with the field name.
- You can add conditions to multiple fields. However, you must place the filtering information for each field in a separate column.
- You can add as many filter conditions as you want.

Filter conditions follow the same rules that you used for search criteria in the data form window. Thus, you can use comparison operators like less than (<) and greater than (>) to create conditions like *<500* (all prices under $500) or *<>Travel* (all products not in the Travel category). If you don't specify a comparison operator, Excel acts as though you chose the equal sign. In addition, it allows partial matches with text criteria. For example, the category criteria T will match both Travel and Tools.

You have total freedom to decide where in the worksheet to place your filter cells. Figure 14-28 shows an example that puts the filter cells at the top of the worksheet. To find the average price of all the products that match these criteria, you use the following formula:

```
=DAVERAGE(A9:D51, "Price", C1:E2)
```

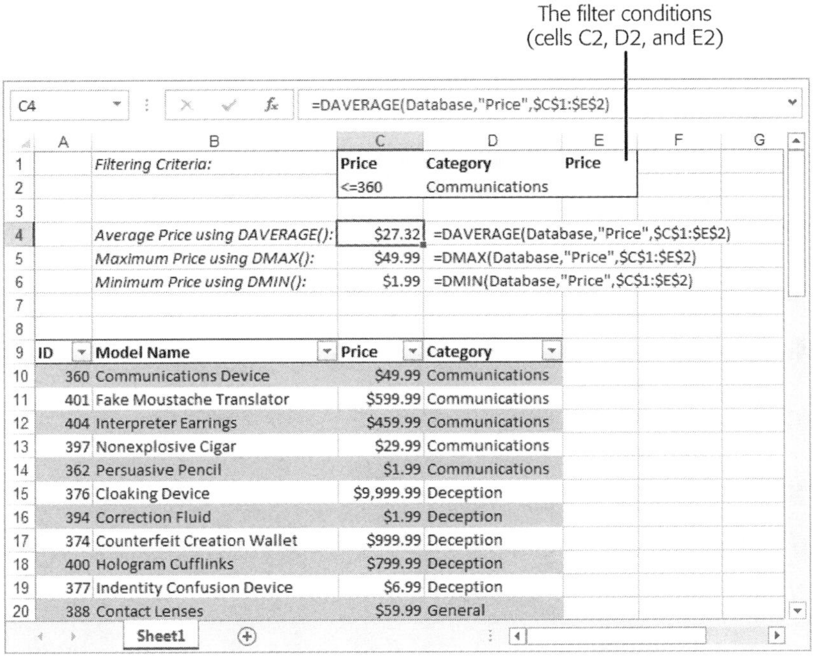

FIGURE 14-28

In this example, you could use cell E2 to add another condition specifying a minimum price. However, because this cell is currently blank, Excel doesn't apply a price filter. Instead, it filters by matching a category and setting a maximum price.

The database functions are nice because they force you to define your criteria in the worksheet. If you want to change the criteria, you simply need to modify these cells, which makes database functions a perfect solution for building dynamic reports.

CHAPTER

15

Grouping and Outlining Data

As you saw in the previous chapter, Excel's tables are great tools for managing big collections of data made up of long, uniform columns (like lists of customers or products). But tables don't work so well if you need to show more complex information, especially if that information is split into separate groups, each with its own subtotals.

Imagine a company sales report that lists a year's worth of quarterly results for each of its regions around the world. If you try to cram all that data into one long list—including subtotals for each region—you're likely to end up with a spreadsheet that looks like a numerical version of Twister. You'd be better off breaking out each region into a separate group of cells, and then tying everything together with another batch of cells that sums up your sales across all regions.

Excel's grouping and outlining features are perfect for dealing with multilayered information like this. They help you quickly and easily expand and collapse big chunks of data and, in the process, make calculating summary information much easier. These tricks are remarkably easy to implement, but they rank as one of Excel's best-kept productivity secrets.

Basic Data Grouping

When you want to simplify your worksheets, you first have to learn how to *group* data. Grouping data lets you tie related columns or rows into a single unit. Once you put columns or rows into a group, you can *collapse* the group, temporarily hiding it and leaving more space for the rest of your data. At its simplest, grouping is just a quick way to help you easily view what you want to see, when you want to see it. It's most handy when you want to show key summary information but not the numbers you used to arrive at these results.

NOTE Excel's grouping settings also affect how your worksheet prints out—collapsed rows or columns don't appear in your printout.

UP TO SPEED

Comparing Grouping and Tables

Overall, grouping isn't as powerful as Excel's tables (covered in Chapter 14). Whereas tables include features for sorting, filtering, and searching, using groups simply makes it easier for you to work with data tables that use one or more levels of subtotals.

Of course, there's no reason you can't use *both* grouping and tables. For example, you can group one or more columns in a big table so that you can see just the columns you want (all the columns that track address components, for instance).

You can also group some of the rows in a table or, more usefully, put all the rows of a table in a single group. (This makes sense if you have a worksheet with multiple tables and you put each one in its own group, so you can collapse the ones you don't want to see.) However, Excel tables grow dynamically, so you could have a problem. If you add a new row at the bottom of a table, the table automatically expands to incorporate the new information. Groups don't display the same behavior. As a result, if your table grows, some of it may slip out beyond an edge of the group.

Creating a Group

To see how grouping can simplify complex worksheets, check out the sales report shown in Figure 15-1. In this example, the information fits easily into the viewable area of the Excel window, but in a real-world company, you could easily end up needing to extend the worksheet with more columns and rows.

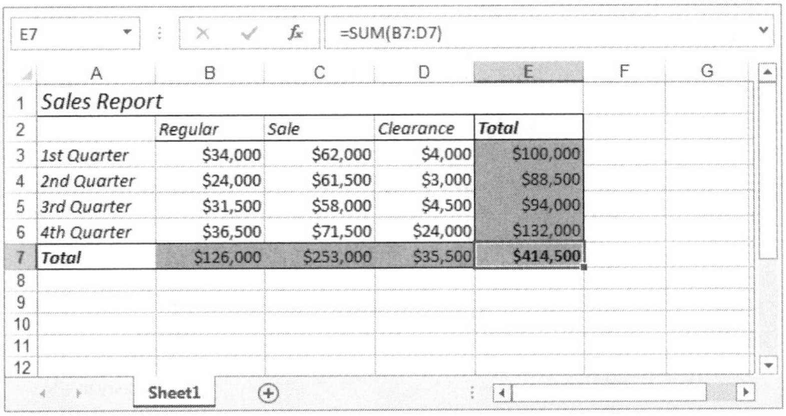

	A	B	C	D	E
1	Sales Report				
2		Regular	Sale	Clearance	Total
3	1st Quarter	$34,000	$62,000	$4,000	$100,000
4	2nd Quarter	$24,000	$61,500	$3,000	$88,500
5	3rd Quarter	$31,500	$58,000	$4,500	$94,000
6	4th Quarter	$36,500	$71,500	$24,000	$132,000
7	Total	$126,000	$253,000	$35,500	$414,500

FIGURE 15-1

This worksheet shows a retail store's revenue, with the numbers broken down two ways: by quarter, and by price point (with merchandise priced regularly, on sale, and as clearance items). The sheet subtotals the revenue by price point so you can tell how much the company sold at a particular price over the whole year (cells B7:D7), how much it sold in a quarter at all price points (cells E3:E6), and how much it sold in total (cell E7).

You could add a variety of columns (representing different types of promotions, different discounts from regular prices, or different departments in the store). Or, you may add more rows to cover sales quarters from more than one year, or to track monthly, weekly, or even daily sales totals. In either case, the data would become fairly unwieldy, forcing you to scroll up and down the worksheet, and from side to side. By grouping columns (or rows) together, you can pop them in and out of view with a single mouse click.

NOTE You may remember from Chapter 5 that you can also use *hiding* to temporarily remove rows and columns from sight. But grouping is a much nicer approach—you can more easily pop data out of and back into view without going hunting through Excel's ribbon. It also makes it more obvious to the person reading the worksheet that there's more data tucked out of sight. People more often use hiding to remove gunk that no one *ever* needs to see. Technically, grouping uses Excel's hiding ability behind the scenes to make grouped cells disappear temporarily.

Here's how you group several columns using the sales report example:

1. **Select the columns or rows you want to group.**

   In most cases, you'll want to group the *detail columns* that provide fine-grained information (like columns B, C, and D in Figure 15-1). You shouldn't include in your group any subtotals (like column E) that summarize your information, because you're likely to want to see those subtotals.

   To make your selection, drag over the column headers, selecting entire columns as you go. This way, Excel can tell right away that you want to group columns. In the sales report example, you'd choose columns B, C, and D.

2. **Choose Data→Outline→Group.**

   If Excel isn't sure which groups of cells you want to group, it shows a Group window that lets you specify whether you're grouping columns or rows. (If you selected cells B3:D3, Excel would consider that an ambiguous selection because it could represent an attempt to group the columns *or* rows.) If the Group window appears, make your selection, and then click OK.

When you group columns, the worksheet doesn't change, though a new margin area appears at the top of the worksheet, as shown in Figure 15-2. This margin lets you collapse and expand your groups (see Figure 15-3). To collapse a group, click the minus sign (–), which then changes into a plus sign (+). To expand a collapsed group, click the plus sign (+).

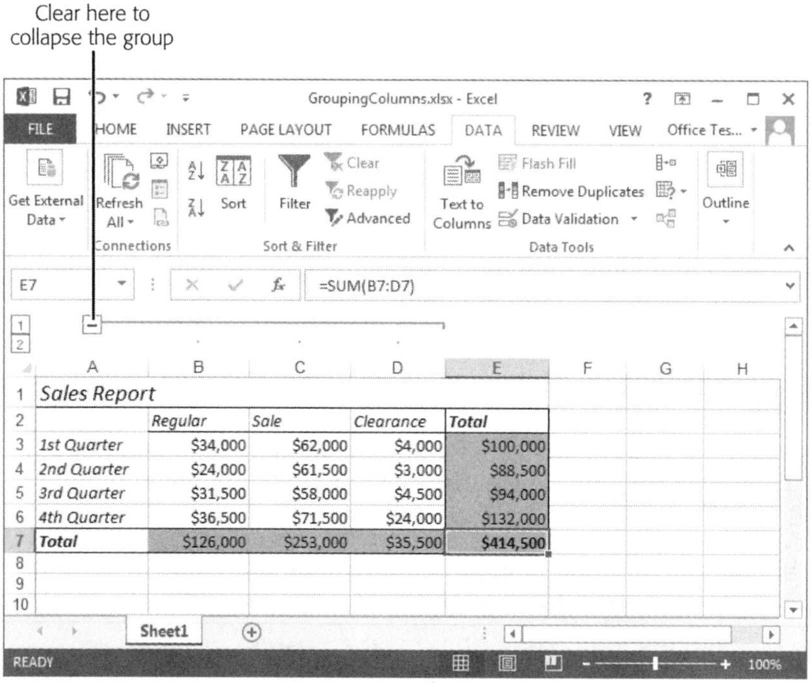

FIGURE 15-2

Here, you've grouped columns B, C, and D.

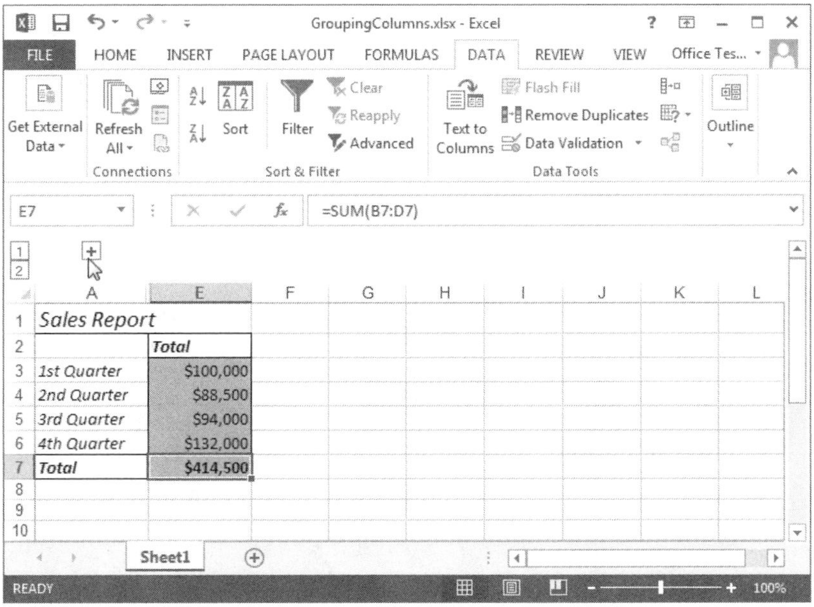

FIGURE 15-3

After clicking the minus sign icon in the worksheet's upper margin (as shown in Figure 15-2), you can quickly collapse this group, hiding columns B, C, and D. When you hide columns, Excel still uses the data in them in calculations (like those in column E).

To remove a group after you've established it, expand the group, select all the columns, and then choose Data→Outline→Ungroup. If you select only some of the columns, Excel removes the selected columns from the group, but leaves the rest of the group intact—as long as at least two grouped columns remain. (If you remove a column from the middle of a group, you're actually left with two groups, one with the columns on the left, and one with the columns on the right.)

NOTE If you're not careful, you may end up ungrouping a set of columns while the group is collapsed. This happens if you select a range of columns that includes a collapsed group, and you use the Data→Outline→Ungroup command. Even though you've removed the group, the columns remain hidden and trapped out of sight! In this situation, you can expose these columns by selecting a range of columns that includes the hidden ones, and then choosing Home→Cells→Format→Hide & Unhide→Unhide Columns.

You can use the same technique to group rows. In the sales report, you may want to group all the detail rows that give the quarter-by-quarter sales numbers, so you can quickly collapse them and see just the totals. To do so, select rows 3 to 6 by clicking the first row number, and then dragging down over all the rows you want to select. Then, select Data→Outline→Group. This time, a margin appears just to the left of the worksheet, letting you quickly hide the grouped rows. You can also have grouped rows *and* grouped columns, as shown in Figure 15-4.

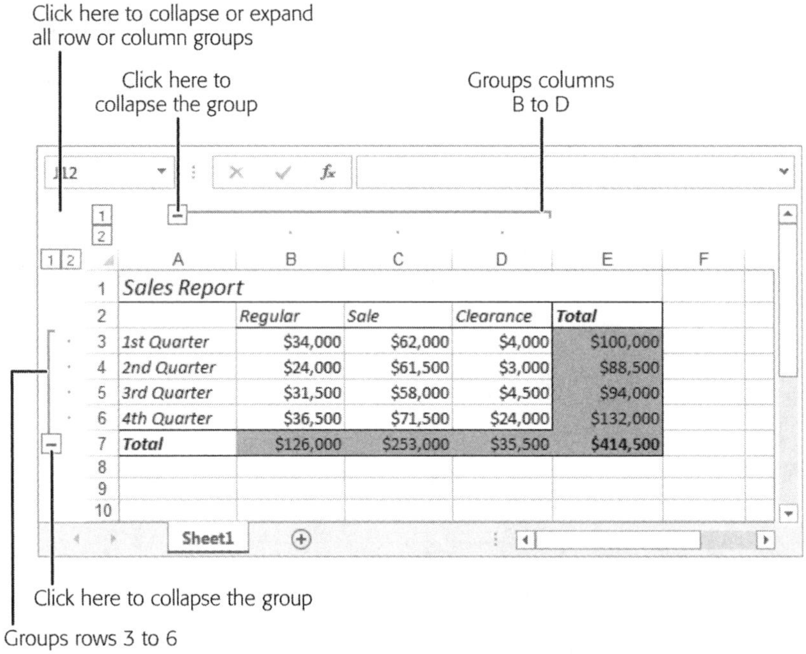

FIGURE 15-4

The trick to mastering Excel's grouping feature is understanding how the grouping bars work. The grouping bars show you the range of cells bound together in a single group. The minus sign (–) icon always appears just outside the group (either over the column to the left, or under the last row). That's because this icon has to remain visible after you collapse the group so you can expand it later.

NOTE If you insert a new row between two grouped rows using the Home→Cells→Insert→Insert Sheet Rows command, Excel automatically places the new row into the group. The same's true if you insert a new column between two grouped columns using Home→Cells→Insert→Insert Sheet Columns.

You can add as many or as few groups as you like. If you have some data with far too many columns, you can put all the extra columns into a single group, or into several separate groups. What's the difference? With one group, you can hide all the extra information with a single mouse click. With multiple groups, you need to do more clicking—but you have the ability to choose exactly what you want to see.

Keep in mind that if you create adjacent groups of columns, you always need to leave at least one column between each group. If you create two groups next to each other (like columns A to C and columns D to F), Excel automatically merges them into a single group. (This little quirk exists because Excel needs a free column to display the expand/collapse icons.) The same holds true for groups of rows.

TIP If you decide to use multiple groups, it makes sense to group related rows or columns. For example, you may group all the columns that have address information into one group.

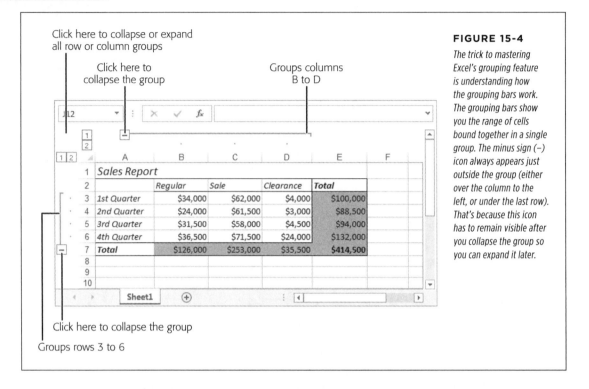

Nesting Groups Within Groups

As you've seen, grouping lets you temporarily shrink the size of a large table by removing specific rows or columns. Grouping becomes even *more* useful when you create a worksheet that has multiple tables of information, like the one shown in Figure 15-5.

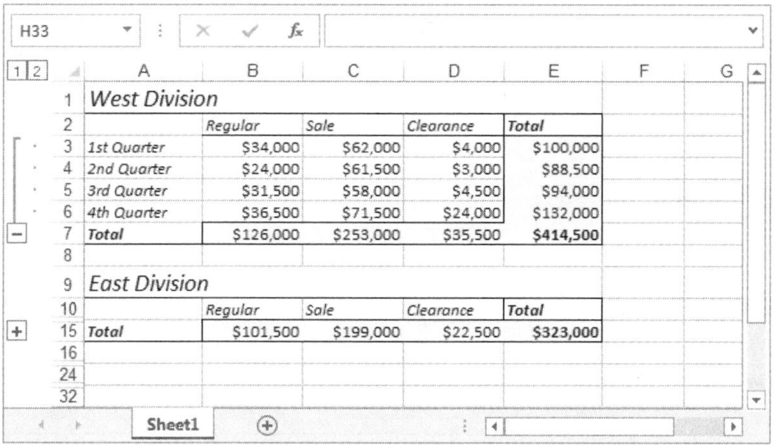

	A	B	C	D	E	F	G
1	West Division						
2		Regular	Sale	Clearance	Total		
3	1st Quarter	$34,000	$62,000	$4,000	$100,000		
4	2nd Quarter	$24,000	$61,500	$3,000	$88,500		
5	3rd Quarter	$31,500	$58,000	$4,500	$94,000		
6	4th Quarter	$36,500	$71,500	$24,000	$132,000		
7	Total	$126,000	$253,000	$35,500	$414,500		
8							
9	East Division						
10		Regular	Sale	Clearance	Total		
15	Total	$101,500	$199,000	$22,500	$323,000		
16							
24							
32							

FIGURE 15-5

This worksheet includes two groups. Currently, the lower group is collapsed, so that you see only the totals. Thanks to grouping, you can fill a worksheet with dozens of tables of detailed information, but see only the summary information for each when you collapse the groups.

NOTE Don't confuse grouping with Excel's structured tables, which you saw in Chapter 14. With grouping, you can use any combination of cells. Here, the data has a tabular structure with easily identifiable rows and columns, but it isn't an official Excel table.

Not only can you create separate groups for different tables, you can also put one group *inside* another. This approach gives you multiple viewing levels. Consider Figures 15-6 and 15-7, which show two views of the same worksheet. This worksheet includes four tables, each of which has two levels of grouping. By collapsing the first-level group for a table, you can hide everything except the summary information (listed in the Total line), as Figure 15-6 shows. By collapsing the second-level group, you can hide the entire table, as you can see (or, rather, *can't* see) in the North Division and South Division tables of Figure 15-7.

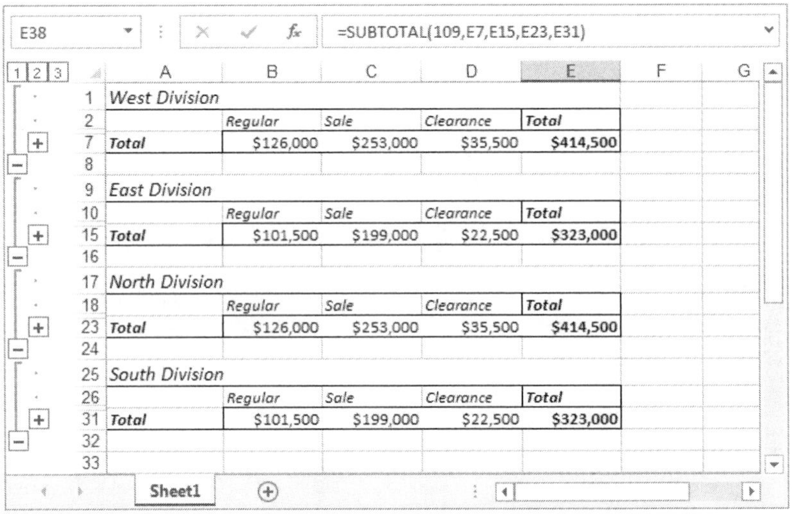

FIGURE 15-6

All four tables are partially collapsed, and each has its second-level groups hidden so that the tables show just the total sales for each region.

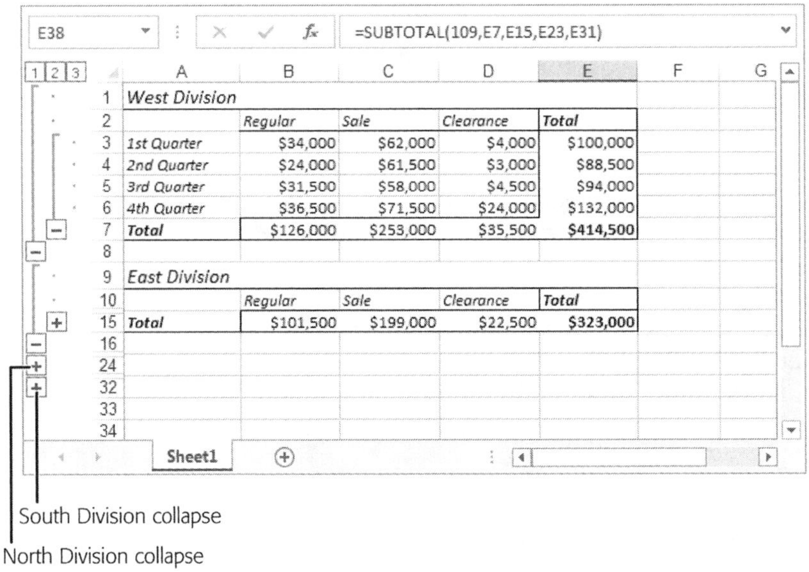

FIGURE 15-7

You see only two tables. The West Division is completely visible, because both its levels are expanded. The East Division is partially visible because its second-level group is collapsed. The North and South Division tables aren't visible at all because the first-level group for each table is collapsed.

NOTE The only drawback to nested grouping is that the more levels of grouping you add, the more room Excel needs in the margins at the side or top of the worksheet to display all the grouping lines.

Technically, when you add more than one level of grouping, you're adding collapsible *outline* views to your worksheet, which let you quickly move back and forth between a bird's-eye view of your data and an up-close glimpse of multiple rows.

TIMESAVING TIP

Collapsing and Expanding Multiple Groups at Once

If you create a worksheet with multiple levels of grouping, you can find yourself doing a lot of clicking to expose all the information you're interested in (or to hide all the details you don't care about). Fortunately, Excel includes a helpful shortcut that lets you expand or collapse multiple groups at once: *grouping buttons* (shown in Figure 15-8).

Each grouping button is labeled with a number that represents a grouping level. If you click number 1, Excel collapses all the column or row groups. If you click number 2, Excel collapses all the groups *except* the top level. If you click number 3, Excel collapses all the groups except the first two levels, and so on. In the sales worksheet in Figure 15-7, you can click 3 to show the whole worksheet, 2 to show just the subtotals, or 1 to hide all the sales tables.

Excel displays a different number of grouping buttons, depending on your worksheet's levels of grouping. The largest numbered button you'll see is 8, because Excel allows a maximum of seven levels of nested groups.

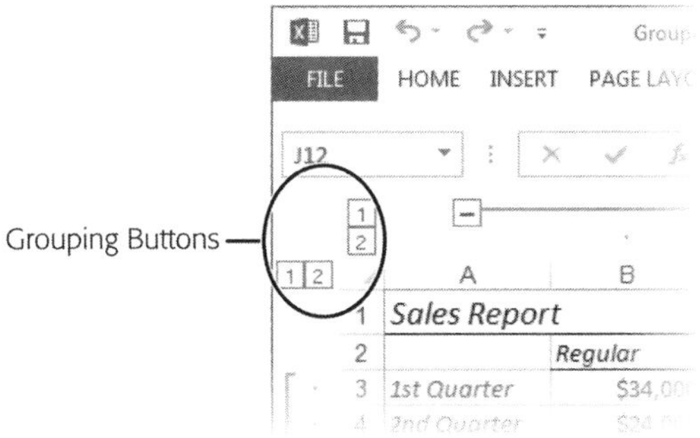

FIGURE 15-8

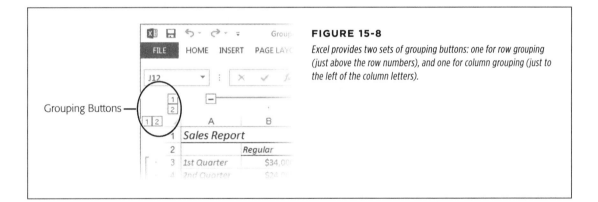

Excel provides two sets of grouping buttons: one for row grouping (just above the row numbers), and one for column grouping (just to the left of the column letters).

Summarizing Your Data

Understanding how to quickly collapse and expand tables is all well and good, but before long, you'll want to *add up* the totals you've collected in these accordion-style tables. In the subtotaled sales report shown in Figure 15-7, the perfect way to complete this worksheet is to add a final table that sums up *all* the Total rows listed in the last row of each division.

To create a grand summary, you need to employ just a few more formulas. They add the separate subtotals (in columns B, C, D, and E) to arrive at a final set of grand totals. The following formula calculates the total sales in all divisions for all quarters for regular merchandise:

```
=B7+B15+B23+B31
```

NOTE You could, of course, also calculate any of these subtotals by using the SUM() function, which is covered on page 267.

Notice that no matter how you expand or collapse the groups in your worksheet, the result of these formulas is always the same. That's because, whether you use straight addition (of multiple cells) or the SUM() function, Excel takes into account visible *and* hidden cells. If you group data sets, however, it may occur to you that it would be handy if you could perform a calculation that deals with only the visible cells. That way, you could choose the portions of a worksheet you want to consider, and the formula could recalculate itself automatically to give you the corresponding summary information.

Good news: Excel gives you the power to build just this sort of formula. All you need is the awesome SUBTOTAL() function. As you may recall from Chapter 14, the SUBTOTAL() function is a useful tool for calculating totals in filtered lists. But it's just as helpful when you apply it to outlines, because it ignores collapsed rows and columns.

As explained on page 445, the first argument (known as the calculation code) you use with the SUBTOTAL() function tells Excel the type of math you want to do (summing, averaging, counting, and so on). If you want to ignore the hidden cells in collapsed groups, you have to use the calculation codes above 100. If you want to perform a sum operation, you need to use the code 109. (For a list of the SUBTOTAL() calculation codes, see page 445.)

Once you choose the calculation code, you need to specify the cells or range of cells you want to add. Here's an example that rewrites the earlier formula to sum only visible cells:

```
=SUBTOTAL(109,B7,B15,B23,B31)
```

Figure 15-9 shows the difference between using the SUBTOTAL() function and the SUM() function.

Combining Data from Multiple Tables

Instead of writing your summary formulas by hand, you can generate a summary table automatically that takes advantage of Excel's ability to *consolidate* data. Consolidation works if you have more than one table with precisely the same layout. You can use consolidation to take the tables shown in the sales report (West Division, East Division, and so on) and calculate summary information. Excel creates a new table that has the same structure but *combines* the data from the other tables. You can choose how Excel combines the data, including whether it totals, averages, or multiplies the numbers, and so on.

NOTE Data consolidation works with any sort of tabular data. You don't need to create the structured tables you learned about in Chapter 14.

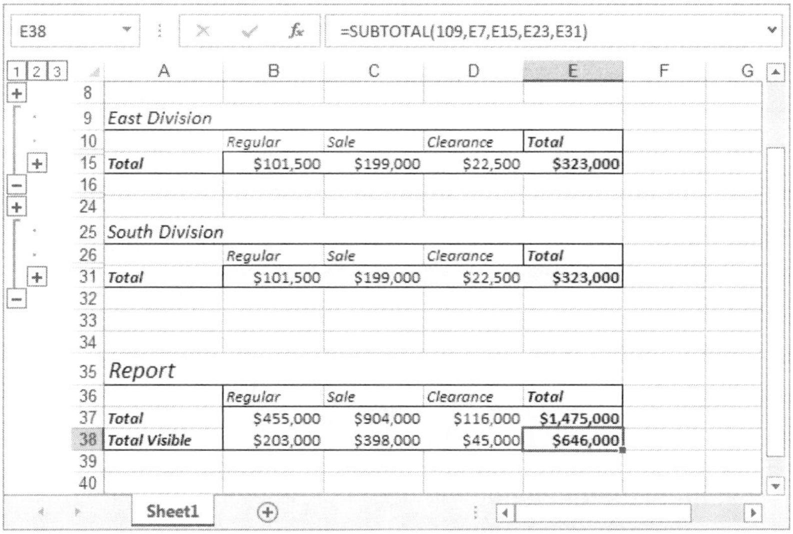

FIGURE 15-9

This worksheet calculates summary information using two different approaches. The formulas in row 37 use the SUM() function, while the formulas in row 38 use the SUBTOTAL() function. In the SUBTOTAL() calculation, Excel doesn't include the subtotals for the completely hidden tables, giving you a different result than that provided by the SUM() function.

Data consolidation works with any worksheet (with or without grouping); you can even use it to analyze data in identically structured tables from different worksheets.

TIP For best results, you should only consolidate data that has the *exact same layout*. Although you can coax Excel into combining differently sized ranges of data, it's all too easy to get confused about what is and isn't combined. To make life easier, only consolidate ranges that have numeric data or identical labels (like column or row titles). Leave out the overall table title, because there's no way to consolidate it.

To consolidate the sales report data, follow these steps:

1. **Move to the location where you want to insert the summary table.**

   Excel inserts the summary table starting at the current cell. Make sure you scroll down past all your data, so you don't overwrite important information.

2. **Choose Data→Data Tools→Consolidate.**

   The Consolidate window appears, as shown in Figure 15-10.

3. **From the Function pop-up menu, choose how you want to combine numbers.**

   In the sales report, Sum is the best choice to calculate total sales. However, you may want to create separate tables that pick out the best or worst sales using Max and Min.

4. **Click inside the Reference text box. Now, drag to select the first table you want to consolidate in the worksheet.**

   If Excel's main window isn't already visible, click the icon at the right end of the Reference text box to collapse the Consolidate window. You have to click this icon again to restore the window when you're done selecting the cells you want.

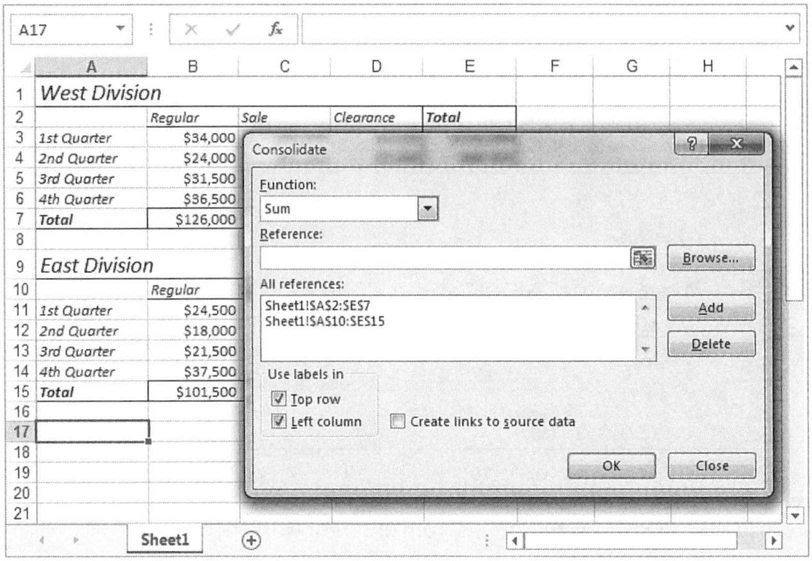

FIGURE 15-10

This worksheet contains two detailed sales tables that are about to be consolidated. Both ranges have been added to the Consolidate window (they're listed in the "All references" list), and the "Top row" and "Left column" checkboxes have been turned on so that Excel can find and use the headings on either side of the table.

5. **Once you select the appropriate cells, click the Consolidate window's Add button.**

   The range appears in the "All references" list.

6. **Return to step 4 to select the next table you want to consolidate.**

   Repeat steps 4 and 5 for each table you want to consolidate.

7. **If your selection includes labels (like row or column titles), select the "Top row" or "Left column" checkbox to tell Excel where the labels are.**

   If you don't tell Excel where the labels are, it ignores the label cells, and the corresponding cells in the summary table wind up blank. But if you use these checkboxes, Excel copies the relevant labels directly to the summary table.

NOTE If the labels don't match exactly in the ranges you're using, you may need to clear the "Top row" and "Left column" checkboxes to perform your consolidation. Otherwise, depending on the placement of these labels, Excel may refuse to consolidate your data.

8. **Click OK to generate the summary table.**

   When creating the consolidated data, Excel copies headings and calculates numbers, but it doesn't copy any of the source formatting. Figure 15-11 shows the result.

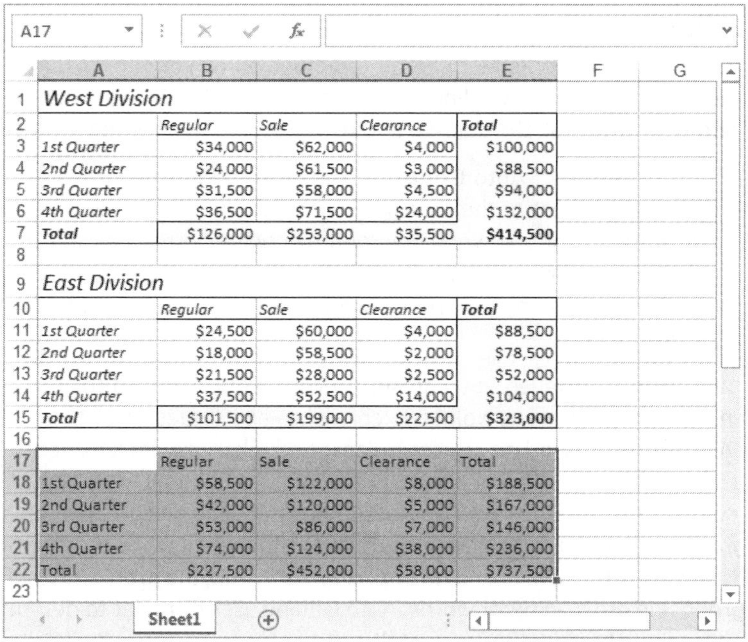

FIGURE 15-11

Here, the newly created consolidated data table is at the bottom of the worksheet. In this case, you used the Sum option, which means that the consolidated data shows the totals you get by adding the values from the separate tables. Cell B18 has the consolidated data for regularly priced merchandise sold in the first quarter in both the West and East Divisions (cells B3 and B11).

Data consolidation's big disadvantage is that it generates a table filled with numbers rather than formulas. Microsoft's engineers probably designed the consolidation feature this way so you can consolidate data from multiple files and not worry about losing the information if the source files move or their structure changes. But this behavior means that if you modify any of the original sales figures, Excel doesn't update the consolidated summary table. To get the correct numbers, you need to generate a new summary table by using the Data→Data Tools→Consolidate command again. Fortunately, the second time around should be quite a bit faster, because Excel keeps track of all the ranges you selected for consolidation, so you don't need to define them again.

Grouping Timesavers

So far, you've learned to tame an intimidating worksheet and neatly organize it into groups. Why stop there? This section covers a few other tools that, along with the grouping tools you just mastered, will make your life easier. These tools include automatic outlining and subtotaling (both of which can create data groups automatically).

Auto Outline

Adding groups to a large worksheet can be tedious. You can leap over that tedium in a single bound with Auto Outline, a feature that gets Excel to examine your worksheet and then create all the column and row groups you need automatically.

Like most automatic features, Auto Outline is a great solution when it works, and it's absolutely no help the rest of the time. Automatic outlining is an all-or-nothing affair, giving you either a grouped worksheet or the unhelpful error message, "Cannot create an outline." You also don't have any ability to configure how many levels of nesting Excel uses, how many groups it creates, and whether it creates column groups, row groups, or both.

With a bit of planning, however, you can set up your worksheets so they're Auto Outline-friendly. Here are the key points. Excel makes all its guesses about how to implement Auto Outline based on any formulas it finds that give it clues about the structure of your worksheet. If you have a formula that uses SUM() to total the cells in multiple columns in the same row, Excel assumes that it can place these columns in a single group so that you can collapse the details and leave just the totals visible. If Excel finds a formula that uses the data in the rows above it, the program assumes that a row group is in order. In other words, Auto Outline uses formulas to determine the grouping levels it should add. If you don't use any summary formulas at all, or if your worksheet uses a table, the Auto Outline feature doesn't work.

To use automatic outlining, select the portion of the worksheet that you want to outline, and then choose Data→Outline→Group→Auto Outline. Generally, it's easiest to select the whole worksheet (click the square just outside the top-left corner of the worksheet) to apply grouping to all your data at once.

If you don't like the results, you can't undo the outlining operation, but you can remove all the groups from your worksheet by choosing Data→Outline→Group→Clear Outline.

Automatic Subtotaling

Auto Outline isn't the only outlining trick that Excel has up its sleeve. The Subtotal tool lets you create groups *and* subtotals all in one click—a feature that can save you scads of time.

To use automatic subtotaling, you need to have a long table of repetitive data (product catalogs, sales transactions, calorie-counting meals on the Atkins plan, and so on). You can't use more than one table—instead, the goal is to get Excel to break your table into summarized subtables for you. Each table gets its own subtotal (for any or all of the columns you choose) and all the subtotals get added together for your very own Grand Total.

To subtotal and outline your data simultaneously, follow these steps:

1. **Sort your data so that the rows you want to group are together in the list.**

   Before subtotaling your data, you may need to sort it into the right order. If you have a list of products and you want to subtotal the product information by category, you need to sort the table by category before you begin. This step ensures that Excel groups all the products in each category together. For detailed information on sorting, see page 424.

2. **Once you have the list in the correct order, select the range of cells that contains the list.**

   Usually, the easiest option is to select each of the columns in your list by dragging across the column headers.

3. **Choose Data→Outline→Subtotal.**

   The Subtotals window appears.

4. **In the "At each change in" pop-up menu, choose the field under which you want the subtotal to appear.**

   The menu provides a list with all the column titles in your selection. If, say, you want to group together (and create subtotals for) products that have the same Category label (as shown in Figure 15-12), you'd choose Category. Excel inserts a subtotal row each time the category label changes. (In the figure, the Communication products subtotal first, the Deception products next, and so on.) For this process to work, you have to sort the list—as you did in step 1—so that all records with the same category are already next to each other.

5. **In the "Use function" pop-up menu, choose the function you want to use to calculate the subtotal information.**

   This list includes everything the SUBTOTAL() function supports, including averages, counts, and subtotals. Unfortunately, you can't total different columns using different functions.

FIGURE 15-12

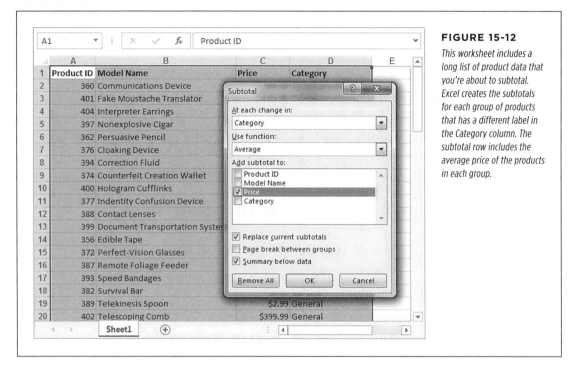

This worksheet includes a long list of product data that you're about to subtotal. Excel creates the subtotals for each group of products that has a different label in the Category column. The subtotal row includes the average price of the products in each group.

6. **The "Add subtotal to" list includes all the column names in your selection. Put a checkmark next to each column you want to generate a subtotal for.**

   To calculate the subtotals, Excel uses the function you chose in step 5.

7. **If you want to start each group on a new page, turn on the "Page break between groups" checkbox.**

   This option works well if you have large groups, and you want to separate them in a printout.

8. **If you want to display the summary information at the end of each group, choose "Summary below data." Otherwise, the totals appear at the beginning of the group.**

   If you're dividing products into category groups, choose "Summary below data" to make sure you'll see the listing of products, followed by the subtotal row.

9. **Click OK to group and subtotal the data.**

   Excel inserts a row in between each group, where it adds the formulas that calculate the subtotals for the group (Figure 15-13). All of the formulas use the SUBTOTAL() function. Excel also calculates grand totals for all the subtotals that it generates.

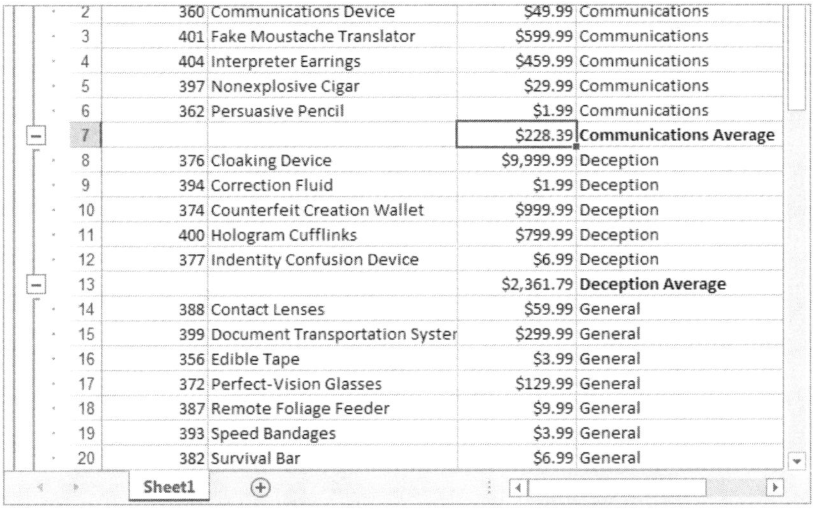

2	360	Communications Device	$49.99	Communications
3	401	Fake Moustache Translator	$599.99	Communications
4	404	Interpreter Earrings	$459.99	Communications
5	397	Nonexplosive Cigar	$29.99	Communications
6	362	Persuasive Pencil	$1.99	Communications
7			$228.39	**Communications Average**
8	376	Cloaking Device	$9,999.99	Deception
9	394	Correction Fluid	$1.99	Deception
10	374	Counterfeit Creation Wallet	$999.99	Deception
11	400	Hologram Cufflinks	$799.99	Deception
12	377	Indentity Confusion Device	$6.99	Deception
13			$2,361.79	**Deception Average**
14	388	Contact Lenses	$59.99	General
15	399	Document Transportation Syster	$299.99	General
16	356	Edible Tape	$3.99	General
17	372	Perfect-Vision Glasses	$129.99	General
18	387	Remote Foliage Feeder	$9.99	General
19	393	Speed Bandages	$3.99	General
20	382	Survival Bar	$6.99	General

Sheet1

FIGURE 15-13

The product list, with subtotaling applied. Rows 7 and 13 contain the newly calculated subtotals. Excel has also added a grand total at the bottom of the list (which isn't shown in this figure).

If you want to remove the subtotals, you have two choices. The easiest is to choose Data→Outline→Subtotals to open the Subtotals window, and then click the Remove All button. Alternatively, you can replace the existing subtotals with new subtotals. To do so, choose different options in the Subtotal window, and make sure you turn on the "Replace current subtotals" checkbox.

CHAPTER

16

Templates

Spreadsheets are rarely one-of-a-kind creations. After you build the perfect sales forecast, expense report, or personal budget, you'll probably want to reuse your hard work instead of starting from scratch. One approach is to save an extra copy of your workbook and just change the data for each new spreadsheet you want to create. That works fine, but it's not terribly convenient.

Excel provides a more streamlined option with *templates*, which are spreadsheet blueprints that you can use to create new files. Templates don't necessarily hold any data (although they can if you want them to). Instead, their main role is letting you format them to your heart's content—adding things like column titles, fancy shading, and complex formulas—so that every time you want a worksheet that looks like your template, all you have to do is select the template and voilà! A new file opens, containing all the design elements you created in the original template.

For example, you could create a monthly expense report template containing all the formulas and formatting you need, and use it to create a fresh report each month. If you ever need to change your report's formatting or calculations, you simply modify the template, and all future expense reports will use the updated version.

In this chapter, you'll use Excel templates two ways. First, you'll consider how you can use one of Microsoft's many prebuilt templates, which are stored on the Office Online website. This massive collection of templates gives you a helpful starting point for all kinds of common spreadsheets. Next, you'll learn how to create your own templates, so you can standardize the types of spreadsheets you create.

Using the Office Online Templates

So far, every example worksheet in this book has started from scratch, with nothing more than Excel's empty grid of cells. This approach is a great way to learn the nuts-and-bolts of Excel, but it's not always necessary. In many cases, you can find a template that's similar to the worksheet you want to create.

You'll have the best odds of finding the template you need if you have lots of templates to choose from. Excel makes this possible through its nifty Office Online website. Office Online provides thousands of free, readymade templates that are just a download away. Its sprawling collection includes the sort of spreadsheet templates you'd expect (ones for creating invoices and financial reports, for example) and many interesting and unusual choices (like templates for baseball scorecards, calorie counters, and wedding planners). Best of all, you can search through this expansive catalog, download the templates you want, and try them out, all without leaving the comfort of Excel's backstage view. The following section leads you through the process.

NOTE Using a template is an obvious tradeoff. If you can find a template that has the exact structure, formatting, and formulas you want, you'll save yourself a good deal of work. But usually, you need to spend some time tweaking a prebuilt template to suit your needs. And in some cases, it's easier to build a new workbook from scratch than rework an ill-fitting template to accommodate your data.

Creating a New Workbook from an Office Online Template

To use a template, begin by selecting File→New to go to the New page in backstage view. (You see a similar screen when you first launch Excel.)

You already know that you choose "Blank workbook" to create a new, empty workbook. But beside the "Blank workbook" image are many more choices, each of which corresponds to a specialized template for a certain type of spreadsheet (Figure 16-1). For example, click "Quarterly budget analysis" to create a workbook with a business-style breakdown of expenses and profits for a single quarter. Choose "Blood pressure tracker" and you'll get a completely different spreadsheet—one that's designed to help you record regular blood pressure readings.

What templates you see in the list depends on various factors. First, Excel makes note of the templates you use, and keeps them close to the top of the list. Second, as long as you have an Internet connection, Excel makes an effort to show you timely templates—for example, an "Election tracker" workbook before a presidential election and a "Holiday budget planner" workbook when the holidays approach. But to really find what you want, you probably need to search for it.

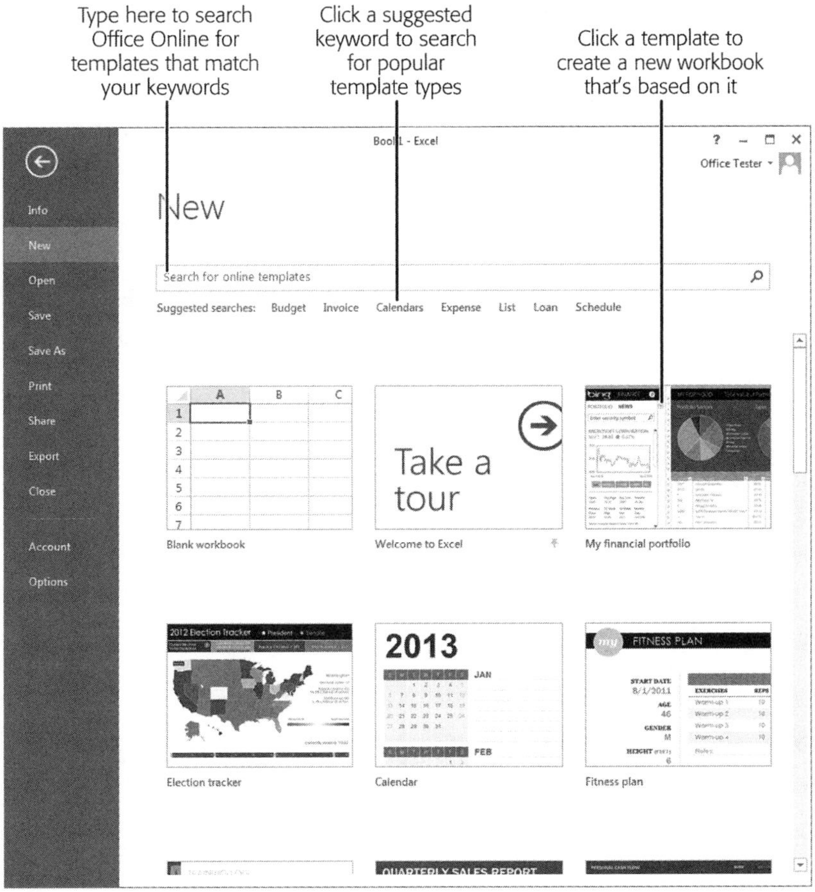

FIGURE 16-1

Excel's New page lists templates you might be interested in. But unless you're just browsing, you'll probably need to turn to the search box to find what you really want.

NOTE Obviously, if your computer doesn't currently have an Internet connection, you can't search for online templates. Instead, you're limited to the templates installed on your computer. However, you can use a trick called pinning (page 476) to download the templates you want when you *are* online, and make sure they remain available even when you're offline.

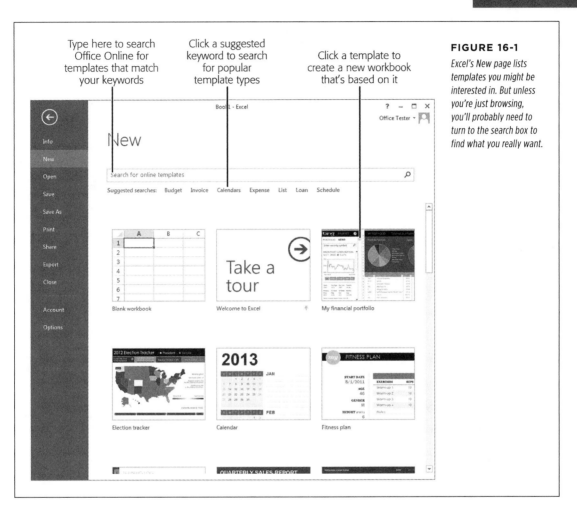

To search by keyword, type one or more search words into the "Search online templates" text box (Figure 16-1), and then press Enter. You can enter as many words as you want, but Excel only shows you templates that contain *all* the words you specify. Try using a word that you think may appear in the template name (like "invoice" or "budget" or "real estate"). If you need some inspiration, click one of the suggested searches links that appear under the text box. These suggestions include templates whose names include some of the most common search keywords.

Depending on the keywords you enter, you may find no templates, just one (Figure 16-2), or a long list of matches (Figure 16-3). For example, if you search for "budget" you'll find templates for personal budgets (including budgets for monthly spending, college, renovations, weddings, and holiday shopping) and templates for business budgets (including marketing plans, business trips, operating expenses, and so on). You can scroll through the list to find what you want, but if it's really long, you might want to limit the results to show only the templates in a specific category, as shown in Figure 16-3.

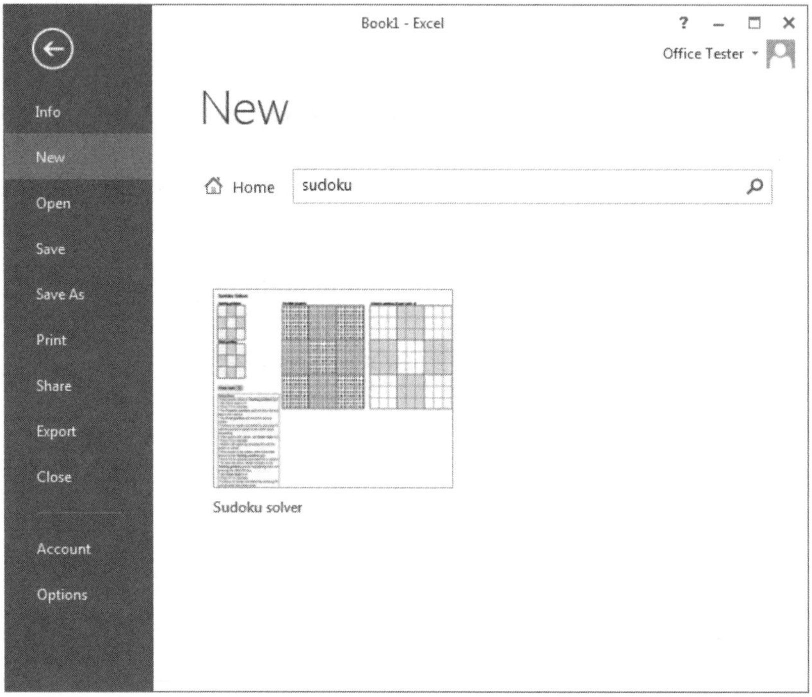

FIGURE 16-2

In this example, a search for the word "sudoku" turns up just one Excel template, the one for solving Sudoku number puzzles.

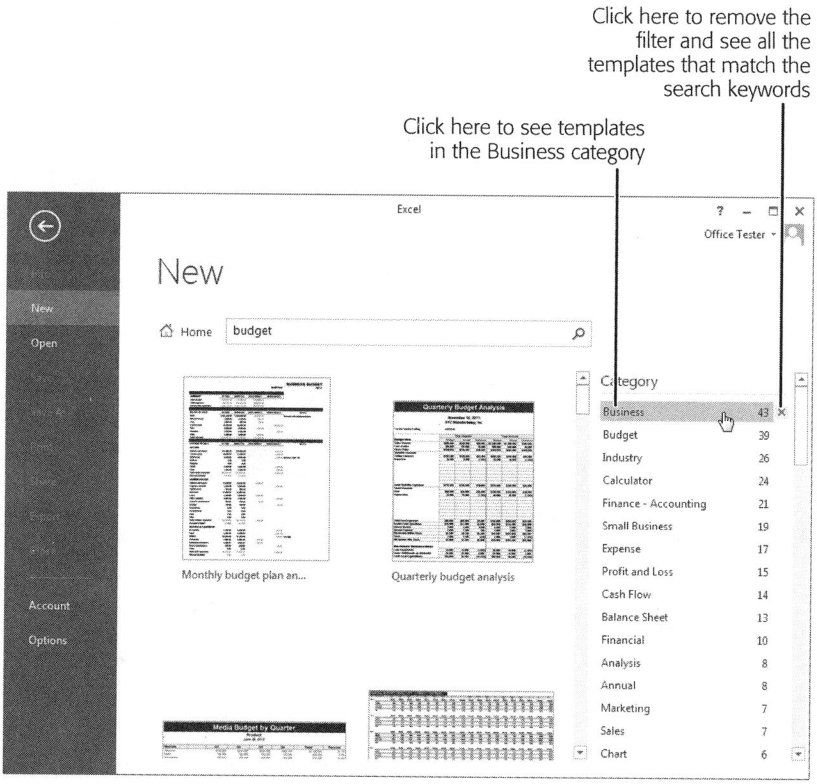

FIGURE 16-3

Here, a search for the word "budget" turns up a long list of templates. On the right are a list of template categories you can use to filter your results. For example, click Business to show only templates in the Business category. Categories aren't exclusive, so a template in the Business category might show up in the Industry category, too. You can even pick more than one category at a time—for example, pick Business and Industry to see only those templates that declare themselves to be a member of both categories. To remove a filter, hover over it and click the tiny X icon that appears to the right of it.

Once you find a template that looks promising, click it to take a closer look. Excel pops open a window that includes the essential template details (Figure 16-4). Then, if you like what you see, click Create to start a new workbook using that template.

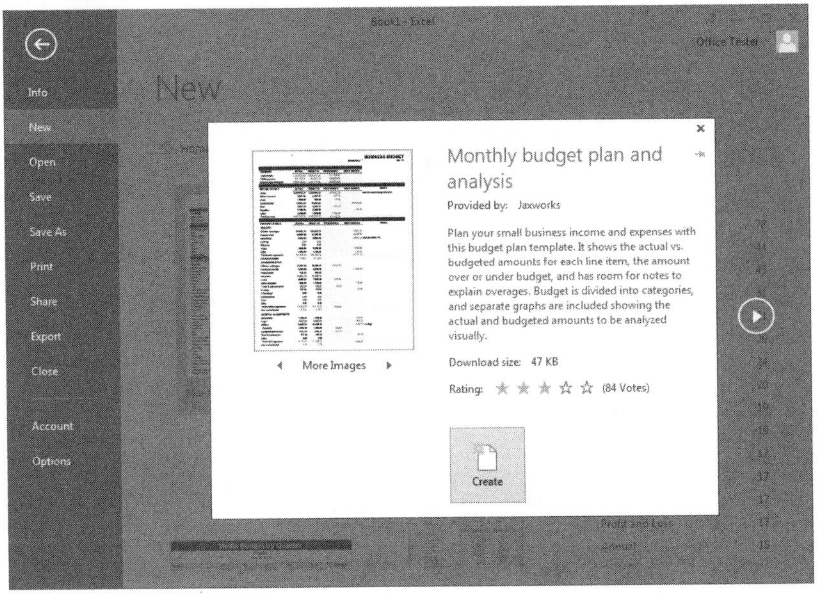

FIGURE 16-4

When you click a template, Excel provides a more detailed description, the name of the person or company that created the template, and the template's star rating (as voted by other Excel fans). You can use this template (click Create), or not (click the X in the top-right corner of the window). And if you want to take a closer look at all the templates in your list, use the left and right arrow buttons on the side of this window to step from one template to the next.

NOTE The template rating plays the same role as customer reviews on Amazon.com—other folks who have downloaded the template can give it a score of up to five stars (but they can't write a review).

Note that you can't rate a template from inside Excel. Instead, you need to surf to the Office Online site to submit a star rating. See page 476 for details.

GEM IN THE ROUGH

Templates for Other Programs

When you perform a template search, Excel doesn't stick to itself. If you scroll to the bottom of the template list, you'll find a section named "Results from your other Office applications" (Figure 16-5). Here, Excel lists templates for other Office programs, like Microsoft Word. This is handy if you aren't sure which program is the best choice for the sort of document you want to prepare.

For example, consider a simple invoice. If you have a lengthy list of items and complex calculations to deal with, Excel is clearly the best choice. But if you want to create an attractively formatted single-page receipt, a Word document with a table might be a better option.

When you click a non-Excel template, you see the same pop-up window with the description and star ranking as you do for an Excel template. But when you click the Create button, the template opens in the appropriate program, like Word.

When you click create, Excel downloads the template you picked. Most Excel templates are very small, so the download process unfolds in a blink—you may not even realize that Excel is fetching the file from the Office Online website.

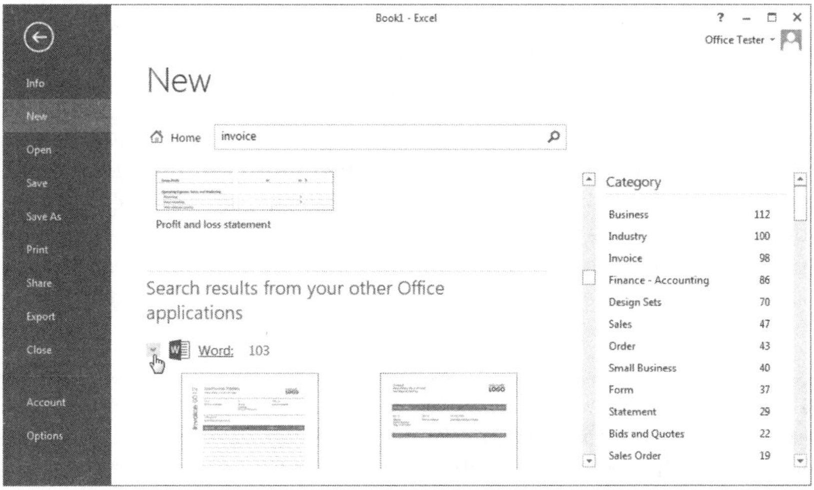

FIGURE 16-5

Here, Excel lets you know that there are 103 invoice templates designed specifically for Word. Initially, these templates aren't shown. But when you click the tiny arrow (or the word "Word"), Excel pops them into view, as shown here.

After Excel downloads the template, it creates a new workbook based on that template (Figure 16-6). You can add your data to this workbook, and, when you save it, Excel prompts you to choose a new file name. Excel suggests a name based on the name of the template. For example, if you select the loan amortization template, Excel suggests a name like "Loan Amortization Schedule1.xlsx" (you can, of course, change this name to anything you want).

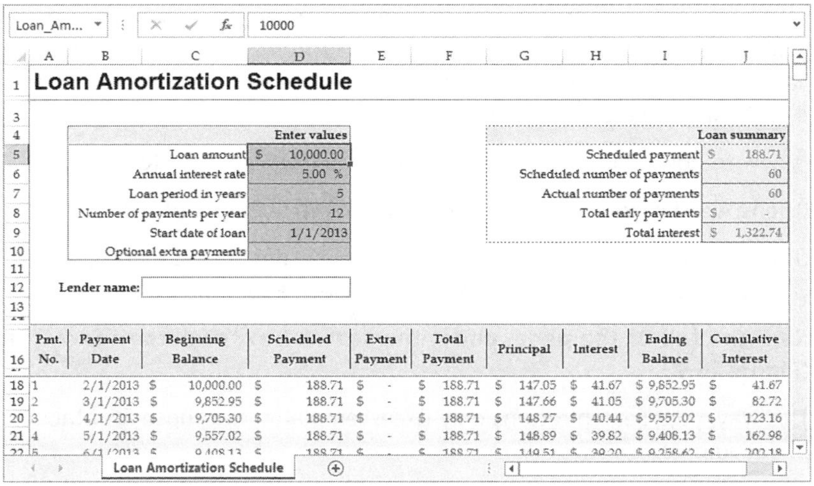

FIGURE 16-6

When you choose this loan amortization template, Excel automatically creates a worksheet with all the formulas you need. You need to enter only the loan amount, interest rate, duration, payment frequency, and start date (cells D5 to D9); Excel calculates the rest automatically, using the financial functions you learned about in Chapter 10.

Make Your Favorite Templates Stick Around

See a template you'd like to use—not just now, but again and again? Excel lets you "pin" your favorite templates to the File→New page, so they're always available, in the same way that it lets you pin frequently used documents (page 41). Just hover over the template in the list and click the small thumbtack icon (you'll see it in the bottom-right corner, under the template preview picture). Or you can pin it from the pop-up window that displays the template details (Figure 16-4)—only now the thumbtack appears in the top-right corner of the window.

Either way, pinned templates stick around. You'll see them at the top of the template list whenever you choose File→New. Pinned templates also behave slightly differently than unpinned templates. When you click one, you won't see the pop-up window with the template details in it. Instead, Excel barrels ahead and creates a new workbook based on the template, without showing you any additional information or asking you to click Create. To remove a pinned template from the list, simply click its thumbtack again.

TIP Pinning is also a handy way to make sure your favorite templates are available even when you don't have an Internet connection. Just pin the template you want and make sure you've used it at least once to create a workbook. If you satisfy these two conditions, the template will be available even when you're offline.

Incidentally, Excel starts with one pinned template, named "Welcome to Excel," which describes the new features of Excel 2013. (Although it's called a template, it's really more of a sample file. You may be interested in reviewing its contents, but you won't use it to build workbooks of your own.) Now that you know how template pinning works, you can remove the "Welcome" workbook if you decide you don't need it anymore.

Downloading Templates from the Office Online Website

Instead of getting all your templates served to you via Excel, you can download them the old-fashioned way, from the Office Online website where they live. You may make the trip to Office Online to download templates because you're on a computer that doesn't have Excel installed, or if you want to rate a template you've found particularly useful (or useless).

Here's how to download a template from the Office Online website:

1. **Open a web browser, and then surf to *http://office.microsoft.com/templates.***

   Use Internet Explorer if you want to open your template in Excel automatically. Otherwise, it'll be up to you to save the template file somewhere and then open it.

2. **Near the top of the page, under the search box, click the "Excel" link (Figure 16-7).**

   This way, your search returns only Excel templates, not those for other types of documents.

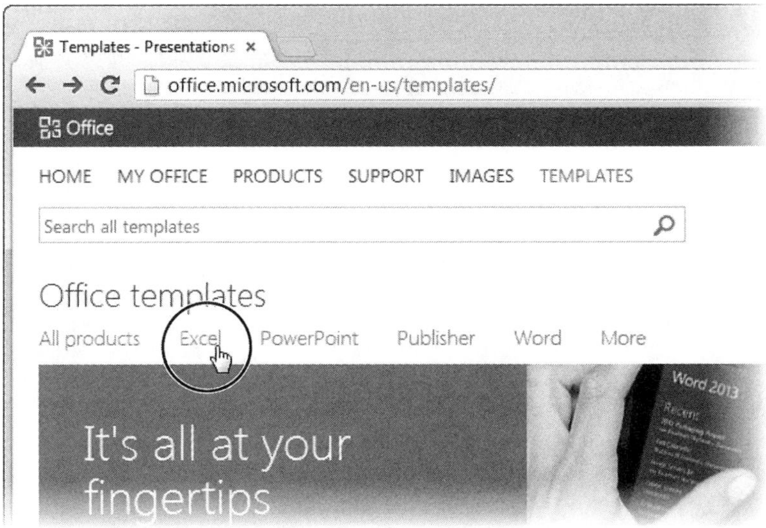

FIGURE 16-7

Click here to zero in on Excel templates. If you don't take this step, your searches will find templates that work with any Office program, including PowerPoint, Publisher, and Word. This is occasionally useful—for example, you might want a way to print out a calendar for 2014, but you don't know whether Excel or Word has the better template.

3. **In the search box, type your search keywords (like "invoice" or "travel") and press Enter.**

   When you search for templates, the search results list the name of each match and the minimum version of Excel that it requires.

4. **Choose a template file from the list by clicking its name.**

   A page appears with detailed template information (Figure 16-8).

5. **If you're still happy with the template, click Download. If you haven't found the right template, click your browser's back button to return to the template list.**

   When you download a template, Microsoft may present you with a license agreement. (This essentially states that you won't sue Microsoft if the template makes your computer explode. Don't worry; it won't.) To continue, click Accept.

6. **If you're using Internet Explorer, a pop-up message appears at the bottom of the page, asking you to install the "Microsoft Office" add-on. To do so, click Install.**

   The "Microsoft Office" add-on simplifies life because it automatically unzips templates (if necessary), launches Excel (if it's installed on the current computer), and opens your newly downloaded template. You only need to install the add-on once.

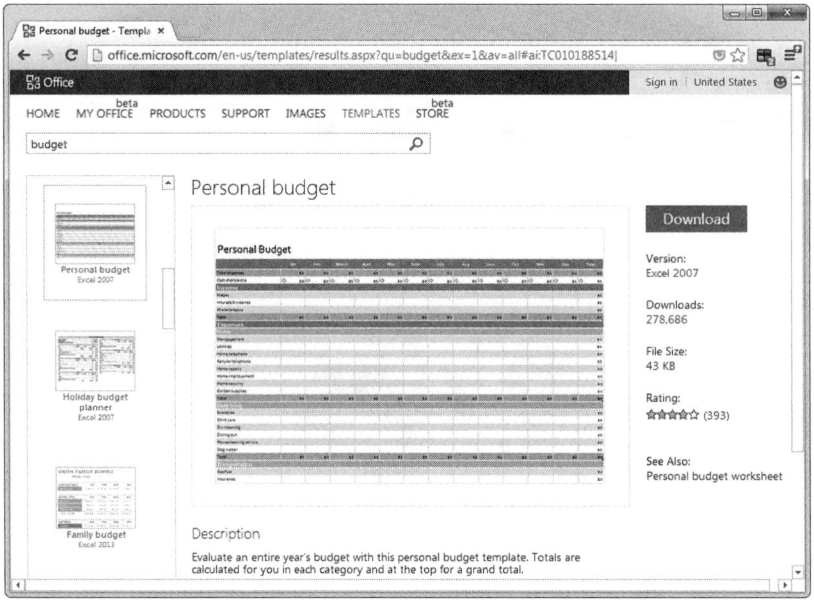

FIGURE 16-8

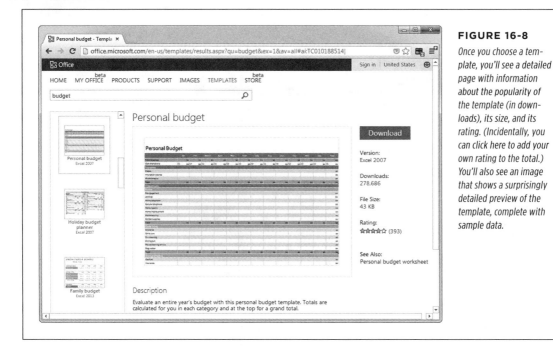

Once you choose a template, you'll see a detailed page with information about the popularity of the template (in downloads), its size, and its rating. (Incidentally, you can click here to add your own rating to the total.) You'll also see an image that shows a surprisingly detailed preview of the template, complete with sample data.

7. **Click Download again to get your template.**

   Your web browser may ask you to approve a pop-up window. If so, click Yes.

   If you're downloading your template with the help of the recommended Microsoft Office add-on, the pop-up window shows you the progress of the download. Once the template downloads (usually, just a fraction of a second later), a Save As window appears. Continue with the next step.

8. **Click Save to save the template in your templates folder.**

   Excel points the window to your personal template folder (page 480), a location on the current computer where you can store all the templates you download and the templates you create. Click Save to accept this location. Then, the Microsoft Office add-on launches Excel and uses your template to create a new workbook, just as if you'd chosen the template in backstage view.

NOTE If you aren't using the Microsoft Office add-on, your web browser downloads your template like a normal file. You can then double-click that template file to open it in Excel. However, if you to use your template to create new workbooks and you want to see it in your list of template choices backstage, it's up to you to copy it to your personal template folder (page 480).

Rolling Your Own Templates

Ready-to-use templates are a fantastic innovation because they provide fine-tuned worksheets without forcing you to write a single formula. Of course, these templates also have a major drawback: No matter how clever Microsoft programmers are, they can't predict your every need.

For example, the Travel Services Invoice provides a generic worksheet that a travel agency might use to bill its customers. But what if you need to group different types of expenses separately, apply different discount rates to various groups, include a late fee, and tack on a few miscellaneous charges to pad your company's bottom line? If that's the case, you need to add your own formulas, restrictions, and formatting to the template. In that case, creating a template from scratch, with the exact features you need, is probably easier.

Templates are particularly useful in large companies. Once the resident Excel genius builds a solid template, everyone else can use that template to create their own workbooks. And spreadsheet experts can create templates brimming with advanced Excel features (things like data validation tools, which you'll learn about in Chapter 21, and fancy formula design). These features help prevent errors (like entering incorrect data or entering it in the wrong place) and provide additional guidance to others who use the template.

UP TO SPEED

Understanding Template Files

Before you begin using and creating templates, it's important to understand what they really are. Many template novices assume that templates are a special sort of file that's *similar* to Excel spreadsheets. However, the crafty individuals who created Excel actually designed template files so that they're *exactly the same* as spreadsheet files. (Whether this feature is a brilliant masterstroke of simple, elegant design or the product of terminally overworked programmers is up to you to decide.)

If you use a file-browsing tool like Windows Explorer to look in a folder that contains spreadsheet files and template files, you'll notice that templates have different files extensions. Whereas ordinary Excel files have the extension *.xlsx* (or *.xlsm* if they contain macro code), templates have the extension *.xltx* (or *.xltm* with macros). In Excel spreadsheets, the *s* stands for spreadsheet (.xlsx), whereas in template files the *t* stands for template (.xltx). For example, Invoice.xltx could be a template for creating invoices, while Invoice01.xlsx would be an actual invoice. However, you can put the exact same type of data in both files: elaborately formatted worksheets, formulas, numbers, text, and so on.

Most organizations and businesses maintain a group of templates that standardize things like layout and formulas for common types of spreadsheets, like invoices and expense reports. Some organizations host these templates in a central location on a network file server or web server (the two best options), or just distribute them to each employee who needs them.

Setting Up a Personal Template Folder

As you'll soon see, it's easy to create a template file. But on its own, a template file isn't of much use. That's because in order to use the template, you need to go hunting for the file, open it up, and then save your work with a new name. It's the same process you go through if you want to take an existing spreadsheet and use it as the starting point for a new workbook. And while that process works, it's not exactly convenient.

To make a template truly useful, it needs to appear in the template list in Excel's backstage view when you choose File→New. To make that happen, you need to set up a *personal template folder*. This is a folder, on your computer or on a company network, that Excel checks for templates *automatically*.

For example, imagine you create a folder named *c:\Templates\Excel* and put three template files inside. If you tell Excel to use this location as your personal template folder, it will find your three templates and offer them as choices in backstage view when you create a new workbook.

TIP Template-sharing is a simple idea that can become incredibly useful in a company environment. Instead of sending template files whizzing back and forth in emails, trying to keep a group of overworked employees in sync each time the template changes, you simply need to modify the templates in the shared location. That way, everybody always has the latest versions available, and there are no distribution headaches.

Here's how you set up a personal template folder:

1. **Decide which folder you want to use as your personal template folder.**

   If you want to use a folder that doesn't exist yet, now's the time to create it. The easiest approach is to use a tool like Windows Explorer.

2. **In Excel, choose File→Options.**

   The Excel Options window appears.

3. **From the list on the left, choose the Save section.**

4. **In the "Save workbooks" section, look for the text box named "Default personal templates location." Type the folder name here (Figure 16-9).**

   Remember, you aren't limited to your local computer. Feel free to use a network drive. The only catch is that you need to know the exact name of the folder, because Excel forces you type it in—it doesn't let you browse to the folder.

5. **Click OK to close the Excel Options window.**

   Now you're ready to start creating templates.

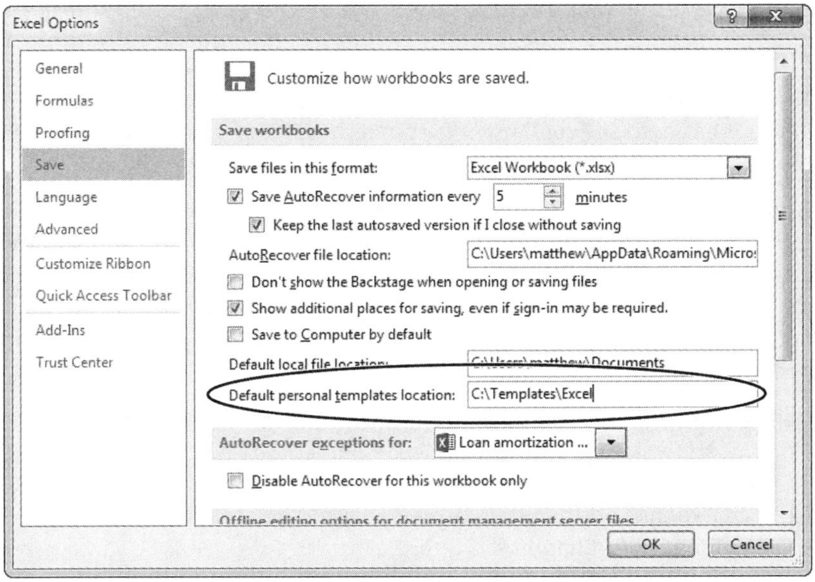

FIGURE 16-9

If you haven't configured a personal templates folder before, the default location setting starts off blank. That's because Office has no idea where to put your templates until you give it the right instructions.

Building a Custom Template

To create a custom template, you simply need to build a new workbook, add any headings, formatting, and formulas you desire, and then save it as a template. You can start this process from scratch by opening a new, blank workbook, or you can refine a built-in template. Either way, you should follow the same process for perfecting your template-to-be. Here are some tips:

- **Clear out the junk.** Your template should be a blank form politely waiting for input. Clear away all the data in your template, unless it's generic content. For example, you can leave your company name or the worksheet title, but it probably doesn't make sense to have sample numbers.
- **Assume formulas won't change.** The ideal template is one anyone can use, even Excel novices who are too timid to edit a formula. If you have a formula that contains some data that might change (for example, a sales commission, interest rate, late fee, and so on), *don't* type that data directly into your formula. Instead, put it in a separate cell, and refer to that cell in the formula. That makes it easy for the person using the template to put different numbers into your calculations. (For example, say your accounting department gives each salesperson a different commission rate. By putting the sales commission in a separate cell and referring to that cell in the sales commission formula, you ensure that there's no need to change the formula for each salesperson.)

- **Don't be afraid to use lists and outlining.** These features are too complicated for many mere mortals (those who haven't read this book, for example), but they make spreadsheets easier to use and more powerful. By adding these frills to a template, other people can take advantage of their organizational powers without having to apply them on their own. Charts and pictures, which you'll learn more about in Part Four, are also good template additions.
- **Turn off worksheet gridlines.** Many templates turn off Excel's gridlines. That makes it easier to see custom borders and shading, which you can use to draw attention to important cells. To turn off gridlines, select View→Show→Gridlines.
- **Add the finishing touches.** Once you have the basics in place—titles, captions, formulas, and so on—it's time to create a distinct look. You can add borders, change fonts, and inject color. (Just remember not to go overboard with cell shading, or the output may be impossible to read on a black-and-white printout.) You may also want to tweak the paper size and orientation to ensure a good printout.
- **Delete extra worksheets and assign good names to the remaining ones.** Every workbook starts with three worksheets, named Sheet1, Sheet2, and Sheet3. The typical template has only one worksheet, and it's named appropriately (such as Expense Form). For information about deleting and renaming worksheets, flip back to Chapter 4.
- **Consider adding shapes with tips.** You can add callouts, word bubbles, and other text containers from the Insert→Illustrations→Shapes list (page 596). You can then type in helpful tips that explain the template and guide the person who's using it. (For example, you might include an arrow that points to a cell and states "Here's where you put the amount of money you borrowed.") Microsoft uses this technique in many of its newer templates.
- **Consider adding custom macros to make a really slick spreadsheet.** For a real treat, you can create a custom macro that performs some sort of task with your worksheet data. You can even add a button to your worksheet that triggers the macro. For more information about how to build macros, see Chapter 29.

TIP You can use one of Excel's templates as a starting point for your own templates. Just follow the process described earlier, edit the template (by adding information, changing formatting, and so on), and then save it as a new template. However, you'll generally find it easier (at least at first) to create your own templates from scratch.

Once you perfect your template, save it. Follow these steps:

1. **Select File→Export.**

   Excel's Export page appears.

2. **Click Change File Type. Then, in the list of file formats, double-click "Template (*.xltx)."**

   The Save As window appears.

3. **Browse to your personal template folder.**

   To make your template appear in backstage view, you need to put it in your personal template folder (the location you configured on page 480).

4. **Name the template, and then click Save.**

   Just like any other Excel file, you can open and edit your template any time you need to make changes. (However, if you change a template, it won't affect any of the workbooks created with the old version of the template.)

To actually use your template, start by choosing File→New to enter backstage view. Excel keeps your templates separate from the sprawling catalog of templates from Office Online. To see them, click the word Personal under the template search box (Figure 16-10).

TIP If you have a huge pile of templates to manage, you can arrange them in subfolders. For example, if your personal template folder is *c:\Templates\Excel*, you can create subfolders like *c:\Templates\Excel\Invoices* and *c:\Templates\Excel\Expenses*, and place template files inside them. You'll see these folders in the personal template list (Figure 16-10).

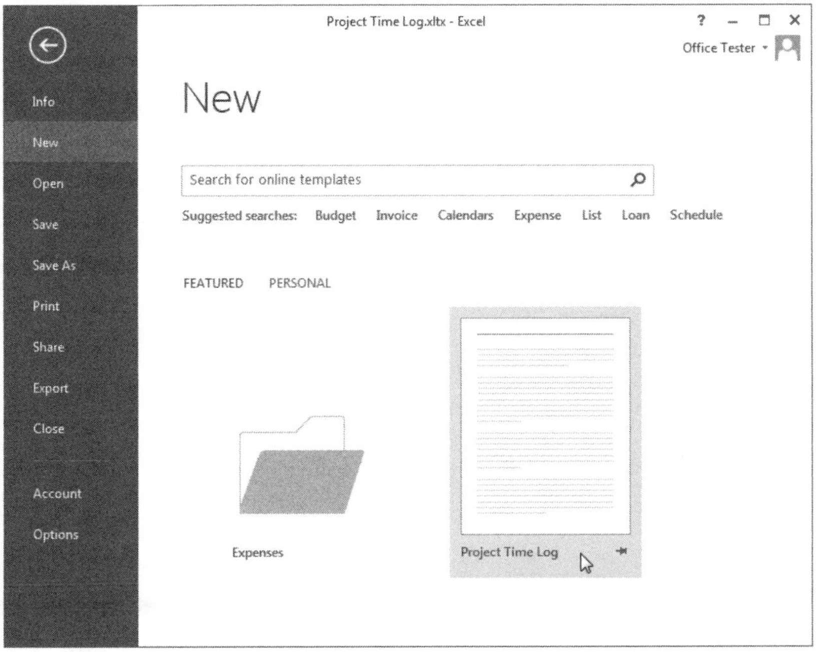

FIGURE 16-10

The Personal category displays all your homemade templates. To use one to create a new workbook (like the Project Time Log shown here), just click it. To browse to a subfolder to look for more templates, click the subfolder (like Expenses here).

WORD TO THE WISE

Creating Bulletproof Templates

By now, you probably realize that templates aren't just a way to eliminate repetitive work when you need to create similar spreadsheets. They're also a way to let ordinary people—those, unlike you, who aren't familiar with Excel's dark arts—to record information, fill out forms, and analyze data. These people need a little guidance, and templates are there to help.

Unfortunately, Excel isn't always forgiving. Even if you craft the perfect template, an Excel novice can accidentally delete or overwrite a formula just by pressing the wrong key. And it's almost as easy for someone to put the wrong information in a cell (for example, by entering a date incorrectly so that it's interpreted as text). Furthermore, a template is no help when the person using it doesn't know where to start typing or what the different headings really mean. All these problems can occur (and regularly do) even if you think your template is a small miracle of straightforward design and organization.

When you want to create a truly bulletproof template, you can use two more Excel features:

- *Data validation* prevents people from entering the wrong type of data in a cell (or warns them when they do). It also lets you set up a handy drop-down list of values that the person editing the worksheet can choose from.
- *Worksheet protection* prevents people from changing certain cells, and (optionally) stops them from viewing the formulas inside.

Microsoft designed both these features for ordinary workbooks, but they make good sense in templates too. To learn more about how they work, skip straight to Chapter 21 for the full story.

PART

4

Charts and Graphics

CHAPTER

17

Creating Basic Charts

As you become more skilled with Excel, you'll realize that entering numbers, organizing your layout, and formatting cells aren't the most important parts of spreadsheet creation. Instead, the real work lies in *analyzing* your data—in figuring out a way to tell the story that lies *behind* your numbers. And one of the best ways to do that is with Excel's charting tools.

Charts depict data visually, so you can quickly spot trends. They're a fabulous way to help you find the meaning hidden in large amounts of data. You can create many different types of charts in Excel, including pie charts that present polling results, line charts that plot rising or declining assets over time, and three-dimensional area charts that show relationships between environmental conditions in a scientific experiment.

Excel's charting tools are enormously flexible: You can generate a simple chart with standard options with a couple of mouse clicks, or you can painstakingly customize every aspect of your chart's appearance (including colors, scale, titles, and even 3-D perspective). This chapter takes the first approach and explains how to generate straightforward charts, which you'll examine in detail. You'll also learn which chart types are out there. In the next chapter, you'll learn how to fine-tune your charts for maximum effect.

NOTE All charts are *not* created equal. Depending on the chart type you use, the scale you choose, and the data you include, your chart may suggest different conclusions. The true chart artist knows how to craft a chart to emphasize the most important information. As you become more skilled with charts, you'll acquire these instincts, too.

Charting 101

Excel provides a dizzying number of chart types, but they all share a few characteristics. In this section, you'll learn basic charting concepts that apply to almost all types of charts; you'll also create a few basic Excel charts. At the end of this chapter, you'll take a chart-by-chart tour of each and every one of Excel's many chart types.

To create a chart, Excel translates your spreadsheet numbers into a visual representation of that data. The process of drawing numbers on a graph is called *plotting*. But before you plot your data, you need to lay it out properly. Here are some tips:

- Structure your data in a simple grid of rows and columns.
- Don't include blank cells between rows or columns.
- Include titles, if you want them to appear in your chart. You can use category titles for each column of data (placed in the first row, atop each column) and an overall chart title (placed just above the category-title row).

TIP You can label each *row* by placing titles in the far-left column. For example, if you're comparing the sales numbers for different products, list the name of each product in the first column on the left, with the sales figures in the following columns.

If you follow these guidelines, you can create the sort of chart shown in Figure 17-1.

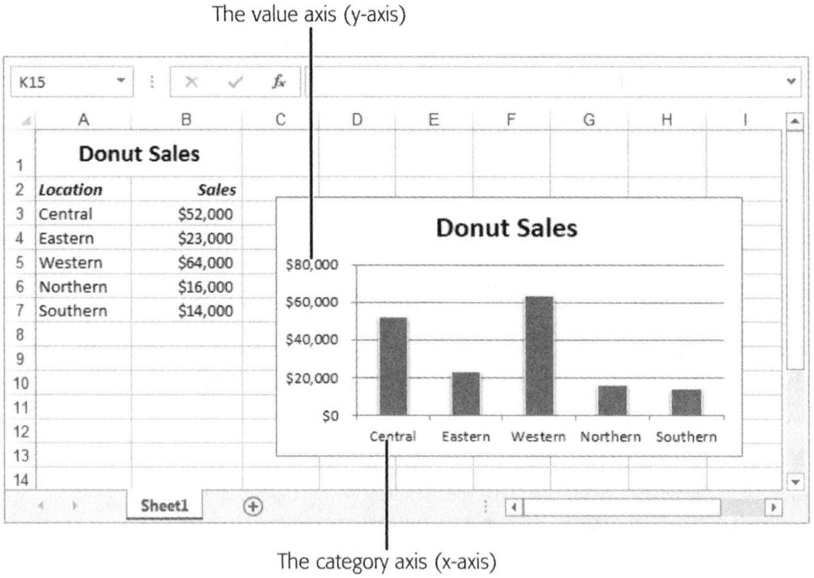

FIGURE 17-1

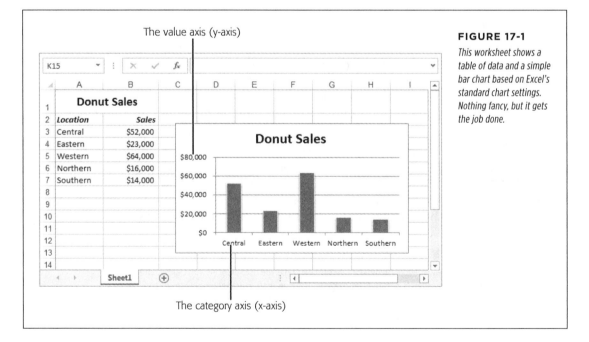

This worksheet shows a table of data and a simple bar chart based on Excel's standard chart settings. Nothing fancy, but it gets the job done.

To create the chart in Figure 17-1, Excel performs a few straightforward steps (you'll learn how to actually create this chart in the next section). First, it extracts the text for the chart title from cell A1. Next, it examines the range of data (from $14,000 to $64,000) and uses it to set the value—or Y-axis—scale. You'll notice that the scale starts at $0, and stretches up to $80,000 (or so) to give your data a little room to breathe. (You could configure these numbers manually, but Excel automatically makes commonsense guesses like these by looking at the data you ask it to chart.) After setting the vertical scale, Excel adds the labels along the bottom axis (also known as the X-axis or category axis), and draws columns of appropriate height.

Embedded and Standalone Charts

The chart in Figure 17-1 is an *embedded* chart. Embedded charts appear in a worksheet, in a floating box alongside your data. You can move the chart by dragging the box around your worksheet, although you may obscure some of your data if you're not careful.

Your other option is to create a *standalone* chart, which looks the same but occupies an entire worksheet by itself. That means that your chart data and your chart reside in separate worksheets. (See Chapter 4 if you need a refresher on creating new worksheets, switching between them, or changing their order.)

Usually, you'll use an embedded chart to create printouts that combine both your worksheet data and one or more charts. On the other hand, if you want to print your charts separately, it's more convenient to use standalone charts. That way, you can print an entire workbook at once and have the charts and the data on separate printed pages.

NOTE If you use embedded charts, you still have the option of printing just the chart, sized so that it fills a full sheet of paper. Simply select the chart, and then choose File→Print. If you create a standalone chart, you don't have a choice—Excel always prints your chart on a separate page.

Adding a Recommended Chart

So how do you create a chart like the one in Figure 17-1? It's easy if you use Excel's Quick Analysis feature. Quick Analysis reviews your worksheet and *recommends* a chart that it thinks suits your data, all in just a few mouse clicks. Here's how it works:

1. **Select the range of cells that includes the data you want to chart, including the column and row headings.**

   If you wanted to chart the data in Figure 17-1, you'd select cells A2 to B7.

   The Quick Analysis icon appears at the bottom-right corner of your selection (Figure 17-2).

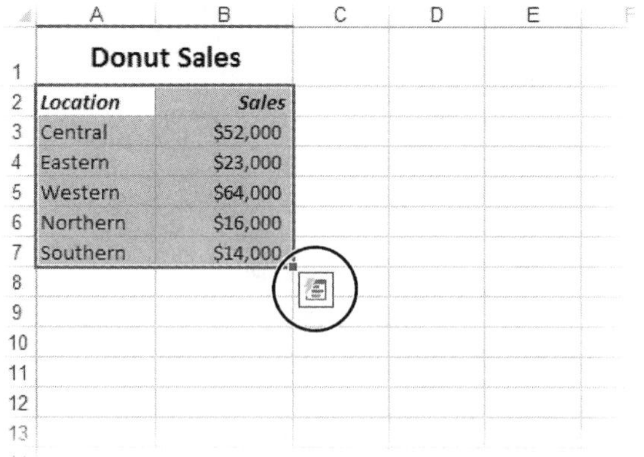

FIGURE 17-2

The Quick Analysis icon (which looks like a worksheet with a lightning bolt in front of it) gives you a shortcut to five of Excel's major analysis features: conditional formatting, charts, formulas that calculate totals, tables, and sparklines. Click Charts to see what Excel recommends for the currently selected cells.

2. **Click the Quick Analysis button, and choose the Charts section.**

   Depending on the data you selected, Excel may recommend different types of charts (Figure 17-3).

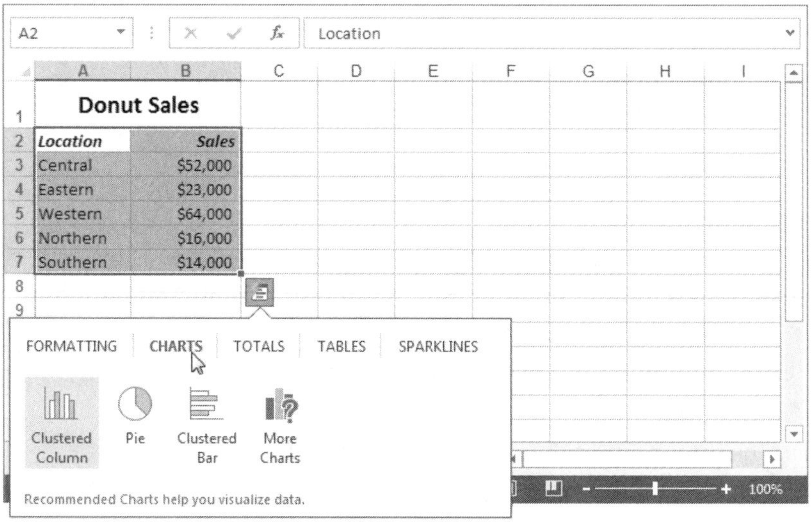

FIGURE 17-3

For this simple data, Excel recommends a clustered column chart, pie chart, or clustered bar chart.

If you see the chart type you want, click it.

To create the chart in Figure 17-1, you'd click Clustered Column. Excel inserts a new embedded chart alongside your data, using its standard options (which you can fine-tune later).

If you don't see the chart you want, click More Charts to pop open the Insert Chart window, which offers many more charting options. The next section explains how to choose from among them.

NOTE The different chart types are explained in more detail later in this chapter. Remember, the chart you pick is just a starting point, because you can configure a wide range of chart details like titles, colors, and overall organization.

Picking from the Full Range of Charts

Excel's Quick Analysis feature gives you a quick way to add a basic chart. But Excel has plenty more charting options, some of which are specialized and bizarre, and may not appear in the list of recommended charts.

Fortunately, it isn't hard to get exactly what you want, provided you understand how Excel categorizes charts. First, Excel divides every chart into one of *nine* general types: charts that have columns, lines, pie slices, bars (they're like columns, but horizontal), points, two-dimensional areas, three-dimensional surfaces, and stock bars. And Excel further divides each of these chart types into chart *subtypes*. For example, if you choose a pie chart as your type, your subtypes include the ordinary pie chart, a pie chart that shows a detailed breakdown for a single slice, a pie chart in the shape of a donut, and so on. (You'll find all of Excel's chart types and subtypes described at the end of this chapter.)

To pick a specific chart type and subtype, start by selecting the data you want to use. But instead of clicking the Quick Analysis button, head to the ribbon's Insert→Charts section. You'll see a separate button for each type of chart, more or less. (Excel groups together the stock, surface, and radar chart types under one button, and adds extra buttons for combination charts and pivot charts, which offer slightly different features.) When you click one of the chart types, Excel opens a drop-down list of subtypes (Figure 17-4).

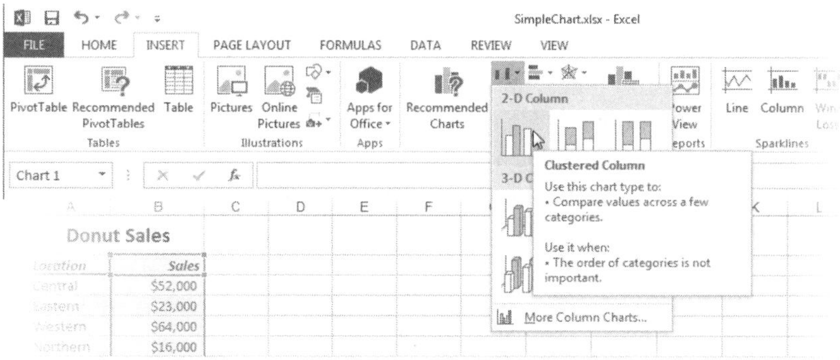

FIGURE 17-4

Under each chart choice, you'll find chart subtypes, which add to the fun. If you select the Column chart (shown here), you'll get subtypes for two- and three-dimensional column charts. Click one to insert it in your worksheet.

If you're trying to find a less commonly used type of chart, or you just want to browse through your chart options before you pick one, you can use the all-powerful Insert Chart window. To see it, click the dialog launcher (the square-with-an-arrow icon in the bottom-right corner) in the ribbon's Insert→Charts section. Or, use the Quick Analysis button: Pop it open, choose Charts, and then click More Charts.

The Insert Chart window has two tabs. The Recommended Charts tab shows the same recommended charts you'd get with the Quick Analysis button. But the All Charts tab (Figure 17-5) list *all* the charts you can create, grouped by subtype.

For example, to add an ordinary column chart from the Insert Chart window, you first click Column (on the left), then click the Clustered Column thumbnail (the first option in the list across the top), then pick the formatting options (by clicking one of the two large thumbnails below), and finally click OK.

NOTE The All Charts tab in the Insert Chart window includes a few extra options: Recent (the charts you recently picked), Templates (charts with custom settings you configure, as described on page 529), and Combo (combination charts that fuse two types of otherwise ordinary charts, as described on page 573). Ignore these for now, and you're left with Excel's nine fundamental chart types.

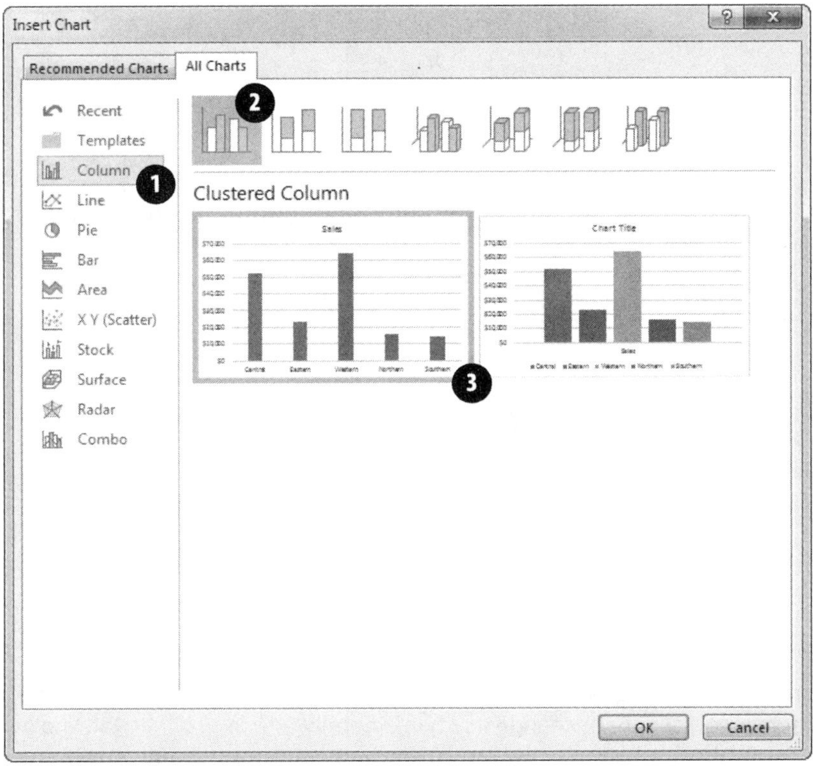

FIGURE 17-5

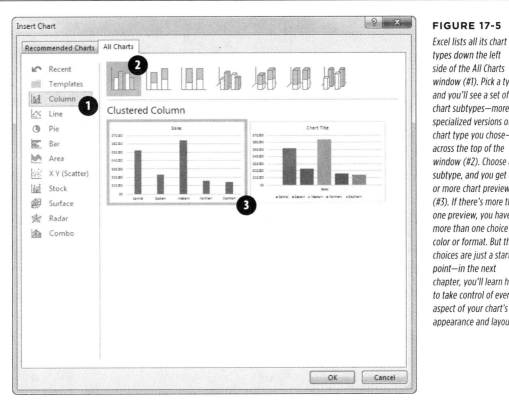

Excel lists all its chart types down the left side of the All Charts window (#1). Pick a type, and you'll see a set of chart subtypes—more specialized versions of the chart type you chose—across the top of the window (#2). Choose a subtype, and you get one or more chart previews (#3). If there's more than one preview, you have more than one choice of color or format. But these choices are just a starting point—in the next chapter, you'll learn how to take control of every aspect of your chart's appearance and layout.

Selecting a Chart

When you select a chart, Excel highlights the worksheet data the chart uses. At the same time, it puts some handy chart-manipulating tools at your fingertips, including three new buttons (Figure 17-6) and two extra ribbon tabs.

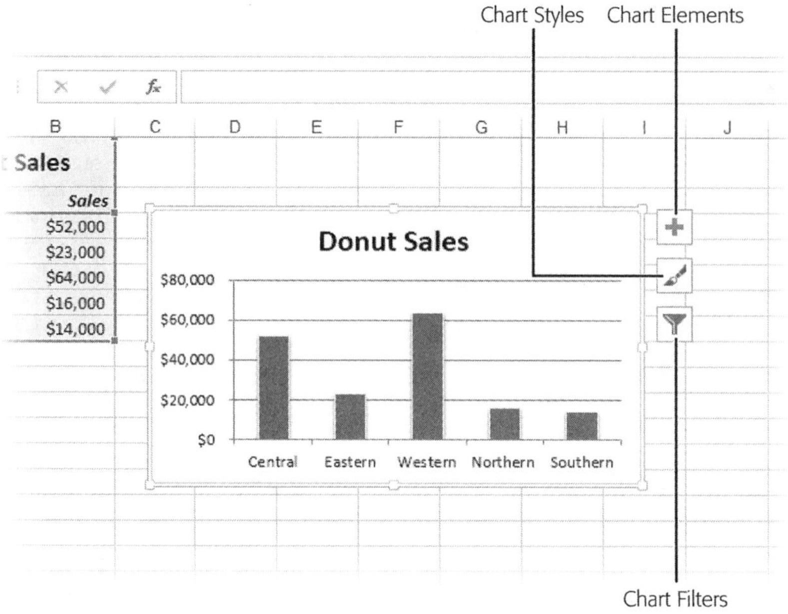

FIGURE 17-6

Select a chart and three new buttons appear, floating above your worksheet. At the same time, Excel stuffs two more tabs filled with chart-tweaking goodness into the ribbon (not shown).

The three new buttons, which show up on the right edge of the chart, let you add new details to your chart, change its style, or apply filtering so that you show only some of your data on the chart. You'll learn about filtering later in this chapter (page 499), and you'll consider the other buttons with the more ambitious chart-customization tasks in Chapter 18.

The two new tabs, which appear in the ribbon under the Chart Tools heading, give you even more chart-customization powers. In this chapter, you'll use the Chart Tools | Design tab to change the chart type and the linked data that the chart uses. In Chapter 18, you'll use the Chart Tools | Format tab to format individual parts of the chart.

NOTE If you've worked with charts in previous versions of Excel, you might be thrown off by Excel 2013's ribbon rearrangement. Both Excel 2007 and Excel 2010 have *three* chart-specific tabs under the Chart Tools heading (Design, Format, and Layout). Excel 2013 removes the Layout tab, and relocates its functionality into the other two tabs. All the same features are there, but now they're more compactly organized.

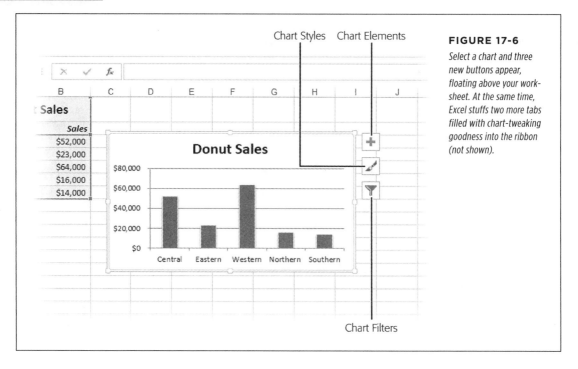

Basic Tasks with Charts

Unlike the orderly rows of numbers and labels that fill most worksheets, charts float *above* your data, locked inside special box-like containers. To take advantage of these chart boxes, you need to understand a little more about how they work.

Moving and Resizing a Chart

When you insert a chart into an existing worksheet, it becomes a floating object, hovering above your worksheet. Depending on where Excel puts it, it may temporarily obscure your data. The chart box doesn't damage your data in any way, but it can end up hiding your worksheet's numbers and text (both onscreen and in your printouts).

You have to learn to grab hold of these floating boxes and place them where you really want them. The process is pretty straightforward:

1. **Click the chart once to select it.**

   You'll know that you've selected the chart when the three charting icons appear along the right side of the chart.

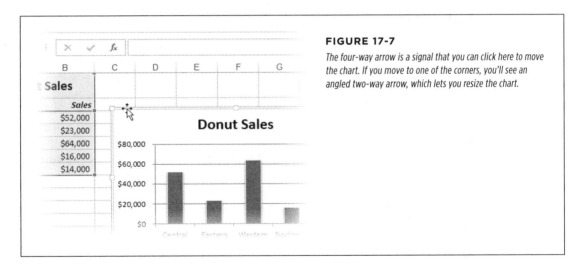

2. **Hover over the chart border until the mouse pointer changes to a four-way arrow (Figure 17-7). Then, click and drag with your mouse to move the chart.**

   Using the four-way arrow, you can drag the chart anywhere on your worksheet, releasing the mouse button when it's in the right spot.

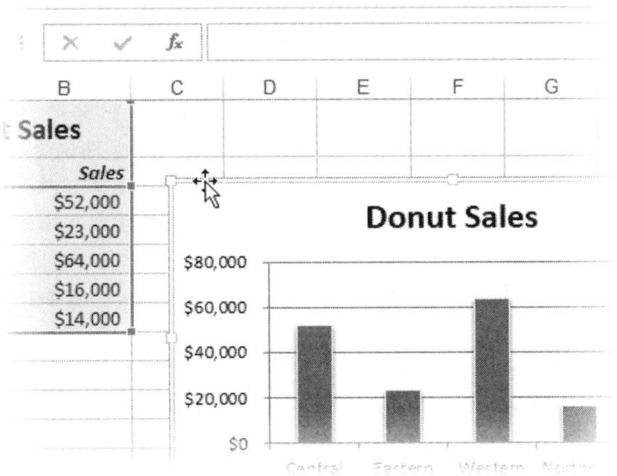

FIGURE 17-7

The four-way arrow is a signal that you can click here to move the chart. If you move to one of the corners, you'll see an angled two-way arrow, which lets you resize the chart.

3. **Move the mouse to the bottom-right corner of the chart box, so the mouse pointer changes to a two-way arrow. Then, click and drag the border to make the chart larger or smaller.**

   Once you resize the chart box, you may also want to resize the individual components inside the chart to better use the available space. Page 543 tells you how to select chart elements and resize them.

TIP To remove a chart in one fell swoop, first select it (the easiest way to select the whole thing is to click somewhere on the border) and then press Delete.

4. **When you finish moving and resizing, click a cell anywhere in the worksheet to go back to your data.**

   At this point, life returns to normal, and the Chart Tools tabs disappear.

TIP You can resize a chart in another, slightly more circuitous way. You can set the Height and Width boxes in the Chart Tools | Format→Size section of the ribbon. Although this isn't as quick as dragging the chart edge, it lets you set the size exactly, which is indispensable if you have several charts on the same worksheet and you need to make sure they're all the same size.

UNDER THE HOOD

How Excel Anchors Charts

Although charts appear to float above a worksheet, they're actually anchored to the cells underneath. Each corner of the chart is anchored to one cell (these anchor points change, of course, if you move the chart around). This fact becomes important if you decide to insert or delete rows or columns anywhere in your worksheet.

For example, consider the chart in Figure 17-1. Its top edge is bound to row 2, and its bottom edge is bound to row 12. Similarly, its left edge is bound to column C, and its right edge to column I. That means that if you insert a new row above row 2, the whole chart shifts down one row. If you insert a column to the left of column C, the whole chart shifts one column to the right.

Even more interesting is what happens if you insert rows or columns in the area that the chart overlaps. For example, if you insert a new row between the current row 10 and row 11, the chart stretches, becoming one row taller. Similarly, if you delete column D, the chart compresses, becoming one column thinner.

If it bugs you, you can change this sizing behavior. First, select the chart, and then head to the ribbon's Chart Tools | Format→Size section. Click the dialog launcher (the square-with-an-arrow icon in the bottom-right corner). When the Format Chart Area panel appears, on the right, click the Properties section to expand it. You'll see three positioning options. The standard behavior is "Move and size with cells," but you can also create a chart that moves around the worksheet but never resizes itself and a chart that's completely fixed in size and position.

Creating a Standalone Chart

You can place a chart in a workbook two ways. You can create an embedded chart, which appears in an existing worksheet (usually next to the appropriate data), or you can create a standalone chart, which appears in a new worksheet of its own (Figure 17-8). Technically, this latter type of worksheet is a *chart sheet*.

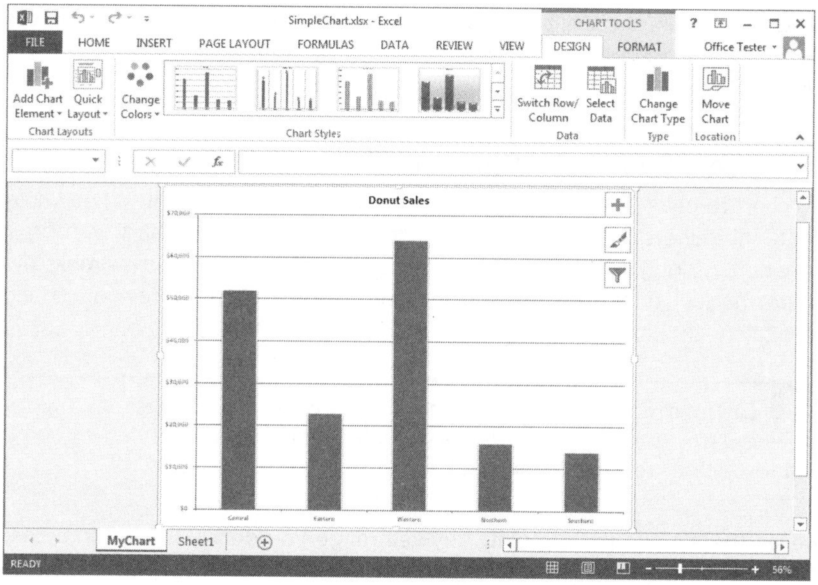

FIGURE 17-8

A standalone chart lives in a separate worksheet that doesn't have any other data in it and doesn't include the familiar grid of cells.

Ordinarily, when you pick a chart type from the ribbon, Excel creates an embedded chart. However, you can easily switch your chart over to a chart sheet if you're running out of room. Follow these steps:

1. **Right-click the chart, and then choose Move Chart (or select the chart, and then choose Chart Tools | Design→Location→Move Chart).**

   The Move Chart window appears (Figure 17-9).

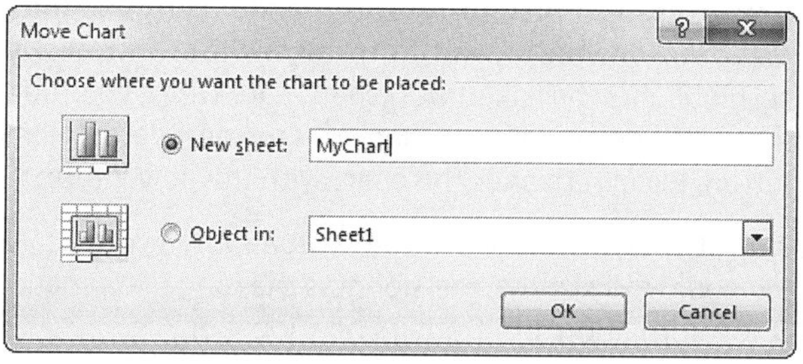

FIGURE 17-9

Using the Move Chart window, you can transfer a chart to a chart sheet (as shown here) or shuffle it over to another worksheet and keep it as an embedded chart. (If you want the latter option, it's just as easy to select the chart, and then use a cut-and-paste operation to move it to a new worksheet.)

2. **Choose "New sheet," and then enter a name for the new chart sheet.**

3. **Click OK.**

   Excel creates the chart sheet and places the chart in it. The chart sheet goes in front of the worksheet that contains the chart data. (You can always move the chart sheet to a new position in your workbook by dragging the worksheet tab.)

NOTE You can only move or resize embedded charts—the ones that appear in floating boxes inside other worksheets. If you create a chart sheet, you can't move or resize your chart. Instead, it automatically shrinks or enlarges to match the Excel window's display area.

Editing and Adding to Chart Data

Every chart remains linked to the source data you used to create it. When you alter the data in your worksheet, Excel automatically refreshes the chart with the new information. As long as Excel is set to automatic recalculations (and it almost always is), there's no such thing as an out-of-date chart. (Page 400 has more about changing Excel's calculation mode.)

NOTE Excel has no restriction on linking multiple charts to the same data. So you can create two types of charts (like a pie and a column chart) that show the same data. You can even create one chart that plots all the data and another chart that uses just a portion of the same information.

However, there's one tricky point. Any cell range you define for use in a chart is *static*, which means that if you add to that range, the chart doesn't reflect the row or column of data you added. So if you add a row at the bottom of the range, that row's data doesn't appear in the chart because it's outside the range you initially set for the chart.

If you *do* want to add data to a cell range used in a chart, you have several options:

- You can use the Home→Cells→Insert→Insert Sheet Rows command. If you do, Excel notices the change, and automatically expands the range to include the newly inserted row. However, this command works only if you add a row to the middle of your data. If you tack a row onto the end, Excel still ignores it, and you'll need to use the solution described in the next bullet point.

- After you insert new rows, you can modify the chart range to include the new data. This approach is the most common, and it's quite painless. First, click your chart to select it. Excel highlights the linked worksheet data with a colored border. Click this colored border, and drag it until it includes the new data When you release the mouse button, Excel refreshes the chart with the new information.

Excel is smart enough to adjust your chart range in some situations. If you drag your chart data to a new place in your worksheet, Excel updates the range automatically, so your chart gets the same information, but from its new location.

GEM IN THE ROUGH

Charting a Table

You can use Excel's table feature (discussed in Chapter 14) with charts. Tables and charts make a perfect match. Tables grow and shrink dynamically as you add or delete records. If your chart is bound to a table, Excel updates the chart as you add new information or remove old data.

You can build a chart based on a table in the usual way—by selecting the data and then clicking the Quick Analysis button. If you've already created the chart with an ordinary range of cells, you can still use a table—all you need to do is convert the linked range to a table. In the sales report example in Figure 17-1, here's what you'd need to do:

1. Select the range of cells that contain all the data, including the column headers but not the chart's title (so select cells A2 to B7).
2. Select Insert→Tables→Table.

Now, as you add new items to the table, Excel adds them to the chart immediately.

If you turn a range of cells into a table, you can tap into the features a table confers, like the ability to sort and filter your data. For example, you can sort your data to change the order in which items appear within a chart, and you can filter the info to hide rows so you chart only a portion of your data.

For more information about filtering and the ever-impressive table feature, refer to Chapter 14.

Filtering Chart Data

As you just saw, your charts aren't married to the data they started out with. With just a few clicks, you can change the selection of data that appears in your chart.

Excel charts also have a complementary feature called *filtering*. Filtering temporarily hides some of the information that belongs to your chart. This comes in handy if you want to dig deeper into your data and search for patterns, without worrying about scrambling your original chart. When you finish exploring your data, you can quickly flip off your filtering settings and return your chart to normal.

You can filter a chart two ways. The first is to use table filtering. In this case, you pick new filtering conditions from the column headers of your table (as described on page 430), and the chart automatically adjusts itself to use the currently displayed data.

The second approach—the one you'll focus on in this section—is to use chart filtering. Chart filtering provides fewer options than table filtering, but it works with every chart, even if your data isn't in a table. Chart filtering has at least one other big advantage over table filtering: It lets you keep all your data visible on your worksheet, even when you plot only some of it in your chart.

NOTE Chart filtering is also more convenient because you filter from the chart box itself, rather than through the column headers. If your data is on a different worksheet than your chart, it's easier to filter via the chart rather than jump back and forth between your worksheets.

Here's how to use chart filtering:

1. **Click the chart once to select it.**

   You'll see three chart-manipulation icons appear outside the right edge of the chart.

2. **Click the Chart Filters icon.**

   It's the third icon, and it looks like a funnel. When you click it, a window pops up with filtering options (Figure 17-10).

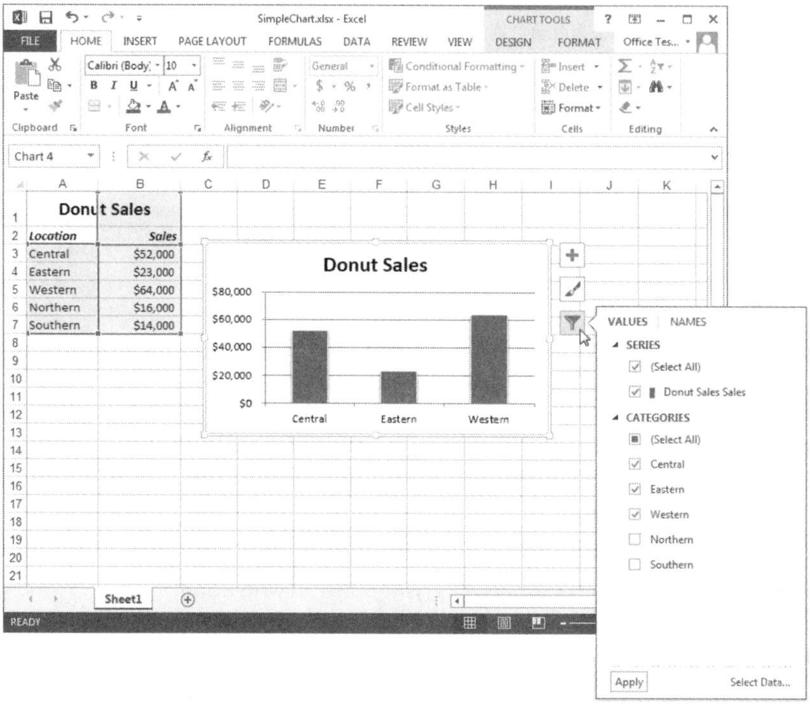

FIGURE 17-10

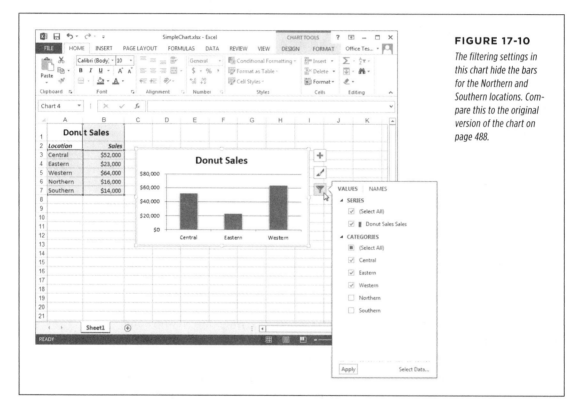

The filtering settings in this chart hide the bars for the Northern and Southern locations. Compare this to the original version of the chart on page 488.

3. **Choose what you want to hide by clearing the checkbox next to that item.**

   You can apply two types of chart filtering.

   - **Category filtering** hides some of the data values. For example, in the Donut Sales chart, you can hide sales at one or more locations (Central, Eastern, Western, and so on).
   - **Series filtering** lets you hide a series, which is a set of numbers plotted on your chart. This isn't much help in the Donut Sales chart, because it has only a single series of sales figures. But if you tracked multiple sets of sales values (for example, for separate locations or products), you could hide some of them. Page 502 has more about building charts with multiple series.

TIP If you're not sure what a given item corresponds to in the chart, hover over it in the filtering box, and Excel highlights the corresponding part of the chart.

4. **Click Apply to make the change official and redraw the chart.**

   To return your chart to normal, click Chart Filters, and add a checkmark next to the "(Select All)" item in the list of series (if you filtered by series) or the list of categories (if you filtered by category). This adds a checkmark next to all the items underneath in one fell swoop.

Changing the Chart Type

When you create a chart, you choose a specific chart type (page 512). But you may want to try out several chart types to see which tells your story better. Excel makes this sort of experimentation easy. All you need to do is click your chart to select it, and then make a different choice from the ribbon's Insert→Charts section. You can use this technique to transform a column chart into a pie chart, for example.

You can also choose Chart Tools | Design→Type→Change Chart Type to make a choice from the Change Chart Type window, which looks just like the Insert Chart window shown in Figure 17-5.

Printing Charts

How you print a chart depends on the type of chart. You can print embedded charts either with their worksheet data or on their own. Standalone charts, which occupy separate worksheets, always print on separate pages.

EMBEDDED CHARTS

You can print embedded charts two ways. The first is to print your worksheet exactly as it appears in the Excel window, with its mix of data and floating charts. In this case, you need to take special care to make sure your charts aren't split over a page break or positioned over data you want to appear in the printout. You can check for both issues using Excel's Page Layout view (choose View→Workbook Views→Page Layout View) or the smaller print preview you see in backstage view when you go to print your worksheet (make sure the chart isn't selected, and then choose File→Print).

You can also print an embedded chart on a separate page, which is surprisingly easy. Click the chart to select it, and then choose File→Print. When you do, Excel prints your chart in landscape orientation (the default), so that the chart's wider than it is tall. Landscape is usually the best orientation, because it lets your chart spread out horizontally, giving it more room to plot your data. For that reason, Excel automatically prints in landscape mode no matter what page orientation you configured for your worksheet. Of course, you can change this as you would with any other printout; just choose Portrait Orientation in the list of print settings before you click the big Print button.

Excel also includes two print options specific to charts. To see them, click the Page Setup link at the bottom of the list of print settings. When the Page Setup window appears, choose the Chart tab. You'll see an option to print a chart using lower print quality, and in black and white instead of color.

STANDALONE CHARTS

Excel always prints standalone charts on a separate page, sized to fit the whole page. To print just the chart page (rather than the whole workbook), switch to the chart's worksheet, and then choose File→Print. Excel automatically sets all chart worksheets to Landscape orientation, which means the chart's long edge runs horizontally across the bottom. If this layout isn't what you want, change the page setting to Portrait Orientation before you print.

If you want to print the entire workbook, choose File→Print from any worksheet. Then, change the first print setting from Print Active Sheets to Print Entire Workbook.

Practical Charting

Figure 17-1 showed you how to chart a list that contains two columns you want to graph—one with text labels and one with numeric data. But in real life, you'll probably need to deal with many types of data in many configurations in your worksheet.

Consider all the possible variations for the simple sales chart in Figure 17-1. You may need to compare the sales figures but, rather than showing region-to-region comparisons, you want to show how well (or poorly) each of your firm's products sold. Or you might want to chart the quarterly performance of different stores over a five-year period, or determine the relationship between sales and profitability. All these charts require a slightly different arrangement of data. In the next section, you'll get a quick introduction to all these possibilities, using only Excel's simple column chart and line chart.

Charts with Multiple Series of Numbers

A *series* is a sequence of numbers you plot on a graph. The chart in Figure 17-1 has just one series of numbers: the sales figures for a company's different regions. Of course, a real chart usually includes more layers of detail. You may want to compare sales over several years, for example. In that case, you'd add a column of sales results for each year you want to compare. Then you'd add each column to your chart as a separate series.

It doesn't take any extra expertise to create a chart that uses multiple series—you just select the right range of cells, and then pick a chart from the ribbon, just as you would for a chart with a single series of data. Different types of charts handle multiple series in different ways. The clustered column chart, for example, creates a separate bar for each value in a row, as shown in Figure 17-11. A line chart, on the other hand, shows a separate line for each series (as you'll see in the next section). For more possibilities, take a look at the "Chart Types" section that starts on page 512.

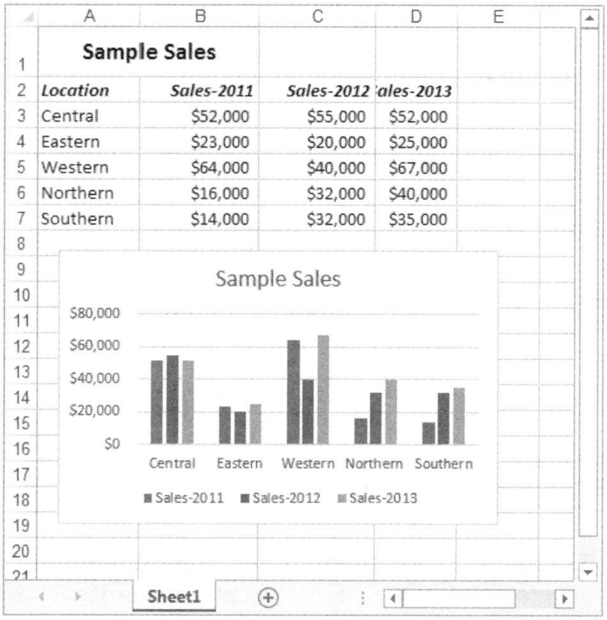

FIGURE 17-11

This chart has three series of sales figures (one for each year) and five sets of columns (one for each region). When you chart these results, you can see that the graph for each region has three bars, one for each data series. The chart's category axis identifies the region, but you need to consult the legend to determine which year each column represents.

TIP You can add multiple series to an existing chart without starting over from scratch. First, select the chart to highlight the linked data. Then click the rightmost edge of the chart, and drag it to the right to expand the underlying cell range so that it includes the new columns (which, of course, you need to have already added to your worksheet).

UP TO SPEED

Data in Different Scales

Remember when your mother told you not to compare apples and oranges? The same rule applies to charts. When you add multiple series of data, each series should use the same *scale*. In other words, the points for each series should be plotted (placed on the chart) using the same measurement system.

The worksheet in Figure 17-11 works perfectly well because the different series of sales figures all use the same unit—dollars. But if one series recorded sales totals in dollars and another recorded them in euros (or even worse, recorded totally different data, like the number of units sold), the chart would be inconsistent.

Excel doesn't complain if your series use different scales—in fact, it has no way of noticing that anything's amiss. And if you don't notice either, you'll create a misleading chart. Your chart may imply a comparison that isn't accurate, for example, or, if the scale is radically different, the chart can get so stretched out that it starts to lose detail. If you have sales figures from $50,000 to $100,000 and units sold from 1 to 100, the scale stretches from 1 to 100,000, and the differences in sales totals or units sold are too small to show up at all.

What's the solution? Don't mix different scales. Ideally, convert values to the same scale (in this case, use the currency exchange rate to turn euros into U.S. dollars before you create the chart). Or just create two charts, one for each data series. But if you really want to compare the changes in different types of data across the same categories, there's a way. Page 573 shows you how to build combination charts that fuse two incompatible sets of data in a logical way.

Controlling the Data Excel Plots on the X-Axis

Excel's charting tool has a dirty little secret. You may not realize it right away, but sooner or later, whether it's your first chart or your 40th, you'll stumble onto the fact that Excel makes a fairly important decision for you about what data shows up on your chart's X-axis. Unfortunately, this decision may not be what you want. Fortunately, you can change it.

So how does Excel decide how to plot your numbers? Essentially, it makes a best guess based on the structure of your data: If you have more rows than columns, Excel assumes that the first column holds the labels for the *category axis* (the X axis). If you have more columns than rows, or if you have the same number of rows and columns, Excel assumes that the first row represents the category axis. The following example shows you how this process plays out.

The two tables in Figure 17-12 have the same sales numbers, but in two different arrangements. When you create a chart for the table on the left, Excel uses the year for the category axis (the X axis). Excel uses the sales income as the *value axis* (the Y axis). Finally, Excel creates a separate series for each region.

Here's the twist: It makes just as much sense to organize the table in a different way. For example, you could turn the table around so it lists the years in the left column and the regions in the top row (Figure 17-12, right). If you create a chart for this table, Excel uses the region for the category axis and creates a separate series for each year! Figure 17-12 contrasts these two different ways of looking at the same data, and shows how they affect the way Excel your data looks in a column chart.

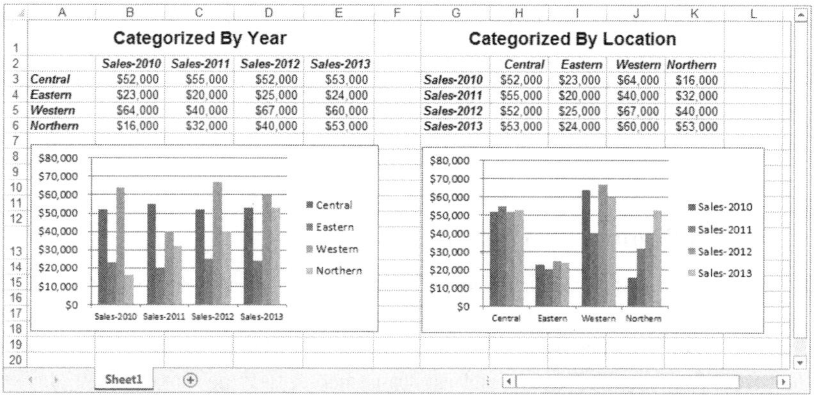

FIGURE 17-12

This worksheet shows the same data charted two ways. In the first table (left), the category axis lists the sales years, which are used to group the regions. In the second table (right), the category axis lists the regions, which are used to group the years.

The column chart example in Figure 17-12 is fairly innocent. Although you may prefer one way of looking at the data over the other, they're relatively similar. However, most Excel charts aren't as forgiving. The line chart's a classic example.

In a line chart, each line represents a different series. If you list the sales years on the category axis (as shown on the left side of Figure 17-13), you end up with a separate line for each region that shows how the region has performed over time. But if you invert the table and make the region the category axis (shown on the right side), you end up with a chart that might make much less sense: a series of lines that compare sales by region in each year. Figure 17-13 shows the problem.

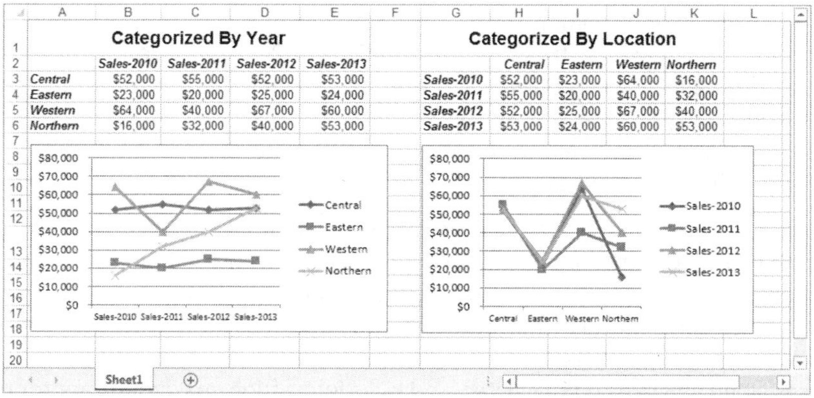

FIGURE 17-13

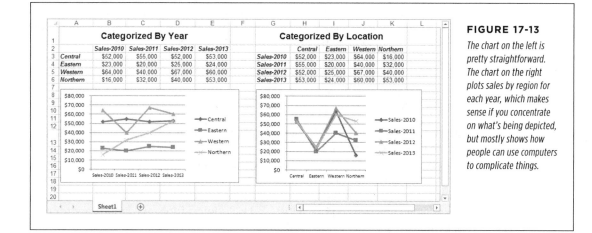

The chart on the left is pretty straightforward. The chart on the right plots sales by region for each year, which makes sense if you concentrate on what's being depicted, but mostly shows how people can use computers to complicate things.

Clearly, when you create a line chart, you need to make sure the chart ends up using the data in a way that makes the most sense to your audience. Fortunately, you can override Excel's automatic plotting choices if you need to. Just select your chart, and then choose Chart Tools | Design→Data→Switch Row/Column. If you try this on the charts in Figure 17-13, you reverse the results. Thus, the chart on the left would group sales into yearly series, and the chart on the right would group sales into regional series. To return them to normal, select each chart, and then click Switch Row/Column again.

UP TO SPEED

The Difference Between a Column and a Line

With simple column charts, life is easy. It doesn't matter too much what data you choose to use for your category axis because your choice simply changes the way the chart groups your data. Other chart types that follow the same principle include pie charts (which allow only one series), bar charts (which are like column charts, but oriented horizontally instead of vertically), and donut charts (where each series is a separate ring).

The same isn't true for line charts and most other types of Excel charts. The category axis you use for a line chart is important because the values in each series are connected (in this case, with a line). This line suggests some sort of "movement" or transition as values move from one category to another. That means that it makes sense to use a line to connect different dates in a region (showing how sales change over time), but it probably doesn't make sense to use a line to connect different regions for each date. Technically, this latter scenario (shown on the right side of Figure 17-13) should show how yearly sales vary as you move from region to region, but it's just too counterintuitive for anyone to interpret properly.

As a general rule, use time or date values for the category axis. You should do this *especially* for chart types like line and area graphs, which usually show how things change over time.

Data That Uses a Date or Time Scale

As the previous example shows, using date or time values for the category axis makes a lot of sense when you want to chart progress over time or spot long-term trends. However, the example in Figure 17-12 does cheat a little. Even though any sentient human knows that the labels Sales-2011, Sales-2012, and Sales-2013 represent consecutive years, Excel is oblivious to what these labels actually mean. You could chart a bunch of years that are far from sequential (like Sales-2007, Sales-2009, and Sales-2013), and Excel would obediently (and misleadingly) place each value on the category axis, spaced out evenly.

This snafu doesn't present a problem in the previous example, but it's an issue if you need to chart years that aren't spread out evenly. Fortunately, Excel offers an easy solution. Instead of entering text labels, you can enter actual dates or times. Because Excel stores dates and times as numbers, it can scale the chart accordingly (this process is sometimes called *category axis scaling*). Best of all, Excel automatically notices when you're using real dates, and kicks into action, making the appropriate adjustments, as shown in Figure 17-14.

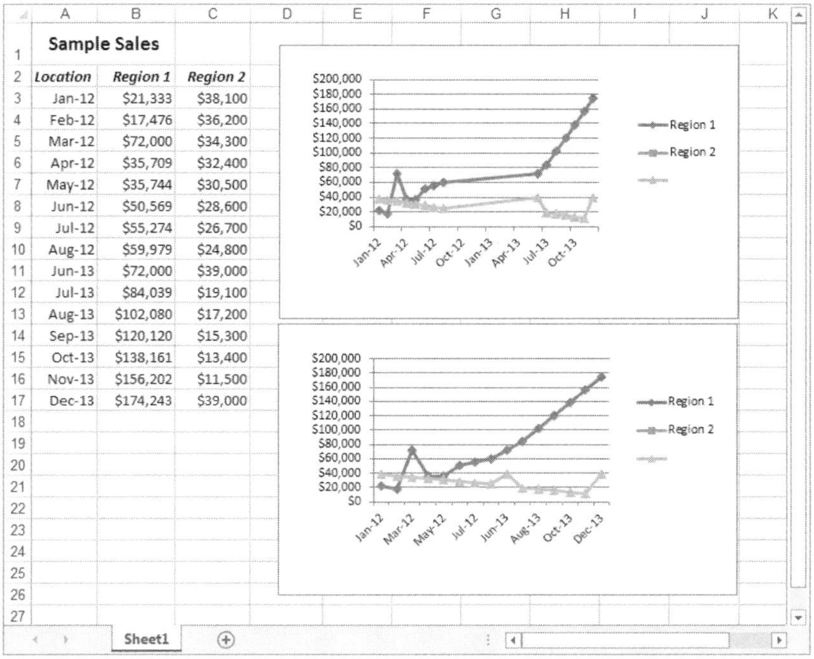

Location	Region 1	Region 2
Jan-12	$21,333	$38,100
Feb-12	$17,476	$36,200
Mar-12	$72,000	$34,300
Apr-12	$35,709	$32,400
May-12	$35,744	$30,500
Jun-12	$50,569	$28,600
Jul-12	$55,274	$26,700
Aug-12	$59,979	$24,800
Jun-13	$72,000	$39,000
Jul-13	$84,039	$19,100
Aug-13	$102,080	$17,200
Sep-13	$120,120	$15,300
Oct-13	$138,161	$13,400
Nov-13	$156,202	$11,500
Dec-13	$174,243	$39,000

FIGURE 17-14

The top chart uses category axis scaling to properly space out dates, even when values are missing. The bottom chart doesn't.

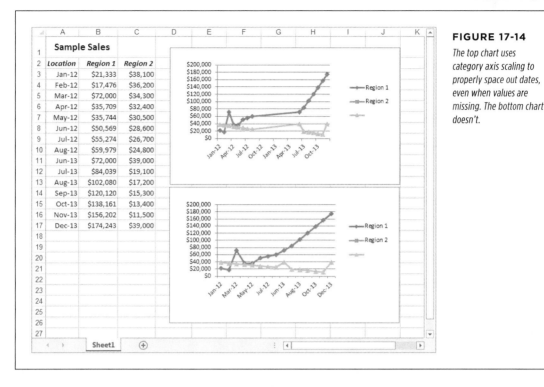

What's happening in Figure 17-14 is worth examining in detail. The worksheet shows two charts that plot the exact same data: a series of monthly sales figures from two regions covering January 2012 through December 2013. The diamonds and triangles on the lines represent data points—in this case, sales—for each month that sales data is available. The twist is that a big chunk of data (the months between August 2012 and June 2013) is missing. To make sure Excel handles this omission correctly, you have to enter real date values (rather than text labels) for the category axis. If you take that step, the chart Excel creates automatically uses a continuous time scale, as shown in the top chart. (As you can see by looking at the data points, no values fall in the middle of the series.)

On the other hand, if you enter the labels as text (as was done in the bottom chart), you get an incorrect result: The data from August 2012 and June 2013 are placed close together—even though they record values that are almost a year apart.

Optionally, you can tell Excel to disregard any values you used in your column or row labels, thereby spacing the dates out evenly, as though they are ordinary text labels. That's how the incorrect chart in Figure 17-14 was created. (Why you'd want to do that is another question, but someone, somewhere, is probably in desperate need of this feature.) To change how Excel scales the category axis, select the chart, and then choose Chart Tools | Design→Chart Layouts→Add Chart Element→Axes→More Axis Options to show the Format Axis panel (Figure 17-15). Under the Axis Type heading, pick one of the following: "Text axis" (treat the category values as labels), "Date axis" (treat the category values as date vales), or "Automatically select based on the data" (let Excel decide based on what it thinks is best).

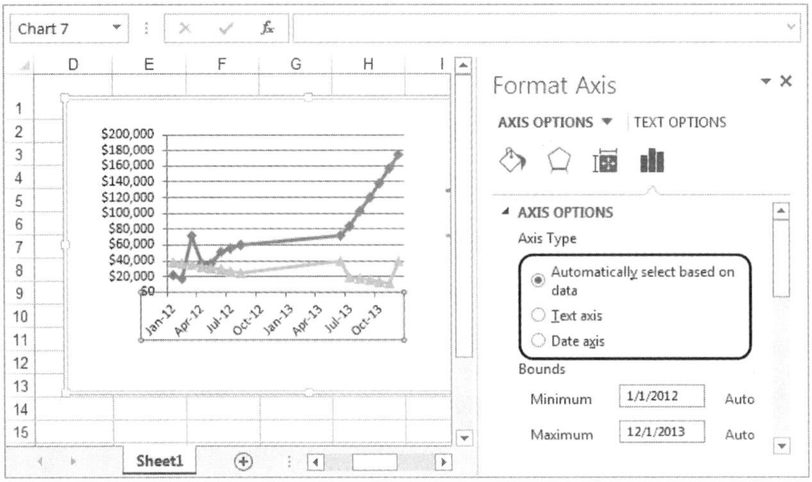

FIGURE 17-15

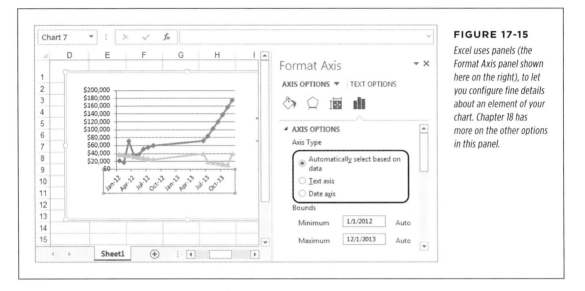

Excel uses panels (the Format Axis panel shown here on the right), to let you configure fine details about an element of your chart. Chapter 18 has more on the other options in this panel.

Category axis scaling works with more than just dates. You can scale any category axis values, as long as they're numeric, which is particularly useful if you're trying to determine the relationship between two different values. If you wanted to determine the relationship between students' IQs and their test scores, for example, you could use the numeric IQ for the category axis, and the test scores for the value axis. If you want to create a chart like this that compares two sets of numbers, you must use a *scatter chart* instead of a line chart. Scatter charts look similar to line charts; see page 518 for more detail.

Noncontiguous Chart Ranges

So far, all the chart examples have assumed that you recorded the data you want to chart in a single, tightly packed table. But what if your information is scattered across your worksheet? This scenario may seem unlikely, but it actually happens quite often when you need to chart only *part* of the data in a table. Say you want to create a chart using two or three columns of data, but the columns aren't next to each other. In this case, you need to take a few extra steps when you create your chart.

For example, imagine you have a table like the one in Figure 17-16. It records the monthly sales of 10 regional offices (labeled Region 1, Region 2, and so on in your worksheet), but you want to create a chart that compares only two of these offices. Your chart will use the category information in column A (which contains the month in which the sales were recorded), along with the values in column C and column D (which contain the total amount of sales for the two regions in which you're interested).

The easiest way to create this chart is to start by selecting the noncontiguous range that contains your data. Chapter 3 describes this technique in detail (page 89), but here's a recap:

1. **First, use the mouse to select the data in column A.**
2. **Hold down the Ctrl key while you drag to select the data in columns C and D.**

   Because you're holding down the Ctrl key, column A remains selected.

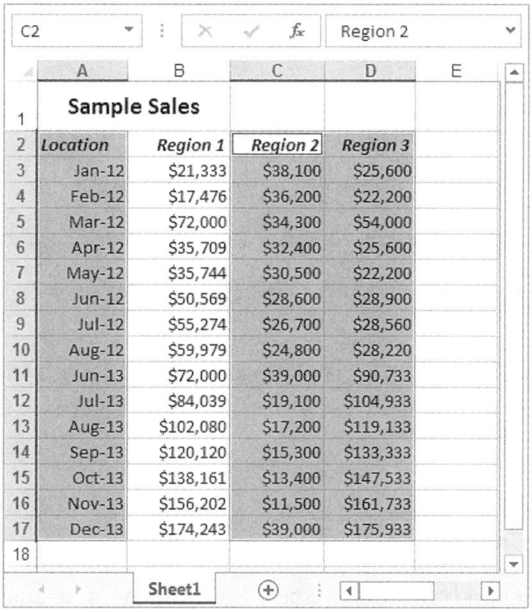

C2 | Region 2

	A	B	C	D	E
1	Sample Sales				
2	Location	Region 1	Region 2	Region 3	
3	Jan-12	$21,333	$38,100	$25,600	
4	Feb-12	$17,476	$36,200	$22,200	
5	Mar-12	$72,000	$34,300	$54,000	
6	Apr-12	$35,709	$32,400	$25,600	
7	May-12	$35,744	$30,500	$22,200	
8	Jun-12	$50,569	$28,600	$28,900	
9	Jul-12	$55,274	$26,700	$28,560	
10	Aug-12	$59,979	$24,800	$28,220	
11	Jun-13	$72,000	$39,000	$90,733	
12	Jul-13	$84,039	$19,100	$104,933	
13	Aug-13	$102,080	$17,200	$119,133	
14	Sep-13	$120,120	$15,300	$133,333	
15	Oct-13	$138,161	$13,400	$147,533	
16	Nov-13	$156,202	$11,500	$161,733	
17	Dec-13	$174,243	$39,000	$175,933	
18					

Sheet1

FIGURE 17-16

This worksheet shows a noncontiguous selection that ignores the numbers from Region 1. When Excel creates a chart from the selection, it includes only two series: one for Region 2, and one for Region 3.

3. **Now choose Insert→Charts, and then pick the appropriate chart type.**

   Excel creates the chart as usual, but uses only the data you selected in steps 1 and 2, leaving out all the other columns.

This approach works most of the time. However, if you have trouble, or if the columns you want to select are spaced *really* far apart, you can explicitly configure the range of cells for any chart. To do so, follow these steps:

1. **Create a chart normally, by selecting part of the data, and then, from the Insert→Chart section of the ribbon, choosing a chart type.**

2. **Once you select a chart, choose Chart Tools | Design→Data→Select Data.**

   The Select Data Source window appears (Figure 17-17).

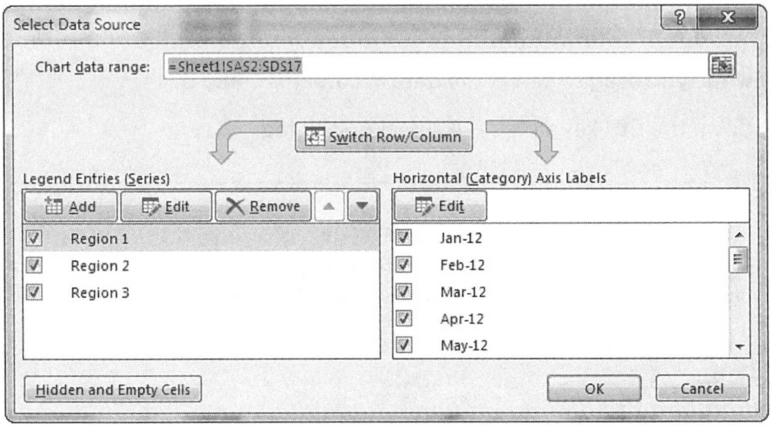

FIGURE 17-17

This window not only identifies what cells Excel will use to create a chart (as shown in the "Chart data range" text box), it also lets you see how Excel breaks that data up into a category axis and one or more series (as shown in the Legend Entries list).

3. **Remove any data series you don't want and add any new data series you do want.**

   To temporarily hide a series, clear the checkbox next to it. (To remove a series altogether, select it in the Legend Entries (Series) list, and then click Remove.

To add a new series, click Add, and then specify the appropriate cell references for the series name and the series values.

You can also click Switch Row/Column to change the data that Excel uses as the category axis (page 504) and you can adjust some more advanced settings, like the way Excel deals with blank values and the order in which it plots series (as explained in the following sections).

Changing the Order of Your Data Series

If your table has more than one data series, Excel charts it in the order it appears on your worksheet (from left to right if your series are arranged in columns, or from top to bottom if they're arranged in rows). In a basic line chart, it doesn't matter which series Excel charts first—the end result is the same. But in some charts, it *does* make a difference. One example is a stacked chart (skip ahead to Figure 17-19 to see a sample stacked chart), in which Excel plots each new series on top of the previous one. Another example is a 3-D chart, where Excel plots each data series behind the previous one.

You can easily change the order of your data series. Select your chart, and then choose Chart Tools | Design→Data→Select Data. Now select one of the series in the Legend Entries (Series) list, and then click the up or down arrow buttons to move it. Excel plots the series from top to bottom.

Changing the Way Excel Plots Blank Values

When Excel creates a chart, its standard operating procedure is to *ignore* all empty cells. The value of 0 doesn't count as an empty cell and neither does text (Excel plots any cells that contains text as a 0).

So what's the difference between an ignored cell and a cell that contains the number 0? In some types of charts, there is no difference. In a bar or pie chart, for example, the result is the same—you don't see a bar or a pie slice for the blank or zeroed cell. However, in some charts, there *is* a difference. In a line chart, for example, Excel plots a 0 value on the chart, but it produces a break in the line when it encounters an empty cell. In other words, the line stops just before the missing data, and then starts again at the next data point. This broken line indicates missing information.

If you don't like this behavior (perhaps because your empty cells really do represent 0 values), you can change it. Select your chart, and then choose Chart Tools | Design→Data→Select Data to get to the Select Data Source window. Then, click the Hidden and Empty Cells button, which pops open a window with three choices:

- **Gaps.** Excel leaves a gap where the information should be. In a line chart, this breaks the line (making it segmented). This option is Excel's default choice.
- **Zero.** Excel treats all blank cells as though they contain the number 0.
- **Span with line.** Excel treats all blank cells as missing information and tries to guess what the value should be. If a line chart goes from 10 to 20 with a blank cell in between, Excel interpolates the data point 15 and plots it.

You can also switch on or off the "Show data in hidden rows and columns" setting to tell Excel whether it should include hidden cells when it creates a chart. This setting determines how Excel deals with data when you use filtering in a table, or when you explicitly hide rows or columns using the Home→Cells→Format→Hide & Unhide menu. Ordinarily, Excel treats these missing values just like blank values, and ignores them.

Chart Types

Although there's a lot to be said for simple column charts—they can illuminate trends in almost any spreadsheet—there's nothing quite as impressive as successfully pulling off the exotic bubble chart (skip ahead to Figure 17-27 to see one). This section covers the wide range of charts that Excel offers. If you use these specialized chart types when they make sense, you can convey more information and make your point more effectively.

NOTE The following sections explain all of the Excel chart types. To experiment on your own, try out the downloadable examples, which you can find on this book's Missing CD page at *www.missingmanuals.com/cds/excel2013mm*. The examples include worksheets that show most chart types. Remember, to change a chart from one type to another, just select it, and then make a new choice from the ribbon's Insert→Charts section, or use the Chart Tools | Design→Type→Change Chart Type command.

Column

By now, column charts probably seem like old hat. But column charts actually come in several variations (technically known as *subtypes*). The main difference between the basic column chart and these subtypes is how they deal with data tables that have multiple series. The quickest way to understand the difference is to look at Figure 17-18, which shows a sample table of data, and Figure 17-19, which charts it using several types of column charts.

Number of Students in Each Room		
	Male	*Female*
Cafeteria	42	24
Lounge	13	16
Games Room	73	40
Lecture Hall	31	40
Library	19	18

FIGURE 17-18

This simple table records the number of female and male students in several rooms at a university. The category axis is the room name, and there are two data series: the numbers of male students, and the numbers of female students. This data is perfect for a column chart, but different subtypes emphasize different aspects of the data, as you can see in Figure 17-19.

NOTE In order to learn about a chart subtype, you need to know its name. The name appears when you hover over the subtype thumbnail, either in the Insert→Charts list (Figure 17-4) or the Insert Chart window (Figure 17-5).

Here's a quick summary of your column chart choices:

- **Clustered Column.** In a clustered column, Excel plots each value as a separate column (Figure 17-19). To form the cluster, Excel groups the columns according to category. If your chart data doesn't include category information, there's no clustering, and you get the plain vanilla chart you created at the beginning of this chapter (page 488).

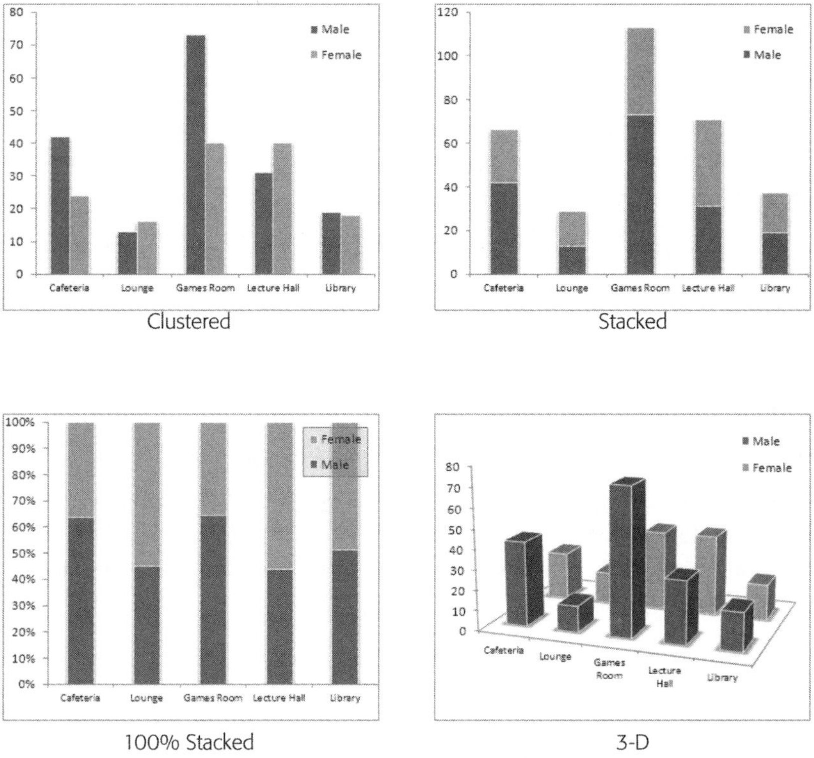

FIGURE 17-19

The Clustered Column chart makes it easy to compare the gender of students in each room, but makes it somewhat more difficult to compare different rooms. The Stacked Column chart is an elegant way to compress the data, and it lets you compare the total number of students in each room without losing the gender information. The 100% Stacked Column chart makes each column the same height, so it's useless for comparing total student numbers, but perfect for comparing how the gender breakup varies depending on the room. (Notice the scale also changes to reflect that you're comparing percentage values.) Finally, the 3-D chart shows you all the data at once by placing the male student counts in front of the female student counts.

- **Stacked Column.** In a stacked column chart, each category has only one column. To create it, Excel adds the values from every series for each category. It also subdivides and color-codes each column so you can see the contribution each series makes.
- **100% Stacked Column.** The 100% stacked column is like a stacked column in that it uses a single bar for each category, and subdivides that bar to show the proportion from each series. The difference is that a 100% stacked column always stretches to fill the full height of the chart. That means 100% stacked columns are designed to focus exclusively on the percentage distribution of results, not the total numbers.

- **3-D Clustered Column, Stacked Column in 3-D, and 100% Stacked Column in 3-D.** Excel's got a 3-D version for each of the three basic types of column charts, including clustered, stacked, and 100% stacked. The only difference between the 3-D versions and the plain-vanilla charts is that the 3-D charts are drawn with a three-dimensional special effect that's either cool or distracting, depending on your perspective.
- **3-D Column.** While all the other 3-D column charts simply use a 3-D effect for added pizzazz, this *true* 3-D column chart actually uses the third dimension by placing each new series *behind* the previous series. That means that, if you have three series, you end up with three layers in your chart. Assuming the chart is tilted just right, you can see all these layers at once, although it's possible that some bars may become obscured, particularly if you have several series.

Bar

The venerable bar chart is the oldest form of data presentation. Invented sometime in the 1700s, it predates the column and pie chart. Bar charts look and behave almost exactly like column charts, the only difference being that their bars stretch horizontally from left to right, unlike columns, which rise from bottom to top.

Excel provides almost the same set of subtypes for bar charts as it does for column charts. The only difference is that there's no true three-dimensional (or layered) bar chart, although there are clustered, stacked, and 100% stacked bar charts with a three-dimensional effect. Some bar charts also use cylinder, cone, and pyramid shapes.

TIP Many people use bar charts because they leave more room for category labels. If you have too many columns in a column chart, Excel has a hard time fitting all the column labels into the available space.

Line

People almost always use line charts to show changes over time. Line charts emphasize trends by connecting each point in a series. The category axis represents a time scale or a set of regularly spaced labels.

TIP If you need to draw smooth trendlines, you don't want to use a line chart. That's because a line chart connects every point exactly, leading to jagged, zigzagging lines. Instead, use a scatter chart (page 518) without a line, and add one or more trendlines afterward, as explained in the next chapter (page 561).

Excel provides several subtypes for line charts:

- **Line.** The classic line chart, which draws a line connecting all the points in the series. The individual points aren't highlighted.

- **Stacked Line.** In a stacked line chart, Excel displays the first series just as it would in a standard line chart, but the second line consists of the values of the first and second series added together. If you have a third series, it displays the total values of the first three series, and so on. People sometimes use stacked line charts to track things like a company's cumulative sales (across several departments or product lines), as Figure 17-20, bottom, shows. (Stacked area charts are another alternative, as shown in Figure 17-22.) Stacked line charts aren't as common as stacked bar and column charts.

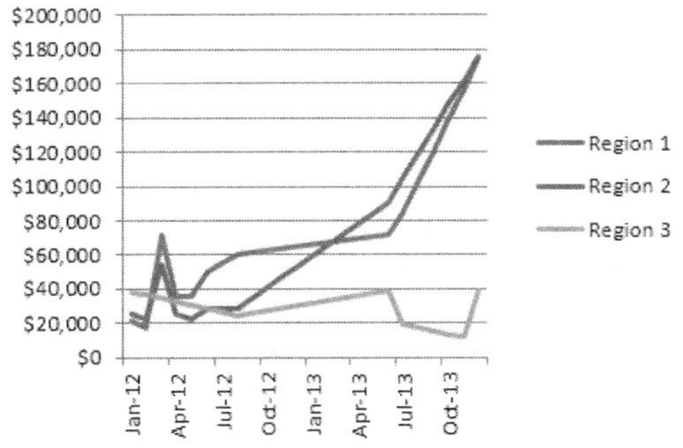

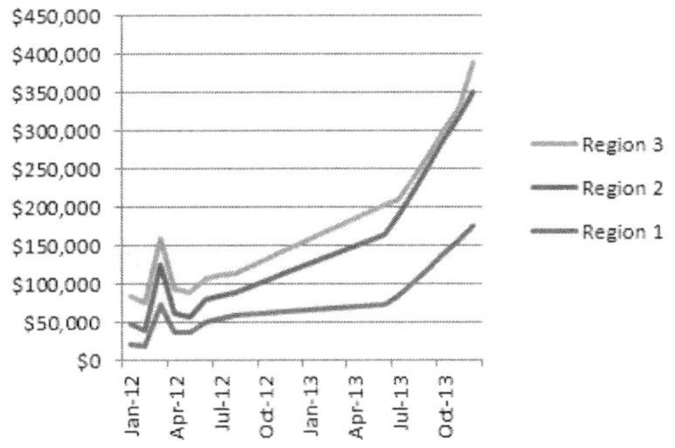

FIGURE 17-20

Here are two line chart variations—both of which show the same information, though you'd never be able to tell that from looking at them quickly.

Top: This chart is a regular line chart that compares the sales for three regions over time.

Bottom: This chart is a stacked line chart, which plots each subsequent line by adding the numbers from the earlier lines. That makes the stacked line chart a great vehicle for showing cumulative totals. For example, sales in Region 3 for April 2013 appear to top $150,000. That's because the Region 3 line is stacked. It shows a total made up from three components—$72,000 (Region 1), $54,000 (Region 2), and $34,300 (Region 3). In this example, the stacked line chart clearly shows that sales spiked early on, and have risen overall, which isn't clear in the top chart. However, the stacked line chart also obscures the differences between regions. You'd never guess that Region 3 is the underperforming region, for example, because this chart reflects the total of all three regions.

NOTE Lines can never cross in a stacked line chart, because Excel adds each series to the one (or ones) before it. You can change which line is stacked at the top by changing the order of the series. To do this, either rearrange your table of data in the worksheet (Excel places the rightmost column on top) or refer to page 511, which describes how you change the order of a series manually.

- **100% Stacked Line.** A 100% stacked line chart works the same way as a stacked line chart in that it adds the value of each series to the values of all the preceding series. The difference is that the last series always becomes a straight line across the top, and the other lines are scaled accordingly so that they show percentages. The 100% stacked line chart is rarely useful, but if you do use it, you'll probably want to put totals in the last series.

- **Line with Markers, Stacked Line with Markers, and 100% Stacked Line with Markers.** These subtypes are the same as the three previous line chart subtypes, except that they add markers (squares, triangles, and so on) for each data point in the series.
- **3-D Line.** This option draws ordinary lines without markers but adds a little thickness to each line with a 3-D effect.

Pie

Pie charts show the breakdown of a series proportionally, using "slices" of a circle. Pie charts are one of the simplest types of chart, and one of the most recognizable.

Here are the pie chart subtypes you can choose from:

- **Pie.** The basic pie chart everyone knows and loves, which shows how a single series of data breaks down.
- **Exploded Pie.** The name sounds like a Vaudeville gag, but the exploded pie chart simply separates each piece of a pie with a small amount of white space. Usually, Excel charting mavens prefer to explode just a single slice of a pie for emphasis. This technique uses the ordinary pie subtype, as explained in the next chapter.
- **Pie of Pie.** This subtype, you can break out one slice of a pie into its own, smaller pie (which is itself broken down into slices). This chart is great for emphasizing specific data; you'll see it in the next chapter.
- **Bar of Pie.** The bar of pie subtype is almost the same as the pie of pie subtype. The only difference is that the breakdown of the emphasized slice appears as stacked bar chart instead of as a separate pie.
- **Pie in 3-D** and **Exploded Pie in 3-D.** These options produce the pie and exploded pie chart types in three dimensions, tilted slightly away from the viewer for a more dramatic appearance. The differences are purely cosmetic.

NOTE Pie charts can show only one series of data. If you create a pie chart for a table that has multiple data series, you'll see just the information from the first series. The only solution is to create separate pie charts for each series (or try a more advanced chart type, like a donut, described on page 522).

Area

An area chart is similar to a line chart. The difference is that the space between the line and the bottom (category) axis is filled in. Because of this difference, the area chart tends to emphasize the sheer magnitude of values rather than their change over time (see Figure 17-21).

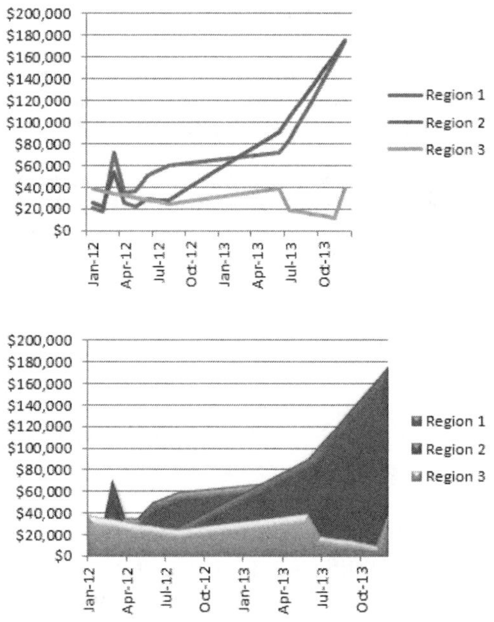

FIGURE 17-21

This example compares a traditional line chart (top) against an area chart (bottom). As you can see, the area chart makes a more dramatic point about the rising sales in Region 2. However, it also obscures the results in Region 1.

Area charts exist in all the same flavors as line charts, including stacked and 100% stacked. You can also use subtypes that have a 3-D effect, or you can create a true 3-D chart that layers the series behind one another.

Stacked area charts make a lot of sense. In fact, they're easier to interpret than stacked line charts because you can easily get a feeling for how much contribution each series makes to the total by judging the thickness of the area. If you're not convinced, compare the stacked charts in Figure 17-20 (bottom) and Figure 17-22. In the area chart, it's much clearer that Region 3 is making a fairly trivial contribution to the overall total.

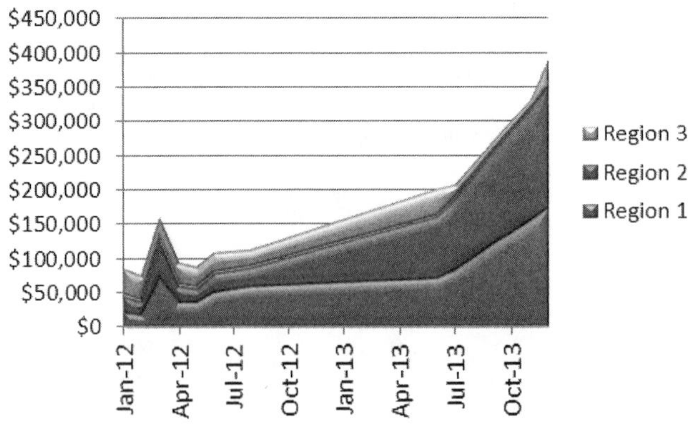

FIGURE 17-22

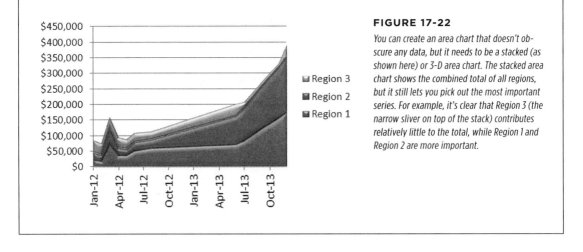

You can create an area chart that doesn't obscure any data, but it needs to be a stacked (as shown here) or 3-D area chart. The stacked area chart shows the combined total of all regions, but it still lets you pick out the most important series. For example, it's clear that Region 3 (the narrow sliver on top of the stack) contributes relatively little to the total, while Region 1 and Region 2 are more important.

Scatter (XY)

Scatter charts, also known as XY charts, show the relationship between two sets of numbers. Scatter charts are common in scientific, medical, and statistical spreadsheets. They're particularly useful when you don't want to connect every dot with a straight line. Instead, scatter charts let you use a smooth "best fit" trendline, or omit lines altogether. If you plot multiple series, the chart uses a different symbol (like squares, triangles, and circles) for each series, ensuring that you can tell the difference between the series.

Why would you want to plot data points without drawing a line? For one thing, you may need to draw conclusions from an inexact or incomplete set of scientific or statistical data. Scientific types may use a scatter chart to determine the relationship between a person's age and his reflex reaction time. However, no matter how disciplined the experimenters, they can't test every different age. In addition, their data will include natural variations from the overall trend. (In other words, if the trend is for older people to have gradually slowing reactions, you're still likely to run across a few exceptionally speedy older folks.) In this case, the best approach is to include no line, or use a smooth "best fit" line that indicates the overall trend, as shown in Figure 17-23.

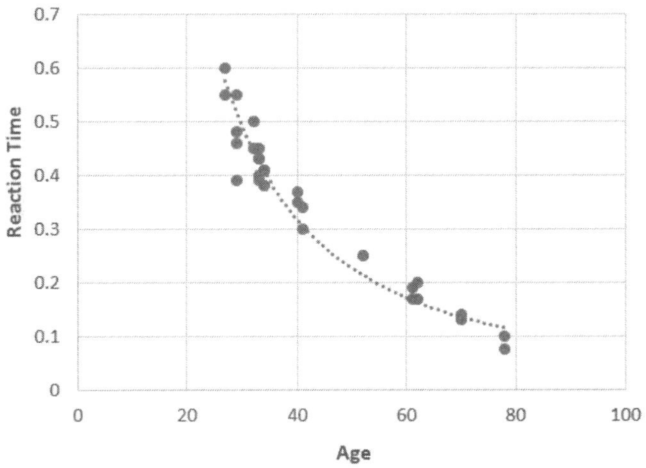

FIGURE 17-23

This XY Scatter chart shows the relationship between a person's age and his reflex reaction time.

Excel offers several scatter chart subtypes, including:

- **Scatter with Only Markers.** This scatter chart uses data markers to show where each value falls. It adds no lines.
- **Scatter with Smooth Lines and Markers.** This scatter chart adds a smooth line that connects all the data points. However, the points are connected in the order they appear in the chart, which isn't necessarily the correct order. You're better off adding a trendline to your chart, as explained in the next chapter.
- **Scatter with Straight Lines and Markers.** This subtype is similar to the scatter chart with smoothed lines, except that it draws lines straight from one point to the next. A line chart works like this, and this subtype makes sense only if you have your values in a set order (from smallest to largest or from the earliest date to latest date).
- **Scatter with Smooth Lines and Scatter with Straight Lines.** These subtypes are identical to the scatter with smooth lines and markers and the scatter with straight lines and markers. The only difference is they don't show data markers for each point. Instead, all you see is the line.

Stock

A stock chart displays specialized charts for stocks. Usually, these charts show how a stock value changes over a series of days. The twist is that the chart can display information about the daytime high and the daytime low of a stock, along with its opening and closing value. Excel uses all this information to draw a vertical bar from the stock's low point to its high point on a given day. If you're really ambitious, you can even add volume information (which records the number of shares traded on a given day).

Stock charts are more rigid than most other chart types. To use one, you need to create a column of numbers for each required value. The type of columns you need and their order depends on the stock chart subtype you select. Here are your choices:

- High-Low-Close
- Open-High-Low-Close
- Volume-High-Low-Close
- Volume-Open-High-Low-Close

In each case, the order of terms indicates the order of columns you should use in your chart. If you select Volume-High-Low-Close, the leftmost column should contain the volume information, followed by another column with the stock's daytime high, and so on. (Technically, you can use the Chart Tools | Design→Data→Select Data command to specify each series, even if it's not in the place Excel expects it to be. However, this maneuver is tricky to get right, so it's easiest to just follow the order indicated by the chart type name.) No matter which subtype you use, a stock chart shows only values for a single stock.

TIP The simplest stock chart (High-Low-Close) is also occasionally useful for charting variances in scientific experiments or statistical studies. You could also use a stock chart to show high and low temperature readings. Of course, you still need to follow the rigid stock chart format when ordering your columns.

Figure 17-24 shows an example of a Volume-High-Low-Close.

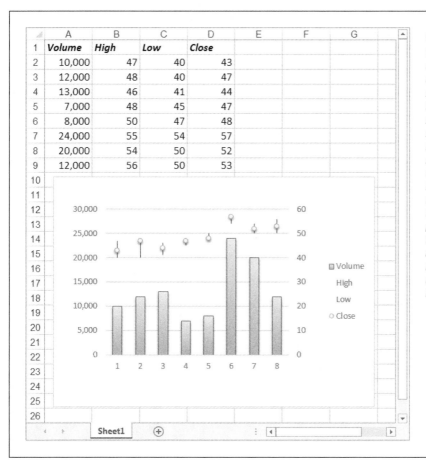

	Volume	High	Low	Close
1	Volume	High	Low	Close
2	10,000	47	40	43
3	12,000	48	40	47
4	13,000	46	41	44
5	7,000	48	45	47
6	8,000	50	47	48
7	24,000	55	54	57
8	20,000	54	50	52
9	12,000	56	50	53

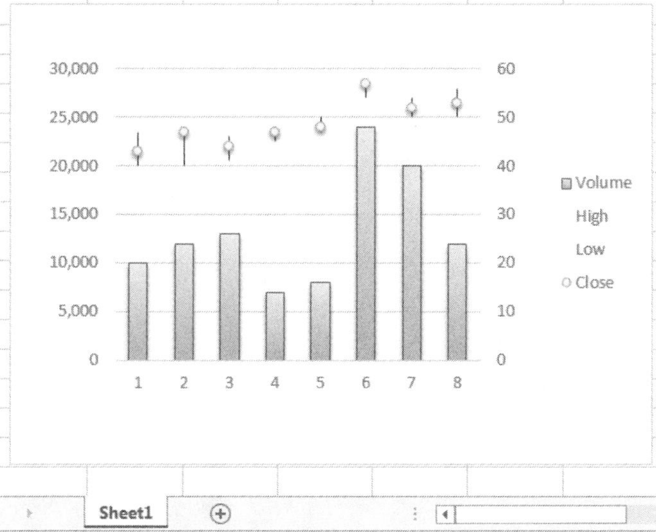

FIGURE 17-24

The Volume-High-Low-Close chart displays several types of related information in the same chart. The columns at the bottom show the number of shares traded (using the value scale on the left). The vertical lines above these columns show the stock price (using the value scale on the right). For each day, the line spans from the stock price's low for the day to its high. The closing price is marked with a tick in the bar. If you like, you can add a trendline to show the movement of the stock price using the techniques explained in the next chapter.

Surface

A surface chart shows a 3-D surface that looks a little like a topographic map, complete with hills and valleys. Surface charts are different from most other charts in that they show the relationship of three values. Two category axes (X and Y) determine a data point's position. The value determines the height of the data point (technically known as the Z-axis). All of the points link to create a surface.

Surface charts are neat to look at, but ordinary people almost never create them, as they're definitely overkill for tracking your weekly workout sessions. For one thing, to make a good surface chart, you need a lot of data. (The more points you have, the smoother the surface becomes.) Your data points also need to have a clear relationship with both the X and Y axes (or the surface you create is just a meaningless jumble). Usually, rocket-scientist types use surface charts for highly abstract mathematical and statistical applications. Figure 17-25 shows an example.

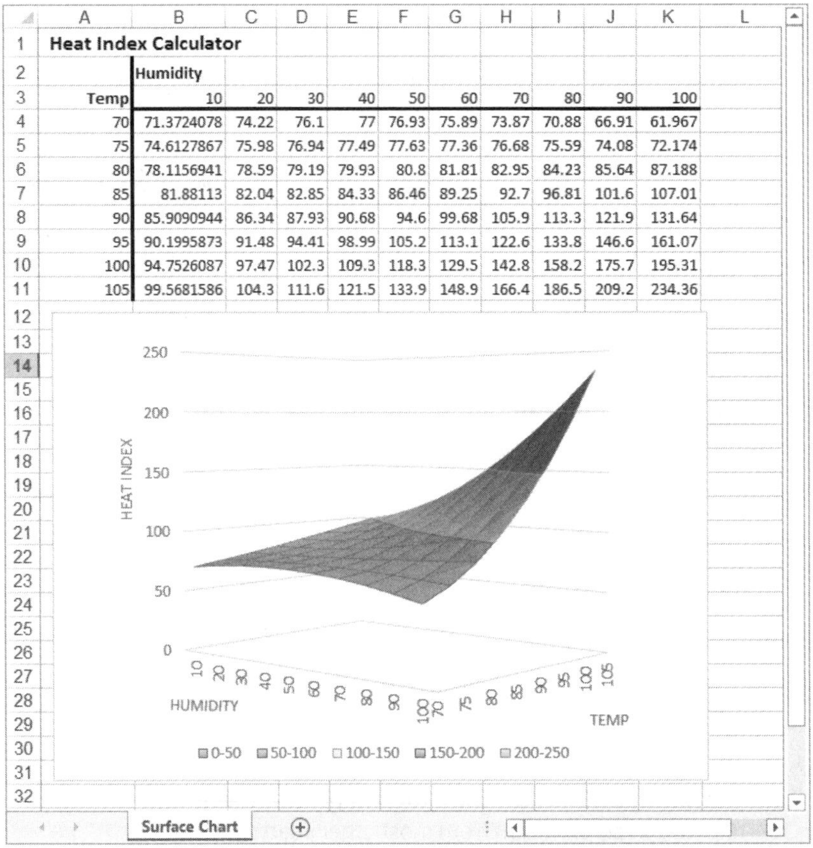

Heat Index Calculator

Temp	Humidity 10	20	30	40	50	60	70	80	90	100
70	71.3724078	74.22	76.1	77	76.93	75.89	73.87	70.88	66.91	61.967
75	74.6127867	75.98	76.94	77.49	77.63	77.36	76.68	75.59	74.08	72.174
80	78.1156941	78.59	79.19	79.93	80.8	81.81	82.95	84.23	85.64	87.188
85	81.88113	82.04	82.85	84.33	86.46	89.25	92.7	96.81	101.6	107.01
90	85.9090944	86.34	87.93	90.68	94.6	99.68	105.9	113.3	121.9	131.64
95	90.1995873	91.48	94.41	98.99	105.2	113.1	122.6	133.8	146.6	161.07
100	94.7526087	97.47	102.3	109.3	118.3	129.5	142.8	158.2	175.7	195.31
105	99.5681586	104.3	111.6	121.5	133.9	148.9	166.4	186.5	209.2	234.36

FIGURE 17-25

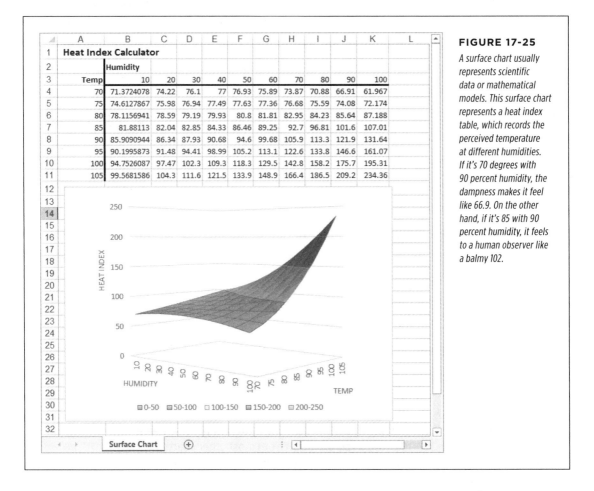

A surface chart usually represents scientific data or mathematical models. This surface chart represents a heat index table, which records the perceived temperature at different humidities. If it's 70 degrees with 90 percent humidity, the dampness makes it feel like 66.9. On the other hand, if it's 85 with 90 percent humidity, it feels to a human observer like a balmy 102.

Donut

The donut chart (Figure 17-26) is actually an advanced variation on that other classic food-themed chart, the pie chart. But while a pie chart can accommodate only one series of data, the donut can hold as many series as you want. Each series is represented by a separate ring. The rings are one inside the other, so they all fit into a single compact circle.

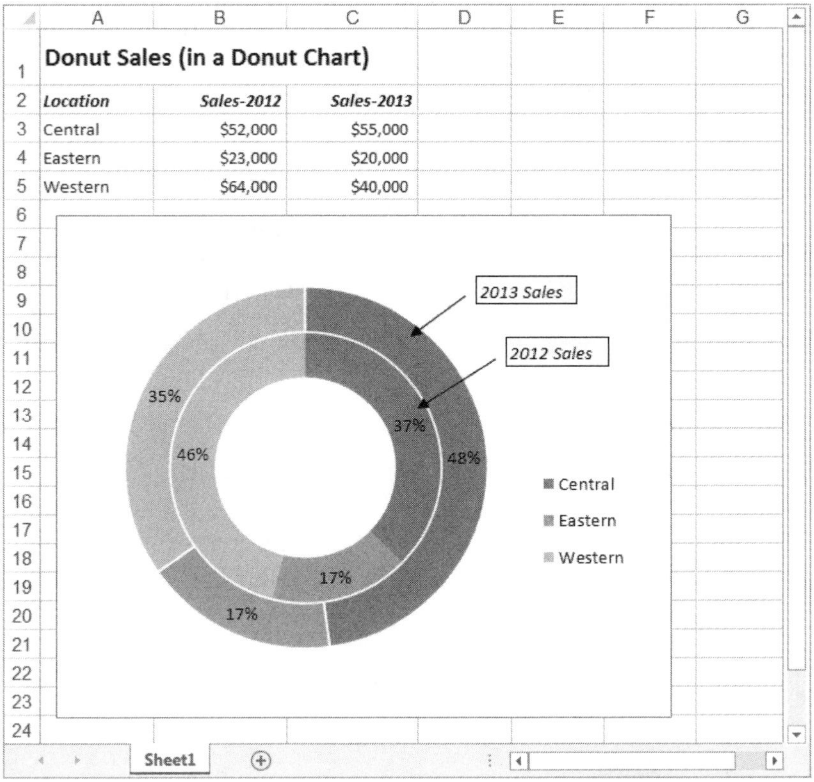

FIGURE 17-26

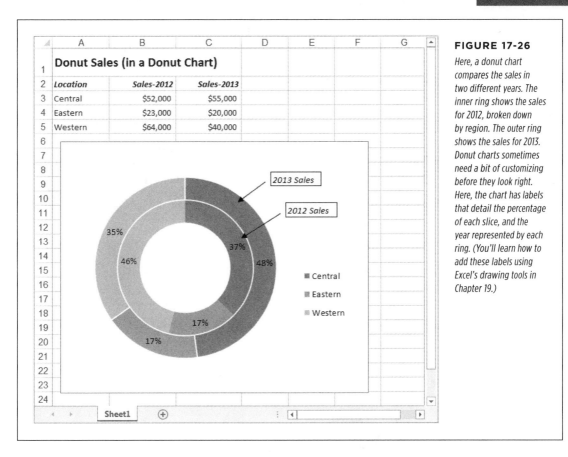

Here, a donut chart compares the sales in two different years. The inner ring shows the sales for 2012, broken down by region. The outer ring shows the sales for 2013. Donut charts sometimes need a bit of customizing before they look right. Here, the chart has labels that detail the percentage of each slice, and the year represented by each ring. (You'll learn how to add these labels using Excel's drawing tools in Chapter 19.)

The donut chart is ideal for comparing the breakdown of two sets of data. However, the data on the outside ring tends to become emphasized, so make sure this series is the most important. To change the order of the series, see page 511.

Donuts have two subtypes: standard and exploded. An exploded donut doesn't suggest a guilty snack that's met an untimely demise. Instead, it's a donut chart where the pieces in the topmost ring are slightly separated.

Although the donut chart can hold as many series as you want, if you add more than two or three, the chart may appear overly complicated. No matter what you do, the center of the donut is never filled in (unless you decide to add some text there using Excel's drawing tools, which are covered in Chapter 19).

NOTE Think twice before you use a donut chart in a presentation. Most Excel gurus avoid this chart, because it's notoriously difficult to explain.

Bubble

The bubble chart is an innovative variation on the scatter chart. It plots only a single series, and it never draws a line. Each point is marked with a circle—either an ordinary circle or a 3-D sphere, depending on the chart subtype you choose. The extra frill is that the bubble sizes change based on a second set of related values. The larger the value, the larger the bubble. In any bubble chart, the largest bubble is always the same size. Excel scales the other bubbles down accordingly. Figure 17-27 shows an example.

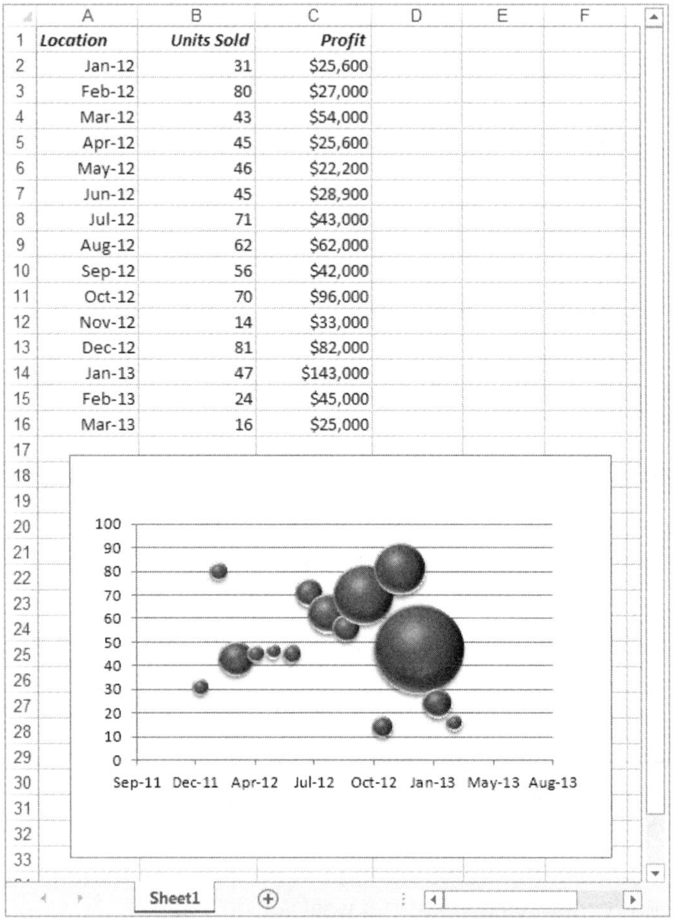

	A	B	C
1	*Location*	*Units Sold*	*Profit*
2	Jan-12	31	$25,600
3	Feb-12	80	$27,000
4	Mar-12	43	$54,000
5	Apr-12	45	$25,600
6	May-12	46	$22,200
7	Jun-12	45	$28,900
8	Jul-12	71	$43,000
9	Aug-12	62	$62,000
10	Sep-12	56	$42,000
11	Oct-12	70	$96,000
12	Nov-12	14	$33,000
13	Dec-12	81	$82,000
14	Jan-13	47	$143,000
15	Feb-13	24	$45,000
16	Mar-13	16	$25,000

FIGURE 17-27

Each bubble's position represents two values: the month (the category axis) and the number of units sold (the value axis). Each bubble's size reflects the profit generated by the units sold.

Radar

The radar chart (Figure 17-28) is a true oddity, and it's typically used only in specialized statistical applications. In a radar chart, each category becomes a spoke, and every spoke radiates out from a center point. Each series has one point on each spoke, and a line connects all the points in the series, forming a closed shape. All these spokes and lines make the chart look something like the radar on an old-time submarine.

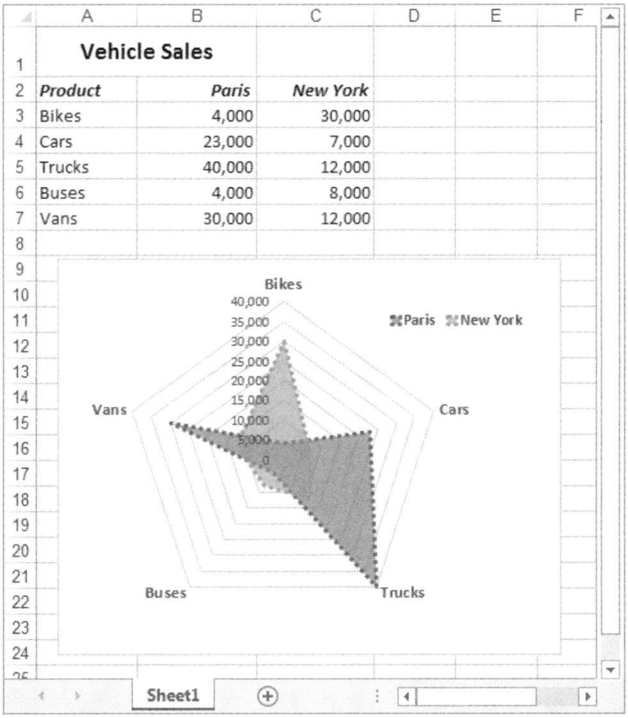

FIGURE 17-28

This filled radar chart compares the products sold in sales offices in two cities. Because all the categories (in this case, the various products) are joined into a closed shape, the radar chart acts somewhat like an area chart, so you can judge the significance of values by looking at the size and shape of the area. It's easy to see that bicycles are selling well with customers in the New York store, while trucks lead the way in Paris. If the two series had similar results, you couldn't effectively use a filled radar chart, because it would obscure some of the data.

You have three radar subtypes: the standard radar chart, a radar chart with data markers indicating each point, and a filled radar, where each series appears as a filled shape, somewhat like an area chart. No matter what subtype you use, choosing data for a radar chart isn't easy.

CHAPTER

18

Formatting and Perfecting Charts

In the previous chapter, you learned how Excel charts work and how you can transform ordinary tables of information into graphical representations, complete with columns, bars, lines, and even bubbles. But creating the right chart is only half the battle. The next step is *refining* your charts so they convey their point more effectively. Often this step means tweaking the chart's formatting, inserting labels, and fine-tuning the scale. But if you're really ambitious, you'll want to tackle more advanced professional charting techniques, like trendlines, overlays, and combination charts. These techniques let you turn plain-vanilla charts into polished graphics—like the ones you see in magazines, annual reports, and brochures.

In this chapter, you'll start by looking at how you can use basic formatting techniques to change the color and font of different chart components. Then you'll learn how to set a chart's scale, unleash 3-D views, and make your data stand out no matter what type of chart you use.

Chart Styles and Layouts

In Chapter 6, you learned how *cell* styles let you take ready-made formatting and apply it to your data to glitz up the dullest worksheet. Excel provides a set of *chart* styles for the same reason—they let you give even the plainest chart a dazzling makeover.

Like cell styles, chart styles draw from the colors, fonts, and shapes that are part of each chart's theme (page 172). For example, if you use the Trek theme, your chart style draws upon a palette of earthy tones, while the Verve theme gives you a more vivid set of colors. When you use a theme, the fonts and colors of your cell styles, table styles, and chart styles are consistent everywhere. You can also swap in a new palette for all these elements just by choosing a new theme.

TIP Before you choose a chart style, it helps to pick the theme you want to use so you can see the real, final result. To change the theme, make a selection from the Page Layout→Themes→Themes list. Page 172 has the full story.

Chart Styles

Chart styles give you a way to apply shake-and-bake formatting to ordinary charts. Excel includes a wide range of chart styles that vary from simple, flat charts with minor accents (like colored borders) to showier styles that include bevel effects and shadows. You can quickly create plain or opulent charts, depending on your needs.

Before you use a chart style, it's important to understand what that style changes (and what it doesn't). Every chart style includes settings that determine:

- The chart's background fill and type of gridlines.
- The shading and fill style of each series (which the chart might display as bars, lines, points, or something else).
- Shape effects, like softly curved or beveled edges and shadows.
- The placement of data labels, which indicate the values on your chart.
- Marker styles (for line and XY scatter charts) that distinguish the points in one series from those in another.

NOTE Some chart styles use a heavy black background with bold colors. This sort of style isn't designed for worksheets because it can tie the best color printer in knots. But these high-contrast styles look good on computer monitors and projection screens, so use them if you want to cut and paste your chart into a PowerPoint presentation. (Chapter 24 has more about transferring chart objects and other data between Excel and other programs.)

On the other hand, chart styles don't change the chart colors or the font that Excel uses for the chart title and labels; instead, Excel bases these elements on the current theme. Chart styles also don't change the layout of the chart or the chart settings Excel uses for the legend, scale, axis titles, error bars, and so on. (You haven't yet seen how to tweak all these details, but you'll learn about them later in this chapter.)

To choose a style, first select your chart. Three icons will appear on the right side of it. Click the Chart Styles icon, which looks like a paintbrush. A window pops open with a list of styles.

NOTE You can also change a chart's style from the ribbon's Chart Tools | Design→Chart Styles section, which provides the same gallery of choices. Click one of the pictures in the Chart Styles section to apply the style to your chart.

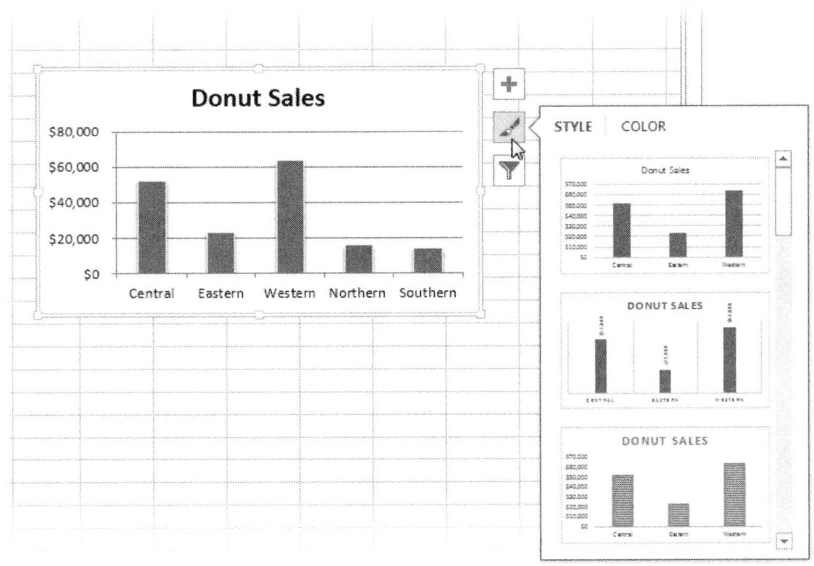

FIGURE 18-1

Click any of the chart pictures to dress up your chart with a different style. Or just hover over a style and Excel shows you a live preview of what the changes will look like, should you choose to apply the style.

NOTE Although you can't create your own chart styles, you can save all your chart layout and formatting choices as a chart template. Simply right-click your chart box and choose Save as Template. (Excel prompts you to save the template as a file with the extension .crtx. Type in a descriptive file name, like "Psychedelic Pie Chart," and click Save.) The next time you create a chart, you can use your template. You'll find it in the familiar Insert Chart window (page 493); just click the All Charts tab and choose the Templates group.

Chart Colors

As you already learned, charts get their colors from your workbook theme (which you pick from the Page Layout→Themes→Themes list). However, every workbook theme includes six colors, and a chart has the flexibility to use these colors in different ways. For example, a chart can use a colorful design that gives each series one of the six colors. Or, a chart can use a monochromatic design, which uses different shades of the same color for each series.

To change the colors in your chart, select it and click the Chart Styles icon. When the window of styles pops open, click the Color link (at the top). You'll see the list of color options shown in Figure 18-2.

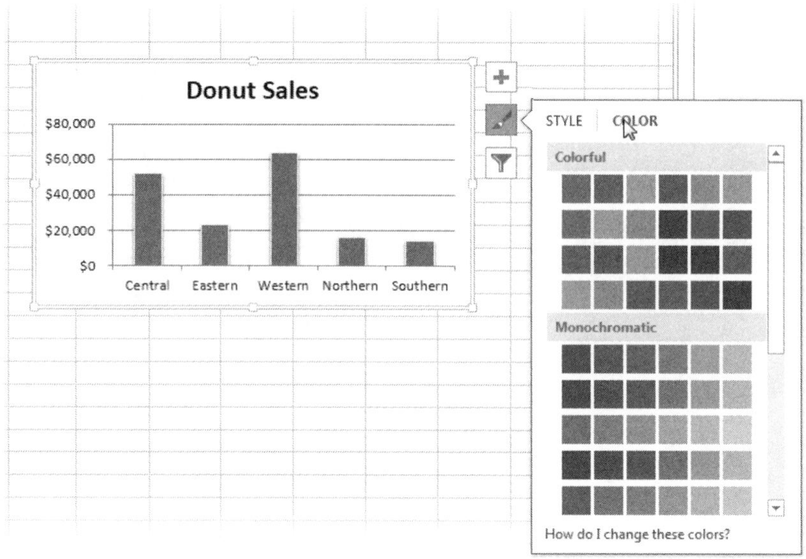

FIGURE 18-2

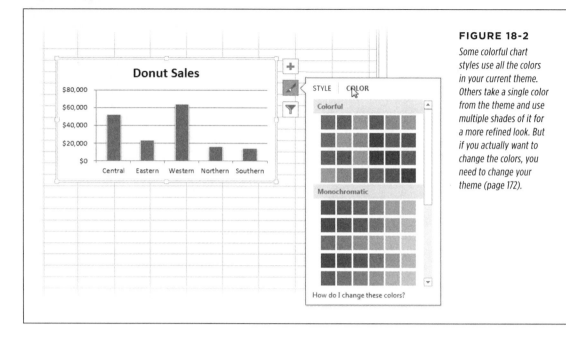

Some colorful chart styles use all the colors in your current theme. Others take a single color from the theme and use multiple shades of it for a more refined look. But if you actually want to change the colors, you need to change your theme (page 172).

Chart Layouts

Chart styles make it easy for you to change the colors and visual styling in a chart. Chart layouts are complementary—they let you control the presence and placement of various chart elements, like the chart and axis titles, and the legend.

As you'll learn in the next section, Excel lets you tweak each of these ingredients separately. However, you can choose a prebuilt layout to do it all in one shot. To try that out, head to the ribbon, and then make a choice from the Chart Tools | Design→Chart Layouts→Quick Layout list. (Or, hover over one of the layouts in the list to preview it in your worksheet.) As with styles, the list of layout choices depends on the chart type. Figure 18-3 shows an example.

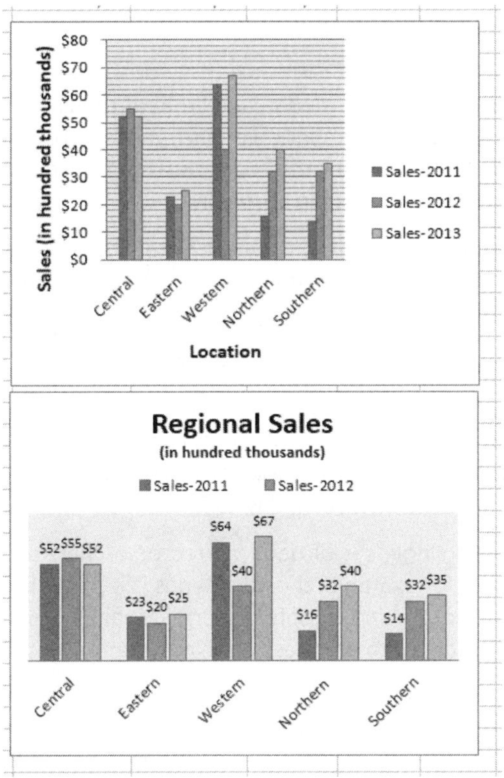

FIGURE 18-3

This worksheet shows two versions of the same chart, each with a different layout. The chart at the top includes heavy gridlines, axis titles, and a legend on the right, while the chart below includes a title and places the legend at the top. It also dispenses with the gridlines and displays the series value above each column.

NOTE To make chart layouts as practical as possible, the creators of Excel reviewed thousands of professional charts and identified the most common arrangements. Most Excel pros still want to customize the various parts of their chart by hand, but a chart layout can provide a great starting point.

Adding Chart Elements

You build every chart out of small components, like titles, gridlines, axes, a legend, and the bars, points, or exotic shapes that represent the data. Excel lets you manipulate each of these details separately. That means you can independently change the format of a label, the outline of a bar, the number of gridlines, and the font and color of just about everything.

Figure 18-4 shows the different elements that make up a chart. They include:

- **Chart and axis titles.** The chart title identifies the chart's topic. You can also title the chart's axes, and style them independently of the chart title.
- **Legend.** The legend identifies each data series on a chart with a different color. A legend's useful only when the chart contains more than one series.
- **Horizontal and vertical axes.** An axis runs along each edge of the chart and determines the scale used. In a typical two-dimensional chart, you have two axes: the category axis (typically on the bottom of the chart, running horizontally), and the value axis (typically on the left, running vertically).
- **Plot area.** The plot area is the chart's background, where Excel draws the gridlines. In a standard chart, the plot area is plain white, which you can customize.
- **Chart area.** The chart area is the white space around the chart. It includes the space that's above, below, and to either side of the plot area.
- **Gridlines.** Gridlines run across the plot area. Once you plot data points, the gridlines give you an idea of the value of each point. Every chart starts out with horizontal gridlines, but you can remove them or add vertical gridlines. You can tell Excel how many gridlines to draw, and even how to format them.
- **Data series.** The data series is a single set of data plotted on a chart across the category axis. In a line chart, for example, the data series is a single line. If a chart has multiple series, you'll often find it useful to format them separately to make them easier to differentiate or to emphasize the most important one.
- **Data point.** A data point is a single value in a data series. In a line chart, a data point's a single dot, and in a column chart, it's a single column. If you want to call attention to an exceptionally important value, you can format a data point so that it looks different from the rest of the points.

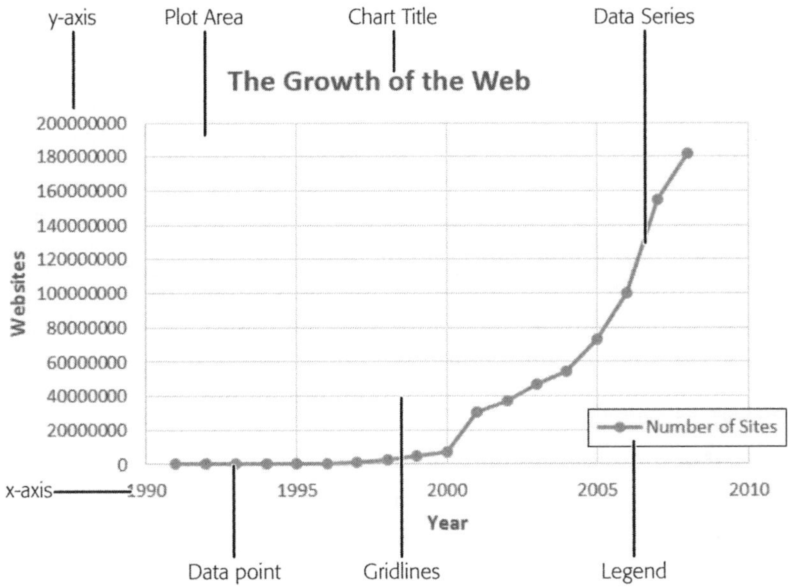

FIGURE 18-4

Before you can begin tweaking your chart's format, you need to know the names of the elements you'll find on a chart.

Not all charts include all these elements. Your chart layout determines whether you have a chart title, a legend, gridlines in the background, and so on. When you first create a chart, Excel gives it a default layout that shows some elements and hides others. If you pick another quick layout (as described on page 530), Excel displays a different arrangement of chart elements.

However, in many cases you'll want to pick and choose exactly the elements you want. The easiest way to do that is to select the chart and click the Chart Elements icon (it's the first icon to the right of the chart, and it looks like a plus symbol). When you click it, Excel pops open the Chart Elements window, with a list of chart elements you can show or hide (Figure 18-5).

Alternatively, you can add and configure chart elements using the ribbon, by picking from the Chart Tools | Design→Chart Layouts→Add Chart Element list. Either way, the result is the same.

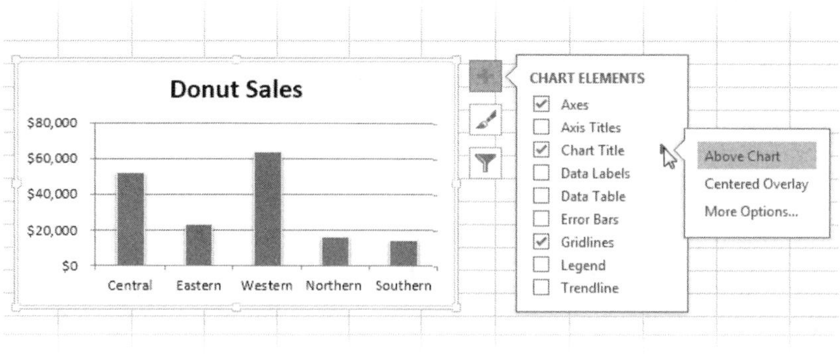

FIGURE 18-5

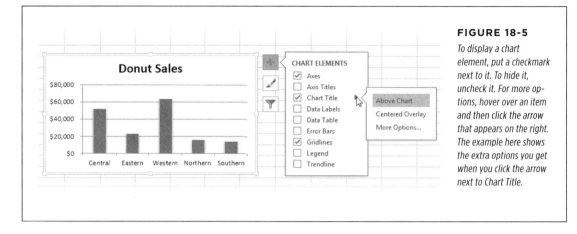

To display a chart element, put a checkmark next to it. To hide it, uncheck it. For more options, hover over an item and then click the arrow that appears on the right. The example here shows the extra options you get when you click the arrow next to Chart Title.

Adding Titles

It doesn't matter how spectacular your chart looks if it's hard to figure out what the data represents. To clearly explain what's going on, you need the right titles and labels.

An ordinary chart can include a main title (like "Increase in Rabbit Population vs. Decrease in Carrot Supplies") and titles on each axis (like "Number of Rabbits" and "Pounds of Carrots"). To show or hide the main title, select the chart, click the Chart Elements icon, and check or uncheck the Chart Title box. And if you click the arrow next to Chart Title, you can choose one of two placement options:

- **Above Chart** puts a title box at the very top of your chart and reduces the size of the chart itself to make room.
- **Centered Overlay Title** keeps the chart as is, but superimposes the title across the top. Assuming you can find a spot with no data, you get a more compact display.

To set your text, click inside the title box and type away (Figure 18-6).

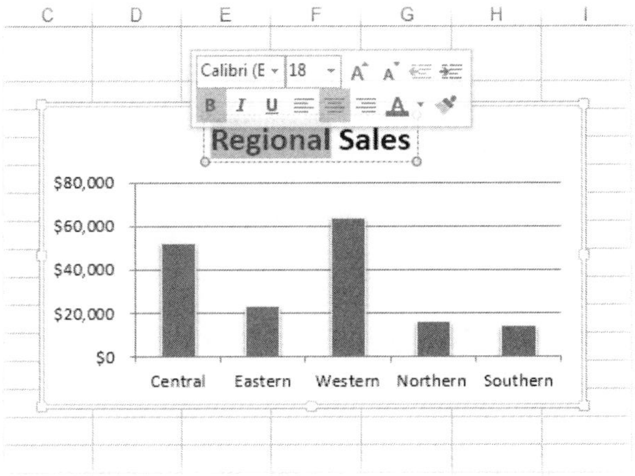

FIGURE 18-6

You can type in whatever text you'd like for a chart title. If you select part of the text with your mouse, a mini bar appears (sadly, of the alcohol-free variety), with formatting options that let you change the font, size, color, and alignment. These commands are the same as those in the Home→Font section of the ribbon, but it's way more convenient to reach them here.

You can just as easily add a title to each axis from the Chart Elements window. Tick the Axis Titles checkbox to add a title to both axes. (Excel rotates the vertical axis title so that it runs neatly along the side of your chart.) To add just one axis title, click the arrow next to Axis Titles and choose Primary Horizontal or Primary Vertical.

Adding a Legend

Titles help explain a chart's overall purpose. Usually, they indicate what a chart compares or analyzes. You may add a chart title like "Patio Furniture Sales" and the axis labels "Gross Revenue" and "Month of Sale" to a chart that shows how patio furniture sales pick up in the summer. However, category labels don't help you single out important data. They also don't let you point out multiple series (like the sales results from two different stores). You can fix this problem by adding additional labels or a *legend*. A legend is a separate box off to the side of a chart that contains one entry for each data series in the chart. The legend indicates the series name, and it adds a little sample of the line style or fill style you used to draw that series on the chart.

If your chart doesn't already have a legend, you can add one from the Chart Elements window by checking the Legend box. You can change the legend's placement, by clicking the arrow next to Legend and choosing a position, but true Excel pros just drag the legend box to get it exactly where they want.

Legends aren't always an asset when you need to build slick, streamlined charts. They introduce two main problems:

- **Legends can be distracting.** In order to identify a series, the person looking at the chart needs to glance away from the chart to the legend, and turn back to the chart again.
- **Legends can be confusing.** Even if you have only a few data series, the average reader may find it hard to figure out which series corresponds with each entry in the legend. This problem becomes more serious if you print your chart out on a printer that doesn't have the same range of colors as your computer monitor, in which case different colored lines or bars may begin to resemble each other.

If you don't want to use a legend for these reasons, you can use data labels instead.

Adding Data Labels to a Series

Data labels are identifiers you attach to every data point in a series. The text in a data label floats just above the point, column, or pie slice that it describes.

Data labels have unrivalled explaining power—they can identify *everything* in your chart. Their only possible drawback is with charts already dense with data—adding labels may lead to an overcrowded jumble of information.

To apply data labels, open the Chart Elements window and click the arrow next to Data Labels to see a list of placement options. If you choose Center on a column chart, each bar's value appears as a number centered vertically inside the bar. On the other hand, if you choose Outside End, the numbers appear just above the top of each column, which is usually more readable (Figure 18-7).

TIP No matter how you choose to label or distinguish a series, you're best off if you don't add too many of these elements to the same chart. Adding too many labels makes for a confusing overall effect, and it blunts the impact of any comparison.

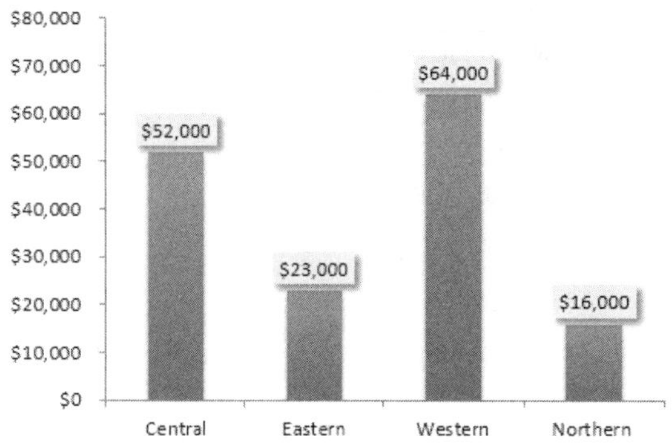

FIGURE 18-7

Here, you can see how a value label adds information to a column chart. Even without the labels, you could gauge regional revenue by running your eye from the top of the bar to the value axis on the left, but the labels make it a whole lot easier to get that information in a single glance. The labels have been customized slightly to shrink their font size and add a simple box with a shadow effect.

If you're in an adventurous mood, you can create even more advanced labels. To do that, right-click one of your data labels and choose Format Data Labels from the pop-up menu. Or, if you haven't yet added your labels, click the Chart Elements icon and choose Data Labels→More Options. Either way, a panel named Format Data Labels appears on the right of the Excel window, with plenty of additional options for customizing the labels (Figure 18-8).

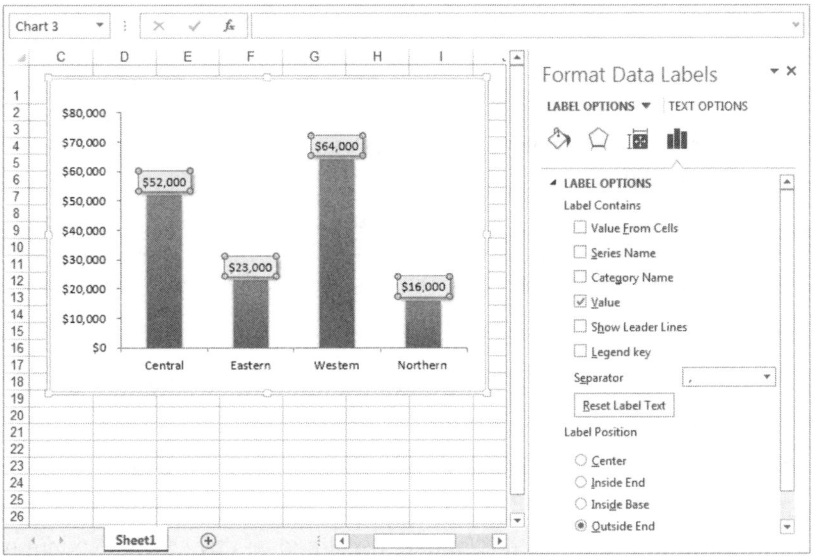

FIGURE 18-8

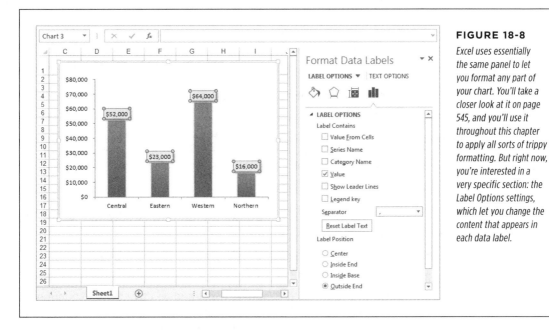

Excel uses essentially the same panel to let you format any part of your chart. You'll take a closer look at it on page 545, and you'll use it throughout this chapter to apply all sorts of trippy formatting. But right now, you're interested in a very specific section: the Label Options settings, which let you change the content that appears in each data label.

Using the Format Data Labels panel, you can choose the data label's position (just like you can when you add data labels via the Chart Elements icon). But the options under the Label Contains heading are more interesting, as they let you choose the information that appears in the label. Ordinarily, that information is simply the value of a data point. However, you can also apply a *combination* of values. Your exact options depend on the type of chart you created, but here are all the possible choices:

- **Series name.** The series name identifies the series each data point comes from. Because most series have multiple data points, using this option means the same text repeats again and again. For example, in a line chart that compares sales between two stores, this option would put the label "Store 1" above each data point for the first store, which is probably overkill.
- **Category name.** The category name repeats information from the category axis. For instance, if you use a line chart to compare sales from month to month, this option adds a month label above every data point. Assuming you have more than one line in your line chart, you'll get duplicate labels, which crowds out the important information in your chart. For that reason, category labels don't work very well with most charts, although you can use them to replace the legend in a pie or donut chart.

- **Value.** Value labels display the underlying value for a data point. If you plot changing sales, for example, this label gives you the dollar amount of sales for a given month. Excel pulls the data from the corresponding cell in your worksheet. Value labels are probably the most frequently used type of label.
- **Percentage.** Percentage labels apply only to pie charts and donut charts. They're similar to value labels, except that they divide the value against the total of all values to find a percentage.
- **Bubble size.** Bubble size labels apply only to bubble charts. They display the value from the cell that Excel used to calculate the bubble size. Bubble labels are quite useful because bubble sizes don't correspond to any axis, so you can't figure out the numeric value a bubble represents just by looking at the chart. Instead, you can only judge relative values by comparing the size of one bubble to another.

NOTE In some charts (including XY scatter charts and bubble charts), the checkboxes "Category name" and "Value" are renamed as "X Value" and "Y Value," though they have the same effect as "Category name" and "Value."

And at the bottom of the list you'll see two more options that let you further refine your data labels:

- **Show Leader Lines.** If you check this option and drag one of your data labels away from its data point, Excel adds a thin line to visually connect the two.
- **Legend key.** If you check this option, Excel adds a tiny colored square next to each data label. The color of this square matches the color used for the corresponding series (and the color that's shown in the legend, if your chart has a legend).

When you use multiple items, you can also choose a character from the Separator list box to specify how to separate each piece of text in the full label (with a comma, space, semicolon, new line, or a character you specify). And if you want to display a mini square with the legend color next to the label, then choose "Include legend key in label" (although most people don't bother with this feature).

Figure 18-9 shows more advanced data labels at work.

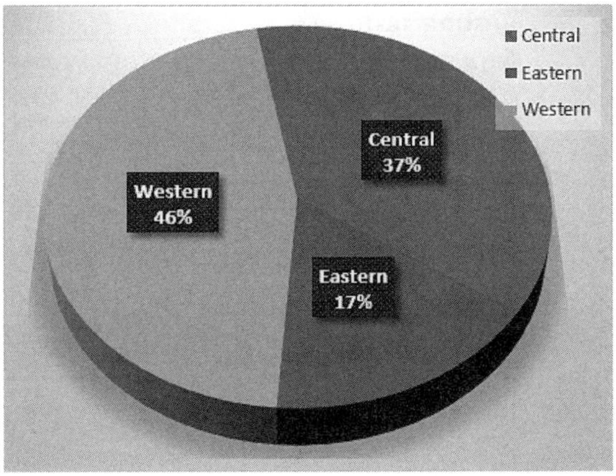

FIGURE 18-9

Here's how you can combine percentage and category information to make a pie chart more readable; with these labels in place, you can now eliminate the legend.

Adding Individual Data Labels

In simple charts, data series labels work well. But in more complex charts, data series labels can be more trouble than they're worth, because they can overcrowd a chart, particularly one that plots multiple series. The solution is to add labels to only a few data points in a series—those that are most important. Figure 18-10 shows the difference.

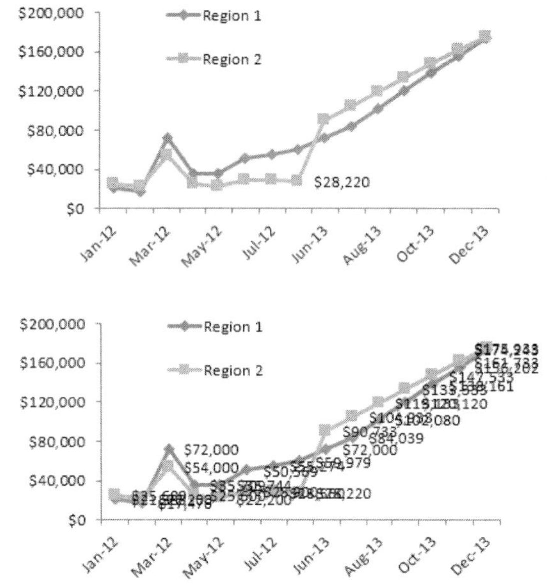

FIGURE 18-10

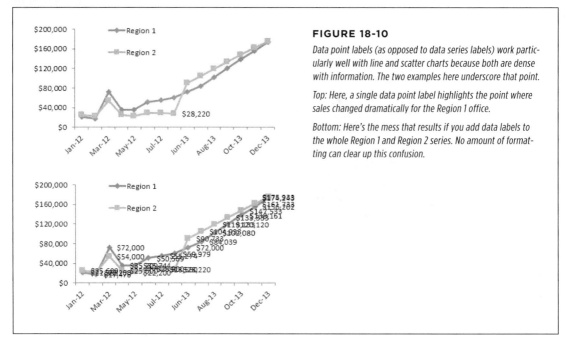

Data point labels (as opposed to data series labels) work particularly well with line and scatter charts because both are dense with information. The two examples here underscore that point.

Top: Here, a single data point label highlights the point where sales changed dramatically for the Region 1 office.

Bottom: Here's the mess that results if you add data labels to the whole Region 1 and Region 2 series. No amount of formatting can clear up this confusion.

To add an individual data label, follow these steps:

1. **Click the precise data point you want to identify.**

   This could be a slice in a pie chart, a column in a column chart, or a point in a line chart.

   Selecting a data point is a little tricky. You need to click twice—the first click selects the whole series, and the second one selects just the data point you want. You'll see handles appear around the specific column or point to indicate you selected it, as shown in Figure 18-11.

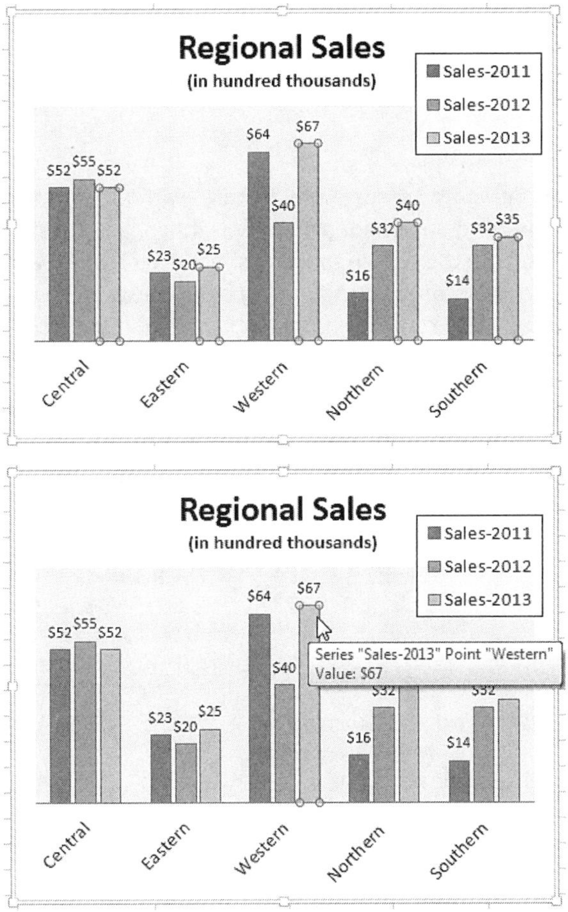

FIGURE 18-11

Top: To select a single data point, click it twice. Here, the first click selects the whole Sales-2013 series.

Bottom: The second click isolates just the data point you want, which is the Sales-2013 data for the Western sales office. In some cases, you may not be able to tell which data point's the one you want, especially if you're creating a dense scatter chart. When that happens, hover over the data point briefly to see a tooltip with the category, series, and value information.

2. **When you have the right data point selected, right-click it and choose Format Data Label.**

   If you don't already have the side panel with the formatting options open, it appears now, with the title Format Data Label. Its options work the same way as the options for a data series, except that these settings will apply only to the currently selected data label.

   To remove a data label, click to select it, and then press Delete. If you want to add several data labels, you're best off adding the data *series* labels (as described in the previous section), and then deleting the ones you don't want.

3. **Optionally, edit the text in your data label.**

   If a data label doesn't have exactly what you want, click inside it and type in new text, just as you would with a chart title.

TIP Instead of using data labels, you can add arrows and text boxes anywhere on a chart to call out important information. To do so, you need Excel's drawing features, explained in the next chapter.

Adding a Data Table

Trying to pack as much information as possible into a chart—without cluttering it up—is a real art form. Some charting aficionados use labels, titles, and formatting to highlight key details, and then use the data in the worksheet itself to offer a more detailed analysis. However, Excel also provides a meeting point between chart and worksheet that works with column charts, line charts, and area charts. It's called a *data table.*

Excel's data table feature places your worksheet data *below* your chart, lined up by category. You can best understand how this feature works by looking at a simple example, like the one in Figure 18-12.

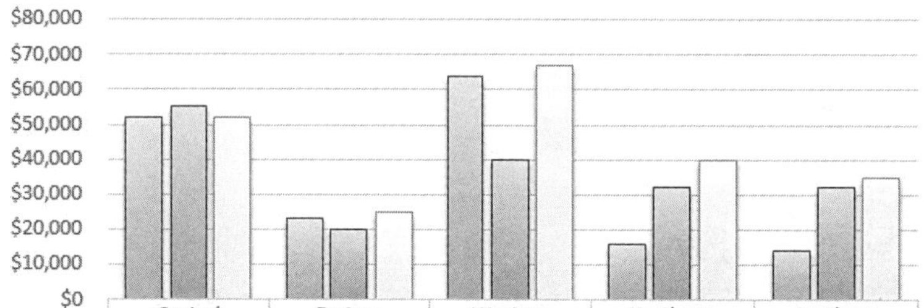

	Central	Eastern	Western	Northern	Southern
Sales-2011	$52,000	$23,000	$64,000	$16,000	$14,000
Sales-2012	$55,000	$20,000	$40,000	$32,000	$32,000
Sales-2013	$52,000	$25,000	$67,000	$40,000	$35,000

FIGURE 18-12

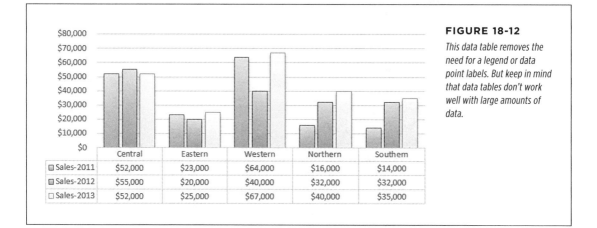

This data table removes the need for a legend or data point labels. But keep in mind that data tables don't work well with large amounts of data.

To add a data table, click the Chart Elements icon and choose Data Table. If you want to complement each series in the table with a small square whose color matches the related data series, click Chart Elements and choose Data Table→With Legend Keys. This way, you might not need a legend at all.

Formatting Chart Elements

Some chart elements, like titles and axes, are hard to miss. Others are a little more subtle. Either way, it's important to realize that everything you add to a chart is its own distinct ingredient, and you can tweak each component independently—even the data labels that identify important values (page 536). That means you can select these elements, move them, delete them, and so on. Understanding this principle is the secret to creating charts that stand out from the crowd.

So far, you've learned how to add the most popular elements to your chart. (You've left out a few, like trendlines and error bars, which you'll consider in the more advanced charting examples later in this chapter). But you haven't learned everything you can do with a chart component once you create it. In the following sections, you'll learn how to grab hold of the element you want and further fine-tune it.

Selecting a Chart Element

If you want to manipulate your chart components, you first have to learn how to select them. The easiest way to do that is to click directly on the element, as shown in Figure 18-13.

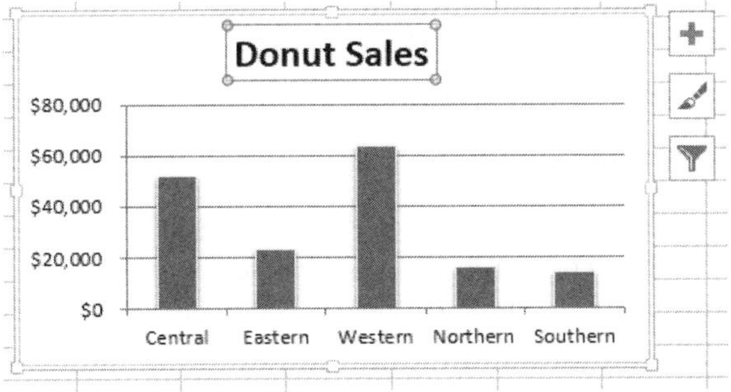

FIGURE 18-13

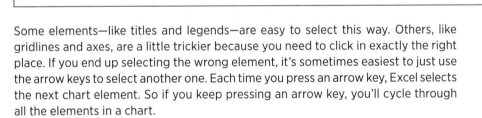

When you select a chart element, a rectangle appears around it, with a circle (known as a handle) in each corner. In this example, you've selected the chart title.

Some elements—like titles and legends—are easy to select this way. Others, like gridlines and axes, are a little trickier because you need to click in exactly the right place. If you end up selecting the wrong element, it's sometimes easiest to just use the arrow keys to select another one. Each time you press an arrow key, Excel selects the next chart element. So if you keep pressing an arrow key, you'll cycle through all the elements in a chart.

You can also select chart elements with the ribbon's Chart Tools | Format→Current Selection section, as shown in Figure 18-14. Using this list, you can select any of the elements described earlier (page 532), except individual data points.

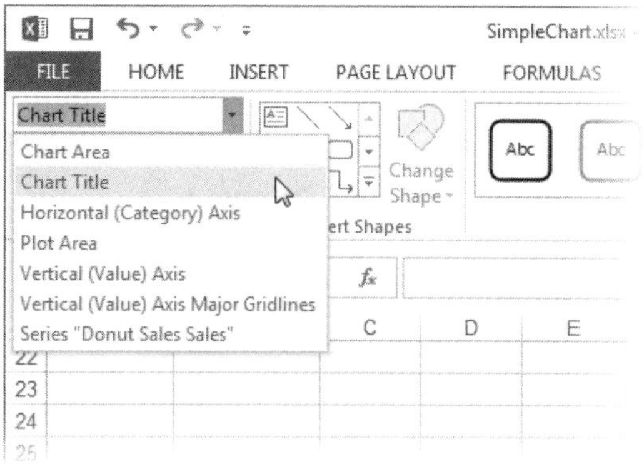

FIGURE 18-14

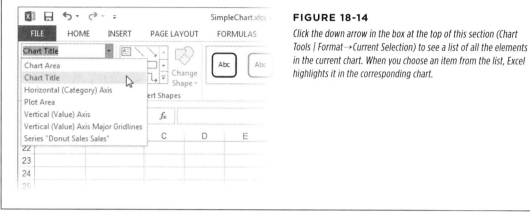

Click the down arrow in the box at the top of this section (Chart Tools | Format→Current Selection) to see a list of all the elements in the current chart. When you choose an item from the list, Excel highlights it in the corresponding chart.

So what do you do with a chart element once you select it? You can perform three basic tasks, although not every element supports every task. The tasks include:

- **Deleting an element.** To remove a selected element from your chart, press Delete. You can delete any chart element, including titles, legends, data series, gridlines, the background, and even an axis. It's possible to restore these elements after you delete them by choosing a new layout (page 530) or using the Undo command (Ctrl+Z) immediately after your gaffe.
- **Moving an element.** You can move a chart element by dragging it, just like you can move the whole embedded chart. You can easily move some elements, like labels, legends, and the whole chart. Other elements—including axes, gridlines, and data points—can't go anywhere.
- **Resizing an element.** You can resize an element by dragging one of the *resizing handles* (the circles that appear in each corner of the element when you select it). Resizing is mainly useful with legends and the overall chart—there aren't many other chart elements you can resize.
- **Formatting an element.** You can change how any element looks—for example, by giving it a different border, font, or color. The quickest way to do that is to double-click the item you want to format. A panel full of formatting options will appear on the right side of the Excel window. Figure 18-15 shows what happens when you double-click a chart title.

TIP If you find that double-clicking a chart item is a bit too awkward, Excel gives you plenty of other options. You can right-click your item and choose the Format command (for example, Format Data Labels). Or you can use the ribbon and pick Chart Tools | Format→Current Selection→Format Selection.

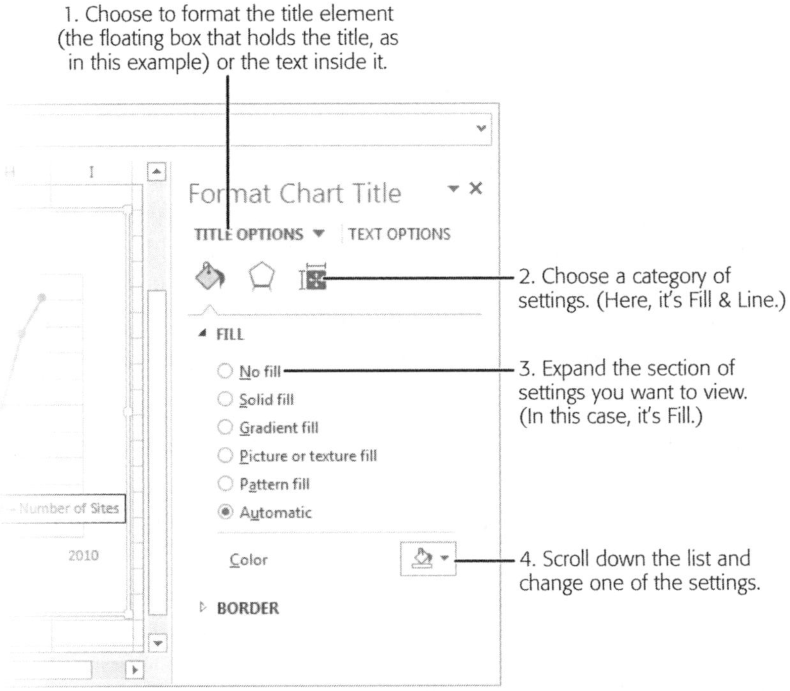
1. Choose to format the title element (the floating box that holds the title, as in this example) or the text inside it.
Format Chart Title
TITLE OPTIONS
TEXT OPTIONS
2. Choose a category of settings. (Here, it's Fill & Line.)
FILL
No fill
Solid fill
Gradient fill
Picture or texture fill
Pattern fill
Automatic
3. Expand the section of settings you want to view. (In this case, it's Fill.)
Color
4. Scroll down the list and change one of the settings.
BORDER
Number of Sites
2010

FIGURE 18-15

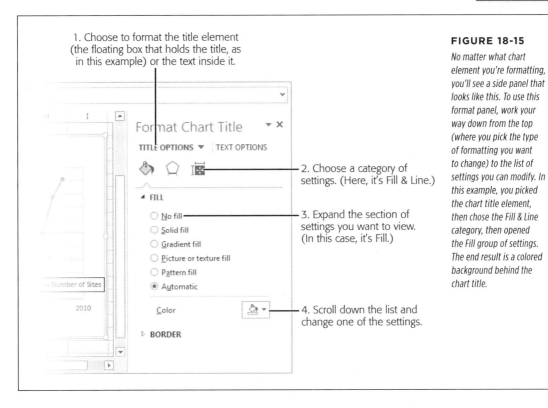

No matter what chart element you're formatting, you'll see a side panel that looks like this. To use this format panel, work your way down from the top (where you pick the type of formatting you want to change) to the list of settings you can modify. In this example, you picked the chart title element, then chose the Fill & Line category, then opened the Fill group of settings. The end result is a colored background behind the chart title.

Once the side panel is open, it automatically adjusts itself to work with whatever element you select in the chart. For example, if you double-click the chart title, the panel appears with the name Format Chart Title (as shown in Figure 18-15). If you then click the horizontal axis, the panel remains visible, and changes its name to Format Axis. Now the panel lists the formatting options for the chart axis. Think of the panel as your formatting sidekick. It's always ready to offer formatting possibilities, no matter what part of the chart you're working on.

TIP You may need to click around the formatting panel a bit before you get comfortable with it, because it stuffs a huge number of settings into different categories and subcategories. Often, you'll see the same settings appear for different chart elements. For example, almost every chart element has a Fill section and a Line section, where you can set the element's color and border.

Coloring the Background

Now you're ready to create spiffy looking, customized charts. The background color is a good starting point. Initially, this color is a plain white, but it's easy enough to change if you want to add a personal touch. Just follow these steps:

1. **Select the plot area.**

   To select the plot area, click the empty space between gridlines, or choose Chart Tools | Format→Current Selection→Plot Area.

2. **Make sure the side panel is visible.**

   If the formatting panel isn't already open from a previous element edit, double-click the plot area (the empty space between the gridlines). If that's too tricky, choose Chart Tools | Format→Current Selection→Format Selection.

3. **In the Fill settings, choose "Solid fill." To choose your color, click the Color button underneath and click the tiny colored square that catches your fancy.**

   For the most flexible formatting, choose one of the theme colors (which appear under the heading Theme Colors). That way, if you choose a new theme, the chart switches itself to one of the new theme colors.

   Don't worry about the other fill options right now—you'll take them on in the following section.

NOTE Remember, if you don't have a color printer, you need to think about how colors convert when you print them in black and white. In some cases, the contrast may end up being unacceptably poor, leading to charts that are difficult to read. As a general rule, the less powerful your printer, the less you should use graphically rich details like tiles, background images, and gradients—unless, of course, you're planning to view your worksheet on-screen only.

The neat thing about this sequence of steps is that you can use exactly the same process to format *any* chart element. That means you now know enough to give a solid fill to a chart title, the gridlines, the columns in a column chart, and so on. And once you learn your way around the rest of the formatting options, you'll be able to really spiff up your chart.

TIP If you run rampant changing a chart element and you just want to return it to the way it used to be, select it, and then choose Chart Tools | Format→Current Selection→Reset to Match Style. Excel removes your custom formatting and leaves you with the standard formatting that's based on the chart style.

Fancy Fills

Coloring the background of a chart is nice, if a little quaint. In the 21st century, charting mavens are more likely to add richer details, like textured backgrounds or gradient fills. Excel gives you these options and more. And although textured fills don't always make sense, they can often add pizzazz to the background of a simple chart. You can apply fancy fills to the chart background (the plot area) or individual chart items, like the columns in a column chart. Figure 18-16 shows some of your fill choices.

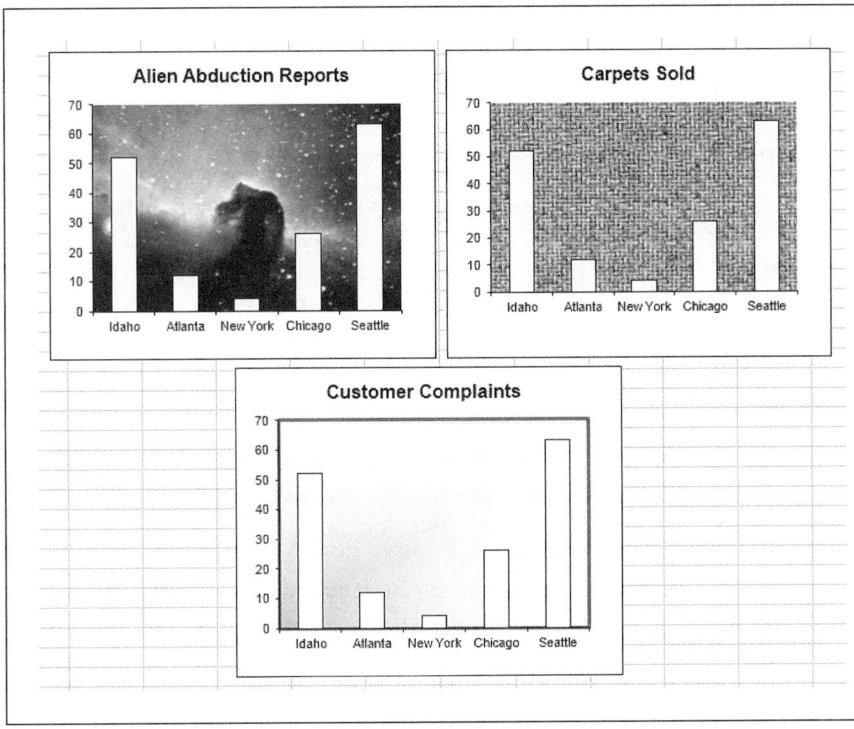

FIGURE 18-16

Depending on the type of fill you use, you can subtly change the message your chart conveys. These figures show a picture fill (top left), texture fill (top right), and gradient fill (bottom), with each graph using the same numbers and chart type. Fancy fills are particularly useful if you want to use your charts in a presentation program like PowerPoint. (Chapter 24 covers how to integrate your Excel worksheets with other programs.)

To apply a fancy fill, double-click the item, which opens the formatting panel. (Or, if the formatting panel is already open, you simply need to click the item once to select it.) Now, in the formatting panel, click the Fill & Line icon (which looks like a paint can that's tipping over), and expand the section of settings named Fill. What you do next depends on the type of fill you want.

GRADIENT FILLS

A gradient is a blend between two or more colors. For example, you can create a black-and-white gradient that gradually fades from black in the top-left corner to white in the bottom-right corner. More complex gradients fade from one color to another to another, giving a 1960s-era tie-dye effect. To set a gradient, choose the "Gradient fill" from the formatting panel's Fill section.

You can tweak two settings for your gradient: the colors it uses and the shading pattern. For the utmost in simplicity, you can choose a prebuilt set of color and shading options by clicking the "Preset gradients" button, and then clicking one of the thumbnail previews in the drop-down list. Make your choice, and Excel applies it to the chart instantly.

If you're not happy with the preset gradients, or you fancy yourself a bit more of an artist, you'll prefer to create your own gradient (or modify one of the presets). Here's how:

1. **From the Type list, choose a gradient type.**

   The type determines how Excel shades the fill. A normal linear gradient shades colors from one side (like the top) to the other (the bottom). The more exotic radial setting shades colors in concentric rings, starting from a single point.

2. **From the Direction list, choose an option.**

   The directions available depend on the gradient type you chose in the previous step. If you opted for a linear fill, you can choose whether the gradient starts at the top, bottom, left, or right. You can also set the angle of the fill (in the Angle text box) to tilt the gradient just a bit, so that it's not completely horizontal or vertical.

3. **In the Gradient Stops section, specify where you want one color to stop and another to begin.**

   A gradient stop tells Excel where to stop using a color in a gradient. In a simple gradient (like the white-to-blue shading in Figure 18-16, bottom), you have two colors, which means you need just two stops, one for each color. For a more complex gradient (like a tacky yellow-green-red number), you need three gradient stops, one to trigger each color. To specify gradient stops, click the "Add gradient stop" and "Remove gradient stop" buttons until you have the right number of stops (Figure 18-17).

   Of course, your gradient stops don't need to be different colors; you could use different tints or shades of the same color. Gradient experts add extra stops even in simple gradients, because that allows them to control exactly how fast the gradient blends from one color to the next.

4. **Modify each gradient stop to suit.**

   Select a stop on the bar (Figure 18-17). Underneath, you can adjust the stop's color and position. The position is a percentage that determines when the gradient switches from one color to another. Say you create three gradient stops for use with the colors yellow, green, and red. You may choose gradient stops of 0%, 50%, and 100% to space them out evenly. That way, the fill is yellow at the starting point (0%), green by mid-point (50%), and red at the end (100%).

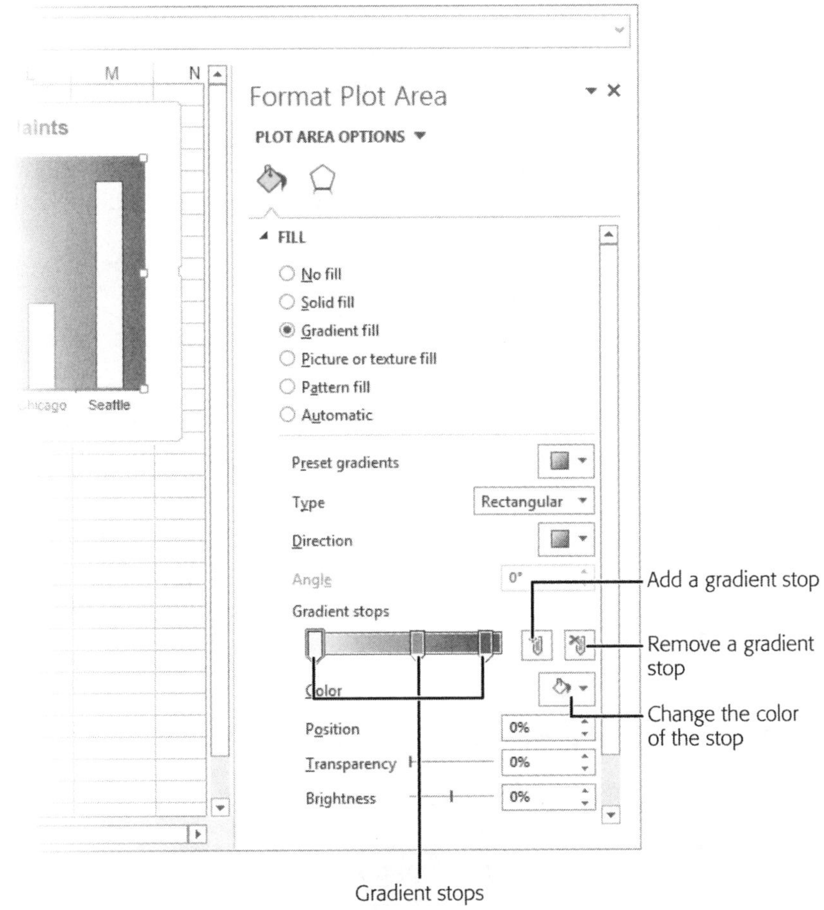

FIGURE 18-17

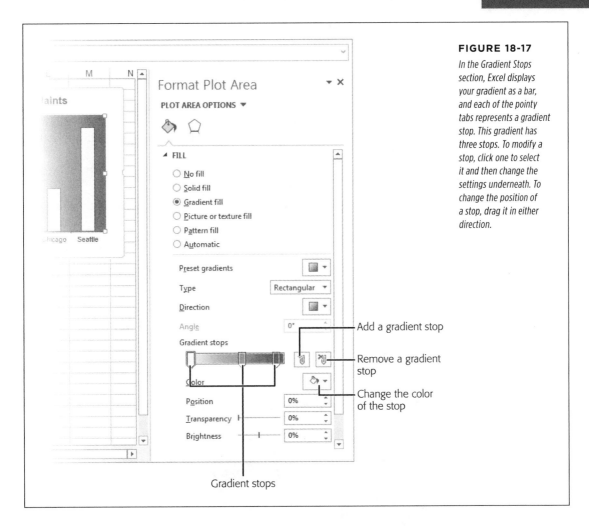

In the Gradient Stops section, Excel displays your gradient as a bar, and each of the pointy tabs represents a gradient stop. This gradient has three stops. To modify a stop, click one to select it and then change the settings underneath. To change the position of a stop, drag it in either direction.

TEXTURE FILLS

A texture is a detailed pattern tiled over a whole chart element. The difference between a texture and an ordinary pattern is that patterns are typically simple combinations of lines and shading, while textures use an image that may have greater, more photographic detail.

To add a texture fill, click "Picture or texture fill" from the list of Fill options. You can get the image for a texture from three places:

- **Your computer.** Click File to grab your texture from a picture file on your computer. You'll use this technique to create picture fills on page 551.
- **The Web.** Click Online to get your texture from Microsoft's Office Online website or a random web page. You'll explore this feature in closer detail when you add pictures to your worksheet on page 578.
- **A ready-made Excel texture.** The quickest way to get a texture is to use one of the ones bundled with Excel. To do that, choose from the drop-down Texture list (Figure 18-18).

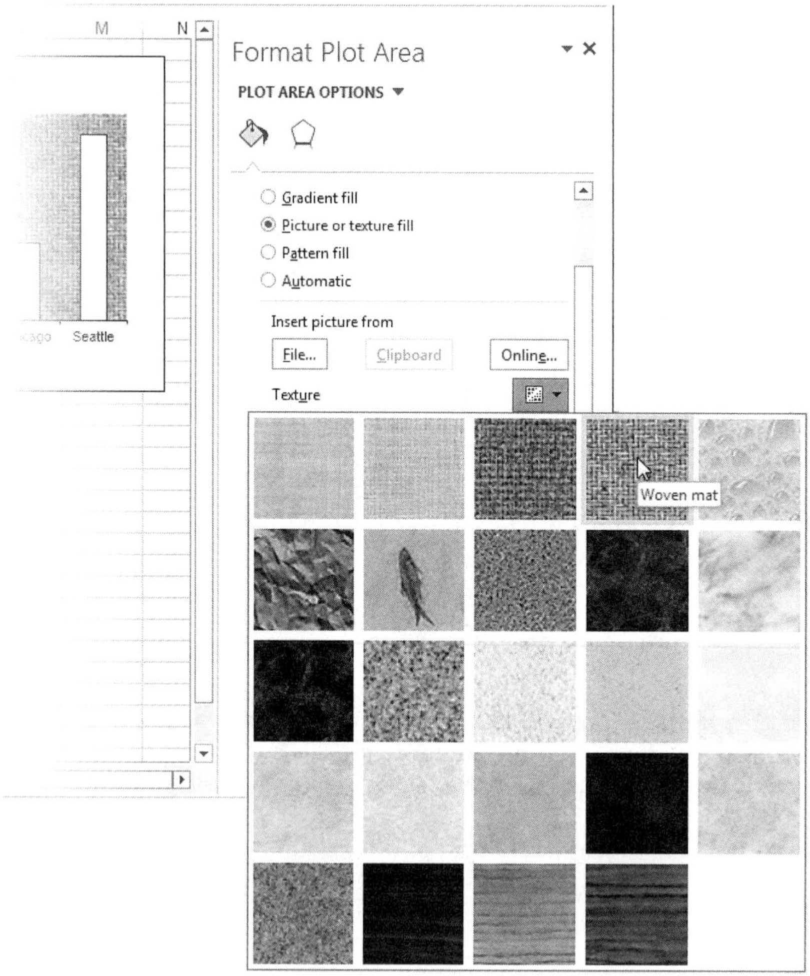

FIGURE 18-18

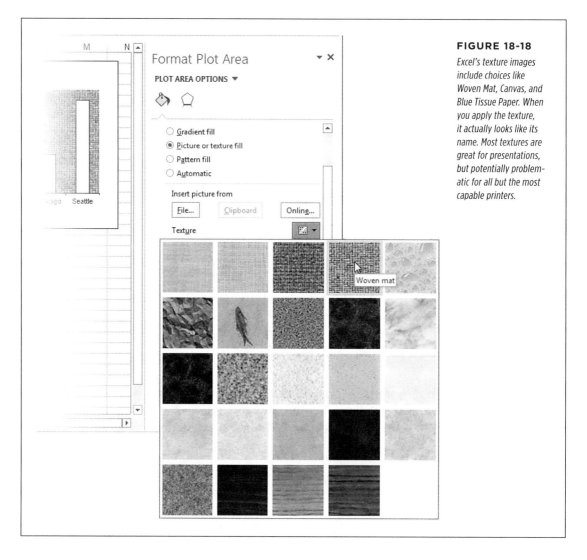

Excel's texture images include choices like Woven Mat, Canvas, and Blue Tissue Paper. When you apply the texture, it actually looks like its name. Most textures are great for presentations, but potentially problematic for all but the most capable printers.

Once you pick a texture, you can tweak it. You can resize it by adjusting the scale percentages, and you can play with the offset settings to alter the overlap of the tiled texture image. You can use the "Alignment" list to pick the edge or corner where the texture starts (Excel will trim the texture to fit along the other edges). And you can use the "Mirror type" list to flip subsequent tiles around, creating a more varied texture. But in truth, all these options are excessive frills, and you'll rarely need to touch any of them once you have a texture you like.

If you find that texture fills just don't thrill you, you can use a picture as a fill, which is the next section's topic.

NOTE You'll notice that the Fill section has a slider bar you can use to set the degree of transparency you want. You can make a fill partially transparent so that other elements show through. You can see a chart background through a partially transparent chart column, for example. But transparency is difficult to get right, and it often makes ordinary charts harder to read. That said, if your boss is out of the office and you need to fill the next hour, go ahead and experiment!

PICTURE FILLS

A picture is a graphical image that goes behind your chart and stretches itself to fit. Excel doesn't provide any ready-made pictures. Instead, you need to browse to a graphics file on your computer (a .bmp, .jpg, or .gif file). This option works well if you need a themed chart—like a beach scene behind a chart about holiday travel choices. If you just want to add a company logo somewhere on your chart, you're better off using the drawing tools described in the next chapter.

To use a picture fill, choose the "Picture or texture fill" option, and then click the File button to browse for the picture you want to use. Once you pick the picture, you can adjust the other options in the Fill section. Start by making sure the "Tile picture as texture" checkbox isn't selected—if it is, Excel tiles your picture just like it tiles the textures you saw in the previous section. (On the other hand, if that's the effect you're looking for, click away.)

Ordinarily, Excel stretches a picture over the surface of the chart. However, if you want your picture to fill just a part of the chart, you can adjust the offset percentages in the Top, Left, Right, and Bottom settings.

NOTE If you just want to add an unstretched image or two somewhere to your chart, you shouldn't use a picture fill. Instead, add the picture as an object, as described in the next chapter.

Fancy Borders and Lines

Now that you've tweaked the background fill to be slick and sophisticated (or wild and crazy), you're ready to modify other details. Along with the fill, an element's border is the next most commonly modified detail. You can add a border around any chart element, and your border can sport a variety of colors, line thicknesses, and line styles (like dashed, dotted, double, and so on).

The border settings are just under the fill settings in the formatting panel. If the Border section is collapsed, click to expand it.

1. **Choose the type of line you want.**

   Usually, it's "Solid line."

   Obviously, "No line" removes an existing border altogether. "Gradient line" lets you create a line that's painted with a gradient fill of colors (page 547). The reason this odd feature exists may never be clear.

   Once you pick a line choice, a pile of new line-formatting settings appear underneath.

2. **Set the line settings, and then click Close when you finish.**

   Figure 18-19 shows your options.

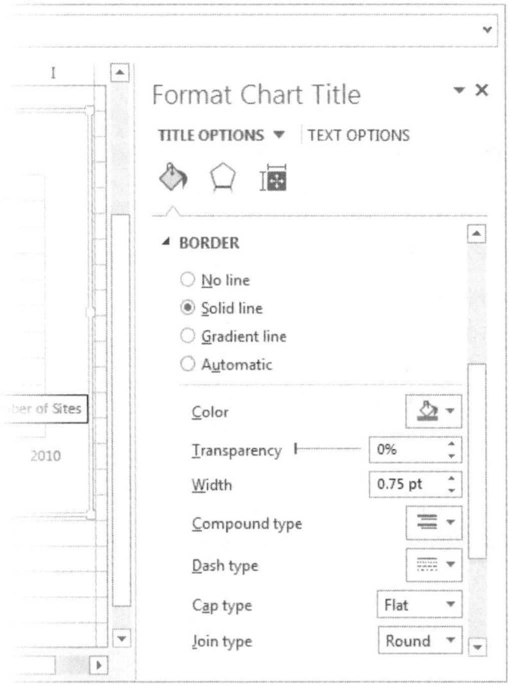

FIGURE 18-19

Using the formatting panel, you can set the line's color and width, choose a fancy double or triple-edged border (from the "Compound type" list), choose between solid and different types of dotted or dashed lines (from the "Dash type" list), and even set what the line corners look like (the "Join type") and what the line ends look like (the "Cap type"). The "Cap type" doesn't have an effect on borders unless you use dashed lines, because that's the only broken line offered, and it has visible ends.

TIP You can use the formatting panel to configure the gridlines that appear behind your chart data, too. First, make sure you have the gridlines visible by picking them in the Chart Elements list. Then double-click any one of them. Finally, adjust the line settings in the formatting panel, just as you would when adding a border.

POWER USERS' CLINIC

Using Shadows

The various formatting windows offer another option. You can choose the Shadow section to apply a shadow effect to a title, data series, or some other part of a chart. (A shadow, of course, is a faint shaded region behind a graphical shape or piece of text. Usually, you use a shadow to make something look more three-dimensional, so it seems to float above the rest of the background.) And although the idea sounds a little strange, a soft shadow can make an ordinary chart seem more professional (Figure 18-20).

To apply a shadow, click the Effects icon at the top of the formatting panel (it looks like a five-sided geometric shape). Then, expand the Shadow section, and choose one of the ready-made options from the Presets list. This list includes thumbnails for a wide range of shadow effects with different degrees of fuzziness and shadow placement. If you're a hard-core artist, you can choose a different shadow color and tweak all the other aspects of your shadow below that, using the sliders that control transparency, shadow size, blurriness, distance from the shadowed chart element, and so on.

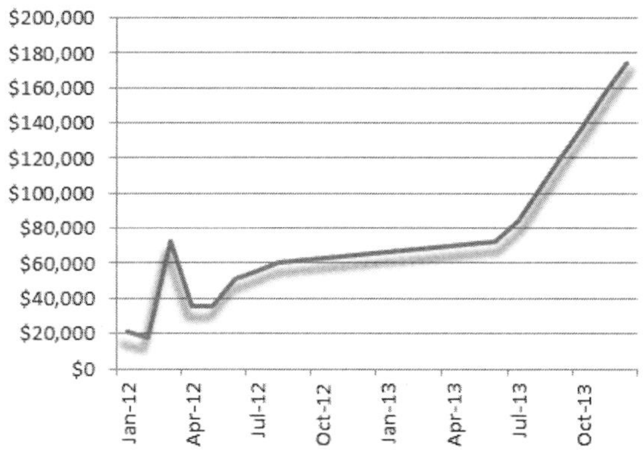

FIGURE 18-20

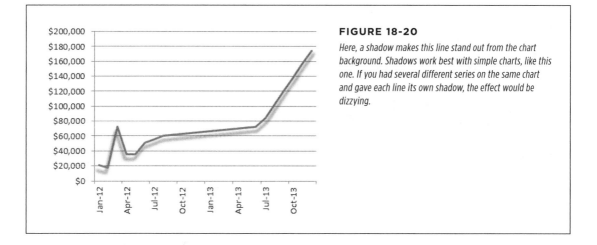

Here, a shadow makes this line stand out from the chart background. Shadows work best with simple charts, like this one. If you had several different series on the same chart and gave each line its own shadow, the effect would be dizzying.

Formatting Data Series and Data Points

Adding labels is one way to distinguish important points in your chart. You can also use color, borders, and patterns. These techniques don't provide any additional information (like the value of a data point), but they're a great way to emphasize information without cluttering up your chart. Figure 18-21 shows two examples.

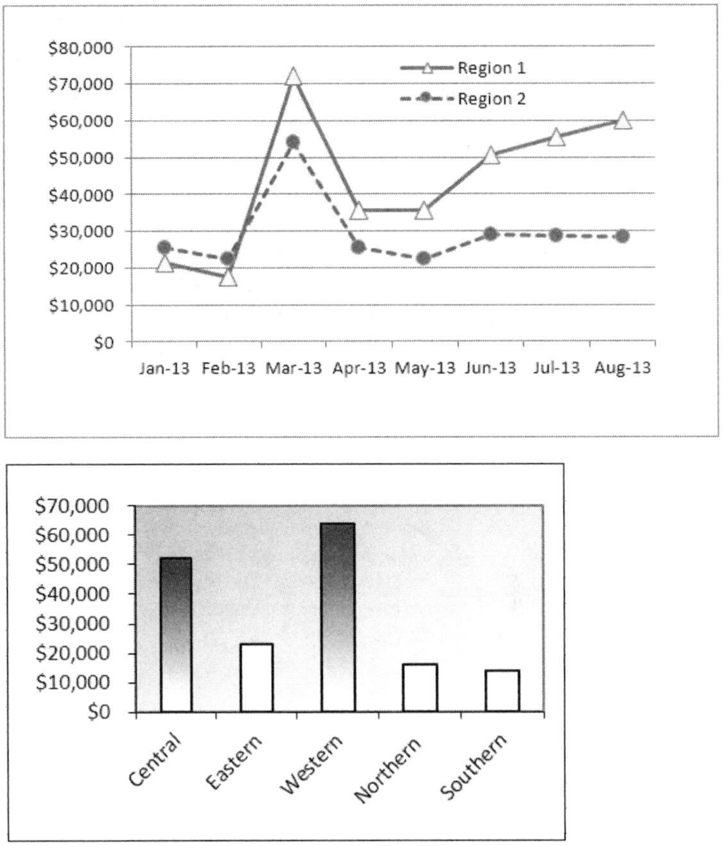

FIGURE 18-21

These figures show two examples of formatting at work.

Top: Here's a line chart where the two lines are carefully distinguished from one another with different shaped markers and line styles. To get this effect, format each series separately.

Bottom: Here's a column chart where a few columns are emphasized with a gradient fill. For this result, you need to format your data points individually.

You could have several reasons for formatting a data series or data point:

- You want to draw attention to specific data.
- You want to make sure that you distinguish between different series.
- You want to make sure your printout is legible, and that you can identify all the important information, even if your printout's black and white.

You already know the basic steps to format a data series, because they're almost identical to the steps you took to format other parts of the chart. First, make sure the formatting panel is open (if it isn't, double-click any item on the chart). Next, select the chart item you really want:

- If you select a data series, your changes affect all the data points in that series. Usually, you use this approach to distinguish each series.
- If you select a single data point (using the two-click technique explained in Figure 18-11), you affect only that data point. Usually, you use this approach to highlight important values.

TIP If you format a data point, and *then* format the series that contains the data point, the new formatting for the series takes over. Therefore, you need to reapply your data point formatting if you want a specific value to stand out from the crowd. To save time, you can use the helpful Redo feature to apply changes over and over again. First, format a data point the way you want it. Then, select a second data point, and press Ctrl+Y to apply the same formatting to the new data point. This technique can save you loads of time.

Here are some formatting ideas:

- For column, bar, or area charts, you can adjust the fill colors and even use gradients and textures to make different series stand out. Click the Fill & Line icon at the top of the formatting panel, and then go straight to the Fill section.
- If you have a line or XY scatter chart, you can change what the line looks like for each series. Click the Fill & Line icon and look at the Line section. If you have more than two or three lines, you may need to get creative with different line styles to make sure you can tell them apart at a glance, particularly if the chart's final destination is a black-and-white printout.
- For line or XY scatter charts, you can change the shape, size, fill, and border of the markers used to indicate each data point (Figure 18-22). For example, one line can use square markers, another triangles, another diamonds, and so on. You can even change the color or size of a single marker to denote a particularly important data point.

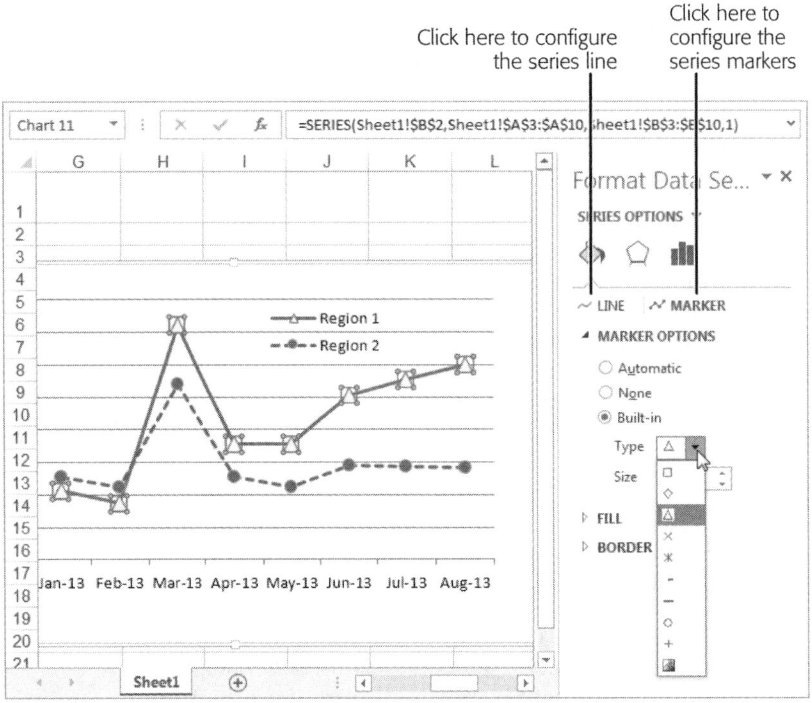

FIGURE 18-22

In line and XY scatter charts, the Fill & Line section gives you twice the formatting options of other charts. Not only can you change the color, width, and dash style of the line for each series, you can also change the shape, size, and color of each marker. To configure markers, click Marker at the top of the settings list. To configure the lines, click Line.

TIP Your use of color and fills is limited only by your imagination, but excessive formatting can be distracting, so it's best to add extra flourishes only when they help you make a point. You could use different colors in a bar chart to help highlight the meaning of the results on a company's annual sales chart, for instance. Red-colored bars could represent losses, while black ones could show profits.

Improving Your Charts

So far, you've learned the key techniques to make sure your charts tell the right story. However, Excel lets you do plenty more, including adding trendlines and error bars, and tweaking 3-D perspectives and shapes. In the following sections, you'll pick up even more tips to help you make the perfect chart.

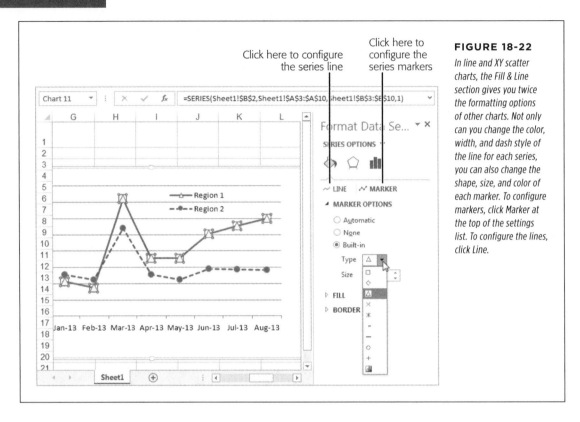

Controlling a Chart's Scale

Many people don't think twice about the scale they use when they create a chart—instead, they let Excel set it automatically, based on the values the chart uses. There's nothing wrong with this laissez-faire approach, but if you know how to take control of your chart's scale, you can make important data stand out and make it easier to spot relative differences in data and understand overall trends.

Usually, you'll be most interested in changing the scale of the value axis that runs up the left side of most charts. You can modify this scale on most charts, including column charts, line charts, scatter charts, and area charts. (In a bar chart, the value axis actually runs horizontally along the bottom of the chart, although you can modify the scale the same way you modify it in these other chart types.) Pie and donut charts don't show a value scale at all.

NOTE It's worth noting that quite a few unsavory individuals try to skew charts with crafty scale tricks. People often show two similar charts next to each other (for example, sales in 2012 and sales in 2013), and use a smaller scale in the second one to make it look like nothing's changed. Once you finish this section, you'll have a good idea of how to spot these frauds. Some companies even have policies that enforce strict scale usage!

To change the scale, start by double-clicking the value axis. This action selects the value axis and opens the formatting panel. (If the formatting panel is already open, there's no need to double-click—just click the value axis once to select it.) You'll know you clicked the right spot when the header on the formatting panel changes to Format Axis.

TIP If you're having trouble finding the value axis and you don't know what part of the chart to click, look for an element with a name like "Vertical (Value) Axis" in the ribbon's Chart Tools | Format→Current Selection section. Then, if the formatting panel isn't already open, choose Chart Tools | Format→Current Selection→Format Selection to show it.

Once you select the value axis, click the Axis Options icon in the formatting panel, and then expand the Axis Options section underneath (shown in Figure 18-23). You have the choice of letting Excel automatically set the scale based on your data, or entering the values you think are appropriate.

NOTE When you set a scale value to Auto, Excel calculates it based on the current chart size and your current data. If you add more data, change the data values, or resize the chart (in which case there's more room to show intermediate values on the axis), Excel may modify the scale. But when you use Fixed, your numbers are hard-wired into the chart, and Excel never changes them (although you may, later).

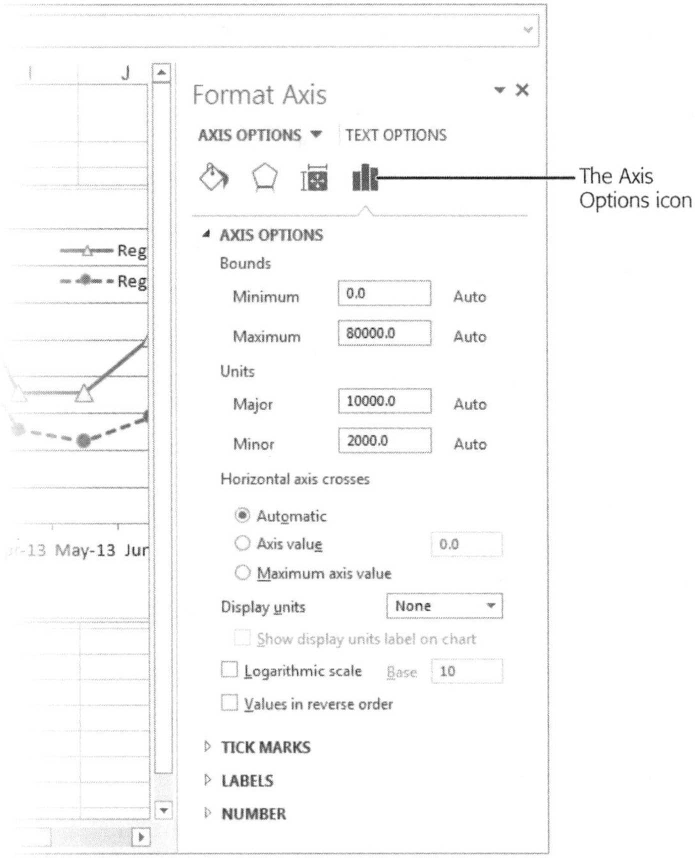

FIGURE 18-23

The Axis Options settings let you change the scale your chart uses. There's an "Auto" option next to each value. If you select it (as in this example), Excel chooses the scale value (and the value it chooses appears in the text box on the right). In this example, the scale currently stretches from 0 to 180,000, with a major tick mark shown every 20,000 units. If you want to take control of the scale yourself, click Fixed instead of Auto (next to the value you want to change), and then edit the number in the corresponding text box.

Several settings determine the scale of your chart. They include:

- **Bounds (Maximum and Minimum).** These values set the range of your scale. The axis starts at the minimum value (at the bottom of your chart), and ends at the maximum value (at the top). Usually, Excel sets these values so that the minimum is 0 and the maximum is just a little bit above your largest data point. However, if your data points are very large and have only minor differences, you can make data comparisons easier by starting the scale at a higher minimum value.

- **Units (Major).** The major unit setting determines how many units the scale is divided into. If you have a scale from 0 to 1,000 and a major unit of 100, gridlines and axis labels appear every 100 units. Altogether, that makes for 11 labels.
- **Units (Minor).** The minor unit setting determines how many **tick marks** are on the scale. (Tick marks are tiny lines added to the axis to help you judge the scale.) Usually, the minor unit is less than the major unit. You may use a major unit of 100 and a minor unit of 10 in a chart that stretches from 0 to 1,000, for example (which generates 11 gridlines and 10 tick marks between each gridline). A readable chart usually comprises five to 10 major units on each axis, and five to 10 minor units for every major unit.

NOTE When you first create a standard chart, minor tick marks are turned off, so the minor unit setting doesn't have any effect. To set whether Excel shows major and minor tick marks, scroll down to the Ticks section and choose an option from the "Major type" and "Minor type" lists. Anything other than None does the trick. (The various options determine exactly what the tick marks look like—for example, whether they're on the inside of the grid, the outside, or if they cross the gridlines completely.)

Along with the settings just listed, you may want to tweak the "Horizontal axis crosses" setting. This number controls where the category axis line crosses the value axis. Usually, this line's right at the bottom of the chart, at the minimum value. But you have two other choices. You can choose "Maximum axis value" to place the category axis at the top of the chart. The scale remains the same (meaning the minimum value is still at the bottom of the chart and the maximum value is at the top).

More interestingly, you can choose "Axis value," and then type in the exact value where the category axis should appear. This choice lets you put the axis somewhere in the middle of your chart. For example, you may want to plot a chart of test scores and draw the axis at a point that would indicate the minimum passing mark. Note that in a column chart, when a column has a value that's less than the axis, it points "downward," as you can see in Figure 18-24, bottom.

Using these basic ingredients, you have a good deal of control over your chart's appearance. Figure 18-24 shows how different scale choices can transform a chart, with the help of a little formatting.

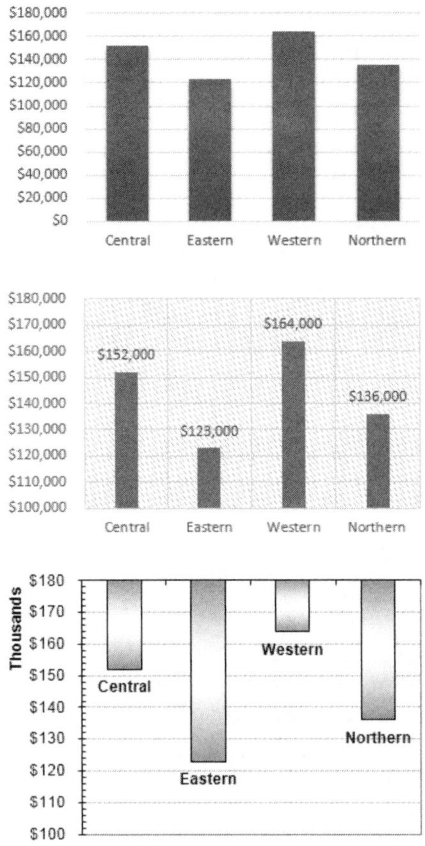

FIGURE 18-24

These charts show the same data prepared three different ways.

Top: Here's a column chart the way Excel creates it. This chart's problem is that the difference between the column values doesn't come across as very substantial when, in fact, it is. The middle and bottom charts solve this problem by setting the minimum value of the axis to $100,000, which shrinks the scale and emphasizes the differences between the columns' values.

Middle: This chart includes data labels that show each column's value.

Bottom: This chart's data labels have been removed from the X-axis, and category labels have been added to the data series so that the region's name shows up just below the bar. This example is further enhanced with gradient fills, minor tick marks, and a vertical scale set to use thousands.

The Axis Options section also provides a few specialized options that aren't as commonly used but are still quite interesting. They include:

- **Display units.** Use this option to shorten the text labels on your axis, which is particularly useful if you have large dollar amounts. Imagine that your value axis stretches from $100,000 to $300,000. If you choose Thousands as your display unit, Excel adds the label Thousands along the value axis and changes the scale values to three-digit numbers, like $100 and $300. The bottom example in Figure 18-22 shows this space-saving trick at work.
- **Logarithmic scale.** A logarithmic scale doesn't increase gradually; instead, every major unit represents an increase by a power of 10. The values 0, 10, 20, 30, 40, and 50 make up a typical scale. The values 0, 10, 100, 1000, and 10000 make up a logarithmic scale. Logarithmic scales lend themselves to scientific

and mathematical applications to help you see certain types of relationships and patterns in your data.

- **Values in reverse order.** This option turns your chart upside down. It places the category axis at the top of the chart (instead of at the bottom), and changes the value scale so that it increases as it stretches down the side of the chart.

NOTE If you use a numeric or date-based category axis, you can format its scale the same way you format the scale of the value axis. You may want this option when you create XY scatter charts or line charts. If your category axis just displays labels, you can still format it, but you have fewer options. You can't change the scale, but you can reverse the order of categories, add tick marks, hide labels, and format the axis line's look.

Adding a Trendline

One of the main reasons people create charts is to reveal patterns hidden inside the source data. A gift card company may look at a historical record of sales to make an educated guess about the upcoming holiday season. Or a researcher might look at a set of scientific data to find out if potatoes really can cure the common cold. In both of these examples, what's most important is spotting the trends that lurk inside most data collections.

One of the easiest ways to spot a trend is to add a *trendline* to your chart. A trendline is similar to an ordinary line in a line chart that connects all the data points in a series. The difference is that a trendline assumes the data isn't distributed in a perfectly uniform pattern. Instead of exactly connecting every point in a series, a trendline best represents all the data on a graph, which means that minor exceptions, experimental error, and ordinary variances don't distract Excel from finding the overall pattern. Figure 18-25 shows an example.

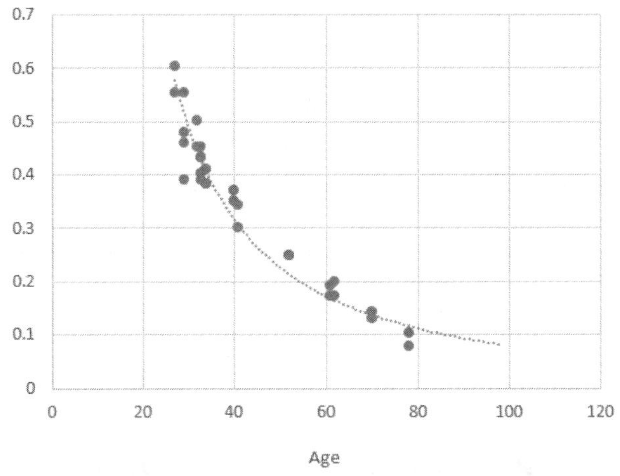

FIGURE 18-25

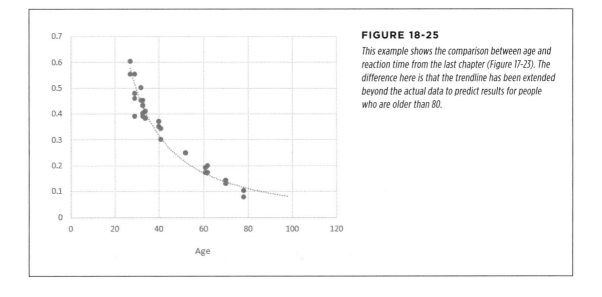

This example shows the comparison between age and reaction time from the last chapter (Figure 17-23). The difference here is that the trendline has been extended beyond the actual data to predict results for people who are older than 80.

The other reason trendlines are important is that they can predict values you don't have. The gift card company can use a trendline to get a good estimate of future sales, while a scientific experimenter can make educated guesses about data that wasn't recorded.

People most often use trendlines in XY scatter charts. They also makes sense in a column chart, and they can work in line, bar, and area charts in specialized circumstances.

To add a trendline, follow these steps:

1. **Select your chart.**

   If you're using an XY scatter chart (the most common choice), make sure you select a subtype that doesn't already include lines. To change the subtype of a chart, right-click the chart, and then choose Change Chart Type.

2. **If your chart has more than one series, choose the series you want to use to create the trendline.**

   If your chart has just a single series, you don't need to go to this trouble—just select the entire chart.

3. **Click the Chart Elements icon, click the arrow next to Trendlines, and then choose one the four most popular types of trendline. Or, click More Options to see all your trendline choices in the Trendline Options section of the formatting panel.**

   The type of trendline you choose depends on the type of relationship you expect to find in your data. Your options include:

   - **A Linear trend** is the simplest possible relationship, and suits data that varies regularly. For example, if you drive at a constant speed, the distance traveled increases linearly as the time increases. This trendline looks like a straight line, with no bends.
   - **A Linear Forecast trend** is similar to a Linear trend, but it extends a little bit further (the equivalent of two data points) to make a guess at where this relationship is going.
   - **A Two Period Moving Average trend** is a line that follows your data, but uses the average-so-far to "smooth out" each data point. It creates an effect that's similar to the line in a simple line graph, but less extreme—the swings up and down are smaller.
   - **A Power and Exponential trend** creates a curve that starts off slowly and quickly ramps up. These types of trends are more complex, but they're more common than linear trends in natural phenomena. Two example exponential relationships are the change in a population size with successive generations, and the distance traveled in a car if you continuously accelerate.

- **A Logarithmic trend** is the inverse of an exponential trend. It creates a curve that starts off rapidly and then levels out.
- **A Polynomial trend** attempts to fit the data by creating an equation with a combination of different terms. The result is a complex curve that can have multiple bends. This trend is the best choice if multiple factors are involved and your data doesn't fit a smooth line or curve.

If your chart has more than one series, you can repeat this process to add a trendline for each one.

After you add a trendline, you can change what it looks like. First, double-click the trendline. Then, click the Fill & Line icon in the formatting panel and change the color, width, and style options in the Line section.

A standard trendline fits the data you have. However, you can extend a trendline forward or backward to fill in values you don't know. This process of estimating data that you don't have (based on data that you do have) is called *extrapolation*. A closely related concept is *interpolation*, which estimates unknown data values *between* known values. If a gift card company has information about sales from 2010 to 2012, you'd use extrapolation to predict sales in 2013. To make an educated guess at what sales were like in March 2011 (a month in which your firm lost its sales data), you'd use interpolation. All trendlines necessarily use interpolation, since there's always, in effect, "missing" data points between the data points you have.

To extrapolate values in a trend, double-click your trendline. In the formatting panel, click the Trendline Options icon and scroll down to the Forecast settings. In the Forward and Backward boxes, specify the number of units you want to add before the start or after the end of your trendline. Figure 18-25 shows an example.

NOTE Don't always trust trendlines. It's quite possible that a relationship holds true only over a limited set of values. If you use a rising sales trendline as the basis for guessing future results, Excel's guesses don't, of course, take into account unexpected developments, like limited inventory or rising production costs. Similarly, if you extend the age versus reaction time comparison in Figure 18-23 too far, you'll wind up with ages and values that don't make sense (like a reaction time of 0 seconds, or a reaction time for a 300-year-old).

Adding Error Bars to Scientific Data

In a typical scientific experiment, you have two important sets of information: the actual results and an estimate that indicates how reliable these results are. This "reliability" number is the *uncertainty*. The uncertainty doesn't compensate for human error, faulty equipment, or invalid assumptions. Instead, it accounts for the limited accuracy of measurements. Think of the typical bathroom scale, which can give you your weight only to the nearest pound. That means there's an uncertainty of 0.5 pounds because any given measurement could be off by that amount. If a scientific experimenter weighs in at 150 pounds, he would record that measurement as 150±0.5 (150 pounds plus or minus 0.5 pounds). Any other calculations based on weight need to take this potential inaccuracy into account.

Because every type of measurement has a different range of accuracy, there's always a certain degree of imprecision that you need to account for before you make a dramatic conclusion. In a scientific chart, you can indicate this uncertainty using error bars, as in Figure 18-25. If you plot 150±0.5 on a chart, you should end up with a point at 150 and an error bar that stretches from that point up to 150.5 and down to 149.5.

To add scientific error bars to a chart, follow these steps:

1. **Click to select the appropriate data series on the chart.**

   If you have more than one data series, each series can have its own error bar settings.

2. **Click the Chart Elements icon, then click the arrow next to Error Bars and choose More Options.**

   Excel guesses how big you'd like your error bars to be, and adds them to your chart. In the formatting panel, you can fine-tune your error bars (Figure 18-26).

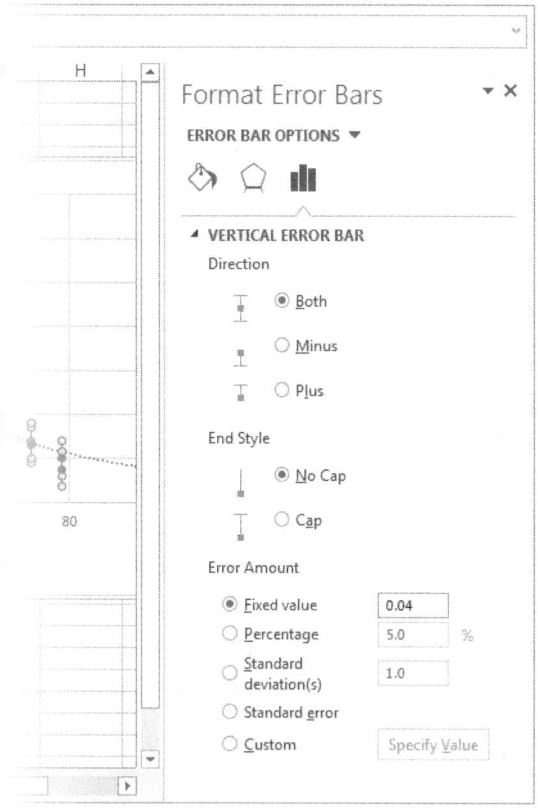

FIGURE 18-26

You can set error bars to use a fixed value (as in this example), a fixed percentage of the value, or you can specify a range of cells in the worksheet that contains the uncertainty value for each measurement.

3. **Choose how large your error bars should be.**

   Two simple and useful choices are "Fixed value" (which lets you specify the same measurement of uncertainty for every value), and Percentage (which lets you specify a percentage uncertainty for every value). You can also supply a different fixed uncertainty for each value. In this case, add a new column beside your column of current values, and list the uncertainty for each of those values in the new column. Then choose the Custom option, and click Specify Value to specify the range of cells that list the uncertainty information (you need one uncertainty value for each data point). Statistics fans can also use two more-advanced options, Standard Deviation and Standard Error. For definitions of these two weighty concepts, consult your favorite statistics textbook.

4. **Click Close to add error bars to your chart.**

   Figure 18-27 shows a chart with error bars added.

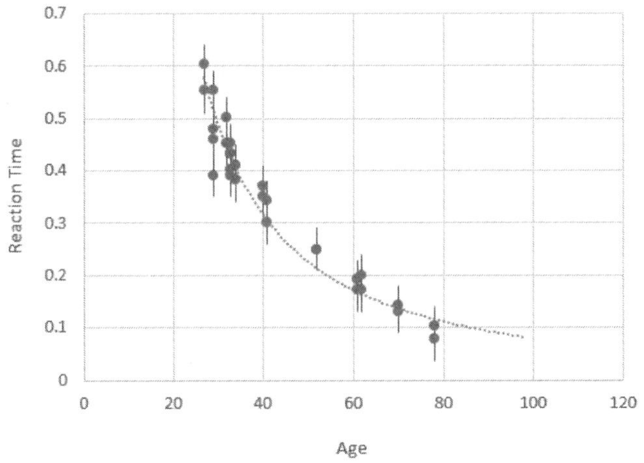

FIGURE 18-27

This graph attempts to show a link between age and reaction time, with the error bars indicating that the reaction time couldn't be measured precisely. The error bars tell us that even though the trendline doesn't fit the data exactly, it lies within the range of measurement error. In this example, you can't distinguish all of the error bars, because sometimes the points and error bars overlap (consider the two data points around age 40). On the other hand, it's easy to see the single data point at age 50 and the error bars above and below it.

Formatting 3-D Charts

As you learned in Chapter 17, many chart types offer subtypes that draw data in three dimensions. Some 3-D chart types are no different from their plainer 2-D relatives. In these charts, a 3-D effect simply gives the chart a more interesting appearance. But true 3-D charts add information by layering data from the front of the chart to the back, with each series' results appearing behind the previous set of results. (The column chart has seven subtypes. The first three are ordinary 2-D charts, the second three use a 3-D effect, and the last one's the only true 3-D chart. For more details about what subtype each chart supports, see the "Chart Types" section that starts on page 512.)

In true 3-D charts, you may need to take special care to make sure that data in the background doesn't become obstructed. A few tricks can help, like reordering the series and simplifying the chart so it isn't cluttered with extraneous data. You may also want to rotate or tilt the chart so that you have a different vantage point on the data.

To rotate or tilt a chart, follow these steps:

1. **Right-click the chart, and then select 3-D Rotation.**

   In the formatting panel, Excel opens the 3-D Rotation section, as shown in Figure 18-28.

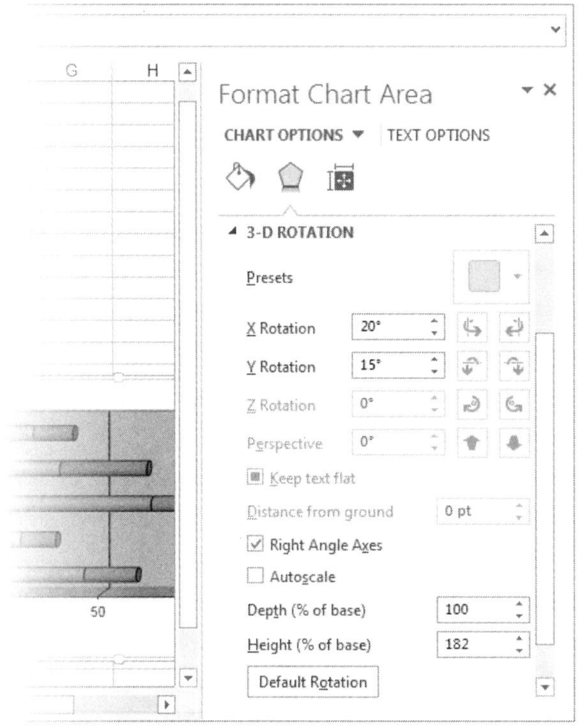

FIGURE 18-28

The 3-D Rotation settings let you twist and turn your 3-D chart. As you make your changes, Excel dynamically updates the chart on your worksheet.

2. **Use the arrow buttons to tilt the chart in various ways, changing the rotation and perspective.**

   You can also edit the individual settings by hand:

   - The X Rotation value lets you turn the chart from side to side.
   - The Y Rotation value lets you tilt the chart up and down.
   - The Perspective value lets you make the chart seem closer or farther away.

   You can also use a few more-specialized settings to fine-tune your chart:

   - Turn on the Right Angle Axes checkbox if you're tired of turning your chart this way and that, trying to find a good vantage point. When you switch this setting on, the Perspective value has no effect. Instead, Excel "straightens" out the chart by squaring it up, face-forward.
   - Turn off the Autoscale checkbox if you want to set the height of the chart using the Height box. The Height box specifies a percentage that's compared against the length of the bottom of the chart (the X-axis). In other words, a Height of 100 percent means the chart will be just as high as the base is wide. A height of 200 percent means the chart will be twice as high as it is wide. Keep in mind that Excel compares the height against the width of the base, not the width of the entire chart. If you rotate the chart, the perspective makes it appear as though the base isn't as wide as it really is. In this situation, Excel still makes the chart just as tall as if you hadn't rotated it.
   - Use the Depth box to set how deep the chart is (from front to back). As with the Height box, you use a percentage that's compared to the base of the chart. That means a depth of 200 percent makes a chart twice as deep as its base is wide. Sometimes, a deeper chart creates a more dramatic 3-D effect.
   - Click the Default Rotation button to return your chart to the just-slightly tilted way it began life.

Changing the Shape of a 3-D Column

Excel provides several subtypes of column and bar charts that use a 3-D effect. Ordinarily, 3-D column and bar charts use 3-D rectangles, but you can change these rectangles into more exotic shapes, like pyramids and cones, with hardly any effort.

It doesn't really make much difference whether you use rectangles, pyramids, or cones—the overall effect is pretty much the same. However, you create a much more dramatic effect by putting more than one shape in a single chart. If you want to compare two series, you could represent one with columns and the other with cones, as shown in Figure 18-29.

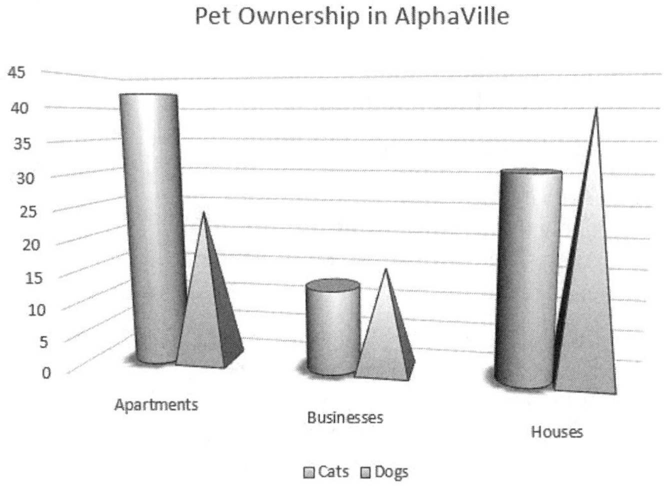

FIGURE 18-29

To make a dramatic point, you can combine more than one shape in a chart. In this example, cylinders represent the cat population and pyramids represent the corresponding dog figures. Creating this chart is refreshingly easy—you just need to change the "Column Shape" setting in the series options.

To try this out, follow these steps:

1. **Create a column chart with two or more data series.**

   Make sure you pick one of the chart subtypes that use a 3-D effect.

2. **Double-click one of the data series.**
3. **In the formatting panel, click the Series Options icon.**
4. **Pick one of the shapes in the "Column shape" section.**

   Click one of the pictures to change your columns into cylinders, cones, pyramids, or something else. Then click Close.

5. **Repeat steps 2 to 4 for any other data series that you want to change.**

Advanced Charting

At this point, you've seen a wide range of tips and tricks for improving almost any Excel chart. But it's worth learning a few advanced charting techniques. Most of these work only with specific chart types, like exploding pie slices and overlaying bar charts. You'll also learn about one of the most interesting chart tricks known to Excel-kind: using a combination chart to fuse together two different chart types into one object.

Exploding Slices in a Pie

Data labeling and formatting help make individual slices of a stand out. But to really accentuate important information in a pie or donut chart, you can separate a piece from the rest of the pie by *exploding* the slice (to use the rather dramatic technical term). You've already seen this feature at work with the pie or donut chart subtypes that explode *all* the pieces. This technique shows you how to explode just a single slice, as shown in Figure 18-30.

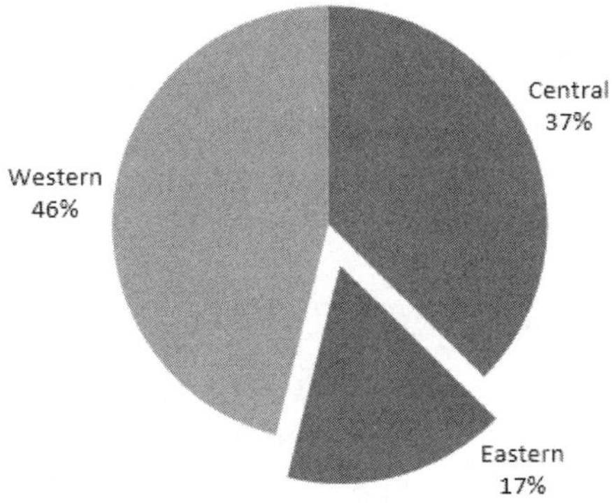

FIGURE 18-30

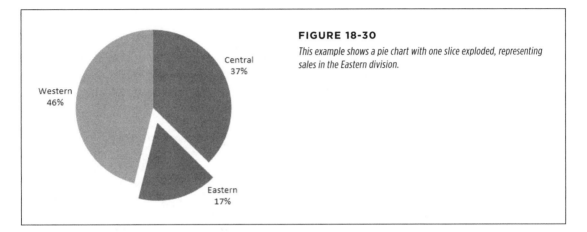

This example shows a pie chart with one slice exploded, representing sales in the Eastern division.

To explode only one slice of a pie chart, just click the slice, and then drag it away from the pie. You can pull it as far away as you want, and you can repeat this process to explode several pieces (although the emphasis works best when you remove just a single slice). Be careful that you don't select the whole data series before you start dragging, or you'll end up exploding the whole pie.

TIP You can also help separate your slices by adding a thin white border around each slice. Double-click any slice to show the Format Data Point panel. Then, click the Fill & Line icon, scroll down to the Border section, and choose a solid white border. Make it as thick as you need to properly separate your slices.

Grouping Slices in a Pie

An even more interesting pie chart feature breaks down a single slice into more detail. You may want to create a pie chart that shows your personal budget by category (including food, living expenses, clothes, and so on). You could then further subdivide a single slice, like food, to show what portion goes to groceries, restaurants, the local hot dog vendor, and ice cream stores. Adding all this information into a single pie would result in too many slices, making the chart less effective.

Creating a pie chart with a single slice broken down is pretty easy, but it's not the most intuitive operation in the world. First, you need to set up your data correctly.

Your table needs to include *all* the information you're putting into the chart in a single series. Imagine you want to create a pie with these slices:

Food	$13,911
House	$18,342
Clothes	$4,790
Fun	$7,980
Computer	$34,010

Now, assume that the slice you want to subdivide is the Computer slice. That means you need to remove the Computer entry and replace this information in the chart with more detailed information. Here's what you might end up with:

Food	$13,911
House	$18,342
Clothes	$4,790
Fun	$7,980
Computer Software	$7,500
Computer Hardware	$6,500
Missing Manual Books	$20,010

Notice that the Computer Software, Computer Hardware, and Missing Manual Books entries add up to the whole computer slice ($34,010), which has been removed from the chart.

NOTE The only limitation to breaking down an individual slice is that you can perform this trick on only one slice in a pie.

Now that you organized your data the right way, create a new pie chart, and choose either the "Pie of Pie" or "Bar of Pie" subtypes. Excel automatically chooses some slices from the bottom of your chart to group in a separate pie or bar chart. Unless Excel makes a lucky guess, this selection doesn't include the same slices that you want. Fortunately, it's easy to change the separation just by dragging.

If you have a "Bar of Pie" chart, you can add a slice to the bar by dragging it from the main pie to the column. If you want to take a slice that's in the column and put it back in the pie, drag it from the column back to the main pie. Continue this process until you've grouped the Computer Software, Computer Hardware, and Missing Manual Books slices into the standalone bar.

Figure 18-31 shows a perfected "Pie of Pie" chart.

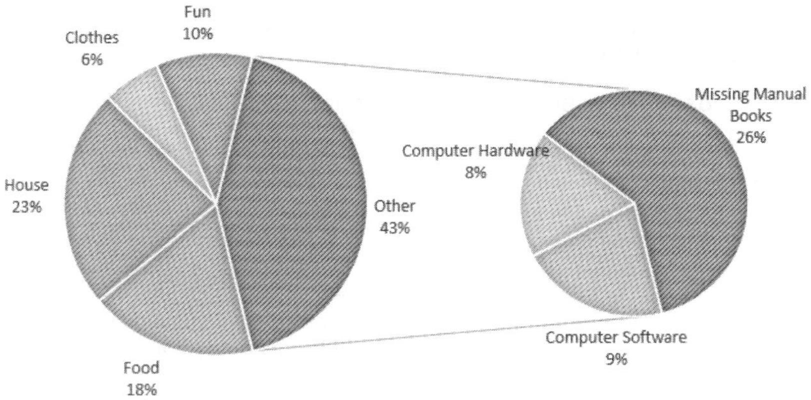

FIGURE 18-31

This example shows a pie chart of expenses, with the Other slice broken down further into a second, smaller pie chart. Excel pie charts often need a fair bit of tweaking before they look respectable. Usually, you want to remove the legend and use category labels, as shown here. If you drag the label a short distance away from the midpoint of the slice, Excel adds a line pointing from the label to the slice. These lines often help to make a pie chart more readable.

Gaps, Widths, and Overlays in a Column Chart

Column and bar charts have their own options for fine-tuning. You can adjust the distance between column groups and the distance between each column in a group. With a little imagination, you can use these settings to create an innovative *overlay chart*, which layers two sets of data on top of each other.

To see these extended column chart settings, double-click a data series in the chart (or just select the series if the formatting panel is already open). You'll see the Series Options section, which provides two settings:

- **Series Overlap** is the amount of overlap between columns in the same category. This setting takes effect only if you have more than one series. The standard option is 0, which means that clustered columns touch each other but don't overlap. With a value of 100, the columns in the same category overlap completely, while negative values put a space between the columns.
- **Gap Width** is the space between each category. In a chart with one series, this setting is the space between each column; in a chart with multiple series, it's the space between each group of columns. The standard value is 150, which leaves a space that's roughly equal to the width of 1.5 columns.

NOTE In a 3-D column chart, you'll find an extra setting: Gap Depth. This is the space between the columns at the front and the columns that appear behind them.

One interesting trick is to use the overlap setting to compare two sets of data. People often use this technique to compare projections against actual results. Here are the steps you need to follow:

1. **Create a bar or column chart with two series.**

   Figure 18-32 shows an example of a bar chart that compares projected sales against actual sales.

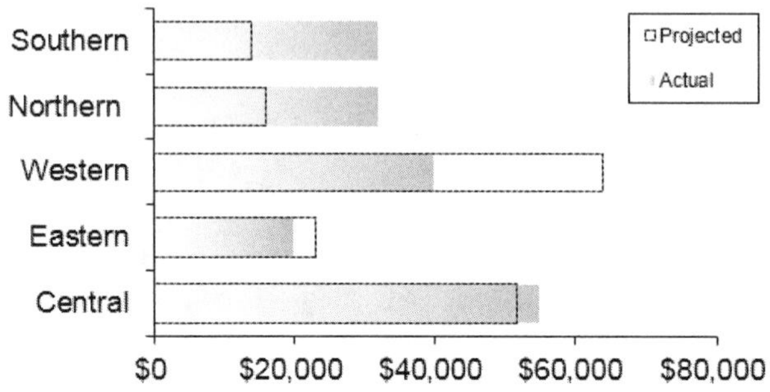

FIGURE 18-32

This example shows an overlay bar chart. The projected sales values have dotted borders and a transparent fill. The actual sales numbers show a gradient fill. Using this model, you can clearly see that the Southern and Northern locations exceeded their expectations, while the Western region fell far short of its predictions, even though it had the second-best overall sales.

2. **Decide which series should be on top of the other.**

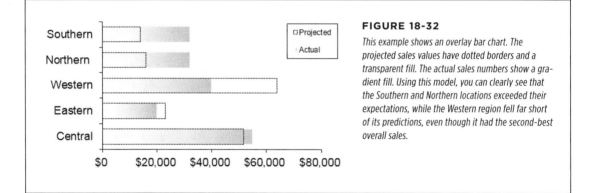

   The series that's on top needs to be transparent, so the other series can show through. In Figure 18-32, the projected sales values are placed on top.

3. **Find this topmost series in the chart, and double-click it.**

   The formatting panel appears, if it's not already visible.

4. **In the Series Options section, change the Series Overlap to 100%.**

   This setting ensures that two series are layered one on top of the other.

5. **Click the Fill & Line icon. In the Fill section, choose "No fill."**

   This tells Excel to make this data series transparent, with only the border visible.

   Next, you want to make sure the right series is on top.

6. **Right-click the chart, and then choose Select Data. Make sure the series that's supposed to be on top is at the bottom of the list.**

   To move a series, select it, and then click the down arrow button. Excel draws the series from top to bottom in this list, so the one it draws last ends up in front.

7. **Now select the bottom series. In the formatting panel, click the Fill & Line icon, head to the Border section, and choose "No line."**

   You can also choose a fill color or fill effect. You may need to try several combinations to get enough contrast between the series for the overlay chart to really work.

Creating Combination Charts

Sometimes, you want to use a chart to compare trends in different but related data. Imagine you create two charts, one to show how many hours you worked in the last few months, and the other to show how much money you spent. After you create these two charts, you start to wonder if there's a link—in other words, do you spend more money when you have a greater workload? Unfortunately, because these two measurements use different units (one records the number of hours, while the other counts the number of dollars), you can't put them on the same chart—or can you?

Combination charts are a well-kept Excel secret. Using them, you can compare trends across different sets of data, even if the units are wildly different. Combination charts are also useful when you need to compare more than one piece of information to tell a complete story. A chart that shows quarterly sales could make it look like your company is meeting wild success. But using a combination chart, you can contrast the sales against another factor (like changing currency exchange rates, or increased business expenses brought about by an irrational 80-percent-off coupon campaign) to tell a different tale.

You make a combination chart by creating a new secondary value axis. This axis appears on the right side of the chart. In other words, you'll end up with two value axes, one that applies to the first series of data, and the other that applies to the second series. Figure 18-33 shows how this process works.

FIGURE 18-33

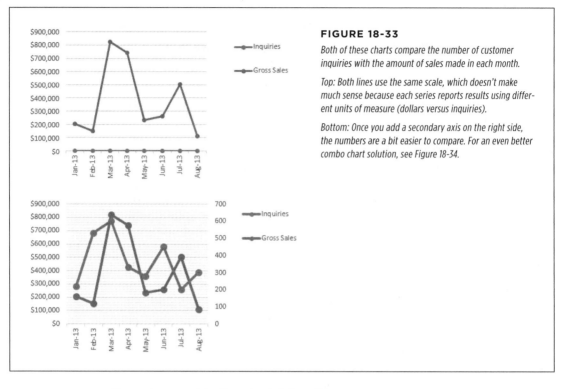

Both of these charts compare the number of customer inquiries with the amount of sales made in each month.

Top: Both lines use the same scale, which doesn't make much sense because each series reports results using different units of measure (dollars versus inquiries).

Bottom: Once you add a secondary axis on the right side, the numbers are a bit easier to compare. For an even better combo chart solution, see Figure 18-34.

To create a combination chart, follow these steps:

1. **Create a chart that includes both sets of data.**

   Initially, the smaller set of data doesn't appear correctly, because the scale is wrong. To solve this problem, you need to plot this data against another axis.

2. **Find the data series that doesn't fit, and double-click it.**

   If the scale difference is really extreme, you may have trouble selecting the data series you want to change, because it may be squashed against the bottom chart axis. In this case, select the series by name from the Chart Tools | Format→Current Selection list.

3. **In the Series Options section, you'll see a Plot Series On setting. Change it from Primary Axis to Secondary Axis.**

   Excel creates a new scale on the right side of your chart and uses this scale to plot the other data series. Excel automatically chooses the best scale, although you're free to change it by formatting the axis.

Combination charts don't just let you compare different units of data. They also help you fuse together two different types of charts. You could plot one series using a scatter chart, and then add columns to represent the values in the second series, as shown in Figure 18-34. When done right, this combo produces an attractive chart with a series of columns and a line above them, which you see commonly in shareholder reports and marketing documents.

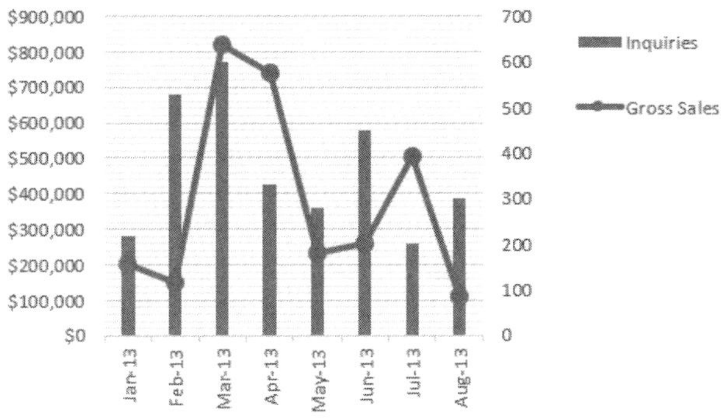

FIGURE 18-34

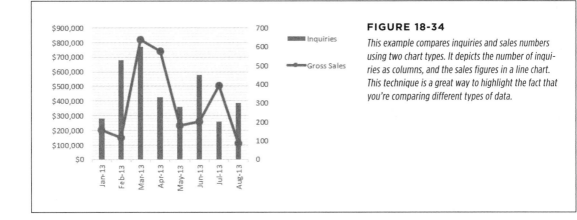

This example compares inquiries and sales numbers using two chart types. It depicts the number of inquiries as columns, and the sales figures in a line chart. This technique is a great way to highlight the fact that you're comparing different types of data.

TIP Some chart types just don't mix. To mix properly, the arrangement of axes should be the same in both chart types. Thus, a combination of a column chart and line chart works great, but a combined line chart and pie chart doesn't make much sense.

To create a combination chart that uses more than one chart type, right-click the *series*, and then choose Change Series Chart Type. Excel recognizes that you're trying to create a combination chart, and automatically switches to the All Charts tab and chooses the last item in the list, Combo. There, you'll see a list of all the series in the current chart. Initially, all your series have the same chart type, but you can pick a different chart type for each one, using the handy drop-down list shown in Figure 18-35.

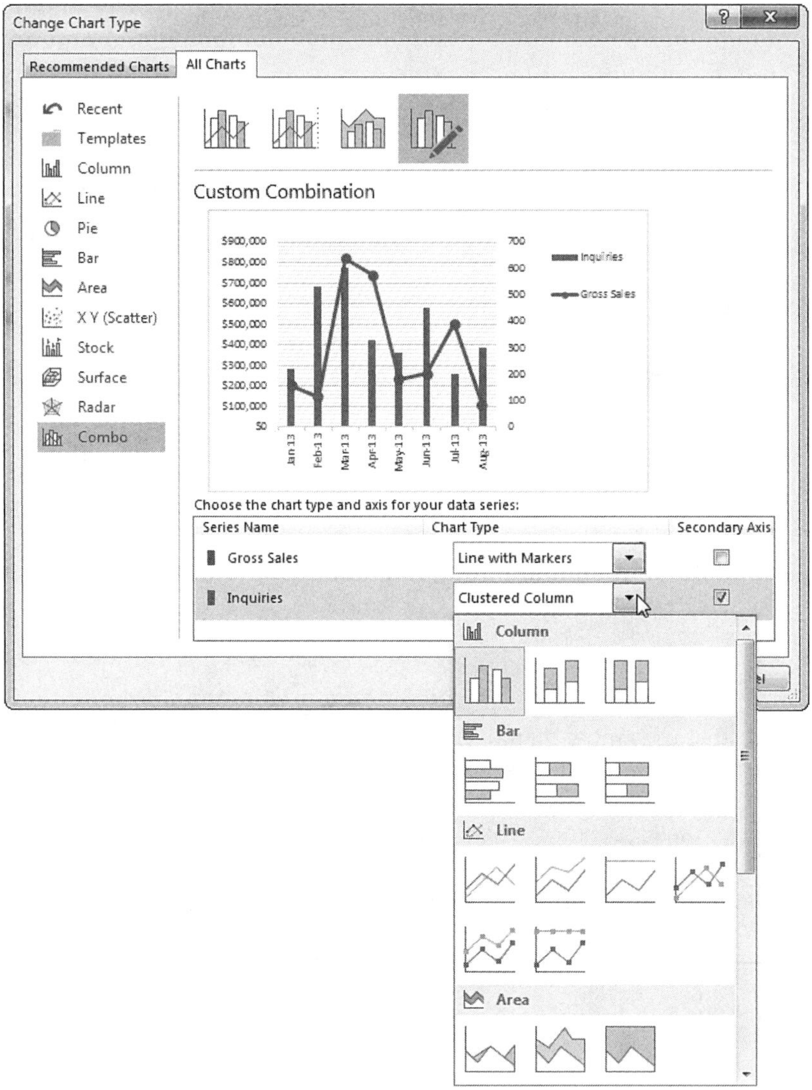

FIGURE 18-35

This chart's two series each use a different chart type.

CHAPTER

19

Inserting Graphics

Most Excel fans concentrate on numbers, formulas, and charts when they create worksheets. But Excel has another dimension—graphics. In fact, Excel includes a slew of drawing tools that may seem like they belong more in an artsy illustration program than in the rigid confines of a spreadsheet. Some of these drawing features are shameless frills that just take up space on the Excel ribbon. Others are genuinely useful, letting you add beneficial touches and highlight important information with real pizzazz.

Excel's drawing capabilities fall into the following four categories:

- **Picture-handling.** These features are what most people think of when they think about graphics. Picture-handling lets you take picture files on your computer and insert them into an Excel worksheet. For instance, if you created the perfect company logo in another program, you may want to place it in a blank spot on your worksheet.
- **Clip art.** Clip art graphics are usually cartoonish, themed pictures (like a stack of dollar bills or a drawing of a globe). While you probably don't need this stuff in most worksheets, Excel's clip art features are still quite impressive. Instead of limiting you to a small selection of preinstalled image files, Excel lets you search an online collection of thousands of images using keywords.
- **Shape-drawing (and fancy text).** Excel's shape-drawing tools let you create images directly on your worksheet. These shapes include arrows, circles, stars, banners, floating text boxes, and captions with zany gradients and 3-D effects. Shape drawing is occasionally useful when you want to highlight information on your worksheet, but it's most practical when you use it with charts.

- **SmartArt.** SmartArt lets you add complete diagrams that combine shapes and text. You can use SmartArt to create organizational charts, simple lists and flow charts, and pyramid-style diagrams. Under the hood, SmartArt uses shape-drawing features to create its diagrams, which means you can use all the same graphical flourishes and fancy effects as you find in the shape-drawing tools mentioned above.

This chapter covers all four kinds of drawing in Excel.

Adding Pictures to a Worksheet

In the previous two chapters on charts, you learned how Excel places charts in special floating boxes that hover above your worksheets. Pictures work in a similar way—they're distinct, floating objects that you can place anywhere. And just like charts, a picture box may hide data underneath it, but it'll never disturb the data.

Common examples of graphics in worksheets include minor embellishments, like a company logo next to the worksheet title, or an exclamation mark icon that highlights a worst-case scenario. You shouldn't go overboard with pictures because they tend to clutter up the real data. A few careful touches, however, can go a long way to making your spreadsheet more readable and more memorable.

To add a picture, you click a button in the Insert→Illustrations section of the ribbon. You can choose to insert a picture from your computer (click Pictures), a piece of Office clipart (Online Pictures), a floating shape (Shapes), a diagram (SmartArt), or a picture of another program that's currently running on your computer (Screenshot). In this chapter, you'll try out all these types of graphics.

Inserting a Picture from a File

To insert a picture file that already exists on your computer, follow these steps:

1. **Choose Insert→Illustrations→Pictures.**

   The Insert Picture window appears (Figure 19-1). It's essentially the same as the trusty Open window you use to open old workbooks, except the "Files of type" list is set to show all the types of image files you can use in Excel. You can change this option to show only the file type you're interested in (for example, bitmap files, JPEG files, GIF files, or something else).

TIP If you're having trouble sifting through piles of pictures, remember to enlarge the Insert Picture window. Just drag the bottom-right corner to stretch the window to more accommodating proportions.

2. **Browse to the picture you want to insert, select it, and then click Insert.**

   Excel lets you use a range of image file formats, including files with the following extensions: .bmp, .gif, .jpeg, .tif, .png, .wmf, and .emf.

   Optionally, you can insert several pictures at once, provided they're in the same folder. The trick is to hold down the Ctrl key while you click each picture. Once you select all the pictures you want, click Insert.

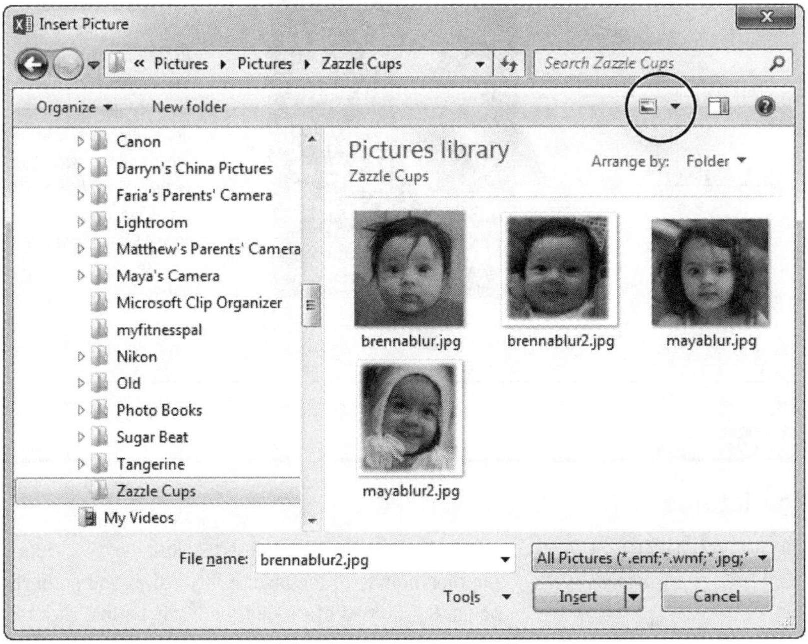

FIGURE 19-1

Depending on the mix of content in the folder you search for an image, the Insert Picture window may or may not show thumbnail previews for each picture it finds. If you don't see the previews but you'd like to have them, click the Views button (circled), and then choose Large Icons.

NOTE Excel includes an odd feature that lets you insert a snapshot of a currently running program instead of a picture file. To try this out, choose Insert→Illustrations→Screenshot, and then pick the window you want from the list of thumbnails. This quirky feature is interesting, but few people are likely to use it—and those who really need screen captures probably won't be satisfied with the way Excel rudely chops off the edges and corner of the window frame. (For a more professional result, you can use dedicated screen capture software like WinSnap—we do.)

When you insert a picture, Excel places it in a new floating box. Figure 19-2 shows the result.

NOTE When you insert a picture this way, Excel copies all the picture data into your worksheet. Even if you change or delete the original picture file, it doesn't have any effect on your worksheet.

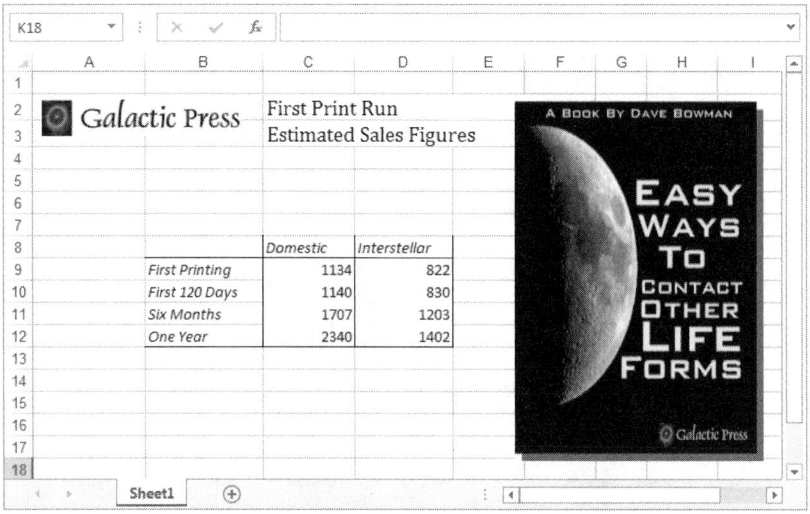

FIGURE 19-2

This worksheet has two picture objects: a logo in the top-left corner, and a book cover image on the right. The picture boxes Excel creates are similar to chart boxes, except that Excel doesn't draw a border around picture boxes unless you insist. Whenever you select the picture, the ribbon sports a new tab named Picture Tools | Format, and you can use that to add a border.

FREQUENTLY ASKED QUESTION

Inserting Really Big Pictures

I want to insert a few really big pictures that I took with my digital camera, but I don't want to have a workbook that's 30 MB in size!

Inserting big pictures into a workbook is often a bad idea. If you do so, you'll have trouble emailing your workbook to other people. Sometimes you can slim down pictures using the Compress Pictures command described on page 591. But slimming down often isn't enough.

Fortunately, Excel has another picture trick up its sleeve. Rather than inserting a full picture, you can insert a *link* to your picture file. This way, your Excel workbook file stays small (and if anyone changes the picture, you'll see the difference the next time you open your workbook). The obvious disadvantage is that if you move, rename, or delete the image file, it disappears from your spreadsheet. (For that reason, it's generally a good idea to keep the picture in the same folder as your Excel workbook.)

To insert a picture link, choose Insert→Illustrations→Pictures, and then browse to the picture file, just as you normally would. But instead of clicking the Insert button, click the down-pointing arrow on the Insert button's right side. That pops open a menu with extra choices. Choose Link to File to add a linked picture.

You have another option. You can choose Insert and Link to insert a picture normally *and* add the link to the original file. This way, if the picture changes, your workbook reflects the new look, but if the picture file disappears (say you mistakenly delete it), your workbook still has its own internal copy. The drawback of Insert and Link is that your workbook still stores a copy of the picture file, so it's still just as large as if you inserted the picture in the usual way.

Positioning and Resizing a Picture

The easiest way to move a picture once you inserted it is to click anywhere on the picture, and then drag it to a new location.

TIP Sometimes you want to move your picture just a small amount so that it lines up perfectly with some other part of your worksheet. To get really fine-grained control over picture positioning, click the picture to select it, and then use the arrow keys. For example, if you press the left arrow key, Excel nudges the picture ever so slightly to the left (one pixel, to be exact).

You can nearly as easily change a picture's size. First, click the picture once so that the *resizing handles* appear. The handles look like small circles and squares, and they show up at each corner and in the middle of each side. Drag one of these handles to one side to expand or shrink the picture.

Depending on which handle you drag, the type of resizing Excel performs changes:

- Use the squares that appear in the middle of each side to stretch the picture in one direction (possibly stretching it beyond all recognition at the same time).
- Use the circles that appear in each corner to resize the picture bigger or smaller without changing its proportions. See the box below for an explanation of the difference.

UP TO SPEED

Resizing Without Distortion

Excel doesn't impose any limits when it comes to resizing pictures, and, if you're not careful, you can completely mangle your image. Watch out for two problems when resizing a typical image.

First, you need to resist the urge to expand or compress your image dramatically. When you enlarge an image, Excel uses *interpolation* to guess the information it should add. (Interpolation is the process by which Excel looks at the existing pixels in your picture, and then uses them to calculate extra pixels that it should add in between. If Excel finds a blue dot next to a yellow dot, for example, it may add a blue-yellow dot in between.) If you expand an image too much, Excel needs to make far too many guesses, and you end up with a poor-quality image (usually the edges of lines and shapes appear blocky or jagged).

Similarly, when you shrink an image, Excel needs to decide what information to discard. In order to minimize the damage, Excel tries to smooth out the new picture. But if you shrink an image too much, you end up with a picture that looks blurry or fuzzy.

To avoid either of these problems, take a careful look at your worksheet (and print it out) after you make your changes to make sure the images remain acceptable.

The second issue to be aware of is *aspect ratio*—the ratio of an image's width to its height. A company logo may be twice as wide as it is tall, giving it an aspect ratio of 2:1. When you resize the picture, you need to keep this sense of proportion in mind. If you change the height of the logo without adjusting its width correspondingly, the image becomes distorted. To avoid these problems, just use the resizing circles at the *corners* of the image (rather than the squares in the middle of each side). These resizing handles let you change the size of the image without altering its aspect ratio. Instead, the height and width change in lockstep, keeping the right proportions.

If your image is what's known as a *vector graphic*—created by a program like Adobe Illustrator that uses formulas rather than bit-by-bit information to draw its pictures—you're in luck. You can resize vector images without any distortion. Excel's clipart and shape-drawing features (both of which you'll use later in this chapter) use fully resizable vector graphics.

If you're not too handy with a mouse, or if you just want to size your picture with exact precision (possibly because your worksheet contains several pictures and you want them all to be consistent), head to the ribbon's Picture Tools | Format→Size section. You'll see two text boxes, which provide the current height and width of the picture box. (The units depend on the computer, but inches and centimeters are two common possibilities.) You can click either of these text boxes, and then type in a new value by hand.

Pictures, like charts, are anchored to specific cells. Excel may move and resize the picture when you insert, remove, or resize rows and columns. The difference between picture boxes and chart boxes is that you can explicitly control how Excel moves and sizes the picture, to make sure it isn't inadvertently moved when you want it to remain firmly in one spot.

To change the *way* Excel positions a picture, follow these steps:

1. **Right-click your picture and choose Format Picture.**

   The Format Picture panel appears on the right side of the Excel window.

2. **In the Format Picture panel, click the Size & Properties icon. If the Size section is collapsed, click it to expand it.**

   In the Size section you'll find the properties that let you adjust the size of a picture and its placement (Figure 19-3).

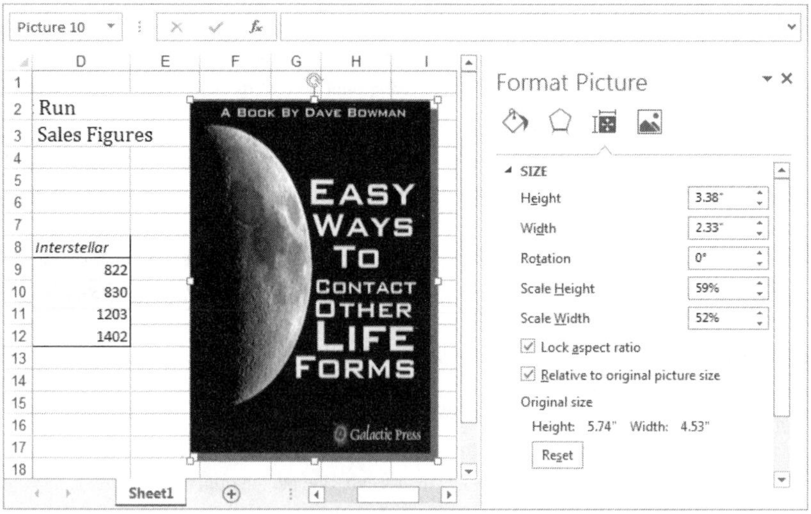

FIGURE 19-3

In the Size section of the Format Picture window, you can use the Height and Width boxes to precisely change the dimensions of a picture, or the Scale Height and Scale Width boxes to change the size as a percentage of the original size. Either way, Excel preserves the picture's aspect ratio, keeping the width and height synchronized as long as the "Lock aspect ratio" box is checked. There's also a Rotation box that lets you turn a picture around its center. (Try an angle of 180° to flip a picture on its head.)

3. **If the Properties section is collapsed, click it once to expand it.**

   The Properties section lets you choose how Excel anchors a picture to your worksheet (see the next step). It also has a useful "Print object" checkbox—turn it off to tell Excel to leave the picture out of your printouts. This option makes sense if you want to include rich graphics that don't look right on your black-and-white printer (or if printing the pic just wastes too much ink). Underneath that is a Locked option, which works in concert with Excel's worksheet protection feature (see Chapter 21).

4. **To change the placement of the picture, choose one of the three options in the Properties section.**

   The "Move and size with cells" option gives pictures the same behavior as charts. If you insert new rows above the picture, the whole picture shifts down. If you insert rows under a picture, the bottom edge stretches down. This behavior usually isn't what you want because stretching a picture could distort it.

   The "Move but don't size with cells" option anchors the top-left corner of the picture. If you insert new rows above the picture, it shifts down. If you insert rows under a picture, Excel doesn't stretch the picture. When you first insert a new picture, Excel uses this option—which makes the most sense if you have a picture you want to position near some related data (but you don't want the picture dimensions to get mangled when you add or remove content).

   The "Don't move or size with cells" option doesn't anchor the picture at all. In this case, Excel doesn't move the picture or resize it no matter where you insert or delete rows. This option makes the most sense if you want a picture to stay put, regardless of wherever the underlying content moves. This is typically a good choice for a graphical headers or company logos.

POWER USERS' CLINIC

Transfer Pictures Quickly with Copy and Paste

You can also insert a picture by copying it from within another program, and then pasting it into Excel. After you select Copy in the source program, select Home→Clipboard→Paste→Paste Special in Excel. When you use the Paste Special command, a Paste Special window appears, with a list of choices. Choose the option that reflects the image format ("Bitmap" if you're pasting a bitmap file, for example), and then click OK.

You must use Paste Special instead of Paste so that you insert the right type of content. Depending on the program you're copying from, Excel may paste the picture as a bitmap or as a *linked* or *embedded object* (page 741). If you use the Paste command, Excel decides which option it thinks is best. If you use Paste Special, you get to decide.

Either way, the picture looks the same in your spreadsheet. The difference is what happens when you select the picture. If it's an ordinary picture, you can manipulate it using Excel's picture tools. If it's a linked object, you can double-click it to edit it with the program that created it. But if you open your worksheet on a computer that doesn't have the required program, you can't edit it. One quick way to tell whether you have an object or a picture is to right-click the object. If you see the option Format Picture, you've selected a picture. If you see the command Format Object instead, you've selected an object.

So which choice is best? It you don't intend to change an image, it's always best to paste it as picture data. This choice also ensures you can share your workbook files with other people without any complications. On the other hand, if you decide that you absolutely need the ability to modify the image using the original program, you can paste a linked object instead. Head straight to Chapter 24 to learn how linked objects work and how to manipulate them.

Picture Touch-Up

Once you get your picture into Excel, you may decide you want to polish it up by changing colors or applying special effects. Depending on the result you're after, you could use a dedicated graphics program (and if you want more features than Excel provides, that's the best choice). But you'll probably be surprised to see that Excel has a wide range of built-in picture-tweaking features. There are two ways to access them:

- **From the ribbon.** When you select a picture, Excel adds the Picture Tools | Format tab to the ribbon. It's stocked with buttons you can use to radically transform your picture.
- **From the Format Picture panel.** If you right-click your picture and choose Format Picture, Excel opens a panel with formatting settings on the right side of the window. If you've ever used Excel's side panel to format a chart (page 508), you've seen many of these settings before.

The Picture Tools | Format tab and the Format Picture panel provide most of the same settings, but they're organized differently. The ribbon is slightly more accessible (requiring fewer clicks for the average task), while the Format Picture panel is slightly more comprehensive (offering a few details that don't turn up in the ribbon).

Which one you use is largely a matter of preference, although in this chapter you'll do most of your work through the ribbon.

The simplest operations you can do with a picture are touch-ups—minor corrections that change the pic's sharpness, color, and contrast. The commands for these operations are in the Picture Tools | Format→Adjust section of the ribbon. They include:

- **Sharpening and softening.** Click the Picture Tools | Format→Adjust→Corrections button and you'll see a gallery of choices that let you emphasize lines and fine detail, or soften them. Under-sharpened pictures can look blurry, but over-sharpened pictures look artificial.
- **Brightness and contrast.** Click the Picture Tools | Format→Adjust→Corrections button and you'll see a gallery of options that let you change the overall brightness of your picture (Figure 19-4), making all the colors lighter or darker. You can also change the contrast, which is the difference between a picture's brightest highlights and its darkest shadows. As you increase contrast, bright colors get brighter and dark colors get darker. As you decrease contrast, all colors start to converge toward a middle-of-the-road gray.

NOTE A brightness of -100% creates a very dark (entirely black) picture. A brightness of 100% creates a very light (all-white) picture. Similarly, a contrast of -100% creates a completely washed out (solid gray) picture, while a contrast of 100% reduces the picture to a high-contrast juxtaposition of black and white. Choose a 0% brightness or contrast to remove your previous brightness or contrast setting and return the image to normal.

FIGURE 19-4

The Corrections button is the key to two types of commonly adjusted picture details. When you hover over one of the thumbnails, a tooltip tells you the exact brightness and contrast changes your choice applies. Here, the choice pumps up the brightness by 20% while reducing the contrast by 20%. If you want more control, choose Picture Correction Options at the bottom of the menu to open the Format Picture panel, where you set these percentages to the exact values you want.

- **Color Saturation.** Click the Picture Tools | Format→Adjust→Color to see a gallery with three sections of picture-changing choices. Use the Color Saturation section to alter how pale or vivid your pictures colors are. Under-saturated pictures look like washed-out watercolors, while over-saturated pictures have a burn-your-eyeballs-out riot of color.
- **Color Tone.** Click the Picture Tools | Format→Adjust→Color to see a gallery with three sections of picture-changing choices. Use the Color Tone section to change the overall tint of your pictures (also known as the *color temperature*), shifting it to be more blue or yellow.

TIP If you don't want to pick from the gallery, choose Picture Tools | Format→Adjust→Color→Picture Color Options to open the Format Picture panel, where you can set saturation as a percentage from 0% to 400% and the color temperature as a number from 1,500 (cool blue) to 11,500 (yellowy orange).

- **Recolor.** Click the Picture Tools | Format→Adjust→Color and look in the Recolor section for more drastic color-changing choices. In the first row of the gallery, you'll see options for Grayscale, which changes every color to a shade of gray (and gives you a good idea of what a picture will look like on a black-and-white printer); Sepia, which does much the same thing as Grayscale but adds a slight brown tone reminiscent of old photographs; Washout, which fades the picture colors (and helps save ink when you print the worksheet); and Black and White, which changes every color to either black or white (a process that ruins all but the simplest of pictures). Underneath these basic options are other options that tint your picture using one of the accent colors from the current theme (page 172).

GEM IN THE ROUGH

Reversing Picture Changes

There comes a point in every picture-tweaker's life when you've made a few changes to many. If it's too late for Excel's Undo command to save you (or if your image is completely messed up), you'll be happy to hear that you can wipe your changes away and start again from scratch. All you need to do is select your picture and click Picture Tools | Format→Adjust→Reset Picture (or Picture Tools | Format→Adjust→Reset Picture→Reset Picture & Size if you want to return your picture to its original size and shape, as well as discard any picture corrections).

The Reset Picture command works because Excel stores the full-size original picture data with your worksheet (unless you've used the Compress Pictures command). The only drawback to the Reset Picture command is that it discards *all* the changes you made. You can't roll back just a single change this way (instead, use Ctrl+Z to undo a change right after you make it).

Removing the Background Behind a Picture

Every picture, no matter how simple or complex, is a rectangle. You might think you have a picture of your company logo, but what you really have is a picture of your company logo over a white background in a white box. This can create a problem when you try to integrate picture content into your worksheet. For example, if you place your company logo next to some cells that have content, its white background may mask the content you want to see underneath.

Excel has a solution: You can make certain portions of an image transparent. If there's worksheet data underneath the transparent regions, it shows through (Figure 19-5).

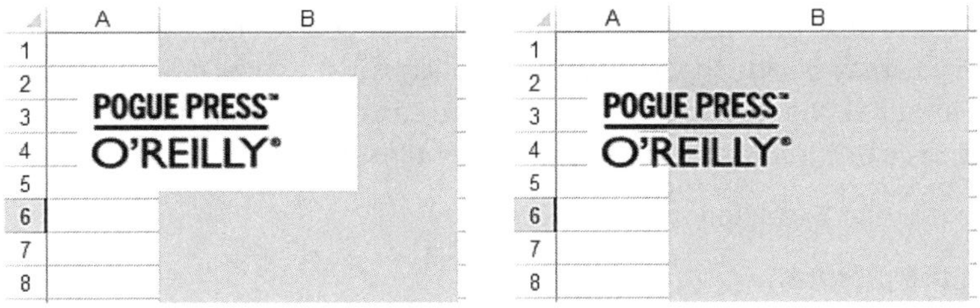

FIGURE 19-5

Using Excel's Set Transparent Color feature, you can make any color in an image transparent. Here are two versions of a graphic, one with no transparent color (left), and one where the background white color is transparent (right). As you can see, in the transparent version, the shaded content of the cell clearly shows through. If there were any data in those cells, it would also show through.

To make part of your picture transparent, choose Picture Tools | Format→Adjust→Color→Set Transparent Color. Next, click the color in the image that you want transparent. If you want a white background to be invisible, for example, click the white portion of the image.

TIP When you make a color transparent, it affects that color no matter where it appears in the picture. For example, if you make white the transparent color, white regions and white lines in your picture will both become transparent. To avoid this potential problem, when you design your image in a graphics program, use a background that doesn't appear anywhere else in the picture.

Excel has another way to create transparent backgrounds that's quicker but gives you less control. To try it out, select a picture and choose Picture Tools | Format→Adjust→Remove Background. Excel tries to identify the background area of your picture and turns it (temporarily) purple. Click away from the picture, and Excel finishes the job and makes the background area transparent. The remarkable part is that the Remove Background feature is smart enough to identify more complex backgrounds—for example, ones that have a blend of colors. However, Remove Background isn't perfect, and it will sometimes obliterate a part of a picture that Excel thinks is part of your background. In this situation, your only option is turn to a more powerful graphics program and do your work outside of Excel.

Cropping and Shaping a Picture

Ordinarily, Excel puts the whole picture you select in your worksheet. However, in some cases you may decide that you want to highlight just a small part of the picture and forget about all the rest. In this situation, you can clip your picture down to size using a graphics program, or you can crop it right inside Excel.

To crop a picture in Excel, follow these steps:

1. **Select the picture.**

2. **Choose Picture Tools | Format→Size→Crop.**

   After you click this button, cropping handles appear in each corner of the picture and in the middle of each side. (If your picture is dark, you may need to look carefully to see the cropping handles, because they're black.)

3. **To crop your picture, click one of the cropping handles and drag it inward.**

   As you drag a cropping handle, Excel hides the outlying part of the picture (Figure 19-6).

4. **Once you finish, choose Picture Tools | Format→Size→Crop again to turn off the cropping handles.**

   Excel keeps the picture data you cropped out in case you want to return the picture to its original size (either by recropping the picture or using the Picture Tools | Format→Adjust→Reset Picture command). If you're sure you don't need this option, you may want to use the Compress Pictures option (explained on page 591) to discard this extra data and cut down on the size of your workbook file. This is a good idea if you crop even a tiny bit out of a very large picture (because your workbook file's storing a lot of excess picture).

FIGURE 19-6

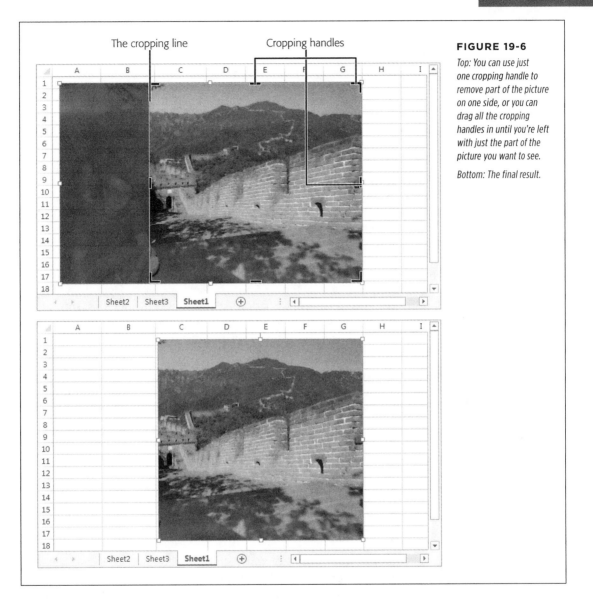

Top: You can use just one cropping handle to remove part of the picture on one side, or you can drag all the cropping handles in until you're left with just the part of the picture you want to see.

Bottom: The final result.

Picture Borders, Effects, and Styles

If Excel's picture coloring, cropping, and shaping features don't keep you busy, you'll be happy to learn that the graphical fun doesn't stop there. Along with the features you've already seen, Excel lets you apply a picture border and a picture effect.

When picking a border, it's up to you to pick the color, thickness, and style. You set all these details by selecting the picture in question, and then using the Picture Tools | Format→Picture Styles→Picture Border list. Here's what to do:

- If you don't want to use basic black for the border, pick a color from the Picture Border list. It's always a good idea to use theme colors (page 174) so your pictures blend in with the scenery.
- To make your border appear, choose a thickness from the Picture Border→Weight submenu; 1/4pt is sleek, while 6pt is thick and heavy.
- If you don't want a solid border, choose another line style from the Picture Border→Dashes submenu. You'll see a variety of dashed and dotted lines.
- To get rid of a border you don't like anymore, choose Picture Border→No Outline.

Picture effects are more exotic, but just as easy to discover. To get picture effects, you need to use the Picture Tools | Format→Picture Styles→Picture Effects list. You'll see submenus for applying shadows, reflections, 3-D rotations, soft edges, or glowing edges. Each of these submenus has a gallery of common options with thumbnail previews. Figure 19-7 shows one example.

TIP The best way to learn about all of Excel's wacky picture effects is to experiment. As you move your mouse over the different picture effects, Excel's live preview changes the picture on your worksheet accordingly. To get a better look, click to apply the change, and then hit Ctrl+Z to undo it if it isn't to your liking.

If you're in a hurry, you don't need to fiddle with the picture shaping, border, and effect settings separately. Instead, you can choose a preset style that applies a combination of these settings from the style gallery in the ribbon's Picture Tools | Format→Picture Styles section. You'll find options that makes your picture look like a postcard, a scrapbook clipping, or a wavy piece of glass that's fallen on its side (which is the current frontrunner for the "Feature Least Likely to Ever Appear in a Real Spreadsheet" award).

Picture effects affect the picture *container*—that's the box in which Excel places the picture. When you choose a different effect, you'll notice that the box gets a different border (one that's softened, shadowed, beveled, and so on). However, it's also possible to use effects that change the picture *content*. To use these, choose from the Picture Tools | Format→Adjust→Artistic Effects list. These effects are similar to what you might see in a picture editing tool like Photoshop. They let you radically transform the picture so it looks like it was drawn in chalk, painted with a brush, placed behind a piece of glass, and so on. These picture effects are fun to play with, though they aren't much help to the average Excel number-cruncher.

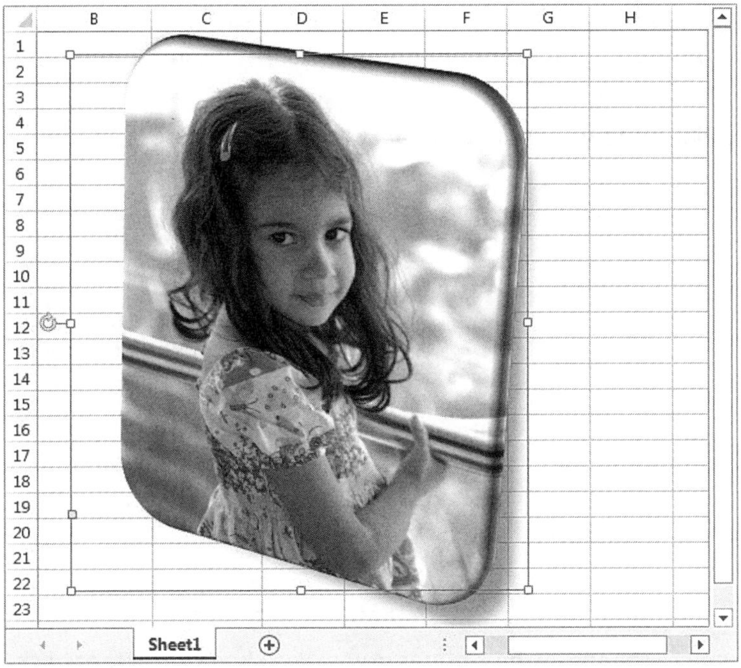

FIGURE 19-7

A 3-D rotation is a dramatic way to make the statement, "I have too much free time."

Compressing Pictures

Pictures increase the size of your spreadsheet file, and if you create a worksheet with dozens of graphics, the file's size can grow significantly. Most of the time, you won't worry too much about the size of your Excel files. However, if you plan to send them through email, you may need to pare them down in size. In a spreadsheet with a number of high-quality bitmap pictures, the images can take up a significant amount of disk space. (On the other hand, vector drawings like clip art and shapes don't use much space at all.) One solution is to cut down the picture data by compressing it.

NOTE Don't compress pictures if you want to change them later. Why? Because compressing a picture discards the original picture information. If you shrink a picture, compress it, and then enlarge the picture back to its original size, you end up with a lower-quality image.

To compress a picture, follow these steps:

1. **Select the picture you want to compress in your worksheet.**

   To compress more than one picture at once, hold down Ctrl while you click each picture. If you want to compress all the pictures in your file, the Compress Pictures window (in the next step) has a shortcut you can use, so just select one picture for now.

2. **Choose Picture Tools | Format→Adjust→Compress Pictures.**

   The Compress Pictures window appears (see Figure 19-8).

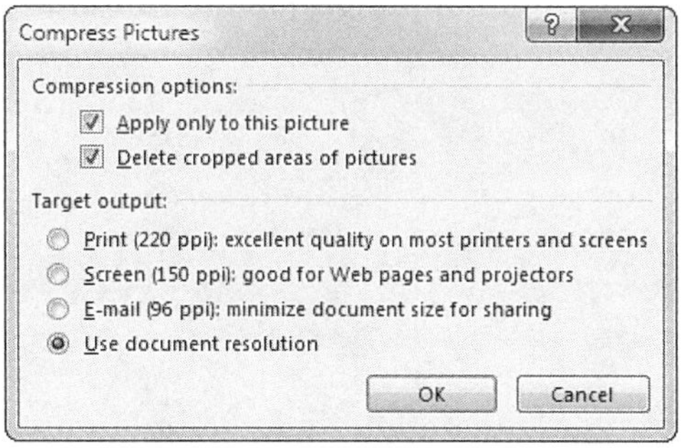

FIGURE 19-8

The Compress Pictures window lets you choose just how compressed your pictures will be. The Print setting (used here) keeps 220 pixels for every square inch of print space.

3. **If you want to change all the pictures in your workbook, clear the check box next to the "Apply only to this picture" setting.**

   This option is useful in a workbook that has plenty of big pictures, because it slims them all down in a single step.

4. **To remove the unused portion of a cropped picture, turn on the "Delete cropped areas of pictures" checkbox.**

   Cropping lets you cut out a smaller part of a larger picture. (There's more on cropping in the next section.) When cropping a picture, Excel ordinarily keeps the full-size original in case you want to change the cropping later on. To throw out that extra information and save space, use this option.

5. **Choose an option in the "Target output" section.**

   When you compress a picture, Excel *resamples* the picture based on its current size. In other words, if you reduce the size of a picture (by dragging the picture handles), Excel saves only enough information for the current, smaller version of the picture.

Exactly how much information Excel stores depends on the resolution option.

- **Print** tells Excel to keep enough information for a decent printout at the current size. However, you may notice a little blurriness if you resize the picture larger later on.
- **Screen** tells Excel to store a lower-quality picture that's sufficient for screen display (in a PowerPoint presentation or an online web page, for instance) but produces a poorer printout.
- **E-mail** tells Excel to store an even smaller picture, which makes sense if you plan to send your workbook in an email and you need to pare it down as much as possible to avoid bloating your recipient's Inbox.
- **Use document resolution** tells Excel to use the standard image compression setting for this document. By default, this is 220 dpi (the same as Print). However, you can change the document resolution at any time using the Excel Options window.

NOTE To change the default document resolution, choose File→Options. Then click the Advanced category (on the left) and scroll down until you see the Image Size and Quality section. Finally, choose a new resolution from the "Set default target output to" list.

6. **Click OK to close the Compress Pictures window and apply your new compression settings.**

   You can now save your new, leaner spreadsheet with the File→Save command.

   Once you compress your pictures, there's no turning back. (Of course, if you keep the original version of a picture somewhere else on your computer, you can always re-insert it later if you need it.)

Excel's Clip Art Library

One of the challenges in using pictures is finding the right image. If you need to use a company logo, you probably have that on hand already. But if you're looking for a picture on a specific subject—say a drawing of French fries for your analysis of fried versus steamed carbohydrate calories—it can take hours of web surfing to find an image that fits your requirements and is legal to use.

Excel answers this challenge with an online library of clip art that, at last count, contained a staggering 150,000 images. Best of all, anyone who owns Excel can search this clip art library and use any of its images for free. And if you still can't find what you want in Excel's picture library, you can use Microsoft's Bing search engine to scour the Web and download what you find straight to your worksheet (provided you don't run afoul of copyright rules).

To insert a picture from the Office clip art library or the Web, follow these steps:

1. **Select Insert→Illustrations→Online Pictures.**

   The Insert Pictures window appears (Figure 19-9).

2. **Choose where you want to search for pictures.**

   Excel gives you several choices:

   - **Office.com Clip Art** lets you search Microsoft's huge library of art. Best of all, it's all free to use however you please.
   - **Bing Image Search** is similar to a Google image search, except that it scours web pages looking for pictures. This gives you access to endless pictures—far more than you can find in Microsoft's catalog—but it comes with a catch. Most of the pictures you'll find are owned by other people. Drop them in a professional publication, and you risk a lawsuit.
   - **SkyDrive** lets you search your SkyDrive account for pictures. This is handy if you maintain your own collection of important images that you want to use in Excel.
   - **Flickr** lets you search your Flickr account, but you need to configure it first. Click the tiny Flick icon at the bottom of the window (it looks like two side-by-side circles) to get started.

   In this section, you'll use the Office.com Clip Art, which is the most useful clip-art repository.

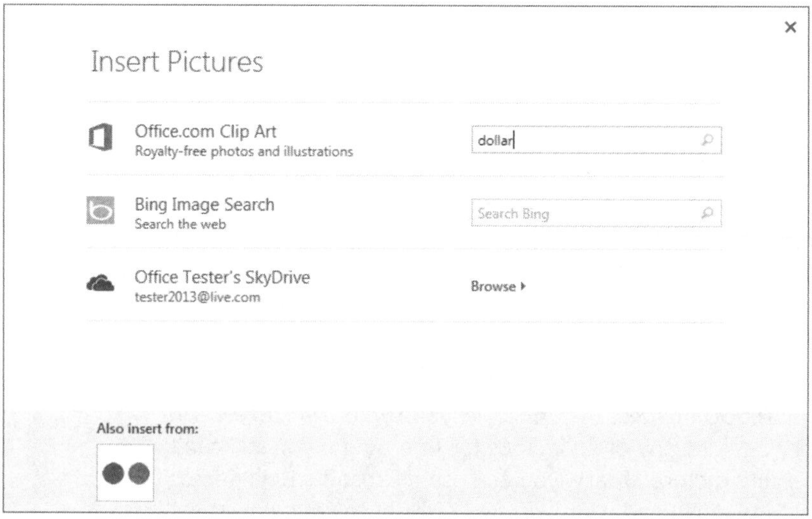

FIGURE 19-9

The Clip Art pane is your doorway to the vast resources of clip art on your computer and on Microsoft's Office Online website. You can search for images using topic keywords, and then drag the pictures into your worksheet.

3. **Enter a few words that describe the images you want to find.**

   Microsoft stores a list of descriptive words for every image in its clip art library. When you perform a search, Excel tries to match the words you enter against the description for each image. If it finds the words in the description, it shows you the picture as a match.

   You can include one word or a combination of words. If you use the search words *banana monkey*, you'll find only pictures that have the words *banana* and *monkey* in their description. On the other hand, if you search for *monkey*, you'll end up with a much larger list of results.

4. **Press Enter to start the search.**

   The results appear as a list of thumbnail images.

5. **If you see an image you want to use, double-click it to insert it into your worksheet (Figure 19-10).**

   Once you add a picture to your worksheet, you can treat it like you would any other picture, so go ahead and resize it, crop it, change the contrast, and so on. When you save your worksheet, Excel adds the picture data to your file, so you don't need to download it again.

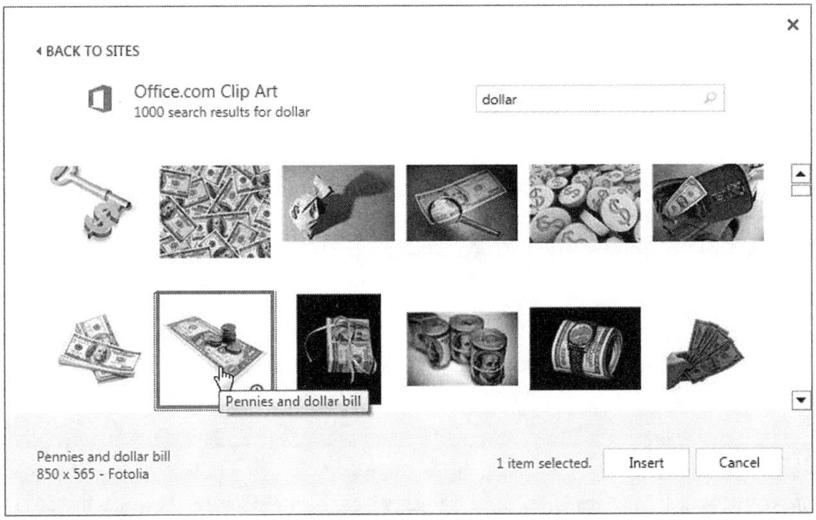

FIGURE 19-10

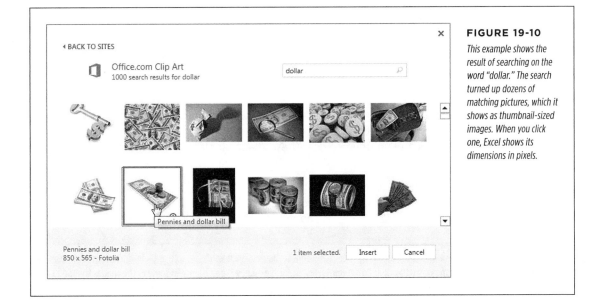

This example shows the result of searching on the word "dollar." The search turned up dozens of matching pictures, which it shows as thumbnail-sized images. When you click one, Excel shows its dimensions in pixels.

Drawing Shapes

If the stock graphics provided in the clip art collection don't satisfy your inner art critic, you can create your own pictures. Excel's drawing features make this process a lot easier than you might expect. In fact, you can create everything from simple shapes to complex art without leaving your worksheet.

The starting point for all drawing activity is the ribbon's Insert→Illustrations→Shapes section, which is filled with potential shapes (Figure 19-11).

Before you can really get started drawing anything, you should understand the basic shape categories. They include:

- **Lines.** This category includes straight lines, curved lines, and arrows.
- **Rectangles.** Albeit ordinary, rectangles are great for storing bits of text or just wrapping themselves around groups of other shapes.
- **Basic Shapes.** This category includes geometric shapes like the square, circle, rectangle, octagon, and more. Leave it to Microsoft to also include not-so-basic shapes like rings, lightning bolts, suns, moons, and even a happy face.
- **Block Arrows.** This category includes a variety of one-way and two-way arrows, as well as shapes with arrows attached to them.
- **Equation Shapes.** This category includes large mathematical symbols, like the multiplication, division, and equal signs.
- **Flowchart.** This category includes shapes often used in flowcharts, like the rectangle (which represents a step in a process) and the diamond (which represents a decision).
- **Stars and Banners.** This category includes the common five-pointed star and other starburst shapes. It also includes different types of banners, like award strips and unfurled scrolls. These shapes look best if you put some text inside them.
- **Callouts.** Callouts are designed to add information to a worksheet. Most Excel callouts are shapes with a connected line. The line points at something important, and the shape contains any descriptive text you want to write.

NOTE Most Office programs feature these shapes. Once you learn to use them in Excel, you can use them the same way in Word or PowerPoint. This fact also explains the existence of some of the shapes that don't make much sense in Excel spreadsheets—they're really intended for other Office applications.

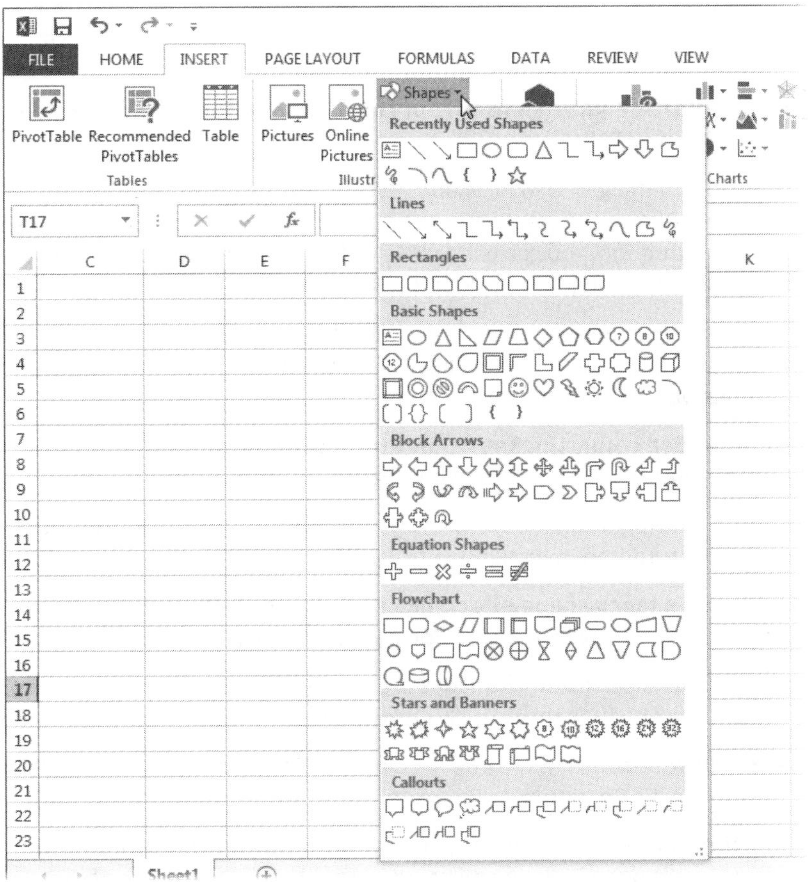

FIGURE 19-11

Click Insert→Illustrations→Shapes for a list of shapes you can add to your worksheet, subdivided into logical sections.

Drawing a Shape

Excel lets you draw a range of shapes, from simple lines and circles to banners and three-dimensional arrows (Figure 19-12). To insert a new shape, follow these steps:

1. **Find the shape you want in the Insert→Illustrations→Shapes section, and then click it.**

2. **Click your worksheet in the spot where you want the shape to appear, and then drag to make the shape as big as you want.**

   Usually, Excel inserts the image as soon as you release the mouse button. However, some shape types, like the curved line or freeform line, have an extended drawing mode. With these shapes, every time you click the worksheet, Excel adds a new curved line segment. To finish the drawing, double-click the last point.

Once the shape appears, Excel selects it, and then adds the Drawing Tools | Format tab to the ribbon.

NOTE The Drawing Tools | Format tab is a lot like the Picture Tools | Format tab you learned about earlier. It includes similar buttons for applying borders and effects, and for arranging and resizing your shape.

3. **Pick a color for your shape from the Drawing Tools | Format→Shape Styles→Shape Fill list.**

   This color fills the inside of all shapes except for lines. You can also choose No Fill to make the shape transparent so that other shapes (and your worksheet data) show through. You can use a circle with no fill to point out some important data on your worksheet, for example.

   Along with the standard color choices, you can use a fancy texture, an existing picture, or a gradient. In fact, shapes offer exactly the same options that you saw when you colored in chart elements (page 546).

4. **Pick a border color, thickness, and dash style from the Drawing Tools | Format→Shape Styles→Shape Outline list.**

   To pick a shape border, follow the same process you did to add a border to an ordinary picture from a picture file (page 590).

5. **If you want a fancy shape effect, like a shadow or 3-D rotation, choose the effect from the Drawing Tools | Format→Shape Styles→Shape Effect list.**

   The effects you can use with shapes are mostly the same as those you can use with pictures (although they usually make more sense with shapes). They include:

   - **Shadow** adds diffused gray shading behind your shape, which makes it look like it's floating over the page.
   - **Reflection** adds a faint copy of part of the image just under the bottom edge, as though it's being mirrored in a pool of water or piece of shiny glass.
   - **Glow** adds a blurry edge in a color you choose.
   - **Soft Edges** adds a blurry edge that softens your border.
   - **Bevel** shapes the surface of the image so that part of its surface appears raised or indented.
   - **3-D Rotation** turns the image around in three dimensions. This trick works best with images that have some depth to them—the thick block shape is a better choice than the flat square.
   - **Preset** lets you choose from some ready-made options that combine more than one effect.

FIGURE 19-12

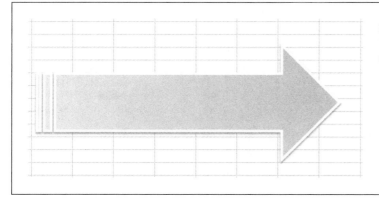

This eye-catching arrow sports a thick white border, gradient fill, and shadow.

TIP If you don't want to pick a separate fill color, border, and effect, you can use one of Excel's preset styles. Just make your choice from the gallery of options (each of which has a tiny thumbnail preview) in the Drawing Tools | Format→Shape Styles section of the ribbon.

6. **Once you perfect your shape, you can drag it to the position you want, and then resize it.**

   When you select a drawing, Excel displays the usual resize handles: a white square at each corner and at the midpoint of each side. It also gives you one or more yellow squares and a circular arrow, as shown in Figure 19-13. You can drag the circular arrow to rotate the image. You can use the yellow squares to change the shape's elements. For example, you can use the yellow squares to change the amount of curve in a curved banner, the width of each point in a star, or the length of a line in a callout. As you drag, Excel superimposes a light copy of the shape to preview how the shape will change.

POWER USERS' CLINIC

Hard-Core Shape Manipulation

If you're feeling very punk rock, you can make dramatic changes to a shape in Excel. In fact, Excel lets you edit a shape like it's a diagram in an illustration program. To do so, select the shape, and then choose Drawing Tools | Format→Insert Shapes→Edit Shape→Edit Points. This shows all the points that make up the shape (where every line and curve connects).

Now you can drag a point to move it somewhere else. As you move the point, Excel "pulls" the rest of the shape along with it. Drag a few points and you can take an ordinary shape like an arrow and transform it into a strangely distorted blob.

Most people find that this feature is an effective way to ruin a perfectly good shape. But your art skills could make the difference in improving a design.

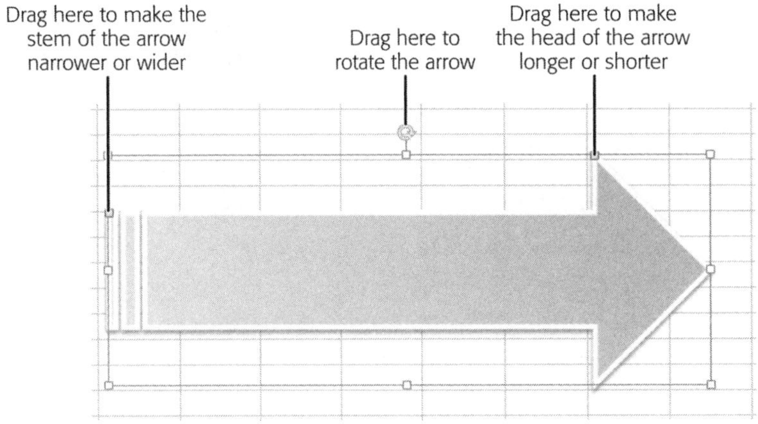

FIGURE 19-13

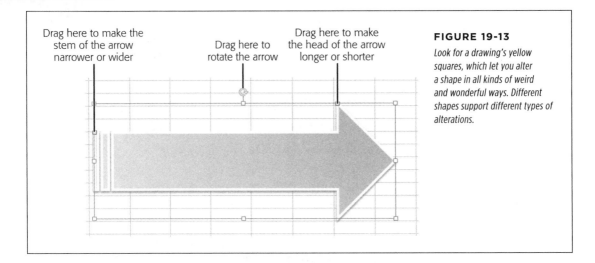

Look for a drawing's yellow squares, which let you alter a shape in all kinds of weird and wonderful ways. Different shapes support different types of alterations.

Adding Text to a Shape

You can add text to almost any shape. It doesn't matter whether you've got a circle, a box, an arrow, a banner, a starburst, or even something weird. Shapes that don't have any interior space, like lines, are the only exceptions.

When you add text to a shape, the text wraps itself to fit neatly inside the shape. Figure 19-14 shows a few examples.

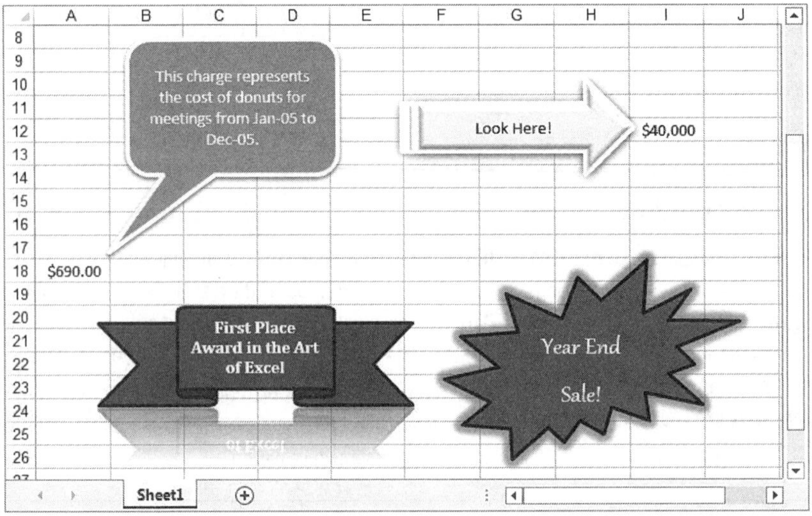

FIGURE 19-14

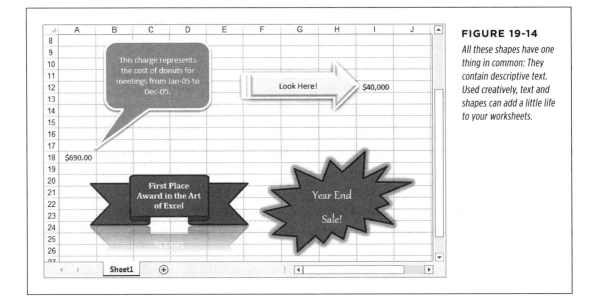

All these shapes have one thing in common: They contain descriptive text. Used creatively, text and shapes can add a little life to your worksheets.

To add text to a shape, follow these steps:

1. **Right-click the shape, and then choose Edit Text.**

   Your cursor moves to inside the shape, and a box appears around the current text, if there is any.

   You can also just click the shape, and then start typing, without bothering to choose Edit Text.

TIP If you want to add floating text that isn't inside a shape, choose Insert→Text→Text Box, draw the text box somewhere on your worksheet, and then start typing. Or, use one of fancy presets from the Insert→Text→WordArt gallery if you want to add a text box that already has some wild formatting in place.

2. **Type the text you want to use.**

3. **If you want to format your text, use the mini formatting bar or the buttons on the Drawing Tools | Format→WordArt Styles section of the ribbon.**

   To use the mini bar to make basic formatting changes, select the part of the text you want to change, and then choose a new font, size, color, and so on from the small toolbar that appears just above.

   To use the WordArt feature to apply eye-catching effects, select the whole shape, and then head to the ribbon's Drawing Tools | Format→WordArt Styles section. You'll find buttons that let you independently apply a fancy fill, border, and various effects (you used these features with shapes and pictures). Or, you can choose a ready-made combination of formatting settings from the Drawing Tools | Format→WordArt Styles→Quick Styles list. Figure 19-15 shows a shape with some WordArt-enhanced text.

FIGURE 19-15

This text uses a dazzling reflection effect to distract spreadsheet readers from abysmal sales numbers elsewhere in the worksheet.

NOTE There's a little-known trick you can use to put a cell reference into the text of shape. Any time you're typing text into a shape (or in a floating text box), click the formula bar. You can then type in a simple cell reference (like *=B3* to show the value that's in cell B3) or a more complicated formula, complete with all the usual Excel functions. This handy-dandy trick lets you pull the current information out of your worksheet, avoiding duplication and making sure your graphics are always up-to-date.

Selecting and Arranging Shapes

If you add enough shapes, you may start to run into trouble manipulating and layering all these objects. Here are some potential headaches you could face:

- **Some shapes are difficult to select.** If you don't click exactly on a line, you end up selecting the worksheet cell *underneath* the line.
- **Some shapes may obscure other shapes.** What if you want to put a starburst shape inside a circle? Depending on the order in which you added the shapes, when you move the starburst over the circle, it could actually disappear *underneath* the circle.

Excel has a handy tool to help you out. It's called the Selection pane (shown in Figure 19-16), and you call it into action by choosing Page Layout→Arrange→Selection Pane. Or, if you have a shape currently selected, you can get the same feature using the Drawing Tools | Format→Arrange→Selection Pane command.

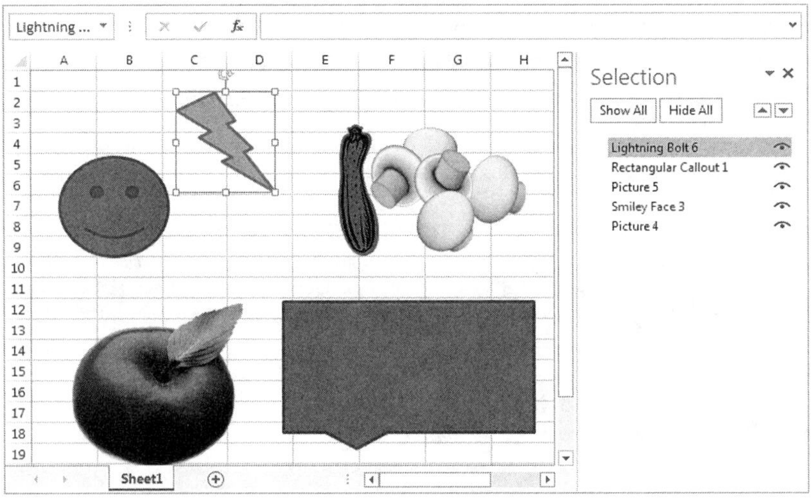

FIGURE 19-16

The Selection pane lists all the floating objects you added to your worksheet. These objects include shapes, pictures, text boxes, and charts. Excel labels the shapes based on the shape type and the sequence in which you added it. The 10th text item you add may have a name like TextBox 10. For pictures, you see the word "Picture," and for charts you see whatever name you set in the ribbon's Chart Tools | Layout→Properties→Chart Name box.

The Selection and Visibility pane lets you do two things: select difficult-to-reach objects, and change the way they're layered.

To select an object, simply click it in the list. This method works even if your shape is buried underneath another shape and therefore impossible to click with your mouse. Once you select your shape, you can move it, resize it, or format it using the ribbon.

TIP To quickly jump from the currently selected shape to the next one, press Tab. The resizing handles appear around the newly selected shape. You can also use Shift+Tab to move back to the previously selected shape, or Esc to return to your worksheet.

Sometimes, you'll want to select several shapes at once. To do so, hold down the Ctrl key while you click each shape in the list. Once you select several shapes, you can move or format them as a group. You use the ribbon the same way as before, but now your changes affect every selected shape.

TIP If you plan to use a group of shapes as a single unit, you can *group* them together. When you do, Excel treats them as one object when you select or move it. To group shapes, select them all, and then choose Drawing Tools | Format→Arrange→Group→Group. The only disadvantage to grouping shapes is that you can't modify the individual shapes unless you first choose Drawing Tools | Format→Arrange→Group→Ungroup to remove the grouping.

The Selection and Visibility pane also shines when you need to change the *layering* in your worksheet (the way that different images overlap one another). Technically, each image on your worksheet exists in its own private layer. Whenever you add a new shape, Excel creates a new layer at the top of your worksheet, and then puts the new shape in this layer. That means that Excel layers new objects on top of older ones—which may not be what you want.

To change the way Excel layers objects, you need to change the order of items in the Selection and Visibility pane list. Objects at the top of the list appear on top of other objects farther down the list (Figure 19-17). To move an item, select it, and then click the up or down arrow button. Figure 19-18 explains how to create transparent shapes—good for when you want the cells beneath your shapes to remain visible.

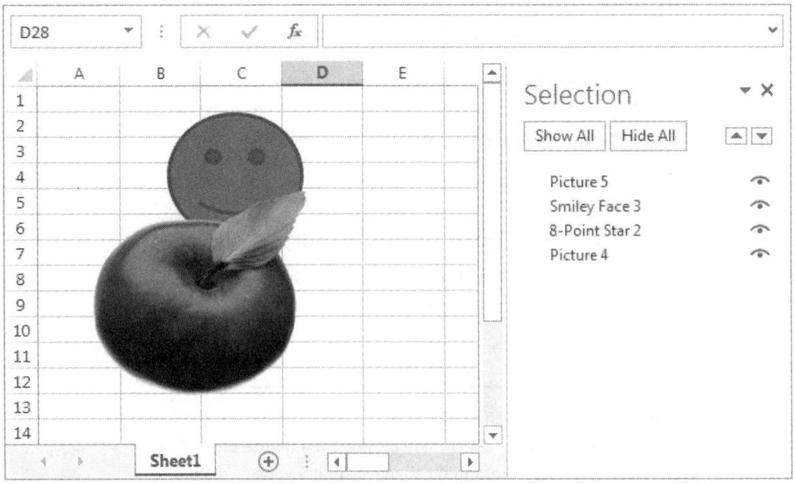

FIGURE 19-17

In this example, the apple (Picture 5) appears on top of the happy face (Smiley Face 3) because it's higher up in the list.

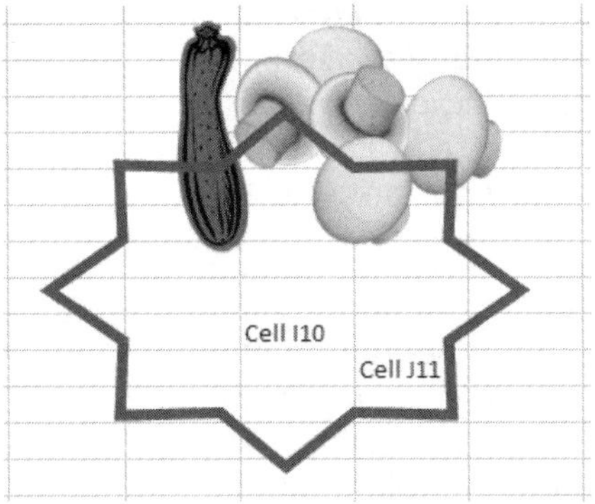

FIGURE 19-18

The starburst shown here is transparent, so the data and shapes underneath show through. To create this effect, select the shape and choose Drawing Tools | Format→Shape Styles→Shape Fill→No Fill.

NOTE You can also change the layering order using the Bring to Front and Send to Back buttons in the ribbon's Drawing Tools | Format→Arrange section. However, the Selection and Visibility pane is much easier to use.

If you have an extraordinarily complex worksheet that's dense with objects, you may find that it helps to temporarily hide the ones that you aren't interested in. You can do so two ways:

- **To hide everything**, click the Hide All button in the Selection and Visibility pane. Now, whenever you click an image label in the list, the image appears. When you finish making changes and you're ready to see all your shapes again, click Show All.
- **To hide just a few items**, click the eye icon next to each item in the Selection and Visibility pane list. Click the eye again to make the item reappear (or use the Show All button to show everything).

TIMESAVING TIP

Lining Up Shapes

When creating a complex piece of Excel art (like a diagram that's entirely made up of shapes), you need a way to line up shapes with precision. Simply dragging each shape into place with the mouse may be too difficult or just take too long. Happily, Excel has an automatic alignment feature that can really help you out.

To use it, begin by selecting all the shapes that you want to line up. (Hold down the Ctrl key, and then select each one on your worksheet or in the Selection and Visibility pane.) Then, make a choice from the Drawing Tools | Format→Arrange→Align section of the toolbar. You can line up shapes along their left, right, top, or bottom edges, or center them so their mid-points line up. And if you selected more than two objects, you can use the Distribute Horizontally and Distribute Vertically commands to space them out evenly, with a consistent amount of space between each shape.

Connecting Shapes

On the one hand, you may notice that the shapes in the Lines category are perfect for connecting one shape to another. The creators of the Office shape-drawing model noticed this, too, and they made it easier for you to snap your lines into place to connect two shapes.

On the other hand, you may wonder if there's really any point to connecting two shapes this way. Why not just drag a line anywhere on the border of a nearby shape? After all, that makes it look like your line is connected to the shape. But the real benefit to using formal connections is when you *move* the connected object. Imagine you have a line that links two squares. If you used connections, when you drag one of the squares to a new place, the line goes along for the ride. If you haven't used Excel's connection-point feature, you have to move the square, and then resize the line every time.

Here's how to connect shapes. Every shape has predefined *connection points*, which are ideal places to connect a line. A basic rectangle has four connection points—one in the middle of each side—and a typical circle has about eight, arranged in even intervals along the border. To use the connection point feature, you click to select a line, and then drag one end of the line over another shape. As you get close, your mouse pointer changes to a cross and Excel shows you all the connection points using small black circles (see Figure 19-19). When you drop the line on one of these points, you create a connection.

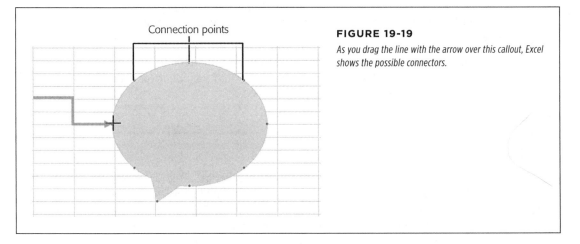

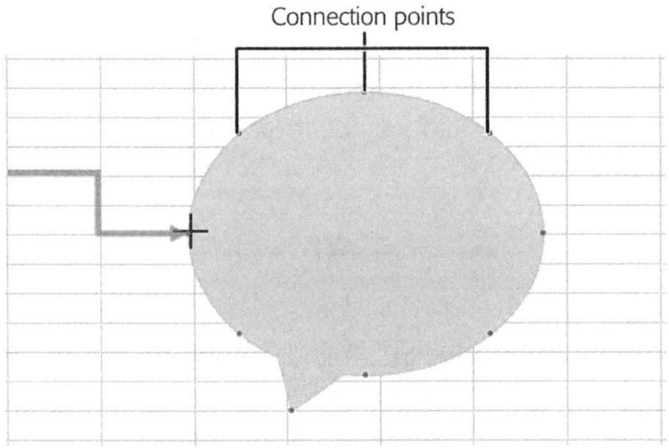

FIGURE 19-19

As you drag the line with the arrow over this callout, Excel shows the possible connectors.

Connections let you take separate shapes and build more impressive diagrams. When you use connections, you may also want to consider using grouping (page 603), too. And if you don't want to connect everything on your own, you may be interested in the SmartArt feature (discussed in the next section), which gives you premade diagrams that include numerous shapes and connecting lines.

GEM IN THE ROUGH

Drawing Graphic Objects in Charts

You may find that shapes are more trouble than they're worth, because they can quickly gunk up a worksheet. But graphic objects become extremely useful in one area: your charts. With the right shapes, you can break out of Excel's limiting rules for labeling and highlighting data and add eye-catching arrows and shapes.

Excel lets you draw on a chart object in the same way you draw on a worksheet—using the tools found on the Insert→Illustrations section of the ribbon. Best of all, once you draw a shape in a chart box, it stays locked into that box. That means that if you move the chart, the shape follows along, remaining in the appropriate position. Figure 19-20 shows some of these techniques.

Here are a few ways that Excel's drawing features can enhance your charts:

- Use arrows to point to important places on a chart. This technique works well if you need to highlight a single data point.
- Use circles or squares around an important region on the chart. This technique works well if you need to highlight a section containing multiple data points.
- Use callouts to add descriptive text explaining why a chart line takes a sudden dive or turns upward suddenly.
- Add picture objects, like logos or a themed background (for example, show a picture of a beach in a chart that tracks favorite vacation destinations).

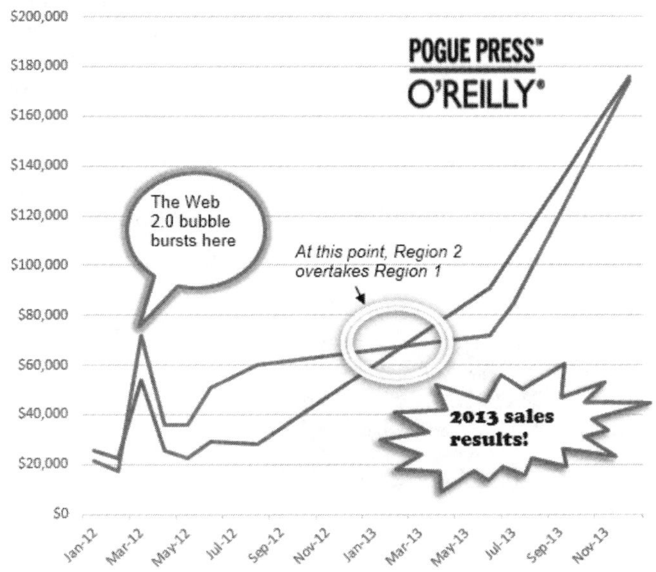

FIGURE 19-20

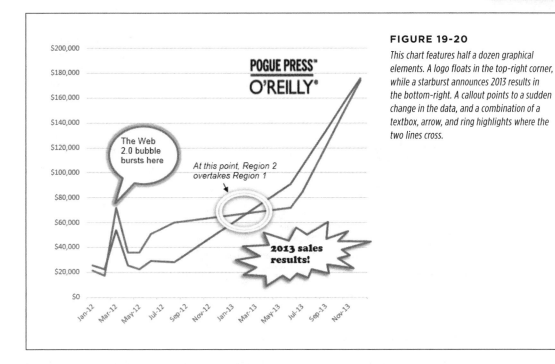

This chart features half a dozen graphical elements. A logo floats in the top-right corner, while a starburst announces 2013 results in the bottom-right. A callout points to a sudden change in the data, and a combination of a textbox, arrow, and ring highlights where the two lines cross.

SmartArt

SmartArt is a feature that lets you create business graphics and place them in your Excel worksheet. Figure 19-21 shows a few examples of SmartArt diagrams.

SmartArt and Excel have a slightly awkward relationship. Although the SmartArt graphics are unarguably attractive (and easy to build), they don't make sense in most Excel workbooks. After all, most people expect to use Excel to record reams of numbers, and analyze them with number-crunching formulas and sophisticated charts. Diagrams make more sense in the company report (a Word document) or a budget presentation (a PowerPoint document). Truthfully, you're more likely to use SmartArt in both these programs than in Excel.

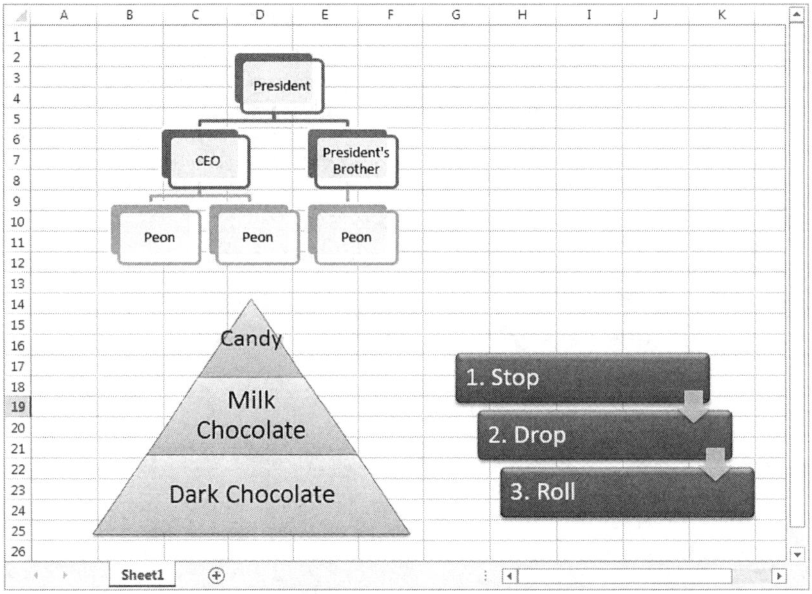

FIGURE 19-21

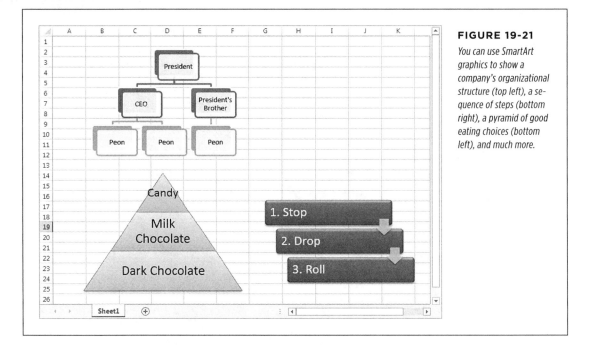

You can use SmartArt graphics to show a company's organizational structure (top left), a sequence of steps (bottom right), a pyramid of good eating choices (bottom left), and much more.

Furthermore, SmartArt diagrams have the same fundamental limitation that all shapes have in Excel—you can't use cell references as part of your text. That means that if you need to include summary numbers or the result of a complex calculation in a SmartArt diagram, you need to copy the values yourself (and you need to remember to update them when the value in the worksheet changes).

Even with all these considerations, SmartArt can still help you create some professional-caliber diagrams in a hurry.

Here's how to create a SmartArt diagram:

1. **Choose Insert→Illustrations→SmartArt.**

   The Choose a SmartArt Graphic window appears (Figure 19-22).

2. **Choose the diagram you want, and then click OK.**

   The Text pane appears where you can enter the text you want to include in the diagram (Figure 19-23). If the Text pane doesn't appear automatically, choose SmartArt Tools | Design→Create Graphic→Text Pane.

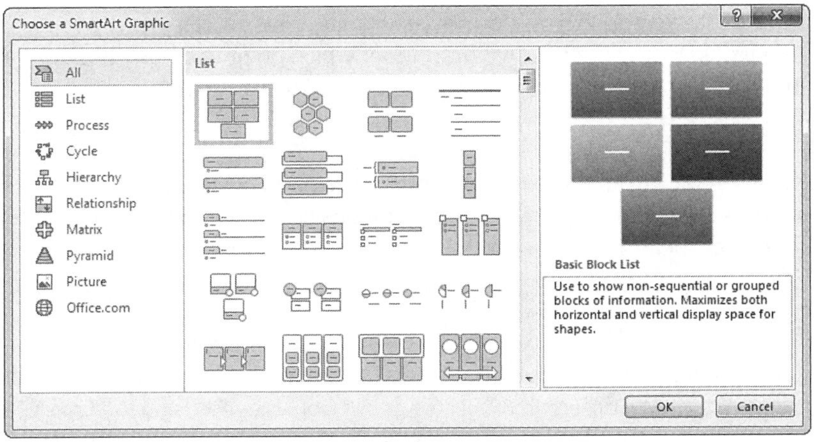

FIGURE 19-22

You can choose from a gallery of about 80 diagram types.

3. **Type the text for your diagram.**

   The Text pane works like a bulleted list. You press Enter to create more lines, each of which is called a *point*. You hit Tab to indent your point one level, which makes it a subpoint. (Press Shift+Tab to turn a subpoint back into a normal point.)

   Each point is always a separate shape. However, different diagrams have different ways of presenting points and subpoints. In some diagrams (like the process diagrams), the subpoints become bulleted points inside each shape. In others (like the organizational diagrams), the subpoints become their own distinct shapes, as shown in Figure 19-23.

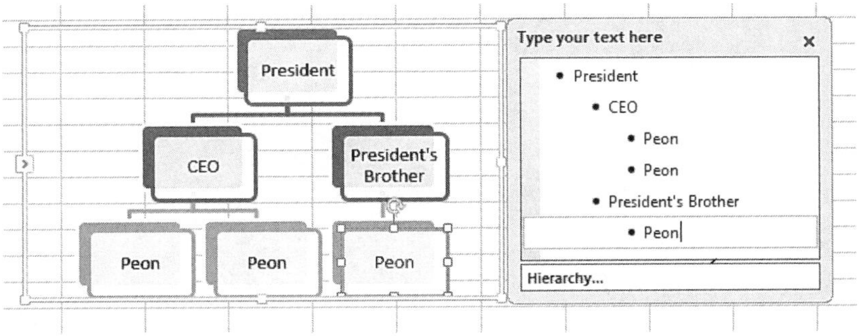

FIGURE 19-23

You don't need to fiddle with individual shapes to create a SmartArt diagram. Instead, you can type in everything you need in a special Text pane (shown here on the right). Excel uses this text to create the diagram.

4. **When you finish, drag your diagram into place, and then resize it as you see fit.**

   You can click anywhere on your worksheet to return to Excel.

Once you create a diagram, you can format and fine-tune it much the way you format shapes. First, select your SmartArt graphic, at which point two new tabs appear in the ribbon: SmartArt Tools | Design and SmartArt Tools | Format.

Here are some tricks you may want to try out:

- Make a choice from the SmartArt Tools | Design→Layouts gallery to switch to a different type of diagram. Excel automatically transfers the text you entered to the new diagram.
- Make a choice from the SmartArt Tools | Design→SmartArt Styles gallery to apply different color, border, and shape effects.
- Click one of the shapes inside the SmartArt graphic (like a single text box). You can then format it differently so it stands out from the rest using the Smart Tools | Format tab. You can, for example, change the type of shape, apply WordArt effects, and move or resize the shape.
- Choose Smart Art Tools | Design→Reset→Reset Graphic to clear your formatting and return everything to normal. The list of points and subpoints you typed in remains.

CHAPTER

20

Visualizing Your Data

Ordinary numbers are fun, but on their own they lack a little pizzazz. That's why, when you need to advertise just how important a set of numbers is, you usually turn to some sort of *data visualization*—a graphical technique that turns part of a worksheet's information into a picture.

You already learned about Excel charts, which are the most obvious type of data visualization. But Excel offers far more than simple line charts to help you see trends in your data. For example, you can add shaded bars, colored cells, or tiny icons to your graphs. Unlike charts, these types of data visualization take place directly on your worksheet. (There's no floating box, as there is with charts.) But as with charts, the goal is the same—to provide visual cues that help the spreadsheet reader interpret the numbers.

The data visualization tools you'll learn about in this chapter fall into two categories:

- **Data bars, color scales, and icon sets.** These three features are more powerful versions of Excel's basic conditional formatting feature, which you considered in Chapter 6. Like all types of conditional formatting, they change the way a cell looks based on the value it contains. For example, data bars draw a shaded bar that's big for big cell values, but small for small numbers. Color scales change the background color of a cell based on its value, but more gradually than ordinary conditional formatting can. And icon sets use tiny pictures to flag important values, wherever they crop up.
- **Sparklines.** These tiny chart-like graphics show basic information (trends, patterns, and changes) without a lot of fuss. Even better, they integrate seamlessly into your worksheet, unlike massive floating charts.

Used with a little bit of thought and experience, both of these features can extract meaning out of the densest jumble of worksheet data and turn otherwise drab spreadsheets into clear and powerful message-makers.

Data Bars

Data bars—a feature that places a shaded bar in the background of every cell you select—are one of the simplest and most useful forms of conditional formatting. The trick is that the data bar's length varies depending on the value of the cell. Larger values generate longer bars, while smaller values get smaller bars.

To see how this works, consider the worksheet in Figure 20-1, which shows a boring grid of numbers with no formatting.

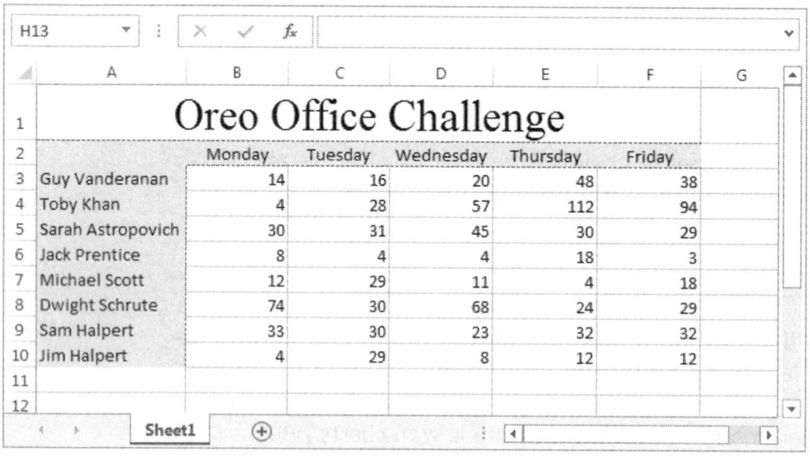

Oreo Office Challenge

	Monday	Tuesday	Wednesday	Thursday	Friday
Guy Vanderanan	14	16	20	48	38
Toby Khan	4	28	57	112	94
Sarah Astropovich	30	31	45	30	29
Jack Prentice	8	4	4	18	3
Michael Scott	12	29	11	4	18
Dwight Schrute	74	30	68	24	29
Sam Halpert	33	30	23	32	32
Jim Halpert	4	29	8	12	12

FIGURE 20-1

This worksheet shows the weekly results of a company's Oreo-eating competition. Right now, it's a densely packed grid of information, so it's hard to see who set the most impressive totals.

To use data bars, select the cells you want to format (in this example, that's cells B3 to F10), and then choose Home→Styles→Conditional Formatting→Data Bars. You see a gallery with several choices of data bar, arranged in two categories:

- **Gradient Fill.** Choose this and you get attractively shaded data bars that grow lighter as they travel from left to right. Not only is this a nice detail, it also has a practical purpose. As you know, Excel aligns numbers against the right edge of a cell. With gradient data bars, the right side of the bar is much lighter than the left side, making your superimposed numbers easy to read.
- **Solid Fill.** Choose this and you get solid, filled-in data bars with no outline. They're plain but functional. Solid data bars work well if you plan to show data bars in one column and the numbers they represent in another column. (To pull off this trick, you need the Show Bar Only setting described on page 617.)

Once you decide on a fill, you simply need to pick the color you want (blue, orange, purple, and so on). Figure 20-2 shows a worksheet that uses a gradient fill.

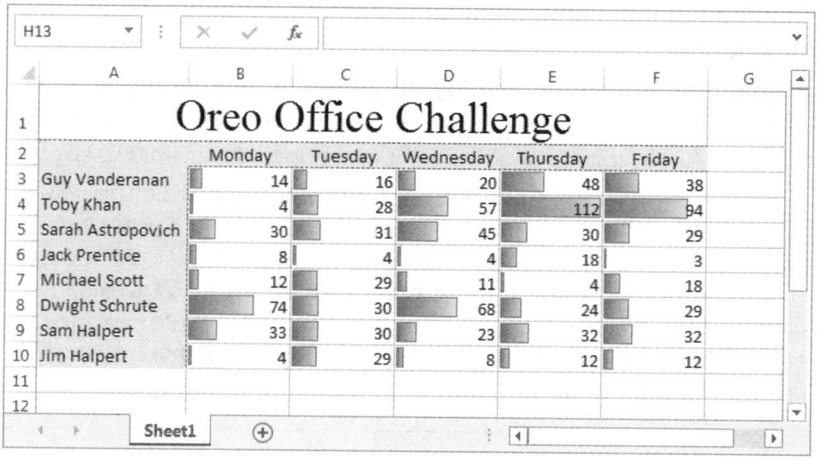

FIGURE 20-2

These data bars let you quickly pick out the largest and smallest values. For example, there's no doubt that Toby's Thursday and Friday totals and Dwight's performance on Monday set the office standard.

When using data bars, Excel finds the largest value and makes that the largest data bar (so it fills the entire cell). Excel fills every other cell proportionately. That means a cell with a value that's half the maximum gets a data bar that fills half the cell, and a cell with a value of 0 has no data bar at all.

Keep in mind that the size of every data bar is relative to the width of the cell that contains it. For example, in Figure 20-2, there are data bars in columns B, C, D, E, and F. If column D is wider than the others, the data bars in it will look longer than those in the other columns, even for cells that have smaller values. To avoid misleading anyone, you should make sure that every column you use in a group of data bars has the same width. That way, Excel will size every data bar consistently.

TIP To make all the columns in a chart the same width, select the widest column, right-click it, choose Column Width, and make note of the number Excel displays. Then select *all* the columns in the chart, right-click any one of the column headers, choose Column Width, and then type in the number you noted earlier. Excel applies that width to all the selected columns.

WORD TO WISE

The Limits of Quick Analysis

If you're in a hurry, you can apply all the features described in this chapter—data bars, color scales, icon sets, and sparklines—using Excel's Quick Analysis feature. (You may remember Quick Analysis from page 489, where you used it to create a recommended chart.)

To use Quick Analysis, you first select the range of cells you want to work with, and then you click the Quick Analysis icon that appears in the bottom-right corner of the range (it looks like a spreadsheet with a lightning bolt on it). This pops open a window packed full of convenient shortcuts for a variety of Excel features. To create a data visualization, you simply make a choice from the Formatting section (for example, click Data Bars or Color Scale). For sparklines, you use the Sparklines section.

Quick Analysis may save you a few steps, but it limits how you can visualize data. For example, if you click Data Bars, Excel gives you the standard blue solid-fill data bars. There are no other formatting choices. Because of this, Excel pros prefer to go straight to the ribbon and get exactly the visualization they want, and that's the approach you'll follow in this chapter.

The best part about data bars is that Excel keeps them synchronized with your data. In other words, if you change the worksheet shown in this example by filling in the numbers for the next week, Excel automatically adjusts all the data bars.

Data bars work best with groups of numbers that are spread out evenly. This feature makes sense for recording the Oreo cookie extravaganza, because the Oreo consumption of most employees falls into the same basic range. However, when you have one or two values that are dramatically higher or lower than the rest, they skew the scale and make it hard to see the variance between the values.

Incidentally, data bars also work with negative numbers. To deal with this situation, Excel draws a dashed vertical line to represent the zero mark in each cell. Then it draws positive values using a shaded bar that stretches from the dashed line to the right, and negative values using a red-colored bar that stretches from the dashed line to the left (Figure 20-3).

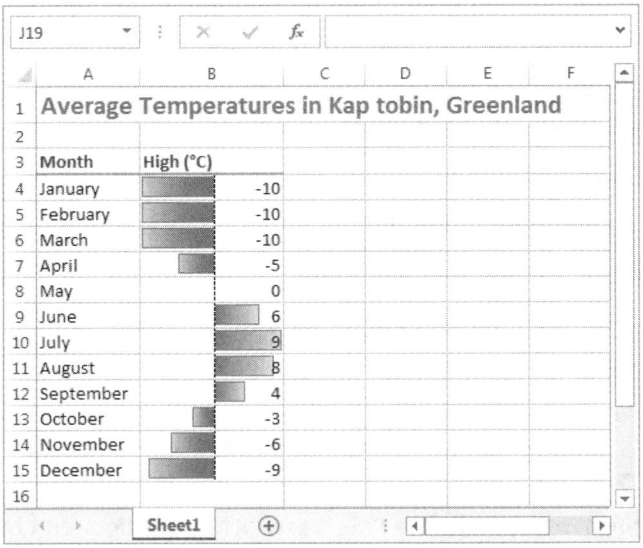

FIGURE 20-3

When visualizing negative numbers, Excel uses a dashed line to show where zero falls. It places this line proportionately between the lowest negative value and the highest positive value and keeps the position the same in every cell, so it's easy to compare numbers at a glance.

The position of the dashed zero-line depends on the scale. For example, if your values range from –10 to 10, the dashed line falls in the middle of every cell. But if your values range from –20 to 10, the dashed line is closer to the right side, because Excel places the zero value proportionately.

TIP It's best not to use red, pink, or purple data bars if your data includes negative numbers. If you do, it becomes more difficult to separate the bars that represent positive values from those that represent negative numbers.

TROUBLESHOOTING MOMENT

Conditional Formatting in Old Versions of Excel

Some conditional formatting tricks—namely, data bars, color scales, icon sets, conditional formatting that overlaps, and cells with more than three conditional formatting rules—don't work in versions of Excel before Excel 2007. So, if you use one of these tricks, export your spreadsheet to the Excel 97–2003 standard (as described on page 31), and then open it in an older version of Excel, you won't see your conditional formatting. Instead, your cells will have the normal, unformatted appearance.

Unless you start fiddling with the conditional formatting settings in an older version of Excel, all the formatting should return the next time you open the spreadsheet in Excel 2013. That's because the information is still there in your spreadsheet file—older versions of Excel just can't deal with it.

Editing a Formatting Rule

When you apply data bars, color scales, or icon sets to a group of numbers, Excel creates a new conditional formatting rule, which tells the program how to format the group of cells you selected.

To fine-tune the way conditional formatting works, you can tweak your rule. Here's how:

1. **Find the section of your worksheet that has the conditional formatting you want to change, and click one of the formatted cells.**

2. **Select Home→Styles→Conditional Formatting→Manage Rules.**

   The Conditional Formatting Rules Manager appears, displaying any conditional formatting rules you previously created. (You learned about this window on page 186.)

3. **Select the rule you want to edit, and then click Edit Rule.**

   The Edit Formatting Rule window appears, which looks exactly the same as the New Formatting Rule window you saw earlier. The top portion of the window lets you change the type of rule (which isn't what you want to do), and the bottom section lets you refine the current rule (which makes more sense).

4. **Modify the settings in the "Edit the Rule Description" section, and then click OK to apply them.**

   You can also click Preview to see what the result of your change will look like on your worksheet.

5. **Click OK again to close the Conditional Formatting Rules Manager.**

   The options in the Edit Formatting Rule window depend on the type of rule you're modifying. The following sections guide you through your choices.

Fine-Tuning Data Bars

If you're editing a data bar (using the steps described in the previous section), you can change several details:

- Use the Show Bar Only checkbox to hide cell value and show just the data bar.
- Use the Minimum and Maximum settings to control how Excel determines the length of each bar.
- Use the Bar Appearance section to set the exact color you want for the data bars and the border Excel draws around them.
- Click the "Negative Value and Axis" button to control the color of data bars that represent negative values and the position of the dashed line that represents the zero point (which can be at the midpoint of the cell or placed proportionately between the smallest and largest value).
- Use the Bar Direction setting to make right-to-left data bars, instead of the standard left-to-right ones.

The following examples show two ways you can use these settings to fine-tune your data bars.

PUTTING DATA BARS IN A SEPARATE COLUMN

Using data bar customization, you can put your data bars and the corresponding numbers in separate columns. Some Excel purists love this trick for the clear, no-nonsense way it presents their data. Figure 20-4 shows this technique on a worksheet of test scores for a top culinary school.

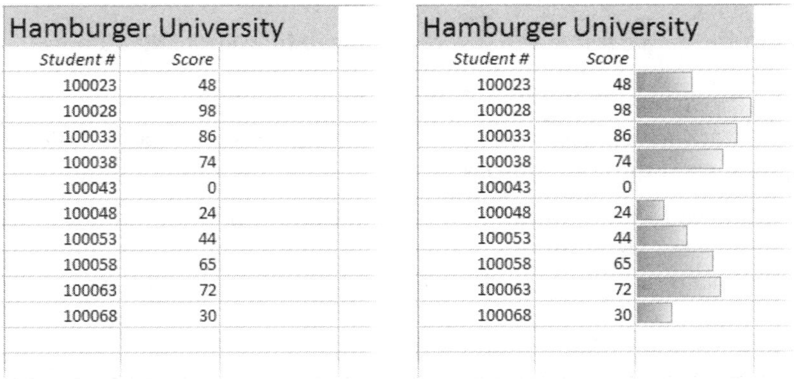

FIGURE 20-4

Left: Initially, you see just test results (in the Score column).

Right: Now you see not only the scores, but their relative values in the data bars in the adjacent column. This makes it easier to compare the data at a glance, and it lets you use solid-color data bars without obscuring their source numbers.

To create the spreadsheet in Figure 20-4, you need two tricks: a column of cell references and the Show Bar Only checkbox. Assume that you start with the values in column B. (If you've already applied data bars, you can remove them by selecting the affected cells and choosing *Home→Editing→Clear→Clear All.)* Then, follow these steps to create the data bars in this example:

1. **The first step is to copy your values. Select the cells in your worksheet (in this case, that's cells B3:B12), and then press Ctrl+C.**

   You can't create data bars unless you put some data in the cells first. So the first step is to copy the underlying data to the right cells—but with a twist.

2. **Move to the first cell where you want to put your data bars (in this case, cell C3).**

   Don't paste your cells just yet! The last thing you want to do is duplicate a bunch of numbers, because the next time you change them you'll wind up with inconsistent data. Instead, you need to use a pasting trick you learned on page 98.

3. **Choose Home→Clipboard→Paste→Paste Link.**

   This pastes a series of cell references. For example, cell C3 gets a formula that points to cell B3, so when you change cell B3, cell C3 refreshes with the new value automatically. Presto: the same values in two places, with no possibility for inconsistency.

4. **Now it's time to add the data bars. Select the newly pasted cells.**

   This is where you want to place the data bars.

5. **Choose a data bar option from Home→Conditional Formatting→Data Bars.**

   Because you're displaying the cell values in column B, you don't need to worry about obscuring them here, so feel free to choose a solid fill.

6. **Now you need to edit the rule to hide the numbers. With the same cells selected, choose Home→Styles→Conditional Formatting→Manage Rules.**

   The Conditional Formatting Rules Manager appears.

7. **Select the data bar rule you just created, and then click Edit Rule.**

   The Edit Formatting Rule window appears.

8. **Put a checkmark in the Show Bars Only setting, and then click OK. Click OK again to close the Conditional Formatting Rules Manager.**

   Although your pasted cells still have the values in them, the values no longer appear in the cells. Even better, because the cells in column C are linked to the cells in column B, when you change the visible data, Excel updates the data bars.

CHANGING THE DATA BAR SCALE

Ordinarily, Excel decides what scale to use when it draws your data bars. In its standard scale, the smallest value is 0 (unless you have negative numbers, as explained on page 614), and the highest value is the highest number in your selection of cells. However, this isn't always the best approach. For example, if most of your values fall into a tight range but include a few super-high values, the outliers will distort the scale. Figure 20-5 illustrates the problem.

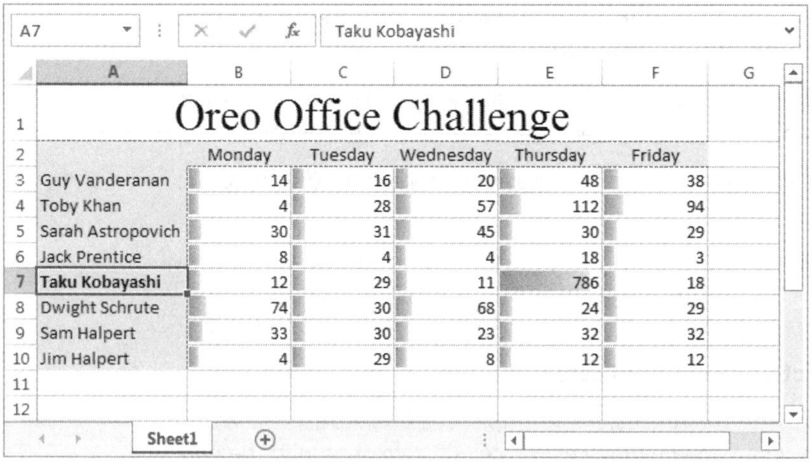

FIGURE 20-5

One challenge with data bars is how to handle off-the-chart values (like Kobayashi's Thursday performance) that make everyone else's numbers look the same. The difference between the smallest value (4) and the largest (786) is much larger than the difference between most other values. See Figure 20-6 for an elegant solution.

To fix this problem, you need to take control of the data bar scale. By manually setting a smaller maximum value, you can focus the scale on the range of values that's most important for your data.

To accomplish this, begin by editing your data bar rule (as described on page 616). Then, in the Maximum section, change the Type to Number, and then set the Value to 100 (Figure 20-6).

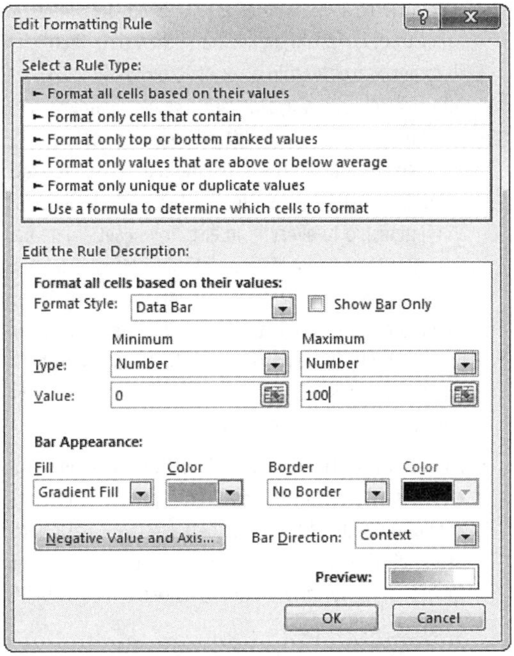

FIGURE 20-6

The data bars in this example use an explicit maximum. Excel treats 0 as the smallest value and 100 as the largest. It represents all the values in between with proportionately filled bars (so 50 gets a half-length data bar). Any value less than the minimum gets the minimum bar size, and any value larger than the maximum gets the maximum bar size. Figure 20-7 shows the result.

UP TO SPEED

Setting the Scale

When you edit a data bar rule, you can set the minimum and maximum of the scale several ways. It all starts with the Type list, which controls how Excel determines these values. You can set the type of both the minimum and maximum, and they don't need to match. Your options include:

- **Automatic**. Excel uses its standard approach to determine scale, making 0 the minimum and using the highest value for the maximum. (One exception: If there are negative values, the lowest value becomes the minimum.)
- **Number**. You supply the number you want to use for the minimum or maximum. Because data bars can't get shorter than the minimum value or longer than the maximum, you use this setting to "cap off" outlying values, as shown in Figure 20-7.
- **Percent**. This option lets you supply the minimum and maximum values as *percentages* instead of fixed numbers. Ordinarily, the lowest value is 0 percent and the highest value is set to 100 percent. So, if you want to cut off the ends of the scale, you might start the smallest bar at 10 percent and cap the highest at 90 percent. If your actual values range from 0 to 500, the bottom value (at 10 percent) becomes 50, and the top value (at 90 percent) becomes 450.
- **Percentile**. This option works similarly to Percent, but in a way that's more satisfying for mathematically minded statisticians. This number arranges all the values in order from lowest to highest, and then slots them into different *percentiles*. In a set of 10 ordered values, the 40th percentile is always the fourth value, regardless of its exact number. In other words, when you use percentiles, Excel isn't all that interested in how high or low the exact value is; instead, it pays attention to how that value falls in relationship to everything else. If you set a data bar minimum to a percentile value of 10, the bottom 10 percent of values get the shortest bar. If you set the maximum to 90, the top 10 percent of values get the longest bar. The nice thing about percentiles is that you always get a good range of short, medium, and long data bars, even if your numbers are spread out unevenly.
- **Lowest Value (for Minimum) or Highest Value (for Maximum)**. Setting Lowest Value for the minimum exaggerates the differences between your data bars, especially if none of your values are close to zero. Setting Highest Value for maximum has no real effect, as that's Excel's default anyway.
- **Formula**. This option is an advanced trick that lets you use a formula to tell Excel what the highest or lowest values should be. Chapter 8 has more about formulas.

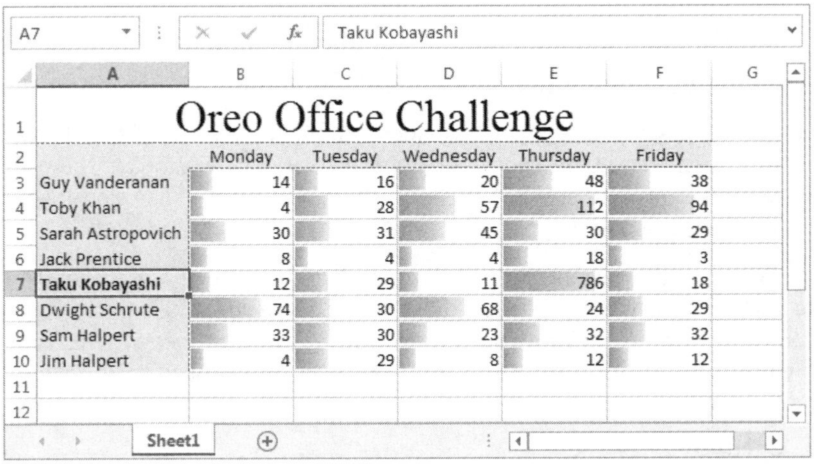

FIGURE 20-7

Now it's easy to see the variation between midrange values. The only tradeoff is that every value above 100 gets the same data bar, so you lose the ability to distinguish between high and extremely high values.

The previous example showed how data with a wide spread can cause problems. A related problem occurs if none of your numbers are close to 0. Once again, the scale tends to wipe out fine distinctions. Figure 20-8 shows the problem and explains the solution.

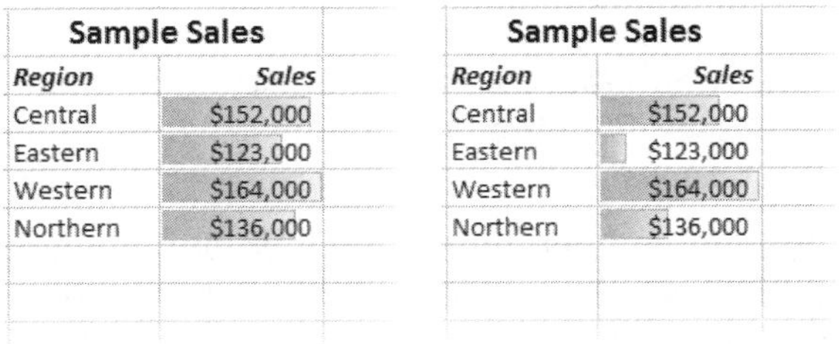

FIGURE 20-8

Left: These sales figures are close together but far from zero. The result is a set of data bars with little obvious difference. If this isn't what you want, you can adjust the data bar scale. But this time, tweak the lower bound of the scale rather than the upper bound.

Right: Here, you set the lower bound at 115,000, and the difference between the bars is obvious—even exaggerated.

Color Scales

Color scales let you format different cells with different colors. As with data bars, Excel automatically chooses the color for each cell. It assigns a predefined color to the lowest value and another predefined color to the highest value, and uses a weighted blend of the two for all the values in between. For example, if 0 is blue and 100 is yellow, the value 50 gets a shade of green.

To apply a color scale, select your cells, choose Home→Styles→Conditional Formatting→Color Scales, and then choose one of the color combinations in the gallery. To test out different color scales, hover over them with your mouse, and then take a look at the live preview on your worksheet.

People don't use color scales as often as data bars, because color scales tend to create a more visually cluttered worksheet. If you do decide to use them, you may want to customize how they work so Excel applies them to specific cells only, or so they use a less obtrusive pair of colors (like white and light red). You'll learn to customize color scales next.

Fine-Tuning Color Scales

You can fine-tune color scales in much the same way you adjust data bars. Here are the settings you have to play with:

- In the Format Style list, choose 2-Color Scale or 3-Color Scale, depending on how many colors you want to use.
- Choose the colors for the minimum and maximum (and, in a three-color scale, the midpoint).
- Set the Type and Value of the Minimum, Midpoint, and Maximum to control the scale explicitly. These settings work exactly the same way they do for data bars, giving you the ability to set the scale with fixed values you supply, percentages, or percentiles, as described on page 620.

One reason you might fine-tune a color scale is to use less obtrusive formatting by setting white as your minimum value color and choosing a light color for the maximum. You can also use percentiles to make a more reserved-looking worksheet, where most values get no color and the highest values get just a tinge (see Figure 20-9).

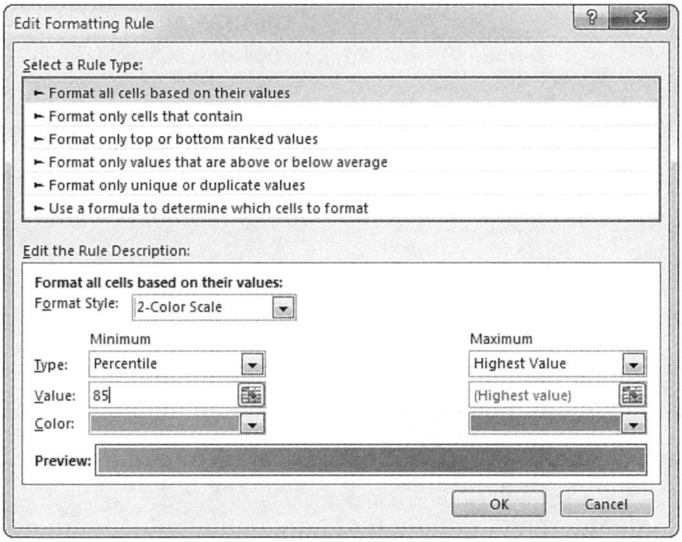

FIGURE 20-9

A two-color scale blends from one color to another, while a three-color scale has a specific midpoint color. Excel blends values in the bottom range between the lowest value color and the midpoint color, and values in the top range between the midpoint color and the highest value color. In this two-color example, the minimum type is set to Percentile and the minimum value is set to 85, which means only the top 15 percent of values have any color.

Icon Sets

So far, you've seen how to graphically represent different values using shaded bars and colors. Both these tricks are called *data visualizations*. Excel has one more data visualization tool that uses conditional formatting: icon sets.

The idea behind icon sets is that you choose a set of three to five icons. Excel then examines your cells and displays one of these icons next to each value, depending on the value. To do this, Excel begins by determining the range of values you have. It then divides that range into equal portions based on the number of icons you're using.

For example, if you choose an icon set with three icons, Excel carves your scale into three segments. If your values range from 0 to 100, cells that have a value from 0 to 33 get the first icon, cells with a value of 34 to 66 get the second icon, and cells with a value of 67 to 100 get the third icon. Similarly, if you pick an icon set with four icons, the first range is 0 to 25, the second is 26 to 50, the third is 51 to 75, and the fourth is 76 to 100. (If this automatic scale setting doesn't work for you, you can set the ranges for each icon manually, as you'll learn on page 626.)

To see the available icon sets, choose Home→Styles→Conditional Formatting→Icon Sets (Figure 20-10).

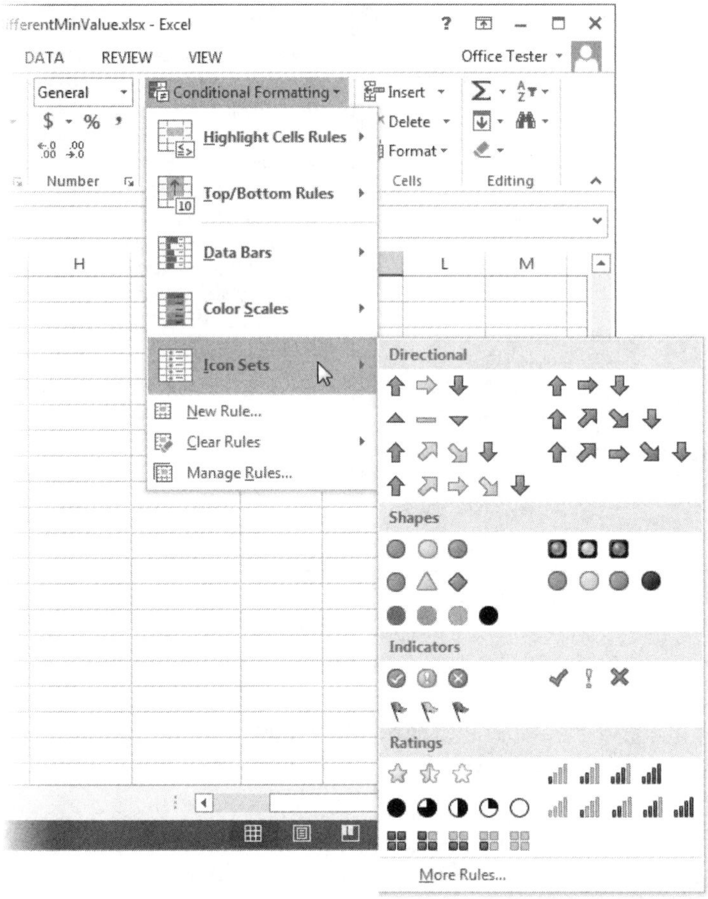

FIGURE 20-10

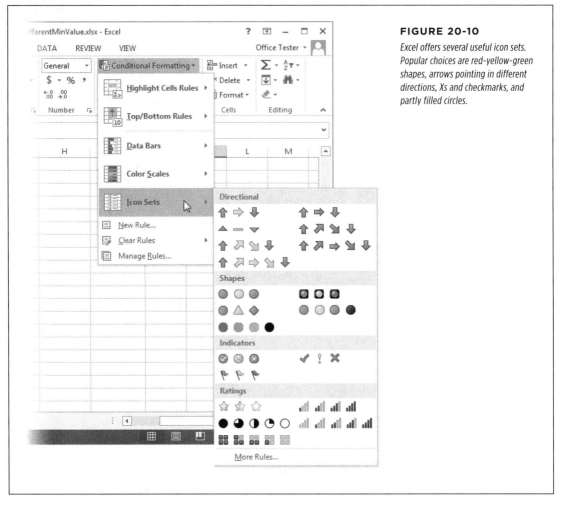

Excel offers several useful icon sets. Popular choices are red-yellow-green shapes, arrows pointing in different directions, Xs and checkmarks, and partly filled circles.

Sadly, you can't create your own icon sets in this version of Excel. However, you can accomplish a lot by using the existing icon sets with a little imagination. Figure 20-11 shows two options with the table of Oreo eaters. The top example ranks each competitor's performance each day, while the bottom one calculates per-person totals (using the SUM() function described on page 267), and then adds icons to those totals.

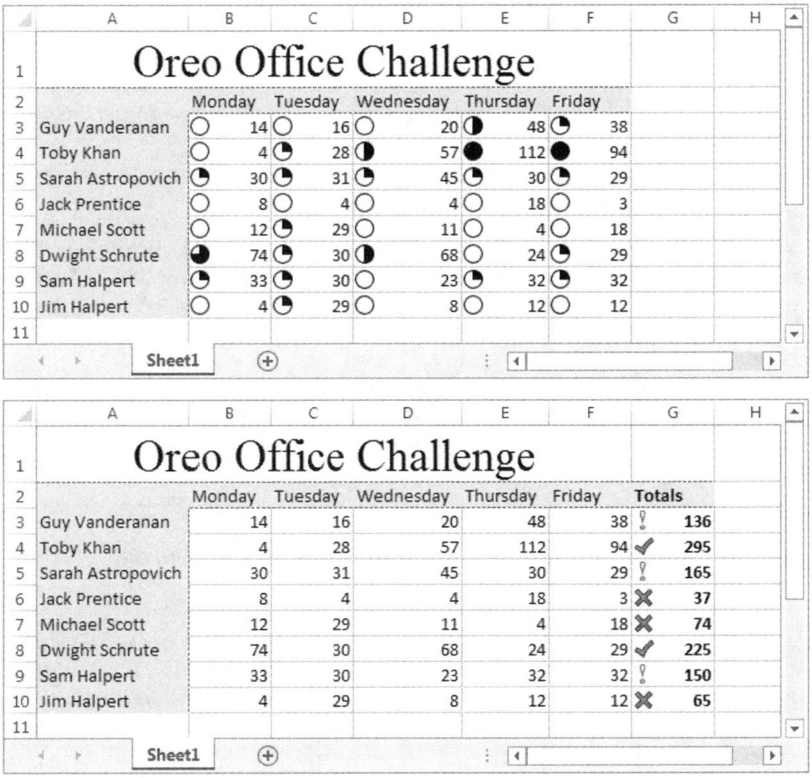

Oreo Office Challenge

	Monday	Tuesday	Wednesday	Thursday	Friday
Guy Vanderanan	14	16	20	48	38
Toby Khan	4	28	57	112	94
Sarah Astropovich	30	31	45	30	29
Jack Prentice	8	4	4	18	3
Michael Scott	12	29	11	4	18
Dwight Schrute	74	30	68	24	29
Sam Halpert	33	30	23	32	32
Jim Halpert	4	29	8	12	12

Oreo Office Challenge

	Monday	Tuesday	Wednesday	Thursday	Friday	Totals
Guy Vanderanan	14	16	20	48	38	136
Toby Khan	4	28	57	112	94	295
Sarah Astropovich	30	31	45	30	29	165
Jack Prentice	8	4	4	18	3	37
Michael Scott	12	29	11	4	18	74
Dwight Schrute	74	30	68	24	29	225
Sam Halpert	33	30	23	32	32	150
Jim Halpert	4	29	8	12	12	65

FIGURE 20-11

Top: The partially filled circles (known by the seemingly contradictory name 5 Quarters) shows how different employees stack up in the Oreo-eating competition. A filled black circle indicates a competition-leading performance, while empty white circles are clear signs of Oreo-haters.

Bottom: It's time to go to round two. Employees with a checkmark icon qualify to move on, while those with an X icon can stay home and drink milk. Employees with an exclamation mark are in the middle ground and can fight for the last remaining playoff spaces in another qualifying round.

Fine-Tuning Icon Sets

With icon sets, you can adjust several settings:

- Use the Icon Style list to change the icons you use. You have all the options you saw in the Home→Styles→Conditional Formatting→Icon Sets gallery.
- Turn on the Reverse Icon Order checkbox to arrange icons in reverse order (so the icon that you previously used for the top values now applies to the bottom ones).
- Use the Show Icon Only checkbox to hide cell values and display just the icon. You can also use this trick with data bars, but it's way more convenient with icon sets. It lets you create a dashboard-like display that indicates the *significance* of different values (for example, good, bad, or neutral) rather than the exact value (which may be of much less interest to the spreadsheet reader).

- Use the Icon section to mix and match your icons. For example, you can use icons from different icon sets to represent different values, and you can even choose not to show an icon for certain values.
- Choose the range of values that Excel uses for each icon. As with data bars and color scales, you can set these ranges using fixed numbers, percentages, percentiles, or a formula.

The following sections show the two most common ways to fine-tune icon sets.

GIVING YOUR ICONS ADDED SIGNIFICANCE

As you've just seen, Excel splits your values into icon groups automatically. If you want icons with no hassle, this seems pretty convenient. But if you want your icons to actually mean something—for example, you want a checkmark to signify a passing grade or an up-arrow to flag a profitable product—you need to define the scale yourself.

Fortunately, it's an easy job. Begin by applying the icon set you want to your data. Then, edit the rule, as described on page 616. Finally, change the ranges that assign icons to cell values, as shown in Figure 20-12.

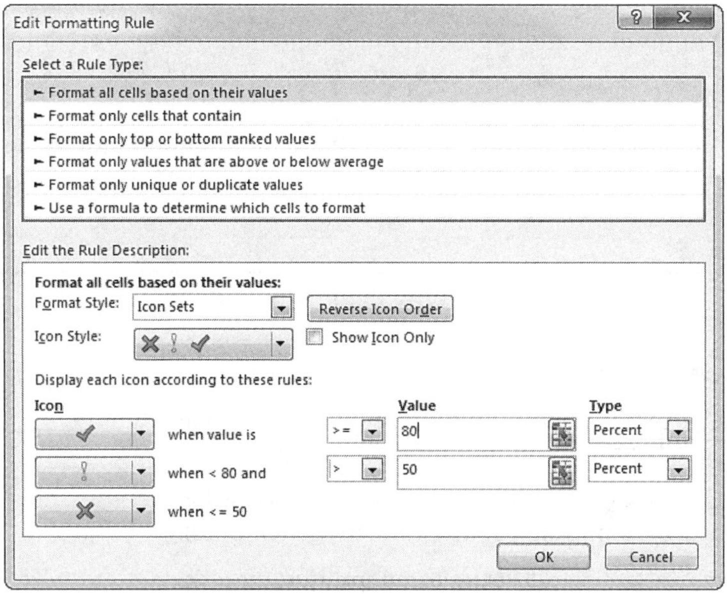

FIGURE 20-12

Ordinarily, Excel splits the range of values into equal groups based on equal percentages. By changing the ranges, you can reserve some icons for narrower ranges of numbers. For example, you could decide to use the X icon for all test scores that fall under 50, and keep the green checkmark for the best performing above-80 scorers (as shown here).

TIP Usually, it's easiest to get the ranges you want with fixed numbers. That means you should set the Type setting for each range to Number (rather than Percent, Percentile, or Formula).

HIDING ICONS FOR SOME VALUES

Icon sets bring a lot of clutter. If you're not careful, your worksheet can dissolve into a jumble of pictures. One way to control the distraction is to use icons for certain ranges, but not for others. (In fact, design experts suggest that icons work best when no more than *10 percent* of your cells use them.)

For example, consider the worksheet with student scores shown earlier. To keep it clear, you want to show an X icon next to all the failing grades, but you don't want to bother showing any icon next to the others. Figure 20-13 shows the difference.

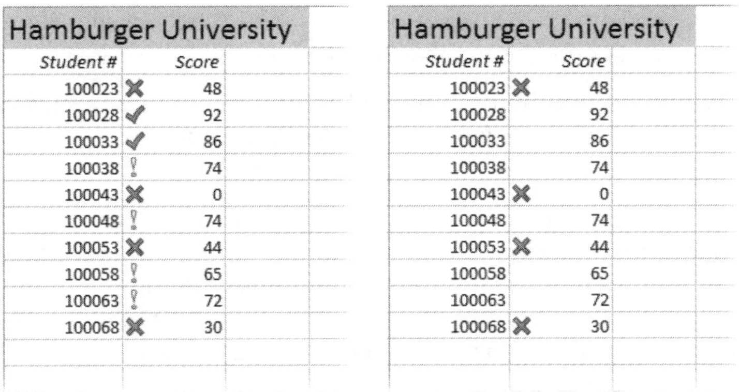

FIGURE 20-13

Left: Tiny icons show the difference between good marks, bad marks, and really bad marks—if you don't go cross-eyed.

Right: If you need to keep track of the really bad marks, the best bet is to hide all the other icons.

You can accomplish this easily by editing the formatting rule. Look at the Icon section in the bottom-right corner of the Edit Formatting Rule window. There, you can click the drop-down arrow next to an icon to pick something different. Or, choose No Cell Icon to leave this range icon-free. To create the worksheet shown in Figure 20-13, set the middle and top ranges to No Cell Icon, while keeping the X icon for the bottom range.

Sparklines

Sparklines are tiny graphics that look like miniature charts, but fit in a single worksheet cell. Compared to charts, they're simplified and stripped down, with no gridlines, borders, legend, or callouts. Interestingly, these limitations make sparklines much more versatile than their graphing big brothers. While a worksheet might feel overburdened with more than a couple of full-fledged charts, you can easily fill its cells with a dozen sparklines, while still keeping it clear and clean.

As you'll soon see, using sparklines is easy. Using them *well* isn't too difficult either, as long as you have a solid understanding of their proper role in life. The key detail you should understand is that sparklines are *not* a poor man's chart. They aren't intended to replace, simplify, or compete with Excel's charting feature. In fact, sparklines have a closer relation to data bars, color scales, and icon sets—the conditional formatting features you explored in the first half of this chapter.

Much like these features, sparklines give your worksheets an at-a-glance overview of your data and its significance. For example, a properly placed sparkline can highlight plummeting profit, a seasonal spike in orders, or an uncanny winning streak in the company bowling league. They might not give you all the details, but they can alert you to trends, patterns, and dramatic changes without forcing you to perform a painstaking review of the numbers.

Currently, sparklines come in just three flavors:

- **Line.** These sparklines chart a series of values with a zig-zagging line that stretches from left to right. It's the same line you see in the familiar line chart.
- **Column.** These sparklines create a series of vertical bars, one for each value, with the bigger columns indicating bigger values. As you've no doubt guessed, it's the sparkline version of the ordinary column chart.
- **Win/Loss.** These sparklines create a series of squares, and Excel puts each square in one of two positions. If the value is positive, Excel puts the square at the top of the cell (win), and if the value is negative, it places the square at the bottom (lose). Unlike the other sparklines, this one simplifies your data. For example, you could use it to take a series of golf scores and show, for each game, whether the golfer beat par.

Figure 20-14 shows all three varieties.

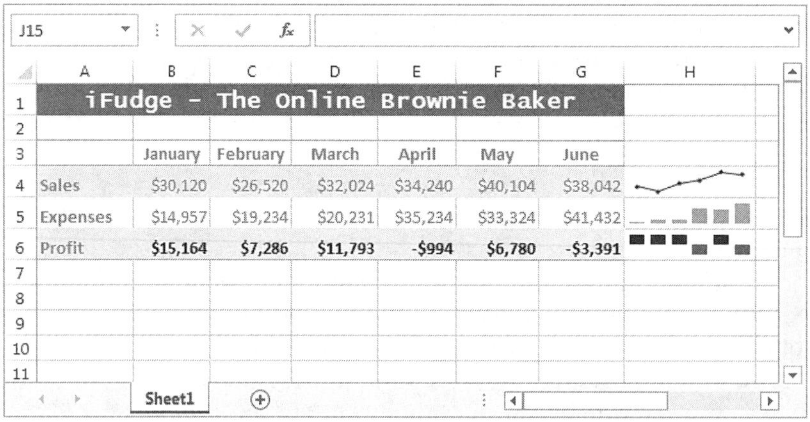

FIGURE 20-14

In this worksheet, a line sparkline (cell H4) shows the changing sales of a web-based baker. Underneath, a column sparkline (H5) shows the worrying increase in expenses. (These two sparklines are essentially interchangeable, so you could use a column sparkline for sales and a line sparkline for expenses.) Finally, a win/loss sparkline (H6) shows the profit or loss for each quarter. A profit counts as a win, while a loss is, well, a loss.

Creating a Sparkline

The easiest way to understand how sparklines work is to create one. Consider the sample spreadsheet in Figure 20-15.

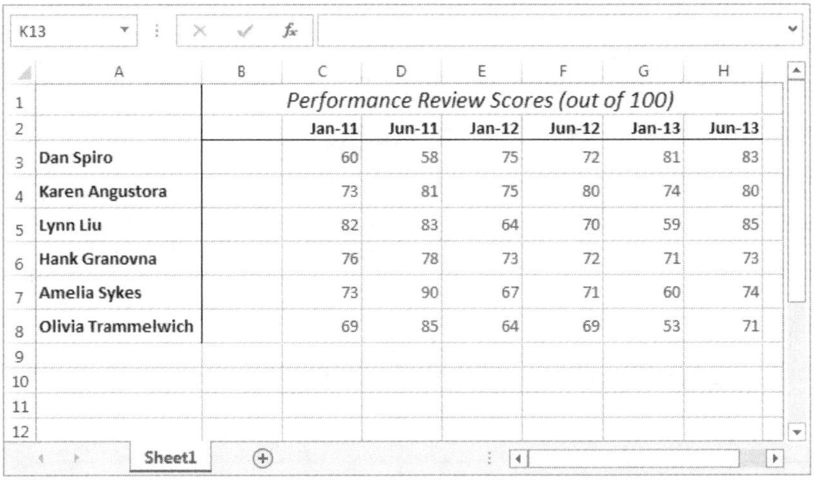

	Performance Review Scores (out of 100)					
	Jan-11	Jun-11	Jan-12	Jun-12	Jan-13	Jun-13
Dan Spiro	60	58	75	72	81	83
Karen Angustora	73	81	75	80	74	80
Lynn Liu	82	83	64	70	59	85
Hank Granovna	76	78	73	72	71	73
Amelia Sykes	73	90	67	71	60	74
Olivia Trammelwich	69	85	64	69	53	71

FIGURE 20-15

This worksheet shows a morass of data: the twice-a-year performance scores for a handful of long-time employees. All the information you could possibly need is here, but it might take some time to dig through it.

In this example, column B (cells B3:B8) is empty and ready for a set of sparklines. If you're working with your own worksheet, you might need to move some cells around to make space. Remember, each sparkline needs just a single cell, so the example in Figure 20-15 has room for a sparkline next to each employee's name.

TIP To save yourself some typing, you can download the spreadsheet in Figure 20-15 from this book's Missing CD page at *www.missingmanuals.com/cds/excel2013mm*. Go to the Chapter 20 section and double-click Sparkline.xlsx. This sample file has the sparklines already set up, but you can delete them to create your own (select cells B3:B8 and then choose Home→Editing→Clear→Clear All).

To create a sparkline for this example, follow these steps:

1. **Move to the cell where you want to place the sparkline.**

   Often, this is next to the data you're charting, but it doesn't need to be. In this example, you can start at cell B3.

2. **Go to the Insert→Sparklines section of the ribbon, and then choose one of the three sparkline types.**

   In this example, click Line. The Create Sparklines window appears (Figure 20-16).

3. **Specify the cells for the Data Range.**

   You can type the range in by hand (in this example, it's C3:H3). Or, click the Data Range box, and then drag on the worksheet to select the cells.

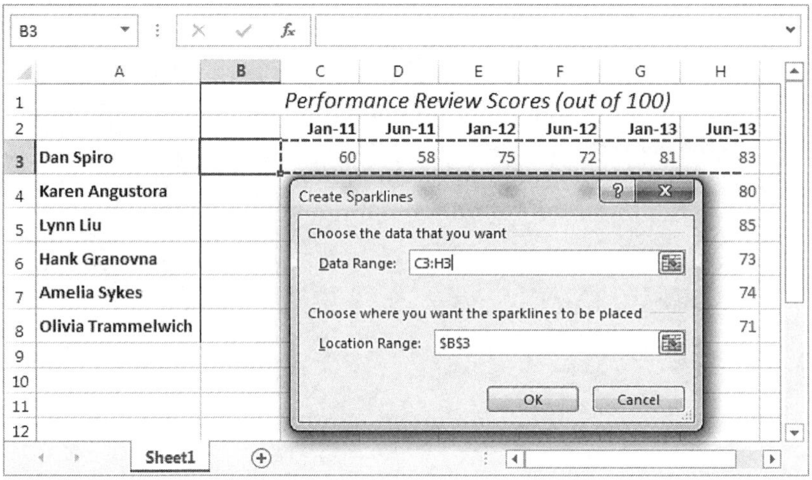

FIGURE 20-16

The Create Sparklines window needs two pieces of information. First is the Data Range: the range of cells with the source data for the sparkline. Second is the Location Range: the cell where you want to put the newly created sparkline. (This box is automatically filled in with the current cell address.)

4. **Click OK.**

   A sparkline appears in the cell.

5. **To add a series of sparklines to the table, copy the newly added sparkline.**

   In the current example, that means you can copy the sparkline in cell B3 (select B3, and then press Ctrl+C), select cells B4 through B8, and then paste the sparkline settings (press Ctrl+V). Much as when you copy a formula, each copy uses adjusted cell references. So, while the sparkline in B3 points to the data in C3:H3, the copy in B4 points to C4:H4, and so on. Figure 20-17 shows the result.

TIP If you're in a real hurry, you can create several sparklines in one fell swoop. It's all in how you fill in the values in the Create Sparklines window. In the current example, you supply the full table (cells C3:H8) for the Data Range and the empty cells where you want to create the sparklines (cells B3:B8) for the Location Range. As a side effect, this approach places all the sparklines into a group, as described on page 632.

6. **Fine-tune the width and height of the cells that hold your sparkline.**

   Each sparkline gets the height and width of its containing cell. If it includes a lot of data points, you might want to widen the column to stretch the line out longer. Or you can heighten the row to better see the variations in value between the points.

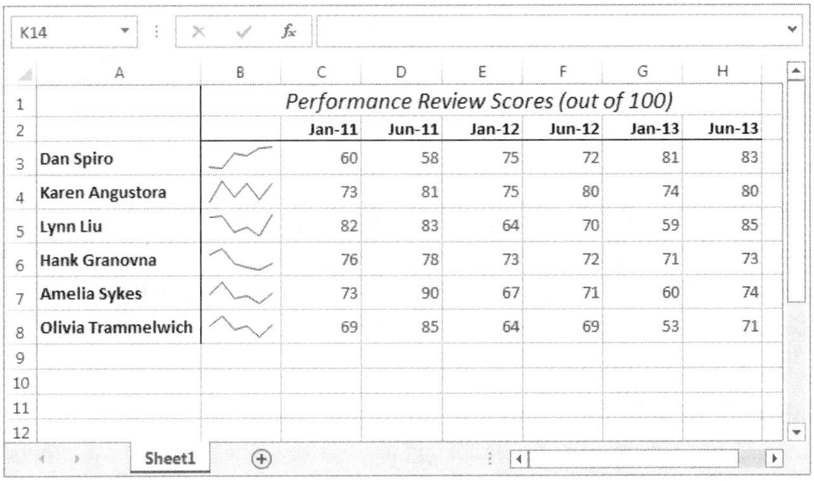

	Performance Review Scores (out of 100)						
		Jan-11	Jun-11	Jan-12	Jun-12	Jan-13	Jun-13
Dan Spiro		60	58	75	72	81	83
Karen Angustora		73	81	75	80	74	80
Lynn Liu		82	83	64	70	59	85
Hank Granovna		76	78	73	72	71	73
Amelia Sykes		73	90	67	71	60	74
Olivia Trammelwich		69	85	64	69	53	71

FIGURE 20-17

These sparklines don't tell you much about the individual scores or whether the scores were satisfactory, but they do show you overall trends—that, is how each employee's scores changed over time. For example, you can quickly tell that Dan Spiro is on the up-and-up.

TIP To make all the rows taller by the same amount, begin by selecting all the row buttons—in this case, that's rows 3 to 8. Then, right-click the selection, and choose Row Height. You can enter a new value in the Row Height window that appears. Figure 20-16 uses a row height of 20 pixels, rather than the standard 15.

7. **Set the color of your sparkline.**

   Whenever you select a cell that has a sparkline, the Sparkline Tools | Design tab appears in the ribbon. To change the color of the sparkline, choose another color from the Style→Sparkline Color list. If you want to change all your sparklines at once, select all the cells that have sparklines, and then choose a new color.

   You can also use the Sparkline Tools | Design tab to modify the data your sparkline uses (choose Sparkline→Edit Data), change the sparkline type (make another selection in the Type section), show markers (page 636), or show a horizontal axis line (page 634).

It's worth noting that, like data bars, color scales, and icon sets, sparklines still leave room for data in the cell. Most of the time, you'll probably keep your worksheet simple and leave the sparkline cells alone, as in Figure 20-17. But for a different effect, you can try adding formatted text, as shown in Figure 20-18.

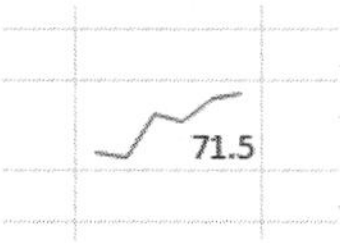

FIGURE 20-18

A cell that has a sparkline can still accommodate cell data, like a number, formula, or piece of text. In this example, the cell value is right-justified and bottom-aligned, so it doesn't get in the way of the sparkline.

As a side effect of the sparkline-and-date design, moving to a sparkline cell and then pressing the Delete key won't remove the sparkline, only the data inside the cell. And if there's no data inside, hitting Delete still won't remove the sparkline. To get rid of it, you have to move to the sparkline cell, and then choose Sparkline Tools | Design→Group→Clear, or Home→Editing→Clear→Clear All.

Changing the Axis

One of the most important principles of sparklines is this: They can tell you something about your data, but not everything. To get the most out of sparklines, you need to decide what it is you want them to say.

For example, the employee review example (Figure 20-17) uses sparklines to show *change*. You can tell, at a glance, whether an employee has been on an upward trend or a downward spiral. However, you can't tell if one employee is doing better than another, because each sparkline uses its own distinct scale. This scale is set so that the maximum value (the best performance-review score) is plotted at the top of the cell, and the minimum value (the worst score) is plotted at the bottom. As a result, Hank Granovna's slight trend down (from 76 to 71) looks nearly as impressive as Dan Spiro's rise up (from 58 to 83).

To correct this, you can configure a group of sparklines to use the same scale. (This change makes sense only for line-type or column-type sparklines, because win/loss sparklines don't use any scale.)

Here's how you do that:

1. **Select all the sparklines you want to have the same scale.**

   In the employee review example, that's cells B3 to B8.

2. **Choose Sparkline Tools | Design→Group→Group.**

   Now Excel treats your sparklines as part of one group, and you can set their axis options as a single unit. Whenever you move to a sparkline cell that's part of a group, Excel displays a blue border around all the grouped cells. You can remove the grouping by choosing Sparkline Tools | Design→Group→Ungroup.

3. **Now it's time to give all the sparklines the same scale.**

   Choose Sparkline Tools | Design→Group→Axis. Under the Vertical Axis Minimum Value heading, choose Same for All Sparklines. Under the Vertical Axis Maximum Value heading, choose Same for All Sparklines.

   This sets the entire group of sparklines to use the same maximum and minimum value for their scale (Figure 20-19). That means the highest score of any employee (90) will become the new maximum, and the lowest score (53) will become the new minimum.

   Alternatively, you can set the scale minimum and maximum manually by choosing the Custom Value option. For example, you could use this technique in the current example to set the scale minimum of 0.

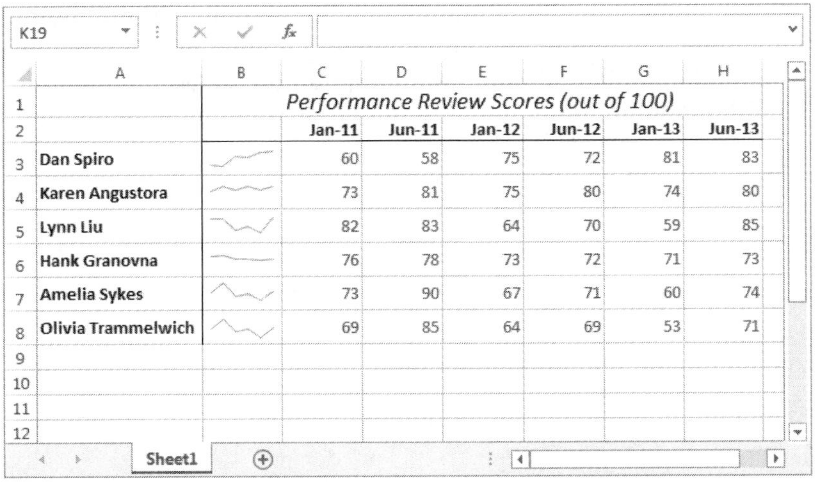

	A	B	C	D	E	F	G	H
1		Performance Review Scores (out of 100)						
2			Jan-11	Jun-11	Jan-12	Jun-12	Jan-13	Jun-13
3	Dan Spiro		60	58	75	72	81	83
4	Karen Angustora		73	81	75	80	74	80
5	Lynn Liu		82	83	64	70	59	85
6	Hank Granovna		76	78	73	72	71	73
7	Amelia Sykes		73	90	67	71	60	74
8	Olivia Trammelwich		69	85	64	69	53	71

FIGURE 20-19

Now that the sparklines use the same scale, it's clear that Hank Granovna has nothing to worry about.

POWER USERS' CLINIC

Even More Axis Options

Although setting the scale is the single most important sparkline change you can make, several other configuration options make a difference in the right situation:

- **Reverse your sparkline**. If you want your sparklines to plot their values in the reverse direction, choose Sparkline Tools | Design→Group→Axis→Plot Data Right-to-Left.
- **Show the horizontal axis**. The horizontal axis is drawn to represent the zero point. To show it, choose Sparkline Tools | Design→Group→Axis, and then select Show Axis under the heading Horizontal Axis Options. Although you won't actually see the horizontal axis unless you have negative values in your sparkline, some Excel gurus get around this by performing an extra calculation, which displays sparklines as shown in Figure 20-20.
- **Use a date axis**. Ordinarily, Excel spaces out the values in a sparkline evenly. That makes sense in the employee review example, because the reviews are performed at regular six-month intervals. However, it's not hard to imagine a different sort of situation, where batches of employees are reviewed in different months. In this case, you can space the values out proportionately by date, as long as you have the corresponding date data in your worksheet. For example, the employee review has the dates (C2:H2) that correspond to the review scores in cells C3:H8. To use these dates to space out the chart, choose Sparkline Tools | Design→Group→Axis→Date Axis Type, select these cells, and then click OK.
- **Deal with empty cells**. Ordinarily, sparklines leave a gap in the line to represent a missing value. If this isn't what you want, you can tell Excel to treat blank values as zeros, or just draw the sparkline straight through to the next value. To change this option, choose Sparkline Tools | Design→Sparkline→Edit Data→Hidden & Empty Cells. You also see the "Show data in hidden rows and columns" checkbox, which lets you configure whether sparklines include data in hidden cells.

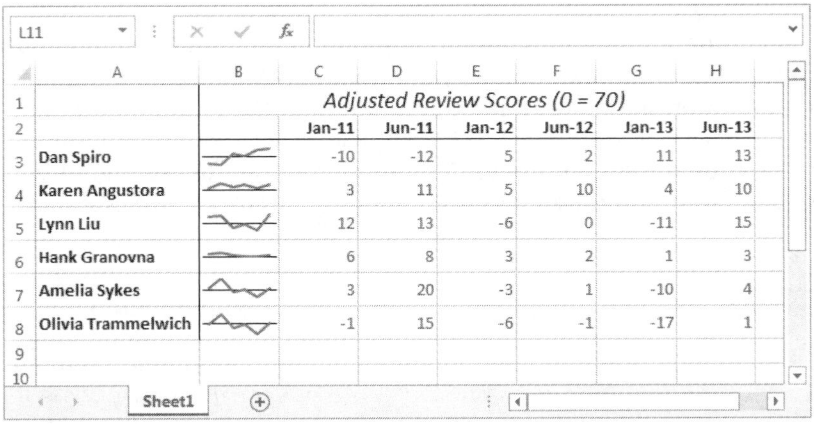

FIGURE 20-20

Here, the horizontal axis is a baseline that indicates whether employees measure up to the minimum threshold (a 70 on each performance review). To get the threshold in the right place, you need to subtract 70 from each performance review score. Some Excel hotshots perform this calculation in a separate set of cells, and then hide those cells so they don't clutter the worksheet. Just remember, if you try this trick, you need to explicitly tell your sparkline to show hidden values, by choosing Sparkline Tools | Design→Sparkline→Edit Data→Hidden & Empty Cells, and then switching on the "Show data in hidden rows and columns" checkbox.

In this example, the same-scale sparklines are the best choice. They prevent people from drawing misleading conclusions about relative performance. However, in many cases, same-scale sparklines don't make as much sense.

For example, if you create a worksheet that tallies the sales performance of different stores for your line of thermal undergarments, you already know that bigger stores sell more underwear. What you really want to see is how sales and profit figures have changed at each location. In this situation, using the same scale will hide the important trend information. And if the stores are dramatically different sizes, the scale will expand so much that some of your sparklines will start looking like horizontal lines. In this situation, relative-scaled sparklines are often more useful than grouped sparklines that share the same scale.

Markers

The line type of sparkline supports *markers*—tiny squares that highlight important data points on the line. The catch is that you need to decide where to add them.

To show markers on a sparkline, select the cells that have the sparklines you want to change, and then go to the Sparkline Tools | Design→Show section of the ribbon. You see a set of checkboxes that let you show different markers. You can show a marker for the greatest data value (select High Point), the smallest (Low Point), all values less than zero (Negative Points), the first value (First Point), the last value (Last Point), or all values (Markers). Once again, it's a case of deciding what story your sparklines should tell. Figure 20-21 shows a stock chart that uses markers.

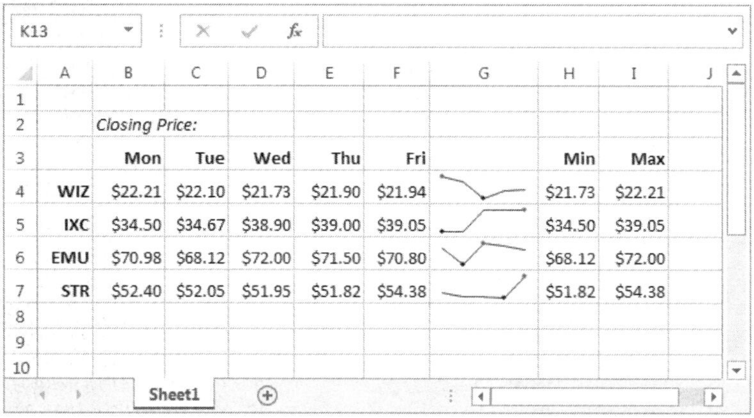

	A	B	C	D	E	F	G	H	I
1									
2		*Closing Price:*							
3		**Mon**	**Tue**	**Wed**	**Thu**	**Fri**		**Min**	**Max**
4	**WIZ**	$22.21	$22.10	$21.73	$21.90	$21.94		$21.73	$22.21
5	**IXC**	$34.50	$34.67	$38.90	$39.00	$39.05		$34.50	$39.05
6	**EMU**	$70.98	$68.12	$72.00	$71.50	$70.80		$68.12	$72.00
7	**STR**	$52.40	$52.05	$51.95	$51.82	$54.38		$51.82	$54.38

FIGURE 20-21

These sparklines show fluctuating stock prices. Each one highlights the highest and lowest value with a marker. The worksheet drives the message home by indicating the exact minimum and maximum numbers in the cells on the right. These cells get their numbers using the MIN() and MAX() formulas you met on page 270.

NOTE You can use markers with column sparklines, but Excel applies them differently than it does with lines. If you choose to show red markers for the largest and smallest values, for example, the largest and smallest columns will be red in color.

You can use any combination of markers. But if you mix and match, you'll probably want to differentiate markers by color. To do so, head to the Sparkline Tools | Design→Style→Marker Color menu. Here you find different submenus for each marker type, where you can pick the exact color you want. Often, Excel pros like to use red markers for bad news (like negative values or the smallest value) and green markers for good news (like the greatest value). If you don't customize the colors, all the markers will use the same color as your sparkline.

PART 5

Sharing Data with the Rest of the World

CHAPTER

21

Protecting Your Workbooks

So far, you've created spreadsheets that are a bit of a free-for-all. You (or anyone else) can open them and change absolutely anything, from the most minor formatting detail to the most critical formula. For everyday Excel use, this freedom makes perfect sense. However, if you're thinking of sharing your carefully crafted work with other people—like colleagues who need to review your numbers—some caution is in order.

In this chapter, you'll consider two tools that can help you build bulletproof spreadsheets: *data validation* and *worksheet protection*. Data validation catches incorrect values. Worksheet protection locks down your worksheets so they accept only certain types of changes in certain areas. Using these features, you can make your workbooks impervious to error (and deliberate fudging).

Understanding Excel's Safeguards

Excel's data validation and worksheet protection give you a number of ways to keep your workbook on the right side of the law. Using them, you can:

- Prevent people from changing a worksheet's structure (inserting or deleting cells, columns, or rows).
- Prevent people from changing a worksheet's formatting (including the number format and other formatting details, like column width and cell color).
- Prevent people from editing certain cells.
- Prevent people from entering data in a cell unless it meets certain criteria.

- Provide additional information about a cell in a pop-up tip box.
- Prevent people from editing—or even seeing—the spreadsheet's formulas.
- Prevent people from moving to cells they don't need to edit or inspect.

You may have different reasons to apply these restrictions. Often, you'll use them to make sure people don't tamper with data. For example, you might have a workbook with a carefully compiled list of sales totals, expenses, and profit calculations. You want to let others update the expense information, but they shouldn't be able to fudge the sales records. Or maybe you want to lock down *all* the data, and let others play only with the summary tables and charts. In both these situations, worksheet protection can prevent unauthorized changes, so that the data in your spreadsheet is just as reliable after it passes a round of revisions as it was when it first left your hands.

In other cases, you might use data validation and worksheet protection to prevent errors, particularly if you share your work with a less-experienced Excel patron. For example, imagine you need to give a copy of your timesheet workbook to all the employees on your team. At the end of every month, they fill out their own copies and pass the finished workbooks on to a manager. Unfortunately, an ordinary workbook is a small minefield for someone who's new to Excel. An Excel novice can accidentally delete or overwrite a formula just by pressing the wrong key, and it's almost as easy to put the wrong information in a cell (for example, by entering a date incorrectly so that Excel interprets it as text). With data validation, you can lock out certain types of errors and guide the people using your workbook to make sure they fill in the right information.

TIP Worksheet protection and data validation also make great additions to Excel templates (Chapter 16). Using these features, you can make sure the people who use your templates put the right information in the right places.

Data validation and worksheet protection are two of Excel's most powerful yet underused features. Once you master them, you'll be able to safeguard your spreadsheets before you share them.

Data Validation

With data validation, you can easily prevent people from entering the wrong data in a cell (or at least warn them when they do). Data validation also helps make Excel a little kinder and gentler for novices by letting you create custom error messages, and add helpful pop-up tips. You need a little time to set up data validation, so usually you'll use it only on your worksheet's most important cells (Figure 21-1).

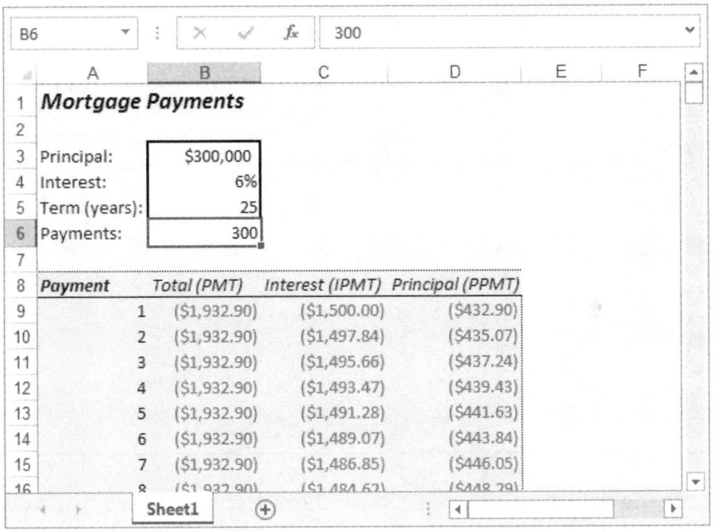

FIGURE 21-1

In this worksheet, which calculates mortgage payments, it makes sense to use data validation on the cells you expect people to change—like the loan amount (cell B3) and the interest rate (cell B4). You can then use worksheet protection, as discussed later in this chapter, to prevent someone from modifying other cells altogether.

To apply data validation, move to the appropriate cell, and then choose Data→Data Tools→Data Validation. A Data Validation window appears with three tabs: Settings, Input Message, and Error Alert. You fill in the settings in these three tabs, and then click OK to put the rule into action. The following sections explain each tab of the Data Validation window.

TIP You can apply validation to a number of cells at once. Just select all the cells before you choose Data→Data Tools→Data Validation.

Settings

Use the Settings tab of the Data Validation window (shown in Figure 21-2) to specify what values you want to allow in a cell. You have two methods at your disposal. First, in the Allow list box, you can set the *type* of value that's allowed. The simplest types include whole numbers, decimal values, dates, times, and text. (Two other types of values—custom and lists—are covered later in the chapter.) For example, if you select "Whole number" from the Allow box, and then try to input a value of 4.3 into the cell, Excel shows an error message and prevents your input.

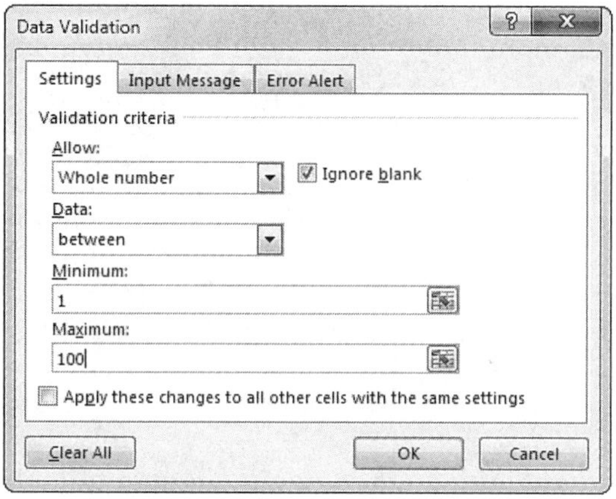

FIGURE 21-2

The options selected here force the person using the workbook to enter a whole number from 1 to 100 (or leave the cell blank). In addition, the "Ignore blank" checkbox in the top-right corner is turned on. This tells Excel to allow empty values, so that it doesn't try to validate the cell if it doesn't contain any data.

Once you choose the data type, you need to set the data *range*. Do so by choosing a comparison from the Data list box, and then specifying the values that you want to use for your comparison. For example, to restrict input to a whole number from 0 to 5, choose "between" and set a minimum value of 0 and a maximum value of 5. Other comparisons you can use include less than, greater than, greater than or equal to, and so on. You set the data range for all data types, including dates, times, and text (in which case you set limits on how many characters can go in the text).

TIP A cell can only have a single validation rule applied to it. However, you can get clever and use a formula to apply an essentially unlimited number of conditions as part of one rule, as you'll see on page 648.

It's easy to remove your validation rule later on. Just select the appropriate cell or cells, choose Data→Data Tools→Data Validation, and then click Clear All.

NOTE Excel begins validating data only *after* you apply a validation rule to a cell. If you apply a rule to a cell that already contains invalid information, Excel doesn't complain.

TIMESAVING TIP

Changing the Validation in Many Cells at Once

If you have several cells that have the same validation settings, you can change them all at once. For example, imagine you have several cells in an expense report that allow prices from $0 to $100. In a fit of generosity, you decide to raise the expense limit from $0 to $200. To do this, select all the price cells, choose Data→Data Tools→Data Validation, and make your changes. (This trick doesn't work if the cells have different validation settings. In such a case, Excel warns you that it will need to erase the current validation settings in the selected cells if you continue to insist on modifying them all at once.)

This feature is handy, but Excel has an even niftier way to make sweeping validation changes. If you have several cells with the same validation settings and you want to change every single one of them, you can get Excel to select the cells automatically. To do this, click one of the cells, choose Data→Data Tools→Data Validation, and then switch on the checkbox that says "Apply these changes to all the other cells with the same settings." If you look at your worksheet now, you'll see that Excel has automatically found and selected every cell with the same validation settings. All you need to do is make your changes, and then click OK to perform a mass update.

Input Message

Once you add data type rules, it's a nice touch to give the person using your workbook (or template) fair warning. You can do so by adding a pop-up message that appears as soon as somebody moves to the corresponding cell.

TIP Use the Settings tab to prevent bad values. Use the Input Message tab to add some helpful information. Sometimes, you'll want to use just one of these two tabs, and other times you'll need them both. The Input Message tab really shines when you share a workbook that someone's likely to copy and reuse in the future, or when you build a template. And it's particularly handy for giving Excel newbies some guidance.

An input message has two components: a title (displayed in bold) and a more detailed message. You enter both of these pieces of information in the Input Message tab of the Data Validation window (Figure 21-3)—just fill in the Title and "Input message" boxes. (While you're there, make sure you have the "Show Input message when cell is selected" checkbox turned on. Otherwise, Excel doesn't show your message at all.)

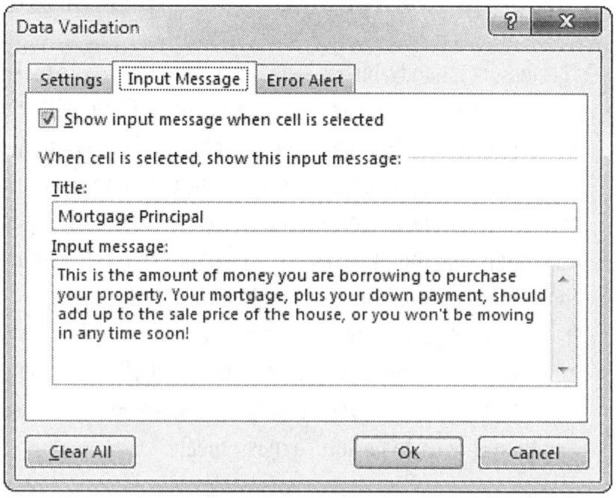

FIGURE 21-3

Here's how you create a helpful and descriptive message to tell whoever's using your workbook what the term "mortgage principal" really means. When you develop an input message, you choose a title for the pop-up box (the title appears in bold) and a descriptive message. Figure 21-4 shows the message in action.

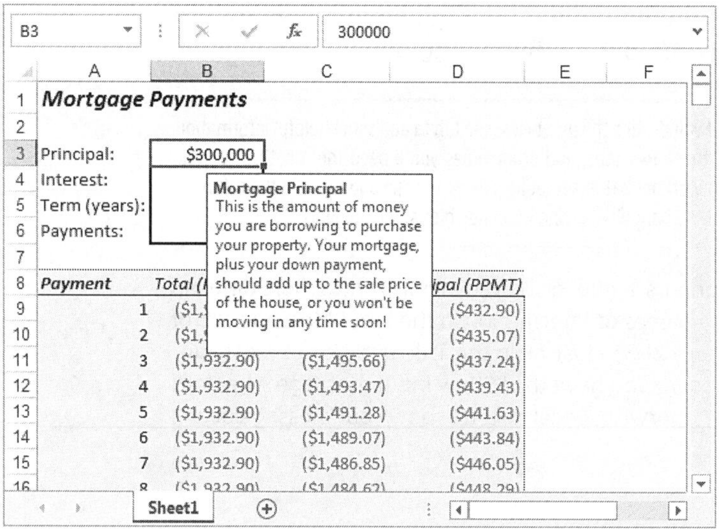

FIGURE 21-4

When a person using your workbook moves to a cell that has an input message, a yellow tip box appears displaying the message. Anyone using the spreadsheet can drag the box to another location on the worksheet if it's obscuring some important information.

Input messages should contain more than a description of your data validation settings. Ideally, your input message *explains* a little bit about the data that the cell is looking for. For example, you may decide to describe the type and format of the information that the cell accepts, and the restrictions you placed on the cell.

For example, for an invoice date cell, you might want a message that says, "This is the date your invoice was submitted to your manager. When you enter a date, use the format day-month-year (as in 29-1-2013 for January 29, 2013), and make sure you don't enter a date earlier than 1-1-2013." For a payment code, you might include a message like "This is the code from the top-right corner of your pay stub. All pay codes start with the letters AZ."

Error Alert

Despite your best attempts, someone, somewhere will probably still type the wrong information in a cell, defying your input messages. In this case, you need to respond by politely explaining the problem. Unfortunately, Excel's standard error message—displayed when someone breaks the data validation rules set down in the Settings tab—leaves a lot to be desired. It's unnecessarily harsh and confusingly vague. Go for a better approach, using the Error Alert tab to define your own error message.

To do so, head to the Error Alert tab in the Data Validation window (Figure 21-5). Begin by turning on the "Show error alert after invalid data is entered" checkbox. This tells Excel to monitor the cell for invalid information. If anyone enters the wrong data, a window appears with an error message. The buttons that Excel uses in that window depend on the style of error message you choose.

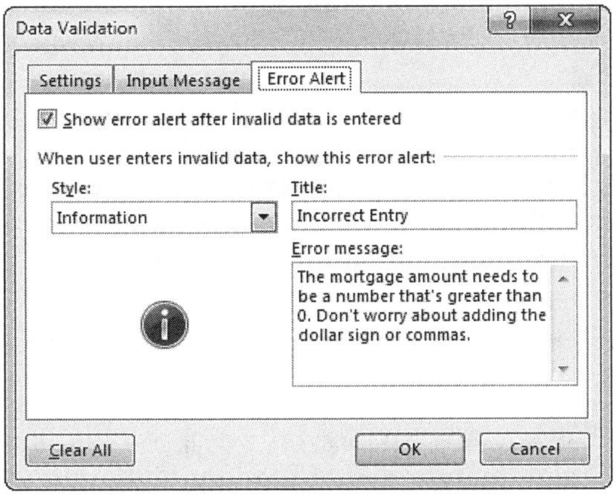

FIGURE 21-5

Helpful error messages, like this one, tell anyone using the spreadsheet what they need to do to fix their mistakes.

To choose an error message style, select an option from the Style list. Excel novices will appreciate it if you use the friendly Information icon, as shown in Figure 21-6, instead of the red X alert icon. But keep in mind that different icons have different effects on whether Excel tolerates invalid input. Here are your choices:

- **Stop.** Excel displays the error message along with a Retry and Cancel button. The person using the workbook must click Cancel to reverse the change (which returns the cell to its last value) or Retry to put the cell back into edit mode and try to fix the problem. The Stop option is the only style choice that completely prevents the person using the workbook from entering invalid data.

- **Warning.** In this case, the error message includes Yes and No buttons that let the person entering the data decide whether to go ahead with their input. Clicking Yes makes Excel accept the data entered into the cell, even if it breaks the validation rules.
- **Information.** This error message comes with Cancel and OK buttons. Clicking OK enters the new (invalid) data in the cell; Cancel leaves the cell unchanged.

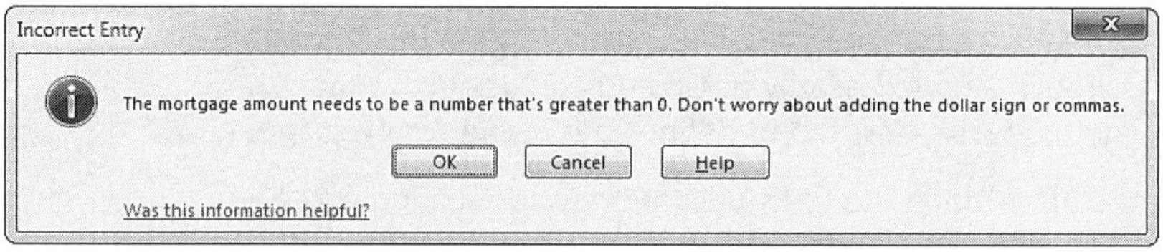

FIGURE 21-6

Because this example uses the Information style, the error message box shows a friendly icon—an "i" inside a circle.

After you set the icon, specify a title and then type a descriptive error message. Remember, you won't know exactly what went wrong, so it's best to reiterate the data type rules you applied, or use a phrase that begins with something like "You probably..." to identify a common problem.

NOTE If you set a data validation rule but turn off the "Show error alert after invalid data is entered" checkbox, the person entering the data won't see any error messages and won't have any idea if she's entered the wrong type of information. You'd switch off the "Show error alert after invalid data is entered" checkbox only if you ever want to temporarily turn off your validation rules but not remove them, so you can apply them again later.

GEM IN THE ROUGH

Quickly Spotting Every Error

Auditing circles are an often-overlooked Excel troubleshooting tool. When you choose the Data→Data Tools→Data Validation→Circle Invalid Data command, Excel draws a red circle around every cell that breaks a validation rule on the entire worksheet (Figure 21-7). You can click Data→Data Tools→Data Validation→Clear Validation Circles to remove the validation circles.

You don't need the auditing circles when you use strict data type validation (in other words, when you reject *all* errors with the Alert message type), because you never end up with invalid data. However, it comes in very handy when you use the warning or Information message type, because these settings still allow invalid values. For example, imagine a scenario where you want to let one person fill out a workbook, but have another person review it afterwards. In this scenario, the auditing circles can help the second person quickly find mistakes.

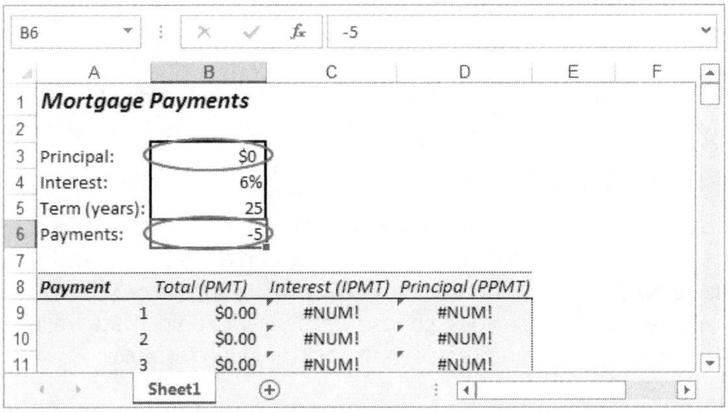

FIGURE 21-7

Validation circles, which Excel automatically displays when you use the Data→Data Tools→Data Validation→Circle Invalid Data command, help you spot troublemaking cells.

Data Validation with Formulas and Cell References

You can create more advanced cell restrictions by using formulas and cell references. Imagine you want people to enter the current date in a form. You want to make sure that the date is no *earlier* than the current date. In this scenario, you can't use a literal date in your data validation rule, because the date limit needs to change each day.

The TODAY() function can help you out. To use it select Data→Data Tools→Data Validation. In the Settings tab, select the Date data type, and require values greater than or equal to *=TODAY()*. In other words, when someone types information into that cell, Excel runs the TODAY() function and compares the result against the cell value. This is one example of how you can embed a function within a data validation rule.

You could also use a formula that contains a cell reference. You might want to make sure that an expense cell always contains a value that's equal to or less than a corresponding budget cell. In this case, you can't put the budget limit directly into the data validation rule, because you don't know what the budget will be until the person using the workbook fills it in. You need to create a data validation rule that uses a formula that references the value of the budget cell. You could specify that the value in the expense cell must be less than or equal to the formula *=C3*, assuming the budget value's in cell C3.

For an even more powerful approach, from the Allow list box, choose the Custom data type. When you use Custom, you must supply a *conditional* formula in the formula box. A conditional formula is simply one that responds with a value of either *true* or *false*. (Chapter 13 tells you all about creating conditional functions.) If the result is true, Excel allows the cell entry. If it's false, Excel displays your custom error window (assuming you turned on the "Show error alert after invalid data is entered" checkbox in the Error Alert tab). The neat thing about conditional formulas is that you can combine as many unrelated conditions as you need, using the conditional functions AND() and OR().

Conditional validation rules are also useful if you need to compare the current cell against the value returned by a function. The following fairly intimidating-looking formula prevents a person using your workbook from entering a date that falls on a weekend. B3 is the cell containing the validation rule, and the WEEKDAY() functions verify that B3 doesn't represent a Saturday (a value of 7) or a Sunday (a value of 1). By using the AND() function, this formula forces B3 to adhere to both restrictions:

```
=AND(WEEKDAY(B3)<>1, WEEKDAY(B3)<>7)
```

You might also use a conditional formula in a data validation rule when you need to make sure that the total of a group of cells doesn't exceed a total you specify. If you don't want the series of expense items in cells B2 to B7 to total more than $5,000, for example, you select all these cells, choose Data→Data Tools→Data Validation, choose the Custom data type, and then supply the following formula:

```
=(SUM($B$2:$B$7)<=5000)
```

Figure 21-8 shows an example that introduces an improvement on this formula. Instead of using an exact budget limit in the data validation rule, the rule retrieves the budget limit from a referenced cell (B10 in this example).

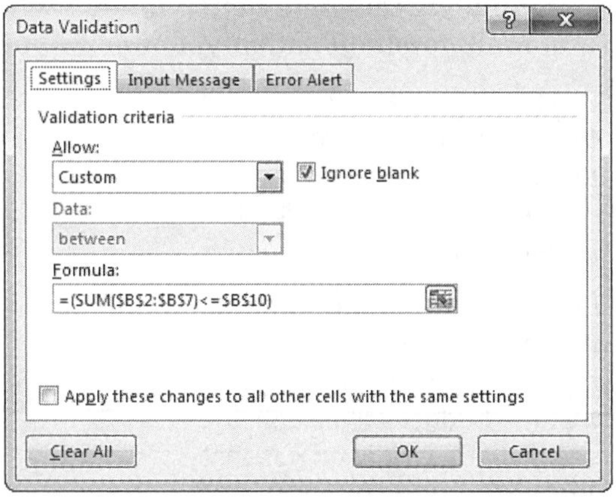

FIGURE 21-8

Here, a custom data validation rule polices the total value of a group of cells. Figure 21-9 shows the result.

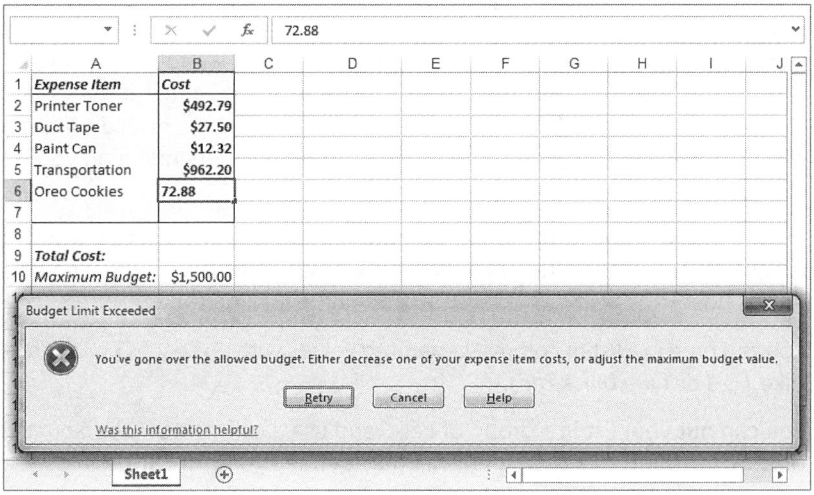

FIGURE 21-9

If the value of cells B2 through B6 is greater than the Maximum Budget cell value (B10), the rule rejects the entry. Of course, you can combine this example with the techniques shown later in this chapter to lock the Maximum Budget cell, preventing other people from changing how much they're allowed to spend.

NOTE You may notice that the SUM() formula uses absolute cell references (for example, $B$2) rather than ordinary references (like B2). You can apply the exact same SUM() formula to multiple cells at once. If you don't take this step, Excel modifies the cell references in each subsequent cell, which isn't what you want. See page 251 for a refresher on the difference between absolute and ordinary cell references.

You may also use the Custom data type to write a conditional formula that prevents duplicates in a range of cells. For example, the formula below checks to see that there's no other instance of the value in cell B3 in the range of cells from B2 to B7. This validation rule goes into cell B3:

```
=COUNTIF(B2:B7,B3)<=1
```

This formula isn't quite as convenient as the summing formula because the SUM() formula applies to all the cells in a range. The COUNTIF() formula needs to be tweaked for each cell. The formula shown above is what you'd use to validate the contents of cell B3, but in order to perform the same check for duplicates in the other cells in the specified range (B2:B7), you need to modify the formula (replacing the cell reference B3 with whatever cell you wanted to check).

Data Validation with Lists

The only other data type choice you have (when filling out the Allow field in the Settings tab) is the List option. The List choice is interesting because it doesn't just restrict invalid values, it also lets you add a handy drop-down list box that appears when anyone using your spreadsheet moves into that cell. The person who's entering data can use the list to quickly insert an allowed value, without needing to type it in. You can also type values in by hand, but Excel assumes that if the value you enter doesn't match one of the entries in the list, your entry's invalid (and it may show an error message or prevent your entry altogether, depending on your Error Alert settings).

To create this list, choose the Data Validation window's Settings tab, and then choose List from the Allow text box. You have three choices for supplying a list in the Source box:

- You can type in a list of comma-separated values with no spaces between them (like *1,2,3* or *blue,black,red*).
- You can put your list in a group of cells, and use a cell range in the Source box (like *=C1:C10*). In this case, the cells that define the list must be in the same worksheet as the cell (or cells) that uses theme for validation.
- You can put your list in a group of cells, give those cells a name (page 384), and then type that name into the Source box (like *=ProductNames*). This approach is especially convenient, because it allows you to place the list on a different worksheet.

If you want the person using the list to be able to choose the entry from a drop-down list in the cell (which is a slick and convenient touch), make sure you keep the "In-cell dropdown" checkbox turned on.

TIP For easy list management, put your list in an official Excel table (Chapter 14). Then, when you add or remove items, Excel automatically adjusts the list of choices to match. And if you don't want the list to appear on the worksheet, you can hide the rows it occupies (page 197) or put the list on a separate sheet and hide the entire worksheet (page 111).

Figure 21-10 shows an example that modifies the lookup worksheet used in Chapter 12. You can create an invoice by choosing products from the drop-down list.

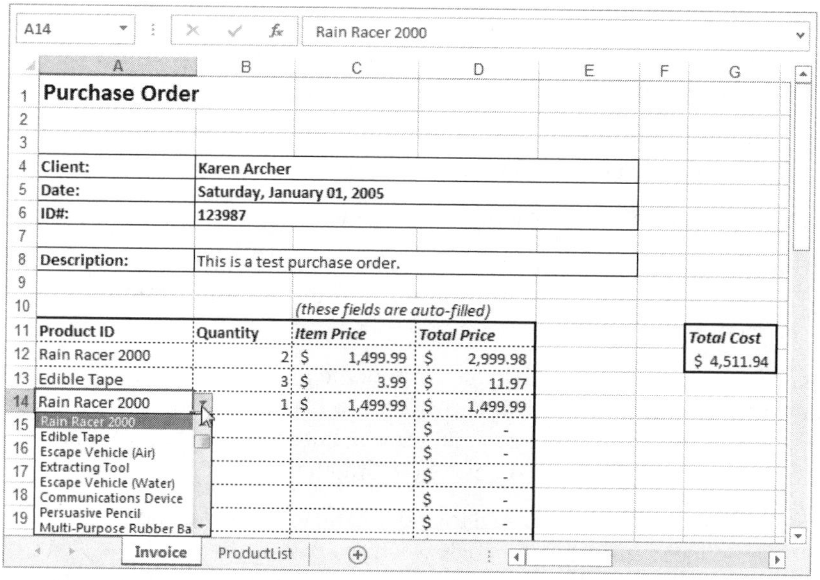

FIGURE 21-10

This worksheet uses list validation. The advantage of this approach is that people using the spreadsheet don't need to remember the name or ID of each product. Instead, there's always a complete list of choices available at their fingertips. Here, the entire product catalog is on a separate worksheet. Figure 21-11 shows the data validation settings that make it work.

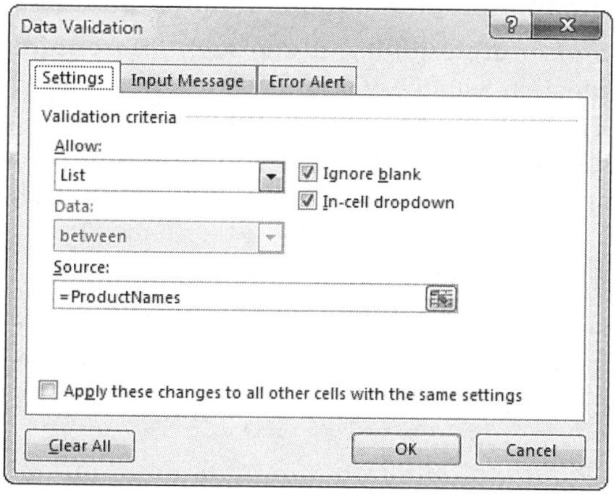

FIGURE 21-11

The list validation settings in this window tell Excel to generate a list of product choices. Excel draws the list from the range of cells named ProductNames, as indicated in the Source box. See Figure 21-10 for what this looks like on the spreadsheet.

Locked and Hidden Cells

Excel's data validation tools help make sure funky data doesn't end up in your worksheet. But they don't protect your worksheets against things like accidentally deleted formulas, mistakenly scrambled formatting, and "unintentionally" modified Maximum Deficit Spending values. To defend against these dangers, you need to use Excel's *worksheet protection* features.

To understand how worksheet protection works, you need to know that each cell can have one of two special settings:

- **Locked.** When a cell is locked, you can't edit it.
- **Hidden.** When a cell is hidden, its contents don't appear in the formula bar. The cell still appears in the worksheet, but if the cell uses a formula, you can't see the formula.

You can use these settings individually or together. When a cell is both locked and hidden, you can't edit it *or* view it in the formula bar. On the other hand, if a cell is hidden but not locked, people can edit the cell but can never tell whether the cell uses a formula, because Excel keeps that information secret.

The most important thing you need to understand about locked and hidden cells is that these settings come into effect only when you *protect* the worksheet. If you don't protect it (and every worksheet begins its life without protection), Excel doesn't use these settings at all. In other words, you need to take two steps to build a bulletproof worksheet. First, you need to specify which cells you want locked and hidden, and then you finish up by protecting the entire sheet so your settings take effect.

Interestingly, every cell in your worksheet starts off in an unhidden and locked state. If you switch on worksheet protection without making any changes, your whole worksheet becomes read-only. Excel uses this approach for a reason. Typically, you'll use worksheet protection to make sure the person using your workbook can edit only a few select cells. It's much easier to designate the few cells that are editable than it is to try to select every single cell that needs to be locked. (Remember, every Excel worksheet boasts millions of cells, most of which are empty.)

NOTE Once you protect a worksheet, you can't change the protection settings of any cells. Of course, you can unprotect a worksheet, as explained below, and *then* change the cells' protection settings.

Protecting a Worksheet

Here are the steps you need to follow to protect your worksheet:

1. **First, *unlock* all the cells into which you want people to type information.**

   You can do this one cell at a time, or you can select an entire range of cells. Once you make your selection, right-click it, and then choose Format Cells. The Format Cells window appears.

2. **Click the Protection tab. Then, turn off the Locked checkbox, and then click OK.**

   Next, you need to hide formulas that you don't want the person using the workbook to see.

TIP You can lock or unlock cells without going to the Format Cells window. Just select the cells, and then choose Home→Cells→Format→Lock.

3. **Select the cell or cells with the formulas you want to hide, right-click the selection, and then choose Format Cells again. This time, click the Protection tab, turn on the Hidden checkbox, and then click OK.**

   If you want, you can change both the Hidden and Locked settings for a cell or group of cells at the same time. Once you finish unlocking and hiding to your heart's content, it's time to protect the sheet.

4. **Select Review→Changes→Protect Sheet (or just right-click the worksheet tab and choose Protect Sheet).**

   The Protect Sheet window appears.

5. **Make sure the checkbox labeled "Protect worksheet and contents of locked cells" is checked.**

   In addition to protecting the contents of unlocked cells, the Protect Sheet window lets you toggle on or off a list of Excel actions that you want to let people using your worksheet perform, as described in the next step.

6. **From the "Allow all users of this worksheet to" list, turn on the things you want people to be able to do.**

   Excel's standard approach is to restrict everything except cell selection (the first two options). Here's a setting-by-setting breakdown of your choices:

   - **Select locked cells.** Turn off this checkbox if you want to prevent people from moving to locked cells.

NOTE Keep in mind that if you can't select a locked cell, there's also no way to copy and paste the information in the cell to another worksheet or program. If you want the people using your workbook to be able to do this, you should keep the "Select locked cells" setting switched on.

   - **Select unlocked cells.** Turn off this checkbox if you want to prevent people from moving to unlocked cells. You won't use this setting very often, but you might use it in conjunction with the "Select locked cells" setting to lock someone out of the worksheet entirely.

- **Format cells, Format columns, and Format rows.** Turn on these checkboxes if people need to be able to format individual cells or entire columns and rows. If you allow row and column formatting, Excel also permits people to hide rows and columns. However, Excel never lets anyone change the locked and hidden settings of a cell while it's protected.
- **Insert columns and Insert rows.** Turn on these checkboxes if you want to let people insert new rows or columns.
- **Insert hyperlinks.** Turn on this checkbox if you want to let people insert hyperlinks in unlocked cells. This setting can be dangerous because a hyperlink can point to anything from another worksheet to a malicious web page. See page 80 for more information about hyperlinks.
- **Delete columns and Delete rows.** Turn on these checkboxes to bestow the ability to remove columns or rows. Use this setting at your peril, because it lets people decimate your worksheet—for example, removing entire ranges of data even if they contain locked cells.
- **Sort.** Turn on this checkbox to let people sort unlocked cells, while keeping locked cells impervious to sorting.
- **Use AutoFilter.** Turn on this checkbox to let people use filtering on any tables in the worksheet. See Chapter 14 for more about tables.
- **Use PivotTable reports.** Turn on this checkbox to let people manipulate any pivot tables in your worksheet. See Chapter 26 for more on pivot tables.
- **Edit objects.** Turn on this checkbox to let people edit or delete embedded objects in the worksheet. These objects can include data from other programs or, more commonly, pictures (Chapter 19), charts (Chapter 17), or slicers (page 434).
- **Edit scenarios.** Turn on this checkbox to let people edit or delete what-if scenarios. See Chapter 25 for more information on scenarios.

7. **If you want to stop other people from unprotecting the worksheet, specify a password in the "Password to unprotect sheet" text box (see Figure 21-12).**

   Once you protect a worksheet, anyone can unprotect it. All a person needs to do is select Review→Changes→Unprotect Sheet. This behavior makes sense if you're just using protection to prevent people from making casual mistakes. But if you're worried about deliberate tampering, or if you want to create a truly invulnerable worksheet, it's a good idea to set a password. If you do, no one can unprotect the sheet without supplying the password.

NOTE Worksheet protection isn't designed to protect your work from data theft and malicious tampering. In fact, there are well-known exploits that let hackers quickly break worksheet protection, no matter what password you use. Instead, worksheet protection is designed to stop ordinary people from changing something they shouldn't. If you need a higher grade of security, consider password-protecting your entire workbook, which automatically triggers Excel to encrypt all the workbook's data, as described on page 36.

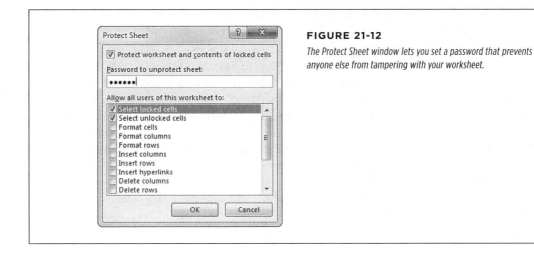

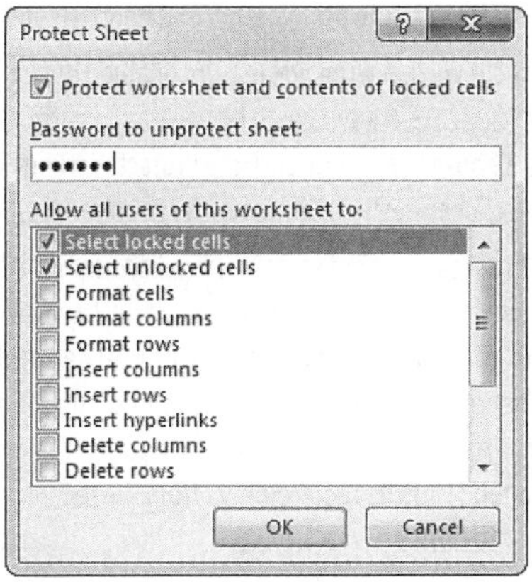

FIGURE 21-12

The Protect Sheet window lets you set a password that prevents anyone else from tampering with your worksheet.

8. **Click OK.**

   The protected worksheet doesn't look any different, but if you try to edit a locked cell, you get an error message explaining that the cell's locked (and explaining that you can unlock the worksheet by selecting Review→Changes→Unprotect Sheet).

TIP Protected worksheets have a nice feature: You can quickly find all the unlocked cells. Just press the Tab key to move from one unlocked cell to the next. When you reach the last unlocked cell, Excel automatically jumps back to the first unlocked cell. If you want to make it even easier to navigate a dense worksheet, consider turning off the "Select locked cells" setting in the Protect Sheet window.

POWER USERS' CLINIC

Exerting Even More Control with IRM

Worksheet protection isn't the only way you can lock down a spreadsheet. Microsoft Office has another technology for controlling what people can do. It's called Information Rights Management (IRM).

IRM is a powerful feature that can exert Big Brother-like control over your spreadsheets. For one thing, it can prevent people from copying data to the Clipboard or printing a workbook. It can also automatically "expire" your workbook, so that it no one else can access it after a date you choose. Most importantly, IRM is user-specific, which means you can give different permissions to different people. When you open an IRM-protected workbook, you need to supply your email address and password. Excel then communicates with the IRM server to find out what you're allowed to do with the document. If you aren't in the list of authorized people, you're out of luck.

To see if you have the IRM feature enabled on your installation of Office 2013, try switching IRM on for the current spreadsheet file. Choose File→Info, click the Protect Workbook button, and then choose Restrict Permission by People→Restricted Access.

IRM makes most sense as a specialized tool for big business. To run IRM on your own, you need to have some seriously high-end software, including SharePoint and Windows Rights Management Server, or you need to sign up for one of Microsoft's pricier Office 365 subscription plans. You can learn more about IRM and its requirements from the technical whitepaper at *http://tinyurl.com/irm2013.*

Protecting an Entire Workbook

You can use one more level of protection: Excel gives you the power to protect an entire workbook. When a workbook's protected, Excel prevents people from inserting, moving, or removing worksheets (tasks covered in Chapter 4).

Workbook protection works hand-in-hand with worksheet protection. If you use workbook protection but not worksheet protection, people can still edit all the cells in your worksheets. However, they can't delete the worksheets or add new ones. On the other hand, if you use workbook protection *and* worksheet protection, people can't tamper with your data or the structure of your workbook.

To turn on workbook protection, select Review→Changes→Protect Workbook. The awkwardly named Protect Structure and Windows window appears, as shown in Figure 21-13.

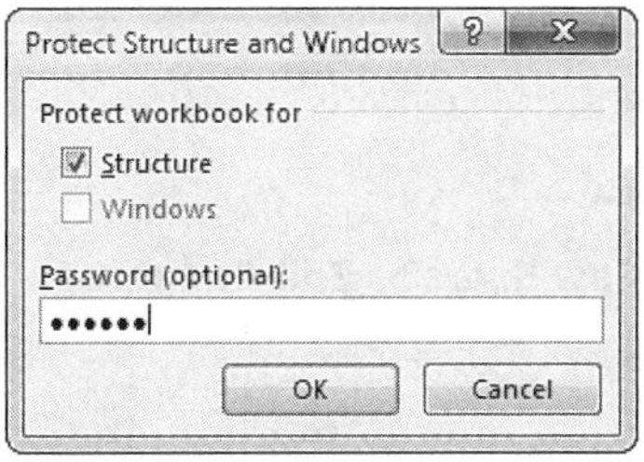

FIGURE 21-13

The Protect Structure and Windows window looks a little like the Protect Worksheet window, but provides fewer options. You still have the chance to lock out miscreants by using passwords, however.

The Protect Structure and Windows window provides two checkboxes:

- **Structure.** When you turn this option on, the people using your workbook can't insert or delete worksheets. They also can't rename an existing worksheet, hide it, or move it from one place to another.
- **Windows.** When you turn this option on, Excel doesn't let anyone change the size or position of your workbook window inside the main Excel window. (Usually, this setting has no effect because the workbook window's *maximized*, which means it's given the largest size that fits in the Excel main window.) In addition, you can't use or change other fancy viewing settings, like frozen columns and split windows (both of which are described in Chapter 7).

NOTE In rare cases, you might use the Windows protection setting to make sure that your workbook viewers don't change specialized view settings you created. However, most of the time it's not worth the trouble, because different people using different computers (with different monitors, different display resolutions, and different eyeglass prescriptions) may have good reasons to want to adjust these settings.

You can also supply a password to prevent people from unprotecting your workbook. You can use the same password that you used to protect a worksheet, or you can choose a new password.

Once you finish, click OK to apply your protection settings. You can remove workbook protection by once again choosing Review→Changes→Protect Workbook, although if you used a password, you'll need to have it handy.

Protecting Cell Ranges (with More Passwords)

As you've already seen, you can use passwords to lock individual worksheets or an entire workbook. For most Excel workers, this is as far as they want to go. But if you're hungering for more protection settings, you do have another option. You can lock up individual cell *ranges*. The ranges you protect can be anything from a single cell to a larger group that encompasses entire rows and columns.

NOTE The ability to protect individual cell ranges sounds great. However, it's often more trouble than it's worth. After all, do you want to manage a workbook with dozens of password-protected areas, each with different passwords? If you can, save yourself some aggravation by separating the data you need to protect and placing it in a dedicated worksheet.

Here's how to add protection to a range of cells:

1. **Select the cells you want to protect.**
2. **Choose Review→Changes→Allow Users to Edit Ranges.**

   The Allow Users to Edit Ranges window appears.
3. **Click New to create your first range.**

   The New Range window appears (Figure 21-14).

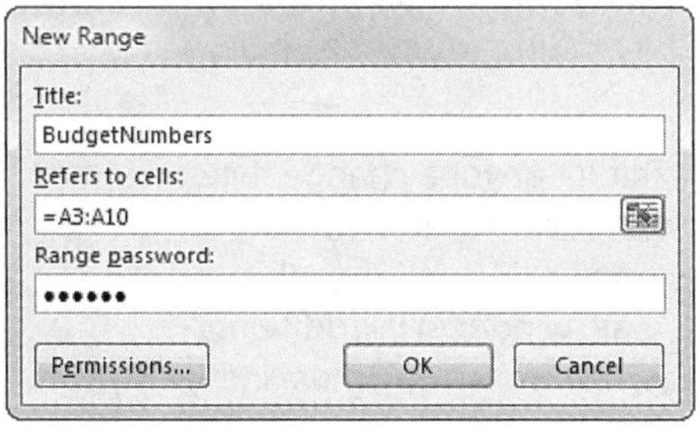

FIGURE 21-14

The New Range window lets you supply three key pieces of information for your range—a title, the cell references, and a password.

4. **Fill in a title and password for your range.**

   You don't need to explicitly set the "Refers to cells" box because Excel automatically fills it in with the cells you selected in step 1. You just have to supply a descriptive title (like "BudgetNumbers") and a matching password that unlocks the range for editing.
5. **Click OK.**

   Excel adds your range to the list in the Allow Users to Edit Ranges window (Figure 21-15).

   You can click New again to create more protected ranges, or click OK to close the Allow Users to Edit Ranges window.

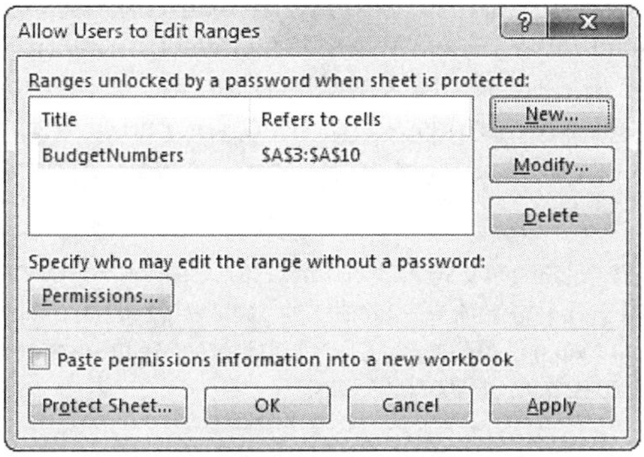

FIGURE 21-15

The workbook associated with this window has a single protected range. Using this box, you can modify a range (click Modify), or remove it (click Delete). You can also add Windows permission settings (discussed in the next section).

6. **Choose Review→Changes→Protect Sheet, enter a master password (that only you know), and then click OK.**

   Remember, your ranges don't become password-protected until you turn on protection for the worksheet.

   Now, if people need to edit certain sections of your worksheet, you can give them the appropriate range password. However, you won't share the password that turns off worksheet protection with anyone. That's for your use only.

Figure 21-16 shows what happens when you start typing in a protected range.

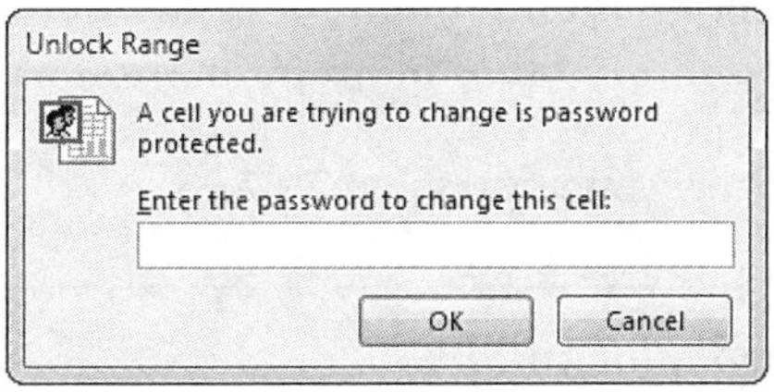

FIGURE 21-16

A nice feature of protected cell ranges is that the person using the workbook doesn't need to explicitly turn off the protection. Instead, when someone starts typing in one of the cells in the protected range, Excel pops up a window asking for the password, as shown here. Fill it in, and you're ready to go.

Allowing Specific Windows Users to Edit a Range

When protecting cell ranges, there's one more wrinkle. As with worksheet and workbook protection, you can restrict access using a password, which the person using your workbook must supply before changing one of the protected cells. Alternatively, you can allow people to edit cells in the range based on their Windows *user account*. (User accounts are the login system Windows uses to let multiple people share a single computer.)

This option is a bit trickier—for it to work right, the person using your workbook needs to log on to the same computer you use, or to the same network server. In other words, this technique works for a small team of people working on a company network, but it's no good for more independent Excel fans.

Keep one other point in mind: The user account permissions bypass the cell range password. In other words, you follow the same process described in the previous section to lock up a range of cells using a specific password. Then, you can give some special people the ability to edit that cell range straight away—no password required.

NOTE If you never intend to actually use the cell range password, you can keep it a secret. However, the password's a good fallback if people need to edit your workbook when they aren't connected to the company network (for example, if someone takes it home on a laptop). At that point, Excel can't recognize the user, so the person using the spreadsheet needs the cell range password to unlock the cells.

Here's how to apply user account permissions:

1. **Choose Review→Changes→Allow Users to Edit Ranges.**

   The Allow Users to Edit Ranges window appears.

2. **Select the range you want to use.**

   If you haven't created the range yet, you can click the New button to add it now. Follow the steps in the previous section to create the range.

3. **Click Permissions.**

   A Windows permission window appears. You may have seen a window like this before if you've ever modified the permissions on your files. The permission window lists all the people allowed to access the range, and can bypass the password. At first, this list is empty.

4. **Click Add to enter your first user.**

   The Select Users or Groups window appears (Figure 21-17).

FIGURE 21-17

You can safely ignore all the buttons in this window. All you need to do to add a user is enter the user name in the "Enter the object names to select" box. In this example, you're adding the user billjones (who logs into the domain Sales).

5. **In the big text box, type in the user name.**

   Excel needs to know two things: where the user logs in (on the local computer, via a network server, or through a Windows domain), and who the user is (the user name). To identify a user correctly, you need to supply both pieces of information, separated by a backslash (\). For example, if billjones logs into the Sales domain, the full user name is *Sales\billjones*.

TIP Forgot your user name? One easy way to get your full user name is to pay attention when you log onto your computer. You'll find all the details in the Windows login box. If in doubt, talk to your friendly neighborhood network administrator.

   Instead of using a user name, you can use a group name to save time and avoid headaches. The box below explains how this works.

TIMESAVING TIP

Put Your Users in Groups

It's easy to get in over your head when giving permissions to specific users. Before you know it, a workbook that you initially planned to share with one person is being passed around an entire company, and you're spending every lunch hour feverishly editing the list of allowed users.

Skilled network administrators use *groups* to simplify this kind of task. For example, *billjones* and everyone else on his team might be assigned to the same *SalesEmployees* group. That way, you can configure your Excel workbook to allow the entire SalesEmployees group to edit your workbook, rather than doing so person by person. This approach is quicker to set up and easier to maintain. Best of all, when you add new hires to the SalesEmployees group, they automatically get access to your workbook. And if Bill goes on a bender and the company gets rid of him, the network administrator can pull him out of the SalesEmployees group. He won't have access to your workbook any longer, and you don't need to waste a second changing your protection settings.

6. **Click OK to add the user.**

   If you make a mistake—for example, type in a user who doesn't seem to exist or isn't defined on the computer or domain you picked—you'll wind up at the Name Not Found window, where you can try to correct the user name.

   If you enter a valid user or user group name, Excel adds it to the list of allowed users, as shown in Figure 21-18.

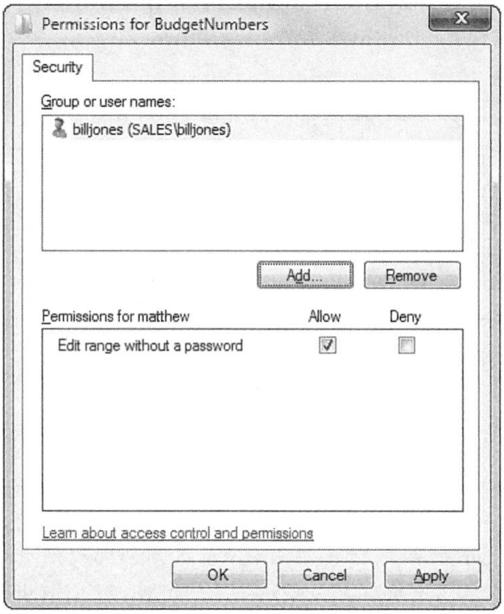

FIGURE 21-18

When you add a new user to the list, that user automatically gets a checkmark in the Allow column, which indicates that he's allowed to edit the range without a password. You can also use the Deny column to explicitly lock out users, but that approach rarely makes sense, because it introduces too many potential security holes.

7. **You can now return to step 4 to add somebody else. When you finish, click OK.**

   Excel returns you to the Allow Users to Edit Ranges window.

8. **Click OK to get back to your worksheet.**

   Remember, you need to protect your worksheet (by choosing Review→Changes→Protect Sheet) for your settings to take effect.

TIP If you want to get a full breakdown of your protected ranges, their passwords, and the people who have access to them, choose the "Paste permissions information into a new workbook" setting before you click OK in step 8. Excel creates a new workbook in a separate window, and copies this information into that workbook.

Once you protect your worksheet, it behaves a little differently. Now, the allowed users don't have any idea that they're typing in a restricted region. For example, if *billjones* starts editing one of the protected cells, Excel quietly checks the user account, sees that it matches your list, and lets him type away without any disruption. On the other hand, if an unsanctioned person tries to make a change to one of the restricted cells, Excel pops up a window asking for the password, just as it did before (as shown in Figure 21-16).

CHAPTER

22

Worksheet Collaboration

Armed with Excel, there's a lot you can do on your own to analyze data. But Excel pros aren't content to struggle in solitude. Instead, they invite their friends, colleagues, and coworkers to join in.

There are plenty of reasons to collaborate on an Excel document. For example, you may want to hand a worksheet off to a friend who can fix a wonky formula or fill in missing data. Or you might want to run your numbers through a review process so your colleagues can comment and flag potential issues. Or perhaps you're even more ambitious, and you're looking for a way that will let your whole team add data to the same spreadsheet *at the same time*. Excel's collaboration features meet all these requirements handily.

In Chapter 21, you saw the first of Excel's collaboration features, worksheet protection. Using it, you can lock down sheets so people can make changes only in specific cells. Along with worksheet protection, Excel has several other collaboration tools you'll learn about in this chapter:

- **Comments.** Excel's comments feature lets you insert questions, suggestions, or other miscellaneous notes that point to specific cells (like "This number's wrong" or "Please boost the sales estimate so we can impress the boss"). The person who created the spreadsheet can then respond to these comments by modifying the spreadsheet.
- **Change tracking.** Change tracking lets you keep track of the edits made by multiple people. You can then choose to apply or reject some or all of the changes. If multiple people make changes to different copies of the same document, you can even merge all their changes back into the original file in one step, saving countless headaches.

- **Workbook sharing.** An ordinary Excel workbook allows one person to edit it at a time. But if you turn on the radical workbook sharing feature and place your Excel file on a network, a whole crowd of people can edit it simultaneously.
- **The Inquire add-in.** The Inquire add-in enriches Excel with features for analyzing workbooks. For Excel collaborators, its most useful feature is its spreadsheet comparison tool, which pinpoints precise differences in data and formatting between different versions of a spreadsheet.

With these features, you'll be able to share your work, team up with other people, and create even greater things *together*. But before you start collaborating, it's important to answer two questions. First: If more than one person works on a spreadsheet, how does Excel know who is who? And, second: What's the easiest way to pass a workbook from one person to another? You'll start this chapter by tackling both these questions.

Your Excel Identity

Excel knows more about you than you might think. Behind the scenes, all of Microsoft's Office applications store some basic information about you, including your user name. This information is set when Office is first installed (even if someone else installed it), and it usually matches your Windows user name (so if you log on as joeZhang, your Excel user name is also joeZhang).

For one-person tasks, it doesn't matter who Excel thinks you are. But your identity becomes much more important when you collaborate with other people. For example, if you add suggestions to a worksheet regarding someone else's work, you want to make sure that anyone who reads your comments knows that *you* made them, not "Excel User 1" or "SalesComputer012."

NOTE If your computer has more than one user account, remember that every Windows user has a distinct set of personal settings. So when someone else logs onto the same computer, the Office applications use a different user name.

The best way to do that is to make sure that Excel correctly identifies you before you make comments or changes. To see the who Excel identifies as the current user, select File→Options and look in the "User name" text box at the very bottom of the Options window. You can edit the name now, and then click OK to apply your change. Spaces are perfectly acceptable, so feel free to replace "smacdo1123" with "Sue MacDonnell."

NOTE Any changes you make to the user name in Excel affect all your other Office applications, including Word, which has its own review and collaboration features. So, in the example above, all of Sue's Word documents will now identify her as the user.

Preparing Your Workbook

Before you go ahead and release your workbook into the wild, you may want to perform a few last-minute tasks (things like giving your spreadsheet a descriptive name, checking whether it's encrypted, and so on). Excel helps you out by grouping some of the most common collaborative-prep tools in its backstage view. To see them, choose File→Info (Figure 22-1).

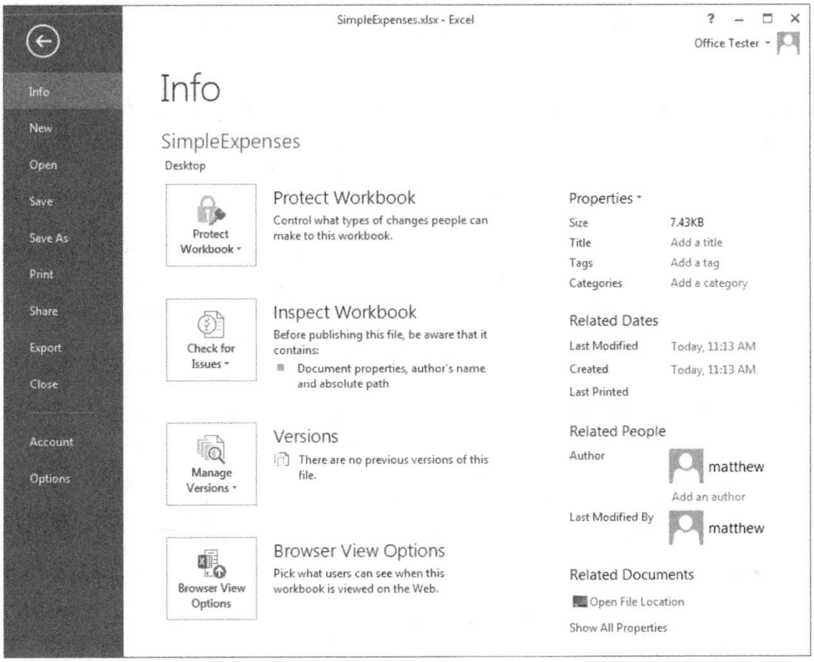

FIGURE 22-1

Before your workbook goes out the door, consider switching on document protection, scouring your spreadsheet for potential issues, and changing its properties. Excel's Info page is the springboard for all these tasks.

The following sections walk you through the most important options in the Info page, and show you to prepare your spreadsheet for a wider audience.

Workbook Protection

Excel's splits the Info page into several sections, each with a large button. The first button, named Protect Workbook, helps you prevent other people from changing things in your workbook.

When you click the Protect Workbook button, a menu pops up with a list of options. You saw some of them in previous chapters. They are:

- **Mark As Final** designates your document as "final," meaning it won't accept any more changes. Once you take this step, Excel's editing commands switch off, you can't type in any cell, and a special icon appears in the Status bar (it looks like a rubber stamp and a sheet of paper). However, it's important to understand that the Protect Workbook→Mark As Final command is really just descriptive. It tells people that you've finished with the workbook, but it doesn't prevent them from "unfinalizing" the workbook and making changes. In fact, anyone can make the spreadsheet editable simply by choosing Protect Workbook→Mark As Final again (to unselect it).

- **Encrypt With Password** lets you scramble your document so absolutely no one can open it without supplying a password. For more information, refer to the detailed steps on page 36. It's also worth noting that the Protect Workbook→ Encrypt With Password command lets you set a "password to open" but not a "password to modify" restriction. If you want to let people *view* but not change your workbook, refer to page 37.
- **Protect Current Sheet** and **Protect Workbook Structure** let you apply worksheet protection, as you learned in Chapter 21. Worksheet protection is a more selective restriction tool than encryption; it can limit edits to certain cells or permit only certain types of modifications.

TIP Encryption and protection play complementary roles, and you may need both. If you're worried about industrial spies cracking your files to steal data or create fake copies of your workbook, you need encryption. But if you want to control the kind of changes that authorized people can make, you need worksheet protection.

- **Restrict Access** lets you add advanced restrictions to your workbook using an add-in called IRM (Information Rights Management). For example, IRM can prevent people from copying worksheet data to the Clipboard or make a workbook inaccessible after a certain date. However, IRM is also more complex to set up, and it depends on SharePoint or Microsoft's web servers to perform authentication. Page 656 has more.
- **Add a Digital Signature** lets you add a special marker to your spreadsheet file that "proves" you created it. The downside's that in order for a digital signature system like this one to be meaningful, you need to set up a complex system of personal certificates and certificate *authorities* that vouch for a given certificate's validity. In other words, unless you're working in a large company (or you're ready to buy a certificate from an online certificate authority), your certificates won't be worth much. (If you *are* ready to buy a certificate, head to the website of a certificate authority like *www.verisign.com* or *www.thawte.com*.)

Checking for Issues

The large Check for Issues button, just under the Protect Workbook button on the Info page, can help you catch any lingering problems before you share your work with the world. When you click the button, you get a menu with three options:

- **Inspect Document** runs the Document Inspector, a tool that helps you track down scraps of information you may not want others to see (Figure 22-2).
- **Check Accessibility** runs the Accessibility Checker, which flags content that people with visual disabilities might find hard to read. For example, people who use screen-reading software won't get much out of pictures unless the images have descriptive text defined (known as alternate, or just alt text). Similarly, they won't find standard worksheet names (Sheet1, Sheet2, and so on) much help when navigating a workbook to find the content they need.
- **Check Compatibility** runs the Compatibility Checker—a tool that flags potential problems if you plan to share your document with people using Excel 2010 or older. Page 31 has the full story.

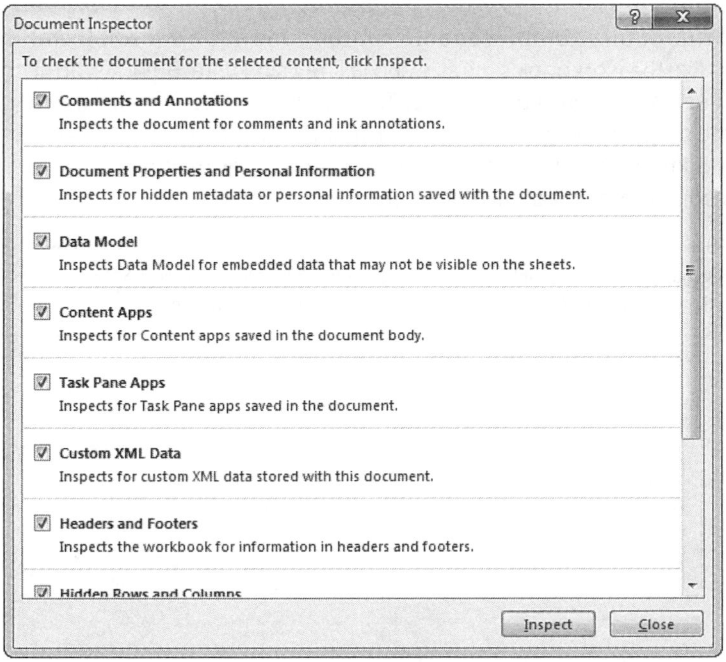

FIGURE 22-2

The Document Inspector is a tool for the truly paranoid. Turn on the checkboxes next to the type of info you want the Inspector to sniff out, and then click Inspect. If the Inspector finds the type of content specified, it lets you remove it sight unseen by clicking a Remove All button. Typically, you use the Document Inspector to create a stripped-down copy of your workbook, lacking any personal information lingering in a comment, page header, or somewhere else. But before you run the Inspector and delete any personal info, make sure you save a separate version of the workbook using a different file name—otherwise, you may lose some information you need. (Like that comment reminding yourself to ask your boss for a raise.)

UP TO SPEED

Two Buttons to Ignore (For Now)

The Info page includes two more buttons that aren't discussed in this chapter:

- **Manage Versions.** This button lets you recover old versions of a workbook after you make changes. This feature can help you recover from a catastrophic editing mistake, but it doesn't have anything to do with document-sharing. It's discussed on page 72.
- **Browser View Options.** This button lets you prepare a workbook so you or a colleague can edit it online, in the Excel Web App. The Excel Web App gives your workbooks a broader reach, but it limits what other people can do with them. You'll start sharing workbooks in the Excel Web App in Chapter 23.

Document Properties

The "Properties" section at the far right of the Info page lists key bits of information about your workbook, like its title and author.

Excel tracks some of these properties automatically, and you can't edit them. They include details like the workbook's file size and last revision date. But you can change other properties, like the workbook's title. To edit one of these details, move your mouse over the property label, which transforms into a text box, which you can click into and start editing. The only exception is the author information, which requires the two-step editing process shown in Figure 22-3.

TIP To set even more descriptive details, click the Properties heading, and then choose Show All Properties. Excel adds entries that let you fill in details like status, subject, company, and comments.

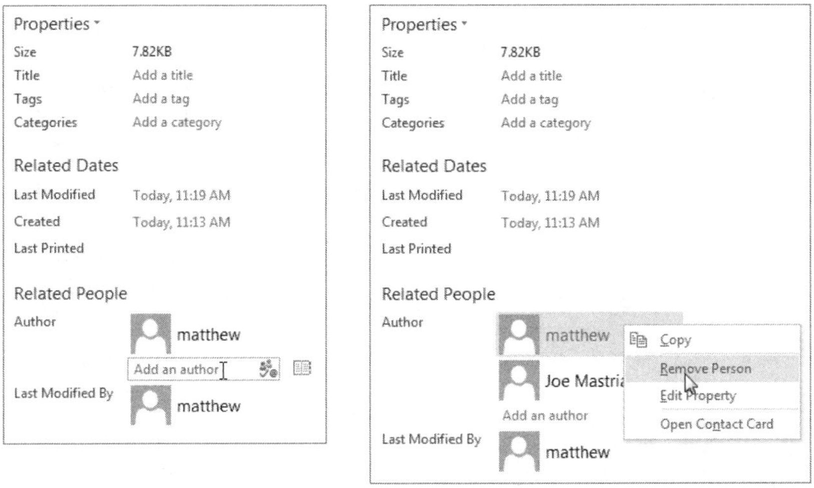

FIGURE 22-3

Left: To change the author, begin by clicking and typing in the "Add an author" text box. This adds a second author to the list.

Right: To remove the original author, right-click that name, and then choose Remove Person. Or, leave the original author if you want to list multiple people.

When you create a new workbook, Excel uses your Excel user name (page 664) to set the author name. It leaves most of the other details—like title, category, company, tags, and so on—blank. It's up to you to add this info if you want to. All of this raises an excellent question: Now that you know how to set the document properties, what do you actually do with them?

The primary role of Excel's document properties is to supply helpful information to other people who might need it. This information turns up in a few interesting places. You'll see it when you hover over a file icon or investigate file properties in Windows Explorer (Figure 22-4). You can also add it to the footers and headers you use in your printouts (page 212). Finally, searching tools (like the one built into Windows) will search the information in the document properties first. In fact, that's the whole purpose of the tags property: You add descriptive keywords, like "budget" and "2013," that someone might use to search for a file. The tags help them locate relevant files quickly.

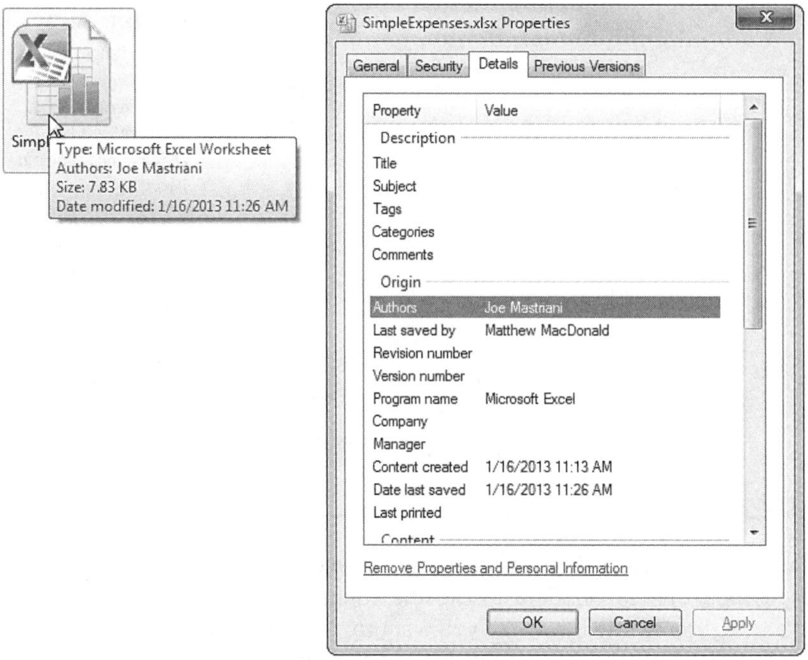

FIGURE 22-4

Left: When you hover over an Excel file on the desktop, a tooltip pops up that lists some of the document properties (assuming they're not blank).

Right: Right-click an Excel file, and then choose properties to get the familiar multi-tabbed Properties window. If you choose the Details tab, you'll see a slew of details about the file, including important dates (when it was last saved, when it was last printed, and so on), and its document properties.

If you find yourself changing document properties often, you don't need to switch to backstage view each time. Instead, you can keep the Document Properties panel open, so it sits just above your worksheet and provides text boxes for quick property editing (Figure 22-5). To show the Document Properties panel, choose File→Info to switch to backstage view, then click the Properties heading (at the far right side of the window), and then choose Show Document Panel.

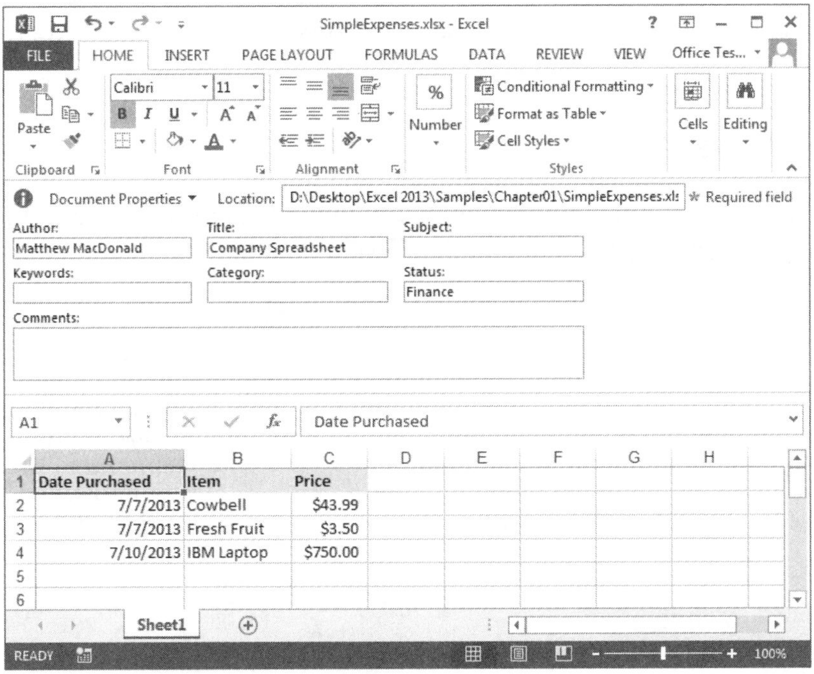

FIGURE 22-5

The Document Properties panel shows key properties of your workbook, including its title, subject, comments, and so on. To fill in this information (or change it), click the appropriate label, and then type away in the text box that appears. To quickly close the Document Properties panel, click the X at the top right. Most people find that the Document Properties panel takes up too much room, and they don't keep it around for long.

Distributing Your Workbook

Once your spreadsheet is ready to go, you have plenty of ways to share it with others. You can distribute your workbook just as you'd distribute any other type of file. Possibilities include:

- Copying it to a memory stick so you can carry it around
- Copying it to a network drive so others can access it
- Uploading it to a SharePoint server
- Uploading it to Microsoft's SkyDrive service (an online storage locker)

All these techniques work perfectly well, and you can carry out many of them from the comfort of Excel's backstage view. Choose File→Save As and pick the location you want, as laid out in Chapter 1 (page 26).

Excel has two more built-in sharing shortcuts: You can send your workbook file to someone in an automatically generated email, or you can spread the word about your work on a social networking site like Twitter, Facebook, or LinkedIn. You'll find both options on the File→Share page.

NOTE The next section describes Excel's emailing abilities. But Excel's social media sharing feature works hand-in-hand with online workbooks and the more restrictive Excel Web App. You'll consider Excel's social media skills in Chapter 23.

Sending by Email

Excel offers several ways to fire your work off in an email message. To use them, you need to have an email program (like Outlook) installed on your computer. Then, choose File→Share, and click Email in the "Share" list (Figure 22-6).

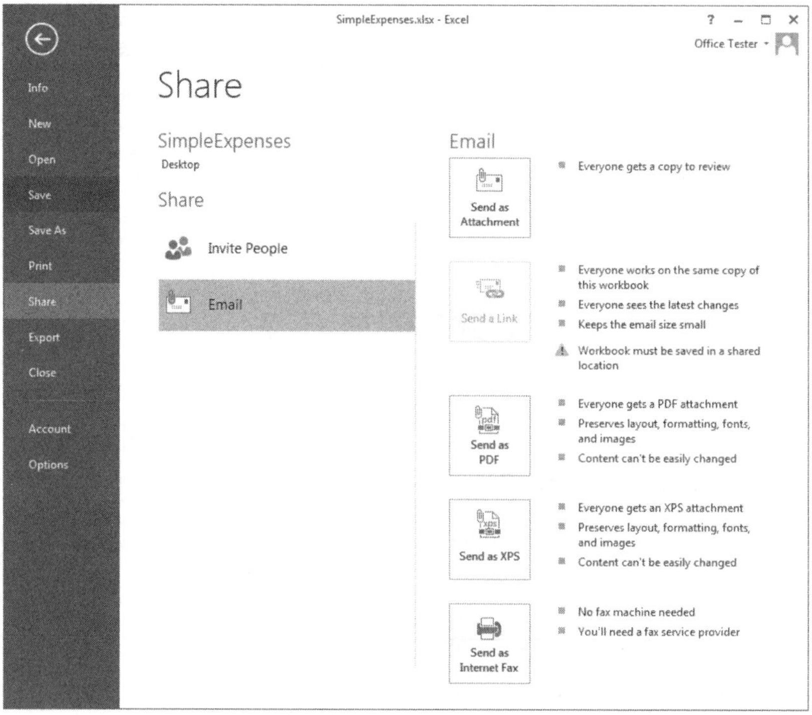

FIGURE 22-6

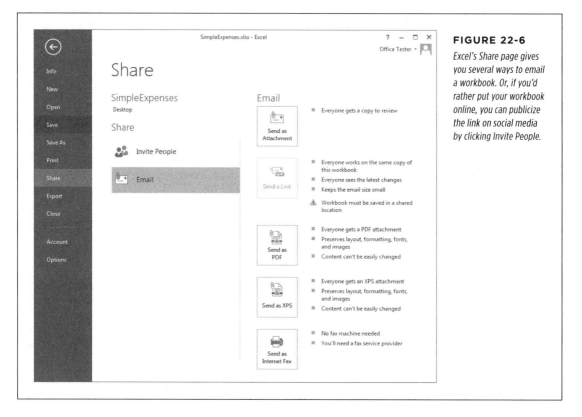

Excel's Share page gives you several ways to email a workbook. Or, if you'd rather put your workbook online, you can publicize the link on social media by clicking Invite People.

Excel provides five email options, each of which has its own button on the Share page. Your choices include:

- **Send As Attachment** creates a new email message (using whatever email program is installed on your computer) and attaches a copy of your workbook file in its full and natural state. It's up to you to fill in the recipient's email address and click Send to dispatch the message (Figure 22-7). Your recipient will need to use Excel to view or edit the file.

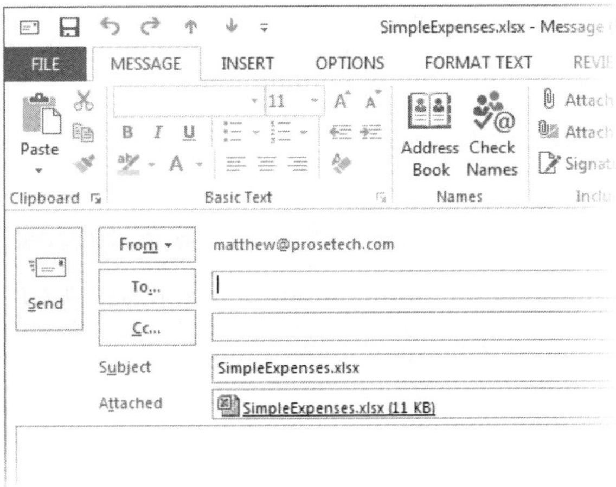

FIGURE 22-7

The Excel workbook file SimpleExpenses.xlsx is attached to this message. Fill in a recipient, subject, and message, and then click Send. You can also cancel the message by closing the window.

NOTE Excel uses the email program specified by your computer's Internet Options control panel. Usually, that's the same program you use on a regular basis, but to make sure, select Internet Options from the Windows Control Panel, choose the Programs tab, and then see which program is specified in the E-mail box. If you'd like to pick a different email program, choose one from the drop-down list.

- **Send a Link** creates an email message with a link that points to your workbook. The idea is that the recipient of that message can click the link to open the original copy of the document, rather than getting a duplicate. However, this button works only if you store the worksheet somewhere public, like a shared folder on a networked computer. It also assumes that the recipient has access to the shared location.

- **Send as PDF** and **Send as XPS** work like Send As Attachment, but they create a copy of the workbook in PDF or XPS format, respectively. This is handy in two cases: if your recipient doesn't have Excel, or if you don't want your recipient to edit your work. Page 34 has more about the PDF and XPS standards.

- **Send as Internet Fax** lets you send the document to a fax number, just as if you'd printed it up and fed it into a fax machine. The drawback is that you need a *fax provider*, which is an Office plug-in that can transmit the electronic data to a real phone number, with no modems or telephone connection required. The first time you click Send as Internet Fax, Excel opens a web page that lists a variety of fax providers you can consider.

Adding Comments

Comments are the simplest form of Excel's collaboration features. Excel displays comments in a floating yellow box that points to a single cell (as shown in Figure 22-8). Place whatever descriptive text you want inside the comment box. For example, you can use comments to flag an error, raise a question, make a suggestion, or praise a particularly brilliant formula.

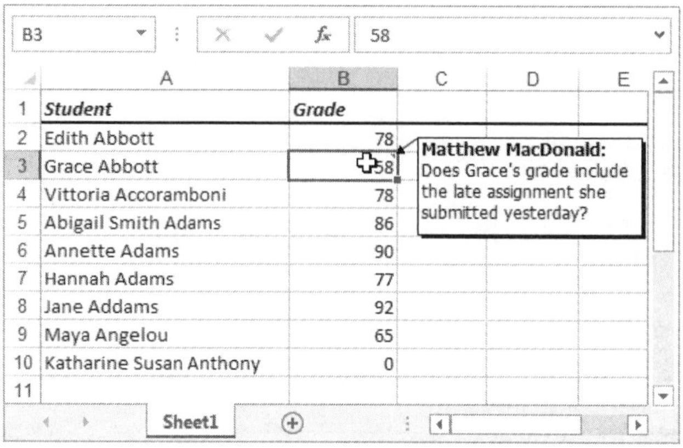

FIGURE 22-8

This worksheet includes a single comment attached to cell B3. You can clearly see the arrow that connects the floating comment box to the cell. Additionally, a tiny red triangle in the top-right corner of the cell indicates it has an attached comment.

The beauty of comments is that you're free to include as much information as you want without modifying the worksheet data. For that reason, comments work perfectly when you send a workbook out for review. An employee can send an expense report to a manager, and the manager can add feedback using comments without altering the original information. Once the manager sends the workbook back, the employee can then decide whether to heed the comments and make some changes, keep the comments for later consideration, or remove them altogether.

Inserting a Comment

Every workbook can include thousands of comments. The only limitation is that each individual cell can have only one attached comment.

To create a new comment, follow these steps:

1. **Move to the cell where you want to place the comment.**

   Every comment anchors to a single cell in a worksheet. You can move the comment to any location you want after you create it, but it always points to the same cell (using a long arrow).

2. **Select Review→Comments→New Comment.**

   A new comment box appears next to the cell. Excel fills in your name on the first line, and positions the cursor inside the text box so you can start typing.

TIP Excel automatically uses the name it has stored for you. You can edit this part of the comment, but rather than change the name every time you add a new comment, it's far easier to change your name information in Excel's settings, as explained on page 664.

3. **Enter the text for your comment.**

   You can space your comment out over multiple lines by pressing Enter to jump to the next line. The comment box scrolls down if you enter more text than can fit in the visible area.

4. **When you finish entering the comment, click the original cell to return to the worksheet, or press Esc twice.**

   Excel marks commented cells with a tiny red triangle in the top-right corner. To see the comment, hover over the cell with the mouse. Figure 22-8 shows an example of a worksheet with a single comment.

Showing and Hiding Comments

Ordinarily, comments appear when you hover over a commented cell with your mouse. When you move somewhere else, they politely disappear from view (although Excel still gives you a clue about which cells have comments, as shown in Figure 22-9). This behavior makes sense if you're dealing with a lot of comments from multiple reviewers. Otherwise, you'd see so many comments that they'd obscure each other—or even important worksheet data.

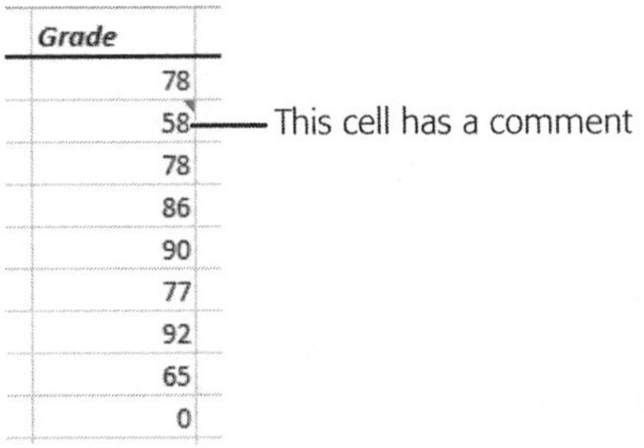

FIGURE 22-9

When comments are hidden, you still know a cell has one thanks to the small red triangle in the top-right corner of the cell.

Sometimes, though, you want to make sure a comment is clearly visible and that no one will overlook it. In that case, you can set a comment so that it's *always* visible, no matter where your mouse is. To do this, move to the cell that has the comment, and then choose Review→Comments→Show/Hide Comment. Use the same command a second time to tuck the comment back out of sight. Alternatively, right-click the cell with the comment and then choose Show/Hide Comments.

TIP You can use the Review→Comments→Show All Comments command to display every comment in your worksheet at once. Comments always appear wherever they were last situated.

Fine-Tuning Comments

Once you create a comment, you can manipulate it the same way you manipulate other floating objects, like charts and graphics. To start off, move to the cell that has the comment. Then, choose Review→Comments→Edit Comment. (Or, if you already used the Review→Comments→Show/Hide Comment command to make the comment visible, just click the comment box to select it.) You'll see resizing handles appear around the comment box. You can now perform the following tasks:

- **Move the comment box.** It's quite likely that the place where the comment box first appears isn't exactly where you want it. The comment may obscure important information on the worksheet. Fortunately, you can easily drag the comment out of the way. Just move the mouse pointer over the border of the comment so that it changes into a four-way resize arrow, and then drag the comment box to a new location. Excel automatically adjusts the arrow that connects the box to the cell.
- **Resize the comment box.** To resize a comment, click one of the resizing handles and drag the box's edge or corner. (The resizing handles look like circles at the edges of each corner and in the middle of each side of the comment box.) You may want to resize a comment box to enlarge it so it can show all the comment text at once. Even though you can scroll through comment box text using the cursor, it's not always obvious that some of the text is out of sight because the comment box doesn't display scroll bars.
- **Edit the comment.** Just click inside the comment box, and then start editing. Or, right-click the cell with the attached comment, and then choose Edit Comment.
- **Delete the comment box.** To delete a comment, click the border of the comment box to select the whole box, and then press Delete. Alternately, you can right-click any cell with an attached comment, and then choose Delete Comment from the pop-up menu.

TIP To delete multiple comments at once, select all the cells that have attached comments, and then select Review→Comments→Delete. But be warned, Excel doesn't ask for confirmation before it removes your comments.

You can also format the text in a comment box. Often, you'll take this step to make your comment stand out (by enlarging or bolding the font) or to fit more text in (by shrinking the font). You may also use a specific color if you know that multiple reviewers will add comments to the same worksheet, and you want to distinguish the comments from different authors at a glance.

To format a comment, select the text you want to format, switch to the ribbon's Home tab, and then use the Font and Alignment sections. You can apply a new font and type size, and different alignment options. You can also change the text color, although to do that you need to select some text in the comment box, right-click it, and choose Format Comment. Figure 22-10 shows a few examples of gussied-up comments.

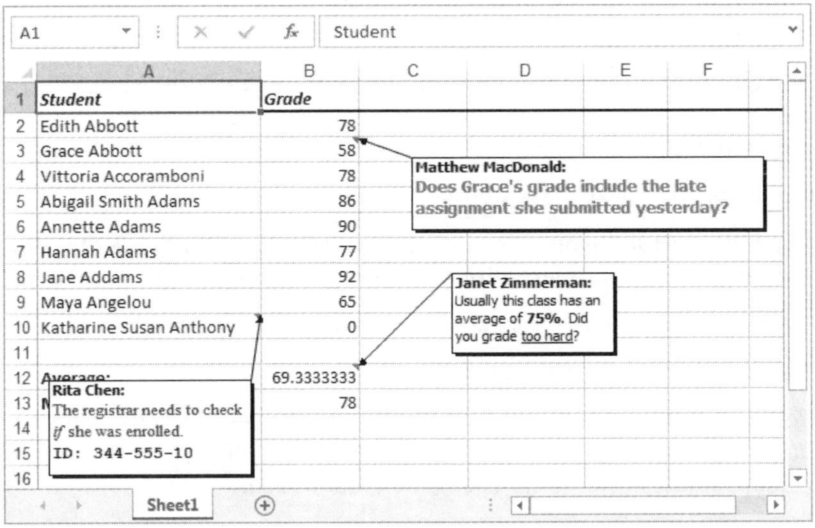

FIGURE 22-10

Formatting helps you tweak all or a portion of your comment text. You can use it to boldface a piece of important information in a comment (like the percentage in Janet's comment), or to distinguish comments from different reviewers.

Reviewing Comments

If it's your job to review everyone else's comments (and make the requested changes), you'll be interested in Excel's buttons for *comment navigation*. These buttons let you move through all the comments in a worksheet, one at a time. Best of all, as you go from comment to comment, Excel automatically opens and closes the comment boxes one at a time, which keeps your screen clutter-free and your sanity intact.

To move through your comments, start at the first cell of your worksheet (A1), and then choose Review→Comments→Next. Excel scans the worksheet starting from the current cell, and then moves to the right, one cell at a time. If it doesn't find any comments in the current row, it scans the next row from left to right, starting in the first column. When Excel finds a comment, it stops the search and, if the comment was hidden, displays it on your worksheet.

To keep moving through the worksheet, click Review→Comments→Next again (or use Review→Comments→Previous to move backward). As you move on, Excel conceals each comment once more.

Printing Comments

Excel's standard behavior is to ignore all comments when it prints a worksheet. Your printed document won't show the comment text or even indicate that a cell has a comment.

If you'd like a printed record of your comments, Excel gives you two options:

- **You can print the visible comments on your worksheet**. In this case, Excel draws the graphical comment boxes in the printout exactly as they appear, potentially obscuring other worksheet information. Hidden comments don't show up.
- **You can print all the comments on a separate page**. In this case, Excel creates a list of comments. Each entry in the list includes the cell reference and comment text.

To change options, follow these steps:

1. **Head to the Page Layout→Sheet Options section, and then click the window chooser (the small square with an arrow in it) at the bottom-right corner.**

   The Page Setup window appears, with the Sheet tab displayed.

2. **Make a selection from the Comments list box.**

   You can choose "None" (the default), "At end of sheet" (which creates a separate comment page), or "As displayed on sheet" (which shows the graphical comment boxes). Figure 22-11 compares your options.

NOTE Excel doesn't let you print just the comment page. If you choose "At end of sheet," you must print the comments page *and* the worksheet data.

3. **Click OK.**

   Excel stores your comment options for this worksheet. You can now use the File→Print command to send your data to the printer.

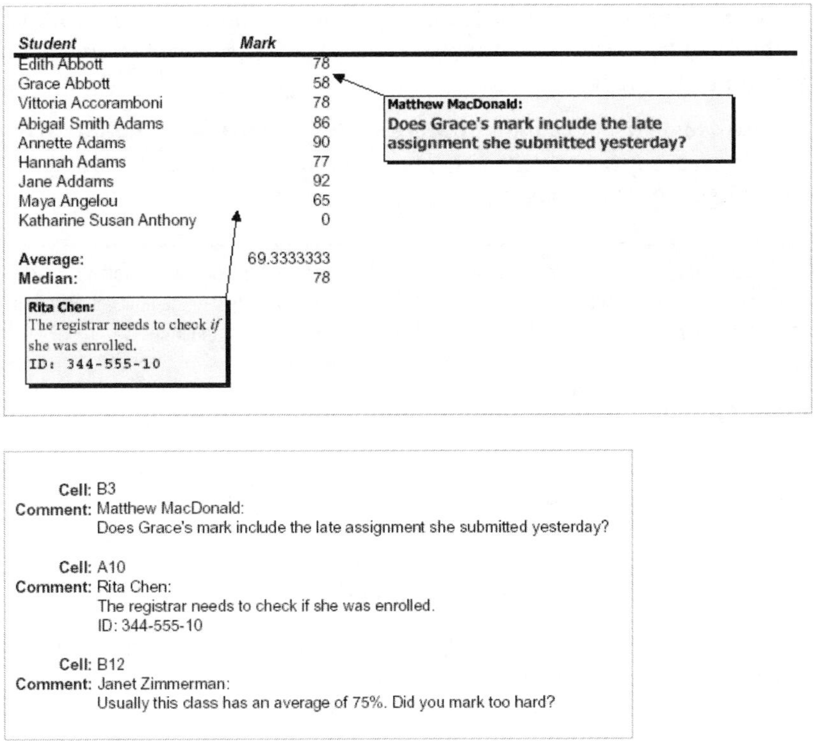

FIGURE 22-11

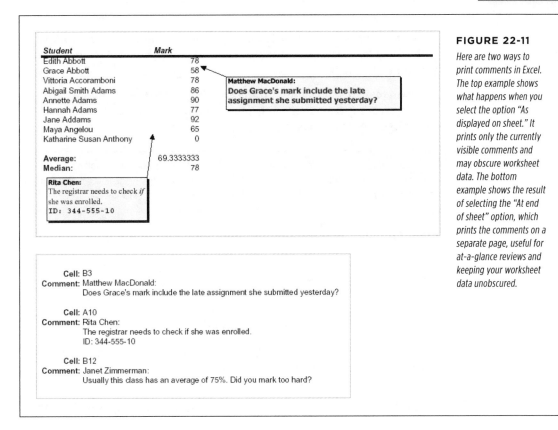

Here are two ways to print comments in Excel. The top example shows what happens when you select the option "As displayed on sheet." It prints only the currently visible comments and may obscure worksheet data. The bottom example shows the result of selecting the "At end of sheet" option, which prints the comments on a separate page, useful for at-a-glance reviews and keeping your worksheet data unobscured.

Tracking Changes

Comments are a great way for people to leave messages for each other in a spreadsheet. However, they become awkward if the workbook requires substantial changes, and they're downright aggravating if more than one person revises a workbook. Imagine a worksheet that tracks a team's weekly progress or one that represents a communal effort to create a business plan. In such situations, where more than one person needs to make substantial additions or changes to a worksheet, comments just can't handle it all.

In cases like those, Excel provides a tool that makes it easier for groups of people to work together—*change tracking*. Change tracking makes sure that the changes made by different people are carefully logged, giving you the power to inspect each person's changes individually and reverse them if you choose. It's a little like keeping several versions of the same worksheet in a single spreadsheet file.

You may consider using change tracking for several reasons:

- **You want to send a workbook to another person for review or editing.** However, you want to be able to quickly spot the changes they make.
- **You want to have the last word on other people's changes to your workbook.** In other words, you not only want to review changes, you want to discard them if they aren't correct.
- **You want to distribute copies of your spreadsheet to several people at once.** Once everyone has made their changes, you want to merge all these changes back into the original copy.

NOTE In one of Excel's most irritating quirks, you can't use change tracking if your workbook includes a data table (like the ones described in Chapter 14). Your only recourse is to move into the table, and then convert it to a group of ordinary cells by choosing Table Tools | Design→Tools→Convert to Range.

Turning On Change Tracking

To turn on change tracking, follow these steps:

1. **Select Review→Changes→Track Changes→Highlight Changes.**

   The Highlight Changes window appears.

2. **Turn on the "Track changes while editing" checkbox.**

   When you turn on change tracking, you also automatically switch on workbook sharing (a separate feature that's described on page 690). There's no way to turn on change tracking without also turning on workbook sharing.

3. **Ignore the Who, When, and Where checkboxes for now, and click OK to return to your worksheet.**

   The Who, When, and Where checkboxes don't affect how change tracking works. They just configure what changes Excel highlights in your document. You'll learn about these settings a little later in this chapter.

   Excel automatically saves your workbook at this point. If you turn on change tracking for a brand-new spreadsheet, you need to pick a file name and location for the workbook. Otherwise, just click OK when Excel prompts you to save an updated copy of your workbook.

To see how change tracking works, enter text in a new cell or edit an existing cell. Excel uses several visual indicators to show that a cell has been changed. Most obviously, it draws a blue outline around the cell and adds a small blue triangle to the cell's top-right corner. Additionally, Excel changes the column headers at the top of your sheet to use red text if that column or row includes changes.

To get the specifics about a change, hover over the cell with your mouse. A yellow box appears that looks just like a comment box. However, you can't edit the text in this box—instead, it contains a message that indicates who last changed the cell, the date and time he made the change, and what the change was. This message disappears as soon as you move the cursor somewhere else. Figure 22-12 shows a closer look.

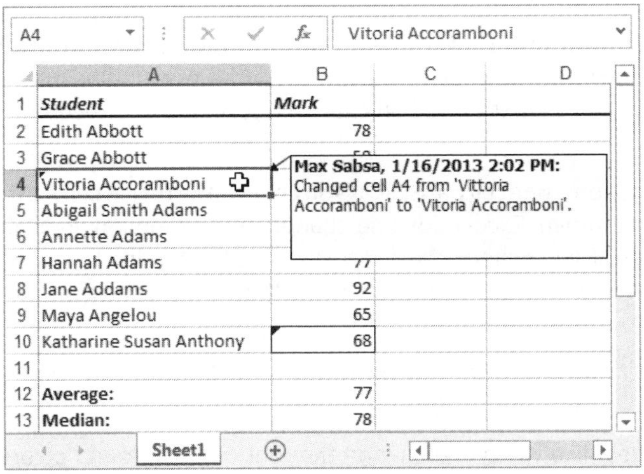

FIGURE 22-12

Cells A4 and B10 have the telltale blue triangles indicating that someone has changed them. To examine a change, position your mouse pointer over the cell. Using this technique, you can see that Max Sabsa changed the name in cell A4 by removing an extra "t" in the word "Vittoria."

NOTE Change tracking applies to the entire workbook. When you switch on change tracking, Excel tracks changes for each cell in every worksheet.

FREQUENTLY ASKED QUESTION

Features That Change-Tracking Affects

I turned on change tracking, and now a bunch of other features don't work—what gives?

Unfortunately, when change tracking is on, Excel automatically prevents you from taking certain actions. This side effect is unavoidable, because change tracking requires workbook sharing (page 690). Workbook sharing always applies a few basic safety restrictions.

As a result, once you turn on change tracking, each of the following changes are off limits:

- Creating a data table, picture, chart, or pivot table.
- Deleting a worksheet.
- Merging cells or splitting merged cells.
- Adding or changing conditional formats.
- Adding or changing data validation.
- Inserting or changing hyperlinks.
- Protecting or unprotecting worksheets.
- Creating, changing, or viewing scenarios.
- Grouping or outlining data.
- Recording, editing, or assigning macros in the current workbook.

In all these instances, you're limited in what you can create or change. If these features already exist in your workbook, they'll continue to function. For example, once you turn on change tracking, you can't add a hyperlink. But if you already had a hyperlink in your sheet, it still works.

Understanding the Change Log

Excel's change tracking is a little quirky, and it often confuses reasonably intelligent people. Even though it's superficially similar to the change tracking features used in other programs (like Microsoft Word), it's subtly different in many ways. In this section, you'll learn how it really works.

Once you turn on change tracking, Excel keeps a *change history log*, which it stores along with your workbook file. The change history log lists every modification you made to a workbook since you first turned on change tracking. It also records who made the change and when.

Excel records all changes on a per-cell basis. So if you change the text in cell A2 from *John Smith* to *Adam Bergman*, Excel adds one change item to the log, indicating the old and new values. If you change the cell text twice, Excel adds two entries. Excel records the change as soon as you commit it (either by pressing Enter or by moving to a new cell).

Excel doesn't track every possible change, however. In fact, it ignores the following changes:

- Formatting changes (like when you change the font or background color for a cell).
- Hiding or unhiding rows or columns.
- Adding, changing, or deleting comments.
- Inserting or deleting worksheets. (However, if you add a new worksheet, Excel does track all changes you make to *that* worksheet.)

Excel also doesn't worry about cells that change indirectly. For example, if you change the value in cell A1 and that causes a formula in cell A2 to display a new value, Excel records the change for cell A1 only. If you think about this approach, it makes perfect sense, because the real content in cell A2—the formula—hasn't changed at all. The only difference is the displayed result.

Changes don't remain in the change history log forever. In fact, once 30 days have passed since a change was made, Excel discards it from the log. Excel checks the date and discards old entries every time you open a file.

TIP If you decide you need more time, you can adjust how long Excel hangs onto the change log. To do so, select Review→Changes→Share Workbook. Select the Advanced tab, and then change the number next to the "Keep change history for" option. That tells Excel the number of days it should keep changes in the log.

You can clear changes from the change history log another way—by turning off change tracking altogether. Just choose Review→Changes→Track Changes→Highlight Changes to show the Highlight Changes window, and turn off the checkmark in the "Track changes while editing" checkbox. You can turn change tracking back on later, but you can't recover the information about the changes you made earlier.

Highlighting Changes

One of the most confusing aspects of change tracking is the difference between how a change is *tracked* and how it's *highlighted*. As you've learned so far, Excel tracks every change you make in a cell. However, it doesn't necessarily highlight these changes so that you can *see* them.

To see what that means, save and close a workbook that uses change tracking, and then reopen the workbook. You'll immediately see that all the blue triangles that flag the changed cells have disappeared. Even though Excel is still tracking these changes, it automatically switches off change highlighting when you open the workbook, because it doesn't know what changes you really want to see.

Confusingly enough, you use the exact same window to configure change highlighting as you do to turn on change tracking—the Highlight Changes window (Figure 22-13). To show this window, choose Review→Changes→Track Changes→Highlight Changes.

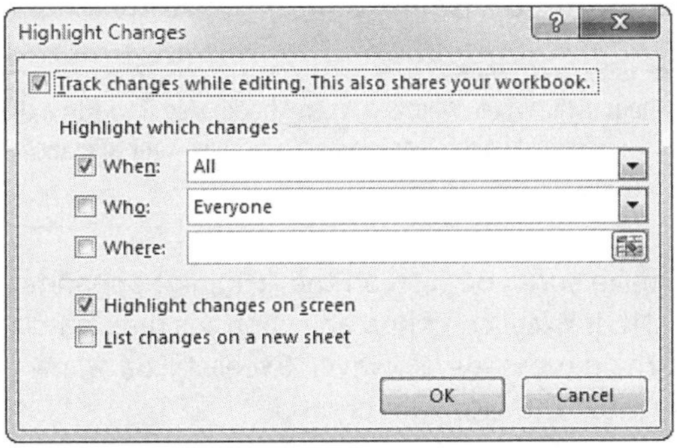

FIGURE 22-13

The Highlight Changes window lets you switch change tracking on or off with the "Track changes while editing" checkbox. You can also configure what changes Excel highlights (with blue triangles and pop-up boxes) by using the When, Who, and Where lists.

What you do next depends on the types of changes you want to see. Here are some of your choices:

- **Show all changes.** In the When list, choose All, which is the default when you first switch on change tracking.
- **Show recent changes.** In the When list, choose "Since I last saved" to show all the changes you made since the last time you saved the workbook (or, if you haven't saved it yet, since you first created or opened the workbook). This is Excel's default setting when you open a workbook that uses change tracking.
- **Show changes since a specific date.** In the When list, choose "Since date..."; Excel automatically fills in the current date, but you can edit it. When you use this option, Excel highlights the changes that were made any time on or after the specified date.

- **Show changes that haven't been reviewed.** In the When list, choose "Not yet reviewed." This option works best when you use Excel's change revision feature to examine each change. When you choose "Not yet reviewed," Excel highlights only the changes you haven't yet reviewed and confirmed. For more about this technique, see page 686.
- **Show changes made by a specific person.** In the Who list, choose the name of the person whose changes you want to see. Excel automatically fills the Who list with the name of each person who's made a change in the workbook. You can also choose to show changes by other people and hide your own changes by choosing "Everyone but me." If your worksheet has changes from several people, you may not see the familiar blue triangles. Instead, Excel tries to color-code the comment flags, so you can tell at a glance which person left which set of comments.
- **Show changes made in specific cells.** Click the Where box, and then drag the worksheet to select the appropriate range of cells. Alternatively, you can type the cell references in range notation (A1:B3) or as individual cell references separated by commas (A1, A2, A3, B1, B2, B3).

TIP You can also use a combination of settings in the When, Who, and Where checkboxes. If you do, a change must meet all the criteria you set in order for Excel to highlight it. For example, you may want to find changes made to a certain range of cells by a certain person after a certain date.

Once you make your selections, make sure you turn on the "Highlight changes on screen" checkbox, and then click OK. If Excel can't find any changes that match the criteria you chose, it displays a warning message. However, Excel still flags any new changes you make, provided they meet the highlight criteria.

NOTE The When, Who, and Where checkboxes determine what types of changes Excel *highlights* in your worksheet, but they don't affect what types of changes Excel *tracks*. Once you switch on change tracking, Excel tracks every change you make—no matter who you are or what cell you modify—until these changes expire and get removed from the log.

Examining the Change Log

Change-highlighting can get a little crowded. If you have a heavily edited document, you'll quickly run into two problems:

- There's no way to distinguish the most recent changes from ones made earlier. You can change the highlighting settings so you don't see all the changes at once, but it's still difficult to figure out the order in which changes were made.
- When you hover your cursor over a changed cell, Excel shows a box with information about the most recent change for that cell. If a cell was modified more than once, you can't see the information about any of the *earlier* changes—in fact, you have no way of knowing whether they were made.

If you need to find out a little more about the changes made to a document, you can create a *change history report*, which presents an ordered list of changes. It's not very useful if you want to see the final product of all the revisions, but it's a great tool if you want to find out what's been modified along the way.

To create a change report, follow these steps with any shared workbook:

1. **Save your workbook.**

   The change report details changes in the currently saved version of your workbook only. If you've made changes but haven't saved your workbook, those new changes won't appear in the change report.

2. **Choose Review→Changes→Track Changes→Highlight Changes.**

   The Highlight Changes window appears.

3. **If you want to create a change report that shows only certain changes, you can adjust the Who, When, and Where checkboxes, as described earlier.**

   To create a change report that shows all the changes made by everyone anywhere in the entire workbook, select All from the Who list, and then make sure the When and Where checkboxes aren't turned on.

4. **Turn on the "List changes on a new sheet" checkbox.**

   This setting tells Excel to create the change report worksheet. This worksheet is new, and Excel copies all the information from the change history into it.

5. **Click OK.**

   Excel adds a new worksheet named History to your spreadsheet file. It contains a list of the changes ordered from oldest to most recent (see Figure 22-14). By reviewing the change report, you can quickly see all the changes made to the worksheet. Using Excel's change highlighting, by contrast, you see only the information for the most recent changes. The bottom of the list has a message indicating when Excel generated the History list.

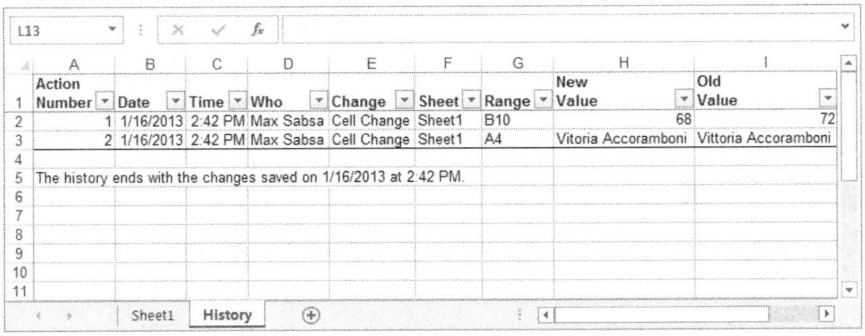

FIGURE 22-14

This change report shows two changes. The change report indicates who made the change, when it was made, where it was made, and what the old and new values were.

Excel doesn't let you delete the History worksheet, but as soon as you save the workbook, Excel automatically removes it. It takes this rather drastic step to ensure that you never end up with an out-of-date change report. If you decide you want to keep a change report, select the cells that make up the History report and copy them to another worksheet.

Accepting and Rejecting Changes

So far, you've learned how change tracking helps you see the history of a spreadsheet's edits, letting you examine who modified what and when they did so. Change tracking is also useful if you want to review changes and make final decisions about whether to keep or discard each change. This review process is called *accepting and rejecting changes.*

When a change goes into the change history log, Excel flags it as a new, unconfirmed edit. If you decide not to review the workbook changes, those changes remain in place. However, if you review the workbook, Excel lets you independently examine each change and decide whether to make the change permanent or discard it. If you decide to discard, or *reject*, a change, Excel restores the previous value for the cell and removes the change from the history log. If you decide to keep, or *accept*, a change, it stays in the history log, but it's flagged as a confirmed edit. Excel will never ask you to accept or reject that change again.

To review the changes in a workbook, follow these steps:

1. **Choose Review→Changes→Track Changes→Accept or Reject Changes.**

   If you haven't saved your workbook yet, Excel prompts you to do so. In Excel, you can't review changes until you save them to the workbook file.

   Once you save the document, Excel displays the Select Changes to Accept or Reject window (see Figure 22-15). This box lets you set filter conditions for the kinds of changes you want to review. These conditions are the same as those you find in the Highlight Changes window.

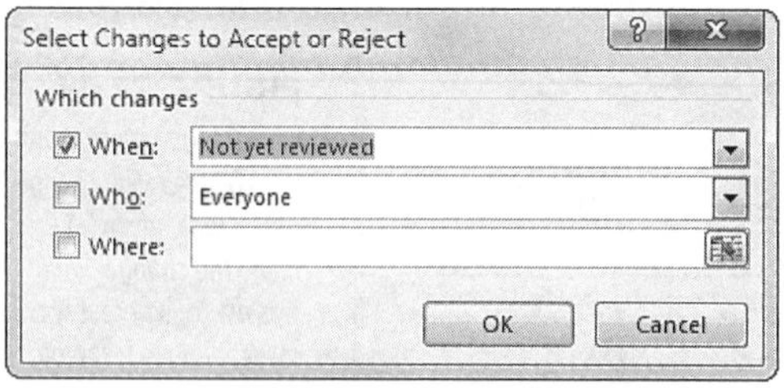

FIGURE 22-15

When you start reviewing changes, you can choose the type of edits you want to examine by turning on the checkboxes and clicking the drop-down menus in the Select Changes to Accept or Reject window. Usually, you'll want to review everything you haven't already confirmed or rejected, as shown in this example.

2. **Adjust the When, Who, and Where lists to indicate the changes you want to review.**

   If you want to see every change you haven't reviewed yet, select "Not yet reviewed" from the When list, and don't make any other selections. (For more information about the When, Who, and Where lists, see page 683.)

   No matter what selection you make, Excel ignores changes you've already accepted.

3. **Click OK to start the review process.**

   If Excel can't find any unconfirmed changes, it informs you that no changes are available and ends the review process. Otherwise, it begins scanning the document from your current position, from left to right, and then from top to bottom, examining one cell at a time. When it reaches the last cell, it starts over at the top of your worksheet to scan the remaining cells, and then continues its search with the other worksheets in your workbook.

   Whenever Excel finds a changed cell, it displays a message describing the change, and then lets you either accept or reject the edit, as shown in Figure 22-16.

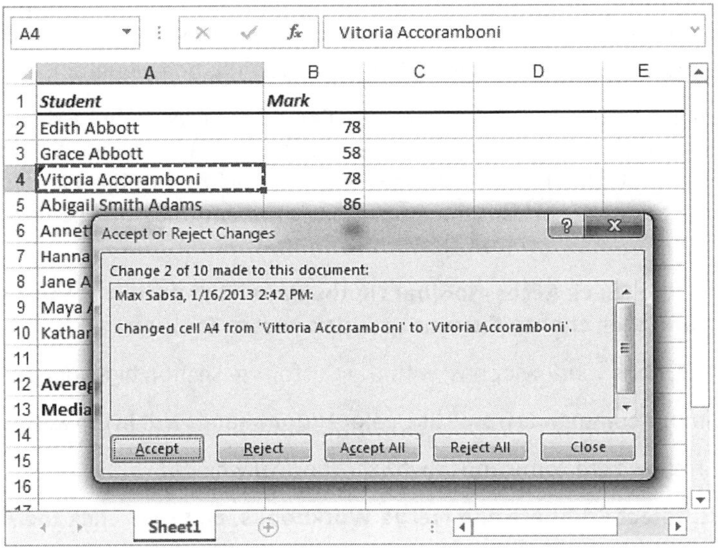

FIGURE 22-16

Excel has found a change made to cell A4. The Accept or Reject Changes window lets you choose to accept this correction—in this case, a minor correction of a misspelled name—or reject it and move on.

4. **Click Accept to confirm the edit, or Reject to discard it and remove the change from the log.**

   If you know that you want to reverse all the changes in a workbook, you can click Reject All to cancel everything in one fell swoop. Similarly, Accept All confirms all the outstanding changes. Be careful, though—if you use these buttons, you can't undo your action afterward.

   After you make your choice, Excel continues its search. When it can't find any more unconfirmed changes, the review process ends, and you return to your worksheet.

NOTE Even after you accept a change, it remains in the change log until the time limit expires. This system differs dramatically from the change tracking you'll find in a program like Microsoft Word, which tracks changes only until you review them.

Merging Multiple Revisions into One Workbook

Change tracking works great when you need to send a workbook from one person to another. Each person can add her insights, and the original author can review all the changes before preparing a final version. Of course, life rarely works so smoothly. More commonly, several people need to work on the same workbook at the same time to get a document revised as quickly as possible. In this case, each reviewer ends up with a separate copy of the original workbook. When they finish their revisions, the original author needs to consolidate all the changes into one workbook file.

This may seem like a guaranteed recipe for hours of manual labor, but Excel provides a neat solution: a special merge feature that combines everyone's changes into a single workbook. Unfortunately, this feature is one of Excel's more specialized commands, and it doesn't appear on the ribbon. If you want to use it, you need to customize the Quick Access toolbar. Here's how:

1. **Right-click the Quick Access toolbar (in the upper-left corner of the Excel window), and then choose Customize Quick Access Toolbar.**

   The Excel Options window opens, with the Customize section highlighted.

2. **In the "Choose commands from" list, select "Commands Not in the Ribbon."**

   This action shows the commands that Excel normally hides.

3. **In the list, select Compare and Merge Workbooks, and then click the Add button.**

   This moves the Compare and Merge Workbooks command to the list on the right, which details all the commands currently in the Quick Access toolbar.

4. **Click OK.**

   Once you add the Compare and Merge Workbooks command to the Quick Access toolbar, you're ready to go. Here's how to combine two spreadsheets and find the differences:

5. **Make sure you turn on change tracking (page 680) before you distribute your document.**

   The compare and merge feature uses Excel's change history log. If you want to compare more than one copy of a spreadsheet, and the changes were made without change tracking turned on, you're out of luck.

TIP You can't merge a document if some of the changes have expired from the change history log. To avoid this problem, it's a good idea to make sure the change history tracks changes for longer than 30 days before you send the workbook out for review. Just select Review→Changes→Share Workbook, and then select the Advanced tab. In the "Keep change history for" setting, enter a really large number, like 500 days. The only disadvantage to keeping change entries for a longer amount of time is that your workbook file becomes larger as it retains additional data.

6. **Make sure each file you want to merge has a different file name.**

   Excel can't open files with the same name at the same time. Usually, you'll give each file a new name based on the reviewer. For example, if your workbook is called expenses.xlsx, you might want to create copies of it with names like expenses_rr.xlsx (for someone whose initials are R.R.), expenses_mj.xlsx (for someone whose initials are M.J.), and so on.

7. **Put all the workbook copies you want to merge into the same folder on your computer.**

   By having all the workbook files in one location, you'll be able to merge all the files in one step.

8. **Open your master copy of the workbook.**

   Before continuing, you should also make sure none of the workbook copies are currently open. If they are, you can't merge them into your master workbook. You may also want to make a backup copy of your original workbook. That's because Excel automatically saves the workbook after the merge, and you can't undo the changes.

9. **In the Quick Access toolbar, click the Compare and Merge Workbooks button.**

   A standard file window appears.

10. **Browse to the folder containing the files, and then select the copies you want to merge.**

    To select more than one file at a time, press the Ctrl key while you click each file name.

11. **Once you select all the copies, click OK.**

    Excel compares each copy and applies all the changes to the current workbook.

    During the merge process, Excel may need to decide between two conflicting changes. If two people have modified the same cell, for instance, or if you modified a cell *after* sending the workbook out for review, you have a conflict. In such a case, Excel uses the most recent change. However, Excel carefully enters every change in the change history log. After you merge all the workbooks, you can use the Accept or Reject Changes command to review all the changes, including those made to cells that have conflicts.

    When you find a "conflicted" cell, Excel displays a message like the one in Figure 22-17; you can then choose which change you want to keep.

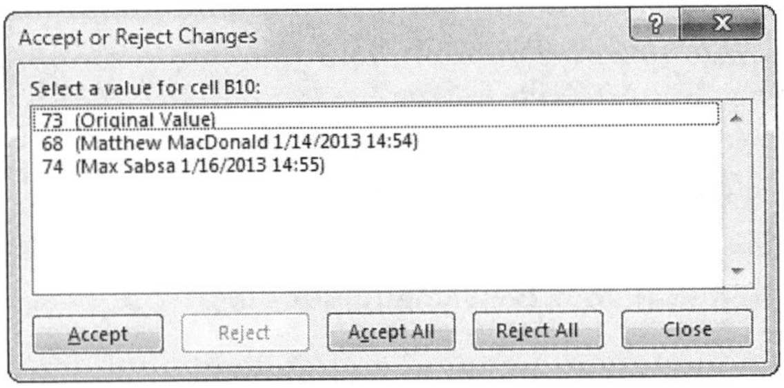

FIGURE 22-17

Occasionally, you may find that more than one change has been made to the same cell. In cases like that, Excel includes all the changes in the change log, and uses the most recent value in your worksheet. When you review the edits made to the battered cell, Excel displays a window asking you which change you want to keep.

NOTE You can also use Excel's workbook merging tool to combine comments from several versions of the same file. Excel automatically adds the comments to your master workbook. Remember, for this plan to work, you need to have change tracking turned on in each file.

Sharing Your Workbook

Change tracking is really just one part of a larger feature known as *workbook sharing*. Workbook sharing makes it possible for more than one person to modify an Excel document at the same time. For sharing to work, the workbook file needs to be somewhere that everyone can access. (The most typical location is somewhere on a company network.)

Workbook sharing is a little risky (as you'll soon see), but it gives you collaboration abilities that you wouldn't otherwise have. To get some perspective on how workbook sharing works, you need to understand what happens when two people fight over a workbook file that isn't shared. Read on.

Multiple Users Without Workbook Sharing

Ordinarily, only one person can open an Excel workbook file at a time. Excel enforces this restriction to prevent problems that can crop up when different people try to make conflicting changes to a file at the same time, and someone's changes get lost.

Figure 22-18 shows what happens when you try to open an Excel workbook that someone else is already using. Excel warns you about the problem and gives you two alternatives:

- **Read Only.** Excel opens a copy of the document. You can make changes, but you'll need to save the spreadsheet as a new file.
- **Notify.** Excel opens a copy of the document (just as though you clicked Read Only), but with a twist. If you wait long enough for the original editor to close the workbook, Excel notifies you (Figure 22-19). At this point, you can ask Excel to open the newly freed-up file. (Now, everyone else will have to wait for you to relinquish the file before *they* can make changes.)

FIGURE 22-18

If you try to open a workbook that someone else is using, you see this message. You can click Read Only or Notify to open a copy of the file.

FIGURE 22-19

If you asked Excel to notify you when a shared file becomes free, it displays this message. At this point, you can click Read-Write to have Excel close your copy and open the original file.

Taking turns editing a file works well enough, but it has one significant drawback: You never know when the file will become available. If someone opens a workbook and then leaves for a two-week vacation without shutting off his computer, you'll be locked out of the workbook. Worst of all, you have no way of knowing when the workbook will be available.

The take-turns approach runs into a more serious problem if you absolutely can't wait to make your changes. Excel gives you an option, but it's a risky one. You can click Notify (Figure 22-18) to open an editable copy of the workbook and make your changes. Then, when you receive the message that the original file is free (Figure 22-19) and you click Read-Write, Excel will attempt to transfer the changes you made to the original file. If the other person (the one who opened the spreadsheet first) was simply reviewing the numbers and didn't make any changes, this process works seamlessly, and Excel applies all your edits. But if the other person made changes to the original file, you're in a sticky situation. Excel notices the discrepancy immediately, and forces you either to save your copy as a separate file or to discard all your hard work before it lets you open the original copy (see Figure 22-20).

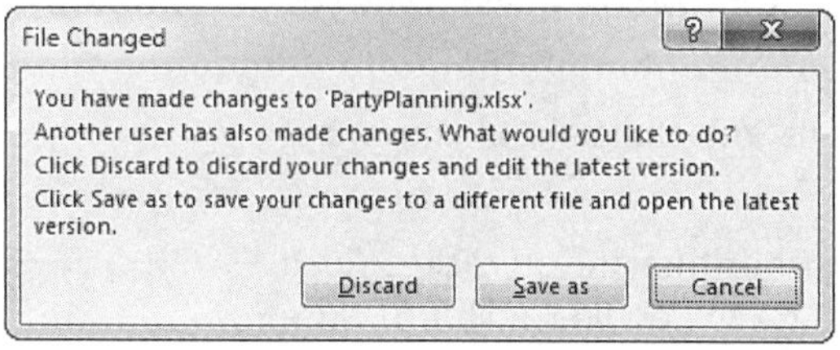

FIGURE 22-20

Here's what happens if you make changes to a copy of a non-shared workbook (like PartyPlanning.xlsx) at the same time that someone else is editing it. When the other person closes the file, you get this unpleasant message.

To avoid headaches like these, don't make changes to a copy of an Excel workbook when someone else has it open. Instead, wait patiently for the first person to finish, or—if waiting isn't practical—use Excel's workbook sharing feature, which is described next.

NOTE Reports differ about the reliability of workbook sharing. Excel experts agree that it's a recipe for failure if you want large groups of people to edit the same file at once. But if you have more modest goals—to manage the work of just a few collaborators, who aren't likely to all fight over the same workbook file at once—it's a reasonably effective option. (If you really do need to have dozens of collaborators making edits simultaneously, you'll have better luck with the collaborative editing feature in the Excel Web App, as described on page 732.)

Turning On Workbook Sharing

It's quite easy to turn on workbook sharing. In fact, it takes only a couple of steps:

1. **Select Review→Changes→Share Workbook.**

   The Share Workbook window appears.

2. **Turn on the "Allow changes by more than one user at the same time" checkbox.**

3. **Select the Advanced tab.**

   Figure 22-21 shows the Advanced tab in action.

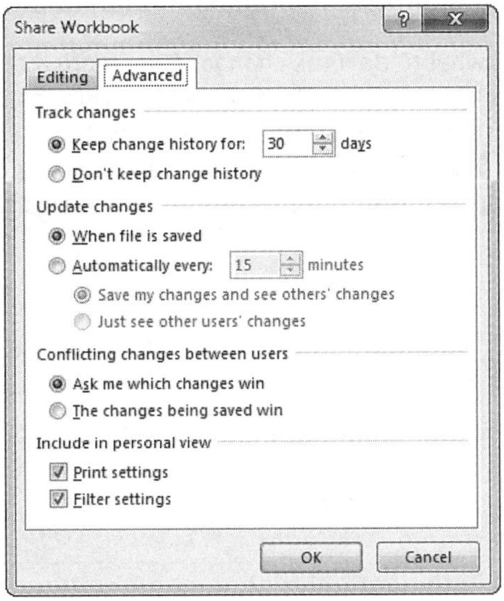

FIGURE 22-21

The Advanced tab lets you configure how Excel handles edits in shared workbooks. The bottom two checkboxes ("Print settings" and "Filter settings") indicate that Excel stores some private information that it doesn't share with the document—namely, your personal printer settings and your view settings (like the current zoom magnification). Excel can't synchronize these settings because they may apply only to your computer.

4. **If you don't want to use change tracking, click the "Don't keep change history" option.**

   When you share a workbook, Excel assumes you want to keep a log of changes. That way, if a conflict arises and one person overwrites another person's changes, you can still find the discarded change in the log if you need it. If you don't want Excel to keep this list of edits, turn this option off.

5. **In the "Update changes" section, choose how often you want Excel to inform you about changes.**

   When you edit a shared workbook, you won't see other people's changed instantaneously. Instead, Excel waits until you save the workbook. Then, it checks for other people's recent changes and refreshes the workbook to include their edits.

   Alternatively, you can tell Excel to check for changes more often to make sure it stays up to date. To switch on this behavior, change the "When file is saved" option to "Automatically every 15 minutes." (If you want to update more or less frequently, change the number of minutes.) Then, select the "Save my changes and see others' changes" option. Now, Excel will save your changes and refresh the workbook every 15 minutes.

   Finally, you can choose to refresh your document periodically without actually saving your changes. Simply change the "When file is saved" option to "Automatically every 15 minutes," and select the "Just see other users' changes" option.

But all of these choices present a problem: How does Excel handle conflicts between edited workbooks? Read on.

6. **If you wish, select one of the settings for "Conflicting changes between users" setting.**

   Here's your chance to tell Excel what to do if the changes from more than one person conflict with each other. Keeping the standard "Ask me which changes win" setting usually makes sense because Excel explains any conflicts and shows you the changes that were made earlier. If you choose "The changes being saved win," Excel automatically overwrites conflicting changes without even alerting you to conflicts or warning you that important data could be lost.

7. **Click OK.**

   Excel saves the workbook automatically. You can tell that it's shared because the word [Shared] appears in the title bar.

When you work on a shared workbook, Excel keeps track of the number of people involved. To see who's working on a workbook at any given moment, select Review→Changes→Share Workbook. Figure 22-22 shows an example.

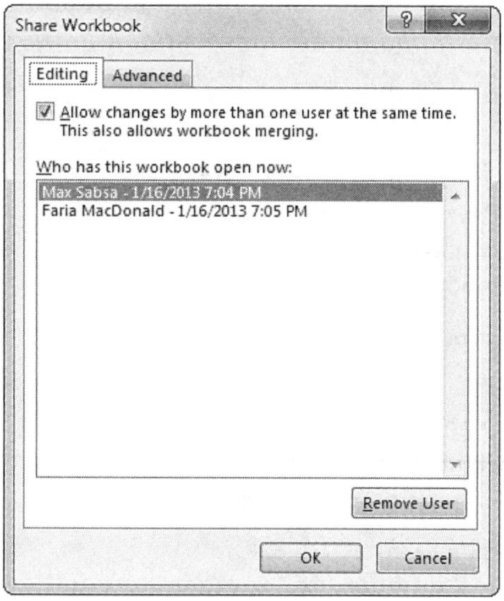

FIGURE 22-22

In this example, two people have the workbook open at the same time. One of Excel's oddest features is the ability to stop people from saving a shared workbook if you select them in the list, and then click the Remove User button. This feature has no limits, which means that, in this example, Matthew can remove Faria and, similarly, Faria can remove Matthew if she gets to the setting first. When you remove someone from the list, they can't save their changes to the shared workbook. Instead, they have to save their copy only under a new file name. This removal process is temporary, however. If Matthew removes Faria, there's no reason that Faria can't open the workbook after Matthew closes it. This anything-goes attitude can make life a bit chaotic if you let multiple people edit the same workbook at once.

NOTE Remember, once you turn on workbook sharing, Excel completely turns off certain features (like inserting charts or pictures). For the full list, see the box on page 681.

Workbook Sharing in Action

When you have workbook sharing switched on, there's no limit to how many people can open the same workbook at once. However, each person has a separate copy of the workbook. Excel synchronizes your copy when you save changes (or at fixed intervals, depending on the "Update changes" option described on page 693).

This approach works well when people change different portions of the workbook. However, it's entirely possible that two people could edit the *same* cell, each in their own copy of the workbook. Sooner or later, both people will try to save their changes.

Imagine that Faria changes cell B5 at the same time that Ricardo modifies B5. Faria saves her changes and doesn't experience any problem. Shortly after, Ricardo tries to save his changes. At this point, Excel warns Ricardo that his changes conflict with the changes someone else made. Ricardo now needs to decide whether to overwrite Faria's changes or discard his own. Figure 22-23 shows an example of the message Excel displays in this situation.

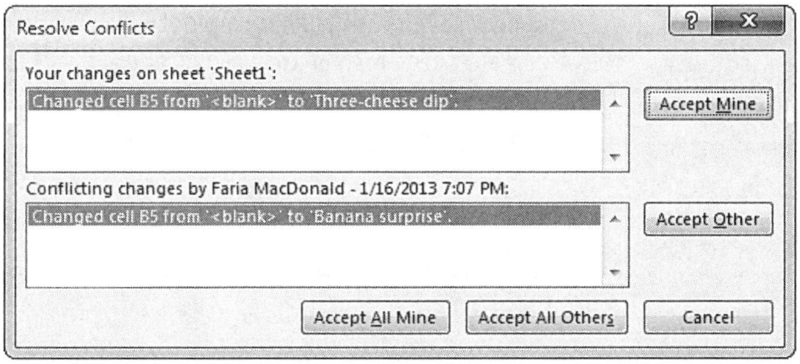

FIGURE 22-23

In this example, Ricardo has just tried to save his copy of a shared workbook. However, one of his changes conflicts with a change Faria made. Ricardo can choose Accept Mine to discard Faria's change or click Accept Other to leave the workbook as it is.

Here's a clear problem—the last person to make changes gets to make decisions about someone else's work. There's no way to avoid this limitation of shared workbooks. Excel doesn't provide any way to stop one person from obliterating a coworker's edits.

In fact, even if changes don't directly conflict, simultaneous edits can still clash. Imagine you have two cells (A10 and B10) that don't quite match up the way they should. (A10 may have the price of a product and B10 may have a discounted price, which—oddly enough—is higher.) One person tries to fix the problem by modifying A10. At the same time, another person tries to resolve the same problem by modifying B10. The end result? Both A10 and B10 get changed, Excel doesn't complain, and the cells still don't match up. These kinds of things make workbook sharing a high-stakes, life-in-the-fast-lane approach.

TIP Workbook sharing works best when multiple people need to read a workbook and only one person needs to edit it. In this situation, the chance of conflicting changes is low, and the workbook editor can still make changes even if someone else has opened the file to check a number or print the data.

FREQUENTLY ASKED QUESTION

The Best Way to Share Workbooks

The Excel Web Application has a collaborative editing feature. Does this replace workbook sharing?

In the next chapter, you'll learn about a whole other way to share workbooks—using collaborative edits in the Excel Web App.

In some respects, the Excel Web App takes a simpler approach than workbook sharing. Edits synchronize almost immediately, while ordinary workbook sharing waits until you save the document or takes place just every few minutes (using the "Update changes" option described on page 693). However, the Excel Web App isn't as good at handling conflicts. If, by some chance, you do change the same cell at roughly the same time as someone else, one person's work will be overwritten, without any warning or notification. (This sounds scary, but it isn't a big concern for many people. Microsoft research shows that in most collaborative situations, different people work with different data and edit different cells.)

Truthfully, the choice between ordinary workbook sharing and the Excel Web App depends on a number of factors. If you work on a home or company network, and if you want to prevent any chance of accidental overwriting, ordinary workbook sharing is the safest choice. But if you want to collaboratively edit with people anywhere, you aren't worried about clashing edits, and you don't mind that the Excel Web App has significantly fewer features than its desktop counterpart, the Excel Web App may be a better choice.

If you're somewhere in between, the decision probably depends on where you want to work—in the full-featured Excel window, or in a slick but less powerful web application that runs anywhere, even on computers that don't have an installed copy of Excel. For more information about the Excel Web App, keep reading.

Reviewing Workbooks with Inquire

As your spreadsheets become increasingly complex and more people get involved editing them, it becomes more difficult—and more important—to keep track of everything that's going on. One tool that can help is Inquire, an add-in that Microsoft includes with Office Professional Plus, the super-premium version of the Office 2013 suite.

NOTE If you don't have Office Professional Plus, you're (sadly) out of luck. Once upon a time, the tools in Inquire were part of a pair of Excel add-ins developed by a company called Prodiance, and their price topped $1,000. In 2011, Microsoft bought Prodiance and began integrating its products into Excel.

Inquire provides a grab-bag of tools that let you explore workbooks in microscopic detail. However, the Inquire add-in isn't really interested in your data. Instead, it's a *meta-analysis* tool that helps you explore how your data is used and how your workbook is structured. For example, Inquire can create a report that tells you how many hidden cells your spreadsheet has, how many of its formulas perform date calculations, and how many times you reference a blank cell. It can also count errors and create diagrams that show exactly how cells, worksheets, and workbooks link together in a complex tangle of formulas.

When you first meet Inquire, you might feel that it's a bit obsessive in its focus on tiny, nit-picky details. But Inquire is a critical tool in big businesses that use spreadsheets to make complex financial decisions. In these environments, an overlooked spreadsheet error—like a formula that refers to a non-existent workbook file, or a formula that references a blank cell where you should have typed in a number—can seriously skew your calculations. This is where Inquire comes in—in skilled hands, it can uncover inconsistencies, outright mistakes, and deliberate fraud. You can think of it as a forensic audit for workbooks.

NOTE Some studies suggest big companies rely on a hodgepodge of complex spreadsheets, and over 90% of them contain some sort of error. See *http://tinyurl.com/spread-errs* for the sobering facts.

Turning on the Inquire Add-In

You'll know the Inquire add-in is active if you see a ribbon tab named Inquire. If you don't, here's how to switch it on:

1. **Choose File→Options.**
2. **In the Excel Options window, pick the Add-Ins category.**

   This shows a list of all your currently active add-ins, and those that are installed but not active.
3. **In the Manage list at the bottom of the window, choose COM Add-Ins, and then click Go.**

   You might expect to pick Excel Add-Ins, but that's not the way Inquire is designed.

   A COM Add-Ins window appears, with a list of add-ins (Figure 22-24).

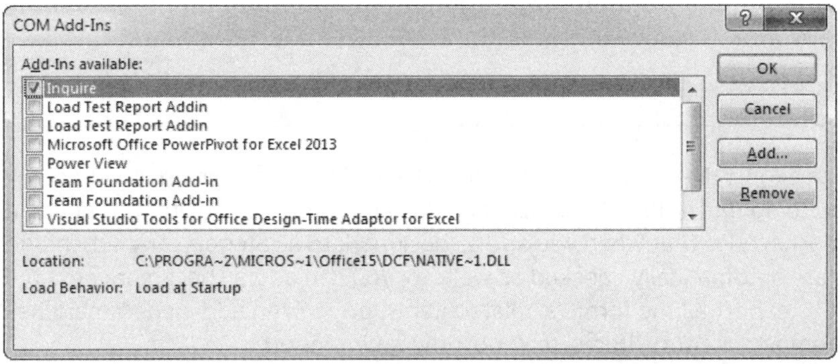

FIGURE 22-24

Every add-in that has a checkmark next to its name is currently turned on. Every other add-in is turned off. Inquire is at the top of the list.

4. **Turn on the checkbox next to Inquire, and then click OK.**

   If you can't find Inquire anywhere in the list, you probably don't have the Professional Plus edition of Office.

Generating a Spreadsheet Report

Inquire's most fundamental feature is its *workbook analysis report*. When you create a report, Inquire studies each sheet, cell, and formula in your spreadsheet, and creates a detailed survey of what it finds. You can use the report as a tool for checking out complex or problematic spreadsheets, or as a starting point if you're trying to understand someone else's work.

To create a report, choose Inquire→Report→Workbook Analysis. Depending on the complexity of your workbook, you may need to wait while Inquire does its work. When it's finished, the Workbook Analysis Report window shows the results. On the left is a tree that places its findings into separate, subgrouped categories. On the right, you'll see the results for the currently selected category (Figure 22-25).

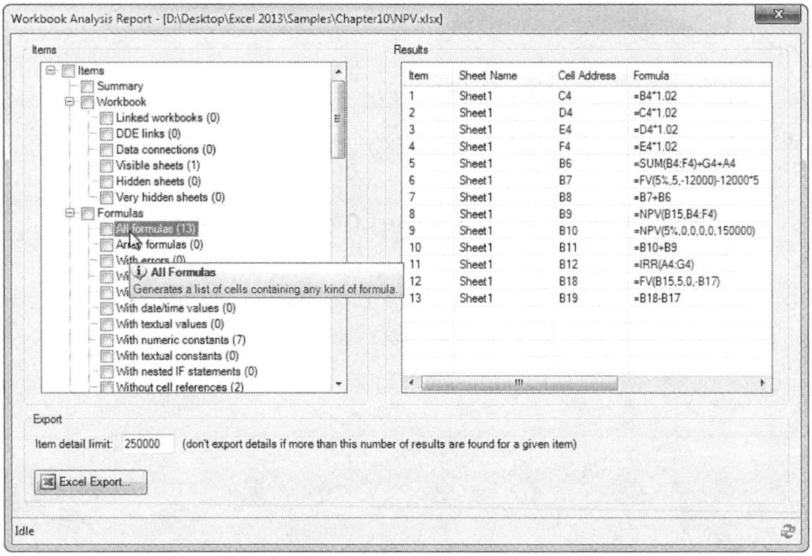

FIGURE 22-25

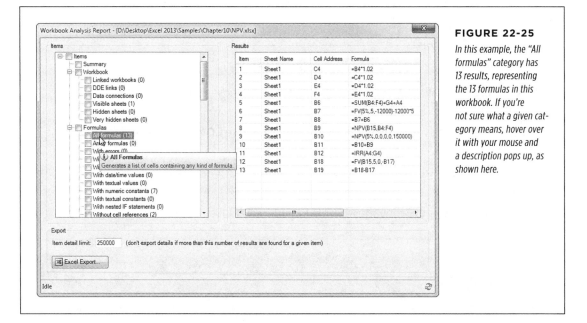

In this example, the "All formulas" category has 13 results, representing the 13 formulas in this workbook. If you're not sure what a given category means, hover over it with your mouse and a description pops up, as shown here.

You can export the workbook report to an Excel file, so you can print it out or review it later. To do that, add a checkmark next to each category with items that you want to export. Notice that when you add a checkmark to a category, any subcategories it has are automatically checked as well. So, you can add a checkmark next to Formulas to export all the formula-related items, or you can add a checkmark next to the topmost category, Items, to export the entire report.

Once you pick the items you want, click Excel Export, enter a file name for your report, and then click Save.

Comparing two Workbooks

One of Inquire's standout features is its workbook comparison tool, which lets you take any two workbook files and generate a detailed report describing their differences.

UP TO SPEED

Change Tracking vs. Workbook Comparison

In many ways, Inquire's workbook comparison tool is more powerful and more flexible than the standard Excel change-tracking feature. Here are some reasons to prefer it:

- **It allows for safer collaboration.** With change tracking, you rely on Excel to coordinate all the modifications into one master copy of your workbook. With workbook comparison, you can let people work on separate copies of a workbook, and *then* integrate the changes yourself, It takes more time, but it's a more disciplined approach.
- **It compares everything.** Change tracking logs changes to the data in your worksheets. Formatting is ignored. But the workbook comparison feature lets you choose what to compare, and it can identify changes in everything from edited cells to formatting tweaks.
- **It doesn't block other features.** As you learned earlier, when you turn on change tracking, you also turn on workbook sharing, and workbook sharing limits what you can do in a workbook in a number of important ways. For example, you can't add new tables or charts (see the sidebar on page 681 for the full list of restricted features).
- **The report is easier to review and understand.** When you use change logging, you get a list of the changes made, in chronological order. It can take a bit of effort to match the changes you see in the log with the cells you're examining. When you use workbook comparison, you get a much clearer report that puts the old and new versions of your data side by side, making the report much easier to navigate.
- **You don't need to enable anything in advance.** With change tracking, you need to remember to turn it on, or you'll have no record of your changes. And even when you have it active, Excel removes the edit history from the change log after a set number of days (page 682). But with workbook comparison, you can explore the changes between different versions of a file any time, as long as you have the old files on hand.

There are also some reasons that Excel pros may prefer change tracking. For instance, change tracking records every modification, even if it's overwritten. That means 10 changes to the same cell result in 10 log entries, and you can follow the edits every step of the way. Change tracking also lets you focus on when changes were made, and lets you ignore all but the most recent modifications. All in all, the choice between change tracking and workbook comparison depends on exactly how you work and what tool feels most comfortable.

Here's how you compare files using Inquire's change tracking:

1. **Open both workbooks you want to compare.**
2. **Choose Inquire→Compare→Compare Files.**

   A window appears where you can pick the files you want to compare (Figure 22-26).

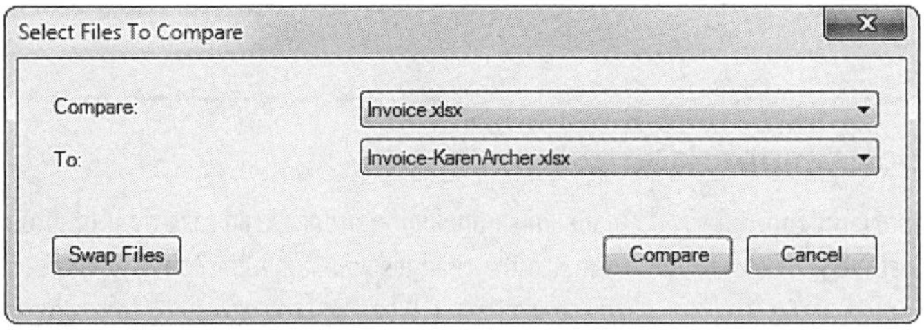

FIGURE 22-26

The Select Files to Compare window has two lists. Each lets you pick from all the currently open workbook files.

3. **Choose the original file from the top list. Choose the more recent, modified file from the bottom list.**

   If you get it backwards, you can click the Swap Files button to switch your two workbooks into opposite places.

4. **Click Compare.**

   If you made any changes to either of the workbooks that you haven't saved yet, the Inquire add-in asks you to save them. Then, it starts the comparison process.

   When it finishes, Inquire displays the results in the Spreadsheet Compare window (Figure 22-27).

   At first glance, the Spreadsheet Compare window is a bit dizzying, because it's packed with information. At the top is a ribbon with commands for changing basic view options and exporting your results to a spreadsheet file. Underneath is a side-by-side look at your workbooks.

   Changes are color-coded, so green cells indicate newly entered values, dark green cells indicated altered formatting, turquoise cells indicate formulas with changed results, purple cells indicate newly entered formulas, and so on. You can scroll your way around the worksheets in the side-by-side comparison, just as you do in Excel, and you can click the worksheet tabs to switch from one worksheet to another. When you click on a cell in one workbook, Inquire automatically shows you the corresponding cell in the other workbook, so you can compare changes.

5. **Choose the changes you want to review.**

   You'll find three more panels under the side-by-side worksheet comparison. The bottom-left one holds a color-coded list of checkmarks that lets you pick the changes you want to see. For example, remove the checkmark next to Structural if you don't care about added or deleted rows and columns. Or clear all the checkmarks except Formulas to look for changed or inserted formula logic.

As you adjust your options, Inquire updates the side-by-side comparison, along with the panels to the right. The bottom-middle panel lists all the cells that have changes that meet your current criteria. The bottom-right panel totals the changes by type, so you can see at a glance which types of changes occur most frequently. For example, in Figure 22-27 the tallest bar represents Entered Values (there are nine new ones), while the second-tallest bar reflects Calculated Values (eight changes). The final bar indicates that there is one new formula, and the absence of any other bars tell you there are no formatting or structural changes. To see the exact count for a given type of change, hover over the corresponding bar with your mouse.

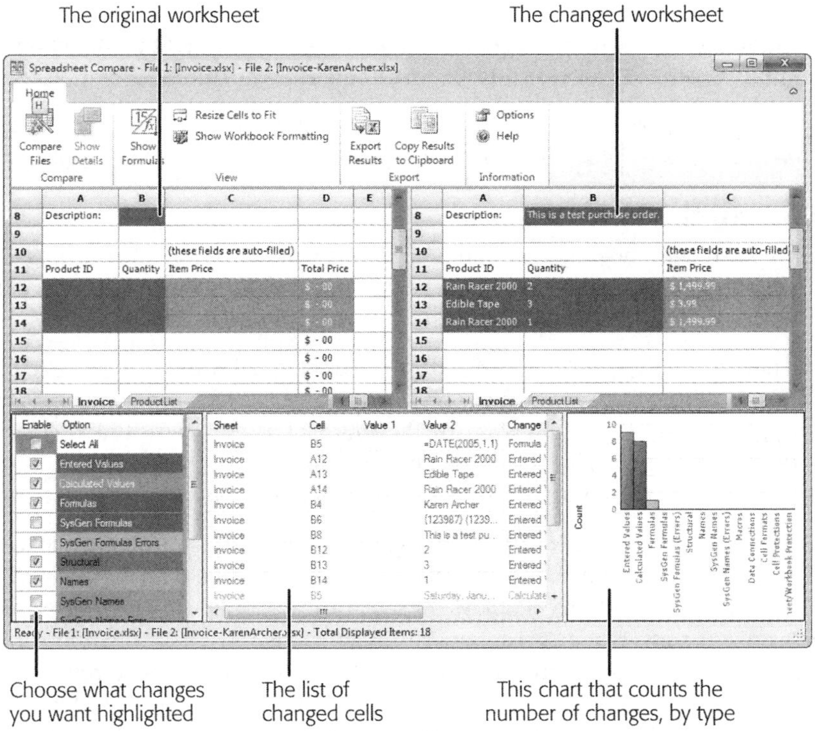

FIGURE 22-27

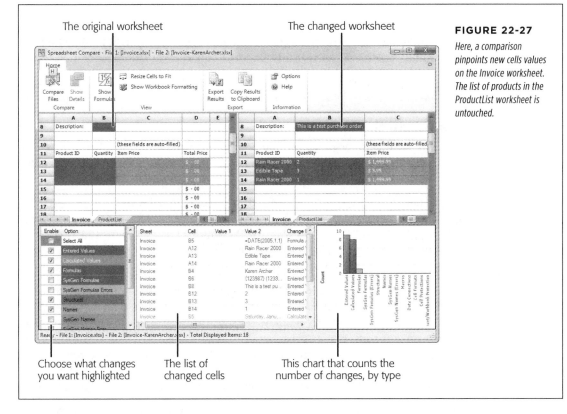

Here, a comparison pinpoints new cells values on the Invoice worksheet. The list of products in the ProductList worksheet is untouched.

6. **Optionally, adjust your viewing options.**

   There are several minor settings you can tweak:

   - If you can't see your data in the worksheet grid, choose Home→View→Resize Cells to Fit. This expands all the columns to fit their data.
   - If you want to focus on formulas, choose Home→View→Show Formulas. Now, Inquire shows the full formula expression instead of the calculated result for each formula in the worksheet.

- If you want to see what the workbook formatting looks like, choose Home→View→Show Workbook Formatting. This turns off the color-coding that highlights different types of changes.

If the changed workbook has added or inserted rows, Inquire records this fact in its change list, but doesn't note each new or removed value. If you want that level of detail, choose Home→Information→Options. Then, turn on the "Process cell contents in inserted rows/columns" setting and the "Process cell contents in deleted rows/columns" setting. Then click OK.

NOTE Inquire isn't intelligent enough to spot when worksheet data has been moved from one place to another. In its change list, Inquire simply assumes you removed data from one place and added it in another place.

7. **Optionally, save the list of changes in an Excel spreadsheet file by choosing Home→Export→Export Results. Choose a name for your file, and then click Save.**

   This action saves an Excel workbook. Inside the workbook are the contents of the change list—the same table of changes you see in the bottom-middle panel.

Following the Formula Trail

So far, you've seen how Inquire can analyze a single spreadsheet or expose the differences between two workbook files. Along with these handy features, Inquire can also create diagrams that show formula relationships.

As you already know, Excel has its own formula tracing feature, which you explored on page 404. And there's nothing wrong with it—in fact, for simple worksheets with relatively few interrelated formulas, Excel's approach is the quickest and clearest. When Excel traces formulas, it draws the relationship arrows right on your worksheet, so you can see how different bits of data are funneled into important equations.

Inquire takes a different approach. It tracks formulas in a separate diagram in a new window, and the diagram shows cell references only (not the data currently in the cells). For a simple workbook, Inquire's tracing is less informative. But in larger, more complex workbooks, Inquire's diagram-based tracing is often easier to understand. That's because, in these situations, it can be difficult to follow Excel's arrows as they crisscross over each other and through your data—and the confusion only gets worse if you have formulas that link to cells on other worksheets or cells in other workbook files.

Here's how you create a diagram in Inquire that shows formula relationships:

1. **Move to the cell that has the formula you want to use as your starting point.**

   Alternatively, you could start at a cell that contains a *value* used in one of your formulas, but it's usually easiest to start with a formula.

2. **Choose Inquire→Diagram→Cell Relationship.**

   Inquire opens the Cell Relationship Diagram Options window (Figure 22-28).

3. **Optionally, change the settings that Inquire uses to create its diagram.**

   - If you want to follow links to different sheets and worksheets, make sure you turn on the "Span sheets" and "Span workbooks" checkboxes.
   - You can choose to include precedents (the cells that a formula uses) or dependents (the cells that use the formula's result to perform additional calculations). By default, Inquire's diagrams feature both. (Page 404 has a more detailed discussion on how precedents and dependents work.)
   - You can choose how many steps the search should take before Inquire stops. For example, if you use 2 (the default value), Inquire finds the cells your formula uses, but it won't find the cells that *those* cells use. However, once Inquire generates the diagram, you can click your way down any branch, so you can continue the search as far as you want.

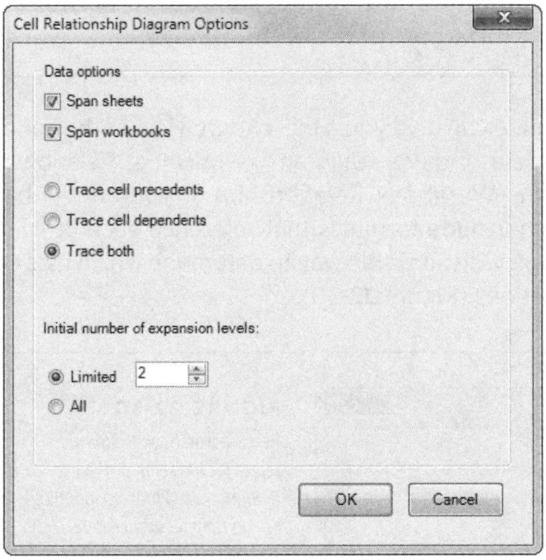

FIGURE 22-28

With the standard settings, Inquire finds all the precedent and dependent cells, but only continues its search for two steps.

4. **Click OK.**

   Inquire generates the formula tracing diagram and displays it in a new window (Figure 22-29). Now you can continue your exploration:

   - If some of the cells in the diagram overlap other cell reports, drag the offenders over to make more space.
   - Hover over an item to see its workbook file name, worksheet name, and cell reference.
   - If you want to dig deeper, click the plus box to expand an item. For example, if you expand a precedent cell, you'll find its precedents. If you expand a dependent cell, you'll find its dependents.

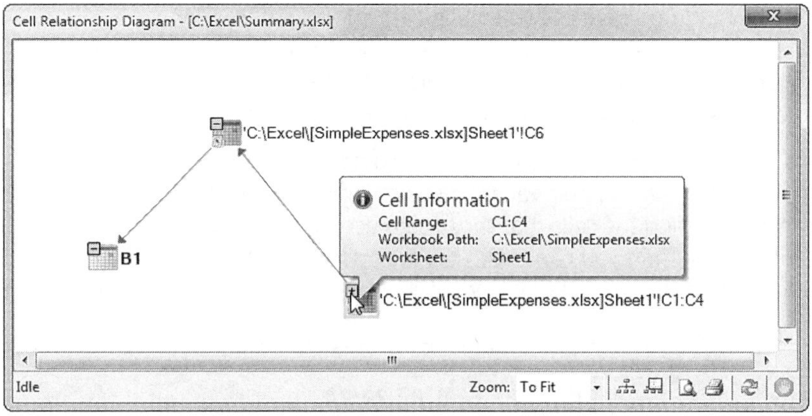

FIGURE 22-29

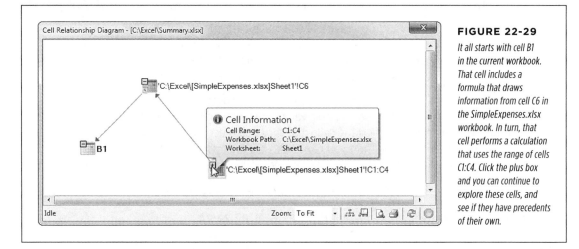

It all starts with cell B1 in the current workbook. That cell includes a formula that draws information from cell C6 in the SimpleExpenses.xlsx workbook. In turn, that cell performs a calculation that uses the range of cells C1:C4. Click the plus box and you can continue to explore these cells, and see if they have precedents of their own.

Along with cell relationships, Inquire can give you a big-picture view of the connections between different worksheets (Inquire→Diagram→Worksheet Relationship) or workbooks (Inquire→Diagram→Workbook Relationship). If you have a batch of workbook files, some of which include formulas that reference each other, the workbook comparison feature is an indispensable way to determine which files each workbook requires for its calculations (Figure 22-30).

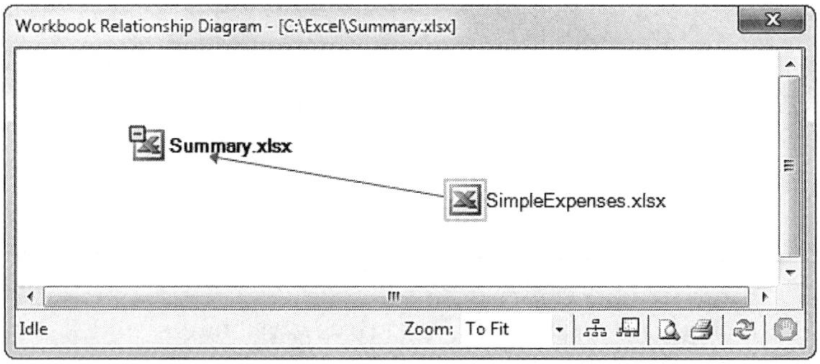

FIGURE 22-30

Here's a workbook relationship report for the same workbook (Summary.xsls) profiled in the cell relationship report in Figure 22-29. The diagram is much simpler—it conveys that Summary.xlsx depends on SimpleExpenses.xlsx. But if you have a chain of linked files, this view prevents serious headaches.

CHAPTER

23

Using Excel on the Web

For almost as long as the Internet has existed, Excel fans have been trying to put their work online. In the past, this was a tedious process that involved converting a spreadsheet into one or more HTML web pages and uploading these pages to a website. Only then could someone else view your Excel masterpiece in a web browser.

Life improved when Microsoft introduced the free Office Web Apps. Not only do the Apps let people view office documents online, with no conversion required, they also let people *edit* Office documents in a web browser. Best of all, no Office software is required, so you can brush up your data on the go, whether you're using a fully decked out laptop or a handy tablet like the iPad. (Smartphone users can't do quite as much—they get tools that let them view Office documents, but not edit them.)

Each web app differs in its exact capabilities, but none matches the extensive functionality of the desktop software. In this chapter, you'll meet the Excel Web App, which is a competent, useful, scaled-down version of its desktop big brother. The Excel Web App lets you edit data, create tables, write formulas, and even build basic charts. Perhaps most interestingly, the Excel Web App adds a live collaboration feature that lets a whole team of people change the same spreadsheet at the same time, with none of the multiuser headaches you encountered in Chapter 22.

Putting Your Files Online

The idea of running an Office program in a web browser seems simple enough. But working on the Web is different from putting spreadsheets together on your own computer, and it raises quite a few new questions. Such as, where do I put my files?

What sort of browser should I run? And what happens if several people try to change a spreadsheet at the same time?

First, before you can do any editing with the Excel Web App, you need to get your workbook online. More specifically, you need to transfer your document to a SharePoint server that has the Excel Web App software installed on it. These are the only files that the Excel Web App can access. It can't open the files on your local hard drive, the files you emailed to a friend, or the files you posted on your personal website.

NOTE SharePoint is a Microsoft product that big businesses use to help people collaborate and share information. You don't need to install SharePoint on your computer to use its features. Instead, you connect to a server that's running SharePoint, in much the same way you connect to a server to buy a book on Amazon or run a Google search.

At first glance, this seems like a Very Big Problem. After all, plenty of Excel fans want to use the Excel Web App, and most of them don't have a spare SharePoint server kicking around. Fortunately, there's an easy solution: You *can* use Microsoft's SharePoint servers. In fact, you can do so for free using a web-based service called SkyDrive.

NOTE If you *are* using SharePoint (either through your company network or through an Office 365 subscription), you can safely skip the introduction to SkyDrive and go straight to page 712 to start uploading files and using the Excel Web App.

FREQUENTLY ASKED QUESTION

Browser Compatibility

Does the Excel Web App need Internet Explorer?

Here's the good news: the Office Web Apps work with virtually all modern browsers, including:

- Internet Explorer 7 and later
- Chrome
- Firefox 3.5 and later on Windows, Mac, and Linux computers
- Safari 4 and later on the Mac

The only gap is the Opera browser. If you use Opera, you'll find that a number of Web App features are broken. Support may improve in the future, but for now you'll need to use a different browser.

The Office Web Apps also work with iPhone, Android, and Windows phones, and the iPod touch. On mobile devices, you're able to browse through complex documents and manipulate them, but you can't edit them. (For example, on a mobile device you can change the sort order of a list or the filter for a chart, but you can't edit the data in that list or chart. Page 716 has more.)

Introducing SkyDrive

SkyDrive began as a handy way to put big files online—for example, so you could back up your computer or share a document with your friends. But SkyDrive's support for the Office Web Apps means that you can upload an Excel spreadsheet, and then start editing it in your browser with the Excel Web App. In this way, SkyDrive actually does two things. First, it stores the Excel files you upload, and second, it hosts the Excel Web App, which lets you (and other people) edit your files.

To use SkyDrive, you need a Microsoft account. If you use Microsoft's Outlook.com or Hotmail email service, Xbox LIVE, or the Office 365 subscription plan, you already have one. To start using your SkyDrive storage space, skip to the next section.

If you don't have a Microsoft account, here's how to sign up:

1. **In your web browser, go to *http://skydrive.com*.**
2. **Click the "Sign up now" link.**

   This brings you to a refreshingly short sign-up page.

3. **Choose an email address.**

   If you want to use an email address you already have, just enter it in the "Microsoft account name" box.

   If you want Microsoft to give you a new Hotmail address, click the "Or get a new email address" link under the "Microsoft account name" box.

4. **Fill in the rest of your personal information.**

   Microsoft asks for relatively few details: a password, telephone number, and ZIP code.

5. **Click the "I accept" button to sign up.**

NOTE At the time of this writing, SkyDrive gives every user a substantial 7 GB of space, although you can pay for more (or just open a second account). Incidentally, 7 GB of space is equivalent to 1,000 songs in MP3 format, eight compressed high-definition movies, or nearly 100,000 average-sized Excel workbooks.

WORD TO THE WISE

Be Careful What You Store

SkyDrive has stringent rules about the content you can store there. In fact, they're considerably stricter than other cloud-hosting services like Dropbox or Amazon S3.

Copyrighted music and movies are obviously not kosher—and Microsoft uses automated tools to scan accounts for offending files. More surprisingly, Microsoft also cracks down on nudity and obscenity, not just pornography. In one case, a German photographer lost his Microsoft account after uploading four partial nudes in a private SkyDrive folder that was not accessible to anyone but him.

Microsoft's response to content violations are far from transparent. It may choose to temporarily disable some features of an offender's SkyDrive account, or lock that person's account completely, effectively banning them from all Microsoft services. (If you use your Microsoft account for email, this is a near death sentence.)

You can read the full legalese at *http://tinyurl.com/skydrive-rules*. If you're in doubt, don't upload content that might fall into a gray area, even if you have a perfectly reasonable explanation for owning it.

Using SkyDrive

Once you have a Microsoft account, you can log into SkyDrive. To sign in directly, visit *http://skydrive.com*. If you're logged into another Microsoft service (like Hotmail), you'll see a SkyDrive link at the top of the web page that can take you there directly.

A new SkyDrive account starts out with three empty folders (Figure 23-1). The first two, "Documents" and "Pictures" are a good place to store private documents and photos that you don't want to share with anyone, or that you want to share with a small group of select individuals. The third folder, "Public," holds files that any web surfer can access, even without a Microsoft account.

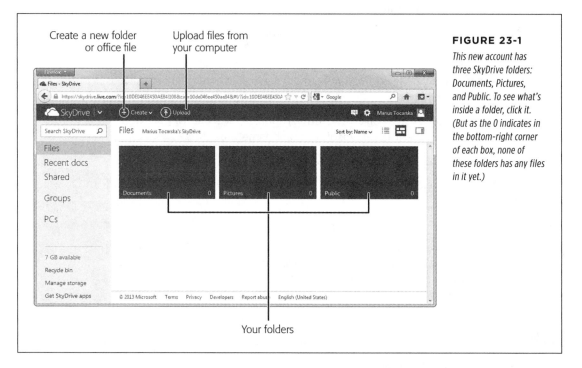

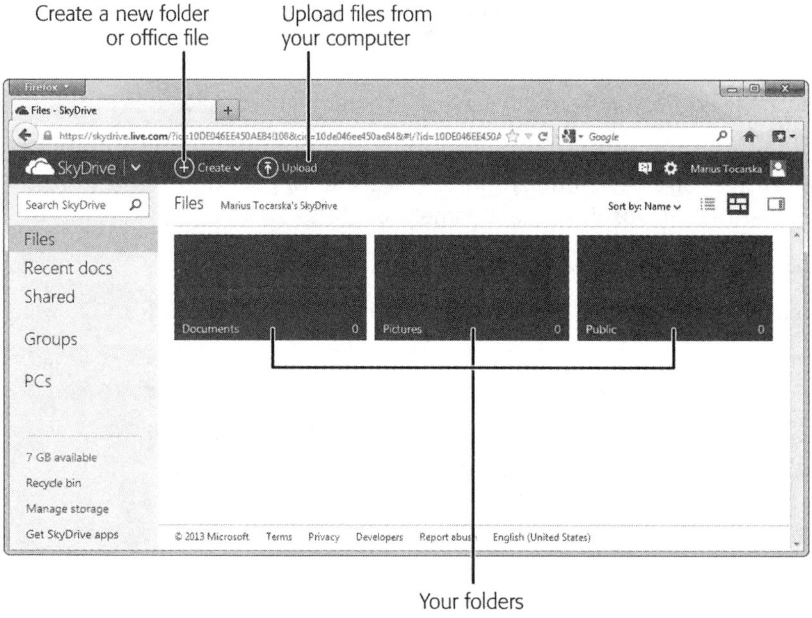

FIGURE 23-1

This new account has three SkyDrive folders: Documents, Pictures, and Public. To see what's inside a folder, click it. (But as the 0 indicates in the bottom-right corner of each box, none of these folders has any files in it yet.)

Microsoft has invested serious effort in improving the SkyDrive interface, and it's far easier to use now than it ever was before. Basic folder and file management tasks are a breeze:

- To add a new folder, click the Create menu at the top of the page, and then choose Folder. Type the folder name you want, and you're done.
- To view the contents of a folder, click it.
- To perform other tasks with a folder, right-click it. The menu that pops up has options for sharing (page 724) as well renaming, deleting, or moving your folder and its contents. The same trick works for files, once you add some.

- To move or delete several folders (or files) at once, click the checkbox in the top-right corner of each folder or file box. (The boxes are the blue rectangles that represent each folder, like the three shown in Figure 23-1.) Once you do, a Manage menu appears at the top of the page. Click it, and choose Delete or "Move to" to finish the operation.
- To recover something you just deleted, click the "Recycle bin" link in the bottom-right corner of the SkyDrive page.

Your Web Workflow

Before you start uploading Excel spreadsheets, you need to give a bit more thought to your *workflow*—that is, the way you want to manage your spreadsheet files and their revisions. Two common approaches incorporate the Excel Web App into your Excel workflow:

- **Use the Web to share a copy of your work.** This approach makes sense if you're the owner and chief maintainer of a spreadsheet that has some important information that other people want to see. You periodically upload a copy of your work, but you keep the main version and revise it on your own computer. In this way of doing things, you're really just using the Excel Web App's viewing capabilities. Other people may edit the copy with the Excel Web App, but there's really no point, as you'll just overwrite it when you upload your next copy.
- **Let your document live online.** In this case, the document that you upload *is* the central version. You (and other people) can edit this document using the Excel Web App or the desktop version of Excel, but changes are always saved to the online file. The creators of the Excel Web App think that this scenario is the most interesting one, because it makes it easier to share information and collaborate on a spreadsheet without needing to designate one person as the official spreadsheet owner. Often, marketing types describe this as putting your documents "in the cloud."

You might want to use both strategies for different files. For example, you could use the first strategy to share copies of a company financial plan, so that everyone can see the info, but no one can fudge the numbers. And you could use the second model for collaborative workbooks—you might, for example, compile a company expense summary and share it with your department heads so they can all enter their numbers into the same workbook. Either way, it's up to you to choose the right strategy and act accordingly, because SkyDrive and the Excel Web App don't distinguish between these two strategies.

NOTE Online workbooks seem like a perfect place to use document protection (Chapter 21), the Excel feature that lets you control who can do what with a workbook. Document protection is fine-grained, which means you can give different people access to different worksheets or different parts of a worksheet, and you can limit the types of changes they're allowed to make. Unfortunately, the Excel Web App doesn't support document protection (at least not yet). That means that everyone who's allowed to edit your workbook has the ability to change anything.

Uploading a File to SkyDrive Using Your Browser

Now that you have a bit of background about the Excel Web App and SkyDrive, you're ready to upload a file. You can transfer a file to SkyDrive in one of two ways: using your browser (in which case you can upload virtually any type of file) or using Excel (in which case you can upload only workbooks).

Usually, you'll find it a bit quicker to upload your workbooks from inside Excel. However, some tasks require your web browser, like deleting files and changing file permissions. In this chapter, you'll learn to use SkyDrive either way.

The following steps show you how to upload a file to SkyDrive with your browser:

1. **Point your web browser (any one will do) to *http://skydrive.com*, and log in.**

   Use the email address and password from your Microsoft account.

2. **Browse to the folder where you want to place the new file.**

   For example, if you want to upload a file to the Documents folder, click Documents. You may want to create a new folder for your document—in this case, use the Create→Folder command first.

3. **At the top of the page, click "Upload."**

   Your browser opens a File Upload window where you can pick your file (Figure 23-2).

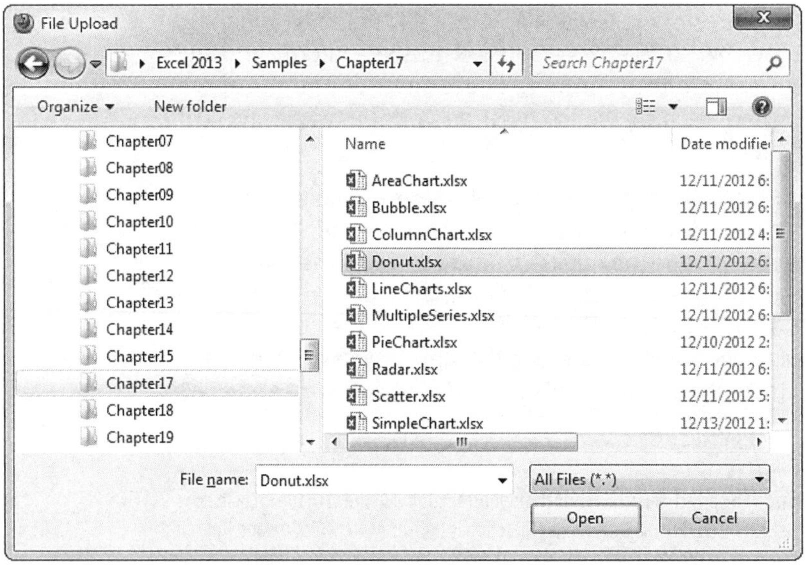

FIGURE 23-2

Here's a nifty secret about the File Upload window. As long as you're using a reasonably up-to-date browser, you can select several files from the same directory, and upload them all at once. Just hold down Ctrl while you click each file name.

4. **Select your file (or files) and click Upload.**

   If you're uploading a large file, you can watch a progress bar tick along as the transfer takes place. When the operation is complete, your browser lists all the files in the folder, including the one you just added (Figure 23-3).

   Managing your new file is easy—just right-click it for a menu of options that let you rename, move, and delete your work. If you want to download your file back to your computer, right-click it and choose Download.

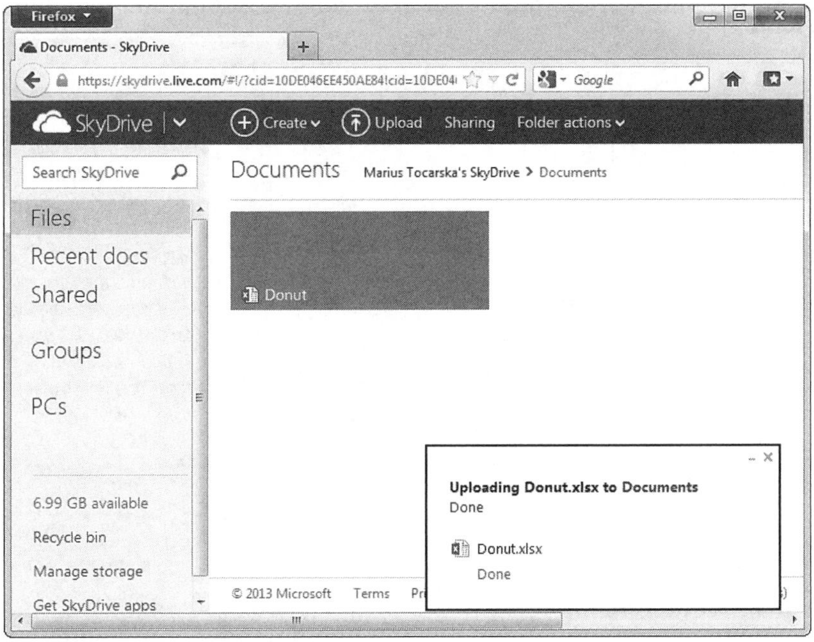

FIGURE 23-3

If you upload an Excel file, like the Donut.xlsx workbook shown here, SkyDrive gives it a green box and the familiar Excel worksheet icon. That way, you can recognize it at a glance.

POWER USERS' CLINIC

Dragging Files from Windows Explorer

If you're the sort of hardcore Windows pro who's often found hanging out in Windows Explorer, you'll be interested in SkyDrive's semi-secret uploading shortcut. Here's how it works:

1. In your browser, head to SkyDrive and browse to the folder where you want to upload your files.
2. In Windows Explorer, browse to the folder with the file (or files) you want to upload.
3. Drag your files from the Windows Explorer window and drop them into the file listing in the web browser window. You can drag one at a time or a bunch at once. As you drop in new files, a box pops up that lists all the files you're copying and the progress of each upload.

Uploading a Workbook to SkyDrive Using Excel

Excel has a nifty SkyDrive integration feature that lets you upload workbooks without leaving the comfort of Excel. The only disadvantage is that Excel limits you to a single upload at a time. Here's how it works:

1. **Open the workbook you want to share.**

2. **Choose File→Save As.**

   This brings you to Excel's backstage view. If you've already configured your SkyDrive account, you'll see it in the list of destinations on the left (Figure 23-4) and you can skip to step 5.

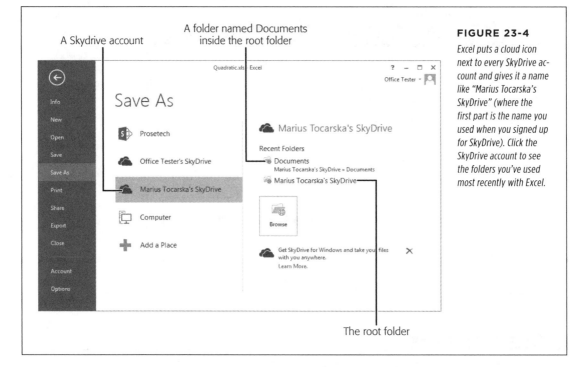

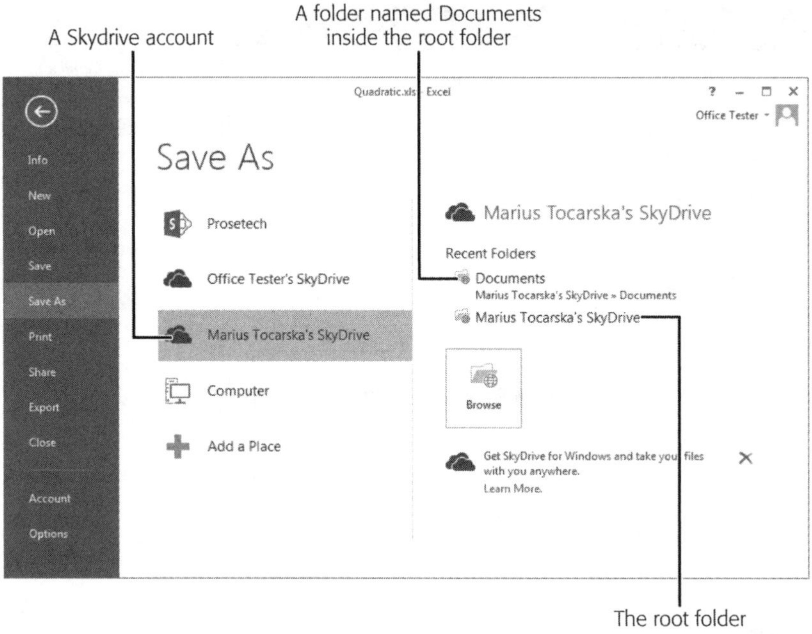

FIGURE 23-4

Excel puts a cloud icon next to every SkyDrive account and gives it a name like "Marius Tocarska's SkyDrive" (where the first part is the name you used when you signed up for SkyDrive). Click the SkyDrive account to see the folders you've used most recently with Excel.

3. **Click "Add a Place." In the "Add a Place" list on the right, choose SkyDrive.**

   Excel invites you to sign in.

4. **Enter the email address and password from your Microsoft account, and then click Sign In.**

   Your SkyDrive account appears in the list of places on the left, ready to use (Figure 23-4).

5. **In the list of places, click your SkyDrive account.**

   Excel displays a list of recently used folders for that account.

   If you just added your SkyDrive account, you'll see just one folder, with a name like "Marius Tocarska's SkyDrive" (assuming your name is Marius Tocarska). This is the *root folder* of your SkyDrive account—any other folder you create will live in a subfolder inside this folder.

6. **Pick the folder you want, or click Browse if you don't see the right folder.**

   Either way, the familiar Save As window appears, where you can pick a folder and set the file name (Figure 23-5).

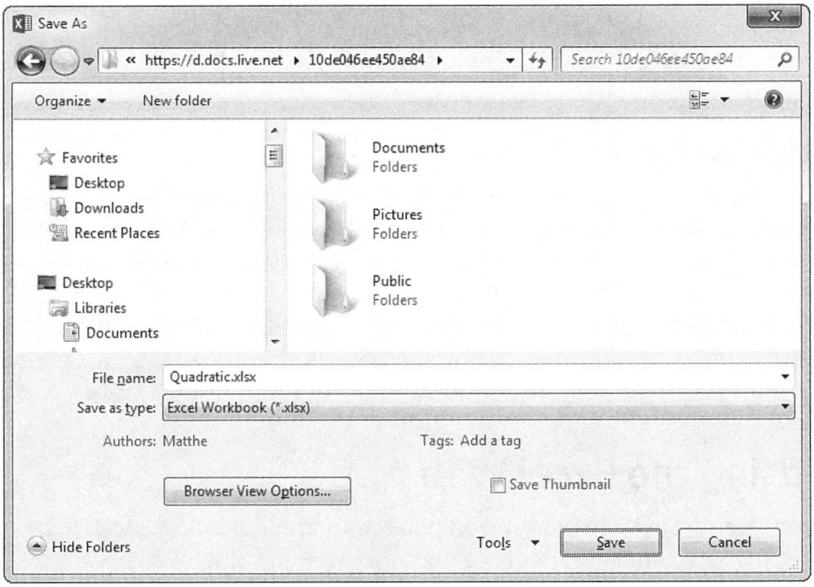

FIGURE 23-5

This Save As window looks a little different from the one you see on your computer, because it's connected to the SkyDrive server. First, the folder pane is a blank box, because you can't switch between folders. Second, the full file path in the box at the top of the window includes a web server name (like https://d.docs.live.net) and a cryptic code (like 10de046ee450ae84) that uniquely identifies your SkyDrive account.

TIP You can create a new SkyDrive subfolder using the Save As window. In fact, you use the same process you use to create a subfolder on your hard drive. First, right-click somewhere in the list of SkyDrive files, but not on a file name itself. Then, choose New Folder, and type in the folder name you want.

7. **Make sure the name in the "File name" box is the one you want for your uploaded file.**

   You should also make sure that you're using the right format. The Excel Web App uses the modern XML-based Excel formats introduced in Excel 2007 (and described on page 28), including .xlsx, .xlsm, and .xlsb. If you upload an older .xls file, you'll be able to view it with the Excel Web App, but not edit it.

8. **Click Save.**

   Excel transfers your workbook to SkyDrive.

From this point on, the copy you're working with in Excel is the SkyDrive copy. If you edit the workbook and save it again, you'll update the online copy. (If this isn't what you want, close the current workbook, and then open the copy that's on your computer.)

TIP Before you make any changes to a shared workbook, make sure you've decided which file is the master version of your spreadsheet: the local copy on your computer, or the online copy on SkyDrive.

Finally, you have to close the workbook before you (or anyone else) can edit it in the Excel Web App. This step is important because the desktop version of Excel takes exclusive control over the files it opens, locking out the Excel Web App.

UP TO SPEED

Uploading a Workbook to a SharePoint Server

The examples in this chapter use SkyDrive. After all, it's free and works for everyone. However, if you're using an instance of the Excel Web App installed somewhere else—on a company SharePoint server, for example, or on a hosted Office 365 plan—your experience remains essentially the same.

As with SkyDrive, you begin by choosing File→Save As. If you see your SharePoint server in the list, click it; if not, choose "Add a Place" to set it up. SharePoint accounts look slightly different from SkyDrive accounts—you'll see an S icon instead of a cloud. (See, for example, the Prosetech location in Figure 23-4.)

Using the Excel Web App

You can open a SkyDrive-stored workbook from inside desktop Excel. If you do, you get the same editing experience you would for any other workbook stored in any other location. But life is more interesting if you leave the comfort of Excel and access the file through your web browser.

To do that, head to *http://skydrive.com* (if you're not there already), sign in, and browse to your file. Once you find it, you can right-click it to perform all the usual file management tasks (downloading, renaming, deleting, moving, and so on). Or, click it once to open it in the Excel Web App (Figure 23-6).

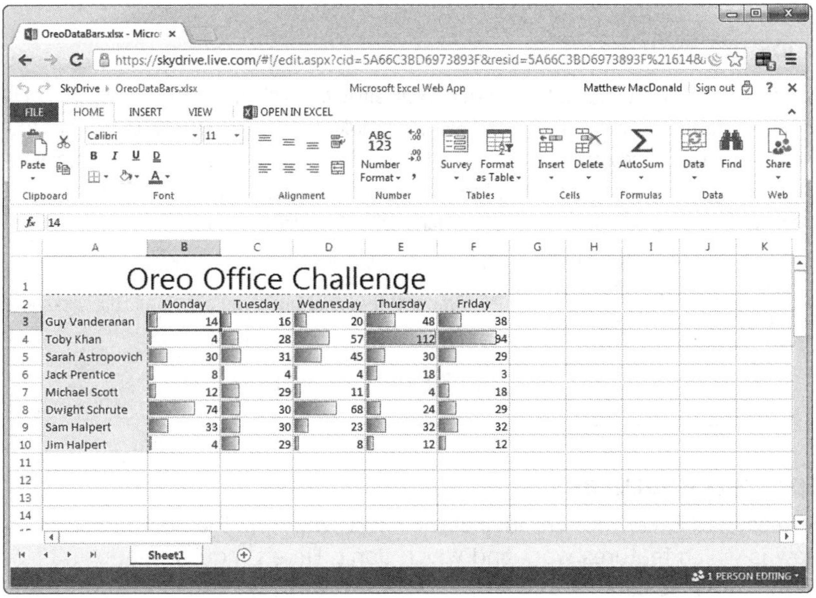

FIGURE 23-6

The Excel Web App lets web surfers view spreadsheets in their browsers, even if they don't have Excel installed. In this example, the Excel Web App is running in the Chrome web browser. Visually, the Excel Web App looks like the desktop version of Excel, and functionally, it behaves the same way (albeit with a reduced set of features).

One of the first things you'll notice is that the Excel Web App looks strikingly similar to the desktop version of Excel, but with a cut-down ribbon that features just three tabs (and two buttons—File on the left and Open In Excel on the right). This resemblance is part of a key feature that the creators of the Excel Web App call *visual fidelity*.

Thanks to visual fidelity, what you see on your worksheet always looks the same, whether you're using the full desktop version of Excel or the Excel Web App. In fact, even if the Excel Web App doesn't fully support a feature, it can usually display it correctly. For example, the Excel Web App doesn't let you create data bars, but if you open a spreadsheet that already has them in place (like the OreoDataBars.xlsx file in Figure 23-6), the data bars appear, with all the right formatting. They even resize themselves appropriately if you change the underlying cell values.

GEM IN THE ROUGH

Creating a Workbook in SkyDrive

You've seen how to create a workbook in Excel, upload it to SkyDrive, and then access it there. This process takes a few steps, but it makes good sense. By creating your workbook in the desktop version of Excel, you get the chance to use some features that you can't access in the Excel Web App. For example, you can add sparklines, conditional formatting, and pivot tables in desktop Excel, and then view them in the Excel Web App, even though you can't actually *create* any of them in the Excel Web App.

However, you sometimes might want to create a workbook for SkyDrive without using the desktop version of Excel. In fact, you might not even have desktop Excel installed on the computer where you're currently working. In this situation, you can create a new workbook in SkyDrive by following a few simple steps:

1. Sign in to SkyDrive at *http://skydrive.com*.
2. Browse to the folder where you want to add the workbook.
3. Choose Create→Excel workbook.
4. Fill in a file name, and then click Create.

Supported Features

When seasoned Excel veterans look at the Excel Web App, the first thing they want to know is which features work and which don't. Here's a quick rundown of what the Excel Web App can do:

- **Cell editing.** You can move around the grid of cells, skip from one worksheet to another, and enter text, numbers, and dates.
- **Worksheet creation.** You can create new worksheets or delete existing ones. However, you can't hide worksheets or rearrange their order.
- **Undo and Redo.** The world's two most useful buttons sit just above the File button (but you can use Ctrl+Z to Undo and Ctrl+Y to Redo without lifting your fingers off the keyboard). As with desktop Excel, the Excel Web App maintains a detailed Undo history, letting you step back through multiple changes, one change at a time. The only limitation is that you can't find out what action the Undo button will reverse until you click it. (The desktop version of Excel is nicer—when you hover over the Undo button, it shows a tooltip that describes the previous action.)

NOTE The Undo and Redo features have a significant limitation. If more than one person is editing a workbook at once (page 732), the Excel Web App switches off both features, leaving you without a safety net.

- **Formula editing.** Just like in desktop Excel, the Excel Web App supports point-and-click formula creation (page 241), where you assemble a formula by clicking the cells you want to reference. The Excel Web App also supports Formula AutoComplete, which pops up possible function names as you type (Figure 23-7). You can also use named ranges in your functions, but the Excel Web App doesn't let you review, create, or change named ranges.

NOTE The formula results that the Excel Web App calculates match those that you get in the desktop version of Excel. If you know a bit about web-page design, this might surprise you. After all, every browser is different, so it seems logical that the results you get on one system might not match those on another. But the Excel Web App doesn't use your browser to perform its calculations. Instead, it talks to the SharePoint server and asks *it* to do the work. This design also has a side effect: With complex formulas and a powerful server, the Excel Web App might get the answer faster than desktop Excel.

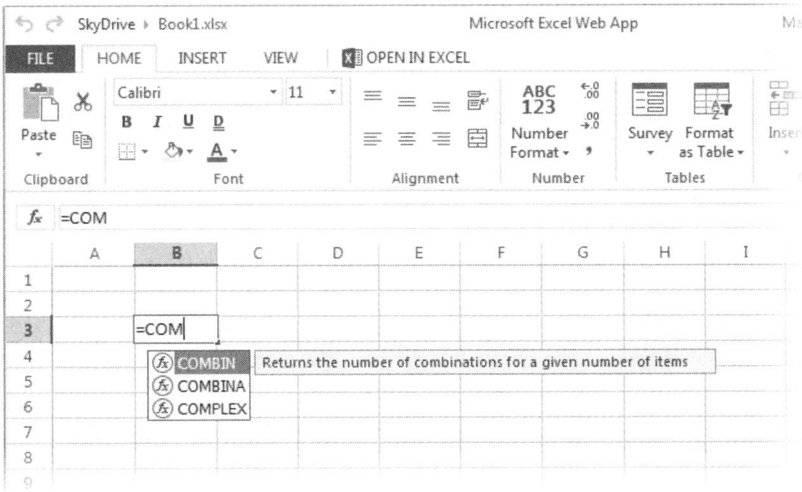

FIGURE 23-7

Here, a drop-down list of suggestions makes it easier to find the right function, just as it does in desktop Excel.

- **Cell selection.** You can drag to select groups of cells, just like in desktop Excel. The only limitation is that you can't select noncontiguous groups of cells (page 89), a little-used feature that lets you select different blocks of cells in different parts of a spreadsheet at the same time.
- **Copy and paste.** Cutting and copying works essentially the same in the Excel Web App as in the desktop version of Excel. However, the Paste feature is more limited, giving you just the four most common pasting options: Paste, Paste Formulas, Paste Values, and Paste Formatting. (Page 97 explains the difference.) As with desktop Excel, when you paste a formula with relative references, it automatically adjusts itself to point to the appropriate cells (page 248).
- **Inserting and deleting rows and columns.** You can use the Home→Cells→Insert and Home→Cells→Delete buttons to add and remove entire cells and columns, just as you do in desktop Excel.

TIP To quickly add a column, right-click a column header and choose Insert Columns. To quickly add a row, right-click the row number and choose Insert Rows.

- **Formatting.** The Home toolbar has all the buttons you need to adjust colors, fonts, and cell borders (in the Font section), text alignment and wrapping (in the Alignment section), and number formats (in the Number section). The Excel Web App even supports *live preview*, which means that when you hover over a new formatting option, you'll see it applied to your worksheet before you go ahead and make the actual change. However, the Excel Web App doesn't support all typefaces, so expect to find that your list of fonts is shorter than in desktop Excel. And the Excel Web App doesn't let you apply or change styles and themes.
- **Find.** The Excel Web App provides a stripped-down version of Excel's find feature (choose Home→Data→Find, or just press Ctrl+F) that simply lets you scan cells forward or backward looking for a specific value. There's no find-and-replace feature.
- **Tables and Charts.** Using the Insert tab, you can add tables (choose Insert→Tables→Table), just as you did in Chapter 14. You can also add charts from the Insert→Charts section, although you'll be forced to pick from a more limited gallery, without 3-D or other specialized charts. Your options for manipulating a chart are also seriously pared down (Figure 23-8).

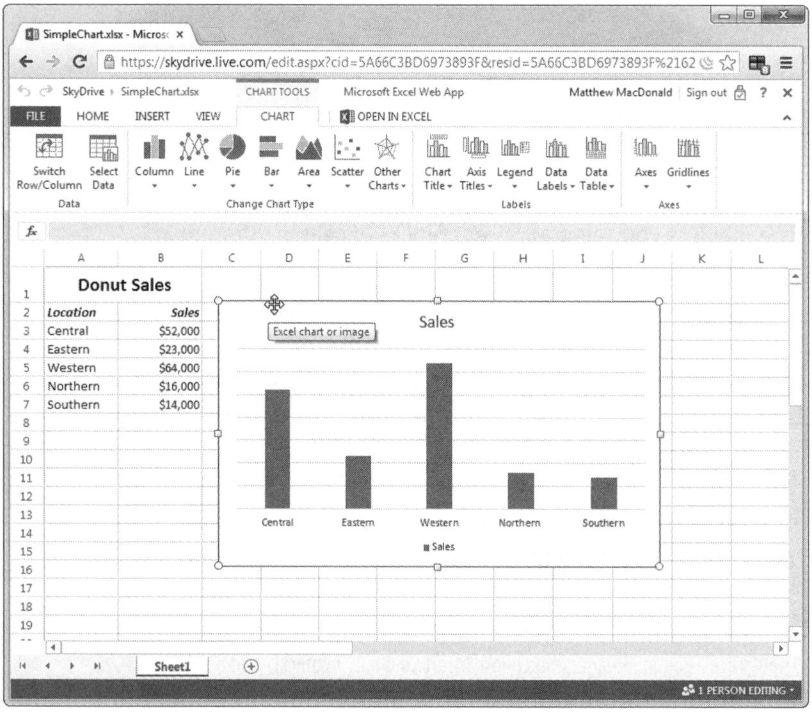

FIGURE 23-8

Once you create a chart, you can select it, drag it around, resize it, or make a small set of changes using the Excel Web App's Chart Tools | Chart tab (shown here). For example, you can edit the title, add data labels, and add a legend. However, the Web App doesn't allow more advanced chart tweaking, like changing the scale or tweaking the color scheme.

- **Hyperlinks.** The Insert→Links→Hyperlink command lets you place a link in a cell that points to another web location. You specify the link text and URL.
- **Printing.** The Excel Web App has a simplified printing feature. To use it, choose File→Print, click the Print button, and choose whether you want to print the current worksheet or the currently selected cells. Excel opens a new browser window with a print preview (Figure 23-9).

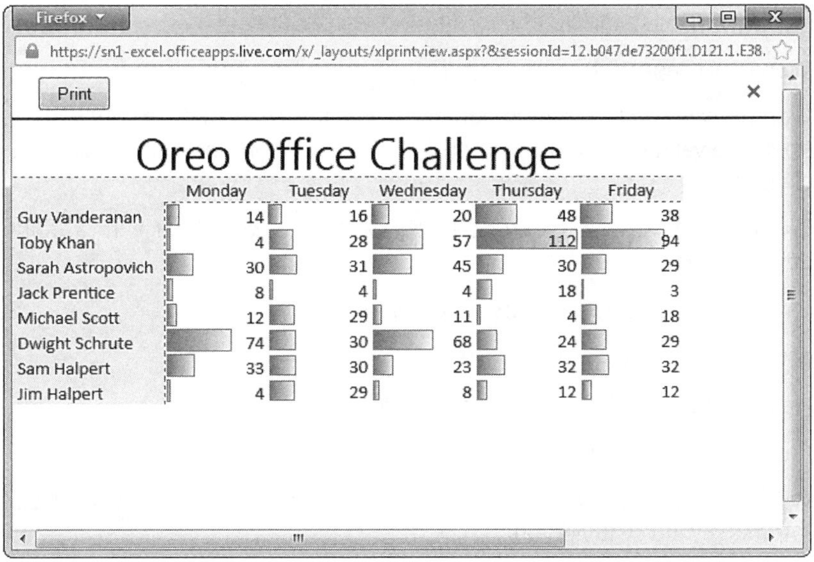

FIGURE 23-9

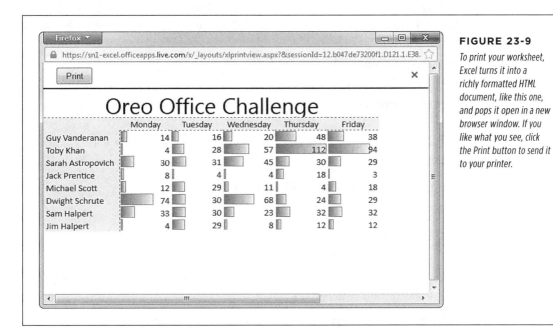

To print your worksheet, Excel turns it into a richly formatted HTML document, like this one, and pops it open in a new browser window. If you like what you see, click the Print button to send it to your printer.

The common theme of the Excel Web App is this: It supports only a subset of Excel's features, but when it supports a feature, it duplicates the desktop approach as closely as possible. In future releases, more features will migrate from Excel into the Excel Web App, and its capabilities will grow.

NOTE The Office Web Apps aren't tied to the desktop software. That means Microsoft can correct problems or add features to the Excel Web App before it releases the next version of Office.

The best way to get a feeling for what the Excel Web App can and can't do it is to give it a test drive. Enter some data, move it around, create a table, and then browse through the simplified ribbon. If you're looking for a simple way to share spreadsheets and work over the Web, the Excel Web App will impress you. But if you're a power user who relies on Excel's premier features, or you spend a lot of time creating charts and graphics, you'll probably miss your favorite features.

Unsupported Features

As you've no doubt already noticed, the Excel Web App lacks the majority of Excel's less essential features. For example, if you want to debug a formula, run a spell check, or fill in missing values with the Solver add-in, you're out of luck. Removing these features is relatively harmless, if a bit inconvenient, but it doesn't affect the basics of opening or editing a workbook.

However, other features, once applied, *do* affect the way a spreadsheet works. If the Excel Web App can't support these features, it won't let you open the workbook at all. Here are the most commonly used forbidden features:

- Scenarios (page 764).
- Workbook protection, digital signatures, and IRM (page 652). If your workbook uses data validation, you can open it in the Excel Web App, but you can't make changes.
- Ink annotations, which are usually "drawn" on a worksheet with a pointing device called a stylus.
- Embedded and linked objects (Chapter 24).
- XML maps (Chapter 28).
- Macros or custom functions (Chapter 29).
- Buttons and other Visual Basic controls (page 916).
- Workbooks you save with the "Show formulas in cells instead of their calculated results" setting switched on.
- Large files. If it's bigger than 5 MB, the Excel Web App won't open it.

If you try to open a file with one of these features, you'll receive an explanatory error message like the one shown in Figure 23-10.

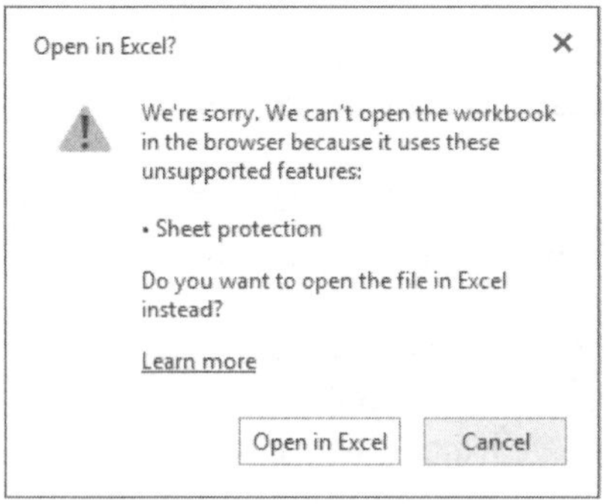

FIGURE 23-10

Because this spreadsheet uses worksheet protection, you can't edit it. However, you can still open it in desktop Excel by clicking the Open in Excel button.

Unfortunately, Excel doesn't include a tool that lets you know if a workbook is compatible with the Excel Web App. Instead, you have to upload it, and then try editing the file in your browser.

Partially Supported Features

There's a second class of features you can't apply with the Excel Web App, but you can keep using if the features are already present in the workbook. Here are the most notable examples:

- **External references.** If you have a formula that points to a cell in another workbook, the Excel Web App uses the most recent value of the cell in its place.
- **Grouping.** The Excel Web App doesn't let you group cells. But if you already set up the grouping in desktop Excel, you can use it in the Excel Web App to expand or collapse columns and rows.
- **Pictures.** They appear as the familiar floating picture boxes. However, you can't move, resize, delete, or add a picture with the Excel Web App. Furthermore, the App doesn't support some types of picture effects, like rotations, shadows, cropping, and 3-D bevels. If your graphics use these effects, the Excel Web App still displays them, but without the extra fanciness.
- **Conditional formatting and sparklines.** The Excel Web App won't let you create conditional formatting rules or sparklines. But if they're already in place, the Excel Web App uses them, refreshing the formatting and redrawing the sparklines as the values in the linked cells change.
- **Pivot tables.** Although you can't create pivot tables or pivot charts, the Excel Web App is surprisingly adept at letting you edit them. That means you can open a workbook that has a pivot table, change its structure, modify filters, and use slicers. To learn more about pivot tables, see Chapter 26.
- **Comments.** If your worksheet has comments, you can view them, but you can't add new ones.

The clear theme here is that these features still work in the Excel Web App; they just need a helping hand from desktop Excel. You can use them, but you may find you have to switch back and forth between the Excel Web App and the desktop version of Excel fairly often.

The routine is simple enough. Every time you need to add (or tweak) the grouping, charts, sparklines, or conditional formatting in your workbook, you use the File→Open in Excel command to bring the workbook into desktop Excel. Once you finish, you close the file to make it available online through the Excel Web App.

Saving Files

If you spend enough time poking around the ribbon and File menu in the Excel Web App, you'll notice that something is missing. No matter where you look, you won't find the Save command.

This omission reflects an important difference in the way the Excel Web App works. Desktop Excel saves changes when you ask it to. But the Excel Web App saves changes continuously as you edit. This way, the Excel Web App ensures that you never lose your work, even if you lose your network connection or your browser crashes—two annoyances that are all too common in the wild world of the Web.

Of course, automatic saving has potential drawbacks too—namely, you can't make casual changes or try out new sample data. Any modifications you make have the potential to replace important data. The Excel Web App includes a collaborative editing feature (described on page 732) that compounds the problem, because other people will see your changes right away.

You might think that the Undo feature can help you out, but it's not quite as protective as you think. If you close the workbook by navigating away, or if someone else starts editing the document at the same time as you, you'll lose your Undo history. So if you need to make potentially dangerous changes—ones that you might want to reverse, or ones that you don't want other people to see yet—your best bet is to open a copy of the workbook in desktop Excel, as described on page 723.

TIP You can protect yourself from accidental edits by switching your workbook into reading mode. To do that, choose View→Document Views→Reading View.

GEM IN THE ROUGH

Digging Up Older Versions of Your Workbook

The Excel Web App does have one feature that can help you recover from rash changes. As you edit your spreadsheet, the Excel Web App makes periodic backup copies of your work. You won't see these files in SkyDrive, but you can access them from backstage view in the Excel Web App.

To hunt for backups, choose File→Info and click the Previous Versions button. The Excel Web App loads a new page, which lists the old copies it has on hand and the date you created them (Figure 23-11). You can then view these old versions, download them to your computer, or *restore* them, in which case the Excel Web App overwrites the current version of your spreadsheet on SkyDrive with the old version you pick.

The previous versions feature is unarguably cool, and it may even help you recover from an Excel editing disaster. However, it also has a limitation: It puts Microsoft in charge of your backups. There's no way to tell the Excel Web App what versions to back up, or how long to keep the backups. This is one reason big companies opt to share their files on a SharePoint server.

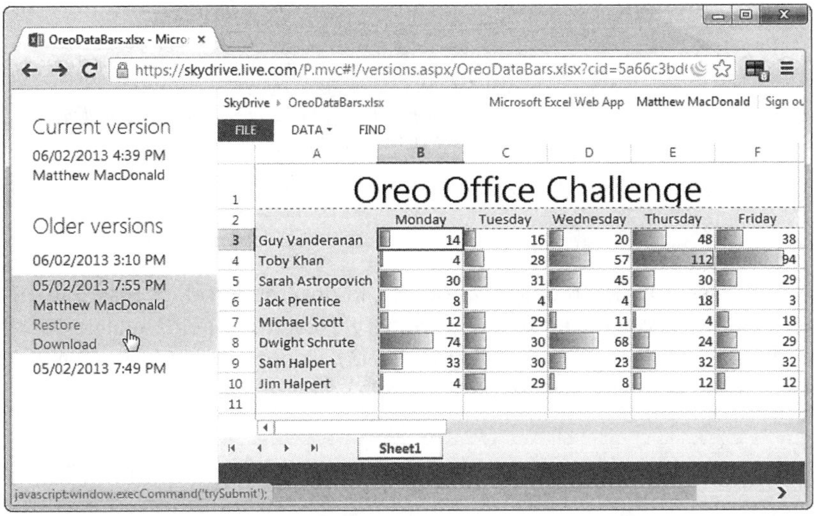

FIGURE 23-11

In this example, you have three old versions of the OreoDataBars.xlsx file. When you pick one of them (on the left), the Excel Web App loads it up so you can look for differences. Then, you can click the Restore link to revert to this version, or the Download link to transfer a copy to your computer.

Taking a Workbook Back to Desktop Excel

The Excel Web App gives anyone an easy way to pop into an Excel document, add some information, and get back to work. It shines if you (or a group of people) need to edit an Excel workbook from multiple computers. It's especially handy for making quick edits on a computer that doesn't have Excel installed.

However, sometimes the Excel Web App isn't the best tool for the job. For example, you might want to use a feature that's available only in the desktop version of Excel (like spell check), or you might want to make changes that are quicker and easier to do offline (like searching and replacing text, or troubleshooting misbehaving formulas). In other cases, you might choose to take exclusive control of the workbook before you make major changes. That way, you're less likely to run into a problem with overlapping edits, and less likely to obliterate something important with an automatically saved change you didn't want to make.

You can deal with scenarios like these several ways. If you use the Excel Web App to share a copy of an important workbook, you can simply change your local version of the file (which is the main version, after all), and then upload a replacement copy. But if your main version is the one online, you need to download *that* version in desktop Excel. You do so by finding the file in Excel's recent document list, or by clicking Open in Excel in the Excel Web App (which appears just to the right of the View tab). Either way, the Excel for Web App downloads the file to your computer, opens it in Excel, and locks the online version. That means that while you're working on the downloaded file, no one can edit the Excel Web App version (Figure 23-12).

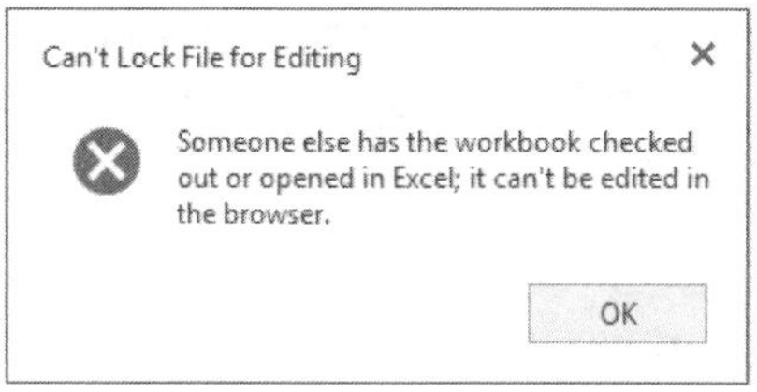
Can't Lock File for Editing
Someone else has the workbook checked out or opened in Excel; it can't be edited in the browser.
OK

FIGURE 23-12

This is the message you get if you try to edit a workbook in the Excel Web App that's open in the desktop version of Excel. Click OK and the Excel Web App opens a read-only version of the spreadsheet that you can look at without making changes.

When you finish editing an online workbook in desktop Excel, choose File→Save (or press Ctrl+S) as you would with any ordinary Excel workbook. Excel uploads the updated file to its online location (Figure 23-13). Choose File→Close when you're finished to release the file and let other people edit it online.

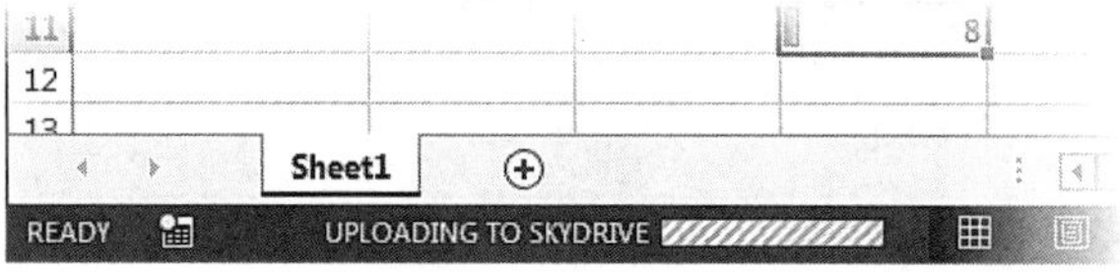
12
Sheet1
READY
UPLOADING TO SKYDRIVE

FIGURE 23-13

In desktop Excel, the status bar tells you when Excel is uploading a file. It does this in the background, which means you can get back to work viewing or editing the workbook while Excel finishes the upload. If you close Excel with an upload underway, it finishes the upload before shutting down.

In some situations, you may want to open a workbook in desktop Excel without locking it. You may simply want a copy of the workbook to use as the starting point for a different file, for instance. There are two easy ways to download a copy of your workbook: In the SkyDrive file listing, right-click the workbook file and choose Download, or, in the Excel Web App, choose File→Save As and then click the Download button.

Sharing Your Files

It's easy enough to view and download one of your own SkyDrive files. All you need to do is log on to your SkyDrive account, and then browse to the right folder. But what if you want to let other people in on the fun?

Initially, every file you upload to SkyDrive (including Excel workbooks) is private. That means only you can see or edit it. However, SkyDrive lets you share your files with a broader audience, and even on social networks.

Workbook sharing revolves around the concept of *links*. If you want someone to be able to view a workbook you uploaded to SkyDrive, you create a viewing link and send it by email. If you want someone to be able to edit a workbook on SkyDrive, you create an editing link. The link serves two purposes: it leads the recipient to the right file, and it allows them to bypass the SkyDrive security system. (Ordinarily, SkyDrive won't let anyone access your workbook files, unless they log in with your email address and password.)

SkyDrive gives you the flexibility to choose who you invite to see your work (individual people, a whole group, or the whole world) and what you allow them to do (edit your files, or just view them). You can even mix and match these two approaches—for example, letting a large crowd of people view your spreadsheet but giving just a few individuals the power to edit them.

Inviting Specific People

The most targeted way to share your workbook is to invite people to come and see it online. You do so from the File→Share page in desktop Excel or the Excel Web App. The process is mostly the same either way. However, the Excel Web App gives the best balance of convenience and features. Here's how to use it:

1. **Choose File→Share.**

   This takes you to the Share page in backstage view.

2. **Click Share with People.**

   A new window opens, packed full of sharing options.

TIP You can get to the same window on SkyDrive without opening your workbook first: Right-click your workbook file and choose Share.

3. **Click "Send email" in the list of sharing options (on the left).**

   The Excel Web App loads up two text boxes, where you type in an email address and an email message (Figure 23-14).

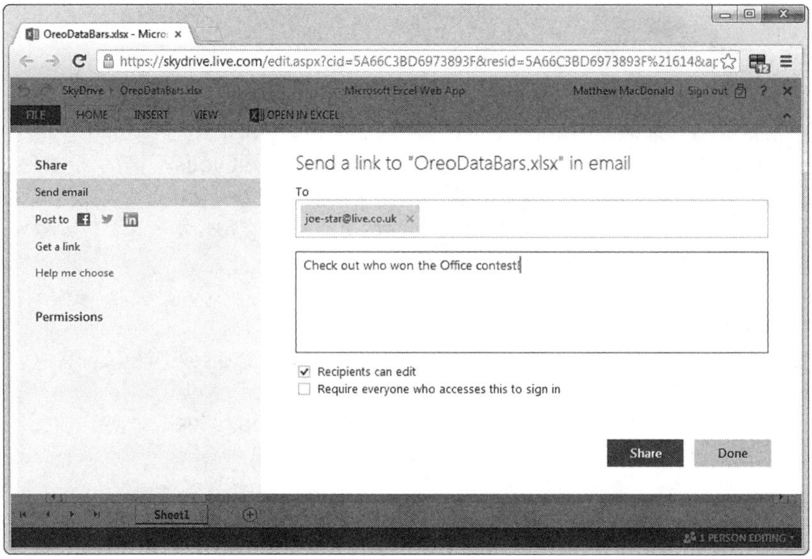

FIGURE 23-14

In this example, you're inviting joe-star@live.co.uk to view or edit OreoDataBars.xlsx, with no SkyDrive sign-in required.

4. **Type in your recipient's email address.**

   To invite several people in one fell swoop, enter multiple email addresses. When you finish typing in the first one, press Tab and then type in a second. Continue this process until you add all the people you want.

5. **Optionally, type a short email message.**

   Your email message always includes a generic bit of text like this: "Charles Samsault has a document to share with you on SkyDrive. To view it, click the link below." If you enter your own message (like "Check out who won the Office contest!"), it appears before the standard copy.

6. **To let your recipients edit the file, turn on the "Recipients can edit" box.**

   This is entirely up to you. But remember, data validation and other workbook safeguards don't work on the Web, so when you let someone edit your workbook, they have control over every detail.

7. **If you want to make sure only one person can use your link, turn on the "Require everyone who accesses this to sign in" checkbox.**

   Even though you may be sending a link to just one person, multiple people can use the link (if your recipient shares it with them).

If you want tighter security, you can tell SkyDrive that your invitation is good for exactly one person by turning on the "Require everyone who accesses this to sign in" checkbox. The downside is that your recipient will then need to have a Microsoft account (page 707), which has the only credentials that SkyDrive accepts.

NOTE SkyDrive doesn't check that the email address you send a link to matches the login address. For example, if you invite *joe-star@company.co.uk*, and he logs in with the email address *joe-star@live.co.uk*, SkyDrive doesn't complain. However, SkyDrive won't allow him or anyone else to use the link a second time, with a different email address.

8. **Click Share to send your message.**

   After you give someone permission to access your workbook, you'll see that person's email address in the sharing window. This is a handy feature, because it lets you remember, at a glance, who has access to a given workbook. It also lets you change permissions and revoke an invitation after the fact (Figure 23-15).

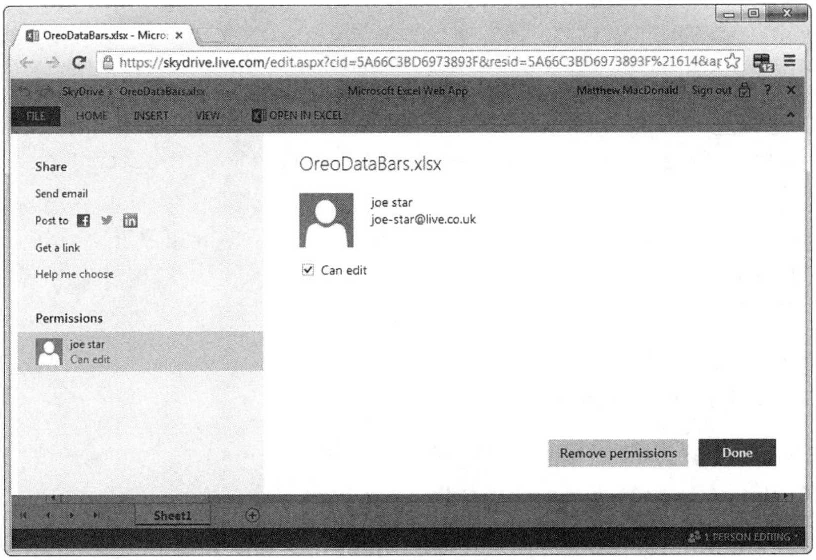

FIGURE 23-15

Every person who has permission to view your workbook appears in the sharing window. (In this example, there's just one.) You can change whether you allow someone to make changes (turn on or off the "Can edit" checkbox) and you can ban them altogether with a click of the "Remove permissions" button.

9. **Click Done.**

   This closes the sharing window so you can get back to work.

When someone visits your workbook using a sharing link, they start out in reading view, regardless of whether you gave them editing abilities. That means they can't make any changes until they click Edit Workbook (Figure 23-16).

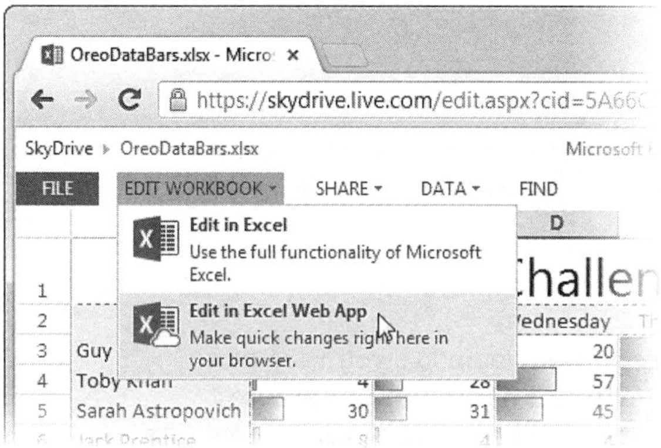

FIGURE 23-16

The first time Joe Star hits up your workbook, he starts in read-only mode. If he wants to make changes, he needs to click the Edit Workbook button shown here, and then choose Edit in Excel Web App.

Creating a Sharing Link

Sometimes you just want to get one of SkyDrive's magic sharing links without sending off an email. Maybe you want to put the sharing link in one of your own emails (like a company newsletter). Or, perhaps you plan to share your document with a large crowd of people, and you want to keep the link on hand so you can reuse it whenever you need it. Maybe you even want to send the link to your contacts on a social network site.

In these situations, you can ask the Excel Web App to create an all-purpose viewing or editing link that will let *anyone* access your workbook (so long as they have the link). Here's how:

1. **Choose File→Share.**
2. **Click Share with People.**
3. **Click "Get a link" in the list of sharing options.**
4. **Click Create next to the type of link you want.**

   The Excel Web App lets you create two types of link: one for viewing only and one for editing (Figure 23-17).

   Excel also provides a third button, named "Make public." Click that to create a viewing link *and* to designate your workbook as a public file. Once your file is public, other people can find it and view it, even if they don't have the link. (The most common way someone finds a public file is by browsing the SkyDrive site of one of their friends or colleagues, but it's also possible for a complete stranger to stumble across one of your public files through a search engine.)

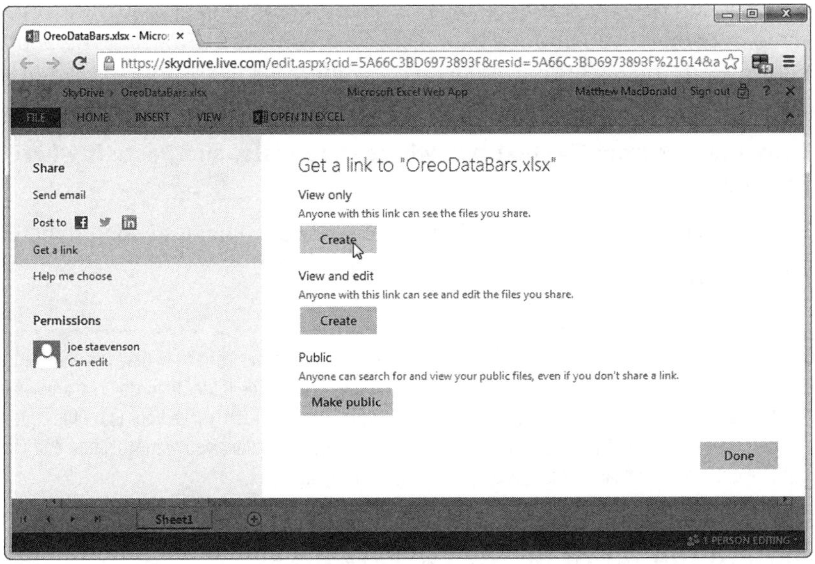

FIGURE 23-17

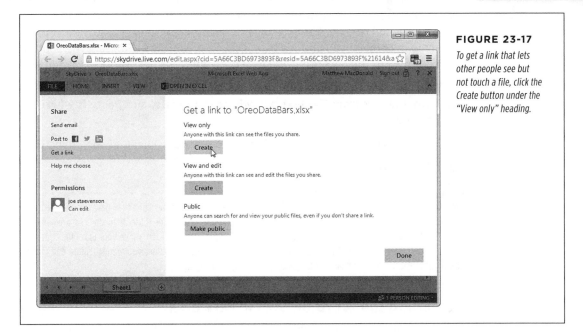

To get a link that lets other people see but not touch a file, click the Create button under the "View only" heading.

When you click one of the link-generating buttons, the Excel Web App takes a brief moment to create the link and then displays it (Figure 23-18).

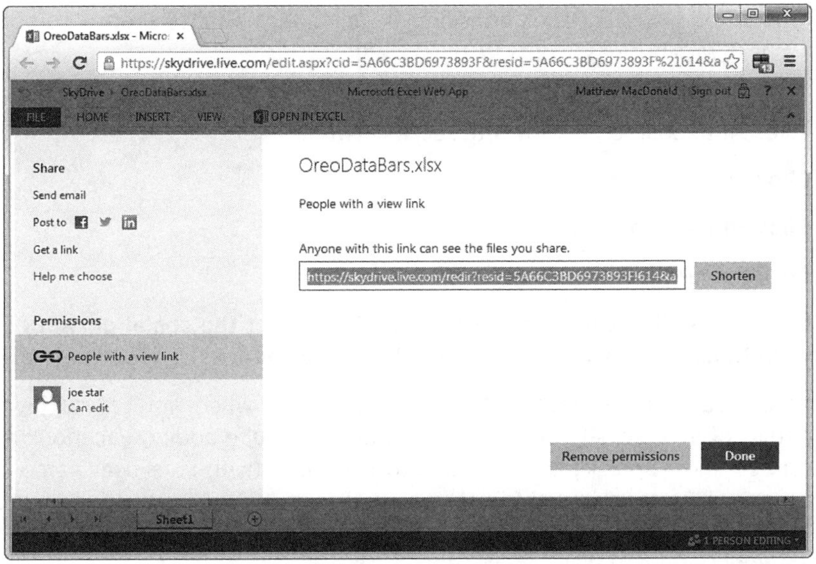

FIGURE 23-18

When you create an all-purpose viewing or editing link, it appears in the Permissions section in the sharing window, alongside any other links you generated. For example, the file in this example has an all-purpose viewing link and an editing link issued to Joe Star. You can remove either permission at any time by selecting it and clicking the "Remove permissions" button.

5. **Optionally, click Shorten to get a smaller link.**

   A typical SkyDrive link looks like this: *https://skydrive.live.com/redir?resid=5A66C3BD6973893F!614&authkey=!AEDk_lIPYnhOHW2U*. It's easy enough to copy that to an email, but not so convenient to jot it down on a scrap of paper. If you prefer a leaner, more streamlined URL, click the Shorten button. You'll be rewarded with a neatly compressed web address like *http://sdrv.ms/XXDMK9*, which uses SkyDrive's dedicated URL shortening service.

6. **Copy the link from the text box where it appears, and paste it wherever you need it.**

   That could be an email message, text file, Word document, or something else.

7. **Click Done.**

TIP Tired of sharing individual files? You can share an entire folder in the same way that you share a single file, but you need to do it using SkyDrive's web interface. Start by creating the folder (choose Create→Folder at the top of the SkyDrive web page, type in a folder name, and press Enter). Then, move your Excel files into that folder, by dragging them onto the blue folder box. Finally, right-click the folder you want to share and choose Sharing. You'll get the same sharing options that are pictured in Figure 23-17.

Spreading the Word on Social Networks

The easiest way to invite someone to use your workbook is with an email message. But as you already know, it's not the email message that's important, but the link it contains—and you can pass that along any way you want.

One way to distribute a link to a large group of contacts is by posting a message on a social network service. And while you're not likely to announce your household budget on your Facebook timeline, you just might want to share a company spreadsheet with business contacts on LinkedIn.

Once again, the sharing window is the hub that lets you advertise your work. Here's how to use it to post to your favorite social network:

1. **Choose File→Share.**

2. **Click Share with People.**

3. **Click the "Post to" link on the left.**

4. **If you haven't yet told the Excel Web App about the social network you want to use, click the "Add services" link and choose the social network.**

   When you do, Excel opens a new browser window where you can supply the details of your social network. For example, if you're adding Facebook as a service, the App asks you to log in to Facebook (with your user name and password, natch) and grant Excel the permission it needs to post on your behalf. When you finish, Excel adds a checkbox for your newly configured social network (Figure 23-19).

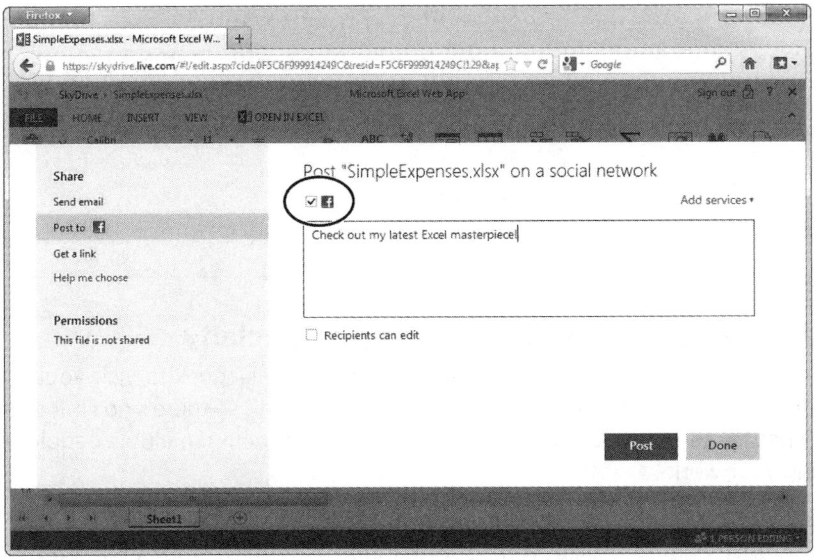

FIGURE 23-19

By turning on the Facebook checkbox, you're sending a workbook link to your circle of Facebook friends.

5. **Click the checkbox next to the social network you want to use.**

   If you added more than one service, Excel lets you simultaneously post to all of them. But that's clearly overkill.

6. **Add the message you want to post.**

   When you post the message, Excel adds the link after your text.

7. **Turn on the "Recipients can edit" setting if you want your social contacts to be able to make changes.**

8. **Click Post.**

   Excel contacts your social network and adds the post, complete with a newly generated sharing link (Figure 23-20).

   As with all the other types of permissions you added in this chapter, your social network link appears in the Permissions list, and you can change whether it allows editing or remove it at any time.

FIGURE 23-20

Here's Excel's Facebook posting for Rob Sampson. Excel-loving Facebookers can now add comments or Like your spreadsheet.

Collaboration: The Excel Web App's Specialty

You've now seen several ways to invite friends and colleagues to visit your Excel goodies. SkyDrive is designed to be speedy and resilient, so there's no limit to how many people can view your work at once. But what happens if multiple people start editing your work?

Excel handles multiple editors with surprising grace, thanks to a nifty feature called *collaborative editing*. Unlike workbook sharing (page 690), you don't need to do anything to turn on collaborative editing in the Excel Web App. In fact, there's no way to stop it. Every file you upload to SkyDrive is automatically available to everyone who has permission to edit it. While you're working on a spreadsheet in the Excel Web App, it lets you know if other people are editing the same file (Figure 23-21).

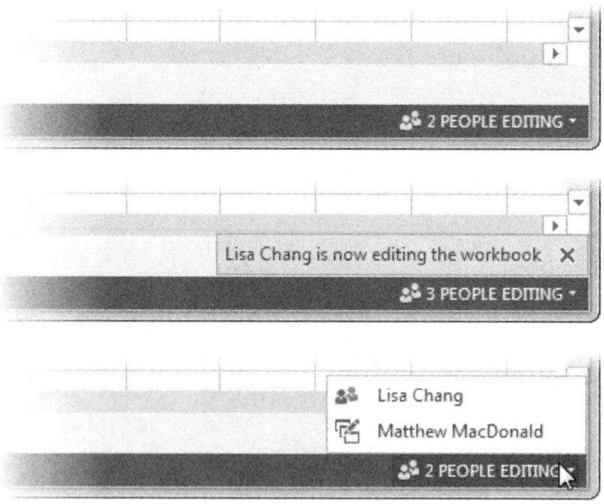

FIGURE 23-21

Top: At any time, you can look to the bottom-right corner of a worksheet to find out how many people are working on the current file.

Middle: Excel alerts you when a new person opens the workbook for editing.

Bottom: When you click the bottom-right corner of the worksheet, the Excel Web App displays the full list of editors, identifying each person by name.

NOTE The desktop version of Excel doesn't play along with the Excel Web App's collaborative editing. As long as the workbook is open in desktop Excel, it's not available for editing in the Excel Web App.

UP TO SPEED

Collaborative Editing Scenarios

The Excel Web App's collaborative editing feature isn't just a way to let a family of accountants review the same figures. It can also serve as everything from a data collection tool to a live chat application. Here are some ideas that show how you can use collaborative editing:

- **Collecting data**. The Excel Web App is perfect for collecting information from a group of people in one place. To prevent the workbook from becoming a data-entry free-for-all (and risking overlapping edits), create a separate worksheet for each person who has information to contribute before you upload the document. That way, everyone can work at the same time, but on completely separate cells.
- **Keeping up-to-date**. If you need to have up-to-the-minute numbers at your fingertips, the Excel Web App may be the answer. You simply leave the workbook open in your Web browser, and the changes that other people make appear on your desktop almost instantly. You could use this approach to monitor everything from current product prices to the status of different members of a team.
- **Chat**. Whether you want to exchange ideas in a meeting, or collaborate on a list of dishes for a company potluck, the Excel Web App makes it easy (in a freewheeling sort of way). And unlike a chat application, the Excel Web App can accommodate mindless banter *and* actual work—that is, numbers and formulas that you save for later.

Whenever more than one person is working on a document, it's possible for changes to clash. You saw this happen with file-sharing on a network (page 691), and the situation can quickly get messy. But the Excel Web App takes a much more relaxed approach to collaborative editing, called *last-in wins* updating. To understand this system, imagine what happens if two people start changing the same cell at once. When the first person finishes and moves to a new cell, the Excel Web App commits the change and updates the cell. But when the second person finishes, the Excel Web App commits the second change, wiping out the first one. The advantages of this approach are no locking and no cryptic error messages. The disadvantage is that your edit can be overwritten almost immediately, and the Excel Web App won't even notify you.

Your opinion about the last-in-wins editing system depends on the way you plan to use the Excel Web App. In tests that Microsoft ran, they discovered that people who wanted to collaborate using the Excel Web App rarely changed the same cells. But if you need a strict versioning system to make sure no data goes missing in a critical workbook, the laissez-faire style of the Excel Web App probably isn't for you.

Creating a Survey

The Excel Web App includes a new survey feature that doesn't exist in desktop Excel. Skeptics argue that it's a bit half-baked, and that it's an obvious copy of a similar function in Google Docs, the search giant's web-based office software. And truthfully, it falls short of the features and reliability of professional survey software.

But if all you need is to ask a small group of people to contribute some information, and a painless way to aggregate that information in an Excel spreadsheet, it works surprisingly well.

The basic process behind the survey feature is this:

- You create a survey by defining a series of simple questions.
- You send out the link to your survey. For example, you can ask all the colleagues on your team to weigh in with their planned contribution to the summer potluck.
- Anyone else who visits the survey sees a basic form where they can type in their responses. (At this point, Excel is nowhere to be seen.)
- As people submit their survey responses, the information is funneled into a table in an online Excel workbook. In fact, if you have the workbook open, you can see the responses as they appear, which is quite possibly the niftiest part of the survey feature.

Here's how to create a survey:

1. **First, create a new workbook.**

   You'll use this workbook to store the data you collect from your survey. You can create it in desktop Excel and upload it (page 712), or you can create a new workbook in SkyDrive (see the sidebar on page 714).

2. **Open your new workbook in the Excel Web App, and choose Insert→Tables→Survey→New Survey.**

   Excel opens a new window where you can design the survey.

   The first order of business is to give your survey a name and description (Figure 23-22).

3. **Add your first question by clicking in the "Enter your first question here" box.**

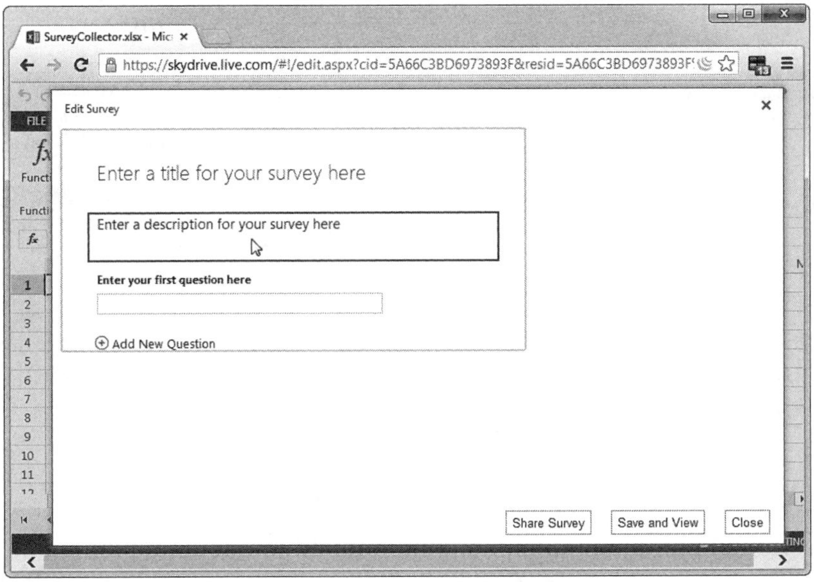

FIGURE 23-22

To set up a survey, you click these boxes to type in a title, description, and your first question. To add more questions, click the plus sign beside "Add New Question."

4. **Fill in the details.**

   Every question consists of a few basic ingredients (Figure 23-23).

   - **The Question.** This is the text of the question, as in "What's your favorite food?"
   - **Question Subtitle.** For more complex questions, you may wish to add extra information in a subtitle, such as "Only include foods you've eaten in the last six months."
   - **Response Type.** The default Response Type is Text, which means survey participants can type in whatever they want. However, text information is also the most difficult to analyze (and you certainly can't feed it into formulas or charts in Excel). Alternatively, you can request numbers, dates, times, or allow a yes or a no response. The most sophisticated Response Type is Choice, which lets you enter a list of predetermined answers from which the participant must select.
   - **Required.** Required questions must be answered before the survey participant can submit the survey.
   - **Default Answer.** If you fill this in, this value appears initially in the answer box, and the survey participant doesn't need to change it.

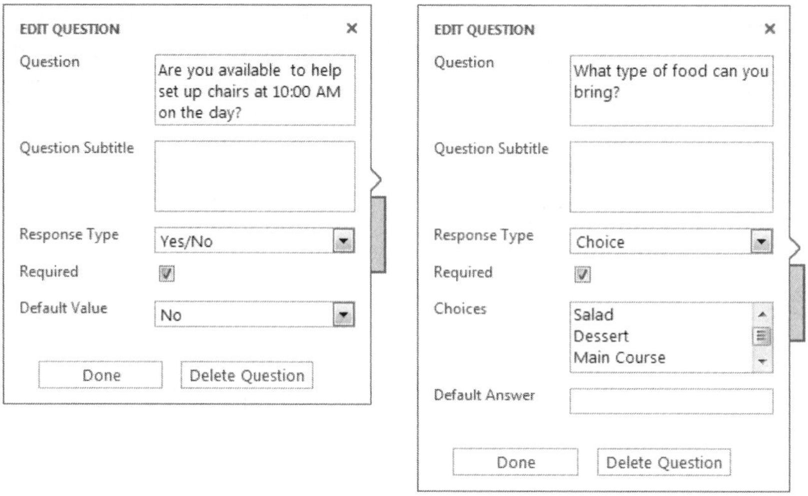

FIGURE 23-23

A Yes/No question (left) gives the survey participant the choice of two answers. A Choice question (right) makes the participant choose from a list of choices you define.

NOTE There's plenty more that you might want to add to a survey, such as questions with detailed instructions, questions dependent on other questions, questions presented in randomized order, error-checking rules that catch spurious mistakes, and so on. However, Excel keeps it simple.

5. **When you finish entering the details for your question, click Done.**
6. **If you have another question to add, click Add New Question and return to step 4.**
7. **When you finish creating your simple survey, you're ready to save it and try it out. Click Save and View.**

   Excel previews what your survey will look like to the people who fill it out (Figure 23-24).

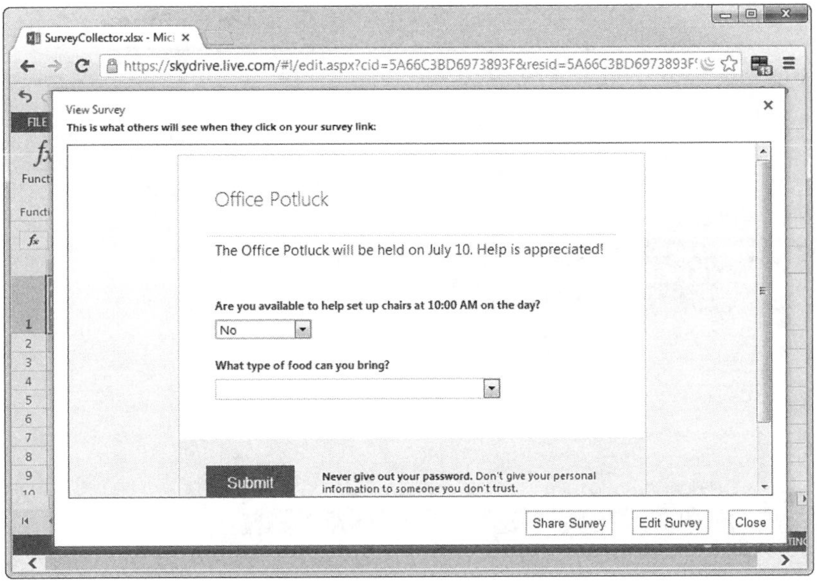

FIGURE 23-24

Excel gives you a live preview of your survey, so you can give it a full test run. Take some time to feel out how it works by scrolling through your questions, typing in some answers, and trying to submit the survey without answering a required question.

8. **To make changes, click Edit Survey. If you're done with the survey and ready to share it with others, click Share Survey.**

   When you click Share Survey, you can generate a survey link in much the same way you create links for viewing and editing your workbooks. Click Create to generate the link and Done to close the window and return to your workbook.

   If you opt not to share your survey yet, you can close your work in progress at any time by clicking the Close button. Excel saves your work so far, and you can pick up where you left off by choosing Insert→Tables→Survey→Edit Survey.

Once you create a survey, there's little to do but wait for people to start answering it. When someone fills it out and clicks Submit, Excel puts the information in the workbook where you defined the survey. The workbook uses a list to keep track of all the survey responses (Figure 23-25).

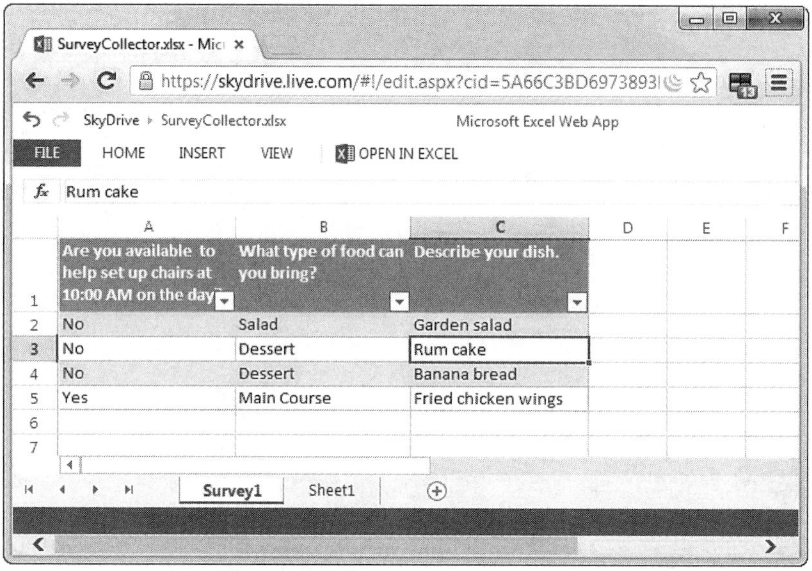

FIGURE 23-25

Excel creates a new worksheet named Survey1 to hold the results for your survey. Here, you've gotten four responses so far.

NOTE Excel lets anyone fill out the survey, even people who haven't logged in, as long as they have the survey link. Sadly, Excel isn't able to prevent the same person from filling out the same survey more than once.

CHAPTER

24

Exchanging Data with Other Programs

No program is an island. Sooner or later, you'll probably want to take your carefully crafted Excel data and insert it into a completely different program. Maybe you want to bolster a presentation with some real data or give some heft to a report. No matter what the reason, you need a flexible way to share Excel tables and charts with other programs.

Fortunately, Microsoft designed the Windows operating system with exactly that idea in mind. Windows lets you integrate different types of data through a pair of features called *embedding* and *linking*. Using these features, you can plant Excel data in other programs. You can also do the reverse, incorporate—objects from other programs into your worksheets.

In this chapter, you'll learn how to use embedding and linking to integrate different types of content into one document. Once you master those techniques, you'll learn how to export and import raw worksheet data.

NOTE Excel is all about data, so it's no surprise that Excel provides a dizzying array of options for importing information. In this chapter, you'll take a look at the simplest—ordinary import operations that can pull data out of old files and paste it into a worksheet. In later chapters, you'll look at more specialized alternatives that can extract information out of massive databases (Chapter 27), and web pages and XML documents (Chapter 28).

Sharing Information in Windows

Every program has its own strengths and weaknesses. For example, Word provides the best tools for formatting long reports, while Excel shines at crunching numbers and charting trends. PowerPoint creates slick slideshows, while Access lets you store and search vast tables of information. Software developers realized long ago that no one could create a single program that was perfectly suited for every type of document.

However, it's not always realistic to separate different types of data. People need ways to integrate the strengths of *all* their favorite programs. Say you want to put an Excel chart in the middle of a Word document (or even attach a Word memo to the end of an Excel worksheet). To build this type of compound document, you need to rely on both Word and Excel. Fortunately, the programmers who built Windows had this type of data linking and sharing in mind from the very beginning, and they wove that ability right into the fabric of your favorite operating system.

Before you attempt any of these maneuvers, it helps to understand that you can transfer information between two programs in two ways:

- **Embedding and linking objects.** Essentially, embedding and linking let you put a document from one program *inside* a document from another program. The trick is that even when you combine these two documents, they both remain in their original format. If you embed an Excel table in a Word document, for example, you can still use Excel to edit the embedded table. And if you link documents, you can refresh the copied information based on changes you make to the source file.
- **Importing and exporting data.** Importing and exporting are more traditional ways of sharing data, but they make good sense in a lot of situations, like when the program you want to work with is *not* part of Microsoft's Office suite. When you import or export data, you convert a document written in one program to a format understood by another program. In some cases, one program may understand another's format so well that you don't need any real conversion. In other cases, the process of importing data changes the data's structure, removes its formatting, or even strips away some information.

So which approach is best? Embedding and linking is the way to go if you want to combine data from two programs into one document (like embedding an Excel chart in a Word report). Even though you need both programs to manage the combined document, you can create the illusion that there's only one document. Linking is the only option if you want to create a document that updates itself automatically when the linked source file changes. If a PowerPoint presentation links to an Excel spreadsheet, for example, the charts in the presentation automatically update when you modify the numbers in the spreadsheet.

On the other hand, importing and exporting data makes sense when you need to process the information contained in one program with the tools provided by another program. For example, if you have a table of information in a Word document that you want to analyze using Excel, you probably want to convert the Word table to Excel's format. If you simply embed the table inside a worksheet, you can see the data, but you can't manipulate it with formulas, charting, and other Excel features.

In this chapter, you'll consider both these approaches. First up: embedding and linking.

Embedding and Linking Objects

Embedding and linking are two tools that let you build *compound documents*, which contain content from two or more programs. Maybe you have a Word file that contains an Excel worksheet. You can save this document as one file and print it as one document, but you need to use both programs to edit its content. Figure 24-1 shows an example.

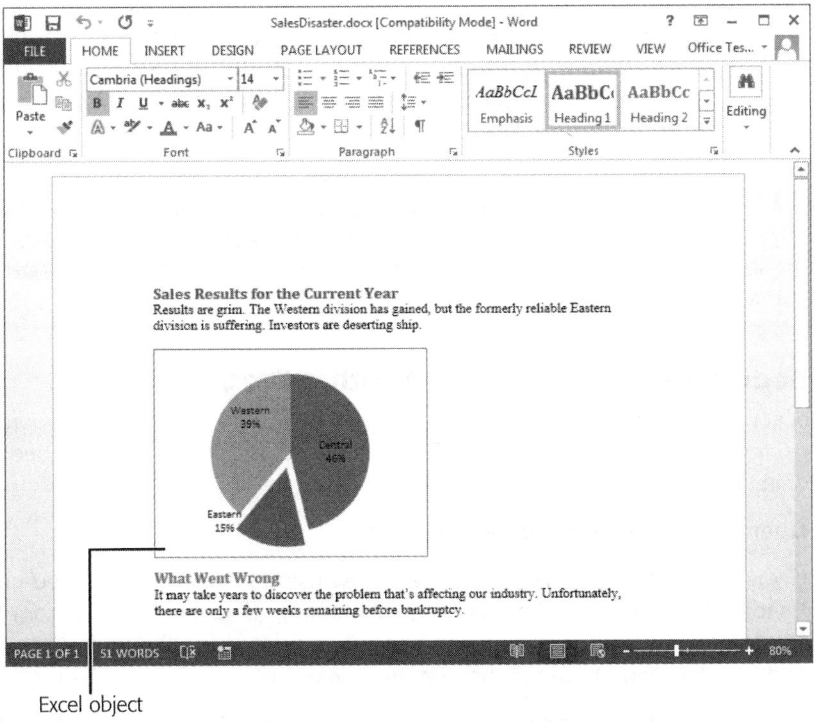

FIGURE 24-1

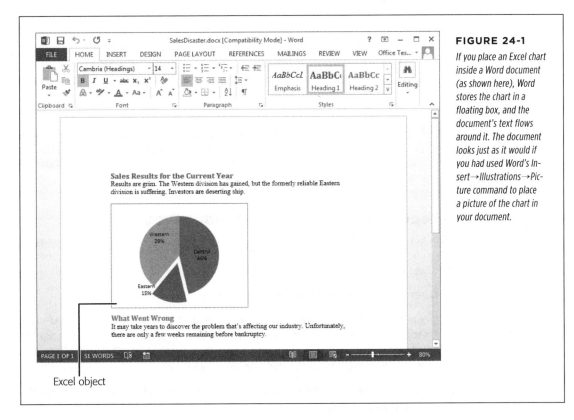

If you place an Excel chart inside a Word document (as shown here), Word stores the chart in a floating box, and the document's text flows around it. The document looks just as it would if you had used Word's Insert→Illustrations→Picture command to place a picture of the chart in your document.

Embedding and linking are really two different, but related, concepts:

- **Embedding** means that you physically store a copy of one document inside the other. If you embed an Excel chart in a Word document, for example, the Word (.docx) file contains all the Word document content *and* all the Excel worksheet data. (This is much like what happens when you insert a picture into a Word document, and Word stores the picture as a blob of binary data in the Word file.)

- **Linking** means that one document contains a *reference* to another document. If you put an Excel chart inside a Word document using linking, the Word file stores the Excel workbook file's name and file location. A linked document stores *some* of the information from the original source, so you have something to show even if the link gets disrupted (if you delete the source file, for instance). However, a linked document's real power is in the link, which you can refresh at any time. When you do, the linked document (in this example, the Word document) grabs the most recent version of the linked content (the Excel chart) and updates itself automatically.

Visually, both embedding and linking give you the same results. Which type of integration you use depends on how you plan to update the document. When you embed an object, like the Excel chart in Figure 24-1, you create a copy of the chart data inside the new document. You can edit that data without having to return to Excel because the chart's no longer attached to the source document. When you *link* a document, any changes you make to the source data automatically appear in the linked document. For example, if you insert a linked chart inside a Word document, then modify that chart in your worksheet, the chart in the Word document also gets updated (once you refresh the link).

NOTE Overall, embedding is easier to manage, but linking is your best approach if your source data changes frequently and you want to make sure the compound document has the latest and greatest information. Linking also makes sense if you want to keep several documents synchronized with the same data (you might, for example, want to show an important worksheet table in four different Word reports).

Embedding an Excel Chart in Another Program

The best way to understand how embedding and linking work is to try them yourself. In the following example, you'll take an Excel chart and use it to create an embedded object in Word:

1. **Open a workbook that contains a chart.**

   If you don't have a chart yet, create it now using the skills you picked up in Chapter 17, or download a workbook containing an example chart from the Missing CD page at *www.missingmanuals.com/cds/excel2013mm*. (You can find the chart workbooks in the Chapter17 folder.)

2. **Select the chart, and then choose Home→Clipboard→Copy, or just use the shortcut key Ctrl+C.**

   The Windows Clipboard is the key to transferring data between all Windows programs. Once you transfer data to the Clipboard, you can retrieve it in another program.

3. **Switch to the program where you want to insert the data. Open the target document (or start a new document).**

   In this example, start by creating a new document in Word.

4. **Use the Paste Special command, if the program provides it. Otherwise, press Ctrl+V to perform a normal paste.**

   Many Windows programs provide an Edit→Paste Special command. When you use it, you see a Paste Special window (like the one in Figure 24-2) that lets you decide whether to embed or link the object, and what format to use. If you're using an Office program with a ribbon (like Word), use the Home→Clipboard→Paste→Paste Special command.

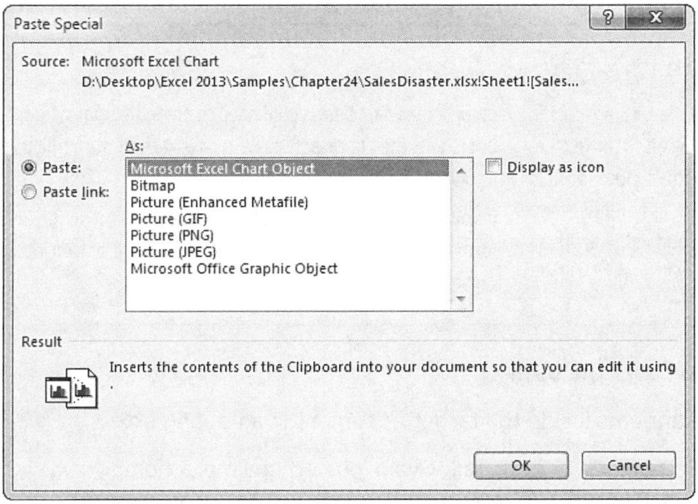

FIGURE 24-2

Many Windows programs provide a Paste Special command that lets you embed or link an object (depending on whether you select "Paste" or "Paste link"). You also have the option of copying the full Excel object or converting it to another format (like a picture).

UP TO SPEED

How Special Is Paste Special?

Different programs differ slightly in how they embed and link files. In Office programs, the Paste Special command gives you the most flexibility, and most Windows programs provide this option. However, a few don't, in which case you have to rely on the less nimble Paste command.

Consider the simple Microsoft Paint drawing program, which comes with just about every version of Windows ever created. (You can run Paint by going to the Start menu and selecting Programs→Accessories→Paint.) If you go to the Paint menu, and then select Edit→Paste with an Excel chart in the Clipboard, Paint inserts a picture of your chart—it doesn't support object embedding or linking at all.

On the other hand, if you use WordPad (from the Start menu, select All Programs→Accessories→WordPad), and then select Edit→Paste, WordPad *embeds* the Excel object. These examples just go to show that different programs make different choices when you use the Paste command. To control exactly what happens, look for a Paste Special command.

5. **Choose either Paste command to insert an embedded object.**

   Remember, an embedded object includes a *copy* of the source data, which gets inserted into your target document.

6. **Choose the format you want to use.**

   The format options you get depend on the type of object you're pasting and the capabilities of the target application. The first option in this example, Microsoft Excel Chart Object, is the only one that performs true object embedding. Choose it to paste the Excel chart, complete with all the behind-the-scenes Excel worksheets that supply the chart data. This gives you unlimited flexibility to change the chart later—for example, you can edit the worksheet data and even save the embedded workbook as a separate Excel file, as you'll soon see.

GEM IN THE ROUGH

Pasting a Chart as a Picture

If you don't plan to change your chart in the future, you can save a bit of time and complexity by choosing one of the picture formats from the Paste Special options. The picture formats take a snapshot of your chart as a picture in one of several graphic file formats. This picture is small and lightweight, so it won't bloat your document or slow it down. If you decide to modify the chart later, you'll need to open the original workbook, edit the chart, and paste a new version of the picture into your document.

If you do decide to paste your chart as a picture, use the PNG format. It's smaller than a bitmap and does a better job of preserving fine detail than a JPEG.

7. **Click OK to paste the object.**

   The object appears inside the target document in a floating box.

To the untrained eye, it's hard to tell if your pasted chart is a homegrown image (stored as raw picture data) or an embedded object. Either way, it looks like a floating box that you can move around as you see fit. The only time you'll notice a difference is when you want to *modify* your chart.

Different programs vary in how they let you edit embedded objects. Usually, you need to right-click the object, and then choose a command like Worksheet Object→Open (which is what you'll see in Word and PowerPoint) or Open Worksheet Object (which is what you see in many non-Office programs, like WordPad). Or, you can double-click the embedded object, which usually has the same effect.

When you open an embedded object, the host program (in this example, that's Word), launches a new instance of Excel and loads a copy of the embedded chart and worksheet data. Interestingly, you'll notice that your workbook doesn't look exactly as it did when you first copied it. That's because, when you paste an embedded chart using the Excel Worksheet Object format, Excel automatically moves the chart to a separate worksheet (Figure 24-3).

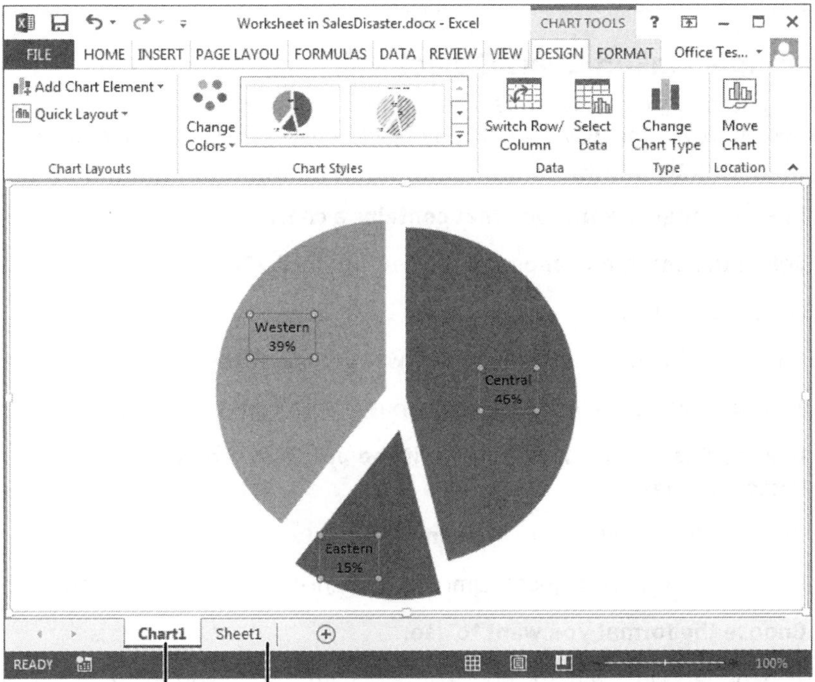

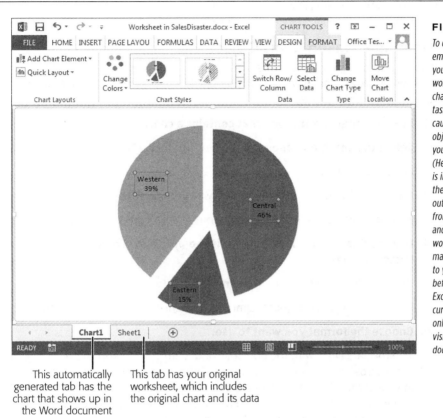

This automatically generated tab has the chart that shows up in the Word document

This tab has your original worksheet, which includes the original chart and its data

FIGURE 24-3

To change the data an embedded chart uses, you need to find the worksheet where the chart's data resides. This task isn't too difficult, because an embedded chart object actually contains your complete workbook. (Here, the original data is in Sheet1, as one of the callouts above points out.) You can switch from one worksheet to another using the familiar worksheet tabs. However, make sure you return to your chart worksheet before you close Excel. That's because the current worksheet is the only worksheet that's visible in your compound document.

When you finish making your changes, close the Excel window. This closes the "virtual" workbook and embeds the new data back into your compound document.

When you edit an embedded workbook in the virtual Excel window, it may seem like you're editing a standalone workbook file. But that's just a clever illusion—in reality, all your Excel data is embedded in another file that belongs to another program (like Word or PowerPoint). And when you save a document that contains embedded objects, the saved file itself doesn't look any different. A Word document with an embedded Excel chart retains the standard .docx file extension. In fact, if you look at the file in Windows Explorer, you can't tell that it contains embedded Excel data in addition to its regular Word content.

NOTE Remember, when you embed an object in another document, you create a copy of your workbook in the target document, while the original Excel workbook file lives on. It's important to realize that these two documents are completely separate. If you modify one, it doesn't affect the other. In fact, you can even delete the original workbook file and still use the embedded object.

Creating a Linked Chart Object

If you want to paste a linked version of an Excel object, you follow a similar series of steps. However, the way your linked object behaves is subtly different. Here's a walkthrough of the process:

1. **In Excel, open a workbook that contains a chart.**
2. **Select the chart, and choose Home→Clipboard→Copy.**

   Or, just press Ctrl+C.
3. **Switch to the document where you want to insert the data.**

   This example uses Word once again, but PowerPoint is no different.
4. **Use the Paste Special command, if the program provides it (or a normal Paste if it doesn't).**
5. **Choose "Paste link" to insert a linked object.**

   Remember, a linked object is simply a reference that points to the original file.
6. **Choose the format you want to use.**

   Two formats work with the object linking feature: Microsoft Excel Chart Object and Microsoft Office Graphic Object. Either way, you'll see the chart appear in your target document, looking exactly as it did in the Excel workbook. And either way, the linked chart is tied to the data in the original workbook—change that and the chart updates itself automatically.

   However, there's a significant difference between the two formats. If you choose Microsoft Office Graphic Object, you create a *duplicate copy* of the chart (but not of the data). That means you can tweak the appearance of the chart in the target document, and it will have no effect on the original workbook file. This isn't true if you use the Microsoft Excel Chart Object format.

   There's another difference between the formats, too. If you choose the Microsoft Office Graphic Object format, you get better integration with the target program. For example, if you use this format when you paste a chart into Word, you'll be able to manipulate the chart in the Word window without needing to launch Excel.

TIP The Microsoft Office Graphic Object format is an Office-only feature. If you're pasting a linked chart into a non-Office program, you won't get this Paste option. But when you can use the Microsoft Office Graphic Object format option, do so—it's the more flexible choice.

7. **Click OK to paste the object.**

   The object appears in a floating box. At first glance, there's no way to distinguish between an embedded and a linked object. But as you'll soon see, embedded and linked objects behave differently when you change them.

The easiest way to change linked content is to modify the original workbook file in Excel. For example, if you paste a linked chart into Word, you can modify the chart's data in the original Excel workbook. Then, the next time you open the Word document, the linked chart grabs the latest data from the source workbook and refreshes itself automatically.

TIP Sometimes, when you change worksheet data, the changes don't appear in the linked object right away. To trigger an immediate refresh, right-click the linked object, and look for a command with a name like Update Link. Or, just close the document that contains the linked object, and then open it up again to force it to get the latest data.

You can also have the program containing the linked object (in this example, Word), open the linked object in its native program (in this case, Excel) so you can edit it there. The exact process for doing so depends on the program that contains the linked object, and they're all a bit different.

If you pasted your linked chart into an Office program (like Word) and you used the recommended Microsoft Office Graphic Object format, you simply need to select your chart to start making changes. When you do, you'll see the Word window go through a slightly miraculous transformation. The familiar quick-access chart buttons will appear on the right side of the chart box, just as they do in Excel. And the two Excel chart tabs will appear in the ribbon, alongside Word's standard ribbon tabs (Figure 24-4). You can use these buttons to change virtually every aspect of the chart's appearance, from its color scheme to its scale, legend, and data labels.

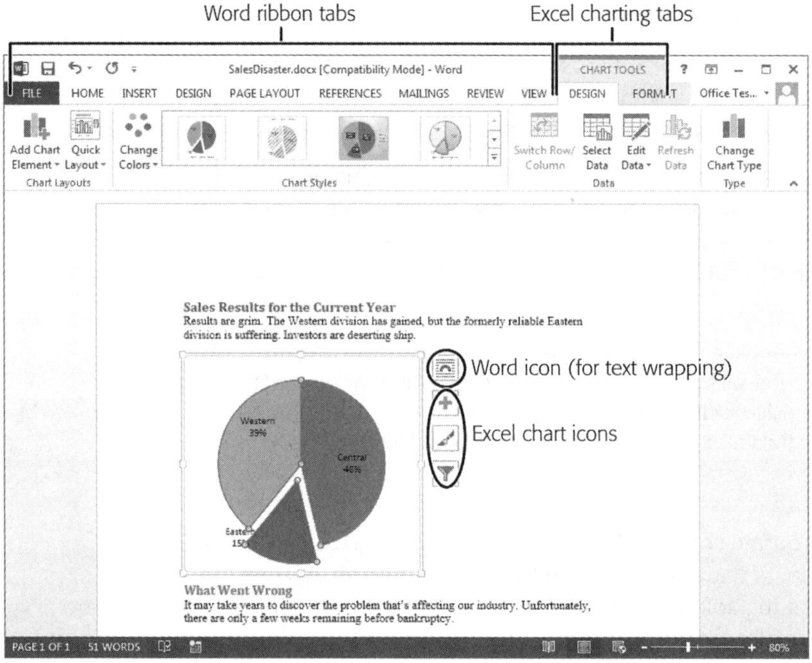

FIGURE 24-4

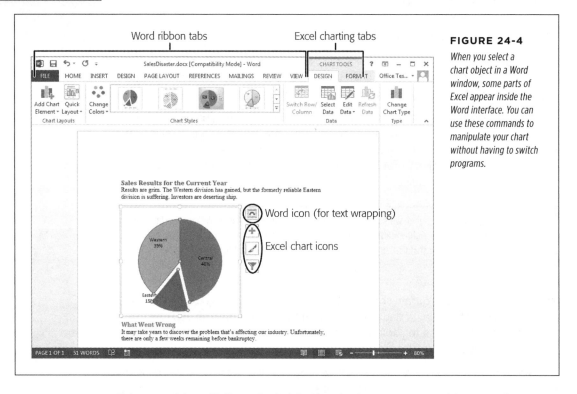

When you select a chart object in a Word window, some parts of Excel appear inside the Word interface. You can use these commands to manipulate your chart without having to switch programs.

If you want to edit the actual data the chart uses, you need to open the source workbook in Excel. To do that, right-click the linked chart and choose Edit Data. A new Excel window appears, with your linked content in it (just as when you edit an embedded object). The difference is that now the workbook is loaded up from the corresponding Excel *file* (rather than from the compound document, as it is with an embedded object). When you finish, just click another section of the compound document. At this point, the linked Excel chart reverts to an ordinary floating box, and the ribbon tabs and chart buttons disappear.

If you're using a non-Office program, or you didn't use the Microsoft Office Graphic Object format, you're interaction is a bit different. You need to open Excel to make your changes, even if you only want to add chart elements or restyle your chart's formatting. The command you use has a slightly different name. Right-click the linked object and choose a command like Object→Edit Link (in Word or PowerPoint) or Open Linked Worksheet Object (in most other non-Office programs).

TROUBLESHOOTING MOMENT

Dealing with Broken Links

Occasionally, links go bad. For example, if you change the file name of a linked Excel spreadsheet or move it to a different folder, the document that contains the linked object won't be able to refresh itself with new data. To correct this problem, you can update the link to point to the new file. However, different programs put this option in different places. In an Office program, you open the document that contains the linked object, choose File→Info, and then click the link named Edit Links to Files (which appears in the bottom-right corner of the Info page). This opens a Links window where you can adjust all the links in the current document. Incidentally, this is the same way that you correct broken Excel formulas that link to missing workbook files (page 257).

Importing Objects into Excel

You can use the same process described in the previous sections to copy objects *out* of other programs and place them inside Excel. When you do, these embedded objects appear as floating boxes (like pictures and charts) that you can position wherever you want.

Embedding doesn't make sense for all types of objects. Although you can technically paste a bunch of text from a Word document as a floating object in Excel, it doesn't integrate all that naturally into a worksheet. However, other types of objects make more sense to import into Excel. One example is an image format that Excel doesn't support. You could paste this image as an embedded object by copying it from the appropriate drawing program. The trick is using Excel's Home→Clipboard→Paste→Paste Special command, which works just like it does in all other Office programs, including Word.

Figure 24-5 shows an example of an object transferred from Visio, a program that creates diagrams.

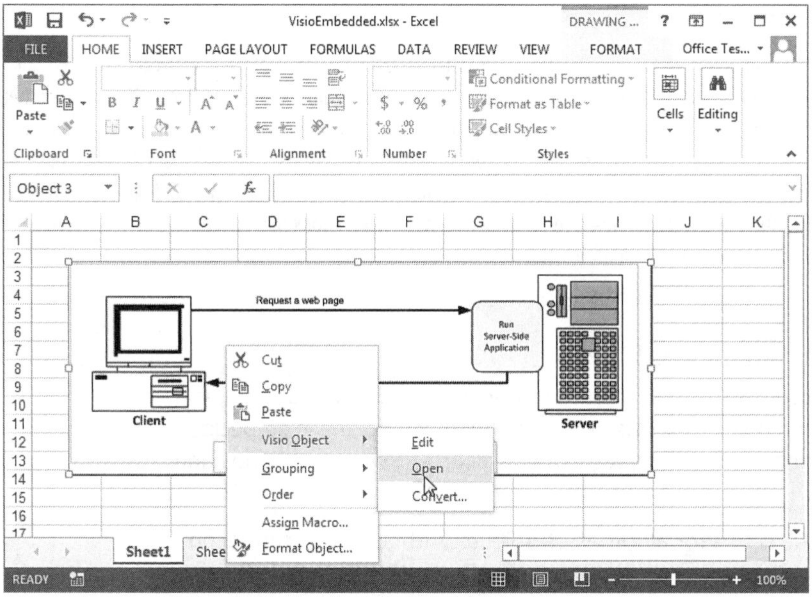

FIGURE 24-5

Visio is a leading diagramming tool. Thanks to linking and embedding, you can integrate Visio objects into your worksheets as easily as charts or pictures. When you select Home→Paste→Paste Special in Excel and there's a Visio drawing on the Clipboard, Excel lets you convert the diagram to a graphic, or paste it as a linked Visio object. If you choose the latter (as shown here), you're able to edit the diagram with Visio at any time.

As in other Office programs, you can use Excel's Links window to inspect all your linked objects and change your links to point to different files. To get there, choose File→Info and click Edit Links to Files (which appears in the bottom-right corner of the Info page).

FREQUENTLY ASKED QUESTION

Super-Size Compound Files

My compound files are gigantic—is there anything I can do to keep the size down?

An embedded chart object contains more than just the chart—it also has the original worksheet's data. You need some of that data to build the chart. To be on the safe side, Excel embeds the entire workbook in the document. Other objects in the Excel file, like pictures and additional charts, also come along for the ride. These accessories are among the reasons a compound document can quickly bloat to an uncomfortably large size.

Before you embed an object, it's a good idea to create a new Excel workbook that doesn't have any unnecessary data or objects. Start by saving a new version of the workbook that contains the chart. Then, delete all the extra information in the workbook. Once you finish paring the workbook down, you're ready to embed the chart in another program.

Transferring Data

With embedding and linking, two or more programs work together to create a compound document. Even though the objects appear side-by-side, different programs actually own them. When you embed an Excel table in a Word document, you can't spruce up any text in your table by using Word's built-in grammar checker.

Sometimes, this level of sophistication isn't necessary, and it may just overcomplicate life. For example, if you have a table of numbers in Excel that you want to show in a Word report, there's no need to use embedding and linking. Word can deal with text and numbers just fine on its own, and gives you all the features you need to arrange and format tables.

In such cases, you could transfer raw *data*, rather than objects. So instead of embedding a worksheet object inside Word, you could simply copy Excel's formatted worksheet data, and then move it into Word. You do lose the ability to update the information with Excel, but you realize a few benefits as well:

- You can edit the data directly in Word without needing access to Excel.
- You can edit the data quickly and more conveniently. This is particularly important if you want to format the data to match the rest of your document.
- The file is smaller than it would be if you used an embedded object.
- You avoid accidentally modifying information if you change the source worksheet (as you would if you used a linked object).

For these reasons, it's worth carefully considering whether you should copy a full-fledged worksheet object, or just transfer the information you want to use.

Exporting Tables of Data

The secret to pasting worksheet data into another program like Word is the same Paste Special command you used to create embedded and linked objects. The following steps walk you through the process.

1. **Select a range of cells from your worksheet, and then choose Home→Clipboard→Copy.**

   For best results, try to avoid selecting empty rows and columns.

2. **Switch to the target document, and then use the Paste Special command.**

   The Paste Special window appears. Figure 24-6 shows what you'd see if you were copying a selection of cells from Excel into Word. In this case, the Paste Special window gives you a slew of choices. In most programs, you have the option to insert formatted or unformatted versions of the text, a linked or embedded object, or even a picture of the text you selected!

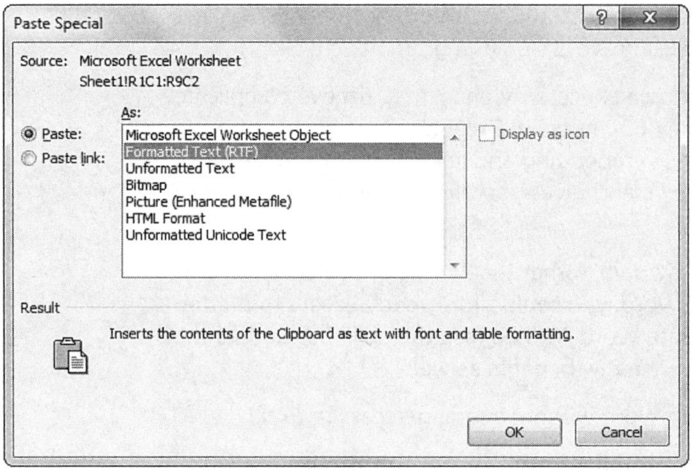

FIGURE 24-6

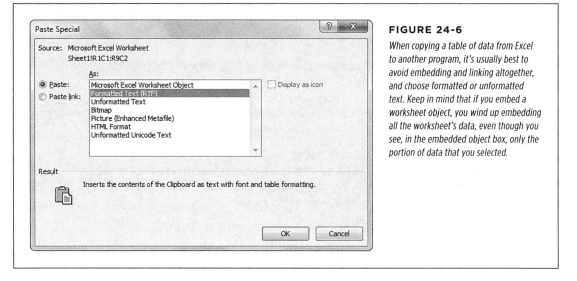

When copying a table of data from Excel to another program, it's usually best to avoid embedding and linking altogether, and choose formatted or unformatted text. Keep in mind that if you embed a worksheet object, you wind up embedding all the worksheet's data, even though you see, in the embedded object box, only the portion of data that you selected.

3. **In the Paste Special window, select the type of object you want to insert.**

   You can choose any supported format from the list. Your choices depend on the type of object you're inserting. For example, Excel lets you paste selected cells as an Excel object, or convert them to unformatted text, HTML text, or even a low-resolution picture.

   You can also choose how Excel synchronizes pasted data with its source. Choose "Paste link" if you want to create a linked object that Excel refreshes based on changes you make to the source file. Choose "Paste" if you want to create an embedded object that you can modify independently.

4. **Click OK.**

   The Excel information appears in the format you chose.

Importing Tables of Data

There's also no reason you can't take text out of another program, and then paste it into Excel. This tactic works best if the information is already arranged in a grid-like structure (for example, a Word table), but Excel can insert the data no matter how you organize it. Figure 24-7 shows an example.

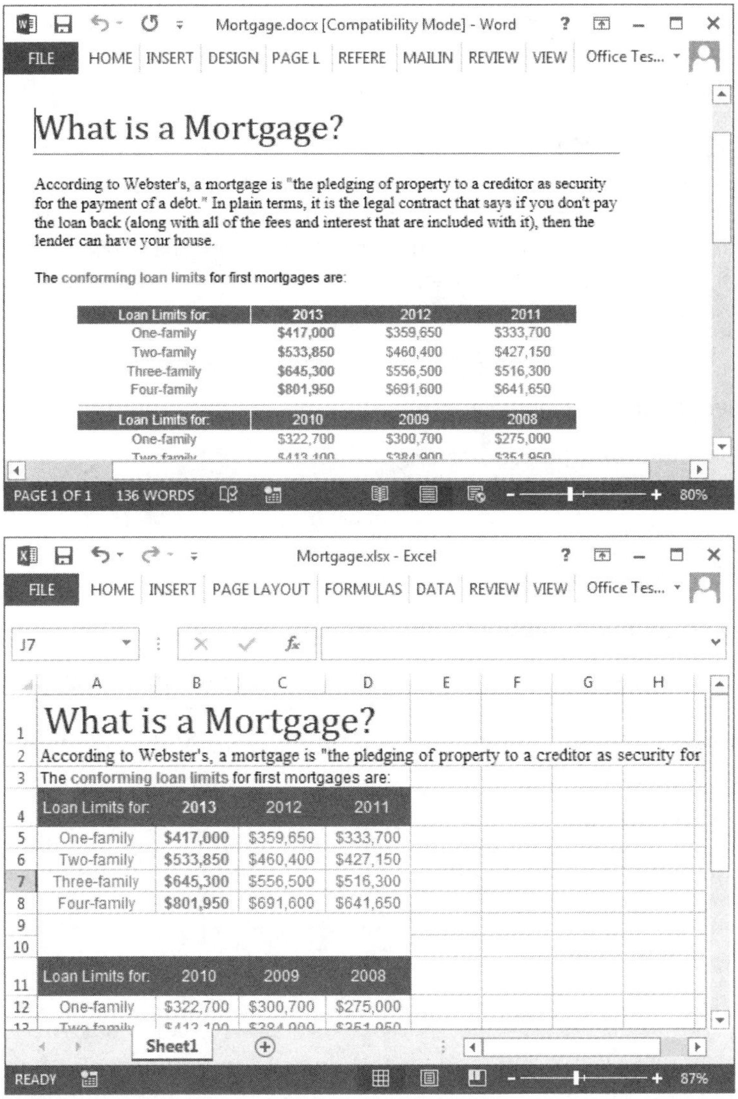

FIGURE 24-7

These examples show some Word content (top) and how it appears when you copy it into Excel (bottom). As you can see, you can transfer large paragraphs, but the result isn't too pleasant. The entire paragraph is crammed into a single cell, and it's hardly readable. On the other hand, tables are much easier to copy and paste. Excel correctly distributes the rows and columns into cells on the worksheet, and it even merges cells in order to match the original document's formatting. This technique works just as well if you copy a table of information from a web page, and then paste it into Excel.

Instead of using Home→Clipboard→Paste Special to paste content into Excel, you can use Home→Clipboard→Paste as a shortcut. When you do, Excel inserts formatted text, and a smart tag icon appears next to the newly inserted content. You can click this icon, and then choose either Keep Source Formatting (which applies whatever formatting you used in the original program) or Match Destination Formatting (which ignores the source formatting and keeps whatever formatting you applied to the cells).

Importing Text Files

Sometimes you want your Excel spreadsheet to use data that's stored in an ordinary text file. In this case, you can import the information into Excel, but you need to go through a special conversion process. This conversion scans the text and splits it into rows and columns so Excel can insert it into a worksheet's cells. Excel provides an intelligent tool, the Text Import Wizard, which does all the work.

To import a text file, follow these steps:

1. **From within Excel, select File→Open.**

   The Open window appears.

2. **From the "Files of type" list at the bottom of the window, select Text Files.**

   Excel looks for files that have the extension .prn, .txt, or .csv. If you have a text file with a different extension, choose All Files instead.

3. **Browse to the file you want to import, and then select it.**

   For a quick and easy test, use the log.txt file included with the downloadable content for this chapter on the Missing CD page at *http://missingmanuals.com/cds/excel2013mm*. This text file contains a list of log entries that reflect system activity on a computer.

4. **Click OK to continue.**

   Excel starts the Text Import Wizard.

UP TO SPEED

Why Text Files Matter

With all the copying, pasting, and formatting features available in Windows, you may wonder why anyone would ever stoop to the lowly level of plain text. In fact, using plain text is more common than you may think, because text files are the lowest common denominator when it comes to data. Even if you have a program that runs on a dinosaur-era operating system like DOS, you can still transfer information, as long as your program includes a text export feature.

Even if you're using a Windows program, you can still find yourself in this situation if the program doesn't provide a way to select and copy objects. You'll often find yourself in this predicament with programs that aren't document-oriented (in other words, programs that aren't designed to help you create, edit, and save some sort of document).

Consider a management tool that lets you assign projects to employees in a company. This tool probably doesn't let you copy employee and project information directly, but it might include an export feature that dumps this information into a text file. Once the text file is ready, you can use Excel's Text Import wizard to bring it into your worksheet.

5. **In step 1 of the wizard (Figure 24-8), choose an option under "Original data type." You have two choices, "Delimited" or "Fixed width," depending on your text file's format.**

   Usually, the program that creates the text file indicates what type of format it's using, or gives you the chance to choose one of several supported formats. If you're unsure of the exported format, you may need to take a closer look at the file by first opening it in a program like Notepad, which should help you figure out what kind of format you're dealing with.

   Delimited means that there's a separator—usually a comma, a tab, or a semicolon—between each column. In a comma-delimited file, the following data would comprise three columns of information, one with the region name (Region 1 is the first name), followed by separate columns containing the month and the number at the end of the line:

   ```
   Region 1,January,43432

   Region 2343,March,839
   ```

   Fixed width means that the columns are separated using a series of spaces. All the columns are spaced evenly. In a fixed-width format, the same information looks like the text below. The problem with fixed-width formats is that a value can't exceed the maximum space allocated to the column:

   ```
   Region  1     January  43432

   Region  2343  March    839
   ```

NOTE Most programs that export data to text use delimited text files. When you import data into Excel, you'll often use the delimited option. To tell whether your text file's delimited, look for its telltale sign—a repeated character that's used to separate each piece of information. Any character can separate columns in a delimited file, but commas and tabs are the top choices.

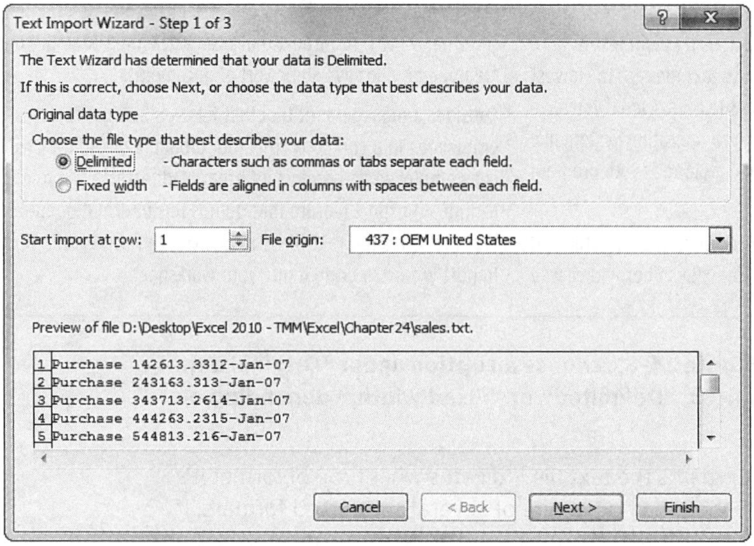

FIGURE 24-8

In this example, you're importing a delimited text file containing a list of purchases. In the first step of the process, pictured here, the file appears as a stream of unstructured information. See Figure 24-9 for the second step.

6. **Click Next, and then complete step 2 of the Text Import Wizard (Figure 24-9).**

   This step varies depending on whether you're importing a fixed-width or a delimited file. If you're importing a delimited file, you need to specify, in the Delimiter box, the character used to separate columns. If you're importing a comma-delimited file (where a comma separates each column), turn on the Comma checkbox. Once you make your change, Excel updates the preview, separating the data into columns using the delimiter you chose.

   If you're importing a fixed-width file, you need to indicate where each column starts. Click the preview window in the appropriate location, once for each column. As you click, Excel adds column dividers between each column.

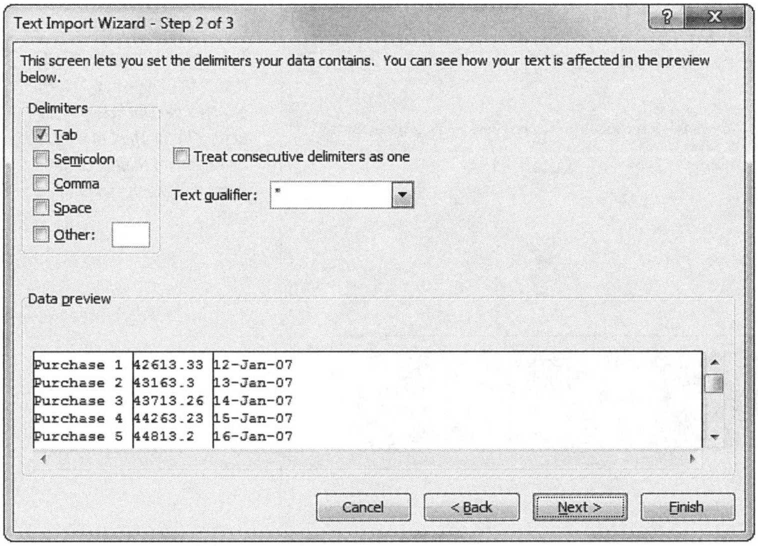

FIGURE 24-9

Life gets better in step 2, which gives you the chance to specify the delimiter that separates columns (in this case, the tab character). Once Excel knows that the file is organized using tab characters, it can parse the file and display it properly in the "Data preview" window.

7. **Click Next to move to the last step (Figure 24-10).**

   The last step lets you specify the data type for each column. Usually, the standard option (General) works perfectly well. If you choose General, Excel examines the content, and then changes it into a text, number, or date entry, depending on the type of values the file contains.

   If you want to override this automatic decision-making process, simply select a column in the "Data preview" section. Then, in the "Column data format" box, choose the data type. You may take this extra step if you have a cell that contains numeric content, but you want to treat it as text.

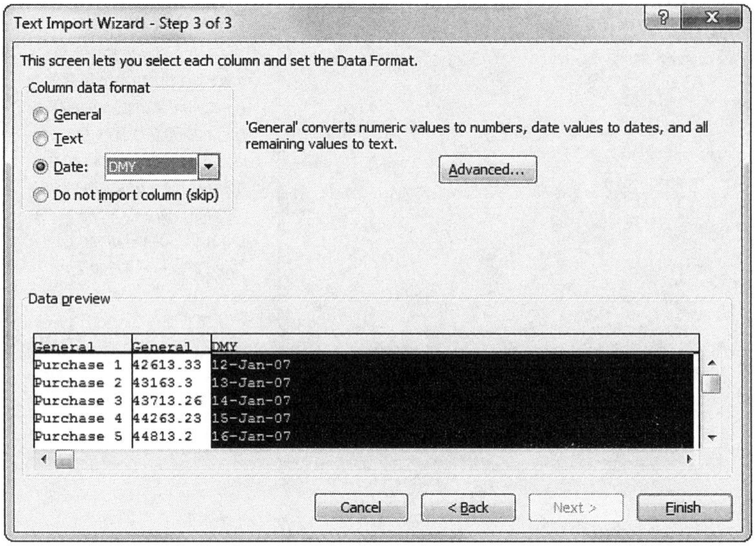

FIGURE 24-10

The third step provides a last chance to change how Excel interprets the data in each column. Here, it's important to tell Excel that the third column contains date information, not ordinary text.

8. **Click Finish to complete the wizard.**

POWER USERS' CLINIC

Importing Text into an Existing File

Rather than using your text file to create a new workbook, you can import its content and place it in an existing workbook. This process uses the same Text Import Wizard—the difference is that once you complete the last step, Excel asks where you want to place the data. (You can use a specific location in the current worksheet, or create a new worksheet.) To launch the process, choose Data→Get External Data→From Text.

At first glance, you may wonder why Excel has two features that seem so similar. But there's a subtle yet important difference in the *way* you use these features. The File→Open command is designed for Excel fans who want to import external data and then change it. On the other hand, the Data→Get External Data→From Text command is for those who just want to *analyze* the information in a text file. Here are two examples that make the difference a bit clearer:

- Your company has oodles of old data created by a Paleolithic piece of mainframe software. This data is stored in bare-bones text files. Now, your company is finally moving into the new millennium. It's up to you to put this data into Excel workbooks, where you can maintain it more easily. In this situation, you need the File→Open command to make the jump from text files to more-capable Excel spreadsheets.
- It's your job to review daily sales transactions and look for emerging patterns or warning signs. To perform this analysis, you use Excel's formula smarts and charting tools. But the data you need to analyze is emailed to you at the end of each day as a text file. It's up to you to pull this information out of the text file and look at it in Excel. In this situation, you need the Data→Get External Data→From Text command. That way, you set up the link once, and you can refresh your connection whenever you need to bring in the newly updated data from the latest version of the file (just choose Data→Manage Connections→Refresh All). Best of all, your linked formulas and charts update themselves automatically when the new data flows in.

Data comes in many forms, and Excel isn't limited to ordinary text files. In fact, the Data→Get External Data→From Text command is part of a broader set of features for creating *data connections*. These connections can link to outside text files, XML files, databases, or even pages on a website. Using the data connection feature, you can perform regular (and even automatic) refreshes so you always have the latest data on hand. For more information about Excel's data connection features, see Chapter 27 and Chapter 28.

PART

6

Advanced Data Analysis

CHAPTER

25

Scenarios and Goal Seeking

Excel formulas are perfect when you need to analyze information from the past, like sales figures, census data, and experimental observations. But life becon [illegible] complicated when you need to plan for the future. Some of the problems y [illegible]

- **Missir** [illegible] om for guessing or est [illegible]
- **Multi** [illegible] single answer. If you [illegible] st-case scenarios into [illegible] same worksheet.
- **Calc** [illegible] jections, you need to *r* [illegible] ed to start with the con [illegible] need to happen for you [illegible] nat score you need on [illegible] erest rate you need to [illegible]

To hel [illegible] pecialized tools that you'll [illegible] use Excel *scenarios* to cor [illegible] ext, you'll learn about Excel' [illegible] for calculating backward [illegible] at one of Excel's most sophis [illegible] or making predictions and o [illegible]

Using Scenarios

People often use spreadsheets to try to predict the future. For instance, in order to plan for the upcoming year, a company may need to make reasonable assumptions about expenses, sales, and profits. However, part of the planning process is considering different possibilities. A responsible company—one that doesn't want to tumble suddenly into bankruptcy, or sell more products than it can make—uses *contingency planning* to prepare for best- and worst-case scenarios.

You can certainly use Excel to create a workbook that includes best- and worst-case information on your own. To do so, however, you need to create duplicate copies of your data. The problem with this approach is that duplicated data is difficult to maintain. If you change the profit calculation formula in a worksheet that calculates the best-case scenario, you need to make sure you track down the same calculation in every other worksheet to make sure your data remains consistent.

Excel provides an easy solution with its *scenarios* feature. Scenarios help you perform multiple calculations on the same set of data—all within the same worksheet. A ski resort may hope for the best and plan for the worst with the scenarios "Projected 2013 Results for a Long Winter" and "Worst Case 2013 Results for a Short Season." You can choose and view the scenarios separately, or generate a summary report with the click of a button.

Creating a New Scenario

You can create a scenario for any worksheet. Start by identifying all the cells specific to your scenario. For instance, if you're creating a business plan that estimates revenue from international sales, you may create different scenarios based on different possible currency exchange rates. In this example, the cell containing the exchange rate's value is a scenario-specific cell. That means that each scenario uses a different value for this cell. As you change from one scenario to the next, Excel modifies the value in this cell but doesn't change any of the other cells (although if they use formulas based on the currency exchange rate, the program recalculates the formula using the new information).

To better understand how this whole process works, consider the worksheet in Figure 25-1.

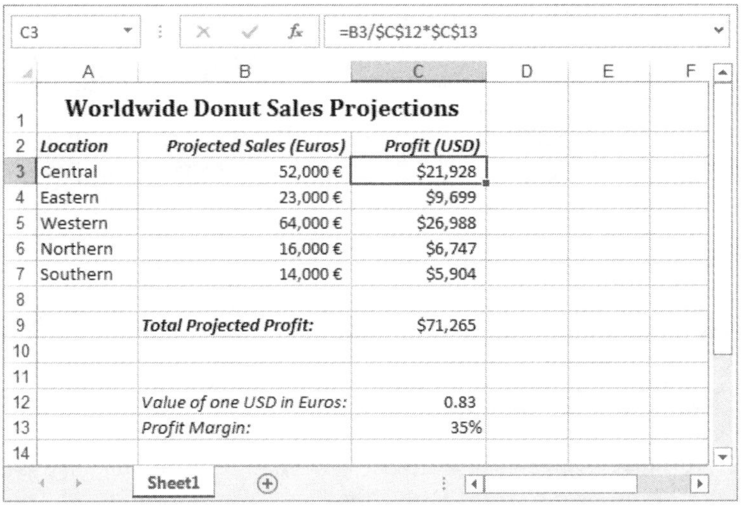

C3 | =B3/$C$12*$C$13

	A	B	C
1	**Worldwide Donut Sales Projections**		
2	*Location*	*Projected Sales (Euros)*	*Profit (USD)*
3	Central	52,000 €	$21,928
4	Eastern	23,000 €	$9,699
5	Western	64,000 €	$26,988
6	Northern	16,000 €	$6,747
7	Southern	14,000 €	$5,904
8			
9		*Total Projected Profit:*	$71,265
10			
11			
12		*Value of one USD in Euros:*	0.83
13		*Profit Margin:*	35%
14			

Sheet1

FIGURE 25-1

This worksheet shows sales predictions for the coming year for five regional divisions of a company. Assuming that the projected sales are correct, it would be interesting to modify two cells in order to see their effect on the projected profits listed in cells C3 through C9: the exchange rate (shown in C12) and the profit margin (C13). How would fluctuations in either of these values affect the profits listed in column C? You can find the answers to those questions using Excel's Scenarios feature.

To try out different possibilities for any formula, you can add scenarios to a worksheet. The following example uses Figure 25-1 as the basis for showing how the scenario tool works.

1. **Select the cells that will change in your scenario.**

   These cells contain the assumptions your scenario makes. You can select any range of cells you want, and you can hold down the Ctrl key to select a noncontiguous range. In the sales projection example, these cells are C12 (the exchange rate) and, optionally, C13 (the profit margin).

2. **Choose Data→Data Tools→What-If Analysis→Scenario Manager.**

   The Scenario Manager window appears.

3. **Click the Add button to create a new scenario.**

   The Add Scenario window opens, as shown in Figure 25-2.

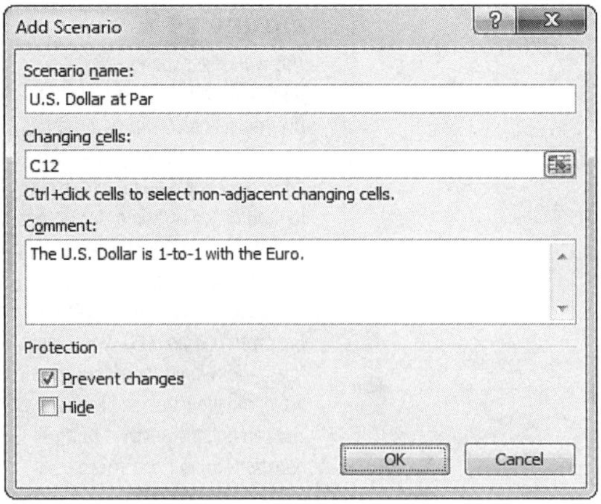

FIGURE 25-2

In the Add Scenario window, choose a name for your scenario. If you like, you can enter a more complete description of the scenario in the Comment text box. You don't need to edit the reference in the "Changing cells" box, because Excel automatically enters whatever cells you select in your worksheet.

4. **Enter a descriptive name for the scenario you're creating.**

   For example, if you plan to create a scenario that explores what happens if the U.S. dollar rises against the euro (thereby causing your profits to plummet), you might use a description like *High U.S. Dollar, Worst Case*, or *Most Likely Case.*

5. **If you need to change the cell references for this scenario, edit the "Changing cells" text box.**

   Excel automatically fills in this text box with references to the cells you selected *before* you started creating the scenario. If you're creating multiple scenarios at once, you may need to change this information. You can edit it directly, so long as you remember to separate each cell reference with a comma. Use a value of *C12, C13* if you want to include both cells C12 and C13, for instance. You can also point and click your way to success. Just click inside the "Changing cells" text box, and then click the worksheet to select the cells you want (holding down Ctrl to select several cells at once).

NOTE You can set your what-if scenario values two ways. First, you can enter the values you want to test in the cells *before* you create the scenario (because Excel uses the current cell values when you do create the scenario). Or, you can adjust the values in the Add Values window when you create the scenario. Both approaches work equally well—it's just a matter of preference.

6. **Optionally, make your scenario tamper-proof by turning on the "Prevent changes" or "Hide" settings.**

   In Chapter 21, you learned how to use worksheet protection to lock down your spreadsheets and prevent changes. Scenarios have two settings that work in conjunction with worksheet protection:

   - **Prevent changes** stops the person using your spreadsheet from modifying any of the scenario values, provided you switched worksheet protection on.
   - **Hide** prevents spreadsheet users from seeing the scenario *at all*. The scenario simply won't appear in the list of scenarios when you have worksheet protection on, and so spreadsheet users won't be able to select it, modify it, or see its values in action.

   It's important to understand that neither of these settings has an effect until you turn on worksheet protection. (You can do that by right-clicking a worksheet tab, choosing Protect Sheet, supplying a password, and then clicking OK. But to understand all the details, refer to Chapter 21.)

7. **Click OK.**

   This action closes the Add Scenario window and opens the Scenario Values window, as shown in Figure 25-3.

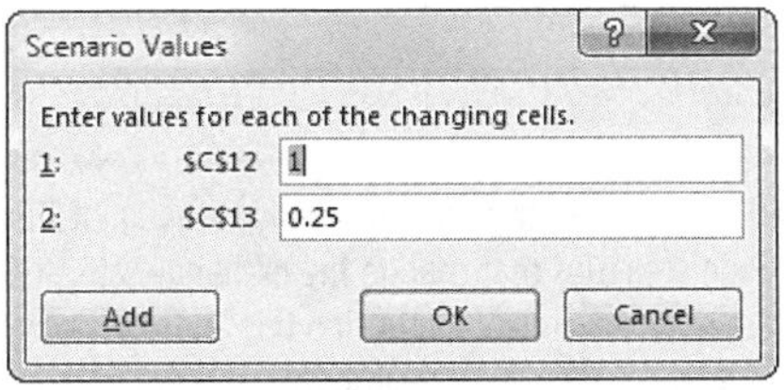

FIGURE 25-3

This particular scenario includes two changing values: the currency exchange rate (first) and the profit margin (second). To examine what happens if the U.S. dollar rises and profit falls, the currency exchange rate is adjusted up to 1 from its original value of 0.83, and the profit margin is reduced to 25%.

8. **Set the values of all the changing cells according to your scenario.**

   Excel automatically inserts the current value of each cell in the Scenario Values window. You can adjust these values or, if they're already correct for your scenario, you can keep them. In the sales projection example, you can adjust the currency rate to make it higher or lower.

9. **Click OK.**

   This action returns you to the Scenario Manager window, which now shows your newly created scenario in the list.

10. **To create more than one scenario, repeat steps 3–8 for each new scenario.**

    There's no limit to the number of scenarios you can create. Remember, you'll also need to create a scenario with your original values (if you want to keep them), because once you've applied a scenario there's no way to revert your cells back to their pre-scenario form. Figure 25-4 shows several scenarios in the Scenario Manager window.

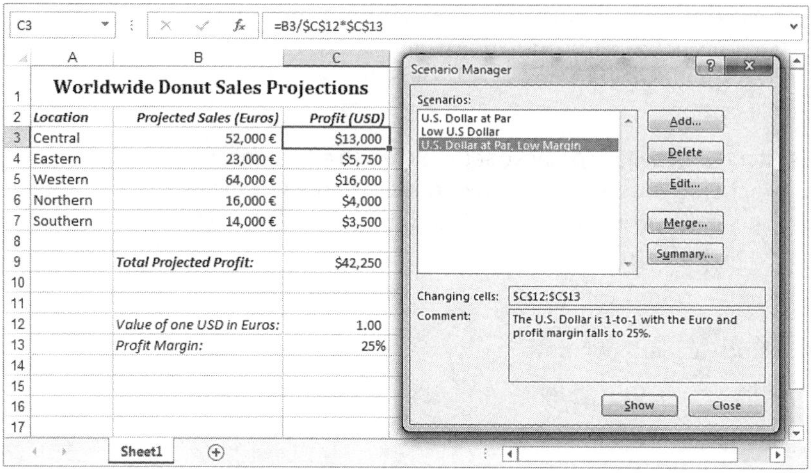

FIGURE 25-4

Scenarios are extremely useful and easy to use. Apply a scenario by choosing it from the list shown in the Scenario Manager window, and then clicking Show. The worksheet updates automatically. Using the scenarios in this example, you can quickly see how the total profit falls from $71,265 to $42,250 in the worst-case scenario.

NOTE Different scenarios don't always need to have the same changing cells, although it simplifies life if they do. In the sales worksheet, you can create some scenarios that change the exchange rate, and others that change both the exchange rate and the profit margin. However, you might find this approach a little confusing if you switch rapidly from one scenario to another. If you change to a scenario that updates both cells, and then switch to a scenario that updates just one of the two cells, the other cell still has the value from the previous scenario—which may not be what you want.

Managing Scenarios

Once you create your scenarios, you probably want to put them to work so you can compare different outcomes. You can switch from one scenario to another using the buttons in the Scenario Manager window. (If you can't see the Scenario Manager window, choose Data→Data Tools→What-If Analysis→Scenario Manager.)

Here are the tasks you can perform in the Scenario Manager:

- **To switch from one scenario to another**, select the scenario you want to view in the list, and then click Show. Excel immediately updates the changed cells (and any cells that reference them).
- **To change a scenario's assumptions**, select it, and then click Edit. The Edit Scenario window that appears looks exactly like the Add Scenario window. It lets

you change the scenario name, modify the changing cells, and edit the description. Click OK to move ahead and adjust the actual values for the changing cells.

- **To remove a scenario completely**, select it in the list, and then click Delete.
- **To return to your worksheet**, click Close at any time. The values from the scenario you applied the previous time remain in effect.

Creating a Summary Report

Scenarios are great for exploring different possibilities, but you're still limited to viewing one scenario at a time. If you'd rather have an at-a-glance look at *all* the scenarios you defined, you can generate an summary report.

To do so, follow these steps:

1. **Choose Data→Data Tools→What-If Analysis→Scenario Manager.**

   The Scenario Manager window appears.

2. **Click Summary.**

   The Scenario Summary window appears, as shown in Figure 25-5.

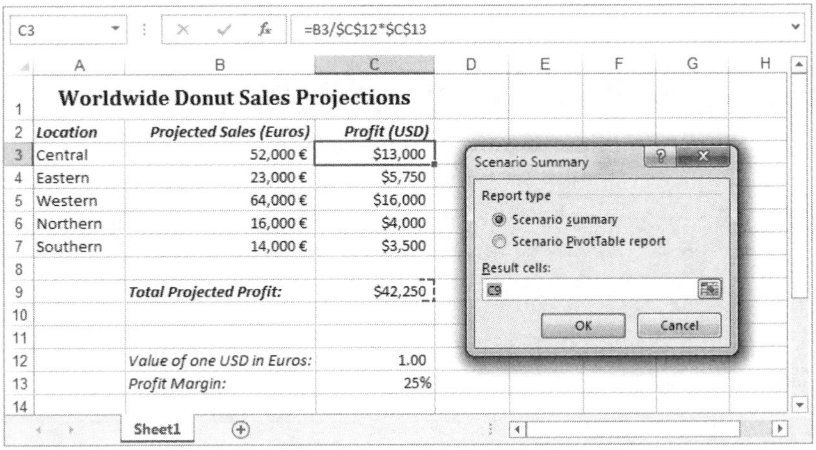

FIGURE 25-5

Once you pick the report type ("Scenario summary" here), you need to specify (in the "Result cells" box) which cells to display in the summary report. Your choices include cells C3 to C7 and C9 (since these cells have values that change depending on the scenario you're considering). You can include all these cells, but you may just be interested in the final total in C9.

3. **Choose the type of summary you want.**

   In most cases, the first option ("Scenario summary") is what you want.

   You can also create a summary *pivot table* instead of a summary report by selecting "Scenario PivotTable report." For more information on pivot tables, which are an advanced feature for summarizing large amounts of data, check out Chapter 26.

4. **In the "Result cells" text box, specify the cells you want to include in the report.**

   These cells fluctuate based on the scenario values you used. When Excel creates the summary, it includes all the values you created for the changing cells, and then shows the resulting value for each of the result cells.

5. **Click OK to create the summary report.**

   The summary report always opens in a new worksheet named Scenario Summary. Excel automatically formats the scenario summary to be readable and gives it basic groupings (Chapter 15) that lets you collapse the summary to show just the portions that interest you. Figure 25-6 shows an example.

NOTE Once Excel creates a summary report, it's completely independent of your data. If you change any of the scenario values or calculations, you won't get an updated summary report (although you can recreate it using the sequence of steps above).

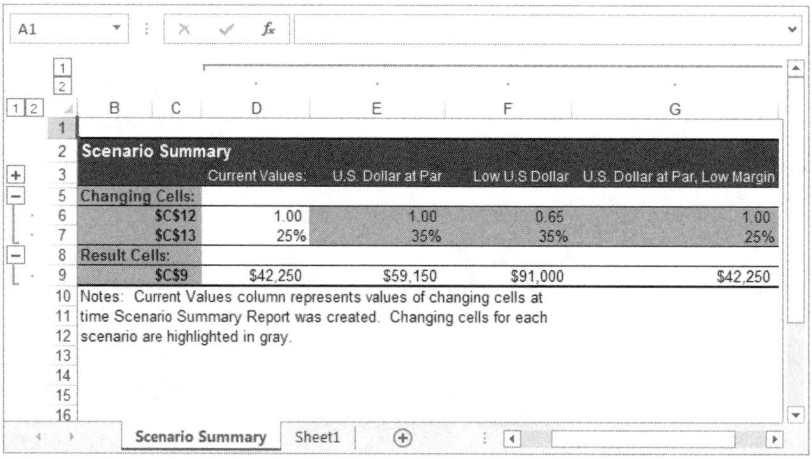

FIGURE 25-6

This report compares different scenarios for the sales projection worksheet. Rows 6 and 7 show the scenario-specific cells. Row 9 gives you the bottom line—the calculated result that appears in cell C9 based on the scenario-specific values.

POWER USERS' CLINIC

Scenarios to Go

When you first create a scenario, it's attached to a single worksheet. However, the Scenario Manager lets you use a little-known trick to *merge* scenarios. This technique lets you transplant your scenarios (and their accompanying cell values) into another worksheet in the same workbook, or another worksheet in a different workbook.

Merging scenarios isn't often useful, but it does come in handy if you need to perform the same analysis with different worksheets that contain the same arrangement of data. For instance, if you have several sales projections worksheets, and the exchange rate and profit margin cells are in the same place in every worksheet, you could copy the same scenarios to each worksheet.

To transfer scenarios, make sure both worksheets are open (the one containing the scenario and the one where you want to copy it to). Then go to the worksheet where you want to place the copied scenarios, choose Data→Data Tools→What-If Analysis→Scenario Manager, and then click Merge in the Scenario Manager window. You can choose the source workbook and worksheet from the lists that Excel provides. Click OK to complete the deal.

When you merge a scenario into a new worksheet, Excel copies the scenario names and the scenario values (the values for all the changed cells). Of course, the merged scenario isn't of much use unless the new worksheet has *exactly* the same structure as the original. Otherwise, when you select the scenario, Excel inserts the changed values in the wrong places.

Using Goal Seek

There are some problems that formulas just can't crack. One of these is solving questions that need trial-and-error guesswork.

In most Excel spreadsheets, you begin with a set of data and use formulas to analyze that data and calculate some conclusions. When you create plans and projections, however, you sometimes invert this process and start with the conclusions. You may begin with a profit projection and calculate "backward" to find out the sales you need to make. Or, you may calculate the rate an investment needs to increase in value in order to meet a set target.

Goal seeking is a fairly simple tool in Excel that can help you answer these sorts of questions, provided your problem meets the following guidelines:

- **There's only one result cell and this cell contains a formula.** You want to make sure the result of this calculation meets a target you specify. The process Excel takes to find the value that meets this target is called *optimization*.
- **There's only one variable cell.** This is the value that Excel adjusts to meet your target in the result cell.
- **There's a valid solution.** If you ask Excel how many years it'll take to pay off a $100,000 loan by making 25-cent monthly payments, you'll end up with an answer—a negative number of years—that makes no sense (since your loan is accumulating interest faster than you're making payments).

To better understand goal seeking, it helps to think about a simple example. Consider the worksheet in Figure 25-7, which shows a list of student grades. Grace Dewitt has the chance to resubmit her assignment, and she wants to determine what grade she needs to increase her final grade from 72 to 80 out of a possible 100.

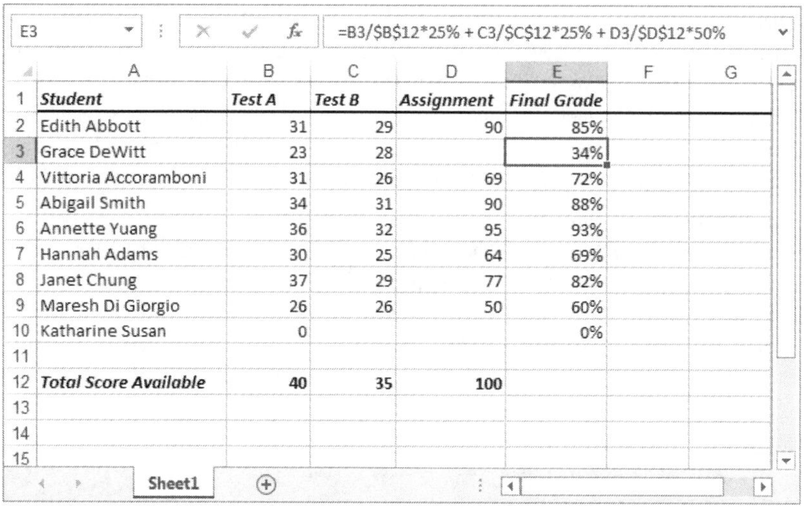

FIGURE 25-7

Grace Dewitt is trying to determine the grade she needs on an assignment to achieve a final grade of 80 percent (which is her target). In this case, the result cell (the one she wants to optimize) is E3. The variable cell (the one that Excel will adjust) is D3.

To use goal seeking in this scenario, follow these steps:

1. **Choose Data→Data Tools→What-If Analysis→Goal Seek.**

   The Goal Seek window appears (Figure 25-8).

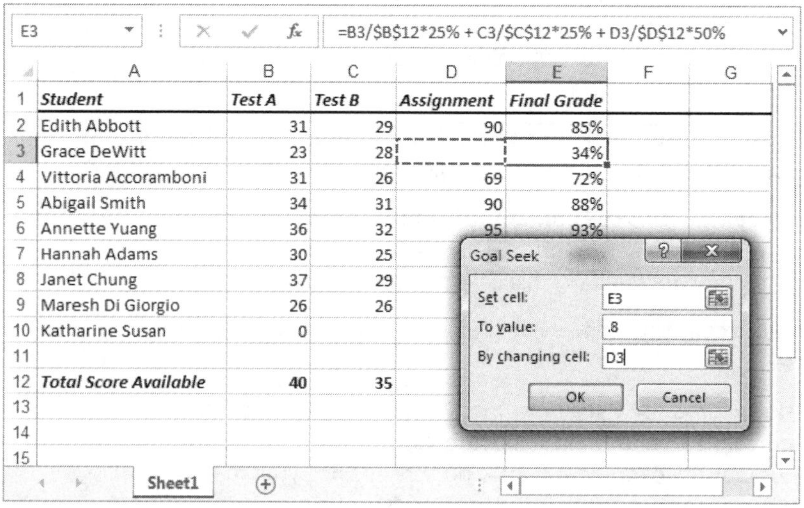

FIGURE 25-8

This example shows the Goal Seek window filled with the values needed to search for the minimum grade Grace needs to increase her final grade to 80. Note that you have to enter the grade as a decimal value (0.80 instead of 80). That's because the cells in column E are formatted to use the percentage number style.

2. **In the "Set cell" text box, enter the cell you want Excel to optimize.**

   In the student grade example, this cell is cell E3, which contains the calculation for Grace's final grade.

3. **In the "To value" text box, enter your target.**

   Grace is seeking a final grade of 80 percent, so the target is *0.80*.

4. **In the "By changing cell" text box, enter the cell that Excel should modify to achieve the target.**

   Cell D3, which contains the assignment grade, is the value that Excel modifies to determine the grade needed to boost Grace's final grade to 80.

5. **Click OK to start goal-seeking.**

   The Goal Seek Status window appears, and Excel cycles through a series of trial values, incrementing the assignment grade and calculating the resulting value.

   If Excel can't find the answer after a series of attempts, the Goal Seek Status window gives you the option to keep trying by clicking Step. If Excel stalls on a long analysis, you can stop it by clicking Pause, although this move's rarely necessary. In most cases, the goal-seeking process ends before you can even take your hand off the mouse to reach for your coffee mug. In a short amount of time, Excel discovers that an assignment grade of 91 (out of 100) raises Grace's final grade to 80 percent. At this point, it stops goal-seeking and shows you the answer.

6. **When an answer appears, click OK to accept the change and return to your worksheet, or click Cancel to return to the original version of your data.**

   Figure 25-9 shows the adjusted worksheet.

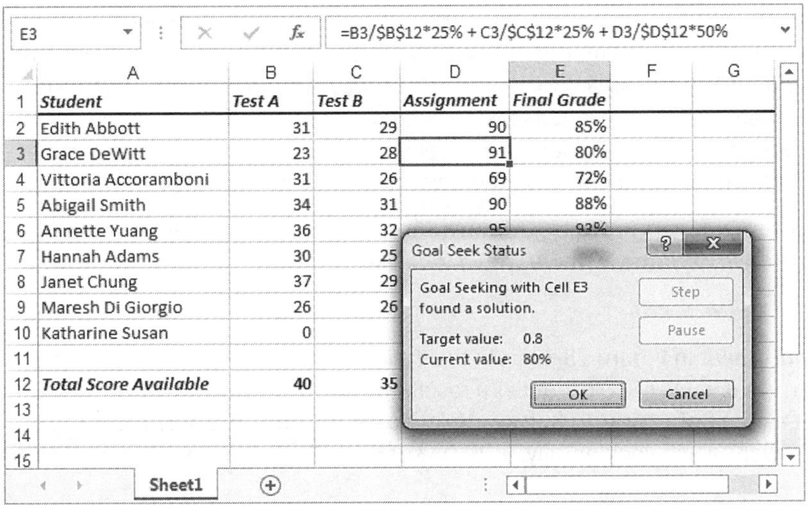

FIGURE 25-9

Usually, goal seeking unfolds in a flash. In this example, Excel has met the target by setting the assignment grade to 91, as shown in cell D3. You can click OK to accept the change permanently, or Cancel to return the cell to its previous value.

Goal Seeking with Complex Equations

In the student grade example, you don't necessarily need to use goal seeking to get the answer you're looking for. You could get the same information by rewriting the equation. To understand how this approach works, take a closer look at the formula that calculates the students' final grade:

```
=(B3/B12)*25% + (C3/C12)*25% + (D3/D12)*50%
```

In this formula, the two tests are each worth 25 percent of the final grade, and the assignment is worth the remaining 50 percent. However, using a dash of high-school math, you can rearrange this formula to find the grade you need on the assignment to get an 80 percent overall grade (assuming you already know your grades on the two tests). Here's the answer:

```
=(80% - (B3/B12)*25% - (C3/C12)*25%)/50%*D12
```

This formula looks a little intimidating at first, but it's really not too difficult to understand. First of all, you start with the 80-percent final grade you're trying to achieve. You subtract the two test scores to find the value you need from the assignment. Finally, you divide that value by 50 percent (the weighting of the assignment) and multiply it by D12 (the total score available on the assignment). The end result is 91.25.

Based on this example, you may assume that goal seeking is just a tool for quickly calculating a number that you could get on your own by rewriting one or more formulas. Although that's often the case, there are some types of formulas that you *can't* reorganize to provide an answer. These formulas often have exponents and use the value in the variable cell more than once. You can find many examples of this sort of equation in the scientific world.

One common example is the *quadratic function*, which shows up in lots of scientific modeling and engineering formulas. A typical quadratic formula looks like this:

```
y = x2 + 5x + 10
```

In this example, it's easy to calculate the result (y) provided you know the input value (x). However, it's much more difficult to perform the reverse task—determining x if all you know is y. Try as you might, there's no way to rearrange the formula to solve the problem. In this case, goal-seeking becomes very useful. It uses a trial-and-error approach that can usually get the answer you need. Excel tries different values of x in succession trying to get closer and closer to the target result.

To put the problem in Excel's formula format, assume that cell B1 contains the x value. Here's what the formula would look like:

```
=B1^2 + 5*B1 + 10
```

The worksheet in Figure 25-10 puts this function to the test. It's easy to figure out that an input value of 20 produces a result of 510. But what input value do you need to get a result of 1,000? In this example, goal-seeking is the only easy way to find the answer (which, incidentally, is 29.06343).

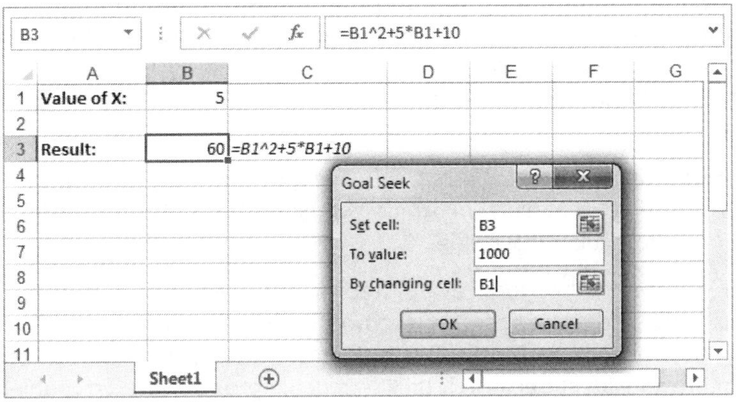

FIGURE 25-10

Figuring out what the value of B1 needs to be to generate a formula result of 1,000 is extremely difficult to resolve without using goal-seeking. Figure 25-11 shows the answer.

NOTE It's often difficult to reverse-engineer a formula in financial calculations, like those that calculate how an investment appreciates in value. However, as you saw in Chapter 10, Excel includes financial functions that can calculate in both directions: the final value of an investment based on a given interest rate, or the required interest rate or investment length based on your desired goal. Of course, you can still use goal seeking with financial functions to find an answer quickly without writing a new formula.

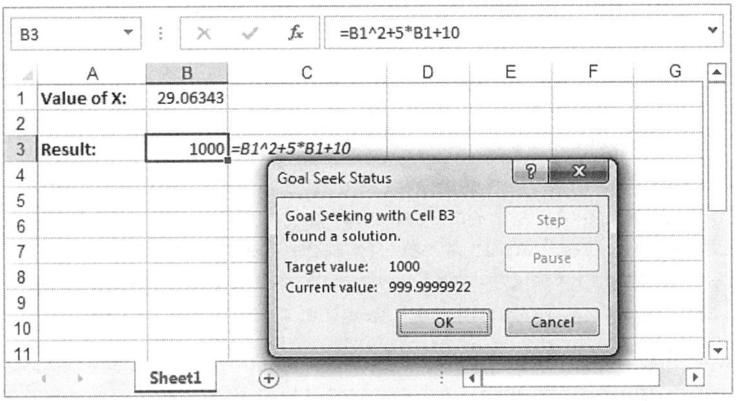

FIGURE 25-11

As you can see in the Goal Seek Status window, the answer isn't perfect (it's 999.9999922 instead of 1000), but it's close enough for Excel to stop searching. When performing goal seeking, Excel doesn't need to match your target exactly.

Solver

Goal-seeking works well for simple problems, but it does have a few limitations:

- **Excel doesn't recognize what you may think of as common-sense limits in your data.** In the earlier student grade example, if you were looking to figure out the assignment grade required to get a final grade of 100, Excel would tell you you'd need a score of 113—even though a grade over 100 percent clearly isn't possible.
- **Excel adjusts only one cell.** There's no way to ask the goal-seeking tool, for instance, to predict the minimum grade combination you'd need on the two tests to get a particular final grade.

Solver is an Excel feature that goes several steps further than goal-seeking. It uses the same basic trial-and-error approach (known to scientific types as an *iterative* approach) as goal-seeking, but it's dramatically more intelligent. In fact, it *needs* to be much more intelligent because it tackles much more complicated problems, including scenarios that have multiple changing cells, additional rules, and subtle relationships. For example, Solver can (with a fair bit of work) suggest an optimal investment portfolio based on a desired rate of return and risk threshold. (Incidentally, Solver is an add-in that you have to turn on the first time you use it; page 777 tells you how.)

NOTE Although it comes as part of the Excel package, the Solver add-in isn't a Microsoft product. Instead, it's provided by a company called Frontline Systems, which sells more enhanced versions of the Solver tool. To find out about these other tools, or to look through a number of interesting (and complicated) sample worksheets that show Solver in action, go to *www.solver.com*.

Understanding Solver

Every problem that Solver is capable of solving contains the same basic ingredients. Altogether, these ingredients make up a *Solver model*. They include:

- **Objective cell.** The objective cell (also known as the *target cell*) is the value you want to optimize. As with goal-seeking, you work with only one objective cell at a time. However, you don't have to set a specific numeric goal for the objective cell. Instead, you can ask Solver to make the target value as large or as small as possible (without violating the other rules of the model).
- **Changing cells.** These cells contain the values (also known as *decision variables*) that Solver modifies in order to reach the target you want. Unlike goal-seeking, you can designate multiple changing cells. When you do, Solver tries to adjust them all at once and gauge the most significant factors. With multiple changing cells, there's a definite possibility for multiple solutions (there's more than one combination of grades that can lead to a final grade of 80 percent, for instance). However, Solver stops when it finds the first matching solution.

- **Unchanging cells.** Unchanging cells can contain values that affect the calculation Solver uses in the objective cell. However, Solver never changes these cells.

TIP Sometimes, it's useful to combine Solver with Excel scenarios. You may, for example, want to create multiple scenarios, each of which has different values for the unchanging cells.

- **Constraints.** Constraints are rules you use to restrict possible solutions. Usually, you apply constraints to changing cell values. People often add constraints that set a maximum and minimum allowed value for each changing cell. You can also use constraints to restrict the target value. You could ask Solver to find the maximum value for the objective cell, but add a constraint telling Solver that the value it finds can't fall within a certain range.

NOTE Solver doesn't enforce constraints absolutely. Instead, it permits a certain *tolerance range*, depending on the configuration options you set. If you specify that a certain changing cell needs to be less than or equal to 100, for example, Solver allows a value of 100.0000001, because that value falls (just barely) in the standard tolerance range of 0.0000001. You'll learn how to adjust the tolerance setting later in this chapter.

You can probably already see that the service Solver provides is similar to goal-seeking, but with a few significant improvements. In the next section, you'll learn how to create a Solver model.

Defining a Problem in Solver

To learn how Solver works, take another look at the student grade example in Figure 25-7. This time, consider what happens when you add a new student named Katharine Susan. This student missed the first test and, as a result, received a score of 0 on it. She wants to know what grades in the second test and assignment she needs to guarantee her a final grade of 70. Excel's goal-seeking tool can't tackle this problem. Not only is it unable to change two cells at once, it doesn't heed any upper limits either, so it cheerily recommends scores greater than 100 percent. Instead, you need Solver.

To create a Solver model for this problem, follow these steps:

1. **If this is the first time you're using Solver, you need to switch it on. Choose File→Options.**

   If this isn't the first time you're using Solver, skip to step 5.

2. **In the Excel Options window, pick the Add-Ins category.**

   This displays a list of your currently active add-ins, as well as those installed but not active.

3. **In the Manage list at the bottom of the window, choose Excel Add-Ins, and then click Go.**

   The Add-Ins window appears, which lets you switch your add-ins on or off.

4. **Turn on the checkbox next to the Solver Add-in, and then click OK.**

   Once you switch Solver on, you'll find an additional entry in the Data tab of the ribbon.

5. **Launch Solver by choosing Data→Analysis→Solver.**

   The Solver Parameters window appears.

6. **In the Set Objective text box, enter the cell you want Solver to optimize.**

   In the student grade example, this is cell E10, which contains Katharine Susan's final grade (see Figure 25-12).

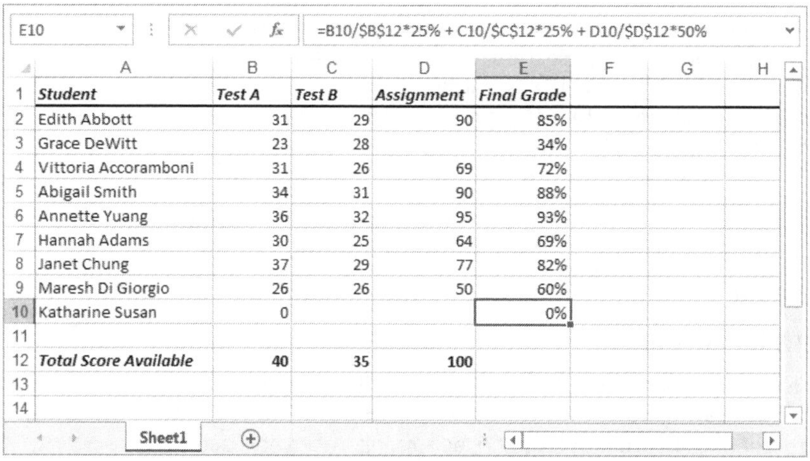

E10 | `=B10/$B$12*25% + C10/$C$12*25% + D10/$D$12*50%`

	A	B	C	D	E	F	G	H
1	*Student*	*Test A*	*Test B*	*Assignment*	*Final Grade*			
2	Edith Abbott	31	29	90	85%			
3	Grace DeWitt	23	28		34%			
4	Vittoria Accoramboni	31	26	69	72%			
5	Abigail Smith	34	31	90	88%			
6	Annette Yuang	36	32	95	93%			
7	Hannah Adams	30	25	64	69%			
8	Janet Chung	37	29	77	82%			
9	Maresh Di Giorgio	26	26	50	60%			
10	Katharine Susan	0			0%			
11								
12	*Total Score Available*	40	35	100				
13								
14								

Sheet1

FIGURE 25-12

The Solver tool helps calculate the values needed in C10 and D10 to boost E10 to 70 percent. A constraint, which you'll add in step 10, ensures that Solver doesn't increase the "Test B" grade above the maximum grade available.

7. **Choose the type of optimization you want by selecting one of the three To options: Max, Min, or Value Of.**

   If you choose Value Of to match a set value, enter the value in the adjacent text box.

   Max attempts to make the value as large as possible. Min attempts to make it as small as possible. Value Of attempts to get the cell to the value you indicate.

   In the student grade example, Katharine is trying to scrape past with a 70 percent grade. So to have Solver figure out the solution, you need to choose the Value Of option, and then set the target to 0.70.

8. **In the By Changing Variable Cells text box, enter the cell references that Excel should modify to achieve the target.**

   You can enter these cell references by hand (separating each reference with a comma), or you can click your worksheet to select the appropriate cells. In the student grade example, the changing cells are C10 and D10, which represent the two grades that are still up for grabs.

Now, you need to indicate the restrictions that Solver follows when it calculates its solution.

9. **If you don't need any constraints, skip to step 12. Otherwise, click the Add button to add a constraint.**

   The Add Constraint window appears (shown in Figure 25-13). In the student grade example, you can use constraints to prevent scores that are above the maximum possible grade (or less than 0).

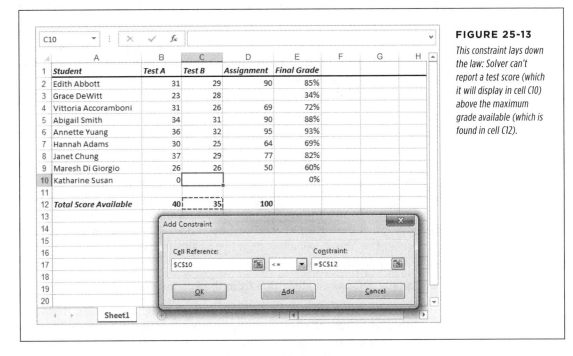

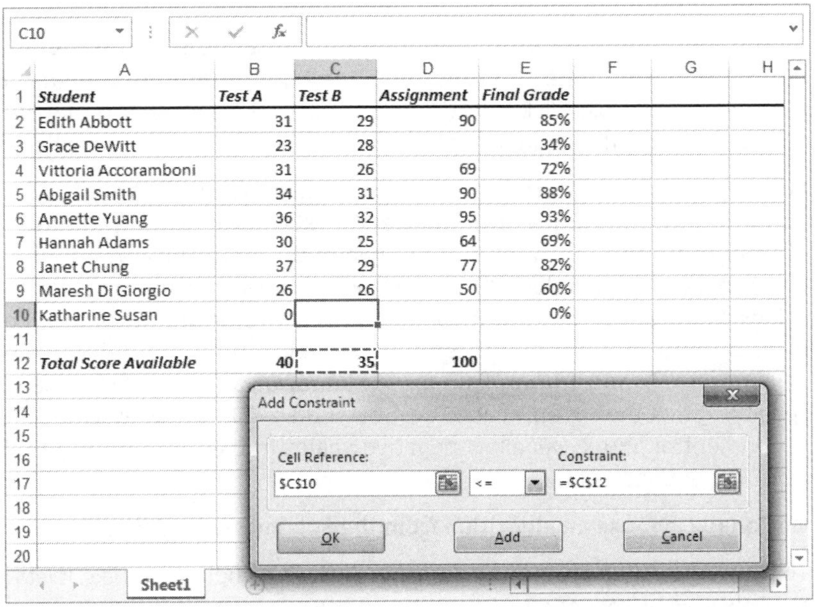

FIGURE 25-13

This constraint lays down the law: Solver can't report a test score (which it will display in cell C10) above the maximum grade available (which is found in cell C12).

10. **Enter the constraint information, and then click OK to add it.**

    Every constraint consists of three details: a reference to a cell, an operator that tests the cell value, and an expression that limits what the cell value can be.

    A basic constraint compares a cell to a fixed value or another cell. You can perform an equal to comparison (=), a greater than or equal to comparison (>=), or a less than or equal to comparison (<=). Figure 25-13 shows one of the constraints used in the student grade example. This constraint uses the less than or equal to operator (<=) to ensure that cell C10 (one of the changing values) doesn't exceed the value in C12 (it's 35 in this example). It's not necessary to set a minimum value in this case because Solver can't solve the problem by lowering the grades.

The Add Constraints window includes three special types of constraint operators. They show up in the list as the words *int*, *bin*, and *dif*. If you apply an int constraint to a cell, Solver allows that cell to contain only whole integer values (with no digits on the right side of the decimal point). If you apply a bin constraint, Solver permits only binary values. If you use dif, Solver makes sure that each cell in the group has a different integer value, so no two cells are alike. In all of these cases, all you need to specify is the cell reference and the operator. You don't need to fill in the third part (the Constraint box) because it doesn't apply.

11. **If you have another constraint to add, return to step 10. Otherwise, continue with the next step.**

    As you've probably already guessed, the Change and Delete buttons let you edit or remove the selected constraint. The Reset All button underneath is slightly less obvious. Click it to delete all your constraints and return all the Solver options to their original values.

    You might also be interested in the Make Unconstrained Variables Non-Negative checkbox, which sits just under the list of constraints. It acts as a sort of super-constraint. When you turn it on (which Excel does initially), Solver limits every variable cell that doesn't already have a lower-limit constraint to positive values. In other words, it's as if you added a "has to be greater than or equal to 0" constraint to each of these cells. However, there's one exception—if you specifically add a lower-limit constraint for a variable cell (for example, specifying that the variable has to be greater than –10), Solver assumes you're taking control and it *will* allow negative values in that cell, as long as they satisfy your constraint.

12. **Optionally, choose an algorithm from the Solving Method list.**

    The Solving Method gives you a peek into Solver's complex internals. It lets you tell Solver what sort of strategy it should use to tackle your problem. Unless you're a Solver expert, you probably won't touch this setting. But if you want to get deeper into the details of how Solver works, jump ahead to page 788.

    Figure 25-14 shows the completed Solver model.

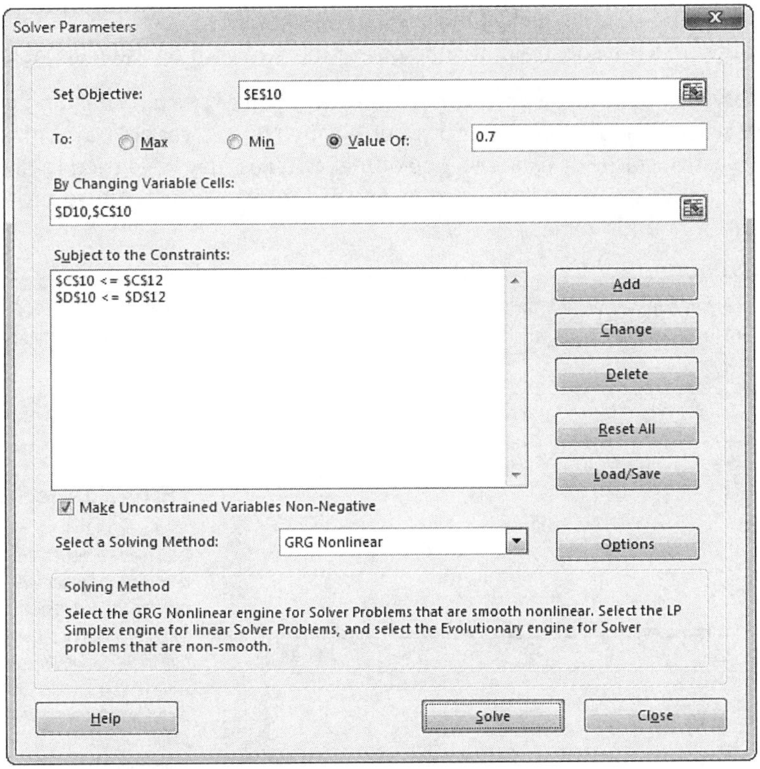

FIGURE 25-14

This completed Solver Parameters window is ready to find out how Katharine Susan can eke out a final grade of 70. It allows for two changing cells (the test and assignment grades in cells C10 and D10), and it sets two constraints to prevent solutions that don't correspond to real-world possibilities—in this case, test scores above 100%.

13. **Click Solve to put Solver to work.**

    When you click Solve, the Solver Parameters window disappears, and the status bar indicates the number of trial solutions in progress. You can interrupt the process any time by pressing the Esc key. If you do, the Show Trial Solution window appears, which lets you abandon your attempt altogether by clicking Stop, or resume the trial-and-error process by clicking Continue.

    When Solver finishes its work, it shows the Solver Results window, which indicates whether it found a solution, and what that solution is. Here are the most common messages:

    - **Solver found a solution** means Solver met your objective and satisfied your conditions. Hooray! Figure 25-15 shows the solution that Solver found for Katharine Susan.
    - **Solver could not find a feasible solution** means that no matter how Solver tweaked the variable cells, it couldn't reach your target value.

- **The Objective cell values do not converge** happens only when you use the Max or Min option (see step 7) to make the objective cell as big or as small as possible. In this situation, Solver may continue to increase or decrease your variable cells to ridiculous values, while continually getting a better and better solution, until it finally gives up. Usually, the problem is that you forget to set a constraint to limit one or more of your decision variables.
- **Solver encountered an error value** means Solver started changing your decision variables and an error value popped up in a variable cell or in the objective cell. (For example, one of the formulas may have tried to divide by zero.) Once again, you probably need to set a constraint to prohibit out-of-bounds values.

TIP If Solver didn't find a solution, switch on the "Return to Solver Parameters window" setting, and then click OK to return to the familiar Solver window that you started at in step 5 so you can set some parameters and retry.

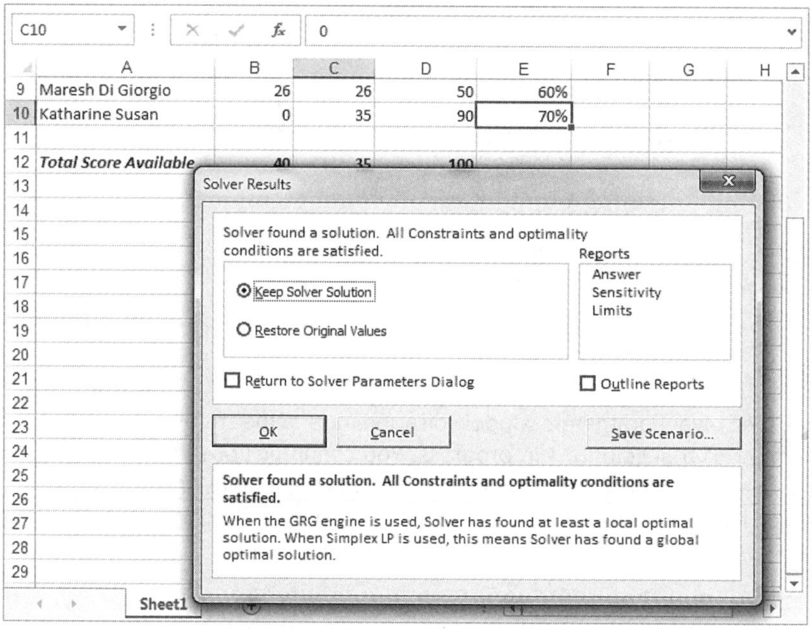

FIGURE 25-15

There's hope for Katharine—provided she does well on the second test and the assignment. Solver identifies a solution by increasing the test score to its maximum (35 points, which translates to 100 percent), and then by incrementing the assignment grade to 90 (out of a possible 100).

14. **Choose Keep Solver Solution if you want to retain the changed values.**

    Or, to undo Solver's work and go back to the previous version, choose Restore Original Values.

POWER USERS' CLINIC

Store the Solver Results in a Scenario

Instead of applying the values that Solver calculates, you can store them so you can refer to them later. Solver helps you out with a nifty feature that stores Solver results in a new scenario.

To use this feature, click the Save Scenario button in the Solver Results window after Solver finishes its calculation. Enter a name for the scenario you want to create, and then click OK. Excel creates the scenario and stores the value of each changing cell. To apply the scenario values later on, select Data→Data Tools→What-If Analysis→Scenario Manager, find the scenario in the list, and then click Show.

15. **Optionally, in the Reports list box, choose a Solver report.**

    Click a report to highlight it. You can choose just one report or as many as you want. These reports show various details about how Solver calculated its answer.

    Solver's reports include Answer, Sensitivity, and Limits. Each report opens in a separate worksheet when you click OK. Most people won't find these reports very interesting because they contain a bare minimum of data, and what they do include are dry statistical calculations. The Solver reports aren't nearly as useful as the scenario summaries described earlier.

16. **Finally, click OK to return to your worksheet.**

More Advanced Solver Problems

The student grade example shows only a hint of Solver's true analytical muscle. To see Solver tackle a more interesting problem, you can add additional constraints. You can, for example, tell Solver to make sure that the assignment grade is always higher than the test score, or that both the assignment and the test end up having equal percentage values. Figure 25-16 shows the latter example.

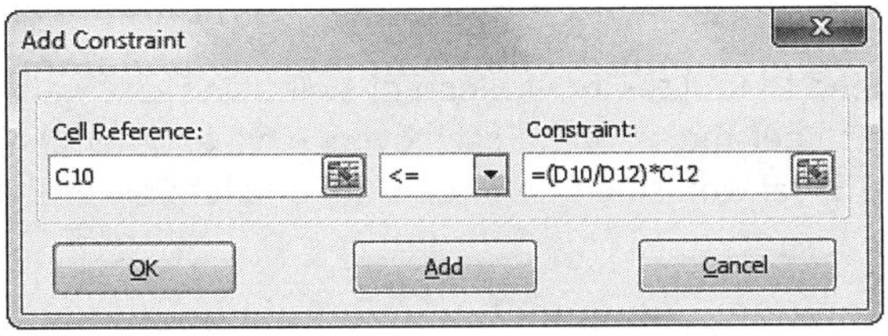

FIGURE 25-16

This constraint calculates the percentage score on the assignment (D10/D12), and multiplies it by the total available test score (C12). The constraint forces a solution in which Katharine has an equal percentage grade on the test and on the assignment. The solution is 33 out of 35 for the test and 93 out of 100 for the assignment, both of which equal 93 percent.

NOTE Solver can't optimize more than one value at a time. You can't tell Solver to calculate the lowest possible grade on test B that can, in combination with the assignment score, still result in a final grade of 80. You can, however, approximate many cases like this with a crafty use of constraints.

Of course, not all problems have a solution. If you repeat the same problem but try to end up with a final grade of 90 for Katharine, you'll find that it's just not possible. Solver increases both changing cells to their maximum allowed values, and then shows the Solver Results window with a message informing you that there's no feasible solution.

Solver is tailor-made for more complicated math problems, like the optimization problems that calculus teachers use to torture their students. Here's a common mind-bending example:

> You're standing at the edge of a slow-moving river which is one mile wide. You're hungry, and you need to return to your campground (which is on the opposite side of the river, and one mile upstream) to get a ham sandwich. To get it, you have to first swim across the river to any point on the opposite bank, and then walk the rest of the way. You can swim at two miles per hour and walk at three miles per hour, and you want to get your sandwich as quickly as possible. What route will take the least amount of time?

As Figure 25-17 shows, the answer isn't obvious.

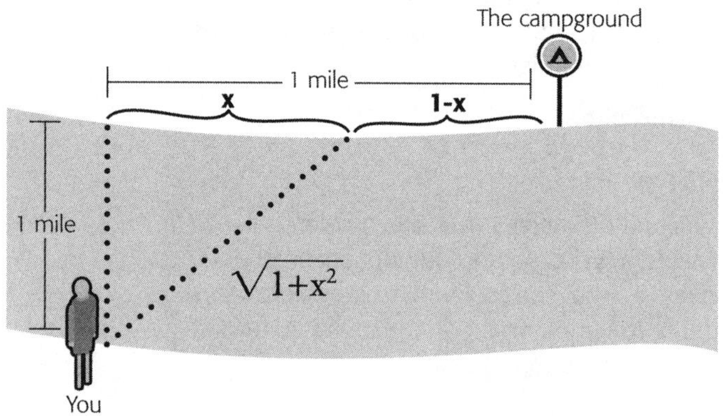

FIGURE 25-17

If you swim straight across the river, you then have a long one-mile walk to get to the campground. If you swim diagonally across to the campsite, you can avoid the walk, but you have to swim a much farther distance. Assuming that x measures the distance upstream from the point to which you'll swim, some basic algebra gives you the total swimming distance and walking distance.

To solve this problem, you need to find the right blend of swimming and walking. Math-heads can use calculus to get the answer. Excel lovers have another choice: Plug all the equations into an Excel worksheet (Figure 25-18) and let Solver do the thinking (Figure 25-19).

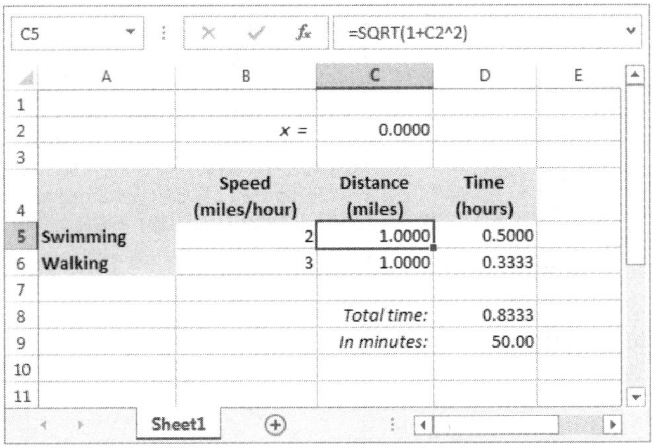

FIGURE 25-18

The vindictive math teacher's scenario tells you the speed you can reach on land and in the water. The diagram above shows you the swimming and walking distances. With these values, you can create formulas that calculate the total time the trip takes. (To calculate the time, you divide the distance by the speed, using the formula time = distance/speed.) Here, you see the results of setting x to 0, swimming straight across the river, and then walking a mile to the campground. But you need Solver to find the best x value—in other words, how far upstream you should swim to get to the campsite in as little time as possible.

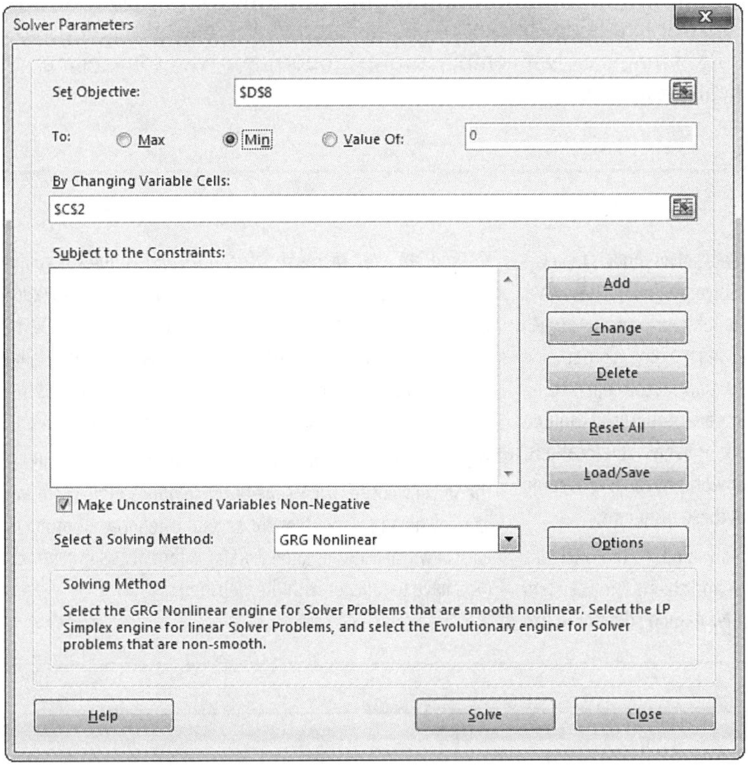

FIGURE 25-19

Using the Min option tells Solver to make the cell with the total time (D8) as small as possible. The only cell that Solver can change is the one that indicates how far upstream you should swim; that's the cell that contains the x value, C2. (You don't need any constraints, because there are no additional restrictions on the solution.) Then click Solve; you'll see the result in Figure 25-20.

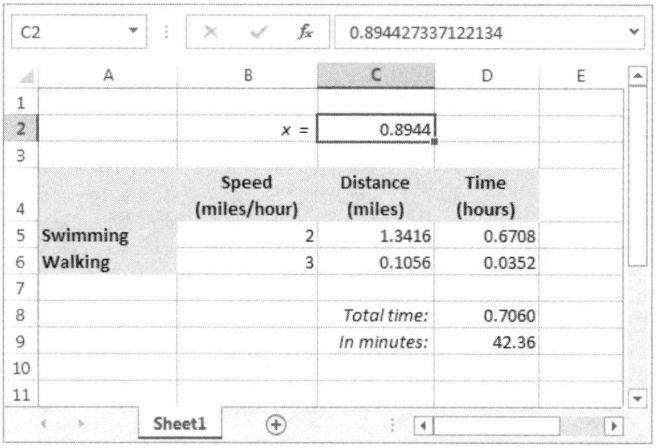

FIGURE 25-20

Solver tells you that you need to swim 0.89 miles upstream, which is most, but not all, of the way to the campground. (To see exactly where this point is, plug in 0.89 for x in the diagram shown in Figure 25-17.) Get out your water wings, because you'll be swimming 1.34 miles, walking a mere 0.11 miles, and getting to the campsite in the shortest possible time, 42 minutes.

As complicated as this example may seem to non-math geeks, it's actually a picnic for Solver. In fact, Solver's genius—which only math majors may appreciate—is its ability to find an answer in a dense thicket of complicated mathematical relationships. To work this sort of magic, Solver combines raw stubbornness with some higher-order mathematical reasoning.

POWER USERS' CLINIC

Solver Examples

With a little imagination, you can create Solver models for a variety of scenarios. People often use Solver to find the best ways to distribute work across multiple manufacturing centers (each of which has its own operating costs and maximum production levels). Or, you could use Solver to plan investments, using constraints to ensure that your assets are properly distributed across different securities, industries, or geographic locations. You can learn a lot about how Solver works by looking at some example worksheets that deal with these problems.

Excel provides a workbook called solvsamp.xls that includes several Solver examples on separate worksheets. (You can find this file on your hard drive in a folder named something like *C:\Program Files\Microsoft Office\Office15\Samples* if you've installed the 64-bit version of Office or *C:\Program Files (x86)\Microsoft Office\Office15\Samples* if you're using the 32-bit version.) Each worksheet has sample calculations and detailed information for using Solver, along with color-coded cells that show the objective cell, changing cells, and constraints.

You can find an even more extensive collection of examples at the Solver website (*www.solver.com/solutions.htm*). There, you can download sample files for several categories of problem, each of which uses the same workbook format as solvsamp.xls. (You have to register with the website.)

Saving Solver Models

Each time you use Solver, Excel keeps track of the settings you've just used. And each time you save your workbook, it also saves the most recent Solver settings. In some cases, however, you may want to keep track of more than one set of Solver settings. That could happen if you're trying to optimize the same data in different ways, for example, or you're using Solver to optimize data in different parts of the same worksheet, or different worksheets in the same workbook.

Fortunately, there is a way to save the key bits of Solver information—the target value, changing cells, and constraints—and use it later. The only catch is that you need to save it in a small block of cells in one of your worksheets. The actual number of cells you need depends on the Solver model you create. Excel uses one cell to store information about the target value and the objective cell, another cell to store the list of changing cells, and one additional cell for each constraint. Excel stacks the cells on top of each other.

To save a Solver model, follow these steps:

1. **If you haven't already started Solver, choose Data→Analysis→Solver.**

   The Solver Parameters window appears.

2. **Click the Load/Save button.**

   The Load/Save window appears.

3. **Click inside the text box. Then, click the worksheet where you want to place the first cell.**

   Make sure that there are enough empty cells underneath the cell you select so Excel can save the information without overwriting any worksheet data. The Load/Save window tells you exactly how many cells you need.

4. **Click Save.**

   Solver writes the information from the current model to your worksheet and returns you to the Solver Parameters window.

   Figure 25-21 shows what stored Solver data looks like. The first cell stores a formula that represents the problem you're trying to solve. In this example, it's *=MIN($D$8)*, because you're trying to minimize the value in cell D8. (In the student grade example, the formula is the somewhat nonsensical *=$E$10=0.7*. This formula doesn't do anything legitimate on its own—it's simply Solver's way of remembering that you want to set cell E10 to 70%.) The other cells track the variables in your Solver model and store miscellaneous Solver settings. They use array formulas to pack multiple pieces of information into a single cell.

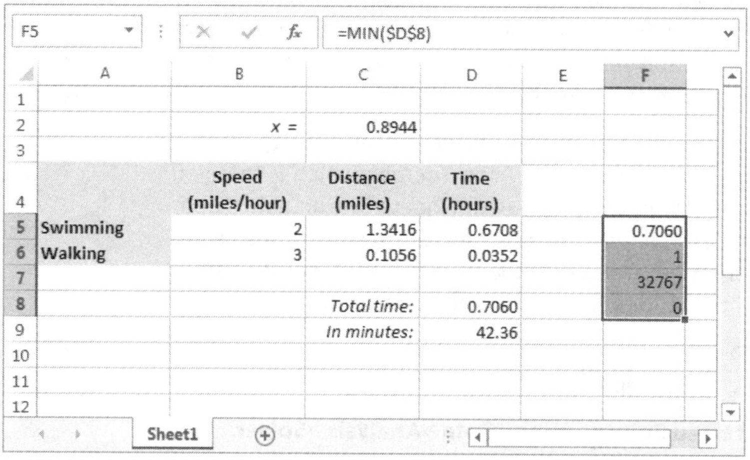

FIGURE 25-21

Solver uses the cells F5 to F8 to store the current scenario information.

To restore a Solver model that you saved earlier, follow these steps:

1. **If you haven't already started Solver, choose Data→Analysis→Solver.**

   The Solver Parameters window appears.

2. **Click the Load/Save button.**

   The Load/Save window appears.

3. **Click inside the text box. Select the worksheet you used earlier, and then select the cells that store the Solver data. Finally, click Load.**

   Solver reads the information from your worksheet and applies it to the current Solver model accordingly. If you already have a Solver model in your current worksheet, Excel asks you if you want to replace the current Solver settings (click Replace), or combine them with the current settings where possible (click Merge), which is certainly more confusing. Finally, Excel returns you to the Solver Parameters window.

Configuring Solver

The standard options that Solver uses are adequate for most situations. However, there's a wealth of options for more advanced tweaking.

To start, you can choose the solving strategy that Solver uses when it attacks your problem. If you have a good understanding of the mathematics underpinning your problem, this may help you get a better or faster answer. You make your choice in the Select a Solving Method list in the Solver Parameters window:

- **Simplex LP** works for simple, linear problems that have only a few variables linked in a straightforward relationship (like the student grade example). When used on the right problem, Simple LP is the fastest approach to a solution.
- **GRG Nonlinear** is Solver's default, and it makes sense if you're not sure what mojo Solver needs to work on your numbers. It's intelligent enough to handle more complex relationships—what mathematicians call *smooth nonlinear functions*—like the campground problem described on page 784. If your objective cell has a formula that uses mathematical operations like log, sine, and cosine, or if it takes the variables and multiples them, divides them, or raises them to a power, GRG Nonlinear is probably your best ticket.
- **Evolutionary** is an advanced approach that uses more complex *genetic algorithms*. This approach is generally slower, but it may let Solver arrive at an answer when other approaches fail. You may need this approach if your objective cell uses a formula that incorporates other Excel functions.

Choosing a solving method is just a starting point. If you want to tinker with some of Solver's advanced settings, you can configure them from Solver's Options window (Figure 25-22). To get there, click the Options button from the main Solver Parameters window.

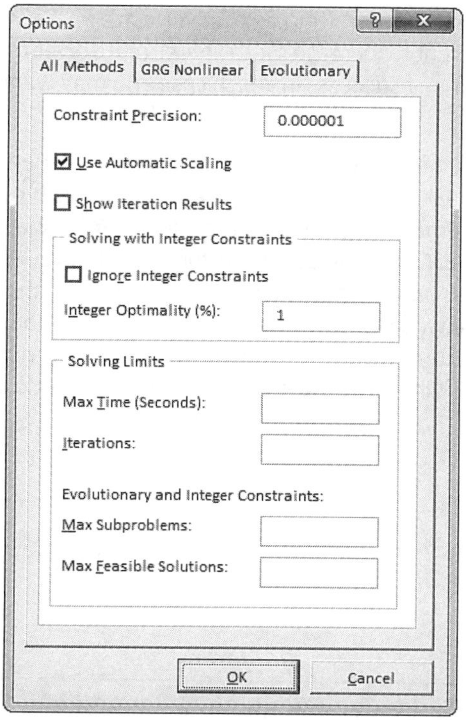

FIGURE 25-22

The Options window helps you tweak some settings that control how Solver attacks a problem. Most of these enhancements are best left in the hands of experienced mathematicians (and even then, they may not improve Solver's rate of success or its performance). The first tab has settings that apply to all solving methods, while the GRG Nonlinear tab and Evolutionary tab have settings that apply to those solving methods only.

The Options window offers a slew of Solver options, all of which you can change. The most useful ones include:

- **Constraint Precision.** This setting indicates how exact a constraint rule is. The smaller the number (the more zeros after the decimal place), the greater the precision, and the more exacting Solver is in trying to meet your constraints.
- **Show Iteration Results.** If you turn this checkbox on, Solver pauses to show the results of each guess it makes in its trial-and-error process. This choice slows down the process tremendously, but it also gives you some interesting insight into how Solver makes its guesses.
- **Integer Optimality.** This setting comes into play when you use *int* constraints to force one or more variable cell values to be integers. For example, if you set the optimality to 1 percent, Solver considers any value that's within 1 percent of a whole number to be an integer.
- **Max Time.** You can use this setting to specify the maximum number of seconds that Solver can take to come up with an answer. You can enter a value as high as 32,767, but Solver rarely reaches the standard limit of 100 seconds in typical small problems.
- **Iterations.** Use this setting to limit how many trial-and-error calculations Solver makes. Once again, the number can be as high as 32,767. The only reason you'd change the Max Time or Iterations setting is if Solver can't find a valid solution (in which case you may want to increase these limits), or if Solver takes an exceedingly long time without any success (in which case you may want to decrease them).
- **Convergence.** This setting is in both the GRG Nonlinear and Evolutionary tabs, because it applies to nonlinear math problems. When solving this type of problem, Solver may have a hard time telling whether its trial-and-error guesses are approaching the best solution. Each time Solver perform a new attempt, it compares its new guess to the last guess. If five guesses pass and the change is always less than the convergence value, Excel decides that it has settled on the closest solution it can find, and returns an answer. If you make the convergence smaller, Solver takes more time trying to refine its solution, and it may deliver a slightly more precise answer.

CHAPTER

26

Pivot Tables

Creating neat, informative summaries out of huge lists of raw data is a common challenge. And while Excel gives you all the tools you need to create such summaries, the actual work of writing formulas, cutting and pasting information, and organizing your totals into a new table can be extremely tedious. Even worse, this approach isn't very flexible. Once you create the perfect summary that compares, say, sales in different regions, you may want to compare sales across different product lines or different customers. But for that, you need to start from scratch and build a whole new report.

Fortunately, Excel has a feature called *pivot tables* that provides a solution. Pivot tables quickly summarize long lists of data, without requiring you to write a single formula or copy a single cell. But the most notable feature of pivot tables is that you can arrange them *dynamically*. Say you create a pivot table summary using raw census data. With the drag of a mouse, you can easily rearrange the pivot table so that it summarizes the data based on gender *or* age groupings *or* geographic location. The process of rearranging your table is known as *pivoting* your data: You're turning the same information around to examine it from different angles.

Pivot tables are a hidden gem in Excel. Many otherwise experienced spreadsheet fans avoid them because they seem too complicated at first glance. The real problem is that pivot tables are rarely explained properly. Most books and the online Excel help use no end of cryptic jargon like "cross-tabulated computations" and "*n*-dimensional analysis." But if you stick with this chapter, you'll discover that pivot tables are really just a convenient way to build intelligent, flexible summary tables—nothing more, and nothing less.

NOTE Pivot tables gain superpowers when you use them in conjunction with Excel's data connection feature, which pulls live information out of a database, web service, XML file, or other type of data source. In this situation, pivot tables can chew through *millions* of rows (far more than could possibly fit in an Excel worksheet) and can amalgamate the information in more than one related table. You'll learn how to use these advanced features in Chapter 27.

Summary Tables Revisited

When you analyze large amounts of data, you can look at the same information many ways. How you organize and group that data often determines whether you find or overlook important trends.

NOTE In Chapter 15, you saw how to tame large tables of data with features like grouping and outlining. Pivot tables offer another approach—they're a little more work to set up, but they give you much more flexibility in rearranging your tables and calculating different summary information on the fly.

Consider the small table of information in Figure 26-1. It lists all the customers of a small business, along with information about their gender, the city they live in, and their level of education. Looking at this table, an important question comes to mind: Is there a relationship between these different pieces of information and the amount of money a customer spends?

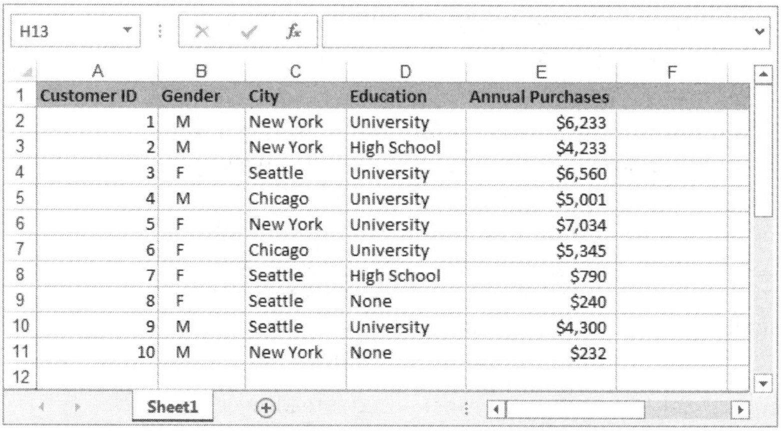

	A	B	C	D	E	F
1	Customer ID	Gender	City	Education	Annual Purchases	
2	1	M	New York	University	$6,233	
3	2	M	New York	High School	$4,233	
4	3	F	Seattle	University	$6,560	
5	4	M	Chicago	University	$5,001	
6	5	F	New York	University	$7,034	
7	6	F	Chicago	University	$5,345	
8	7	F	Seattle	High School	$790	
9	8	F	Seattle	None	$240	
10	9	M	Seattle	University	$4,300	
11	10	M	New York	None	$232	
12						

FIGURE 26-1

This example has only 10 records, so it's pretty easy to spot patterns. But if you extended this list to hundreds or thousands of rows, you'd definitely need a summary table to spot relationships.

To look for trends and patterns in the customer list, it helps to build a *summary table*—a table that tallies key amounts, like the average amount a customer spent in a specific city, at a particular education level, or by gender. However, there are several potentially important relationships, and, therefore, several types of summary tables, you could create. Pivot tables are the perfect summary-building tool because they give you almost unlimited flexibility when you want to search for relationships in your data. But before you learn about how to build pivot tables, it first helps to understand what life is like in Excel *without* them—because only then can you see why pivot tables make sense and decide whether you need them in one of your own workbooks.

Life Without Pivot Tables

The most basic way to calculate summary information is to use the SUMIF(), COUNTIF(), and AVERAGEIF() functions described in Chapter 13. To find the average annual purchases for an individual in New York using the worksheet shown in Figure 26-1, you use a formula like this:

```
=AVERAGEIF(C2:C11, "New York", E2:E11)
```

This formula scans the City column (C2 to C11) looking for the text "New York". Every time it finds a match, it adds the corresponding purchase amount from the Annual Purchases column (E2 to E11). The final result is the average of all these amounts.

Next, you can make this formula generic so you don't have to write a new one for each city. Instead, you change the formula so that it retrieves the text it should match (the city's name) from a cell just to the left of where you're going to place the formula. For example, this formula gets the city name from cell A15:

```
=AVERAGEIF($C$2:$C$11, A15, $E$2:$E$11)
```

Note that in this formula, all the search ranges are fixed as absolute references using the dollar sign ($). The search text isn't fixed—that way, when you copy the formula to a new row, the formula searches the text in that row.

Figure 26-2 shows the result of these "city" formulas, which reside in cells B15, B16, and B17. It also includes formulas that total up the table's numbers using different criteria (like the values in the Education and Gender columns).

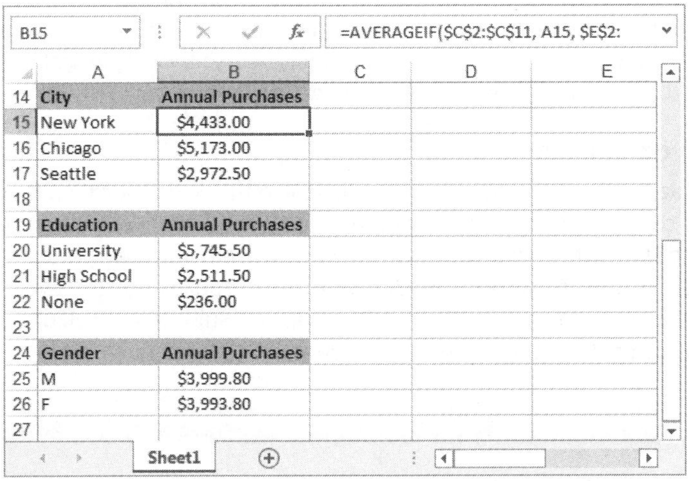

FIGURE 26-2

These three summary tables retrieve their data from the table shown in Figure 26-1 and calculate average purchases by grouping the customers into different categories. The purchase-by-city summary shows that there isn't a significant amount of difference based on location (although Seattle customers tend to spend a little less). The purchase-by-education summary shows a dramatic difference, with less educated individuals making smaller purchases. Finally, the purchase-by-gender comparison turns up no variance at all.

In this example, each table isn't terribly difficult to build, but the situation clearly becomes more tedious the more ways you want to compare the same data. It's not difficult to imagine a more realistic scenario where you want to look at customer purchases based on age bracket, income level, and answers to customer survey questions, for example. To get the full picture with this information, you need to build each table from scratch. In a worksheet that could have thousands of rows of data, that's a tall task.

In fact, in some of these more complex scenarios, you may need to group and then *subgroup* your information. Figure 26-3 shows a more advanced example of a table that calculates the variance in average annual purchases by city, and then shows the subdivided totals in each city by gender.

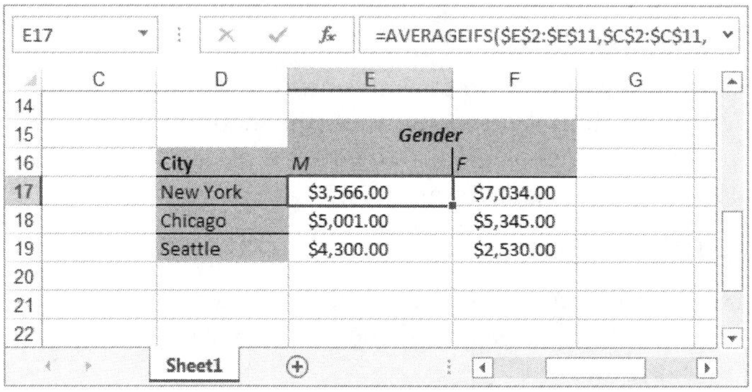

FIGURE 26-3

This summary table is a little more advanced than the ones shown in Figure 26-2. It groups and then subgroups data, which lets you find hidden trends. In this case, it identifies New York females as the best purchasers. Of course, this example has far too few rows for the results to be truly persuasive. In a table with thousands of rows, however, a grouped and subgrouped breakdown becomes much more meaningful.

The summary in Figure 26-3 performs a *two-dimensional* comparison. In other words, it compares two groupings—one by city (in different rows), and one by gender (in different columns). This is a step up from the one-dimensional summary tables you saw earlier, but it's also more difficult to correctly calculate. You could use the AVERAGEIFS() functions (page 382), or create the table in two steps (first grouping the records by city, and then totaling them by gender). In either case, life gets much more complicated, and that's when pivot tables really shine.

Life with Pivot Tables

With a pivot table, you can create summary tables like the ones shown so far just by choosing the columns you want to compare. And once you build your summary, you don't need to stick with it—instead, you can transform a purchase-by-education table into a purchase-by-city table just by dragging and dropping. You can even drill down into the details, apply filters, and apply advanced subtotaling calculations. The following sections describe all these techniques.

UP TO SPEED

Pivot Tables vs. Grouping and Subtotals

When should you use pivot tables instead of other Excel features? In Chapter 15, you learned about two techniques for grouping and organizing data:

- **Grouping**. Excel's grouping tools let you collapse a table's detail information so you see only its summary information. Grouping is the perfect solution when you have a worksheet that contains both detail and summary information and you want to make it more manageable. However, you still need to write all the summary formulas and decide how you want to organize the information.
- **Automatic subtotaling**. Automatic subtotaling generates subtotals for grouped data according to a column you choose. It's a good technique for building a quick-and-dirty summary report, but it doesn't provide a lot of flexibility. It also breaks up the structure of your list so that you can't effectively edit it any longer.

Compared to either of these features, pivot tables are more flexible and more dynamic. A single pivot table can group and subtotal the same list in different ways—all you need to do is drag and drop your columns. Thanks to this flexibility, pivot tables are a much more flexible tool for analyzing your information and discovering hidden relationships.

Building Pivot Tables

Now that you've learned the role that pivot tables play in summarizing data, it's time to create your own. Before you begin, you need to have a long list of raw data that you want to summarize. You could use the customer list from the previous example, but it's too small to really show the benefits of pivot tables. A better example is something like the list of order information shown in Figure 26-4.

TIP The best way to learn about pivot tables is to perform the steps in this chapter, and then start experimenting. If you don't happen to have a table with hundreds of records on hand, you can download the workbook in Figure 26-4 from the Missing CD page at *www.missingmanuals.com/cds/excel2013mm*. It gives you 2,155 rows to summarize and pivot to your heart's content.

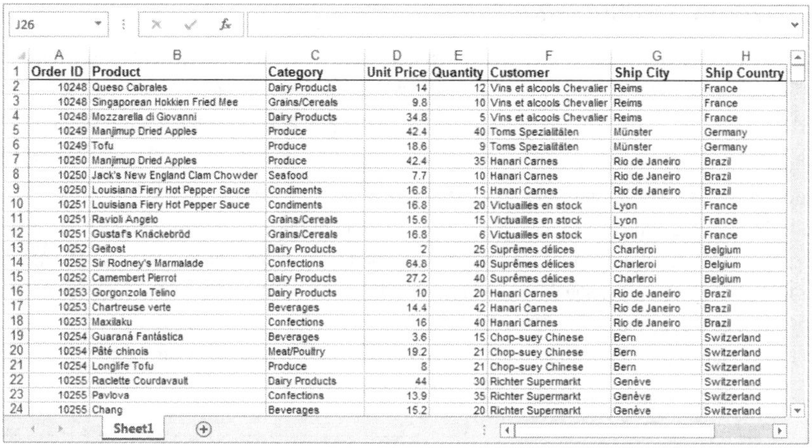

	A	B	C	D	E	F	G	H
1	Order ID	Product	Category	Unit Price	Quantity	Customer	Ship City	Ship Country
2	10248	Queso Cabrales	Dairy Products	14	12	Vins et alcools Chevalier	Reims	France
3	10248	Singaporean Hokkien Fried Mee	Grains/Cereals	9.8	10	Vins et alcools Chevalier	Reims	France
4	10248	Mozzarella di Giovanni	Dairy Products	34.8	5	Vins et alcools Chevalier	Reims	France
5	10249	Manjimup Dried Apples	Produce	42.4	40	Toms Spezialitäten	Münster	Germany
6	10249	Tofu	Produce	18.6	9	Toms Spezialitäten	Münster	Germany
7	10250	Manjimup Dried Apples	Produce	42.4	35	Hanari Carnes	Rio de Janeiro	Brazil
8	10250	Jack's New England Clam Chowder	Seafood	7.7	10	Hanari Carnes	Rio de Janeiro	Brazil
9	10250	Louisiana Fiery Hot Pepper Sauce	Condiments	16.8	15	Hanari Carnes	Rio de Janeiro	Brazil
10	10251	Louisiana Fiery Hot Pepper Sauce	Condiments	16.8	20	Victuailles en stock	Lyon	France
11	10251	Ravioli Angelo	Grains/Cereals	15.6	15	Victuailles en stock	Lyon	France
12	10251	Gustaf's Knäckebröd	Grains/Cereals	16.8	6	Victuailles en stock	Lyon	France
13	10252	Geitost	Dairy Products	2	25	Suprêmes délices	Charleroi	Belgium
14	10252	Sir Rodney's Marmalade	Confections	64.8	40	Suprêmes délices	Charleroi	Belgium
15	10252	Camembert Pierrot	Dairy Products	27.2	40	Suprêmes délices	Charleroi	Belgium
16	10253	Gorgonzola Telino	Dairy Products	10	20	Hanari Carnes	Rio de Janeiro	Brazil
17	10253	Chartreuse verte	Beverages	14.4	42	Hanari Carnes	Rio de Janeiro	Brazil
18	10253	Maxilaku	Confections	16	40	Hanari Carnes	Rio de Janeiro	Brazil
19	10254	Guaraná Fantástica	Beverages	3.6	15	Chop-suey Chinese	Bern	Switzerland
20	10254	Pâté chinois	Meat/Poultry	19.2	21	Chop-suey Chinese	Bern	Switzerland
21	10254	Longlife Tofu	Produce	8	21	Chop-suey Chinese	Bern	Switzerland
22	10255	Raclette Courdavault	Dairy Products	44	30	Richter Supermarkt	Genève	Switzerland
23	10255	Pavlova	Confections	13.9	35	Richter Supermarkt	Genève	Switzerland
24	10255	Chang	Beverages	15.2	20	Richter Supermarkt	Genève	Switzerland

FIGURE 26-4

This worksheet shows some entries from an order list of 2,155 grocery store items. Lists like this make great pivot table candidates.

Not all data is suited for a pivot table. To work well, your data needs to meet a few criteria:

- **It has to include at least one column that has duplicate values.** In the order table in Figure 26-4, there are multiple orders from the same customer—in other words, the Customer column has duplicate values. Accordingly, you can create a separate group that lists the items each customer ordered.
- **It has to include some numeric information.** You'll use this information to create subtotals. Often, you'll be interested in generating a simple count, total, or average, although you can also find maximum, minimum, and standard deviation. On top of that, you can use your own formulas on the data.

NOTE It's technically possible to create subtotals without using a numeric column. In this case, the subtotals just count the number of values in the group. This approach is occasionally useful, but it's not as powerful as other types of subtotals.

The order information table is perfect for a pivot table, because it has several columns you can use to group the order rows. These include:

- **Product and Category.** Find out how well specific products are selling or what the hottest product categories are.
- **Customer.** Find out who's making the most purchases.
- **Ship City and Ship Country.** Find out where the majority of your customers reside.

A pivot table can handle all these comparisons. You don't need to choose one column or another before you start building the pivot table.

Preparing a Pivot Table

Creating a pivot table is a two-step process. First you need to run the PivotTable and PivotChart wizard, which asks you to identify the data you want to summarize and select the location where you want to place the pivot table. The next step is to actually define the structure of the pivot table and try out different ways of organizing and grouping your data.

The following steps lead you through the first step in creating a new pivot table:

1. **Select the range of cells you want to use for your pivot table.**

   If you plan to add more rows later, consider using a table (Chapter 14) instead of selecting a range of cells. That way, when you add rows to the data list and refresh the pivot table, Excel automatically adds your new rows to the pivot table.

2. **Select Insert→Tables→PivotTable.**

   If you're creating a pivot table for a table you defined with the Insert→Tables→Table feature (page 414), there's a shortcut. Just move anywhere inside your table, and then choose Table Tools | Design→Tools→Summarize with Pivot.

   Either way, the Create PivotTable window appears (Figure 26-5). Excel automatically chooses the "Select a table or range" option, with the table name or cell range you selected.

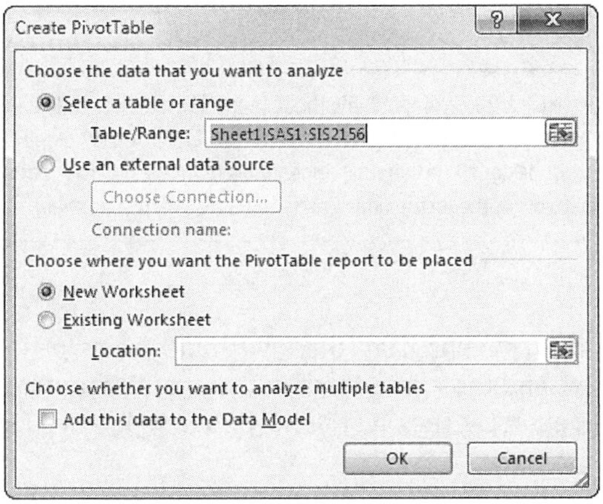

FIGURE 26-5

The Create PivotTable window asks where your raw data is (in a table, cell range, or external data source) and where you want to put the pivot table that summarizes it.

NOTE You can also build a pivot table based on records you select from an external database. But before you take this step, you must configure your database as an Excel data source. To learn how to do so, see page 833.

3. **Select "New worksheet" to create a new worksheet for your pivot table, which is usually the easiest option.**

   Pivot tables are fairly complex creations, so the easiest way to manage them (and keep them separate from the rest of your data) is to pop them into a new worksheet. Alternatively, you can choose "Existing worksheet" to insert your pivot table in a worksheet that's already in your workbook. In this case, you need to specify the cell reference for the top-left corner of the pivot table. If there's data under this cell or to the right of it, Excel may overwrite it as it generates the pivot table. Usually, the best approach is to place a new pivot table on a separate worksheet.

   Don't worry about the setting underneath, "Add this data to the Data Model." You'll learn how to use it on page 846, when you add Excel's data connection features into the mix.

NOTE If you choose to create a new worksheet, Excel gives the worksheet an unhelpful name (like Sheet5), and then places it before the worksheet that contains your data. You can rename the new worksheet, and then drag it to a better spot using the techniques described in Chapter 4.

4. **Click OK.**

   Excel inserts the new pivot table. Because you haven't defined the columns it should use for grouping and analyzing rows, this pivot table appears as an empty placeholder, as shown in Figure 26-6.

NOTE If you create an empty pivot table in Excel 2003 compatibility mode (page 33), it looks a little different from Figure 26-6. Instead of the graphical box shown there, you get a series of linked white boxes, with messages inviting you to drop fields in each one. Microsoft designed this strange appearance to mimic the way that blank pivot tables appeared in Excel 2003. But don't worry—the instructions in this chapter work just as well.

Pivot Table Regions

To build a pivot table, simply drag columns from the PivotTable Fields pane on the right side of the Excel window, and then drop them into one of the four boxes underneath. As you work, Excel generates the pivot table, updating it as you add, rearrange, or remove columns.

NOTE Excel refers to all your source data's columns as *fields*.

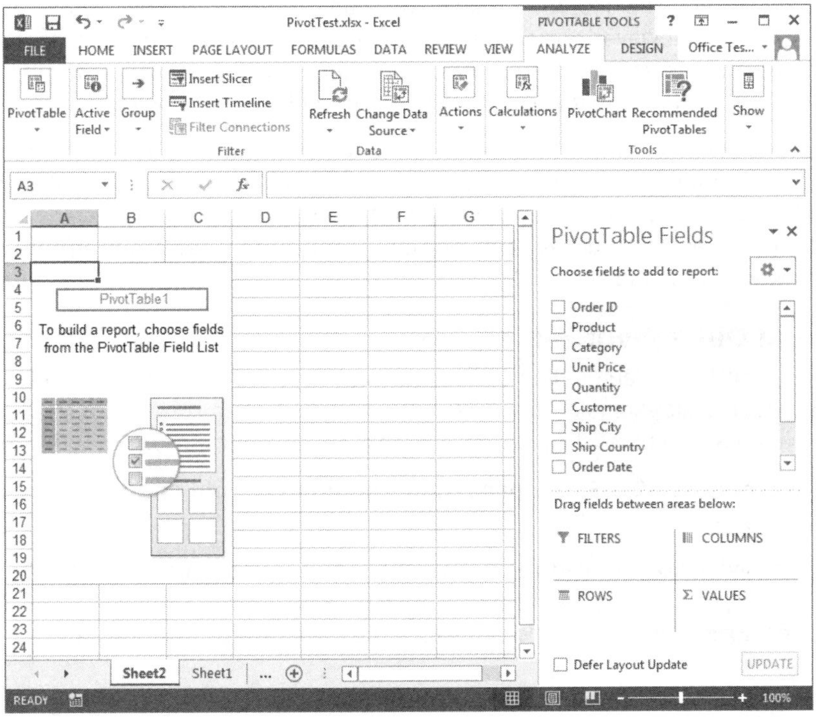

FIGURE 26-6

This worksheet shows a newly created pivot table that doesn't yet contain any information. When you move to a cell inside the pivot table, Excel displays the PivotTable Fields pane on the right, which contains a list of all the columns in the data you're summarizing.

To understand how to fill a pivot table with data, you need to know how each region works. Altogether, a pivot table includes four regions:

- **Values.** These are the fields that you want to subtotal and display in your pivot table. Usually, this is the numeric information you use to build averages and totals.
- **Rows.** These fields let you break down the data into categories. The pivot table uses the row fields to create separate groups, and puts the information for each group into a single row. Using the product list in Figure 26-4, you could group products into categories by dropping the Category field here.
- **Columns.** Often, you want to subdivide your data in more than one way at once. You can use column fields to create groups in the same way that you use row fields. The difference is that these groups are displayed in separate columns. If you use Category for a row field and Ship Country for a column field, you wind up with a table that divides sales figures into rows by product category, and then divides each category row into columns by country.

- **Report Filter.** These fields filter the data the pivot table displays. If you want to look at a breakdown of sales by category, but want to consider U.S. sales only, you could add Ship Country as a page field and configure it accordingly.

Whether you use a field for row grouping or column grouping, the pivot table shows the same data. However, one approach may be more readable than another. If you have a field with extremely long names, it probably works better as a row field than as a column field (where it would stretch out the width of the whole column).

Also, consider how many different groups you want to create. If you want your pivot table to compare sales by category and country, and your list features five categories and 20 countries, you'll probably be best off if you use the country field as a row field and the category field as a column field. That keeps the table long and narrow, which is easier to read and print.

Laying Out a Pivot Table

To get a better understanding of how to create a pivot table, it helps to follow along with a basic example. These steps lead you through the process of creating a summary that compares the products and shipping locations shown in Figure 26-4.

1. **In the PivotTable Fields pane, drag the Product field into the Rows box underneath.**

   When you drop the field, Excel fills in the names of all the products from the list from top to bottom, in alphabetical order (see Figure 26-7). When you finish this step, Excel creates one row containing the subtotals for each product.

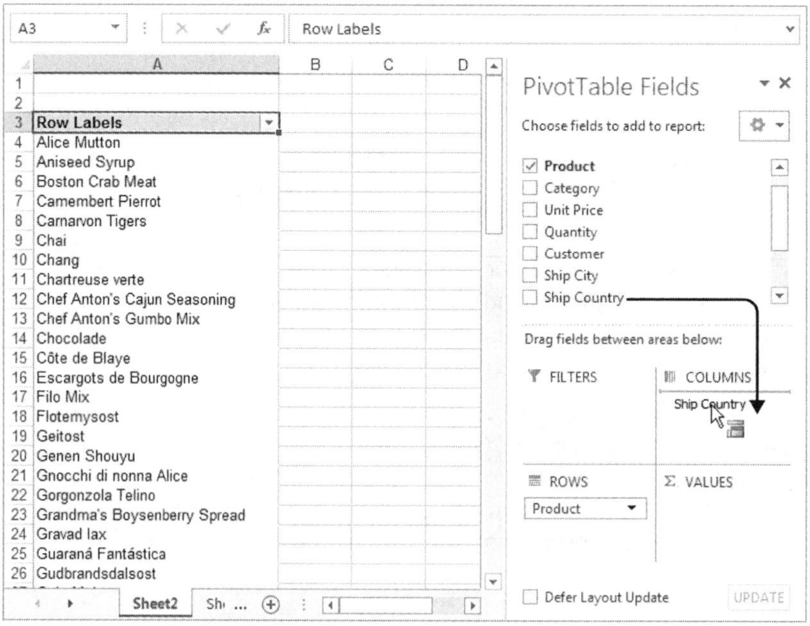

FIGURE 26-7

In this example, Excel has already added the list of products to the row area (it appears in column A), and you're dragging the second grouping criteria (the list of countries you ship to) into the Columns box. Notice that once you link a field, Excel lists its name in boldface in the PivotTable Fields pane.

2. **From the PivotTable Fields pane, drag the Ship Country field to the Columns box.**

   When you drop the field, Excel fills in the names of all the countries from the list from left to right, in alphabetical order. In other words, Excel lists each country in its own column.

3. **Now you need to choose the data you want to examine. Drag the Quantity field to the Values box.**

   This step is designed to actually fill the table with data—specifically, with the numbers of products customers in various countries ordered. It's helpful to remember what's in the table just prior to this step: a list of products in column A and, from column B on, columns labeled with a different country.

   Once you complete this step, Excel generates the pivot table using its standard calculation option, which is to sum all the fields in the Values box. In this example, it adds all the values in the Quantity field for a given group, which tells you how many units of a specific product you shipped to a specific country. Figure 26-8 shows the result.

NOTE Pivot tables also calculate row and column subtotals. If you want to find the total number of units shipped for a given product across all countries, scroll to the far right end of the chart. If you want to find the total number of units sold in a given country, scroll to the totals at the bottom of the chart.

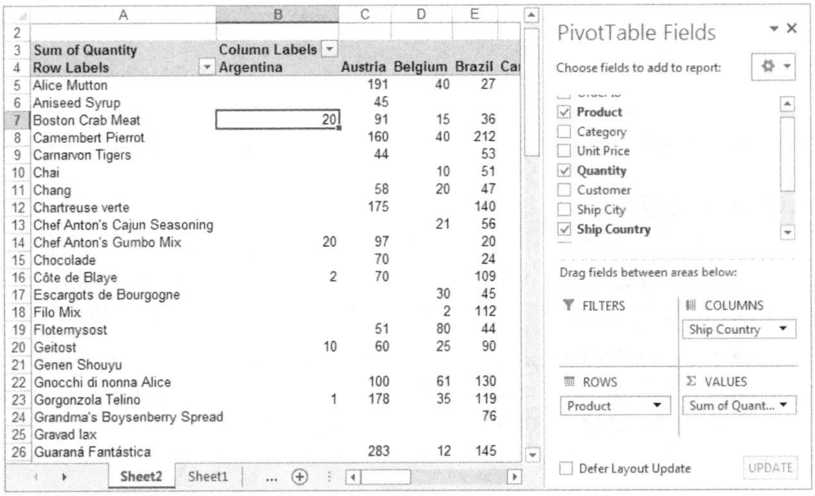

FIGURE 26-8

This pivot table totals the quantity of product units in every order. For example, it tells you that 20 units of Boston Crab Meat were shipped to Argentina.

This example built a fairly sophisticated two-dimensional pivot table, which means that it compares two groupings (one represented in rows, and the other represented in columns). Most of the pivot tables you'll see in real life are two-dimensional, but there's no reason you can't create simpler one-dimensional pivot tables. All you need to do is leave out the fields in either the Columns box or Rows box. Figure 26-9 shows a pivot table that simply totals the number of units sold for particular products.

Unlike most other elements in Excel, pivot tables don't refresh themselves automatically. That means that if you change the source data, the pivot table may show out-of-date totals. To correct this problem, you can refresh the pivot table by moving to one of its cells, and then selecting PivotTable Tools | Analyze→Data→Refresh (or the keyboard shortcut Alt+F5). This action tells Excel to scan the source data and regenerate the pivot table.

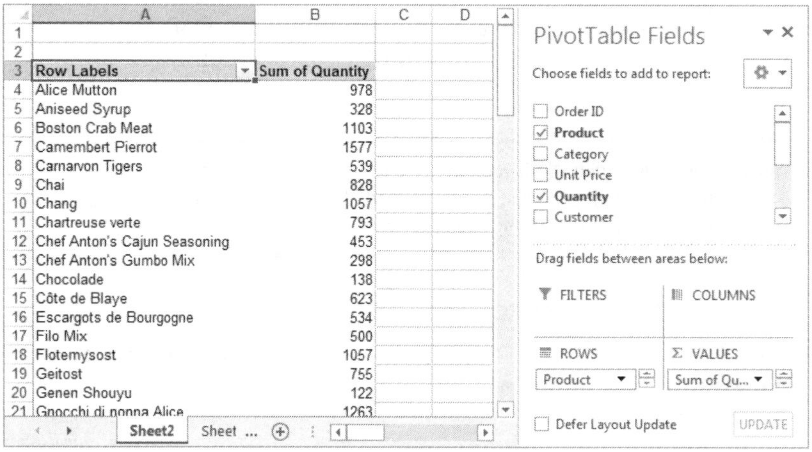

FIGURE 26-9

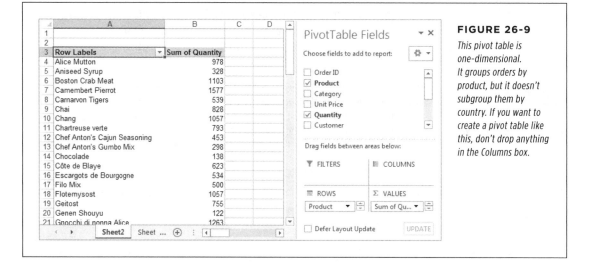

This pivot table is one-dimensional. It groups orders by product, but it doesn't subgroup them by country. If you want to create a pivot table like this, don't drop anything in the Columns box.

Formatting a Pivot Table

As you've probably noticed, when you move into one of the cells of a pivot table, two new tabs spring up in the ribbon under the PivotTable Tools heading. These are similar to the tabs that appear when you select a chart, picture, or table.

You can use the PivotTable Tools | Analyze tab to access a few advanced features that you've yet to consider, like grouping, pivot table formulas, and pivot charts. You'll consider these features in the rest of this chapter. The PivotTable Tools | Design tab is more modest; you use it to format and otherwise fine-tune the appearance of your pivot table.

The PivotTable Tools | Design tab is carved into three sections. At the far right, you'll find the PivotTables Styles section, with a familiar style gallery. If you choose one of the entries here, Excel adjusts your PivotTable automatically, giving it new colors and shading that can range from subtle to dramatic.

TIP The colors Excel uses in the pivot table styles actually come from your workbook theme (page 172). So if you want a different set of accent colors for your pivot table, choose a new theme from the Page Layout→Themes→Themes gallery.

Some pivot table layouts use *banding*—a pattern of shading alternate rows or columns to distinguish one row or column from the next. Banding works well in some pivot tables, but you may find the effect overwhelming in others. To give you more control over your pivot table's formatting, Excel lets you apply just a portion of the full pivot table style. You can do so by using the checkboxes in the PivotTable Tools | Design→PivotTable Style Options section of the ribbon. If you want to use a specific style but you don't want to apply its banding effects, clear the Banded Rows and Banded Columns checkboxes. Similarly, if you don't want to apply the style formatting to headers, clear the Column Headers or Row Headers checkboxes.

Finally, the PivotTable Tools | Design→Layout section lets you choose from various preset options that control spacing and subtotals. This section contains four submenus:

- **Grand Totals.** Pick an option from this list to show or hide the totals at the end of each row and column.
- **Subtotals.** Pick an option from this list to show or hide subtotals at the end of every group. This setting works only if you subdivide your groups—in other words, only if you have more than one field in the Rows section or more than one field in the Columns section. Otherwise, the group "subtotals" are actually the grand totals.
- **Report Layout.** Pick an option from this list to choose how tightly packed your pivot table is. By default, Excel shows pivot tables in "compact" form, which keeps columns as narrow as possible. (Typically, the column is just wide enough to fit the data inside and the column header.) Old versions of Excel (like Excel 2003) made each column as wide as the widest column, which takes considerably more room. If you still want this space-chewing display choice, choose PivotTable Tools | Design→Layout→Report Layout→Show in Outline Form.
- **Blank Rows.** Pick an option from this list to add a blank line between groups. This option works only if you have more than one field in the Rows section.

Rearranging a Pivot Table

So far, you've seen how to use a pivot table to quickly build a summary table. However, pivot tables have another key benefit: flexibility. There's no limit to how many times you can move fields or recalculate your summary so that it performs different analyses.

To change a pivot table, use the following techniques in the PivotTable Fields pane:

- **To remove** a field from a pivot table, click the field header (in the appropriate box), and then drag it out of the PivotTable Fields pane. The mouse pointer changes to an X symbol to indicate you're removing the field.

- **To move** a field from one position to another, just drag the field header from one box to another. You can reverse the example shown earlier by dragging the column field (Country) to the Rows box, and dragging the row field (Product) to the Columns box.

Figure 26-10 shows one way you could rearrange the pivot table shown in Figure 26-8.

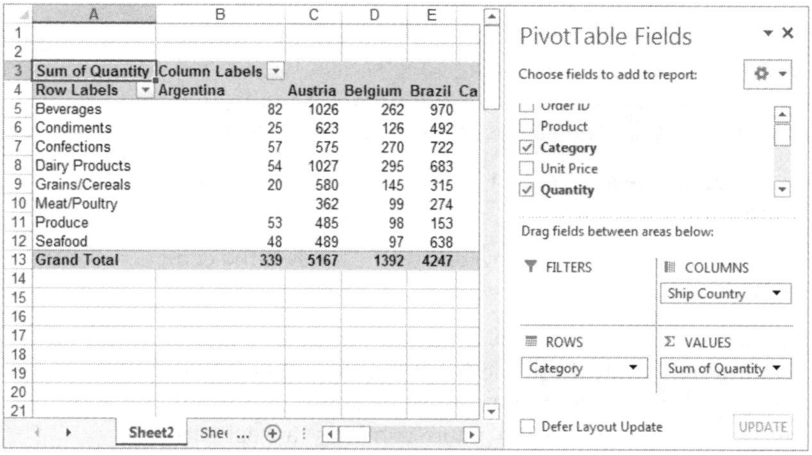

FIGURE 26-10

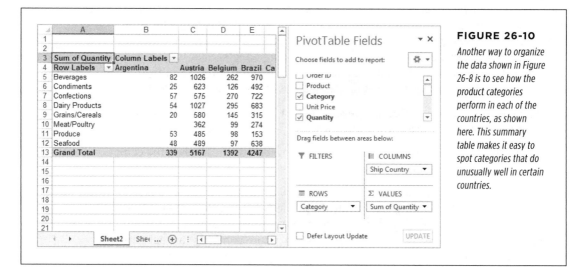

Another way to organize the data shown in Figure 26-8 is to see how the product categories perform in each of the countries, as shown here. This summary table makes it easy to spot categories that do unusually well in certain countries.

Getting to the Source

As you review the summarized information in a pivot table, you just might discover trends and relationships you didn't expect. For example, the pivot table in Figure 26-10 exposes a fact you probably wouldn't have realized by just looking at the raw data—namely, Austrians love their dairy products.

When faced with a fact like this, it's often worthwhile to dig a little deeper. For example, you might wonder exactly how Excel calculated the high value in cell C8. Did customers in Austria place a huge number of orders, or were there just a few orders that were unexpectedly large? Now that the pivot table has done its number-crunching job by highlighting this sort of information, you need to return to the source data to further your investigation.

Although you could flip back to the worksheet that has your source data and search for the corresponding records, Excel has an easier solution. If you double-click any value in a pivot table, Excel adds a new worksheet. In this worksheet, it copies the records that were used to calculate the pivot table cell in question, and nothing else. For example, if you double-click cell C8 in Figure 26-10, Excel adds a worksheet that shows all the Austrian dairy sales (Figure 26-11). Excel pros call this *drilling down* into your data.

Once you finish reviewing the data, you can delete the worksheet Excel created. After all, the source information is in your original worksheet. To remove the worksheet, right-click the corresponding worksheet tab at the bottom of the window, and then choose Delete.

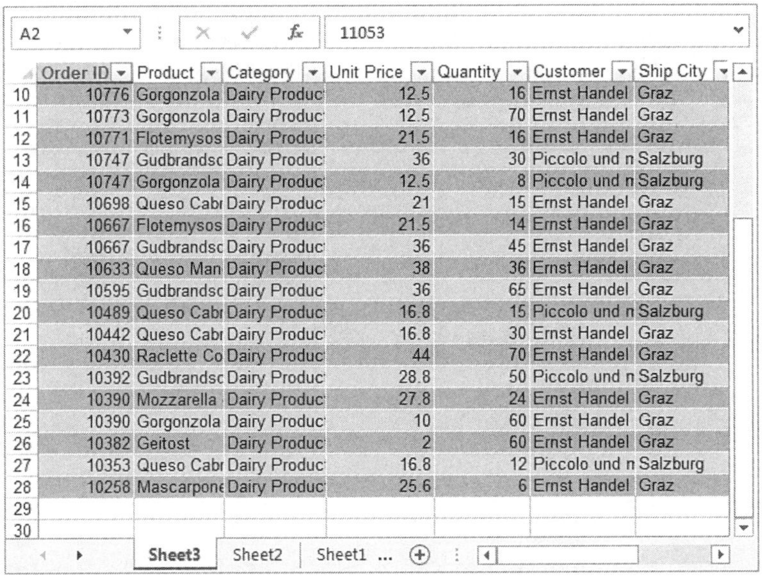

A2 | 11053

	Order ID	Product	Category	Unit Price	Quantity	Customer	Ship City
10	10776	Gorgonzola	Dairy Produc	12.5	16	Ernst Handel	Graz
11	10773	Gorgonzola	Dairy Produc	12.5	70	Ernst Handel	Graz
12	10771	Flotemysos	Dairy Produc	21.5	16	Ernst Handel	Graz
13	10747	Gudbrandsc	Dairy Produc	36	30	Piccolo und n	Salzburg
14	10747	Gorgonzola	Dairy Produc	12.5	8	Piccolo und n	Salzburg
15	10698	Queso Cabı	Dairy Produc	21	15	Ernst Handel	Graz
16	10667	Flotemysos	Dairy Produc	21.5	14	Ernst Handel	Graz
17	10667	Gudbrandsc	Dairy Produc	36	45	Ernst Handel	Graz
18	10633	Queso Man	Dairy Produc	38	36	Ernst Handel	Graz
19	10595	Gudbrandsc	Dairy Produc	36	65	Ernst Handel	Graz
20	10489	Queso Cabı	Dairy Produc	16.8	15	Piccolo und n	Salzburg
21	10442	Queso Cabı	Dairy Produc	16.8	30	Ernst Handel	Graz
22	10430	Raclette Co	Dairy Produc	44	70	Ernst Handel	Graz
23	10392	Gudbrandsc	Dairy Produc	28.8	50	Piccolo und n	Salzburg
24	10390	Mozzarella	Dairy Produc	27.8	24	Ernst Handel	Graz
25	10390	Gorgonzola	Dairy Produc	10	60	Ernst Handel	Graz
26	10382	Geitost	Dairy Produc	2	60	Ernst Handel	Graz
27	10353	Queso Cabı	Dairy Produc	16.8	12	Piccolo und n	Salzburg
28	10258	Mascarpone	Dairy Produc	25.6	6	Ernst Handel	Graz
29							
30							

Sheet3 | Sheet2 | Sheet1 ...

FIGURE 26-11

When you double-click the calculated total for Austrian dairy sales, Excel creates this worksheet, which shows the 27 records it added together to produce the pivot table result.

GEM IN THE ROUGH

Recommended Pivot Tables

Most Excel pros like to hand-design their pivot tables, using the techniques you just explored. But if you're in a hurry, you can pick from one of Excel's *recommended* pivot tables.

Normally, when you create a pivot table, you start with the blank view you saw in Figure 26-6. But when you create a recommended pivot table, Excel creates the pivot table *and* chooses what fields to put in the Columns, Rows, and Values boxes.

Excel recommends pivot tables that it thinks will suit your data (although its insights are necessarily limited, because Excel doesn't really know what each field really represents). To see Excel's suggestions, start by selecting the data you want to use to create the pivot table. Then click the Quick Analysis icon, which appears next to the bottom-right corner of your selection, and then choose Tables. Excel offers four prebuilt pivot table choices (Figure 26-12).

Alternatively, you can select your data and choose Insert→Tables→Recommended PivotTables to see an even longer list of choices in the Recommended PivotTables window.

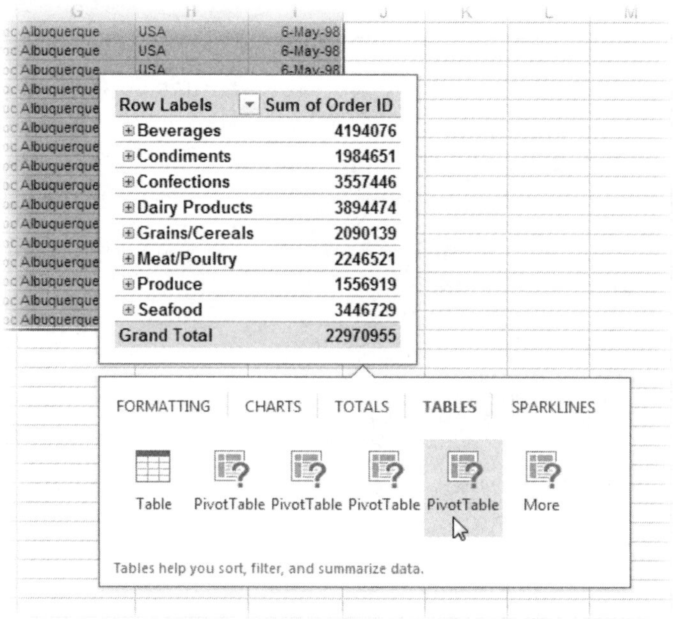

FIGURE 26-12

Excel offers you a choice of four recommended pivot tables. To preview what your data will look like in each, hover over the corresponding icon. Some recommended pivot tables make great sense, while others are useless—like this one, which calculates the total of the OrderID for the records in each product category. If you find something you like, click the icon to create the pivot table. You can always rearrange the fields and customize the pivot table once you add it.

Multi-Layered Pivot Tables

So far, you've seen examples of how to create one- and two-dimensional pivot tables. But the fun doesn't need to end there. In fact, there's no limit to the number of groupings you can add to a pivot table. To add additional levels of grouping, simply drag the appropriate fields from the PivotTable Fields pane onto the row or column area of the pivot table. Each time you add a new grouping, Excel *subdivides* your current groups.

If you add Product to the row area of your pivot table, Excel groups all your records into rows so that each row totals the information for a separate product. Next, say you add *another* field to the row area—this time, the Order Date field. Excel responds by dividing each product row into *multiple* rows. Each individual row shows the total units for a given product sold on a given day.

The problem with subdividing is that it can needlessly enlarge the size of your summary table. If you're not careful, your summary table may not be a summary at all! Consider the table in Figure 26-13, which shows the Category and Order Date fields in the row area, and the Ship Country field in the column area. The problem here is that there aren't many orders that fall on the same date. Even when they do, they're often for products in different categories. As a result, many of the rows aren't true totals—instead, they display only the results for a single order.

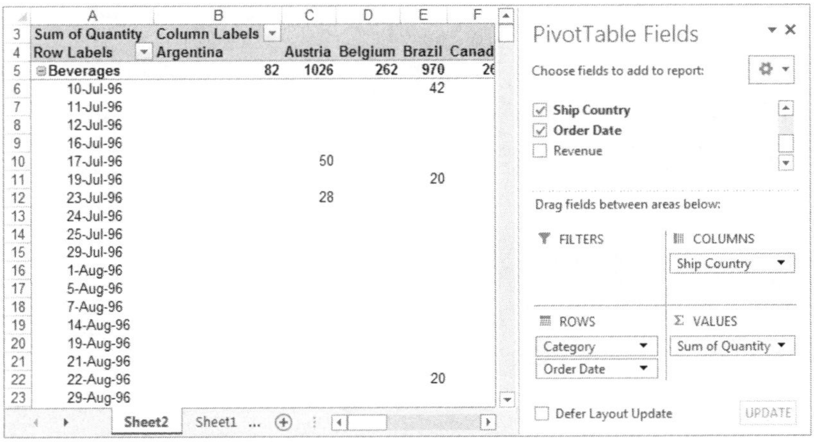

FIGURE 26-13

In this pivot table, you've grouped rows by category and subdivided the categories by order date. That means that each row shows information for the orders made for a given product category on a given day. Each row is further broken up into columns by country. At the bottom of each group (not shown), Excel subtotals all the rows for that product across all days.

One hint that the table isn't performing a good summary is the number of rows in the pivot table. At 1,621 rows, it's not much smaller than the total 2,155 rows of source data in the original table. You'll also notice that the table is quite sparse, because each row is further broken down into columns (by country). The end result is a lot of blank, wasted space.

This example may lead you to conclude that pivot tables with more than two groupings aren't much use—unless you have a staggering amount of data (thousands or even tens of thousands of records). However, subgrouping does come in handy if you have *related* fields. Two good examples of related fields in the orders table are:

- **Categories and Products.** Each product is a part of one category. Thus, you can group first by category, and then subdivide each category by product. This subgrouping appears in Figure 26-14.
- **Ship Country and Ship City.** Each city is located in one country. You can group first by country, and then subdivide each country into cities.

In both examples, it's important to make sure that you add the fields in the correct order. You don't want to group by product and then group by category, because each product is only a part of one category. Instead, you want to group by category, and *then* list products within these categories. Figure 26-15 shows the difference.

Row Labels	Sum of Quantity
Alice Mutton	**978**
Meat/Poultry	978
Aniseed Syrup	**328**
Condiments	328
Boston Crab Meat	**1103**
Seafood	1103
Camembert Pierrot	**1577**
Dairy Products	1577
Carnarvon Tigers	**539**
Beverages	539
Chai	**828**
Meat/Poultry	828
Chang	**1057**
Beverages	1057
Chartreuse verte	**793**

Row Labels	Sum of Quantity
Beverages	**9243**
Carnarvon Tigers	539
Chang	1057
Chartreuse verte	793
Côte de Blaye	623
Guaraná Fantástica	1125
Ipoh Coffee	580
Lakkalikööri	981
Laughing Lumberjack Lager	184
Outback Lager	817
Rhönbräu Klosterbier	1155
Sasquatch Ale	506
Steeleye Stout	883
Condiments	**4547**
Aniseed Syrup	328
Genen Shouyu	122

FIGURE 26-14

Top: When subgrouping, make sure you place your fields in the correct order. Here, the pivot table groups the records by product, and then subdivides the products by category, which really doesn't make sense. The result is a table where each group contains a single subgroup.

Bottom: This pivot table's rows are grouped by category, and then subdivided by product, which makes much more sense.

To make sure you have the right grouping, look in the Rows box (if you're grouping rows) or the Columns box (if you're grouping columns) in the PivotTable Fields pane. In the example shown in Figure 26-14, bottom, the Category field should appear above the Product field in the list. If it isn't, you can drag the Category field into place, or you can click it, and then choose Move Up from the pop-up menu.

GEM IN THE ROUGH

Avoiding Slow Refreshes

If your pivot table involves a huge amount of information, and you plan to use multiple levels of grouping, you may not like Excel's standard behavior. Every time you drag a field to a box in the PivotTable Fields pane, Excel regenerates the pivot table with your new settings. This refresh takes a bit of time, and it can make designing a complex pivot table seem just a little sluggish.

If you're tired of waiting, Excel has a solution. Before you make any changes to your pivot table, switch on the Defer Layout Update setting, which appears at the bottom of the PivotTable Fields pane. While the Defer Layout Update is on, Excel doesn't refresh your pivot table as you build or change it. If you're a fast mover and you're dealing with a massively large pivot table, this lets you work much faster.

When you finish making your changes (or you just want to see what the pivot table looks like so far), click the Update button to perform a one-time refresh. Or, turn off the Defer Layout Setting to go back to normal, and let Excel refresh the pivot table automatically.

Of course, there's one disadvantage to using Defer Layout Update. You don't see the effects of your changes until you're done. As a result, the Defer Layout Update setting is a great tool for pivot table pros, but you'll probably want to stay away from it while you're learning.

Hiding and Showing Details

Subgrouping gives you another interesting ability—you can hide or show individual groups. This feature lets you show detailed information for just the part of the table you're interested in, while hiding the rest. In fact, this feature works just like the collapsible outlines you learned about in Chapter 15.

Imagine you create a pivot table that uses the Category and Product fields to group rows. When you create this table, Excel shows you every product in every category. But what if you want to show only the products in a specific category? In this case, the trick is to hide every category you *don't* want to see.

- **To hide** (or **collapse**) the products in a specific category, click the plus/minus icon next to the category name. You can repeat this process to collapse as many categories as you want. All you'll see is the row with the category totals.
- **To show** a collapsed category, click the plus/minus icon again.

TIP For an even quicker shortcut to hide or show a category, double-click the cell with the category name (like *Beverages* in A6). When you double-click an expanded category, Excel collapses it. When you double-click a collapsed category, Excel expands it. This feature helps you quickly drill down to the most interesting parts of your summary.

- **To collapse** all the categories in your pivot table, right-click any category, and then choose Expand/Collapse→Collapse Entire Field.
- **To expand** all your categories, right-click any category, and then choose Expand/Collapse→Expand Entire Field.

Figure 26-15 shows a pivot table that takes full advantage of Excel's ability to hide and show details.

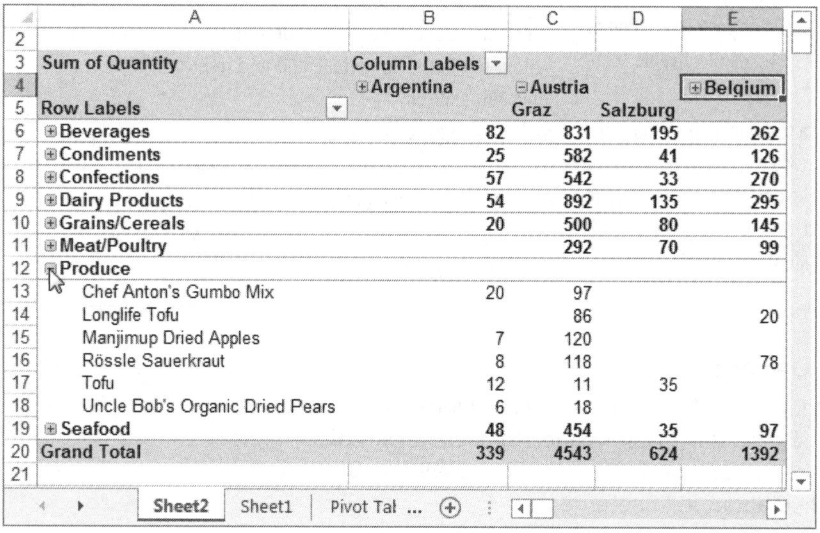

	A	B	C	D	E
2					
3	Sum of Quantity	Column Labels			
4		⊞Argentina	⊟Austria		⊞Belgium
5	Row Labels		Graz	Salzburg	
6	⊞Beverages	82	831	195	262
7	⊞Condiments	25	582	41	126
8	⊞Confections	57	542	33	270
9	⊞Dairy Products	54	892	135	295
10	⊞Grains/Cereals	20	500	80	145
11	⊞Meat/Poultry		292	70	99
12	⊟Produce				
13	Chef Anton's Gumbo Mix	20	97		
14	Longlife Tofu		86		20
15	Manjimup Dried Apples	7	120		
16	Rössle Sauerkraut	8	118		78
17	Tofu	12	11	35	
18	Uncle Bob's Organic Dried Pears	6	18		
19	⊞Seafood	48	454	35	97
20	Grand Total	339	4543	624	1392
21					

FIGURE 26-15

In this pivot table, you grouped rows by Category and subgrouped them by Product. Then you grouped Columns by Country and subgrouped them by City. All the category groups are collapsed except for Produce, and all the country groups are collapsed except for Austria. This way, the pivot chart highlights produce sales in Graz and Salzburg, two picturesque Austrian cities.

There's no limit to how many levels of grouping you can add. If you use the Show Detail command to try to expand the last level of your pivot table, Excel prompts you with a Show Detail window that lists all the fields you aren't currently using. If you choose one of these fields and then click OK, Excel adds another layer of grouping to the pivot table, as shown in Figure 26-16.

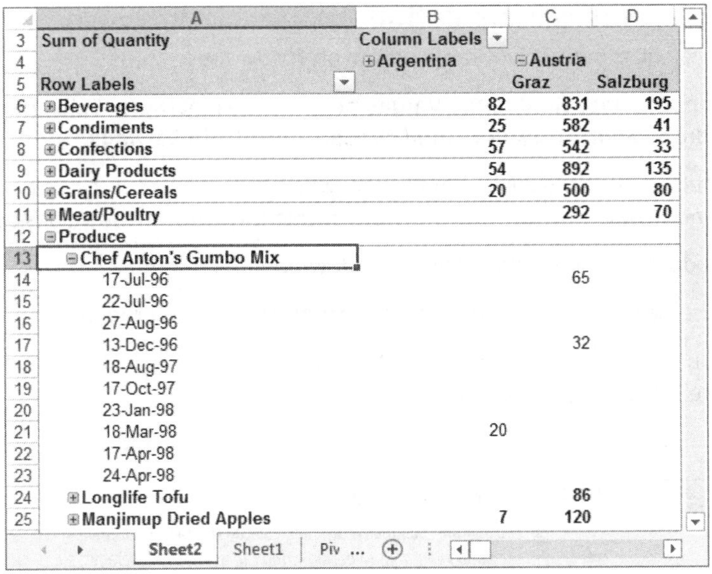

	A	B	C	D
3	Sum of Quantity	Column Labels		
4		⊞Argentina	⊟Austria	
5	Row Labels		Graz	Salzburg
6	⊞Beverages	82	831	195
7	⊞Condiments	25	582	41
8	⊞Confections	57	542	33
9	⊞Dairy Products	54	892	135
10	⊞Grains/Cereals	20	500	80
11	⊞Meat/Poultry		292	70
12	⊟Produce			
13	⊟Chef Anton's Gumbo Mix			
14	17-Jul-96		65	
15	22-Jul-96			
16	27-Aug-96			
17	13-Dec-96		32	
18	18-Aug-97			
19	17-Oct-97			
20	23-Jan-98			
21	18-Mar-98	20		
22	17-Apr-98			
23	24-Apr-98			
24	⊞Longlife Tofu		86	
25	⊞Manjimup Dried Apples	7	120	

FIGURE 26-16

This pivot table drills down through three levels of row groupings. It shows a detailed breakdown that indicates when Chef Anton's Gumbo Mix was ordered, and exactly where the shipments were headed.

Fine-Tuning Pivot Table Calculations

As you saw earlier, when you add a field to the Values box, Excel guesses what calculation you want to perform. In most cases, it assumes you want to use a sum operation to total up all the values in the field. However, this calculation isn't always the right one. Consider the sales summary pivot table you've been exploring in this chapter. Although it makes sense to examine the total units sold, you may be just as interested in the maximum, minimum, or average order size, or the order *count* (the number of times a product was ordered, without considering the number of units in each order).

Fortunately, Excel makes it easy to change the type of calculation you use. And as you'll see in the following sections, you can even perform more than one calculation in the same pivot table, and throw your custom formulas into the mix.

Changing the Type of Calculation

To modify the calculation the pivot table performs, follow these steps:

1. **Find the appropriate field in the Values box of the PivotTable Fields pane. Click the drop-down arrow, and then choose Value Field Settings.**

   If you want to change the current operation, which sums together the Quantity value for each row in a group, click the "Sum of Quantity" item in the Values box.

   When you do, the Value Field Settings window appears (Figure 26-17).

2. **In the "Summarize by" tab, choose a different option from the list.**

   Choose Count to add up the number of different orders for a product, or Average to calculate the average order size.

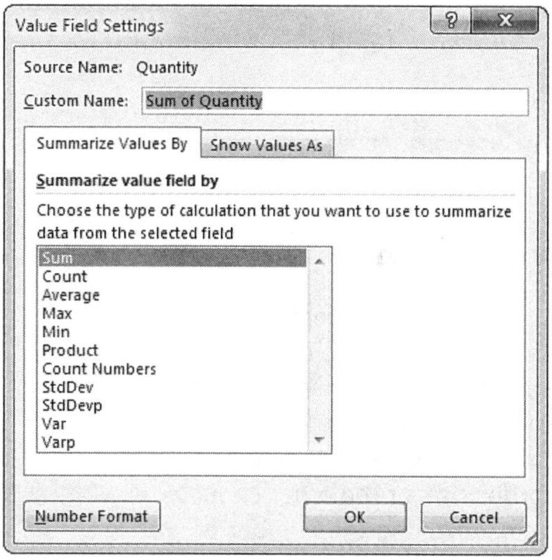

FIGURE 26-17

Using the "Summarize by" tab, you can choose the subtotaling calculation you want to perform. You can use counts, averages, sums, or find the maximum value, minimum value, or standard deviation. The "Show Values as" tab lets you configure more complex calculations that compare fields (like differences, percentages, and so on) or calculate running totals.

3. **If you want to change the number format to display the new summary information, click the Number Format button, choose a new format, and then click OK.**

   When you click Number Format, Excel shows a slimmed-down version of the Format Cells window, which only includes the Number tab. You can use this tab to change the number of decimal places, get a currency symbol, and so on.

4. **Click OK to close the Value Field Settings window.**

   Excel refreshes the pivot table with the new settings.

TIP The column headings used for data values can use up valuable space. To get narrower columns, you can apply a shorter custom column name. To do so, click the field in the Values box, and then choose Value Field Settings. In the Value Field Settings window, enter a new field name in the Custom Name box.

POWER USERS' CLINIC

Adding Multiple Values

As you've seen, you can add more than one field to the Rows and Columns boxes. You can use the same technique to add multiple fields to the Values box. When you do, Excel calculates each field and displays it in the pivot table in a separate column, as shown in Figure 26-18.

You could decide to show the total for the Quantity field *and* the average of the Unit Price field. To do so, drag both fields into the Values box. Then, follow the steps on this page to configure the type of calculation Excel performs for each field.

You can also use this technique to perform multiple calculations on the same field. If you want to average and total the Quantity field, drag the Quantity field into the Values box twice. You'll end up with two separate items, which you can configure separately.

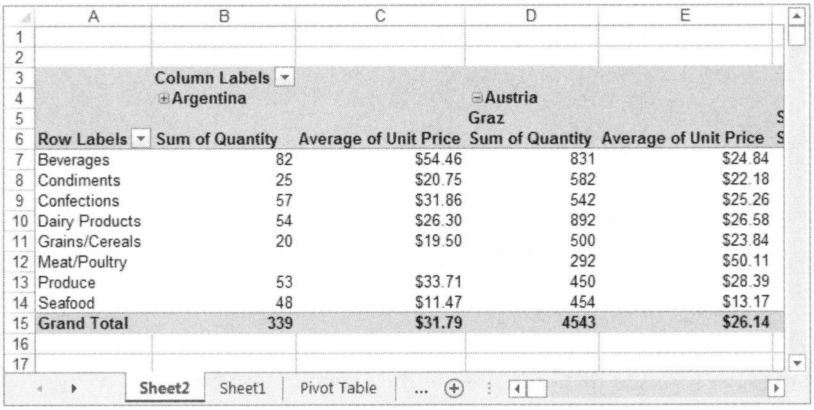

	A	B	C	D	E	
1						
2						
3		Column Labels				
4		⊞Argentina		⊟Austria		
5				Graz		S
6	Row Labels	Sum of Quantity	Average of Unit Price	Sum of Quantity	Average of Unit Price	S
7	Beverages	82	$54.46	831	$24.84	
8	Condiments	25	$20.75	582	$22.18	
9	Confections	57	$31.86	542	$25.26	
10	Dairy Products	54	$26.30	892	$26.58	
11	Grains/Cereals	20	$19.50	500	$23.84	
12	Meat/Poultry			292	$50.11	
13	Produce	53	$33.71	450	$28.39	
14	Seafood	48	$11.47	454	$13.17	
15	Grand Total	339	$31.79	4543	$26.14	
16						
17						

FIGURE 26-18

When your pivot table contains multiple values, they appear in different columns with headings like "Sum of Quantity" and "Average of Unit Price."

Adding a Calculated Field

Using the pivot tables you've learned about so far, you can perform a variety of operations on any field, including averages, sums, and other preset calculations. But what if you want to branch out a little further and create a *custom calculation?* You could alter the source data, add a new column containing your calculation, and then recreate the pivot table. But Excel provides a much easier option by letting you define a calculated field.

The following steps show how to create a calculated field within a pivot table. Using these steps, you can modify a pivot table that shows a list of orders so that it totals the amount of revenue generated instead of just adding up the number of units shipped.

1. **Move anywhere inside the pivot table.**
2. **Choose PivotTable Tools | Analyze→Calculations→Fields, Items, & Sets→Calculated Field.**

   The Insert Calculated Field window appears, as shown in Figure 26-19.

NOTE You may have noticed the other options in the Calculations section of the PivotTable Tools | Analyze toolbar tab (OLAP Tools and Relationships). Both of them are turned off, because they apply only when you pull your information out of a high-powered database, as you'll learn in Chapter 27.

3. **Enter a name for the new field in the Name text box.**

   In this case, the new name is Revenue.

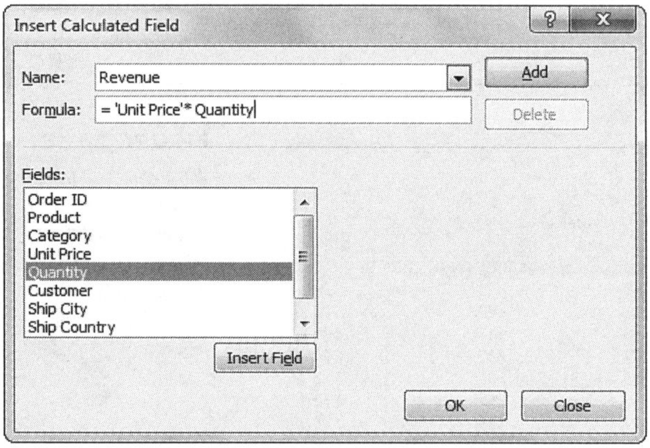

FIGURE 26-19

Here, Excel creates a new field named Revenue to calculate how much money you make on any given order. To arrive at the total revenue, you have Excel multiply the Unit Price field by the Quantity field.

4. **Enter the formula this field uses in the Formula text box.**

   (This is a standard Excel formula that modifies one or more of the other fields provided in the Fields list.)

   Your formula can use Excel's built-in functions, or you can enter a formula that alters or combines one or more of the fields in the Fields list. The new Revenue field calculates the total revenue generated by multiplying the price of the item by the quantity purchased. It uses the following formula:

   ```
   ='Unit Price'* Quantity.
   ```

   Note that you need to enclose field names that include spaces or special characters, like Unit Price, in apostrophes. If you're in any doubt, double-click the field name in the list to have Excel insert it into the Formula text box with apostrophes if they're necessary.

5. **Click OK.**

   Excel automatically adds the calculated field to the PivotTable Fields pane, and then inserts it in the Values box, so that it appears in the pivot table (Figure 26-20).

   As with any other numeric field, Excel assumes you want to perform a sum calculation that totals up your formula for every row. If you want to perform a different calculation, you can customize your field as described in the previous section.

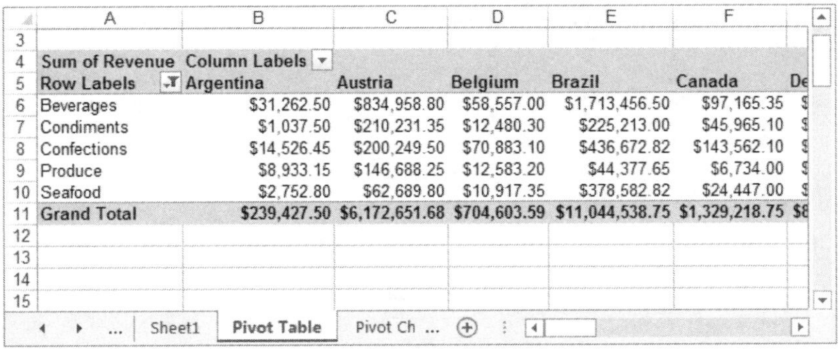

	A	B	C	D	E	F	
3							
4	Sum of Revenue	Column Labels					
5	Row Labels	Argentina	Austria	Belgium	Brazil	Canada	De
6	Beverages	$31,262.50	$834,958.80	$58,557.00	$1,713,456.50	$97,165.35	$
7	Condiments	$1,037.50	$210,231.35	$12,480.30	$225,213.00	$45,965.10	$
8	Confections	$14,526.45	$200,249.50	$70,883.10	$436,672.82	$143,562.10	$
9	Produce	$8,933.15	$146,688.25	$12,583.20	$44,377.65	$6,734.00	$
10	Seafood	$2,752.80	$62,689.80	$10,917.35	$378,582.82	$24,447.00	$
11	Grand Total	$239,427.50	$6,172,651.68	$704,603.59	$11,044,538.75	$1,329,218.75	$8
12							
13							
14							
15							

FIGURE 26-20

The worksheet now shows the total revenue by category and customer country.

NOTE Even if you drag your custom field out of the Values box to remove it from the pivot table, it remains in the field list. If you want, you can drag it back to the Values box later on.

Filtering a Pivot Table

As you've seen, pivot tables are a miraculously powerful tool for creating detailed summary tables. The only problem is that sometimes these reports are too detailed—leaving you with summaries that are nearly as detailed as the original table.

To simplify your pivot tables, you may want to restrict them so that they show only a *portion* of the total data. This process is known as *filtering*, and you can do it in four ways: report filtering, slicers, timelines, and group filtering.

NOTE As you already know, you can create a pivot table that draws its data from a table (the kind you learned to create in Chapter 14). Excel tables support filtering, but their filtering settings have no effect on linked pivot tables. In other words, even if you apply a filter to hide some of the raw data in your source table, all the data still appears in the pivot table. If you want to filter information from the pivot table, you need to use one of the four methods of pivot table filtering.

Report Filtering

Report filtering lets you filter your data so that your pivot table uses only the rows that really interest you. For example, you may want to narrow your sales summary to a specific country. To do so, you need to drag the appropriate field (in this case, Ship Country), to the Filters box in the PivotTable Fields pane. You'll see it appear on your worksheet as shown in Figure 26-21.

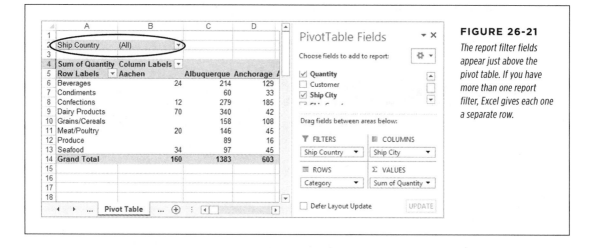

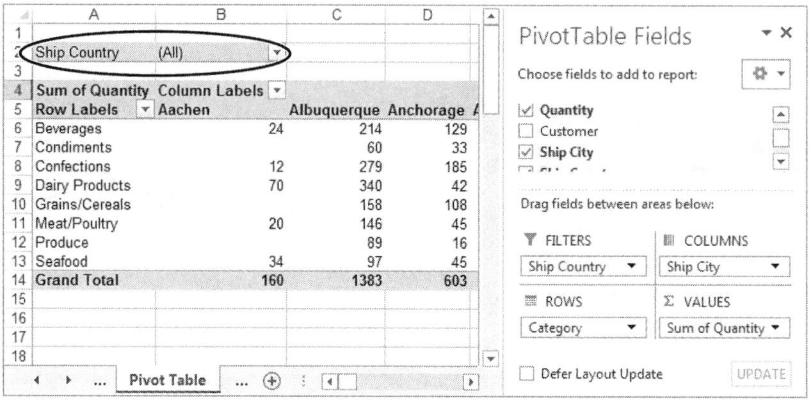

FIGURE 26-21

The report filter fields appear just above the pivot table. If you have more than one report filter, Excel gives each one a separate row.

NOTE Before you go any further, it's important to understand one basic fact about report filtering. You can't use grouping on any field you want to use to filter your report. So if you're filtering by Ship Country, you can't also group by Ship Country. (If you try to, Excel removes your grouping when you add the report filter.) This limitation doesn't apply to the slicers or group filters that you'll learn about in the following section.

Once you add a field to the Filters box, you can use it to filter your report. To actually *set* the filter, click the drop-down arrow in the field box. This pops up a list showing all the values currently in that field. You can then choose the one value you want to display. Figure 26-22 shows an example.

If your report filter offers a long list of potential filtering values, there's no need to spend all day scrolling. Instead, type the first few characters of the value you want in the search box that sits at the very top of the filter list (Figure 26-22). As you type, Excel reduces the options in the list. For example, type "Po" into the Ship Country filter and you'll see a list that includes just two choices: Poland and Portugal.

If you want, you can filter for several values at once. To do so, switch on the Select Multiple Items checkbox at the bottom of the list. When you do, a checkbox appears next to every entry in the list, with a checkmark. Excel uses checked values to create the pivot table, and ignores unchecked entries. Figure 26-23 shows an example.

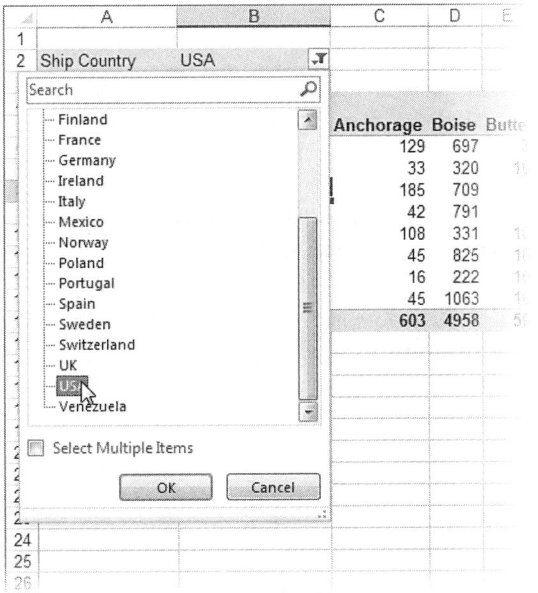

FIGURE 26-22

In this example, you used report filtering to hide every country except the U.S. using the Ship Country field. (Ship Country isn't used as a grouping field, although Ship City is.) The resulting pivot table shows only U.S. cities. You could also add the Customer field to the Filters box to show an order summary for specific customers.

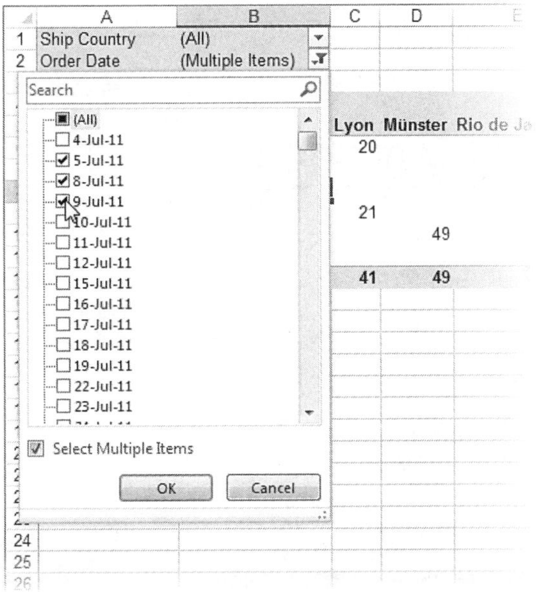

FIGURE 26-23

Clear the checkbox next to items you don't want to see in your pivot table. In this example, the pivot table is using the sales records from three specific days.

To quickly remove a report filter, choose the first item in the report filter list: "(All)."

FREQUENTLY ASKED QUESTION

Choosing the Right Filtering

Should I use report filters or slicers?

Slicers create a sort of "data dashboard" effect. They're perfect if you need a way to quickly switch between different filtering choices. For example, if you frequently compare sales in different product categories, slicers make it easy and intuitive. And unlike report filters, you can create slicers for the same fields you're using to group your pivot table.

However, slicers aren't a clear-cut replacement for report filters. In fact, they have two potential drawbacks. First, slicers take a lot of space in your Excel window, and they can easily obscure parts of your pivot table data, making it difficult to read. This is particularly true if you want to filter on multiple fields—in this case, the report filtering lists are far more compact than the floating slicer windows. Second, slicers don't work well where single fields have a lot of possible values, because all the possibilities won't fit into the floating slicer window at once. You can scroll your way through the list, but there's no handy search box, as there is with report filters.

Finally, if you want more power from your filters—for example, the ability to intelligently pick out ranges of data—neither report filters nor slicers will cut it. Instead, you need the more advanced group filtering feature described on page 823.

Slicers

The first thing you need to understand about slicers is that they don't do anything you can't already accomplish with report filters. (And they're a fair bit *less* powerful than the advanced filters you'll learn about in the next section.) However, slicers show filter settings in a unique way—right in the Excel window, so you can change them with a single click (Figure 26-24).

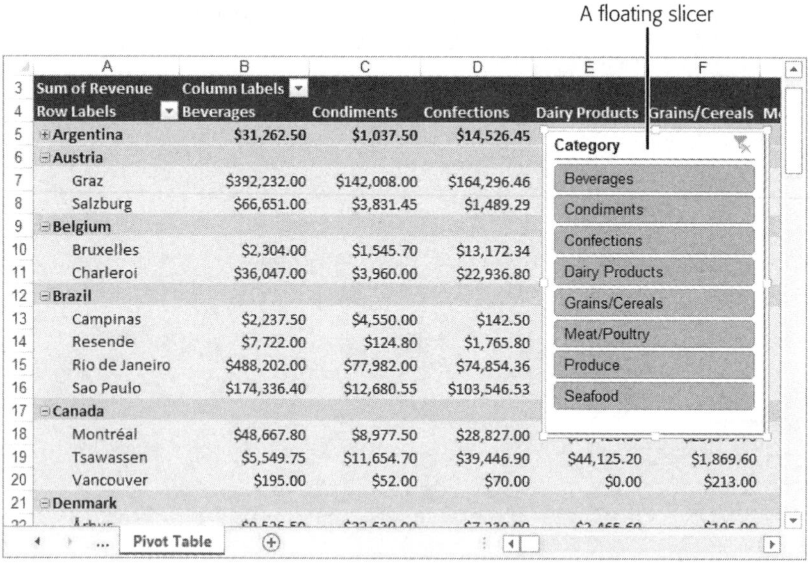

FIGURE 26-24

Each slicer gets its own floating window, which you can format, and then drag around the main Excel window. This makes sure your filtering options remain at your fingertips all the time, but it can also clutter your display.

To get a closer look at a slicer, you need to create one of your own. Here's how:

1. **Click somewhere inside your pivot table.**
2. **Choose PivotTable Tools | Analyze→Filter→Insert Slicer.**

   The Insert Slicers window appears, with a list of all the fields in your pivot table (not including any calculated fields you created). Next to each one is a checkbox.

3. **Add a checkmark next to the field you want to use for filtering.**

   For a field to make a good slicer, it should have a relatively small number of values. For example, the Category field makes a great pivot table slicer, because there are only a handful of different category values. The Product field works too, but not as well, because the list of products is much longer. On the other hand, Unit Price and Order Date are poor choices, because there are far too many different values. They just won't fit well in the floating slicer window.

   If you want to add several slicers, add a checkmark next to several fields.

4. **Click OK.**

   Excel adds your slicers.

5. **Drag the floating slicer box (or boxes) wherever you like.**

   You can drag or resize a slicer just as you move and resize a chart or picture. Ideally, you'll position each slicer in a place where it won't obscure important pivot table data.

6. **Use the slicer to apply your filter.**

   The floating slicer box shows a list of all the unique values in the field you chose. In the case of the Category field, for example, you'll see a list of all the categories. Excel displays each category as a separate button, and shades in the categories that are currently visible. When you first create a slicer, there's no filtering in place, so Excel shades every value. Here's how you filter it:

   - To filter the pivot table to a single value, click the corresponding button.
   - To filter the pivot table to show multiple values, hold down the Ctrl key while you click each value (see Figure 26-25).
   - To clear the filtering (and show everything), click the tiny funnel-with-an-X icon in the top-right corner of the slicer box.

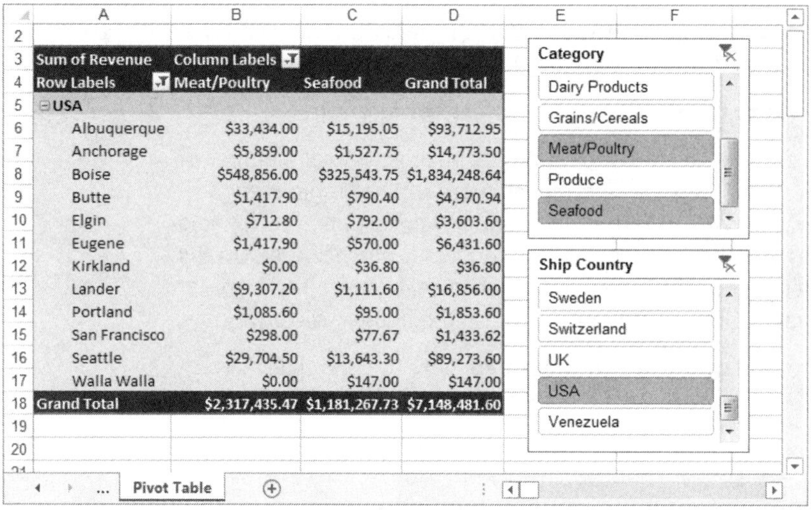

Sum of Revenue	Column Labels		
Row Labels	Meat/Poultry	Seafood	Grand Total
USA			
Albuquerque	$33,434.00	$15,195.05	$93,712.95
Anchorage	$5,859.00	$1,527.75	$14,773.50
Boise	$548,856.00	$325,543.75	$1,834,248.64
Butte	$1,417.90	$790.40	$4,970.94
Elgin	$712.80	$792.00	$3,603.60
Eugene	$1,417.90	$570.00	$6,431.60
Kirkland	$0.00	$36.80	$36.80
Lander	$9,307.20	$1,111.60	$16,856.00
Portland	$1,085.60	$95.00	$1,853.60
San Francisco	$298.00	$77.67	$1,433.62
Seattle	$29,704.50	$13,643.30	$89,273.60
Walla Walla	$0.00	$147.00	$147.00
Grand Total	$2,317,435.47	$1,181,267.73	$7,148,481.60

FIGURE 26-25

Here, the Category slicer limits the pivot table summary to the Meat/Poultry and Seafood categories. In addition, the Ship Country slicer displays U.S. sales only. Changing either of these filters requires nothing more than a quick click, making slicers a great tool for exploring your data.

7. **To get that finishing touch, format your slicer.**

   If you plan to keep your slicer around as a permanent part of your pivot table, it's worth the effort to make it fit in. Here are some ways you can refine its appearance:

   - To change the button colors in your slicer, pick a new style from the Slicer Tools | Options→Slicer Styles gallery.
   - To change the title that appears at the top of your slicer, go to the Slicer Tools | Options→Slicer section, and then change the text in the Slicer Caption box. To hide the title altogether, choose Slicer Tools | Options→Slicer→Slicer Settings, and then remove the checkmark from the "Display header" setting.
   - To make a slicer more compact, you can shrink the size of the buttons or tile them into multiple columns (Figure 26-26). To do so, go to the Slicer Tools | Options→Buttons section of the ribbon, and then change the numbers in the Columns, Height, and Width boxes.
   - To sort the values in reverse order, right-click the slicer, and then choose a different sorting option (like Sort Z to A for alphabetical values or Sort Largest to Smallest for numeric values).

At any point, you can repeat the first four steps to add new slicers. To remove a slicer, click it, and then press Delete.

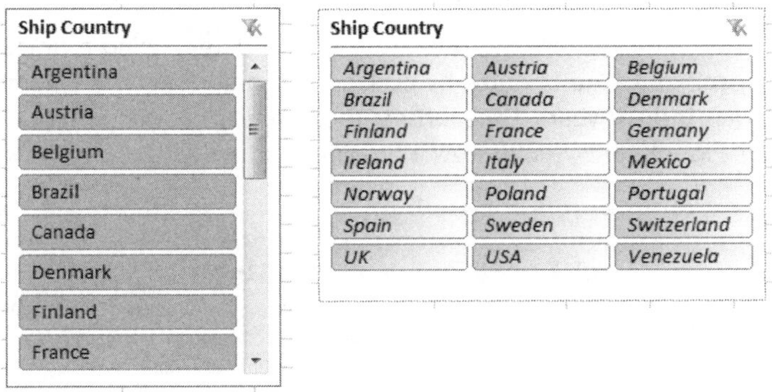

FIGURE 26-26

On the left is the Ship Country slicer as it first appears. On the right is the revamped version that uses three columns, smaller buttons, and slightly different styling.

POWER USERS' CLINIC

Custom Slicer Styles

To get even more control over your slicer formatting, you can create a *custom slicer style*. Best of all, you only need to create the style once, because you can reuse it with as many slicers as you want. Here's how:

1. Click the drop-down arrow in the Slicer Tools | Options→Slicer Styles section of the ribbon, and then choose New Slicer Style.

   The New Slicer Quick Style window appears.

2. In the Name box, give your slicer style a name (like "High Contrast Slicer Style").

3. Pick an entry from the Slicer Element list.

   Each item lets you configure how a specific part of the slicer looks in a specific state. The most useful options are at the top of the list: Whole Slicer (which applies formatting to the whole shebang) and Header (which formats the title at the top of the slicer). Underneath are more specialized choices that let you set how an item looks when someone selects it, when they hover over it, and when there's no corresponding data for that value in the pivot table.

4. Click the Format button to format your selected element.

   The Format Slicer Element window appears. It looks a lot like the Format Cells window but contains only three tabs, which let you change the font, border, and fill.

5. Once you finish formatting the slicer element, click OK.

   If you want to format another element in the slicer, return to step 3.

6. Click OK to finish creating the style.

   Your custom style appears in the Slicer Styles gallery. You can now apply it to any slicer. You can also right-click it, and then click Modify (to edit your formatting settings), Delete (to remove the style), or Duplicate (to create another style with the same settings, which you can then fine-tune).

Timelines

Timelines are a specialized variation of a slicer. Like slicers, every timeline exists in a floating box you can position wherever you want. And like slicers, timelines are there to help you quickly change the filtering settings of your pivot table.

The difference is that timelines are designed for filtering dates. Using a timeline, you can quickly specify a range of dates by clicking and dragging over a number of days, months, quarters, or years. Excel orders these values on a line (hence the name "timelines"). Figure 26-27 shows how a timeline works.

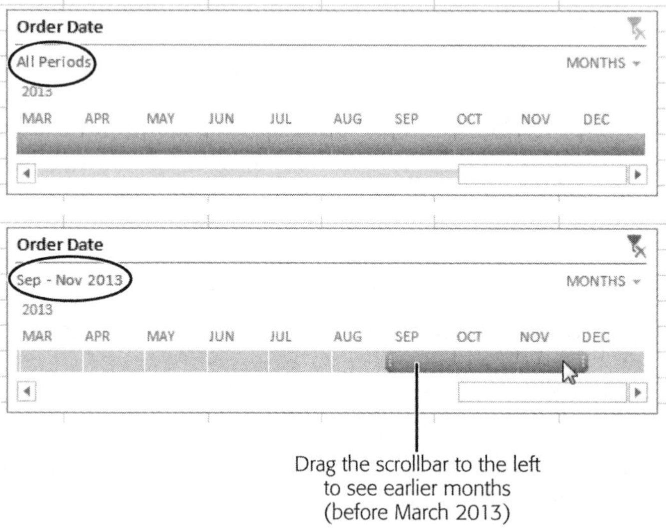

FIGURE 26-27

Top: This newly created timeline for the Order Date field doesn't apply any filtering (as indicated by the "All Periods" text).

Bottom: To select a range of months, click on the first month, and then drag along the line until you reach the final month. This timeline includes September, October, and November of 2013.

Here's how to add a timeline:

1. **Click somewhere inside your pivot table.**
2. **Choose PivotTable Tools | Analyze→Filter→Insert Timeline.**

   The Insert Timelines window appears, with a list of all the fields in your pivot table that contain date data. In the current order list example, there's just one date field, called Order Date.

3. **Add a checkmark next to the field you want to use for your timeline.**

   If you want to add several timelines, you can add a checkmark next to several fields.

4. **Click OK.**

   When you add a new timeline, Excel examines your data and adds a range of months that covers the span of your values. For example, if your earliest date value is February 3, 2008, and the latest is December 19, 2013, you'll get a timeline with months from February 2008 to December 2013.

5. **Drag the floating timeline box wherever you like. Optionally, resize it.**

   The best place to put a timeline box is above or below your pivot table, so you can widen it. The wider you make your timeline, the more months you can see at once, and the easier it is to select a large range of dates.

6. **Use the timeline to apply your filtering.**

   You've already seen how to select a range of months in a timeline (see Figure 26-27). What you might not realize is that timelines work equally well for selecting ranges of days, quarters, or years (Figure 26-28).

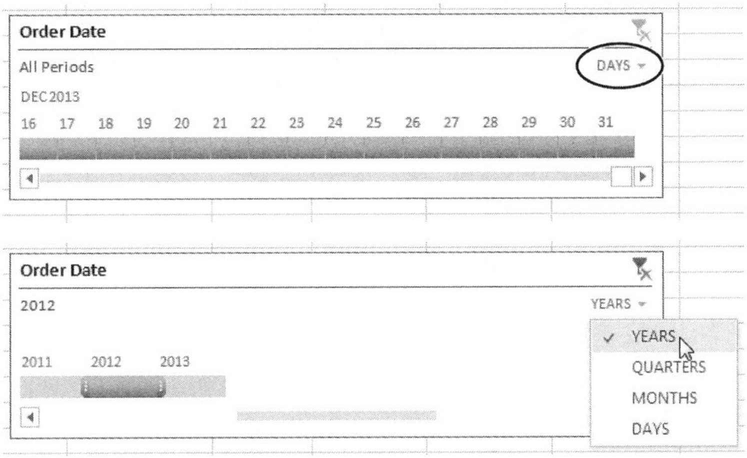

FIGURE 26-28

To switch the timeline's selection mode, click the word "Months" in the top-right corner of the timeline box, and pick something else. For example, if you pick Days (top), the timeline stretches from the first day in your data to the last. This makes for a much wider timeline, and will necessitate more side-to-side scrolling. But if you pick Years (bottom), you'll have a more compact timeline where you can select an entire year of data with a single click.

7. **Optionally, format your timeline.**

   When you click a timeline, Excel adds a ribbon tab named Timeline Tools | Options, which is similar to the Slicer Tools | Options tab you used before. Using this tab, you can hide parts of the timeline and change its colors.

Group Filtering

Excel also lets you apply filtering to the fields you use to group your pivot table. (We call it *group filtering*, but Excel doesn't have an official name for this feature.)

Group filtering gives you two abilities. First, it lets you hide and show specific items, just like a report filter does. This is a handy feature, because you can't create a report filter for a grouping field.

Second, group filtering lets you create much more powerful filter conditions. For example, you can pick out numbers that fall in a specific range or names that contain a specific snippet of text, and so on. Using this sort of filter condition, you can home in on the exact subset of data that interests you.

NOTE Pivot table filtering is *additive*, which is a fancy way of saying that Excel applies every filter you create at the same time. For example, imagine you create a pivot table that analyzes a decade's worth of chocolate sales. Using a report filter, you can focus on sales at a specific store. Using an advanced grouping filter, you can ignore sales of less than $5.

To apply group filtering, click the drop-down arrow at the right of the Column Labels or Row Labels cell. Figure 26-29 shows exactly where to go.

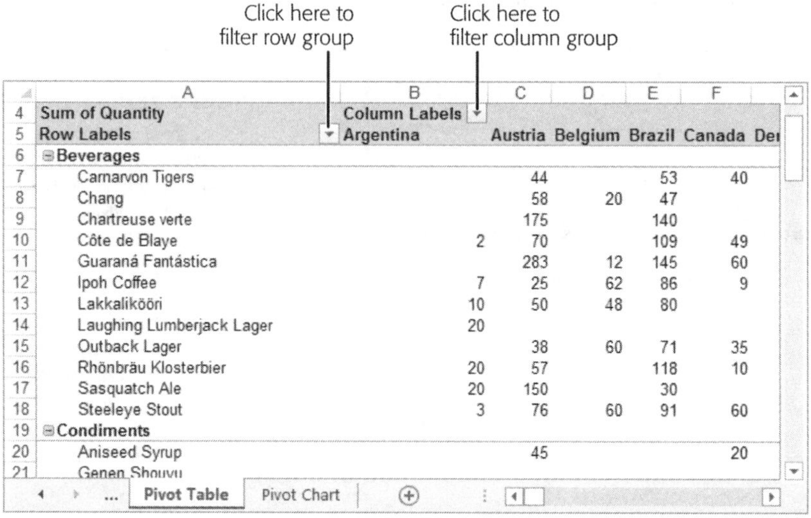

Sum of Quantity	Column Labels					
Row Labels	Argentina	Austria	Belgium	Brazil	Canada	Del
⊟Beverages						
Carnarvon Tigers		44		53	40	
Chang		58	20	47		
Chartreuse verte		175		140		
Côte de Blaye	2	70		109	49	
Guaraná Fantástica		283	12	145	60	
Ipoh Coffee	7	25	62	86	9	
Lakkalikööri	10	50	48	80		
Laughing Lumberjack Lager	20					
Outback Lager		38	60	71	35	
Rhönbräu Klosterbier	20	57		118	10	
Sasquatch Ale	20	150		30		
Steeleye Stout	3	76	60	91	60	
⊟Condiments						
Aniseed Syrup		45			20	
Genen Shouyu						

FIGURE 26-29

To filter by Category, you need to click the drop-down arrow next to the Row Labels cell. Figure 26-30 shows the drop-down list that appears.

You can add filter settings to more than one field to hide certain categories and certain products. However, you need to configure them separately. Here's how:

1. **Click the drop-down arrow to show the filter list (see Figure 26-30).**
2. **In the "Select field" box at the top, choose Category.**
3. **Now uncheck the categories you don't want to see, and then click OK to make it official.**
4. **Click the drop-down arrow to show the filter list again.**
5. **Now, choose Product in the "Select field" box.**
6. **Hide the products you don't want to see (by clearing the checkboxes), and then click OK.**

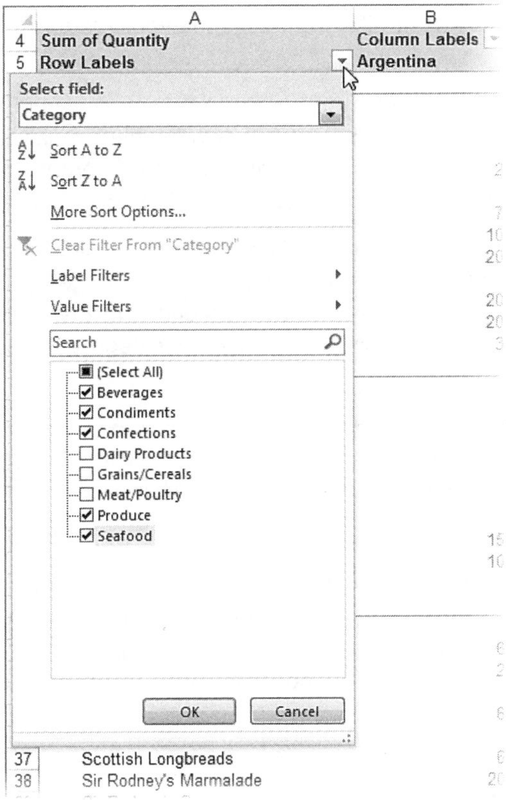

FIGURE 26-30

Because this table has two row fields (Category and Product), you need to start by choosing the one you want to use for your filter. Then, hide the items you don't want to see by clearing the checkbox next to them in the list. In this example, only five categories appear in the pivot table. Excel also adjusts the subtotals and grand totals accordingly.

The drop-down filter menu has additional options that let you filter out groups according to more sophisticated criteria. You could use these options to show or hide categories (or products) that contain specific text, for example, start or end with a certain letter, and so on. To set these options, click the drop-down arrow next to the Column Labels or Row Labels cell, pick your field, and then choose an option from the Label Filters submenu. For example, to show only categories that begin with a "C," choose Label Filters→Begins With, and then type *C* into the window that appears.

NOTE The filtering options in the Label Filters submenu work the same way as the filtering options for structured tables (tables you create with the Insert→Tables→Table command). To learn more about your filtering options, refer to page 430.

You'll also spot a similar submenu named Value Filters. The Value Filters menu lets you filter out information based on *calculated data*. If, say, you calculate the sum of all your product orders, you can filter out the products that sold fewer than 500 units. Just choose Value Filters→Less Than, and then fill in the number 500 when asked. Once again, you've seen this sort of filter before—when you created tables in Chapter 14.

Filtering can be a bit tricky at first, particularly if you have several row fields or several column fields to play with. Before you set a label or value filter, make sure you pick the right field. The Value Filters→Less Than command has a different effect depending on whether you apply it to the Product field or the Category field.

If you apply it to the Product field, you'll see slow-selling products, those that sold fewer than 500 units. If you apply it to the Category field, you'll see only categories that have fewer than 500 units of sales across *all* their products. In the current example, this action would hide every category, because every category has sold significantly more than 500 units.

NOTE If you apply a filter on a row field (like Products), your column fields have no effect. Thus, in this example, it doesn't matter that you subdivided your product sales by country. When evaluating the filter condition, Excel considers the *total* sales for that product.

You can remove your filters using the Clear Filter command in the filter menu. However, if you added filters to more than one field, you need to remove each filter separately. A faster alternative is to choose PivotTable Tools | Analyze→Actions→ Clear→Clear Filters. Doing so removes every filter and returns your pivot table back to normal, so it shows all the data.

Pivot Charts

Excel lets you create charts based on the data in a pivot table. These charts work more or less the same way as ordinary Excel charts (Chapter 17). However, pivot charts are typically very dense, so they warrant a couple of extra considerations:

- Because pivot charts are so dense, many of the specialized chart types don't work well. Instead, stick with simple chart types like column charts and pie charts. One popular choice is the stacked column chart, which helps you see the breakdown of your various groups.
- Before you create a pivot chart, it's often useful to limit the amount of information in your pivot table. Too much information can lead to a chart that's hard to read. Avoid using too many levels of grouping, and use filtering (as described in the previous section) to cut down on the total amount of information displayed in the pivot table.

Figure 26-31 shows a sample pivot chart.

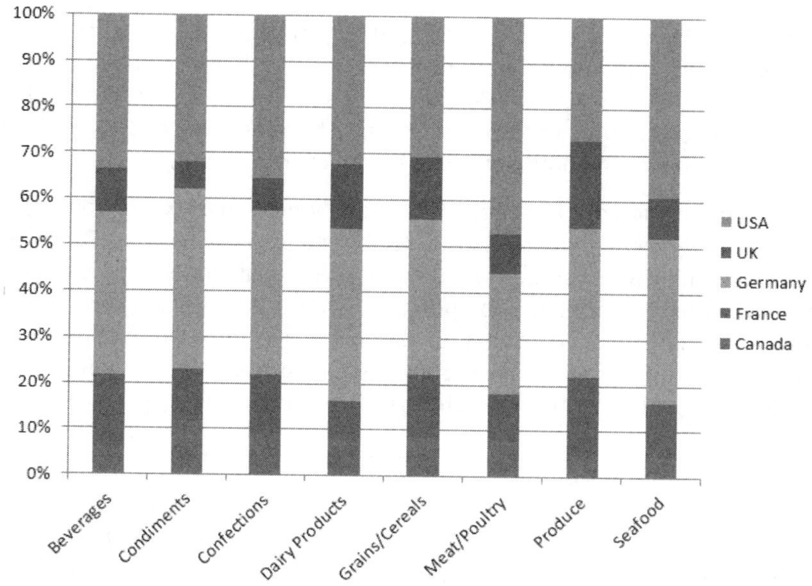

FIGURE 26-31

In this example, a stacked column chart shows the breakdown of orders by product category and country. Each bar represents a different category and is subdivided into color-coded sections that represent a country (as detailed in the legend). A pivot chart doesn't necessarily show all the data, because you can use filtering to show just a subset of the total information.

Creating a Pivot Chart

To create a pivot chart, follow these steps:

1. **Choose PivotTable Tools | Analyze→Tools→PivotChart.**

   The Insert Chart window appears.

2. **Choose the type of chart you want, and then click OK to generate it.**

   Your pivot chart appears in the worksheet.

   When you create a new pivot chart, Excel places it in a floating box. If you want to move it to a separate worksheet, select it, and then choose PivotChart Tools | Design→Location→Move Chart. When the Move Chart window appears, choose "New sheet," pick a sheet, and then click OK.

Manipulating a Pivot Chart

When you select a pivot chart, Excel adds several new tabs to the ribbon under a PivotChart Tools heading. These tabs are similar to the charting tabs you learned about in Chapter 18. They let you change the formatting and layout of the chart, and configure chart elements like titles, axes, and gridlines.

Like pivot tables, pivot charts are *interactive*. That means you can rearrange your pivot chart on the fly, simply by dragging the fields in the PivotTable Fields pane from one section to another. (If you don't see the PivotTable Fields pane, choose PivotChart Tools | Analyze→Show/Hide→Field List.) As you make your changes, Excel regenerates the pivot table *and* your pivot chart, because the two are inextricably linked.

Excel changes the names of the sections in the PivotTable Fields pane to help you understand how it uses the different parts of your pivot table to create the chart. The Rows section becomes "Axis (Categories)." Excel uses these fields to create the different chart categories. The Columns section becomes "Legend (Series)," and Excel uses them to create different series for the chart.

You can also change your filter settings (or apply new ones) while working with your pivot chart. There are two ways to do so. One is to use the PivotTable Fields pane. First, find the appropriate field; then click the small funnel icon that appears next to it (on the right side) to pop open the familiar list of filtering choices. If you want to tweak your filter settings without using the PivotTable Fields pane, you can add filtering buttons to your chart, as shown in Figure 26-32. To add these buttons, choose PivotChart Tools | Analyze→Show/Hide→Field Buttons.

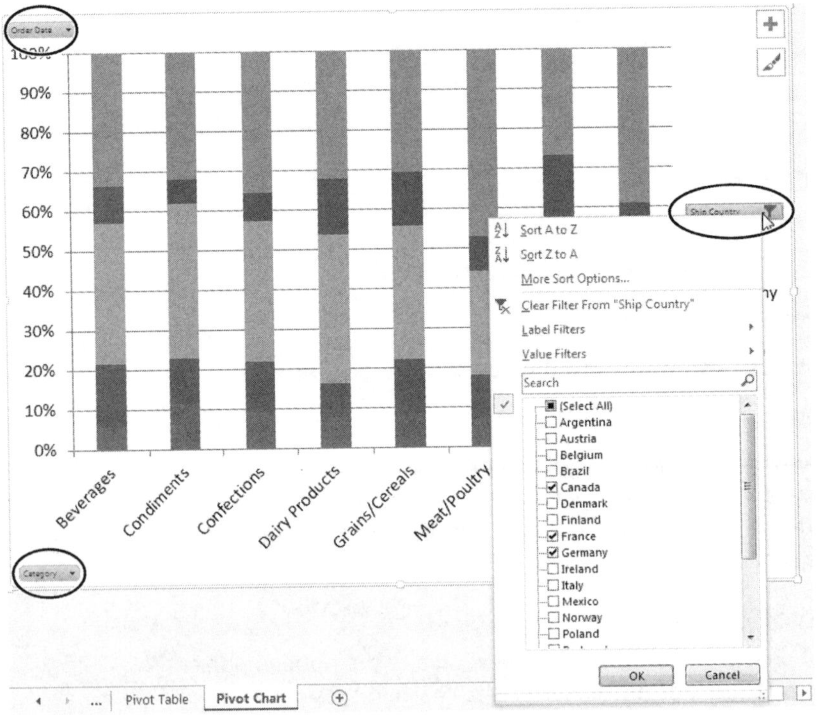

FIGURE 26-32

If you want to change pivot chart filtering right from your chart, you can add some or all of these filter buttons from the PivotChart Tools | Analyze→Show/Hide→Field Buttons menu. Here, they let you filter by Order Date (the report filter, in the top-left corner), Category (the row field, in the bottom-left corner), and Ship Country (the column field, above the legend).

It makes no difference whether you adjust filter settings on the chart, through the PivotChart Filter pane, or on the original pivot table in the worksheet. No matter the approach, Excel applies the new filtering settings to your pivot table and pivot chart.

Overall, pivot charts are a specialized tool. You're likely to use pivot tables much more frequently than pivot charts. However, if you need a way to quickly visualize the numbers and get a feel for the most important groups in a summary, a pivot chart can help you out.

CHAPTER

27

Analyzing Databases

An ordinary Excel workbook stores a bunch of information, and uses Excel tools (like formulas and charts) to analyze it. However, a great deal of the world's business information isn't stored in Excel files. Instead, it sits inside *databases*—organized catalogs of information managed by high-powered computer software. Databases are extremely fast, secure, and durable. They're the best place to put mission-critical information.

At first glance, this approach (storing big volumes of information in a database) seems to cut Excel out of the loop. However, Excel's greatest strength isn't storing information, but *analyzing* it, no matter where that information lives.

Say, for example, that your company has a decade of sales records stored in a database. Using Excel, you can extract this raw data and start working with it, using all of Excel's awesome data analysis tools, from charts to pivot tables. However, the data you get is a *copy* of what's in the database, and you can't alter the original records.

This approach offers the best of both worlds, because it lets your database do what it does best (store massive amounts of data) and lets Excel do what it does best (summarize, chart, and analyze that data). Best of all, you can refresh your workbook any time to get the latest information from the same database, so your workbook never goes out of date.

Excel and Databases

Databases provide the best way to store huge amounts of data, like product catalogs for online stores or customer lists for mail order companies. Databases break this info into separate tables and let you search it with unrivaled flexibility. They're particularly adept at answering questions like "What products did this customer order last week?" and "How many employees have completed sensitivity training?"

The world has two basic types of database:

- **End-user databases** are designed for small-scale or single-person use. They store data and provide people-friendly tools for searching and managing the information they contain. Microsoft Access, which comes with some versions of Office, is the best-known consumer database.

TIP For the full scoop on Microsoft Access, check out *Access 2013: The Missing Manual.*

- **Server-side databases** work on a larger scale by storing data and feeding it to other programs and websites. Ordinary mortals don't use server-side databases directly. Instead, they use applications that, in turn, rely on databases. For example, when you browse Amazon.com, the Amazon web page code is hard at work getting product information and customer reviews from some of the most high-powered databases on the planet. Microsoft SQL Server is one well-known server-side database.

In Excel, you can extract information from a small-scale database like Access just as easily as you get it from a full-fledged database server running SQL Server. You'll find a few minor differences—for example, if you want to use Access data, you need to supply only the file name, whereas you need to know the server name, user ID, and password to get into a typical SQL Server database. However, the process of searching and importing the information is the same in both cases.

NOTE Data querying is a one-way street. You can extract data and analyze it, save a copy on your computer, and even modify the information in your worksheet. But Excel doesn't provide any tools that let you route your changes back to the original source.

UP TO SPEED

Getting Data from Other Places

Excel's data connection features were designed with databases in mind. After all, databases are the most common place for businesses to store information. But over the years, Excel has broadened its data connection features to work with other, more specialized data sources. Nowadays, you can use Excel to fetch information from a web page, an XML file, or even a web server on the Internet (through a sophisticated technology called OData; see page 882).

No matter what data source you use, Excel's data connection feature remains essentially the same (and the overarching vision of Excel as supreme analyzer of all your information, no matter where it comes from, remains unchanged). In this chapter, you'll begin by connecting to databases. As you continue through this chapter and onto the next, you'll see examples that fetch data from more exotic data sources.

Creating a Data Connection

Before you can get information out of a database, you need to create what's known as a *data connection*. The connection tells Excel how to connect to your database server (or database file) so that it can extract the information it needs. You need to do this only once for each data source you want to use.

If you want to try out Excel's data connection features but don't have a database server in your basement, you'll run into a small stumbling block. Fortunately, there are several places to get free database information. The following sections use an Access database named Northwind.accdb, which you can download as a single and relatively small file from the Missing CD page (*http://missingmanuals.com/cds/excel2013mm*). Later, you'll learn how to use a similar process to create a data connection for an SQL Server database.

Connecting to an Access Database

Access databases are refreshingly simple, because they put all their information in one file. If you have a copy of Access, you can open this file directly. And even if you don't, you can get at the information inside using Excel. Just follow these steps:

1. **Choose Data→Get External Data→From Access.**

   The Select Data Source window appears, which lets you browse through the files on your computer.

2. **Find the Access file you want to use, select it, and then click Open.**

   Access database files have the file extension .mdb or .accdb.

NOTE Keep in mind that this connection remains valid as long as you don't move the database file. If you do, you'll need to modify the connection, as explained on page 843.

Once you pick a database file, the Select Table window appears (Figure 27-1).

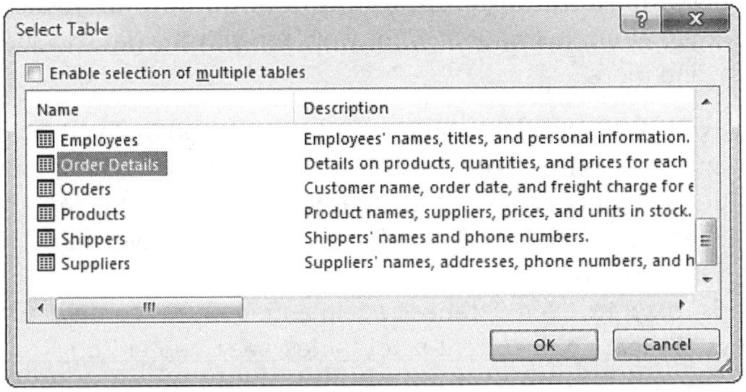

FIGURE 27-1

A typical database includes several tables. Each contains a set of records structured in a particular way. For example, the Northwind database (which you can find on the Missing CD page at http://missingmanuals.com/cds/excel2013mm) includes a table named Order Details, which is selected here.

NOTE Along with the list of tables, you may also see some Access *queries*. Queries present a customized view of a table, which can sort the data, hide columns, or filter out unimportant records. Queries are a great shortcut for getting combined results from separate tables and for calculating and summarizing database information before it reaches Excel. For example, a worksheet shown later (in Figure 27-4) uses a query to get a list of sales summarized by product category.

3. **Choose a table from the list, and then click OK.**

   If you're using the Northwind.accdb database from the downloadable samples, you can use any of the tables, including Customers (for a list of customers with contact information) and Order Details (for a list of purchased items from every order made by every customer). Don't worry about the "Enable selection of multiple tables" option just yet. You'll learn to use this feature later, when you dig into the data model (page 846).

   Once you choose a table, Excel's Import Data window appears (Figure 27-2).

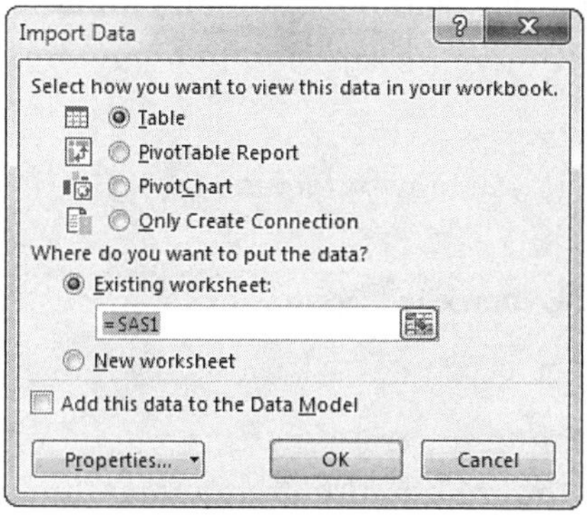

FIGURE 27-2

After you pick a database and a table, use this window to tell Excel where in your workbook it should put the data.

4. **Choose whether you want to see the data as an ordinary table or as a pivot table.**

   Usually, you'll choose to insert the data as a table. That choice gives you all the features you learned about in Chapter 14 for working with the data, including sorting, filtering, and more.

   If you're dealing with extremely large amounts of information that you want to summarize, a pivot table is more practical. That way, your worksheet doesn't actually store the raw data (which would bloat your workbook file, and slow down Excel). Instead, it uses the information to create the pivot table. This method's only disadvantage is that if you decide to rearrange your pivot table later, Excel needs to contact the database again and fetch all the data, which can be a bit slow. (To learn more about pivot tables, see Chapter 26.)

TIP If you decide to use a pivot table with a slow database, you should consider using the Defer Layout Update option, which is discussed on page 809.

5. **Choose whether you want to place the data in a new worksheet.**

   You can choose "Existing worksheet" to place your table somewhere in the existing workbook. Then, switch to the worksheet you want to use (using the worksheet tabs), and click the top-left corner where your data should appear. Be sure to leave plenty of space for all your data.

   You'll find it easier to choose "New worksheet," which keeps your imported data separate from the data that's already in your workbook. If you opt for this choice, you'll probably want to move and rename the worksheet after Excel creates it, as described in Chapter 4.

6. **Click OK.**

   Excel pulls the information out of the database and inserts it into your workbook, as shown in Figure 27-3. Next you can apply formulas, create charts, and start analyzing. You can also use the Table Tools | Design tab to format the table by applying a different table style.

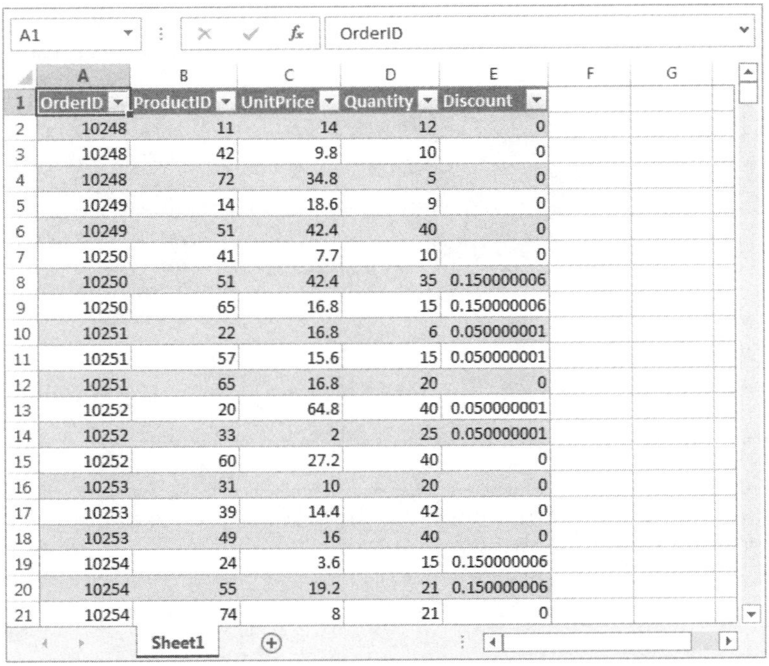

	A	B	C	D	E	F	G
1	OrderID	ProductID	UnitPrice	Quantity	Discount		
2	10248	11	14	12	0		
3	10248	42	9.8	10	0		
4	10248	72	34.8	5	0		
5	10249	14	18.6	9	0		
6	10249	51	42.4	40	0		
7	10250	41	7.7	10	0		
8	10250	51	42.4	35	0.150000006		
9	10250	65	16.8	15	0.150000006		
10	10251	22	16.8	6	0.050000001		
11	10251	57	15.6	15	0.050000001		
12	10251	65	16.8	20	0		
13	10252	20	64.8	40	0.050000001		
14	10252	33	2	25	0.050000001		
15	10252	60	27.2	40	0		
16	10253	31	10	20	0		
17	10253	39	14.4	42	0		
18	10253	49	16	40	0		
19	10254	24	3.6	15	0.150000006		
20	10254	55	19.2	21	0.150000006		
21	10254	74	8	21	0		

FIGURE 27-3

This worksheet shows a portion of the results extracted from the Order Details table of the Northwind database. As you can see, Excel isn't smart enough to determine the proper number formats for your data, so it's up to you to apply the Currency format to the UnitPrice column and the Percentage format to the Discount column. Furthermore, a table might not have all the information you want—the Order Details table, for example, doesn't tell you your customer's shipping address. To get that sort of information, you need to import multiple tables, as you'll see on page 851.

Refreshing Data

Once you pull information out of a database, you can work with it in the same way you work with ordinary Excel data. You can edit cells, apply conditional formatting, cut and paste chunks of data, and so on. Assuming you put your data in an Excel table, you can also use sorting, filtering, and all the other handy table features described in Chapter 14.

One of the nicest aspects of Excel's database support is that it lets you refresh the data at any time. If you suspect that the data's changed in the database, just move somewhere in the list, and then choose Table Tools | Design→External Table Data→Refresh All. When you do, Excel wipes out your current table and replaces it with the up-to-the-minute information taken from the database, without disturbing any other content that might be in your worksheet. You can use this technique to build a "window" that can analyze the most recent information in your database, as shown in Figure 27-4.

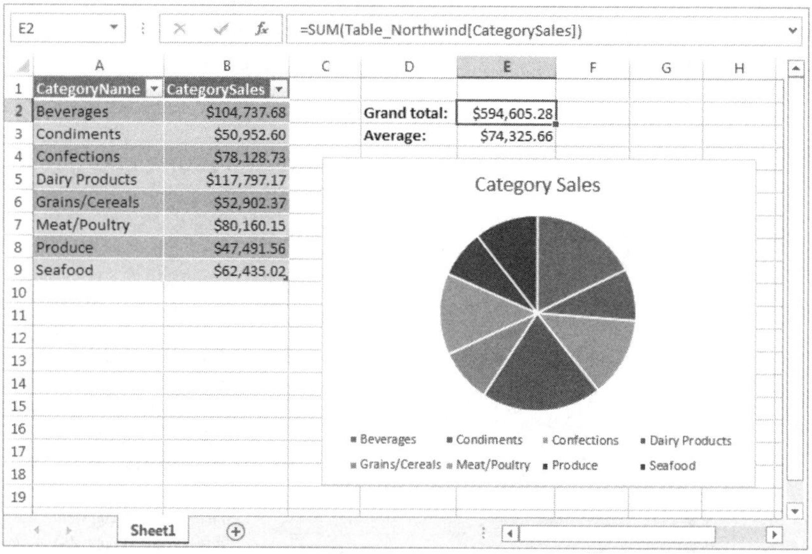

FIGURE 27-4

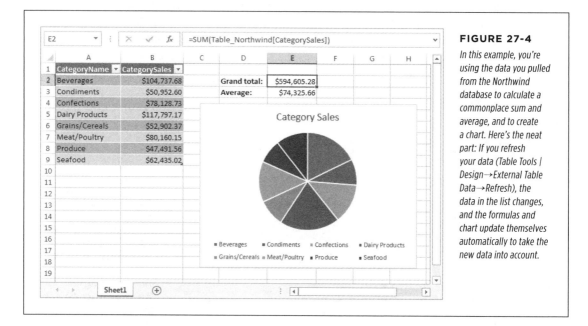

In this example, you're using the data you pulled from the Northwind database to calculate a commonplace sum and average, and to create a chart. Here's the neat part: If you refresh your data (Table Tools | Design→External Table Data→Refresh), the data in the list changes, and the formulas and chart update themselves automatically to take the new data into account.

TIP A workbook can have as many connections as you want. To refresh them all at once, choose Table Tools | Design→External Table Data→Refresh→Refresh All.

If you're using a database that you can access quickly (like an Access file on your computer), the update process happens almost instantaneously, and you might not even notice the refresh. If you're grabbing a large amount of information from a heavily taxed server on your network, this process takes more time.

The Excel database features' only limitation is that you're always working with a *copy* of the data stored in the database. Even if you change the information in your worksheet, you can't change anything in the database. As a result, the next time you refresh your data, Excel wipes out any changes you made and replaces them with whatever content is currently in the database. Interestingly enough, this limitation doesn't apply to formatting, which Excel preserves even after you update. In other words, if you format a few rows in bold and then refresh the data, you'll see the same rows boldfaced even after the new data appears.

NOTE Remember, Excel's database features are designed to let you analyze information, not change it. If you need to modify a database, you need a different tool. For example, if you want to modify the information in an Access database, you need to use the Access software.

If you ever get tired of your database and decide to break free, just click somewhere in your table and choose Table Tools | Design→External Table Data→Unlink command. This action changes your database-linked table into an ordinary table. In other words, you can't use the Refresh command any longer. Before you take this step, be certain that you don't want to connect to the database any longer. Once you use the Unlink command, all the database information disappears from your workbook, and there's no going back. (If you do want to get the most recent data from the database, you have to create the connection all over again.)

POWER USERS' CLINIC

Controlling the Refresh Process

You can change a few details about the refresh process using Excel's External Data Properties window (Figure 27-5). To get there, move into your table, and then choose Table Tools | Design→External Table Data→Properties. You'll see a series of check boxes:

- **Include row numbers.** If you switch on this setting, Excel adds a new column to the left of your data, which it uses to sequentially number each row (starting at 0). One reason you might use this option is to restore the original order of your data after you've sorted it on another column. (To do that, just sort on the row number column, which is named *_RowNum.*)
- **Adjust column widths.** If this checkbox is on, whenever you refresh your data, Excel automatically widens columns so they can display all the information they contain. If you turn off this setting, Excel lets your columns keep their current widths.
- **Preserve column sort/filter/layout.** If this checkbox is on, Excel keeps your sorting, filtering, and column ordering settings, even when you refresh the data. In other words, the new data slides right in to your existing table layout.
- **Preserve cell formatting.** If this checkbox is on, Excel keeps the formatting you applied to your rows when you refresh your data. However, this might not work the way you expect, because the formatting you apply doesn't move *with* your data. For example, imagine you give the cells in row 6 a bright yellow background. If, as a result of the refresh process, your data gets bumped down from row 6 to row 8, row 6 keeps its yellow background, even though it now contains different information.

The final option in External Data Properties window tells Excel what to do if it finds that someone has removed or added records when it refreshes your table. Ordinarily, Excel inserts the new data and removes anything that's been deleted (the first option in the list), which is by far the simplest choice. Alternatively, you can choose one of two much more complex options that insert the new information in new rows, and leave blank spaces to denote deleted information. This lets you take stock of what's changed, although it messes up the structure of your table.

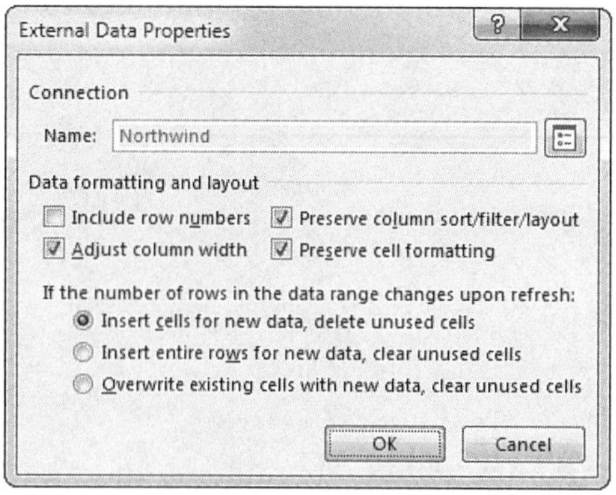

FIGURE 27-5

Here are the standard settings that Excel gives every new data connection. It opts to keep your sorting, filtering, and formatting settings when you refresh, while expanding columns to fit new data and inserting or removing rows as necessary.

Data Source Security

Excel stores the data connection information in your Excel file. You can save your workbook, open it later, and refresh the data to get the most recent information.

Unfortunately, Excel is also relentlessly paranoid. When you open a workbook that has a data connection in it, Excel keeps the connection closed and displays a security warning (Figure 27-6). It does so because it knows there's an incredibly slim chance that you're opening a workbook created by a devious computer hacker. This workbook could contain a database connection that doesn't just read data, but somehow executes a command that changes or even deletes it. To guard against this possibility, Excel stops you, temporarily, from using the connection.

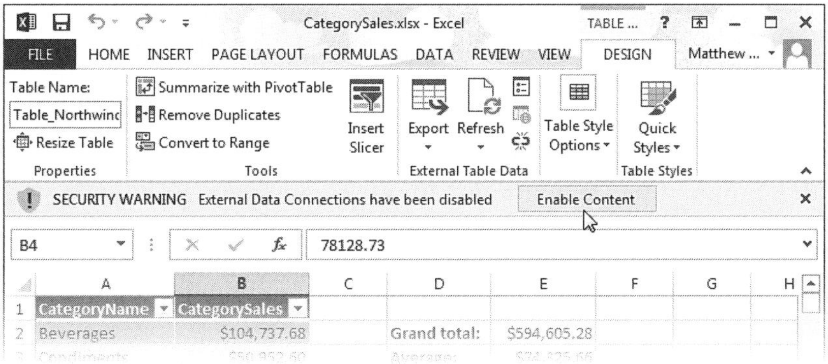

FIGURE 27-6

This warning tells you your workbook contains one or more data connections, and that Excel closed them just to be safe. You can switch them back on by clicking Enable Content.

Of course, if you created the workbook yourself (and you know that you aren't a computer hacker), there's no way your workbook could contain any devious trickery. Therefore, your connections are safe, and there's no reason you shouldn't turn them on. To do so, click the Enable Content button. This tells Excel to treat your workbook as a trusted document, so it won't hassle you the next time you open it. (Page 904 has all the details about Excel's trusted document system.)

Connecting to a SQL Server Database

The process for connecting to a full-fledged SQL Server database is similar to the process for connecting to an Access database—you just need to supply more information. To get the process going, follow these steps:

1. **Choose Data→Get External Data→From Other Sources→From SQL Server.**

   Excel launches its Data Connection Wizard (Figure 27-7).

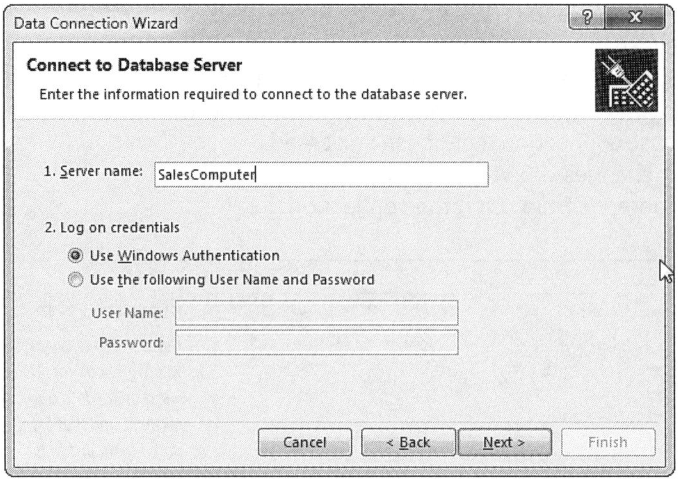

FIGURE 27-7

In the first window of the Data Connection Wizard, you need to choose your database server and supply login information.

NOTE SQL Server isn't the only server-side database you can connect to using Excel. In fact, you can pull information out of just about any database created in the last 10 years. Get started by choosing Data→Get External Data→From Other Sources→From Data Connection Wizard. Choose Other/Advanced from the Data Connection Wizard, and then click Next to see a long list of supported databases. To get the exact settings you need, check with your organization's resident network administrator.

2. **Enter the database server's name.**

   The server is the computer that runs the database software; Excel has to be able to access it on your network. (Check with the nearest network administrator for help.) If the SQL Server database happens to be on your computer, just enter the word *localhost*, which is code for "this computer right here." If you've installed the slightly scaled-down but absolutely free version of SQL Server that's known as SQL Server Express (and it's on your computer), you should use the server name *.\SQLEXPRESS*. Reminder: Don't forget the initial period.

TIP You can learn more about SQL Server Express (and download it for free) at *www.microsoft.com/express/sql*. However, you may need the help of a SQL Server guru to guide you through the setup process, which features a series of technical questions.

3. **Supply your login information.**

   Usually, you'll choose Use Windows Authentication, which tells Excel to log into the database using your current Windows account. Depending on the setup of your network and database, that option may not work, and you may need to choose "Use the following User Name and Password" instead. If so, supply the correct user name and password in the appropriate boxes.

4. **Click Next to move to the next step.**

   Now you need to pick your database (Figure 27-8).

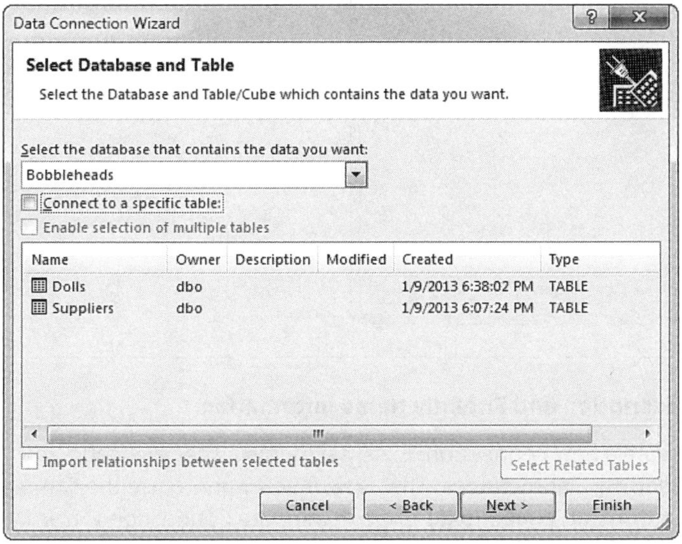

FIGURE 27-8

A database is chock-full of information. You need to pick the database you want to use using the drop-down list at the top. In this example, you're establishing a connection to the Bobbleheads database, which contains two tables (Dolls and Suppliers).

5. **Choose the database you want from the "Select the database that contains the data you want" list.**

   A SQL Server computer can hold hundreds (or more) databases. Every database is a collection of tables. You need to pick the database that has the table you need.

6. **Make sure the checkbox next to the "Connect to a specific table" setting is *unchecked.***

   When you choose a database, Excel lists all the tables in the database (see Figure 27-8). However, don't pick the table you want just yet. You may want to reuse this connection to connect to different tables in the same database.

7. **Click Next.**

   This move gets you to the last step (Figure 27-9).

FIGURE 27-9

In the final step, you describe your connection.

8. **Fill in the Description and Friendly Name information.**

   When you create a new connection, Excel saves it in a special location on your computer called My Data Sources. That way, if you want to use the same connection again, you don't need to go through the Data Connection Wizard. (See page 844 for the full details.)

   To make the connection easier to identify, fill in the Description and Friendly Name boxes. (The "friendly name" is a name that makes sense to ordinary humans. The file name is the name of the actual file that stores the data connection info on your computer. You don't need to worry about this detail, although you're free to change it, too.)

9. **Click Finish to end the wizard.**

   Now, Excel shows you all the tables in your database and asks which one you want to use (Figure 27-10).

10. **Pick a table, and then click OK.**

    Excel shows the Import Data window that you saw earlier (Figure 27-2), which lets you choose where to store the new data. Once you make your selection, Excel contacts the database server, fetches the contents of the table you selected in the previous step, and then inserts it into your workbook. From this point on, you can refresh the data and modify the connection using the techniques you learned earlier in this chapter.

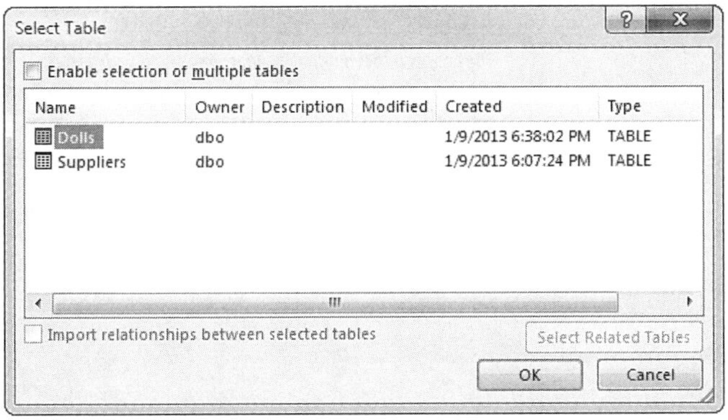

FIGURE 27-10

The Bobbleheads database has two tables. In this example, Excel will insert the contents of the Dolls table into the worksheet.

POWER USERS' CLINIC

Creating a Data Source That Updates Automatically

Excel leaves a few of its advanced database connection options off the Data Connection Wizard, including a nifty timesaving tool: the ability to have Excel automatically suck in a fresh load of data at regular intervals. To make Excel do this updating, follow these steps:

1. Choose Data→Connections→Connections. The Workbook Connections window appears, with a list of all of the connections in your workbook.
2. Select the connection you want to modify.
3. Click the Properties button to open the Connection Properties window, which has every setting you can change (Figure 27-11).
4. If you want to tell Excel to refresh the data in your workbook periodically, add a checkmark in the "Refresh every" box, and then enter your preferred number of minutes. Excel performs these updates automatically, without bugging you, so you can keep working on other tasks.

Of course, if you change the data that you've imported into your spreadsheet, you'll lose those changes when Excel refreshes the data. So use "Refresh every" with caution. In addition, don't use it with an extremely slow database, or the performance of your workbook may suffer. Finally, don't make the refresh interval too small, or you'll create an unnecessary amount of work for your database server. (Remember, there's always the Data→Connections→Refresh All button to trigger an immediate refresh.)

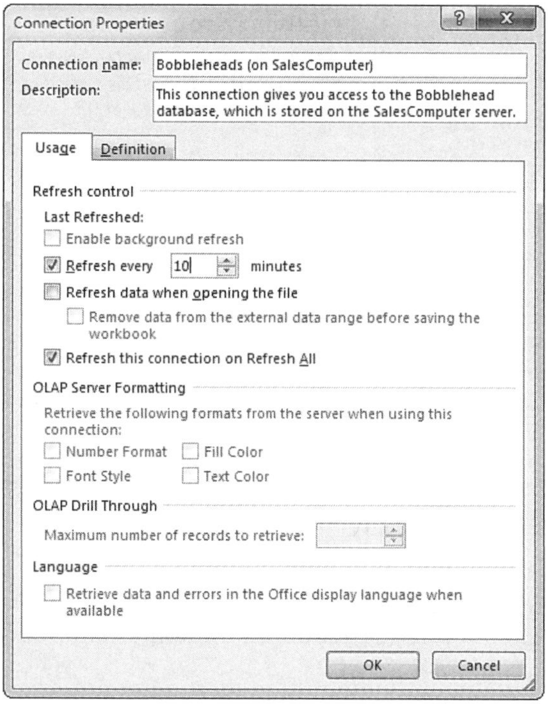

FIGURE 27-11

The Connection Properties window has several advanced database connection options. You can, for example, have Excel retrieve the latest information from the database whenever you open the workbook using the "Refresh data when opening the file" setting. You can also tell Excel to automatically refresh your data every few minutes using the "Refresh every" setting.

Reusing Your Database Connection

Once you create a connection, Excel stores it in your workbook so you can reuse it—a real timesaver if you want to grab another table from the same database. To do so, just click on a cell anywhere outside of your data table, and choose Data→Get External Data→Existing Connections. The Existing Connections window appears (Figure 27-12). You'll find your existing connection(s) in the "Connections in this Workbook" section at the top of the list. Select it and then click Open to use it again, without being forced to re-enter all the same settings.

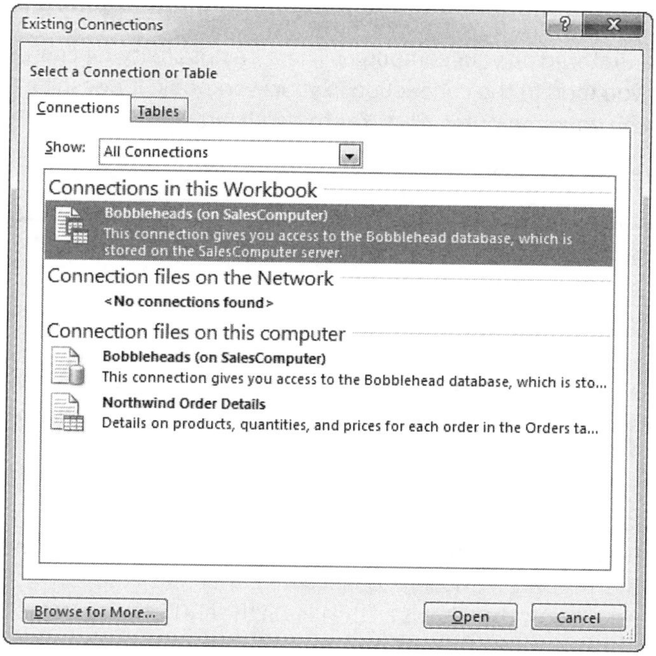

FIGURE 27-12

The Existing Connections window gives you a head start for connecting to the Bobblehead database you created previously. If you go ahead and click Open, Excel asks which table you want to use. If you want, now's the time to import a different table in a different place in your workbook.

This technique works for all connections, whether they point to Access databases or more powerful server-side databases like SQL Server. However, if you're using a server-side database, there's one more trick you can use. You can tell Excel to make your connection information available to *other* workbooks on your computer. So you have yet another way to cut down on the amount of time you spend creating (or recreating) database connections. Here's what you need to do:

1. **Choose Data→Connections→Connections.**

   The Workbook Connections window appears, with a list of all of the connections in your workbook.

2. **Select the connection you want to reuse, and then click the Properties button.**

   This action shows the Connection Properties window (Figure 27-11), where you can tweak all the connection details you supplied in the Data Connection Wizard (plus a few more).

3. **Choose the Definition tab, and then place a checkmark in the "Always use connection file" checkbox.**

4. **Click OK to save your changes.**

   Excel warns you that you'll now actually have two connections (one in your workbook and one stored on your computer). There's a possibility for confusion here because if you modify the connection in your workbook, it doesn't affect the copy stored on your computer. Click Yes to go ahead.

5. **Click Close to return to Excel.**

Now you can use the Data→Get External Data→Existing Connections command from any workbook. In the Existing Connections window, you'll see your connection in the "Connection files on this computer" section.

NOTE Behind the scenes, Excel stores your database connections in a special My Data Sources folder deep within the Documents folder on your computer. For example, if your user name is MattG, you might find the database connection created in the previous example in the file *C:\Users\MattG\Documents\My Data Sources\SalesComputer_Bobblehead.odc.*

To delete a connection, you need to remove the connection file from the My Data Source folder. The easiest way to do this is to open the Existing Connections window (choose Data→Get External Data→Existing Connections). Then, click the "Browse for More" button to open a window that shows all the files in the My Data Sources folder. When you spot the file for your data connection, right-click it, and then choose Delete.

The Data Model: Boosting Pivot Tables

Over the years, Excel has gradually morphed from a number-crunching tool loved by accountants everywhere to a *data analysis tool* that lets big businesses spot trends, detect anomalies, and predict the future. With each version of Excel, its data connection tools have become faster and more reliable. Excel 2013 introduces the biggest behind-the-scenes change yet: a new data model that can handle larger amounts of data and deal with interrelated tables.

Before you go any further, it's important to understand a key fact: The new data model is all about *pivot tables*, the miraculously flexible data analysis tool you explored in Chapter 26. Although the data model is at work in almost every workbook that has a data connection, you won't gain any benefits from it unless you're creating a pivot table, pivot chart, or Power View report.

So, assuming you're fetching your information from a database and you're planning to create a pivot table, what benefits does the new data model provide? There are three advantages:

- **Big data.** An ordinary Excel worksheet tops out at about one million rows. If your database has more, you'll have to leave some records behind. But the data model lets you feed *millions* of rows into a pivot table. (The only quirk is that you can't see these individual records in your workbook.)
- **Relationships.** Databases break data down into multiple, independent tables. To analyze that information, you need to fuse these tables back together. (For example, if you combine a list of sales data with customer address information, you can spot city-specific sales trends.) Excel's data model lets you create relationships between your tables, and combine their data for analysis in a single pivot table.
- **Rich reporting.** The new data model can work in conjunction with the Power View add-in to create rich data visualizations—everything from fancy charts to dashboards and colorized maps. With the help of a SharePoint server, you can even put these visualizations on a website. That said, Power View is a complex product best suited to data analysis junkies. And the only way to get it is with Office Professional Plus, the super-premium version of Office marketed to big companies in volume licensing packages. If you're using one of the many lesser versions, including Office Professional, you'll be forced to do without.

NOTE The data model features were available to previous versions of Excel through a separate Microsoft add-in called Power*Pivot.* (The name emphasizes that these features were designed to help Excel fans build better pivot tables.) Excel 2013 borrows the best parts of PowerPivot, and smoothes out some of the wrinkles.

Dealing with Big Tables

Ordinarily, if you try to import data that exceeds what Excel can fit in a worksheet, you'll get a warning message (Figure 27-13).

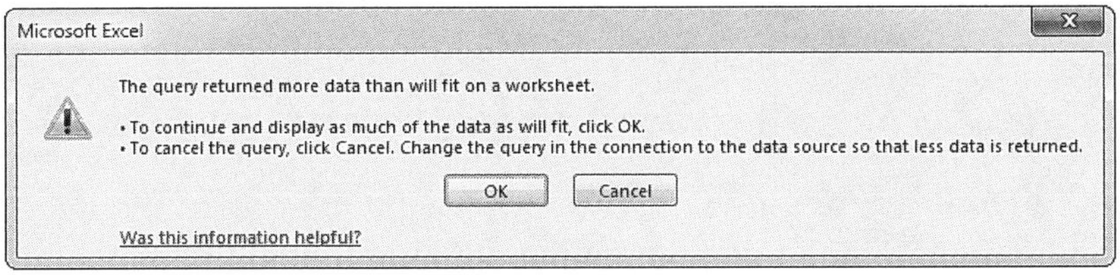

FIGURE 27-13

Excel shows this message if you attempt to fill your worksheet with more than 1,048,576 records.

One solution is to create a query that extracts a subset of the data. For example, you might create a query in your database that fetches the most recent year of sales, rather than the entire contents of the Sales table.

But creating a query requires some database smarts and, more significantly, you might really want to include all the data in your analysis. The solution is to use the data model and funnel your data directly into a pivot table, bypassing your worksheet. Here are the steps you need to follow:

1. **First, find a big database.**

   To test Excel's data model, and its ability to deal with huge quantities of information, you need a big database. One good candidate is Microsoft's Contoso sample, which features an Access database file that weighs in at roughly 100 MB. You can download it from *http://powerpivotsdr.codeplex.com*.

2. **Click the Data→Get External Data button, and choose the type of data source you're using.**

   For example, if you're using the Access database from the Contoso sample, you'd pick Data→Get External Data→From Access. If you're using SQL Server, you would choose Data→Get External Data→From Other Sources→From SQL Server.

3. **Continue normally, until you reach the point where Excel asks you to pick a table. Then, choose the table you want, and click OK.**

   If you're using the Contoso database, choose the FactSales table, which includes more than 2 million records.

4. **In the Import Data window (Figure 27-14), choose PivotTable Report.**

   PivotTable report tells Excel that you want to build a collapsible, multilayered pivot table. If you prefer to graph the results in a chart, choose PivotChart instead.

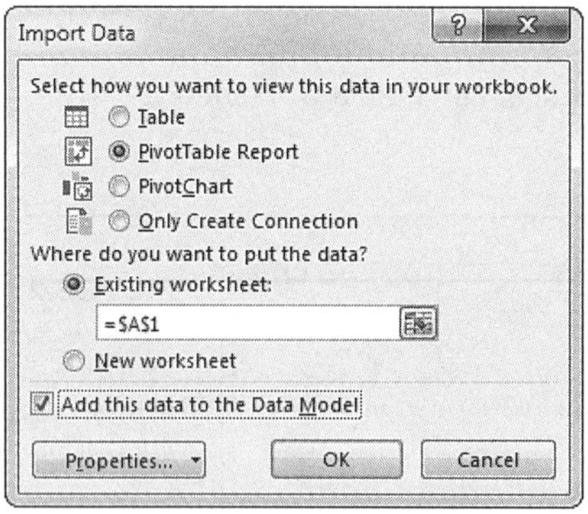

FIGURE 27-14

Here's where things take a different turn. In previous examples, you chose Table, which tells Excel to add your data to an ordinary worksheet. That option won't work with huge amounts of data.

5. **Turn on the "Add this data to the Data Model" checkbox.**

   This settings tells Excel that you want to use the data model to deal with the avalanche of data.

6. **Click OK to continue.**

   Excel makes the connection, and starts to retrieve your data. While it works, you'll see the message "Running Background Query (Click Here to Cancel)" in the Excel status bar. When it finishes, you'll be rewarded with a blank pivot table, which looks just the same as when you create a new pivot table with ordinary worksheet data (page 797).

   You won't see any trace of the imported data (the contents of the FactSales table) in your workbook. Excel keeps all this information behind the scenes, in a highly optimized, compressed form.

NOTE The hard, cold reality is this: On a modern computer, Excel is fast and efficient enough to manipulate millions of records on its own. However, it *isn't* powerful enough to manage millions of records on a worksheet, where you can scroll through them, edit them, format them, and so on. That's why Excel keeps its data model tucked out of sight.

7. **To actually see your data, add some fields to the pivot table.**

   If you're using the FactSales table from the Contoso database, here's how to get to a quick start:

   - **Drag ProductKey to the Columns box.** This tells Excel to create a separate column for each product.
   - **Drag PromotionKey to the Rows box.** This tells Excel to create a separate row for each promotion.
   - **Drag TotalCost to the Values box.** This tells Excel to calculate the total sales of each product in each promotion category.

   Figure 27-15 shows the result.

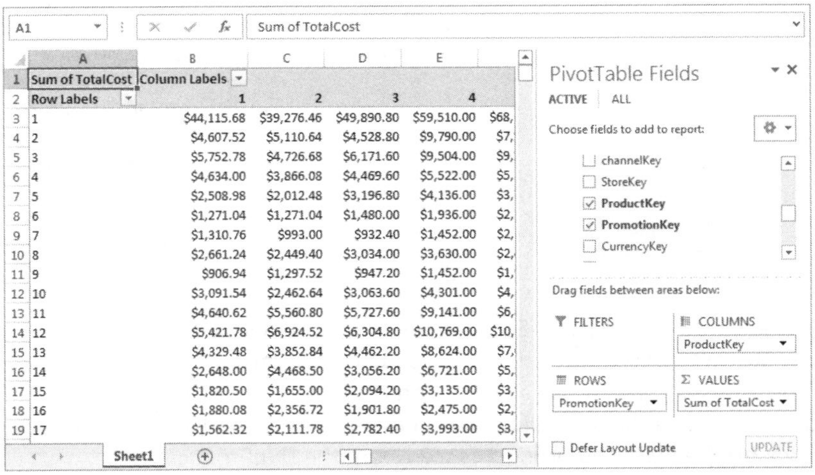

FIGURE 27-15 *This pivot table summarizes 2 million records from the FactSales table. In its current form it's not terribly helpful, because the FactSales table identifies each product and promotion with a numeric number instead of a descriptive name. (You'll learn to fix this problem in the following section.)*

TIP If you need a refresher to remember how pivot tables work, jump back to page 798 for all the gory details.

Understanding Relationships

The sheer muscle of Excel's data model is impressive. In the Contoso example, it can analyze the 2 million records in the FactSales table and create a subgrouped summary for your pivot table, all in surprisingly short time. But the pivot table Excel creates is underwhelming, because it lacks important contextual information. The problem isn't Excel, but the underlying FactSales table, which dutifully records each sale but doesn't supply any additional information about what was sold or who bought it.

These omissions aren't the result of bad database design. In fact, all these details *are* in the Contoso database, but they're stored in separate tables (see the diagram in Figure 27-16). This rigorously structured design is common in databases. To assemble the full picture, you need to combine the information from different tables using a database feature called *relationships*.

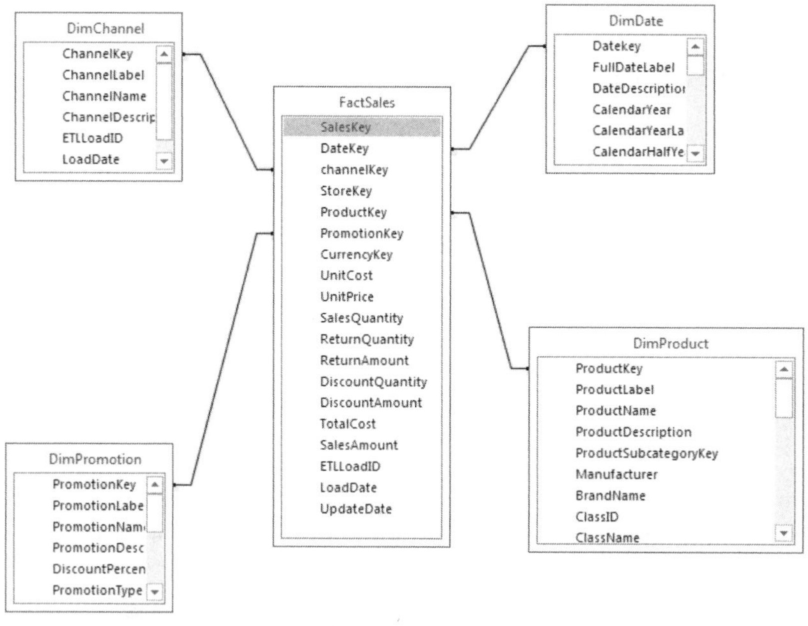

FIGURE 27-16

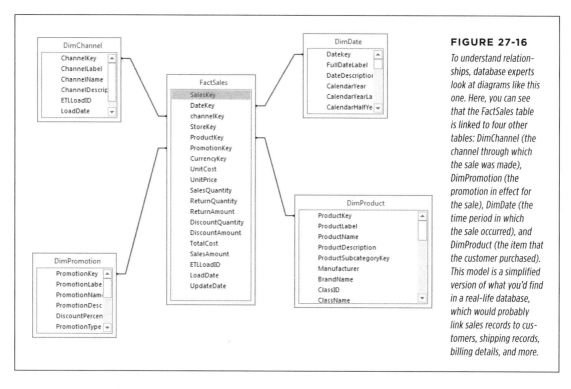

To understand relationships, database experts look at diagrams like this one. Here, you can see that the FactSales table is linked to four other tables: DimChannel (the channel through which the sale was made), DimPromotion (the promotion in effect for the sale), DimDate (the time period in which the sale occurred), and DimProduct (the item that the customer purchased). This model is a simplified version of what you'd find in a real-life database, which would probably link sales records to customers, shipping records, billing details, and more.

To properly interpret the FactSales table—or just about any other table in a relational database—Excel needs to combine the data from several related tables. For example, consider the FactSales table Contoso database. It includes a field named ProductKey that records the unique ID number of each product. Using this ID, you can look up the matching product record from the DimProducts table, which lists all the products on offer. Then, you can extract other product information, including its name and description. Similarly, if you want to understand what each ID number in the PromotionKey field represents, you need to match it up to the corresponding promotion record in the DimPromotion table. Then you can find out the name of promotion, the dates that it ran, and several additional details. There's no limit to this pairing up, and most databases feature tables that connect to one another in a tangled web of relationships.

There are two ways to create relationships in an Excel data model:

- **Define the relationship by hand.** This is the most flexible approach, but also the most time-consuming. You'll learn how to use it first.
- **Import the relationship from your database.** If the bond between your tables is already defined in the database (and it usually is), Excel can detect it and use it automatically in your workbook's data model. You'll try this feature out on page 854.

Defining a Relationship

Before you can create a relationship, you need to make sure your workbook has a connection to *both* of the related tables. This process is easy enough—you simply need to follow the steps starting on page 839 twice, once for each table. Once you've imported both tables into your workbook, you need to tell Excel how the two tables are related.

You can try this out with the Contoso database example. You already have a connection to the FactSales table, so now you need to add a connection to another table, like DimPromotion. The following steps walk you through the process of adding a connection for DimPromotion, creating a relationship, and using that relationship to improve your pivot table.

1. **Create a new worksheet.**

   You'll use a new worksheet to import your second table of data.

   You can't create a new data connection while you're inside the pivot table that belongs to the first connection. (If you try, you'll see the Get External Data button grayed out and unclickable.)

2. **Click Data→Get External Data→From Access, pick the database file, and choose the DimPromotion table.**

   This part of the process is the same as when you created the first connection.

3. **At the Import Table window, turn on the "Add this data to the Data Model" checkbox and click OK.**

   However, you don't need to create a new pivot table. Instead, you can choose the standard Table option to copy the new data into a worksheet. That's because all the other tables in the Contoso database are smaller than Excel's 1 million record maximum and will fit handily in a worksheet, including DimPromotion.

4. **Click OK to import the table.**

   The promotion records appear in your worksheet, in an Excel table.

   Now you have the DimPromotions data, and you imported it into the same data model, together with the FactSales records. However, there's a problem—Excel doesn't know that FactSales and DimPromotion are related. It's up to you to define the relationship.

5. **Choose Data→Data Tools→Relationships.**

   The Manage Relationships window appears. Initially, it's empty, because you haven't created any relationships.

6. **Click the New button to begin adding your first relationship.**

   The Create Relationships window appears. Here, you need to tell Excel how the two tables are linked. First, pick the two tables you want, one from the Table drop-down list and one from the Related Table list (it doesn't matter which you pick first). Then, choose the linked fields using the Column and Related Column lists (Figure 27-17).

NOTE Don't be confused if the list of tables includes some tables with similar names, like DimPromotion and Table_DimPromotion. The first item (DimPromotion) represents the data you're pulling out of your database, while the second item (Table_DimPromotion) represents the table displayed in the Excel worksheet. Usually, both choices are equivalent, but it's best to stick with the version that doesn't have the *Table_* prefix.

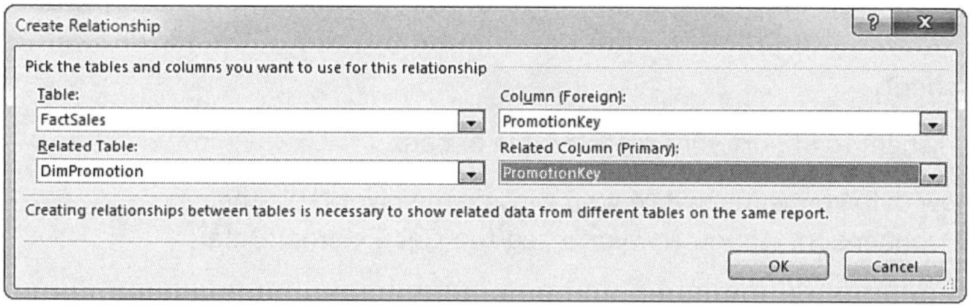

FIGURE 27-17

Every table relationship has the same anatomy. A field in one table links to a field in another table. Often, both fields have the same name. For example, the PromotionKey field in the FactSales table matches up with the identically named PromotionKey field in the DimPromotion table.

7. **Click OK to create the relationship.**

   Excel returns you to the Manage Relationships window. Now you see your one and only relationship in the list.

8. **Click Close.**

   This closes the Manage Relationships window and returns you to your workbook.

9. **Click somewhere inside your pivot table.**

   Now it's time to use the related data in your pivot table.

10. **Click the All link at the top of the PivotTable Fields panel (Figure 27-18).**

    Initially, the PivotTable Fields panel lists only the fields that are in the FactSales table. The All link lets you see the fields from the other tables.

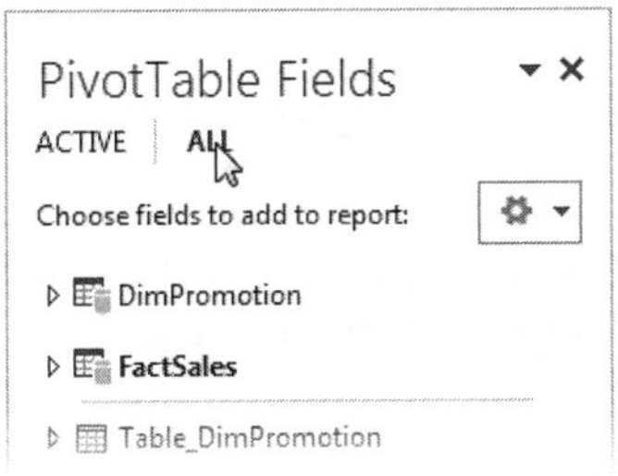

FIGURE 27-18

Click All to see all the tables in your data model. Here, the data model includes the original FactSales table and the related DimPromotions table. To see the fields inside a table, click the table name.

11. **Adjust your pivot table by adding the related data you want.**

    Drag the PromotionKey field out of the Rows box. Then, drag the PromotionName field from the DimPromotions table into the Rows box. This swaps the difficult-to-decipher ID numbers in your table with more meaningful text (Figure 27-19).

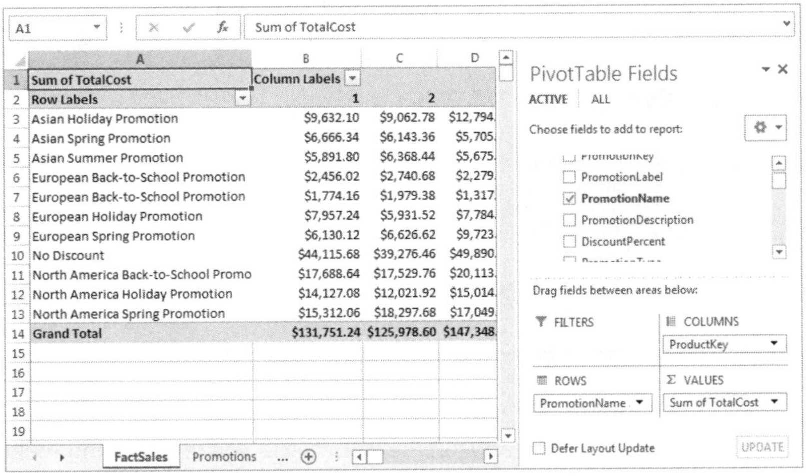

FIGURE 27-19

This pivot table uses the same grouping as the pivot table in Figure 27-15, but now, it's obvious what each promotion represents. You can repeat this process to import and link the DimProduct table to get its product information.

Now that you know how to create a relationship the hard way, you have unlimited power. For example, you can extract tables from different databases or completely different data sources, and then unite them in your Excel data model. Big organization are notorious for keeping different sets of data in different places, and the capability to take down these walls and bring multiple sources of data together in a spreadsheet has Excel data analysts drooling.

Importing Relationships

The problem with defining relationships by hand is that it's tedious. It's a particular chore if you need to connect a whole batch of tables together, because you need to add each table and definite its relationship separately.

However, Excel has a near-miraculous feature that can help you out. If you want to import related tables from a single database, Excel may be able to spot the relationships and set them up automatically. Here's how to try out this timesaver with the Contoso database:

1. **Start with a new, blank workbook.**

2. **Use the Data→Get External Data button to begin creating a new connection.**

   In the case of Access, you start with the familiar Data→Get External Data→From Access command.

3. **When you reach the Import Table step, switch on the "Enable selection of multiple tables" setting. Then, select all the tables you want (Figure 27-20).**

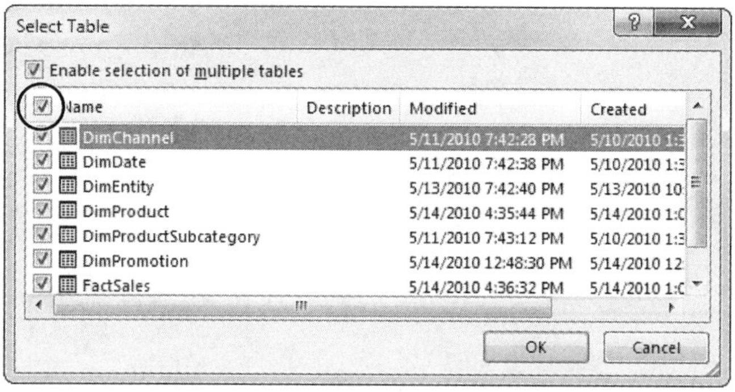

FIGURE 27-20

To import a table, add a checkmark next to it. To import all the tables, click the checkbox in the top-left corner of the table (circled). This example grabs all the tables from the Contoso database, which ensures that no valuable resources are left out.

4. **Click OK.**

   The Import Data window appears next. Because you're importing multiple tables, Excel automatically chooses PivotTable Report (instead of Table) and checks the "Add this data to the data model" setting.

5. **Click OK to create the connection and fetch your data.**

   Depending on the size of your database, this step may take a minute or two. When Excel finishes, you'll see an ordinary blank pivot table. But you'll see all your tables listed in the PivotTable Fields panel.

6. **Create your pivot table.**

   Now you can build your pivot table by dragging the fields you want into the appropriate boxes (Figure 27-21). Best of all, you don't need to create any relationships, because Excel already knows about them. However, you *do* still need to understand how your database is structured in order to use its tables correctly. (For example, if you create a pivot table that attempts to group your product parts list by customer name, you'll end up with a nonsensical pivot table that doesn't tell you anything, because the two tables aren't directly related.)

NOTE If you add fields from tables that don't appear to be related (or are related, but Excel doesn't know about it), Excel shows a yellow warning message at the top of the PivotTable Fields panel, which states "Relationships between tables may be needed." If you think you can fill in the missing relationship, click the Create button under this warning to go to the Manage Relationships window (page 852).

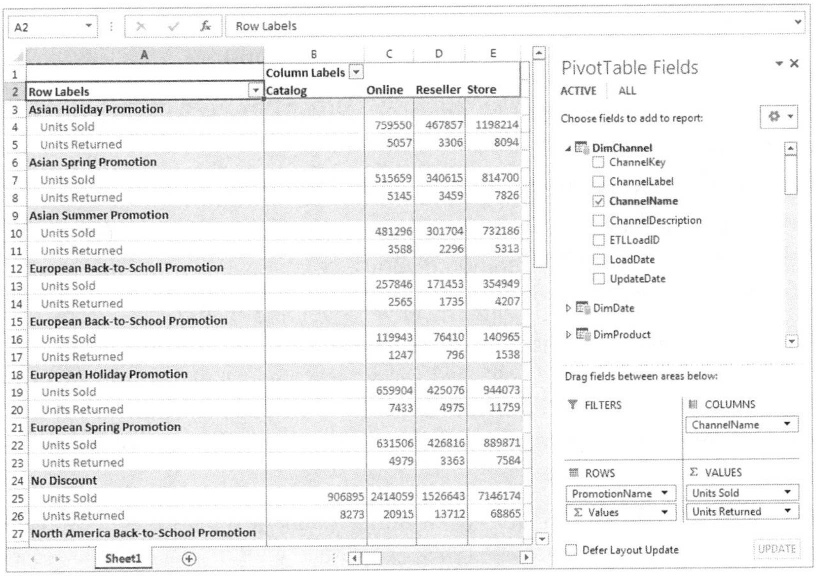

FIGURE 27-21

This pivot table explores how different promotions fare in different sales channels. It uses the PromotionName and ChannelName fields (from the linked tables), rather than the less descriptive PromotionKey and ChannelKey fields stored directly in the FactSales table.

Going Behind the Scenes with PowerPivot

You've now explored the full extent of Excel's data model. However, Microsoft has a few more goodies in store for businesses that use the Office Professional Plus edition of Excel. Many of these features are aimed at professional data analysts, who spend entire days poring over business data and building data visualization spreadsheets for big companies. However, even ordinary Excel fans will find a few useful options.

The gateway to these features is an add-in called PowerPivot, which Microsoft bundles with Office Professional Plus. In the not-so-distant past, you needed to use PowerPivot to get any of the data model features you just learned about, including table relationships and support for tables with more than 1 million rows. Excel 2013 changed that by embedding the best parts of PowerPivot inside Excel. However, PowerPivot still lives on, with some of the specialized features Microsoft left behind.

Before you can use the PowerPivot add-in, you need to activate it:

1. **Choose File→Options.**
2. **In the Excel Options window, pick the Add-Ins category.**

   This shows a list of all your currently active add-ins, and those that are installed but not active.

3. **In the Manage list at the bottom of the window, choose COM Add-Ins, and then click Go.**

   The COM Add-Ins window appears, with a list of add-ins.

4. **Turn on the checkbox next to "Microsoft Office PowerPivot for Excel 2013," and then click OK.**

   Excel adds a new tab to the ribbon, named PowerPivot.

   If you can't find PowerPivot anywhere in the list of add-ins, you probably don't have the Professional Plus edition of Office.

The first thing you'll want to do with the PowerPivot add-in is check out the data in your data model. As you already learned, if your data model includes a table with more than 1,048,576 records, Excel can't show it in a worksheet. Instead, Excel holds that data in memory, out of sight. But PowerPivot lets you peek behind the scenes, so you can take a look at these gargantuan tables and see the information that Excel uses to build your pivot table.

To take a look, choose PowerPivot→Data Model→Manage. PowerPivot opens a new window, which lets you browse the full set of data in your model (Figure 27-22).

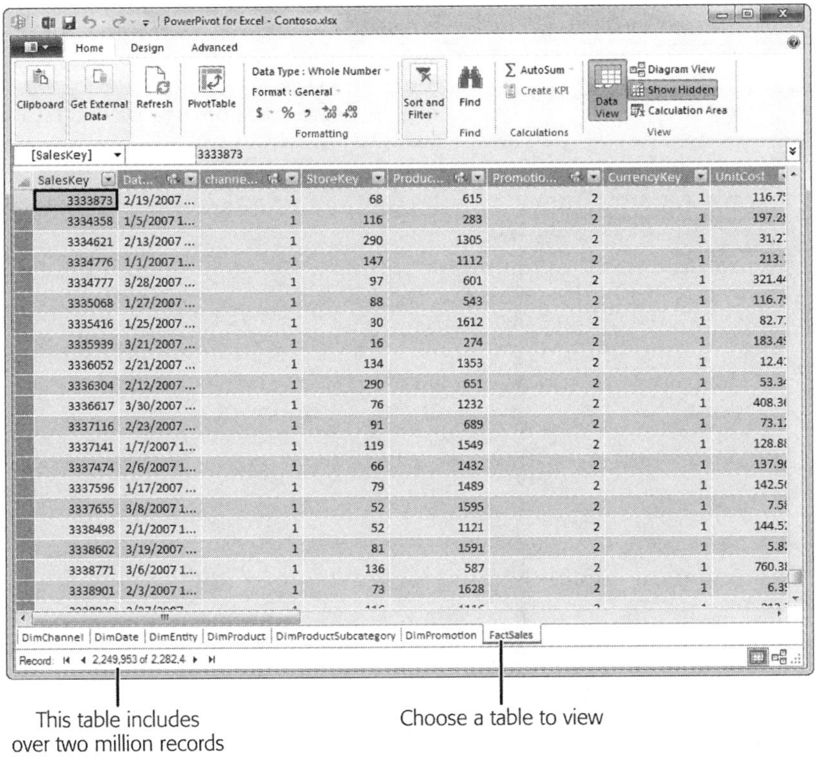
This table includes over two million records
Choose a table to view

FIGURE 27-22

This data model includes all seven tables from the Contoso database. You can scroll through the data in any of these tables, including the full set of over 2 million records in the FactSales table. However, you can't format, edit, or print this data. This compromise lets you browse your data without overtaxing your computer.

TIP The PowerPivot window can happily coexist alongside the Excel window. If you want, you can switch back and forth between your workbook in Excel and the data display in PowerPivot.

PowerPivot's data display is interesting, and it can help you orient yourself if you open a workbook someone else created, and you're not sure what its data model contains. However, you probably won't spend much time looking at individual records. After all, the whole point of importing these records into Excel is so you can group them together, perform summary calculations, and look at the big picture.

Along with its data display, the PowerPivot window includes a few pro-level features unavailable in Excel. One is the sorting and filtering options, which you can show by clicking the drop-down arrow in any column header (Figure 27-23).

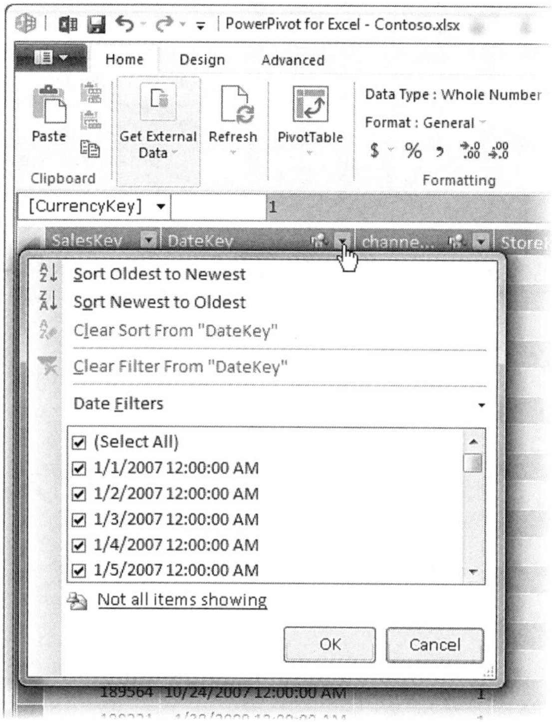

FIGURE 27-23

PowerPivot's sorting and filtering choices should look familiar. They work the same way as the sorting and filtering menus you use with ordinary Excel tables in a worksheet, as described on page 424.

You might wonder why you'd bother to sort or filter your data when your pivot table gives you a similar set of sorting and filtering features. One reason is that you may have a complex workbook with several pivot tables that use the same data model. If you want to filter your data differently in each pivot table, pivot table filtering works best (page 815). But if you want to add filter conditions that affect all your pivot tables, it's much faster to apply the filtering in PowerPivot. That's because each time you update a pivot table, you force Excel to review the underlying data. If your data model holds millions of rows, that process takes time. For hardcore data analysts, it's a serious difference.

Creating a Calculated Field with PowerPivot

One useful feature that PowerPivot adds to Excel is the ability to add calculated fields to the tables in your data model. You may remember that pivot tables have a feature for creating calculated fields (page 813), but you can't use this feature when you link your pivot table to multiple tables in a data model. Fortunately, PowerPivot picks up the slack.

Here's how to create a calculated field in PowerPivot:

1. **In the PowerPivot window, browse to the table where you want to add your calculated field.**

   Remember, you can switch from one table to another using the tabs at the bottom of the PowerPivot window.

2. **Scroll all the way to the right edge of the table.**

   After the last column, you'll see a blank column that has the heading "Add Column."

3. **Click any cell inside the "Add Column" column.**

   It doesn't matter where you click; PowerPivot will copy the formula you create to every record.

4. **Type the equals sign (=) and begin entering a formula (Figure 27-24).**

   Your formula can include numbers, text, Excel's basic math operators, functions, and column names. However, it's important to remember to wrap every column name in square brackets. If you want to find the number of days between two dates, for example, your formula might look like this:

   ```
   =[SubmittedDate]-[ProposedDate]
   ```

   If you don't want to type in a column name, just click the column you want. PowerPivot will insert the column name into your formula.

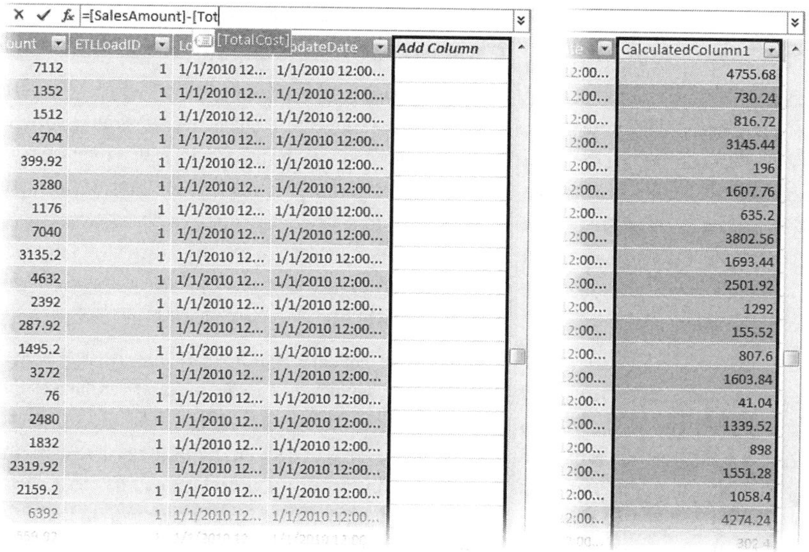

FIGURE 27-24

Left: Entering a formula in PowerPivot is similar to doing so in Excel. There's even an AutoComplete function that suggests formula expressions.

Right: The finished formula calculates the difference between Sales-Amount and TotalCost for all records.

5. **When you finish writing the formula, press Enter.**

   PowerPivot copies your formula to every record.

6. **Double-click the heading at the top of your calculated field, and then type in a new name.**

   PowerPivot assigns a name like CalculatedColumn1 to your new field. You should change it to something more meaningful, like NetProfit.

7. **Press Enter to confirm the new field name.**

   Now your calculated field is part of the data model, and you'll see it in the PivotTable Fields panel. To show it in your pivot table, drag it into the Values box, just as you would with an ordinary field.

Calculated fields get plenty more complex. That's because PowerPivot supports a language called DAX (which stands for Data Analysis Expressions). Using DAX, you can create formulas that pull together related data and perform complex aggregations. In fact, there's an *entire book* written on the subject. Data nerds can check out *DAX Formulas for PowerPivot*, or Microsoft's terse but detailed DAX reference at *http://tinyurl.com/dax-reference*.

POWER USERS' CLINIC

Exploring More Features in PowerPivot

There's still more in the PowerPivot tool. Here are a few specialized features that are worth exploring:

- **Relationships.** You already learned how to use the Manage Relationships window to review the relationships in your data model and add new ones (page 851). But if your data model has dozens of tables and relationships, it can be hard to figure out exactly how everything ties together. PowerPivot can create a diagram (like the one shown on page 850) that shows how your tables relate. You can even add relationships while reviewing a diagram, simply by dragging a field from one table to the matching field in another table. To see a diagram of your data model in PowerPivot, choose Design→Relationships→Manage Relationships.
- **Perspectives.** A perspective is a subset of the tables and fields in your data model. For example, in the Contoso example in Figure 27-22, you could create a perspective that includes just the FactSales and DimPromotion tables (and you could leave out some of the FactSales fields that don't interest you). Perspectives are a useful convenience if you have a complex data model with a pile of tables. To create one in PowerPivot, choose Advanced→Perspectives→Create and Manage. To pick the perspective that's currently active, choose Advanced→Perspectives→Select.
- **Fancy pivot table worksheets.** PowerPivot makes it easy to create worksheets that combine more than one pivot table in a nice grid arrangement, or ones that combine pivot tables and pivot charts side-by-side. Excel pros use these options to create densely packed analysis worksheets (although it's still up to you to fill each pivot table with data). To create one of your own, make a selection from PowerPivot's Home→PivotTable list.

And if you're planning to launch a new career as a data analyst, you can dig even deeper into the tricks and techniques that make a PowerPivot master by reading a dedicated book on the topic. If you're ready to wade into the deep end, try *PowerPivot for the Data Analyst*. Or, if you want to create database-driven reports with PowerPivot and Power View, check out *Visualizing Data with Microsoft Power View*.

CHAPTER

28

Analyzing XML and Web Data

An ordinary Excel workbook stores a bunch of information, and uses Excel tools (like formulas and charts) to analyze it. However, a great deal of the world's business information isn't stored in Excel files. Instead, it sits inside *databases*—organized catalogs of information managed by high-powered computer software.

Typical mid-size (or bigger) companies store product catalogs, customer lists, and purchase orders in databases. When they need to change this information (or just take a look at it), they use a program that talks to the database. Databases are extremely fast, secure, and durable. They're the best place to put mission-critical information.

At first glance, this approach (storing big volumes of information in a database) seems to cut Excel out of the loop. However, Excel's greatest strength isn't storing information, it's *analyzing* it. In fact, Excel is the perfect tool for analyzing information, no matter where it comes from. Your company might track orders using a custom application that dumps its results into a database. If you want to find out what all the numbers amount to and make a prediction about your company's future, you can pull that info out of a database (using a process called *querying*), and then start charting away. In other words, your Excel workbook copies information stored in the database so you can put that data under the microscope. Best of all, you can refresh your workbook any time to get the latest information from the same database, so your workbook never goes out of date.

In this chapter, you'll learn how to pull information out of a database so you can analyze it in a workbook. Then, you'll consider how to pull information out of an *XML* (Extensible Markup Language) file, which gives you even more options for plugging business data into Excel. Next, you'll look at a messier but occasionally useful technique called web queries, which let you extract information from a web page and transfer it to your worksheet. Finally, you'll learn about a more structured way to grab information from other computers on the Web, using a technology called OData. All these approaches have one thing in common: They use Excel to analyze information stored in another place.

Understanding XML

Databases aren't the only place you can find massive amounts of information. All kinds of specialized programs store vast quantities of data in their own ways. More often than not, when you need to get information out of (or into) one of these programs, you'll use *XML*.

XML is an all-purpose system for structuring and organizing data in a file. XML lets you exchange information with just about anyone, so you can send your spreadsheet data to other businesses that don't use Excel, or analyze raw information created with other programs.

For example, instead of saving data in Word documents, Excel spreadsheets, or ordinary text files, you can save it in an XML file. XML alone *sounds* pretty modest, but this simplicity is deceiving. Two factors make XML really special:

- **XML is flexible.** You can tailor XML to store pretty much any type of information: pictures, product catalogs, invoice data, receipts, catalog listings, the maintenance specs for every Dodge minivan ever built, and on and on.
- **XML is widespread.** Computer programs written in different programming languages (Java, Visual Basic, C++, and so on), or running on different operating systems and computer hardware (Windows, Mac, Linux, and so on), can all use XML in exactly the same way. XML is a perfect solution for exchanging information between people, companies, and even computers programmed to send data to one another automatically. (Features like this last one cause supply-chain management types to start drooling when they talk about XML.)

What Is XML, Really?

Contrary to what many people believe, XML is *not* a data format (as is, for example, HTML, the format used to create web pages). If XML were an ordinary data format, it wouldn't be nearly as useful, because no matter how good a format is, it can't suit everyone. Even though almost every company needs to create invoices, most companies wouldn't be happy with a generic format for storing invoice information. One company might need to track customer names, while another needs to track customer IDs. The bottom line is that most companies need to store slightly different data in slightly different ways. A one-size-fits-all solution is pretty much always doomed to failure.

So if XML isn't a data format, what is it? Technically, XML is a *meta-language*, which is a fancy way of saying that XML is a language for creating *other* languages. XML does this by setting out a few simple rules that let you build your *own* data format that's just right for *your* data.

For example, Acme Company can build an XML format for invoices and call it Acme-Invoice. Meanwhile, Budget Company can build *its* own XML invoice format and call it BudgetInvoice. Even though both these formats are designed to store invoice information, they can contain completely different kinds of data. XML's strength is its flexibility.

At the same time, XML's flexibility can create problems. Imagine that a bank named Worldwide Green sets up a system to automatically process XML invoices that arrive in a specific format. The system works smoothly until Acme Corporation sends along its own homegrown invoice. Even though Acme's invoice uses XML, it doesn't conform to the XML that the bank expects, and so it gums up the bank's automated invoice-processing application. Suddenly, XML doesn't look so useful.

The bottom line: XML holds the *promise* of universal data sharing—but if you don't create some rules and follow them, you're left with a bunch of incompatible formats.

NOTE XML is really quite simple. However, you'll find a slew of other standards with names like XML Schema and XSLT that work in conjunction with XML, and provide solutions for validating XML, searching XML, transforming XML, and so on. These other standards are complex and outside the scope of this book. For more information, pick up a book like *Learning XML* by Erik Ray (O'Reilly), or see the website *www.w3schools.com/xml.*

Three Rules of XML

To better understand how to configure Excel to handle XML, look at a simple example. Technically, you don't need to know what XML looks like in order to use Excel's XML features, but the more you understand, the less confusing life will be. In this section, you'll learn the three most important rules that shape all XML documents. If you already know a little about XML, feel free to skip ahead to page 867.

By the way, good news before you even start: XML is written in a text-based, human-readable format. That means you can use a program like Notepad to crack open an existing XML file and get a basic idea of its format and structure. You can even write an XML file from scratch using Notepad. You can't do the same with the average Excel spreadsheet file, because Excel stores its worksheets in a binary format that you can read only when you look at the file in Excel. (If you open an ordinary Excel file in Notepad, you see a jumble of indecipherable symbols.)

THE PROLOG

All respectable XML documents start with something called a *document prolog*. This bit simply announces that you're looking at an XML document. It can also indicate the *encoding* of the document, which sometimes specifies that the document uses a special character set (for example, a non-English alphabet).

Here's a typical document prolog, indicating that this document uses Version 1.0 of the XML standard (the most prevalent version):

```
<?xml version="1.0" ?>
```

If you create an XML document by hand, make sure you include the document prolog as the very first line of your file.

ELEMENTS

The *element* is the basic building block of any XML document. Elements are information containers. If you want to store a person's name, for instance, you might create an element called Name. (For more on the infinite variety of elements anyone can create, see the box on page 865.)

A typical element is composed of a start tag and an end tag. The actual information goes between these two tags. You can easily recognize start tags and end tags because they use angle brackets <>. For example, here's one possible start tag:

```
<Name>
```

This tag marks the start of the Name element. The end tag looks almost identical, except it begins with the characters </ instead of just <. Here's what ends the Name element:

```
</Name>
```

To actually store some information in an XML document, you insert the content between the start and end tag of an element. Here's how you might store someone's name in an XML document:

```
<Name>Patrick</Name>
```

You could create a list of names by putting one <Name> element after the other, or you could add other elements that store different types of information, like address, title, employer, and so on. You put all these tags together in a file to make an XML document.

NESTING

So far, you've seen examples of XML elements that contain text. You can also create an element that contains one or more additional elements. This is a basic principle for organizing information in XML.

Imagine you want to keep track of several people's names and ages. The following format isn't especially clear, because it's hard to tell which person connects to which age:

```
<Name>Lisa Chen</Name>
<Age>19</Age>
<Name>Bill Harrison</Name>
<Age>48</Age>
```

UP TO SPEED

A Closer Look at Tags

Tags follow fairly strict naming rules. They can be of any length, are case-sensitive, and can include any alphanumeric character and hyphens (-), underscores (_), and periods (.). You can't use other special characters, including spaces, and the tag name *must* start with an underscore or letter. XML documents also support characters from non-English alphabets.

The most important thing you should understand about tags is that it's up to you to create them. If you decide that you need to store a list of names, you might create an XML format that uses a <Name> tag. Meanwhile, someone else might decide to track name information by creating another XML format that uses elements like <firstName> and <lastName>. These two elements might store the same type of information as your <Name> element, but they're different, and a document written with the <firstName> and <lastName> tags isn't compatible with your document.

Because so many possible XML formats exist, a lot of intelligent people have invested a lot of time and energy in trying to create ways to define and manage different XML formats. Also, companies and organizations have come together to define specific XML standards for different industries. (If you search on the Internet, you'll find predefined XML formats for law, science, real estate, and much more.) When you use an XML document in Excel, you probably won't be responsible for creating it. Instead, you'll be given a document that's already in a specific XML format, and you'll just be interested in retrieving the information the document contains.

Better to group the <Name> and <Age> elements together for each person, and put them inside *another* element. Here's an example:

```
<Person>
    <Name>Lisa Chen</Name>
    <Age>19</Age>
</Person>
<Person>
    <Name>Bill Harrison</Name>
    <Age>48</Age>
</Person>
```

Here, the two <Person> elements each represent a distinct individual. Information about each person is stored in <Name> and <Age> elements that are *nested* inside the appropriate <Person> element.

There's no limit to how many layers deep you can nest information, making this method of organizing information extremely flexible. In fact, it's part of the reason that XML can work with so many different types of data.

XML imposes one more rule. Every document must start with a single element that you place right after the document prolog. You place all the other content inside this element, which is called the *root* or *document element*. So far, the examples you've seen are only excerpts of XML. The following listing shows a complete, valid XML document—a list with information about two people—that starts off with the document element <PeopleList>:

```
<?xml version="1.0" ?>
<PeopleList>
    <Person>
        <Name>Lisa Chen</Name>
     <Age>19</Age>
    </Person>

    <Person>
        <Name>Bill Harrison</Name>
        <Age>48</Age>
    </Person>
</PeopleList>
```

You could enhance this document by adding more <Person> elements, or by adding different elements to track additional information about each person.

You've probably noticed that the XML examples above indent each level of element. That indentation makes the overall structure easier to read, but it's not required. In fact, applications that read XML (including Excel) ignore all the white space between elements, so it doesn't matter if you add spaces, tabs, or blank lines. In fact, as far as computers are concerned, the previous document is exactly the same as the following, much less human-friendly version:

```
<?xml version="1.0" ?>
<PeopleList><Person><Name>Lisa Chen</Name><Age>19</Age>
</Person><Person><Name>Bill Harrison</Name><Age>48</Age>
</Person></PeopleList>
```

XML Files and Schemas

As you already learned, a file is one place you can store XML documents. But you can just as easily place XML documents in databases or other storage locations. In fact, sometimes XML data isn't stored anywhere—instead, you just use it to send information between applications over the Internet. However, when you use XML with Excel, you're always using XML files (unless your company's created a custom solution using Excel's heavy-duty programming features). Most XML files have the extension .xml. It makes perfect sense to take the person list document shown earlier and place it in a text file named PersonList.xml.

TIP The Excel XML features make the most sense when you have information that's already in an XML format. If you *don't* have XML information that you need to work with, there's really no reason to play around with Excel's XML features.

There's another type of XML document that's extremely important: XML *schemas*. Schemas are designed to solve a common problem—namely, defining the rules for a specific XML-based format. A schema may indicate the element names you can use, how you can arrange the elements, and the type of information each element can contain. An XML-friendly application like Excel can use the schema to verify that an XML document uses the right structure and contains the appropriate content. In an ideal world, every time a company created an XML format, they'd write an XML schema that defines it. (You probably won't be surprised to learn that this doesn't always happen.) Excel doesn't include schemas of its own, so it's up to you to supply the schema based on the XML you want to use.

This book doesn't look at XML schemas in detail, because they're a more complicated standard than XML. However, even if you don't know how to build your own schemas, you can still use other people's schemas with Excel. In fact, you'll find that doing so actually simplifies your life. To use a schema, you simply need to have a copy of it in a file (schemas themselves are complex and ugly, and beyond the scope of what a typical office needs—or wants—to learn). Usually, schema files have the extension .xsd.

TIP For a more comprehensive beginner's introduction to XML and XML schemas, check out the excellent online tutorial provided by W3 Schools at *www.w3schools.com/xml*.

Retrieving Information from XML

XML is a great way to exchange data between different programs. But what does that have to do with Excel, which already has its own perfectly good file format? Here's the deal: Today, more and more companies use XML to pass data back and forth. For example, when companies exchange business orders, news organizations post stories, or real estate firms list properties for sale, chances are they're using an XML-based format. If you want to crack open these documents and analyze their data using all of Excel's features, including formulas and charts, you need to use Excel's XML tools.

There's another side to this story. Instead of trying to get XML information *into* Excel, you may need a way to get your worksheet data *out of* Excel. You might want to take an expense worksheet, export it to XML, and then feed that XML into an automated expense-processing program. That program could then track your expenses, submit them to your supervisor for authorization, and notify the payroll department when a payment is required. In a small company, it could be just as easy to print out the expense report and deliver it by hand (or email it). But in a large company, an automated application can help the whole process flow seamlessly, without forcing anyone to sort through stacks of paper or dozens of email messages. In these situations, XML really shines.

NOTE Experts estimate that Excel spreadsheets contain more data than all the world's relational databases combined. Excel's XML features can help you extract information that's trapped in your spreadsheet files and use it in other automated applications.

Because XML is so flexible, there's no single-step solution to importing and exporting XML. You can't just perform an *Open XML* command because Excel doesn't know *which* XML format you're using. Instead, you first need to give Excel some information about that format, and then tell it how to extract the data you need.

Excel makes this possible through a set of features called *XML mapping*. XML mapping lets you link a specific XML format to a specific spreadsheet. Once you set up this link, you can use it in two ways: to export data *from* your worksheet into an XML document, or to import the contents of an XML document *into* your worksheet.

Some of the options for Excel's XML features are tucked away on a special tab that doesn't ordinarily appear. Before you do anything with XML and Excel, you need to display this tab. To do so, choose File→Options, and then choose the Customize Ribbon section. On the right of the window, a large box lists all the tabs currently shown in the ribbon. Near the bottom, you'll see an unchecked item named Developer. To show the Developer tab, check this box, and then click OK.

Mapping a Simple Document

The simplest way to map an XML document is to link each element in the document to a corresponding cell in a worksheet. Then, when you import the document, the data flows out of the elements and into the linked cells.

NOTE You can find all the XML files used in this chapter on the Missing CD page at *www.missingmanuals.com/cds/excel2013mm*. You can use these files to map your own worksheets.

To try this out, you can use the simple Student.xml document shown here, which stores the test and assignment scores for a single student:

```
<?xml version="1.0" ?>
<Student>
    <Name>Lisa Chen</Name>
    <StudentID>45349920</StudentID>
    <Test1_Score>75</Test1_Score>
    <Test2_Score>63.23</Test2_Score>
    <Assignment1_Score>94</Assignment1_Score>
    <Assignment2_Score>90</Assignment2_Score>
</Student>
```

Keep in mind that in real life, you wouldn't create this document by hand. Instead, you might extract it from a database or, even more likely, generate it using some sort of automated student-grading program.

Before you can map an XML document to an Excel workbook, you need to prepare the workbook. Simply follow these steps:

1. **Create a new blank Excel document.**

   You could map to an existing workbook, but, in this case, it's easier to start from scratch.

NOTE Excel worksheets can contain a mix of linked cells (those that'll be receiving the XML file's content) and nonlinked cells containing other information (like your own descriptive labels, or formulas that use the imported data). Excel doesn't include these nonlinked cells in any import or export operation.

2. **Choose File→Open.**

   This brings you to the Open page in backstage view.

3. **Choose Computer from the list on the left, and then click the Browse button.**

   The Open File window appears.

4. **Browse to the Student.xml file, and then open it.**

   Excel shows an Open XML window with three options (Figure 28-1).

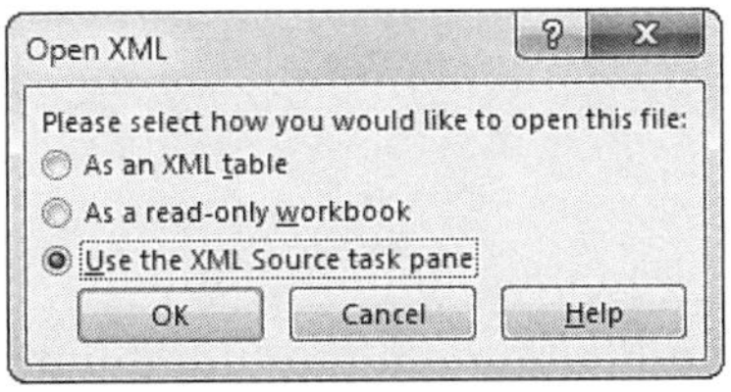

FIGURE 28-1

You have three choices when it comes to opening a basic XML document. You can import the data into a basic table, dump all its content into the worksheet in read-only mode, or take full control of the linking process. The last option is the best for this example, because it lets you choose where you want to display the imported data.

5. **Select "Use the XML Source task pane," and then click OK.**

6. **Excel warns you that you're mapping a document without a schema. Click OK to continue.**

   A schema defines the structure of an XML document, as explained on page 866. Using a schema is the best way to link XML documents to worksheets because its strict rules prevent errors. You can, however, get away without using a schema, and, because you don't have a schema file for the Student.xml file, you can proceed without it.

   When you click OK, Excel doesn't yet import the data into your document. Instead, the XML Source pane appears, showing a "tree" that includes all the elements Excel found in your XML document (see Figure 28-2). At this point, you're ready to start the mapping process.

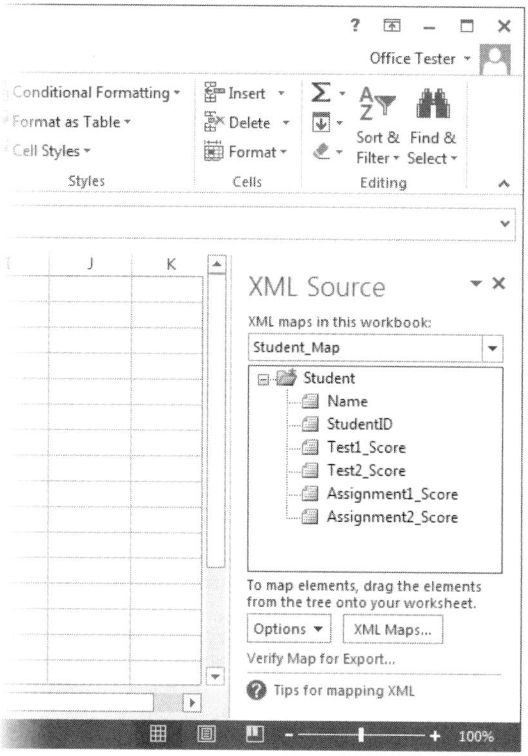

FIGURE 28-2

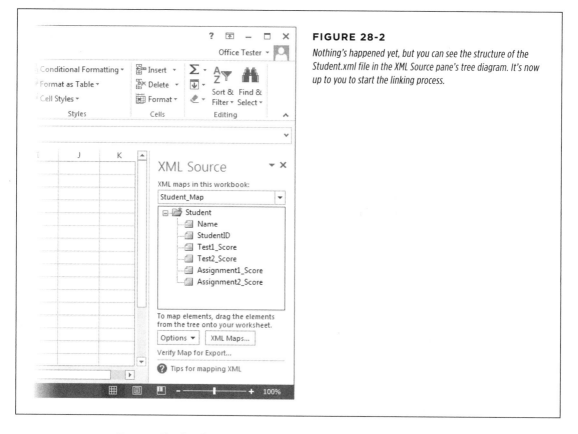

Nothing's happened yet, but you can see the structure of the Student.xml file in the XML Source pane's tree diagram. It's now up to you to start the linking process.

To map the Student.xml elements to your spreadsheet, follow these steps:

1. **In the XML Source pane, select the element you want to link.**
2. **Drag the element from the XML Source pane to the appropriate place in your spreadsheet.**

   You may want to place the student's name in cell B1 (leaving room for a label in cell A1). Simply click Name in the XML Source pane, drag it over cell B1, and then release it, as shown in Figure 28-3. Excel indicates linked cells with a blue outline.

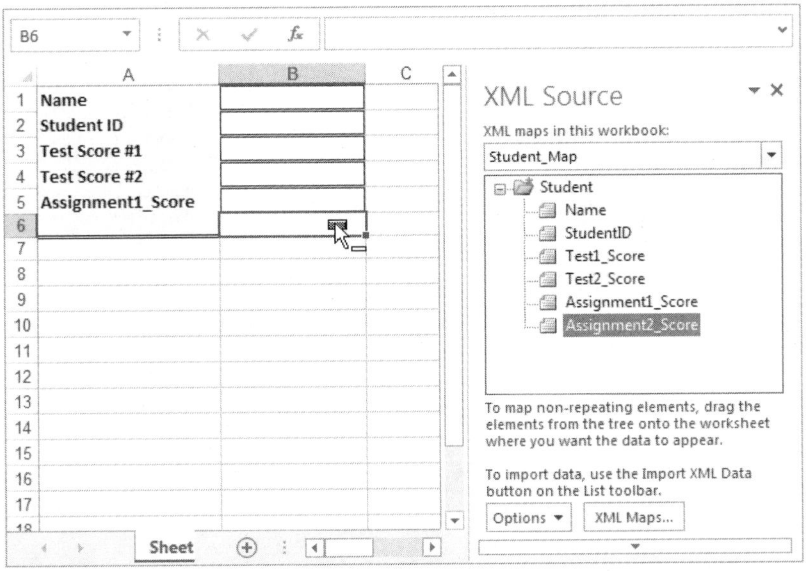

FIGURE 28-3

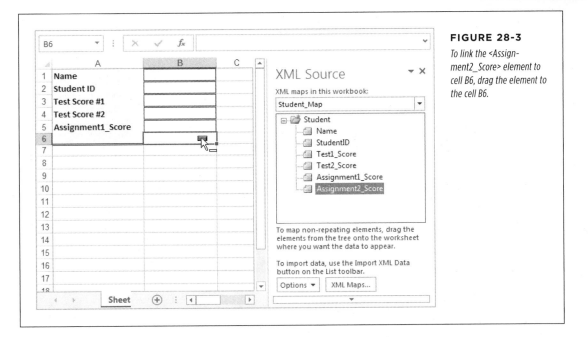

To link the <Assignment2_Score> element to cell B6, drag the element to the cell B6.

3. **Optionally, add a caption to your element by clicking the smart tag icon that appears next to the newly mapped cell.**

   The smart tag gives you two caption choices: "Place XML Heading to the Left" or "Place XML Heading Above," as shown in Figure 28-4. When you choose one of these options, Excel inserts a piece of static text with the name of the linked element in bold formatting. You can use this technique to insert the caption "Name" in cell A1 after you link cell B1 to the <Name> element.

NOTE Excel doesn't immediately insert any information in a linked cell. You won't see the student's name appear when you drag the <Name> element to cell B1, for example. Instead, you need to import the XML data once you finish mapping the cells. You'll learn how to import in a moment.

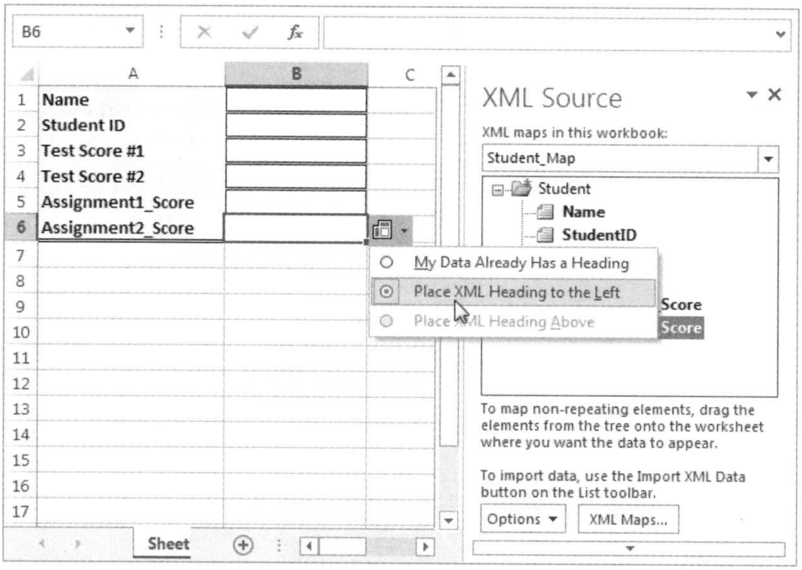

FIGURE 28-4

Once you link an element, Excel displays a smart tag. You can use this tag to quickly insert a caption for the linked data. This step is optional, because you can add your own labels. However, using the smart tag helps you quickly create the basic structure of your mapped worksheet. In this case, you still need to do some cleanup to make the XML element names more attractive; you might want to replace Assignment1_Score with Assignment Score #1, for instance.

4. **Return to step 1, and then repeat the process until you map all the elements.**

   You don't need to map every element. It's quite possible that you want to work with just a portion of your XML file's data. In that case, you'd want to map only the elements you need. Of course, if you don't map an element, you can't extract its data and put it into your worksheet. Similarly, if you eventually export the Excel file as an XML document, that element won't be included.

   If you change your mind while mapping, you can remove any element by right-clicking the corresponding element in the XML Source pane, and then choosing Remove.

Once you finish mapping the document and adding your headings, it's time to import the XML. Choose Date→Connections→Refresh. Figure 28-5 shows the worksheet with the XML data imported.

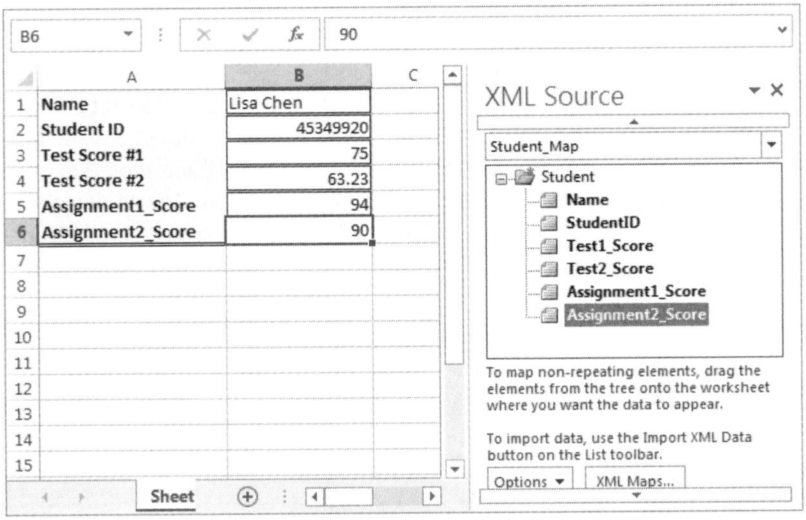

FIGURE 28-5

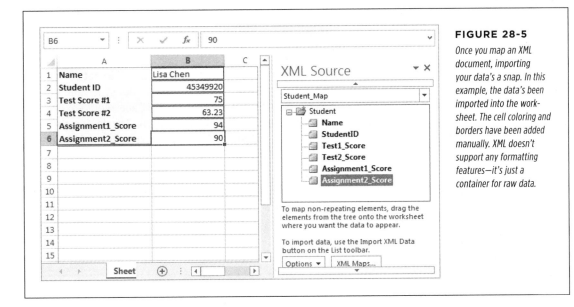

Once you map an XML document, importing your data's a snap. In this example, the data's been imported into the worksheet. The cell coloring and borders have been added manually. XML doesn't support any formatting features—it's just a container for raw data.

Importing and Exporting XML

Now that you mapped the Student.xml file, you've not only extracted some information from the XML document, you also gave yourself a range of options for managing the link between your spreadsheet data and the world of XML. The real magic of XML lies here.

Once you define a link between your worksheet and a specific XML format, you can perform three tasks:

- **Refresh.** If the XML source changes, you can easily refresh your worksheet with the new content. Just click any linked cell, and then select Data→Connections→Refresh, or Developer→XML→Refresh Data (both buttons have the same effect).
- **Export.** You can export the data to a new XML document. Click any linked cell, select Developer→XML→Export, and then choose a new XML file. Optionally, you can choose to replace the original XML data with the new XML file. (You might want to use this option if you edited the XML content inside your Excel spreadsheet.)
- **Import.** You can import XML data from another file that has the same structure. In this case, click any linked cell, select Developer→XML→Import, and then choose a new XML file. The new XML data flows into the existing worksheet, replacing the original data.

This ability to import means that in the Student.xml example, you could import a student's information, modify it, and then save it back to a *different* XML document. In fact, you could use your spreadsheet as a way to create dozens of different student documents in separate XML files, just by exporting different data to different files. A crafty developer could, for example, create a custom application that scans student XML files, and then automatically generates and mails report cards.

All you need to do is export the XML. In fact, the whole process could get even easier if someone develops a little piece of Excel macro code to handle the XML export. In that case, you'd just click a button on the worksheet, and Excel would export the student data to XML and submit it to the custom application. Developing this type of workflow takes a fair bit of work, and the first step's learning Excel's VBA macro language, which is introduced in Chapter 29.

NOTE Remember, if you save a mapped workbook, you're saving only the Excel spreadsheet file, with whatever data it currently contains. If you want to save the content to an XML file, you need to Export the data in XLS format. Choose Developer→XML→Export.

POWER USERS' CLINIC

XML Mapping with a Schema

Serious XML gurus don't map a worksheet using an XML document. There are too many possible problems, including optional elements that Excel might ignore, data type rules that it doesn't enforce, and certain types of structures that Excel might misunderstand.

A better way to map a worksheet to XML is to use an XML schema. A schema defines the structure of the XML document you want to import. If you create a worksheet to analyze lists of student grades, for example, you could define the elements you'll use, along with document's structure, in a file called StudentList.xsd.

XML mapping works more or less the same way with a schema as it does with an actual document. The key difference is that the schema removes the possibility for error. To map a schema, follow these steps:

1. Open the workbook in which you'd like to add the XML schema, or create a new workbook.
2. Select Developer→XML→XML Source to show the XML Source pane. In the XML Source pane, click the XML Maps button.
3. In the XML Maps window, click the Add button.
4. Browse to your XML schema file, and then click OK.
5. Click OK to close the XML Maps window. You now see the schema-defined elements in the XML Source pane.
6. Drag the elements from the XML Source pane to the worksheet.
7. When you finish, you need to import an XML document that has the same structure as the schema. To do so, select Developer→XML→Import, and then browse to the XML file.

When using an XML schema, Excel can perform validation with the schema data types to prevent invalid input. If you want to use this feature, you have to turn it on for the document. Select Data→XML→Map Properties. In the list of options, turn on the first checkbox, "Validate data against schema for import and export." Now, every time you import or export XML data, Excel checks it against the rules defined in the schema.

Mapping Lists

Excel's XML features really get interesting when you need to map XML documents that contain *lists* of information, like product catalogs, order tables, and—as in the following example—a class report. As you've no doubt noticed, most Excel documents use lists of some kind. Whether you track student grades, monthly expenses, or employee contact information, you rarely have just one piece of information.

XML documents are often designed to hold repeating elements. The Student.xml file, in contrast, held information for only a single student. But you can readily create a document that holds a list of students, each one in separate <Student> element containers.

Here's an example (available in the StudentList.xml file, which you can find on the Missing CD page at *www.missingmanuals.com/cds/excel2013mm*). Only two students are shown here, but the actual StudentList.xml file contains many more:

```
<?xml version="1.0" ?>
<Students>
    <Student>
        <Name>Lisa Chen</Name>
        <StudentID>45349920</StudentID>
        <Test1_Score>75</Test1_Score>
        <Test2_Score>63.23</Test2_Score>
        <Assignment1_Score>94</Assignment1_Score>
        <Assignment2_Score>90</Assignment2_Score>
    </Student>
    <Student>
        <Name>Edwin Albott</Name>
        <StudentID>45349921</StudentID>
        <Test1_Score>85</Test1_Score>
        <Test2_Score>73.23</Test2_Score>
        <Assignment1_Score>94</Assignment1_Score>
        <Assignment2_Score>95.6</Assignment2_Score>
    </Student>
    ...
</Students>
```

When you try to map this document, Excel quickly notices that the <Student> element repeats. Instead of mapping the <Student> element to a single cell (as it did in the previous section), Excel creates a mapped table that you can use to manage the list of students with filtering, sorting, and searching the data.

NOTE This example, in fact, creates the same type of table you studied in Chapter 14. So why bother mapping the info to an Excel table? Doing so gives you all of Excel's fancy table tools, like sorting, filtering, alternating row formatting, and so on.

To map the StudentList.xml file, follow these steps:

1. **Choose File→Open.**

   The Open File window appears.

2. **Browse to the StudentList.xml file, and then open it.**

   If you haven't already gotten this file, download it from the Missing CD page at *www.missingmanuals.com/cds/excel2013mm*. Excel shows an Open XML window with three options for the file.

3. **Select "Use the XML Source task pane," and then click OK.**

   Excel warns you that you're mapping a document without a schema.

4. **Click OK to continue.**

   The XML Source pane appears, with the structure of the StudentList.xml file. It looks similar to the previous example, but there's a difference now. When you drag an element onto the worksheet, Excel creates a table column complete with a header that has a drop-down list. Why? Because Excel recognizes that the StudentList.xml file contains multiple students, and it can't store all these student names in a single cell on your worksheet.

5. **Click the Student element, and then drag it to cell A1.**

   When multiple columns belong to the same XML list, it's often easiest to drag these elements onto your spreadsheet in one operation. You can select multiple elements by holding down the Ctrl key while you select items in the XML Source pane or by selecting the *parent* element (the element that contains all the elements you want to insert).

   In the student list example, if you select the Student entry in the XML Source pane, you also select *all* the elements that contain student information. You can then drag them all at once. It's entirely up to you whether you create your table as a series of contiguous columns (the easiest approach) or as separate columns spread out over your spreadsheet. Either way, the data is equivalent.

6. **Choose Data→Connections→Refresh All.**

   Now the student information flows into the table, filling it up automatically, as shown in Figure 28-6.

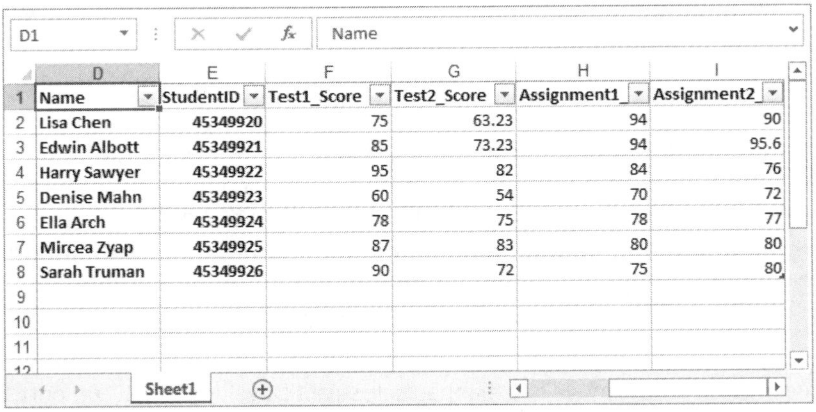

Name	StudentID	Test1_Score	Test2_Score	Assignment1_	Assignment2_
Lisa Chen	45349920	75	63.23	94	90
Edwin Albott	45349921	85	73.23	94	95.6
Harry Sawyer	45349922	95	82	84	76
Denise Mahn	45349923	60	54	70	72
Ella Arch	45349924	78	75	78	77
Mircea Zyap	45349925	87	83	80	80
Sarah Truman	45349926	90	72	75	80

FIGURE 28-6

This example shows a worksheet mapped with the table of student information. You can insert new students, remove existing ones, and edit student data before you export the information back to XML.

TIP In this example, all the XML data contains a repeating list of students. However, XML documents often use hybrid structures, where some information repeats, like the list of students here, and some information appears only once, like the name of the class and the name of the instructor teaching it. In this case, you'd probably link individual cells in the top portion of your worksheet, and then add the table a little lower down.

Gaining the Benefits of XML Mapping

Regardless of whether you want to import or export XML, you should always save a copy of your mapped spreadsheet. Excel stores the mapping information in that file. Essentially, you should think of this spreadsheet as a window that lets you analyze any XML file, as long as it has the same structure as the XML document you mapped.

For example, at the end of a semester, you might use an automated student-grading application that generates a new XML document with the most up-to-date information. Fortunately, you don't need to map this document, as long as its structure matches that of the grading document you used initially—you can import the new XML document with a couple of mouse clicks. The new information flows seamlessly into your existing workbook.

In a very real sense, you can reuse a mapped workbook to examine different XML files in the same way you can use a database query to get and analyze the most up-to-date information from a table in a database (as shown on page 836).

For example, consider the StudentList.xml workbook you created earlier. To make it a better tool for analyzing student grades, you'd probably add a few extra ingredients. Here are some possibilities:

- A calculated column in the table that determines each student's overall grade.
- A calculated field outside the table that determines the average or median grade.
- A chart that shows the distribution of grades in the class.

The beauty of XML mapping is that once you add these extra touches, you can *reuse* them with the data from other XML documents, provided these documents have the same structure as the document you used to map your worksheet. For example, you might receive a new file, called StudentList_Geography2010.xml, with a whole series of grades for another class. This document uses the same elements, so you don't need to go through the whole mapping process again.

Instead, you can just import this new information into your existing worksheet. All you need to do then is move to a mapped cell, select Developer→XML→Import, and then choose the StudentList_Geography2010.xml file. The student information flows into the linked cells on your worksheet, and Excel immediately updates the extra information you added to your worksheet, including the total grade calculation, average grade calculation, and the chart that shows grade distribution (see Figure 28-7).

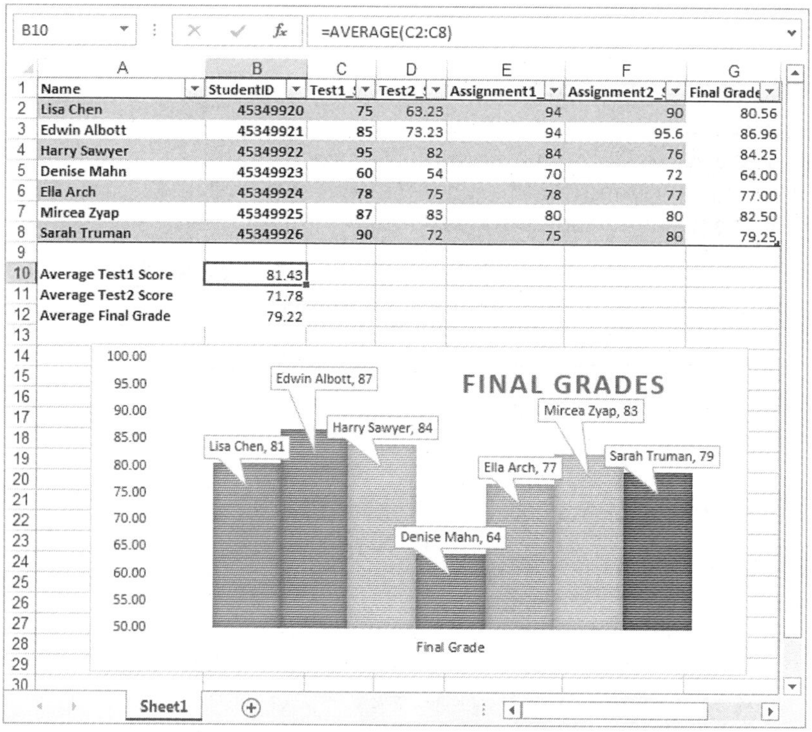

FIGURE 28-7

Here, you enhanced the linked table with a new column that calculates a student's final grade, performs a few summary calculations, and adds an attractive chart. Best of all, you can import another XML document with the exact same structure into your worksheet, potentially saving you hours of work.

Creating Web Queries

The Internet's greatest attraction (other than its ability to help Uncle Charlie auction his *The Y2K Bug Will End Life As We Know It* T-shirts) is that it provides a huge mass of continuously updated information. If you know where to look, you can find up-to-the-minute product prices, stock quotes, and sports scores.

And if you're like most web surfers, you can see this information only by using a web browser. That approach works well most of the time, but it limits what you can actually *do* with the information you find. Because one of Excel's strengths is helping you analyze data—whether it's in your worksheet, a relational database, or an XML document—you'll be glad to know that Excel can also help extract important information right off a live web page. This feature is called a *web query*.

When you perform a web query in Excel, you suck the data out of one or more tables on a web page and insert it into the cells in a worksheet, where you can work with them just as you do any other data. Excel also stores the web address you used and some information about the table you queried. That way, when you refresh a web query, Excel returns to the web page, grabs the new information from the same location, and then replaces it in your worksheet. That definitely beats copying and pasting!

The Limitations of Web Queries

Excel web queries seem downright miraculous. After all, who could pass up the ability to insert and update information from across the globe? But beware: Web queries are notoriously fragile. Due to the always changing nature of the Internet, a web query that works one day may not work properly the next. Here are some of the pitfalls:

- **Web queries are tied to specific web addresses.** If the website owner moves the information somewhere else, your web query can't find it.
- **Web queries find information based on the structure of a web page.** Minor changes in that web page (like adding a new table or even rearranging the order of elements) can throw Excel off, so it may download the wrong information or fail altogether.
- **Web queries rarely work on websites that require authentication.** That's because you need to log in before you can retrieve data. Excel can't tell that you haven't logged in, and its attempt to get the information fails.

NOTE Most of these shortcomings are factors that limit the *repeat use* of web queries. In other words, web queries usually work great the first time you use them. Just don't assume that you'll be able to easily update the information in the future, unless you're using a website that never changes.

So, what types of web pages are good candidates for web queries? Ideally, you'll use a page that has a simple, rigid structure, and puts the information you need in a table. Unfortunately, you often can't tell how complex a page is (or whether it uses tables) just by looking at it, so you may want to try a web query to assess whether it'll work. Also look for web pages where the structure and formatting never change, unless you're willing to create a new web query each time the web page you're drawing from changes. Some examples you may want to try include getting a temperature from a city-specific web page, reading a stock quote from a financial site, or getting the list price of a book on Amazon.com.

Creating a Web Query

Now that you're forewarned, you're ready to create a web query of your own. Follow these steps:

1. **Decide where you want to go to get the data you want to import into Excel.**

   Although you can actually browse different websites from within Excel (more on that in step 3), it's usually easiest to find the correct address using your web browser *before* you create a web query. That's because Excel's New Web Query window doesn't let you access your favorite Internet shortcuts.

   Excel finds a page based on its web address. So once you find the website you want using your web browser, just copy all the text in the address bar. You'll be able to paste it right into Excel's New Web Query window.

2. **Open the worksheet you want to use, or create a new worksheet.**

   You can place as many web queries as you want in a single worksheet, and you can freely mingle web queries with ordinary data.

3. **Choose Data→Get External Data→From Web.**

   The New Web Query window appears, shown in Figure 28-8. This window provides many of the conveniences of Internet Explorer, including an address bar and basic buttons for refreshing, stopping, and going forward and backward. The difference is that Excel automatically scans the page when you surf to it in the New Web Query window, looking for data that it can import. Every time it finds a table of information, it adds a tiny yellow arrow box next to the table. You click these arrow boxes to tell Excel what data you want to extract.

TIP The New Web Query window is resizable, so stretch away if you can't see all the information on a web page.

4. **Enter the web address for the page you want to use in the Address box. Hit Enter or click Go to load the page.**

   Optionally, you can enter the address for a search engine like Google (*www.google.com*), perform a search, and then browse to the page you want. But the quickest and most reliable approach, as discussed previously, is to find the page in a standalone browser first (like Internet Explorer), and then copy that page's web address to the New Web Query window.

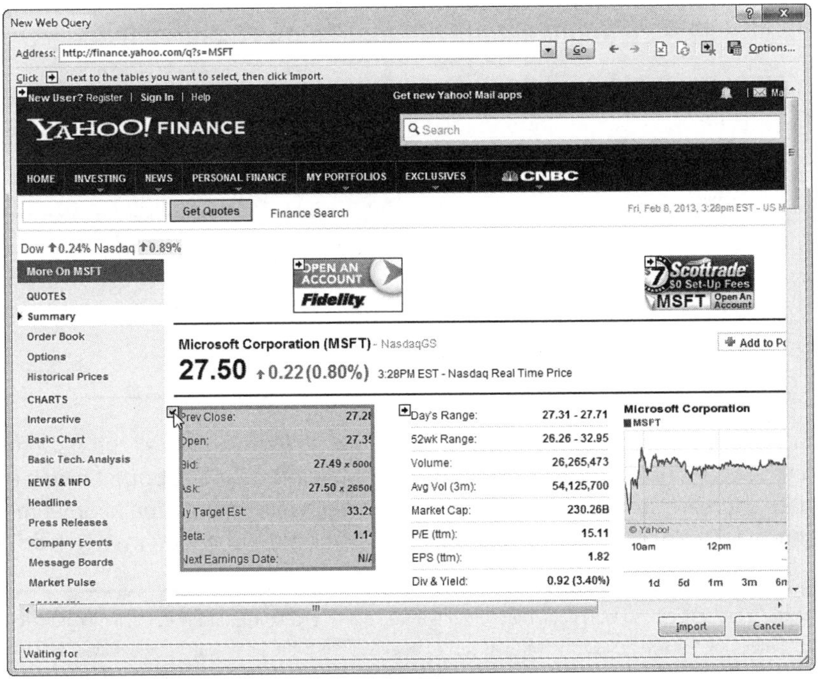

FIGURE 28-8

Here's the New Web Query window with a page from Yahoo! Finance. Each arrow-in-a-box represents a table of info that Excel's capable of importing. To give Excel the go-ahead, click any arrow to transform it into a checkmark, like the one shown here next to the table of data about Microsoft's stock performance.

5. **Select the table you want to extract.**

   When the page appears in the New Web Query window, Excel adds yellow arrow boxes next to every table you can import. As you hover over each arrow box with your mouse, Excel draws a bold blue outline around the related table.

   Once you find the table you want to extract, click the arrow box (which then changes to a green checkmark). To deselect a table, just click the box again.

6. **When you finish selecting all the tables you want, click the Import button at the bottom of the New Web Query window.**

   The Import Data window appears.

7. **Choose where you want your data to go, and then click OK.**

   To insert the extracted information into your current worksheet, select the "Existing worksheet" option, and then enter a cell reference. If you use the cell reference $A$1, Excel starts the first column of the first row in cell A1.

   If you want to insert the information into a new worksheet, select the "New worksheet" option.

Once you click OK, Excel retrieves the information and inserts it into your worksheet, as shown in Figure 28-9.

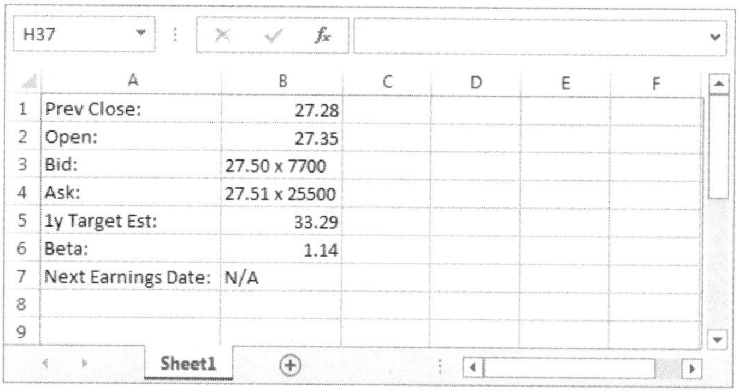

FIGURE 28-9

Excel pulls the data out of the formatted HTML page and converts it into a plain text-and-numbers table you can analyze to your heart's content.

When you save a worksheet that uses a web query, Excel stores all the data that's now in the cells of your worksheet, along with some information about the web query's data source. You can grab the latest version of your information at any time by moving to any one of the linked cells and choosing Data→Connections→Refresh All.

NOTE When you open a workbook that contains a web query, Excel turns off the Refresh All command and shows the message bar with a security warning, just to be safe. (This is the same watchdog behavior you learned about on page 839 with databases.) To turn on your web query, just click the Enable Content button to designate your workbook as a trusted document (page 904).

The Web world changes quickly, and a web query that works fine today may fail tomorrow for trivial reasons. For example, the page you're querying may be renamed, or the data you want may be pushed into a different table. Depending on the extent of the changes, you may be able to modify your web query so that it keeps working. Follow these steps to make your changes:

1. **Choose Data→Connections→Connections.**

   The Workbook Connections window appears. It lists all the connections that link to outside data, including databases, XML files, and web queries.

2. **Find your web query connection in the list (which is probably the only connection you've created so far), and then click Properties.**

   The Connection Properties window appears. Here you can give your connection a better name and description, and then set it to refresh your data periodically (either every time you open the file or after a certain number of minutes). Page 843 has more on Excel's automatic refresh feature.

3. **Click the Definitions tab, and then click the Edit Query button.**

   This opens an Edit Web Query window, which looks exactly the same as the New Web Query window. Using this window, you can choose a different table, or even enter a different web page URL.

4. **When you finish, click Import.**

   Click OK to close the Connection Properties window, and then click OK again to close the Workbook Connections window and return to your worksheet.

Connecting to Online Data Services with OData

When web queries work, they're wonderful. There's no need to join a company network or fiddle with a database connection—instead, you get real-time information straight from the Internet.

The disadvantage of web queries is that they're fragile. Web pages were designed to present richly formatted information in a web browser. They're not the best way to share data. As a result, the web query that works for you today may fail tomorrow, and you'll need to rebuild it all over again (and possibly restructure your workbook, too).

For the past decade, large technology companies like Microsoft, Google, Apple, and IBM have been hard at work on standards that provide better ways for programs to share information over the Web. Their goal has been to combine a clean, universal data exchange format (like XML) with the simple networking of the Internet. One of the most recent attempts in this endeavor is a Microsoft-sponsored technology called Open Data Protocol (or OData for short).

It's too soon to tell if OData will become a widely adopted standard. However, it's not too early for you to start *using* OData, because Excel handles all the hard work. It has the ability to talk to an OData service anywhere on the Internet, fetch the information you want, and then download it to your workbook. In fact, Excel can talk to an OData service just as easily as it communicates with a database (page 833).

UP TO SPEED

Understanding OData

You don't need to understand the technical underpinnings of OData to use it. Instead, all you need is a link to an OData service and a copy of Excel. If you're trying to evaluate whether OData is a good fit for your organization, or you're just plain curious, it's worth a closer look.

OData allows *clients* (which can include custom software or Excel spreadsheets) to communicate with *web services* (programs that run on high-powered web servers). They talk to each other over HTTP, the same protocol that lets browsers request web pages.

The first step in an OData interaction is for the client to send a request message. For example, a common request is to ask the web service for some data (like a list of product sales from 2013). When the server receives the message, it sends back the data. This exchange is similar to the way web queries work, but with a critical difference: The messages sent back and forth contain clearly organized data in a specific XML language. There's no fancy formatting or extra web page junk.

OData isn't the only technology that uses this approach of sending XML-encoded messages back and forth over an HTTP connection. In fact, virtually *all* web querying technologies use this approach. (Example includes RESTful web services, XML-RPC, and SOAP.) The key difference is that OData doesn't just standardize the way web services talk to each other, it also standardizes the way that common data operations, like filtering, sort, and updating, work. For all the techy details, you can visit Microsoft's OData site at *www.odata.org.*

Creating an OData Query

Before you can create an OData query, you need to find an OData service that provides the information you want. If you get data from a large company or organization, they may already have an OData service you can work with. (And it that case, they'll give you a link that points to it.) But you can also find more than a few free, public OData services on the Web and use them to test Excel's OData features. You may even find a public OData service that provides genuinely useful information.

Microsoft provides a list of live OData services that you can play with at *www.odata.org/ecosystem*. The following example uses the OData service for Netflix, which lets you explore its huge catalog of movies. For specific information about the Netflix OData service, visit *http://tinyurl.com/netflix-odata* (Figure 28-10).

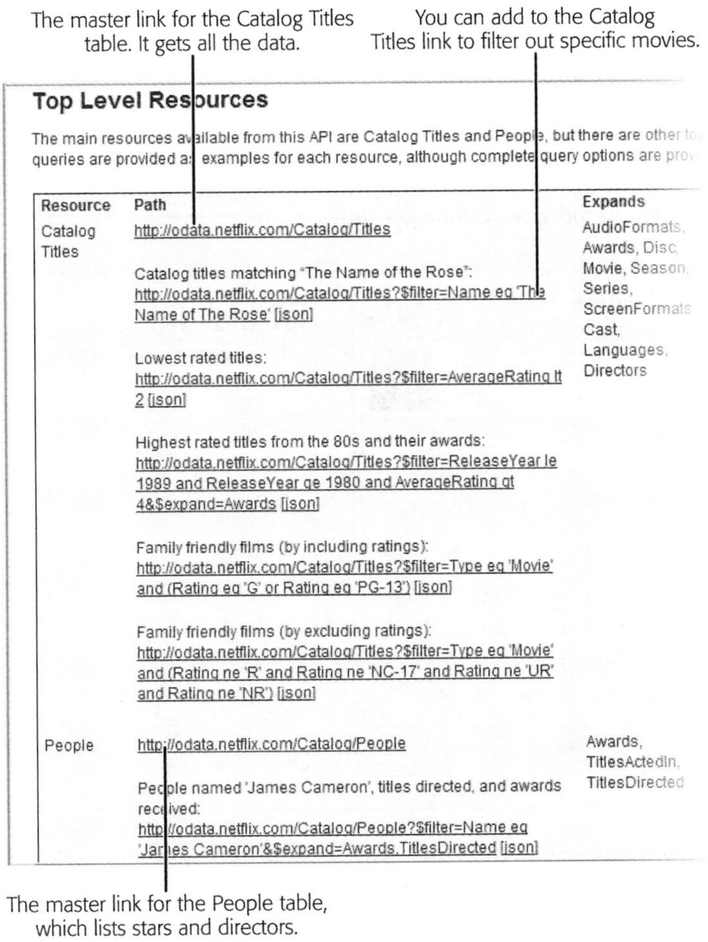
The master link for the Catalog Titles table. It gets all the data.
You can add to the Catalog Titles link to filter out specific movies.
Top Level Resources
The main resources available from this API are Catalog Titles and People, but there are other
queries are provided as examples for each resource, although complete query options are
Resource
Path
Expands
Catalog Titles
http://odata.netflix.com/Catalog/Titles
AudioFormats, Awards, Disc, Movie, Season, Series, ScreenFormats, Cast, Languages, Directors
Catalog titles matching "The Name of the Rose":
http://odata.netflix.com/Catalog/Titles?$filter=Name eq 'The Name of The Rose' [json]
Lowest rated titles:
http://odata.netflix.com/Catalog/Titles?$filter=AverageRating lt 2 [json]
Highest rated titles from the 80s and their awards:
http://odata.netflix.com/Catalog/Titles?$filter=ReleaseYear le 1989 and ReleaseYear ge 1980 and AverageRating gt 4&$expand=Awards [json]
Family friendly films (by including ratings):
http://odata.netflix.com/Catalog/Titles?$filter=Type eq 'Movie' and (Rating eq 'G' or Rating eq 'PG-13') [json]
Family friendly films (by excluding ratings):
http://odata.netflix.com/Catalog/Titles?$filter=Type eq 'Movie' and (Rating ne 'R' and Rating ne 'NC-17' and Rating ne 'UR' and Rating ne 'NR') [json]
People
http://odata.netflix.com/Catalog/People
Awards, TitlesActedIn, TitlesDirected
People named 'James Cameron', titles directed, and awards received:
http://odata.netflix.com/Catalog/People?$filter=Name eq 'James Cameron'&$expand=Awards,TitlesDirected [json]
The master link for the People table, which lists stars and directors.

FIGURE 28-10

The information page for the Netflix OData service is filled with sample links. The links shown here get movie titles and actor names, but there are many more choices farther down the page. (You can click the links to view the data in your browser, but the data will appear in an XML document, which isn't terribly easy to read.)

You can create an OData connection just as easily as you add a connection to an Access database file or a SQL Server database server. Here's the process:

1. **Choose Data→Get External Data→From Other Sources→From OData Data Feed.**

   The Data Connection Wizard starts up.

2. **In the "Link or File" box, type in the URL that points to the OData service you want to use (Figure 28-11).**

   For example, to download the full set of movie information from Netflix, you'd use *http://odata.netflix.com/Catalog/Titles.*

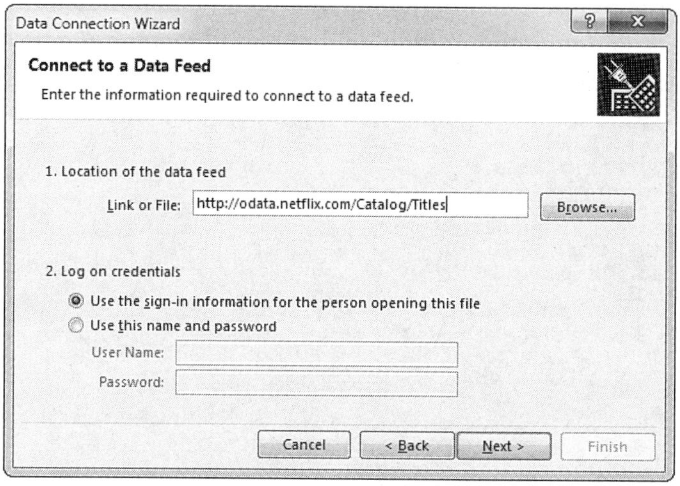

FIGURE 28-11

This URL tells Excel to download the movie catalog from Netflix.

3. **If the service requires you to supply a user name and password, click "Use this name and password" and type in your credentials.**

   The other option, "Use the sign-in information for the person opening this file", means that Excel will attempt to use your currently logged in Windows user account to gain access to the OData service. However, if you use a public service like Netflix, you don't need authorization, so this setting is of no importance.

4. **Click Next.**

   Excel contacts the OData service and shows you a list of the tables you can import (Figure 28-12).

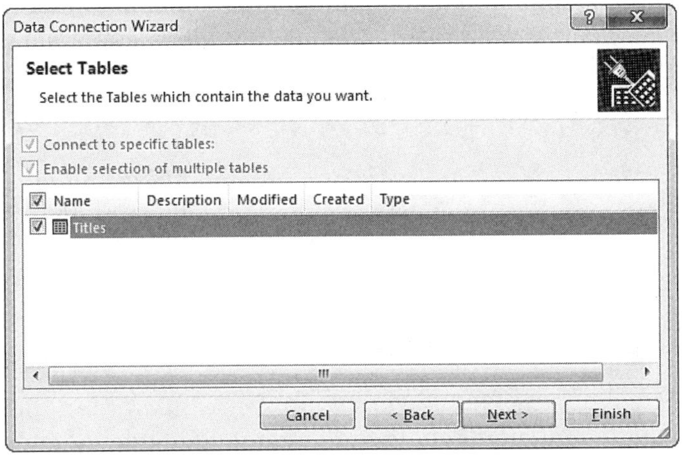

FIGURE 28-12

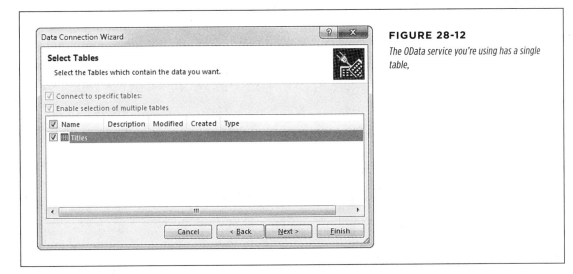

The OData service you're using has a single table,

5. **Add a checkmark next to the table you want to download.**

   If you see more than one table, add a checkmark next to each one you want to import.

6. **Click Next.**

   Excel offers to save your connection.

7. **Optionally, fill in some descriptive information for your connection in the Description and Friendly Name boxes.**

   The friendly name should be a short meaningful name, like "Netflix Movie Titles." The description can include any information that you think describes your connection.

   Once Excel saves your connection, you'll be able to reuse it in other workbooks (page 844).

8. **Click Finish.**

   Excel asks where you want to put the data from the OData service.

9. **Choose the standard option, Table, to insert the data into one of your worksheets.**

   In the rare case that you're importing more than 2 million records, you'll need to use a pivot table or pivot chart instead, as explained on page 847.

10. **Click OK.**

    Excel begins to fetch the information it needs. During this time, you'll see a "Retrieving data" message in the Excel status bar (Figure 28-13). If the query is taking a long time, you can click this message to cancel it. Otherwise, Excel continues working until it receives all the data, which it then inserts into your worksheet (Figure 28-14).

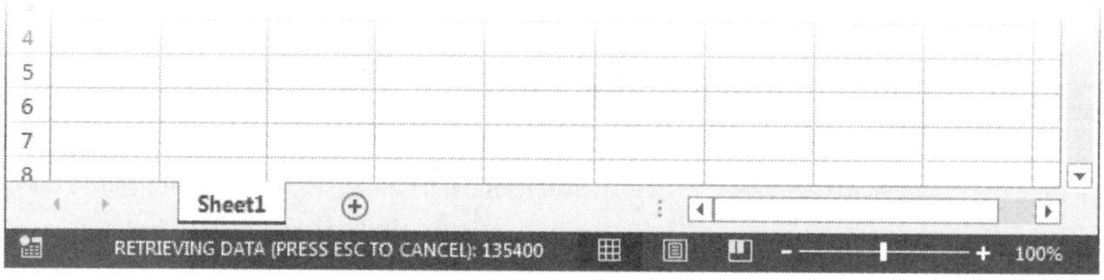

FIGURE 28-13

Excel uses the status bar to keep you to up to date on its download progress. Here, Excel has retrieved 135,400 records, but it's not finished.

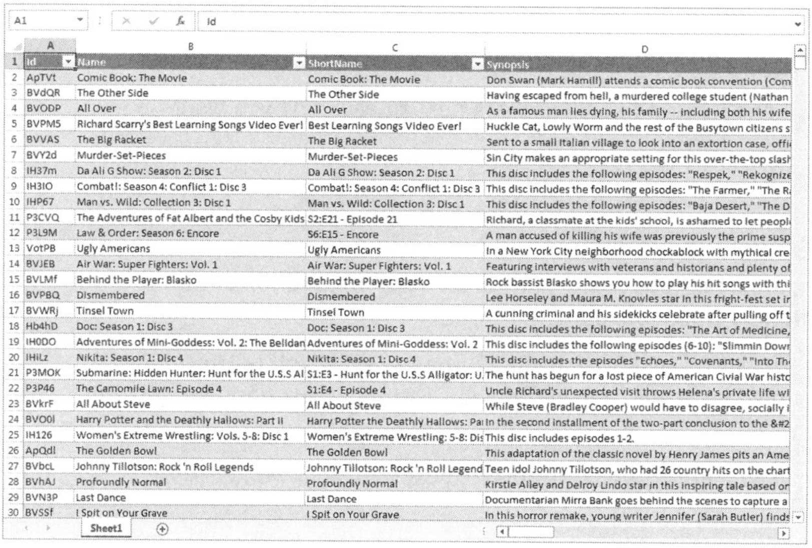

FIGURE 28-14

Here's the result of the Netflix query—a long list of movies that includes titles, release dates, brief summaries, and even a link to the movie's box art image.

POWER USERS' CLINIC

The Web Service Functions

Excel includes a small set of functions that can call simple web services (ones that provide small amounts of information and don't require authentication). They are:

- **WEBSERVICE()** calls a web service (at the web address you supply) and returns the full text of the response message. Usually, this response takes the form of a lengthy and difficult-to-interpret XML document, which isn't much use to you. (That's where the next function comes in.)
- **FILTERXML()** hunts through an XML document looking for a specific element at a specific location you specify. (To pull this off, you need to understand XPath, the XML search-and-navigation standard.) You can use FILTERXML() with the response message returned by WEBSERVICE() to find the one piece of information you actually want. You can then show that information in a cell or use it in a calculation.
- **ENCODEURL()** takes a small piece of information and converts it into a form that can be safely used in a web URL. This function works in conjunction with WEBSERVICE() in cases where you need to send some information *to* a web service. For example, if you're calling a web service that tells you the current temperature for a given city, you might use ENCODEURL() to convert the name of the city to a URL-friendly format, which you can then tack onto the end of the URL you're using with WEBSERVICE().

The advantage of these functions is that you can use them directly from your worksheet—you don't even need to delve into Visual Basic code. Unfortunately, the idea is great in theory, but awkward in practice. The web service functions are complex, and require a deep understanding of XML. They don't support complex web services, and they often need to be used in combination—for example, when creating a formula that calls a web service you might need to use ENCODEURL() inside WEBSERVICE(), and then put the whole thing inside FILTERXML(). All in all, Excel's web query and data connection features are easier to use than these web functions. But if you'd like to learn more, you can review the functions in Excel's online documentation at *http://tinyurl.com/webfuncs*.

PART 7

Programming Excel

CHAPTER

29

Automating Tasks with Macros

No one wants to repeat the same task over and over again. Excel gurus especially hate the drudgery of repetitious work like data entry and formatting cell after cell after cell. Fortunately, Excel offers serious time saving tools called *macros*—miniature programs that automatically perform a series of steps within any workbook.

Excel macros are written in a full-blown programming language called *VBA* (short for Visual Basic for Applications). VBA is a scaled-down version of the incredibly popular Visual Basic programming language, and it's fined-tuned for Excel and other Office programs. Fortunately, you don't need to be a programmer to use VBA. In fact, you can create a simple macro using a special Excel tool called the *macro recorder*. The macro recorder works like a tape recorder, but instead of recording audio, it records keystrokes and mouse actions as you perform them.

In this chapter, you'll learn how to use the macro recorder, how macros work, and where Excel stores them. You'll also learn how to attach macros to shortcut keys, the Quick Access toolbar, and buttons in your worksheet. In the next chapter, your exploration goes one step further and plunges into the VBA language.

Macros 101

Macros can automate everything from simple tasks to complex operations, making your life immensely easier. Here are examples of tasks people commonly use macros for:

- Quickly inserting a group of cells you need often (like a company header for a report).
- Applying complex formatting to multiple rows or columns.
- Cleaning up text, rearranging cells, or transferring information from one place to another.
- Printing data in a specific format. This operation could involve switching to a custom view, selecting part of a worksheet, and then choosing specific print options (like paper size or the number of copies).
- Analyzing a selection of cells, perhaps by adding a set of functions or even by generating a specialized chart.

These examples are just the tip of the macro iceberg. When you create a macro, you can use the full range of Excel's features. It's like having a personal assistant, skilled in the ways of Excel, ready to carry out whatever instructions you provide.

Excel gives you two ways to create a macro:

- **Write the macro by hand, using pure VBA code.** This option isn't as difficult as you may think, but it isn't easy either. The problem isn't learning the *syntax*, or rules, of the VBA language (which are fairly basic), it's learning how to find all the Excel features you want to use. When you want to enter text in a cell, create a new worksheet, or print a selection, you need to find the right Excel *object* to handle the job. Objects are programming tools that let you get at features you need. For example, if you want to write macro code that spell-checks your spreadsheet, you need to know the name of the spell-checker object.
- **Record the macro using the Excel macro recorder.** You turn the recorder on, and then go about your business, entering text, navigating a worksheet, and selecting choices from Excel's ribbon. While you work, Excel records each operation and translates it into the corresponding VBA code. When you finish, you can stop the recorder, save the macro, and replay it to repeat all the actions you just performed.

Using the macro recorder is the simplest approach, particularly if you've never used a programming language before. However, writing macros by hand is much more powerful and flexible. It lets you create macros that can make decisions, repeat actions in a loop, and even prompt whoever's viewing your worksheet to enter some information.

In the next chapter, you'll take a closer look at the intricacies of VBA and start digging through the vast collection of Excel objects. In this chapter, you'll get right to work creating simple macros with the macro recorder.

NOTE There's a middle ground between writing macros yourself and having Excel record your actions. You can record a macro with the macro recorder, and then tweak the VBA code with the Visual Basic editor to make your macro more powerful. At the start of the next chapter, you'll take a look at what a recorded macro looks like from inside the Visual Basic editor.

Macro-Free and Macro-Enabled Workbooks

In Chapter 1, you took your first look at Excel's file formats (page 29). So far, you've stuck with Excel's *.xlsx* file type, the format of choice. However, .xlsx files have a serious limitation when it comes to macro writing—they can't store macros. That means you need to either choose a different format for your workbook (one that does support macros), or store your macros elsewhere, in a workbook that does have macro-storing abilities (which you can then use in conjunction with the macro-free workbook that houses your data).

Fortunately, Excel has two perfectly good file formats that support macros and all the same features as their macro-free counterparts:

- **.xlsm files** are macro-enabled workbooks. They're identical to .xlsx files, except they have the added ability to store macro code. Like .xlsx files, .xlsm files are stored using XML.
- **.xlsb files** are workbooks stored in binary format, which is more efficient for certain types of files (like very large spreadsheets). They also allow macro code.

Microsoft recommends that you use the .xlsm format. In some situations, extremely complex files may load faster if you store them in the .xlsb format. To review the difference between Excel's XML-based formats (like .xlsm) and its binary formats (like .xlsb), see page 29.

FIGURE 29-1

Excel gives macro-enabled workbooks (both .xlsm and .xlsb files) a different icon, with a superimposed exclamation mark. This icon lets you recognize a macro-enabled workbook—like the MacroWorkbook shown here on the Windows desktop—before you open it. But don't get too paranoid just yet. As you'll discover on page 903, Excel's macro security features make sure there's little to fear about malicious macro code.

FREQUENTLY ASKED QUESTION

A Reason to Like Macro-Free Workbooks

Why doesn't everyone use .xlsm files? Whose idea was it to create a file format that supports fewer features?

At first glance, it seems that Microsoft could have avoided a lot of confusion if it had just created a single file format and made sure that file format was able to store macro files. After all, why encourage people to use a file format that can't do everything?

The reason Microsoft created .xlsx files (and the reason they're standard when you don't need macro support) is security. In recent years, Microsoft's become increasingly paranoid, as have the thousands of companies using Excel in a business setting. Their nightmare is that one day the company accountant opens an innocent-looking Excel spreadsheet, and a malicious macro toasts the computer.

Of course, evil Excel macros are fairly rare, and you're guaranteed to stay safe if you avoid opening spreadsheets that come from mysterious sources (like a "Get Well Endowed" email message). But as more companies use Excel to deal with sensitive, mission-critical information, even a small risk is too high. As you'll learn a little later (page 904), Microsoft automatically disables macros when you open a macro-enabled workbook for the first time. It's up to you to re-enable them and accept the risk.

So what does all this have to do with the two file formats? These formats let network administrators quickly distinguish between macro-free files (.xlsx), which are always safe, and potentially risky macro-enabled files (.xslm). And thanks to the different file extensions, administrators can create spam-blocking rules that automatically remove macro-enabled workbooks that are attached to email messages. In other words, a little bit of extra complexity makes it easier to keep company systems safe.

The Macro Recorder

Excel's macro recorder is easy to use, but keep a few key points in mind as you record so that you end up with a great collection of really useful tools:

- **Excel is watching you.** Excel captures every ribbon command or keyboard shortcut you use. In other words, don't do anything that you don't want the macro to do, unless you're willing to edit the VBA macro code after the fact. Also, try to avoid switching to another program while you record an Excel macro. Even though the macro recorder ignores anything you do outside of Excel, it's easy to confuse yourself and inadvertently add macro code you don't want by jumping back and forth.
- **You don't need to work fast.** The macro recorder doesn't record anything in between each action you perform. If you browse through the ribbon for 20 minutes before you eventually select Home→Clipboard→Paste, Excel just adds a single line of VBA code to your macro—the line it needs to invoke the Home→Clipboard→Paste command. As a result, macros tend to execute very quickly when you replay them—much more quickly, in fact, than when you perform the actions yourself.

- **Try to be generic.** The ideal macro is general enough that you can reuse it in a wide range of scenarios. If you make a macro so specific that you can use it only once, the macro won't get much use, and all your hard work will be wasted.

Before you jump into the macro-recording studio, it helps to understand the difference between recording modes and to know where Excel saves your macros. The next two sections cover these topics in detail.

Relative and Absolute Recording

When you click a command in the ribbon, Excel's macro recorder knows exactly what you're doing. However, sometimes Excel needs a little guidance from you in order to decide how to interpret some of your actions. When you type in text, Excel can interpret your action in two different ways, depending on which of two recording modes you're in (page 901 tells you how to change modes):

- **Absolute reference mode.** In absolute reference mode, Excel stores absolute references (the ones with the dollar signs) for the cells you modify (for a refresher on absolute cell references, see page 251). When you play the macro again, the macro affects only these cells.

- **Relative reference mode.** In relative reference mode, Excel tracks how far you move from your starting position. That means that when you play the macro again, Excel takes your *current* location into account.

You can most easily understand the difference between the two modes by following an example. Imagine you move to cell A1, and then start recording a macro. You then move two columns to the right to cell C1, type in the number 42, and then save the macro.

If you used absolute reference mode, here's the series of instructions that Excel stores in your macro:

1. Move to cell C1.
2. Enter the number 42.

On the other hand, if you used relative reference mode, Excel stores this list of instructions:

1. Move two columns to the right (from wherever the active cell is).
2. Enter the number 42.

You'll see the difference if you clear the worksheet, move to cell E10, and play the macro. If you used absolute reference mode when you recorded the macro, the macro always returns to cell C1 to enter its information. If you used relative reference mode, Excel enters the number 42 two cells to the right of the current cell, cell G10 in this example.

NOTE Absolute reference mode works if your data always needs to be in the same position. This need arises most often when you have to add some sort of header information at the top of a worksheet. Relative reference mode works if you need to repeat a task in several places—like bolding, italicizing, and enlarging the font in a series of cells you choose. It's the most common approach.

Where Macros Live

Once you craft the perfect macro, you need to make sure Excel stores it so you can find it later on. In Excel, every macro's attached to a workbook and saved in that workbook's .xlsm file. When you open a workbook that contains a set of macros, Excel makes them available instantly.

Excel beginners often assume that before you can use a macro in a particular workbook, you need to store the macro inside *that* workbook. In fact, macros have a much greater range. As soon as you open a workbook that contains macros, Excel makes those macros available to every other workbook that's currently open.

In other words, imagine you're editing a workbook named SalesReport.xlsx, and you open another workbook named MyMacroCollection.xlsm, which contains a few useful macros. You can use the macros contained in MyMacroCollection.xlsm with SalesReport.xlsx without a hitch. Once you close MyMacroCollection.xlsm, those macros are no longer available to SalesReport.xlsx.

This design makes it easy to share and reuse macros across workbooks (and between different people). It's up to you whether you want to store macros in your most commonly used workbooks or create standalone workbooks that hold collections of useful macros.

When you record a macro, Excel gives you three slightly different storage options:

- **This Workbook.** If you choose this option, Excel stores your macro in the current workbook. Remember, you need to save this workbook as a macro-enabled .xlsm file or a binary .xlsb file, or you'll lose your macros.
- **New Workbook.** If you choose this option, Excel automatically creates a new workbook (which it opens in a separate window) and stores your macro there.
- **Personal Macro Workbook.** If you choose this option, Excel stores your macro in a special hidden workbook named Personal.xlsb. When you record a macro in the personal workbook, you have a choice. You can save it permanently, so that it's always at your fingertips when you're using Excel, no matter what workbook you're editing. Or, you can use it temporarily, and then toss it away when you're finished. Excel asks you whether you want to save your personal workbook macros when you close the program.

Just because you place a macro in a specific location doesn't mean it needs to stay there. In fact, it's quite easy to copy a macro from one workbook to another, or even move it into and out of the personal macro workbook. All you have to do is fire up the Visual Basic editor and learn a little bit about how it organizes macro code. You'll get an introduction to the editor in the next chapter.

TIP One useful place to put macros is in an Excel template. That way, every time you or anyone else creates a new workbook based on the template, you have immediate access to the macros. To store macros in a template, record them inside the template using the This Workbook option. See Chapter 16 for more on templates.

FREQUENTLY ASKED QUESTION

Locating the Personal Macro Workbook

Where's the personal macro workbook hidden?

It makes sense to save your most useful macros in your personal macro workbook so they're always available, without requiring any extra steps. Excel stores the personal macro workbook in a file called Personal.xlsb, which lives in a folder named XLStart.

You can find the XLStart folder in a location like *C:\Users\UserName\AppData\Roaming\Microsoft\Excel\XLStart*, where UserName indicates the account name of whomever is currently logged on to Windows. So if you're logged in as the user billjones, you'll find the personal workbook in *C:\Users\billjones\AppData\Roaming\Microsoft\Excel\XLStart.*

Each person with an account on your PC has a separate personal workbook, so if you log on as someone else, you won't have the same collection of macros. Also, keep in mind that Excel doesn't actually create the personal macro workbook until you add record your first macro and exit Excel. So, unless you recorded at least one macro for the personal macro workbook to hold, there's no point hunting for it or the XLStart folder.

But if you're in the habit of placing a lot of important macros in the Personal.xlsb file, you should search it out. That way, you can easily back it up so you don't lose all your hard work when the next computer virus strikes.

Recording a Macro

Now that you know the basics of Excel macros, it's time to try creating one:

1. **Choose View→Macros→Macros→Record Macro.**

   The Record Macro window appears (Figure 29-2).

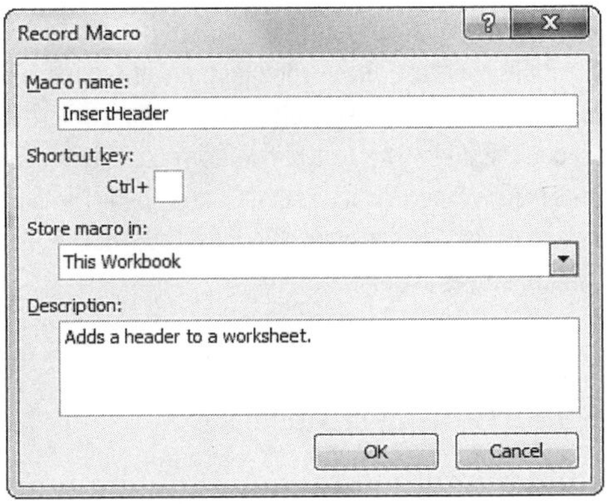

FIGURE 29-2

Here, Excel is about to start recording a macro named InsertHeader. Excel will store this macro in the current workbook, along with an optional description. Since you left the "Shortcut key" box blank, Excel won't assign a shortcut key to the macro.

TIP For an even faster way to start recording a new macro, click the macro recording button, which appears on the left end of the status bar. It looks like a worksheet window with a tiny circle superimposed on top. If you don't see the button, right-click the status bar and make sure the Macro Record item is checked.

2. **Type in a name for your macro.**

   The macro name must begin with a letter and can include letters, numbers, and the underscore character (_), but it can't include spaces or other special characters. Use a descriptive macro name like CompanyHeader or CreateSalesChart, because you'll identify the macro based on the name later on. (The macro name is also the name Excel uses when it records the VBA instructions.)

3. **If you want to create a keyboard shortcut, choose one now.**

   Shortcut keys let you launch your macros in a hurry. The only shortcut keys you can use are Ctrl+*letter* combinations. You can use uppercase or lowercase letters, as in Ctrl+A (which means hold down the Ctrl key, and then press A) and Ctrl+Shift+A (which means hold down the Ctrl and Shift keys, and then press A).

WORD TO THE WISE

The Dangers of Macro Shortcuts

Using shortcut keys can be dangerous because Excel doesn't warn you if you choose a shortcut key that corresponds to another Excel task.

If this sort of conflict happens, Excel always uses the shortcut key for the *macro*. This habit can cause confusion if other people use your macros and you replace a common shortcut key. Imagine their surprise when they hit Ctrl+S to save a document and end up triggering a macro that turns all negative numbers positive.

Here are some common key combinations that you should *never* assign to macro shortcuts, because people use them too frequently:

- Ctrl+S (Save)
- Ctrl+P (Print)
- Ctrl+O (Open)
- Ctrl+N (New)
- Ctrl+X (Exit)
- Ctrl+Z (Undo)
- Ctrl+Y (Redo/Repeat)
- Ctrl+C (Copy)
- Ctrl+X (Cut)
- Ctrl+V (Paste)

To avoid problems, always use Ctrl+Shift+*letter* macro key combinations, because these combinations are much less common than the Ctrl+*letter* shortcut keys. And if you're in doubt, don't assign a shortcut key when you create a new, untested macro, especially if you think it may conflict with an Excel shortcut key. You can always assign a shortcut key later if the macro proves extremely useful.

4. **Choose a storage location from the "Store macro in" list.**

   This option determines where Excel saves the macro.

5. **In the Description text box, type a description for the macro.**

   You can use the description to help you identify macros later on. Excel also adds the description to the macro code as a series of comments.

6. **Click OK to start recording the macro.**

   At this point, macro recording begins. If the macro record button is visible on the Status bar, it changes to a nondescript white square (Figure 29-3).

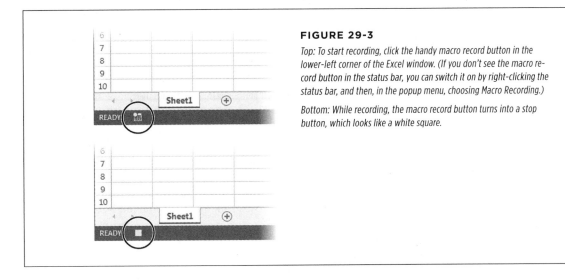

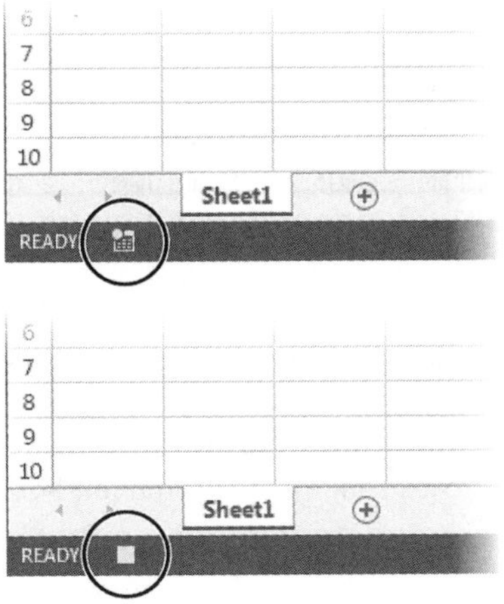

FIGURE 29-3

Top: To start recording, click the handy macro record button in the lower-left corner of the Excel window. (If you don't see the macro record button in the status bar, you can switch it on by right-clicking the status bar, and then, in the popup menu, choosing Macro Recording.)

Bottom: While recording, the macro record button turns into a stop button, which looks like a white square.

7. **Decide whether you want to use absolute or relative cell references.**

   To use relative references, make sure you select the View→Macros→Macros→Use Relative References button. To use absolute references, make sure the Use Relative References button is ***not*** selected.

   Remember, if you use absolute references, Excel always replays your actions on the same cells. If you use relative references, Excel executes your actions according to where you are at the time you launch the macro (see page 897 for a description of the difference between the two modes).

NOTE It's possible to create a macro that performs some actions in relative reference mode, and some in absolute reference mode. You just click the Relative Reference button on or off while you record the macro. However, this approach can lead to much confusion, so unless you're very comfortable with macros, you'll probably want to pick one system before you start recording, and then stick with it.

8. **Perform the actions you want Excel to record.**

   The macro recorder records all the actions you take, from worksheet editing and formatting to ribbon commands (like switching views, printing a document, creating a chart, and so on).

NOTE The macro recorder stores code, not your specific actions. That means it doesn't matter whether you activate a feature using a shortcut key, the Quick Access toolbar, or the ribbon. In all cases, the macro code is the same.

9. **Choose View→Macros→Macros→Stop Recording to save the macro (or click the stop square in the status bar).**

   Excel stops recording and quietly stores your macro. Excel doesn't show any confirmation message—the only way you can tell that the macro recorder is off is by looking at the ribbon or status bar, where the record button replaces the stop button.

10. **Save the workbook that has your macro in it.**

NOTE If you try to save a workbook that contains a macro using Excel's macro-free .xlsx file format, you receive an error message warning you that you'll lose your macros. Instead, choose File→Save As, and then, from the "Save as type" list, pick "Excel Macro Enabled Workbook (*.xlsm)."

If you opted to save your macro file in the personal macro workbook (in step 4), your macro isn't stored permanently until you close Excel. At that point, Excel asks you if you want to save the changes you made to the personal macro workbook. Click Save and Excel stores your macro permanently, so it's available the next time you need it.

Playing a Macro

Once you've recorded a macro, it's even easier to play it back. Just follow these steps:

1. **Move to the location where you want to play the macro.**

   The location doesn't make a difference if your macro doesn't modify the worksheet, or if it uses absolute reference mode. On the other hand, if your macro uses relative reference mode and it modifies or formats cells, it's important to select the cell where you want to apply the changes.

   If you want to test your macro in a completely new workbook, select File→New to create a new file. Just remember to keep your original workbook open if it contains the macro you want to use.

2. **Choose View→Macros→Macros. Keyboard lovers can also use the handy Alt+F8 shortcut.**

   The Macro window appears, with a list of all the macros in your personal workbook and in any open workbooks (see Figure 29-4). You can filter this list (to show things like only macros in the current workbook or those in the personal macro workbook) by choosing a different option from the "Macros in" list.

NOTE If you get an error message informing you that Excel has turned off the macros in your workbook (which it does automatically when you close and reopen it), you need to take a few extra steps. The next section has the scoop on macro security.

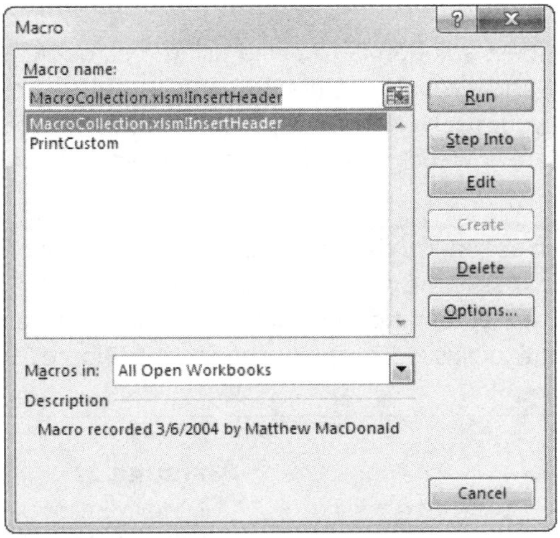

FIGURE 29-4

The Macro window lists all the macros in every open workbook, as well as those in your personal workbook. This example has two available macros. The first one, InsertHeader, is located in another workbook. Excel uses a name that starts with the name of the workbook file to indicate this fact (MacroCollection.xlsm!InsertHeader). The second macro, PrintCustom, is in the current workbook, so the file name isn't present. The Macro window also includes a Delete button that lets you remove a macro, and several additional buttons for editing and debugging macro code, which you'll learn about in the next chapter.

3. **Select a macro from the list, and then click Run.**

   Excel closes the Macro window and runs the macro. Don't blink—99 percent of all macros replay so quickly that you can't see the changes being made. Instead, the modifications seem to appear all at once.

CAUTION Once you play a macro, you're stuck with the changes. Sadly, the Undo feature can't reverse a macro, so make sure you save your worksheet before trying out an untested macro.

Using the Macros window, you can attach a shortcut key to an existing macro. Just select View→Macros→Macros, and then select the macro you want to modify. Click Options, and then type in (or change) the shortcut key. Once your macro has a shortcut key, you can trigger the macro by pressing the appropriate key combination, without making a return visit to the Macros window.

Macro Security

Excel's macro language is surprisingly powerful. In fact, the VBA language packs enough power for both expert gurus *and* hackers who want to design malicious worksheet viruses. Unfortunately, macros aren't limited to moving from cell to cell, entering information, formatting data, and so on. Instead, macros can use full-fledged VBA code (which you'll consider in the next chapter) to delete files and even lobotomize your operating system.

NOTE Excel macro viruses are adept at spreading—they work by copying themselves from an infected workbook to other currently open workbooks. But only a few Excel viruses exist, and almost none are destructive. They may annoy you, but they aren't likely to trash your computer. You can find a catalog of macro viruses that affect Office programs at *http://tinyurl.com/lgmls.*

To keep your machine clean, the best solution is to avoid using macros in Excel spreadsheets that you don't trust. (And if you do get infected, antivirus software can help you out.) Happily, Excel's got your back—whenever you open a macro-enabled workbook, Excel automatically disables all the macros it contains. In fact, this is even true for the workbooks *you* create.

To see Excel's automatic security in action, try this test. Create a new workbook (or open an existing one), record a macro, save the workbook (as a .xlsm or .xlsb file), and close it. Now try opening it again. Excel automatically disables the macro you created and pops open a message bar that explains (sort of) what happened (Figure 29-5).

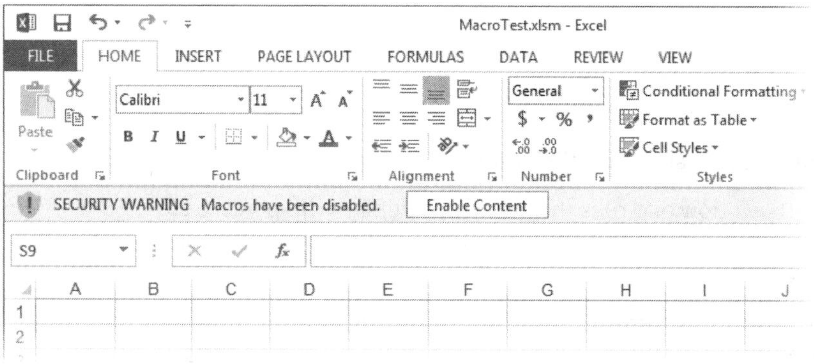

FIGURE 29-5

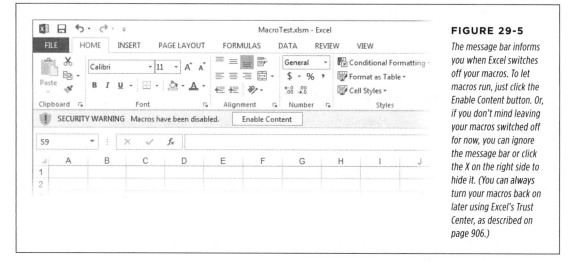

The message bar informs you when Excel switches off your macros. To let macros run, just click the Enable Content button. Or, if you don't mind leaving your macros switched off for now, you can ignore the message bar or click the X on the right side to hide it. (You can always turn your macros back on later using Excel's Trust Center, as described on page 906.)

Trusted Documents

The first time you open a workbook with macros, data connections (page 833), or linked formulas (page 254), Excel shows you the security warning. But if you click Enable Content, Excel remembers that you trust this workbook, and it won't ask you the next time you open the file (even if you change the macro code). This feature is called *trusted documents.*

Here's how the trusted document system works. Every time you decide to trust a workbook, Excel stores the information about that document in the Windows registry. (The registry is a massive catalog of settings that every Windows computer uses.) The next time you open that document, Excel looks in the registry and discovers that you already trust it.

However, Excel *will* turn off your macros and show the message bar again if you rename the file, move it to another folder, or move it to another computer, because in these situations it can't be sure that it really is the same document. Similarly, Excel won't trust your document if you log into your computer as another user, and you can't fool Excel by replacing a trusted workbook with another file that has the same name. (This sneaky strategy fails because Excel stores other details about the file, like its size and creation date. If these don't match, Excel knows that something's up.)

NOTE You may wonder why Excel doesn't wait until you try to run a macro before it warns you. Some macros can be set to run even if you don't explicitly use the View→Macros→Macros command. These macros run automatically in response to certain Excel events (like opening a document). To further complicate life, nefarious macros can sometimes hide or password-protect their code, making it difficult to find out that a problem even exists.

There's one exception to Excel's trusted document system, and it happens when you open a macro-enabled workbook from a network drive. When you click Enable Content on a network file, Excel turns on the macros but it doesn't automatically designate the workbook as a trusted document. Instead, it shows an additional warning message (Figure 29-6) that asks if you want to make this workbook a trusted document. If you're certain that you do, click Yes. If you want to turn on the macros for this session only, click No. All the macros will work, but Excel switches them off again the next time you open the document.

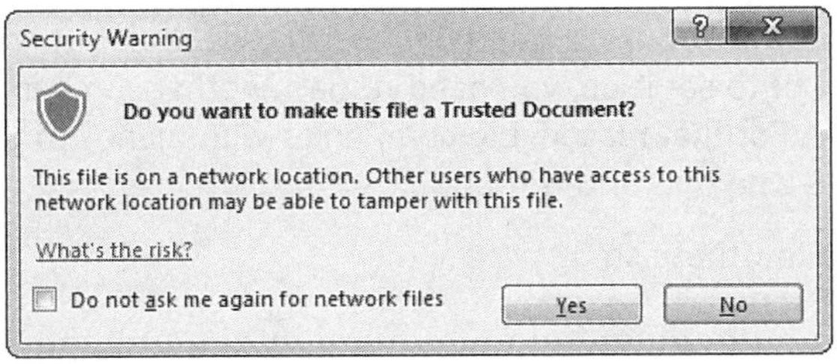

FIGURE 29-6

Network documents represent a different type of risk. Because they aren't stored on your computer, it's possible that someone else might modify the file after you decide to trust it. If you're worried about this scenario, click No to turn on the macros but refrain from designating the file as a trusted document. If you're not so paranoid, and you're opening the file from a personal or company network, you're probably safe to click Yes.

You can also give temporary trust to a macro-enabled workbook stored on your own hard drive, but it's a lot less common and requires a little more work. The following section shows you how.

Temporary Trust

Usually, the trusted document system is exactly what you want. Excel locks up potentially dangerous files until you check them out, and then click Enable Content. After that, the files are family, and Excel lets them run their macro code. However, it's possible that you might decide to trust a document just temporarily—in other words, turn on its macros for one time only.

If this is what you want, don't click the Enable Content button. Instead, follow these steps:

1. **Click File→Info.**

   This switches you to backstage view.

2. **Click the big Enable Content button, and then choose Advanced Options.**

   A new window appears, with two options: Keep the macros disabled or let them run just this once.

3. **Choose "Enable content for this session," and then click OK.**

   Now the workbook can run its macros—at least until the next time you close and reopen it.

The Trust Center

If you want more control over Excel's macro security settings, you need to visit Excel's Trust Center. It gives you several options to make it even easier to work with files that contain macros:

- You can lower the Excel security settings to allow macros. This approach isn't a great idea, because it allows all code to run—even potentially malicious code in other files.
- You can tell Excel to trust the files in certain folders on your computer (or on other computers). This option is the most convenient way to go.
- You can tell Excel to trust workbooks created by a *trusted publisher*. This option's the most secure, but to set it up, you need to pay another company to get a security certificate. For that reason, big companies with money to burn are usually the only ones who opt for this route.

To get to the Trust Center, follow these steps:

1. **Choose File→Options.**

   The Excel Options window appears.

2. **In the list on the left, choose Trust Center.**
3. **Click the Trust Center Settings button.**

   The Trust Center window appears (Figure 29-7).

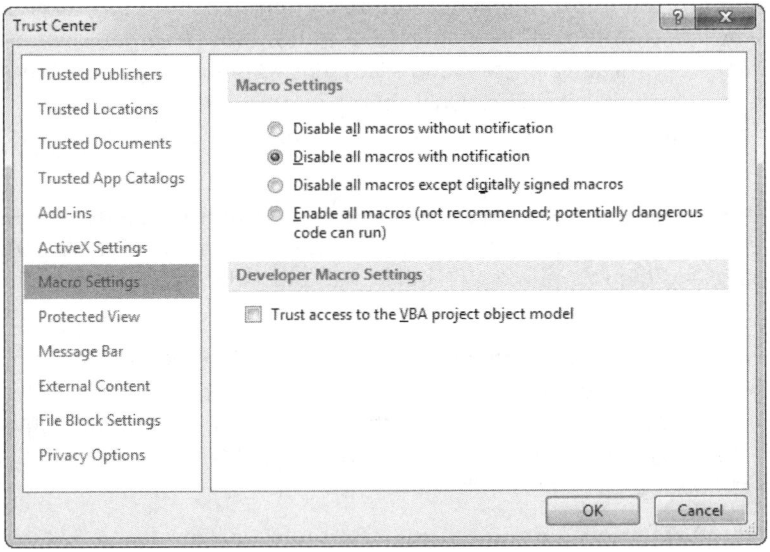

FIGURE 29-7

The Trust Center window is divided into several sections. (You move from one section to another using the list box on the left.) The Macro Settings section lets you decide how Excel reacts to macros. You can choose to turn macros on or off, and you can choose whether Excel should notify you when it turns something off.

The Trust Center has several sections:

- **Trusted Publishers** lets you tell Excel to trust workbooks that are *digitally signed* by certain people. To use this feature, your company needs to buy a digital certificate from a company like VeriSign (*www.verisign.com*). Then, when you open a signed workbook, Excel contacts the company that issued the certificate and checks that it's valid. If it's valid, everything's kosher, the workbook is trusted, and Excel allows all macros. Digital certificates are outside the scope of this book, but you can learn about them at *http://tinyurl.com/digcerts*.

NOTE If you dig around long enough, you'll discover that Microsoft has a tool (known as *MakeCert.exe*) for generating your own digital certificates. However, this tool is only for testing purposes, as the certificates it generates don't work on anyone else's computer.

- **Trusted Locations** lets you pick out the places on your hard drive where you store **your** workbooks. That way, Excel knows to trust *your* workbook files but not anyone else's. You'll learn how to set up a trusted location in the following section.
- **Trusted Documents** lets you switch off the trusted document feature altogether, or switch it off for network documents only. You can also remove the current list of trusted documents (in other words, you can "untrust" everything you've trusted so far) by clicking the Clear button. However, Excel doesn't provide a list of the documents you trust.

- **Trusted App Catalogs** lets you choose to trust catalogs from which you can install Excel apps. Apps are a new system that lets experienced coders build Excel plug-ins. You can learn more at *http://tinyurl.com/excel-dev*.
- **Add-ins** lets you adjust whether Excel add-ins (mini programs that extend the features in Excel) should be supported even if a supported publisher didn't create them. Ordinarily, Excel allows all add-ins. (After all, if you don't trust a specific add-in, don't install it!) Only people in corporate environments, where they need to lock down Excel severely to prevent any chance of a problem, use this setting.
- **ActiveX Settings** lets you adjust how Excel treats ActiveX controls. ActiveX controls are graphical widgets (like super-fancy buttons) that developers create (or buy), and then plop into workbooks and other documents. People don't often use ActiveX controls with Excel.
- **Macro Settings** lets you configure how Excel deals with macros. You can make protection more rigorous (so that you don't let in any macros, unless they're from a trusted publisher), or less (so that all macros are allowed, no matter what they may do). By far the best choice is leaving this option at the standard setting: "Disable all macros with notification."
- **Protected View** configures the way Excel's protected view feature works. As discussed on page 42, Excel uses protected view to open unknown documents in a carefully limited window, ensuring that potentially dangerous files can't do any damage. Using these settings, you can choose whether Excel should use protected view automatically on workbooks you download from the Web, workbooks you receive in your email, workbooks you open from potentially risky folders (like the Temporary Internet Files folder), and so on.
- **Message Bar** lets you set whether Excel shows the message bar when it blocks macros in a suspicious workbook. It's best to keep this feature on, so you know when your macros have been put out of commission.
- **External Content** lets you configure how Excel deals with formulas that link to other workbooks (page 254) and data connections that pull information from other sources, like databases (page 833). Ordinarily, Excel is a bit cautious with both these ingredients. When you open a workbook that uses these features, Excel turns off its links and data connections, and shows the security warning in the message bar. (You can then click Options, and then click Enable Content to tell Excel to switch these features back on.) If clicking the Enable Content button sucks too much time out of your life, the best way to remedy this inconvenience is to use a trusted location.
- **File Block Settings** lets you prevent Excel from opening or saving certain file types. It's up to you to prevent Excel from opening restricted file types altogether or simply force Excel to open them in protected view (page 42). The standard settings configure Excel to use protected view for Excel file formats that are older than Excel 95.

- **Privacy Options** lets you tweak a few options that aren't related to macros at all. You can choose whether Excel checks the Web for updated Help content, and whether it sends troubleshooting information to Microsoft when a problem occurs (so that Microsoft can spot bugs and learn how to improve Excel in the future). If you're paranoid about Internet spies, you may want to turn off some of these options. Most of the time, these settings are for conspiracy theorists only.

Setting Up a Trusted Location

Wouldn't it be nice to have a way to distinguish between your workbooks, which contain perfectly harmless code, and other workbooks, which may not be so nice? Excel lets you designate a specific folder on your hard drive as a trusted location. If you open a workbook stored there, Excel automatically trusts it. And if one of these workbooks contains macros, data connections, or links, Excel switches on all these features right away.

NOTE Of course, it's still up to you to make sure that you place only *your* workbooks in the trusted location. If you put a potentially dangerous workbook in the trusted location, you don't have any protection when you open it.

Here's how you set up a new trusted location:

1. **Open the Trust Center window.**

   If you're not there already, follow the steps on page 906.

2. **Select the Trusted Locations section.**

   A window lists all your trusted locations (Figure 29-8), including a few you didn't assign. That's because, when you first install Excel, it creates a few trusted locations so it can store templates, add-ins, and other important files that it uses.

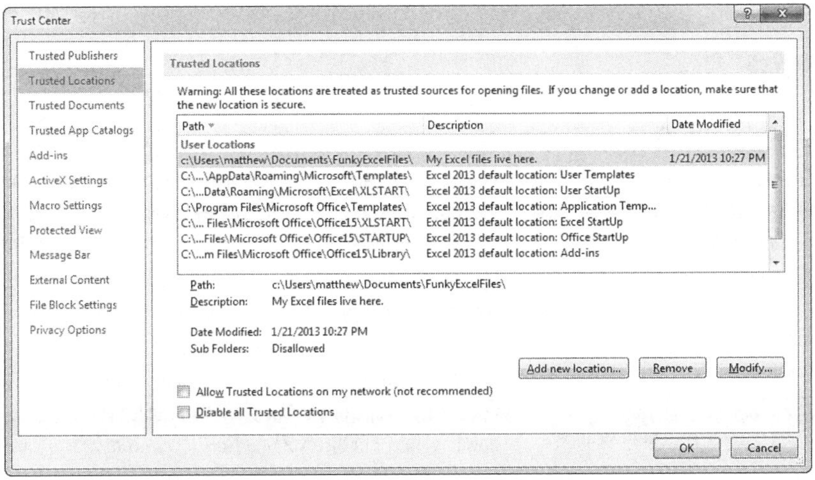

FIGURE 29-8

In this example, there's only one user-added trusted location (selected here). It's the Funky-ExcelFiles folder in the hard drive's Documents location.

3. **To have Excel trust a specific folder on your company or home network, turn on the "Allow trusted locations on my network" checkbox before you go any further.**

   You're taking a bit more of a risk when you turn this setting on, because a network location is out of your control. A hacker could sneak a virus-laden workbook into that location without you noticing. However, if you're reasonably certain that the network's secure (and the other people who use the folder aren't likely to download workbooks from the Web and place them there), you probably don't need to worry.

4. **Click "Add new location."**

   Excel asks you to fill in a few pieces of information, as shown in Figure 29-9.

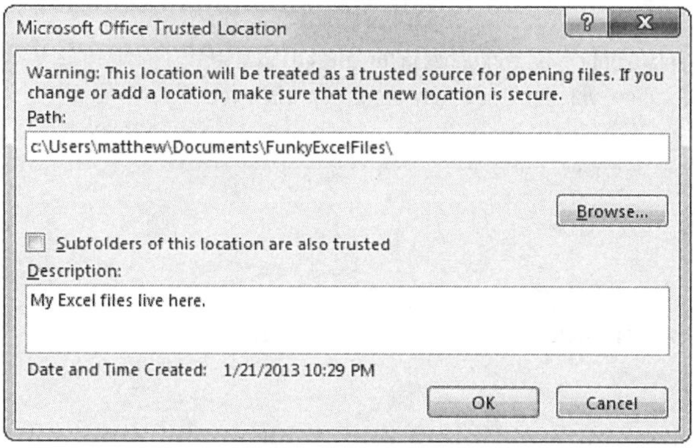

FIGURE 29-9

To configure a trusted location, you need to specify its path (click Browse to hunt it down). You can also choose whether Excel should automatically trust all this folder's subfolders, and you can fill in an optional description that appears in the list of trusted locations.

5. **Click OK to add the location to the list.**

   You can configure or remove the location any time by selecting it in the list, and then using the clear-as-a-bell Modify and Remove buttons shown in Figure 29-8.

POWER USERS' CLINIC

Authenticode Macro Signing

If your company frequently creates and distributes workbooks that have macros, you may want to use an advanced Excel option called Authenticode signing. With Authenticode, you sign all your macros with a digital signature. When someone opens the workbook, their computer checks the signature, and verifies that it's from a known, trusted source. If it's not from a trusted source, the Security warning window appears (if Excel's using the standard Medium security level), or Excel turns the macro off (if it's using High or Very High security).

Authenticode macro signing is problematic, because the person who opens the document needs a way to verify that the digital signature's trusted. You need to create a *digital certificate* for the person who writes the macro, and register this certificate with everyone who needs to use macros this person creates.

This process can be complicated, and large organizations that use macros heavily go through it. Authenticode signing is far outside the scope of this book, but you can learn more about how it works from Microsoft at *http://tinyurl.com/macro-sign*.

Creating Practical Macros

If you're still wondering what macros can do for you, it helps to look at a few straightforward examples. In this section, you'll learn about some helpful macros you can create for practice and profit.

Inserting a Header

A really simple macro to start out with is one that inserts some boilerplate information into a group of cells. Consider the header at the top of a company spreadsheet, which typically includes a company's name, the spreadsheet's author, the date the spreadsheet was created, and a title. If you're often adding this same information to many worksheets, you can automate the task with a macro.

Here's what you need to do:

1. **Fire up the macro recorder (select View→Macros→Macros→Record Macro).**

   The Record Macro window appears.

2. **Name your macro.**

   Choose a memorable name (like InsertHeader), and then click OK to get started with the actual macro recording.

3. **Make sure you're in absolute reference mode (the View→Macros→Macros→Use Relative References button should *not* be selected).**

   You want absolute reference mode because you always want Excel to place the header in the same few cells at the top of the worksheet.

4. **Move to cell A1, and then insert a generic title (like "Sales Report").**

   You can of course pick whatever title you want to use.

5. **Select cells A1 to C1, right-click the selection, and then choose Format Cells.**

   In the next step, you're going to create a little more breathing room for your title by increasing its size.

6. **Change the font to something large and dramatic.**

   In the Alignment tab, turn on the "Merge cells" checkbox to group these three cells into one larger cell that can accommodate the title. Click OK once you're done.

7. **Move to cell A2 and enter the text "Created." Move to cell B2, and then type the formula *=TODAY()*.**

   The TODAY() function inserts the current date. However, you want this cell to reflect the creation date, so that Excel doesn't update the date every time someone opens the spreadsheet. To make sure the date can't change, you need to replace the formula with the calculated date value. Press F2 to put the cell in edit mode, and then F9 to replace the formula with the result. Press Enter to commit the change.

8. **Optionally, add any extra text you'd like to include (like a company slogan or a copyright message).**

   Feel free to tweak column sizes as well.

9. **Choose View→Macros→Macros→Stop Recording to save your macro.**

   To try out your macro (Figure 29-10), replay it in a different worksheet in the same workbook.

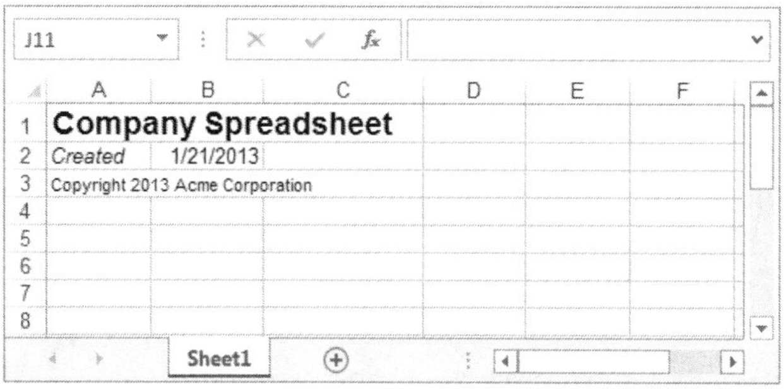

FIGURE 29-10

The InsertHeader macro (which you can download from the Missing CD page at http://missingmanuals.com/cds/excel2013mm) inserts a generic header at the top of a worksheet and then automatically grabs the current date and inserts it as text.

Alternating Row Formatting

A custom macro is a useful tool for complex and unusual formatting tasks. Macros are particularly useful if you want to apply a pattern of formatting to a large block of cells. For example, if you want to format every other row with a different background color, a macro comes in quite handy. In this case, the easiest approach is to create a macro that formats just a few rows; you can then replay this macro multiple times to format a whole table of data.

Here's how to build a macro for applying alternating row formatting:

1. **Move to the cell where you want Excel to start before you begin recording.**

   In this example, it makes sense to use relative reference mode. Therefore, it doesn't matter which cell you start from; Excel doesn't record the cell address as part of the macro.

2. **Choose View→Macros→Macros→Record Macro, and then choose a name you'll remember (like FormatRow).**

   You can also specify a shortcut key (like Ctrl+Shift+F). The FormatRow macro described here is much more practical with a shortcut key, because you'll want to use it multiple times in quick succession. When you finish, click OK.

3. **Make sure you're in relative reference mode.**

   Click the View→Macros→Macros→Use Relative References button so that it's highlighted. You want this button selected since you're going to repeatedly apply this macro across your worksheet.

4. **Click the row number button at the left of the current row to select the entire row. Right-click the selection, and then choose Format Cells.**

   The Format Cells window appears.

5. **Select the Patterns tab, choose a new color, and then click OK.**

6. **Press the down arrow key twice to move down two rows.**

   If you're in row 1, move down to the third row.

7. **Choose View→Macros→Macros→Stop Recording to save your macro.**

The neat thing about this macro is that you can replay it multiple times to format unlimited expanses of data. To try this trick out, start at the top of a table of data. Press the macro shortcut key (if you created one) to format the first row and automatically move down two rows. Then press the macro shortcut key again to format the current row and move down again. (If you haven't used a shortcut, you'll have to use the more awkward approach of selecting View→Macros→Macros, and then selecting the macro from the list of available macros.) You can continue this process for as long as you want. The end result is a table where every second row is highlighted with a different background color.

A Combined Task

Really sophisticated macros don't just add data or format cells, they perform a whole *series* of operations. To get a better feeling for these types of macros, try out the following example, which figures out the average and median values for a list of numbers.

1. **Before you start recording the macro, create a list of numbers in an Excel spreadsheet. These numbers are the ones the macro will analyze.**

   If you don't want to type in your own numbers, you can open an existing worksheet, like the student grade worksheet from Chapter 9 (which you can download from this book's Missing CD page at *http://missingmanuals.com/cds/excel2013mm).*

2. **Select the numbers.**

   Note that you select the numbers *before* you create the macro. That's because the macro you're creating is designed to analyze a selection of cells. Before you replay the macro, you need to select the range of cells you want the macro to analyze.

3. **Choose View→Macros→Macros→Record Macro.**

   Choose a suitable name (like AnalyzeSelectedCells), and then click OK.

4. **Before you take any other steps, define a new name for the selected cells.**

   In the formula bar's Name box, type AnalyzedCells. (The name box is at the extreme left side of the formula bar, and it usually displays the reference for the active cell.)

5. **Press the right arrow key once or twice to move to a free column.**

6. **Enter the formula *=AVERAGE(AnalyzedCells)* to calculate the average of the named range you created in step 4.**

7. **In a cell underneath, enter the formula *=MEDIAN(AnalyzedCells)*.**

   This formula calculates the median value for the named range you created in step 4.

8. **Add labels next to the cells with the two formulas, if you want.**

9. **Choose View→Macros→Macros→Stop Recording to save your macro.**

To test this macro, select the group of cells you want to analyze before you play the macro. The neat thing about this macro is that you can use it to analyze any number of cells, as long as you select and name them all. The only limitation is that you can have just one range with the same name in a worksheet, so you can't use this macro in more than one place on the same worksheet. If you wrote the same macro by hand in VBA code, you could circumvent this limitation.

Placing a Macro on the Quick Access Toolbar

Once you create a useful macro, you may want to attach it to the Quick Access toolbar at the top of the Excel window so that it's conveniently available when you need it. You'll especially want easy access if you create a macro that you're going to use frequently (and it helps if you save the macro in the personal macro workbook, since that ensures you can use the macro in any workbook, as explained on page 898).

NOTE If you attach a macro to the Quick Access toolbar and the macro isn't in your personal macro workbook, you could run into trouble. If you rename or move the workbook that contains the macro later on, the button won't work anymore.

Adding a Quick Access toolbar button that activates macros isn't difficult. Just follow these steps:

1. **If the macro isn't in the current workbook, start by opening the workbook that contains it.**

   Ideally, you'll store the macro in your personal macro workbook. (If you want to copy a macro from another workbook into your personal workbook, jump ahead to page 923 in the next chapter.)

2. **Right-click the Quick Access toolbar, and then choose Customize Quick Access Toolbar.**

   The Excel Options window appears, with the Customize section chosen (see Figure 29-11).

3. **In the "Choose commands from" drop-down list, choose Macros.**

   Underneath, a list appears with all the macros available in the personal macro workbook and any other currently open workbooks.

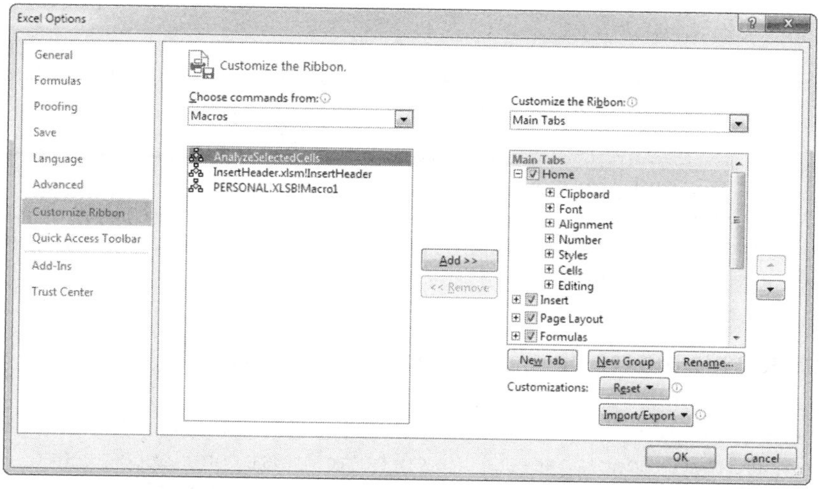

FIGURE 29-11

Choose the category of commands you want to see by picking from the "Choose commands from" list. The right side of the window shows the Quick Access toolbar's current contents. You can move items on or off the toolbar using Add and Remove, and you can change the order of items by selecting them and using the arrow buttons.

4. **Choose the macro you want in the list, and then click Add to place it in the Quick Access toolbar.**

   The item appears in the box on the right, which shows the current list of Quick Access commands.

5. **Choose the newly added macro (at the bottom of the list), and then click Modify.**

   The Modify Button window appears.

6. **Choose a new icon and display name.**

   Initially, all macros use a hideously bizarre icon and a tongue-twisting display name that includes the name of the workbook where they're stored. You can do better.

   The icon's the miniature picture that appears in the Quick Access toolbar. Pick one of the ready-made icons, all of which look better than the stock macro icon.

   The display name is the pop-up text that appears when you hover over the icon in the Quick Access toolbar. Try using a more understandable name. Instead of SuperMacroWorkbook.xlsm!MySuperMacro, consider "My Super Macro" or "MySuperMacro from SuperMacroWorkbook" or "Formats Alternating Rows."

7. **If you don't like your macro button's positioning, select it, and then use the up and down arrow buttons.**

   When you add a new item to the Quick Access toolbar, it heads straight to the end of the list (which means it appears at the toolbar's right edge). If you want, you can move it to a more prominent position.

8. **Click OK.**

   Your macro appears in the Quick Access toolbar. If you tire of it, right-click the button, and then choose Remove from Quick Access Toolbar.

TIP When you customize Excel's Quick Access toolbar, Excel stores your custom settings on your computer, but not in any workbook file. People who use your workbook files on other computers don't see your new button. They need to rely on the Macros window or the macro shortcut key. You can get around this limitation by attaching a macro to a worksheet button instead, as described in the next section.

Attaching a Macro to a Button Inside a Worksheet

Only a few extremely useful macros will ever be worth space on the Quick Access toolbar. But if you create a macro that you use frequently with a specific workbook—say, a macro that produces a special printout or performs a complex calculation—you may want it easily available, but only when you use that workbook.

The solution? Use a *button control*. You can place this button anywhere you want on your worksheet and configure its text. When the person using the spreadsheet clicks the button, the linked macro runs automatically. This behavior is particularly useful if a lot of people use the worksheet; not everyone can remember a specific macro name or shortcut key, but nobody has any trouble clicking a large inviting button.

To add a button to a worksheet, you need the Developer tab (Figure 29-11), which doesn't appear until you ask Excel to show it. To do so, choose File→Options, and then choose the Customize Ribbon section. On the right of the window, a large box lists all the tabs currently shown in the ribbon. Near the bottom, you'll see an unchecked item named Developer. To show the Developer tab, check this box, and then click OK.

The Developer tab has buttons for recording and playing macros (which duplicate the options from the View→Macros section of the ribbon), along with more advanced programming commands, most of which you'll never use unless you become a hard-core code jockey. Although you can record and play macros with status bar buttons, it's a good idea to show the Developer tab before you continue any further. The Developer tab includes a few more options, like the ability to control whether the macro records relative or absolute references (page 897), and a way to manage Excel's macro security settings (page 907).

Once you make the Developer tab show up in the ribbon, you're ready to add a button to your worksheet and attach a macro to it. Just follow these steps:

1. **If the macro isn't in the current workbook, start by opening the workbook that contains it.**

   Ideally, you stored the macro in the workbook where you want to add the button, or in the personal macro workbook. Otherwise, you're probably complicating your life unnecessarily.

2. **Choose Developer→Controls→Insert→Button (*not* the similarly named Command Button).**

   When you choose Developer→Controls→Insert, a list of controls appears (Figure 29-12).

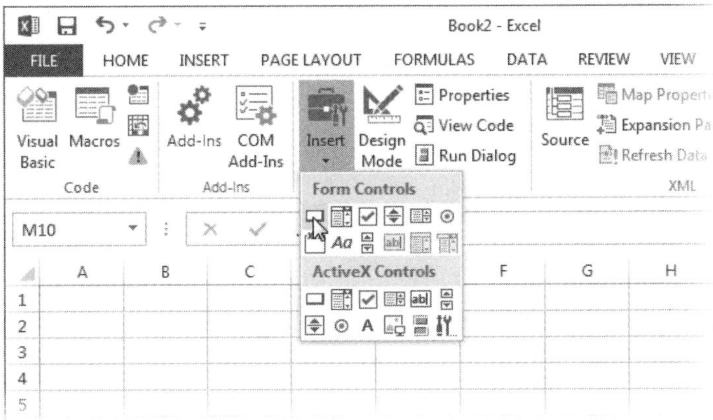

FIGURE 29-12

If you don't spot the Button icon right away, move your cursor over all the icons until the tooltip text Button appears. Then click the icon.

3. **Drag to "draw" the button on your worksheet.**

   There's no restriction as to where you can place a button, or how large it can be. However, you don't want to obscure important data in the cells underneath. Once you finish drawing the button, the Assign Macro window appears, with a list of available macros.

4. **Select a macro, and then click OK.**

   Ideally, you should choose a macro stored in the current workbook or your personal workbook. Otherwise, the button won't work if you move or rename the workbook where the macro resides.

5. **Right-click the button, and then choose Edit Text. Replace the standard text (Button 1) with something more descriptive (like Update Totals).**

6. **Click the worksheet.**

   Click anywhere on the worksheet to finish this procedure. At this point, the button is fully functional, and you can click it to run the linked macro (see Figure 29-13).

   If at any point you want to change the button text or move it somewhere else, start by right-clicking the button to select it. You can then drag it, resize it, delete it (by pressing the Delete key), or click to change the button text, without inadvertently triggering the linked macro.

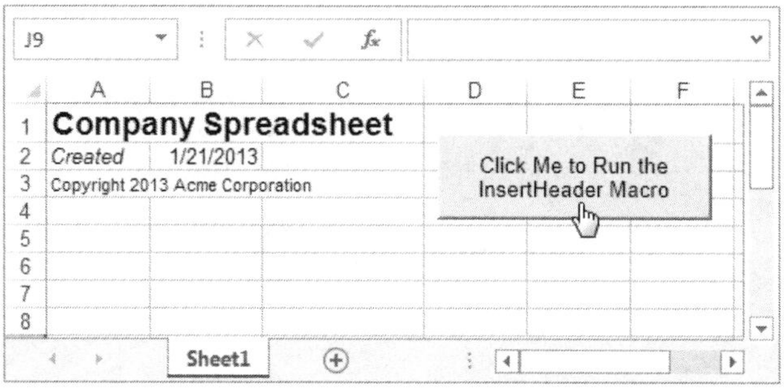

FIGURE 29-13

This worksheet includes a custom button that runs a linked macro. When you move your mouse over the button, it changes into a hand, indicating that you can click the button to unleash the macro.

CHAPTER

30

Programming Spreadsheets with VBA

When you use Excel's macro recorder (covered in the previous chapter), you actually build a small program. Excel translates every action you take, from selecting a menu item to editing a cell, into a line of *VBA* code (short for Visual Basic for Applications), and inserts it into your new macro. The obvious benefit is that you can use the macro recorder without knowing the first thing about programming. However, this free pass has limitations.

You'll find that you can record only actions that you can perform yourself. If you want to create a macro that inserts a column with 100 identical cell values, you need to go through the drudgery of typing in each cell value so that the macro recorder knows what to capture. A more serious problem is that when you record a macro, you can respond only to the worksheet that's in front of you. If you want to make a more flexible macro that has the ability to examine a variety of cells and the intelligence to respond to different conditions, you need to tap into some of VBA's more advanced capabilities.

Sooner or later, every Excel guru delves into macro code. Often, you first work with macro code when you need to enhance an existing recorded macro to make it more nimble or to correct a problem. Depending on your preference, these encounters may be the only time you come face to face with VBA, or it could be the start of a new career path as an Excel programmer extraordinaire.

There's no way to explain a complete programming language in one chapter. Instead, this chapter walks you through the Visual Basic editor, explains some important coding techniques, and shows a few useful macros. By the time you finish this chapter, you'll know enough about VBA to grab a useful snippet of macro code from an Excel website (and understand what it's supposed to do), or dive into an advanced book that's dedicated to VBA programming.

The Visual Basic Editor

Before you can modify a macro, you first need to find it. The tool you use to edit macros isn't actually part of Excel. It's a separate program called the Visual Basic editor.

The easiest way to get to the Visual Basic editor is to use Excel's Developer tab. The only problem is that Excel likes to hide its high-powered coding features from ordinary people. To ask Excel to show the Developer tab, you need to choose File→Options, and then choose the Customize Ribbon section. On the right of the window, a large box lists the tabs currently shown in the ribbon. Near the bottom, you'll see an unchecked item named Developer. Check this box, and then click OK to reveal the Developer tab. Now you can switch to the Visual Basic editor window at any time by choosing Developer→Code→Visual Basic. When you do, Excel launches the standalone window shown in Figure 30-1.

TIP Alternatively, if you already created a macro, you can jump straight to its code using the familiar Macros window. Just choose View→Macros→Macros, select the macro in the list, and then click Edit.

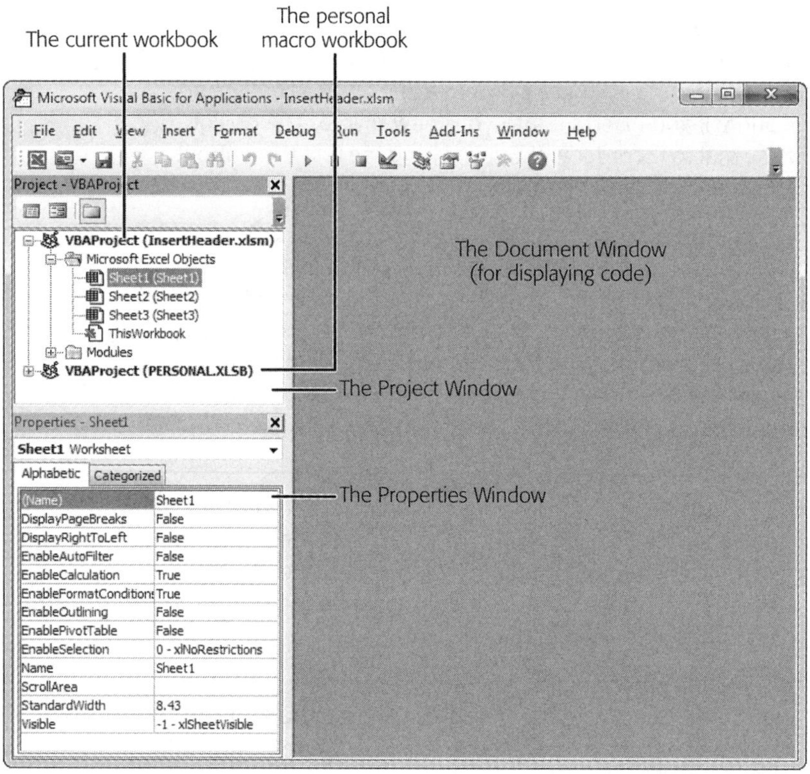

FIGURE 30-1

Microsoft divides the Visual Basic editor window into three regions: the Project window, the Properties window, and the Document window. The Document window is where your code appears (it starts off blank). The Project window lists all your projects (two are shown here: InsertHeader.xlsm and the personal macro workbook). The Properties window lists the individual settings you can change for the currently selected project.

The Project Window

The best way to orient yourself in the Visual Basic editor is to start by looking at the Project window in the top-left corner. It shows a directory tree representing all your currently open workbooks. Each open workbook becomes a separate VBA project, which means that it contains its own set of macro code.

Along with the workbooks you currently have open, you may also find in the Project window a few workbooks you don't recognize. Don't panic—these interlopers are completely kosher. They correspond to *hidden workbooks*—workbooks that Excel opens but doesn't show you or let you edit. Often, a hidden workbook loads when you activate an add-in like Solver (page 776). That's because all the code and specialized functions that the add-in provides are actually written using VBA *modules* (code files). A little later in this chapter, you'll see how you can use modules to not only create macros, but also to define your own specialized functions.

Some of the unexpected workbooks you may find in the Project window include:

- **PERSONAL.XLSB.** This project is your personal macro workbook (page 898); it contains the macros you share between all workbooks. If you haven't recorded any macros to the personal macro workbook, you won't see this project because Excel hasn't created it.
- **SOLVER.XLAM.** This project contains the code for the Solver add-in, if you've turned it on (page 776).
- **SUMIF.XLAM.** This project contains the code for the Conditional Sum wizard add-in, if you've turned it on.

NOTE Don't try to open the add-in projects. They're password-protected so you can't modify (or even look at) any of the code they contain. However, you can change the macros you create, as well as your personal macro workbook.

Each workbook in the Project window contains one or two folders. The first one, Microsoft Excel Objects, is always present and contains a separate entry for each worksheet in the workbook. You use these entries to attach code that reacts to a specific worksheet event. For example, you could create a task that springs into action every time someone opens the worksheet. The Microsoft Excel Objects folder also contains a single workbook object—called ThisWorkbook—where you can write code that's triggered when something happens to the workbook (for example, when it's saved, opened, or printed).

NOTE Creating code that reacts to events is an advanced Excel technique. For example, you could use an Excel event to run some code every time your workbook is opened. This book doesn't cover events.

Modules is the second folder in a workbook project. It appears only if you've created a macro for this particular workbook. Figure 30-2 details the action inside one particular Project window.

NOTE As you open new workbooks, they automatically appear in the Visual Basic editor's Project window. Similarly, as you close workbooks, they disappear from the Project window.

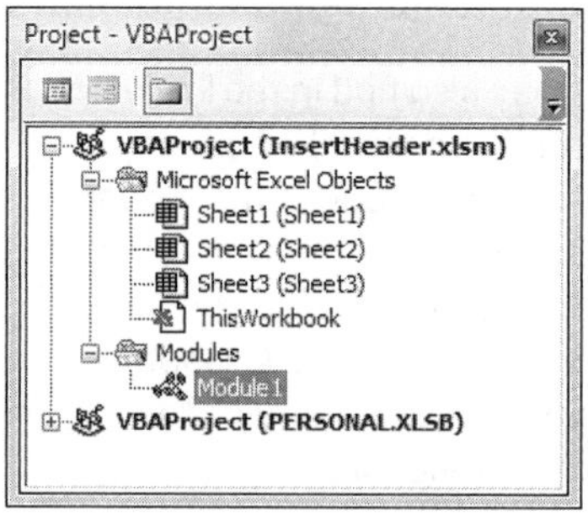

FIGURE 30-2

This window has two VBA projects. The first, InsertHeader.xlsm, is an Excel workbook file with three worksheets and one module for macro code. The last, PERSONAL.XLSB, is the personal macro workbook, which may also contain worksheets and macro modules (although that branch of the tree is collapsed, so you can't see these objects).

Modules and Macros

Modules contain macro code. Ordinarily, Excel creates a new module the first time you record a macro, and names it Module1. Excel then places every macro you record for that workbook into Module1. If you want, you can separate macros into different modules for better organization. However, the number of modules you create, or the module you use for a given macro, has no effect on a macro's function.

Every module contains one or more VBA *subroutines*. Each subroutine is a named unit of code that performs a distinct task. In the VBA language, subroutines start with the word Sub followed by the subroutine's name. They end with the statement End Sub. Here's an example:

```
Sub MyMacro
    ' Your macro code goes here.
End Sub
```

This small snippet of VBA code illustrates two important principles. First, it shows you how to start and end any subroutine (by using the statements Sub and End Sub). And it shows you how to create a *comment*. Comments are special statements that Excel ignores; they're notes to yourself (like explaining in plain English what the following or preceding line of code actually does). To create a comment, you just place an apostrophe (') at the beginning of the line.

TIP Master programmers always leave comments in their code (or at least they feel terribly guilty when they don't). Comments are the best way to clarify what you want your code to do, so you can remember your intentions when you review it a few months later.

In Excel, each macro is a separate subroutine. (In some cases, you may want to break a macro down into more than one subroutine to make your code easier to understand and edit, but the macro recorder doesn't do this for you automatically.)

When you record a macro using the macro recorder, Excel generates a new subroutine using the name you supply. It also includes adds comments that use the description text you type in. Then, Excel places all the code it generates into the subroutine.

Here's the basic skeleton for the InsertHeader macro you created in the last chapter:

```
Sub InsertHeader()
    '
    ' InsertHeader Macro
    ' Macro recorded 3/6/2013 by Matthew MacDonald
    ' (Code goes here.)
End Sub
```

To look at the subroutines in a module, double-click the module in the Project window. The Module opens in a new window, as shown in Figure 30-3. You can scroll through this window to see all the macro procedures it contains.

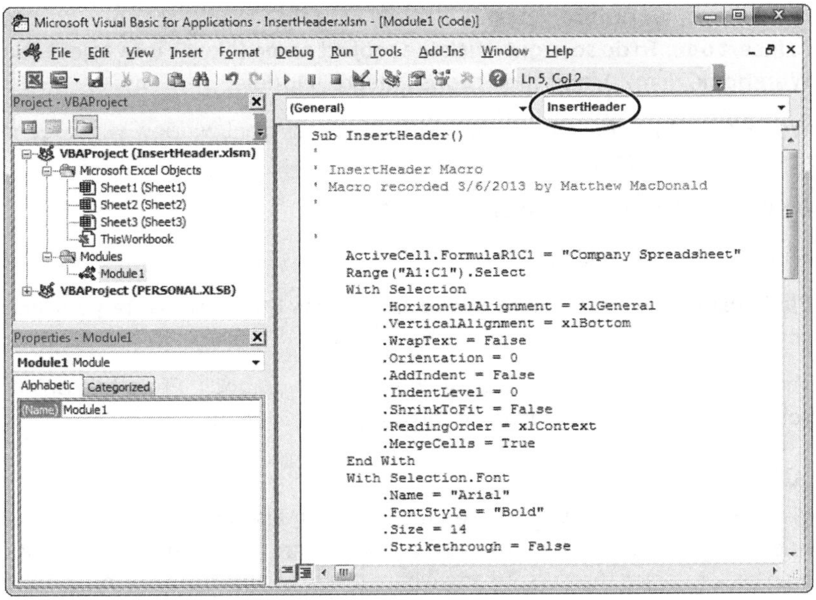

FIGURE 30-3

In this example, the Visual Basic editor shows a portion of the code for the InsertHeader macro. If you scrolled down, you'd see additional macros in separate modules (providing the workbook contains additional macros, of course). Excel separates the subroutines with a solid line (not shown). You can also jump directly to a subroutine that interests you by selecting the subroutine's name from the drop-down list in the top-right corner of the code window (circled).

Finding and Moving Macros

With your new knowledge of VBA, you can transfer a macro from one workbook to another. Just follow these steps:

1. **Open both workbooks in Excel.**

   Before you start, you need to open the workbook that contains the macro you want to move or copy (that's the *source workbook*), and the workbook where you want to move the macro to (the *target workbook*).

2. **Switch to the Visual Basic editor window.**

   If it's not already open, use the View→Macros→Macros→View Macros command, pick a macro, and then click Edit.

3. **Using the Project window, expand the source workbook until you see the module where the macro is stored (this module is usually named Module1). Double-click the module.**

   The code window appears with the macro code for the source workbook.

4. **Scroll through the code window until you find the macro you want to copy or move. Select it all, from the starting Sub line to the concluding End Sub statement. Press Ctrl+C to copy, or Ctrl+X to cut the macro code.**

   If you use Ctrl+X, you remove the macro code from the source workbook, and the macro's no longer available in that workbook.

5. **Using the Project window, expand the target workbook.**

6. **If the target workbook doesn't already contain a macro module, you need to insert one. To do so, right-click the project name (like "VBA Project (New-Workbook.xlsm)"), and then choose Insert→Module.**

   When you add a new module, it appears in the project window with a generic name (like Module1).

7. **Double-click the new module.**

   A blank code window appears.

8. **Click inside the code window, and then press Ctrl+V to paste your macro code.**

   This action places the macro code in the new workbook. From this point on, you can use the macro whenever this workbook is open.

Debugging a Macro

The Visual Basic editor isn't just for editing. You can also use it to *run* any macro. Just open the module that has the macro you want, scroll through the code window, and then click to place the cursor somewhere inside the macro. Now, on the Visual Basic toolbar, click the Run button (which looks like the play button on a DVR). If you have a long-running macro, you can click the pause button to temporarily halt the code, or click the Stop button to abort the macro altogether.

NOTE You may assume that Excel performs the macro on the workbook that *contains* the macro code, but this scenario isn't necessarily true. Instead, Excel runs the macro on the *active workbook*, which is the one you looked at *most recently*. In other words, if you have two workbooks open and you use the Windows task bar to switch to the second workbook, and then you go back to the Visual Basic editor, Excel runs the macro on the second workbook.

Macro debugging is another neat trick you can perform from the Visual Basic editor. This feature lets you walk through your macro code and run it one line at a time. After each line executes, you can take a look at what's happened so far in the workbook. Macro debugging is a great tool for finding mistakes or diagnosing bizarre behavior. It's also a good way to learn what each statement in a macro actually does.

To debug a macro, follow these steps:

1. **Find the macro you want to debug, and then click anywhere inside the code.**

   Excel's debugging tools aren't limited to misbehaving macros. You can use them to watch any macro in action, just for the fun of it.

2. **From the Visual Basic editor menu, select Debug→Step Into, or press F8.**

   Excel highlights the first line of the macro (the Sub statement) in yellow, and places an arrow next to it. The arrow indicates that this line is ready to run.

3. **Press F8 to run the highlighted line.**

   Once Excel runs this line, it moves to the next line (skipping any comments), and highlights *it* in yellow. Then it moves you to the first actual line of code in the macro, as shown in Figure 30-4.

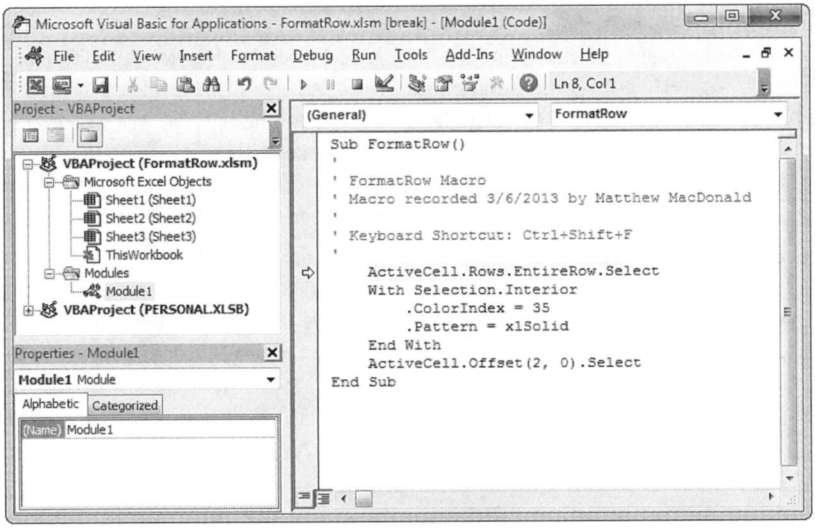

FIGURE 30-4

When you press F8, Excel runs the line that's highlighted in yellow and marked with an arrow. Then it moves to the next statement and pauses again.

4. **Press F8 to run the highlighted line.**

   Excel runs the highlighted line, moves one line down to the next line, highlights it, and waits for your command. At this point, you can switch back to the workbook to see if the first line of code produced any visible effect. Be careful not to change anything in your worksheet, however. If, for instance, you clear the current selection or move to a different place in the worksheet, you could throw the macro off completely.

When you finish looking at the worksheet, switch back to the Visual Basic editor.

5. **Return to step 4, and keep repeating it for each line in the macro.**

   You can stop stepping through your code at any point, and run everything that's left by clicking the Play button, or you can cancel the remainder of the macro commands by clicking the Stop button. When you reach the last line, the macro ends.

TIP Excel gives you a way to jump right to a macro that interests you. From the Excel window, choose View→Macros→Macros→View Macros to see a list of available macros. Select one, and then click Step Into to open it in the Visual Basic editor and begin debugging it, running one line at a time.

POWER USERS' CLINIC

Adding New Modules

If you fill a single module with dozens of macros, you can quickly end up bogged down in a murky pool of macro code. In this situation, why not simplify your life by adding more modules to your workbook? For example, you might decide to organize your macros by purpose by creating modules named ChartMacros, FinancialCalculations, and FormatCleanUp. Remember, Excel can find and use your macro subroutines with the same ease, regardless of whether they're concentrated in one module or spread out in several.

You can easily add new modules to a workbook. All you do is right-click the name of your project in the Project window, and then choose Insert→Module. Once you create a new module, you can follow the steps shown earlier to transfer the macro from one module to another.

Of course, if you create multiple modules with generic names (like Module1, Module2, and so on), you'll have a hard time keeping track of what's what. So once you create your module, change the name to something descriptive by selecting the module in the Project window and looking at the Properties window underneath. In Figure 30-4, that window shows one entry, (Name). You can click this entry and type in something more specific. Module names have all the same restrictions as macro names, which means they have to start with a letter, and use only letters, numbers, and the underscore character.

If you end up with a module you don't want, it's easy enough to remove it. Just right-click the module in the Project window, and then choose Remove. (At this point, the Visual Basic editor asks if you want to export your macro code to a separate file so you can import it back into some other workbook. If you just want to get rid of your module for good, choose No.)

Understanding Macro Code

Now that you've learned how macros are organized, it's time to dive in and tackle the actual macro code. In the following sections, you'll take your first look at VBA code and learn how Excel uses a special programming tool called *objects*. (Objects are programming tools that you use to trigger Excel features. You'll learn more about them on page 928.)

The Anatomy of a Macro

A good place to start learning about the guts of a macro is the FormatRow macro shown in the previous chapter, which automatically highlights every other row with a light green background.

The complete VBA code for the FormatRow macro is below. To make it easier to analyze, each line of code has been numbered, and the code has been simplified a little from what Excel would generate automatically:

```
1  Sub FormatRow()
2      '
3      ' FormatRow Macro
4      ' Macro recorded 3/6/2013 by Matthew MacDonald
5      '
6      ' Keyboard Shortcut: Ctrl+Shift+F
7      '
8      ActiveCell.EntireRow.Select
9      Selection.Interior.ColorIndex = 35
10     Selection.Interior.Pattern = xlSolid
11     ActiveCell.Offset(2, 0).Select
12 End Sub
```

Line 1 starts the macro and defines its name. Lines 2–7 are simply comments. They appear in green in the editor and don't actually do anything (other than convey information to the person reading the code).

The action gets started in line 8. Here, the code accesses a special object called ActiveCell, and uses it to select the entire current row. Next, line 9 changes the background color of the selected cells (to light green), and line 10 sets the type of background fill (to solid). Both lines 9 and 10 use the Selection object.

Finally, line 11 returns to the ActiveCell object, and uses its Offset command to jump down two rows from the current cell. Line 12 marks the end of the macro.

Altogether, this macro doesn't do much, but the code is quite dense, and fairly difficult to read on first sight. The problem isn't the VBA language—in fact, the only language-specific details in this example are the Sub and End Sub statements (not to mention all those odd periods, which are explained in the next section).

The real complexity comes from understanding all the different objects you can use in macros. To write a macro like this one, you need to know that there's an ActiveCell object that lets you select rows and a Selection object that lets you adjust the rows' formatting. These details (and many more that aren't shown in this macro) make up Excel's *object model*. To perform any task using a macro, from printing a document to saving a worksheet, you need to first figure out which object can do your bidding.

Objects 101

In many programming languages, including VBA, everything revolves around objects. So what, exactly, is an object?

In the programming world, an object is nothing more than a convenient way to group together some related functionality. In the FormatRow macro, two objects are front and center: one named ActiveCell, and one named Selection. The ActiveCell object bundles together everything you may want to do with the currently active cell, including editing it, selecting it, and moving from this cell to another. The Selection object offers other features for modifying a group of selected cells, including ways to change their borders, background colors, and font.

Programmers embraced objects long ago because they're a great way to organize code (not to mention a great way to share and reuse it). Objects also make it easier for developers to discover new features. For example, once you learn about ActiveCell, you immediately know what object you need to use for any task related to the current cell.

You can use objects in a number of ways. Altogether, you interact with objects three ways:

- **Properties.** Properties are pieces of information about an object. You change properties to modify the object or how it behaves. The FormatRow macro uses the ColorIndex property to change the background color of a row.
- **Methods.** Methods are actions you can perform with an object. The FormatRow macro uses the Select method to select the current row.
- **Events.** Events are notifications that an object sends out that you, as the macro programmer, can respond to. This chapter doesn't look at events, but you can use them to react to certain actions that someone using your worksheet takes (like saving a workbook).

In the next section, you'll take a closer look at how to use properties and methods.

Using Properties and Methods

So how do you change properties or use methods? The answer is the lowly period. Imagine you have a Car object that provides a StartIgnition method. In this case, you use the following syntax to start your engine:

```
Car.StartIgnition
```

The same technique works with properties, but it tends to look a little different. With properties, you typically want to perform one of two actions. Either you want to retrieve information about the property, or you want to change the property. To change the property value, you use the equal sign (=). The following line of code changes the number of people in a car by modifying the Passengers property:

```
Car.Passengers = 2
```

NOTE Think of the equal sign as an arrow pointing to the left. It takes whatever information's on the right side (in this case, the number 2) and stuffs it in whatever receptacle is on the left side (in this case, the Passengers property of the Car object).

Surprisingly, this information is just about everything you need to know about objects. Of course, if you look back at the FormatRow example, you'll notice that none of the lines look quite as simple as the previous two Car object examples. That's because you need to use multiple objects at once to accomplish many Excel tasks. Excel is so feature-laden that its developers needed to divide and subdivide its features into dozens of different objects to make them more manageable.

Consider the following statement (line 9 from the FormatRow macro):

```
Selection.Interior.ColorIndex = 35
```

In this example, two objects are at work. The Selection object contains another object named Interior. Technically, Interior is a property of the Selection object. Unfortunately, the Selection object doesn't give you any way to change the background color of the selected cells. To do that, you need to use the ColorIndex property, which is a part of the Interior object. That's why this statement has two periods. The first one accesses the Interior object, and the second one accesses the ColorIndex property.

The same mechanism is at work in line 8:

```
ActiveCell.EntireRow.Select
```

In this case, the ActiveCell object has a property called EntireRow, which is also an object. The EntireRow object provides the Select method that highlights the current row.

In short, understanding the basics of objects really isn't that difficult, but you could spend days wandering around Excel's family of objects trying to find the ones you need. Excel includes objects that represent worksheets, workbooks, cells, ranges, selections, charts, the Excel window, and more. The next section tells you how to get started.

UNDER THE HOOD

The With Statement

Once you find the right object, you'll probably need to use several of its properties or methods. To save yourself the effort of typing in the object name each time, you can use a *With block*. A With block starts off by identifying an object you want to use. The following statements (up until the final End With) don't need to include the object name. Instead, they skip straight to the period, and use it to start the line.

The FormatHeader macro uses the following statements to set the formatting of the current selection:

```
Selection.Interior.ColorIndex = 35
Selection.Interior.Pattern = xlSolid
```

You can rewrite this statement using the With statement as follows:

```
With Selection.Interior
    .ColorIndex = 35
    .Pattern = xlSolid
End With
```

Either way, the result is the same. But it helps to be familiar with the With statement, because the macro recorder uses it frequently. In fact, if you look at the original FormatHeader code the macro recorder generated, you'll find that it uses a With block.

Hunting for Objects

Finding the objects you need isn't trivial, and if you do more than a little bit of macro code editing, you'll want to invest in a dedicated reference book. However, the Visual Basic editor tries to help you out as you type code with a feature called IntelliSense. Every time you press the period after typing in a valid object name, a pop-up menu appears with a list of all the properties and methods for that object (see Figure 30-5). If you don't know the exact name of the property or method you want to use, you can scroll through the list, and then select it. Of course, you still need to know *how* to use the property or method, but this feature helps you get started.

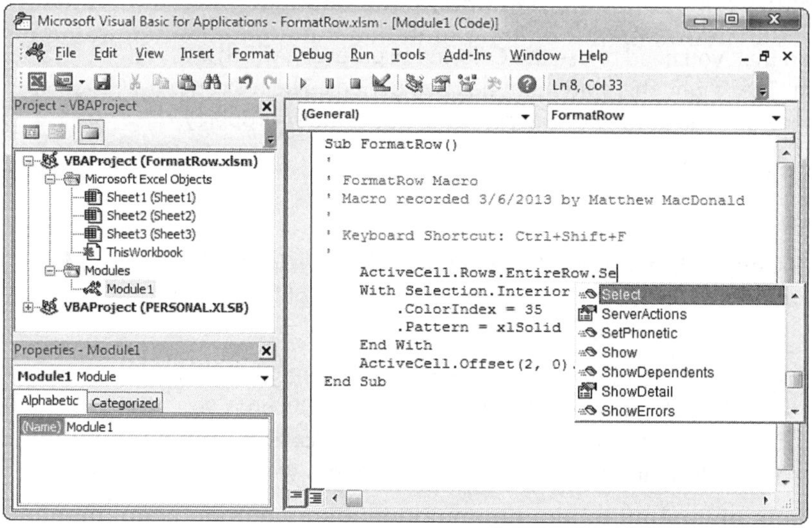

FIGURE 30-5

When you press the period key, a Visual Basic feature called IntelliSense shows you the available properties and methods for the current object. It represents properties with a hand-and-page icon, and methods with what appears to be a flying green eraser.

Exploring the VBA Language

Now that you've learned a bit about the Visual Basic editor and how Excel uses objects, it's time to jump right in and get some firsthand experience with VBA. First, you'll see how custom-programmed macros can perform some basic editing and formatting. After that, you'll learn how you can use simple macro code to solve problems you can't tackle with the macro recorder alone. In these sections, you'll see how to manipulate data more flexibly, make decisions, and repeat actions.

Before you get started, here are a few helpful tips:

- For easier macro coding, try to arrange your windows so you can see the Excel window and the Visual Basic editor window at the same time, side-by-side.

- To play a macro, move to the position in the worksheet where the macro should execute, and then switch to the Visual Basic editor. In the Visual Basic editor, move to the appropriate subroutine, and then click the Play button.
- Make sure you type in every command and object name correctly. Minor differences cause mysterious errors.
- If Excel finds some invalid code when it runs a macro, it stops executing it and highlights the problem line in yellow. At this point, you can correct the line and press Play to keep going, or stop and give up altogether (many programmers find long walks on the beach or guzzling a jug of Mountain Dew a helpful way to clear their heads).

Entering Text in the Current Cell

A few examples can go a long way to showing you how a typical macro works. First of all, check out the following macro subroutine, which represents one of the simplest possible macros you can create. It inserts the text "Hello World!" in the current cell (replacing whatever content may already be there):

```
Sub MyMacro
    ActiveCell.Value = ''"Hello World!'"
End Sub
```

With a little more effort, you can *edit* the current cell value instead of replacing it with new content. Imagine you want to take the current text value, and add the message "INVALID:" before the text. To accomplish this feat, you can use the following macro code:

```
Sub MyMacro
    ActiveCell.Value = '"INVALID: '" & ActiveCell.Value
End Sub
```

In this macro, Excel begins by joining together two pieces of text: the word "INVALID:" and whatever content is in the current cell. It then takes that combined piece of text and places it back into the cell. In this macro, the ampersand symbol (&) is key. It's a *concatenation operator*, which means it glues together different pieces of text.

You can use a similar approach to adjust a cell that has a number in it. In this case, you can use all the ordinary numeric operators, like +, –, /, *, and ^. Here's an example that multiplies the current cell value by 2, subtracts 1, and then enters the new value:

```
Sub MyMacro
    ActiveCell.Value = (ActiveCell.Value * 2) - 1
End Sub
```

TIP When using arithmetic operators, make sure the current cell contains a valid number. Otherwise, your code fails with a cryptic "type mismatch" error, which is a reminder that Excel can't perform numeric calculations with text.

Interacting with Other Cells

The ActiveCell object is the starting point for everything you want to do with the current cell. However, it doesn't let you change the content of *other* cells. If you want to do that, you need to access those cells by using the Offset property.

The property looks a little more complicated than other properties because it needs two pieces of information: a row offset and a column offset (in that order). The row offset tells Excel how many rows down you want to move. The column offset tells Excel how many columns to the right you want to move. If you want to move up or left, you need to use a negative number.

The following macro places the phrase *Top cell* in the current cell, and then places the phrase *Bottom cell* in the cell immediately underneath it.

```
Sub MyMacro
    ' Change the top cell.
    ActiveCell.Value = '"Top cell'"

    ' Change the bottom cell.
    ActiveCell.Offset(1,0) = '"Bottom cell'"
End Sub
```

You need to note one important factor about this code. Although it uses the Offset() property to change the value in the cell under the current cell, it doesn't actually *move* to that cell. Instead, when the macro ends, you're still positioned in the top cell.

If you actually want to move to the new cell, you need to use the Activate or Select method, as shown here:

```
Sub MyMacro
    ' Change the top cell.
    ActiveCell.Value = '"Top cell'"

    ' Move down one cell.
    ActiveCell.Offset(1,0).Select

    ' Now this changes the bottom cell.
    ActiveCell.Value = '"Bottom cell'"
End Sub
```

TIP If you look at the code that Excel creates when you record a macro, you'll see that it often uses the Select method to move around the worksheet. However, when you write your own macros from scratch, it's much simpler—and a far better design—to stay in one place. You can still change cells throughout the worksheet, but you rarely need to actually go there.

Editing Specific Cells

Using Value and Offset, you can romp around your worksheet changing cells as you please. However, you probably remember from the last chapter that you can edit cells in two ways—using relative or absolute references. The example macros you've seen so far use relative references, which means that they start working in the current position in the worksheet. However, in some situations you want to move to a specific cell. To do this in macro code, you use the Range object.

The basic technique is easy. You supply the cell address (like A2) as an argument to the Range object. This points Excel to the cell you want to manipulate. Then, you can do anything you want, including modifying the cell's value, changing its formatting, and so on, all without leaving your current position. Here's an example that shows this technique:

```
Sub MyMacro
    ' Change cell A1.
    Range('"A1'").Value = '"This is A1'"
End Sub
```

Interestingly, you can even modify multiple cells at once using a range reference (like A1:A2). In this case, when you set the Value property, that value appears in every cell in the range.

```
Sub MyMacro
    ' Insert the text '"Hello'" in ten cells
    Range('"A1:A10'").Value = '"Hello'"
End Sub
```

For a little more excitement, take a look at the next macro. It starts by creating a new worksheet for your workbook, and then it fills in several cells in that worksheet.

```
Sub MyMacro
    ' Create the worksheet using the Add method.
    ActiveWorkbook.Worksheets.Add

    ' Enter several cell values.
    Range('"A1'").Value = '"Company Report'"
    Range('"A2'").Value = '"Generated by an Excel macro'"

    ' Get the name of the person who owns this copy of Excel
    ' using the UserName property of the Application object.
    Range('"A3'").Value = '"Generated for '" & Application.UserName
End Sub
```

Formatting Cells

Conceptually, using macros to format cells is just as easy as using them to edit text. The difference is that you need to think about many more properties, because you can format a cell in dozens of different ways.

Before you can apply any formatting, you need to start off by finding the cells you want to change. If you know the exact reference, you can use the Range object (as shown in the previous section). If you know where the cells are relative to your current cell, you can use the ActiveCell.Offset property (as shown on page 932).

And once you have the object that represents your range of cells, you can use a variety of properties to format it, including HorizontalAlignment, VerticalAlignment, and MergeCells. You can also use some properties that are themselves objects, and so provide a slew of sub-properties, including Interior (which lets you set fills and patterns) and Font (which lets you configure the typeface and font size).

Here's an example that shows some of the code from the InsertHeader macro:

```
Sub InsertHeader
    With Range('"A1:C1'")
        'Note that the alignment properties take special constant values.
        .HorizontalAlignment = xlGeneral
        .VerticalAlignment = xlBottom
        .MergeCells = True
    End With

    ' Change the font of the selected cells.
    With Range('"A1:C1'").Font
        .Name = '"Arial'"
        .FontStyle = '"Bold'"
        .Size = 14
    End With

    ' (Other code omitted.)
End Sub
```

This code grabs a range of three cells (A1 to C1) and changes their alignment and font.

Using Variables

Every programming language includes the concept of *variables*, which are temporary storage containers where you can keep track of important information. In an Excel macro, you can use variables to get around problems that you just can't avoid with the macro recorder.

Imagine you want to swap the content in two cells. On the surface, this operation seems fairly straightforward. All you need to do is copy the text in one cell, place it in the other, and insert the other cell's text in the first cell. Unfortunately, once you paste the first cell's content into the second cell, you overwrite the content in the second cell, which is the content you wanted to put in the first cell. The easiest way around this problem is to use a variable to keep track of the information you need.

To create a variable in VBA, use the oddly named *Dim* keyword (short for *dimension*, which is programmer jargon for "define a new variable"). After the word Dim, you enter the name of the variable.

Here's how you'd create a variable named CellContent:

```
Dim CellContent
```

Once you create the variable, you're free to put information in it and take information out. To perform both of these operations, you use the familiar equal sign, just as you would with properties.

Here's an example that stores some text in a variable:

```
CellContent = '"Test text'"
```

The following macro puts it all together. It uses a variable to swap the content of two cells.

```
Sub SwapTextWithCellOnRight()
    ' Create the variable you need.
    Dim CellContent

    ' Store the content that's in the current cell.
    CellContent = ActiveCell.Value

    ' Copy the value from the cell on the right
    ' into the current cell.
    ActiveCell.Value = ActiveCell.Offset(0, 1).Value

    ' Copy the value from the variable into the
    ' cell on the right.
    ActiveCell.Offset(0, 1).Value = CellContent
End Sub
```

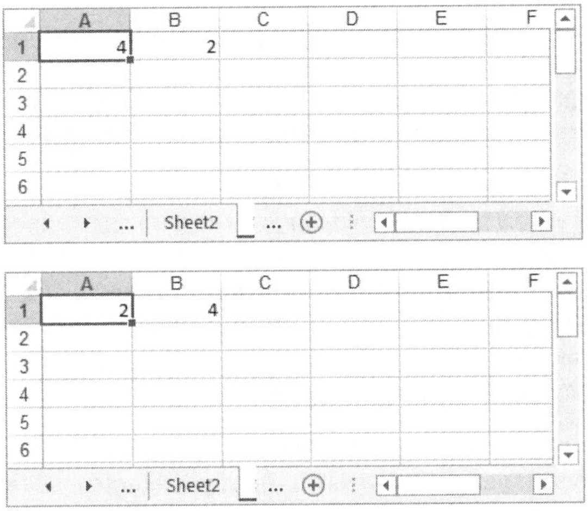

FIGURE 30-6

Top: To try out the SwapTextWithCellOnRight macro (included with the downloads for this book at http://missingmanuals.com/cds/excel2013mm), type number 4 in cell A1 and the number 2 in cell A2. Now move to cell A1 and run the macro.

Bottom: The macro moves the number 2 into cell A1 and the number 4 into cell A2. It isn't rocket science—but it's almost impossible to do without using variables.

POWER USERS' CLINIC

Variable Data Types

The variable examples in this chapter are a bit lazy. They don't specifically tell Excel what type of information the variable will hold. This approach works perfectly well, but real programmers frown on it, because it lets certain types of errors slip into your code undetected. For example, you might inadvertently store the wrong type of data in a variable.

A better approach is to add the As keyword after your variable name, followed by the variable's *data type*. The only problem is that in order to do this, you need to know what data types VBA supports. Some common data types include String (for storing text information, which you have to enclose in quotation marks), Integer (for storing positive and negative whole numbers), Single (for storing fractional numbers), and Date (for storing dates). Here's an example:

```
Dim MyText As String
MyText = "This is string data."
Dim MyNumber As Integer
MyNumber = 42
```

Simple data types are easy enough, but the Excel objects also have their own data types. For example, to define the CellContent variable in the previous example, which represents the content in a cell, you need to use the Range data type:

```
Dim CellContent As Range
```

As you can imagine, you need a fair bit of experience before you know when to use the right data type. In Microsoft's online VBA documentation, you can learn about all the basic data types at *http://tinyurl.com/vba-data-types*. (This covers everything you need for text and numeric data.) To get the scoop on more specialized Excel objects, like the Range object shown above, visit *http://tinyurl.com/excel-objs*.

Making Decisions

Conditional logic is another programming staple, and it's code that runs only if a certain condition is true. There's no limit to the number of ways you can use conditional logic. You could perform a different calculation based on the value of a cell, apply different formatting based on the number of cells, or create a different printout depending on the date. Conditional logic lets you do all this, and a lot more.

All conditional logic starts with a *condition*, a simple expression that can turn out to be true or false (programmers call this process *evaluating* to true or false). Your code can then make a decision to execute different logic depending on the outcome of the condition. To build a condition, you need to compare a variable or property using a logical operator like = (equal to), < (less than), > (greater than), and <> (not equal to). ActiveCell.Value = 10 is a condition. It can be true (if the current cell contains the number 10), or false (if the current cell contains something else).

On its own, a condition can't do anything. However, when you used it in conjunction with other code, it can become tremendously powerful. Once you create a suitable condition, you can put it inside a special structure called the *If block*. The If block evaluates a condition, and then runs a section of code if the condition is true. If the condition isn't true, Excel ignores the code.

Here's a macro that looks at the current cell value. If that value exceeds 100, Excel changes the value in the cell to 100. If the cell value is less than 100, nothing happens, and the current value remains:

```
Sub MyMacro
    If ActiveCell.Value > 100 Then
        ' This value is too big. Change it to the maximum of 100.
        ActiveCell.Value = 100
    End If
End Sub
```

Note that the If block always starts with If and ends with End If. Everything in between runs only if the condition is true.

An If block can also evaluate several different conditions. Here's an example that considers the current value of a cell. Depending on the cell's value, the If block uses a different calculation to arrive at the sales commission, which it places in another cell:

```
Sub MyMacro
    If ActiveCell.Value > 1000 Then
        ' Use the 5% commission rate.
        ActiveCell.Offset(0,1).Value = ActiveCell.Value * 0.05
    ElseIf ActiveCell.Value > 500
        ' Use the 2.5% commission rate.
        ActiveCell.Offset(0,1).Value = ActiveCell.Value * 0.025
    Else
        ' Give a basic $5 comission.
        ActiveCell.Offset(0,1).Value = 5
    End If
End Sub
```

Here, only one segment of code runs. Excel works its way through the If block, testing each condition until one matches. If the cell value is greater than 1,000, it runs the first conditional block of code, and then jumps down to the closing End If statement. It then continues with any other code in the macro. If the cell value is less than (or equal to) 1,000 but greater than 500, the first condition is false, and Excel tries the second one, which is true. If no If block condition matches, Excel runs the code in the final clause, the Else clause.

These examples scratch only the surface of what careful conditional logic can do. You can use *And* and *Or* keywords to combine conditions, put one conditional block inside another, and much more. To learn more about these approaches, you may want to consult the Web or a dedicated book about VBA programming. Those ready to dive right in to the nitty-gritty can try *Excel 2013 Power Programming with VBA*, by John Walkenbach (Wiley).

Repeating Actions with a Loop

Computers work particularly well when you need to automate a tedious task. While you may tire out after typing in your 100th cell value, an Excel macro has no such weakness, and can perform thousands of operations without pausing.

The *loop* is one of the best tools for repeating operations. A loop is another type of block, one that repeats itself over and over again. Here's an example:

```
Do
    ActiveCell.Select
    Selection.Interior.ColorIndex = 35
    Selection.Interior.Pattern = xlSolid
    ActiveCell.Offset(1,0).Select
Loop
```

When Excel reaches the Loop statement at the bottom of this loop, it automatically jumps back to the beginning and repeats your code. However, there's one problem—this process continues infinitely! That means that if you make the mistake of running this macro, your worksheet is locked up indefinitely (until you press the emergency-stop key combination Ctrl+Break).

To avoid this situation, you should build all loops with an *exit condition*. This condition signals when the loop should end. Here's a rewritten version of the loop above that stops running the code as soon as it finds an empty cell:

```
Do Until ActiveCell.Value = '"'"
    ActiveCell.Select
    Selection.Interior.ColorIndex = 35
    Selection.Interior.Pattern = xlSolid
    ActiveCell.Offset(1,0).Select
Loop
```

This technique is quite powerful. Consider the following macro, which uses a loop to format all the rows in a table. It gives each row an alternating color and stops when there are no values left:

```
Sub FormatAllCellsInColumn
    Do Until ActiveCell.Value = '"'"
        ' Format the first row.
        ActiveCell.EntireRow.Select
        Selection.Interior.ColorIndex = 35
        Selection.Interior.Pattern = xlSolid

        ' Move down two rows.
        ActiveCell.Offset(2,0).Select
    Loop
End Sub
```

This macro is really an enhanced version of the FormatRow macro shown in the previous chapter. Unlike FormatRow, you need to run this macro only once, and it takes care of all the rows in your worksheet that contain data.

Excel actually has different types of loops. The For Each loop is another useful loop, which repeats itself once for every item in a collection of objects. For Each loops come in handy if you need to process all the cells in the current selection.

Imagine you want to fix up many cells that have a jumble of upper-and lowercase letters. As you learned on page 324, the Excel PROPER() function can do the trick and convert a string like "hElLo THERE" to a respectable "Hello There." The downside is that you need to write a separate formula for each cell you want to change. A much better solution is to use the PROPER() function from inside a macro to make the changes automatically.

The following macro does the trick. It accesses the PROPER() function through the Application.WorksheetFunction object:

```
Sub FixText()
    ActiveCell.Value = Application.WorksheetFunction.Proper(ActiveSheet.Value)
End Sub
```

This useful macro quickly cleans up the current cell. However, if you select *multiple* cells and run the macro again, you're likely to be disappointed. The FixText macro changes only the current cell. It ignores all the other selected cells.

To take these other cells into account, you need to create a loop using For Each. That's because the For Each block lets you scan through all the selected cells, and then run a series of code statements once for each cell.

Here's the revised macro, which cleans up every selected cell:

```
Sub FixTextInAllCells()
    ' This variable represents the cell you want to change.
    Dim Cell

    ' Change all the cells in the current selection.
    For Each Cell In Selection
        ' This code repeats once for each cell in the selection.
        Cell.Value = Application.WorksheetFunction.Proper(Cell.Value)
    Next
End Sub
```

This code works even if you don't explicitly select any cells. That's because Excel treats the current cell as though it's selected. In this situation, the For Each loop performs just one pass. Figure 30-7 shows the result.

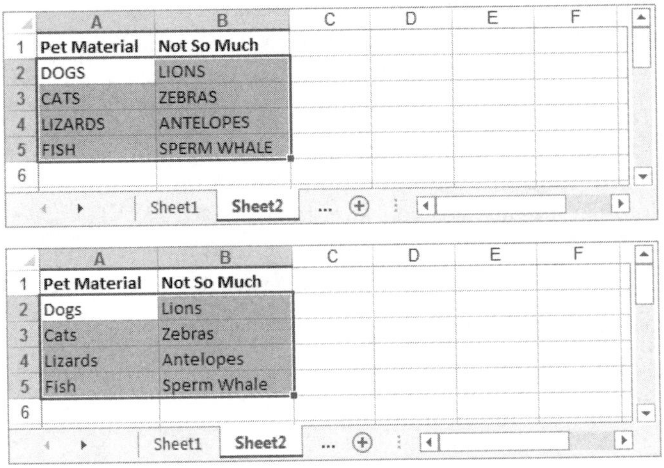

FIGURE 30-7

Loops are one of the handiest tools for fixing up large tables in a hurry. Here, a loop transforms a table crammed with text in all capital letters (top) into something much more palatable (bottom). The best part? You need to select the cells and run the FixTextInAllCells macro only once.

Creating Custom Functions

So far, you've seen how you can use code to create powerful macros that take control of Excel. But you have another option for plugging your logic into Excel: You can create custom functions (known in programmer-ese as *user-defined functions*). Essentially, a custom function accepts some information (through arguments), performs a calculation, and then provides a result. Once you create your custom function, you can use it in a formula in a cell, in exactly the same way that you use Excel's built-in functions.

You create custom functions in the same place as you create macros—in modules. In fact, any number of macros and functions can exist side-by-side in a module. The difference is that macros start with the word *Sub*, and custom functions start with the word *Function*.

Here's an example of one of simplest possible custom functions:

```
Function GetMyFavoriteColor()
    GetMyFavoriteColor = '"Magenta'"
End Function
```

Every function needs to provide a result, which is what appears in the cell when you use the function. To set the result, you use the name of the function, followed by an equal sign and the value, as shown here:

```
GetMyFavoriteColor = '"Magenta'"
```

The function provides the text "Magenta" as its result. If the function provided a number instead of a piece of text, you wouldn't use the quotation marks, just the number.

To use the function in your worksheet, just create a formula that uses the function. Figure 30-8 shows you how.

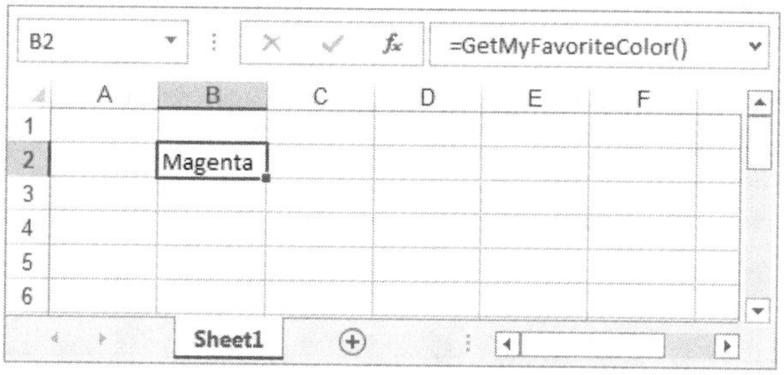

FIGURE 30-8

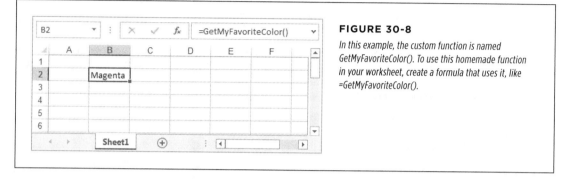

In this example, the custom function is named GetMyFavoriteColor(). To use this homemade function in your worksheet, create a formula that uses it, like =GetMyFavoriteColor().

The GetMyFavoriteColor() function is particularly simple because it doesn't use any arguments. But there's no reason you can't get a little fancier. Consider the following custom function, which takes two arguments—length and width—and calculates the total area by multiplying them together:

```
Function Area(Length, Width)
    Area = Length * Width
End Function
```

The two arguments are defined in the parentheses after the function name. You can add as many arguments as you want, as long as you separate each one with a comma.

Now, to use this function in one of your worksheet cells, you can use this formula:

```
=Area(100,50)
```

This formula uses literal values, but you can easily go one step further and use cell references instead.

Neither the GetMyFavoriteColor() nor Area() function shows you anything you couldn't already achieve on your own. The following example shows a much more practical function that does something you *can't* otherwise achieve in Excel—*banker's rounding*. As discussed on page 266, Excel's rounding can contribute to biases when adding numbers. To avoid this problem, accountants sometimes use other types of rounding. Banker's rounding is one example—it sometimes rounds 0.5 up and sometimes rounds it down, depending on whether the preceding number is even or odd. Therefore, 1.5 always rounds up to 2, while 2.5 always rounds down to 2. With ordinary rounding, 0.5 is always rounded up, and that can slightly inflate long columns of numbers.

Implementing banker's rounding by hand is tricky, and it requires some conditional logic. The VBA language, however, gives you a powerful shortcut. It provides a built-in Round() function that always uses banker's rounding, unlike Excel's ROUND() function.

Here's the complete function you need:

```
Function BankerRound(NumberToRound)
    BankerRound = Round(NumberToRound)
End Function
```

To test it out, try the following two formulas. The first one produces a result of 0, while the second one has a result of 2:

```
=BankerRound(0.5)
=BankerRound(1.5)
```

POWER USERS' CLINIC

Power Programming

If this taste of Excel programming has whet your appetite, there's no need to stop now. The next logical step is to read a book that's all about Excel programming. Two good choices are *Excel 2013 Power Programming with VBA* (Wiley) and *Programming Excel with VBA and .NET* (O'Reilly). If possible, look for an edition that's updated for Excel 2013, but don't worry if you're stuck with an older copy. Other than a few additions to cover new Excel features, the VBA language really hasn't changed over the years.

If you already have solid programming skills, you might be interested to know that the VBA macro language isn't the only game in town. For example, just about any Windows programming language can communicate with—and take control of—Excel using COM. (COM, or Component Object Model, is a Microsoft technology for sharing useful objects between different programs.) For example, a Visual Basic developer can use this technique to build a standalone program that "drives" Excel—creating worksheets, inserting data, and performing calculations. The best part is that you still use the same set of Excel objects, methods, and properties that you would in a macro, but you place your code in a standalone program that has much greater power. This approach gives you the ability to create large-scale solutions, like programs that generate Excel documents or websites that read Excel data.

COM has "oldie but goodie" status. It's been around for much more than a decade, and while it still works, cutting-edge developers have newer and slicker tools. In Office 2013, there's a brand-new model called Apps for Office, which lets you build Excel plug-ins using Web standards like HTML and JavaScript. To learn more about Apps for Office, and all your other development options, visit Microsoft's Excel Developer Center at *http://tinyurl.com/excel-dev*.

PART

8

Appendix

APPENDIX A

Customizing the Ribbon

APPENDIX

A

Customizing the Ribbon

When Microsoft introduced the ribbon in Office 2007, they clamped down on letting people customize it. Quite simply, the designers of Office were concerned that overly creative fans would replace the standard arrangement of buttons with a jumble of personal favorites. Their worst fear was that Excel customizers would transform Excel so completely that no one else would be able to use the program on their computers, and the instructions in books like this one would be useless. To prevent this crisis, Microsoft made it extremely difficult to customize the ribbon. In fact, ribbon customization was only available to programming gearheads willing to work with the intimidating RibbonX standard.

Excel 2013 isn't nearly as paranoid. It lets anyone rename tabs, hide them, add groups, and remove them. It even lets you create an entirely new tab with your own buttons. When used carefully, this feature gives you a great way to speed up your work and put your favorite commands in a central spot. In more reckless hands, it's a great way to confuse friends, family, coworkers, and even yourself.

Along with its surprisingly powerful ribbon customization ability, Excel 2013 lets users customize the Quick Access toolbar—the sequence of tiny buttons that sits just above the ribbon and its tabs. If you're not so ambitious that you want to create your own custom tab, the Quick Access toolbar is a convenient place to stick your favorite buttons. That's the task you'll consider first.

Adding Your Favorites to the QAT

You've already seen the Quick Access toolbar (known to Excel nerds as the QAT). It's the micro-size toolbar above the ribbon. The QAT uses only icons, but you can hover over any of them to see the name of the command it triggers.

When you first start out with Excel, the Quick Access toolbar is a lonely place, with buttons for quickly saving your workbook and undoing or redoing your last action. But Excel gives you complete control over the space, including the ability to add new buttons. You can most quickly add stuff by clicking the down-pointing arrow at the right side of the toolbar. Figure A-1 shows you how.

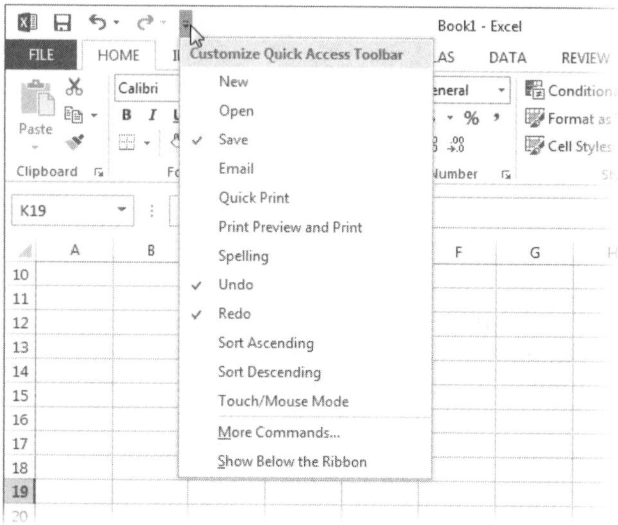

FIGURE A-1

When you click the drop-down arrow in the Quick Access toolbar, Excel lists often-used commands that you can add by just clicking them. The commands include those for creating a new workbook, opening an existing workbook, sending your workbook to a printer with no questions asked, and firing up Excel's spell-checker. To see all the possibilities (or to rearrange commands you already added), choose More Commands.

TIP If you don't like the Quick Access toolbar's placement, Excel gives you one other option. Click the drop-down arrow and choose "Show Below the Ribbon" to move your toolbar underneath the ribbon so your mouse has less distance to travel.

You might add buttons to the Quick Access toolbar for two reasons:

- **To make it easier to get to a command you use frequently.** If it's in the Quick Access toolbar, you don't need to memorize a keyboard shortcut or change the current ribbon tab.
- **To get to a command that the ribbon doesn't provide.** Excel has a small set of less popular commands that it doesn't keep in the ribbon. Many of them are holdovers from previous versions of Excel. If you have a long-lost favorite Excel feature that's missing in Excel 2013, you just might be able to add it to the Quick Access toolbar.

Keyboard lovers can also trigger the commands in the Quick Access toolbar with lightning speed thanks to Excel's KeyTips feature (page 16). When you press the Alt key, Excel superimposes a number over every command in the Quick Access toolbar (starting at 1 and going up from there). You can then press the number to trigger the command. In the Quick Access toolbar in Figure A-1, for example, Alt+1 saves the current workbook, Alt+2 opens the Undo list, and so on.

You've seen how to customize the Quick Access toolbar in a few places in this book—you used it to get to the Compare and Merge Workbooks feature in Chapter 25, for example, and to get quick access to macros in Chapter 28.

TIP To add a command in the ribbon to the QAT, here's a shortcut: Find the command in the ribbon, right-click it, and then choose Add to Quick Access Toolbar.

Adding Buttons

To add a button to the Quick Access toolbar, follow these steps:

1. **Click the drop-down arrow in the Quick Access toolbar, and then choose More Commands.**

   The Excel Options window opens on the Quick Access Toolbar page (Figure A-2).

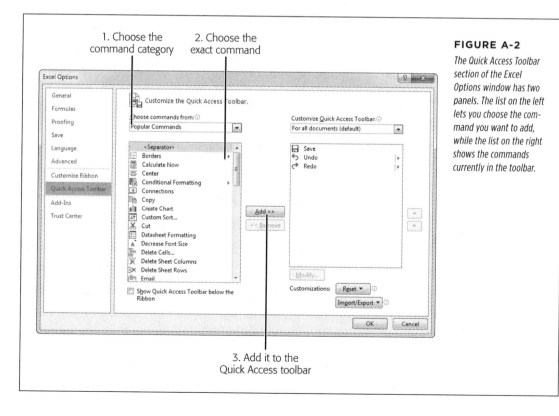

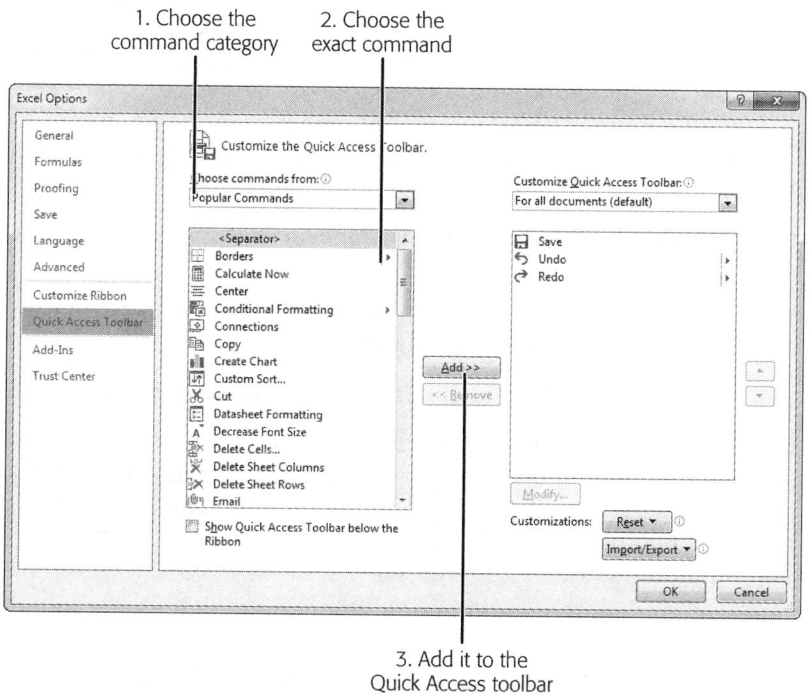

FIGURE A-2

The Quick Access Toolbar section of the Excel Options window has two panels. The list on the left lets you choose the command you want to add, while the list on the right shows the commands currently in the toolbar.

2. **Choose a category from the "Choose commands from" list.**

   The library of commands you can add to the Quick Access toolbar is enormous. To make it easier to find what you want, it makes sense to choose a specific category. Many of the categories overlap—Excel simply provides them to make finding what you want easier. Here are the top choices:

   - **Popular Commands** gives you a short list of commands that Excel jockeys love. If you want to add a button for a commonly used feature, you just might find it here.
   - **Commands Not in the Ribbon** provides all the leftovers—commands that Microsoft didn't consider useful enough to include in the ribbon. This list holds some commands that are superseded or partially duplicated by other commands, commands included in other windows, and commands used in previous versions of Excel but put out to pasture in this release.
   - **All Commands** includes the full list of choices. As with the other categories, it's ordered alphabetically.
   - **Macros** shows all the macros in the currently open workbooks, including the personal macro workbook. Be careful about adding a macro that's not in your personal macro workbook—if you move the macro file, Excel can't run it when you click its button.

     Excel puts several additional categories under these categories that correspond to the File menu and various tabs in the ribbon. For example, you can choose the Insert tab to see all the commands that appear in the ribbon's Insert tab. The File tab tops the tab list, and it includes the commands from the File menu and backstage view. At the bottom of the list are the "Tools" tabs—tabs that appear only when you select certain objects in a worksheet, like charts, pictures, or images.

3. **Once you choose a category, pick a command from the list, and then click Add.**

   The command moves from the list on the left to the list on the right, placing it on the Quick Access toolbar (Figure A-3).

4. **To add more commands, repeat this process starting at step 2.**

   Optionally, you can rearrange the order of items in the Quick Access toolbar. Just pick a command from the list on the right, and then use the up and down arrow buttons to move it. Excel displays the topmost commands in the list to the left on the Quick Access toolbar.

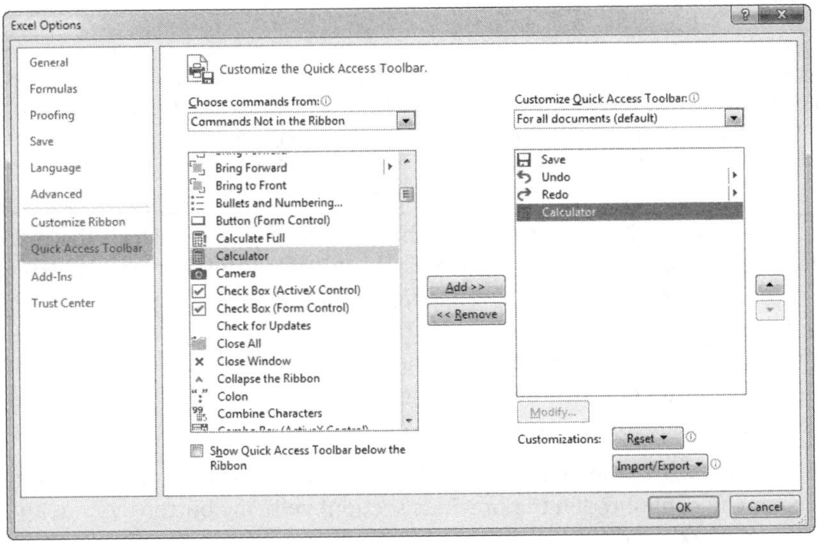

FIGURE A-3

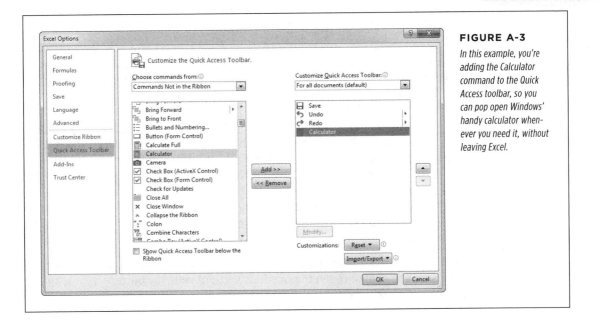

In this example, you're adding the Calculator command to the Quick Access toolbar, so you can pop open Windows' handy calculator whenever you need it, without leaving Excel.

TIP If you customized the heck out of your Quick Access toolbar and want to go back to a simpler way of life, click the Reset button.

5. **When you finish, click OK to return to Excel and its revamped Quick Access toolbar.**

   Adding to the Quick Access toolbar isn't a lifetime commitment. To get rid of a command you don't want anymore, right-click it, and then choose Remove from Quick Access Toolbar.

NOTE You might notice the tempting Modify button, which lets you change a command's name and picture. Unfortunately, it works only for macro commands.

Customizing Specific Workbooks

Do you have a button or two you use incessantly, but just for a specific workbook? In such a situation, it may not make sense to customize the Quick Access toolbar in the normal way. If you do, you'll get your extra buttons in *every* workbook you use, including those where the extras aren't useful.

Excel has a great feature to help you out. You can customize the Quick Access toolbar for *individual* workbooks. That way, whenever you open the workbook, the buttons you need appear in the Quick Access toolbar. When you close it (or open another workbook in a separate window), the buttons disappear.

NOTE Customizing individual workbooks has advantages and disadvantages. The disadvantage is that you need to customize the toolbar for every workbook, which can take a lot of time. The advantage is that your customizations are recorded right in your workbook file. As a result, they stick around if you open the workbook on someone else's computer (or if you log onto your computer as a different user).

To customize the toolbar for a single workbook, follow the same steps in the "Adding Buttons" section above. Start by clicking the Quick Access toolbar's drop-down arrow and choosing More Commands. Then, before you add any commands, change the selection in the Customize Quick Access Toolbar list, which appears just above the list of commands in the Quick Access toolbar. Instead of using "For all documents (default)," choose your workbook's name (as in "For SecretSanta.xlsx"). The list starts off empty, so follow the steps above to add buttons.

When Excel displays the Quick Access toolbar, it combines the standard buttons (the ones you configured in the previous section) with any buttons you define for the current workbook (Figure A-4).

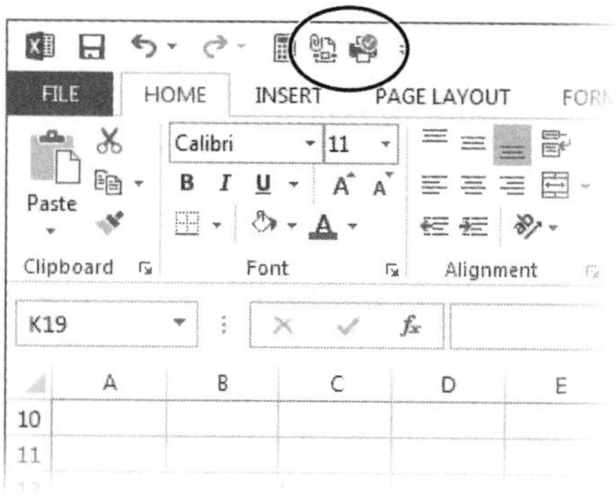

FIGURE A-4

Workbook-specific buttons, like the two circled here, always appear after Excel's standard buttons. You can define the same button as a standard button and a workbook-specific button, in which case it appears twice.

Customizing the Quick Access toolbar for a specific workbook is a handy trick. It makes great sense with macros (Chapter 28) because it lets you create a single workbook that has a useful set of macros and handy buttons for running them. It's also great with templates (Chapter 16); if you customize the Quick Access toolbar for a specific template, every workbook you create with that template gets the buttons you added.

Personalizing the Ribbon

Customizing the Quick Access toolbar gives you one-stop access to a bunch of commands, but if you really want to streamline your Excel experience, you can customize your ribbon, too, tailoring it to the tasks you perform most often.

Ribbon customization takes place in the same Excel Options window you used to change the Quick Access toolbar. The easiest way to get there is to right-click the ribbon, and then choose Customize Ribbon. Excel opens the Excel Options window and sends you straight to the Customize Ribbon section (Figure A-5).

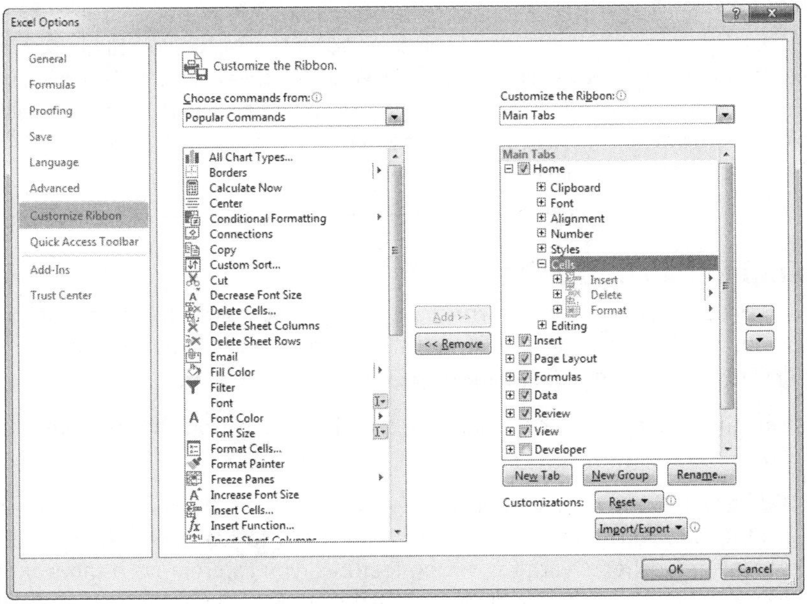

FIGURE A-5

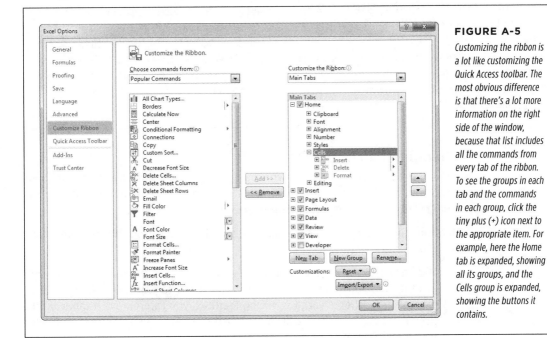

Customizing the ribbon is a lot like customizing the Quick Access toolbar. The most obvious difference is that there's a lot more information on the right side of the window, because that list includes all the commands from every tab of the ribbon. To see the groups in each tab and the commands in each group, click the tiny plus (+) icon next to the appropriate item. For example, here the Home tab is expanded, showing all its groups, and the Cells group is expanded, showing the buttons it contains.

There's a lot you can do to fine-tune your ribbon. The next sections show you how.

NOSTALGIA CORNER

What Happens to Excel 2003 Toolbars?

Using the customization features in Excel 2003 (or before), you might have designed your own specialized toolbars (which you could then attach to a workbook file). The bad news is that Excel no longer provides this feature, so you can't enhance or modify the toolbars you configured in Excel 2003 and before. The good news is that you can still access those custom toolbars, just in a slightly different way.

All the buttons from old custom toolbars and custom menus end up on a separate tab in the Excel 2013 ribbon, named Add-Ins. This tab appears only if you had a custom toolbar or custom menu in the workbook. When it appears, it ends up at the end of the series of standard ribbon tabs. This arrangement may not be the prettiest, but it makes sure that old solutions keep working in the newest version of Excel.

If you want to keep your custom commands closer at hand, you can add them to the Quick Access toolbar. You need to look for three items (in the All Commands list): Custom Toolbars, Menu Commands, and Toolbar Commands. When you add these to the Quick Access toolbar, they appear as drop-down menus that, when clicked, offer all the custom commands in your current workbook.

Changing Existing Tabs

Tired of Excel's standard tabs? Surprisingly, you can do quite a bit to change them. Of course, *can* doesn't mean *should*, and if you're overly ambitious, you may end up hiding something you need, and making Excel much more difficult to use.

Here are the changes you can make to an existing tab from the ribbon-editing window:

- **Hide a tab.** If you're absolutely positive you don't need any of the commands in a tab, or if you're a system administrator trying to prevent users from messing up spreadsheets with the wrong features, you can remove a tab from the ribbon. To do so, clear the checkbox next to the tab name. To restore it later, turn the checkbox back on.
- **Remove a group.** A similar, but more fine-grained strategy, is to remove a group of commands from a tab, leaving more room for tabs that are presumably more useful to you on that tab of the ribbon. To remove a group, click the plus (+) icon to expand the tab that has it, select the group, and then click the Remove button (located between the two lists).
- **Change the order of tabs.** If you use one tab far more often than another, you might decide to change the tab order. Select the tab you want to move from the list on the right, and then click the up arrow button (to move the tab toward the left side, or start, of the ribbon) or the down arrow (to move the tab toward the right side, or end, of the ribbon). You can find both arrow buttons just to the right of the list.

- **Change the order of groups in a tab.** This works the same way as changing the tab order does, but it lets you rearrange the sections *within* a tab. Click the plus (+) icon to expand the appropriate tab, select the group you want to move, and then use the up and down arrows to shuffle its position. Be warned: Though this seems like a small change, it can seriously throw off other Excel fans, because people tend to remember the general position of the commands they use.

NOTE If you keep pressing the up arrow when you reach the top of the group list (or the down arrow when you reach the bottom), Excel moves the group to the next adjacent tab.

- **Rename a tab or group.** Select either a tab or a single group under a tab. (You can't rename individual buttons.) Then click the Rename button under the list. A small window pops up where you can type in the new name. Then click OK.
- **Add a new group to an existing tab.** First, expand the tab where you want to place your group. Select an existing group, and then click the New Group button. Excel places your new group immediately after the group you selected, but you can use the arrow buttons to move it. Now give your group a good name (click Rename), and then fill it up. To do that, select the command you want from the list on the left, and then click Add, just as you did when adding commands to the Quick Access toolbar.

NOTE The ribbon changes you make are linked to your Windows user account. If someone else logs on to your computer with a different user name and runs Excel, that person gets the standard ribbon.

And here's the much smaller list of changes Excel *doesn't* let you make:

- **Delete or rearrange commands in a standard group.** You can delete a group wholesale, but you can't modify it. Of course, nothing stops you from removing a standard group altogether and creating a similar-looking custom group that has just the commands you want.
- **Add custom commands to a standard group.** If you want to add new commands, you need to place them in a custom group in a standard tab or, even better, a custom group in a custom tab.

If you find you've gone too far, Excel lets you return the ribbon to its original state by clicking the Reset button, and then choosing "Reset all customizations." Alternatively, you can reset just a single tab: Select it in the list, click the Reset button, and then choose "Reset only selected Ribbon tab."

UP TO SPEED

Ribbon Tweaking: Too Much of a Good Thing?

Before you begin a wild bout of customization, it's worth asking which changes are really worth the effort. Here's the rundown:

- Hiding tabs and removing groups makes sense if you're trying to simplify Excel. However, you risk losing features you may need later, which is usually far more inconvenient.
- Changing tab and group names doesn't make you more efficient, but it could confuse other people, so it's usually a bad idea.
- Rearranging groups is a worthwhile strategy if you want to move the features you never use to the far right end of the tab, so they won't distract you.
- Adding new groups is a great way to get important features at your fingertips, but it probably makes even more sense to put your custom-picked buttons in a brand new tab you add from scratch, as you'll do in the next section.

Any ribbon customization is a tradeoff between personalization and consistency. You already know that a revamped ribbon can confuse other Excel fans when they use your computer. But you might not realize the more insidious reverse effect—namely, you'll be embarrassingly slow when you switch to a normal Excel installation on a colleague's computer or at the local copy shop. For that reason, it's best to practice a bit of restraint and follow these ribbon-customization guidelines:

- Customize only when you're absolutely sure it will make your life easier and more convenient.
- If you want to add more than two or three new commands to the ribbon, consider putting them all into a new tab, so they're clearly separate from the standard buttons.
- If you want to customize something just so you can express your own personal design aesthetic, stick to your computer's background wallpaper and desktop icons.

Creating Your Own Tab

The safest way to customize the ribbon is to put your custom buttons in a separate tab. This lets you keep the rest of the Excel user interface in its normal state (and ensures that you'll be able to use the instructions in this book). It's also oddly satisfying to have a ribbon tab all to yourself, to fill with your favorite shortcuts, as shown in Figure A-6.

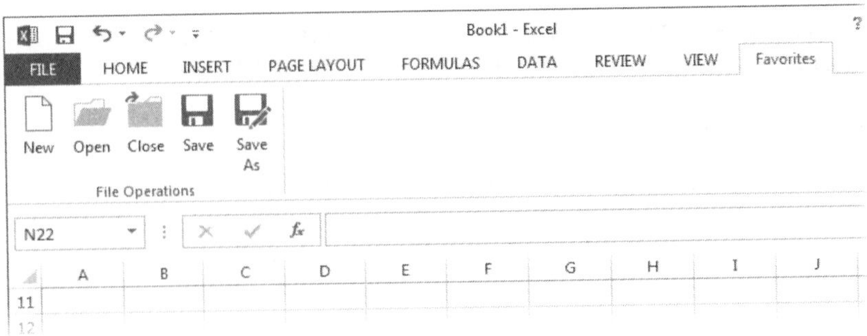

FIGURE A-6

You can fit quite a bit more into a custom ribbon tab than you can fit in the Quick Access toolbar. Here, the custom tab (named Favorites) has a few items from the File menu, like Open, Save, and Close.

You probably already know how to create a custom tab and add commands to it. But if you're unsure, follow this sequence of steps:

1. **In the Excel Options window, select the last tab in the list, and then click the New Tab button.**

   Excel adds a tab, named "New Tab," at the end of the ribbon. (You can move it using the arrow buttons.) Inside the new tab, Excel adds a single new group named "New Group."

2. **Change the tab and group names.**

   First, select the new tab, click Rename, and then fill in a new name. Then, select the new group, click Rename, and give it a new name. For example, in Figure A-6 the tab is named Favorites and the first group is named File.

3. **Now add your favorite commands.**

   The Customize Ribbon section of the Excel Options window works the same way as the Quick Access Toolbar section. You pick commands in the list on the left, and then click Add to transfer them over to the currently selected custom group.

   For example, to add the Open command shown in Figure A-5, pick "File Tab" from the "Choose commands from" list, select Open, and then click the Add button.

NOTE The command list includes many variations of each command. For example, along with Save, you'll find Save As, Save As Other Format, Save as Another File Type, Publish as PDF or XPS, and so on. Although you can do just about everything with Save As, these variations are slightly more convenient. You may want to explore a little and try the different variations before you settle on the exact commands you want.

4. **Optionally, add more groups.**

   To create each new group, click Add Group. You can use the arrow buttons to re-arrange them.

5. **Once you finish, consider saving your ribbon layout so you can reuse it on other computers or quickly switch between different custom layouts.**

   The following section shows you how.

Exporting Your Custom Ribbon

Dedicated Excel customizers can expend a lot of effort getting exactly the right arrangement of tabs and buttons. After doing all that work, it's natural to wonder if you can reuse your ribbon on another computer. Fortunately, Excel has an export feature that preserves all your hard ribbon-customization work. It copies your ribbon settings to a special file (with the clunky file extension *.exportedUI*), which you can then apply to a copy of Excel installed on another computer.

Here's how to use Excel's ribbon export feature:

1. **Start by perfecting your ribbon in the Excel Options window.**
2. **When you finish, click the Import/Export button, and then choose "Export all customizations."**

   A File Save window appears.
3. **Browse to the folder where you want to place your file, and then give it a suitable name, like DavesCustomRibbon. Then click Save.**

   Excel adds the file extension .exportedUI, so if you type in DavesCustomRibbon, Excel actually saves a file named DavesCustomRibbon.exportedUI.
4. **Now go to the computer where you want to replicate your ribbon, and take your file with you. In the Excel Options window, click the Import/Export button, and then choose "Import customization file."**

   A File Open window appears.
5. **Browse to your file, select it, and then click Open.**

   Before it imports your ribbon, Excel gives you a last-minute confirmation warning, because the settings that are stored in your file will overwrite any custom ribbon settings that are already applied.
6. **Click Yes to seal the deal and import your custom ribbon.**

   Presto—Excel replaces the standard-issue ribbon with your personalized version.

FREQUENTLY ASKED QUESTION

Troublesome Tabs

Help! There's a tab in my Excel ribbon that I can't remove.

Sometimes, a tab may appear in the Excel ribbon but not in the Excel Options window. In this situation, the culprit is almost always an add-in—a program that plugs into Excel, extending it with new features and (sometimes) a ribbon tab that just won't go away. The only way to remove this sort of tab is to turn off the add-in.

To do that, go to the Add-Ins section of the Excel Options window, choose the appropriate add-in type from the Manage list (if you're not sure what type it is, try both Excel Add-ins and COM Add-ins), and then click the Go button. You'll see a list of add-ins that you can disable or remove. If you're not sure which one is at fault, you can try disabling them all, and then add them back one by one until the culprit appears.

Index

Symbols

A

D

F

G

H

I

J

K

L

M

S

X

Excel 2013

THE MISSING CD
There's no
CD with this book;
you just saved $5.00.
Instead, every single Web address, practice file, and
piece of downloadable software mentioned in this
book is available at *missingmanuals.com*
(click the Missing CD icon).
There you'll find a tidy list of links,
organized by chapter.

Don't miss a thing!
Sign up for the free Missing Manual email announcement list at missingmanuals.com. We'll let you know when we release new titles, make free sample chapters available, and update the features and articles on the Missing Manual website.